David R. Godine, Publisher
Page 536

The Atlantic Monthly, page 354
The Atlantic Monthly Press, page 518

# 1 9 8 6
# FICTION
# WRITER'S
# MARKET

Edited by
Jean M. Fredette

**Writer's Digest Books**
Cincinnati, Ohio

Managing Editor, Market Books Department: Constance J. Achabal

Endpaper photos of publishing houses by Michelle Fredette

International Standard Serial Number 0275-2123
International Standard Book Number 0-89879-216-9

# ACKNOWLEDGMENTS

The editor thanks the following writers for their original contributions to *Fiction Writer's Market 1986*:

Michael A. Banks, "Writers' Organizations: the Great Support System."
Barbara Wernecke Durkin, "Congratulations! It's a Book."
David Groff, "Superior Bambini and Other Samples From Slush."
Ben Nyberg, "The Serious Business of Choosing Literary Fiction."
Peter R. Stillman, "A Writer's Potpourri."
J.N. Williamson, "Scare Tactics—the Guts and Bolts of Horror Writing."


The editor of *Fiction Writer's Market* gratefully acknowledges the following publishers, authors and agents for granting permission to publish their articles and book excerpts:

Barbara Bauer and Robert F. Moss, "Feeling Rejected? John Updike, Mailer, Oates," from *The New York Times Book Review*, July 21, 1985.
Lawrence Block, "The Carrot and Some Tricks," from *Telling Lies for Fun and Profit* (two articles/columns from *Writer's Digest*), Arbor House; copyright (1981) by Lawrence Block.
Raymond Carver, "Fires," published in a collection of the same title by Capra Press. Copyright © 1983 by Raymond Carver. Reprinted by permission of Raymond Carver.
Anton Chekhov, "On Writing a Short Story," from *The Story and Its Writer*, by Anton Chekhov, translated by Constance Garnett. Reprinted with permission by the Estate of Constance Garnett and Chatto & Windus, The Hogarth Press, London.
Bill Downey, "The Writing Process Vs. the Block," from *Right Brain . . . Write On!*; copyright © 1984. Reprinted by permission of Prentice-Hall, Inc., Englewood Cliffs NJ 07632.
John Gardner, abridged from "The Writer's Training and Education," from *On Becoming a Novelist*, by John Gardner. Copyright © 1983 by the estate of John Gardner. Reprinted by permission of Harper & Row, Publishers, Inc.
Gail Godwin, "A Diarist on Diarists," *Antaeus* Magazine, © 1976, from *First Person Singular, Writers on Their Craft*, edited by Joyce Carol Oates, Ontario Review Press.
Lynn Gray, "Harriet Doerr," from *Fm. Five*, June, 1985.
Caryn James, "The Phenomenon of James Michener," from *The New York Times Book Review*, September 8, 1985.
Michael Larsen, "Introducing: the Literary Agent," from *The Basics of Selling Your Writing*, *Writer's Digest*, 1983.
Arnold Lobel, "A Good Picture Book Should . . ." from *Celebrating Children's Books*, edited by Betsy Hearne and Marilyn Kaye. Copyright © 1981 by the Zena Sutherland Lectureship Fund. By permission of Lothrop, Lee & Shepard Books (A Division of William Morror & Company).
June & William Noble, "Spicing the Story," from *Steal This Plot*. Reprinted with permission of Paul S. Eriksson, Publisher, Middlebury VT.
Shannon OCork, "The Truth, More or Less, As Long As It Makes a Good Story," from *Murder Mystique*. Reprinted with permission of Ann Elmo Agency, Inc. Copyright © 1982 by Shannon OCork.
Marge Piercy, "For the Young Who Want to," from *The Moon is Always Female*; copyright © 1980 by Marge Piercy. Reprinted by permission of Alfred A. Knopf, Inc.
Maxine Rock, "Riches From Research," by Maxine Rock from *The Fiction Writer's Help Book*, Writer's Digest Books; copyright © 1982 by Maxine Rock.
Sharon Rudd, "The Break-in: An Inside Look at a First Fiction Sale," from *Writer's Yearbook 1985*.
John Updike, "The Importance of Fiction," from *Esquire*, August 1985.

# Table of Contents

## To Begin . . .

## WRITING TECHNIQUES

### INSPIRATION

### THE WRITING LIFE

### RESEARCH

### WRITING THE SHORT STORY

# 628 CATEGORY INDEX

# 647 MARKETS INDEX

# To begin . . .

This is a book all about *fiction*. *Fiction Writer's Market* is a reference to assist you in writing better short stories and novels; it's also a market guide to show you how and where to publish them.

The book's message, however, is completely *nonfiction*: Develop your writing talents and hone your skills as part of the long and time-consuming process to publish. And with hard work, proper direction and determination, publishing your writing is indeed possible.

Like a great many nonfiction books today, we'd like to offer you the one-minute miracle to success, or tell you that you can become a famous novelist in 30 days, in the great modern American tradition. Unfortunately, there are no fast formulas or guaranteed roads to success; we'd be leading you down the garden path in that regard. To become an accomplished writer of fiction may take years, perhaps a lifetime. Hemingway described the writer's plight when he said, "A writer is an apprentice in a craft where no one ever becomes a master."

Despite his lofty and perhaps exaggerated definition, Hemingway himself was a master. In fact, few writers can realistically expect to emulate his level of achievement. But you *can* set realistic objectives. Probably as an unpublished writer, or even a writer with a few publishing credits, you're playing it safe. As bestselling novelist Jean M. Auel said of her own career a few years ago when she was starting out, "You don't tell anyone you're writing—in case you fail at it. But there comes a point when you say to yourself, 'I'm serious. I'm going to give this every bit of effort I have.' " That time finally came for Jean Auel; she worked hard; she succeeded.

When you've set your goal and decided to make that effort, you can start with this book. In the sixth edition of *Fiction Writer's Market*, we offer how-to articles from writers with different approaches, suggestions, and points of view on the craft of fiction. This year to complement our other editions, we've assigned articles to be written on subjects you have requested. There is original information on writing horror; the value of writing clubs and organizations; how a literary editor selects short fiction for a little magazine; what an editor from a large commercial publishing house finds in the slush pile; the first-hand experiences in writing and publishing a first novel; and a potpourri of sage writing advice and thoughts by a longtime expert. Twenty-three articles in all by familiar novelists and short story writers. There are also 14 close-up interviews with editors and writers, an agent and a writing conference instructor, who offer help and insight to understand and break into this crazy, confusing publishing business.

In 1986, again at your request, we've added more new listings, designated this year by the dagger (‡) preceding the magazine, publisher, contest or agent—about 350 additional opportunities in the US, Canada and abroad for placing your novel, short story, novella or short story collection. Again we bring you the category index, this time with a new section on agents and their preferences in genres or subjects.

To help you connect with the most appropriate market, we've ranked each listing according to its accessibility for a beginning, established or specialized writer. We've also described the formats of the magazines and books to give you a better idea of the physical appearance and quality of the publication in which your work may appear. In all, a better book, we hope, a blend of art and commerce, with additional and completely updated information.

Let us help you get started—if you haven't already. Like Jean Auel you have to decide to get serious and give your fiction writing every bit of effort you have. That time has come.

*—Jean M. Fredette*

 *It is art that makes life, makes interest, makes importance, for our consideration and application of these things, and I know of no substitute whatever for the force and beauty of its process.*

*—Henry James*

# For the young who want to

## by Marge Piercy

Talent is what they say
you have after the novel
is published and favorably
reviewed. Beforehand what
you have is a tedious
delusion, a hobby like knitting.

Work is what you have done
after the play is produced
and the audience claps.
Before that friends keep asking
when you are planning to go
out and get a job.

Genius is what they know you
had after the third volume
of remarkable poems. Earlier
they accuse you of withdrawing,
ask why you don't have a baby,
call you a bum.

*Marge Piercy has authored eight novels and ten volumes of poetry. Well known and highly acclaimed in both poetry and fiction for her diversity and timeliness in subject and style, Piercy has been a prodigious writer since high school. At present she is at work on a long novel about World War II.*

The reason people want M.F.A.'s,
take workshops with fancy names
when all you can really
learn is a few techinques,
typing instructions and somebody else's mannerisms

is that every artist lacks
a license to hang on the wall
like your optician, your vet
proving you may be a clumsy sadist
whose fillings fall into the stew
but you're certified a dentist.

The real writer is one
who really writes. Talent
is an invention like phlogiston
after the fact of fire.
Work is its own cure. You have to
like it better than being loved.

**"** *Artists are the antennae of the race.*

*—Ezra Pound* **"**

# The importance of fiction

### by John Updike

Well, when the importance of something has to be proclaimed, it can't be all that important. And certainly most of the people in the United States get along without reading fiction, and more and more of the magazines get along without printing it. Even *Esquire*, which used to run short stories as automatically as he-men smoked unfiltered cigarettes, has to whip itself up and cheer itself on to give us a special fiction issue.

The old throwbacks still producing fiction should be grateful, and we are. It's hard to believe that this fragile business ever had any muscle, but it did. In Gutenberg's Gymnasium, Dickens and Balzac worked out on the high rings and the Brontë sisters did back flips in unison on the balance beam and Harriet Beecher Stowe bench-pressed more kilos than Herman Melville, while Flaubert and Mark Twain were just a double blur on the parallel bars and the bourgeoisie in the bleachers went wild. Even in the days of network radio, fiction put hair on Hemingway's chest and gin in Fitzgerald's glass and that far-off starry look in Faulkner's eye, those days when the mules weren't running. But after Hitler's coonskin was nailed to the barn door and the boys came back to make babies and put on gray flannel suits, something went out of fiction. Those good folks who sat around in the kitchen near the wood stove reading about Mr. Tutt and Perry Mason in the *Saturday Evening Post* had slipped out the back door and bought oil burners and television sets, and the aura of the party being over was so pervasive that Norman Mailer tried to be a party all by himself. Saul Bellow kept winning the prizes, but there was something effete and professorial about his appeal, compared with the way Sinclair Lewis and John Steinbeck had reached down and given Main Street a shake, and the way those two-dol-

*John Updike has received most major awards for his prolific literary work—short story and essay collections, volumes of verse, plays, and his 12 well-known and critically acclaimed novels, including the bestselling* Rabbit *trilogy;* The Bech *books and his latest novel,* The Witches of Eastwick. *Updike wrote the article above for* Esquire's *annual summer fiction issue.*

lar books of theirs had stood fading on the sunny windowsills of every small-town piano
teacher's front parlor.

## Dearth mother and beautiful bards

The '60s were when the demise of fiction became something to crow about. Philip
Roth told us that life in America had become so barbaric and bizarre that no fiction could
hold a candle to the grotesque truth. Truman Capote allowed as how he had invented a
new kind of narrative treat, the nonfiction novel, that made the un-non kind as obsolete
as hand-churned ice cream. Tom Wolfe (the younger) let us ineluctably know that his
New Journalism was zippier, grabbier, funnier, wilder, and truer-to-life than any old
wistful bit of fiction published by, say, those tiny giants over at *The New Yorker*. Even in
*The New Yorker*, as the old two-column departments died off and were replaced by learned specialists whose exhaustive poop overflowed the narrow columns like freshly singed
popcorn, there was less space for fiction than there had been in the days of Bob Benchley
or even the days of Nat Benchley. The Revolution had little use of fiction: Fiction was
sublimation, it was Leavis and Trilling, it was graduate school; it was the civilization and
its discontents, it was the lonely crowd. Fiction was how you consoled yourself in the
dark ages before love beads and "Lucy in the Sky With Diamonds." A revolution sings
songs and trashes chain-store windows; it does things in a bunch, and nothing is more an-
tisocial and nontribal than one individual sitting in a quiet room coding make-believe for
another individual to decipher in a quiet room maybe tens of years and thousands of miles
away.

Accordingly, the Revolution left us rock music and co-ed dormitories but not much
in the way of fiction. Who now remembers Marge Piercy's *Dance the Eagle to Sleep* and
Gurney Norman's *Divine Right's Trip*? I do, because I reviewed them. Otherwise, there
were Pynchon and Kesey, who have subsequently tended to imitate the sound of one
hand clapping. The postrevolutionary anticlimax, though, has not lacked for bards, beginning with the beautiful Ann Beattie, who found the right filtered tone to let the lack of
sunshine in, and who, young as she is, has played dearth mother to a vast, fresh bevy of
delicate/tough female talents, such as Bobbie Ann Mason, Laurie Colwin, Elizabeth Tallent, T. Gertler, Andrea Lee, Deborah Eisenberg, to name but a few. The young males
aren't quite so vivid, since having made their entry splash, they tend to sink into full time
extraliterary employment or to sidestroke toward Hollywood, like John Sayles. But even
the most diffident such inventory insults the intelligence and the fundamental wonder of
fiction, its fundamental irresistibility even in an age when the very sidewalks are heated
by television cables. Its fundamental importance, I suppose one has to say.

Fiction is nothing less than the subtlest instrument for self-examination and self-dis-
play that mankind has invented yet. Psychology and Xrays bring up some portentous
shadows, and demographics and stroboscopic photography do some fine breakdowns,
but for the full *parfum* and effluvia of being human, for feathery ambiguity and rank fac-
ticity, for the air and iron, fire and spit of our daily mortal adventure there is nothing like
fiction: It makes sociology look priggish, history problematical, the film media two-di-
mensional, and the *National Enquirer* as silly as last week's cereal box.

## Humility on eternal record

In fiction everything that searchers for the important tend to leave out is left in, and
what they would have in is left out. Stendhal had served devotedly under Napoleon and
was one of the most lucid thinkers in Europe, but what Fabrizio, in *The Charterhouse of
Parma*, makes of Waterloo is sheer confusion, highlighted by a conversation with a *can-
tinière* steering her cartful of brandy through the thick of the battle. For Tolstoy, Napo-

leon was an excuse for the Moscow aristocrats to gossip and to push on with their spiritual searches; for Jane Austen, Napoleon was the reason the English countryside was so sparsely equipped with prospective husbands. Thus a vast historical presence refracts down into little lives that are precious only because they resemble our own. Kutuzov, Tolstoy's splendidly fictionalized version of an actual Russian general, reads French romances while the steppes around him tremble at the approach of the superman, the master strategist, the general of supreme genius. Romances safeguard the importance of our sentiments, our spiritual dignity, amid the uncontrollable large-scale surges that constitute history; the inner lives of the obscure, as Erich Auerbach points out in his *Mimesis*, have been from the New Testament on the peculiar and precious burden of the Western narrative imagination.

The fiction writer is the ombudsman who argues our humble, dubious case in the halls of eternal record. Are defecation, tipsy bar babble, days of accumulating small defeats, and tired, compromised, smelly connubial love part of our existence? Then put them into literature alongside Homer, says *Ulysses*. Has a life been ill-spent in snobbery, inaction, neurasthenia, and homosexual heartache? Then make that life into a verbal cathedral, says *Remembrance of Things Past*. Do pathetic and senseless-seeming murders appear daily in the newspapers? Then show the humble aspirations and good intentions and small missteps that inexorably lead to such ruin, say *Tess of the D' Urbervilles* and *An American Tragedy*. Feeling nervous and as though things don't quite add up? Then write like Virginia Woolf, and give us actuality in its sliding, luminous increments. Feeling worse than nervous, and certain that the world is a mess? Then write like Céline, and wake up the French language. Want a taste of Latin American backcountry blues? Try Graham Greene or Gabriel Garcia Márquez. Want to know what goes on in those tacky developments just beyond the cloverleaf? Let Raymond Carver or Bobbie Ann Mason tell you. Curious about the condo life in the new, homogenized Deep South? Here comes Frederick Barthelme. No soul or locale is too humble to be the site of entertaining and instructive fiction. Indeed, all other things being equal, the rich and glamorous are less fertile ground than the poor and plain, and the dusty corners of the world more interesting than its glittering, already sufficiently publicized centers.

## Fiction's shapely lies

Yet we do not read fiction for information, informative though it can be. Unlike journalism, history, or sociology, fiction does not give us facts snug in their accredited truth, to be accepted and absorbed like pills, for our undoubted good; we *make* fiction true, as we read it. Fiction can poison our minds, as it did those of Madame Bovary and Don Quixote. It extends our world, and any extension is a risk. The self we are left with when we close the book may not be a useful, marketable one. Fiction offers to enlarge our sense of possibilities, of potential freedom, and freedom is dangerous. The bourgeois capitalist world, compared with the medieval hierarchies it supplanted and with the communist hierarchies that would supplant it, *is* a dangerous one, where failure can be absolute and success may be short-lived. The novel and the short story rose with the bourgeoisie, as exercises in democratic feeling and in individual adventure. *Pamela, The Pilgrim's Progress, Robinson Crusoe*—what do they tell us but that our entrepreneurism, on one level or another, may bear fruit? If fiction is in decline, it is because we have lost faith in the capacity of the individual to venture forth and suffer the consequences of his dreams. Myself, I feel that this most flexible and capacious of artistic forms still holds out its immense space to our imaginations, still answers to a hope within us of more adventure. What is important, if not the human individual? And where can individuality be better confronted, appraised, and enjoyed than in fiction's shapely lies?

# Fires

## by Raymond Carver

Influences are forces—circumstances, personalities, irresistible as the tide. I can't talk about books or writers who might have influenced me. That kind of influence, literary influence, is hard for me to pin down with any kind of certainty. It would be as inaccurate for me to say I've been influenced by everything I've read as for me to say I don't think I've been influenced by any writers. For instance, I've long been a fan of Ernest Hemingway's novels and short stories. Yet I think Lawrence Durrell's work is singular and unsurpassed in the language. Of course, I don't write like Durrell. He's certainly no "influence." On occasion it's been said that my writing is "like" Hemingway's writing. But I can't say his writing influenced mine. Hemingway is one of many writers whose work, like Durrell's, I first read and admired when I was in my twenties.

So I don't know about literary influences. But I do have some notions about other kinds of influences. The influences I know something about have pressed on me in ways that were often mysterious at first glance, sometimes stopping just short of the miraculous. But these influences have become clear to me as my work has progressed. These influences were (and they still are) relentless. These were the influences that sent me in this direction, onto this spit of land instead of some other—that one over there on the far side of the lake, for example. But if the main influence on my life and writing has been a negative one, oppressive and often malevolent, as I believe is the case, what am I to make of this?

## Coincidental rightness

Let me begin by saying that I'm writing this at a place called Yaddo, which is just outside Saratoga Springs, New York. It's afternoon, Sunday, early August. Every so often, every 25 minutes or so, I can hear upwards of 30,000 voices joined into a great out-

*Raymond Carver, one of America's greatest contemporary short story writers, is "the chronicler of blue-collar despair," the basis for his three short story collections:* Will You Please Be Quiet Please?, What We Talk About When We Talk About Love, *and* Cathedral. *His recent five-year grant from the American Academy and Institute of Arts and Letters has enabled him to leave his creative writing position at Syracuse University to write fulltime.*

cry. This wonderful clamor comes from the Saratoga racecourse. A famous meet is in progress. I'm writing, but every 25 minutes I can hear the announcer's voice coming over the loudspeaker as he calls the positions of the horses. The roar of the crowd increases. It bursts over the trees, a great and truly thrilling sound, rising until the horses have crossed the finish line. When it's over, I feel spent, as if I too had participated. I can imagine holding pari-mutuel tickets on one of the horses that finished in the money, or even a horse that came close. If it's a photo finish at the wire, I can expect to hear another outburst a minute or two later, after the film has been developed and the official results posted.

For several days now, ever since arriving here and upon first hearing the announcer's voice over the loudspeaker, and the excited roar from the crowd, I've been writing a short story set in El Paso, a city where I lived for a while some time ago. The story has to do with some people who go to a horse race at a track outside El Paso. I don't want to say the story has been waiting to be written. It hasn't, and it would make it sound like something else to say that. But I needed something, in the case of this particular story, to push it out into the open. Then after I arrived here at Yaddo and first heard the crowd, and the announcer's voice over the loudspeaker, certain things came back to me from that other life in El Paso and suggested the story. I remembered that track I went to down there and some things that took place, that might have taken place, that *will* take place—in my story anyway—2,000 miles away from here.

So my story is under way, and there is that aspect of "influences." Of course, every writer is subject to this kind of influence. This is the most common kind of influence—*this* suggests that, *that* suggests something else. It's the kind of influence that is as common to us, and as natural, as rain water.

But before I go on to what I want to talk about, let me give one more example of influence akin to the first. Not so long ago in Syracuse, where I live, I was in the middle of writing a short story when my telephone rang. I answered it. On the other end of the line was the voice of a man who was obviously a black man, someone asking for a party named Nelson. It was a wrong number and I said so and hung up. I went back to my short story. But pretty soon I found myself writing a black character into my story, a somewhat sinister character whose name was Nelson. At that moment the story took a different turn. But happily it was, I see now, and somehow knew at the time, the right turn for the story. When I began to write that story, I could not have prepared for or predicted the necessity for the presence of Nelson in the story. But now, the story finished and about to appear in a national magazine, I see it is right and appropriate and, I believe, esthetically correct, that Nelson be there, and be there with his sinister aspect. Also right for me is that this character found his way into my story with a coincidental rightness I had the good sense to trust.

## Stripped to minimal

I have a poor memory. By this I mean that much that has happened in my life I've forgotten—a blessing for sure—but I have these large periods of time I simply can't account for or bring back, towns and cities I've lived in, names of people, the people themselves. Large blanks. But I can remember some things. Little things—somebody saying something in a particular way; somebody's wild, or low, nervous laughter; a landscape; an expression of sadness or bewilderment on somebody's face; and I can remember some dramatic things—somebody picking up a knife and turning to me in anger; or else hearing my own voice threaten somebody else. Seeing somebody break down a door, or else fall down a flight of stairs. Some of those more dramatic kinds of memories I can recall when it's necessary. But I don't have the kind of memory that can bring entire conversations back to the present, complete with all the gestures and nuances of real speech; nor can I recall the furnishings of any room I've ever spent time in, not to mention my inability to remember the furnishings of an entire household. Or even very many specific things about a race track—except, let's see, a grandstand, betting windows, closed-circuit TV screens, masses of people. Hubbub. I make up the conversations in my stories. I put the furnishings and the physical things surrounding the people into the stories as I need those things. Perhaps this is why it's sometimes been said that my stories are unadorned, stripped down, even "minimalist." But maybe it's nothing more than a working marriage of necessity and convenience that has brought me to writing the kind of stories I do in the way that I do.

None of my stories really *happened*, of course—I'm not writing autobiography—but most of them bear a resemblance, however faint, to certain life occurrences or situations. But when I try to recall the physical surroundings or furnishings bearing on a story situation (what kind of flowers, if any, were present? Did they give off any odor? etc.), I'm often at total loss. So I have to make it up as I go along—what the people in the story say to each other, as well as what they do then, after thus and so was said, and what happens to them next. I make up what they say to each other, though there may be, in the dialogue, some actual phrase, or sentence or two, that I once heard given in a particular context at some time or other. That sentence may even have been my starting point for the story.

## Plenty after 20

When Henry Miller was in his 40s and was writing *Tropic of Cancer*, a book, incidentally, that I like very much, he talks about trying to write in this borrowed room, where at any minute he may have to stop writing because the chair he is sitting on may be taken out from under him. Until fairly recently, this state of affairs persisted in my own life. For as long as I can remember, since I was a teenager, the imminent removal of the chair from under me was a constant concern. For years and years my wife and I met ourselves coming and going as we tried to keep a roof over our heads and put bread and milk on the table. We had no money, no visible, that is to say, marketable skills—nothing that we could do toward earning anything better than a get-by living. And we had no education, though we wanted one very badly. Education, we believed, would open doors for us, help us get jobs so that we could make the kind of life we wanted for ourselves and our children. We had great dreams, my wife and I. We thought we could bow our necks, work very hard, and do all that we had set our hearts to do. But we were mistaken.

I have to say that the greatest single influence on my life, and on my writing, directly and indirectly, has been my two children. They were born before I was 20, and from beginning to end of our habitation under the same roof—some 19 years in all—there wasn't any area of my life where their heavy and often baleful influence didn't reach.

In one of her essays Flannery O'Connor says that not much needs to happen in a writer's life after the writer is 20 years old. Plenty of the stuff that makes fiction has already happened to the writer before that time. More than enough, she says. Enough things to last the writer the rest of his creative life. This is not true for me. Most of what now strikes me as story "material" presented itself to me after I was twenty. I really don't remember much about my life before I became a parent. I really don't feel that anything happened in my life until I was 20 and married, and had the kids. Then things started to happen.

# Washed out

In the mid 1960s I was in a busy laundromat in Iowa City trying to do five or six loads of clothes—kids' clothes, for the most part, but some of our own clothing, of course, my wife's and mine. My wife was working as a waitress for the University Athletic Club that Saturday afternoon. I was doing chores and being responsible for the kids. They were with some other kids that afternoon, a birthday party maybe. Something. But right then I was doing the laundry. I'd already had sharp words with an old harridan over the number of washers I'd had to use. Now I was waiting for the next round with her, or someone else like her. I was nervously keeping an eye on the dryers that were in operation in the crowded laundromat. When and if one of the dryers ever stopped, I planned to rush over to it with my shopping basket of damp clothes. Understand, I'd been hanging around in the laundromat for 30 minutes or so with this basketful of clothes, waiting my chance. I'd already missed out on a couple of dryers—somebody'd gotten there first. I was getting frantic. As I say, I'm not sure where our kids were that afternoon. Maybe I had to pick them up from someplace, and it was getting late, and that contributed to my state of mind. I did know that even if I could get my clothes into a dryer it would still be another hour or more before the clothes would dry, and I could sack them up and go home with them, back to our apartment in married-student housing. Finally a dryer came to a stop. And I was right there when it did. The clothes inside quit tumbling and lay still. In 30 seconds or so, if no one showed up to claim them, I planned to get rid of the clothes and replace them with my own. That's the law of the laundromat. But at that minute a woman came over to the dryer and opened the door. I stood there waiting. This woman put her hand into the machine and took hold of some items of clothing. But they weren't dry enough, she decided. She closed the door and put two more dimes into the machine. In a daze I moved away with my shopping cart and went back to waiting. But I remember thinking at that moment, amid the feelings of helpless frustration that had me close to tears, that nothing—and, brother, I mean nothing—that ever happened to me on this earth could come anywhere close, could possibly be as important to me, could make as much difference, as the fact that I had two children. And that I would always have them and always find myself in this position of unrelieved responsibility and permanent distraction.

I'm talking about real *influence* now. I'm talking about the moon and the tide. But like that it came to me. Like a sharp breeze when the window is thrown open. Up to that point in my life I'd gone along with thinking—what, exactly, I don't know, but that things would work out somehow—that everything in my life I'd hoped for or wanted to do was possible. But at that moment, in the laundromat, I realized that this simply was not true. I realized—what had I been thinking before?—that my life was a small-change thing for the most part, chaotic, and without much light showing through. At that moment I felt—I knew—that the life I was in was vastly different from the lives of the writers I most admired. I understood writers to be people who didn't spend their Saturdays at the laundromat and every waking hour subject to the needs and caprices of their children. Sure, sure there've been plenty of writers who have had far more serious impediments to their work, including imprisonment, blindness, the threat of torture or of death in one form or another. But knowing this was no consolation. At that moment—I swear all this took place there in the laundromat—I could see nothing ahead but years more of this kind of responsibility and perplexity. Things would change some, but they were never really going to get better. I understood this, but could I live with it? At that moment I saw accommodations would have to be made. The sights would have to be lowered, I'd had, I realized later, an insight. But so what? What are insights? They don't help any. They just make things harder.

## Bend or break

For years my wife and I had held to a belief that if we worked hard and tried to do the right things, the right things would happen. It's not such a bad thing to try and build a life on. Hard work, goals, good intentions, loyalty—we believed these were virtues and would someday be rewarded. We dreamed when we had the time for it. But eventually we realized that hard work and dreams were not enough. Somewhere, in Iowa City maybe, or shortly afterward, in Sacramento, the dreams began to go bust.

The time came and went when everything my wife and I held sacred, or considered worthy of respect, every spiritual value, crumbled away. Something terrible had happened to us. It was something that we had never seen occur in any other family. We couldn't fully comprehend what had happened. It was erosion, and we couldn't stop it. Somehow, when we weren't looking, the children had got into the driver's seats. As crazy as it sounds now, they held the reins, and the whip. We simply could not have anticipated anything like what was happening to us.

During these ferocious years of parenting, I usually didn't have the time, or the heart, to think about working on anything lengthy. The circumstances of my life, the "grip and slog" of it, in D.H. Lawrence's phrase, did not permit it. The circumstances of my life with these children dictated something else. They said if I wanted to write anything, and finish it, and if ever I wanted to take satisfaction out of finished work, I was going to have to stick to stories and poems. The short things I could sit down and, with any luck, write quickly and have done with. Very early, long before Iowa City even, I'd understood that I would have a hard time writing a novel, given any anxious inability to focus on anything for a sustained period of time. Looking back on it now, I think I was slowly going nuts with frustration during those ravenous years. Anyway, these circumstances dictated, to the fullest possible extent, the forms my writing could take. God forbid, I'm not complaining now, just giving facts from a heavy and still bewildered heart.

If I'd been able to collect my thoughts and concentrate my energy on a novel, say, I was still in no position to wait for a payoff that, if it came at all, might be several years down the road. I couldn't see the road. I had to sit down and write something I could finish now, tonight, or at least tomorrow night, no later, after I got in from work and before I lost interest. In those days I always worked some crap job or another, and my wife did the same. She waitressed or else was a door-to-door saleswoman. Years later she taught high school. But that was years later. I worked sawmill jobs, janitor jobs, deliveryman jobs, service station jobs, stockroom boy jobs—name it, I did it. One summer, in Arcata, California, I picked tulips, I swear, during the daylight hours to support us; and at night after closing, cleaned the inside of a drive-in restaurant and swept up the parking lot. Once I even considered, for a few minutes anyway—the job application form there in front of me—becoming a bill collector.

In those days I figured if I could squeeze in an hour or two a day for myself, after job and family, that was more than good enough. That was heaven itself. And I felt happy to have that hour. But sometimes, I couldn't get the hour. Then I would look forward to Saturday, though sometimes things happened that knocked Saturday out as well. But there was Sunday to hope for. Sunday, maybe.

I couldn't see myself working on a novel in such a fashion, that is to say, no fashion at all. To write a novel, it seemed to me, a writer should be living in a world that makes sense, a world that the writer can believe in, draw a bead on, and then write about accurately. A world that will, for a time anyway, stay fixed in one place. Along with this there has to be a belief in the essential *correctness* of that world. A belief that the known world has reasons for existing, and is worth writing about—is not likely to go up in smoke in the process. This wasn't the case with the world I knew and was living in. My world was one that seemed to change gears and directions, along with its rules, every day. Time and again I reached the point where I couldn't see or plan any further ahead than the first of next month and gathering together enough money, by hook or by crook, to meet the rent and provide the children's school clothes. This is true.

I wanted to see tangible results for any so-called literary efforts of mine. No chits or promises, no time certificates, please. So I purposely, and by necessity, limited myself to writing things I knew I could finish in one sitting, two sittings at the most. I'm talking of a first draft now. I've always had patience for rewriting. But in those days I happily looked forward to the rewriting, as it took up time which I was glad to have taken up. In one regard I was in no hurry to finish the story or the poem I was working on, for finishing something meant I'd have to find the time, and the belief, to begin something else. So I had great patience with a piece of work after I'd done the initial writing. I'd keep something around the house for what seemed a very long time, fooling with it, changing this, adding that, cutting out something else.

This hit-and-miss way of writing lasted for nearly two decades. There were good times back there, of course; certain grown-up pleasures and satisfactions that only parents have access to. But I'd take poison before I'd go through that time again.

The circumstances of my life are much different now, but now I *choose* to write short stories and poems. Or at least I think I do. Maybe it's all a result of the old writing habits from those days. Maybe I still can't adjust to thinking in terms of having a great swatch of time in which to work on something—anything I want!—and not have to worry about having the chair yanked out from under me, or one of my kids smarting off about why supper isn't ready on demand. But I learned some things along the way. One of these things I learned is that I had to bend or else break. And I also learned that it is possible to bend and break at the same time.

## Common language

I'll say something about two other individuals who exercised influence on my life. One of them, John Gardner, was teaching a beginning fiction-writing course at Chico State College when I signed up for the class in the fall of 1959. My wife and I and the children had just moved down from Yakima, Washington, to a place called Paradise, California, about ten miles up in the foothills outside Chico. We had the promise of low-rent housing and we thought it would be a great adventure to move to California. (In those days, and for a long while after, we were always up for an adventure.) Of course, I'd have to work to earn a living for us, but I also planned to enroll in college as a part-time student.

Gardner was just out of the University of Iowa with a Ph.D. and, I knew, several unpublished novels and short stories. I'd never met anyone who'd written a novel, published or otherwise. On the first day of class he marched us outside and had us sit on the lawn. There were six or seven of us, as I recall. He went around, asking us to name the authors we liked to read. I can't remember any names we mentioned, but they must not have been the right names. He announced that he didn't think any of us had what it took to become real writers—as far as he could see, none of us had the necessary *fire*. But he said he was going to do what he could for us, though it was obvious he didn't expect much to come of it. There was an implication, too, that we were about to set off on a trip, and we'd do well to hold onto our hats.

I remember at another class meeting he said he wasn't going to mention any of the big-circulation magazines except to sneer at them. He'd brought in a stack of "little" magazines, the literary quarterlies, and he told us to read the work in those magazines. He told us that this was where the best fiction in the country was being published, and all of the poetry. He said he was there to tell us which authors to read as well as teach us how to write. He was amazingly arrogant. He gave us a list of the little magazines he thought were worth something, and he went down the list with us and talked a little about each magazine. Of course, none of us had ever heard of these magazines. It was the first I'd known of their existence. I remember him saying during this time, it might been during a conference, that writers were made as well as born. (Is this true? My God, I still don't know. I suppose every writer who teaches creative writing and who takes the job at all seriously has to believe this to some extent. There were apprentice musicians and composers and visual arts—so why not writers?) I was impressionable then, I suppose I still am, but I was terrifically impressed with everything he said and did. He'd take one of my early efforts at a story and go over it with me. I remember him as being very patient, wanting me to understand what he was trying to show me, telling me over and over how important it was to have the right words saying what I wanted them to say. Nothing vague or blurred, no smoked-glass prose. And he kept drumming at me the importance of using—I don't know how else to say it—common language, the language of normal discourse, the language we speak to each other in.

## Grown but not gone

Recently we had dinner together in Ithaca, New York, and I reminded him then of some of the sessions we'd had up in his office. [Gardner died in 1982.] He answered that probably everything he'd told me was wrong. He said, "I've changed my mind about so many things." All I know is that the advice he was handing out in those days was just what I needed at that time. He was a wonderful teacher. It was a great thing to have happen to me at that period of my life, to have someone who took me seriously enough to sit down and go over a manuscript with me. I knew something crucial was happening to me, something that mattered. He helped me to see how important it was to say exactly what I wanted to say and nothing else; not to use "literary" words or "pseudopoetic" language. He'd try to explain to me the difference between saying something like, for example, "wing of a meadowlark" and "meadowlark's wing." There's a different sound and feel, yes? The word "ground" and the word "earth," for instance. Ground is ground, he'd say, it means *ground,* dirt, that kind of stuff. But if you say "earth," that's something else, that word has other ramifications. He taught me to use contractions in my writing. He helped to show me how to say what I wanted to say and to use the minimum number of words in a short story. He made me see that absolutely everything was important in a short story. It was of consequence where the commas and periods went. For this, for that—for his giving me the key to his office so I would have a place to write on the weekends, for his putting up with my brashness and general nonsense—I'll always be grateful. He was an influence.

Ten years later I was still alive, still living with my children, still writing an occasional story or poem. I sent one of the occasional stories to *Esquire* and in so doing hoped to be able to forget about it for a while. But the story came back by return mail, along with a letter from Gordon Lish, at that time the fiction editor for the magazine. He said he was returning the story. He was not apologizing that he was returning it, not returning it "reluctantly"; he was just returning it. But he asked to see others. So I promptly sent him everything I had, and he just as promptly sent everything back. But again a friendly letter accompanied the work I'd sent to him.

At that time, the early 1970s, I was living in Palo Alto with my family. I was in my early 30s and I had my first white-collar job—I was an editor for a textbook publishing firm. We lived in a house that had an old garage out back. The previous tenants had built a playroom in the garage, and I'd go out to this garage every night I could manage after dinner and try to write something. If I couldn't write anything—and this was often the case—I'd just sit in there for a while by myself, thankful to be away from the fracas that always seemed to be raging inside the house. But I was writing a short story that I'd called "The Neighbors." I finally finished the story and sent it off to Lish. A letter came back almost immediately telling me how much he liked it, that he was changing the title to "Neighbors," that he was recommending to the magazine that the story be purchased. It was purchased, it did appear, and nothing, it seemed to me, would ever be the same. *Esquire* soon bought another story, and then another, and so on. James Dickey became poetry editor of the magazine during this time, and he began accepting my poems for publication. In one regard, things had never seemed better. But my kids were in full cry then, like the racetrack crowd I can hear at this moment, and they were eating me alive. My life soon took another veering, a sharp turn, and then it came to a dead stop off on a siding. I couldn't go anywhere, couldn't back up or go forward. It was during this period that Lish collected some of my stories and gave them to McGraw-Hill, who published them. For the time being, I was still off on the siding, unable to move in any direction. If there'd once been a fire, it'd gone out.

Influences. John Gardner and Gordon Lish. They hold irredeemable notes. But my children are it. Theirs is the main influence. They were the prime movers and shapers of my life and my writing. As you can see, I'm still under their influence, though the days are relatively clear now, and the silences are right.

*In every good writer is the willingness to say that unspeakable thing which everyone else in the house is too coy, or too frightened, or too polite to say.*

—*Tobias Wolff*

# A diarist on diarists

## by Gail Godwin

*This inescapable duty to observe oneself: If someone else is observing me, natural-ly I have to observe myself too; if none observes me, I have to observe myself all the closer.*
— Kafka, *November 7, 1921*

*I fall back on this journal just as some other poor devil takes to drink.*
—Barbellion

*I am enamoured of my journal.*

—Sir Walter Scott

Diarists: that shrewdly innocent breed, those secret exhibitionists and incomparable pur-veyors of sequential, self-conscious life. How they fascinate me and endear themselves to me by what they say and do not say. If my friends kept diaries, and if I read them, would I know them as well as I know Kafka, standing in front of his mirror, playing with his hair? And Virginia Woolf, languishing because of a snide remark made about her novels by an undergraduate. And poor Dorothy Wordsworth, trying valiantly to stick to descriptions of sunsets while losing all her teeth. And Pepys, giving a colorful account of his latest fight with his wife. And Camus, coolly observing, "Whatever does not kill me strengthens me." Or plantation owner William Byrd, "dancing his dances" and "ro-gering his wife" (code words for bowel movements and sexual intercourse). Or the anonymous Irish scribe driven to confide into the margin of a medieval text: "I am very cold without fire or covering . . . the robin is singing gloriously, but though its red breast is beautiful I am all alone. Oh God, be gracious to my soul and grant me a better hand-writing."

---

*Gail Godwin is the author of seven novels and one collection of short stories; her two lat-est books are the critically acclaimed* A Mother and Two Daughters *and* The Finishing School. *Godwin's stories and essays have appeared in* Harper's, Esquire, The Atlantic *and many other magazines and anthologies. The selection above was written in 1976.*

In the old days everybody kept diaries. That's how we know that "Carlyle wandered down to tea looking dusky and aggrieved at having to live in such a generation": from Caroline Fox's diary; and that Henry James "kept up a perpetual vocal search for words even when he wasn't saying anything": from his 19-year-old nephew's diary; and that when Liszt played, he compressed his lips, dilated his nostrils and, when the music expressed quiet rapture, "a sweet smile flitted over his features": from George Eliot's diary. People came home from their dinners and visits and wrote down what others said and how the great men looked and who wore what and who made an ass or a pig of himself ("A little swinish at dinner," the diligent Dr. Rutty wrote of himself in his 18th-century diary). Those who stayed home alone also documented their evenings. ("I dined by myself and read an execrably stupid novel called *Tylney Hall*. Why do I read such stuff?" wrote Macaulay.) Even a literate body-snatcher gave an account of himself before he turned in at night: "March 16, 1812, Went to Harps got 3 Large and 1 Large Small & 1 Foetus, took 2 Large to St. Thomas', 1 Large to Guy's."

## Sense of accountability

Are there fewer diarists now? It seems so, to me, but perhaps I'm unusual in that I have not one friend who keeps a diary—or at least who admits to it. Sometimes I'll happen upon a diarist and we greet each other like lonely explorers. Last spring I discovered a fellow diarist over lunch, and what a time we had discussing the intricacies of our venture-in-common, our avocation . . . specialty . . . compulsion? We confessed eccentricities (he has a pseudonymn for the self that gambles; I often reread old journals and make notes to my former selves in the margin). We examined our motives: Why keep these records, year after year? What would happen if we stopped? *Could* we stop? We indulged in shop talk: hardbound or softcover? lined or unlined? about how many pages a night? proportion of external events to internal? Did one write more on bad days than on good? More or less on quiet days? (More, we both decided.) Did we feel honorbound to report in at night, even when exhausted—or intoxicated? Ah, it was a good lunch we had.

"I should live no more than I can record, as one should not have more corn growing than one can get at. There is a waste of good if it be not preserved." This, from Boswell, expresses the aspect of duty that many diarists typically feel. Queen Victoria continued her diary strictly as a duty from the age of thirteen to eighty-two. Unfortunately, much of it reads like it. Many diaries, left by long-forgotten owners in attic trunks, describe neither affairs of state nor the table talk of great geniuses nor the growing pains of profound souls. But a sense of *accountability* emanates from these old books. ("Went with Maud to Chok's for a soda. J.L. lost two heifers from shipping disease . . . nothing of interest to record today.") Man and woman were beholden to the *recording* of God's hours, be they interesting or not.

No mighty deeds, just common things,
The tasks and pleasures each day brings.
And yet I hope that when I look
Over the pages of this book,
Twill be (and, if so, I'm content)
The record of five years well spent

This, from the title page of my mother's college diary, offers captured memory as incentive to daily diligence. *Nulla dies sine linea*, it orders, and my mother obeyed, detailing in tiny handwriting, in a variety of inks, the social and mental highlights of 1932-36. People seemed to go to the movies every day, sometimes twice in one day. They ate a lot of spaghetti—but, of course, there was a Depression. No longer a diarist, my mother offered the little blue and gold book to me (we had to pick the lock—she had no idea it was even hers until we opened it). Her parents had given her the five-year diary as a going-away present for college, and she felt she owed it to them to write in it. I'm glad she did. How many daughters can read—in purple ink—about the night they were conceived?

## Byron, Scott, Woolf, Kafka

Now I'm the only practicing diarist in my family. Not one of my friends keeps a diary, as I've mentioned. "To tell the truth, I've never thought I was that interesting," says one. "I'm not a *writer*," says another. A third writes letters, sometimes three or four every evening, and says this serves the purpose of a diary. Another person who is a very prolific writer has advised me to "put all that material into stories rather than hide it in your journals. When you feel haunted or sad, write a story about a person, not necessarily yourself, who feels haunted or sad. Because, you see, it's the feelings that are universal, not the person."

Art, fiction, if it is to be public, must tap the universal. A diary by its very nature is the unfolding of the private, personal story—whether that story be told from a distance (the "I" in a political diary, observing affairs of state; the "I" in the captain's log, marking latitude, longitude, and the moods of the sea-changes exist inside his own head. I need to write a diary, just as I need to write fiction, but the two needs come from very different sources. I write fiction because I need to organize the clutter of too many details into some meaning, because I enjoy turning something promising into something marvelous; I keep a diary because it keeps my mind fresh and open. Once the details of being me are safely stored away every night, I can get on with what isn't just me. So, as I explained to my friend, the fictional and the diary-making processes are not interchangeable. I had to keep a diary for many years before I could begin writing fiction.

Like Victoria, I, too, began keeping track of my days at the age of thirteen. But it was not because I felt the young queen, whose comings and goings would one day be read by the world. Nor did anyone make me a present of a sumptuous diary with a lock and key that cried out to be made the repository of secrets. I made my first diary, with half-sheets of notebook paper, cardboard, and yarn, and I wrote in it passionately, because I felt there was nobody else like me and I had to know why—or why not. "I don't believe people exist whose inner plight resembles mine; still, it is possible for me to imagine such people—but that the secret raven forever flaps about their head as it does about mine, even to imagine that is impossible." That is Kafka at 38, speaking for me at 13—and for diarists not yet born.

There are many books about diarists, and some of them make fascinating reading. What is odd, however, is that many of the authors do not seem to be diarists themselves: *They* write with the air of scientists, observing this peculiar organism called a "diarist" from the other side of a polished lens. F.A. Spalding states in *Self-Harvest, a Study of Diaries and Diarists* that we seldom if ever find development within the individual diary, either in what is recorded or in the manner of recording it. Also that "diarists who hope to aid memory continue to the end to complain of the lack of it." Also that diaries do not seem to teach diarists "how the better to spend my time for the future," even if they read over their diaries, "and few do so." Spalding also says that, except for Scott and Byron, "there is hardly an example of a diary written out of a first class creative mind." "We cannot imagine a Shakespeare keeping a diary," he says. In fairness to Mr. Spalding, he wrote his book before access to the Kafka diaries was possible—or Virginia Woolf's;

though maybe he wouldn't have considered these writers first class creative minds. As for Shakespeare, that enigma, who can say with certainty whether he did not jot down his moods and plots for plays into a little book that lies crumbling in the earth or awaiting its finder in some forgotten cranny?

## Two lives at once

Every true diarist knows that having a relationship with a diary is like having a relationship with anyone or anything else: the longer it lasts, the more it is bound to change. When I began my diary, at age 13, I traversed that naked space between my mind and my little book's pages as hesitantly as a virgin approaching a man who may or may not prove trustworthy. Now, two-and-a-half decades later, my diary and I have an old marriage. The space between us is gone. I hardly *see* my diary anymore. And yet, there is a confident sense that we are working together. We have been down many roads together, my diary and I (I used the singular, but what I call "my diary" resides in many separate books—some of them lost, others maimed or destroyed [more on this later], and I have been neglectful and insincere and offhand and have not always shown respect in regard to this fellow-traveler of mine. In adolescence, I weighed him down with feelings of gloom and doom; in late teens, I wasted his pages cataloguing the boys who fell into, or eluded, my snare; in my 20s, I drove him to near death-from-boredom with my lists of resolutions, budgets, and abortive plans for "the future." Sometimes I shunned the sight of him, and I wrote my secrets on sheets of loose paper—not wanting to be bound by him—and, of course, those pages are now lost. In my 30s, as my craft of fiction was consolidated and I felt I had "something of my own," I returned to him with new respect. I told him when good things happened, and shared ideas for future work. As I became less trapped in my universe of moods and recognized my likeness to other people and other things in the universe-at-large, my entries began to include more space. Now there are animals and flowers and sunsets in my diary, as well as other people's problems. As a rule, I complain less and describe more; even my complaints I try to lace with memorable description, because . . . yes, Mr. Spalding, diarists do reread their diaries, and how many times I have exclaimed aloud with rage when I looked up a year or a day, hoping to catch the fever or the flavor of the past, and found only a meager, grudging, "I feel awful today." So now I write for my future self, as well as my present mood. And sometimes, to set the record straight, I jot down a word or two in old diaries to my former self—to encourage, to scold, to correct, or to set things in perspective.

As for memory, I don't complain of the lack of it or use my diary to improve it, as Mr. S. would have me do. It is rather that I know one of us has it—my diary or me—and so, if I can't remember something, I look it up. (Though, as I've said, sometimes nothing's there except a mood nobody wants anymore.) Yet, though I frequently look things up, or sometimes browse through a year, I have never read my diaries straight through, and possibly never will. I have tried, a couple of times, but there are simply too many of them, and, after a while, I get the peculiar dizziness that comes from watching a moving train while on another moving train. One cannot live two lives at once, for long periods of time.

## The unedited self

Early, or late, there comes a time in every diarist's life when he asks himself: "What if someone should read this?" If he truly recoils at the thought, he might take measures to prevent it, writing in cipher like Pepys, or in mirror-writing (da Vinci's notebooks) or in a mixture of foreign languages. One century schoolmaster wrote his diary in a notebook so small as to be illegible without a magnifying glass, the whole in abbreviated Latin. (The diary was four inches by two and a half inches; and there were 70 lines to the page!)

But far, far more prevalent, I think, is the breed of diarist who writes for *some* form of audience. This audience may be God, it may be a friendly (or unfriendly) spirit (witness the way some diarists must justify their self-contradictions and shortcomings); or it may be one's future self (at 38, Virginia Woolf wrote in her journal that she was hoping to entertain herself at 50) or . . . in many cases, more often than we may care to admit . . . we write for some form of posterity. How many diarists can honestly say they have never once imagined their diaries being "discovered," either before or after their deaths? Many of us hope we will make good reading. (I occasionally catch myself "explaining," in my diary: putting in that extra bit of information that I know quite well but cannot expect a stranger to know.)

In *The Golden Notebook* Doris Lessing writes about a pair of lovers, each of whom keeps two diaries. It is understood tacitly between them that one diary must be "secretly read" but the second diary, the really private one, may not. Of course, one of the partners cheats and the couple is sundered forever because of this unpardonable breach. I know perfectly well that if I had a partner who kept a diary (or two diaries) I would probably cheat. Several times over my diary-keeping years, people have read my journals. Some sneaked and were caught (perhaps others sneaked and were not); a few let me know about it, in a variety of ways. One left a cheerful note: "Enjoy the halcyon days!" Another tore out a handful of pages. Another tossed the whole book into the Atlantic Ocean. On several occasions I have actually read parts of my diary aloud to someone. But too much "publicity" is destructive to a diary, because the diarist begins, unconsciously perhaps, to leave out, to tone down, to pep up, to falsify experience, and the *raison d'être* of the undertaking becomes buried beneath the posings.

The prospect of people reading my diaries after I am dead does not disturb me in the least. I like to think of pooling myself with other introspective hearts: madmen (and women), prudes, profligates, celebrities, outcasts, heroes, artists, saints, the lovelorn and the lucky, the foolish and the proud. I have found so many sides of myself in the diaries of others. I would like it if I someday reflect future readers to themselves, provide them with examples, warnings, courage, amusement even. In these unedited glimpses of the self in others, of others in the self, is another proof of our ongoing survival, another of the convenants eternity makes with the day-to-day.

*My whole interest is in the act of writing itself.*

—*John Fowles*

# The writer's training and education

### by John Gardner

One of the most common questions asked by young writers is whether or not they should study creative writing and literature in college or graduate school. If the writer means only: "Will these courses help me become a better writer?" the answer is generally, Yes. If he or she means: "Will they improve my chances of supporting myself, for instance by getting a Master of Fine Arts degree and then getting a job teaching writing in college?" the answer is, Possibly. The world has far more writing teachers than it needs, and as a rule it is publication, not the MFA degree, that impresses employers, though an MA or MFA from a good school may help.

It's common for students to think of their college and/or grad school education in practical terms, as preparation for making a living. In many fields it is reasonable to think in this way, but not in the arts. European and English writers receive a good deal of support from the state, but in America, though federal, state, and local governments make feeble gestures of support (the whole National Endowment for the Arts comes to, I think, the cost of one frigate), it seems clear that nobody quite knows what to do with artists. In former times, when artists were church- or patron-supported, things were simple. Not now. Today, true, serious artists in all fields (music, visual arts, literature) are something like an alternative culture, a group set apart from all other groups, from theology to professional pornography. They sacrifice the ordinary TV-watching pleasures of their society to pursue an ideal not especially valued by the society, and if they are lucky, they bring the society around, becoming culture heroes, but even the successful pay dearly. Both in the world of grants and in the marketplace, the novelist probably has a better chance than any other artist—certainly a better chance than the serious actor, poet, or

*John Gardner, a devoted teacher of writing for much of his life, wrote* On Becoming a Novelist *and* The Art of Fiction, *in which he maintained that writers are not born but self-made—with training. Gardner also authored ten volumes of criticism, five books for children, two works of poetry, two collections of short stories and eight novels before his untimely death in 1982.*

composer. But very few novelists can support themselves by their writing. The study of writing, like the study of classical piano, is not practical but aristocratic. If one is born rich, one can easily afford to be an artist; if not, one has to afford one's art by sacrifice. On this, more later.

## Community support

Let us turn to the benefits and dangers of going through a creative writing program and of studying literature in college.

It is true that most writers' workshops have faults; nevertheless, a relatively good writers' workshop can be beneficial. For one thing, workshops bring together groups of young writers who, even in the absence of superb teachers, can be of help to one another. Being with a group of serious writers at one's own stage of development makes the young writer feel less a freak than he might otherwise, and talking with other writers, looking at their work, listening to their comments, can abbreviate the apprenticeship process. It cannot be too strongly emphasized that, after the beginning stages, a writer needs social and psychological support.

When a writer first begins to write, he or she feels the same first thrill of achievement that the young gambler or oboe player feels: Winning a little, losing some, the gambler sees the glorious possibilities, exactly as the young oboist feels an indescribable thrill when he gets a few phrases to sound like real music, phrases implying an infinite possibility for satisfaction and self-expression. As long as the gambler or oboist is only playing at being a gambler or oboist, everything seems possible. But when the day comes that he sets his mind on becoming a professional, suddenly he realizes how much there is to learn, how little he knows.

The young writer leaves the undergraduate college, where everyone agrees he is one of the best writers there, and he goes to, say, the Iowa Writers' Workshop, or Stanford, Columbia, or Binghamton. There he finds nearly every one of his classmates was a writing star at his or her college; he finds famous teachers who read his work and seem largely unimpressed; and suddenly the young writer's feelings are mainly alarm and disappointment. Why did his undergraduate teachers so mislead him? he wonders. I'm not sure myself why undergraduate reputations are inflated even by good teachers with high standards; perhaps because outside the specialized, nationally known writers' workshops one encounters relatively few young writers of real promise; or perhaps because at this early stage of a writer's work, the teacher believes that encouragement and praise seem more beneficial than a rigorous assessment of the writer's skill.

In any event, the writer adjusts (or else he gives up). He accepts the truth that he is not as great as his teachers and classmates imagined. He recognizes that the success he hopes for will take work. What a writer in this gloomy situation needs above all is a community that values what he values, a community that believes, rightly or wrongly, that it is better to be a good writer than to be a good executive, politician, or scientist. Good writers are after all intelligent people. They *could* have been executives, politicians, or scientists. They might not like or want such jobs, but they could do them, and in some ways any of those jobs might be easier. What keeps the young writer with the potential for success from turning aside to some more generally approved, perhaps easier path is the writing community.

## Writer talk

No doubt the truth is that as often as not the writing community saves the writer by its folly. It is partly made up of fools: Young innocents who've not yet had the experience of valuing anything other than writing, and maniacs who, having considered other things, think writing the only truly valuable thing the human mind can do. It is partly made up of born writers: People who value other human activities but have no wish to do anything but write. (Asked why she wrote fiction, Flannery O'Connor once said, "Because I'm good at it.") Some members of every writing community are there because they're snobs: Writing, or just being around writers, makes them feel superior; others are there because they think being a writer (though they may not have much talent) is romantic. Whatever their reasons or reasonings, these various contingents form, together, a group that helps the young writer forget his doubts. However good or bad the writing teacher, the young writer can count on close attention from all these kinds of people, not to mention a few chemists who enjoy going to readings. The young writer writes, feels uncertain about his work, and gets praise or, at very least, constructive criticism—or even destructive criticism, but from people who appear to care as much about writing as he does himself.

It's the same in all fields, of course. A young businessman in a society of people who can see only wickedness in business cannot easily remain a young businessman. We're social animals. Few born and bred Republicans remain Republicans in a context where everyone they know and respect is a Democrat. I've said that stubbornness is important for writers. But stubbornness can carry one only so far. If you grow up in a happy family and move to a community of pessimists—for example, if you grow up on a fortunate and peaceful farm in Indiana and move to New York City—you can stubbornly hold out, but only because you have, in your memory, something real to hold out for. (The same is true in reverse. Born and bred in Manhattan, you cannot easily shift to the less cynical attitudes of rural Ohio.) I don't mean to slight the complications. You may be by nature a pessimist, even though born to a happy family in Indiana. But in hostile circumstances—that is, in the exclusive company of optimists—you cannot easily make art of your pessimism, you can only be odd and miserable.

So the first value of a writers' workshop is that it makes the young writer feel not only not abnormal but virtuous. In a writer's community, nearly all the talk is about writing. Even if you don't agree with most of what is said, you come to take for granted that no other talk is quite so important. Talk about writing, even in a mediocre community of writers, is exciting. It makes you forget that by your own standards, whatever they may be, you're not very good yet. It fills you with nervous energy, makes you want to leave the party and go home and write. And it's the sheer act of writing, more than anything else, that makes a writer.

## The right teacher

On the other hand, the writer who avoids writers' workshops (or some other solid community of writers) is probably in for trouble. One can be fooled by the legend of, say, Jack London, and imagine that the best way to become a writer is to be a seaman or lumberjack. Jack London lived in an age when writers were folk heroes, as they are not now, and an age when technique was not quite as important as it is now. Though a tragic and noble man, he was a relatively bad writer. He could have used a few good teachers. Hemingway once remarked that "the best way to become a writer is to go off and write." But his own way of doing it was to go to Paris, where many of the great writers were, and to study with the greatest theorist of the time, and one of the shrewdest writers, Gertrude Stein. Joseph Conrad, though we tend to think of him as a solitary genius, worked in close community with Ford Madox Ford, H. G. Wells, Henry James and Stephen Crane, among others. Melville had Hawthorne and his circle. Great writers are almost always associated with a literary dynasty. It's hard to find an exception. (Incredibly, even Malcolm Lowry was part of a group.) So for psychological reasons, if for no other, even a bad workshop may be better than none.

If a bad writers' workshop is worth attending, a good one is more so. If I could, I would tell you what the good workshops are. Iowa, being the oldest and best known, always attracts good students and sometimes has fine teachers. Binghamton has a good program in fiction, which is why I teach there. I've already mentioned others I consider dependable—Columbia and Stanford; and the list might easily be expanded. But it's hard to give sure advice. For one thing, workshops change from year to year, as skillful writing teachers come and go, and for another, what makes a good workshop for one writer may be a disaster for another. I myself am not very interested in so-called experimental writing, though I do it sometimes and have occasionally been moved or delighted by works of fiction by William Gass (who does not normally teach writing) or Max Apple (with whom one can study at Rice). When I find I have in one of my writing classes a student who has no interest in the more or less traditional kind of fiction I favor, I know that both the student and I are in trouble. Much as I want to help him, I am the wrong kind of doctor. On the other hand, John Barth, who heads the writing program at Johns Hopkins and has gathered around him an interesting group of writers who, like himself, favor the new and strange, can have a crippling effect on the young realist. What all this suggests, of course, is that the student should select his writing program on the basis of its teachers, hunting out those whose interests seem closest to his own.

One of the things that make a good writers' workshop beneficial is that it has at least one or two brilliant students (also five or six solid, sensible ones, and then several who are either pretentious or ploddingly conventional). Even in the best writers' workshop one is likely to learn more from one's fellow students than from one's teachers. A workshop perceived to be better than most attracts good students, and because they are at the apprentice stage, these people can be counted on for careful scrutiny of one's work, for encouragement, and useful criticism. Teachers in the well-known workshops may or may not prove helpful. They tend to hire the more famous writers, but not all famous writers are good teachers. Moreover, the main commitment of famous writers is, as a rule, to their own work. However deeply they may care about their students, their main business is to work on a form that takes a great deal of time. Often their solution is to concentrate on the very best of their students and give the rest short shrift. There is no doubt, I think, that good teachers can be helpful to the young writer; but in practice it turns out that the student either encounters good writers who teach on the side and do not work as hard as they might at it, or good teachers who are not very good writers, so that what they teach is partly wrong, or good writers who cannot teach at all.

## Technically correct

Whatever the quality of their teaching, famous writers do a good deal for writing programs. Perhaps the chief value of the famous writer is his presence, his contribution as a role model. Just by being around him day after day, the young writer learns how the famous man reads, and what he reads; how he perceives the world; how he relates to others and to his profession; even how he schedules his life. The famous writer's presence is vivid proof that the young writer's goal is not necessarily unreasonable. If the student is extraordinarily lucky, the famous writer may also be a good teacher: He not only knows what real art is but can explain it.

I must add that at some of the creative writing programs where I've visited or taught I've found excellent teachers who are not creative writers at all, really, though they may have published a story or two, or one novel years ago, or several mediocre novels. Some people can catch mistakes in student writing that they cannot see in their own, and some writers who have excellent minds write, by some quirk of personality, books unworthy of them. Sometimes the excellent writing teacher is a critic rather than a fiction writer;

sometimes he is a person without literary credentials, perhaps a freshman English teacher who, drafted to teach a low-level creative writing course, has proved to have a gift for it. How to find such teachers only luck or the grapevine can tell you. One can ask writers one admires where they would go if they were just starting out; or one can simply set out for a generally respected university and hope. The odds are good that one will find, in any major university, someone who can help.

One of the oddities of creative writing courses is that there exists no standard theory on how to teach creative writing. Many people ask—even some creative writing teachers—"Can writing really be taught?" No one asks that about painting or musical composition. Writing has been identified so strongly with "genius" or inspiration" that people have tended to assume that the art cannot be passed on by such methods as the other arts have used. That perception may be partly right; the writing of fiction may be a less specific, detectable skill than painting or musicianship.

In any case, within the past 20 or 30 years, with the rise of creative writing programs in the United States, a pedagogy for the art has begun to develop, and with every passing year the general level of teaching improves. There are those who deplore this fact, claiming it as the main reason for the dreary sameness of so much of our fiction and poetry; and no doubt there is something to be said for that view. But at least at the technical level, it seems to me, fiction has never been better off. Probably the truth is that in any age there are only so many writers of genius, and teaching a writer not to make mistakes—teaching him to avoid those forms of vagueness or clumsiness that impair the vivid and continuous dream—cannot make him a more interesting or original person than he is. Perhaps the one great danger that the student in a good creative writing course ought to guard against is the tendency of good technical theory to undermine individuality and the willingness to take risks.

## Constructive criticism

A bad workshop in creative writing has one or more regular features. If the student notices several of them in the workshop he has chosen, he should drop the course.

In a bad workshop, the teacher allows or even encourages attack. It is common in writers' workshops for the student to read a story (usually one he's gone over beforehand with the teacher), then get comments from his teacher and classmates. In a good workshop, the teacher establishes a general atmosphere of helpfulness rather than competitivenss or viciousness. Classmates of the writer whose work has been read do not begin, if the workshop is well run, by stating how *they* would have written the story, or expressing their blind prejudices on what is or is not seemly; in other words, they do not begin by making up some different story or demanding a different style. They try to understand and appreciate the story that has been written. They assume, even if they secretly doubt it, that the story was carefully and intelligently constructed and that its oddities have some justification. If they cannot understand why the story is as it is, they ask questions. A common fault poor teachers inculcate in students is the habit of too quickly deciding that what they have failed to understand makes no sense. It takes confidence and good will to say, "I didn't understand so-and-so," rather than, belligerently, "So-and-so makes no sense." It is the nature of stupid people to hide their perplexity and attack what they cannot grasp. The wise admit their puzzlement (no prizes are given in heaven for fake infallibility), and when the problem material is explained they either laugh at themselves for failing to see it or they explain why they couldn't reasonably be expected to understand, thus enabling the author to see why he didn't get his point across.

Good workshop criticism, in other words, is like good criticism anywhere. When we read what is generally acknowledged to be a great work of art, we try to understand, if we have sense, why intelligent people, including the writer, have thought the work esthetically satisfying. In a good fiction workshop one recognizes that even if a work seems bad at first glance, the writer sat writing and thinking about it for a fair amount of time and deserves a generous response. It is true, of course, that some of the fiction one hears read in a workshop is bad, and often there is no real question about its badness. The story is patently melodramatic, vague, pretentious, inadequately thought out, overloaded with detail, sentimental, uninterestingly vulgar. I myself think really bad fiction should never reach a reading in the workshop; it cannot teach much or sharpen students' critical skills, and it is likely to embarrass the writer. If bad fiction does reach the workshop, it should be dealt with quickly and politely, its mistakes made clear so that neither that writer nor any other in the workshop is inclined to repeat them, and its virtues acknowledged. But in most fiction that reaches workshop reading, the badness is not so obvious. The business of the teacher and the writer's classmates is to figure out (or if necessary ask) the purpose and meaning of the piece and only then to suggest carefully, thoughtfully, why the purpose and meaning did not come through.

A writer does not become better by being scorned. It is helpful if a class, as it listens to a writer's story, makes careful notes of apparent mistakes or weaknesses and read them to the writer after the story has been read, but it is helpful only if the class generally understands that anyone's work could have similar shortcomings. If a class regularly attacks its members, and the teacher allows it, the course is counterproductive. The only final value of class criticism is that it teaches each member of the class to criticize and evaluate his own work and appreciate good fiction different from his own. Often class criticism can show the writer that he has at some specific point written misleadingly or has failed to evoke some important element of a scene—mistakes the writer could not catch himself because, knowing what he intended, he thinks his sentences say more than they do. He may imagine, for instance, that the bulge in his female character's coat clearly indicates that she is carrying a gun, whereas a listener not privy to the writer's mental image may imagine that the woman is pregnant. Seeing the effects of his mistakes makes the writer more careful, more wary of the trickery words are capable of. Or again, class criticism may make a writer aware of his unconscious prejudices, for instance his notion that fat people are easygoing, or that all hellfire fundamentalists are mean, or that all homosexuals try to seduce boys. The wide range of opinion a class affords increases the writer's chance of getting a fair hearing—especially the writer whose style, goals, and attitudes differ radically from his teacher's—and the focus of the whole class on the writer's work increases the odds that most of his mistakes or ineffective strategies will be noticed. At its best, class criticism can help everyone involved, as long as that criticism is basically generous. Vicious criticism leads to writer's block, both in the victim and in the attacker.

## Basics and values

In a bad workshop, the teacher coerces his students into writng as he himself writes. The tendency is natural, though not excusable. The teacher has worked for years to figure out his style and has persistently rejected alternatives. The result is that if he is not careful he is likely to be resistant to writing markedly unlike his own or, worse, written in a style opposed to his own, as in the case of the elegant stylist confronting a rough, demotic prose. The teacher's purpose ought to be to help students find their *own* way. This is the point teacher and poet Dave Smith is making when he says, "My object is to catch right now what will embarrass my students when they look at their poetry ten years from now." His object, in other words, is not to impose some strictly personal standard but to notice, within the implicit laws of the student poet's standards, what will not stand up in time. The poetry teacher who by force turns a light, anapestic, lyrical poet into an ode writer in stern Anglo-Saxon rhythms, the fiction teacher unwilling to tolerate experimental writing of a kind he himself hates to read—the teacher who consciously or unconsciously seeks to make fundamental changes in his student's personality—is, at least for that student, an inadequate if not a destructive teacher.

In another kind of bad workshop, there are no standards of goodness. I mentioned earlier one common set of standards for good fiction—creation of a vivid and continuous dream, authorial generosity, intellectual and emotional significance, elegance and efficiency, and strangeness. Another teacher of writing may have other esthetic values—though I hope most teachers would admit the general validity of these. If the teacher has no basic standards, his class is likely to develop none, and their comments can only be matters of preference or opinion. Writers will have nothing to strive toward or resist, nothing solid to judge by. As I've said, undue rigidity can be destructive; but even a rigid set of standards, if it's clear and at least more or less valid, can be useful in giving the student something to challenge. An individual style is developed as much by resistance as by emulation. Students of a teacher who refuses to set standards are in danger of falling into the philistine persuasion that all literary success is luck or public whim. In that class, the student who writes an excellent story about fishermen and dolphins will be open to the objection that some particular classmate hates all stories of the sea. This is not to say that standards cannot change, adapting themselves to new successes. The moment I propound my principles, I can count on it that some clever student will consciously, perhaps even brilliantly, defy them. In that case, as a serious teacher I must determine without guiding rules—nothing but my honest thought and emotions—whether or not the story works, that is, interests me and moves me. The workshop teacher who has no basic theory, no set of esthetic values conscientiously worked out, is probably doomed to mediocrity, as is his class. There is in the end no substitute for a critical understanding of fiction—which is not to claim that fiction is philosophy.

## Close analysis

No experienced teacher underestimates how hard it is to see a student's work in its own terms. Since I generally teach fairly advanced courses, mainly graduate school level, I've often seen student work I thought to be quite bad and then later learned that the same piece was singled out for praise or even publication by other teacher-writers I respect. Recently I was given a story (a work sample on the basis of which I was to decide whether or not the student should be admitted to my course) that had been praised by two earlier writing teachers, both of them firmly established writers reputed to be good teachers. I did admit the student; the energy and vividness of the work were undeniable. But I thought the story execrable. It was a first-person story told inside the head of a madman, a tour de force of violence and scatology, seething with malice, frighteningly cynical, ending in the same place it began. It did none of the things I think art ought to do, except that it was vivid and (in a nasty, discomforting way) interesting. And the sentences were carefully made. When I said, with restraint, that I did not like the story very much, the student sighed and confessed that he didn't like it, either. Some of the verbs were too low-key, he said, and when he tried to put in more lively verbs they seemed to call undue attention to themselves. At this point, of course, I saw that I hadn't been thinking well. The student really was a gifted writer, fully conscious of what he was doing, earnestly looking for help from a teacher whose standards are about as applicable to his project as the rules of pinochle or the gladiator's oath.

. One forgets the extent to which esthetic standards are projections of one's own personality, defensive armor, or wishful thinking about the world. If there are objective laws of esthetics, not all of them apply in every instance, and none of them finally have to do with purpose. One can argue, as I've done elsewhere, that—descriptively speaking—the fiction that lasts tends to be "moral," that is, it works with a minimum of cynical manipulation and it tends to reach affirmations favorable rather than opposed to life. One can argue on this basis that a writer is generally unwise to fake despair and nihilism he does not really feel. One cannot argue that the writer's purpose should be the creation of moral fiction, or any other kind; one cannot even argue that his purpose should be to create something beautiful or pleasing or even honest or universally interesting. A given writer may wish to set such standards for his students; but insofar as he means to be a teacher, he must leave room for intelligent rebellion.

In a bad workshop, the teacher takes the place of the student's critical imagination. This is the one great danger in a workshop where the teacher is not only an impressive writer but also a skillful and articulate teacher, one who can figure out narrative or stylistic problems, solve them, and make his mental processes clear to students. This fully articulate teaching implies, of course, a close teacher-student relationship—not just one in which the teacher jots an occasional comment on the student's writing but rather one in which the teacher goes over each of the student's works with meticulous care, missing neither the virtues of the piece nor the defects. How it is that the best teacher's help and concern can impede the student's progress—how the virtue of showing students ways of evaluating and correcting their fiction can press over into the defect of making student minds clones of the teacher's—is a matter both teacher and student need to become sensitive to.

The best kind of writing teacher, it seems to me, not only meets his regular workshop classes but deals with each student individually, half an hour or an hour each week or so, in tutorial sessions, like a violin instructor. The teacher closely analyzes the student's work and shows him, not on the basis of the teacher's own personal preferences but in terms of the inherent logic of the student's fiction, what is right and wrong and what needs to be done. This is not a matter of opinion or individual feeling. In any true story, certain things have to be shown dramatically, others can be summarized or implied. In general the rule is simply this: Anything necessary to the action's development must be shown dramatically. For instance, if a man is to beat his dog, it is not enough for the writer to *tell* us that the man is inclined to violence or that the dog annoys him: We must see how and why the man inclines to violence, and we must see the dog annoying him. For young writers it is sometimes hard to recognize what has to be dramatized or how it can be done. And here the problem arises.

## Ground for judgment

Nothing is easier than to give the student specific actions, even specific sentences, that will solve his story's problems; and at a certain point in the young writer's development it may perhaps be valuable to do such things, so that the student can get the hang of it. But basically, what teachers need to teach students is not how to fix a particular story but how to figure out what is wrong with the story and how to think about alternative ways of fixing it. At the Bread Loaf Writers' Conference I've frequently worked with writing assistants—young writers with successful first novels—whose inexperience as teachers led them to focus on finding the best solution to problems in the writing placed in their care, led them, in other words, to show the student writer what to do to make his fiction work. In case after case, when I myself looked at the student's work later, I felt there were a number of possible solutions to the problems—alternative solutions whose relative value must depend on the student writer's preference—and that in suggesting only one solution, the one he himself would choose, my assistant had done an unwitting disservice to the student. What the beginner needs to learn is how to think like a novelist. What he does not need is a teacher who imposes his own solution, like an algebra teacher who tells you the answer without showing how he got there, because it is *process* that the young writer must learn: Problems in novels, unlike problems in algebra, may have any number of solutions. At some point—the sooner the better, some would say—the teacher's job is simply to say so, "Not good enough," and vanish.

Finally, a bad fiction workshop is "workshoppy." It tends to emphasize theme and design over feeling and authentic narrative. Working too much with too many young writers, or having no teaching talent in the first place, the teacher may slide into simplifying his work by forcing original ideas into what all good editors immediately recognize as workshop formulas. The evil is perhaps most easily described in the case of poetry: Rather than helping the student poet to feel out the natural development of his poem, the writing teacher may rest on some simpleminded habit of design—for instance, the notion of "orchestration," the idea that the end of a poem should somehow bring back, like a musical comedy, all its main ideas and images in a final stanza. The same mistake is possible in fiction. Beware of the teacher who cries, "Reprise! Reprise!" The reader who encounters a reprise ending—if he's not very good at reading poetry or fiction—feels a superficial thrill of recognition. The more experience he gets, the more annoyed he is by such foolishness.

A story may be "workshoppy" because the writer (or the teacher) has too often thought from the literature student's point of view rather than from the writer's, so that instead of working like a storyteller, beginning with what happens and why, and only gradually moving (in his thought process if not in the actual writing) to the larger issues (how this story is in some way every human story, an expression of a constant or universal theme), the student writer begins with theme, symbolism, etc., in effect working backward from his imagined New Criticism analysis of a story not yet in existence. One can quickly spot this tendency in a workshop. Class discussion of a story begins in the wrong place, not with the immediate virtues of good fiction (an interesting and original but not distracting style, a clear and well-designed plot, vivid characterization and setting, an interesting and expressive use of a particular genre) but with the kinds of things normally central to a class in literature (theme and symbol). It is of course true that in a given story these less immediate matters may be the appropriate starting point; indeed, one mark of the first-rate writing teacher is his ability to move discussion swiftly to what happens to the most important ground for judgment of the story at hand.

## The novel approach

Another reason workshops become "workshoppy" is that often teachers slide unconsciously into overprizing the kind of narrative writing that teaches well, undervaluing and even dismissing work that does not. This sometimes gives an advantage to, for instance, the symbolic or allegorical story over the straightforward, well-crafted realistic story, and to almost any short story over the more sprawling prose of a novel-in-progress. For the teacher, a well-made allegorical story is a delight, a puzzle he and the class can, if they wish, play with for hours. In the fiction workshop I am teaching this semester I encountered a story entitled "Jason." Early in the story, a child, Jason loses one shoe; much later in the story, we come to a huge old Vermont inn, many-storied and circular, whose hallways wrap around like the coils of a snake (the idea is better expressed in the original). The story is told so cunningly, with such realistic detail, that only one member of this well-read graduate class caught on to the writer's use of the Jason and the Medea myth. Once the secret was out, the class pounced on one allusion after another, and after that members of the class delighted in turning over, with subtlety almost equal to the writer's, the story's deconstructionist (or revisionist) tricks. I think no one who attended the class or has read the story would deny that it's an interesting and effective piece. But the point is, the first chapter of Tolstoy's *Anna Karenina* probably could not have stirred such lively discussion.

Short fiction in the symbolic or allegorical mode can no more compete in the arena of well-constructed full-length novels than a batamweight can hope to compete in the ring with a skillful heavyweight. (It goes without saying that each has its/his place.) But in the writers' workshop the heavyweight may not fare well. For practical reasons (the fact that young novelists try out their wings on the short story, for one thing), most creative writing workshops are oriented toward short fiction. For the young novelist, this can be troublesome. His talent may go unnoticed: His marathon-runner pace does not stir the same interest as the story writer's sprinter's pace; and the kinds of mistakes workshops focus on are not as important in a novel as in a short story. Poets and short story writers must learn to work with the care of a miniaturist in the visual arts. Novelists can afford to stand back now and then and throw paint at the wall. Granted, they must throw well; but there can be no comparison between the skillful paint thrower and the Japanese master who touches his brush to the surface between heartbeats. Sometimes it happens that the young novelist distorts his art in an attempt to compete with the short story writers in his class. He tries to make every chapter zing, tries dense symbolism and staggeringly rich prose; he violates the novelistic pace.

Ideally, he belongs in a novel-writing workshop. The young novelist is as different from the young short story writer as the young short story writer is from the poet. The esthetic problems he must work out are different from those that confront the story writer, and the novelist's whole character and way of working are different. (Granted, some people write both good novels and good short stories. I am speaking of extreme examples of the two types of writer.)

## Happy to be there

In the last novel workshop I gave I had ten students. I asked that they work up a novel outline, which we would go over in class, and then that they present me, each week after that, with a new chapter and also a revision of the former chapter (revised in the light of conference discussion of it). I didn't believe anyone could really hold to this schedule; I presented it only as an ideal to work toward, pointing out that the farther they were able to get on their novels, the more I would be able to show them about episode rhythm, overall construction, and so on. All but one of the students kept to the schedule. The exception, a town woman with a fulltime job, was hospitalized as a result of overwork. I pushed these students no harder than I push students in other workshops. (In fact, I hardly push at all. If the student doesn't feel like writing, I don't have to read his work.) The novelists pushed themselves, as novelists characteristically do. The true young novelist has the stamina, patience, and single-mindedness of a draft horse. Those novel-workshop students who were involved with other college courses that semester dropped those other courses. Of the ten students in the course, eight later published their novels.

Students like these have no very comfortable place in the elegant, leisurely world of poets and short story writers. In the usual creative writing course, the potentially fine young novelists may even look rather dull. One of the best young novelists I ever taught, now a successful writer, got bad grades in high school and entered college (as a rugby player) with one of the lowest verbal aptitude scores on record at that university. His grammar was awful and his social adjustment was less than might have been desired. He stands for me as a kind of symbol of the young novelist, even though some are in fact witty, classy, and petite.

You know you're in a good writers' workshop if nearly everyone in the class is glad to be there, if writing and talk about writing become, in the course of the term, an increasingly exciting business, and if the writers in the workshop become increasingly effective as writers. The chief mark of a bad writing class is teacher meanness. Beware of the teacher who scoffs at "little magazines," claiming that they promote and proliferate mediocrity: You are dealing with a snob. Beware of the teacher who loves little magazines and hates *Esquire*, *The New Yorker*, or the *Atlantic*. You are looking at the same snob in drag. If you feel miserable in your writers' workshop, you should talk about your misery in private with the teacher, and if things don't improve, you should quit. A bad writing class doesn't only fail to teach writing, it can make one give up.

*Everywhere I go I'm asked if I think the university stifles writers. My opinion is that they don't stifle enough of them. There's many a bestseller that could have been prevented by a good teacher.*
—*Flannery O'Connor*

# The carrot and some tricks

## by Lawrence Block

I've found over the years that the mechanics of writing appear to be endlessly fascinating to writers and non-writers alike. Perhaps because the creative process is so utterly incomprehensible, even to those of us who are personally involved in it, it is easier for us to focus on more tangible aspects of writing. Do we write in the morning or at night? At the typewriter or in pencil—or with a crayon, for those of us who are not allowed to use anything sharp? Do we outline in advance or plot things out as we go along?

Somewhere in the course of this sort of conversation, one is apt to be asked just how many hours a day he tends to put in. The answer, whether it's two or twelve hours a day, is apt to be followed by a qualification. "Of course that's just time spent actually writing. Of course that doesn't include the time I devote to research. Of course, when you come right down to it, a writer is working from the instant the alarm clock goes off to the moment when he goes to bed. For that matter, the process doesn't stop when I'm asleep. The old subconscious mind takes over then and sifts things around and sets the stage for the next day's work. So I guess it's safe to say that I actually practice my craft twenty-four hours a day, seven days a week."

I suppose most of us deliver some variation of that speech at some time or other, and I suppose some of the time we even believe it. A certain part of me, however, does not buy this load of pap for a minute. As far as that stern writer's conscience of mine is concerned, I'm only really working if I'm sitting at my desk tapping my typewriter keys and turning out pages of finished copy. Thinking about writing isn't work, and research isn't work, and reading proof isn't work, and meeting with publishers isn't work, and talking

*Lawrence Block is a prolific writer in and on fiction. The author of countless novels, including his mystery series with popular heroes Matthew Scudder and Bernie Rhodenbarr, Block also writes a monthly column for* Writer's Digest *on fiction and promotes his writing philosophy throughout the US via his writing seminar Write for Your Life. The fiction expert's latest novel is* When the Sacred Ginmill Closes.

on the phone isn't work, and not even rewriting and editing are work. Unless I can actually see a manuscript of mine getting further from the beginning and closer to the end because of what I'm doing, I'm not entirely capable of regarding the task I'm performing as work.

## Burglarizing the neighborhood

Understand, please, that I *know* better. I realize intellectually that the non-writing chores I've enumerated above are directly related to my profession, that they take time and energy, that I can't slight them without adversely affecting the quality and/or quantity of my writing. But this knowledge doesn't seem to help me much. Unless I've put in my daily stint at the typewriter, and unless I've got something to show for it, I feel as though I've played hookey.

This attitude probably serves a purpose. My mind is sufficiently fertile that I can almost always dream up some worthwhile occupation which will keep me away from my desk. There's always a book it would pay me to read, a neighborhood I could profitably explore, a person whose expertise I should seek. None of these extramural activities is as hard as actually sitting down and writing something; thus, but for the conscience that hounds me, I could happily go months on end without wearing out a typewriter ribbon.

Sometimes, though, I find myself backed into a corner, locked into a no-win situation, damned if I do and damned if I don't. This happened quite vividly when I was working on *The Burglar Who Liked to Quote Kipling*. Bernie Rhodenbarr, the burglar of the title, had just hied himself off to Forest Hill Gardens, an upper-middle-class enclave in the borough of Queens. It occurred to me that I had not been to Forest Hill Gardens in over 20 years, at which time I had visited it very briefly. I had only dim memories of the neighborhood and had no way of knowing if it had changed in the intervening years.

I had two choices. I could trust my memory while taking comfort in the fact that every work of fiction takes place in its own alternate universe anyway. Or I could spend an afternoon zipping out there on the F train and walking aimlessly around to see what I could see.

Either way I was determined to feel guilty about it. If I stayed home and worked, I'd beat myself up for slacking on research. If I went out there, I'd accuse myself of wasting time on pointless research when I might have been tapping typewriter keys and producing finished pages. Once I was able to see that I was in a double bind, I tossed a mental coin and went to Forest Hill Gardens.

As it turned out, my memory was sound and the place hadn't changed a bit. But I felt my time had been profitably spent; I'd refreshed my impressions, picked up a little local color, and certainly enabled myself to write the scene with increased confidence.

It doesn't always work out that way. Sometimes hours devoted to this sort of research are a waste, and sometimes there's no way to determine in advance whether this will be the case. American Tobacco's George Washington Hill used to say that fifty cents of every dollar he spent on advertising was wasted. The trouble was, he went on to explain, that there was no way of knowing which fifty cents it was, so he'd go on spending the whole dollar all the same. It's that way with research, and with all the other tasks that take me away from my desk.

## Woolgathering into a yarn

One factor in the operation of my personal Jiminy Cricket mechanism is, I'm sure, that I *don't* spend all that many hours at my desk. Years ago I was given to putting in long stretches at the typewriter; I was younger then, which may have had something to do with it, and I was a less meticulous writer, which must have had plenty to do with it. In any event, I could work effectively for five or six or eight hours at a clip.

I can't do that now. I don't structure my work in terms of hours, finding it more useful to aim at producing a certain amount of work, usually somewhere between five and ten pages depending on the sort of material I'm working on, the deadline I'm facing, and phases of the moon. My work usually takes me somewhere between two and three hours. If I'm done in an hour, I'm delighted to call it a day. If I'm not done in three hours, I generally call it a day anyway, though I'm by no means delighted about it. There's a point at which it becomes counter-productive for me to continue to work, on a par with running a car's ignition when the gas tank's empty. You don't get anywhere and you just run down the battery.

Most workers, I've been told, don't really spend more than two or three hours a day actually doing anything. They take breaks, they file their nails, they daydream at their desks, they talk baseball, and two hours get stretched into eight. It's comforting to know this, but it doesn't change the fact that I think of myself as putting in a shorter working day than the rest of the world.

I've found a couple of things I can do to make my writing life as guilt-free as possible, and I pass them on for whatever they're worth.

1. *I Make Writing The First Thing I Do.* Over the years, I've written at every possible time of day and night. For some time now I've written immediately after breakfast, and it's by far the best system for me. There are several advantages—I'm freshest then, my batteries recharged after a night's sleep—but the most important reason for me is that once I've got my day's work done, I'm able to give myself permission to do as I wish with the remainder of the day.

2. *I Try to Work Seven Days a Week.* Again, there are other reasons why this is useful. With a novel, for example, working every day keeps the book from slipping away from my subconscious mind. Whatever I'm working on, novels or short stories, daily production helps me keep from feeling profligate over working so few hours per day. By the same token, when I do take an unscheduled day off, I can do so with a clear conscience; after all, I'm still working six days that week.

3. *I Save Routine Work for Later.* I'm frequently tempted to answer my mail the minute it arrives, to proofread galleys as soon as they hit my desk. These chores enable me to be practicing my profession without actually having to write anything. But they're of secondary importance, and I don't have to be at my sharpest to deal with them. They'll still be around when I've got my daily five pages finished. Lately, for example, I've been getting packages, parcels chock-full of entries in a short story contest. My natural inclination is to drop everything and read these stories as they appear, but instead I stay at my typewriter and save those stories for late at night when I can't sleep. After I've read a couple dozen, I sleep like a baby.

Finally, I allow myself to make occasional use of that old reliable copout—i.e., that writers are really working 24 hours a day. Because in certain respects it's undeniably true. Just the other day, for example, I did my daily quota of pages in the morning, spent the afternoon in the gym lifting heavy objects, and then wandered around for an hour or so. In the course of my wandering I watched a car enter an apartment building's underground garage, and it suddenly occurred to me how Bernie Rhodenbarr could get into an otherwise impregnable apartment building by first locking himself in an automobile trunk.

Will I ever use that little bit of business? I probably will, as it happens, but almost every walk I take produces some comparable bit of woolgathering, and most of the wool

I gather never gets spun into a yarn. Is it work? And does it matter if it is or not?

Points to ponder. For my part, I've spent a shade over three hours writing this article, and I'm done now. I think I'll give myself permission to enjoy the rest of the day.

## Swat with the stick

"So you're a writer," she said, spearing a cocktail frank. "You know, I'd *love* to be a writer, but I know it's impossible. I lack the discipline."

I suppose I could have offered to supply the missing ingredient, perhaps by lashing her nude to a desk chair and flogging her with a flail, but I only muttered something inoffensive and went off in search of the stuffed grape leaves. Because everybody would love to be a writer, and everybody lacks the discipline, and it's a good thing, because the profession is crowded enough as it is.

Imagine, for instance, if every dreamer with an urge to see his byline on a book jacket actually went so far as to roll a sheet of paper into his typewriter and start filling it up with words. Imagine, further, if all the people who started novels had the effrontery to finish the bloody things. Imagine if everybody with an itch and an idea took the trouble to turn the idea into a plot, and then sat down and wrote the story.

Why, we'd be up to our nostrils in literature, for heaven's sake! Forget the trees that would be pulped to facilitate such a gush of literary productivity. Think instead of the editors who would be the recipients of it all. They all have too much to read as it is, and it takes forever to get an answer from them, and just consider how much worse the situation would be if their daily reading load were increased by a factor of ten or twenty or two hundred.

You lack the discipline to write, sir?

Well, good for you. Stick with it.

Ah, but for *you*, Gentle Reader, the situation is rather a different matter. You, let it be said, are a writer, not a bore at a cocktail party or some similar sort of ship passing in the night. The last thing I want to do is discourage you from putting words on paper. You, clearly, are Serious About Your Work. Haven't you purchased this book? Are you not reading this very page? If that's not a commitment to one's art, a dedication to one's craft, whatever is?

It's my belief that self discipline is a problem for the vast majority of writers, however productive and successful they may be. In order to get his work done, the writer has to be every bit as much of a self-starter as the chap they're always looking for in those ads for door-to-door widget salespeople. He doesn't even have the advantage of an early morning pep talk from the divisional sales manager. He has to supply all his motivation himself. Ultimately, he has to tempt with the carrot and swat with the stick—and at the same time he's the poor old donkey pulling the cart.

## The bee and the ant

Novelists are especially assumed to require a full measure of self discipline, and for good reason. It takes a lot of hard work over an extended period of time merely to complete a book-length work of fiction. A poem can be dashed off in a matter of minutes. A short story can be hammered out at a single sitting. In both cases, inspiration can carry the writer through the completion of the work.

This is simply not true with the novel. Inspiration alone will not get the thing written, any more than sheer speed will carry anyone to the finish line in a marathon. To continue the analogy, a novelist, like a marathon runner, receives praise simply for having completed his task irrespective of how well he's performed it. No one (except perhaps the runner's mother) congratulates a last-place sprinter for having survived to the finish line of a hundred-meter dash. Nor do people hail one as some sort of conquering hero for having typed the last line of a poem or a short-short.

All this notwithstanding, I submit that the short-story writer has every bit as great a need to apply the carrot and the stick in order to be either productive or commercially successful. While seeing one story through to completion may be a less than Herculean task, it takes no end of discipline to do the same thing repeatedly, coming up with idea after idea, grinding out story after story, and working throughout at the top of one's form.

The novelist has the advantage of momentum; once into a book, he can give it its head and follow where it takes him. He knows, when he gets up in the morning, what he's going to be writing that day. The writer of short fiction, on the other hand, has to keep developing new projects and developing enthusiasm for them as he does so. And he has to do so while marketing previously completed efforts, shrugging off the inevitable rejections that are a part of that marketing process and refusing to allow them to interfere with his steady production of new stories.

Are there tricks of self-discipline? Is there a particular distance to extend the carrot, a special way to apply the stick?

I'm sure there must be, and I live in hope that one day I'll find the formula. Because I've been indefatigably productive over the years, turning out more books than anyone should reasonably have to read, people tend to assume me to be a model of self discipline. Yet I frequently look at other more industrious writers and castigate myself for my dilatory nature. Doubtless they in turn berate themselves for falling short of their role models—the bee and the ant, I would imagine. And does the ant in turn worry that he's a closet wastrel? I wouldn't be a bit surprised.

## Only a pack of lies . . .

Here are a few tricks of the trade:

1. *Give Writing Top Priority.* At executive training programs they like to tell the story of Charles Schwab, then president of US Steel. He told an efficiency expert that he didn't have time to listen to him at length but wondered if the man had any quick suggestions for him. "Every morning," the expert said, "make a list of the things you have to do that day. List them in order of importance. Then concentrate on the first task until it's finished, without diverting your attention to anything else. Then go on to the second task, completing as much as you comfortably can in the course of the day." Schwab looked at him, shrugged, and asked what he wanted for the suggestion. "Try it for a month," the man said, "and then pay me what you think it's worth to you." Thirty days later, Schwab put a check in the mail for $25,000.

The expert's advice is as good as it ever was, and as much so for writers as for steel company presidents. I would suggest that you put writing at the head of each day's list. Make it the first thing you do. Give it priority, not letting yourself be sidetracked until the day's writing is done.

2. *Set Goals For Yourself.* I work mornings, generally putting in two or three hours a day; when I work more than three hours my concentration flags and the work suffers. My objective, however, is not to put in a certain number of hours but to produce a certain quantity of work. More often than not, the goal I set myself is five pages a day.

If I get my five pages written in a flat hour—which does happen now and again—I'll generally call it quits then and there. I may do an extra page or two, if the words are flowing nicely and I want to leave off at a natural stopping point. But I'll feel under no obligation to put in all the hours allotted for purpose of writing.

On the other hand, if I don't reach my five-page goal within three hours, I may stay at the typewriter a little longer and see if I can't fulfill my quota. I'm not absolutely compulsive about this, but I know I'll feel better during the rest of the day if I get my pages written, and I do so when possible.

I can usually manage it—in part because I've had the foresight to set easily attainable goals for myself. I rarely find five pages a day to be a strain; if I did, I'd adjust the quota accordingly. I avoid the trap of raising the goal as I go along, like an assembly line speedup. The object's not to test myself. It's to get my work done.

3. *Stay in the Now*. The most important single element in enabling me to concentrate on today's work is the ability to make that the *only* thing I'm concentrating on. If I let myself worry about tomorrow's work and next Tuesday's work, I'm not going to do my best work today. If I'm writing a short story, I can't let myself get diverted into worrying about what story I'll write next, or where I'll send this one when I'm finished with it, or what I'll do if it's rejected, or what I'll buy for myself when it sells. I can only do today's work today, so why waste energy?

4. *Just Get It Written*. Frequently I find myself convinced that all I'm doing is turning perfectly good bond paper into garbage. Sometimes I'm right. Sometimes it's an illusion. When I feel this way, it's impossible to tell which will prove to be the case.

The answer, I've found, is simply to get it written, giving myself permission to throw it out later on if it turns out I've produced swill. This is occasionally easier said than done. It's hard to persevere when I'm convinced that the last sentence I typed is utterly wooden. But I frequently find afterward that what seemed horrible while I was writing it looks perfectly fine the next day—or at least no more horrible than the rest of my work. And, on those occasions when I do wind up tearing it up the next morning, at least I've done some work and the momentum of my writing is undisturbed.

5. *Don't Take it Too Seriously*. The work of any artist requires a certain degree of doublethink. In order to practice my craft day in and day out, I have to be very serious about it. But if I take it too seriously I'll clutch, rendering myself incapable of the relaxed approach necessary for optimum creativity.

Here's a story for illustration. Two retired gentlemen meet, and one complains that he's going nuts. "You need a hobby," the other one says. "Something to give you an interest in life and a reason for living."

The first is skeptical. "You mean like pasting stamps in a book? Doing needlepoint? What kind of a hobby?"

"I'll tell you," says the other, "it doesn't even *matter* what the hobby is so long as you got one. My hobby, just as it happens, is bee-keeping."

"You keep bees? You, living in two and a half rooms on Pitkin Avenue? How many bees do you have, anyway?"

"Oh, it's hard to say, but about twenty thousand."

"Where do you keep 'em?"

"In a cigar box."

"But . . . but, don't they get all crushed and dead and everything?"

"So? Listen, it's only a hobby."

*It's only a book*, I've told myself time and time again. *Sometimes it feels like the most important thing in your life, and it seems to be what you do to justify your own existence, but don't take it so seriously. It's just words on paper, it's just a pack of lies. Listen, it's only a book.*

That takes the pressure off. Knowing it's only a book, knowing empires won't rise and fall on the strength of it, I'm able to breathe in and breathe out and get the thing written. Ahem. Usually.

# The writing process vs. the block

## by Bill Downey

The great nemesis for right brain creativity is writer's block, a subject as topical for well-known authors as for beginners. Here some of the best-known writers verbalize their feelings on how they deal with writer's block. Several speak out on the state of the art in general. And even those who declined had interesting responses:

For *Joan Didion* and her husband, *John Gregory Dunne*, to discuss writer's block at mid-stage of the new books they were writing would have been something akin to a curse, she confided: ". . . too fearful to talk about the process out loud."

*Eudora Welty*, nestled in her Jackson, Mississippi, home, said, "I am not able to help you in right brain creativity discussions. I don't know a thing about it. I am sorry."

This is ironic, because Miss Welty's work is about as right brain and creative as any in print and has been a pattern for writers in America and around the world.

*Alistair Cooke*, obviously immune to writer's block, said: "I'm sorry—I myself have never had writer's block. I learned early on that being a writer is like being a plumber. You work every day at the same time; write when you don't feel like it. Imagine a plumber who couldn't turn off a raging faucet because he had plumber's block."

Those writers who did contribute speak out on how to overcome the problems; in some cases they address as well the issue of holistic power and the spiritual forces that can develop in writing.

**Ted Berkman** is a Santa Barbara writer with New York roots. He was critically applauded for the biography *To Seize the Passing Dream*, which captured the life and times of

---

*Bill Downey is the author of* Uncle Sam Must be Losing the War, Black Viking, Tom Bass: Black Horseman *and* Right Brain . . . Write On. *An instructor at Santa Barbara City College in California, Downey teaches creative and "right brain" writing courses.*

James Whistler. Berkman has also written many other books and screenplays, including Ronald Reagan's *Bedtime for Bonzo*, a romping satire in which he shared the spotlight with a chimpanzee.

In reply to the question, "Have you had writer's block?" Ted Berkman said, "Yes," with no hesitation.

**Berkman:** I had wanted to do a medieval Spanish novel, but someone suggested it should be a romantic novel. I gave that some thought, and then other things came up. But if I wanted to do the thing, I know I would have done something by now. I am listening to my gut and it says, Hey, you probably don't want to do this damn thing right now. This is a serious message from inside causing this resistance, and maybe I should listen and realize it might not be the greatest project for me.

*But how do you deal with the block?*

If I encounter resistance, I take a long walk on the beach and take a pad with me, then wait for something to happen. Very often it does. If the thing has been rattling around in my unconscious it is very likely to occur when I am moving my body physically, as with a long walk or a swim. I've written some very good sentences in the water. I memorize them and probably look strange to the people swimming alongside me. They look and wonder and I say something I memorized and they really wonder. I learned to do that at the YMCA in New York, a very good place to work, particularly when I was stuck.

Sometimes the block occurs out of sheer fatigue, when I have done all I could do. Then I take a break. Sometimes I go to the piano for half an hour or so and let the thing revolve in my head. I strongly believe in the workings of the unconscious and keep a pad beside my bed. I find, for me, the most creative time might be when I wake up and before I am fully awake. A sort of amorphous dream state. And before I really fix on the sequence of the day's events, things seem very fluid for me. That's when I grab a holistic-type structure of total concept: Many writers have said they feel closer to their work at early hours or when they first awaken. Holistic study indicates that we are closest to our conditions of mind, body, and spirit, when we first wake up. The external factors are then least realized.

*Have you had times when the writing took over?*

You mean a total immersion into the thing and it goes on its own? Sure. The prime example is Mozart's letter in a book called *Creative Process*. Mozart said he is simply a vehicle through which the whole thing passes. That does not mean to me that he didn't think about it a lot. He probably gave his music a good deal of intellectual thought. Putting the thing down is the final act.

Ian McClelland Hunter, a motion picture film writer, said most of the writing is done in his head before he writes. The experience for him is a lot like Mozart's. I think, with time, one might come closer to that. The novice won't be able to do it, but with a grasp of structure and the process becoming more familiar, it's something akin to driving a car and shifting gears. You know when you are in high; that's when the thing is taking over.

Another feeling with the block is that you have to examine yourself and your own emotionality. Ask, Why am I slowing up? Why is it so difficult? Am I really terrified? Remind yourself that every time the painter faces a canvas the same white paper confronts him as well the writer.

*Newspaper writers have said there is no such thing as the block.*

Writing a quick journalistic piece about a fire down the block is not the same, other than groping for the right lead.

*Is there a level of concentration the newswriter does not need or realize?*

Absolutely. There are levels of function. Much of newswriting [Berkman has written for the *Christian Science Monitor*] is a relatively mechanized, left brain operation. You take the pyramid shape, the classical form for a news story which allows the editors to strike out any part of the story without loss of the information. You tell it in such fashion that if everything got knocked out but the top, you could still understand the story. But that's mechanized. You don't need a right brain for that. But you don't write a novel that way. I don't even write a news story that way.

*Have you even been aware of a spiritual element in your writing at some time in your career? In other words, did Whistler guide your hand?*

In one case I can recall, I was writing about Whistler in great length. His full name was James McNeill Whistler. But I began writing about him as Jimmy all the time. To his buddies, he was Jimmy. But he also became a presence. When I was doing the novel that won the awards, he almost became a collaborator. I never thought of it consciously, but when I sat down to the typewriter it was with Jimmy.

There were no conflicts with him, and I felt great with his presence. To a large extent I became Whistler. I was me but yet like an actor, outside the character, a part of it. I suspect, though, that a good novelist like Styron, however much he was visited, would still be consciously directing. You never give yourself over totally to the force guiding you.

The left brain is doing something like steering. But there will be moments when the right brain takes over and there is no direction at all—it is pure emotionality. You have to learn to ride two horses at the same time. Neither one can dominate, and the right brain horse has to know that when he hits a good stride the other horse will ride along with him. And the left brain horse has to know as well that the right won't run away.

Sometimes talking with good friends will help with severe writer's block, but we all know the danger of that. You don't generally discuss your work. But I have found that calling old buddies with whom you can let your hair down helps. Or to walk around the block with them talking and then maybe coming into an idea.

Sometimes a psychiatrist helps. I've been in situations when scientists or psychologists were able to point out the resistance. Maybe you don't want to do this and you don't like this guy and no matter how much the publisher says he wants you to do it, inside, you resist.

Almost everyone I know has been to an analyst for help with writer's block. I am talking about Meyer Levin, after he did *Compulsion* and had that terrible experience with the Anne Frank diary. He claimed it was stolen from him and that Anne Frank's father got tied up with the Communist party; this paralyzed Meyer's writing for two years. He was in and out of law courts fighting this case. Only therapy got him back on course.

So many people, by nature of the same sensitivity that enables them to write, find themselves vulnerable. The pores have to be open all the time, but they don't always receive good messages.

**William Manchester** is adjunct professor of history at Wesleyan University. He has published an enviable list of fiction and nonfiction, including *American Caesar*, the story of General Douglas MacArthur. *Goodbye Darkness*, an account of World War II in the Pacific theater with the US Marines, became one of the bestselling war stories ever written. A former marine himself, Manchester is sympathetic with those who suffer writer's block, but is not too threatened himself:

**Manchester:** I don't believe I have ever had a serious block but in 1959 I was in what can only be described as heavy labor. At the time I was writing the last of four serious novels which the critics admired. They predicted a great future for them. They were dead wrong. The customers turned away. The most difficult books to write were *The Death of a President* and *Goodbye Darkness*. They tore me apart. I wept as I wrote.

*What do you do when you labor?*

In rough passages I use a fountain pen. I write a word in the center of the page. Then I circle it with other words until a pattern appears. That works for me.

*What do you tell other writers?*

We have a writers' workshop at the university every summer. Young writers come and we discuss problems. I try to discourage them. If they *can* be discouraged, they aren't going to make it anyway. There is a whole cobweb of misunderstandings about writers. In the public view, the writer, unless he achieves fame, lacks the status of doctors, generals, or corporation executives. And no two writers are alike. Even their working habits defy classification. John Hersey is matutinal (a morning person) but Balzac began at midnight. Wolfe was nocturnal. I write afternoons.

*Does this mean anyone can become a writer?*

No. The author belongs to a separate species and may be spotted by his plumage. Perhaps his most striking aspect is his detachment. He is apart from society. "Writing," said Hemingway, "is the loneliness trade." And the critics are like horseflies; they sting but don't help with the plowing.

If you describe the life of any writer you are likely to find that he has already been a man aloof. He has learned the greeter's smile and winks the genial wink, laughs the deep-chested laugh, and shakes the manly handshakes because he needs a protective screen. Behind that screen lives a man within himself, as withdrawn as a catatonic schizophrenic. The chief difference is that he writes about it. Because despite all circumstantial evidence, he really is sane and his sanity tells him that no personality is complete without the understanding of others; that a darkened room is unseen and the tree falling in the deserted forest cannot in fact be heard.

*Does the writer have a different start?*

I learned that early fascination with words is a telltale sign of a child marked for my craft. Reverie is another. Delighted with fables of Stevenson, Twain, Lewis Carroll, the future author lapses into glassy-eyed trances and spins a few yarns of his own. Daydreaming is not confined to novelists. That explains why so many people say so frequently, "If only I had time to write." We are all Walter Mittys. I doubt there is a man here who hasn't broken through the defensive unit of the New York Giants (NFL football team) at 2 a.m. some sleepless morning.

*And then comes writer's block?*

Most writers experience the eve-of-battle tension at the very least. The writer knows the writing ahead will be a real battle and the bloodshed will be his own; he will be battling himself. E.M. Forster said that a writer dips a bucket into the subconscious and is amazed at what he dredges up. Wild things happen over the keyboard at midnight. Talking and quarreling with oneself is an endless strain.

The psychoanalytic patient lies on the couch an hour a day for perhaps two years and spends the rest of his time telling his friends what an ordeal it was; but the writer undergoes self-analysis forever. Others may build a thick floor between the conscious mind and the murk below. The writer cannot. We must peer downward, always trying to make out the dim and ghostly shapes below. Some of them are not agreeable. Aspects of his own personality are unpleasant and sometimes even loathsome. Self-protective instincts intervene. The mind casts a shrouding veil. *The writer has a block.*

The fear of running dry is constantly in the back of every artist's mind. Renewed each time he gets stuck. But he goes on groping through the cloaking, soaking fog until he sees the way and the shape and makes the thing right.

*Do you share this with anybody?*

The late Bernard De Voto once reported that he had discovered a sure-fire way of getting novelists to talk about their work. It consisted, he said, of refraining from speaking for 30 seconds. There are such writers, but I am not one of them.

*Do you try to protect the novel you're working on?*

I'm of the breed who believes if you talk about it you lose it. For such a one as I the question: "What's the new novel about" is discomfiting. I generally answer that I'm writing a thinly veiled exposé of the questioner.

You must understand that while the novelist is indispensable to the novel, his role is limited. He decides the rules and exercises a certain control. The writer is God; he determines climate, temperature, and rainfall; he can even assassinate a troublesome character. But those who remain are not intimidated by him. They are imaginary people but they *are* people with wills of their own, and any of them can knock the novelist's plot into the wastebasket. The phenomenon of the character coming to life is often treated as a great mystery. It's not really. If the character has been thoughtfully conceived, he has certain strong traits and his behavior must be consistent with them. At the outset the writer's people are puppets. Then his Pinocchios come alive. Their wood is now flesh; they move without strings.

*You seem to have very strong feelings about all aspects of writing. Are you that assured yourself?*

Success [laughing] has not affected me very much because I was 40 years old when it happened. I used to be jealous of Norman Mailer because he made it so young. But then it disrupted his whole life. I live in a Spartan existence by comparison and don't need much. I make money now, but the spenders are my family, not me.

*What do you do to keep your confidence and avoid writer's block?*

One thing I do is play a game whenever I drive long distances. I'll take a year like 1956 and try to remember everything that happened that year—including obscure phone numbers. Once I remembered an old telephone number that took me an hour to recall. But I got it all. Remember, it's all in the memory bank. It's there to get.

**Saul Bellow** expounds on life and philosophy from offices at the University of Chicago, as a member of the Committee on Social Thought. Among his best-known works are *The Adventures of Augie March*, *Herzog*, and the perennial *Henderson the Rain King*, a book of enormous acclaim and recognition.

**Bellow:** I have had my bad times, but I never describe them to myself as blocking. It seems to me this is work, or pleasure, that I have freely undertaken, and if it went well I was delighted. But I never thought of it as a form of impotency. When I was younger you went to the analyst to be unblocked, so I could not help but consider it [writing block] as something of the same type.

*What did you feel?*

First I was miserable and tried to find something else to do, or else changed my topic and maybe blamed it on the manuscript, and wondered if I had chosen a bad topic and should turn to other work. But I can't say I ever described my incapacity to myself as a block—particularly because I thought of it as a harmful description.

*Were some of your books more difficult than others?*

Some were more difficult. But I had asked for it, hadn't I? And I got into trouble on my own. I found the remedy somehow, I don't know how. But I have abandoned many projects. I didn't abandon a book, though, until I was through and then realized it was awful; that I didn't want to read it myself, so how could I presume to expect it to hold other people's attention? So I spared them as I would have wanted to be spared.

*Was* Henderson the Rain King *difficult?*

Well, I had difficulty when I was writing it. It was an oppressive time and there was great misery about me. And death was around me too, but I kept writing the book. I turned to it with relief.

*Was it an escape?*

No, not an escape, I think it was a vacation from everything. The more abuse I was subjected to, the sunnier the book seemed to me. There was a difference in escape and in transcendence.

*What kept you going when you began writing and what do you tell young writers to keep them going?*

I tell them what a hard life they have chosen for themselves. I tell them I can understand how it is when they face the blank page. The panic. But after all, it isn't that they want only a word of encouragement. But I also know the pain that overcomes the writer when he faces the task of getting something out of nothing. In the early days I felt that panic, but I think it was caused by ambition, not writer's block. I had decided to do great things and found I was incapable of it. After all, who was asking me to do great things?

*What do you feel now when you sit down to write?*

I feel like quoting Isadora Duncan to you. When asked why she danced as she did, she said, "The dance is the explanation. I have no words for this. It involves so much of my life it would be foolish to try and formulate it."

*Have you ever felt you were drawing on some spiritual force when you write?*

I find myself in a state where I feel deeply moved by what I have done. In after thought, I feel it was a spiritual, invisible grace, but at the time I only know that I was terribly worked up over it. If it comes to me in an unnatural form, I put it aside as pretentiousness. If I find myself saying it is some spiritual quality, I say baloney. The way a woman uses her hands or a man pushes back his hair can tell you as much about their spiritual pleasure as any kind of tissue under the spiritual microscope.

**Irving Wallace** is the Chicago-born product of Williams Institute in Berkeley, California. He wrote and sold his first story for five dollars at age fifteen. Since then he has published fiction and nonfiction, along with hundreds of articles and screenplays, with much success. Of his best-known stories *The Prize*, and its revelations about the Nobel Prize and *The Chapman Report* are continuing favorites. It would be out of character for a prolific producer like Irving Wallace to have writer's block. This he confirmed:

**Wallace:** As far as I can say, I have never had writer's block. You can't write a book with writer's block.

*What about those parts of a book that are tough sledding?*

I have found that keeping a journal—not writing to great depths, but covering something of the day—will help. I learned quite by accident that not overwriting has made the creative things more available. My children, Amy Wallace and David Wallechinsky, perhaps by my example have both kept daily journals; as a consequence, the transference of one form to another has led them into writing.

The whole thing is to put ideas into black and white. I feel that it comes of the whole idea of having stuff in your head and getting it down. This overcomes a great deal of the fright of writing.

*How does this apply to your own work?*

When you get to something tough, like a book I just finished last week, first draft . . . well, I had bad days. I've not formulated this before, but what I do is the night before I'm facing a scene—or sometimes the day before, especially if it's a scene I'm afraid of—I will start making notes in pencil on a scratch pad. I have no pressure there. I can throw them out. And I will start by saying where the logical place for these people to confront each other has to start. And I will put down the logical sequence and then I invariably, by the following day, will have started something in my head.

*What does this accomplish?*

The next day I will have triggered something. I see it really should have begun in another place, and it all will have happened the night before, things I didn't think of the night before. This gets me going, and another thing, you come right into the scene with a good deal of background woven into it.

*Can you give an example of this?*

Suppose I have a woman coming into the scene who is a psychologist. I drag out my files and then start making one-liner notes. The notes rather define what Wallace wants from this character, and I get all this down. These are some places where I will skip to factual stuff, as in research, to continue with the imagined stuff. I want to keep the momentum going, and knowing I go back to the factual stuff makes it all right. Sure, there are places where I need more information or more correct information, but I let it go and come back to revise it. Sort of fatten it up somewhat. A lot of writers do that.

*How do you keep track of all this, marginal notes?*

No, no, what I do is keep rewrite notes. They might say, "Hey, you forgot to do this for yourself," and now, when I am done, as I will be Monday on this novel, I will go back and read the notes and plan to revise. I don't read what I have done when I am writing. When I finish I read the novel for the first time. I spend about ten days reading the novel and then make notes. But I don't reread when I am writing. I like for it to come out pretty raw. When I read and make notes on the second revision, I start fixing the holes, writing and rewriting.

*Your system seems to be designed to prevent writer's block more than cure it.*

Maybe that's why I don't like to go to bed with something on my mind. If I have to I will stay up till two or three in the morning fixing things. I'll try to get everything on my mind on paper. Once it is on paper it is safe and I don't have to think about it. I don't want to have a little self-debate when I go to bed.

*Some writers don't have a block with writing, but do have trouble plotting. Could there be such a thing as plot block?*

Constantly. Most writers I know work with an outline and will sit right down to see what happens—especially with a character. I feel that's death. You might turn up with the wrong novel. What I like to do is have a flexible outline. I might even write five outlines. Some have been as long as 60 pages, single-spaced. And in the final form I break this down into chapters, marking down the logical places for various things to happen. I have always done this and perhaps this does keep me going. But I must say that the writing is not as difficult as the fiction part. A lot of writers I know dread the creative part.

I remember a novel I wrote that had an ending I was not satisfied with, and I struggled with it off and on until one day, about three months later, lo and behold, it happened by itself. There was a sensational yet believable last and final act. I had to go back and repair some areas due to the change around, but it turned out to be marvelous. I couldn't have been happier.

*Do you believe there is a greater power or outside force that influences your work?*

Not really, except in the sense that there is something mysterious going on. I don't understand, but something happens without your knowledge. I am not religious, although I have finished a book on religion. In respect to spirituality, you have to be open to those things happening. It could be something peculiar to writers. Somehow you wake up and something is there. I can't imagine where it comes from.

**John Leggett**, Jack to his friends, is recognized as one of the high craftsmen of writing, and thus his position at the University of Iowa as director of the Writers' Workshop is well deserved. A graduate of Yale, editor for Houghton Mifflin and Harper and Row, he was one of the founding members of the Santa Barbara Writers' Conference staff. His biography *Ross and Tom*, captured the tragedies of Ross Lockridge and Thomas Heggen, both young authors who rose to fame and then crashed in self destruction.

**Leggett:** I don't know that I have writer's block, but I do have a hard time getting started. I find that the most intimidating thing is the clean sheet of white paper. And if I have a bad hangover or a bad cold and my mind seems filled with oatmeal, I use the back of an old envelope or a dirty scrap of paper for notes. It helps me, and I write my messiest thoughts and get started. Something out of the wastepaper basket this way is not wasted. I am not spoiling a nice piece of paper with my thoughts.

*Has any single book given you more trouble than the others?*

The one I am working on right now. [laughs] I think like other books, its trouble and pain ends once it is over. Then it's not so bad. But when the work is in progress, it is difficult.

*What makes some stories easier than others?*

I believe that the subject matter has a lot to do with how you are going. When you run out of enthusiasm you do slow down. I did well with my first book *Wilder Stone* because the subject matter basically was my own family origin. An abstract idea can take so long that you lose enthusiasm.

I take up to five years to do a book. I always think the next book will take a year and at the outside two years. If you are not very smart, which I'm not, then it takes longer than you plan to write a book.

*Do you discuss writer's block at the workshop?*

Students in the workshop do have writer's block. Maybe it's the competitiveness. One of the ways you get writer's block is you become so critical. Every time you think of something you start crossing it out before you get it on the page. You get very critical and that is self-inhibitive.

We have a staff psychiatrist here, and she said my problem was that I write with the left side of my brain. She did a study to show the extent writers were schizophrenic.

*Did this study prove anything?*

Yes, [laughs] it shows that each individual writer differs. I can remember one who said he loved the act of writing. Just sitting down with his pen and going scribble, scribble, made him feel good. That was strange to me, but I think he was sort of one extreme. In fact, any extreme in writing is bad. If you are facile and sit down without thinking very much it comes forth as thin writing without much depth.

*Is this evident in the workshop writing?*

In the Writers' Workshop at Iowa City, the people are so winnowed they are already of professional caliber. They know they must become accustomed to discouragement. They don't expect to mail something and have it published. They realize the apprenticeship is ten years, and they accept that. Sometimes they come to me and say, "I've been here two years and I want you to tell me if you think I am good enough to be a writer." And I tell them that if you have to ask me, then you don't have it. Don't have the grit for the task. You don't ever ask anybody. If you don't feel it in your anklebones, then you better go sell Toyotas.

*Does this mean the surest writers become the most successful?*

In looking back on students who have made it and the ones who dropped out of sight, I remember many of the bright ones and they are heard from, while others who had the energy seem to have made it. A little talent, a lot of intelligence, and a lot of energy is the better combination.

**Budd Schulberg** is a Dartmouth graduate; as a student there, he was president of the school's prestigious newspaper. His father was one of Hollywood's most powerful producer-barons. Yet Schulberg has shown throughout his illustrious career one of the most sensitive social consciousnesses of record. His first novel, *What Makes Sammy Run*, and the acclaim that followed made him the country's most celebrated young writer. But during the Watts riots in Los Angeles he was one of the first to rise to the cause; he founded the Watts Writers' Workshop, which gave black talent a piece of the action. Schulberg's many books are consistently at the forefront of required American literature.

**Schulberg:** I'm not troubled with what is commonly known as writer's block. I don't have too many days a week when I feel that I simply can't move. At times I distract myself by trying to do too many things, which is a different kind of writer's block. I'm off covering boxing or doing things, then I look up and a year or two has gone by and I try to do a book every two or three years.

*Have you had difficult books?*

My most difficult book to write was about a Latin revolution called *Sanctuary V, 1970*, which I started and stopped, moving around trying to find a more congenial spot to work on it. I was so involved in the Watts workshop at the time that I had started the projects stemming from the workshop and was trying to write the book at the same time.

A book was published from the work in Watts. It is called, *From the Ashes: Voices of Watts*. After that I had to get away, and I went to Florida and Italy, Lake Como, to take two or three months' vacation from the workshop and the book. At the same time it was rather a complicated book with its politics and so forth.

*Based on your experience with this, what do you tell writers now?*

I teach at the Southhampton College and what I suggest about writer's block is that you get into the habit of writing, so if you feel stumped, feel blocked, just write something. Even a letter to a friend or even in a notebook. Even write, "I can't understand what is making me unable to write today." At least you are going through the process of putting your fingers on the keys and attempting to write. Sort of forcing your way through it instead of walking around wringing your hands and saying, "God, I'm blocked."

*Some writers credit their fluency with reaching a spiritual level. Are you aware of this?*

I don't think in terms of spirituality in relation to writing. But I do think of morality. I think if you scratch an honest writer you will find a moralist. I don't think you are in this work, writing, really to entertain the reader or write a page turner. I think you have to write what you believe in and want to convince other people to believe in too. You are, in a sense, teaching as you are writing.

**Alex Haley** is the author of two books, one of which had a profound effect on publishing—*Roots*—which documented the tracing of Haley's ancestry from slavery in this country to Africa, where his Mandinka origins are as old as the land. A second, *Autobiography of Malcolm X*, has been regarded as one of the few exact accounts of the American Muslim movement. If ever a writer had to write his way out of obscurity to fame, Alex Haley is that writer.

*Before you wrote* Roots *and you told about owing thousands of dollars for research expenses. You weren't able to write and you told of crossing the Atlantic in the hold of a freighter to search out the feelings of thousands of slaves who also came that way. You could hear the slaves as you lay there in the dark and felt like stepping off the fantail into the sea. How did you shed this feeling to write?*

**Haley:** The depression absolutely was there. I never thought of it as writer's block; it was kind of circumstantial—a low point. I have always interpreted writer's block, from what I've heard, as something where you simply find yourself unable to get on with it. You just sit and stare at the page and, in a sense, I feel that is writer's block. I have always felt myself blessed that I have never experienced something like the block.

*Do you have a writing problem?*

Yes, my big problem since *Roots* has been trying to find the time to write the way I used to write. At the time I was on that ship I wasn't really involved in writing; I was researching. But when I get into the writing part, I am truly blessed. Give me the clear time, immersion time, and I get almost high off writing. It's euphoric.

*What is that like?*

I get tunnel vision about what I'm doing, and I tend to average anywhere from two to three times my normal output. I'm an incurable rewriter. I might rewrite from five to eight times on almost everything.

*Doesn't that much rewrite cause you an enormous amount of work?*

Right now I'm making some large changes. I have always felt inhibited by word processors—I'm so used to the typewriter. But almost every major writer I know tells me I am a fool if I don't make the transition.

*You travel so much, Alex. Could that be a means of escaping? Avoiding the writing?*

We all do that unless we get into what I was talking about—the creative euphoria. But when you are on the periphery, trying to get into writing, you find all kinds of reasons to get up and do this, that, or the other.

*What would you tell beginning writers?*

The beginning writer has no legitimate reason to say he has writer's block; he's not a writer yet.

*You mean it's doubly tough without credits. So how did you do it?*

For the beginning writer it's like looking into a maze, a mist, or a fog, not knowing which way to go. His block is something else entirely. I was always fascinated with the intrigue of writing, and when I was a sailor (I was a cook) I would finish the dishes and look forward to writing after I had taken a shower and then a nap. About the time everyone else was going to sleep I was going to my typewriter to write for two or three hours each night before I slept. That became a habit with me. I love writing at sea. It helps me to write every day.

*Is this one of the things you want to change in your life?*

If I could organize my life as I would ideally like it, I would spend one month at sea and one month ashore, alternating around the year. That way I would get my maximum output because I would write at sea and do all other things I need to do when I was ashore. I've got almost too many subjects to write about. I keep coming back to being obviously blessed, especially when I hear about what other people go through.

*A number of the writers I talked to mention a spiritual element or awareness when they write. Are you aware of this?*

I live on the spiritual element. Again, when I go back to the euphoria I mentioned, it's absolutely spiritual. It's a force I feel that is with me in a way I don't understand; I simply accept it. It's just something that happens, like for days I will just feel cloaked and I'm turning out pages like magic. I especially felt this when I was writing that part in *Roots* where Kunta is in his village as a boy, and certainly parts of the book when he was in the slave ship crossing the ocean. I tend to find that when the research has been intense, the writing will also be intense.

Another spiritual experience would be when Kunta was first in this country and he was set into a cultural conflict—this was a kind of high moment to write.

*You mention research—do you always research as intensively as you did for* Roots?

Generally, I spend so much time and effort in research I have probably over-researched. I rarely use two thirds of the material I've gathered. I like to feel I know what I'm writing about.

*Have any of your books been easy to write?*

I've only written two books, and neither of them was easy. The *Autobiography of Malcolm X* and *Roots* were not easy, nor would any book be if it was a good book.

*Why do you continue to push yourself to write when your life and time are so intensely in demand?*

I love my work. I love to write. One of the biggest problems beginning writers have is that they don't appreciate how much work goes into being a professional writer. Writing looks easy to people who don't write. *The better the writing the easier it looks*. But writing is hard. It is so easy for a beginner to think that he can write because he writes good letters or he got good grades in composition or his aunt says what he writes is great. Most people say, if they write two months or six months—and some are generous enough to say a year—some magazine or book publisher might accept their stuff. That's utterly far-fetched. My view is that it takes about as much time to become a professional writer as it does to become a surgeon. You have so many people entering writing—I would compare it to someone with first-aid capability for acceptance as a surgeon.

Beginning writers must appreciate the prerequisites if they hope to become writers. You pay your dues—which takes years.

**Margaret Millar** is the Canadian-born author of over 20 books. She is a University of Toronto graduate and was the 1965 *Los Angeles Times*' "Woman of the Year." An enthusiastic birder and nature lover, Maggie Millar wrote one of her few nonfiction books, *The Birds and the Beasts*, then returned to her first love, fiction. Though she is legally blind with a retina dysfunction, Millar continues to write, and until July 1983, to regularly tend as well to her famous husband, Kenneth Millar (Ross Macdonald), who was ill.

*Have you ever had writer's block?*

**Millar:** I've never had writer's block, but I am being troubled but that is different. I see no connection. Usually for me it's a matter of plot or I've been on the wrong track. When this is the case all you have to do is do something about it.

*Have you always been so sure of your writing?*

I've retired a couple of times, but I always unretire because I have the habit. But I think this thing about creativity is strange. As soon as I finish a book or compose a poem I make up a song on the piano and it's always the thing that keeps on going. It touches every part of my life because I don't do things the way other people do them.

*Have you thought much about how some books come so much easier than others?*

Certainly. Sometimes I get a first-class idea and carry it all the way through. That makes it a tour de force. I think, *Ask For Me Tomorrow* was one I carried all the way through. That kind of book had a lot in it that was difficult.

*What's your system?*

I keep enough notes ahead of time to learn which of my characters are going to carry all the way through and which are not. Say I write 50 pages, then I find which ones are going to last and which are dull and ought to be dropped. You have to do this or else you end up writing about someone who was only a minor character.

*How would you describe your books?*

I don't think my books have any heroes or heroines. I like to avoid that.

*How would you describe your nature book?*

It was a pleasure, but the research was difficult. It was a fact book, and I don't like to stick to the facts. I am a fictioneer, as you say. I will never write another fact book, I guess. I am a natural-born liar or fictioneer.

*What if I were a beginner and asked you what to do for my writing block?*

I'd say don't come to me, kid. I got problems of my own. And I get a chance to say that about once a week. Ken was always the teacher and critic. He enjoyed helping people. And I do too. I'll help them across the road and help them with their animals, but I'll be damned if I'll help them with their writing because I don't feel I have it in me.

*Did Ken ever have writer's block?*

That blabbermouth? No, no, he never did. He considered writing a real privilege. That is how he always acted. He worked for years without taking a holiday.

*Do you think Ken was free of the block because he paced himself? You know, he always worked for about three hours a day writing in longhand using a board on his lap.*

Yes, that's right. But when he had the urge he would write longer. But when you want to make it a steady thing you have to pace yourself.

*What keeps you so vigorous, keeps you writing?*

I'm able to swim a half mile every day of my life and I don't try to show off, but try and pace myself. Another thing, if you had to live by writing, I'd say you pretty well have to have both people in it and you both have to write very hard.

*You mean husband and wife?*

If you are going to make a living at it, yes. If one of us was doing books, we understood. Once in a while we were both finished at the same time and that was great. Usually, we were between books.

*Did you help each other?*

I was never able to exchange editing with Ken, but I did when he started his first two books. I always thought that when he was writing and I was reading along with him that he could not write dialogue. He was writing everybody as if they were speaking the same way he was. And I take credit for one thing, because I really think I taught Ken to write dialogue.

*Do you feel strongly about dialogue?*

My ambition is to write a book so that when people read it and hear one sentence, they will know which character is speaking. That, to me, would be great. Dialogue is my forte and I like people to talk the way I think they should talk.

*Do you listen to people when you are out?*

I am a terrible eavesdropper. You are not safe having me around when you are talking. Every restaurant and elevator I have been in—I listen in on everything I can. There are oftentimes some very personal conversations. And if you think I don't listen to them you're nuts. Once I was out with Ken and he said to me, "I'll bet you can tell me what everyone in the restaurant said but me."

*How has writing come so easily for you?*

Ken and I both had a very strong Canadian education. And with a background like that you don't have to wonder too much if you are punctuating right or not. You know damn well you are. And I am sorry that we are getting away from that. Now when I go to court and listen to some of the lawyers speak, whatever God-knows-what tongue they are using, I begin to concentrate on their errors and redundancies and I stop listening to what they are saying. I actually find myself correcting their language.

*Would you say correct language is a problem with writers?*

Of course. Illiteracy? Yes, indeed. You see they have gone too far the other way with it. It is not too readable.

*Why is mystery writing your favorite genre?*

I prefer to write mysteries because, within certain limits, you can say what you have to say: life, love, and the pursuit of happiness. All you need is a bit of framework.

*Your husband [deceased 1983] would be proud of you, soldiering on and writing in the old tradition.*

Yes, he would, he always was. And that's a nice feeling. But if I couldn't write today—oh boy!

# A writer's potpourri

## by Peter R. Stillman

I am thinking about a line from Faulkner—not in itself a memorable line, the kind that shimmers or thunders. It is simply, "It was just before sundown and they were not trailing, they were making the noise dogs make when they want to get out of something." I'm reasonably sure no one else would be stopped by it, bother to jot it down. But in its very ordinariness—its lumpish syntax, doubtful punctuation, its artless tone—you hear *story* and you quicken.

I am a storyteller; so are you. It is an unavoidable part of being human. And so when I come to a line like this one (which is actually about halfway through the story "Was"), it can never be for the first time; I have heard, used it before. So have you. There is a story embedded in it; it is a familiar matrix. It is one of those oddly uncomplicated, commonplace constructions that is also a miracle, an infinite source of narrative.

I've just spent a half-hour playing with the thing—long enough to satisfy myself that you can't get out of it without having a dozen tales come boiling into being. Or maybe, in rough, quick form, parts of the same one. For example—

It was long into morning and he wasn't working, he was drinking the way people drink when they need to forget something.

It was near to home but she was worried, she was walking the way old women walk just before they decide to walk faster.

It was dark on the stairs and he was not moving, he was crouching the way you crouch when you're going to spring at someone.

How much of the narrative's compelling influence lies in its syntactical shapes is a moot and eventually pointless question. But it's fascinating to wonder at a supremely good

---

*Peter Stillman has written nine books on various subjects including writing (*Writing Your Way), *plus many articles and stories. Poetry is his first love, however; his most recent book,* Gilead, *is a compilation of poems and journal entries about a rural mountain hamlet. Stillman is also editor for Boynton/Cook, Publishers, and frequently conducts writing seminars and workshops throughout the US.*

writer's ways—to discover in an audaciously homely sentence the essence of his craft, which is to put it so that it is *inescapably* story.

The line for me concedes that he knows I'm a storyteller too, that we both know the old shapes—that they've been borrowed and re-borrowed and don't belong to him or me or anyone except for the moment when we fill them with our own particulars. (Ironically, in all the years I taught English I never came across a sentence like this one in a composition text, which as a genre are fervidly narrow-minded. So, unfortunately, are most English teachers, who would promptly classify such a construction as a comma splice.)

But aren't there a considerable number of syntactical alternatives that lend themselves equally well to narrative? Of course. I don't want to deal with them, however. I'm writing about just one sentence, because it is a marvelous one and easy to consider. I do not mean to be instructive. If you would take from this the obvious and hardly novel point that some very fine writers pay us the exquisite compliment of listening to us long and attentively, learning our cadences and rhythms, then telling us back our own stories in familiar shapes, fine. That's instructive enough. *Write a story as if you were telling it* is only tautological until you deeply consider the distinctions.

*It was . . .* Every story begins this way. Often the construction is invisible, but we know it is there, when we read or write or speak a story. It is the most irresistible, forever fresh phrase in fiction. It may be, for that matter, fiction's heart, for it makes everything that follows it a story.

I have always thought it somewhat foolish and ultimately disabling for beginning writers to seek out tricks of the trade of the "Six Surefire Ways to Start Your Stories" ilk. Because there are no such ways, beyond using a capital letter, any more than there are surefire ways to end them. Yet I think a writer would be safe to begin every story with "It was . . . ," especially if he didn't have the faintest idea where it would take him. It is not a gimmick; it simply amounts to starting at the beginning, discovering what and where the beginning is. I don't know of a better way to enter the landscape of your own imagination. Nor is there a cleaner, more eloquent way to address a reader. Listen:

It was in a bar, a quiet little hole in the wall. It was four o'clock in the afternoon. (Eudora Welty, "The Purple Hat")

It was a magnificent July day, one of those days which come only when the weather has been fair for a long time. (Ivan Turgenev, "Byezhin Meadow")

It was raining that morning and still very dark. (Carson McCullers, "A Tree • A Rock • A Cloud")

It was getting into June and past eight o'clock in the morning, but there was a fire—even if it wasn't a big fire, just a fire of chunks—on the hearth of the big stone fireplace in the living room. (Robert Penn Warren, "Blackberry Winter")

It was a serene summer night; the harbor lay like a darkened mirror at our feet. (James Joyce, "After the Race")

It was Sunday afternoon, and from her bedroom Amy could hear the Beardens coming in, followed a little while later by the Farquarsons and the Parminters. (John Cheever, "The Sorrows of Gin")

Lovely stuff, all of it. Simple, clean, tingling with possibilities. They take us someplace we know we'd like to be. And it's not just because the lines have been composed by master writers; it's also because, like you, like me, like all storytellers, they revert to a form that tends magically to fill itself with story, to become the thing it talks about. You may write an execrably bad story that begins with "It was . . ." (just as you can by starting off with "Once upon a time . . .," of which "It was . . ." is the modern equivalent), but you will find it nearly impossible to write a bad first line.

This is all a metaphor, of course. What I've meant all along is only that stories begin themselves at the beginning if you let them.

\* \* \*

*"I go from one step to another and say 'How I got there I do not know.' " (Joyce Carol Oates).*

\* \* \*

In Joseph Conrad's *Heart of Darkness* his narrator Marlow begins, "I was thinking of very old times, when the Romans first came here, 1,900 years ago . . ." It seems an oddly unremarkable way for a short story to start; you sense that Marlow is casting about, isn't at all certain about where the next line will take him, or the one after that. It is the way we strive to discover the way—a pushing out of words to see where they may lead and what we may learn from them. It is how nearly all stories begin when you tell them for the very first time—when, indeed, they are not yet stories, honed, formulaic narratives easy and familiar on the tongue, but are instead inchoative first formings. Marlow isn't attempting primarily to *convey* a story but to forge its meaning for himself. It will never, in subsequent tellings, take similar shape.

I don't know if there is anything for the writer in such an observation. Certainly it isn't meant to be an argument that one should set out to tell a story as if he or she didn't know what its outcome will be or even if it will be of interest to another. I do think, though, that serious writers have probably come to know that a story rarely *presents* itself—has a pre-existence of sorts that needs only a bit of tightening and buffing to make it work as literature; or even that some "stories" aren't—they are at best the nearly ineffable, tortured elements of human experience disguised as conventional narrative.

Marlow is not a yarn spinner. His listeners are familiar enough with his ways to dread what's coming. "We knew we were fated," one of them observes, "to hear about one of [his] inconclusive experiences." He will say whatever occurs; his eloquence will be overlaid with indirection, slowed and weighted by his obsession for detail. Always he will frustrate our expectations. But this is reasonable, for Marlow is attempting with mere words to re-enter the heart of his own particular darkness, to shed light on it, make it knowable. Eventually, this is what a serious storyteller must do, aware that it is hopeless, impossible—that you cannot always ravel out the tangle and make a meaning.

But it is not really futile, not for the writer at least. Some huge matters of the mind and heart are untellable as stories, and in the struggle to make them otherwise, we can *evoke*, even if we cannot explain. *Heart of Darkness* is a long, complex narration. In the end Marlow will let it all evaporate. But by the time the bottle is empty and the evening chill has settled over the *Nellie*, he will have made so vivid for his listeners the confusion and guilt and pride involved in being human that to press for conclusion—for an *answer*—would be unthinkable. This is the kind of writing that can make a reader's mind go Woof! as if he had been butted by God.

\* \* \*

*"Against the disease of writing one must take special precautions, for it is a dangerous and contagious disease."* (Abélard to Héloïse)

\* \* \*

I know that in the swirling galaxy of words into which I was born and out of which I make a living, there must be a few that say it perfectly once you find the way to fit them together—a handful of sentences you can trust to have a socko effect no matter where or when you trot them out.

The other morning I tracked some terrifically malodorous dog feces into the dentist's office. I didn't realize it, of course—it would be despicable as a premeditated act, unless you were trying to draw people's attention away from something even worse—until the dentist had most of his hand in my mouth. Then it came wafting up. His nose twitched three or four times and his left eye started to water, and I began hoping to myself that it was on his foot and not mine. The drill fell auspiciously silent, and he spoke out of the miasma that had enveloped us, "Life is a very serious business." It struck me as incongruous, even irrational for a moment, but that is only because novocaine tends to bring out the superficial in me.

It is a honey of a line. I wished in a minute that I had thought to say it, not only because it is one of those rare observations that loses nothing for being uttered through another person's fingers, but also because it is a pronouncement you can use just about anywhere without ever using it up. So I wrote it down on the back of my appointment card and exited across the waiting room's burnt-orange carpet, my right heel elevated just enough to cause the receptionist to call after me, "Did you hurt your leg in there?"

On the way home I considered how you could end any novel you would ever want to write with that sentence, if you didn't use the one I got from my wife's favorite soap opera, which is also nearly unbeatable. I doubt even Nathaniel Hawthorne could do any better at electrifying readers than to have one of his characters observe, "I've got to put the past behind me and get on with my life." It feeds right into the other line I got from *Guiding Light* that threw off such sparks I ran right into my office and jotted it down: "I'll always be there for you."

It is a good bet that Tolstoy would have been a nobody if he hadn't stumbled across the Russian equivalent of lines like that, and if I had it to do over again, I'd never stick a word on paper without its having to do with somebody being there for somebody else who is getting on with the very serious business of life by putting the past behind him or her where it belongs. Some things you come across too late in life to get the most good out of. I can only in a somewhat melancholy moment of generosity be happy for the many, many writers who have made such important discoveries early in the game.

\* \* \*

"*. . . for imperfection is the language of art . . .*" (Robert Lowell)

\* \* \*

These are merely some things I think I know—random gleanings from 25 years of editing and writing and working with writers young and not so young. I take them to be true, although they are ventured in the knowledge that about no other business is it as reckless to issue truisms.

● Writers as a species are not distinguishable from the rest of humankind by virtue of natively superior insight, sensitivity, intelligence, wit, or imagination. They were not, in other words, blessed at birth with an enviable array of genes. They have, most of them, simply bothered to write, almost always against the odds of their succeeding at it and in the increasing knowledge that it's a very taxing business and unlike many others gets no easier with experience. But they have also necessarily discovered through writing, I believe, a validity about their own perceptions—a sense of living ever a bit closer to understanding how the whole thing works. And this is sufficiently glorious to drive anyone again and again at the task. Put another way, if you would be more insightful, intelligent, imaginative, write. There is no better way to make the most of being human.

\* \* \*

● You can believe that F. Scott Fitzgerald occasionally wrote a superb story in a couple of hours, if you want; I don't. Because *no* decent story is ever written; it is always *re*written—composed from wrong words thrown down and reworked until they are less wrong—not dug whole and shining from the muck of imagination.

● If you can outline a story *completely* before you begin writing it, it will probably be a godawful story.

● There is a double irony at work concerning writer and reader: Writers are driven by the need to make a work's meaning unmistakable, which is patently impossible. And readers strive to *know*—to get the meaning exactly right. Yet all readings are necessarily *mis*readings, for reading is a marvelously messy, inexact experience. You come at it with your visions, expectations, uncertainties, I with mine. (I can't imagine a worse blight afflicting the world than our absolute *agreement* about its metaphors.) Meaning—hence joy, enrichment—lies in an ill-defined ground somewhere between story and reader, not within the text. We stumble over it, suspect always that it's the wrong meaning—that everyone but us has got it right, take away what of it we would, attempt to fit it to what we know to be so, what we need to believe. It won't be the same tomorrow, and it will change still again the day after that. It is much the same with writing, thank goodness. We may lament, along with Prufrock, that "It is impossible to say just what I mean!" but it would be tragic, paradoxical if we could. To tell a story is necessarily to tell it imperfectly; it is the nature of the art that it is kept alive by the writer's inability to flatten it once and for all on a page.

● For the most part and possibly excepting dialogue, it isn't worth your worrying about where to begin a new paragraph. Indenting is primarily a typographical device; it has nothing at all to do with what you're saying. (And never ever waste a minute attempting to frame a topic sentence. They are no less mythical than the unicorn.)

● Faulkner was a heavy drinker. So was Hemingway and so, notoriously, was Fitzgerald. Between us we could probably come up with a score of other eminent writers who drank. Most would have died before their time (which I admit has a dark panache about it), but most also would have exhibited a diminution of power in later years. While you can take from this that booze fosters a genius in a person long before it kills the sting in his prose, it is probably the wrong thing to take. I have had it from at least a hundred people that you can't drink and write. I have also wasted time on occasion trying to do both or one right after the other. I am not moralizing; I'd be all for it if I could get it to work. The trouble is, you *think* it does—until you read your stuff over the next morning and discover that something terrible has happened to it overnight. I don't know how those fellows got away with it, but I'm guessing they were geniuses first and drinkers second until the two got going neck and neck, and then one eventually pulled ahead of the other.

● It is immoral to fail to encourage your children to write stories, even and especially before they can spell or make their letters right; and it is doubly reprehensible to fail to upbraid the teacher who will inevitably come along and try to stamp out the joy they've discovered in it.

● A word processor won't improve your writing. It will make it faster and perhaps easier to correct simple errors and even to revise what's already there. But it will not help good writing happen, no matter what the machine or the program. The thriving pastime of debating the relative merits of this word processor or that amounts mostly to the willfull self-delusion that one of the many programs on the market is Mr. Right—that you and your novel are going to find each other via some miraculous mechanical means.

● Do not despair your imperfect memory. For fiction writers especially, near-total recall would be a cruel handicap. You cannot write imaginatively about past moments if you remember them too clearly. Their details become too burdensome, and hence their essences escape. It is only *apparently* easier to transcribe than to re-create, to prune back a thicket of particulars than to imagine the right ones. A commonplace belief about fiction by inexperienced writers is that it's often flawed by indiscriminate excesses of detail. I think this comes in great part from a mistaken reliance on recall rather than invention, allowing the past to own us, when it should, of course, be the other way around.

\* \* \*

One night years back I came upon the *quintessential American sentence* while I was lighting a lantern. It is only about an inch and a quarter long, yet it encompasses our vast nation, resonates with its past glories, bespeaks with a native terseness the very spirit of America. Within it swarm our noblest moments and their heroes. It is the ultimate, portable edition of the American myth, and how, by God, I wish I'd written it!

It was one of those big, sturdy boxes of Ohio Blue Tip kitchen matches. "Strike anywhere," it said. *Anywhere!* Think of that. *Anywhere at all*, from sea to shining sea. On a dinosaur bone in the Badlands, on a wall of the Alamo, on the notched grip of a six-gun, on the seat of your buckskin trousers, on the Statue of Liberty. *Anywhere*. Find me a sentence that looks as good by the dawn's early light, would be more at home on the range, is as downright *salutable*. (I've had people argue that "Don't tread on me" is a superior piece of work, when if you had half a brain you'd know it wouldn't make a speck of sense to anybody living outside of rattlesnake country.)

The author of that ringing imperative must've been looking west out the window of the Ohio Blue Tip match factory when it hit him—the whole sunburnt limitlessness of it all. And then, like any good writer, he sat down and gave it his very best shot, knowing damn well it was going to tear the heart and soul right out of him and it would be all downhill from there.

I don't know what's happened to sentiments as brawny as that or the writers brave enough to frame them. I do know, though, that nearly every container you pick up today says it's all done and over—that it's all fenced in and tamed down and there's no place left to go. "Open here" is all you're ever told, and it's followed by a chubby little arrow to nail you right to the spot.

*An idea is a naked and shivering thing until it is clothed in words.*
—*James Stephens (poet)*

# Riches from research

## by Maxine Rock

Research is the soul of writing. It's the writer's way of educating himself, building a solid foundation for his fiction, and having fun at the same time. Editors warm to writers who are careful reporters, too, and when they find a writer who won't do research, they consider him lazy.

You need research on history, location, dress, mannerisms, and social mores to pump authenticity into your novels and short stories. Dates, times, accurate descriptions of places—even correct snatches of songs—all lend weight to your words. Professional writers spend considerable time on research. It's the amateurs who prefer to philosophize about life, to pen essays on personal ideals. Such work rarely sells.

Many professionals start with market research. Before they begin to write, they may contact publishers to find out what types of books are selling best. Then they construct a story to fit current market needs. Surveys say most books are now bought by women. So novels, for, by, and about women are usually the most successful.

## Fact sheets on fiction

Getting information like that is the most basic form of research. Many publishers put out fact sheets, listing their primary markets (who buys their books); their favorite subjects (what to write about); and the most successful style (how to write it). The fact sheets are yours if you request one from a publishing house and include a self-addressed, stamped envelope. If you collect and study several fact sheets, you'll have a good idea of what the market will bear at the time you're writing.

Other ways to find out what's hot these days is to ask the manager of local book-

---

*Maxine Rock has published more than 800 articles and stories in* The New York Times, McCall's, Smithsonian, *and many other publications. A longtime freelancer, she has taught writing at Georgia State University and the University of Maryland. Rock co-authored,* Gut Reactions *and recently published* The Marriage Map, *a book about the stages of marriage.*

stores. You should also devour newspaper and television ads for books. Read *The New York Times Book Review* every Sunday and invest in a subscription to *Publishers Weekly*, a trade magazine for writers and other professionals in the publishing field. The address is R.R. Bowker Co., 205 E. 42nd St., New York NY 10017.

# Know your subject

The next step is to know as much as possible about your subject. Fiction is usually dull and unimpressive without facts to back it up and give it life. The bestselling novels are often those which satisfy the reader's curiosity with rich detail such as how a war was won or lost, how crime rings are broken, or how something actually works. Arthur Hailey's *Hotel* was enchanting because he included behind-the-scenes facts about hotels; for example, the way poor people are hired to sift through the muck and rescue silverware that is carelessly tossed down garbage chutes. Pulitzer Prize winner James A. Michener's books, such as *Hawaii* or *Centennial*, deeply probe the real history and social patterns of a geographic area. Norman Mailer, in writing his "true-life" novel, *The Executioner's Song*, plowed through reams of convict Gary Gilmore's letters and court documents, interviewing almost everyone who ever knew the man. Mailer needed research assistants to help him do the job. In his afterword to the novel. Mailer tells the reader what his research entailed:

> This book does its best to be a factual account of the activities of Gary Gilmore and the men and women associated with him. In consequence, *The Executioner's Song* is directly based on interviews, documents, records of court proceedings, and other original material that came from a number of trips to Utah and Oregon. More than 100 people were interviewed face to face, plus a good number talked to by telephone. The total, before count was lost, came to something like 300 separate sessions . . .

This stubborn research gave Mailer the facts he needed to build a heart-thumping account of Gilmore's brutal life and death. It's the little truth—lines of Gilmore's poetry, letters detailing his love and loyalty to his girl friend, and real people recounting the way he developed his vicious temper—that keep the reader going through Mailer's 1,050-page novel. The book is more than entertainment. It's an education in psychology, sociology, criminal law, and prison life. Readers like to know they're learning something real while they turn the pages. And they depend on you, the author, to do the research that will help them.

# Primary and secondary sources

There are two ways to do research: through primary sources, and secondary sources. Primary sources are ways to find information that nobody has yet written down. They are your own observations, experiences, and interviews with people upon whom you wish to base your characters. You should also talk to people who have had the experience about which you want to write.

Secondary sources are written. They can usually be found in the library. They are references books, subject books, dissertations, and newspapers, magazines, and other periodicals.

Most writers use a combination of primary and secondary sources. I go to secondary sources first, so I can bone up on a subject before I start asking people questions. That means I spend time in the library before taking my tape recorder and venturing into the field.

# Love your library

James Michener says he visits the library more than once a week. He makes a beeline for the card catalog or computer terminal, which will help you locate a book by author or title. If you go through the catalog by subject headings, you'll come across exciting books you never dreamed were there. Browse along the library shelves, too. New books will pop out at you like unexpected treasures. They'll give you information and ideas.

There are all sorts of subject indexes—Art Index, Business Periodicals Index, and the Social Sciences Index, to name a few—which will tell you where to find specific information. And there are endless biographical sources. These can start your mind clicking on a character.

One day while browsing through a 1969 edition of *Current Biography*, I found a tiny photo of blind singer and guitarist Jose Feliciano. Along with the photo was heart-rending story about how the singer started his career. He begged restaurant owners to let him, "a simple poor blind kid," come in out of the cold and tune up his guitar. Of course, instead of tuning, he played for the guests.

What guts! what an inspiration for a fictional character!

In the *Dictionary of American Biography*, I found a four-page story on the life of Clara Barton, who started the American Red Cross. The biographer described Barton as a spoiled child who grew into a determined, strong-willed woman, "unable to act as a subordinate gracefully or to cooperate easily." She was even physically described as a petite, slender woman who marched—not walked—into a room, with her head held high. These traits apparently made Barton an unusual woman for her times, and if I wanted to do a short story or novel on a spunky lady who lived during the period of (1812-1912), I couldn't find a better source for initial inspiration and information than that dictionary.

# Research is fun

Library research is just one source for fiction writers. Some writers use it only sparingly. They have more fun with on-the-spot research. So they rely on travel for detail and authenticity; on interviewing to catch the sounds and sights of people as they react to news or emotions; on personal experience; and on astute observation of everyday events.

This type of research can be expensive, because you invest time and money traveling to locations about which you want to write. But it pays off. There's usually no good substitute for *being* where your imaginary action takes place, or talking to real people who live there. It would be hard to believe that novelist Leon Uris wasn't in Cyprus when he described it in the first few pages of *Exodus*:

> The flatness, the yellow stone houses with their red tiled roofs, the sea of date palms. The road ran alongside the ancient Venetian wall which was built in a perfect circle and surrounded the old city. Mark could see the twin minarets that spiraled over the skyline from the Turkish section of the old city. The minarets that belonged to St. Sophia's, that magnificent crusader cathedral turned into a Moslem mosque. As they drove along the wall they passed the enormous ramparts shaped like arrowheads.

Descriptions like this spice fiction with details that attract and hold reader interest, and draw readers into your story. And they show that the author knows something about what he's seeing: Uris researched the origin of the minarets, and informed the reader they belonged to a cathedral that was turned into a mosque.

Why go to all that trouble? Because research provides a strong footing for your fiction and makes readers identify with what you say. They feel part of the times, places, and people in your story.

Yes, fiction writers do make things up. They create characters and events. But fiction writers also need the anchor of reality, provided only by research.

Research provides a learning experience for you and your readers. It can be an exciting, fun-filled part of your writing, And, there's another reason why research is important: Well-researched fiction is the kind that sells best.

**Research does pay off,** says author Francis Statham, who invests at least several months of reading, travel, and library research in each of her romance stories or Gothics. Gothics are novels usually characterized by the use of desolate, remote settings and mysterious incidents. They have complicated historical plots. Statham says she wouldn't dream of doing such a book without research to give her a full and accurate picture of the lifestyle and events of the times.

"To be a good writer, you can't be lazy about your research. A lot of people won't write about something that didn't happen to them, because they don't want to struggle with bits and pieces of information. But you have to do that, because publishers appreciate—and pay for—books that give the reader a little history lesson along with the plot.

"Even if you're not doing history, you must be correct about statements and events, or you'll lose credibility. I once read a novel by a British writer who had a female character in his book get into an auto accident. She had a head injury. This girl, the heroine, was taken to the hospital and given a sedative.

"I put the book down right there. As the former wife of a doctor, I know that you don't give sedatives to people with head injuries. That writer didn't do his research, and I lost faith in his writing."

**Educate yourself during research.** In the book, *Creation*, Gore Vidal traces the life of a fifth century Persian politician. To do it, he devoted six years to the study of history, religion, and philosophy.

Vidal said he chose a Persian hero because he thought the Persians were superior in many ways to the Greeks. And the Persians appealed to him because theirs was a more gentlemanly society and more settled, apparently, than Greece. "Also, I chose a Persian point of view from a desire to know more about the people, leaders, and culture of the times. I can only write about what interests me greatly . . . I've always been fascinated by Confucianism and Buddhism and as I taught myself, I put what I learned in the book."

**Writers must love to learn,** believes historian Elizabeth Stevenson. She writes biographies, such as the huge Macmillan book on Frederick Law Olmstead, *Park Maker*, and says fiction writers must be just as careful as she is about their facts.

"I'm a writer of nonfiction, but I know that fiction suffers greatly if it lacks authentic detail. It isn't hard to find those details. You know what I do when I research? I sit very quietly in the library, spying on the personal lives of others, getting stuff on people I'm going to write about. I concentrate on secondary sources, because since I'm doing history, all the people I'd talk to are dead.

"I start with a person's birth and slip in a three-by-five inch card for each important event in the person's life. Everything is done chronologically on little cards that I put neatly into files. I stack the files in an old bathtub in my home. Before I'm ready to write, I may have six or seven boxes or files in the tub. But that means I'm never stumped for a fact, so I don't have to put off my writing, once I do get to it, to go and hunt down the answer to a research question."

**Hunting for answers** intrigues readers. If you've done careful research, your plot is likely to include enough fascinating facts to keep readers turning the pages. Perhaps few authors know that better than Martha Hennissart and Mary Jane Latsis, who write mystery novels together under the pseudonym Emma Lathen. These writers pick a complicated—and shady—business deal as their subject and build a murder mystery around it. In the process, they teach readers about banking, real estate, and other aspects of our industrial society. Books like *Banking on Death* earned the writers a review in the *Wall Street Journal* in March 1981:

> The authors say that most of their research for a new book involves living in a place awhile to get ideas for scenes and talking with people involved in an industry. (For their hockey book, they bought season tickets to the Boston Bruin games.) "It's a form of impression-gathering rather than fact-finding," Miss Hennissart says. "We're gathering types for our characters, sort of an aura . . . Especially if you have the whiff of an academic researcher, it's amazing how much people will tell you.

**Check on what people tell you,** advises Pat Watters, a veteran magazine and book writer. He warns that interviews aren't always accurate because people love to make up things when they're talking to writers.

"My biggest project was a book on the Coca-Cola company, and it kept me in the library seven days a week, ten hours a day, for two months. Then I interviewed salespeople, executives, bottlers, and so on. All of it went down on tape. I also took a notepad, which I used to jot down descriptions of the person, what his office looks like, what gestures he makes—stuff you can't get on a tape recorder.

"I always ask for anecdotes. I was doing non-fiction, but what I got was enough for a lifetime of novels, too. I learned what the owners went through to keep Coke's formulas a secret, and odd ways people tried to steal the secret.

"I discovered people love to tell you 'inside' stories, but you have to check on them. One guy told me he knew the original driver of the first Coke wagon. Sure, I wanted to interview the old fella! But when I told the public relations person at Coke how excited I was about it, he just cracked up. He said, 'Oh, that makes about 125 men who drove the first wagon.' "

**Readers tour story worlds** through research. Terry Kay relied heavily on his knowledge of the rural American South to write *After Eli*. Kay feels that readers want to be led into times and places that are new and exciting for them. To do that, your research must be accurate.

"Why do people read? Mostly, for fun. They want to escape from their everyday lives. They want to be transported to places they might never visit in real life; they want to go back and forth in time. The writer is their tour guide. Nobody trusts a tour guide who isn't at home with the locale or who stumbles with the language. If you want to make the reader's trip enjoyable, you'd better bone up on where you're taking him."

**Don't rush research,** admonishes French-educated Rosemarie Simpson. If you devote enough time to researching your book, you'll produce a better product. You will know more about your subject and be more enthusiastic about it.

"It took me five years to complete the research for my novel, *The Seven Hills of Paradise*. Of course, I was teaching at the time, as well as writing. Unless you're rich, you can't afford to drop everything and hide away in the library all the time. But every bit of time spent on that research was well worth it. My book is set in the 13th century, and it's not possible to learn about life in that period unless you really dig into it.

"Even more important, you must *feel* what life was like in the time period about which you wish to write. It took weeks of research before I could *feel* the slimy stone wall of a dungeon, and *feel* the cold drafts blowing through a castle.

"You must feel as if you're living every minute of the action that takes place in your novel. That feeling will come if you spend time researching."

**Your emotion lives in characters.**  Editor/writer Jack Lange dug into daily newspaper reports of 1913 to research his fictionalized account of the Leo Frank case, in which an innocent Jewish man was lynched for the murder of a little Southern girl.

"First, I read several books on the case. Then I went through the day-by-day reports in three different newspapers. By following the story closely, I was able to get into the skins, into the heads, of the people involved. So I could *feel* their anguish and pain, *feel* what was going on in society at that time.

"When I wrote, this feeling made my characters more believable. They came alive almost by themselves. Words jumped from their mouths because I was inside them, feeling everything that was going on. Obviously, I was fabricating, but my research was what made the fabrication possible. I had learned so much about my subject that I was able to see the scenes, hear the words, smell the smells.

"I was living in 1913 through my research."

**Personal observations serve as research.**  R.V. Cassill advises writers to pay close attention to sounds, smells, and body language. This helps writers tune in to the emotional environment of a place or person. He calls this type of research a "search for signals," in that it teaches writers to pick up on important details and discard those which are insignificant.

"Because you are looking specifically for material that will fit into and enchance your writing, you want to do some specific observing, some specific research. Some writers research first, then write. Others, who are more concerned with feeling their way through the plot and characters, might find the best technique is to start writing first, before you research, and let the research follow the needs of the character.

"For example, if the main character is going to go to Colorado to ski, that may be the time for the writer to go—not before. In nonfiction the research most often comes first, and is more organized. Fiction may not be planned. Its research may rely more on immediate need rather than long-range planning.

"But no matter how you do it, it's important to remember the search for signals, the tiny details of life, is a research tool that cannot be overlooked, no matter how well you think you know your subject."

**Knowing your subject gives a head start,**  states multitalented Dr. John Feegel. He is a physician, attorney, and novelist whose interests come together in writing mysteries with medical and legal elements in the plot. He started writing in 1972 "for my own enjoyment," publishing *Autopsy* in 1975. Since then he's also written about the CIA (Central Intelligence Agency), the Bay of Pigs, and trouble in a small Georgia town.

"My novel *The Dance Card* took about a year of research, since it concerned the Bay of Pigs affair, and I wanted to get precise information and dates into my book. For that, I went to the periodic literature of the times, such as newspapers and news magazines.

"*Malpractice* was done off the top of my head because it's about medicine; I had a big start there because I'm a physician. My research was already part of my general fund of knowledge. I'd advise other writers who want to be accurate about precise fields, such as medicine, to consult with someone who is accustomed to the work and who can talk knowledgeably about it. Then, go back and check the texts to make sure the information is accurate and you aren't getting a slanted point of view.

"Better yet, stick to what you know. You may still have to do some research, but it won't consume you. Of course, there are some very fine writers who can go out, learn someone else's craft, and write and about it. I'm thinking of Arthur Hailey (*Airport, Hotel, Wheels*) who can dive into the hotel or airline business and really devour all that information and detail. But most of us do best selecting a subject we know and care about, and supplementing our own knowledge with careful research."

**Your interest in the research subject will grow,** contends science fiction writer Michael Bishop. Once you learn about a subject, you can do several books, drawing on and enlarging your fund of knowledge as you go along.

"Anthropology fascinates me, so I've done several books that use the information I have on the subject. Every time I tackle a new story idea, I learn more about the same subject, so the research gets easier as I go along. It also gets deeper; you become almost an expert in the field. That's wonderful, because your interest will grow.

"My novel, *No Enemy But Time*, amounts to an in-depth study of human evolution. A character goes back in time to learn about the first humans. Even though I already knew a lot about the subject, I found it necessary—and enjoyable—to spend a good deal more time on research. I read about 25 books on anthropology, and at least 30 magazine articles. I also toured a primate research center with a professional anthropologist.

"The book took three years of research and one year of writing. I got more and more interested. It won't be hard to write more books on the same subject. Knowledge doesn't dry up. It expands, and so does your mind. That's a good reason to do research. It's a joy."

> ❝ *The novel germination process means thinking it out in broad terms, not trying to plot every zig and zag in the storyline. I don't bother with the details because I like to be agreeably surprised by what I write.*
> —*Saul Bellow* ❞

# On writing a short story

## by Anton Chekhov

## From a letter to Alexander P. Chekhov

In my opinion a true description of Nature should be very brief and have a character of relevance. Commonplaces such as, "the setting sun bathing in the waves of the darkening sea, poured its purple gold, etc."; "the swallows flying over the surface of the water twittered merrily"—such commonplaces one ought to abandon. In descriptions of Nature one ought to seize upon the little particulars, grouping them in such a way that, in reading, when you shut your eyes, you get a picture.

For instance, you will get the full effect of a moonlight night if you write that on the mill-dam a little glowing star-point flashed from the neck of a broken bottle, and the round, black shadow of a dog, or a wolf, emerged and ran, etc. Nature becomes animated if you are not squeamish about employing comparisons of her phenomena with ordinary human activities, etc.

In the sphere of psychology, details are also the thing. God preserve us from commonplaces. Best of all is it to avoid depicting the hero's state of mind; you ought to try to make it clear from the hero's actions. It is not necessary to portray many characters. The center of gravity should be in two persons: him and her.

[1886]

## From a letter to Aleksey S. Suvorin

You abuse me for objectivity, calling it indifference to good and evil, lack of ideals and ideas, and so on. You would have me, when I describe horse thieves, say: "Stealing horses is an evil." But that has been known for ages without my saying so. Let the jury judge them; it's my job simply to show what sort of people they are. I write: You are deal-

---

*Anton Chekhov, the great Russian dramatist and short story writer of the last century, wrote* The Seagull, Uncle Vanya, The Cherry Orchard, The Three Sisters *and hundreds of short stories, which have immensely influenced the art of fiction. Chekhov often described his theories of literature and his practices as a storyteller in letters, such as the three here, to his older brother, his publisher and a younger author whose work he admired.*

ing with horse thieves, so let me tell you that they are not beggars but well-fed people, that they are people of a special cult, and that horse-stealing is not simply theft but a passion. Of course, it would be pleasant to combine art with a sermon, but for me personally it is extremely difficult and almost impossible, owing to the conditions of technique. You see, to depict horse thieves in 700 lines I must all the time speak and think in their tone and feel in their spirit; otherwise, if I introduce subjectivity, the image becomes blurred and the story will not be as compact as all short stories ought to be. When I write, I reckon entirely upon the reader to add for himself the subjective elements that are lacking in the story.

[1890]

## From a letter to Maxim Gorky

More advice: When reading the proofs, cross out a host of terms qualifying nouns and verbs. You have so many such terms that the reader's mind finds it a task to concentrate on them, and he soon grows tired. You understand it at once when I say, "The man sat on the grass"; you understand it because it is clear and makes no demands on the attention. On the other hand, it is not easily understood, and it is difficult for the mind, if I write, "A tall, narrow-chested, middle-sized man, with a red beard, sat on the green grass, already trampled by pedestrians, sat silently, shyly, and timidly looked about him." That is not immediately grasped by the mind, whereas good writing should be grasped at once— in a second.

[1899]

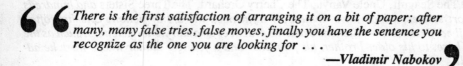

> *There is the first satisfaction of arranging it on a bit of paper; after many, many false tries, false moves, finally you have the sentence you recognize as the one you are looking for . . .*
>
> *—Vladimir Nabokov*

# The serious business of choosing literary fiction

## by Ben Nyberg

To take, or not to take: That's the bottom-line question we editors are always asking. When I first became a practicing editor back in 1966—picking stories, poems, and essays for *Kansas Magazine*—I had no complicated set of criteria to help me answer that question, and fortunately, I didn't need many. If something was publishable, *Kansas Magazine* wanted to publish it. Not that we didn't reject plenty of stories. We had our standards. But they were like a homeplate umpire's—a story was a strike or a ball; if a strike, we took it.

A year later, Harold Schneider and I found ourselves editing *Kansas Magazine*'s successor, *Kansas Quarterly*, with four times the space to fill. I don't think we've ever "widened the strike zone" to make up our quota of pages. From the start, I believe *Kansas Quarterly*'s standards have been consistently high (or at any rate consistent). But I know that at first it was still possible to make editorial decisions largely on the toggle basis of printworthiness: publishable, green light; not publishable, red light. Sometimes I yearn for those good old days, when I could feel that every deserving submission we screened saw print.

But only sometimes. Most of the time I'm happier being an editor besieged by deserving writers, deluged by worthy material. I like knowing there's so much good stuff out there, so many wordsmiths crafting diligently away, quite a few of them eager to be published in our magazine. I'm also glad I've had to become a better editor. When you can print only a few of many deserving submissions, you have to refine your critical sensitivity and establish your esthetic priorities beyond the simple toggle level. You have to know—well enough to explain and justify it to fellow editors—why you value one publishable work over another.

*Ben Nyberg is an associate professor of English at Kansas State University and an editor of* Kansas Quarterly. *He has published his own stories in various literary magazines—* South Dakota Review, Quartet, Texas Review *and others—and is currently on sabbatical in England at work on a story-writing textbook,* The Fiction Primer, *and a play.*

## Special affects

You ask: What *are* the standards literary magazine fiction editors try to apply to the steady, welcome stream of unsolicited mss? As a fairly representative literary editor, I can explain. But before getting down to criteria, a disclaimer: No matter how hard I, or any other editor, may try to make purely objective judgments, there are always X-factors muddying our objectivity. This doesn't make our decisions less just, only more human. When the late John Gardner judged *KQ*'s fiction awards for 1977, he admitted candidly: "My fifth standard is pure blind prejudice." Meaning that he, like the rest of us, had his quirks. I know we editors sometimes seem to behave like soulless robots, handing down death sentences with icy indifference. But we're really pretty normal humans with a full set of personal passions and phobias, and a fair measure of fallibility.

These X-factors are the main reason magazines need editorial boards. Without X-factors, we could simply codify selection guidelines and hire a technician to screen submissions. A few magazines do operate with a single editor as judge-jury-executioner. This eliminates all the weary wrangling sessions and speeds the waiting author's trial. But editors are too scrupulous a lot, generally, to like one-man shows. Consensus judgment rather than individual taste holds sway. That means more hurdles for your ms to leap, but less chance you'll be rejected (or accepted) because of X-factors.

One other thing to keep in mind: a publication's "special interests." Of course, some of them are obvious enough. *Ellery Queen's Mystery Magazine*, not surprisingly, "accepts only mystery, crime and detective fiction." *Rod Serling's Twilight Zone* is interested in "experimental, fantasy, horror, psychic/supernatural." A waste of time and postage to send mainstream fiction to either of them. But most general-interest magazines have a slant, too, and you'll have to dig beneath their names to find it. Reading a magazine before you submit to it is the only way to know for sure what its editors want. But descriptions of objectives and needs, like those in this directory, can help narrow your list. You'd think *Road King Magazine*, for instance, might be every bit as macho as *Hustler*, but its editors warn: "Remember that our magazine gets into the home and that some truckers tend to be Bible belt types. No erotica or violence." *Seniority Magazine*, whose audience is the "55 and over group," offers this caution: "No stories about coping with retirement, entering nursing homes, dealing with tired marriages, etc." So be sure you really know the special needs of any magazine before you ship your work off to it.

Some magazines also strive for some kind of thematic unity in each of their issues, so that unless your story has the particular focus they're featuring it will be returned unconsidered. But keep your eyes open and you can also take advantage of such special topics. I've heard of magazines doing issues that featured epistolary fiction, Edgar Allen Poe spoofs and parodies, stories about children, rural fiction. The best thing about submitting to such "specials" is that there's just not as much competition. It won't mean a better chance of getting shoddy work published, but good work won't have so far to rise to the top. Invitations to submit to features are normally found in the magazines, themselves. But most editors seek variety rather than unity of effect, so that once they've taken several stories with a similar theme (like marital infidelity), tone (brightly comic, steely grim), or even setting (shopping mall, darkest Africa) they're unlikely to want another until they've seen the accepted one into print.

## Baited breadth

Still, after all the X-factors and special interests, it's the literary excellence of your work more than anything else that brings acceptances. Regardless of our individual whims and cranks, we editors are all looking for the same thing—fiction masterpieces. No wonder the commonest piece of advice to writers in sourcebooks like *FWM* about "how to break in" is: Send us your best. Now we know, given the choice, you'd rather have your story appear in, say, *The New Yorker* than in *Boondocks Review*; you get more visibility and the pay's better. But don't suppose the editors of *Boondocks* will be any easier to satisfy than *The New Yorker*'s. Rumor has it that name writers send out their junk to *Boondocks*, whose editors snap it up because they'll do anything for a little status. But of course name writers don't want trash published under their name, in *Boondocks* or elsewhere, and *Boondocks* doesn't want condescension from anyone. So send only your best to any magazine and hope the editors are discriminating enough to appreciate it.

And keep sending it. Even if your work deserves print, given the odds against you on any one submission it probably won't make the grade if you don't persist. You've heard of shrinking violet geniuses who never showed their stuff to anyone and left a trunkful of masterpieces in the attic of posthumous publication. Such pathological modesty is no virtue for you to imitate. Better model yourself on the old fisherman who baited up a dozen poles along the bank, and when he was accused of taking unfair advantage of the fish, replied, "Hell, I'm just giving myself a fighting chance!" Use your own poles and bait, but keep as many hooks baited as you can to keep yourself in circulation.

Your best stuff, and only your best stuff. But that really presents the tough question—what is your best stuff? And how do you know when it's good enough? Maybe that's not even something a writer should ponder much. You can start brooding about "actualizing your creative potential" and wind up spooking yourself right out of the game. But you do need to have a firm grip on just who you are and what you know that merits a reader's attention. If you don't know your own mission, vision, habits, scruples, and quirks, you're not on familiar enough terms with yourself to self-criticize. Only if you're a "conscious artist," working from technique rather than "inspiration," can you use any advice about how to improve.

## Playing god

Now to those criteria. Mine work like a system of screens, from coarsest to finest or, in another sense, most basic to most refined. To be acceptable, stories need to pass the first two screenings. To be actually accepted, probably three or four. The first, most fundamental screening must be for the most essential virtue:

**Honesty.** What, honesty in a craft dedicated to artifice? Yes, because only sincere lies will do. Your imaginary details must come from an alternative environment so real that you're not alibiing when you talk about it. Building air-castles is fine, but unless you create the ground they stand on and the beings that live in them as well, you're not going to convince anybody that they exist. Your first duty as a fiction writer is to know that other place like a native, not just an occasional visitor. Trollope was so well acquainted with Barsetshire that he knew what its people were doing even when they weren't in the story. Faulkner "lived" in Yoknapatawpha County as surely as he did in Jackson, Mississippi. You've got to do the same. Being familiar with the setting is the only way to cover the doings and sayings, goings and comings of your imagined world's residents accurately and thoroughly enough to take us there with you. That's the essence of honesty—giving the reader a direct view of the lives of people who exist only in your unique mindland.

Obviously all the stories *KQ* has printed over the years felt honest, at least to us. Probably half our submissions have this basic virtue. But that still leaves half of them "dishonest" in one way or another. How does an editor know when a story is dishonest? The same way you'd spot any con-job—it smells fishy. As an example, let me recap my first attempt at fiction writing. Twenty-five years ago I knew little of fictional honesty. What I did know was that I could give *Good Housekeeping*'s readers a better story than they were used to getting. I'd have to sacrifice some seriousness and subtlety, but with just a little scaling down of my lofty standards, I'd treat them to a real gem of a yarn. So I went and wrote a slanderously false account of a gawky high school intellectual's helpless infatuation with a glamorous cheerleader. The story bore no resemblance to life as it is lived. Worse, it was insufferably patronizing, strutting and swaggering, casting snide glances at a presumed throng of enchanted admirers. The sad moral of this bad fable: Don't write out of pride or greed, and don't write about what you can't believe in. In short, be honest.

Efficiency comes right after honesty. I mean the principle that in fiction, nothing's there for nothing. Fiction may look like straight life, but the resemblance is superficial. Scratch a story and you get, not blood, but contrivance: structure, logic, symbolism, all sorts of synthetic goodies. Events happen only because some author-god makes them happen. In the real world, we seem to enjoy a measure of free will, but the world of fiction is driven entirely by the will of author-gods. Authors can literally make anything happen. They can say, "Let there be light," and there will be light. Because they are all-powerful, author-gods have an absolute responsibility to play fair with both their puppet characters and their show's spectators. And the basic rule of fair play is: Give readers as much as, but no more than, they need to know to get the point of the story. So the presentation of evidence in fiction is highly selective—what helps the reader *get it* belongs; what doesn't, doesn't.

## 3-D efficiency

I've returned hundreds of potentially strong stories that failed mainly because of inefficiency. Every year I read dozens of narratives that seem to be nothing but records of actual experience. The raw data can't be doubted, but I always have to wonder why a reader should be curious about the random episodes of somebody's personal life he doesn't know from Adam or Eve. Such a confessional ego trip is a waste of editorial time. We try to pretend it's really fiction and so to make sense of the authorial persona's spiritual journey, only to find in the end the joke's on the reader, there's no real point after all.

Of course nothing done by fallible humanity is ever perfectly anything. So no story is ever perfectly efficient. But some *KQ* stories have come close. I recall with a shudder the stern, cruel efficiency of James Hashim's "The Party" (*KQ*8.1.), that John Cheever praised for its total control. Or Phil Schneider's sure-footed, closely felt "Traps" (14.3.), a saga of self exile and isolation that won both our *KQ* (national) and Seaton (Kansas only) awards for 1982/83. As Lee Zacharias said, "It is a rare story which can so successfully close in on itself." Or Jack Matthews' "Quest For an Unnamed Place" (13.3/4), which Natalie Petesch called "an exquisitely-rendered story of the yearning for lost innocence and the days of our youth, with a gently-heroic ending that is unforced and honest." Honest and efficient both! What makes me cite these stories for efficiency is their refusal to waste a single moment of the reader's attention. They never quit pushing ahead, never relax their search for answers to the questions they raise. The result is a rich, dense illusion of life that manages to pack large meaning into a few pages.

Few, but not necessarily very few. Efficiency isn't simply brevity. The shortest of these efficient stories needed nine *KQ* pages. And some of the classical masterpieces of efficiency like Joyce's "The Dead" and Chekhov's "The Lady With the Pet Dog" would take 30 or more. Efficiency isn't pure velocity either. For sheer speed Ian Fleming's spy novels are hard to top, but for real pace—that feeling of powerful purpose unfolding, surging inevitably on like a great river to spill finally into a vast resolving sea—give me Conrad's *The Secret Agent* any day. Pace is set by the rate a story's central idea develops, not by the noise level of the plot. So if you're tempted to introduce some sex or violence just to liven things up, ask yourself instead why your story's so dull. If it's not going anywhere anyway, no amount of gratuitous hype will save it.

**Complexity** is the third screen I sift stories through. Eudora Welty says a good story is a "continuing mystery." That means, no matter how often you read it, a story worth reading will always be larger than your comprehension of it. You can't wear it out because its central question is the question life itself asks, Life gets more profound the more we know of it, and so does the expanding universe of serious fiction. What gives a story this quality of complexity is its author's determination to accept no easy fixes, to settle for no less than the depth and range of actual experience. Specifically, this means 3-D characters involved in 3-D predicaments.

It's so tempting to sell out. Human nature yearns for simplicity, because life's so complicated. We want fairy tale solutions—"and they lived happily ever after." It's tough enough to live problems, we feel. Why should we have to face them in our stories too? Because stories, the best stories, are the finest life-problem decoders and life-crisis stabilizers available. Of course there'll always be escapist fiction too, for those times when we really need to run rather than cope. Nobody's up to fighting trim every day. But nobody with any gumption wants to spend more time running than coping. Hence, the mission of serious fiction: to see life steadily and see it whole (thank you, Matthew Arnold).

## Authority, authority

When I was trying to work myself up to read *The Lord of the Rings*, I asked those who'd read and liked it what there was to get interested in. Fan after fan told me, without hesitation, I'd be fascinated by Gollum. When I got into it, I saw why: Gollum is Tolkein's little go at Dostoevsky. No Raskolnikov, but still a truly tormented soul that makes us ponder Faulkner's everlasting problem of the human heart in conflict with itself. Stories that fail the Complexity test do so because they try to deny human nature, to tell us life is a bowl of pitless cherries. Good fiction gives us the cherries, pits and all.

Of the many *KQ* stories deserving blue ribbons for complexity, the first to come to mind is Winston Weathers' "The Man Who Was Tricked By God" (2.1.). There is a magical resonance about its narrator's spiritual journey that moves me, just thinking of it now, some 15 years later. Even longer ago, George Blake's "A Modern Development" in 1.1, a natural microcosm complete with Everyman trying to fight off the inevitable, was an O.Henry Prize winner. Natalie Petesch's allegory, "The Bathhouse & Leprosarium" (8.3/4.), returns to haunt me with dismal regularity. As David Madden wrote, "Ms. Petesch approaches perfection in her handling of all this story's elements." Which hints at the essence of complexity: quality workmanship throughout, uniformly top-of-the-line components, no skimping on characters or theme or plot or setting. Henry James recommended that you try to be one on whom nothing is wasted. If you practice that kind of sensitivity, and add honesty, you've got complexity.

**Authority**, my fourth screen, is hard to define, but easy to feel. The honest story that lacks authority may well be the single biggest category of rejected fiction. Because poor authority is so tough to describe, writers often think editors capricious, arbitrary, or evasive when they report, "Your story didn't quite come off," or "Interesting, but not quite compelling." Such remarks usually mean, "Close but no cigar"—a compliment. If you're new to the craft, be encouraged. A little more experience should bring the authority you need.

But what is this mysterious "authority" and where does it come from? I'd call it a wise and easy authorial confidence that both guides a reader's attitude and spurs his thinking. How to get it? Exercise. Practice, I mentioned earlier that you had to be able to live in the elsewhere of your story. The air of that elsewhere is words, and you've got to breathe words. When you've made and remade enough sentences that the scribal act is the most natural and familiar routine of your life, you ought to feel comfortable enough with words to write with authority. Not that the verbal flow ever turns smooth or steady, but its trickle/gush can become as mundane as heartbeats.

## Original drumbeat

The common name for authority is, of course, *style*. But style is really authority in action, authority showing itself verbally. Or concealing itself: The best style is usually invisible. When writing calls attention to itself, ordinarily it's a case of words upstaging ideas, which puts cart before horse. Poor style of any kind—from "purple" to sloppy—is a distraction, and so an enemy of concentration, and so an enemy of good writing, fiction or otherwise. Of course there are exceptions to this rule. H.E. Francis' stories, several of which *KQ* has had the good fortune to publish, are always very gaudy stylistically. But only because they reflect the tortured minds of their main characters. Rodney Nelson used poetic diction in "John Root Is Gone" (9.1.) to capture the aura of his Roethke-like central figure. Stephen Dixon's "Cy" (8.1.) can't very well keep his strangeness from showing itself in his narrative voice. But the rule stands: *Good style is* normally a colorless, odorless, textureless medium of conveyance. What's conveyed may have color, odor, texture, but style shouldn't be a distorting lens the reader has to correct for.

When a reader's under the influence of style/authority, it's like following the Pied Piper. About Jerry Bumpus' "A Morning in Arcadia" (9.3.) John Gardner wrote, "it wears its learning with a beautiful indifference, wastes not a word, not an image, convinces me against my will." That's authority. He went on, "Bumpus can lay down a line of prose—his sentences have the authority of a Zen painting or a Mozart transition." That's style. Anne Tyler said of H.E. Francis' "Two Lives" (11.1/2.), "I felt I was not so much reading [it] as becoming absorbed into it. Returning from it took hours." No finer tribute to authority than that.

**Originality** is the ultimate test of worth. Nothing is rarer than genuine originality, nothing artistically finer. Of course it's easy to be different. Anyone can perform a weird masquerade and get folks to point at him. What's hard is to be different and still get folks to hear and believe. That takes genius. Meaning it's out of reach for most of us? On a daily basis, probably yes. Beethoven, Shakespeare, Michelangelo—a handful of creative giants seem to have enjoyed steady runs of original vision. But for most of us garden-variety specimens it's a case of now-and-then, off-and-on flashes of "inspiration."

The most important thing to remember about originality is that it absolutely can't be forced. Try to force it and you'll get nothing but oddity. The most you can actively do is to cultivate your eccentricity. Don't let your natural uniqueness die of neglect. If you spend your life imitating others, socially or artistically, you can't expect to turn out very original. It's not even necessary to be a recluse in some isolated garret. Just don't lose your identity in the crowds. Hold fast to your observer status, to that perspective that sets you apart. You needn't look down on people or think you're a privileged character. But you can't hop on the bandwagon and also march to a different drumbeat.

Some young fiction writers worry about a lick of freshness in their plots or unusualness in their characters or novelty in their style or format. Remind yourself that Shakespeare's plots were all derivative and his dramatic technique was conventional, and quit worrying. If you have the potential of originality, be yourself and it will show through.

## Cool the coffee

Having claimed so much for originality, I'm not suggesting that most *KQ* stories achieve it. But we have printed several that convince me anew each time I read them that they really do break fresh ground. I'll mention only two of them: first, yet another H.E. Francis gem, "A Chronicle of Love" (7.1/2.), our most "prized" and anthologized story, of which William Gass wrote: "a splendidly ambitious piece, full of emotional power, real song, and impressive verbal energy. One is at once aware of a writer going somewhere very special in a high-performance vehicle." It is indeed a trip worth taking. The other story I'll credit with originality went largely unnoticed, so far as I can tell, except by *KQ* editors—"Mary" (2.1.) by J. Johnson, who may have published nothing before or after, but who made her indelible mark on our consciousness with this eerie tale of a transfigured reality as potent as a black-and-white Bergman film.

From originality you can only go back to honesty and start over. Originality is simply the highest avatar of honesty, the ultimate expression of authority. True complexity is possible only within a context of full efficiency, which must be practiced upon a groundwork of honesty. And so it goes, up and down—and around—the scale. Five benchmarks of quality, five gradations. You must be honest to pass. Honest and efficient gets you a C. Add complexity for a B. And authority for an A. Originality is that exceptional A+ that's really off the scale.

In closing, let me give you an affective criterion that sums up all the descriptive ones. One final bit of personal history. I recall the Sunday afternoon I finished reading the submitted ms. of Steven Allaback's "It's Never Bad in the Mountains" (14.1.) and turned to find a full cup of cold coffee beside me. The neglected cup of coffee: not too bad a figure for the subjugating mesmerism of strong fiction. The intensity of this experience a powerful story inflicts on us comes, I am convinced, from our being forced to face its issues so directly we adopt them as our own. We are, in a word, *implicated* in the depicted action. In the Allaback story I was caught up superficially on the level of adventure, wondering if anyone was going to fall to his death, and if so, who. But I was more surely held by the battle of wills, the moves and countermoves of its three conflicting quests. I was made to care so deeply about the lives of these imaginary beings that I forgot they were only performers on a stage and took their case to heart.

That's always the way with working fiction. No wandering idly through a zoo, noting with detached amusement the alien oddities of some other species. Rather, listening for dear life to crucial news about humanity's struggle for high ground. We don't so much escape into great fiction as come home to it. We don't lose ourselves in some exotic adventure, we find ourselves challenged by our own uncertainties, disturbed by our own cussedness, supported by our own determination. And when we're all done, our coffee's gone cold. Make an editor forget his coffee and you're a long way toward making him take your story.

---

 *My aim is to put down what I see and what I feel in the best and simplest way I can tell it.*

—*Ernest Hemingway*

# The break-in: an inside look at a first fiction sale

## by Sharon Rudd

While working as assistant editor in the fiction department at *McCall's*, I once dreamed I was surrounded by unsolicited manuscripts. Stacks of stories, all waiting to be read. They grew taller and taller, threatening to topple and bury me beneath a blizzard of *SASE*s and unread prose. Trying to keep them at bay, I woke up, relieved to find myself pushing the bedclothes away instead.

I never fell as far behind in my manuscript reading as that dream suggested. Yet, keeping up with all the submissions *McCall's* received was a constant challenge. And sometimes I had the sensation I was reading the same four or five stories again and again. Birth stories, mother-daughter stories, disgruntled housewife stories, divorce stories— after a while I could almost predict what would happen in them. What made all the time I spent reading worthwhile was finding a story that offered something fresh and compelling in its handling of familiar themes. If a story showed some spark that set it apart from other submissions—even if it didn't fully succeed in accomplishing what it set out to do or in meeting our editorial requirements—I might be able to work with the writer to improve it. Each time I sat down to read, I hoped to discover some seed of promise that could be nurtured into a story for *McCall's*.

## "David went to Woodstock . . . a week late"

What did I look for in a story? And how might I help the writer improve its chances for publication? I can answer these questions, in part, by telling what happened with an

---

*Sharon Rudd is assistant editor of* Writer's Digest *and has also worked on the editorial staffs of* McCall's *and* St. Martin's Press. *Her work has appeared in* McCall's *and* Writer's Yearbook 1985.

over-the-transom story about a single mother and her son. Titled "Nobody's Woman-folk," it opened like this:

> "David told me a great joke today, Mom. Wanna hear it? . . . David says I can go fishing with him someday. Fly-fishing. In the mountains . . . David thinks Jane Fonda's prettier than Bo Derek . . . David says . . ."
>
> David . . . David . . . David. . . David . . . Now this. Diana frowned, shaking her long, dark hair loose from its confining bun. David was coming to supper. Never mind that Logan had invented him from the whole cloth of his mind. David was coming, and no amount of arguing could convince Logan that he wasn't.
>
> She had spent a month steeped in the lore of David. "David went to Wood-stock," Logan had told her. "Only, he got the date wrong so he was there a week late." Diana had stared at Logan then, trying to decipher the limits of her son's fertile imagination. He had invented the perfect hero to replace his father—a man complete with motorcycle and a past that would charm any six-year-old.

In just three paragraphs, I could see this story had energy and a certain charm. The story's premise, the imaginary friend, was intriguing, if not especially unusual. And I could see the writer was going to do something special with it. This David fellow wasn't your typical talking teddy bear. He rode a motorcycle, was opinionated about movie stars—he was even prey to human foibles. I was immediately drawn to the precocious little boy who would invent such an outlandish hero, and I wanted to find out what he'd come up with next.

The more I read, the more I liked Logan's mother, too. She's not quite sure what to make of Logan's chatter about David and his Harley, but she was willing to humor her son nonetheless. The writer had done a nice job of catching Diana's skeptical amusement toward Logan in this scene, for instance, where he pesters her about getting supper ready for his "friend":

> "What are we having?" [Logan asked.]
>
> "TV dinners." [Diana said.]
>
> "TV dinners?" Logan was appalled. "We can't have TV dinners. Besides, there's only two of them." So David was still coming, Diana thought, glancing at Logan's painfully disapproving face. She had expected an imaginative cancellation—a secret mission for the President, perhaps—but if that was how Logan was planning to save face, he certainly was playing his timing very close.
>
> "OK. There's one frozen pizza. Do macho, he-men like pizza?" There was also a crabmeat casserole put aside for an emergency—that rare, impromptu situation demanding elegance—but she wasn't about to waste her emergency casserole on a man who didn't exist . . .
>
> "Yeah. He'd probably like the pizza OK," Logan agreed, though his tightly puckered forehead warned that she wasn't coming up to David's standards.
>
> Diana stripped the cellophane wrapper off the pizza and dropped it with a clunk onto a metal cookie sheet. "I'll pop it in and go wash up," she offered "Why don't you turn on the tube or read your bulldozer book?"
>
> "Naw, I think I'll pick up the living room." He slid off the chair and headed for the living room, but he turned back before he reached the door. "Do you think we could have a vegetable?"
>
> "Sure." Diana stared after him. Something green, and he had asked for it himself. Maybe David could be useful.
>
> "Hey, monster child," she called out, "Do you think David would like spinach?"

"Naw. Nobody likes spinach."

Spinach was too much to expect, Diana thought pragmatically . . . Green beans were a start.

This story was really fun to read. I enjoyed those apt bits of detail, and the breezy, whimsical dialogue rang true. I could hear the rise and fall of Logan's indignation and disappointment in those lines as clearly as I could hear the frozen pizza drop with a thud onto the cookie sheet. And when I read that by the end of the week Diana was down to her last two TV dinners, one "emergency" casserole and a pizza, I knew she was someone I—and many *McCall's* readers—could relate to.

## "James Cagney, right?"

For characters to really involve a reader in a story, they must be believable as well as likable. With touches like the ones I've just mentioned, the writer had etched a wryly sympathetic picture of this working mother stretched thin by her responsibilities. Logan's six-year-old antics were equally endearing and convincing.

The story earned good marks for commerciality by being not only realistic but also nicely upbeat. The warmth between Logan and Diana was a refreshing change from many of the harried housewife stories I read at *McCall's*. I especially enjoyed the easy give and take between them that the writer showed in this light-hearted scene, when Diana comes of the shower and sees how pleased with himself Logan is for tidying up the living room:

Logan sat in the wing-backed chair beside the window looking for all the world like a child who had just been crowned the local king. His bowl-cropped hair was neatly combed, and he had changed into his most becoming, ironed, shirt . . .

"[You] look gorgeous." She stopped halfway across the room to grin at her cherubic son. Funny that he seemed so terribly grown-up sometimes . . .

"You're going to change, aren't you?" His smile faded as she stood in the middle of the room wondering whether to tell him what she felt. He'd probably find it horribly embarrassing.

"In a minute. . . . I've got something very important to tell you first."

"Can you tell me later? It's going to be slushy, isn't it?"

"Yes. It's going to be slushy." Diana caught him up and dragged him from his chair. "Now listen to me, kid, and listen good," she muttered in a gravelly voice, "'cause if you don't listen, you're going to end up in the river wearing a pair of cement overshoes, see? The warden in this joint loves you to distraction. So there!" She planted a raspberry kiss against the giggling youngster's cheek.

"James Cagney, right?"

The voice came from the ktichen doorway, deep and masculine and every bit as amused as the brown eyes that met hers unexpectedly.

So David wasn't a figment of Logan's imagination after all! That sort of twist can be fun to come across in a story, but it's difficult to pull off convincingly. There's a fine line between having it seem to come out of nowhere and so clearly telegraphing it that the reader feels insulted the writer expected it to be a surprise. This writer had succeeded, however, and earned my respect in the process. Looking back, I could see that Logan's description of David had been too detailed, too idiosyncratic for even the most imaginative six-year-old to have conjured from thin air. But I'd been enjoying the friendly repartee between Logan and Diana so much that I was carried right along, unsuspecting.

Since I was as surprised as Diana, I could understand her puzzled dismay to be standing there, still in her bathrobe, face to face with a leather-jacketed stranger. Especially one who is so much more in command of the situation than she: "I found one beer and about half a glass of wine in your refrigerator," David tells Diana. "Plenty of apple juice, though. I think we're set for apple juice until the turn of the century. Do you want the wine or the beer?"

Taken aback, Diana warns David that he'd better leave, then marches off to the bedroom to change out of her bathrobe. David goes after her a few minutes later, hoping to talk her into changing her mind. But he aggravates the already tense situation by striding into the bedroom before she has finished dressing. Diana tells him she doesn't like the fact that her son has taken up with a total stranger—a scruffy-looking biker, of all things. But David finally wins her over in this scene (one of my favorites), explaining that, far from being a Hell's Angel, he's actually an investment counselor.

"I'm serious." He pulled out his wallet and handed her a card. "Here's my ID."

There he was, serious and reflective, dressed in a dark gray suit and impeccably correct blue tie. He certainly looked like a man who could be trusted with one's money.

He flipped through his wallet. "My driver's license. I'm licensed for everything except tractor trailer rigs and I don't need corrective lenses . . . My library card . . . I read occasionally. . . .My uniform donor's card. . . . If I drop dead in your living room, just call this number and they'll come divide me into my most useful parts. . . . Do you think I can stay for supper, or do I have to show you my credit cards, too?"

Diana relents, and while the three of them eat dinner, David spins silly stories that give further evidence for why Logan adores him.

After Logan goes off to bed, David and Diana talk for a while. Finally David gets on his motorcycle to go home, but he stops at the end of the driveway to make a rambling, embarrassed speech about how much he's wanted to kiss Diana all evening. Here's how Diana responds:

Something had to stop his idiotic flow of words. Diana kissed him. His arms hung loose for a startled half-second before he caught her up, taking her breath away with the ferocity of his embrace.

"Yeah, well. . . . that's what I wanted to do," he whispered when he let her go. . . . "I own a sidecar. Have you ever seen a sidecar?"

"No."

"Well, you will. Tomorrow. I'll pick you both up at 10. Be ready. I like my womanfolk to be on time." He kicked down hard to start the engine.

"David! There's just one more thing you've got to know if we're going to see each other," she shouted above the engine's rasping blare. "I will not be called a womanfolk. I'm nobody's womanfolk!"

"The hell you aren't!" His triumphant voice was swallowed by the screeching gurgle of the engine as he soared down the street.

Now, I liked Diana and David, and I'd sort of hoped they would hit it off. But that conclusion seemed a bit much. They had decided they were going to be seeing each other after just one evening? Like most readers, I enjoy a little romance and a happy ending. But in this case (as in many of the stories I received at McCall's), I felt the writer was forcing the story to end on a more optimistic note than it warranted.

There were so many things I liked about the story—the zippy dialogue, Logan's exuberance, David's offbeat sense of humor, Diana's rapport with her son. Where had the story lost me?

## "Worth seeing, sidecars"

To get a clearer sense of why I had trouble swallowing that ending, I went back to the scenes that led up to it. In some places, I felt the story lacked sufficient motivation for the character's actions. In others, I saw that the writer had provided more explanation than necessary. Two scenes in particular I found awkward and unconvincing: One was right after David's appearance, where Diana tries to get him to leave. The other was when David goes into her bedroom to talk.

Now, I could understand Diana's being startled to discover that David was real. But she seemed to be over-reacting to the situation. David was such an amusing, good-natured fellow that I couldn't see why she was so determined to get rid of him. And since Logan was so proud of himself for inviting David to dinner, it seemed out of character for Diana to go against his wishes.

The impropriety of David's barging in on Diana also struck a sour note. He was a bit outrageous, but nothing else in the story suggested he was ill-mannered. If he really wanted to gain Diana's good graces (and I believed he did), he certainly seemed shrewd enough to pick a more comfortable setting for their conversation.

Despite its problems, the story exhibited a freshness that I didn't come across often in the manuscripts I read for *McCall's*. These basic situations and relationships the story dealt with were certainly appropriate for our audience, and Logan, David and Diana were people I thought our readers would find especially appealing. I thought the story had promise. So I passed it on to Helen DelMonte, the fiction editor, for another reading.

She shared my feeling that the story had spark, and agreed that it didn't yet live up to its potential. We discussed the elements of the story we liked, as well as those that made us uneasy. Our job was not simply to point out the story's faults, but to figure out concrete ways they could be corrected. How could individual scenes be made to work better, and how would these changes affect the overall shape of the story.

The main problem was that the story tried to cover too much emotional ground. I couldn't believe that a reasonably level-headed woman like Diana would undergo such an abrupt change of heart in the course of one evening—and one short story. On page nine, she was trying to throw David out of her house. Just ten pages later, she was falling head over heels in love with him. The story didn't seem to demand either of those extremes of emotion—both Diana's initial antagonism toward David and that extravagantly romantic conclusion seemed false. If, on the one hand, the writer would temper Diana's hostility (and cut that scene where David makes matters worse by bursting into her bedroom) and, on the other, tone down the certainty of their love affair, the story wouldn't have to travel so far to get where it was going. And it would be much more convincing. We decided to ask the author to revise the story with those things in mind.

The writer, Sharron Cohen, didn't have an agent, and she'd never published fiction. In fact, this was the first time we'd seen her work. Encouraging a writer to rework a story and then let us see it again wasn't terribly uncommon. But we knew that, unfortunately, only a small percentage of those revisions would find their way into the magazine. What made us think that it would be worth our time—and Sharron Cohen's—to work on revising this story?

It offered a lot of material to work with, and contained certain essential ingredients, like vivid, sympathetic characters. (It's much harder for an editor to guide a revision of a story that has shadowy characters—you can raise questions that such a story begs to have answered about the people in it, but that's no guarantee the writer will succeed in making them come alive.) Sharron Cohen had conveyed such a strong sense of the kinds of people Diana, David and Logan were that we could pinpoint places in the story where their actions were out of character, throwing the story off track. As a result, we could offer her specific suggestions for making the characters more consistent and believable, and the story, as a whole, more satisfying.

We also decided to pursue this story because it gave indications the writer was capable of making the kinds of changes we would ask for. Essentially, we wanted her to pull back a bit, to be more subtle. The light touch she had brought to those first pages (in drawing Diana's relationship with Logan, for instance) gave us hope that she could accomplish what we thought the story needed.

So I wrote Sharron Cohen a letter that included these comments:

"Nobody's Womanfolk" is fresh, charming, and full of wit and humor. Logan is a cute kid and there's a nice quality to the relationship between mother and son. But rather than make this a full-blown love story, the *suggestion* of an attraction between David and Diana is really all that's needed, and that's what the story should build toward.

Diana shouldn't be so hostile when David turns up—maybe just puzzled and flustered—and she shouldn't try to throw him out of the house. (After all, she's too sensitive to her son's feeling to be mean to his "best friend.") You should also avoid having David come into her bedroom—it's just not convincing that he would barge in on her like that.

Of course, there has to be some initial tension here, and a resolution of it. You should emphasize David's humor and their common consideration for Logan's feelings in easing Diana's reluctance toward David and in making her willing to make the best of an awkward situation . . .

All you need after Logan goes off to bed is to bring the story to conclusion— the reader should get the idea that Diana and David are interested in each other, that romance is in the air, but they shouldn't be diving headlong into a relationship quite so obviously.

I sent the letter off, not knowing what sort of response I would get. I had given the writer a general outline of what I thought the story needed. It was her job—if she was willing to entertain my suggestions—to figure out how, specifically, to implement them.

When I received Sharron Cohen's revision a few weeks later, I was delighted to find she'd taken my advice . . . and run with it. She had seen what I was getting at and, without diminishing the spark and vitality of the original version, had reshaped the story to make it much more persuasive. She hadn't been afraid to substantially alter problem scenes, yet she had been careful to weave those changes into the fabric of the story. She had done some cutting, some adding—and she had sometimes taken elements from the first version and recast them for a subtly different effect. Here, for instance, you can see what a different turn she gave to that final conversation between Diana and David, right down to the sidecar references:

You've raised a fine, well-mannered boy," David said as Diana followed him to the porch.

"So I'm discovering. Thank you for being so nice to him."

He retrieved his helmet . . . and turned it nervously in his hands . . .

"It's a nice motorcycle," Diana said, searching for something to say in the awkward silence. And searching too, she realized, for some way to prolong the moment before he said good night and drove away.

"Do you know about motorcycles?"

"No. Just what Logan tells me."

He shifted his weight from one foot to the other and frowned down at the helmet in his hands. "I have a sidecar, too. Have you ever seen a sidecar?"

"Only in the movies."

"They're worth seeing, sidecars," he murmured as he pulled on his helmet and backed down the walk. "I use it to do my grocery shopping. I should be coming down this street about 10 tomorrow morning. In case Logan wants to see the sidecar."

He kicked down hard to start the engine, then turned back to shout above the motor's rasping blare. "Maybe I can repay Logan for the supper invitation some night . . . And you. Good night."

"Good night."

She locked the kitchen door behind her, catching sight of the widening shimmer of her smile in the mirror beside the pantry door. She'd remember to tell Logan. David would be by at 10.

## "We've gotta get his supper!"

I was impressed by the solid, thoughtful work Sharron Cohen had put into the story. It worked much better now. Best of all, I still found the story charming and fun, although I had long since lost track of how many times I'd read it. But I knew my enthusiasm alone wouldn't get the story published. It would have to receive approval from the fiction editor, several senior editors, and finally the editor-in-chief. All of those people except Helen DelMonte would be reading the story for the first time. Now that the contours of the story were in place, I had to try to imagine what it would be like to read this story for the first time. Were the details presented in a way that was easy to read and follow?

Rereading those first three paragraphs, I realized they might confuse a reader coming to the story cold. It was hard to tell when or where the action was taking place, and it took a while to figure out what the relationship between the people were. I knew that a reader who had to work too hard to figure out what was going on in a story would likely put it down. Although those opening paragraphs contained important information—*and* were fun to read—they would have to be modified for the sake of the story.

The main action began almost three pages into the manuscript when Diana approaches the house on the night David will turn up for supper and calls out to Logan, "Hey, Slugger!" Three pages was too long to expect a reader to wait. Since most of the first two pages seemed to refer to remarks Logan had made about David in the last month, why not open the story with the "Hey, Slugger" scene—which was firmly anchored in the present and would immediately orient the reader to the story's action—and then have Diana flash back to what she'd heard Logan say about the motorcycle man?

As I experimented with rearranging the manuscript, I realized that to begin in the present and then flash back all at once to the first two pages would pull the reader too far away from the story line. Because the first two pages consisted of snippets of several different recalled conversations, I decided to use a series of flashbacks and to intersperse them with the ongoing scene when Diana gets home that evening.

The reorganization I had in mind would require occasional bridges between past and present. And I was sure the writer could provide transitions that would be far more graceful and better suited to the story than I could. As a rule, we didn't send an unpurchased story back for a second revision. If it didn't overcome our objections after one re-write, it probably wouldn't be worth our time—or the writer's—to ask for a second. But the substantial work Sharron Cohen had already put into the story did solve its major problems. Now it needed fine-tuning. So I wrote her a letter that included these comments:

> You've done an excellent revision of "Nobody's Womanfolk." The story is much stronger now, and you've turned the romance between Diana and David with a very nice touch. But we would like you to do a bit more polishing.
>
> I've already done some editing and am enclosing my working copy of the manuscript. None of this is graven in stone, of course, but it will give you some idea of what we think needs to be done. Your introductory paragraphs are a bit confusing. It's not quite clear what's happening or when the action takes place. We think it would be better to start right off with Diana's arrival at home on Friday night. I've reorganized the first four pages, interspersing present and past in a way that gives the reader the essential background information without getting too far away from the scene at hand. In many cases, as you'll see from my marginal comments, all we're asking is that you supply a line or two of transition or stage directions to get the characters from place to place.

Sharron Cohen went to work on the story again. Our combined efforts produced an opening that in part read:

"Hi, Slugger!" Diana waved at the dark-haired child who waited expectantly beside the gate.

"Hi, Mom! You're finally home! We've gotta hurry." Logan came at his mother like a wheeling, dark-eyed crow. "David will be here at 6. We've gotta get his supper!"

David, David, David. Logan talked of nothing else these days. "David told me this great joke today, Mom . . ." "David says I can go fly-fishing with him some day . . ." "David thinks Jane Fonda's prettier than Bo Derek . . ." And now this. David was coming to supper. Never mind that Logan had invented him from the whole cloth of his mind. David was coming, and that was that.

"David said he'd come over on his motorcycle." Logan's eyes glittered with excitement as he slipped his hand into his mother's to tug her along.

"C'mon, Mom. Hurry up. David likes his womanfolk to be quick with his supper."

Womanfolk?" He says things like *that?*

"He says womanfolk are meant for cooking and nursing. He's real pleased you're a nurse. And pretty. He says he like pretty, green-eyed nurses. Almost as much as motorcycles . . ."

## Sold: a first short story

Our final job was to cut the story. At a magazine like *McCall's* where limited space is allotted to fiction, almost every manuscript must be shortened somewhat. Cutting this story wasn't something Helen and I relished, but we knew we had to do it if the story were to have a shot a publication. By the second revision, every scene had an important function. So we couldn't remove whole chunks of text without damaging the story. Some scenes could be speeded up, though. And from there on out, it was a matter of trimming a nonessential word or phrase here, an occasional sentence there. The idea was to tighten the story throughout, without losing anything that was especially fun to read or necessary to lead the reader through the story. I had asked Sharron Cohen to do as much cutting as she could, and she'd done quite a bit. But, as she wrote me when she returned her second revision, "I went at 'Nobody's Womanfolk' with grim determination and managed to cut only half of what you wanted, so I'll leave the rest of the cutting to your discretion. I'm also enclosing a copy of the story before my cuts, in case you disagree and think some parts should be restored." Helen and I thought most of her cuts worked just fine. Then we found places where we could make a few more.

All of the substantial changes to the story had been made by the writer herself. I had tackled the manuscript only to reorganize her material in the early pages and to do some cutting. Beyond that, I had offered her suggestions, but she had done the real work—the rewriting, recasting, reshaping.

Although the problems this story eventually overcame were typical of the kinds of things we might work with a writer to correct, we seldom asked a writer to do so much work on a single story. In many cases where a story needed this much work, we would simply write a letter explaining why the story didn't work for us and asking the writer to let us see more of her work. We felt that few writers would have the willingness or skill to rework a story so thoroughly, and we knew that it was asking a lot of a writer to put so much time into revisions when we couldn't promise that the story would be accepted for publication.

But I had seen something special in this story that made me willing to take a chance on it. My persistence and the writer's paid off. Sharron Cohen's story appeared as "The Man on the Motorcycle" in the April 1984 issue of *McCall's*. She had sold her first short story.

---

> ❝ *Writing a short story is like fitting a delicate ship into a bottle.*
> —*Gordon Lish* ❞

# The phenomenon of James Michener

## by Caryn James

The elderly gentleman sitting quietly in an Austin, Texas, restaurant, hands folded before him, tends to stare straight ahead into space. It is impossible for someone who has just met him to know whether this signals shyness, boredom, the self-absorption of an obsessive writer or the natural distraction of a 78-year-old, tired and hungry at the end of a long day. But it is the most surprising of James A. Michener's many unexpected traits—this author, renowned for his curiosity, does not seem curious about other people; he rarely meets your eyes.

Yet moments later, he is chuckling, with a modesty and a teasing sense of humor that are endearing. An apologetic waiter has returned to say the kitchen is out of the roast duck Michener ordered, and the dinner becomes part of a running joke between the author and his right-hand man, John Kings. Michener has a knack for choosing the most popular item on a menu. Indeed, a few days later, he misses out on the last of the shrimp at a private club, and on both evenings Michener, on stage in his own low-key way, responds with the same laugh and the same line: "Harris and Gallup don't have to make all those phone calls to find out what people think. They should just call me. I'm the average guy."

No one doubts Michener's instinct for popular taste, but he was never average. *Tales of the South Pacific*, his first published fiction, won the 1948 Pulitzer Prize, but only when he moved from small stories of people to monolithic tales of places—beginning with the fictionalized history of *Hawaii* in 1959 through Israel in *The Source*, South Africa in *The Covenant*, *Poland*, *Chesapeake* and *Space*—did he become the kind of brand-name author whose books hit the bestseller lists before they reach the bookstores

---

*Caryn James has worked as an editor for* The New York Times Book Review *for a year. After her graduation from Brown University, she freelanced for several years and wrote frequently on literary subjects.*

# Detachment with appeal

The Michener formula might seem an unlikely one for the media age: big, old-fashioned narratives weaving generations of fictional families through densely documented factual events, celebrating the All-American virtues of common sense, frugality, patriotism. Yet these straitlaced, educational stories are so episodic that they are perfectly suited to the movie and television adaptations that have propelled Michener's success; his newest epic, *Texas,* which was published last fall, was as much a media event as a novel from the start, and a measure of Michener's unique place among today's writers. What other author would be officially invited, as Michener was in 1981 by Gov. William Clements, to write about Texas? Or offered a staff and office by the University of Texas to help him along? How many average guys have more than two years of time and upward of $100,000 of their own money to travel the state in borrowed planes, talking with scholars, tycoons and just plain folks? The product of this extravaganza is the heftiest Michener work yet, weighing in at 1,096 pages, moving from 16th-century Spanish explorers to 1980's cattle barons. Random House says its first printing of 750,000 is the largest in its history; ABC bought the television rights for a miniseries before a word was written.

All this hoopla seems out of character for the sedate man who likes to say of his work: "Whatever I did, there was always someone around who was better qualified. They just didn't bother to do it." But the Michener persona is not always consistent. Five minutes after playing down his accomplishments, he is apt to boast, "Every one of my books is still in print in hardcover. They just go on and on." He has been an adviser to NASA and an unsuccessful Congressional candidate. He is a millionaire who picks up rubber bands from the sidewalk, saying, "I can use these." Yet the role Michener delights in the most is that of the average American blessed with slightly-more-than-average brains, tenacity and luck.

Mari Michener, to whom the novelist has been married for 30 years, has an easy explanation for her husband's success, which is consonant with his Quaker upbringing. "He works very, very hard," she says with a summary nod. As with so much of what the Micheners say, the determined simplicity hints at a more complex truth. For a Michener novel is a tribute to the industriousness of both author and reader; and, in addition to the easy-to-swallow data, it contains a morality tale about the heroism of hard work and guts. His thick, fact-filled books seem thoroughly impersonal, but several days in Michener's company show the novels to be perfect expressions of their author's anomalies—moral without being stern, methodical yet digressive, insistently modest yet bursting with ambition, full of social conscience yet grasping at facts as a way to avoid emotion.

Michener is equally anomalous away from his typewriter. Day after day, he puts on his cowboy hat to accommodate photographers, autographs books when he has sworn to do no more, answers interviewers' wornout questions as if they were fresh. Every time a fan compliments his books, he replies with evident sincerity—"Thank you very much. That's good to hear"—in his deep, still-strong voice. But not one of these strangers says, "I feel I know you," or reacts with the warmth they might offer an I. B. Singer or the first-name familiarity they'd accord a Norman Mailer.

In his novels, Michener assumes the same distanced manner. As the literary critic Leslie Fiedler says, "Some writers are read because they have a voice like that of an old friend; Michener doesn't have that. His is as close to a neutral or nonstyle as you can get." Yet that detachment is part of his appeal to readers, Fiedler suggests: "He puts a book together in a perfectly lucid, undisturbing way, so that even potentially trouble-

James Michener, prolific author of *Texas, Poland, The Covenant, Chesapeake, Space* and other bestselling novels.

photo by John Kings

some issues don't seem so. *Hawaii* is about the problem of imperialism, yet one never senses that. *The Source* is about the Middle East, one of the most troublesome political issues in the world, but he's forgotten all the ambiguities. His approach is that if you knew all the facts, everything would straighten out, so it's soothing and reassuring to read him.''

Michener's polite reserve has fostered the legends that surround him—of childhood poverty, of enormous research staffs and novels written by committee, of a man impatient with small talk and wary of introspection. Some are true, some are myths Michener refutes; others, myths he helps along.

## Depression deep-felt

The official Michener biography, the story he tells and approves for Random House to distribute, is perfectly Dickensian. As an infant, he was taken in by Mabel Michener, a poor, young widow in Doylestown, Pa., and raised as her son alongside many foster children who came and went. At times, he recalls, reduced circumstances forced her to send him to the local poorhouse, but at home he felt loved and was inspired by her reading aloud from 19th-century novels, particularly Dickens. Not until he was a 19-year-old scholarship student at Swarthmore College did he learn, from an acquaintance, that he was adopted. He has never learned who his real parents were.

These facts are accurate, though slightly less melodramatic than they appear. John Hayes, in his biography of the author, claims that Michener was, in fact, Mabel's illegitimate son. Michener replies to that possibility: "I don't know whether it's true or not. I have no idea who I am. I know what I was told at the time, that I, like all the others, was a foundling. When I applied for a passport in 1931, there was no birth certificate, so the procedure was for the Government to establish with reputable people who I was. Nobody could trace me back farther that two years old; the investigation went on for a long time. They did establish that I was in Pennsylvania at the age of two. Now, whether people masked the truth or whether that's the case, I don't know, but that is the legal case." This explanation illustrates Michener's fundamental approach to life and art—tackle a problem, research it thoroughly, then put it aside (resolved or not) and don't brood about it. "I don't think about that much," is a frequent response to unsettling questions.

But the facts of Michener's early years are not so easily discovered and put aside. His childhood poverty was real, although it did not involve the abandonment the poorhouse story might suggest. One of Mabel Michener's sisters was married to the superintendent of the poorhouse, and the entire family occasionally stayed with her. Michener is hazy when discussing his aunt. "She worked there as a public nurse, and was the agent by which I got in." he says, insisting, "I was in the poorhouse on several extended occasions." At times, he may have been housed in the men's dormitory, but even someone as fond of Michener as John Kings believes the story is an exaggeration.

Whatever the details, the impact of those early years was so strong that discussing them even now evokes a rare emotional tone: "An experience like this is overwhelming. I can't remember how old I was, maybe 13, 14, and to see these fellows and hear their stories and to see life come to such a drab ending—my God, a poorhouse in those days was something. You would have to be inert not to respond to it. Maybe the most important aspect of my life."

Michener escaped poverty through education, becoming a social studies teacher in private schools and college and eventually a textbook editor at Macmillan. He became financially independent as a result of the stories he began while in the Navy stationed on the Pacific island of Espiritu Santo during World War II. That book never became a bestseller, but it was turned into the hit Broadway musical "South Pacific." (Michener liked to advise struggling writers on the key to success: "Make sure Rodgers and Hammerstein read your first book.") Yet he recalls of the Depression years, "They have a deeper impact on someone like me than people realize. It makes you more dour, more tightly grained, it inhibits you. If you don't turn it to anger, which I never did, you are always aware that it could come back. You know, the chain of bank failures a while ago, that strikes terror in my heart. If the damn thing ever got a little bit out of hand—wooh, we're back again. I don't think that's a desirable attitude, but it has motivated me. I live as if I had stayed at my job and retired on a small pension and some savings and security, because I need to know what it's like."

## Taking care

Of his childhood poverty, Michener says, "I'm very conscious of the effect of it, but it never soured me. I'm very similar to my wife. She went to detention camps in the most cruel and totally unwarranted way. She hates it and she's terribly outspoken, but there's no great bitterness or revenge motive at all. It's just something that happened. And I was always that way."

Mari Michener is a woman able to turn fierce loyalty to her husband into spirited charm. She and Michener call each other "Cookie," but their marriage seems more a happy balancing of opposites than of similar types. When Mari Yoriko Sabusawa married the twice-divorced Michener, she was 35, an editor for the American Library Association and a graduate of Antioch College. The American-born daughter of Japanese parents, she had been in a detention camp during World War II. Mari Michener sounds more bitter about that experience than her husband allows. One reason their extensive million dollar 20th century art collection was donated to the University in Texas, she explains, is that, "I was in a detention camp on the West Coast and we had *no* interest in seeing it go to the West."

Offering coffee to visitors, chatting about the weather and politics, she is as forthright and social as her husband is withdrawn. Herman Silverman, a Pennsylvania businessman who has been one of Michener's closest friends for nearly 40 years, says that the greatest change in the author's life is attributable to his marriage to Mari: "She's his secret weapon. She's his opposite, exuberant and buoyant, and she made him enjoy life more." Mari Michener cites the names of friendly literary critics and warns, "My husband never reads reviews, but I read them all. And nobody better say anything bad about my husband." One Saturday afternoon when Michener heads off for a barbecue, she sends regrets; she has to stay home and wait for the plumber to arrive. It is, perhaps, the kind of convenient excuse any homemaker might rely on, but the Micheners' way of life allows her to use it plausibly.

And while she handles all the household details and daily finances, she says, "My job is to make sure the man I love is around for a long, long time." Michener's health is good for a man his age, but he had a serious heart attack in 1964. On his daily walks, he favors a sometimes painful arthritic hip. He seems weary after a morning schedule of interviews and meetings, but resists slowing down. So it is Mari who makes sure he takes his afternoon nap and worries that the television lights are too hot during an interview in their den.

## Instinct for a good source

Despite his wife's protectiveness, Michener has not slowed down much for *Texas*, traipsing through old forts, following the Brazos River, reading hundreds of books to make sure the wildcatters, plantation owners and religious leaders who inhabit the novel are historically accurate. He listened to music of the region, from Mexican dances to songs by Charley Pride and Willie Nelson. (The music Michener says he listens to "every day" is more likely to be classical—"everything from Brahms to Stravinsky—it's really a part of my life.") As always, Michener consulted dozens of experts. But in the past, he did not have fulltime help—with some notable exceptions, such as *Centennial* and nonfiction works like *Kent State*. For *Texas,* Michener employed the kind of well-oiled staff he has been rumored to have had all along. In addition to the secretary and office space, the university provided two graduate students in history as part-time research assistants. John Kings, who first worked with Michener on *Centennial* in 1972, signed on at Michener's own expense as fulltime coordinating editor—that is, he organized trips and drove the car, ran the office and fielded so many requests for Michener's time that he pinned a button on his bulletin board, reading. "NO! Mr. Michener CAN'T!"

Michener's longtime pattern has been to block out the plot and write one section while continuing to research another. "It does not get easier," he says of the writing. "When I start one of these projects, I am painfully aware of my inadequacy. But the arrogance of the artist is a very profound thing, and it fortifies you." Michener kept his own arrogance under wraps for half a lifetime. *Tales of the South Pacific* was not written until he was nearly 40. "Partly because I'd had such a hard childhood, I was quite content just to go along," he says in explaining his hesitancy about writing. "There must have been a factor of fear—I didn't want to face the big challenges, was perfectly happy the way it was." Even now, he says, he counterbalances his mammoth efforts by thinking, "Let's just get through Friday afternoon."

If the writing has remained difficult, the research has become easier in proportion to Michener's fame. These days, "I just drop a hint that I want to know how the building of Houston is financed and first thing you know, eight people fly up here or I fly down there, and we have a seminar for a weekend and talk. I set up hypothetical situations and they fill them in completely." For *Texas* the graduate students fetched his books, checked his facts, wrote reports and accompanied him into the field, though Michener's well-developed instinct for a good source was still crucial. Robert Wooster, one of those staff researchers, recalls that on a typical trip to the Brazos, Michener stopped for directions. "He went to a house and talked to this elderly black woman. He not only got detailed directions, but three generations of her family history."

## A steady flow

When not on the road he kept to his routine of sitting at the typewriter from early morning until noon. But this time, Michener's typed drafts were photocopied for the staff—the administrative secretary Lisa Kaufman, Kings, Wooster and the second researcher, Frank de la Teja—which would have lengthy meetings with the author. They offered suggestions on everything from character consistency to style, which Michener frequently incorporated into revised drafts. Michener credits Kaufman with saving him from using sexist terms like "coed." And Kings, who may know his boss better than anyone except Mari Michener, had a very free editorial hand in making cuts and stylistic changes. In one chapter of *Texas,* for example, Kings' suggestions toned down some of Michener's phrases. The "barbarism of the frontier" became the "roughness of the frontier," and a "rich and notable piece of land" came to print as a "varied parcel of land."

Just as Mari Michener protects the author on the domestic front, Kings does likewise in Michener's professional life. He also has a contract with Random House to write Michener's biography, and while it has become a cliché to call any biographer a Boswell, the novelist's life truly subsumes that of this middle-aged Englishman who is nearly always at his side. Anyone who wants to contact Michener must first get past Kings.

The point at which the lines of defense and all the heavy editing turn a novel into a team effort may be fuzzy, and perhaps irrelevant for Michener's readers. He insists that every word is his, but he admits, "I don't think the way I write books is the best or even the second-best. The really great writers are people like Emily Brontë who sit in a room and write out of their limited experience and unlimited imagination. But people in my position also do some very good work. I'm not a stylist like Updike or Bellow, and don't aspire to be. I'm not interested in plot or pyrotechnics, but I sure work to get a steady flow. If I try to describe a chair, I can describe it so that a person will read to the end. The way the words flow, trying to maintain a point of view and a certain persuasiveness—that I can do."

## Deep in the heart of . . .

*Texas*, of course, is long since finished for Michener, but wherever he goes, there are Texans impatient to learn how this famous outsider has treated their state. Michener seems to enjoy the chauvinism, adopting just a trace of it now that Austin is home. He takes along his cowboy hat as he and Kings go off to the nearby town of Dripping Springs, out toward the hill country and the ranch of the real-estate developer and longhorn breeder H. C. Carter. One of Michener's informal expert sources, Carter provided advice about breeding cattle and lent him a private plane. Michener seems comfortable, even grandfatherly, in the understated affluence of the Carters' small, Spanish-style house. He makes a fuss over the dog and calls out to a longhorn whom Michener has named after his novel's antihero, "Quimper, you old fraud, you look just like your namesake."

The occasion is a barbecue for Carter's employees, and when the crowds arrive Michener is suddenly among a cross section of his readership—they defy categorization by age, sex or class, but these are people who read for information. They may dismiss most fiction as fantasy, but Michener's books offer the satisfaction of acquiring a lot of predigested information. Sitting in the sun among them, Michener looks like a tourist, in a Far Eastern style yellow print shirt never meant to go with a Stetson, and people approach him shyly. A junior college teacher says she assigns part of *Centennial* to liven up American history; a young man says, "My grandmother can't wait to read *Texas*; Michener grills Carter, for reasons known only to Michener, about why sink stoppers in hotel bathrooms don't work. "You never really know when he's picking your brain and when he's just visiting with you," says Carter.

Although Carter has known Michener for just a few years, he illustrates the way Michener surrounds himself with people who understand him. For example, Carter recognized Michener's dual need both for privacy and adulation: "He wants to be recognized, but in a very low-key way. He'd never push himself forward and say, 'You probably don't know who I am, I'm James Michener.' But nobody can be that good without having a big ego. He didn't have to stay here in Texas for three years to write one book, but if you feel the book *can't* be unsuccessful, that's what you do. He wants to be popular and he wants people to think he's good, but he does the best job of saying it doesn't matter. I don't believe that, but I love to see a guy have it down so perfect."

## Taking it all in

Asked if there is a hero in this novel, full of fictional Texas rangers and explorers and real-life heroes from the Alamo, Michener surprisingly cites a heroine, Emma

Larkin: "The young woman who is stolen by the Comanches at the age of 12 or 13, horribly abused for six or eight years, has her ears and nose cut off, survives through courage that few of us would have, and attains a very beautiful life in later years. That kind of person represents what I think."

The most unexpected aspect of Emma's character, though, is that she turns away the boy born as a result of her rape by the Comanches, a rejection that her Quaker missionary husband cannot comprehend. It is hard not to see these two characters as different sides of Michener himself, who has no natural children but who, for a very brief time during his second marriage, was father to two adopted children.

In 1953, Michener and his second wife, Vange Nord, had adopted two little Amerasian boys from Welcome House, an orphanage founded by the novelist Pearl Buck. The next year, their marriage ended, and the younger child was returned to the orphanage because his adoption had not yet become final. Michener's former wife received custody of the older boy, Mark. But in 1956, after Michener had married Mari Sabusawa and was traveling abroad, Pearl Buck sent word that Vange Nord had returned Mark, then nearly four years old, to the orphanage. Michener says he cabled Pearl Buck and offered to take in the boy. "I always wanted the child, but it didn't work out. I didn't get back for half a year. Meanwhile, I had already arranged for the child to stay with my aunts in Doylestown, but nothing ever happened," he says. Asked why, he is vague—"The whole thing became rather muddled." He says of the boy, "I cabled that I would take it, and I didn't question that it would be moved to my aunts'. But it never happened," he repeats sadly. "It went back into the system. It was the ward of the orphanage, and it was simply easier for the orphanage to let the abandonment to go through, and they found another home for it."

Michener insists he never regrets anything in his life, except perhaps some books he has not written; he denies connections between his fiction and his biography. But the attitude he attributes to his heroine in *Texas* seems to be an odd, even if inadvertent, reflection of his own rational response to disappointments. "I find it entirely reasonable, entirely reasonable," he says of Emma's rejection of her child. "I think we reach a point at which the errors of the past are just done with. And everything associated with them is wiped out. It's harsh, even cruel, but I do think it represents a lot of life experience."

Those close to Michener realize how difficult it is to get to know him, and some anticipate the charges of coldness his vagueness about his past might bring. Owen Laster, his agent of 17 years recalls that the distracted tendency that strangers notice is nothing new: "When we first started working together, he sometimes seemed preoccupied, as if he was not interested in anything you had to say. Not knowing him at the time, I interpreted that as coldness, but it wasn't. It's just that his mind never stops. He was taking everything in, but wasn't reacting. I came to realize he is as warm and generous as anyone I've ever known."

## Full circle

Michener sits in his Austin study two days before setting off on an extended trip to Alaska, the setting of his next novel. At the joint invitation of the governor and of Sheldon Jackson College in Sitka, he will give the Michener treatment to the largest state, coming full circle, he says, and returning to the Pacific. This novel will, he promises, go back further in time than any of his other works—further than *Hawaii* with its famous beginning. "Millions upon millions of years ago"—and since he expects to be 80 when it is completed, he says this will probably be his last big book.

On balance, the novelist's reaction to his monumental success would have to be called humble. Again and again, Michener's conversation turns to the difficulties facing young writers. He recently donated $2 million to Swarthmore and endowed a $500,000 fund for the Writers' Workshop at the University of Iowa. True to Michener's let's-get-results approach, the fellowships at Iowa are not for beginning students; they primarily support those at the end of their studies who have proven themselves with nearly publishable manuscripts.

Contemplating art and artists, he recalls Hemingway's suicide: "The death of Hemingway raises a fabulous number of questions. It was so contrary to his public image, there is a failure to mesh with this enormous tragedy. I didn't know Hemingway well, but I knew his work and I knew his public figure. It fooled me."

Guiding the discussion easily between himself and Hemingway, this man who claims not to care about his own posterity warns about the deceptions of public images and at the same time presents an image of himself that is as pure and simple as the message of his books. "You must remember, you've heard all these guesses about me. I am a far more simple mechanism than the guesses would imply. With somebody like Hemingway, there is a temptation to try to construct a theory, and oftentimes it is not relevant."

Yet he says, with a command of his public persona that Hemingway might have admired, "I'm just a guy up on a hill writing."

 *I wrote the story I wanted to read. I didn't write it for critics or for a mass audience. To me it's very serious fiction: It's about adventure, love, danger, fear, loneliness, jealousy and belonging. I like stories that pick me up and put me down somewhere else. 'What if'—that's the great thing fiction writers work with.*

**—Jean Auel, about The Mammoth Hunters**

# Spicing the story

## by June and William Noble

Say what you wish about the literary pinnacles achieved by writers such as John O'Hara, Kenneth Roberts, Thomas Costain, Dashiel Hammett, Margaret Mitchell . . . the appeal of writers such as Rosemary Rogers, Robert Ludlum, Danielle Steele. The literary establishment is prone to scratch its collective head and wonder just what *is* it that makes people want to read such apparently simpleminded stuff.

But the truth is there in plain view: Each of these writers, and hundreds of others who have gone before or will come after, mastered the essence of story writing—*they've learned how to tell a good story*! Convoluted circumstances, two- and three-dimensional story lines, lengthy explorations into metaphysical questions may offer the intellectual a comfortable, perhaps an exciting exercise, but for most of us, a good story is a good story is a good story.

What is the writer *saying*? Critics ask this all the time. Clearly, a book that delves into broader areas than simple entertainment is entitled to be judged by standards appropriate to its aims. If the author wishes to explore the sheer obscenity of war and its consequences, as Dalton Trumbo does in *Johnny Got His Gun*, then his book must be held up against others that have tried to do the same thing. Or if an author wants to show how war and revolution can corrupt even the seemingly incorruptible, as Robert Stone does in *A Flag for Sunrise*, then here, also, a measure can be made.

But every story must have a plot, and it is only after creating it that the author can turn attention to working out what it is he or she wants to say. The literary intellectual may choose books that go beyond basic story telling, such as the various works of William Faulkner portraying the decay and decadence of the South, but even so there is a story line and plot, too. Sometimes a bit frail perhaps, but without plot and story line all the literary intellectual would be feasting on is a literary essay.

But for a story to be a *good* story, now that's what we're after. Plot motivators will give us the story line, that much is clear. Whether it's a story about vengeance or betrayal

*June and William Noble have co-authored several books, including* The Psychiatric Fix, The Private Me, How to Live With Other People's Children *(a Book-of-the-Month Club Alternate),* The Custody Trap, *and* Steal This Plot, *from which this excerpt is taken. William Noble is a former attorney.*

or rivalry, or a combination of all three, we come away with the bare construction. We have the framework put together, but there is no paint, no finish, no landscaping.

That's where story spicers come in. They make a story a good story, they act with plot motivators to give a richness and fullness not otherwise achieved. A story about vengeance is okay, but what if the story is about vengeance achieved through deception? Or what if the story is about ambition, and we spice it with elements of mistaken identity? It doesn't make things more complicated. Just more interesting.

Think of story spicers as road signs that can guide us on a book-writing journey. Using deception, for example, will turn a story in one direction. Using suspicion may turn it in another direction. And keep in mind that combinations of story spicers may also work. In fact, it is a rare book that doesn't have more than one story spicer.

Here, then, are the story spicers that seem to appear and reappear through the literary ages. Some work better with one plot motivator than another, some work better in one genre than another. (For example, suicide would hardly seem appropriate in a light-hearted romance, but it would most certainly be effective in a mystery.) To the author we leave the question of when and where and what and how to apply . . . as we would with any accomplished *chef de cuisine*.

## Deception

The literary antecedents here go all the way back to the legend of the Trojan Horse. "I fear Greeks even when they bring gifts," Vergil wrote in the *Aeneid*, and, of course, he was referring to the deception practiced on Troy by the Greeks with their huge wooden horse. Deception as a literary tool has been common for as long as the written word has been used. The Greek legends abound in stories of deception, as with Prometheus in his quarrel with Zeus over the division of sacrificial meats. Prometheus tries to hide the good meat inside skin and the bones inside fat. Zeus, possibly deceived by the outer wrapping of fat, chooses the bones. The legend then proposes that from this time on, men will always keep for themselves the flesh of sacrificial animals, always offering the fat or inedible parts to the Gods. Zeus, however, is aware of the deception, and in his anger begins to hold the gift of fire from mortals.

Deception is trickery; it's double dealing, fraud and cheating. It doesn't have to spring from dark-hearted motivation; there are deceptions clearly justified, such as the actions of Alec Leamas, the protagonist in John Le Carré's *The Spy Who Came in From the Cold*. For most of the book we see him as a case of spook burnout, and only near the end do we realize he's been deceiving the Russians and playing possum. Deception in the name of honor is effective as a story spicer but, of course, it doesn't have to be honorable. Heinous actions such as the commission of a crime (blackmail and extortion, even murder fit pretty well here), character assassination, unbridled ambition, greed and lust also work. Deception is a good springboard for rounding off a story; it carries with it the elements of conflict and tension. The reader wonders whether the deception will succeed, how it will succeed, when it will succeed.

## Material well-being

Like the plot motivators they work with, story spicers provide movement for a story. They keep things from stagnating. If people are seen either losing or gaining economic worth, the way it happens becomes an important part of the story. As a story spicer, material well-being involves both the increase *and* the decrease of the things that make a prosperous life. We say *material* because we want to keep everything fairly narrow. Material well-being means an emphasis on things, on creature comforts, as opposed to less tangible effects such as emotional stability. Not that one can't flow naturally from the other, but for purposes of this story spicer we believe the emphasis should be on the physical, on items one can touch.

A classic example of the use of material well-being as a story spicer is Margaret Mitchell's *Gone With the Wind*. It is truly an epic of decline and destruction of the South, a harsh splintering of one family's material of well-being. Two major plot motivators are present here—rebellion and survival—and material well-being certainly fits neatly. In fact, whenever the plot motivator is rebellion or survival, the chances are that material well-being will be there, somewhere.

Just as material well-being can go down, it can also go up. In Jeffrey Archer's novel, *Kane and Abel*, we have the story of two men born on the same day, one to a life of comfort and position, the other to poverty and anonymity. How this latter character rises from such mean circumstances to a life of power and wealth, while carrying on an intense rivalry with someone he has never set eyes on, is the essence of the story. Abel's drive for financial success (translation: material well-being) spices up a story hinged on the plot motivator, rivalry. The wealthier Abel becomes, the more power he acquires in his struggle to outdo Kane. The story is immeasurably strengthened in this way.

## Authority

*L'état c'est moi!* stated Louis XIV almost 300 years ago, and ever since we have had a measure to gauge absolute power. "The state is me," and by that Louis meant that he and he alone was the fountain of all authority. He was the living embodiment of everything French. The authority of France started with him and ended with him.

As a story spicer, authority is an artful technique to establish an immediate conflict situation. Either one bows to authority or one challenges. There really is no middle ground.

Shakespeare plays with the pulls of authority in many of his tragedies. In most cases it is an us-versus-them scenario. Either the characters are behind the authority of the ruler or they are against him. In *King Lear* the king's authority is slowly eroding because of his growing senility. In *MacBeth* the king's authority is challenged because of the ambition of MacBeth. In *Hamlet* the king's authority is challenged because he had killed Hamlet's father, the rightful king. The fact that in each story it is a king who is being challenged makes everything so much more intense and serious. The ultimate authority is the king, and this authority is in danger of toppling.

Authority, of course, can appear in many other circumstances. It can be institutionalized as in the armed services, government, church, school, hospitals; it can be morally based as with a parent or a spouse or any other respected person; it can be physically based through fear or terror or simple intimidation. Authority is the power to command through behavior or thoughts or opinion. A plot which is spiced with elements of authority—whether supported or opposed—provides a concrete story line to follow. Authority is touchable, palpable; we can recognize authority when we see it.

## Making amends

This might be called the guilty-conscience story spicer. We wrong someone, and then we have to decide whether to make it up to them. Do we recompense them, and if so, how?

In Theodore Dreiser's *An American Tragedy*, a young man impregnates a young woman, not out of love but in a moment of lust and passion. Afterwards, he is torn. His true love would be so shocked by what he has done that it would be over between them.

Still, he feels something for the other woman, and he is so sorry about what happened. They go out in a small boat in the moonlight, and the young man wants the young woman to try and understand, try to see things from his position. He is so sorry about everything . . . The young woman goes overboard (helped to an extent by the young man) and is drowned. Eventually the young man is accused and later convicted of murdering her. He wanted to help her. He thought about making amends for getting her pregnant. He tried, he really did.

Sometimes making amends is more successful. In Goethe's *Faust* it takes a lifetime of orgiastic pleasure-seeking for Faust to realize that helping others and providing for their happiness and contentment is the only true source of joy and fulfillment. After taking, taking, taking he finally sees that giving is by far the happier alternative. He makes his amends that way.

Amends-making works best with plot motivators which focus on someone suffering or hurt or otherwise wronged. Betrayal, persecution, vengeance, catastrophe would fall into this category. Of course, the amends-maker need not be the one who did the foul deed. While we may not like it when the sins of the father are visited on the son, human nature is not always so discriminating.

## Conspiracy

Two or more people meet, they plot, they plan to do something, they have an end in mind—some definite goal. They *conspire*.

The key is that the entire scheme must result in something wrongful being done. Even if we meet in secret, even if we keep everyone else in the dark, it's not really a conspiracy if what we want to accomplish is perfectly legal and the way we do it is perfectly legal. A conspiracy implies illegality, and that's what makes this story spicer.

Because people doing anything against the law is, in itself, an effective story tool. Conspiracy can be a criminal act, and so it can be linked with criminal action, another story spice.

But conspiracy doesn't have to be overtly criminal. It can be economically motivated, as with consumers deciding to boycott a certain product or certain business; it can be socially motivated, as with a well-directed snub or shunning.

The great bulk of conspiracy-laden stories, though, are politically motivated. Look at Shakespeare's work: conspiracy after conspiracy in *Othello, Julius Caesar, MacBeth, Richard the Third*—each with some political end. Two or more people get together and they dream of political change, and they act to achieve it. In their actions we see the essential nature of conspiracy; they twist or bend the natural political forces to suit their own ends, they lie, they falsely accuse, they even murder and persecute. The way conspiracy operates, the wrongful aims and the wrongful ends are the necessary ingredients for building tension and conflict. Imagine *Julius Caesar*, for example, if Brutus had decided to kill Caesar on his own, without being urged by Cassius or anyone else. Brutus' reasons might have been just as sound, but the entire nature of the story would have been changed. Brutus would stand out as a lone assassin and not as personifying the groundswell of public objection to Caesar's ambition. Could Brutus be so sympathetic under these circumstances? Could his character be so evened-off as it is by contrast with the motivations of the other conspirators?

The modern political novel is replete with conspiracy and counter-conspiracy. We need only read Robert Ludlum (*The Holcroft Covenant*, for example) or Steve Shagan (*The Circle*) to see how effective conspiracy can be at spicing up a story. Take any plot motivator, sprinkle a dash of conspiracy and—voilà! A story line.

# Rescue

Most commonly, this story spicer can be found when the plot involves physical danger or peril. Will he/she make it? Will the rescue work? Plot motivators such as catastrophe, persecution, survival are natural tie-ins with rescue because each can be founded on some element of physical danger. Is there ever a catastrophe without physical danger? When persecution is in the air, isn't there danger all around? When we survive some traumatic event, aren't we rescued?

Typical of this kind of story is Hammond Innes' *The Land God Gave to Cain*, published in 1958. The action takes place in Labrador following an eerie radio message received by a ham operator in London. The message is sent by a man supposedly killed in an airplane crash, and it begins a tale of search and rescue that slogs its way through unbelievably rugged wilderness which compounds the constant physical danger. It is a story of survival with the hope of rescue spurring the characters on.

In most stories involving rescue, the presence of another story spicer—searching—can be found. To rescue someone or something, there first has to be a search. Then comes the rescue. Even where the rescue consumes the story almost in its entirety, a search for some type of final absolution or honor will generally occur. In Walker Percy's fine novel, *The Second Coming*, for instance, the rescue of a schizophrenic girl from her mental strait jacket consumes much of the book, but as the protagonist performs his rescue, he also searches for some divine order in the events as they unfold. The search is there as the rescue takes place. And the rescue, of course, is not so much from physical danger as from emotional turmoil. Danger is no less severe when it is directed in the mind, and a rescue from that kind of circumstance is no less intriguing as a story spicer.

# Mistaken identity

It started with the gods and goddesses in the earliest Greek legends. Zeus and Hera and Apollo and Athena and Aphrodite—all would assume mortal roles for some specific purpose, and then, after they had accomplished their goal, they would return to being gods and goddesses. In the *Odyssey*, Homer writes: "Owl-eyed goddess Athena smiled at (Odysseus') words and stroked him with her hand; she was in the likeness of a woman fair and tall and accomplished in glorious works, and she spoke winged words to him. . ."

Or Apollo, taking the shape of a dolphin in *The Hymn to Apollo*, jumps aboard a ship from Crete and diverts it to the bay of Crisa where he finally reveals himself and demands that those around him build a temple in his honor. "I declare to you that I am the son of Zeus; I am Apollo," he says. "I brought you here over the great gulf of the sea with no evil intent, but you shall possess here my rich temple held in much honor among all men, and shall know the counsels of the immortals and by their help be continually honored for all your days . . ." Thus the Delphic Oracle is born.

Adventure stories seem a natural home for plots which are spiced with mistaken identity. Stories of vengeance, for example, where one of the prime characters is not who the others think he is. Or stories of love and hate where mistaken identity has precipitated such deep feelings. Or stories of a rivalry which might never have existed if there hadn't been a misstep about who was who. In Daphne du Maurier's *The Scapegoat* an Englishman meets a Frenchman by chance in a railroad station in Le Mans. They bear an amazing likeness to one another, and the Englishman is forced to assume the Frenchman's identity and move into his household where he is surrounded by hate and suspicion and rivalry. Mistaken identity is the story spicer that moves this plot along because the Englishman has no choice but to play his role, and the remainder of the household continue in ignorance as the entire story unfolds.

Mistaken identity works from two directions: We see it from the point of view of the one assuming the wrong identity or from the aspect of those relying on the wrong identity. Either way we have a built-in-story advantage: Will anyone discover the mistaken identity? How will he/she continue to cover up the mistaken identity? What happens when the mistaken identity is revealed?

## Unnatural affection

The Greek legends abound with this type of spicer. From Zeus transforming himself into a bull in order to make love to Danae, the mother of Perseus, to the act of love performed between Pasiphae, wife of Minos, King of Crete, and a bull to the passion of Phaedra, wife of Theseus, for her stepson, Hippolytus (which is further dramatized by Euripedes in his play, *Hippolytus*) . . . to the incest between Oedipus and his mother, Jocasta (also further dramatized by Sophocles in his *Oedipus Tyrranus*).

The Point is that any form of passion, whether physical, emotional or both, that steps out of the normal man-woman, adult-adult, non-blood-related framework has a claim to be called "unnatural," and this surely creates an intriguing story line. It's different, it's unusual, it's interesting. John Irving could have a brother and sister in wild bouts of passion in *Hotel New Hampshire*, and lend a wacky tilt to a story about a family who runs a hotel. Survival, perhaps even discovery, may have been the prime plot motivators, but doesn't it add an air of intrigue and sheer anti-establishment nose-thumbing to have a running account of incest?

Of course the ultimate question of what is "natural" and what isn't depends on the lean of the observer. Is homosexuality or lesbianism or even transvestitism natural? To some they are, though it's safe to say that the large majority might not think so.

Yet a work of fiction where homosexuality (see, for example, E.M. Forster's *Maurice*) or lesbianism (see, for example, Marge Piercy's *Small Changes*) plays an important part might shower the reader with aspects of unnatural affection and carry a fairly conventional story line. In Thomas Mann's *Death in Venice*, we have a story of a reknowned author on vacation who gradually falls in love with a young Polish boy, his feelings ultimately consuming him so that he even ignores the threat of an impending cholera epidemic. Survival, discovery, and love and hate are the major plot motivators, and if we erase the unnatural affection, we have a conventional story line without much passion. But when we add pederasty to the mix, things become not so conventional, then!

## Criminal action

Any act against the law makes a good story. The conflict is built in, the black hats against the white hats. And it doesn't matter from which side one writes the story or which plot motivator we use. They all work here. We sympathize with the bouts of conscience Macbeth suffers even though we know him to be a murderer and a political outlaw. We applaud the unselfishness and higher motives of Brutus even as we read about his plunging his dagger into Caesar's body. One the other hand we find it easy to identify with those intrepid characters who hunt down the criminals—private eyes, police detectives, federal government spooks—and while genre fiction on this side of the law enforcement ledger appears to have a monopoly, let's not forget one crucial fact above all— it's a *good* story we're really after, and we have to be good storytellers! Genre fiction or no, criminal action spices up a story.

Murder, treason, larceny, rape, assasination, extortion, blackmail, counterfeiting, arson—these and many more are the types of events that add body to a story. Imagine a Shakespearean tragedy without at least one murder. Or any of the great adventure novels such as Jules Verne's *20,000 Leagues Under the Sea*; or Charles Nordhoff's *Mutiny on the Bounty*; or a great political novel such as Robert Penn Warren's *All the King's Men*—without a criminal act taking place. The plot motivators may hinge on ambition or vengeance or self sacrifice or survival, but when someone plans or commits a criminal act in the course of the story, it means so much more in terms of characterization, plot direction and ultimate story resolution.

Look at it this way. What if . . . an upstanding citizen of a major city is quietly arrested for shoplifting. There's no police record and no medical record or emotional instability. The shoplifter is successful in business, has a fine, attractive family, is well respected within the community and offers no reason for the crime. Is this not an intriguing plot concept? Would it be less intriguing if there had been no shoplifting? Does it matter which side this story is written from? Don't we want to know *why?*

You bet we do.

## Suspicion

This story spicer occurs in the minds of the characters rather than as an overt event. If we suspect someone of doing or not doing something, the process by which we get there is based on things happening that move us into an area of distrust. Distrust. That's the bottom line with suspicion. If we suspect someone, we distrust them, and if we distrust them, we have a natural conflict to work with.

Obviously, suspicion is always present with the police procedurals, the detective stories, the suspense genre. Suspicion—or distrust—is what makes this type of book go because it sets up (as with criminal action) the good guys-bad guys format.

Yet suspicion is really a preliminary step to criminal action. It's in the head, a surmise, a guess, but in no way does it confirm that something criminal or against the law has taken place.

And that's why it has its intellectual side. Is the suspicion justified, we can ask. What *actually* has happened to create the suspicion, and are we seeing those events in their proper perspective? What's the motive for the suspicion? Perhaps the one doing the suspecting is the one we should suspect. There are many variables with suspicion, many levels and approaches we can take. For example, in Daphne du Maurier's *Rebecca*, suspicions abound over just who Rebecca was, what happened to her and why. The story moves from one ominous circumstance to another, leaving behind a growing pile of suspicions with little resolution until the end. Distrust is palpable throughout the book, even though the plot motivator fluctuates between survival and love and hate. Suspicion is what really gives it substance.

For the most part suspicion works best with motivators like betrayal, vengeance, rivalry, survival, rebellion and persecution. That's because these plot motivators demand strong conflict situations, and suspicion is in itself a conflict-laden condition. If we suspect someone of something, we sure don't want to make ourselves vulnerable, do we?

So we step back, button ourselves up and watch our suspicions grow and grow.

## Suicide

This is a corollary to the story spicer, criminal action. When we commit a crime, we are doing something unlawful to someone else; when we commit or try to commit suicide, we are doing the same thing to ourselves. (Actually, attempting to commit suicide is, in itself, a crime and a violation of most state statutes. But the law is rarely enforced in this connection.)

The idea of suicide comes in many forms: as a political statement, as the ultimate despair in a failed love affair, as the only release from degradation and horror, as a form of penance, as a compulsive pursuit of unlimited earthly pleasures. Motivations are as varied as the ways we set about killing ourselves, but one thing is clear: The act of suicide conjures up an unsettling barrage of questions. How can someone do that to himself! What's the *real* reason! Did he/she have to go *that* far?

It seems to us that the truth of suicide is this: It's embarrassing to family and friends; it's a final clutch at some form of reality; it's rarely without pain; it's an extremely self-centered act; it's the ultimate rebellion.

It's also a fine technique for spicing up a story, and it works best with plot motivators that can strip a story line to its raw, emotional edge, such as catastrophe, grief and loss, love and hate, persecution, betrayal. Suicide is a catastrophic event, and the feelings it engenders can be equally as substantial.

Suicide, of course, doesn't have to be a single, lone event, happening without warning. There can also be a process to suicide, a slow disintegration that culminates in death. In Gustave Flaubert's *Madame Bovary*, we see moral degeneration taking place, one step after the other, a slow sinking into despair, the result of trying to survive the sheer boredom of provincial life. Joan Didion in *Play It as It Lays* also picks up the theme of a character in the midst of an arid life. In this case Didion has her character indulging herself with pills, drugs, sexual experimentation—anything, in fact, to numb her to the pain of living. Survival is the plot motivator in both these works, but suicide is what is happening. Survival, in fact, fights a losing battle.

## Searching

Most often this story spicer should be used in conjunction with rescue. If we search, we hope to find. And if we find, the chances are we're going to be doing some rescuing. Searching implies that something or someone is lost or must be found. Note the difference, though: Just because we find something doesn't mean it's been "lost." Some people—such as the waterclerk in Joseph Conrad's *Lord Jim*—don't want to be found. So when we search, it may not be for someone or something that's been lost. Just missing would be better.

Searching works well with plot motivators such as discovery, survival and the chase. Story lines that move the action quite a bit seem natural here because a search implies a series of events that carries us in one direction or another. Of course, we can search not only for someone or something, but for ourselves. That is, we can hope to discover who we are when set against events that are destined to test us. It is one of Hemingway's favorite themes, one he propounds in a variety of works, from Jake Barnes in *A Farewell to Arms* to Robert Jordan in *For Whom the Bell Tolls*. We face a series of tests, and they turn us into a better, stronger human being or they don't. We come to know ourselves and to discover what we can do and can't do.

Searching for ourselves or for someone or something else, has strong antecedents in Homer's *Odyssey* and *Iliad*. The journey of Odysseus after the fall of Troy is the picture of a massive search, set against a backdrop of survival and discovery. The Lotus-eaters, Polyphemus the Cyclops, Aeolus, king of the winds, the huge Laestrygonians, Circe, Scylla and Charybodis, the cattle of the Sun, Calypso's island—these and more are the tests for Odysseus as he makes his way home in the years following the Trojan War. Odysseus is searching for home and in the process he finds himself.

# Honor and dishonor

This is perhaps the simplest and easiest of the story spicers to use. It works with every plot motivator because it deals with human nature and its changeable form. In a story of betrayal, for example, how the characters act with one another could be hinged on how they honor one another; in a story of grief and loss, is there honor in the aftermath of the mourning? In a story of self sacrifice, is there dishonor in the ultimate demise?

Honor and dishonor have reference to esteem, both public and private. If we have a sense of honor, it's generally because we have a feeling of self esteem. We respect ourselves, and thus we can share the respect in our feelings for others. We honor ourselves as we honor others. And the world honors us in return.

Take *Julius Caesar*. Brutus tells Cassius as they converse about Caesar's worrisome ambition that honor is something he holds higher than almost anything else. "For let the gods so speed me as I love the name of honour more than I fear death." Brutus says. And Cassius responds, "I know that virtue to be in you Brutus . . ."

It is a story of honor even in the commission of a crime. Brutus remains an honorable man. He is driven to kill Caesar *because* he is an honorable man. He looks for nothing for himself, no rewards of any kind. At the funeral orations, Mark Antony calls Brutus an "honorable man" over and over, implying, of course, just the opposite. But regardless of how the reader ultimately feels, the point is that honor and dishonor have been used as a means to add depth to the story. Suppose, for example, Brutus is not so honorable. What kind of story would there be? Little sympathy for the conspirators, much more identification with Caesar . . . and probably a much less well-balanced drama. It is in Brutus' sense of honor that we see Caesar and his ambition unveiled, for if such an honorable man as Brutus is moved to kill, perhaps Caesar deserved such a fate.

The story line may have been founded on ambition, but it is in the clash between concepts of honor and dishonor that substance and spice have been added. Honor and dishonor . . . public and private esteem . . . it's how we feel about ourselves and about others that turns the trick.

> 66 *A narrative is like a room on whose walls a number of false doors have been painted. The skillful author leads us past the many apparent choices of exit to the only door that opens.*
> —*John Updike* 99

# Superior bambini and other samples from slush

### by David Groff

It's late Friday afternoon. I have written jacket copy for three novels, calmed two anxious authors, discussed a pending contract with an agent in need of Valium, dickered with the Production Department for a rush job on a blurry author photograph, and consumed four cups of coffee. Now I turn to the stack of manuscripts beside my desk and plan my weekend.

Before me are four piles of novels, each pile 18 inches high. That makes six feet of fiction. Novels from Nashville, novels from Nome, novels from 95th Street. I should be able to read two feet this weekend, and, if I'm lucky, still be able to finish Milan Kundera's *The Unbearable Lightness of Being*, which work forced me to put aside two weeks ago. For me, it's a rare pleasure to read a book with a spine.

From Louisville, Kentucky, a novel about "two competing intelligence bureaus, the international bond market, and the call of mankind to God." Heavens. That one I can put off for a swift browse on Monday morning.

From Rochester, New York, the story of a young woman psychotherapist and her eccentric patients, including a lawyer who wears a boa constrictor wrapped around his shoulders. It's badly typed, but not in a while have I read about a snake in court. Will see.

An M.D. in Florida has sent a medical thriller about a gastroenterologist who uncovers a hospital scandal while he's resectioning bowels. Ick. But the writer has been

*David Groff is an assistant editor at Crown Publishers, Inc., in New York, where he edits both fiction and nonfiction. While studying at the Iowa Writers' Workshop he was poetry editor of* The Iowa Review. *His poems and prose have appeared in* The New York Times, The Georgia Review, The Missouri Review, North American Review *and other magazines.*

published in small magazines and colon quarterlies, so it's worth a look. The novel might well be too "genre" for my publishing house, but maybe it could be a paperback original, assuming the writing is decent.

From another doctor—when do all these M.D.'s find time to play golf?—comes the story of his Texas boyhood, a "fictional novel." Uh oh. That's another one for early Monday morning.

A former screen actress I've never heard of submits a "romance" concerning a young nurse who goes to Hollywood and ends up ministering to an alcoholic film star, with whom she falls in love just as she lands a role in a famous director's new musical movie. The drunk actor grows suitably jealous. The story sounds suspiciously like *A Star Is Born*. Still, everybody loves to read about Hollywood, including me.

A top literary agent has sent me a novel about the first Irish princess to visit the Ottoman Empire. I flip to page 23: "Mohammed let his robe fall to the tiled floor as Elaine lay breathless beneath him like an octopus out of water, panting. 'Come to me,' she cried, even as she knew her lover could barely understand her English. He fell willingly against her, centuries of desire visible in his shortening breaths. 'Ah,' Mohammed cried as he licked her seashell-like ear, his voice as piercing as a rapier. 'You shall today become one of my wives. Together we shall sire a race of superior bambini!' "

The agent says she wants big money for this one. Like a good boy I put Mohammed, the nurse, the Rochester therapist and the crusading gastroenterologist into my backpack. After taking an hour to work off my frustrations on the Nautilus machines at my gym, I go home and read until Sunday evening.

## On watch for the Rolex

I shouldn't leave the impression that most editors hate their jobs and would prefer to live on Fiji surrounded by charming islanders who don't know a book from a brick. While the Fiji part sounds nice, editors on the whole adore their jobs, work long hours for relatively low pay, and enjoy a pleasure rare among working people: They get to see the product of their labors. They assist in a kind of birth, watching a novel evolve from a jumbled stack of pages to an ordered stack of pages, then to a copyedited manuscript, proofs, and finally a *book*—a book they can hold in their hands, a book that a few and sometimes many people will enjoy and benefit from. Few jobs can be this rewarding.

Nor is reading manuscripts, either solicited or unsolicited, an onerous task. Certainly it's often frustrating, not because so many are bad but because so many are mediocre—decent ideas for novels that lack wit, spark, singularity, authority. Nevertheless, reading manuscripts in search of the one that's dazzlingly publishable isn't like looking for a needle in a haystack. It's more like burrowing through a haystack in search of something slightly larger and much more valuable—a Rolex watch, say, that needs only a once-over or twice-over before it ticks like a charm. I like that analogy because a novel, like a watch, is useful.

Useful? How can fiction be *useful*?

Some months ago there was a cartoon by William Hamilton in *The New Yorker*: Two well-to-do young women are in a bookstore doing some serious browsing, when one says to the other, "Fiction's nice, but it doesn't get you anywhere."

That cartoon hit home for me. As a young editor involved in publishing both fiction and nonfiction while trying to stay in tune with the readership out there, I'm constantly amazed at the difficulty inherent in getting even the most commercial fiction across to a larger audience. Few novels sell as well as *The One-Minute Manager*, *In Search of Excellence*, *Iacocca*, *Entertaining*, or *Smart Women, Foolish Choices*. Often, a publisher's leading fiction titles—especially from new authors—will sell no better than so-called "mid-list" nonfiction dealing with women alcoholics, say, or jet lag, or how to get a corner office, thin thighs, or loving mate in 30 days. Fiction is always a hard sell. People want to spend $18.95 on a book that tells them something they can *use*.

Booksellers are saying that fiction sales have begun to improve, not just for blockbusters like Stephen King and Jean M. Auel, but also for modest commercial and literary fiction. Still, editors remain very cautious in choosing fiction to take on. A novel has to be truly extraordinary to garner much attention. That's probably a good thing. What is also a good thing is that editors of fiction have taken a leaf from nonfiction. They know now that people read fiction not only to be entertained but to learn something useful that gets them somewhere.

The pundits say this is the age of information. Every day we're engulfed by facts about new software, yuppie eating habits, Shiites, and Elizabeth Taylor's love life. Sure, we can sometimes drown in fact, but most of the time we wallow happily in our trivial and not-so-trivial pursuits.

## For peat's sake

Readers want a good story, fascinating characters, and some refreshing sex; but they also want to know about polo ponies in Palm Beach, the lives of the natives of Egypt, Maine, the revolutions in the record industry, the strained routine of Marines in Vietnam, and the drugs of choice among Hollywood wives.

I believe that if a writer can weave a whole world with drama, immediacy, and authority, then he or she is halfway along to competing with *Iacocca*. If there's one thing editors are looking for, it's a vivid, authoritative engagement with the world. Editors don't want much; they just want the world.

The fatal flaw in most manuscripts I read is a lack of engagement and intimacy in describing and evoking a very particular world. Few novels I read are vivid enough in their physical detailing to create a physical response in me. Few are full of information engaging and useful enough for me to remember.

As a positive example, consider that First Lady of popular fiction, Judith Krantz. Ms. Krantz is not only a glamorous jetsetter who wakes in Beverly Hills and dines in Paris. She is a hard worker and a dogged researcher. Most of *Mistral's Daughter* is a romp between three passionate generations; it's also a carefully plotted (and most important) convincing protrait of avant-garde 20th century worlds of art and fashion. Writers tend to believe they can reel off a Judith Krantz sort of novel, but it takes that one thing called talent. Her novels are sweet cream, factual, informative, and fun, with characters you care about because they're sexy and glamorous and *real*—existing in a genuine world genuinely painted.

Currently, I'm working on a new novel by Morgan Llywelyn, whose novels of Irish history have won her an enthusiastic following. *Grania: She-king of the Irish Seas* is the story of a real-life Irish woman pirate, a sort of Queen Elizabeth I with estrogen, who captains a shipping empire, staves off the invading English, and learns how to love a man. Grania is a terrific character, and I see her so sharply because Morgan Llywelyn knows Ireland inside out. I can smell the peat burning. (Do you know where the phrase "keep a straight face" comes from? When you dig out peat, you must make the spade thrust perfectly vertical—and so keep a straight face.)

The creation of a convincing, engaging world is a vital ingredient of every kind of fiction. Earlier this year my company, Crown Publishers, bravely brought out a book of short stories: *Easy in the Islands*, by Bob Shacochis. The book succeeded because Shacochis was able to put across his intimate knowledge of the Caribbean with terrific drama and style. His is not the Club Med Caribbean but the Caribbean of fishing boats, canny natives, shanties, jazz clubs, and dissolute, scared Americans. After reading Shacochis I felt I could wander the islands without a map. [Editor's note: *Easy in the Islands* won the American Book Award for 1985.]

## Vinyl imagination

You don't need an exotic locale or esoteric knowledge to succeed in engaging your reader, however. Michael Cunningham's *Golden States*, for example, is a magnificently detailed, quiet novel of a young boy coming of age in southern California. You sympathize with this character and come to love him; and you learn exactly what it's like to sip coffee in a Burger King at dawn.

Few of the novels I read possess this sort of intrigue and detail. Sure, the characters may feel real, and they may have interesting thoughts, actions, and neuroses. The dialogue may be sharp and the people may not all sound alike (this last is a rare phenomenon). But if the people I'm reading about don't startle me into paying attention and don't exist in an environment that fascinates me intrinsically, then I'm going to start longing for Fiji.

Let's go back to one of the novels I took home for the weekend—the one about the nurse who comes to Hollywood, mops up after the drunk star, and then hits the big time. It's a rehash, but that's okay; writers are constantly writing versions of what they have read, and publishers often publish last week's pot roast. The dialogue is nice, even occasionally witty, and the nurse has more guts than Florence Nightingale.

But I do not believe for a second that this author has ever jaywalked across Santa Monica Boulevard. She does mention a Jacuzzi once or twice, but I don't learn a damn thing about the movies, or how Malibu feels at dusk. I might as well be in Newark, New Jersey. Her setting, and the overall physical circumstances of her fiction, are utterly generic.

Even when writers think they are stocking their novels with detail, they usually aren't. I'll read all about how our heroine makes love with a Maytag repairman in the back seat of a 1969 Oldsmobile Cutlass parked on a radiant cliff at Big Sur. But, for example, what kind of sound does our heroine's buttocks make as Maytag lifts her off the sweaty vinyl seat? Beats me. And although I'll hear a lot about the crashing Pacific surf, nothing in the writing will send the spray into my eyes.

An author may write with what he or she feels is sharp focus, but usually the camera doesn't linger long enough or zoom in with any style. Most writers fail to treat their readers with enough intimacy. They seem to assume that readers can feel exactly what the writers feel themselves, but most readers really need a strong jump-start to ignite their imaginations.

## To wit ironically

In his book *After Virtue*, the philosopher Alasdair MacIntyre posits that any ethical position in the 20th century cannot be the result of theory or abstract reasoning. Ethical stands must spring out of complicated, real situations seen fully and honestly, in all their complications. Only with *thick description* can someone make a virtuous ethical choice.

And only with *thick description* can a novelist render character and situation with the virtue that is authority.

All of this comes down, of course, to language. If a writer can zoom in on a scene, or a feeling, using language that transcends the simplifications inherent in everyday language, then he or she will write with that element that is so unteachable, so impalpable, and so necessary: style.

I have no idea what style is. At the Iowa Writers' Workshop I took a course in Prose Style and while I did learn that Joan Didion writes with an immense number of periodic sentences, I ended up with even less concept of style. I don't think even Joan Didion knows for sure what style is.

I did learn enough, though, to encourage all writers (myself as jacket-flap writer included) to master all the forms of classical rhetoric, from periodic sentences to anaphora. Even many of the best writers I know write too sparely, too blandly. It's always best, I think, to pile on everything in the first draft and then to hone in on dialogue, actions, and descriptions that truly resonate stylistically and textually. Too many writers, moreover, tend to slap sentences together so as to make their meaning clear and their rhetorical impact nil. Style works much as music does rendering feelings too deep for tears. Cicero, for one, knew a hell of a lot we don't.

There is one element of style and attitude that is in fact definable, and, while not always overtly necessary, a big help to any writer. Wit.

I have plodded through thousands of manuscripts that are as somber and arid as Death Valley. Presumably, most are written by people who can make amusing dinner conversation, but who confuse sobriety with seriousness. These novels, about being rich, or female, or gay, or American, may reveal earnestness, pain and sensitivity—and also induce in the reader not only bouts of giggling but narcolepsy as well.

Sure, human life is nasty, brutish, and short. But far too many authors have been convinced by some Miss Thistlebottom that fiction must be as solemn as an undertaker's funeral. This is nonsense. Tragedy is not superior to comedy. Ask Shakespeare.

To our gastroenterologist, there is nothing inherently funny about resecting a bullet-ridden bowel. True enough. But it turns out our hero is as singleminded and aggressive as Caspar Weinberger. Even when he lies beside the fire with his girlfriend he doesn't crack a smile. Nobody jokes; nobody (including the author, it seems) finds anything ironic in the story. Since the novel isn't fun, and the plot a little improbable and icky, I'll decline on this one.

But Gert, our Rochester therapist, is thoroughly human, likable, easier to take. She has two crazy cats named Boris and Natasha. At the local natural history museum, one of her patients tails her. It's the mayor; he is dressed like a nun. Gert treats her mayor with all the perplexity, irony and wit owed to a public official, who believes he is Sister Maria Dolorosa.

I'm not in the business of giving prescriptions to writers' sensibilities. Part of the pleasure of editing is the chance to help a writer shed his or her particular angle of light on the world. But I do believe in wit—not gut-busting jokes necessarily, but wit as John Donne might define it: the use of all your intellectual, emotional and creative faculties, together with a sense of proportion and a modest taste for irony.

Those same pundits who call our era the age of information also declare it the age of irony. What is irony after all but the recognition that all is not as it appears to be? We receive that message several hundred times a day. And all fiction writers are in the business of revealing not what seems to be simple and true but what is complicated and true.

## Looking for . . .

Beyond wit, style, thick description, and characters to care about, what does an editor look for?

Editors don't know what they are looking for. They are basically readers, and they like to be surprised. They also like neatness, a snappy cover letter (with the manuscript), and an addressed return envelope with the stamps already in place. You should also keep in mind the following when submitting fiction for publication:

1. Know your publisher. If you've written a romance novel about an 18-year-old girl who falls in love with an international photographer and lives happily ever after, you shouldn't send it to Knopf. Knopf doesn't publish romance. Neither do most other hardcover houses. Ask yourself what kind of novel you have written, and write away for the publisher's catalogs so that you know exactly what you're getting into, or check the book racks in your favorite bookstore.

2. Ask yourself if you're really ready to publish a book. Maybe your epic novel of Greenland could work well initially as a series of short stories. By publishing extensively in magazines, you could garner a bit of cash, some recognition (editors do take notice of an author's credits and they try to keep abreast of magazine fiction), and possibly an agent.

3. Agents. Like a dishwasher or a Cuisinart, an agent is nice to have, but you can do the job yourself. Novels submitted by agents generally get read first, but most editors pay attention to work from unagented writers as well—where the quality and originality are often just as high.

4. Write a wonderful query letter. It may be difficult—it may seem easier to write another novel—but it's worth the effort. A query letter is a great opportunity to write your own jacket copy. Your letter should be a succinct, entertaining and informative introducion to your fiction and its author. Spend time on it. Don't be cute, just human.

5. Sample chapters. I personally don't mind when an author sends along several sample chapters with an initial query. But I'm infuriated when those chapters are either taken from the middle of a manuscript or are nonconsecutive. Supposedly, nonconsecutive chapters give an editor the chance to see the writer's overall style and plot, but the editor reads your work with no context. Send the first three or four chapters of your story. If you don't think they represent your entire novel, rewrite them until they do—until they make an editor quiver from scalp to toenail, demanding to read more.

6. Manuscript mechanics. If you're sending in hundreds of pages, put them in a box. Don't ever bind your manuscript; that means I can't take home only a hunk of it at a time. Don't send loose stamps and please don't enclose a check for return postage; that's a pain. It's fine and dandy to submit a clean photocopy; everybody does it; and I would feel terrible if I dropped an original typescript in the bathtub. Computer-generated text is fine too, just as long as it's not dot-matrix on perforated paper, in which case I will ruin my eyes and barely resist the temptation to return the manuscript in dot-sized pieces.

7. Never, ever, send a manuscript addressed to "the Editor" or "Fiction Editor." There is no such person. Your novel will be read in 30 seconds by an overworked assistant and not even Henry James could survive that. Check the directories (*Literary Market Place, Writer's Market, Fiction Writer's Market,* or *Publishers Weekly,* etc.) for the name of an editor whose specialties and previously published books indicate he/she might be interested in your work. This is worth the hassle of researching. You still might receive a form rejection slip, but at least you've done everything you can.

8. Give the editor time to read your manuscript. I'm generally about four weeks behind in my reading. If an editor holds onto your novel for a long time, it may mean that many editors are reading it. It may also mean your novel has been lost in the mail. That sometimes happens. Feel free to query a publisher after the stated time elapsed and hope that the publisher has kept a record of your submission.

9. Don't operate in a vacuum. After three years at Iowa, I don't quite believe a writ-

ers' conference or creative writing program can create a writer, but contact with other literary toilers certainly can make the process of writing more professional and less lonely. Read everything you can and feel free to imitate; everybody does it ("Bad writers borrow and good writers steal," said one of my teachers). And try your work out on people around you who won't try to keep you happy with pacifying answers. Rewrite and rewrite and then, after five months, rewrite again. Most of the novels I read would have been much more successful if they'd gone through the typewriter or word processor once more, or at least had an objective reader early on. Why do I feel so often that the author and I are the only ones who have ever read the author's novel?

## Super baby

I can't encourage anyone to be a writer. Writing and publishing are still mannerly occupations, without the high-stakes viciousness of the movie biz or arms-control talks—and the rewards are concurrently small. Few books make anyone much money; fewer people buy bestsellers than gyrate to Madonna. Become a rock star or a television evangelist—you'll have a better shot at posterity. Writing is a long, lonely, grinding and often unsuccessful endeavor.

So is editing. I spend hours reading manuscripts despairing at the amount of mediocrity in circulation. But editing is a craft, not an art, and compared with the toil of writing, it's child play, requiring just politeness and an ability to see the forest for the trees.

Sometimes, late on a Sunday afternoon when manuscripts sprawl like autumn leaves on my living room floor, I open to page one of a new novel and realize suddenly, viscerally, from the first sentence, that I'm in the presence of a wonderful, talented, publishable writer: "Gert had always hated her name. It rang in her ears like the noise a duck would make as it froze slowly on the snowy lawn of the Kodak building. Gert. She sat pinned in her sweaty office chair listening to the unfortunately-named Thomas G. Hardy, a wholesale lingerie salesman, explain why he could no longer sleep with his wife. He was discussing gardenia perfume with Gert. As he leaned forward, sniffling slightly, Gert felt a feathery, damp terror tumble into the cavern of her body as soundlessly as an eyelash."

A little overwritten, maybe. But nice sounds, great imagistic contrasts, and two fascinating characters in one paragraph. I keep on reading, until dusk, past dinner, toward bedtime, until Gert's story is complete. I go to bed and even dream of Gert.

On Sunday night, Mohammed, the Hollywood nurse, and the crusading gastroenterologist are boxed and replaced in my backpack, all to be politely returned on Monday morning.

Gert stays with me. I'll write a report on the novel, trying to be as savvy as Gert's creator. I'll walk down the hall to the office of another editor, cradling Gert. If I'm lucky, and other editors love this novel too, this will be the first of many trips down the hall with Gert, until at last I am carrying a finished book, ready for the rest of the world.

Now I burst into the editor's office, carrying something that's alive. "Barbara," I say, as the editor looks up. "A superior bambino!"

*In literature as in love we are astonished at what is chosen by others.*
*—André Maurois*

# Congratulations! It's a book!

## by Barbara Wernecke Durkin

It's a lot like operations or childbirth: Everybody who's published a first novel has a story to tell, and to the uninitiated, each one is unique, fascinating, and shining with rainbow promise. If he/she did it, so can I, the heart and mind believe. And why not? It's happened to some of the unlikeliest characters.

It's happened to me.

True, it all occured somewhat later than I'd originally planned—I was 38 years old when I got the good news—but nothing could lessen its impact or diminish its dazzlement for me. My husband Bill (the Lone Engineer) was happy but unfazed.

"I knew it would happen," he said calmly, reasonably, as I stood shaking in the tiny foyer of our modest home, dazed and afraid to believe it had happened.

"I can't believe it," I panted.

"Believe it," he said, "and get busy."

As you may surmise, that's not the beginning or the end of this story. Let me paint in a little background and detail.

## Can't you publish the *Polka*?

In high school, all I wanted to do was write. Other kids ate cereal for breakfast; I munched sugar-coated melancholy. Other kids went out for cheerleading and student government; I hung out at home making poems out of my personal melodrama. One appeared in the school's literary magazine and subsequently won a prize from the local women's club—five bucks and a rhyming dictionary. I was on my way.

The theatre and the study of American Lit got in my way for a time, and then ten

*Barbara Wernecke Durkin sold her first short story to* Seventeen *in 1981. In five years her byline has appeared in* Lady's Circle, Woman's World, Upper Room, Grit, YM, *and other publications. Her first novel,* Oh, You Dundalk Girls, Can't You Dance the Polka? *was published in 1984, and she recently completed its sequel,* The Waltz of the Slowdancing Bear.

years of teaching English, speech, and drama in a public high school, and then marriage, followed by two baby boys in quick succession and several years of serious illness. Suddenly I was 37, haggard, restless, and weary. Weary not only of life and its rigors, but also of trying to fight off the overwhelming *need to write* despite all the world's contention that a writing career was an impossible dream. I fought it until I couldn't anymore.

Bewitched, bothered, and bemused, I tapped out halfhearted short stories and sent them off accompanied by pathetic, and as I see now, negative, little cover letters, the text of which generally ran something like, "You probably wouldn't want to buy this, but if you'd only just please look at it, sir or madam, as the case may be . . ."

Three or four a year, maybe, I sent away like that, and when they came back with those little photocopied thanks-but-no-thanks notes paperclipped to them, I would whine and sniffle and say, "See? It's no use. You've just got to know somebody, or else you've go to be Norman Mailer before they'll even look at your stuff."

On New Year's Eve, 1980-becoming-1981, Bill said, in effect, "Fish or cut bait. Be professional for once. Get as many things out as you possibly can, and the law of averages promises that eventually you will sell something. If, after a decent period of time, say 18 months, you haven't sold anything, then drop the dream and be done with it."

Good advice. Within two months, I'd sold my first story to a national magazine, and that gave me the impetus to go on and on, and as soon as I had ten or so solid sales, I took advantage of a friend's recommendation to his agent. To my astonishment, she liked my work, and believed in my talent. I cried with joy when she said she'd represent me. I'd sent her the first hundred pages of *Oh, You Dundalk Girls, Can't You Dance the Polka?*, and she loved it.

## Big deal

It was early summer when I returned from our annual family vacation, and my trusty phone recorder held a cryptic message for me from my agent. When I returned her call, she answered laughing.

"Are you sitting down?"

The book sold, on the strength of the first 100 pages, to William Morrow, with a $3,000 advance.

"Now send the rest of it along as soon as you can," she said. I gulped and promised I would. I did not feel it wise to mention that the rest of it did not quite exist. That was what Bill meant when he said, "Now, get busy."

I got busy. Within a few weeks, I had the rest of it finished and mailed off in a fever of great expectation.

And then I waited. I was expecting maybe a contract or something, I said hesitantly in about August. True, my agent agreed, there should have been a contract around somewhere. Phone calls to the publisher produced, finally, the unhappy information that their contract person had been on a lengthy vacation, and then had been fired upon her return and no replacement had been found as yet. Oh.

Golly, I hoped I wasn't bothering anybody with all my pesky questions. What did I know about the mysterious publishing business? Zilch, like most new writers (and a lot of old ones). Of course, no advance money was making its way to my bank account until the contract was signed, so my first half of the advance was delayed by six months, since the papers were never signed until December. But that was all right with me; even though friends and family had been asking for months when the book would be out, I hung on and smiled and said, "Soon."

Ha. There's no word for it but "Ha."

My faint heart sank when my beloved first editor decided to take a Giant Step over to another big deal house and be an even bigger honcho. Where did that leave me? In a better position than some, I've since found out, because I inherited the new senior editor at Morrow, which was incredibly fortunate. The new man had never even read my manuscript. Naturally, he was unavailable for comment from December through January, because a hard-earned vacation to parts unknown came between us, and he hadn't thought to take my book along with him to fill in those empty hours at the beaches and casinos, or whatever.

## Bouncing baby book

I got the manuscript back in March, along with a four-page single-spaced letter chock full of suggestions, improvements. Again, I was almost in tears.

"I don't know why you're so upset," Bill said in his scientist's voice. "After all, the only things he doesn't like are the plot, the characters, the setting, the language, the structure, and the style." All the pages were meticulously red-penciled so that they looked like individual road maps, and all the roads led to Yukville. He didn't seem to like it much.

What now? Was I supposed to take all his "suggestions" and lose what seemed to me to be the spice and flavor of my story and its people, or should I take a stand and insist that they print it as it was? How could I maintain my integrity without risking the publisher's wrath and disgust?

I carefully reread all my editor's comments, then made what I believe was a fortunate decision. Relying on something I'd read in Flannery O'Connor's biography, I decided to follow those directions that seemed to enhance and improve my own concepts, and to reject those that were at odds with what I was trying to accomplish. To this day, I am grateful for the painstaking editing that kept me from faking love scenes with honey drips of stream-of-self-consciousness drivel and from endless repetitions of simple ideas and phrases I could never quite trust the reader to get on his/her own.

The result was a carefully-edited, more mature, harder-hitting manuscript, and a book I liked even better than the original. Now it would be a bona fide published book, and soon.

Again, Ha.

Copyediting took a long time. Then it was my turn to re-edit the copyeditor's edited manuscript. Is everyone still with me here? Good. Now it would soon be a real live published book. Soon. Real. Published.

In the beginning of July, toward the end of our annual family vacation (yes, the years managed to fly by), a quietly frantic phone call left me trembling. The editor's assistant wanted to know if I'd ever received the copy-edited manuscript, mailed to me weeks before, registered mail. Registered in the Twilight Zone, apparently, since it never arrived at my doorstep.

Back to Square Three. The copy editor started again, the new edited version came to me, I re-edited that, and back it went to Morrow. Now, surely, it wouldn't be long. Countless inquiries from family and friends were answered confidently now: soon. Soon.

Spring, 1984 was the date the publisher settled on, just under the wire of the time limit specified in my contract.

"It takes about nine months, appropriately enough," my editor said patiently when I complained about how long this thing had been in the making. "Those are just the simple facts of publishing," he assured me.

I've never been able to explain why I so enjoyed being pregnant that I could cheerfully have carried each baby for a year or more without effort, and yet the wait for this damned, infernal book was making me into a wretched, nervous, fretful, crabby old hag. I finally came to believe that it would never come out, and forgot about it. In January, the first copy arrived in the mail, with a cover I (miraculously) liked and a dedication to my parents and brothers that made me choke with real emotion.

To herald its arrival I had a friend, a printer, make about 100 or so "baby announcements" that read:

Barbara Wernecke Durkin
is proud to announce
the birth of her first novel . . .
*Oh, You Dundalk Girls, Can't You Dance the Polka?*
on March 1, 1984
(William Morrow, New York)
Weight: 15 ounces   Length: 311 pages

The total cost for printing and postage was about $50, but it was money well spent, since it amused and enlightened friends—and it kept the book foremost in their minds when it first came out.

The book itself was beautiful, just like my other two babies. Beautiful and perfect.

## High time

Not everyone agreed with the "perfect," of course. The first two reviews I saw contained a few minor criticisms, but they were qualified by phrases like, "but for a first effort . . . fine . . . funny . . . like a *Catcher in the Rye* of the '80s . . . hilarious . . ." and subsequent reviews seemed to get better and better. The old hometown (Baltimore) major papers got behind me and the book, and then the Rochester dailies here, and then I did a two-week tour in Baltimore. Noontime news shows on the three big channels, local cable shows, personal appearances and book signings—it was wonderful, and just like Old Home Week, considering the (literally) thousands of people I know there. Still, I was separated from the people I love most in Rochester, and it was wearing, a time of too many strangers, too many parties, too much attention, too many commitments on too tight a schedule, and I got tired.

Tired and crazy. First of all, some people I expected to welcome me home with banners and balloons shoveled compost onto my head and shouted, "Boo." I was absolutely stunned. It had never once occurred to me that anyone from home would read anything but love in my book. In all innocence, I believed that every reader would feel my devotion in the book to the people and places of my youth. Instead, some chose to perceive insult and injury therein, and I suffered mightily from their criticism.

On the other hand, I was not prepared for the adoration of the multitudes, for more loved the book than resented it. Do you know how hard it is to listen to several weeks of praise? Oh, no, I found myself protesting—it's not that good, folks! It's only a book, after all. Shucks.

For a somewhat flamboyant character who'd learned a bit of subtlety over the years, it was a struggle to maintain my equilibrium. After a while, it's easy to start believing that you're Hot Stuff, and it's definitely time to get back home to the people who know you're only you.

"Come and get me," I wailed long distance from Baltimore to the Lone Engineer back home. "And bring one of the kids," I begged. Nobody can put you in your place like your kids.

All that transpired slightly over a year ago as I write this. Now what I most recall about those first few marvelous months of celebrity was the high-flying feeling that I had conquered all—truly all—by proving that even a chubby houseperson who was not from The Big Apple or Los Angeles had things to say that people found valid and moving, as well as genuinely funny. It was enough for me, a high to last a lifetime.

## Household what?

But that lifetime was, in reality, only a few weeks in all. Before long, the urge to do it again came chasing after me, and I've been a slave to it ever since. Everyone asked for a sequel, and so I dove into that project with a vengeance. Six months and three false starts later, I realized that my attempts to write a sequel were dismal failures, and I stared dejectedly at hundreds of pages of dead-end crap.

"I'm all washed up," I said to Bill, as I imagined the dialogue might run in a 1948 movie starring Joan Crawford and Van Johnson.

"Balderdash," Bill said. "You're just on the wrong track. Try something new."

I did, and sure enough, the Big Second Novel is now almost finished. I know now from talking to others in the same canoe that there is always that day of reckoning for every novelist, that terrible day when you believe with all your heart, mind, and spirit that there is nothing more in you, that you were a one-trick pony, a day-tripper, a fluke.

Allow me one more ha. Ha. It's not true. There's plenty more where the first came from. The trick is to peel off all the hyped-up power and glory after your first success, and get down to the business of producing something more, something better, something finer and sharper . . .

And there's absolutely nothing more encouraging than winning recognition from People Who Know. I was thrilled to the soul when I learned that *Dundalk Girls* was among the American Library Association's "Best of 1984" for YA readers. Realizing that experts in the field of reading and books found my work superior restored my flagging spirits.

As a result, I now make it a point to be available as a speaker for libraries, literary clubs, any group, and have been paid anywhere from $25 to $500 for these appearances. Audiences have been beautiful, and my love for this aspect of the writing life grows in breadth and depth.

I would have been gratified to see more national publicity and a bigger "push" for *Dundalk Girls* from the publisher, since the reviewers who have seen it are surprised that there was no hoopla, no excitement accompanying the book. Most of them sort of stumbled upon it in a cloud of serendipity, and this disturbs me, because it seems that known and well-established writers receive tons of expensive publicity they probably don't need, and we who are struggling don't seem to rate much of the publisher's advertising dollar. I've had to do most of my own "pushing," and it doesn't come naturally.

There's also the disappointment, probably inevitable, of not becoming rich and famous as soon as the world discovered my talent, pizzazz, and personal charisma. I envisioned a house overlooking the lake (Ontario), a piece about me in *People*, a few moments in that chair next to Johnny Carson's desk, and a minor fling with David Letterman. In case you hadn't noticed, my name has not become the household word Spiro Agnew's (also from Baltimore, originally) did. Sometimes that still hurts, but mostly I've gotten back to wordsmithing and tried to brush such nonsense aside.

## Even Evens

Don't think, however, that mine is the "normal" saga of publishing a first novel. Actually, there is no normal or average story. Here are a few others to enlighten you as to the myriad possibilities for a first novelist:

*LORI HAHN EVENS* had always written, but hadn't thought of herself as a writer, even though she'd won awards in high school and had had several poems and articles and a short story published over the ten years after her graduation. Her life goals were simple: husband, a couple of kids, and a two-story house in the country.

One day, her goals accomplished according to plan, she sat in her remodeled farmhouse in upstate New York and said to herself, "Now what? You've done it all and you're only 30 years old. Is this it?"

That day she became a writer.

"Over the next four years, my postage bill rivaled the national debt," she said. "Most of what I wrote came right back, but I kept on mailing. I read nearly every book I could get my hands on about fiction writing, and one day I found *Writer's Market* on the library shelf. I was delighted at the difference it made in my time, typing, and postage."

Gradually, the rejection letters became more personal and helpful, and Lori had the courage to start writing novels and trying to sell them. In January of 1983, she did what many of us do when we feel we're at a crisis point; she prayed.

"God, if I supposed to be a writer, let me publish something this year. If I don't, I'll do something else."

In a village library, she picked up a light romance in hardcover from Avalon Books. She knew it was the kind of thing she could write, and she checked out every Avalon romance they had. After reading 25 of them, she wrote one that she called *Stranger at Cole Junction*. She wrote about a chapter a week, then rewrote each one again, and again.

The hardest part was typing it on a faulty electric typewriter with no carriage return and a cranky line-spacer. No amount of fixing seemed to faze this machine, so Lori found herself typing at a snail's pace and promising herself that if her book sold, she'd spend the money on a new machine.

A friend who'd sold books to Avalon in the past submitted the manuscript for her in October, and on December 23, 1983, just two days before the end of her year, she had a contract, and by March, the book was in the library. Now it was entitled *Autumn Kisses*, but it was still Lori's own book, with only a few minor changes.

"Although I made very little money from the book, I deliberately chose a small, low-paying, but long-established and reputable publisher because I hoped the competition wouldn't be as fierce. I wanted to set an attainable goal. Now, when I go into a library and find my name in the card catalog, someplace between Evening and Everything, I want to yell, 'Hey—that's my name!' *Autumn Kisses* is my first book, but not my last. I've set another goal."

## Rhapsody in pink

From upstate New York to East Coast metropolitan, hopes and dreams soar. *BEN HERMAN* has the unique distinction of having published a first novel twice. Twice? Yes.

A native of Baltimore, Ben Herman writes with a delicate touch, painting his words in water colors. He evokes the Baltimore of the '30s and '40s through the eyes of an unassuming Jewish kid with rare wit and insight.

"In 1972 I gave some dozen or so New York publishers the chance to publish my first book, *Sunday After Sunday After Sunday*. When none of them jumped at this opportunity, I decided to publish it myself. After all, I was in good company. Henry David Thoreau paid for his first book. Walt Whitman brought out *Leaves of Grass* himself, so why not me?"

Ben met with one of the top commercial artists in Baltimore, a representative of a typesetting company, and the president of Bay Printing Company. They worked out a ballpark figure for producing 2,500 paperback copies of the book—$2,000.

"I told the president I wanted the same print used in Hemingway's *In Our Time*, and the artist did ten delightful line drawings. He also suggested ivory paper to, as he put it, enhance the warmth of the book. I can still feel the warmth of that handsome pink book as it rolled off the presses. (Some people referred to the cover as "lox-colored".) Then all the good things began to happen."

The *News-American* and the *Sun* did major stories and publicity. Reviews were good. Radio interviews and word-of-mouth advertising did wonders. Confident regarding his novel's worth, Herman packed boxes of books into the trunk of his green Mustang and had no trouble placing them in the Walden's, Gordon's, and Remington bookstores. All in all, he was able to pay off the book's producers easily, and made about a thousand dollars in profit from this venture.

Was this a happy experience? "Yes. Terrific," Ben said. "I loved every minute of it."

"Regular" publication first came in 1981, when Herman's novel *The Rhapsody in Blue of Mickey Klein* was brought out by Stemmer House. "This experience was just as much fun, just as exciting, just as rewarding, as the first book, but in a different way."

This time, Herman had "the luxury of having a great editor, Barbara Holdridge, whose suggestions made it a better book. The distribution was national as well as local. Reviews, too. Then *Library Journal* asked me to do a piece about writing the book. Best of all, I woke up one morning to learn that the book had been nominated for a National Jewish Book Award (thanks to my publisher)."

Herman pitched in when it came to promotion. He contacted old friends and writers he knew, and made it known that he was available for interviews and TV and radio appearances. Maryland Public Television featured him on a half-hour interview program, and also included him in a special series on Maryland writers.

All things considered, Ben Herman felt that his work was well-respected in both instances, since he still doesn't consider his first "first book" a vanity press publication. "But it did feel fine the second time around to have somebody else take care of all the publicity details I'd handled myself the first time," he says. "Besides, the first book made money, and the second didn't. Its success was only modest, but it was still a step in the right direction for me. Now my new novel, *Green Dust of the Milky Way*, is making the rounds of the New York publishers."

## Mountain mover Monroe

Our last success story for first-timers is remarkable and inspirational, to say the very least. Hannelore Hahn, director of IWWG (International Women's Writing Guild) recommended a new novelist whose story might move mountains for others who feel they're at the end of their inner resources: Mary Monroe.

**MARY MONROE** of Oakland, California, wrote her first novel, *The Upper Room*, in two months. It is a novel rich in the lore and legend of black America, with characters as wild and improbable as they are real. Because of her nine-to-five job, she wrote to and from work on her commuter bus, weekends, and a couple of hours each day before and after work, sometimes completing several chapters in an hour.

"The original title was *My Sister, My Brother*, and the story was a weak, badly-structured 'romance,' " says Monroe. "I rewrote the book eight times before it was published."

For four years, Monroe tried to get a publisher without benefit of an agent. After all the agents in directories rejected her several times each, she looked for additional sources, and found an agent listed in *Scriptwriter's Newsletter* in March, 1982, and with him, Monroe struck gold.

"Rejections? I received my thousandth rejection letter in March of '82," she said. "*The Upper Room* alone was rejected 80 times over a period of six years."

When she was finally offered a contract, Monroe was "so desperate any contract would have looked good to me." But her agent spent a lot of time going over it, revising and negotiating until he was satisfied with the terms. "I'm very happy with my contract with St. Martin's," Monroe says now. They must have done a good job of publicizing, because many major newspapers reviewed the book.

"I'm glad now that I had to struggle so much," she says. "I appreciate the rewards and truly feel that I earned all this recognition. I ended up with the best agent and editor a beginning novelist could get. Both worked with me far beyond the call of duty even before the novel was accepted."

The newspaper articles about Mary Monroe and her work tell a real Cinderella tale of courage and determination. Time after time her efforts, from her first childhood autobiography (age 7, 400 pages) to her adult stories and books, have met with ridicule from family and friends, and with little commercial success.

"But publishing my first novel brought more than I expected," she says. "My life has changed drastically. Friends and relatives pester me and demand everything from financial assistance to a lock of Stephen King's hair."

Ah, fame. What about fortune?

Advances range from zero to lots. According to the most recent Authors Guild survey results, advances of $5,000 to $20,000 are most common, but the survey makes no distinction between first and subsequent books, so it's difficult to know what to expect. First runs of first books could be 5,000 or 25,000 copies—who knows why publishers do what they do? The whole business seems to the writer like a Chinese fire drill. Editors, assistants, contract people, seem to go in and out of revolving doors in a mad rush, and bewilderment sets in. That's why so many of us rely heavily on agents for love, support, and guidance. Others prefer to go it alone. More power to us all, I say. Go for it any which way you can, I say.

> *What wins over the reader is a cleansing and continous laughter, sometimes so intense that in itself it becomes astonishingly painful.*
> —*Philip Roth*

# Harriet Doerr

## Interview by Lynn Gray

Harriet Doerr was born in Pasadena in 1910. She entered Smith College in 1927, graduated from Stanford in 1977, and continued there in the graduate writing program until 1984. She has received numerous grants and awards in connection with her writing, including a Wallace Stegner Fellowship (1980-81), a *Transatlantic Review*-Henfield Foundation Award (1982) and a NEA grant (1983). This year she received The American Book Award for First Fiction for her novel, *Stones for Ibarra*, as well as an award from the Bay Area Book Reviewers Association (B.A.B.R.A.) for the same work.

**Lynn Gray:** Is *Stones for Ibarra* your first novel, or have you written others that weren't published or that you didn't try to have published?
**Harriet Doerr:** I've not written extensively before this book; this is my first novel, published or unpublished. In grammar school, high school and college I always loved to write, but I didn't know as E.B. White did, at age seven, that I would be a writer. I was a history major in college, not an English major. I haven't been writing all this time, all these many, many years, and worse than that I haven't kept a journal. I'm trying to now. I did not keep a journal in Mexico and I'll regret that forever, because you do forget.
**LG:** What was the impetus for writing *Stones*? It has a strongly autobiographical feel; is this an accurate perception?
**HD:** I think everything anyone puts on a piece of paper is autobiographical in some degree because it comes *through* you; it's your impression and insight. Three separate people will give three different stories about the same incident; everyone notices and emphasizes something different. As far as the characters being real, they aren't. Eudora Welty, in her book *One Writer's Beginnings*, states that when you care deeply about an individual you find it impossible to fictionalize that person. It's an invasion of privacy for one

---

*Lynn Gray is features editor for the San Francisco-based literary, Fm. Five, for which she conducts interviews. A former editor of* Esencia, *she has also published in* The Goodfellow Review *and* Akwesasne Notes.

photo by Bonnie Schiffman

Harriet Doerr, winner of the American Book Award for First Fiction for *Stones for Ibarra*.

thing. What you have to do is put yourself in that person's skin, and think and behave and feel the way he or she does, and if you can make a whole person in that fashion, the character then comes to life. As far as the dialogue in the book is concerned, only one sentence was ever spoken in real life.

**LG:** Was the book written in the US or elsewhere? Is there a value, especially for the artist, in placing oneself in a foreign culture for a period of time in order to gain a certain perspective?

**HD:** I have spent time in Mexico, the setting of my book, and I think it's an astonishing and fascinating country. I did try to write there once or twice and found it didn't work; I was too close to what I was writing about. Besides that, no matter how hard I tried to secure my privacy, and I was quite far away from civilization, no one seemed to believe I truly wanted to be alone. Even if I asked to have time to myself for three hours they felt I couldn't have meant it. It's hard for me to write when I don't have any distance and things are right in front of me. So I think the best thing, when you feel something will make a story or a novel, is to take copious notes and then refer to them later with a different perspective.

**LG:** Sara Everton, one of the main characters in *Stones*, is interesting because she obviously is a deeply feeling person, yet she maintains an inner equilibrium that carries her through the knowledge of her husband's inevitable early death. How did Sara evolve in your mind?

**HD:** She evolved little by little. I have to tell you this book is extremely untraditional in the way it was written. I went back to school and took a writing course, and I started writing Mexican stories which I chose because I had recently returned from there and the images were very sharp in my mind. I started writing tales of people in a small town and I added Sara and Richard Everton later. This is *not* the way to write a novel. I had six or seven of these tales and someone in the writing class suggested I put them together to make a novel. I tried to figure out how to tie all these in and create a little suspense and so I added the Evertons. I wanted to explore the encounter between the Mexicans and the Americans. I didn't plan any of the plot in advance; I had no design about Sara's or Richard's character or what would happen to them when I started out. The book really proceeded chapter by chapter; but there was no overall concept before I started.

**LG:** As an older writer what role do you think memory plays in the creative process?

**HD:** I think even a 16-year-old writer needs memory to get anything written. Without memory you have no way to express even your immediate feelings. If you start out without any images in your head and try to write a paragraph about something even very intense, I think it would be impossible to describe that circumstance or feeling. Everything builds and you take from it as you go. Eudora Welty described memory as "a wonderful interior vision." Certainly anyone's memory is faulty, but it's still a vision. Gabriel García Márquez commented one time about his writing of *One Hundred Years of Solitude* that he clearly remembered going to live with his grandparents and added that nothing interesting had happened to him since he was eight. I love that remark. Much, much later he was on the road from Mexico City to Acapulco with his family on vacation, and suddenly he turned around halfway there and went back to Mexico City, because this vision came to him and he saw the book, or enough of the book, to begin writing. So he drove back home and sat down at his desk and began to write. Which must have been a slight blow to his children who were looking forward to the beach.

**LG:** Why do *you* write? What do you think is the purpose of writing?

**HD:** I think one writes because one sees or hears some small, astounding thing (writers are always spying and eavesdropping, you know; otherwise, inspiration might elude you) and suddenly what matters most in the world is to get it down on paper. Caring is the important thing. Eudora Welty spoke of "a writer's own emergency." You have a need, a compulsion even, to put something down. Grace Paley said that to write without pressure is hard, if not impossible. You have to feel you have a story you *must* tell. You must think that if you can somehow get something down perfectly, so that it's absolutely right, all the problems of the world will be solved, including man's fate.

As for the purpose of writing fiction, well, sometimes I really do wonder if there's a purpose. But I think perhaps the purpose is to transmit a feeling or an insight of yours to other people. There is the consideration of entertaining people, but I never put that at the top of my list. If you can expose something that everyone has seen all his life, show it in a different, clearer light, that's the reason. And that's why I read, that's what I look for when I read. And I also look for language. You know, when a sentence makes you gasp, or an insight puts a searchlight on something you've ignored, that's what it's all about.

**LG:** What I felt was very impressive in your book was your delicate treatment of what could have been a typical sentimental situation of loss and grief . . .

**HD:** I'm relieved you said that because I really hoped that it wasn't sentimental. It's very hard to handle the theme of illness and of death, and of course the word "leukemia" is like flashing a card: Everyone is supposed to burst into tears immediately. Actually, it's only part of the human condition; everybody faces something sooner or later.

**LG:** Did you rewrite the book much?

**HD:** Oh lots. I can't tell you how many times. One chapter I rewrote six or seven times. As far as words and phrases there's no end to the revisions. In fact I have a copy of the published book where I've written corrections, which only I will ever see, in the margins. I have a bit of a perfectionist problem, which makes me a very slow writer.

**LG:** I think if you are trying to create a strong tone, which your book definitely has, the writing must be necessarily slow. If tone is at least as much of a component as plot then you have to weigh each word in order to sustain that atmosphere.

**HD:** Once I started and knew how it was going to go, I would find myself facing a piece of paper and concentrating, almost as though I were listening to music or tuning an instrument, trying to find the right key. You sit there and wait until you have that, and then you start.

**LG:** Did you have trouble getting an agent, or having the book published?

**HD:** I got an agent while I was in the writing class at Stanford. A classmate of mine, Ron Hansen (author of *Desperadoes* and *The Assassination of Jesse James by the Coward Robert Ford*) sent a few of my stories to his agent, and she took me on. And then for all those years, from 1978 to 1984, when the book was published, I worried about her because she didn't make enough from me to pay for telephone calls and stamps. The publishing of the book came by chance, too. I sent it out as a collection of linked stories and it was rejected by three publishers. I became very discouraged. They all liked the writing but they didn't know what it was: a collection of stories, a novel or neither. Then there was a competition, The Henfield Award, for college writers all over the country. I was extremely lucky and tied for first place. Prior to that I'd had a whole year of rejection and despair. I felt I'd never have anything published. Then a letter came from an editor at Viking in London suggesting that I send the three Henfield award stories (which this editor had somehow read) to a Viking editor in New York. Then two months later a letter came asking me to send the entire manuscript, and then two months after that a phone call came saying they wanted to take it as a novel.

So I "featherdusted" strenuously for three months, straightening out the chronology, eliminating and strengthening characters, eliminating superfluous events and places, making bridges between chapters, adding a chapter, making sure certain historical dates were accurate, and just generally turning it into a novel. But basically I think I have an enormous lucky star. Otherwise, I might have been discouraged and not persevered to get published.

**LG:** Who do you read and enjoy?

**HD:** I think you are influenced by everything you see, hear, touch, read, from the moment you're born, whether you're aware of it or not. As for specific writers, I especially enjoy the Latin American writers, Juan Rulfo, who may not yet be translated, Garcia Márquez, of course, and Cortazár. I like William Trevor, Mavis Gallant, Raymond Carver. I think Grace Paley is a wonderful writer, and Eudora Welty. William Maxwell and Peter Taylor. There are so many.

I think as a writer you take a little bit from everything and it comes out in your writing. All you have is your experience and your imagination and your perspective. If you're old, like me, you have a very long view, and maybe what you write becomes a little too measured. It has a different urgency from the work of someone young. And you have to love words. That's the best part, don't you think, when four or five of them come together just right. It's wonderful.

 *I have been told, both in approval and in accusation, that I seem to love all my characters. What I do in writing of any character is to try to enter into the mind, heart, and skin of a human being who is not myself. Whether this happens to be a man or a woman, old or young, with skin black or white, the primary challenge lies in making the jump itself. It is the act of a writer's imagination that I set most high.*
*—Eudora Welty*

# The truth, more or less, as long as it makes a good story

## by Shannon OCork

If, long ago, back in Lyndon, Kentucky, where I was born, I murdered Johnny Williams and got away with it, I could not admit it now, could I? The case is still on the books there in Jefferson County, and in Kentucky there is no statute of limitation on murder. But maybe I did. I wrote a novel about it once. Or, better, maybe I can make you think I did. I'd like to put the possibility of it and a little suspicion in your mind. The truth of the matter, as truth usually is, is a mix of fact and fancy. Of reportage and fiction. Truman Capote said all novelists are liars. And I say all big lies begin with little truths.

Johnny Williams was 22 years old in 1959. Curly-haired. Golden-chested. He died in Lover's Hollow alongside Beargrass Creek. He was stabbed with a potato knife. Within two minutes, his blue eyes faded to gray. A potato knife is a sharp, long-bladed knife used in the field to cut potatoes out of the ground, cut them free from the earth-loving roots that can run deep as coffins. And be hard to cut through as bone. Everyone said Johnny's girl friend, Margaret Mary Dillman, did it. She didn't. Monsignor Roland started that rumor. Margaret Mary was pregnant and she was ashamed. She ran away after. I heard she never did come back. Isabelle Williams, Johnny's sister, said she'd wait for Margaret Mary. Swore she'd be layin' for her. Far as I know, and it's been years now, Izzard still is. Izzard always was mean-spirited like that; the kind of person who thought *The Ox-Bow Incident* was a comedy. I was only 15 at the time, but I remember it well. In

*Shannon OCork is the author of the widely-acclaimed mystery series featuring sports photographer T.T. Baldwin, including* Sports Freak, End of the Line, *and* Hell Bent for Heaven. *OCork has written fiction and nonfiction for various publications; she also has recently completed a full length mystery play* Tuned in to Murder; *and she is now at work on a modern suspense novel.*

my time around Lyndon, Kay-wy, the killing of Johnny Williams was the biggest thing ever happened.

## Telling detail

To write the story of Johnny Williams' murder, I'd re-create the characters, the situation, and the scene as exactly as I could. That's called focusing, locating the event precisely where you want it. I'd intensify a few details and eliminate those that didn't affect the story. I'd add in, painterly, some chosen-for-effect touches. I'd want to make dramatic the reason I killed Johnny, and I'd want you to like him and care that he died. I'd want you to like me, too, the narrator-character and murderer. So, through the writing, I'd lace in reader wooing; that is, I'd talk to you confidentially, one on one, as to a friend. That's likable, and I'd hope you wouldn't notice it was purposeful.

I'd keep the year it happened the same as it really was, 1959, so that everything I remembered would fit properly into the time. When I think of the summer Johnny Williams died, here are some of the things I remember, fresh as mint at Derbytime: the general store-post office in Lyndon, and Mrs Ada Guthrie, and the exotic look of a first-class stamp. The signs that cautioned us from riding the horses on the new, concrete sidewalks along Beech Drive into town. The ice house. What we talked about at supper. How we prayed. The limestone quarry where Johnny used to meet my mama, other side of Beargrass Creek, other side of Lover's Hollow. The action of the novel would take place among those remembered things. The things time, not people, change. The things that change when you aren't looking, the things you didn't realize were special and one-time-only until after they are gone for good and final. In writing, it's called putting in the local color. It's particularizing the environment.

Since I would be looking back, I could foreshadow events to come. And if I wanted, I'd be able to prophesy. That's called narrator omniscience or less grandly, Monday-morning quarterbacking.

I'd not forget the *telling detail*, the particular and peculiar characteristics of a time or a place or a character. One telling detail I'd use would be the dress I wore the night Johnny died; its collar, and how it tore on the knot of barbed wire, and what that meant after.

There was a long way and a short way to Bickel's quarry. The shortcut was through our cow pasture. That night I was bellying under the barbed-wire fence, looking for my mama. I saw Johnny up the hill of the hollow, in the pussy willow weeds with Margaret Mary. I forgot I was still stretched under the bottom strand. I lifted my head and caught my collar behind on a wire knot, on the three spiny barbs they leave sticking out to turn the cow back if she leans on the fencing too hard.

The reason the torn collar was important was because Auntie 'Phine always starched my collars and cuffs too much. One of the things I hated about Sacred Heart Academy was having to peel open the starched breast pocket of my white uniform blouse every Monday morning when I dressed. The whole blouse felt like cardboard until Friday, and Friday nights it got washed and starched again. And long before my dresses wore out, the collars frayed and the cuffs cracked. I'd have to go on wearing the dresses that way because they were basically still good. When I complained, Auntie 'Phine said pride was a devil's toy, but it was her lack of understanding of a young girl and her dresses that was the problem, not my pride. I begged her every time, "Please, Auntie, no starch." The reader would want to know about the overstarching because it was a *telling detail* in the killing of Johnny. It was what made no one think of me as anything other than an innocent witness to an especially savage murder.

Of course, I'd have to explain how that all worked out. It would be one of the *plot devices* in the novel, a thread of continuity. And I could use it to show character: Auntie 'Phine starching collars and cuffs was scary. She was dedicated to her task. (Give her any worthy task and she would quickly grow dedicated to it. You should have seen her on Sunday mornings, listening to Mass on the radio, gutting the dinner chicken with her bare hands.)

Auntie 'Phine was righteous as only a country virgin spinster can be. She liked the *Jack Benny Show*, but she had no sense of humor. What she had was a dressing mirror, oval, and rosewood, and tall as I was. In the evenings after prayers, Auntie 'Phine would go into the front parlor room Dad converted into her and Aunt Agnes' bedroom. (Twin beds and, between, a statue of the bleeding heart of Jesus on a round oak table, a votary candle burning before in a thick, blood-red glass. The statue stood on a doily starched stiff enough to cut your fingers.) Auntie 'Phine would sit herself on the piano stool in front of the mirror and brush her never-cut gray hair. The hair was long as Rapunzel's. Auntie 'Phine would sit a long time, counting brushstrokes in whispers, smiling at something inside the mirror only she could see. I asked her once if she'd ever had a lover. Aunt Agnes heard. She beat me until the yardstick broke.

## Thick and full of life

What I've done here is called *character delineation*. Through visual description, if I did it right, the reader caught a glimpse of Auntie 'Phine's soul. At its best, character delineation should be *heuristic*; that is, it should interest the reader and lead him or her to read on and learn more.

The story would have a provincial period flavor, then, of the American South in the late 1950s. For the action scenes, I would want *immediacy*; a you-are-there feeling for the reader. I would not want the novel to read like history. I'd want the reader to follow the 15-year-old girl, the first-person narrator. I'd want the reader to mentally participate in her emotions and actions and reactions. I'd want the reader, male or female, to *identify*.

To get *immediacy*, vividness, into the murder scene, I'd use Roysie and what happened to him last August. Roysie's stabbing is still startling in my mind. The killing of Johnny has grown warm and soft like a favorite blanket; I've slept with the killing of Johnny for a long, long time. I'd merge the two actual crimes into one fictional one. I'd work out the sequence of events of what happened to Johnny, and exactly how. That would be the *plot*. And then I'd overlay the stabbing of Roysie, about which I learned through effective *reportage*.

That way, I'll get the *objective* and the *subjective* together. I'll lace how it was (the objective) with how it looked (the subjective). They'll form a pattern, called the *author's style*.

I'll try to stay away from the *banal* and the *extraneous*. An example of the banal would be what my sister said when she heard about the death of Johnny. She said something forgettable like: "Gee, and he was so cute, too. Conceited, but cute."

An example of the extraneous would be whoever was walking on the other side of the street when Roysie was borne that night, under a bloodied white sheet, out of our apartment building on a stretcher by paramedics. There was no moon. The sheet glowed astrally in the mercury-green-of the streetlamps. On the stretcher, Roysie sat straight as a corpse coming out of rigor mortis. He said to me, me just out of a cab and dumbfounded: "Hope *you* had a nice night, dear." He was smoking a Marlboro. He was naked and white as Moby Dick. His hair hugged his forehead in sweaty little wisps. His face was the color of wet concrete. Roysie was slid, then, like a greased thermometer, into the gray anus of the ambulance. The ambulance door closed, quiet. The people on the other side of the street and what they thought, for this scene, are *extraneous*. They are without importance or effect. This scene is about Roysie, and, underneath, about Roysie and me.

Roysie is my neighbor. He lives just above me with his roommate, Morris, in 2-A. Roysie will tell you: "When I want to be, I'm the sweetest person in the world." Usually, when I'm sweet (unless I love you) it's because I'm after something I can use in my fiction. I'm after *reportage*. I want to yank away at a life and hold the vital parts of it in the long claws of my memory. And then use it sometime in the telling of a tale. And so it was that I got sweet with Roysie last August.

It was about 1 a.m. of a muggy, cloud-hiding-moon, hot Wednesday. Roysie was mugged in his apartment. Roysie had the top window open and the air conditioner on full. He fell asleep on the blue velvet sofa waiting for Morris to get home from Roosevelt Hospital, where Morris works as a nurse's aid. All Roysie was wearing were his favorite jogging shorts, the pink satin ones with the little slits on the thighs, and his tank watch from Cartier. And a little Royal Copenhagen, which was no help at all, he said.

Apartments 1-A and 2-A of the brownstone where we live face the street behind a curlicued wrought-iron fence. A young black man, a teenager really, Roysie and the witnesses agree, climbed from the fence to the lintel of the door of the attached apartment house next to us. From the arch there, the burglar long-stepped to the ledge under the second-story windows of our place. Then, one sneaker on the air conditioner box and up. He slithered into Roysie's apartment through the open top window. Roysie was robbed, of course. Worse, he was slashed deeply in the abdomen, down and into the lower intestine. The gouge in the bowel alone took 90 minutes of surgery to repair. When I asked, concerned friend of Roysie's that I was, the doctor explained it to me: The bowel is round and slippery, and the tear was long and jagged-lipped and uneven. Roysie's thigh was sliced to the bone. The femoral artery was severed. This is what almost killed him. Roysie remembers the attack. Remembers his blood spurting from his thigh like sap out of a ripe maple tree. The blood was astonishingly red, he says, and thick, and full of life.

## Easy for effect

Seeing his own blood, Roysie says, excited him. His attacker was small and young. Almost frail, Roysie said. As I, arms curved like scimitars, out of my dress collar caught on the barbed wire, must have seemed frail and harmless, running toward Johnny. Johnny's eyes had been on my white, dressless body and not on the potato knife he himself had sharpened for me the day before on the flintstone wheel behind the barn.

Roysie says he struck with his fist, that he was bigger, but with the knife his assailant was better. "He cut me down," Roysie told me, "As I flailed at him. Attacking, he never said a word. His breath in my ear was terrifying; rhythmic and muffling, like water rushing over me. And then there was a pounding in my head that was my blood pulsing out of my body." I listened carefully. Later, alone, I made notes. *Reportage*.

After his attacker left, Roysie came out on the between-floor landing. His life was bleeding away. He lit a cigarette, a Marlboro. Roysie was high from shock or loss of blood. He is not sure why, but he was euphoric, he said, beyond pain and into celestial pleasure. He sang, a capella, Kenny Rogers' "The Gambler." The mugger had cut the telephone cord, cut the curled cord between the receiver and the body of the telephone. So Roysie stumbled out onto the first-floor landing, starkers in his ripped satin boxers, bloody as Julius Caesar. Singing country and calling for me.

He got no answer. While Roysie has being ravaged, I was downtown. At Sardi's.

Being rushed by a Hollywood producer's talent scout, who wanted, for a kiss and a promise, the film rights to a novel I'd written. I was sipping anisette and Colombian expresso slicked with lemon oil. Talking the big money. Getting stroked. Feeling wonderful.

The night Johnny was murdered, the potato knife found his heart. Veins, not arteries, were cut. Veins do not gush with pent-up force as arteries do. Veins take the blood toward the heart and lungs, and the color of the blood is not so brilliantly crimson. Arteries carry the blood away. Arterial blood is fresh with oxygen and very red and explosive when freed.

Learning these biologic facts, if one did not know them before and wants to use them in a story for *authenticity* or for *effect*, is called *research*. *Authenticity* in fiction is writing with probability on your side, writing as close to actuality as one is able to. *Effect* is, simply, emphasis. Effect is tricky, though, because it can tilt a story all the way from serious to funny.

My writing is deceptively simple. It looks easy until the reader gets into it. And then the writing winds, gracefully devious, and slithers off to strange places. Like a diamondback rattler, or so I like to think. (This is called *self confidence*. In the writing game you cannot have too much of it.) So for me, things like *authenticity* and *effect* and *research* are best when they are simple. Simple and vivid. If the research is too complicated, the story either gets lost in the research or the story is being written by the wrong writer. There will ever be stories, good stories, that are not for me. I leave them despite their temptation. One was a beauty, the story of a Scots woman who killed her husband. He stayed away too long on offshore oil rigs in the North Sea. He did it for love of her. For the extra money. Because he did it, she grew to hate him. Cooked him a carrot souffle and put him in the ground. The tale was mine for the asking, and it had the black humor I like and the irony. The contract was generous: carte blanche, within reason, on expenses. I would go to the town for research and reportage. But it would have meant, for me, too much of both. I did not know the territory, hers or his. I would have come, and stayed, a stranger. The story, in my hands, would not have been as wonderful as it could be. Some day it will get told, better told, by someone else.

## Life and death matters

For simple things, one can consult an expert, in which case one has a *source*, an authority in the field or in that area of expertise. I file my sources in a *source book* and remember the persons from time to time. This is called keeping one's contacts open. To have an open contact is to have *access*, and *access* is what all storytelling, *reportage* (which is supposed to be true), and *fiction* (which is supposed to be imaginary) are based on. Whether you are creating or reporting, access to a story is the crucial first door if the story is not your own. This is why writers write so often in the first person. We always have access to ourselves.

When Johnny was stabbed, he was lying on his back in brown Kentucky grass, surrounded by pussy willows. His blood did not spurt like Roysie's. Johnny's blood seeped like tidewater over his white T-shirt, like a huge ketchup mistake for Rosie, the quicker picker-upper, to wipe up with her Bounty paper towels. After Johnny was stabbed, I dreamed of mopping up Johnny's blood with Bounties, and the paper towels finally shredding from the effort the way, in the TV ads, the competitions's do. Brand X. Or did the dreams come later, long later, after I went away. After I knew Margaret Mary had been blamed and would never come back and that they wouldn't chase her and hound her home. They knew she would come to a bad end. Everyone who knew Margaret Mary

Dillman concurred in that. It was the way she wore her blouses made them think it. You know, a size too small. Growing up, we've all known girls like her. Usually they whistle, too, and they laugh at anything.

Now Roysie was stabbed on his blue velvet sofa. The blood sprayed all over it. Roysie said, like room deodorant. The blood misted his eggshell-white walls. Dappled Tova, the crippled mahogany-coated dachshund Roysie's not supposed to have. The blood ruined his sofa. Morris, Roysie's roommate, neglected to get the sofa cleaned right away, and the stains set. Morris is not the domestic type. Away from the hospital where he works, Morris fancies himself an engineer, a conductor, and is into electric trains. Clever intersecting tracks crisscross their apartment floor, and are what made the assailant stumble and wake up Roysie and slice him like baloney. After Roysie got out of the hospital, he tried Lysol on the blue velvet. What he got was bleached halos around the blood spots. An unbecoming polka dot effect, he says. For Christmas last year, Roysie and Morris bought a Chesterfield divan from Sloan's that's a smash. They pay on it a little a month. Three years it'll take, Roysie says.

The intruder was seen catwalking our building's second-story ledge. In the act of lifting himself over Roysie's window frame, he waved at a couple who noticed him. They were looking for a place to park their red Datsun. The couple identified themselves as Ms. Evangel Cuevas, 23, a flight attendant on her way the next morning to Brazil, and Mr. Pedro Garcia-Rodriquez, 28, a computer programmer with Apple Electronic, Games Division. They thought, they said, the man probably lived in the apartment he was so unorthodoxly entering and had mistaken them as neighbors he knew. But they were not naive to the ways of New York City. Cuevas and Garcia-Rodriquez talked it over. They decided no harm would be done if the police were told and asked to check. So, after finding a parking space in the next block, Cuevas and Garcia-Rodriquez strolled up to Central Park West and a police call box there and reported the man to the 20th Precinct. The man, they said, was to all appearances breaking and entering the second-floor front apartment at _____ West 7 _____ Street.

The police did not come in time to interrupt the burglary or the assault. But the fact that they did come, Detective Sergeant Michael Reardon of the two-oh let me know, got the third charge reduced from murder three to attempted. That's how close Roysie came.

As it was, Roysie was in surgery for two days; five hours immediately after he arrived at Roosevelt emergency and seven hours the next day because the sutures in the bowel leaked after. Overall, Roysie was in the hospital eight weeks.

## Fact and fancy

So Roysie lived and Johnny died.

The night Roysie lived, it was August. The night Johnny died, it was August, too. After the potato harvest. In October, after my 16th birthday, I lit out, convinced Margaret Mary Dillman, poor Margaret Mary Dillman, wasn't coming back. Besides me, Margaret Mary was the only one knew the truth. Johnny had been killing her. Punching her baby-full belly. That's why I went for him. Johnny was nothing to me, and I hadn't meant to kill him. Seeing me coming toward him, out of my dress, pale in the taffeta slip, must have frightened him. He fired that little hand pistol he had right at my bosom. Missed by a mile. When I jumped him, he hit me in the eye. And then the world went red, and Johnny was dead. Stabbed with a potato knife.

And one daybreak, in October, I gunned away toward all my tomorrows in a hundred-dollar '49 Hudson I bought from V. V. Wynner. From Jurl back home, I hear V. V. is in jail now. Tax evasion. At the time, V. V. had three used-car lots and a slogan I liked: "I caught you smilin', neightbor." To this day, I think I got a good buy from V. V. Metallic green that Hudson was, with a wasp back and a buzz in its carburetor. And five pretty good tires, which was the important thing. I was traveling alone, and I was going a thousand miles. I piled the rear seat with all I owned and cared about. There were three cardboard suitcases, a box of paperback books, and a Royal portable typewriter. In the front there was only me and $500 cash and a load of to-be-forgottens.

I made it to New York City, to Far Rockaway, Queens, to be exact. I parked that old Hudson in front of a fire hydrant so the city would take care of it for me and walked away from Lyndon, Kay-wy. Rented a bungalow smack dab on the ocean. The little house stood on stilts about 20 feet from the boardwalk and the high-water mark. The time was after season. The shack was unheated. Winter was coming, and I got her cheap. The landlord's name was Pearlstein, Irving Pearlstein. He was the first Jew I ever met, and I thought his name was magical, and omen that boded well for me. Pearlstein was a hairdresser in Manhattan. He dreamed of going to Hollywood and doing Kim Novak and Arlene Dahl. He said they needed him to become the stars they deserved to be. I hope he got there.

Trying to forget, on weekends I waitressed in a diner. Slinging hash, the pros called it. I called it *reportage*. I met a hairy-chested man. I called it research. He moved in, and I studied him. He kept me warm that winter. He was handy around the house, too.

Trying to remember, weekdays I wrote the novel. My first novel. I called it *Johnny Goodbye*. It was about missing my daddy and loving Malcolm. About Mama and the two old-maid aunts. About Johnny Williams and Margaret Mary Dillman. About Monsignor Roland saying he couldn't remember me coming to his door, late, late, beat up and shot at and begging him to come and save Margaret Mary from her doom. He didn't come. Considering what happened, how could he have forgot?

The lady at Random House was nice. She corrected my grammar. She asked me to write it again, please, changing Monsignor Roland, changing Margaret Mary Dillman. Maybe now, after Roysie, I will.

Personal history, you say. Well, fact and fancy. But if *esthetic distance* is established, individual history becomes *reportage*. It can give you the background and material for a third-person-voice novel. Achieving *esthetic distance* means not taking what happens to you personally, no matter how personal what happens is. *Esthetic distance* objectifies the personal experience. Done right, it makes for unique *reportage*. It makes your fiction read like truth and resonate like art.

# The vicarious scoop

If you get too close to your own materials, though, you lose perspective. That's what I did the first time I wrote about Johnny. The writing turns *self-indulgent* and sloppy. It gets weepy, drippy, and readers don't like that. Readers don't want to feel worry or happy or excited for writers. They want to be swept away. One way a writer gets them there is by establishing esthetic distance and letting the reader close the gap himself. The reader does that by *identifying*.

If a writer makes it possible for a reader to identify, that writer has succeeded in one basic purpose of storytelling, the *vicarious experience*. A vicarious experience is an experience we imagine we have as opposed to one we actually have. A *vicarious experience* is often as satisfying as a real one, and some people prefer them. Most of us like to go where we have never been, especially if it's safe and scarfree. And, no small thing, we can go away and come back without even having to change our clothes. Along the way we may laugh, cry and grow lustful, become excited. We may get an inkling of what it is like to be beautiful, brilliant, privileged, strong, loved. We exercise and entertain the soul through emotions, the mind through ideas, and the body through adventures. After a good read, for a while, the inner beasts quiet down.

A writer is ever after a new story, a fresh experience to give the reader. So when Roysie awoke from the anesthetic, the first thing he saw and the first thing he smelled were the roses I'd sent. And the first thing he found was his favorite thing, a half-pound bar of Hershey's with almonds under his pillow. I'd put it there while he was in the OR. As soon as Roysie was able to talk, while he was still in intensive care, as Roysie's closest living friend, I visited. Heard all about his ordeal, detail by detail, while the terror was strong in him. I met the investigating detective, Sergeant Reardon. Had the man to my apartment for tea. Gave him a book I wrote. Roysie calls my conduct friendship. It was more and less than friendship. You know what it was. It was *reportage*, And I scooped; nobody got Roysie's whole story but me. Not even Sergeant Reardon got as much out of Roysie as I did. So I got a new story, some good new facts, and a new source in Sergeant Reardon. Roysie's misery proved invaluable to me.

Roysie knows the sorry truth. He doesn't mind. Or he forgives me. He says he's looking forward to seeing his story transmogrified and in print. Dear Roysie. He's doing fine now, thank you.

## Just a ring of truth

The truth is that the faculty of *reportage* is an artistic flaw. (I call it a flaw because it is not normal and makes living harder.) Somehow, a writer will record, by some means, all the life and people he or she can. That's just how it is. It's tax on the talent, and we all pay.

This strange compulsion, this warp, terrifies some writers. What happens is that one feels insincere at a certain life moment because one is taking note of one's own and/or others' responses so as to be sincere in the amount of fiction. If you're not careful, the flaw can drive you crazy. It's had me in dark water most of my life. André Gide was aghast at himself monitoring the dying of his long-suffering wife, but he couldn't stop. Ernest Hemingway, supposedly self-mocking, did it to himself, in diaries, during his last illness. Anne Frank did it unquestioningly, beautiful doomed child. One way or another the writer does it. We have to.

*Reportage* is, at best, a filtered truth, a mix of fact and fancy filtered through a writer. It is the truth as perceived, but only more or less and only as long as it makes a good story. The novelist, when the truth gets boring, begins artfully to lie.

As I did, by the way, about Johnny. I made the whole thing up. But you knew that all along. You know I'm too nice a person to have done a thing like that.

Regarding reportage in fiction, I pass along to you some guidelines I use, with the reminder they are, and any and all, to be changed as the need arises.

1. Do anything you have to, excepting detectable crime, for a good story. There is nothing you can do for a great story. Great stories are either lived or dropped in your lap. Great stories are fated. On the other hand, do anything, anything at all, for a great story.

2. Cultivate people to whom things happen. Pry. Self-important people love it, and most people who are important think they are.

3. All roads lead to Rome. This means there is no only, or best, way to write. Each of us, all of us, each time, uncovers a way to come to Rome.

4. Coming to Rome means completing the project, telling the story, writing the novel. It may or may not bring you money, fame, praise, satisfaction, and hap-

piness—all of which are, in the short run, why we do it. In the long run, what is necessary is that each time we come to Rome, we arrive better at our craft. Sometimes it is only by a smidgin. Sometimes it's by a hectare.

5. It is the nature of truth to become muddy. Move away from the truth as soon as you can into clean and beautiful lies.

6. Ground your lies in little, verifiable truths. This way you fool most of the people all the time.

7. If you want to know something, try living it first or experimenting. If you can't do either, ask an expert. If you can't find an expert, make up whatever you like. No one will publicly gainsay you. Those who know better are usually too busy.

8. Visualize, visualize. And then write what you see simply and specifically. Avoid simile and metaphor, unless you are seeking effect. Do not seek often or hard for effect.

9. For the ring of truth which resonates, throw away most adjectives. Especially "very" and "really" and "super" and such.

10. In a writer, it is considered a better thing to be amusing than accurate.

---

> **66** *Like poetry, the detective story makes order out of chaos.*
> —*Frederic Dannay (Ellery Queen)* **99**

# Scare tactics—the guts and bolts of horror writing

## J.N. Williamson

Detective fiction contains mystery and probably suspense but rarely romantic sex, science, or horror. Romance stories may incorporate sex, or mystery, rarely detection or suspense, science or horror. Science fiction can be suspenseful, use mystery or techno-horror, but rarely sex—and romance is almost never an SF concern. Good, which is to say entertaining and readable, horror fiction regularly utilizes elements of all these. At its finest, it offers abundantly more.

The most remarkable surprises in literature today are the amount and range of skill-fully-created horror writing and the degree to which it contains those qualities sometimes even lacking in "serious" fiction: original ideas; tight plotting; viewpoint; and moral stand-taking. It's ironic that one of the most welcoming realms for writers is often seen as narrow and inevitably bloody. That misjudgment is advanced mainly by those who confuse the fiction of fear with filmed imitations, most of which give a different and thoroughly unpleasant meaning to the word "horror."

Yet the confusion also stems from what comedian George Carlin joked about in quite a different context; call it *word squeamishness*: "Fantasy" conjures images of tiny, elfin beings or unicorns gamboling on the green. "Science fiction," given our love-hate

*J.N. Williamson is an all-purpose writer and editor with a special interest in horror. Since 1979 he has written and edited at least 30 books, including the Balrog award-winning* Masques, Ghost, The Longest Night, Wards of Armageddon (*in collaboration with John Maclay*), *and* The Second Devil's Dictionary. *The recent recipient of the Dale Donaldson Memorial award for Service from the Small Press Writers and Artists Organization, Williamson has also published more than 50 short stories in major commercial and little magazines.*

relationship with the nuclear "community," sounds authoritative, no-nonsense, crisply prophetic. "Mystery" brings to mind English drawing rooms, plus Edward Gorey damsels-in-distress swooning with radar posteriors upon convenient tombstones.

## Creature in the closet

But—"occult?" It smacks of crystal balls, cults, witches—of *real* evil. To some, then, "horror" suggests bathtubs overflowing with bare blondes and blood; red-eyed things chuckling like laughtracks in your plumbing; or bullet-proof madmen running amok in neighborhoods populated exclusively by persons under twenty-one. Offhand, I recall very few fright fables about such improbabilities which have earned the respect of writers or discerning readers.

Truth is, *alarums*—an old word of mine for horror—are as varied as mystery tales. There's the classical or period piece, generally told in the first person. "Thematic" or myth and ancient, belief-system horror, often my own preoccupation. Fiction about ordinary folks whose life goes *slightly* askew, who meet weird, terrible, or displaced persons. Subtle, psychological fiction and the worlds of vision, dream, nightmare. Monster-oriented yarns, not all awful. Overt horror emphasizing what Stephen King terms the "gross-out." Fictionalizations of people with paranormal gifts. Techno-horror. The fiction of hauntings, itself a diverse subset. While they all move in and out of vogue, it is publishers who, primarily, declare a vogue—not the readers, who are as insatiably eclectic as 'tec and SF fans, if not more so.

This creature called Horror is a vastly more intriguing, intelligent entity than the general public has understood until recently. And he works in your office, lives down the street, or maybe he's related—the people whom he imperils are just like us. At times, in the story, he may *be* us. But whether he wears his mother's garb as he did in Robert Bloch's inceptional *Psycho* or your brother's face as in Ray Bradbury's "Mars is Heaven" or shroud-like clothes covering a skeletal form as with the Pumpkin Man in Robert R. McCammon's *Usher's Passing*, or the sometimes unseeable faces in Peter Straub's *Ghost Story*—even if he wears whatever face he chooses, as in Dean R. Koontz' terrifying *Phantoms* . . . the creature's coming out. And nobody can ever put him back into the closet again.

Horror tends to be based upon a frightening, fresh premise or a portentous theme and is particularly dependent upon mood, conflict, danger, suspense, and revelation. The same is often true for other kinds of good reading. Someone who avoids this genre because it is scary risks drowning in the mainstream. *Jaws, In Cold Blood, Lord of the Flies, Magic, The Godfather*, and *First Blood* chill you. So do treatments of those with multiple personalities, and accounts of society's sociopaths and psychopaths.

Check a bestseller list. Half the novels are either exploitative, moodily and ultimately boring, or self-consciously "important," while the other half is fanciful, fantastic, mysterious, or intentionally thrilling. Critics who quest for symbolic values in *Moby Dick, Robinson Crusoe, Huckleberry Finn* or even the *oeuvre* of Hugo, Dumas, Kafka, Wells, Orwell and Vonnegut, may forget that people continue to read them because they're full of ideas and obstacles. Of people in peril. Thrill, as in "thrillers."

A key distinction between King's *Pet Sematary* or Bari Wood's *The Tribe* or Whitley Streiber's *Wolfen* and a widely-reviewed thriller-in-disguise is said to be that horrific danger has a fantastic, improbable origin. Yet how many of us will encounter a killer shark, or whale; crazed killers; persons marooned on desert islands; schizophrenic ventriloquists or the Mafia?

A major reason readers *do* like horror fiction is that the characters in much of the work by Bradbury, Richard Matheson, King, McCammon, Koontz, F. Paul Wilson, Mort Castle and Al Sarrantonio are *recognizable*. Readers and characters alike are aware of the loss of loved ones, and hazard to their young; of the silent, battered wife; of drug abuse; of mental illness; of being fired, alone, *scared*. They wonder about the natures of good and evil; about the hereafter. What writers of the "occult" create may well seem a logical extension of day-to-day terror. But because of that extension, that not-so-far reach into fantasy, the reader escapes the protagonist's peril and, for a time, is *less* afraid.

The significant distinction between dark fantasy and mainstream is that the former takes people like us, places them in ultimate peril, and thereby demands of the creative author the utmost imaginative and persuasive skills in determining ways for the characters to be saved. And just as it is in real life, they may *not* be . . .

## Blood and guts?

Those who aren't "into" peril-for-pleasure sometimes seem to have a fixation on gore which some low-budget movie-makers may share but the enduring authors of horror do not.

Let's analyze some truths about dark fantasy written since 1982, approximately the year when publisher-coroners declared the horror "boom" of the '70s muffled and moribund—and when basically one-book writers of slight merit began disappearing from the paperback shelves. Since I'm not one who advocates that most horror be psychologically motivated, or obscure and muted, my books will serve to answer questions about the quantity of blood, the body count and extent of killing. From '82 through '85, I published 11 novels plus a short novel, *Hour*. One, with a fresh prologue, was the first publication of what had been my initial novel. Three were ghost stories. The facts: In *Brotherkind*, no blood is seen, one person dies—the villain. Two men perish in *Horror Mansion*, one gruesomely. People are "vampirized" in two of my books featuring the 3,000-year-old Lamia, yet live; several die offstage; six are murdered visibly, four shedding blood, copiously. In *Playmates, The Evil One*, and the finally-published *Offspring*, most of the carnage occurs in the prologues. House editors appreciate something ghastly early on. Otherwise, that trio totaled three natural passings—nine that weren't. Of the nine, one-third bled.

This leaves *Ghost*; my two Dell novels; and *The Longest Night*. Two good folks are, in the first, killed by an agent of Hell—no blood spills, and each, literally, goes to Heaven at story end. In *The Dentist*, I have an offstage death plus two villains who quite luridly expire (one, in a nice variation on decapitation: a blow that drives his head *into* his shoulders). With *Longest Night*, many brutally die in the prologue to become the ghosts who furnish the plot for the rest of the novel. Another man dies. In *Babel's Children*, no human being is killed at all. The only seepage is from a broken leg. Now, the totals:

In my last eleven horror books—post-prologue—blood flows ten times—often from perfectly terrible characters, and to the assumed cheers of my readers. Six die naturally; twenty-one characters are slain. The result of this morbid accounting: On the average, gross-outs occur gorily fewer than *once per book*. Described for you to read, to *see*, *1.9* characters are killed. You read about that many fatalities in your daily paper, see that much blood, frequently, in televised news. And in most so-called "horror movies"—the adjective shape-changes to euphemism—there're more gore and lives taken *before the end of the titles and credits*!

## Into the foreshadows

Writers of this weird genre depend, arguably, more upon imagination and imagery, suspense, convincing writing and psychological insight than the majority of wordsmiths in any other genre. That's why it *seems* so graphically, persuasively . . . horrifying. And progressive editors appreciate the literary skill.

Not that writers and editors of dark fantasy *don't want* to scare readers! A guideline of mine for *Cold Sweat*, my second collection, was that material should frighten me. In the absence of violence, that can happen when the writer is always *on the verge of threatening to describe awful things that haven't been shown before*. Often, these are revulsive; more often, they are clever ideas and observations. The finer talents in horror constantly *hint at* their readers, slyly suggest that—any page now—an inexorable build-up will begin to that climactic revelation, terrible deed, or unbearable force they've hitherto shown *in flashes*: glimpses of dreadful actions, plots, or persons in a distant place; loved ones undergoing radical personality change; unguessable family secrets, whispered or scribbled on envelopes . . .

Or nothing more ominous than rats, restlessly scuttling; dogs barking, growling, howling; drifting snow, unexpected rainfall, glaring noontime sunlight, shadows with *no source* . . .

Foreshadowing. Standing on the brink of that moment when you'll be shown the face of darkness. William F. Nolan's "Lonely Train A'Comin' " tells of the cowboy Ventry, whose sister has disappeared, or died, who was last seen riding on a "beautiful old train"; Ventry must learn what *happened* to Amy but the train only makes "night runs . . . about a month apart"; and when he boards the train of mystery, is *locked in*, and *sees Amy*—only it *isn't* Ventry's sister, it's—it's . . .

There are many masters of this, the thumping heart of the contemporary horror technique, some gone now and others still writing. Most of them excel in that hardest of forms, the short story: Beaumont, Bradbury, Richard Matheson, Fredric Brown, Bloch, Ray Russell, Ardath Mayhar, Al Sarrantonio, Janet Fox, Roald Dahl. John Keefauver, Paul Olson, Castle, Richard Christian Matheson, James Kisner, Tom Sullivan, Charles L. Grant, Nolan.

Examples: Picture an all-night diner down south; family place. Sheriff drops by for coffee, chats with the owner; terrible murders south of there, the killer escaped. Enter a thin, wasted man who seems exhausted, also has an air of ominous about him. Conversation; sheriff loses his temper. Imagine the customer not only a Nam vet but one who carries the terror of what he experienced everywhere he goes. Learn that he was exposed to an experimental gas in Nam; learn how guilty he feels because he, alone, from his squad, escaped hideous death. Remember that he carries that terror with him—and you know some of the foreshadowings, the suspenseful "on the verge of threat" I mentioned in Robert R. McCammon's "Nightcrawlers."

Or the late Charles Beaumont's "In His Image" which begins with a man at a train station, annoyed by a woman with a religious tract. He shoves her into the path of a train—but a page later, he's an attentive, gently wry fiancé. You look back to the story's start to be sure you read it right. And when this nice fellow returns to his hometown, the author threatens to show you the *Awful*, coming up—but what you get is the man's growing bewilderment. His town has *changed*, but he left it only a week and a half ago; "it was as though Couerville had aged 20 years." Only the consummate writer could match that build-up. Charles Beaumont *topped* it.

# Taboos and terror—the technique of horror

Horror could be said to be written best while you're reliving what has recently scared you; when you learn what has *always* made you panic; and when you can at last admit to yourself what it is that you *dread* the most. That holds true both for what you read, and what you might wish to write in this genre.

Unlike other genres—the western, for example, very possibly set in an era long before you were born—you quite likely begin an alarum, as reader or writer, in the home, or a locale with which you are entirely familiar: a hotel, motel, hospital or church; an office, a farm, or accompanying people reminiscent of your own family on vacation, or motoring into a sleepy little town. Horror, you see, is a genre that seeks and speaks the truth, remorselessly—if often in fantastic terms. Steady readers expect the no-holds-barred, grim intimacy and understand that it's frequently necessary to use a shorthand for good and evil, God and Satan, the powerful and smothering Organization and the loyal but imperiled family. Or, on occasion, the loyal but endangered organization and smothering, covert family. It's in the sense that horror is popular due to its conservatism, its preserving values. The good person stands athwart symbols of bleak menace which tend to represent giant corporations as much as they represent the minions of Hades. More often than not, the good guy blunders into his/her confrontation—and wins.

Because, in part, horror is part of the umbrella called *fantasy*, writers have fewer taboos and more freedom of imagination than in most genres today. Once, SF had such an argument; but with the advent of writers and readers who are scientifically better informed, it must rely heavily upon extrapolation from actual science. An alarum author who wishes his villain to fly has only to provide creatively convincing "reasons" from lore, and then write more persuasively than the wordworkers of other kinds of fiction.

Still, a vampire or werewolf cannot be shown on page 221 toppling the Empire State or growing to 40 feet; they've never been credited with such abilities. The fantasist must play fair with the reader. Yet the liberty to invent is so great that, if the writer declares in chapter two that *his* creature is endowed with unique skills and furnishes an explanation for them, the reader is both satisfied, and pleased that something *different* has been created for his entertainment.

In horror there may be the brand-new, never-recorded inspirations—some the products of current national concerns—and the clever twists on time-honored themes. Among the former, I think of Bob Bloch's *then*-fresh transvestite schizophrene, in *Psycho*; F. Paul Wilson's entire mythical structure for *The Keep*; Ray Russell's hideous rictus, in *Sardonicus*; Sol Stein's frightening hotel, in *The Resort*; King's regenerating burial grounds, in *Pet Sematary*; Matheson's paradise-revealed in *What Dreams May Come*; my own hermaphroditic horror in *The Offspring* and Pythagorean immortality in *Death-Coach*. Among the latter, fresh twists: Peter Straub's unsurpassable blending of secret and spook in *Ghost Story*; McCammon's deft updatings of *Baal* and the Poe-etic *Usher's Passing*; my combination of idioglossalia was reincarnated Atlanteans in *Babel's Children*; Bari Wood's recall of the Jewish *golem* (*The Tribe*); Matheson's end-of-the-world mutants of *I Am Legend* and James Herbert's end-of-the-world rats in *Domain*; Bernard Taylor's *Bad Seed*-snapping *Godsend*; King's prefiguring use of the paranormal, in *Carrie*; the absorbing explorations into reincarnation of *Damon*, by C. Terry Cline, Jr., as well as Terrel Miedaner's *Soul of Anna Klane*; and Ira Levin's germinal *Rosemary's Baby*. Should the inventions of short story writers such as Bradbury, Joe Lansdale, Vincent McHardy, Douglas E. Winter, David Silva, Richard Christian Matheson, Stanley Wiater, Steve Rasnic Tem, Castle Keefauver, Kisner, or Ray Russell—who may be the most original short story writer in fiction—be explored, we would be here forever.

Perhaps the major taboo in alarums is employing a protagonist with no resemblance to someone we know. Ray Bradbury's children are the kids we once were, or believe we were. Dean Koontz' endangered sisters in *Phantoms* are bright young modern women we know or would like to meet. Virtually all of King's characters are identifiable. My novels include a widowed mother of three; a sportswriter; a pubescent girl who just discovered she is telepathic; a lawyer and a lady teacher; small publishers; a little girl transplanted to Ireland; an editor; a divorced novelist. Whatever the age, characters in horror tend to be middle-class Americans, of either sex.

If your imagination is rich and wild enough, weirdwork permits you a wide range of opportunities for exploring your *own* strange, new worlds, beginning with familiar but partly-fantasized difficulties and carrying your creations through a maniac's minefield of terrors to a stunning outcome. It's your chance to examine the human spirit at its most basic, at the crucial instant when our beliefs—in God; in loved ones; in pursuit of order over chaos; in oneself—are most severely and ingeniously tested.

## The alchemy of alarums

Most of what has been published in the genre fits, surprisingly, into what has been reproachfully, even condemnatorially, called "formula fiction." In his introduction to my collection *Nevermore!*, author Mort Castle (*The Strangers*) imagined himself vaulting atop a table in an ardent defense: "Edgar Allan Poe wrote formula fiction. He figured *out* the formula!" Which isn't, in any genre, as simple a proposition as it might seem. Castle, added that, after all, Melville, Dickens, Twain, Aiken, Beaumont, Harlan Ellison, and Bradbury also wrote formula fiction; their work contains "beginnings, middles, ends," the requisites of a good story. To write good horror, you stress certain features. From the start of a fresh idea or twist, guided both by your individual beliefs and your insight into what frightens, you accentuate (a) your selected viewpoint, (b) step-by-step plotting, (c) intriguing atmosphere, and (d) suspense leading to confrontation.

In the case of (a), I mean either weaving your yarn in the detached third person or intimate first person, and if you'll inform readers about the exact nature of the dark power or if you'll *build* toward revelation. Prologue often serves as a teasing peek at the evil force, after which the book reveals little more about it for possibly half the novel. McCammon's *Bethany's Sin*, King's *The Shining*, Straub's *Ghost Story* and my own *Playmates* are steady "escalators"; bit by bit, you learn the half-dreaded truth. Stoker's *Dracula* Bob Bloch's *Night of the Ripper*, Herbert's *Lair* or *The Fog* and most of Koontz' chilling novels begin with a bang. Early on, much of the fantastic, occult, or horrifying device is somewhat spelled out.

By (b), I refer to the sort of event-packed plotting that may be possible only with a detailed outline, or incessant revision. Outlines for my first two novels ran, respectively, 30,000 and 20,000 words; my most recent one comprised over four-thousand. With (c), atmosphere, a writer of rue has a friend in a developed skill for shading even the most innocuous scenes with that threat-to-start-showing-you I've cited. Atmosphere also refers to the uses of weather, pets, furnishings, color and shadow and shadings; as well, dependent upon the writer's observational ability, it includes the *way* characters are described by one another: "When I asked her what was wrong, she whispered, 'Nothing,' but her voice was a distant whisper." "I watched my teenager Billy sit carefully beside Susan and caught his oddly-furtive glance in her direction." "What's wrong with Mom tonight, sport? You get into it with ol' Stanley again?" "After Ted got home, the strangest thing happened. Sport wouldn't go near him, even when we ate dinner; and you *know* how that dog absolutely *worships* my husband . . ."

The suspense-leading-to-confrontation element (d) is harder to create when readers have the entire background told to them upfront. Then, the writer must place the protagonist in even more steady peril—and create a character who especially evokes the reader's empathy—to sustain tension. Where mystery writers plant clues, alarum writers move the evil closer, and closer, to home. Suspense works especially well when the main character's chances look dim and he or she isn't even *aware* of the danger. Confrontation, the second part of my equation, is often horror's version of the 'tec tale dénouement and has many of the same features. Whereas in mysteries, most sleuths solve the case and something very much like living-happily-ever-after is set up, horror stories may eliminate everyone but the protagonist and leave a shuddery, cautionary aftertaste. Even he or she is not guaranteed safe passage (unless the protagonist is a *series* character).

For formula to work neatly, clichés must be avoided. Ferocious, feral children as well as those unfortunates who were born only to be maimed or possessed are *passé* these days. Amnesia has been buried for two decades. Beheadings. Excessive use of flashbacks. Gratuitous sex, without which a newcomer could scarcely place a novel six years ago, is disdained—at least, by most authors. Unnecessarily stupid or helpless heroines will quite rightly risk feminine wrath. Monsters seem to be enjoying a renaissance of sorts, but they'd better be original—watch not only the reasons provided for the Big Fella's powers but the *extent* of them. If we want to see a creature that only atomic blasts or, worse, bathwater can destroy, there are always the so-called "sci-fi" flicks of yore—most of which were, actually, techno-horror with bad science.

## Horrific history

The gross-out, a scene of detailed shock carried to a revulsive extent, is to horror's past what sex and swearing were to the D.H Lawrences and Henry Millers of the '50s.

Past horror masters such as Shelley, Stoker, Stevenson, Poe, M.R. James, Jacobs, Lovecraft, and Dunsany who were as explicit as possible won't be analyzed here because, by modern publishing standards, they're deader than something left behind by Dracula; or Lacey in Clive Barker's "Pig Blood Blues," or Vic in Ellison's "Boy and His Dog." Quite apart from the gross-out, craftsmen of the crypt today enjoy the freedom to peer into every human heart—even if they have to *remove* it first! And because of the freedom, horror and supernatural writers are, heresy though it may be, considerably more skilled—and interesting—than most of those who wrote generally about the same emotions prior to three decades ago.

It's possible then that after 40 years plus of nuclear threat, the *exact* emotions are *not* at risk—or that they have been stretched by our internalized, pregnant shrieks until, for alarums to involve us, they must *match the menace* we see, intuit, or expect. More likely, modern horror is best because both writers and readers know more about the bizarre psychology of our kind. Through advanced communications, we are instantly aware of the newest-to-surface, mad individual's inventive inhumanity. As a consequence that the fiction which most convincingly attracts and engages the individual appears, for awhile, realistic.

Even when our stories become fantastic, lay readers who fret about the modern-day horrors of break-ins and muggings, terrorists, and economic complexities, may not even notice. After all crazies are crazies, deceit is deceit; *all* that is monstrous. And dying is dying. We may wish to escape to simpler times of 1899 and the tidy enigmas of Sherlock Holmes—on those rare occasions when we are able to recall the past but not despise it. But the *Now* of life is so pressure-packed and hectic that we may suspend incredulity only when we read of people in peril. *Other* people; for we can always close the book, turn the page.

Thus today's author alarmists have to be better than those of decades ago. Risking oversight, the modern era progresses, with overlaps, basically this way: Bloch, Brown, Bradbury, Dahl; *Playboy*'s Henry Slesar, Herbert Gold, Jack Finney, Nolan, Russell,

Beaumont; "Twilight Zone's" Beaumont, Dick Matheson, Jerome Bixby, George Clayton Johnson; the seminal Levin, Koontz, Tom Tryon, William Peter Blatty; the crystalizations of Stephen King and Peter Straub; and the rest of us, who have helped lay the foundations for the scope of horror fiction which continues to be published and for the widespread reader acceptance.

Other authors are emerging and bringing subtle changes no one could have expected: The women writers of wrath have arrived, and the British are coming! The grand dames of the diabolical include Anne Rivers Siddons, Tabitha King, Ardath Mayhar, Janet Fox, Anne Rice, Jeannette Hopper, Jessica Salmonson, Tanith Lee, Cezarija Abartis, Chelsea Yarbro, Mona Clee, Mignon Glass, Bari Wood, and Lisa Tuttle. Among the ice-veined invaders from the U.K.—and the Aussies aren't far behind—are Jim Herbert, Ramsey Campbell, and Clive Barker.

## Bright future in dark fantasy

Just how welcoming *is* that haunted house on the hill and the editor-alien who stirs just behind that faintly fluttering curtain, you ask? Because they played out the horror boom of the late '70s and most were convinced they could almost create another King, McCammon, John Saul or V.C. Andrews—with the perfect alchemical mix of title and cover art—publishers are more choosy in the mid—'80s. Yet major publishing houses, such as Doubleday, New American Library, William Morrow, Viking, St. Martin's and Holt, Rinehart, Winston have presented a lot of horror. Small press people are receptive to newcomers (see Category Index) with the exception of a few—Maclay & Associates, Scream Press, and Evening Star Press—who prefer to stick with their established pros, who comprise their small title list.

Among paperback houses, those which survived the '82 horror de-emphasis in preference for romance and seem to be "reading again" include Leisure, TOR, Zebra, Dell, NAL, Signet, Fawcett, Pocket, and the vast Berkley Group. The first three-to-five have demonstrated enough enthusiasm for the genre to make some acquisitions their lead books.

The market for short stories of the sinister is simultaneously extensive, although somewhat unsure of its future footing, but they are a marvelous, possible means to getting published—particularly the little magazines and anthologies which encourage new blood. Here, if anywhere, you may find acceptance or encouragement, excitement, belonging—even fun!

And there are the familiar commercial mass market publications *Fantasy & Science Fiction*, *Isaac Asimov's SF* or *Omni*, actively seeking imaginative horror stories plus the newly-revived, *Weird Tales* which requests just what the name suggests with variety.

That may prove to be less true of *Twilight Zone*, which under new editor Michael Blaine plans to "de-emphasize more overt horror" and "to broaden the definition." Perhaps the fastest-selling new magazine of horror is *Night Cry*, *TZ*'s sister publication. Editor Alan Rodgers, suggests that potential contributors read a couple of issues and the "scare me—it's that simple; you should make me scared."

The first published short stories of six writers occurred in my own anthologies. Just as intriguingly, a total of 16 artisans of awe were first published in hardcover in those books I've edited so far.

Scare tactics, people in peril. Whether you call it horror, occult, dark fantasy of the supernatural, terror and suspense or alarums, the open door attitude tends to be the rule. The creature sidles forth from the shadows, beckoning the imaginatively gifted craftsman—and his embrace may well be warmer than you had believed.

# A good picture book should . . .

## by Arnold Lobel

One night a while ago, as I was watching the late news, I saw a brief bit of reportage on Dr. Seuss' 75th birthday. There was a party given for him somewhere in California. There were lots of children and balloons. Everyone looked very tanned and healthy and West Coast. The good Doctor, bearded and handsome, was there in the middle of it all. A reporter shoved a microphone up to his face.

"Don't you feel that the general quality of children's books is quite low?" asked an off-screen voice.

Dr. Seuss looked startled. He took a few backward steps.

"Now don't ask me to denigrate children's books," he said. "You're not going to make me do that." He turned away sharply and the interview was over.

I was cheered by this little exchange, Here, obviously, was a man who was not going to be made to bite the hand that had been feeding him. And I like to think that Dr. Seuss, having been around children's books for a long time, was well aware of their real worth. Perhaps he was just tired of hearing his profession endlessly bad-mouthed.

The fact is, anyone who has been involved with the field and who has followed it for a period of time can see that each year brings along a really decent portion of good stuff. Since the late '30s when Dr. Seuss began working (and before, as well), we have been bestowing an embarrassment of riches on the young readers of the world. Sure, the junk is there, mediocrity is rampant, but there is enough quality around to permit us, as a group of artists, to be proud of what we have been producing.

Proud I may be, but, in the matter of my work and of children's books in general, articulate I am not. There seems to be a loud clamor and demand for those of us who make

---

*Arnold Lobel is a children's author and illustrator, whose work has earned him the Caldecott Medal, the Newbery Award and the National Book Award. His books include the enchanting* Frog and Toad *series and many other picture and beginning reading books. Most recently Lobel wrote and illustrated* Whiskers and Rhymes.

picture books to haul our bodies up onto the podiums of America. We are asked to talk at length about what we do.

## The best medicine

A good picture book should have a narrative that is simple. But this narrative must be composed skillfully. It must retain its interest with the repetition of many readings. Solid characterization, humor, drama, poetry . . . all these things contribute much.

A good picture book should have drawings that are neither too cartoony cute at one end of the scale, nor too sophisticated and adult at the other.

A good picture book should have artwork that is appropriate to the mood and subject matter of the story. In terms of pacing and selection of images, the artwork should be well integrated into the narrative.

A good picture book should be true. That is to say, it should rise out of the lives and passions of its creators. A book that is created as a commodity will remain just that, however successful that commodity may turn out to be.

That about completes my standard list of remarks on the subject of children's books. There is hardly enough material there to keep an audience waiting through a salad, a plate of creamed chicken on toast, and a fruit cup.

I can pad a little. I can throw in a few amusing anecdotes about the domestic life of the artist. I can divulge a bit of technical information. I can display a color separation, maybe a proof or two. I can drop some lofty names from the arts and literature of the past and present to give some tone to the sources of my inspiration. But all of this falls into the category of making a short story exceedingly long. It disguises the simple fact that the picture book speaks for itself. Its qualities or lack of them are as plain as the print on its pages.

Picture books are nice. The best ones are enormously satisfying. They are objects of pleasing self-containment, somehow capable of suggesting everything that is good about feeling well and having positive thoughts about being alive. They are filled with light and color. The paper is wonderful to the touch.

Not too many bad things happen in picture books. If they do, they usually find their way to a happy resolution at the end. I like them that way. When I feel the morbid need for unpleasantness and despair, I can read the newspaper or watch the news on television or just look out of my window. Picture books are a sanctuary from all of that.

When I am brought low by the vicissitudes of life, I stumble to my bookshelves. I take a little dose of Zemach or Shulevitz. I grab a shot of Goffstein or Marshall. I medicate myself with Steig or Sendak, and the treatment works. I always feel much better.

I often wonder how we end up doing this work, those of us who have dedicated our lives to the making of picture books for children. We are artists, but what has pulled us away from painting large, serious canvases to hang in museums? Why are we not drawing whiskey bottles for magazine ads? As a group we seem to cling to the need for the kind of imaginative playing that childhood allows.

## Say uncle

The cellar in the house in Schenectady where I grew up was often converted into a theater. I painted scenery on old bedsheets and put on plays for my little friends. The gratification that I obtained in producing these enterprises must have been immense for me. I have refused to bring down the curtain. The hair has turned to silver, the body sags, but my show goes on and on.

For their authors, the best books are there for a reason. Doing a book just to have something for a publisher's fall list is, of course, not the most valid of reasons. Granted, a certain amount of economic expediency can be a factor. I have, on a number of occasions, completed a book to keep the pot bubbling and fires burning. Seldom have I been pleased with the results.

It is those books that have a subjective importance to their authors that turn out to be the good ones. When I can put myself into a frame of mind to be able to share with the reader my problems and my own sense of life's travail, then I discover that I am working in top form. It is a devious process. It involves some amount of duplicity, this transformation of adult preoccupation into stories to which children will respond.

At the moment, there is my grandmother. My parents were divorced shortly after I was born. My mother went off to work each day and I was left in the capable hands of Grandma. It worked out fine. Grandma was strong and well organized. She had enough energy to deal with a circumstance that surely could not have seemed ideal to her.

Now Grandma has grown old. Very old. She is 93 and her body has become enfeebled. Her mind is gone. As I make the hour drive to the nursing home where she lives, I know that upon arrival I will not be recognized. It is a grim ordeal for me and I find that my visits to her are becoming less frequent. It is so difficult to witness life's last joke displayed with such cruelty.

I am deeply saddened by this situation. In an effort to exorcise my feelings, I have written a book. This is a book about an old person who is not feeble and who has all his faculties very much intact. I have written a book about the elderly person that I would wish my grandmother to be. The book, *Uncle Elephant*, has somehow dissipated some of my bitterness. That my character turns out to be a pachyderm has absolutely nothing to do with Grandma. I can be forgiven. I like elephants. I enjoy drawing them and I am a compulsive anthropomorphist.

I think the reader will be able to sense my emotional involvement here. If this book has weight and depth, it is because it is not arbitrary. It is an animal story for children but it has worked its way out of the fabric of my life.

For years, I've been convinced that there is an overwhelming separation between the creator of picture books and the children who read these books. This is a natural gulf caused by the age of the readers and the manner in which the books are used. Fan mail is only a partial indication of appreciation since much of it is prompted by a teacher or a librarian. But in the past months I've come to realize that the children are out there and anxious to indicate their responses. I need only to bolster my courage and present myself before them.

## Lobel and kids are friends

For one who is not used to large groups of children, this is not easy. Recently I've done it. I armed myself with big pads of paper and felt-tipped markers for drawing pictures. I arranged my features into a benevolent expression and sallied forth.

I found the third graders standing in the hall, waiting for me, as I entered the door of the school. They stood in several rows according to height. The tallest children in the back were holding a large banner on which was painted in big, red letters, "WELCOME MR. LOBEL." We were all nervous and we greeted each other stiffly, with the kind of formality that one associates with the meeting of diplomats at airports.

A procession was formed. We marched into the classroom. Posted on the walls of the corridor, all along the way, were many smaller signs and drawings. I saw the repetition of my name crayoned into various forms and designs. I caught glimpses of green and brown frogs and toads cut out of colored paper. I was stunned for an instant by a cartoon of my own face, small eyes, ample aquiline nose, bushy mustache . . . all accurately captured by some fledgling Daumier.

There was a special chair waiting for me. It had been wrapped in purple crepe paper. I was guided to it and was happy to sit down. The welcoming ceremony was over and I settled myself to the task of facing my public.

Miserable recluse that I am, this is not an experience that I have often allowed myself. At some point in my career, I made the decision that to create books for children was to live a life of necessary isolation. My art was to grow in atmosphere of lonely introspection. Inspiration was not to be found in the noisy and unpredictable company of children, but in the safe, dark confines of my imagination, among the dusty pages of my book collection.

I would guess that I am correct in making this assumption. It is doubtful that my muse would be able to work for me while sitting in that third grade classroom, even in a chair of royal purple. Any ideas would be quickly obliterated by all the exuberance and enthusiasm around me. But I am becoming aware that inspiration can certainly be nourished by this kind of appreciation.

At the end of the day I staggered out of that school in a state of complete exhaustion but high with the feeling that my work was being consumed, ingested, chewed-up, and loved. The books were being *used* and I felt the need to keep on making them. After 20 years of sustained effort, I think that is called a strong second wind.

66 *When I do a book, I have only one person in mind. I'm writing it for myself. Like all my books, I don't know if this is a children's book for adults or an adult's book for children. If I do it for myself, it usually comes out about halfway between the two groups.*

—*Dr. Seuss* 99

# Feeling rejected? Join Updike, Mailer, Oates . . .

## by Barbara Bauer and Robert F. Moss

On a bleak day in the winter of 1843-44 in New York City a dark, slender, fine-boned man with a look of frayed elegance presented himself at the offices of *Graham's Magazine*, a journal he himself had edited until recently, and submitted to his former boss, George Graham, some verses he had written. Graham found no merit in them, but when the poet protested that he and his wife were nearly destitute, the publisher charitably decided to let his staff deliver the final verdict. And so, before an impromptu jury of editors, office boys and pressmen, the poet declaimed his work. Graham's employees were no more enraptured than Graham, but taking pity on their old colleague, they softened the rejection by collecting $15 to ease his poverty. Such was the earliest known flight of Edgar Allan Poe's poem "The Raven."

Poe's excruciating experience at *Graham's* is only an extreme example of a conflict that has probably gone on, in some form or other, since the invention of the printing press. Laurence Sterne's *Tristram Shandy* went begging (publishers, as was said at the time, would not have anything to say to it, nor would they offer any price for it") until the author could raise a partial subsidy. Charles Lamb was driven to a fury by dismissive editors ("When my sonnet was rejected, I exclaimed, 'Damn the age.' "). And Emily Dickinson's verse was scorned by Houghton Mifflin as "queer—the rhymes were all wrong" when it was submitted after her death.

Genius has not been any more readily recognized in the 20th century. D.H. Lawrence's *Women in Love* made a full, and futile, circuit of English publishing houses ("Nobody will print me nowadays," the author complained) and was finally published in America by private subscription. Sherwood Anderson's *Winesburg, Ohio* passed through many hands before reaching a publisher who did not find it too gloomy and too prurient. Thomas Wolfe's *Look Homeward, Angel* was sent to several distinguished publishers before its now-celebrated arrival on Maxwell Perkin's desk at Scribners. The more unconventional and uncommercial a writer's work, the more he needs a "name" to sell it, a fact Doris Lessing underscored last year when she hid her eminence under a nom de plume and saw a novel rejected by her English publisher, Jonathan Cape.

## Rebound from rebuffs

Inviting contemporary authors to share their experiences with rejection might seem potentially hazardous, provoking only irritation or unhappy memories, but the topic actually elicits animated and diverse responses. Of the 16 writers we questioned, only William Styron and Arthur C. Clarke claimed never to have been rejected. For such writers as John Updike and Joyce Carol Oates, acceptance and recognition came swiftly. Precocious talents, both were off to running starts by midadolescence, and their disappointments mostly came from the submission of juvenilia. "I collected many rejection slips, for cartoons, poetry and prose, since the age of about 15," Mr. Updike says. "When my first acceptance came from *The New Yorker*, I was 22 and felt I was due." Miss Oates' story is that of an astonishing prodigy: At 14, she submitted a 250-page young adult novel about drug addiction to a New York publisher and at 19 or 20 a fullscale work of adult fiction; though neither was accepted, the latter effort led to an option on her next book, and she also reached print at 22.

For other writers, the yearned-for rendezvous with success was delayed only briefly. John Irving reports that his first three books were published without any difficulty; as everyone knows, his fourth, *The World According to Garp*, made him rich and famous. Before *Garp*, however, the novel's much praised story-within-a-story, "The Pension Grillparzer," was submitted to the *Paris Review* and was brusquely disposed of with the comment that it was "only mildly interesting" and that Mr. Irving managed to contribute "nothing new to either language or form." Ann Beattie's apprenticeship was not much more grueling: "I got a lot of rejections—nothing but rejections from national magazines for more than a year, maybe two years—but I was prolific in those days." Finally she was "pulled out of the slush pile at *Esquire*, *The New Yorker* and *The Atlantic*." From *Dangling Man*, on, Saul Bellow's novels were bought immediately, although he does remember a publisher who told him "he couldn't afford to bring out a book of mine because he was saving the paper to publish his own memoirs." With his short stories, Mr. Bellow had the same casualty rate as other authors. "I discovered that rejections are not altogether a bad thing," he observes. "They teach a writer to rely on his own judgment and to say in his heart of hearts, 'To hell with you.' "

Other writers have had more punishing encounters with failure. Gail Parent's *Sheila Levine Is Dead and Living in New York*, a book that cheered up millions of single women, went to five publishers before anyone saw its potential. "Luckily, my agent was a friend of mine from college who stuck by me," the author recalls. Gail Godwin was not so fortunate. Her first novel, *The Perfectionists*, inspired enough resistance among the editors to whom it was submitted that her agent gave up on her. As a short-story writer, she endured a barrage of rejections, though mostly the kind that fan a writer's hopes, such as long, encouraging letters from the fiction editor of *The New Yorker*. Stephen King has become so much the reigning monarch of the horror novel that it is surprising to learn that he had 60 stories and four novels turned down on his way to the top. But, as he notes, that quantity could only seem prodigious to "someone who doesn't write as much as I do."

## Tiny tremors

In the grimmest cases, some smirking deity appears to have decreed that success should be withheld as long as possible. Ursula K. Le Guin's career seems to have called an exceptional amount of stoicism. She submitted short stories for six years without an acceptance and novels for 11 years. Among those for whom a spectacular jackpot lay ahead, no one had a harder time reaching it than Richard Bach, whose *Jonathan Livingston Seagull* was returned to him by his exhausted agent ("Look, they're not interested in a talking seagull") after more than 20 refusals. Coincidentally, Mr. Bach says, the same batch of mail contained a letter "from Eleanor Friede at Macmillan asking if I had a book she would be interested in." Finding its home at last, *Seagull* went on to vindicate its creator's never-say-die philosophy by selling a million copies in hardcover.

Failure can be bilingual and trans-Atlantic as well. "I was rejected many times in Poland and later in this country," Isaac Bashevis Singer says. "Some of my very best stories were turned down again and again." *Satan in Goray*, Mr. Singer's first novel (and generally regarded as one of his finest) "was rejected the first time around in Yiddish and then years later in English translation," he says. Still, he was a respected figure in Yiddish culture from the 1930s onward. By contrast, Cynthia Ozick languished outside the portals of the literary world for nearly 20 years, with scarcely a sign of approval from anyone within. "When I finished my long novel, *Trust*," she says, " I was already deep in my 30s. One afternoon I went to *The New York Review of Books* to try to get an assignment for a book review. I stood at the open door, on the threshold, and was dismissed by someone sitting at a desk. I was not even invited across the doorsill."

There are now few literary doors from which Miss Ozick would be turned away, yet even the most widely venerated authors discover that fame is not necessarily a defense against rejection. Perhaps some would expect the Nobel Prize to insure success every time out, but according to Mr. Singer, it does not. "All my life I have received rejection," he says, "before I won the Nobel Prize and after." Mr. Bellow, another Nobel laureate, says much the same and supplies a graphic illustration. *The New Yorker*—which rejected "Seize the Day" in 1956 ("It violated some of their tenets," he explains "it ended with a funeral")—also turned down his lovely short story "Cousins" only last year. "One would think that after 40 years in the trade one could at least expect *The New Yorker* to publish a story like that," Mr. Bellow says. "I was astonished. Then I was indignant. Then I said, 'The hell with them.' "

These are tiny tremors in major careers, of course, but king size disaster can strike too, shaking the foundations of a seemingly secure reputation. Julius Lester made an enviable literary debut with *Look Out Whitey! Black Power's Gon' Get Your Mama!* in 1968, published several other books and was nominated for a National Book Award in children's literature for *Long Journey Home* in 1973. Yet by the mid 1970s, his fortunes, along with those of many other black male writers, had nose-dived so sharply that, he says, "not only couldn't I get a book published, I had trouble getting an agent." Happily, he rebounded impressively with such books as his recent *Do Lord Remember Me*.

## Scar tissue

We are so used to thinking of Norman Mailer as a literary colossus it is amazing to reflect on the crisis his publisher, Stanley Rinehart, created for him in 1954 by abruptly withdrawing *The Deer Park* from production after advance publicity had gone out. The bone of contention was six salacious lines Mr. Mailer would not remove. The author of *The Naked and the Dead* was then compelled to lug his manuscript along publisher's row—eliciting assessments like "This novel will set publishing back 25 years" (Bennett Cerf)—until, at last, G.P. Putnam's Sons accepted it unconditionally.

Although not many writers of renown have been manhandled quite as spectacularly as Mr. Mailer, most have exceedingly good recall when asked about similar pummelings. In her long, arduous climb, Miss Le Guin has been baffled by the almost standardized reaction to her work—that it was "well written" but that "the material seems remote." "They always said material and remote," she remembers. "What do editors mean when they say you write well? That they didn't understand what you wrote?" Many writers see editors as pontificators, and indeed there is an *ex cathedra* quality to a judgment Miss Beattie received sometime in the mid 1970s: "I must say that I've rarely encountered a writer with such generous gifts who at the same time has greater trouble coalescing these in the service of her aim to make a drama. Beattie seems to slip off the mark out of what now looks like habit." Such remonstrances almost seem like love taps compared to the treatment inflicted on Miss Ozick, punishment that suggests the followers of Dr. No are still among us. She recalls that when the better part of *Trust* was submitted to a "certain editor (well known and admired even today)," he "wrote back so woundingly that I could not proceed for most of the following year."

What sort of scar tissue, if any, does the experience of rejection leave on a writer? For the majority, early struggle does not appear to have wrought any permanent damage or dramatic transformations of character. For Mr. Mailer, however, the trauma that enveloped him when Stanley Rinehart rejected *The Deer Park* was the inspiration of his campaign against bourgeois respectability, the origin of his metaphysical rebellion. "I felt something shift to murder in me," he writes in *Advertisements for Myself.* "I felt . . . that I was an outlaw, a psychic outlaw, and I liked it.

## Stout heart

Positive thinkers and silver-lining watchers will assume rejection must have some salutary attributes, as a character builder or, minimally, as a source of constructive criticism. But Miss Ozick dismisses the idea that rejection is an experience in which the uses of adversity can ever be sweet. "One can never catch up to the confidence early publication instills," she says; "the missed train leaves a permanent loss." Mr. Irving also sees no value in rebuffs or in the critiques that are sometimes appended to them: "I have never learned anything from criticisms of my work; I think the only thing to be learned from criticism is a little something about the critic." Miss Godwin concedes that "I can imagine benefiting from a certain caliber of criticism accompanying a rejection, but in my case I'm afraid all I have learned is to trust my own instincts."

Of those who find some dividends, or compensations, in rejection, Miss Oates and Mr. Singer take the most affirmative stance. "One good thing about rejection," Mr. Singer says, "is that it tells me I am still active, still writing. If I stopped working, I wouldn't get rejected anymore. But would that be good? Also, I see rejection as proof that my work is being judged for its quality and not simply because I have a name." And Miss Oates says, "If and when poems of mine are rejected, I usually use the opportunity to rewrite them."

Mr. Singer admits to occasionally revising his stories in response to intelligent criticism, and Miss Beattie has come to acknowledge a glint or two of acumen in editorial dictums she once disparaged. "Way back when," she remembers, "a fiction editor wrote 'Plumbers know and suffer too,' in response to a story I wrote about an unhappy artiste. I knew that, and was angry that he'd think I didn't. I thought I could write about writers if I wanted to. I now think that plumbers know and suffer too. He was right." Joseph Wambaugh reveals that "everyone rejected my short stories, which, in turn, made me go to novel writing," where, of course, he made his mark. Mr. King is half-serious, half-whimsical on this subject: "I think being rejected can be very beneficial, especially if the work really isn't good. If it gets published, you are almost certain to find yourself looking back with great embarrassment!"

Mr. King's attitude is rare, however, since a writer's autopsy on his rejections is always more likely to fault the editor than the work, and in their books novelists are quick to pounce on their old tormentors. In the autobiographical *Martin Eden*, Jack London has his hero punch out a whole office full of editors. In *Garp*, Mr. Irving takes a less flamboyant revenge by simply reaching back to his rejection at the *Paris Review*. "I actually had Garp's story rejected in just that [same] way," he says. "Later, the story was published in a Pushcart Prize anthology; I guess it's in 15 languages now—and so is that classically bitchy rejection (it's been translated 15 times, too)."

The ratio of aspiring writers to available outlets makes it likely that rejection will always be a part of the literary life. A stout heart seems as essential as a skillful pen. The one article of faith that unites all successful writers, however diverse their work and temperaments, is the necessity of inextinguishable belief in oneself. "I believe every writer has a family out there," Mr. Bach says with conviction, "a group of people who share his vision and his dream. If he persists, he will find them—or perhaps I should say, they will find him." In her more cautious and austere voice, Miss Oates sounds a similar refrain: "The only question for most writers must be: When to give up?—or should one *never* give up?"

" *A publishing decision is often like a love affair. It seems good at the time. It's only later that you regret it.*
—*Walter Meade* "

# Writers' organizations—the great support system

## by Michael A. Banks

Writing for publication is a lonely business. We spend most of our time working in a vacuum. The excitement, if any, is all in our mind. Feedback may be months or even years in coming.

Given this situation, and the fact that we are, after all, in the business of communicating, it is no surprise that writers' groups exist in almost all parts of the country. No one can work forever in a total isolation; as with any profession, writers need peer contact. Just knowing that you are not the only one experiencing the rigors of writing life—as well as the joys and the triumphs—goes a long way toward making the tough times more bearable.

It is rare, however, that a local writers' group consists of writers with the same specialized interests. In an average group, you may find a sprinkling of poets, a couple of romance writers, a mystery novelist, perhaps, and maybe a few who are writing children's fiction. But what if you are concentrating on writing, say, science fiction, or westerns? Does a local writers' group provide all the support and information you would like? Probably not. The best you can hope for is good criticism of your style, and maybe some occasional market information.

Fortunately, there exist national organizations that cater to the special requirements of category fiction writing. You may have heard of them—the Mystery Writers of

*Michael Banks has published fiction in major science fiction magazines and several anthologies. He is co-author of* The Odysseus Solution, Joe Mauser, Mercenary *and five other books. Banks, a member of the Science Fiction Writers of America and the Computer Writer's Association, has also published more than 600 articles and several interactive books and computer adventures.*

America, the Western Writers of America, and others. If you're wondering what these are, and how joining one or more of them can benefit you, read on.

The primary reason for joining a writers' group is, as stated earlier, contact with other writers, those with whom you can share information and the experience of being a writer. There are more advantages, however.

## Grief briefs

Inside market information is perhaps the most valuable benefit from a membership with a writer's club. Most national organizations provide information on magazine editorial changes, original anthology requirements, publisher requirements, and agents interested in your field, on a regular basis. The market information provided is always timely, accurate, *and may not be obtainable elsewhere*. The usual vehicle for such information is a newsletter or magazine published for members only.

But that's just the beginning. Other tangible benefits that a national organization may provide include guidance on contracts and other business matters, group discounts, health insurance programs, and legal representation in matters of mutual interest. (Some organizations even go to bat for their members in supporting legislation, blocking moves by publishers that may adversely affect the interests of the membership as a whole, or auditing problem publishers).

On an individual basis, some of the larger writers' groups will also aid a member in handling a grievance with a publisher. The Science Fiction Writers of America, for example, provides its members with assistance in matters involving slow or non-payment, enforcement or contract terms, or other legal cases.

SFWA, whose grievance procedures have served as a model for other writers' organizations, does not provide direct legal representation. Instead, SFWA Grievance Committee chairpersons act as legal advisors and liaisons between member and publisher. Among other support activities, SFWA's "Griefcom," as it is known, interprets contracts and issues, advises members on their rights and possible actions, and, in many cases, attempts to resolve the problem by directly contacting the publisher involved.

And just how effective is this type of service? According to Dr. Dean R. Lambe, who handles grievances involving short fiction for SFWA members, "In the past year and a half, I've aided in the collection of over two thousand dollars for ten writers."

Lambe stresses that getting action involves more than just writing a letter. "As in most other things," Lambe says, "it's a question of who you know. The majority of publishers will meet their contractual obligations and pay their writers, but you have to know who to contact when payment is late. In one instance, contacting the lawyer of a major publisher was what finally brought action."

## Contacts for contracts

Time is of the essence in this type of situation, too, according to Lambe. "In terms of the value of this whole procedure to the membership, the grievance committee has got to respond by taking an action and letting the writer know immediately. In many cases, writers wait too long before complaining, anyway, and they don't need the extra grief of a delay from the Grievance Committee. So, to be effective in dealing with members' problems, an organization must have a grievance committee that will respond quickly."

Thus far, SFWA's grievance committee has an excellent record. This is due in part to the competency of the volunteer advisors, and to the fact that publishers in the science fiction and fantasy field recognize that the organization has a history of standing up for authors' rights.

A highly visible activity of national writers' organizations, as far as non-members are concerned, is the presentation of awards. Some groups sponsor peer awards, such as the Science Fiction Writers of America's "Nebula" Award, or the Mystery Writers of America's "Edgar." These awards, which can only go to members, can quite often help launch a new writer's career, and the resulting exposure and publicity may be invaluable.

National writers' organizations are, at the very least, mutual support groups, and sources of information vital to the writer. And quite often, it isn't a direct market listing in a writers' group newsletter that provides a boost to a member's career, but a bit of gossip, an idea, a tip, or contact with a fellow writer.

Contacts are very important in any business, and writers' organizations are an ideal way to develop editorial contacts directly or by referral. Most organizations hold regional or national meetings at least once a year, and make available to members the names and addresses of all members, so joining one gives you a direct pipeline to almost everyone working in your field—often including the "big names of authors," and some editors. (The fact is, many editors belong to the organizations we're discussing here, and frequently solicit work or referrals from their contacts therein.)

If all of this isn't enough to convince you that membership in a national writers' organization can be of benefit to you, consider the words of prolific short story writer Ralph Roberts, a member of the Mystery Writers of America, the Private Eye Writers of America, the Science Fiction Writers of America, and other writers' associations.

"Just being able to put 'Member: SFWA' or 'Member: MWA' on my manuscripts," Roberts says, "is worth the membership dues, if it encourages even one editor to pull my story out of the slush pile and give it serious consideration."

## Professional edge

Roberts also maintains that membership in writers' organizations can improve a writer's professional image. "Belonging to organizations like SFWA or MWA shows that you've met at least their basic requirements for membership, that you are a professional. It enhances, even if only marginally, your professional standing. In today's exceptionally competitive market, even a *tiny* edge is worthwhile."

In addition to the immediate benefits provided their members, writers' organizations have the same positive effects on their fields as any trade group. That is, through the combined efforts of their membership and officers—and sometimes by their very existence—they help improve the lot of the writer by policing publishers and encouraging fair standards of conduct.

The following are organizations catering to fiction writers in general, and fiction writers in specific genres. Some have specific qualifications for membership, or have more than one level of membership. Complete information (dues, membership requirements, activities, etc.) can be obtained by contacting the organizations.

HORROR WRITERS OF AMERICA (HWA)
Karen Lansdale
608 Christian St.
Nacogdoches TX 75961

Horror writers are encouraged to write the secretary-treasurer, Karen Lansdale at the address above for information and an application to join the organization. HWA, recently restructured with a name change (from HOWL), plans to publish a newsletter in the future. Also in the offing is an annual hardcover anthology of horror stories, contributions from master writers and members of the organization.

## MYSTERY WRITERS OF AMERICA, INC. (MWA)
150 5th Avenue
New York NY 10011

"An organization dedicated to the proposition that the detective story is the noblest sport of man," the Mystery Writers of America's motto is "Crime Does Not Pay—Enough!" Membership includes active members who have made at least one sale in mystery, crime, or suspense writing; associate members who are novices in the mystery field; editors, publishers, and affiliate members who are interested in mysteries. Publishes monthly newsletter, *The Third Degree*. Presents the "Edgar" and "Raven" awards annually for outstanding fiction in the field. Dues: $50 per year.

## NATIONAL WRITERS CLUB (NWC)
1540 S. Havana, Suite 620
Aurora CO 80012

Founded for the purpose of informing, aiding, and protecting freelance writers worldwide. Associate membership is available to anyone seriously interested in writing. Qualifications for professional membership are publication of a book by a recognized book publisher, or sales of at least three stories or articles to national or regional publications. Sponsors contests, periodic conventions, and a home study magazine writing course. Publications include *Authorship*, *Flash Market News*, *NWC Newsletter*, and *Freelancer's Market*. Dues: $40 associate, $50 professional. $15 initiation fee.

## PRIVATE EYE WRITERS OF AMERICA (PWA)
Robert Randisi
Box 1930
Longwood FL 32750

Membership is composed of writers of fiction featuring private investigators. Publishes *Reflections of a Private Eye* quarterly. Sponsors the "Shamus" Award for the best P.I. fiction of various lengths. Dues: $15 per year.

## ROMANCE WRITERS OF AMERICA (RWA)
Patricia Hudgins, Executive Secretary
5206 F.M. 1960 W.
Suite 207
Houston TX 77069

The Romance Writers of America strives to make romantic fiction a recognized genre, to support and encourage writers in their careers, and to provide market information. Presents the Golden Heart, Golden Treasure, and Golden Medallion Awards annually, and publishes *Romance Writers Report* bimonthly. Has 75 chapters throughout the country, and sponsors national and regional conferences. Writers need not be published to join. Current membership over 2,500. Dues: $35 per year.

## SCIENCE FICTION WRITERS OF AMERICA, INC. (SFWA)
Peter D. Pautz, Executive Secretary
Box H
Wharton NJ 07885

Professional organization of writers of science fiction and fantasy. Two levels of membership—active and affiliate. One novel or three short story sales required for active membership; one story sale qualifies for affiliate membership. Publishes SFWA *Fo-*

*rum* ("insider's" newsletter for active members only) and *Bulletin* (for all members, or by subscription). Grievance committee, other services. Presents Nebula Awards for outstanding science fiction and fantasy. Dues: $50 per year active, $40 per year affiliate.

**SMALL PRESS WRITERS AND ARTISTS ORGANIZATION (SPWAO)**
Audrey Parente, Secretary/Treasurer
411 Main Trail
Ormond Beach FL 32074
    Active membership is open to anyone who has been published in the small press, paid or not. Associate membership is open to those interested in writing. Publishes *The SPWAO* bimonthly. Sponsors various awards for excellence in writing. Dues: $10 per year.

**SOCIETY OF CHILDREN'S BOOK WRITERS (SCBW)**
Box 296
Mar Vista Station
Los Angeles CA 90066
    An association of children's book writers, editors, publishers, illustrators, and agents that serves to exchange information and improve conditions in the children's book field. Publishes bimonthly *Bulletin* and sponsors annual Golden Kite Awards. Convenes annually in August, and sponsors regional meetings. Write for membership information.

**WESTERN WRITERS OF AMERICA, INC. (WWA)**
Jeanne Williams
Box 355
Portal AZ 85632
    For freelance writers who specialize in western fiction or nonfiction of all forms, including books, short pieces, scripts, and juvenile material. Presents the Golden Saddleman and Spur Awards annually. Publishes *Roundup* monthly. 500 members in the US. Dues: $50 per year.

---

*Everybody is a regionalist. Tolstoy is a regionalist—one is where one lives, where one writes.*

*—Paul Horgan*

# The Markets

## Find your market

When looking for a specific publication or publisher for your manuscript, check the index of listings. Or if you are unsure of a market, but have an idea for a story or a manuscript already prepared, first refer to the category index immediately preceding the market index. Fiction subjects are listed alphabetically by category or genre and contain those markets requesting short stories or novels in that field.

After finding a market to pursue, *read the entire listing carefully*, before submitting a manuscript. In occasional letters to FWM, editors tell us they still receive too many manuscripts inappropriate for their magazine or publishing house, and they would prefer not to be listed. Writers, they say, are not doing their homework, checking the individual specifications carefully. Returning misdirected manuscripts wastes an editor's precious time. And Canadian editors have pulled their listings out because American contributors failed to send IRCs with their manuscripts. Only Canadian stamp collectors benefit from American stamps.

We have included magazines and publishers that buy or accept fiction from the US, Canada and abroad (foreign listings this year are at the end of each section). To designate the new listings this year in each section, there is a dagger (‡) printed before the title. We have also coded the listings (excluding agents) by markets with (I), (II), (III), and (IV). The editors have ranked their publications, presses and contests and awards according to the level of writers they are receptive to. Those markets with a (I) are open to beginning writers; publications, publishers, contests and awards ranked with (II) accept submissions from beginning and established writers, depending on the quality; those ranked with a (III) are prestige markets, harder to break into, and they accept mostly established or agented authors and the occasional quality first-timers; and markets with (IV) are those specialized publications, presses, and contests limited to contributors from designated regions or with specialized subjects or themes.

## Unlisted markets

On occasion we receive letters asking why a certain magazine, publisher, contest, award or agent is not listed in *Fiction Writer's Market*. Chances are we have already contacted the party in question, but the editors have elected *not* to list with us for several reasons:

• The magazine or publisher may use very little fiction, be over-inventoried with manuscripts for the year, use only agented, or in-house material or manuscripts by their select corps of writers. Or the publication may be a one-shot fiction issue.

● The magazine or press may be in financial difficulty or in a state of flux with their staffs or policies at our press time, and is therefore unable to state their needs for the coming year.

● A listing in *Fiction Writer's Market* means additional manuscripts. Some magazines or publishers are grateful for the choice of material and exposure to new talent; others may not be adequately staffed or have the time or money to respond to additional submissions or those that may be inappropriate because the writer has not read the listing.

● The decision is a personal, arbitrary one with no reason given.

The decision not to list a market may also be ours—to protect you, the writer. If we receive complaints about unfair treatment to writers, misrepresentation of the information in the listing or unethical or unprofessional action in their dealings with writers, and if after thorough investigation we find these reports to be true, we will delete the listing. Or sometimes if the information is not complete because the publication is too new to formulate specific requirements or we feel the needs are too limited to encourage submissions, we will not add this market to our list.

## Let us hear

The listings in *Fiction Writer's Market* are based on correspondence, questionnaires, phone conversations with editors, publishers, agents, and the information is updated annually and is as current as possible. The publishing industry is a volatile one, however, and changes in addresses, policy, editorial staffs, needs and submission requirements occur frequently, and sometimes after we have gone to press.

To keep abreast of these changes we suggest you check the Markets section each month in Writer's Digest for updated information during the year. We also ask your help. If in your writing and publishing endeavors, you are aware of differences, changes, or problems with a particular market, or know of a new magazine or press publishing fiction—or have suggestions on how we can publish a better book, we encourage you to let us hear from you.

---

### Important

● Listings are not paid advertisements; although the information therein is as accurate as possible, the listings are not endorsed or guaranteed by the editor of *Fiction Writer's Market*.

● *Fiction Writer's Market* reserves the right to exclude any listing that does not meet its requirements.

---

# Manuscript mechanics

It's a grand thing to dream of seeing a story with your byline in one of the major national or literary magazines, or to envision your novel in a publisher's catalog. The actual *writing* of it may be a bit difficult, but once you have it down in good shape in a rough draft, the rest is a snap . . . you *think*. There is still one very important—though often irksome—chore to do: preparing the final manuscript for submission to an editor.

It's irritating. It's bothersome. But it's a necessary evil and the quicker you start using the right way, the easier it is to live with.

**Type of paper.** One of the things to consider is the paper. It must measure 8½x11 inches. That's a standard size and editors are adamant; they don't want offbeat sizes—or colors. White is right.

There's a wide range of white, 8½x11 papers. The cheaper ones are all wood content. They will suffice but they are not recommended. Your best bet is a good 25 percent cotton fiber content paper. It has quality feel, smoothness, shows type neatly and holds up under white-outs and erasing. Editors almost unanimously discourage the use of erasable bond for manuscripts, as it tends to smear when handled. Where weight of the paper is concerned, never use onionskin or anything less than a 16-pound bond; 20-pound is preferred.

**File copies.** Always make a carbon or photocopy of your manuscript before you send it off to a publisher. You might even want to make several photocopies while the original manuscript is still fresh and crisp looking—as insurance against losing a submission in the mails, and as a means of circulating the same manuscript to other editors for reprint sales after the original has been accepted for publication. (Inform editors that the manuscript offered for reprint should not be used before it has first appeared in the original publication buying it, of course.) Some writers keep their original manuscript as a file copy, and submit a good-quality photocopy of the manuscript to an editor, with a personal note explaining that it is *not* a simultaneous or multiple submission. They tell the editor that he may toss the manuscript if it is of no interest to him, and reply with a self-addressed postcard (also enclosed). This costs a writer some photocopy expense, but saves on the postage bill—and may speed the manuscript review process in some editorial offices.

**Type characters.** Another firm rule: For manuscripts, always type double space, using either elite or pica type. The slightly larger pica type is easier to read and many editors prefer it, but they don't object to elite. They *do* dislike (and often will refuse) hard-to-read or unusual typewritten characters, such as script, italics, Old English, all capitals, unusual letter styles, etc.

**Page format.** Do not use a cover sheet; nor should you use a binder—unless you are submitting a play or television or movie script. Instead, in the upper left corner of page one list your name, address and phone number on four single-spaced lines. In the upper right corner, on three single-spaced lines, indicate the approximate word count for the manuscript, the rights you are offering for sale, and your copyright notice (© 1986 Chris Jones). It is *not* necessary to indicate that this is page one. Its format is self-evident.

On every page after the first, type your last name, a dash, and the page number in the upper left corner (page two, for example, would be: Jones—2). If you are typing a novel, indicate the chapter sequence as well as page number on each page in the top left location, beginning each chapter halfway down on a new page one. Chapter three, page five would have the following "slugline": Jones—III/5. Then drop down two double-spaces and begin copy.

**How to estimate wordage.** To estimate wordage, count the exact number of words on three interior pages of your manuscript (in manuscripts up to 25 pages), divide the total by three and multiply the result by the number of pages (your first and last pages are likely to be less than full). Carry the total to the nearest 100 words. For example, say you have a 12-page manuscript with totals of 265, 316 and 289 words on the three inside pages. Divide your total of 870 by three to get 290. Now multiply 290 x 12 pages and you get 3,480. Your approximate wordage, therefore, will be 3,500 words. On manuscripts over 25 pages, count five pages instead of three, then follow the same process, dividing by five.

Now, flip the lever to double-space and center the title in capital letters halfway down the page. To center, set the tabulator to stop in the exact left-right center of the page. Count the letters in the title (including spaces and punctuation) and back-space half that number. Centered one double-space under that, type "by" and centered one double-space under that, your name or pseudonym.

Margins should be 1¼ inches on all sides of each full page of typewritten manuscript. Paragraph indentation is five or six letter spaces, consistently.

Now after the title and byline block, drop down three double-spaces, paragraph indent and start your story; or if you are typing a novel, center the words Chapter One on this line, then double space twice, indent and begin your novel.

**Concluding page.** Carry on just as you have on the other pages after page one. After your last word and period on this page, however, skip three double-spaces and then center the words "The End" or, more commonly, the old telegrapher's symbol of —30— meaning the same thing.

**Special points to keep in mind.** Always use a good dark black (*not* colored) typewriter ribbon and clean your keys frequently. If the enclosures in the letters a,b,d,e,g, etc. get inked-in, your keys need cleaning. Keep your manuscript neat *always*. Occasional retyping over erasures is acceptable, but strikeovers are bad and give a manuscript a sloppy, careless appearance. Sloppy typing is viewed by many editors as an index to sloppy work habits—and the likelihood of careless research and writing. Strive for a

Jones--2

Title of Manuscript (optional)

Begin the second page, and all following pages, in this manner--
with a page-number line (as above) that includes your name, in case
loose manuscript pages get shuffled by mistake.  You may include the
title of your manuscript or a shortened version of the title to identify
the Jones manuscript this page 2 belongs to.

Chris Jones
1234 My Street
Anytown, U.S.A.
Tel. 123/456-7890

About 3,000 words
First Serial Rights
©1986 Chris Jones

YOUR STORY OR NOVEL TITLE HERE

by
Chris Jones

The manuscript begins here—about halfway down the first page.
It should be cleanly typed, double spaced, using either elite or
pica type.  Use one side of the paper only, and leave a margin of
about 1-1/4 inches on all four sides.

**NEATNESS COUNTS. Here are sample pages of a manuscript ready for submission to an editor. If the author uses a pseudonym, it should be placed on the title page only in the byline position; the author's real name must always appear in the top left corner of the title page—for manuscript mailing and payment purposes. On subsequent pages, list the real name, then the pen name in parentheses, followed by a dash and the page number.**

clean, professional-looking manuscript that reflects pride in your work.

**Computer submissions.** We ask editors if they are open to receiving computer printout or disc submissions. If the reply is affirmative, that information is included in the listing—be sure to follow these directions carefully.

**Mailing your manuscript.** Except when working on assignment from a magazine, or when under contract to do a novel for a publisher, always enclose a self-addressed return envelope (SASE) and the correct amount of postage with your manuscript. Manuscript pages should be held together with a paper clip only—never stapled together.

For foreign publications and publishers, including the Canadian markets, always enclose an international reply coupon (IRC), determined by the weight of the manuscript at the post office. Editors in Canada and other foreign countries generally accept IRC's but not money in check form. Canadian banks charge $1.50 to cash foreign checks. Small presses and little magazines are on low budgets, so to be safe, send a SASE or IRC with all correspondence.

Most editors won't object too much if manuscripts under five pages are folded in thirds and letter-mailed. However, there is a market *preference* for flat mailing (in large envelopes) of manuscripts over four pages. You will need two sizes of large gummed or clasped mailing envelopes—9x12 for the return envelope, and 9½x12½ or 10x13 for the one used to send out the manuscript and return envelope. Or you may buy two 9x12 envelopes, fold the return one and use the other for the outgoing manuscript, a less expensive method in the long run.

Mark your envelope, as desired with FIRST CLASS MAIL, or SPECIAL FOURTH CLASS RATE: MANUSCRIPT. First Class mail costs more but assures better handling and faster delivery. Special Fourth Class mail is handled the same as Parcel Post, so wrap it well. Also, the Special Fourth Class rate only applies in the US, and to manuscripts that weigh one pound or more; otherwise there is no price difference. Third class is the alternative for anything over five ounces, but it is very slow.

For lighter weight manuscripts, First Class mail is recommended because of the better speed and handling. First Class mail is handled the same as Air Mail.

Insurance is available, but payable only on the tangible value of what is in the package, i.e., writing paper, so your best insurance is to keep a copy at home of what you send. Moreover, publishers do not appreciate receiving (and signing for) unsolicited manuscripts marked Certified or Registered or Insured.

First Class mail is forwarded or returned automatically; however, Special Fourth Rate mail is not. To make sure you get your submission back if undeliverable, print "Return Postage Guaranteed" under your return address.

**Cover letters.** You may enclose a personal letter with your manuscript sent at the Special Fourth Class Rate but you must also add enough First Class postage to cover the letter and mark *FIRST CLASS LETTER ENCLOSED* on the outside.

In most cases, a brief cover letter is helpful in personalizing the submission. Nothing you say will make the editor decide in your favor (the story must stand by itself in that regard), so don't use the letter to make a sales pitch. But you may want to tell an editor something about yourself, your publishing history, or any particular qualifications you have for writing the enclosed manuscript. If you have written to the editor earlier, he probably already has the background information—so the note should be a brief reminder: "Here is the story we discussed earlier. I look forward to hearing from you at your earliest convenience."

If the manuscript is a photocopy, be sure to indicate whether or not it is a multiple submission. An editor is likely to assume it is, unless you tell him otherwise—and many are offended by writers using this marketing tactic (though when agents use it, that seems to be OK).

**Mailing book manuscripts.** Do not bind your book manuscript pages in any way. They should be mailed loose in a box (a ream-size stationery box is perfect) without binding. To ensure a safe return, enclose a self-addressed label and suitable postage in stamps clipped to the label. If your manuscript is returned, it will either come back in your original box, or—increasingly likely today—in an insulated bag-like mailer, with your label and postage used thereon. Many publishing houses open the box a manuscript is mailed in, and toss the box (if it has not been damaged in the mails, or in the opening already); they then read and circulate the manuscript as necessary for editorial consideration, and finally route it through the mail room back to you with a letter or rejection slip. This kind of handling makes it likely that a freshly typed manuscript will be in rough shape even after one or two submissions. So it is wise to have several photocopies made of a novel-length manuscript while it is still fresh—and to circulate those to publishers, rather than risk an expensive retyping job in the midst of your marketing effort. As mentioned before, indicate in a cover note that the submission is not a multiple submission if such is the case.

Book manuscripts can be mailed Special Fourth Class Book Rate, but that can be slow and have an additional mauling effect on the package in the mails. When doing so, if you include a letter, state this on the outer wrapping and add appropriate postage to your manuscript postal rate. Most writers use First Class, secure in the feeling that their manuscript is in an editorial office within a few days. Some send book manuscripts using the United Parcel Service, which can be less expensive than First Class mail when you drop the package off at UPS yourself. The drawback here is that UPS cannot legally carry First Class mail, so you will have to send your cover letter a few days before giving UPS the manuscript, and both will arrive at about the same time. Check with UPS in your area to see if it has benefits for you. The cost depends on the weight of your manuscript and the delivery distance.

The tips and recommendations made here are based upon what editors prefer. Give editors what they prefer and you won't be beginning with a strike or two against you before the manuscript is even read.

**The waiting game.** The writer who sends off a story or book manuscript to an editor should turn immediately to other ideas and try to forget about the submission. Unless you are on assignment, or under contract to do a book—in which case a phone call to your editor saying the manuscript is in the mail is quite appropriate—it's best to use your time productively on other writing projects, and let the submission take care of itself. But one day you realize it's been too long. According to the *Fiction Writer's Market* listing, your editor responds to submissions in a maximum of four weeks—and it's been six already, and you haven't heard a word. Will inquiring about it jeopardize a possible sale? Are they really considering it, or has the editor had an accident and your manuscript is at the bottom of a huge stack of unread mail?

If you have had no report from a publisher by the maximum reporting time given in a *FWM* listing, allow a few weeks' grace period and then write a brief letter to the editor asking if your manuscript (give the title, a brief description, and the date you mailed it) has in fact reached his office. If so, is it still under consideration? Your concern at this point is the mails: Is the manuscript safely delivered? Don't act impatient with an editor—who may be swamped, or short-handed, or about to give your manuscript a second reading. The wrong word or attitude from you at this point could be hazardous to your manuscript's health. Be polite, be professional. Enclose another SASE to expedite a reply. This is usually enough to stir a decision, if matters are lagging in an editorial office, even during rush season (which is year 'round).

If you still hear nothing from a publisher one month after your follow-up, send the editor a short note asking if he received your previous follow-up, and include a photocopy of that second letter. If, after another month, you are still without word, send a polite letter saying that you are withdrawing the manuscript without consideration (include the title, date of submission, and dates of follow-up correspondence), and ask that the manuscript be returned immediately in the SASE your original correspondence included. You are now free to market the manuscript elsewhere.

Even though matters have not worked out, and you have lost months of precious marketing time—never write in anger. Be cool, professional, and set about the business of finding another publisher for your work. The advantage of having a clean photocopy of the manuscript in your files at this point cannot be overstated. Move on to another editor or publisher with it, using a personal cover letter and the same methods outlined before. In the meantime, continue working on your own writing projects.

At times like these, the advantage of having an agent who can insulate you from such marketing discouragement is considerable. See our section on Agents for guidelines on getting and working with a literary agent, especially if you are working on book-length projects.

# Literary/little magazines

History tells us of the important role literary/little magazines have had in launching some of our greatest names in literature—Faulkner, Hemingway, T.S. Eliot, Henry James, Flannery O'Connor, Joseph Heller. As recent as 20 years ago, John Gardner told his protégé Raymond Carver that the best fiction in the world was published in literary magazines.

Such a claim holds true today. Check the table of contents of 20 or so of the best, most reputable literaries in the US, Canada and even abroad, and you'll find a lineup as auspicious—and often with the same names—as *The New Yorker*, *Esquire* or *Atlantic Monthly*. Joyce Carol Oates, Raymond Carver, John Updike, Andre Dubus, Saul Bellow, Alice Munro and many others regularly submit their stories to little magazines. They know their stories will appear in their original length and form, untouched and unaltered because there will be no space problems or potential conflicts of interests with advertisers as in the commercial magazines. On occasion they are willing to forego even a four-figure payment for the sake of good fiction.

The once-wide gap between the commercial publications and little magazines has narrowed; in fact, in some respects, the tables have turned. Commercial publishers even acknowledged literary/little magazines' role (along with the small press) as the future of serious fiction. Today *Harper's*, the old, esteemed commercial publication, has begun excerpting fiction *from* literary magazines. And B. Dalton, one of the largest bookstore chains in the country, following the example of the small progressive independent bookstores, now carries litmags like *Antioch*, *Paris Review*, *Antaeus*, and *Yale Literary Review*—and sales are encouraging, even surprising. Such a sales ploy is a breakthrough for literary/little magazines, which have long been underestimated, misunderstood or ignored because of lack of visibility or accessibility.

## With energy

Such credibility in the literary world is heartening, but let's not forget the raison d'être of the little magazine—the freedom to create, experiment, and take risks with new, unusual forms and styles with new, untried writers, those often unable to publish in commercial magazines. Litmags offer opportunities to build writing careers. Indeed as one editor says, "Writers look to small magazines in much the same way performers look to the Catskills and the 'comedy shops.' " Publishing in a literary magazine may be just the necessary apprenticeship for new writers to authenticate their work, and help them find their creative voice and appropriate audience, which for many serious writers *may always be* the literary magazines and small press.

Why such direction and faith, even borderline altruism, in literature, particularly fiction, we asked editors of little magazines. Why publish fiction today when fewer commercial magazines are willing to take it and there's so little financial gain? "For the pure love of it"; "to keep fiction and its traditions alive"; "it's our duty to society," they report. Fiction reflects life and reveals more about truth and the human condition or man's/women's fate; it's the backbone of literature. Or more basically these editors explain, their readers simply love the short stories; and they balance their publications. Why publish fiction today? Why doesn't everyone? wonders one editor.

Such endorsement has helped create the recent upsurge in short fiction, a "renaissance," even "hunger for it," by one editor's observation. "This is as interesting, as vital a time for fiction as any in the last 30 years," states one of the editors of *Kansas Quarterly*. "It's a great time for fiction writers and readers to be alive," says Richard Peabody of *Gargoyle*.

Fiction of the '80s is more varied, more alive and energetic, than the predominant abstract style of the '70s. Fiction's growth is also far-reaching; in various areas of the US and Canada there's a "new regionalism," grass roots fiction (and poetry, nonfiction) indigenous to specified areas. At the same time there is evidence of transcultural awareness; writing in the literary magazines has transcended geographic boundaries. Such development or expansion means more publishing outlets in all types of literature.

## Literary specialties

This year *Fiction Writer's Market* brings you more than 100 additional little/literary magazines. Some are established publications that are just now accepting fiction; others are beginning their publishing programs. These are in addition to the 400 plus magazines already represented, including those like the *Greenfield Review* which plans to feature more fiction, and others that this year are able to increase their writing fees.

Literary/little magazines generally fall into three categories: general interest, special subject/interest and regional publications. General literary reviews defy classification. They seek their own identity or personality through individuality and quality literature, and hence establish their reputations. They include magazines, quarterlies, journals like *Triquarterly, Epoch, Antaeus, Shenandoah, Mississippi Review*, for example, or lesser-known publications like *Swift Kick*, which simply requests "the unusual story." Special interest magazines espouse a cause or social issue or promote a hobby or interest or a segment of the population. Thus to write for these special magazines, you should know your subject well—or at least be willing to do research for a related story in, say, a publication like *Spitball* (baseball) or *Grue* (horror). There are also the "zines," semiprozines, fanzines for genres (western, horror, science fiction, fantasy) which may pay reasonably well to nothing at all. In regard to the regional magazines, like *Cold Drill* (Idaho), or *The Azorian Express* (rural Montana), you should be a resident of the magazine's prescribed area or at least be familiar with the locale. Most Canadian publications, literary or regional, have a bias for their local writers.

This year there are noticeably more special interest magazines in such subjects as horror, fantasy and feminism. Specialization is particularly obvious in publications like *Reborn*, which mixes SF and fantasy with horror with a Biblically Christian point of view—and the fiction must reflect this special focus. Occasional small magazines are so specialized as to require the author (or his family) to be handicapped (*Handicap News*); a student (*Merlyn's Pen*); under 13 (*Stone Soup*); or over 60 (*Muscadine*).

Frequently litmags, like *Ploughshares* last year and *Antioch* this spring, publish all-fiction issues or one-time anthologies with special themes—thus offering additional space for short stories (check your listings or a sample copy, or query for information). Longer fiction, today a rare commodity especially in commercial magazines, has its outlets, too, in *Long Story*, for example, which asks for longer stories and novellas.

## Target time

The exciting, creative writing process got you interested in publishing, but now the marketing of your story may seem anti-climactical. You can shorten your time and travails in finding a "home" for your short story, with careful research and "targeting."

First it's important to understand that each magazine differs in policy and submissions requirements as much as the publication itself differs from others. Diversity is what little magazine publishing is all about. Therefore each listing is to be read *carefully*.

Understand at the beginning of your search, that "little" may refer to payment. The writer's fee may be an honorarium, a minimal reward, contributor's copies or nothing at all. Generally these magazines are low-budget, nonprofit publications that can afford little more. Accept the fact that you're approaching a literary for the experience, the exposure, an opportunity to see your work in print—not for the financial gain.

Start with the Category Index as a "targeting" base, if you have a story already written. Decide the kind or category of your story and check that section of the Category Index (science fiction, romance, religious/inspirational, children's), which in turn refers you to publications that accept that type of fiction. If you have just an idea for a story or one that cannot be adequately categorized (literary, serious), check the listings themselves.

In the listings check the established date. Magazines like *Chicago Review* and *Antioch* have published for 40 years or so and are stable markets that will remain in business during your publishing search. Other magazines with a 1984 or 1985 established date don't have the assured track record. Therefore before you send off your manuscript to a new publication, we recommend you obtain a sample copy to ascertain that it is in business. Or at least query to check its status.

Next, check the required submissions period. Some college/university-based literaries do not read manuscripts in the summer. You can also avoid losing valuable time by querying the editor for future themes for the magazine, if it has special issues or issues alternating with poetry, which sometimes happens. Preference to writer-residency, nationality, sex, age or status may be a submission requirement, as buying a magazine subscription may be before manuscript submission.

## Support system

To assist you in matching your manuscript with the appropriate publication, this year in the listings we have added information about the physical appearance and format of each publication: the size, number of pages, quality of paper and cover, the type of printing and whether there are photos or illustrations. Also with the editor's help we've ranked each publication (with the exception of a few) regarding the editorial policy in accepting beginning or established writers. If you're a beginning writer you should try magazines with (I) after the title, like *Red Bass*, whose editor states simply, "We're in the business of publishing new writers"; or *Square One*, which encourages new writers interested in "expanding fiction writing." Magazines like *The Agni Review* or *Calyx* rank themselves with (II), inviting established *and* beginning writers of quality. And publications like the *Paris Review* and *Partisan Review* are traditionally prestige publications and very hard to break into, unless your story is outstanding, and are ranked with (III). Those publications marked with a (IV) are special interest and regional publications; their requirements are self-explanatory. Also this year notice the listing with the daggers preceding the title—they are new markets.

If you plan to submit to literary/little magazines, your support is *vital* to their health and longevity. Send for sample copies, or better yet, subscribe to one or several for a year. Then exchange copies with writer-friends and change subscriptions the following year. It's important to understand the financial plight of a literary journal—often a long, discouraging struggle to stay alive in a business where sometimes there are more submissions than subscriptions. Lending support and becoming familiar with the magazines are parts of the writer's apprenticeship. In addition to your financial support, heed the wise advice of Pam Painter, short story writer and instructor at the New England Writers' Conference, who suggests volunteering to proofread manuscripts at a nearby literary publication. This is a method she used years ago as one of the founding editors of *Story Quarterly*, which greatly helped to improve her own story construction. Working with a magazine also offers contacts so useful later.

Literary/little editors this year speak with optimism; read the Tips section at the ends of the listings: "Quality will be recognized" (*Cross-Canada Writers Quarterly*): "See your rejections as an opportunity to grow" (*Yellow Silk*); and remember the wisdom of *Triquarterly*'s editor Reginald Gibbons: "Nobody's work suits everybody."

"Suitable" markets for your special short story can be found in the list that follows.

**ADRIFT (II), Writing: Irish, Irish American and . . .**, #4D, 239 E. 5th St., New York NY 10003. Editor: Thomas McGonigle. Magazine: 8x11; 32 pages; 60 lb stock paper; 65 lb cover stock; illustrations; photos. "Irish-Irish American as a basis—though we are interested in advanced writing from anywhere." Semiannually. Estab. 1983. Circ. 1,000+.
**Needs:** Contemporary, erotica, ethnic, experimental, feminist, gay, lesbian, literary, translations. Receives 40 unsolicited mss/month. Buys 3 mss/issue. Length: open. Sometimes critiques rejected ms. Sometimes recommends other markets.
**How to Contact:** Send complete ms. Reports as soon as possible. SASE for ms. Photocopied submissions OK. Accepts computer printout submissions. Sample copy $3.50.
**Payment:** Pays $7.50-300.
**Terms:** Pays on publication for first rights. Publication copyrighted.
**Tips:** "The writing should argue with, among others, James Joyce, Flann O'Brien, Juan Goytisolo, Ingeborg Bachmann, E.M. Cioran, Max Stirnon, Patrick Cavanagh." Published new writers within the last year.

**AGADA (II, IV), A New Jewish Literary Magazine**, 2020 Essex St., Berkeley CA 94703. (415)848-0965. Editor-in-Chief: Reuven Goldfarb. Magazine: 7x10; 48 pages; "good quality" paper; heavy cover stock; illustrations; photos. "Poetry, stories, midrash, Torah interpretation and translation, the Letters themselves, drawings, photos, essays, and exhortations. Arts and letters. Visions into words, mystical revelation, description of life as a Jew in our time, in our place, in this world. *Agada* seeks to share the insights, memories and vision of creative Jewish people with people everywhere." Semiannually. Estab. 1981. Circ. 600.
**Needs:** Literary, religious/inspirational, excerpted novel, and translations. "We prefer Jewish orientation or relevance from the particularistic to the universal. Not overly political." Receives 10-12 unsolicited mss/month. Accepts 6 mss/issue; 12 mss/year. Length: 500-2,000 words average; 6,000 words maximum. Occasionally critiques rejected mss.
**How to Contact:** Send complete ms and cover letter with brief bio. Reports in 3 months. SASE. Simultaneous, photocopied and previously published submissions OK. Publishes ms an average of 6 months after acceptance. Sample copy for $5.75; back issue, $4.75.

**Payment:** 2 free contributor's copies; $3 charge for extras.
**Terms:** Acquires one-time rights. Occasionally accepts reprints. Publication copyrighted.
**Tips:** "Read previous issues; know what you are writing about—depend on personal insight or experience; where necessary, research should be thorough; revise carefully. The quality of submissions has improved as more and more Jews are becoming aware of the strength and beauty of their heritage. There are various perfectly legitimate kinds of fiction being written today. What makes any fiction stand out is the style of its author, not its subject matter or philosophical stance. If you can get inside your character, you can grab the reader's attention. Published new writers within the last year."

**THE AGNI REVIEW (II)**, The Agni Review Inc., Box 660, Amherst MA 01004. Editor-in-Chief: Sharon Dunn. Magazine: 5½x8½; 164-188 pages; 55 lb booktext paper; glossy cover stock; occasional illustrations; occasional photos. "Eclectic literary magazine publishing first-rate poems and stories." Semiannually. Plans special fiction issue. Estab. 1972.
**Needs:** Stories, excerpted novel, and translations. Receives 150 unsolicited fiction mss/month. Accepts 4-7 mss/issue, 8-12 mss/year. Rarely critiques rejected mss. Recommends other markets.
**How to Contact:** Send complete ms with SASE and cover letter with previous publications. Simultaneous and photocopied submissions OK. Accepts computer printout submissions. Reports in 4 weeks. Sample copy $4.
**Payment:** 3 contributor's copies; extra copies 60% of retail price.
**Terms:** Pays on publication for first North American serial rights. Sends galleys to author. Publication copyrighted.
**Tips:** "Read *AGNI* carefully to understand the kinds of stories we publish. Our fiction might be described as highly literate (but not literary). At times experimental, always crafted with great attention to language and to telling a story." Published new authors in the last year.

**AHNENE PUBLICATIONS, Poetry 'N Prose**, Ahnene Publications, Box 456, Maxville, Ontario KOC 1T0 Canada. Editor-in-Chief: M. Williams. Magazine of poetry and prose for the general public, poetry lovers. Bimonthly. Estab. 1982. $10 (Canadian funds) for 1 year subscription.
**Needs:** Contemporary, experimental, fantasy, horror, humor/satire, literary, mainstream, prose poem, religious/inspirational, romance (contemporary), women's, and poetry group news items. "No science fiction, cops 'n robbers or whodunits." Receives "too many" unsolicited short story mss of poor quality. Occasionally critiques rejected mss. Charges $10 critique fee.
**How to Contact:** Send complete ms with SASE or IRCs. Photocopied submissions and previously published work OK (where rights have reverted to authors). Accepts computer printout submissions. Reports in 2 months on mss. Publishes ms 2-4 months after acceptance. Sample copy $2 and 2 first class Canadian stamps (or 2 IRCs).
**Payment:** 1 contributor's copy. Charges $1.50 for extras (special rate for contributors only).
**Terms:** Pays on publication for first rights, second serial rights. Occasionally buys reprints. Publication copyrighted. Tear sheets sometimes supplied when available.
**Tips:** "We are especially interested in beginning, unknown writers. We won't turn you down just because we've never heard of you, but do let us know something about yourself that could be used in our 'About Our Contributors' section."

**ALASKA QUARTERLY REVIEW (II)**, University of Alaska, 3211 Providence Dr., Anchorage AK 99508. (907)786-1327. Contact: Ronald Spatz, Fiction Editor. Magazine: 6x9; 146 pages; 60 lb Glatfelter paper; 10 pt. C15 black ink varnish cover stock; photos on cover only. Magazine of "contemporary literary art and criticism for a general literary audience." Semiannually. Estab. 1982.
**Needs:** Contemporary, experimental, literary, prose poem, and translations. Receives 50 unsolicited fiction mss/month. Publishes short shorts. Accepts 5-8 mss/issue, 15 mss/year. Does not read May 15-August 15. Occasionally critiques rejected mss.
**How to Contact:** Send complete ms with SASE. Photocopied submissions OK. Reports in 2

months. Publishes ms 6-12 months after acceptance. Sample copy $4.
**Payment:** 2 free contributor's copies.
**Terms:** Pays on publication for first rights. Publication copyrighted.
**Tips:** "We have made a significant investment in fiction—15 stories included in our two 1985 issues. The reason is quality; serious fiction *needs* a market. Try to have everything build to a single-ness of effect." Published new writers within the last year.

**THE ALCHEMIST**, Box 123, Lasalle, Quebec H8R 3T7 Canada. Editor: Marco Fraticelli. "We publish prose in every issue with no prejudices in regard to style, but we tend to favor the experimental rather than the traditional." Published irregularly. Estab. 1974. Circ. 500.
**Needs:** Literary, feminist, gay, lesbian, and psychic/supernatural/occult. Buys 1 ms/issue.
**How to Contact:** Send complete ms with SASE or IRC. Accepts computer printout submissions. Accepts disc submissions compatible with Apple. Prefers hard copy with disc submission. Reports in 1 month. Publishes ms an average of 6 months after acceptance. Sample copy $1.
**Payment:** Free author's copies.
**Terms:** Pays on publication. Rights remain with author. Publication copyrighted.
**Tips:** "Please—no American stamps on the SASE."

**ALDEBARAN (II)**, Roger Williams College, Ferry Rd., Bristol RI 02809. Editor: Stephen Martovich. Magazine: 5½x8½; 60-80 pages; illustrations; photos. Literary publication of prose and poetry for a general audience. Published annually or twice a year. Estab. 1970.
**Needs:** Will consider all fiction. Short stories preferred. Receives approximately 10 unsolicited fiction mss each month. Does not read mss in summer. Also publishes short shorts, 10-15 pages or shorter. Critiques rejected mss "when there is time."
**How to Contact:** Send complete ms with SASE and cover letter ("information for possible contributor's notes, but cover letters will not influence decision on publication)." Accepts computer printout submissions. Reports in 1 month. Sample copy $1 with SASE.
**Payment:** 2 free author's copies.
**Terms:** Pays on publication. Publication copyrighted. Copyright reverts to author on publication.
**Tips:** Mss are rejected because of "incomplete stories, no live character, basic grammatical errors; usually returned with suggestions for revision and character change."

**‡ALLEGHENY REVIEW (IV), A National Journal of Undergraduate Literature**, Box 32, Allegheny College, Meadville PA 16335. (814)724-6553. Editor: Thomas J. Stout. Magazine: 6x9; 100 pages; 60 lb White Wove paper; illustrations; photos. "The *Allegheny Review* is an annual journal composed entirely of undergraduate contributions selected from submissions from colleges across the nation. Short fiction topics are open, the only restriction being status as an undergraduate student. Volume is aimed at the undergraduate student with an aim towards providing the missing communications link between undergraduate writers in this nation." Annually. Estab. 1983. Circ. 1,000.
**Needs:** Confession, contemporary, experimental, humor/satire, literary with any topic, mainstream. "All mss must possess adequate literary merit to be regarded as serious literature. Topics are open. The *Review* is intended primarily as a creative outlet for the undergraduate writer, and is suitable as a creative writing text. In the past three issues we have found the content to be extremely interesting to all levels of readers." Accepts 10-15 fiction mss per volume/year. Length: 5,000 words average. "Length necessary to tell the tale." Also publishes short shorts. Recommends other markets.
**How to Contact:** Query first or send complete manuscript with cover letter (name of school author currently attending; some background on the evolution/creation of the piece). Reports in 2 weeks on queries; 2 months on mss following Jaunary 31 deadline. SASE for query and ms. Pho-

---

 **The double dagger before a listing indicates that the listing is new in this edition. New markets are often the most receptive to freelance contributions.**

tocopied submissions OK. Accepts computer printouts including dot-matrix. Sample copy for 8x11 SAE and 3 first class stamps.
**Payment:** Free subscription to magazine; contributor's copies; and charge for extras.
**Terms:** Acquires first rights. Publication copyrighted.
**Tips:** "Selected story judged most outstanding by editors receives $50 award and possible invitation to Symposia with nationally recognized authors (ex. Margaret Atwood). *Review* is ideal for developing writer to see how and what others in peer group are creating. It helps develop a sense of identity."

**ALPHA ADVENTURES SF&F (II)**, Shoestring Publications, 3001 N. 2nd St., Fargo ND 58102. Editor: John Postovit. Magazine: 5½x8½; 32 pages; bond paper; heavy cover stock; illustrations. "We use science fiction and fantasy fiction and poetry" for SF/F readers. Published 3 times/year. Estab. 1981.
**Needs:** Fantasy, horror, humor/satire, psychic/supernatural/occult, and science fiction. No media-based fiction. Receives 40 unsolicited mss/month. Buys 3 mss/issue; 9 mss/year. Publishes short shorts. Length: 6,000 words average; 500 words minimum; 11,000 words maximum. Occasionally comments on a rejected ms.
**How to Contact:** Send complete ms. Reports in 2 weeks on mss. SASE and cover letter with short bit about the author is fine—but no synopses of the submission please. Photocopied submissions OK. Accepts computer printout submissions. Prefers letter-quality. Sample copy $1.50. Fiction guidelines for SAE; business envelope and 1 first class stamp.
**Payment:** $1-25 plus contributor's copy; charge for extras: $1.50.
**Terms:** Pays on acceptance for first North American serial rights.
**Tips:** "Fantasy seems to be dominating science fiction these days . . . as such we have a hard time getting enough SF to balance the fantasy we use. We're most eager to get mid-length stories from 2,000 to 8,000 words. Shorter (to 500) or longer (to 11,000) will be considered, but we look more to the mid-length stories." Published new writers within the last year.

**AMELIA (II)**, 329 E St., Bakersfield CA 93304. (805)323-4064. Editor-in-chief: Frederick A. Raborg Jr. Magazine: 5½x8½; 96 pages; 60 lb high quality moistrite matte paper; kromekote cover stock; original illustrations; b&w photos. "A general review using fine fiction, poetry, criticism, belles lettres, one-act plays, fine pen and ink sketches and line drawings, book reviews and translations of both fiction and poetry for general readers with catholic tastes for quality writing." Quarterly. Plans special fiction issue each July. Estab. 1984. Circ. 1,000.
**Needs:** Adventure, contemporary, erotica, ethnic, experimental, fantasy, feminist, gay, historical (general), humor/satire, lesbian, literary, mainstream, prose poem, regional, science fiction, senior citizen/retirement, suspense/mystery, translations, western, and women's. Nothing "obviously pornographic or patently religious." Receives 60-80 unsolicited mss/month. Buys up to 6 mss/issue; 12-20 mss/year. Length: 2,500 words average; 1,000 words minimum; 3,500 words maximum. Usually critiques rejected ms. Recommends other markets.
**How to Contact:** Send complete manuscript. Cover letter with previous credits if applicable to AMELIA and perhaps a brief personal comment to show personality and experience. Reports in 1 week on queries; 2 weeks-2months on mss. SASE for ms. Photocopied submissions OK. Accepts computer printout submissions; prefers letter-quality. Sample copy for $4.75 ppd. Fiction guidelines free for #10 SAE and 1 first class stamp.
**Payment:** Pays $35-50 plus 2 contributor's copies; extras with 20% discount.
**Terms:** Pays on acceptance. Buys first North American serial rights. Sends galleys to author "when time permits." Publication copyrighted.
**Tips:** "Write carefully and well, but have a strong story to relate. I look for depth of plot and uniqueness, and strong characterization. Fiction is still the backbone of literature. *Amelia* is intended to be a *reader's* magazine, something to act as a companion, something its readers will wish to spend time enjoying and, hopefully, *re*exploring. There is a sameness—a cloning process— among most magazines today that tends to dull the senses. Magazines like *Amelia* will awaken those senses while offering stories and poems of lasting value." Published 2 new writers within the last year.

**THE AMHERST REVIEW (II)**, Students of Amherst College, Box 486, Station 2, Amherst MA 01002. Editor-in-Chief: Ruth Abbe. Fiction Editor: Kate Garrison. Magazine: 7½x8½; 100 pages; 70 lb dull paper; 65 lb white cover stock; illustrations; photos. "We are a college literary magazine publishing work by students, faculty and professionals. We seek submissions of poetry, fiction, essay, photography and art work for the college community." Annually. Circ. 1,000.
**Needs:** Adventure, confession, contemporary, ethnic, experimental, fantasy, feminist, gay, historical, horror, humor/satire, lesbian, literary, mainstream, prose poem, psychic/supernatural/occult, regional, romance, science fiction, suspense/mystery, translations, and western. Receives 10-20 unsolicited mss/month. Does not read March-August. Publishes short shorts. Length: 4,500 words average; 7,200 words maximum. Sometimes critiques rejected ms.
**How to Contact:** Send complete ms. Reports in 4 months on mss. SASE and brief one sentence bio. Photocopied submissions OK. Accepts computer printout submissions; prefers letter-quality. Sample copy $5 and SAE ($1 postage). *Prefers two copies* of ms.
**Payment:** 2 contributor's copies; $5 charge for extras.
**Terms:** Pays on publication for first rights. Publication copyrighted.
**Tips:** "Submit. Persist." Published new writers within the last year.

**ANNEX**, Annex Press, 2417 Londonderry, Ann Arbor MI 48104. Editor: Tod Kabza. Magazine: 8x8; 10-100 pages; good paper and cover stock quality; photos on cover. Poetry, fiction (experimental), and translation for general audience.
**Needs:** Experimental, literary, prose poem, and translations. Receives 2 unsolicited mss/month. Buys 3 mss/issue. Length: variable. Sometimes comments on rejected ms.
**How to Contact:** Query first. Reports in 2 months on queries; 2 months on mss. SASE for query and mss. Photocopied submissions OK. Does not accept computer printout submissions. Sample copy for $6 and 8x11 SAE and 5 first class stamps.
**Payment:** Pays $5-25; subscription and 5 contributor's copies.
**Terms:** Pays on publication for one-time rights. Publication copyrighted.
**Tips:** "Send sample of work and SAE."

**ANTAEUS**, The Ecco Press, 18 W. 30th St., New York NY 10001. (212)685-8240. Editor-in-Chief: Daniel Halpern. Managing and Associate Editor: Katherine L. Bourne. Literary magazine of fiction and poetry, literary documents, and occasional essays for those seriously interested in contemporary writing. Quarterly. Estab. 1970. Circ. 5,000.
**Needs:** Contemporary, literary, prose poem, excerpted novel, and translations. No gothic romance, romance, science fiction. Receives 200 unsolicited fiction mss/month. Rarely critiques rejected mss.
**How to Contact:** Send complete ms with SASE. Photocopied submissions OK. Accepts computer printout submissions. Prefers letter-quality. Reports in 6-8 weeks. Sample copy $6. Fiction guidelines free with SASE.
**Payment:** Pays $5/page minimum and 2 free contributor's copies. 40% discount for extras.
**Terms:** Pays on publication for first North American serial rights and right to reprint in any anthology consisting of 75% or more of material from *Antaeus*. Publication copyrighted.
**Tips:** "Read the magazine before submitting. Unless stories are extremely short (2-3 pages), send only one. Do not be angry if you get only a printed rejection note; we *have* read the manuscript. Always include an SASE. Keep cover letters short, cordial and to the point."

**ANTIETAM REVIEW (II)**, Washington County (MD) Arts Council, Room 215, 33 W. Washington St., Hagerstown MD 21740. (301)791-3125. Editor: Ann B. Knox. Fiction Editor: Ellen Ternes. Magazine: 8½x11; 42 pages; illustrations; photos. A literary journal for short fiction, poetry and black and white photographs. Annually. Estab. 1982. Circ. 1,000.
**Needs:** Contemporary, ethnic, experimental, feminist and literary. "We read manuscripts from our region—Maryland, Pennsylvania, Virginia, West Virginia and Washington D.C. only. We read from October 1 to March 1." Receives about 100 unsolicited mss/month; accepts 7-9 stories.
**Length:** 3,000 words average.
**How to Contact:** "Send ms and SASE to *Antietam Review* at above address with a cover letter,

# Close-up

**Robert Fogarty**
*Antioch Review*

Traveling east from Dayton you pass fields of corn, pigs and lazy cows before you reach Yellow Springs, Ohio. The home of Antioch College since 1855, this sleepy little town is also an unexpected oasis of poets and writers and the setting for the *Antioch Review*, one of the oldest, most reputable literaries in the US.

From his book-lined basement office in the ivy-covered historic main building on the college campus, editor Robert Fogarty speaks with pride about the *Review*. "We're a magazine that likes to surprise people," he says. "Each issue is different." But the mix is the same; that is, there are social and political essays, 12 to 16 pages of poetry, and two to four short stories, depending on the length. *Antioch* takes an eclectic approach in subject matter—and staff. Those associated are not purely literary. Fogarty is an author of books on communal societies and a professor of social history—with an intense interest in literary work. He also has a bias for short stories.

In early 1986 *Antioch* published another of its all-fiction issues featuring both established writers and several first-timers. For example, there's a 30-page contemporary social analysis by Joyce Carol Oates, and a macabre, comic story by Gordon Lish. In general, *Antioch* fiction demonstrates no "house preference" except that the writing be "highly charged, particularly vivid." Fogarty tries to avoid topical stories, preferring timeless, lasting work. The fiction is not terribly experimental, nor must there be a strong story line. The editor favors a more traditional style, however, but not necessarily with a beginning, middle and end.

According to Fogarty and his current associate editor Nolan Miller, the former editor and one of *Antioch*'s founders, most manuscripts don't say much. One of the obvious pitfalls they see is the failure to engage a reader early. Short fiction demands that you get on with the story quickly, stresses the editor. Also the characters should be self-contained and "jump off the page" within the narrative construction. "We want stories people remember five to ten years from now, ones with emotions that remain in the mind."

There is no need to solicit material at *Antioch*; if anything the reverse is true. Agents contact one or two contributors each issue as potential novelists. The magazine accepts short fiction on a roll-in basis. Of the 2,400 or so stories that *Antioch* receives a year, Fogarty says, "We see an enormous number of perfectly-crafted stories, with a professional understanding of plot and character development." Improvement in craft is a reflection of the growing number of writers out of writing workshops. In addition, in the last ten years, Fogarty adds, the quality in general has improved "astoundingly. . . . We've helped create this situation—and we've benefited. But the volume is difficult to manage."

*Antioch*'s diversity and quality in the writing and its graphically-appealing format have contributed to its effective distribution, including recent representation in B. Dalton bookstores. That the quarterly has never missed an issue in 45 years is an affidavit of success in an industry fraught with problems. But crossover into the commercial world is a breakthrough the literati genuinely applaud. "It's well worth the effort," says Robert Fogarty of his 40-plus hours on the magazine each week in addition to his college teaching. The former Brooklyn native is pleased with life in the Midwest. "It's lovely work. I thoroughly enjoy it."

letting us know if you have published before and where, is welcome." Photocpies OK. Accepts computer printout. Prefers letter-quality. Reports in 4 to 8 weeks. "If we hold a story we let the writer know. Occasionally we critique returned ms or ask for rewrites." Sample copy $3. Sends pre-publication galleys if requested.

**Payment:** "We believe it is a matter of dignity that writers and poets be paid. In 1985 we were able to give $100 a story and $25 a poem and hope to continue. Also 2 copies." Prizes: "We offer a $200 annual literary award for the best story."

**Terms:** Acquires first North American serial rights. Publication copyrighted.

**Tips:** "We look for well-crafted writing that shows attention to clarity, precision and language. We like relevant detail but want to see significant emotional movement within the course of the story—something happening to the characters. We look for tight and careful crafting. This journal was started in response to the absence of fiction markets for emerging writers. Its purpose is to give exposure to fiction writers, poets and photographers of high artistic quality who might otherwise have difficulty placing their work."

**THE ANTIGONISH REVIEW**, St. F.X. University, Antigonish, Nova Scotia B2G 1C0 Canada. (902)867-2157 or 867-3962. Editor: George Sanderson. Literary magazine for the educated and creative. Quarterly. Estab. 1970. Circ. 800.

**Needs:** Literary, contemporary, and translations. No erotic or political material. Buys 6 mss/issue. Receives 25 unsolicited fiction mss each month. Length: 3,000-5,000 words. Sometimes comments briefly on rejected mss.

**How to Contact:** Send complete ms with SASE or IRC. Accepts disc submissions compatible with Apple and Macintosh. Prefers hard copy with disc submission. Reports in 8 weeks. Publishes ms 3-12 months after acceptance.

**Payment:** 2 free author's copies, $5/page.

**Terms:** Acquires first rights. Publication copyrighted.

**Tips:** "Learn the fundamentals and do not deluge an editor." Rejects mss because of "poor style—usually foggy, dull or unclear. The number of manuscripts is greatly increased and the quality is somewhat better."

**ANTIOCH REVIEW (II)**, Antioch Review, Inc., Box 148, Yellow Springs OH 45387. (513)767-7386. Editor: Robert S. Fogarty. Associate Editor: Nolan Miller. Magazine: 6x9; 128 pages; 60 lb book offset paper; coated cover stock. "Literary and cultural review of contemporary issues in politics, American and international studies, and literature for general readership. Quarterly. Published special fiction issue last year; plans another. Estab. January 1941. Circ. 4,000.

**Needs:** Literary, contemporary, translations, and experimental. No children's, science fiction or popular market. Buys 3-4 mss/issue, 10-12 mss/year. Receives approximately 175 unsolicited fiction mss each month. Approximately 1-2% of fiction agented. Length: any length the story justifies.

**How to Contact:** Send complete ms with SASE, preferably mailed flat. Accepts computer printout submissions. Prefers letter-quality. Reports in 2 months. Publishes ms 6-9 months after acceptance. Sample copy $3; free guidelines with SASE.

**Payment:** $10/page; 2 free author's copies. $2.70 for extras.

**Terms:** Pays on publication for first and one-time rights (rights returned to author on request) Publication copyrighted.

**Tips:** "Our best advice, always, is to *read* the *Antioch Review* to see what type of material we publish. Quality fiction requires an engagement of the reader's intellectual interest supported by mature emotional relevance, written in a style that is rich and rewarding without being freaky. The great number of stories submitted to us indicates that fiction apparently still has great appeal. We assume that if so many are writing fiction, many must be reading it." Published new writers within the last year.

**APALACHEE QUARTERLY (II)**, D.D.B. Press, Inc., Box 20106, Tallahassee FL 32316. (904)878-1591. Editors: Monica Faeth, Allen Woodman, and Barbara Hamby. Magazine: 50-100 pages; heavy paper quality; illustrations; photos. Contemporary journal of fiction, poetry and drama. Quarterly. Published special fiction issue last year; plans another. Estab. 1972. Circ. over 500.

**Needs:** Literary and contemporary. "We want high quality, modern fiction." Buys 15 mss/issue, 60 mss/year. Receives 200 unsolicited fiction mss month. Length: 700-6,000 words. Also publishes short shorts. Critiques rejected mss "when there is time." Does not read mss in summer. Recommends other markets.

**How to Contact:** Send complete ms with SASE. Accepts computer printout submissions. Prefers letter-quality. Reports in 3 months. Sample copy $3.50, includes postage.

**Payment:** 2 free author's copies. Payment when funds are available.

**Terms:** Acquires first rights. Publication copyrighted.

**Tips:** "We sometimes sponsor regional or statewide contests, depending on grant money. Don't send early drafts. Polish your work. Read modern fiction. And work on finding your own voice." Published 5 unpublished writers within the last year.

**ARBA SICULA (II, IV)**, ARBA Sicula, Inc., Box D, Brooklyn NY 11204-0328, USA. (718)331-0613. Editor: Alissandru Caldiero. Magazine: 6x9; 61-138 pages; top grade paper; good quality cover stock; illustrations; photos. Bilingual ethnic literary review (Sicilian-English) dedicated to the dissemination of Sicilian culture. Published 2-4 times a year. Plans special fiction issue. Estab. 1979. Circ. 1,500.

**Needs:** Accepts ethnic literary material consisting of various forms of folklore; stories both contemporary and classical; regional, romance (contemporary, historical, young adult), and senior citizen. Material submitted must be in the Sicilian language with English translation desirable. Critiques rejected mss "when there is time." Recommends other markets.

**How to Contact:** Send complete ms with SASE and bio. Reports in 2 months. Publishes ms 1-3 years after acceptance. Sample copy $8 with 8½x11 SASE and 90¢ postage.

**Payment:** 5 free author's copies. $4 for extra copies.

**Terms:** Acquires all rights. Buys reprints. Publication copyrighted.

**Tips:** "This review is a must for those who nurture a love of the Sicilian language." Mss are rejected because of "poor Sicilian language. Provide both Sicilian and English. If you have good clean stuff for a literate market, we're interested." Published new writers within the last year.

**THE ARGONAUT (II)**, Box 4201, Austin TX 78765-4201. Editor: Michael Ambrose. Magazine: 8x5; 48 pages; 60 lb paper; varied cover stock; illustrations; photos. "*Argonaut* is a weird fantasy/science fiction magazine. The word 'fantasy' carries few restrictions here. *Argonaut* readers want original, literate, unusual stories." Semiannually. Estab. March 1972. Circ. 500.

**Needs:** Science fiction, fantasy, horror. Buys 5-8 mss/issue, 10-15 mss/year. Receives 40-50 unsolicited fiction mss each month. Length: 2,500-10,000 words. Critiques rejected mss "when there is time." Sometimes recommends other markets.

**How to Contact:** Send complete ms with SASE. Reports in 1-2 months. Sample copy $3.

**Payment:** 2 copies plus 3-issue subscription. $3 charge for extras or 5 copies or more at 40% discount.

**Terms:** Pays on publication for first North American serial rights. Publication copyrighted.

**Tips:** "Know the fields of weird fantasy and science fiction thoroughly, and remember, most of it has already been done in one form or another. Read the professional magazines and sample *Argonaut* and other small press magazines before submitting anything. Don't submit more than one story at a time, and keep trying when rejected. The field is wide open to new writers who have the skill and perseverance to keep at it. *Argonaut*'s infrequent publishing schedule compels me to be very selective of the stories I receive. It takes more than a polished style with no originality of idea, or all idea with no style on the other hand, to get me interested." Published new writers within the last year.

**ARIZONA QUARTERLY (I, II)**, The University of Arizona, Tucson AZ 85721. (602)626-1029. Editor: Albert F. Gegenheimer. Magazine: 6x9; 96 pages. Quarterly. Estab. March 1945.

**Needs:** Literary, contemporary, feminist, regional, and translations. Receives approximately 25 unsolicited fiction mss each month. Length: 3,000-4,000 words. Critiques rejected mss "when there is time." Sometimes recommends other markets.

**How to Contact:** Send complete ms with SASE. Accepts computer printout submissions. Prefers letter-quality. Reports in 1 month; slower reports in July-August. Publishes ms an average of 2 years after acceptance. Sample copy $1.50. No multiple submissions.

**Payment:** Subscription and 20 author's copies.

**Terms:** Acquires all rights. Publication copyrighted.

**Tips:** Mss are rejected because they are "badly written; formula stories; stories that say nothing and get nowhere." Annual award for best short story published in *AQ*. "We recognize a duty not only to writers, but also to readers, to encourage the art of fiction." Published new writers within the last year.

**‡ARTEMIS (II, IV), Artists and Writers from The Blue Ridge Mountains**, Artemis, Box 945, Roanoke VA 24005. (703)774-8440. Fiction Editor: Jeanne Larsen. Magazine: 6x6; 80 pages; heavy/slick paper; colored cover stock; illustrations; photos. "No theme. We publish poetry, art, and fiction of the highest quality and will consider any artist/writer who lives or has lived in the Blue Ridge." General adult audience with literary interest. Annually. Estab. 1976. Circ. 1,000.

**Needs:** Literary. Wants to see "the best contemporary style." Receives 15 unsolicited fiction mss/year. Accepts 2-3 mss/issue. Does not read mss Jan.-Aug. Publishes ms 4-5 months after acceptance. Length: 1,500 words average; 2,000 words maximum. "Sometimes" critiques rejected mss.

**How to Contact:** Submit unpublished ms between Sept. 15-Nov. 15 with SASE, name on each page, short bio. Reports in 2 months. SASE for ms. Photocopied submissions OK. No multiple submissions. Accepts computer printout. No dot-matrix unless high quality. Sample copy $4.60.

**Payment:** Discount for extra copies.

**Terms:** Acquires first rights.

**‡THE ARTFUL CODGER AND CODGERETTE (I, II)**, Snowy Egret, 205 S. 9th St., Williamsburg KY 40769. (606)549-0850. Editor: Humphrey A. Olsen. Mini-tabloid: 7x8 ½; 8 pages; good quality paper; illustrations (line drawings). "Especially appeals to older persons but contains much material equally interesting to ages senior high and up. New material and encores (reprints). Articles, current events, fiction, poetry. Faces realistically problems of older persons: "no euphemistic references to the golden years; years not golden for many people;" for persons with at least average education. 10 issues/year. Estab. January 1984. Circ. 450.

**Needs:** Adventure, contemporary, historical (general), humor/satire, literary, regional, senior citizen/retirement, special interest (nature). No science fiction, sexual-oriented ms, light romance. Accepts 10 fiction mss/year. Publishes ms 3 months (or shorter) after acceptance. Length: 400-500 words average; 200 words minimum; 1,200 words maximum. Occasionally critiques rejected mss. Recommends other markets "if we know of any in that area."

**How to Contact:** Send complete ms with cover letter with SASE. SASE for query and ms. Reprints OK. No computer printouts. Sample copy for SASE (1 first class stamp).

**Payment:** Free subscription to magazine and contributor's copies.

**Terms:** Pays on publication for one-time rights.

**Tips:** "We can be optimistic to a beginning fiction writer."

**ARTFUL DODGE (II)**, Artful Dodge Publications, Box 1473, Bloomington IN 47402. (812)332-0324. Editor-in-Chief: Daniel Bourne. "There is no theme in this magazine, except literary power. We publish primarily first appearances in English of original and translated works. Readers are interested in both American and foreign literature in translation." Semiannually. Estab. 1979. Circ. 500.

**Needs:** Experimental, literary, prose poem, science fiction, serialized/excerpted novel, and translations. "We judge by literary quality, not by genre. We are especially interested in translations of significant contemporary prose writers." Receives 30 unsolicited fiction mss/month. Accepts 2-3 mss/issue, 5 mss/year. Length: 10,000 or so words maximum; 2,500 words average. Occasionally critiques rejected mss.

**How to Contact:** Send complete ms with SASE. Photocopied submissions OK. Reports in 2-3 months. Sample copy $2.75. Free fiction guidelines for legal-sized SAE and 1 first class stamp.
**Payment:** 1 free contributor's copy (subject to change for the better).
**Terms:** Pays on publication for first North American serial rights. Publication copyrighted.
**Tips:** "If we take time to offer criticism, do not subsequently flood us with other stories no better than the first. We sometimes work on revisions. If starting out, get as many readers, good ones, as possible. The voice of your story is as important as the plot; learn when you are disclosing your story effectively. And above all, read!"

‡**THE ASYMPTOTICAL WORLD (II)**, The Asymptotical World, Box 1372, Williamsport PA 17701. (717)322-7841. Editor: Michael H. Gerardi. Magazine: 8½x11; 54 pages; glossy stock paper; illustrated cover; b/w illustrations. "*The Asymptotical World* is a *unique* collection of psychodramas, phantasies, science fiction, poems and illustrations which elucidates the moods and sensations of the world created in the mind of men, for 18 year olds and older; those who enjoy work completed in style and mood similar to Poe." Annually. Plans special fiction issue. Estab. 1984. Circ. 1,300.
**Needs:** Experimental, fantasy, horror, psychic/supernatural/occult, science fiction. Receives 10 unsolicited fiction mss/month; accepts 5 fiction mss/issue. Publishes ms 6-12 months after acceptance. Length: 1,000 words minimum; 2,500 words maximum. Comments on rejected mss.
**How to Contact:** Query first. SASE for ms. Reports in 1-2 months on queries; 3-4 months on mss. Simultaneous and photocopied submissions OK. Accepts computer printouts including dot-matrix. Sample copy $6.95 with SAE and 8 first class stamps. Fiction guidelines for 4x9 SAE and 2 first class stamps.
**Payment:** Pays $20-50.
**Terms:** Pays on publication. Acquires first rights. Publication copyrighted.
**Tips:** "*The Asymptotical World* is definitely unique. It is strongly suggested that a writer review a copy of the magazine to study the format of a psychodrama and the manner in which the plot is left 'open-ended.' The writer will need to study the atmosphere, mood, and plot of published psychodramas before preparing a feature work."

‡**ATLANTIS (II), A Women's Studies Journal**, Institute for the Study of Women, Mt. St. Vincent University, Halifax, Nova Scotia, Canada B3M 2J6. (902)443-4450. Editors: Susan Clark, Deborah Poff, Margaret Conrad. Magazine: 5½; 7½ pages; matt quality paper; glossy cover stock; b&w illustrations and photos. "Interdisciplinary women's studies journal, accepts feminist fiction and nonfiction in French and English for academics, people interested in feminism, students." Semiannually. "We would consider a special fiction issue in future." Estab. 1975. Circ. 800.
**Needs:** Feminist, historical (general) feminist, lesbian feminist, literary feminist, social/science feminist, science fiction feminist. No sexist, male-identified mss. Receives 20 unsolicited fiction mss/month. Accepts 3-4 mss/issue; 6-8 mss/year. Publishes ms 6 months after acceptance. Publishes short shorts. Critiques rejected mss. Recommends other markets.
**How to Contact:** Send complete ms with cover letter. Reports in 6-8 weeks. Photocopied submissions OK. Accepts computer printouts including dot-matrix. Sample copy free.
**Payment:** Pays in contributor's copies.
**Terms:** Sends pre-publication galleys to the author. Publication copyrighted.

**AURA Literary/Arts Review (II)**, University of Alabama in Birmingham, 117 Campbell, University Station, Birmingham AL 35294. (205)934-3216. Editor: Andrea Mathews. Magazine: 8½x8½; 100 pages; illustrations and photos. "We publish various types of fiction with an emphasis on short stories. Our audience is college students, the university community and literary-minded adults, the arts community." Semiannually. Special fiction issue in 1985. Estab. 1974. Circ. 1,000.
**Needs:** Literary, contemporary, science fiction, regional, romance, men's, women's, feminist, and ethnic (black). No mss longer than 7,000-8,000 words or pornographic material. Buys 2-3 mss/issue. Receives 15-20 unsolicited fiction mss each month. Length: 2,000-8,000 words.

Publishes short shorts; length according to editor's decision. Critiques rejected mss "when there is time."

**How to Contact:** Send complete ms with SASE. No simultaneous submissions; please include biographical information. Reports in 2 months. Publishes ms 1-2½ months after acceptance. Free sample copy with 9x12 SASE and 90¢ postage.

**Payment:** Free author's copies.

**Terms:** Pays on publication for first North American serial rights.

**Tips:** "If it's fiction and shows evidence of craft, we will consider it. Many writers try 'experimental' fiction before they have mastered the basics of telling a story. Many stories need tighter weave; stories with too many digressions are rejected; those that are grammatically sound with coherent themes and clear story lines yield high reader impact." Published new writers within the last year.

**AURORA, Speculative Feminism**, SF3, Society for the Furtherance & Study of Fantasy & Science Fiction, Box 1624, Madison WI 53701-1624. (608)233-0326. Head: Diane Martin. Magazine of "feminist-oriented science fiction and fantasy; fiction, poetry, articles, reviews, drawings, photographs and black and white art work for science fiction and fantasy fans and feminists." Published irregularly. Estab. 1975. Circ. 500.

**Needs:** Fantasy, feminist/lesbian, gay, humor/satire, literary, psychic/supernatural/occult, science fiction, serialized/excerpted novel, translations, and women's. "Send for a list of upcoming themes and guidelines for submissions before sending mss. Nothing over 5,000 words or mss having nothing to do with science fiction or fantasy." Receives 10 unsolicited fiction mss/month. Accepts 1-2 mss/issue, 3-6 mss/year. Length: no minimum, 5,000 words maximum, 3,000 words average. Occasionally critiques rejected mss.

**How to Contact:** Query first. Send complete ms with SASE. Simultaneous and photocopied submissions OK. Accepts computer printout submissions "as long as double spaced." Reports in 2 weeks on queries; 6-8 weeks on mss. Publishes ms from 2 months to 2 years after acceptance. Sample copy $4. Free guidelines.

**Payment:** 1 free contributor's copy.

**Terms:** Pays on publication for first North American serial rights. Publication copyrighted.

**Tips:** "Read a sample copy first. Make sure you know what kind of market you are sending to. Always enclose return postage. Feel free to send a follow-up if you haven't heard from us in two months."

**‡THE AZORIAN EXPRESS (II, IV)**, Seven Buffaloes Press, Box 249, Big Timber MT 59011. Editor: Art Cuelho. Newsletter: 8½x11; 8 pages; 60 lb book paper; 3-6 illustrations; photos rarely. "My overall theme is rural; I also focus on working people (the sweating professions); the American Indian and Hobo; the Dustbowl era; and I am also trying to expand with non-rural material. For rural and library and professor/student, blue collar workers, etc." Semiannually. Estab. 1985. Circ. 600.

**Needs:** Contemporary, ethnic, experimental, humor/satire, literary, regional, western, rural, working people. Receives 10-20 unsolicited mss/month. Accepts 2 or 3 mss/issue; 4-6 mss/year. Publishes ms 1-6 months after acceptance. 3% fiction agented. Length: 1,000-3,000 words. Also publishes short shorts (500-1,000 words; "I take what I like; length sometimes does not matter, even when longer than usual. I'm flexible." Recommends other markets.

**How to Contact:** "Cover letter with ms; general information, but it can be personal, more in line with the submitted story. Not long rambling letters." Reports in 1-4 weeks on queries; 1-4 weeks on mss. SASE for query and ms. Photocopied submissions OK. Accepts computer printouts including dot-matrix. Sample copy $1. Fiction guidelines "send stamped envelope for editor's reply."

**Payment:** Contributor's copies "depends on the amount of support author gives my press."

**Terms:** Pays on publication for first North American serial rights. "If I decide to use material in anthology form later—I have that right." Sends pre-publication galleys to the author upon request. Publication copyrighted.

**Tips:** "Style to me is what each individual develops on his or her own; if it is theirs . . . they are a writer, if not they are still play-acting with a pen. I have been a fiction writer for 22 years and a fiction editor and publisher for 12 years. There would not be magazines like mine if I was not optimistic. But literary optimism is a two way street. Without young fiction writers supporting fiction magazines . . . the future is bleak because the commercial magazines allow only formula or name writers within their pages. My own publications receive no grants. Sole support is from writers, libraries, and individuals."

**BA SHIRU (II, IV), Journal of African Languages and Literature**, Ba Shiru, 866 Van Hise Hall, University of Wisconsin, Madison WI 53706. (608)262-2487. Editor: Margaret Brualdi. Fiction Editors: Margaret Brualdi and Barbara Peters. Magazine: 6x9; 120 pages; 20 lb bond sulphite paper; 65 lb cover stock; b&w illustrations; b&w photos. "African themes only: scholarly articles, book reviews, fiction, poetry, short drama, and renderings of African oral narratives." Audience has "special interest in African topics; mainly academic." Semiannually. Published special fiction issue last year. Estab. 1970.
**Needs:** Short stories with African theme. Occasionally critiques rejected mss.
**How to Contact:** Query first or send complete ms. Reports in 2 weeks on queries; 6 weeks on mss. SASE for ms. Photocopied submissions OK. Accepts computer printout submissions. Prefers letter-quality. Publishes ms an average of 1 year after acceptance. Sample copy $3.
**Payment:** 2 contributor's copies; ½ price up to 10 extra copies.
**Terms:** Acquires first rights. Sometimes sends galleys to author. Publication copyrighted.
**Tips:** "We recently published a couple of original short stories which brought several positive responses. We hope to publish more short stories with African themes. We are interested in all aspects of African literature and wish to encourage creative as well as critical writing." Published new writers within the last year.

**‡BACKBONE MAGAZINE (II), A Journal of Women's Literature**, Backbone, Inc., Box 95315, Seattle WA 98145. (206)547-7173. Editor: Lauren Fortune/Melane Lohmann. Magazine: 5½x8½; 80-120 pages; excellent paper quality; 80 lb cover stock. "Feminist publication—we encourage women who have never been published to submit work that inspires poetic, feminist, spiritual and political dialogue." Semiannually. Estab. 1984. Circ. 1,000.
**Needs:** Contemporary, ethnic, experimental, feminist, lesbian, literary, regional, translations. "We're looking for new models for women. No violence or degradation." Receives 12 or more unsolicited mss/month. Accepts 15 or more mss/issue; 30 or more mss/year. Length: 2,000-4,000 words. Publishes essays, poems, and short shorts. Occasionally comments on rejected mss.
**How to Contact:** Send complete ms with cover letter and SASE. Reports in 4 weeks on queries; 1 month before publication on mss. SASE for query and ms. Simultaneous submissions and photocopied submissions OK. Accepts computer printouts. Sample copy $4.50; writer's guidelines free.
**Payment:** 1 contributor's copy. "If there is cash payment it varies depending on funding source."
**Terms:** Pays on publication. Publication copyrighted.
**Tips:** "Well-crafted stories are accepted. Good spelling is a must."

**BALL STATE UNIVERSITY FORUM (II)**, Ball State University, Muncie IN 47306. (317)285-8412. Editors: Frances M. Rippy and Bruce Hozeski. Magazine for "educated non-specialists." One issue a year devoted to fiction of all types. Quarterly. Estab. 1960. Circ. 600.
**Needs:** Adventure, condensed novel (30 pages or less), confession, contemporary, ethnic, experimental, fantasy, feminist, gothic/historical romance, historical/general, humor/satire, literary, mainstream, men's, prose poem, psychic/supernatural, religious/inspirational, romance (contemporary), science fiction, excerpted novel, suspense/mystery, translations, western, and women's. Receives 20 unsolicited fiction mss/month. Accepts 15 mss/year. Length: 200 words minimum, 6,000 words maximum, 4,000 words average. "Only occasionally" critiques rejected mss.
**How to Contact:** Send complete ms with SASE. Photocopied submissions OK. Accepts computer printout submissions. Prefers letter-quality. Reports in 4 months. Sample copy $2.50.

**Payment:** 3 free contributor's copies.
**Terms:** Pays on publication for all rights. Publication copyrighted.
**Tips:** "Send an original, polished story in a clean copy. If it is rejected, we tell you if the vote was close and suggest sending another. Read broadly, write carefully, revise painstakingly, submit mss persistently." Short stories from the *Forum* have been listed in the Houghton Mifflin edition of *Best American Short Stories* and reprinted in *Prize Stories O'Henry Awards*."

**B-CITY (II)**, B-City, Inc., 619 W. Surf, Chicago IL 60657. (312)871-6175. Editor: Connie Deanovich. Magazine: 8½x11; 75-80 pages; bond paper; glossy cover stock. Magazine of "innovative, city-inspired work for those interested in progressive writing." Annually. Plans special fiction issue. Estab. April 1984. Circ. 500.
**Needs:** Contemporary, ethnic, experimental, fantasy, feminist, gay, historical (general), horror, humor/satire, literary, prose poem, science fiction, and suspense/mystery. No romance, pornography, or political mss. Receives 10 unsolicited mss/month. Accepts 0-3 mss/issue. Publishes short shorts of 1-5 pages. Length: 1,000 words maximum.
**How to Contact:** Query first or send only 1-7 pages with brief bio. Reports within 6 weeks on queries; in 4 months on mss. SASE for query and ms. Photocopied submissions OK. Accepts computer printout submissions. Prefers letter-quality. Sample copy $4. Fiction guidelines for SASE.
**Payment:** 1 contributor's copy; $4 charge for extras.
**Terms:** Acquires one-time rights.
**Tips:** "We are interested in *all* fresh writing. Beginners are welcome here."

‡**BEATNIKS FROM SPACE (II), (A Book You Can Really Shake Your Head At)**, The Neither/Nor Press, Box 8043, Ann Arbor MI 48107. Editors: Denis McBee, Jock Henderson. Magazine: 7x8½; 48 pages; varied cover stock; illustrations; photos. Saddle-stitched. "We seek a literature that speaks to the modern mind . . . whammy whip-snake wheeze cleverly disguised as intelligent writing . . . outrageous texts that drive hot pointed needles smack dab through the middle of your mind. . . ." Bimonthly. Published special fiction issue last year. Estab. 1980. Circ. 600.
**Needs:** Receives 20-30 short-story mss/month. Accepts 3-4 fiction mss/issue; 20 mss/year. Length: 250-1,500 words average; 2,500 words maximum. Publishes short shorts.
**How to Contact:** Reports in 4 weeks on queries; 4 months on mss. SASE necessary with background information on author. Simultaneous and photocopied submissions OK. Accepts computer-printout submissions; prefers letter-quality over dot-matrix. Sample copy $3.50.
**Payment:** 1 free contributor's copy.
**Terms:** Acquires one-time rights upon acceptance; all other rights revert to the author upon publication.
**Tips:** "Keep at it . . . persistence and lots of practice do pay off. We like to read and write fiction, and so does our audience." Published new writers within the last year.

**THE BELLINGHAM REVIEW (II)**, 412 N. State St., Bellingham WA 98225. Fiction Editor: Knute Skinner. Magazine: 8x5½; 64 pages; 60 lb white paper; varied cover stock; photos. "A literary magazine featuring original short stories, novel excerpts, short plays, and poetry of palpable quality." Semiannually. Estab. 1977. Circ. 700.
**Needs:** Literary, contemporary, psychic/supernatural/occult, regional, science fiction, fantasy, horror, feminist, gay/lesbian, erotica, gothic, mystery, humor, ethnic, serialized novels, and translations. Buys 1-2 mss/issue. Publishes short shorts. Submission period: September 15 to June 1. Length: 5,000 words. Critiques rejected mss "when there is time."
**How to Contact:** Send complete ms. Reports in 2 months. Publishes ms an average of 1 year after acceptance. Sample copy $2.
**Payment:** 2 free author's copies plus 2-issue subscription. $1.50 for extras.
**Terms:** Acquires first North American serial and one-time rights. Publication copyrighted.
**Tips:** Mss are rejected for various reasons, "but the most common problem is too much *telling* and not enough *showing* of crucial details and situations." Published new writers within the last year.

‡**BELLOWING ARK (II), A Literary Tabloid**, Bellowing Ark Society, Box 45637, Seattle WA 98145. (206)545-8302. Editor: R.R. Ward. Tabloid: 11½x16; 12-24 pages; electro-brite paper; electro-brite cover stock; illustrations; photos. "We publish material which we feel addresses the human situation in an affirmative way. We do not publish academic fiction. We address anyone who can respond to what we publish." Bimonthly. Plans special fiction issue. Estab. 1984. Circ. 500.

**Needs:** Contemporary, literary, mainstream, serialized/excerpted novel. "Anything we publish will be true." Receives 12-20 unsolicited fiction mss/year. Accepts 1-2 mss/issue; 7-12 mss/year. Time varies, but publishes ms not longer than 6 months after acceptance. Length: 3,000-5,000 words average. Publishes short shorts. Critiques rejected mss. Recommends other markets.

**How to Contact:** Send complete ms with cover letter and short bio. Reports in 2 weeks on queries; 6 weeks on mss. SASE for ms. Sample copy for 9x12 SAE and 2 first class stamps. Fiction guidelines for 9x12 SAE and 2 first class stamps.

**Payment:** Pays in contributor's copies.

**Terms:** Pays on publication. Acquires first rights. Publication copyrighted.

**Tips:** "We are trying to offer a venue. Most material is rubbish. Good writing will always find an outlet. The myth of the overlooked genius is great copy but poor history."

‡**BELOIT FICTION JOURNAL (II)**, Box 11, Beloit College WI 53511. (608)365-3391. Editor: Clint McCown. Magazine: 6x9; 104 pages; illustrations rarely; photos rarely. "We are interested in publishing the best contemporary fiction and are open to all themes except those involving pornographic, religiously dogmatic or politically propagandistic representations. Our magazine is for general readership, though most of our readers will probably have a specific interest in literary magazines." Semiannaully. Estab. 1985.

**Needs:** Contemporary, literary, mainstream. No pornography, religious dogma, political propaganda. Receives 75 unsolicited fiction mss/month. Accepts 8-10 mss/issue; 16-20 mss/year. Does not read mss in summer. Publishes ms within 6 months after acceptance. Length: 5,000 words average; 2,500 words minimum; 10,000 words maximum. Critiques rejected mss. Recommends other markets.

**How to Contact:** Send complete ms with cover letter. Reports in 1 week on queries; 2-4 weeks on mss. SASE for ms. Simultaneous and photocopied submissions OK, if identified as such. Accepts computer printouts including dot-matrix. Sample copy $5. Fiction guidelines free for business envelope and 1 first class stamp.

**Tips:** "We believe the short story is an important art form and hope to contribute to its survival in the marketplace. Read the contemporary masters; Ray Carver, Bobbie Ann Mason, etc. Better yet, buy literary magazines and get a cross-section of what is working well in contemporary fiction."

**BIFROST**, Southern Circle Press, Box 1180, Milford DE 19963. (302)335-4848. Editor: Ann Wilson. Magazine: 8½x11; 100 pages; 20 lb bond paper; 90 lb cover stock; illustrations. Magazine of "experimental science fiction and fantasy with an eye to material that would not be found in pro publications. New authors who are willing to tread fresh ground; no safe plots in which the reader receives nothing for the effort he/she has put forth. We have readership of all ages, but with a taste for the innovative." Quarterly. Estab. 1978. Circ. 1,500.

**Needs:** Science fiction and fantasy, including humorous/satirical. No X- or hard R-rated material. Receives 20-30 unsolicited fiction mss/month. Accepts 6-8 mss/issue, 30 mss/year. Publishes ms 3-9 months after acceptance. Occasionally recommends markets.

**How to Contact:** Send complete ms with SASE. Photocopied submissions OK. Accepts computer printout submissions. Prefers letter-quality. Reports in 3-4 weeks. Sample copy $5.50. Free fiction guidelines with business-sized SASE.

**Payment:** Free contributor's copies (number depends on length of piece).

**Terms:** Pays on publication for one-time rights. Publication copyrighted.

**Tips:** "Tell a good, original story with characters who involve the reader. Get the mechanics right: Format, spelling, punctuation, etc., that are incorrect detract from the content of the story, sometimes badly enough to cause rejection in themselves."

‡**BIG TWO-HEARTED**, Mid-Peninsula Library Cooperative, 424 Stephenson Ave., Iron Mountain MI 49801. (906)774-3005. Editor: Gary Silver. Magazine: 9x6; 50 pages; 20 white bond paper; 60 wt. bristol cover stock. General magazine. Frequently (spring, winter, fall). Estab. Oct. 1985. Circ. 200.
**Needs:** Experimental, humor/satire, literary, translations from Spanish. No profanity, erotica. Receives 3 unsolicited fiction mss/month. Accepts 1 or 2 stories/issue. Length: 2,500 words average; 750 words minimum; 5,000 words maximum. Occasionally critiques rejected mss.
**How to Contact:** Send complete manuscript. Reports in 3 months on mss. SASE for ms. No simultaneous or photocopied submissions; reprints OK if credited. No computer printouts. Sample copy $3 and 8¾x11¼ SAE and 1 first class stamp.
**Payment:** 2 contributor's copies.
**Terms:** Acquires one-time rights. Publication copyrighted.
**Tips:** "For the reason that many commercial markets no longer are available for the neophyte author, we've chosen to publish fiction. We are biased toward fiction. Also, there are few places to publish the long piece of 'short' fiction—we'll consider these. Write simple, entertaining stories—do not write self-serving confessions or substitute letters addressed to your own ego. Our audience, though small, considers reading to be a supreme pleasure—don't bore them with yourself."

**BILINGUAL REVIEW (II, IV)**, Bilingual Review Press, Box M, Campus Post Office, SUNY—Binghamton, Binghamton NY 13901. (607)724-9495. Editor-in-Chief: Gary D. Keller. Magazine of US Hispanic life: poetry, short stories, other prose, and theater. Published 3 times/year. Estab. 1974. Circ. 2,000.
**Needs:** US Hispanic creative literature. "We accept material in English or Spanish. We publish original work only—no translations." US/Hispanic themes only. Receives 50 unsolicited fiction mss/month. Accepts 3 mss/issue, 9 mss/year. Often critiques rejected mss.
**How to Contact:** Send 2 copies of complete ms with SAE and loose stamps. Simultaneous and high-quality photocopied submissions OK. Reports in 4 weeks on mss. Publishes ms an average of 1 year after acceptance. Sample copy $6.
**Payment:** 2 contributor's copies. 30% discount for extras.
**Terms:** Acquires all rights (50% of reprint permission fee given to author as matter of policy). Publication copyrighted.
**Tips:** "Write about events reinforced by deep personal experience or knowledge."

**BLACK JACK (II)**, Seven Buffaloes Press, Box 249, Big Timber MT 59011. Editor: Art Cuelho. "Main theme: Rural. Publishes material on the American Indian, farm and ranch, American hobo, the common working man, folklore, the Southwest, Okies, Montana, humor, Central California, etc. for people who make their living off the land. The writers write about their roots, experiences and values they receive from the American soil." Annually. Estab. 1973. Circ. 750.
**Needs:** Literary, contemporary, western, adventure, humor, American Indian, American hobo, and parts of novels and long short stories. "Anything that strikes me as being amateurish, without depth, without craft, I refuse. Actually I'm not opposed to any kind of writing if the author is genuine and has spent his lifetime dedicated to the written word." Buys 5-10 mss/year. Receives approximately 10-15 unsolicited fiction mss/month. Length: 3,500-5,000 words (there can be exceptions).
**How to Contact:** Query for current theme with SASE. Reports in 1 week on queries, 2 weeks on mss. Sample copy $4.
**Payment:** Pays 1-2 author's copies.
**Terms:** Acquires first North American serial rights and reserves the right to reprint material in an anthology or future *Black Jack* publications. Publication copyrighted. Rights revert to author after publication.
**Tips:** "Enthusiasm should be matched with skill as a craftsman. That's not saying that we don't continue to learn, but every writer must have enough command of the language to compete with other proven writers. Save postage by writing first to the editor to find out his needs. A small press magazine always has specific needs at any given time. I sometimes accept material from country

writers that aren't all that good at punctuation and grammar but make up for it with life's experience. This is not a highbrow publication; it belongs to the salt-of-the-earth people."

**THE BLACK SCHOLAR,** The Black World Foundation, Box 7106, San Francisco CA 94120. (415)541-0311. Editor: Robert Chrisman. Magazine on black culture, research and black studies for Afro-Americans, college graduates and students. "We are also widely read by teachers, professionals, and intellectuals, and are required reading for many black and Third World Studies." Bimonthly. Estab. 1969. Circ. 10,000.
**Needs:** Literary, contemporary, men's, women's, juvenile, young adult and ethnic. No religious/inspirational, psychic, etc. Receives approximately 75 unsolicited fiction mss each month. Sometimes recommends markets. Length: 2,000-5,000 words.
**How to Contact:** Query with clips of published work with SASE. Reports in 3 weeks on queries, 1 month on mss. Free sample copy with SASE.
**Payment:** 12 author's copies.
**Terms:** Pays on publication for all rights. Publication copyrighted.

**BLACK WARRIOR REVIEW (II),** Box 2936, University AL 35486. (205)348-4518. Editor-in-Chief: Chief: Lynn Domina. Fiction Editor: Tom Chiarella. "We publish contemporary fiction, poetry, reviews, essays, and interviews for a literary audience." Semiannually. Estab. 1974. Circ. 1,300-2,000.
**Needs:** Contemporary, experimental, literary, mainstream, and prose poem. No types that are clearly "types." Receives 75 unsolicited fiction mss/month. Accepts 5 mss/issue, 10 mss/year. Approximately 25% of fiction is agented. Length: 7,500 words maximum; 3,000-5,000 words average. Occasionally critiques rejected mss.
**How to Contact:** Send complete ms with SASE. Photocopied submissions OK. Reports in 2 months. Publishes ms 2-3 months after acceptance. Sample copy $3.50. Free fiction guidelines for SAE and 1 first class stamp.
**Payment:** $10/page and 2 contributor's copies. "We began paying by the page in early 1985."
**Terms:** Pays on publication. Publication copyrighted.
**Tips:** "Send only your best work, after reviewing past issue(s). We are not a good bet for 'commercial' fiction. Each year the *Black Warrior Review* will award $500 to a fiction writer whose work has been published in either the fall or spring issue of the *BWR* to be announced in the fall issue. Regular submission deadlines are Oct. 1 for fall issue, Feb. 1 for spring issue.

**THE BLOOMSBURY REVIEW (II),** Owaissa Publishing Co., Box 8928. Denver CO 80201. (303)455-0593. Editor-in-Chief: Tom Auer. Fiction Editor: John Roberts. "*The Bloomsbury Review* is a book magazine. We publish book reviews, essays, poetry, and interviews with book-related persons." 10 issues/year. Estab. 1980. Circ. 10,000.
**Needs:** Contemporary, literary, and mainstream.
**How to Contact:** Send complete ms with SASE. Simultaneous and photocopied submissions OK. Reports in 2 months on queries and mss. Sample copy $2.50 with 8x10 SASE and 70¢ postage. Guidelines for legal-sized envelope and 1 first class stamp.
**Payment:** $5-25; $10/year subscription to magazine and 10 free contributor's copies.
**Terms:** Pays on publication for first rights. Rights revert back to writer. Publication copyrighted.
**Tips:** "Can be experimental or traditional. The bottom line is good quality writing."

**BLUELINE (II, IV),** Blue Mountain Lake NY 12812. (518)352-7365. Editor-in-Chief: Alice Gilborn. Magazine: 6x9; 56 pages; 70 lb white stock paper; 65 lb smooth cover stock; illustrations; photos. "*Blueline* is interested in quality writing about the Adirondacks or other places similar in geography and spirit. We publish fiction, poetry, personal essays, book reviews, and oral history for those interested in the Adirondacks, nature in general, and well-crafted writing." Semiannually. Estab. 1979. Circ. 700.
**Needs:** Adventure, contemporary, humor/satire, literary, prose poem, regional, reminiscences, oral history, and nature/outdoors. Receives 4-6 unsolicited fiction mss/month. Accepts 3-4 mss/issue, 6-8 mss/year. Does not read May-July; November-January. Length: 500 words minimum;

2,500 words maximum; 2,200 words average. Occasionally critiques rejected mss. Sometimes recommends other markets.
**How to Contact:** Send complete ms with SASE and brief bio. Photocopied submissions OK. Submit mss Feb. 1-Apr.15; Aug. 1-Oct. 15. Accepts computer printout submissions. Prefers letter-quality. Reports in 2-10 weeks. Publishes ms 2-10 months after acceptance. Sample copy $2.75. Free fiction guidelines for 5x10 SASE with 1 first class stamp.
**Payment:** 1 contributor's copy plus 1 year subscription. $1.75 each for 3 or more extra copies; $2 each for less than 3.
**Terms:** Pays on publication for first rights. Publication copyrighted.
**Tips:** "We look for concise, clear, concrete prose that tells a story and touches upon a universal theme or situation. We prefer realism to romanticism but will consider nostalgia if well done. Pay attention to grammar and syntax. Avoid murky language, sentimentality, cuteness or folksiness. We would like to see more good fiction related to the Adirondacks. Please include short biography and word count. If manuscript has potential, we work with author to improve and reconsider for publication. Our readers prefer fiction to poetry (in general) or reviews. Write from your own experience, be specific and factual (within the bounds of your story) and if you write about universal features such as love, death, change, etc., write about them in a fresh way. Triteness and mediocracy are the hallmarks of the majority of stories seen today." Published new writers within the last year.

**BOGG (II), A Magazine of British & North American Writing**, Bogg Publications, 422 N. Cleveland St., Arlington VA 22201. (703)243-6019. US Editor: John Elsberg. Magazine: 8½x11; 60-64 pages; 50 lb white paper; 50 lb cover stock; line art illustrations. "American and British poetry, short fiction, reviews, and essays on small press." Published 3 times a year. Estab. 1968. Circ. 600.
**Needs:** Comics, contemporary, erotica, experimental, humor/satire, literary, prose poem, and science fiction. Nothing over 5 typewritten pages. Receives 25 unsolicited fiction mss/month. Accepts 2-3 mss/issue; 6-8 mss/year. Publishes short shorts of 1-5 pages. Length: 1,000 words average. Occasionally critiques rejected mss.
**How to Contact:** Query first or send complete ms with SASE. Photocopied submissions OK. Accepts computer printout submissions. Prefers letter-quality. Reports in 1 week on queries; 2 weeks on mss. Publishes ms 6-12 months after acceptance. Sample copy $2.50.
**Payment:** 2 contributor's copies. Reduced charge for extras.
**Terms:** Acquires one-time rights. Publication copyrighted.
**Tips:** "Read magazine first. We are most interested in work of experimental or humorous nature. Good fiction can be short fiction. Many mixed mags have no room for shorts." Published new writers within the last year.

**‡BOGUS REVIEW (II)**, Bogus Books, #10A, 120 West 97th St., New York NY 10025. Editor: Kirk McElhearn. Fiction Editor: Jay Goldberg. Magazine: 5½x8½; 40-44 pages; 20 lb stock paper; 110 lb/raw cover stock; illustrations (b&w encouraged); photos. "Literary experimental, contemporary, with a hint of humor/satire" for open-minded, literary audience. Annually. Plans to publish a special fiction issue. Estab. 1983. Circ. 50-300.
**Needs:** Contemporary, experimental, fantasy, humor/satire, literary, science fiction, translations. No work over 3,000 words. Receives 2-10 unsolicited mss/month. Accepts 3-6 mss/issue. Does not read June-September. Publishes ms 3-9 months after acceptance. Length: 800-1,000 average; 3,000 words maximum. Publishes short shorts of approximately 600 words. Critiques rejected ms. "Brief, may pertain to our wants and needs more than writers attributes and style."
**How to Contact:** Send complete ms with cover letter. Reports in 3 weeks on queries; 3 months on mss. SASE for ms. Photocopied submissions OK. Accepts computer printouts including dot-matrix. Sample copy for $1 and 6x9 or 8½x11 SASE. Fiction guidelines for any size envelope and 22¢ stamp (in US).
**Payment:** Pays in contributor's copies.
**Terms:** Acquires first North American serial rights and anthology rights. Publication copyrighted.

**Tips:** "Our magazine contains a mix of poetry, art and short-short fiction. Short stories, of which we have not received many, provide a necessary balance to our 40-48 page yearly publication. They in fact are highlighted (more or less) in a given issue due to our small size."

**BOSTON REVIEW (II)**, Boston Critic Inc., 33 Harrison Ave., Boston MA 02111. Publisher: Margaret Ann Roth. Managing Editor: Matthew Gilbert. "A bimonthly magazine of the arts and culture." Tabloid: 11x17"; 32-48 pages; jet paper. Estab. 1975. Circ. 10,000.
**Needs:** Contemporary, ethnic, experimental, humor/satire, literary, mainstream, regional, serialized/excerpted novel, and translations. Receives 100 plus unsolicited fiction mss/month. Buys 4-6 mss/year. Approximately 25-35% of fiction is agented. Length: 3,000 words maximum; 2,000 words average. Publishes short shorts. Occasionally critiques rejected ms.
**How to Contact:** Send complete ms with SASE. Simultaneous and photocopied mss OK. Accepts computer printout submissions. Reports in 2-3 months on mss. Publishes ms an average of 6 months after acceptance. Sample copy $3.
**Payment:** $50-200 and 2 contributor's copies.
**Terms:** Pays on publication for first rights, second serial (reprint) rights, one-time rights and assignments on work-for-hire basis. Publication copyrighted.
**Tips:** "We believe that original fiction is an important part of our culture—and that this should be represented by the *Boston Review*. There seems to be a dearth of high quality short fiction, which leaves this as a major opening for new fiction writers." Recently published new unpublished writers.

**BOTH SIDES NOW, An Alternative Journal of New Age/Aquarian Transformations (II)**, Free People Press, Rt. 6, Box 28, Tyler TX 75704. (214)592-4263. Editor-in-Chief: Elihu Edelson. Magazine. Estab. 1969. Circ. 2,000.
**Needs:** Fantasy, feminist, humor/satire ("including political"), psychic/supernatural, and religious/inspirational ("much preferred"), fables, parables. "No violence (including S/M), prurience (pornography), or fascistic views." Receives various number unsolicited fiction mss/month. Accepts various number mss/issue. Length: "about 4 magazine pages at most." Occasionally critiques rejected mss with "brief note."
**How to Contact:** Send complete ms with SASE. Simultaneous submissions, photocopied submissions and previously published work OK. Reports in 3 months on mss. Sample copy 75¢.
**Payment:** 6 free contributor's copies. Charges 75¢ each for extra copies.
**Terms:** Pays on publication. "Authors retain rights." Publication copyrighted.
**Tips:** "Heed our editorial interests."

**BOTTOMFISH MAGAZINE (II)**, Bottomfish Press, Language Arts Division, De Anza College, 21250 Steven Creek Blvd., Cupertino CA 95014. (408)996-4550. Editor-in-Chief: Frank Berry. Magazine: 7x8½; 50-100 pages; b&w high contrast illustrations and photos. "Contemporary poetry, fiction (under 5,000 words), excerpts of novels, black and white graphics and photos for literary and writing community." Annually. Estab. 1976. Circ. 500.
**Needs:** Experimental, literary, and prose poem. "Literary excellence is our only criteria. We will consider all subjects except pornography." Receives 3-5 unsolicited fiction mss/month. Accepts 2-3 mss/issue. Does not read mss in summer. Length: 500 words minimum; 5,000 words maximum; 2,500 words average.
**How to Contact:** Send complete ms with cover letter, brief bio and SASE. Photocopied submissions OK but no multiple submissions or reprints. Accepts computer printout submissions. Prefers letter-quality. Reports in 6 weeks on queries and mss. Publishes ms an average of 6 months-1 year after acceptance. Sample copy for 8x10 envelope and 2 first class stamps.
**Payment:** 2 free contributor's copies. Charges $3 for extra copies.
**Terms:** Acquires one-time rights.
**Tips:** "Strive for orginality and high level of craft; avoid cliched or stereotyped characters and plots. We don't print slick, commercial fiction, regardless of quality." Published new writers within the last year.

**BOX 749 (I)**, The Printable Arts Society, Inc., Box 749, Old Chelsea Station, New York NY 10113. Editor: David Ferguson. "We publish fiction and poetry of every length and any theme; satire, belles-lettres, plays, music, and any artwork reproducible by photo-offset. We have no particular stylistic or ideological bias. *Box 749* is directed to people of diverse backgrounds, education, income and age—an audience not necessarily above or underground. Such an audience is consistent with our belief that literature (plus art and music) is accessible to and even desired by a larger and more varied portion of society than has generally been acknowledged." Annually. Estab. 1972. Circ. 5,000.

**Needs:** Literary, contemporary, fantasy, humor, and translations. "Fiction in any of the categories here could be art. If so, we would consider it for publication. We ask that all translations be accompanied by 'translation history' of the work: Has this work ever been translated into English? If so, when? By whom? Where did the translation appear?" Receives approximately 15 unsolicited fiction mss/month. Buys 10-15 mss/issue. Critiques rejected mss "when there is time," Occasionally suggests other markets.

**How to Contact:** Send complete ms with SASE. Accepts computer printout submissions. Prefers letter-quality. Reports in up to 3 months or longer on ms depending on length. Publishes ms an average of 1 year after acceptance. Sample copy $3.25 for mail orders.

**Payment:** Author's copies. Charge for extras: regular $2.50 cover price unless buying in bulk.

**Terms:** Acquires all rights, but "we reassign rights to author after publication." Publication copyrighted.

**Tips:** Mss are rejected because of "lack of imagination for character, not well written or not about anything that is worth sharing with the general public. Readers are often surprised at how much they enjoy the stories. There's a tendency toward details that distract from real movement of stories. We notice a lack of depth and real humor."

**‡BREATHLESS MAGAZINE (II)**, Breathless Magazine, Inc., 910 Broad St., Endicott NY 13760. (607)785-7790. Editor: Ronald Joseph. Fiction Editor: Dorinda Trumble. Magazine: 8½x11; 50-55 pages; 10 lb white paper; 20 lb glossy cover stock; illustrations; photos. Theme: Reflects the exhilaration and freshness of life through new points of view or interesting aspects of literary style. Material published: short fiction, literary/political essays, poetry, cartoons, photos, art. Literary/semi-literary. Annually. Plans special fiction issue. Estab. 1985. Circ. 500.

**Needs:** Adventure, contemporary, ethnic, experimental, historical (general), humor/satire, literary, translations. No "catchy" or gimmicky kinds of stories. "Be sincere and true to life or don't bother to send us your work." Receives 10 unsolicited mss/month. Accepts 3 mss/issue. Does not read mss June-August. Publishing ms depends on editorial needs at the time. Length: 2,000 words average; 500 words minimum; 4,000 words maximum. Publishes short shorts of 500-1,000 words. Critiques rejected mss.

**How to Contact:** Send complete ms with "cover letter of other published works, return address (with postage); how he/she found out about our magazine. Brief bio information." Reports in 4-6 weeks on queries; 3-8 weeks on mss. SASE for ms. Photocopied submissions and reprints OK. Accepts computer printouts including dot-matrix. Accepts electronic submissions via disc if compatible with IBM XT with 256 KB memory. Sample $2. Fiction guidelines free.

**Payment:** Pays in contributor's copies; charge for extras.

**Terms:** Acquires first North American serial rights. Rights revert to author on publication. Publication copyrighted.

**Tips:** "We see some rather well done manuscripts from time to time. We just hope that in the future the situation will favor the more serious writer. We can be very optimistic to the beginning fiction writer; their ideas are usually the freshest."

**BRILLIANT STAR/CHILD'S WAY (II)**, National Spiritual Assembly of the Baha'is of the US, 5010 Austin Rd., Chattanooga TN 37343. (615)875-5443. Editor: Deborah L. Bley. "Children's magazine: 8½x11; 133 pages; matte paper; slick cover; b&w illustrations and photos. Promotes such principles of the Baha'i faith as harmony of races, religions and nationalities, equality of sexes." For children, ages 5-12. Bimonthly. Estab. 1968. Circ. 2,000.

**Needs:** Preschool and juvenile. "Especially appreciate material emphasizing values, though nondidactic in tone." No "preachy or superstitious stories; or too great emphasis on unpleasant truths." Receives 30 unsolicited fiction mss/month. Accepts 1-2 mss/issue; 6-12 mss/year. Length: 100 words minimum; 1,200 words maximum; 800 words average.
**How to Contact:** Send complete ms with SASE. Simultaneous and photocopied submissions OK. Accepts computer printout submissions. Prefers letter-quality. Reports in 6-8 weeks on mss. Recommends other markets. Publishes ms no sooner than 6-8 months after acceptance. Sample copy for 11x14 SAE and 88¢ postage.
**Payment:** "We make no payments; all manuscripts are considered donations."
**Terms:** "Writers can secure and retain copyright if they choose to, otherwise it reverts to us." Publication copyrighted.
**Tips:** "Keep trying. Fiction we feel is a potent vehicle for reaching children." Published new writers in the last year.

**BROOMSTICK (II), A Periodical by, for, and About Women Over Forty**, 3543 18th St., San Francisco CA 94110. (415)552-7460. Editors: Mickey Spencer and Polly Taylor. "Our first priority in selecting and editing material is that it convey clear images of older women that are positive, that it take a stand against the denigration of older women which pervades our culture, and that it offer us alternatives which will make our lives better." For "women over forty interested in being part of a network which will help us all develop understanding of our life situations and acquire the skills to improve them." Bimonthly. Estab. 1978. Circ. 3,000.
**Needs:** Humor, ethnic, feminist experience in political context, senior citizen/retirement, and women's. No mss of "romantic love, saccharine acceptance, about men or young women." Receives 10 unsolicited fiction mss/month. Accepts 2-3 mss/issue; 20 mss/year. Recommends magazine subscription before reading ms. Occasionally critiques rejected mss.
**How to Contact:** Send complete mss with SASE. Simultaneous, photocopied and previously published submissions OK. Accepts computer printout submissions. Prefers letter-quality. Accepts disc submissions compatible with 8" SD CP/M WordStar. Prefers hard copy with disc submissions. Reports in 3 months on queries and mss. Sample copy for $3.50. Fiction guidelines for $2.50.
**Payment:** 2 free contributor's copies; $3 charge for extras.
**Tips:** "Read our writer's packet." Published new writers within the last year.

**BUFF**, S.U.N.Y. at Buffalo, Dept. of English, 306 Clemens Hall, Buffalo NY 14260. (716)636-2570. Fiction Co-Editors: Edmund Cardoni and Alan Bigelow. Magazine of "artful and entertaining fiction and poetry inclined towards the avant garde for literate readers, other writers, and the university community." Semiannually. Estab. 1981. Circ. 500.
**Needs:** Contemporary, experimental, and excerpted novel. No "formula fiction of any kind." Receives "a large number of fiction mss but it varies each month." Accepts 10 mss/issue. Length: no minimum; 3,600 words maximum; 1,250-1,500 words average. Occasionally critiques rejected mss.
**How to Contact:** Send complete ms with cover letter and "short bio" with SASE. Photocopied submissions OK. Accepts computer printout submissions. Prefers letter-quality. Reports in 3 months on mss. Sample copy for SAE and 4 first class stamps.
**Payment:** 2 free contributor's copies; postage charge for more than 2 copies.
**Terms:** Acquires first rights, one-time rights. Publication copyrighted.
**Tips:** "Readers are excited, enthusiastic, and critical of short stories. Expect a critical reading by graduate student editors at a university English department renowned for its celebrated (and predominantly avant garde) faculty of writers and critics."

**BYLINE**, McCarville Publications, Box 30647, Midwest City OK 73140. (405)733-1129. Editor-in-Chief: Mike McCarville. Magazine for the "encouragement of writers and poets, with emphasis on inspiring beginners." Monthly. Estab. 1981. Circ. 3,100.
**Needs:** Literary, suspense/mystery, and "short stories with a writing or literary twist or setting."

No science fiction. Receives 400 unsolicited fiction mss/month. Accepts 2-3 mss/issue, 60-75 mss/year. Length: 3,500 words maximum, 2,500 words average. Occasionally critiques rejected mss.

**How to Contact:** Send complete ms with SASE. Photocopied submissions OK. "All fiction must be original and unpublished previously." Reports in 6-8 weeks on mss. Publishes ms 3-9 months after acceptance. Sample copy $2.75. Fiction guidelines for #10 envelope and 1 first class stamp.

**Payment:** $60-200. 1 free contributor's copy; $2.75 for extras. Offers 50% kill fee on articles only.

**Terms:** Pays on acceptance for first rights. Publication copyrighted.

**Tips:** "Try us, work with us, don't get discouraged, and never quit. Study the magazine. Submit a professional manuscript with SASE; story line must be strong, include a writing or literary twist and have an ending (surprise preferred)." Sponsors short story and poetry contests several times a year.

**CACHE REVIEW (II)**, Cache Press, Box 3505, Tucson AZ 85722. (602)748-0600. Editor: Steven Brady. Magazine: 8½x11; 50 pages; 24 lb bond paper; classic laid cover stock. Magazine which publishes "quality writing of all styles and modes for anyone interested in good writing." Semiannually. Estab. 1982. Circ. 200-500.

**Needs:** Experimental, fantasy, feminist, gay, historical (general), horror, humor/satire, lesbian, mainstream, prose poem, psychic/supernatural/occult, regional, romance, senior citizen/retirement, science fiction, serialized/excerpted novel, suspense/mystery, and translations. "We will look at anything. The only criterion is excellence." Receives 10-20 unsolicited fiction mss/month. Accepts 3-6 mss/issue, 6-12 mss/year. Does not read June-August. Approximately 10% of fiction is agented. Length: 10,000 words maximum. Publishes short shorts. Recommends other markets.

**How to Contact:** Send complete ms with SASE and cover letter with short bio and example of publication history. Photocopied submissions OK, "but we prefer the original." Accepts computer printout submissions. Prefers letter-quality. Reports in 2 weeks on mss. Publishes ms 6-12 months after acceptance. Sample copy $2 with 9x12 envelope and 4 first class stamps. Fiction guidelines free with legal-sized envelope and 1 first class stamp.

**Payment:** 2 free contributor's copies; $1.50 charge for extras.

**Terms:** Pays on publication for all rights. Publication copyrighted. "Cash awards may be presented for the best pieces of fiction and/or poetry in each issue."

**Tips:** "Send your best. We are looking for excellence and authenticity of voice. Give us an honest story, not one manipulated for a specific market. Don't play any games. Tell the story truthfully and honestly and get out. Don't be afraid to experiment, but remember that editors have seen all the tricks. Listen to your voice; learn to trust it." Published new writers within the last year.

**CALIFORNIA QUARTERLY**, 100 Sproul Hall, U.C. Davis, Davis CA 95616. Editor: Elliot L. Gilbert. Fiction Editor: Nixa Schell. Magazine for fiction, poetry, and graphics. Estab. January 1985.

**Needs:** Contemporary, experimental, and literary. Receives approximately 300 mss/month. Length: 8,000 words average.

**How to Contact:** Send complete manuscript. Reports in 4-6 weeks on mss. SASE. Photocopied submissions OK. Accepts computer printout submissions. Prefers letter-quality. Sample copy free for $2 and 50¢ postage.

**Payment:** $3/page and 2 contributor's copies.

**Terms:** Pays on publication for first North American serial rights. Publication copyrighted.

**Tips:** "Read publication thoroughly before submitting a manuscript."

**CALLALOO (II, IV), A Journal of Afro-American and African Arts and Letters**, Callaloo/Callaloo Poetry Series, Callaloo Fiction Series, Dept. of English, University of Kentucky, Lexington KY 40506-0027. (606)257-6984. Editor: Charles H. Rowell. Magazine: 7x10; 200

pages. Scholarly magazine. Triannually. Plans special fiction issue in future. Estab. 1976. Circ. 1,000.

**Needs:** Contemporary, ethnic (black culture), feminist, historical (general), humor/satire, literary, prose poem, regional, science fiction, serialized/excerpted novel, translations, and women's. Accepts 3-5 mss/issue; 10-20 mss/year. Length: 2,500 words average.

**How to Contact:** Submit complete ms and cover letter with name and address. Reports on queries in 2 weeks; 2-3 months on mss. Simultaneous, photocopied and previously published work "occasionally" OK. Accepts computer printout submissions. Prefers letter-quality or dot-matrix. Sample copy $5.

**Payment:** Contributor's copies.

**Terms:** Acquires all rights. Sends galleys to author. Publication copyrighted.

**Tips:** "Submit clean copy—finished work with serious literary intent."

**CALLIOPE (II, IV)**, Creative Writing Program, Roger Williams College, Bristol, RI 02809. (401)253-1040, ext 2217. Advisory Editor: Martha Christina. Magazine: 5½x8½; 40-56 pages; 50 lb offset paper; vellum or 60 lb cover stock; occasional illustrations; occasional photos. "We are an eclectic little magazine publishing contemporary poetry, fiction, interviews, and occasionaly reviews of other little magazines for those who appreciate fine contemporary writing." Semiannually. Estab. December 1977. Circ. 300.

**Needs:** Literary, contemporary, experimental/innovative. "We are now doing thematic issues and writers should query with SASE for current needs. We try to include 3 pieces of fiction in each issue." Receives approximately 10-20 unsolicited fiction mss each month. Does not read mss mid-March to mid-August. Length: 3,750 words. Publishes short shorts under 15 pages. Critiques rejected mss "when there is time."

**How to Contact:** Send complete ms with SASE. Reports immediately to 3 months on mss. Sample copy $1.

**Payment:** 2 free author's copies and year's subscription beginning with following issue. $1 charge for extras.

**Terms:** Rights revert to author on publication. Publication copyrighted.

**Tips:** "We are not interested in reading anyone's very first story. If the piece is good it will be given careful consideration. Reading a sample copy of *Calliope* is recommended." Mss are rejected because of "poor characterization, too much summary narration, not enough dialogue. Concentrate on telling a story with interesting, engaging characters and believable dialogue. Episodic is fine; story need not (for our publication) have traditional beginning, middle and end." Published new writers within the last year.

**CALLI'S TALES (I, II)**, Box 1224, Palmetto FL 33561. (813)722-2202. Editor: Annice E. Hunt. Magazine: 8½x11"; 18-20 pages; 20 bond paper and cover quality; clip b&w art. Quarterly for "animal lovers of all ages; those who care about pets, wildlife, and the environment." Plans fiction issue in future. Estab. 1981.

**Needs:** Adventure, fantasy (wildlife), historical (general), juvenile (5-9 years), preschool, and young adult/teen. "Stories must relate to animals. No gory details about dying animals; no profanity." Accepts 8-10 unsolicited mss/year. Length: 600 words average; 450 words minimum; 800 words maximum. Publishes short shorts, 800 words or less. Occasionally critiques rejected mss. Sometimes recommends other markets.

**How to Contact:** Query first or send complete ms. Reports in 3 weeks on queries; 1 month on mss. SASE. Simultaneous, photocopied and previously published submissions OK. Publishes ms an average of 6 months after acceptance. Sample copy $2. Fiction guidelines free.

**Payment:** 1 free contributor's copy; $2 each for extras.

**Terms:** Acquires one-time rights only. Publication copyrighted.

**Tips:** "A writer can make an editor's job easier by deleting unnecessary words and typing neatly. Keep revising and rewriting." Published new writers within the last year.

**CALYX (II), A Journal of Art & Literature by Women**, Calyx, Inc., Box B, Corvallis OR 97339. (503)753-9384. Managing Editor: M. Donnelly. Associate Editors: Rebecca Gordon, Jo Alexander, Eleanor Wilner, Lisa Domitrovich, and Cheryl McLean. Publishes prose, poetry, art, essays, interviews and and critical and review articles. *Calyx* editors are seeking innovative and literary fiction works of exceptional quality. Triannually. Estab. 1976. Circ. 2,000.
**Needs:** Accepts 2-3 mss/issue, 9 mss/year. Receives approximately 100 unsolicited fiction mss each month. Length: 5,000 words maximum.
**How to Contact:** Send ms with SASE and biographical notes. Reports in up to 6 months on mss. Publishes ms an average of 1 month after acceptance. Sample copy $6.50.
**Payment:** Pays in copies.
**Terms:** Publication copyrighted.
**Tips:** Most mss are rejected because "the writers are not familiar with *Calyx*—writers should read *Calyx* and be familiar with the publication. Feb. 1-Nov. 1, 1986, only accepting work for our Asian-American anthology. Queries welcome. All other work will be returned. Nov. 1, 1986-Feb. 1, 1987 will again receive general submissions for spring issue."

**CANADIAN AUTHOR & BOOKMAN**, Canadian Authors Association, 24 Ryerson Ave., Toronto, Ontario M5T 2P3 Canada. Fiction Editor: Geoff Hancock. "We are mainly a craft magazine for Canadian writers, publishing articles that tell how to write and where to sell. We publish half a dozen poems and one short story per issue as well as the craft articles. We aim at the beginning or newly emerging writer who reads us to find out how to create the salable article (story or poem) and reap the benefits of his seminal imagination and feverish activity." Quarterly. Estab. 1921. Circ. 4,000.
**Needs:** Literary, contemporary, science fiction, fantasy, horror, men's, women's, feminist, gothic, romance, western, mystery, adventure, and humor. "No porn, near-miss inspirational, personal essays masquerading as short stories, formula writing with tired blood or whatever else is trite, banal, or just dull." Buys 1 ms/issue, 4 mss/year. Length: 2,000-3,500 words. Occasionally recommends other markets. Fiction must be by a Canadian.
**How to Contact:** Send complete ms with SASE or IRC. Accepts computer printout submissions. Prefers letter-quality. Reports in 1 month on mss. Sample copy $3.50.
**Payment:** $125. Free author's copy.
**Terms:** Pays on publication for first rights.
**Tips:** "Send Geoff Hancock a story that will dominate memory and you are in business. He reads with an eye for originality, flair, and imaginative work. He asks, whatever the form or procedure of the story, that it succeed in the author's intention. To write good stories, you must read great stories, and read them from the inside out. The writer's strategy must be examined, from the overall structure, to the rise and fall of the sentences, to the placement of the punctuation. For more specific information send $1.50 to Canadian Authors' Assoc. with your request for a reprint of 'The Green Glad Bag Review,' by Geoff Hancock (CAB, *November 1979*)."

**CANADIAN FICTION MAGAZINE (II)**, Box 946, Station F, Toronto, Ontario M4Y 2N9 Canada. Editor: Geoffrey Hancock. Magazine: 6x9; 148-300 pages; book paper overweight cover stock; 16-32 page portfolio. "This magazine is a quarterly anthology devoted exclusively to the contemporary creative writing of writers and artists in Canada and Canadians living abroad. Fiction only, no poetry. The ideal reader of *CFM* is a writer or somebody interested in all the modes, manners, voices, and conventions of contemporary fiction." Quarterly. Published special fiction issue last year; plans another. Estab. 1971. Circ. 1,800.
**Needs:** Literary. "Theme, style, length, and subject matter are at the discretion of the author. The only requirement is that the work be of the highest possible literary standard. Each issue is ap-

 **The double dagger before a listing indicates that the listing is new in this edition. New markets are often the most receptive to freelance contributions.**

proximately 148 pages. Buys 10 mss/issue, 35 mss/year. Publishes short shorts. No restriction on length.

**How to Contact:** Send complete ms with SASE or IRC. Reports in 6 weeks on mss. Publishes ms up to 18 months after acceptance.

**Payment:** $10/page plus one-year subscription.

**Terms:** Pays on publication for first North American serial rights. Sends galleys to author.

**Tips:** "It is absolutely crucial that three or four issues be read. We sell back issues up to 1976 for $3; current issue $5.50 (postage included). Some double issues are $7.85. *CFM* publishes Canada's leading writers as well as those in early stages of their careers. A wide knowledge of contemporary literature (in English and in translation) plus expertise in creative writing, modern fiction theories, current Canadian literature, and the innovative short story would be of great help to a potential contributor. *CFM* is an independent journal not associated with any academic institution. Each issue includes French Canadian fiction in translation, interviews with well-known Canadian writers on the techniques of their fiction, forums and manifestoes on the future of fiction, as well as art work and reviews. $250 annual prize for the best story submitted in either French or English. Previous winners include John Metcalf, Mavis Gallant, Leon Rooke, W.P. Kinsella, Anne Copeland, Keath Fraser, Guy Vanderhaege, Matt Cohen, Patrick Roscoe, Douglas Glover." Published 15 new writers within the last year.

**‡CANDLE (I), A Working Person's Ragazine**, Tiptoe Publishing, Box 206-OH, Naselle WA 98638-0206. (206)484-7722. Editor: A. Grimm-Richardson. Magazine: 8½x11; 24 pages; G-print tukwila matte paper and cover stock; illustrations. Interests of working people and small business—political and general interest subjects of western hemisphere. International audience of diverse ethnic backgrounds, middle class and lower income. 10 times annually. Estab. 1985. Circ: "Thin, coast to coast and international, and growing."

**Needs:** Adventure if non-sexist, ethnic, fantasy, historical (general), humor/satire, juvenile (5-9 years), regional, science fiction, senior citizen/retirement, suspense/mystery if not violent, young adult/teen (10-18 years), travel. Needs a variety of material. Non-sexist, non-agist, written from various ethnic backgrounds. No erotica, macho, horror, violence, jock sports. Accepts 3 mss/issue; 35-40 mss/year. Publishes ms up to 3 months after acceptance. Length: 1,000 average; 250 words minimum; 1,800 words maximum. Publishes short shorts, short enough to still cover the subject. Comments on rejected mss.

**How to Contact:** Query first or send complete ms with cover letter. A biographical note is sometimes used to introduce new contributors. SASE for query and ms. No IRC. Simultaneous, photocopied, and reprint submissions OK. Accepts computer printout including dot-matrix. Sample copy $1.75. Fiction guidelines for any size SAE and 1 first class stamp.

**Payment:** Pays in contributor's copies, or extension to subscription (or discount on advertising).

**Terms:** Pays on acceptance unless non-subscriber is only to receive copy of one issue. Acquires one-time rights. Publication copyrighted.

**Tips:** "Our readers are well-traveled, are often bilingual, do not live in large city highrise apartments. Any geographic location and ethnic treatment of a subject is fine—but the story must be in language understandable by most who speak English, even as a second language."

**THE CAPILANO REVIEW (II)**, 2055 Purcell Way, North Vancouver, British Columbia V7J 3H5 Canada. (604)986-1911, loc 496. Editor: Dorothy Jantzen. Fiction Editor: Bill Schermbrucker. Magazine: 13½x20½; glossy paper; illustrations; photos. Magazine of "fresh, innovative art and literature for literary/artistic audience." Quarterly. Published special fiction issue last year; plans another. Estab. 1973. Circ. 850.

**Needs:** Contemporary, experimental, literary, and prose poem. Receives 20 unsolicited mss/ month. Accepts 1-2 mss/issue; 4 mss/year. Length: 2,000-6,000 words. Publishes short shorts. Occasionally recommends markets.

**How to Contact:** Send complete ms. Simultaneous and photocopied submissions OK. Sample copy $3.

**Payment:** Pays $40 and 2 contributor's copies.

**Terms:** Pays on publication. Publication copyrighted.
**Tips:** Published "lots" of new writers within the last year.

**CARIBBEAN REVIEW (IV)**, Caribbean Review, Inc., Florida International University, Tamiami Trail, Miami FL 33199. (305)554-2246. Editor: Barry B. Levine. Magazine: 8'x11"; 56 pages; glossy paper; 60 lb cover stock; illustrations and photos. "Dedicated to Latin America, the Caribbean and their emigrant groups for anyone interested in that part of the world." Quarterly. Special fiction issue in 1985; plans another. Estab. 1969. Circ. 5,000 +.
**Needs:** Literary, regional, excerpted novel, and translations. "Must relate to Latin America, Caribbean and emigrant groups." Length: 3,000 words average; 5,000 + words maximum.
**How to Contact:** Query first or send complete ms with cover letter. Reports in 6 weeks. Photocopied submissions OK. Accepts computer printout submissions. Free sample copy.
**Payment:** No payment.
**Terms:** Publication copyrighted.
**Tips:** Published new writers within the last year.

**CAROLINA QUARTERLY (II)**, Greenlaw Hall 066A, University of North Carolina, Chapel Hill NC 27514. (919)962-0244. Editor-in-Chief: Emily Stockard. Fiction Editor: Robert Rubin. "Literary journal: 90-100 pages; illustrations; photos. Fiction, poetry, graphics and some reviews, for that audience—whether academic or not—with an interest in the best in poetry and short fiction." Triquarterly. Estab. 1948. Circ. 1,000.
**Needs:** No pornography. Receives 150-200 unsolicited fiction mss/month. Buys 3-6 mss/issue, 12-18 mss/year. Publishes ms an average of 10 weeks after acceptance. Length: 7,000 words maximum; no minimum; no preferred length. Also publishes short shorts. One story at a time. Occasionally critiques rejected mss.
**How to Contact:** Send complete ms with cover letter (no synopsis of story) and SASE to fiction editor. Photocopied submissions OK. Reports in 2-4 months. Sample copy $4; SASE and $1 postage for writer's guidelines.
**Payment:** $3/printed page; 2 free contributor's copies. Regular copy price for extras.
**Terms:** Pays on publication for first North American serial rights. Publication copyrighted.
**Tips:** "We publish a good many unsolicited stories and yes, I love publishing a new writer for the first time; *CQ* is a market for newcomer and professional alike. Write 'Fiction Editor' on envelope of submitted manuscript. Keep story to decent length—it's hard to publish very short and very long stories. Also—read what gets published in the journal/magazine you're interested in. Make your packet look professional yet modest."

**CEILIDH (I, II), An Informal Gathering for Story & Song**, Ceilidh, Inc., 986 Marquette Lane, Foster City CA 94404. (415)341-6228. Editors: Patrick S. Sullivan and Perry Oei. Magazine: 8½x5½; 32-64 pages; illustrations; photos. "We are a growing literary magazine looking for deep literary fiction, drama, and poetry." Quarterly. Plans special fiction issue. Estab. 1981. Circ. 500.
**Needs:** Experimental, literary, prose poem, science fiction, serialized/excerpted novel, and translations. No romance, juvenile, erotica, preschool, or young adult. Receives 5 unsolicited mss/month. Accepts 3 mss/issue; 9 mss/year. Length: 3,000 words average; 6,000 words maximum. Also publishes short shorts. Sometimes recommends other markets.
**How to Contact:** Send complete ms with SASE. Reports in 6 weeks. Photocopied submissions OK. Accepts computer printout submissions. Publishes ms 2-3 months after acceptance. Sample copy $3.50. Fiction guidelines for legal-sized SASE with 1 first class stamp.
**Payment:** 2 contributor's copies; $2 charge for extras.
**Terms:** "At this point we cannot pay for every piece, but we usually have a contest for each issue." Acquires one-time rights. Publication copyrighted.
**Tips:** "We lean toward experimental, more serious fiction, with a sense of voice, rather than merely a story. Send a neat manuscript with a descriptive cover letter, SASE. Fiction is a good voice for our times. Poetry is also, but people seem to enjoy a short story over a long poem."

**THE CELIBATE WOMAN (IV), A Journal for Women Who Are Celibate or Considering This Liberating Way of Relating to Others**, 3306 Ross Place NW, Washington DC 20008. (203)966-7783. Editor: Martha Allen. Journal for women interested in the issue of celibacy. Published irregularly. Estab. 1982.
**Needs:** Celibacy. Receives 10-15 unsolicited ms/issue.
**How to Contact:** Send complete ms with SASE. Reports in weeks on queries and mss. Simultaneous, photocopied and previously published submissions OK. Accepts computer printout submissions. Sample copy $4.

**CENTRAL PARK (II), A Journal of the Arts and Social Theory**, Neword Productions, Inc. Box 1446, New York NY 10023. (212)362-9151. Editors: Richard Royal, Stephen-Paul Martin, Eve Ensler. Magazine: 7½x10, 100 pages; glossy cover stock; illustrations; photos. Magazine of theoretical essays, poetry, fiction, photos, and graphics for intellectual audience. Semiannually. Estab. 1981. Circ. 1,000.
**Needs:** Contemporary, erotica, ethnic, experimental, feminist, gay, historical (general), lesbian, literary, prose poem, serialized/excerpted novel, and translations. Approximately 10% of fiction is agented. Receives 15 unsolicited mss/month. Publishes short shorts of 5-10 pages. Accepts 3 mss/issue; 6 mss/year. Occasionally critiques rejected mss. Recommends other markets.
**How to Contact:** Send complete ms and cover letter with "publications credits, relevant personal data, reasons for sending to us." Reports in 2 months. SASE. Simultaneous and photocopied submissions OK. Accepts computer printout submissions. Publishes ms an average of 3 months after acceptance. Sample copy $5.
**Payment:** 1 contributor's copy; $5 for extras. Acquires first rights. Publication copyrighted.
**Tips:** "We would like to publish more short fiction, especially if it is experimental, aggressively sexual and political in nature. Write what seems to be an authentic representation of how *your* feelings interact with the social world. Let your imagination have free reign in evolving the form your work takes. Be aware of, *but not harnessed by*, conventions. We like to know who our writers are: what they do, their literary background and activities. Writers should include a cover letter and expect a personal letter in response." Published new writers within the last year.

**‡CHARIOT (II)**, Ben Hur Life Association, Box 312, Crawfordsville IN 47933. (317)362-4500. Magazine: 8½x11; 24-32 pages; 80 lb semi-gloss paper; self cover; illustrations; photos. Material for fraternal benefit society for members of organization. Quarterly. Estab. 1985. Circ. 10,800.
**Needs:** Contemporary, historical (general), humor/satire, juvenile (5-9 years), mainstream, men's, preschool (0-4 years), religious/inspirational, senior citizen/retirement, women's, young adult/teen (10-18 years). "Story must have a 'fraternal thread.' Winter issue features first fiction ever run. It's about a volunteer worker fixing up a child's wagon, presenting it to a crotchety old man in a nursing home, and how this caring act changes the old man's outlook on life. *No* smutty, gay, etc. works. Do not want anything unsuited for family-oriented publication." Receives 10 unsolicited mss/month. Buys 4 fiction mss/year. Length: 2,000 words average; 1,500 words minimum; 3,000 words maximum. Also publishes short shorts; 500-1,000 words. Occasionally critiques rejected mss. Occasionally recommends other markets.
**How to Contact:** Send query or complete ms. Reports in 3 weeks on queries; 5 weeks on mss. SASE for query and ms. Simultaneous, photocopied submissions and reprints OK "as long as we know where we stand in other publications." Accepts computer printouts including dot-matrix; prefers letter-quality. Sample copy free for 9x12 SAE and 4 oz. postage. Fiction guidelines free for #10 SAE and 1 first class stamp.
**Payment:** Pays 3-20¢/word.
**Terms:** Pays on acceptance for first North American serial rights "usually, but will not keep us from buying if it's appeared elsewhere first."
**Tips:** "Too much stuff comes in that wanders all around in a fog without going anywhere. I've even had some that shifts from 3rd to 1st party viewpoint in the middle. Ask for, then R-E-A-D the writer's guidelines. L-I-S-T-E-N to any critique. Remember that you're not a Stephen King or Ernest Hemingway—yet (which wouldn't make a difference, anyway. I look at *content* and *style*, not name or credits)."

**THE CHARITON REVIEW (II)**, Northeast Missouri State University, Kirksville MO 63501. (816)785-4499. Editor: Jim Barnes. "We demand only excellence in fiction and fiction translation for a general and college readership." Semiannually. Estab. 1975. Circ. 700 +.
**Needs:** Literary, contemporary, and translations. Buys 3-5 mss/issue, 6-10 mss/year. Length: 3,000-6,000 words. Critiques rejected mss "when there is time." Sometimes recommends markets.
**How to Contact:** Send complete ms with SASE. Reports in less than 1 month on mss. Publishes ms an average of 6 months after acceptance. Sample copy $2 with SASE.
**Payment:** $5/page. Free author's copy. $2 for extras.
**Terms:** Pays on publication for first North American serial rights; rights returned on request. Publication copyrighted.
**Tips:** "Write well and study the publication you are submitting to. We are interested only in the very best fiction and fiction translation. We are not interested in slick material. We do not read photocopies or carbon copies."

**THE CHATTAHOOCHEE REVIEW (II)**, DeKalb College, 2101 Womack Rd., Dunwoody GA 30338. (404)393-3300, ext. 185. Editor: Lamar York. Fiction Editor: John Chiang. Magazine: 6x9; 100 page; 60 paper quality; 70 cover stock; illustrations (b&w, ink, pencil, pastels); photos. "No specific theme. We publish the best poetry, fiction and nonfiction that comes to us for a general audience. Quarterly. Estab. 1980. Circ. 1,000.
**Needs:** Contemporary, erotica, ethnic, experimental, feminist, gay, historical, humor/satire, lesbian, literary, mainstream, men's, prose poem, regional, and women's. No juvenile. Receives 100 unsolicited mss/quarter. Accepts 4 mss/issue; 16-20 mss/year. Length: 5,000 words average. Considers good short shorts. Seldom critiques rejected ms.
**How to Contact:** Send complete ms with SASE. Prefers cover letter (name, address, bio, past publications). Reports in 2-3 months on mss. Accepts computer printout submissions. Prefers letter-quality. Free sample copy and fiction guidelines.
**Payment:** Pays in contributor's copies.
**Terms:** Buys first rights. Publication copyrighted.
**Tips:** "We see a return to the conventional. Send us the kind of fiction you most like to *read*. Strong mix of unpublished and published writers. Try to offer, if not resolution or conclusion at least an ending to a story."

**CHELSEA (II)**, Chelsea Associates, Inc. Box 5880, Grand Central Station, New York NY 10163. Editor: Sonia Raiziss. Magazine: 6x9 trim; 185-235 pages; 60 lb white paper; glossy cover stock; individual artwork illustrations; occasional photos. "We have no consistent theme except for single special issues. Otherwise, we use general material of an eclectic nature: poetry, prose, artwork, etc. for a sophisticated, literate audience interested in avant-garde literature and current writing, both national and international." Annually. Estab. 1958. Circ. 1,000 +.
**Needs:** Literary, contemporary, and translations. No humorous, scatological, purely confessional, or child/young-adult experiences. Receives approximately 8-12 unsolicited fiction mss each month. Publishes short shorts of 4-6 pages. Approximately 1% of fiction is agented. Length: not over 25 printed pages. Critiques rejected mss "when there is time."
**How to Contact:** Query with SASE and cover letter with previous credits. Accepts computer printout submissions. Prefers letter-quality. Reports in 3 weeks on queries, 2 months on mss. Publishes ms within a year after acceptance. Sample copy $4 plus postage.
**Payment:** 2 free author's copies.
**Terms:** Pays on publication for one-time rights. Publication copyrighted.
**Tips:** "Familiarize yourself with issues of the magazine for character of contributions. Manuscripts should be legible, clearly typed, with minimal number of typographical errors and cross-outs, sufficient return postage. Most mss are rejected because they are conventional in theme and/or style, uninspired, contrived, etc."

**CHICAGO REVIEW**, Chicago Review, Box C, University of Chicago, Chicago IL 60637. (312)753-3571. Editor: Robert Sitko. Fiction Editor: Victor King. Magazine for a highly literate general audience: 5½x9½; 120 pages; offset white 60 lb paper; illustrations; photos. Quarterly. Estab. 1946. Circ. 2,000.

**Needs:** Literary, contemporary, science fiction, fantasy, and especially experimental. Accepts 5 mss/issue, 20 mss/year. Receives 50-100 unsolicited fiction mss each month. No preferred length. Critiques rejected mss "when there is time." Recommends other markets.

**How to Contact:** Send complete ms with cover letter (author's background, circumstances under which he/she wrote piece), SASE. Simultaneous submissions OK. Accepts computer printout submissions. Reports in 4 months on mss. Sample copy $4. Free guidelines with SASE.

**Payment:** 3 free author's copies and subscription. 40% discount for extras.

**Terms:** Publication copyrighted.

**Tips:** Mss are rejected because they are "predictable and boring. Authors give too much 'background' explanation."

**‡CHICAGO SHEET (II), Chicago's Fine Print**, Box 3667, Oak Park IL 60303. (312)383-0277. Editor: Jeremy A. Pollack. Magazine: 11x17; 8-12 pages; 50 lb bookstore paper and cover; illustrations; photos. "The theme is popular-literary; publishing an open range of topics while concentrating on the arts and the city for well educated, serious adult readers." Monthly. Estab. 1984. Circ. 200.

**Needs:** Confession, erotica, humor/satire, literary, special interest: city of Chicago. No juvenile. Receives 5 unsolicited fiction mss/month. Accepts 1-2 mss/issue; 12-24 mss/year. Publishes ms 6-8 months (average) after acceptance. Length: 3,000 words average.

**How to Contact:** Send complete ms with cover letter (with general salutation and introduction to writer) and ms enclosed. Reports in 4-6 weeks on mss. SASE for ms. Simultaneous and photocopied submissions OK. Accepts computer printouts including dot-matrix. Sample copy free. Fiction guidelines for standard SAE and 1 first class stamp.

**Payment:** Pays in contributor's copies.

**Terms:** Acquires one-time rights and one-time anthological rights. Publication copyrighted.

**CHIRICÚ**, Ballantine Hall 849, Indiana University, Bloomington IN 47405. Contact: Editor-in-Chief. "We publish essays, translations, poetry, fiction, reviews, interviews, and artwork (illustrations and photos) that are either by or about Hispanics. Recent issue had an interview with Jorge Luis Borges and a translation from Virgilio Pinero. We have no barriers on style, content or ideology, but would like to see well-written material." Annually. Estab. 1976. Circ. 500.

**Needs:** Contemporary, erotica, ethnic, experimental, fantasy, feminist/lesbian, gay, humor/satire, literary, mainstream, prose poem, science fiction, serialized/excerpted novel, translations, and women's. No fiction that has nothing to do with Hispanics (when not written by one). Length: 7,000 words maximum; 4,000 words average. Occasionally critiques rejected mss. Sends mss to editors of other publications. Sometimes recommends markets.

**How to Contact:** Send complete ms with SASE. Photocopied submissions OK. Reports in 5 weeks on mss. Publishes ms 6-12 months after acceptance. Sample copy $4.50.

**Terms:** Publication copyrighted.

**Tips:** "Realize that we are an Hispanic literary review so that if you are not Hispanic, then your work must reflect an interest in Hispanic issues or have an Hispanic bent to it in literature. Mss rejected "quite simply because beginning writers force their language instead of writing from genuine sentiment and natural language."

**CHUNGA REVIEW (II)**, Chunga Press, Box 158, Felch MI 49831. Editor: Mike Felten. Magazine: 5x7; 40 pages; b&w photos. "Freewheeling magazine—folksy to avant garde for self-educated to college level/college educated." Irregularly. Circ. 250-500.

**Needs:** Adventure, contemporary, erotica, ethnic, experimental, humor/satire, literary, mainstream, regional. Receives 30-40 unsolicited mss/month. Accepts 20-30 mss/issue. Length: 2,500 words average; 250 words minimum; 5,000 words maximum. Publishes short shorts. Sometimes critiques rejected ms. Recommends other markets.

**How to Contact:** Send complete ms. Reports in 2 months. SASE. Photocopied submissions

OK. Sample copy $3. Fiction guidelines for 6x8 envelope with 40¢ postage.
**Payment:** 2 contributor's copies.
**Terms:** Acquires one-time rights. Publication copyrighted.
**Tips:** "We are currently revamping our entire operation—changing from a hobby to a business. We are contemplating a line of fiction/poetry titles." Published new writers within the last year.

**CIMARRON REVIEW (II)**, Oklahoma State University, 208 LSE, Stillwater OK 74078. (405)624-5663. Editor: Neil John Hackett. Managing Editor: Jeanne Adams Wray. Magazine: 6x9; 64 pages; varied 60 lb paper; Satony Lustro finish cover stock; illustrations on cover. "Poetry and fiction on contemporary themes; personal essay on contemporary issues that cope with life in the 20th century for educated literary cognoscenti. We work hard to reflect quality." Quarterly. Estab. 1967. Circ. 500.
**Needs:** Literary and contemporary. No collegiate reminiscences or "juvenilia." Accepts 5-6 mss/issue, 20-24 mss/year. Recommends other markets.
**How to Contact:** Send complete ms with SASE. Accepts computer printout submissions. Prefers letter-quality. Reports in 1 month on mss. Publishes ms 6-9 months after acceptance. Free sample copy with 6½x9½ SASE and 65¢ postage.
**Payment:** 10 free author's copies. $1.50 charge for extras.
**Terms:** Acquires all rights on publication.
**Tips:** "Short fiction is a genre uniquely suited to the modern world."

**CITY PAPER (II)**, Washington's Free Weekly, Inc., 919 6th St. NW, Washington DC 20001. (202)289-0520. Editor: Jack Shafer. Associate Editor: Kara Swisher. Newspaper. Alternative, urban weekly for ages 20-45 "young." Estab. 1981. Circ. 65,000.
**Needs:** Contemporary, literary, mainstream, and science fiction. No experimental. Receives 10 mss/month. Buys 7 mss/year. Length: 1,500-3,000 words average; 1,500 words minimum; 3,000 words maximum. Occasionally comments on a rejected manuscript.
**How to Contact:** Send complete ms with SASE. Simultaneous submissions OK; no photocopied submissions or previously published work. Accepts computer printout submissions. Prefers letter-quality. Sample copy free with SAE (8x10 envelope and 56¢ stamp).
**Payment:** Pays $75 maximum.
**Terms:** Pays on publication for first rights. Publication copyrighted.
**Tips:** "Re-read your copy. There *are* no typos—only misspellings. Clean mss, please. Steer clear of autobiographical fiction."

**CLIFTON MAGAZINE (II)**, Communications Board, 204 Tangeman University Center, Cincinnati OH 45221. Address all fiction to Editor. Magazine: 8x11; 48 pages; 60 lb enamel coated paper; same/self-/coated cover stock; illustrations; photos. "*Clifton* is the magazine of the University of Cincinnati, presenting fiction, poetry, and feature articles of interest to the University community. It is read by a highly literate audience of students, academics and professionals looking for original and exciting ideas presented in our award winning format." Quarterly. Estab. 1972. Circ. 7,000.
**Needs:** Literary, contemporary, science fiction, fantasy, feminist, gay/lesbian, erotica, humor, psychic/supernatural/occult, regional, and ethnic. "Will consider anything we haven't read a thousand times before. We try to have no preconceptions when approaching fiction. Accepts 1-2 mss/issue, 5 mss/year. Publishes short shorts. Receives approximately 25 unsolicited fiction mss each month. Length: 6,000 words.
**How to Contact:** Send complete ms with SASE. Reports in 1 month on mss. Sample copy $1.50. Free guidelines with legal-sized SASE.
**Payment:** 5 free author's copies.
**Terms:** Acquires first rights. Publication copyrighted.
**Tips:** "*Clifton* often publishes work by unpublished authors and is quite open to any fiction. We have previously published Allen Ginsberg, Richard Price, Jonathan Valin and James Wright, as well as unpublished writers who now are professionals. We look forward to continuing the publi-

cation with both young and established writers. *Clifton* tries to find mechanically sound, intricate, original work for publication. The unusual is popular. Be unique. Don't give up. Send at least one follow-up letter."

‡**CLOCK RADIO (II)**, 116 Northwood Apts., Storrs CT 06268. (203)429-7516. Editor: Jay Dougherty. Fiction Editor: Anke Wienand. Magazine: 5½x8½; 24 pages; 20% rag paper; hard card cover stock; illustrations sometimes. "*Clock Radio* publishes fiction and poetry. Fiction published tends to be somehow off-beat and short. For progressive literary audience. Semiannually. Estab. 1984. Circ. 500.
**Needs:** Contemporary, experimental, humor, literary. Receives about 50 mss/month. Accepts 2-3 mss/issue; 5-6 mss/year. Publishes ms up to 2 months after acceptance. Agented fiction: 2%. Length: 500-2,000 words average; 2,000 words maximum. Publishes short shorts. Critiques rejected mss. Recommends other markets.
**How to Contact:** Send complete ms with cover letter. Reports in 1 week on queries; 1-2 weeks on mss. SASE for ms. Photocopied submissions OK. Accepts computer printouts. Sample copy for $1.75, 6x9 SAE and 3 first class stamps. Fiction guidelines for $1.75, 6x9 SAE and 3 first class stamps.
**Payment:** Contributor's copies; charge for extras.
**Terms:** Pays on publication. Acquires first North American serial rights. Publication copyrighted.

**CLOCKWATCH REVIEW (II), A Journal of the Arts**, Driftwood Publications, 737 Penbrook Way, Hartland WI 53029. (414)367-8315. Editor: James Plath. Magazine: 5½x8½; 64 pages (average); coated stock paper; coated heavy cover stock; illustrations; photos. "We publish stories which are *literary* as well as alive, colorful, enjoyable . . . stories which linger like shadows" for a general audience. Semiannually. Estab. 1983. Circ. 1,500.
**Needs:** Contemporary, experimental, humor/satire, literary, mainstream, prose poem, and regional. Receives 25-30 unsolicited mss/month. Accepts 2 mss/issue; 4 mss/year. Length: 2,500 words average; 1,200 words minimum; 4,000 words maximum. Occasionally critiques rejected mss if requested.
**How to Contact:** Send complete ms. Reports in 2 months. SASE. Photocopied submissions OK. Accepts computer printout submissions. Prefers letter-quality. Publishes ms 3-12 months after acceptance. Sample copy $3.
**Payment:** 2 contributor's copies; $2 for extras. "We offer a cash prize for the best short story published in *CR* each year."
**Terms:** Acquires first serial rights. Publication copyrighted.
**Tips:** "Give us characters with meat on their bones, colorful but not clichéd; give us natural plots, not contrived or melodramatic, with *something to say*. Rewrite. Let a story cool before revising and sending it off. I get the feeling that half of the stories we receive are put in envelopes immediately after they're pulled from the typewriters. Above all, give us your *best* work." Published new writers within the last year.

‡**COLD-DRILL MAGAZINE (IV)**, English Dept., Boise State Univ., 1910 University Dr., Boise ID 83725. (208)385-1999. Editor: Tom Trusky. Magazine: 6x9; 150 pages; Beckett text paper; illustrations; photos. Material submitted must be by Idaho authors *or* deal with Idaho for adult audiences. Annually. Estab. 1970. Circ. 500.
**Needs:** Adventure, contemporary, erotica, ethnic, experimental, fantasy, feminist, gay, horror, humor/satire, lesbian, literary, mainstream, men's, science fiction, serialized/excerpted novel, suspense/mystery, translations, western, women's, Idaho topics. "Manuscripts are selected in December for the annual issue in March. Authors may submit any time, but they will not be notified unless they are selected; if they are, notification will be in late December, early January." No children's literature, romance, gothic, true confession, psychic, religious or inspirational. Receives 10 fiction mss/month. Accepts 5-7 mss/issue; 5-7 mss/year. Publishes March 1. Publishes short shorts. Critiques rejected mss. Recommends other markets.

**How to Contact:** Query first. Reports in 2 weeks. SASE. Simultaneous and photocopied submissions OK. Accepts computer printouts including dot-matrix. Sample copy $5. Fiction guidelines for legal size SAE and first class stamp.
**Payment:** Contributor's copies.
**Terms:** Pays on publication. Acquires first rights. Publication copyrighted.
**Tips:** "We publish the best in Idaho literature, regardless of the genre. Know the publication."

**COLORADO-NORTH REVIEW (I, II),** University of Northern Colorado, Greeley CO 80639. (303)351-1360. Magazine: 6x9; 64 pages; 70 lb paper; 80 lb cover stock; illustrations; photos. Magazine of poetry, short fiction, translations, photography and graphic arts for writers or those interested in contemporary creativity. Published in fall, winter and spring. Published special fiction issue last year; plans another. Estab. 1968. Circ. 3,000.
**Needs:** Contemporary and literary. Receives 350 unsolicited fiction mss/month. Accepts 70 mss/issue, 210 mss/year. Length: 2,000 words maximum. Critiques rejected mss by request.
**How to Contact:** Send complete ms with SASE and brief biographical info for contributor's section. Photocopied submissions OK. Reports in 3 months. Publishes ms 2-3 months after acceptance. Sample copy $2.50; free guidelines with SASE.
**Terms:** Pays in contributor's copies. Sends galleys to author. Publication copyrighted.
**Tips:** "We print primarily poetry; however, the short fiction is well received and very competitive. We strive for variety and short stories of different themes. Too often the best two or three stories are of the same theme and so we pick only one. Too many writers are confined to the novella, or bare character studies. It's rare to find a complete story anymore in 2,000 words or less. We are glad to read anything you feel worthy of submission. We take seriously the writer's efforts and support the creative process. Space is limited but we do attempt to provide a quality forum for both students and nonuniveristy writers. We appreciate your best." Published new writers within the last year.

**COLORADO REVIEW (II),** English Department, Colorado State University, Fort Collins CO 80523. (303)491-6428. Managing Editor: Bill Tremblay. Fiction Editor: Steven Schwartz. Magazine: 80-100 pages; 70 lb book weight paper; gloss cover stock. Literary magazine. Fiction issue published annually. Published special fiction issue last year; plans another. Estab. 1977. Circ. 300-500.
**Needs:** Contemporary, ethnic, experimental, literary, mainstream, translations, and women's. Receives 100 unsolicited fiction mss/month. Accepts 8-10 mss/issue; 8-10 mss/year. Under 6,000 words. Does not read mss Jan. 1-July 30. Occasionally critiques on rejected mss. Recommends other markets.
**How to Contact:** Send complete ms with SASE and brief bio and previous publications. Accepts computer printout submissions. Prefers letter-quality. Reports in 3 months. Publishes ms 3-6 months after acceptance. Sample copy $2.
**Payment:** $5/printed page; 1 subscription to magazine; 2 free contributor's copies; $2 charge for extras.
**Terms:** Pays on publication for first North American serial rights. "We assign copyright to author on request." Sends galleys to author "when time permits." Publication copyrighted.
**Tips:** "We are interested in manuscripts which show craft, imagination, and a convincing voice. Character development, strong story lines, and thematic insight are always desired. If a story has reached a level of technical competence, we are receptive to the fiction working on its terms. The oldest advice is still the best: persistance. Approach every aspect of the writing process with pride, conscientiousness—from word choice to manuscript appearance." Published new writers within the last year.

**COLUMBIA: A MAGAZINE OF POETRY & PROSE (II),** 404 Dodge Hall, Columbia University, New York NY 10027. (212)280-4391. Editors: Climeen Wirkoff, Patrick Godon. Fiction Editors: Chris Newbound, Rick Moody. Magazine: 5¼x8¼; 180 pages approximately; coated cover stock; illustrations; photos cover only. "We accept quality short stories, novel excerpts,

translations, interviews, nonfiction, and poetry." Annually.
**Needs:** Literary and translations, but "although we only mention 2 categories, we will consider anything of literary merit." Accepts 3-10 mss/issue. Receives approximately 30-40 unsolicited fiction mss each month. Does not read mss March 1 to August 31. Publishes short shorts, 25 pages maximum.
**How to Contact:** Send complete ms with SASE. Accepts computer printout submissions. Reports in 2 months.
**Payment:** Sends galleys to author. Author's copies. $3 charge for extras.
**Terms:** Publication copyrighted.
**Tips:** "We will consider all mss." Mss are rejected because of "limited, rambling story lines; inability to zero in and concentrate on why it's being written." Editors' Fiction and Poetry Award; entry fee $5 with submission, award $200 in each genre. Published one or two unpublished writers within the year.

**COMET HALLEY MAGAZINE (II)**, Comet Halley Press, #22, 376 W. Park, El Cajon CA 92020. Editor-in-Chief: Brian C. Clark. Assistant Editor: Sheila Clark. Magazine: 8½x11; 22 pages; standard paper; heavy cover stock; pen and ink illustrations; occasional b&w photos. Literary magazine emphasizing science and humor; publishes mostly poetry, 3 or 4 stories per issue. Quarterly. Plans special fiction issue. Estab. 1984. Circ. 250.
**Needs:** Comics, erotica, experimental, literary, science fiction, and translations (with original French/Spanish). Receives 30 unsolicited fiction mss/month. Accepts 2-4/issue, 8-15/year. Length: 3,000 words average. Publishes short shorts. Always critiques rejected ms. Recommends other markets.
**How to Contact:** Send complete ms with a personal letter describing "something about the author—philosophy, political convictions, or schooling." Reports in 2 weeks. SASE. No simultaneous submissions. Photocopied and previously published submissions OK. Accepts computer printout submissions. Prefers letter-quality. Sample copy $2, (payable to editor).
**Payment:** 1 contributor's copy; discount for extras.
**Terms:** Acquires one-time rights. Publication copyrighted.
**Tips:** "Fiction is the highest form of art, if done well. I'd like to see more science-oriented fiction; I think our technology requires that we assimilate and examine it through the ancient mode of storytelling. Learn a style sheet and stick to it; don't be afraid to try new markets that have a small circulation and/or a weird name." Published 3 new writers within the last year.

**COMMON LIVES/LESBIAN LIVES (I), A Lesbian Quarterly**, Box 1553, Iowa City IA 52244. (319)353-6265. Contact: Tess Catalano and Tracy Moore. "*CL/LL* seeks to document the experiences and thoughts of lesbians for lesbian audience." Illustrations; photos. Quarterly.
**Needs:** Adventure, comics, contemporary, erotica, ethnic, experimental, fantasy, feminist, historical (general), humor/satire, juvenile, lesbian, prose poem, psychic/supernatural/occult, regional, romance, science fiction, senior citizen/retirement, suspense/mystery, western, women's, and young adult/teen. "All pertaining to lesbian culture." Publishes short shorts (4-10 pages). Occasionally critiques rejected mss.
**How to Contact:** Send complete ms with cover letter; a short bio sketch is required. Reports in 4 months. SASE. Photocopied submissions OK. Accepts computer printout submissions. Publishes ms up to 4 months after acceptance. Sample copy $3.50.
**Payment:** 2 contributor's copies. Publication copyrighted.
**Tips:** "Readers relate stories to their lives; fiction is an interesting and accesible way for lesbians to document their experience and express their opinions." Published new writers within the year.

**COMMUNITIES: JOURNAL OF COOPERATION (II)**, Communities Publications Cooperative, 126 Sun St., Stelle IL 60919. Editor: Charles Betterton. "Features articles on intentional communities, urban collectives, rural communes, politics, health, alternative culture and workplace democracy for people involved in cooperative ventures." Quarterly. Estab. 1973. Circ. 4,000.

**Needs:** Feminist, science fiction, Utopian, and cooperative. Accepts "maybe 1 manuscript in 2 years (would do more if we got them)." Length: 1,000 words minimum; 5,000 words maximum. Occasionally critiques rejected ms.

**How to Contact:** Query first or send complete ms. Reports in 4 weeks on queries; 6 weeks on mss. Simultaneious, photocopied and previously published submissions OK. Accepts computer printout submissions. Prefers letter-quality. Sample copy $2.50.

**Payment:** Pays 1 year subscription and 3 contributor's copies.

**Terms:** Pays on publication for one-time rights. Publication copyrighted.

**CONDITIONS: A Feminist Magazine With an Emphasis on Writings by Lesbians (II)**, Box 56, Van Brunt Station, Brooklyn NY 11215. "Collective of editors." A magazine of work "by published and unpublished writers of many different backgrounds for women of all ages and backgrounds who feel that a commitment to other women is an integral part of their lives." Semiannually. Estab. 1977.

**Needs:** Ethnic, feminist, lesbian, literary, prose poem, translations, and women's. Wants to see mss "which reflect the experiences and viewpoints of Third World, working-class, and older women." Receives 10 unsolicited fiction mss/month. Accepts 5 mss/issue, 10 mss/year. Length: 500 words minimum, 10,000 words maximum, 5,000 words average. Occasionally critiques rejected mss.

**How to Contact:** Send complete ms with SASE. Photocopied submissions OK. Reports in 2 months. Sample copy $6.

**Payment:** 2 free contributor's copies.

**Terms:** Pays on publication. Publication copyrighted.

**Tips:** "Buy a copy first to understand purpose of magazine."

**THE CONFLUENT EDUCATION JOURNAL**, 833 Via Granada, Santa Barbara CA 93103. (805)569-1754. Editor: Aaron W. Hillman. Magazine: 8x11; 86 pages; bond paper; heavy, non-stick cover stock; illustrations. Magazine about education, psychology and creative work from the humanist viewpoint. Semiannually. Estab. 1972. Circ. 5,000.

**Needs:** Contemporary, ethnic, experimental, fantasy, feminist, historical (general), humor/satire, literary, prose poem, psychic/supernatural, regional, and science fiction. No romance or "escapist that has no intellectual content." Receives 6-12 unsolicited ms/month. Accepts 1 ms/issue; 2 mss/year. Length: 2,500 words average; 3,000 words maximum. Occasionally comments on rejected ms. Sometimes recommends other markets.

**How to Contact:** Send complete ms. Reports in 3 months on mss. Simultaneous, photocopied and previously published submissions OK. Accepts computer printout submissions. Prefers letter-quality. Free sample copy and fiction guidelines.

**Payment:** Pays subscription to magazine and contributor's copies.

**Terms:** Pays on acceptance for one-time rights. Sometimes sends galleys to authors. Publication copyrighted.

**Tips:** "We notice insufficient attention to the whole. Fiction writing is a circle. You must love the elegance of words. Fiction often says explicitly what academic journals say obscurely." Published new writers within the last year.

**CONFRONTATION (I, II)**, Long Island University, English Dept., C.W. Post L.I.V., Greenvale NY 11548. (516)299-2391. Editor: Martin Tucker. Fiction Editor: William Fahey. Magazine: 6x9; 190 pages; 70 lb paper; illustrations; photos. "We like to have a 'range' of subjects, form and style in each issue and are open to all forms. Quality is our major concern. Our audience is literate, thinking college students, educated and self-educated lay persons." Semiannually. Published special fiction issue last year; plans another. Estab. 1968. Circ. 2,000.

**Needs:** Literary, contemporary, science fiction, confession, gothic, humor, feminist, gay, lesbian, regional, senior citizen/retirement, and translations. No "proselytizing" literature. Buys 30 mss/issue, 60 mss/year. Publishes short shorts of 500-1,000 words. Receives 300 unsolicited fiction mss each month. Approximately 10-15% of fiction is agented. Length: 500-3,000 words. Cri-

tiques rejected mss "when there is time." Sometimes recommends other markets.
**How to Contact:** Send complete ms with SASE. Accepts computer printout submissions. Prefers letter-quality. Reports in 6 weeks on mss. Publishes ms 3-12 months after acceptance. Sample copy $2.
**Payment:** $10-$100. 1 free author's copy. Half price for extras.
**Terms:** Pays on publication for all rights "with transfer on request to author." Publication copyrighted.
**Tips:** "Study the magazine. We believe a literary magazine is fiction as well as poetry." Published "several" new writers within the last year.

**CONJUNCTIONS (II)** ,33 W. 9th St., New York NY 10011. Editor: Bradford Morrow. Magazine: 6x9; 284 pages; 55 lb woven paper; heavy cream laid paper cover stock; illustrations; photos. "*Conjunctions*: a conjoining of texts by many diverse writers: a forum of work-in-progress by both well-known and new writers. We represent no clique but are concerned solely with publishing works of high artistic and technical calibre. Recent issues have included new work by Sorrentino, Busch, McElroy, Loewinsohn, Davenport, Creeley, Levertov, Gass, Hawkes, Abish, Duncan, Tarn, Lauterbach, and many others." Semiannually. Estab. 1981. Circ. 5,500.
**Needs:** Experimental, literary, and translations. Receives 100 unsolicited fiction mss/month. Accepts 65 mss/year. No preferred length.
**How to Contact:** Send complete ms with SASE. Reports in 8-12 weeks on mss.
**Payment:** 3 free contributor's copies; extra copies available at 40% discount to contributors.
**Terms:** Pays on publication for one-time rights. Sends galleys to author. Publication copyrighted.
**Tips:** "We desire to present a balance of what is being accomplished both in poetry *and* fiction. A writer writes because he/she must. If he/she writes fiction it is because of the absolute compelling *need*. Published new writers within the last year.

**THE CONNECTICUT WRITER (II)**, Connecticut Writers League, Inc., Box 10536, West Hartford CT 06110. Editor: Betty Hoffman. Magazine: 100 pages; excellent paper; slick cover stock; illustrations or photos on cover. Magazine "interested in providing a forum for the new writer in the fields of fiction." Published special fiction issue last year; plans another. Annually. Estab. 1974. Circ. 500.
**Needs:** "We consider everything. Submissions must be typed and adhere to the guidelines furnished upon request. We receive about 500 mss/year through the contest and through general submissions."
**How to Contact:** "Write for contest guidelines with SASE. Contest closes July 1." Sample copy $5. Fiction guidelines free for SASE.
**Payment:** Cash prizes for contest winners; other payment in copies.
**Terms:** One-time rights. Publication copyrighted.
**Tips:** "We are a non-profit organization and the longest, continuous forum for new writers of poetry and fiction in Connecticut. Our publication offers a new writer opportunities to be published. All our short stories run fewer than ten typed pages (with a few exceptions). Short shorts have a better chance than long ones. A short story should be just that. I'm not interested in mood pieces with no plot, or in thinly disguised autobiographies." Published new writers within the last year.

**CORNERSTONE MAGAZINE (II)**, Jesus People USA, 4707 N. Malden, Chicago IL 60640. Editor: Dawn Herrin. Magazine about "the faith of the ages in the culture of today with social issues, interviews with musicians and artists, investigative reporting and fiction for the 18-35 age group." Bimonthly. Estab. 1972. Circ. 95,000.
**Needs:** Comics, condensed novel, contemporary, experimental, fantasy, humor/satire, literary, mainstream, prose poem, religious/inspirational, science fiction, and young adult/teen (10-18 years). No erotica or romance. Receives 20 unsolicited mss/month. Accepts 1 ms/issue; 4-6 mss/year. Length: 2,500-3,000 words average; 2,000 words minimum; 3,500 words maximum. Occasionally critiques rejected ms.

**How to Contact:** Query first or send complete ms. Reports in 4-5 weeks on queries; 1-2 months on mss. SASE. Accepts computer printout submissions. Prefers letter-quality. Accepts disc submissions compatible with Kaypro II (C/PM). Sample copy $1.50.
**Payment:** Pays $50-250.
**Terms:** Pays on publication for first rights. Publication copyrighted.
**Tips:** "We're looking for fiction which expresses a Christian world view in highly original ways. The sky's the limit."

**CORONA (II), Marking the Edges of Many Circles**, Department of History and Philosophy, Montana State University, Bozeman MT 59717. (406)994-4395. Magazine: 7x10; 128 pages; 60 lb "mountre matte" paper; 65 lb hammermill cover stock; illustrations; photos. "Interdisciplinary magazine—essays, poetry, fiction, imagery, science, history, recipes, humor, etc., for those educated, curious, with a profound interest in the arts and contemporary thought." Annually. Estab. 1980. Circ. 2,000.
**Needs:** Comics, contemporary, experimental, fantasy, feminist, gay, lesbian, humor/satire, literary, preschool, prose poem, psychic/supernatural/occult, regional, romance, and senior citizen/retirement. "Our fiction ranges from the traditional Talmudic tale to fiction engendered by speculative science, from the extended joke to regional reflection—if it isn't accessible and original, please don't send it." Receives varying number of unsolicited fiction mss/month. Accepts 6 mss/issue. Publishes short shorts. Occasionally critiques rejected mss. Sometimes recommends other markets.
**How to Contact:** Send complete ms with SASE. Accepts computer printout submissions. Prefers letter-quality. Reports in 4 months on mss. Sample copy $7.
**Payment:** Minimal honorarium; 2 free contributor's copies; discounted charge for extras.
**Terms:** Pays on publication for first rights. Sends galleys to author upon request. Publication copyrighted.
**Tips:** "Be knowledgeable of contents other than fiction in *Corona*; one must know the journal." Recent contributors include Frederick Turner, William Irwin Thompson, Donald Hall, Richard Hugo (Pulitzer Prize for Poetry), and Richard Brautigan.

**COSMIC LANDSCAPES (I)**, An Alternative Science Fiction Magazine, Dan Petitpas, 6 Edson St., Hyde Park MA 02136. (617)361-0622. Editor: Dan Petitpas. Magazine: 7x8½; 32-56 pages; white bond paper and cover stock; illustrations; photos occasionally. "A magazine for beginning science fiction writers—fiction is published and then critiqued by readers and editor; also articles and news of interest to writers and SF fans." Quarterly. Published special fiction issue. Estab. March 1983. Circ. 100.
**Needs:** Science fiction. Receives 5-6 unsolicited mss/month. Accepts 6 mss/issue; 36 mss/year. Length: 2,500 words average; 25 words minimum. "Every manuscript receives an evaluation." Recommends other markets.
**How to Contact:** Send complete ms with info about the author. Reports usually in 1 week. SASE. Photocopied submissions OK. Accepts computer printout submissions. Sample copy $3. Fiction guidelines free.
**Payment:** 2 contributor's copies; charge for extras: $1.50.
**Terms:** Buys one-time rights. Publication copyrighted.
**Tips:** "We see TV plots, clichéd or old ideas, *Star Wars* ripoffs. Have a strong, fresh, new idea or theme in story. Slice-of-life pieces are not enough; a good short story should have not only a beginning, middle and end but also have meaning."

**COTTONWOOD MAGAZINE (II)**, Cottonwood Press, Box J, Kansas Union, Kansas University, Lawrence KS 66045. Editor: George F. Wedge. Fiction Editor: Tamara Dubin Brown. Magazine: 6x9; 80 + pages; flat-spined cover; illustrations; photos. "*Cottonwood Magazine* is a literary magazine that publishes new and well-known writers. We have no theme aside from quality. For readers of fine literature, poetry and fiction in the Midwest and the nation." Triannually. Estab. 1965. Circ. 500.

**Needs:** Literary, contemporary, men's, and women's. "We are not interested in contrived, slick material." Accepts 4-8 mss/issue, 10-12 mss/year. Receives 25-30 unsolicited fiction mss each month. Length: 500-3,000 words. Critiques rejected mss "when there is time."

**How to Contact:** Query, send complete ms with cover letter (previous publications). SASE for query, ms. Accepts computer printout submissions. Prefers letter-quality. Reports in 1 month on queries, 2 months on ms. Publishes ms an average of 6 months after acceptance. Sample copy $3 (back issues only).

**Payment:** 1 copy.

**Terms:** Acquires one-time rights. Publication copyrighted.

**Tips:** "Read sample issues. *Rewrite.* Many of the manuscripts we reject are not polished. Be certain your story is as 'finished' as you can make it before you submit. We will probably publish even more fiction—perhaps 4-8 stories per issue." Published new writers within the year.

**COYDOG REVIEW (II), A Journal of Poetry, Short Fiction, Essays and Graphics**, 203 Halton Lane, Watsonville CA 95076. (408)688-2794. Editor: Candida Lawrence. Magazine: 7x9; 140 pages; Xerox paper; fine press cover; b&w art and photos. "*Coydog Review* has no theme and seeks honest original work on any subject, in any style for a literate audience that enjoys reading about everyday experiences." Annually. Estab. 1984. Circ. 200-500.

**Needs:** Erotic, ethnic, experimental, feminist, gay, humor/satire, lesbian, literary, mainstream, prose poem, regional, science fiction, excerpted novel, women's, and autobiographical. No obvious porn. Receives 30 unsolicited ms/month. Accepts 20 mss/issue. Length: under 10,000 words average. Also publishes short shorts, 5,000 words. Occasionally critiques rejected ms. Recommends other markets.

**How to Contact:** Send complete ms with SASE. Reports in 2 months on mss. Simultaneous and photocopied submissions OK. Accepts computer printout submissions. Sample copy $4, and $1 postage.

**Payment:** 2 contributor's copies. Offers prize money for special themes.

**Terms:** Acquires one-time rights. Publication copyrighted.

**Tips:** "Write about what you know, not what you think you ought to know or feel, and do not imitate a sophistication which is false. Risk reading your work out loud to yourself before sending. The editor is especially interested in work which tips towards autobiography but avoids self-indulgence. Getting published *anywhere* is a thrill for a beginning or continuing writer. The thrill translates into more devotion to craft. Avoid over-explanation of motive or character. Dramatic flashbacks are becoming *very* trite and ho-hum." Published new writers within the year.

**CRAB CREEK REVIEW (II)**, Crab Creek Review Association, 806 N. 42nd, Seattle WA 98103. (206)634-3199. Editor: Linda Clifton. Magazine: 6x10 minitab; 32 pages; ultrabright newsprint paper; self cover; line drawings illustrations. Magazine publishing poetry, short stories, art, and essays for adult, college-educated audience interested in literary, visual, dramatic arts and in politics. Triquarterly. Estab. 1983. Circ. 350.

**Needs:** Contemporary, humor/satire, literary, and translations. No confession, erotica, horror, juvenile, preschool, religious/inspirational, romance, or young adult. Receives 10 unsolicited mss/month. Accepts 2 mss/issue; 6 mss/year. Length: 3,000 words average; 1,200 words minimum; 3,500 words maximum. Publishes short shorts. Occasionally critiques rejected mss.

**How to Contact:** Send complete ms with short list of credits. Reports in 2 months. SASE. Photocopied submissions OK "but no multiple submissions." Accepts computer printout submissions. Prefers letter-quality. Sample copy $3.

**Payment:** 2 free contributor's copies; $2 charge for extras.

**Terms:** Acquires first rights. Rarely buys reprints. Publication copyrighted.

**Tips:** "Send us a story that compels the reader, by the energy and authenticity of its voice and the experience it portrays, to read all the way through without wanting to stop. Read the magazine first. We have more stories to choose from, so we can be quite selective. Be sure to type name and address on submission. Stick to guidelines of length. We want to offer our readers a balance of poetry and prose, both fiction and essay." Published new writers within the last year.

**CREAM CITY REVIEW (II)**, University of Wisconsin-Milwaukee, Box 413, Milwaukee WI 53201. Editor: Peter Hickey. Magazine: 8½x5½; 100 pages; 60 lb offset/perfect bound paper; 65 lb cover stock; illustrations; photos. National as well as regional audience. Semiannually. Published special fiction issue last year; plans another. Estab. 1975. Circ. 1,000.
**Needs:** Contemporary, avant-garde. Accepts 6-8 mss/issue. Receives approximately 50 unsolicited fiction mss each month. Length: 1,000-10,000 words. Publishes short shorts. Critiques rejected mss "when there is time." Recommends other markets "when we have time."
**How to Contact:** Send complete ms with SASE. Photocopied submissions OK. Reports in 2 months. Sample copy $3.50.
**Payment:** 1 free author's copy.
**Terms:** Acquires first rights. Sends galleys to author. Publication copyrighted.
**Tips:** "*CCR* has always published fiction and will continue to, because we feel that the small press market is the best place for fiction (and poetry) writers to get started." Published new writers within the last year.

**‡CREATIVE YEARS (I, II), Writer's Opportunities**, Coronado Publishers, #40, 2490 SW 14th Dr., Gainesville FL 32608. (904)373-7445. Editor: Eloise Cozeus Henderson. Magazine: 7x12; 32 pages; "best" paper; slick cover stock; illustrations. Inspirational content for mixed audience. Target is "beautiful people over 50." Bimonthly. Estab. 1980.
**Needs:** Historical, literary, religious/inspirational, senior citizen/retirement, retirement. Nostalgia, health-related dealing with age—death (not morbid). Receives 5-20 unsolicited fiction mss/week. Accepts 4 mss/issue; 25 mss/year. Publishes approximately 3 months after acceptance. Length: 1,500 words average; 1,500 words maximum. Publishes short shorts of 750 words maximum. Critiques rejected mss. Recommends other markets when there is time.
**How to Contact:** Send complete ms with cover letter. Reports in 3-6 weeks on queries; 3-6 weeks on mss. SASE for ms. Simultaneous submissions OK. Accepts computer printouts. Sample copy $2. Fiction guidelines for large SASE.
**Tips:** "We hope to help restore interest in wholesome, clean romance." Prefer stories by older persons of "I remember" romance. "We are paying at this time only in copies, but we feel that if a new writer is sincere he/she will know that bylines are helpful in future contacts."

**‡THE CREATIVE WOMAN (I)**, Governors State University, University Park IL 60466. (312)534-5000, ext. 2524. Editor: Dr. Helen Hughes. Magazine: 8½x11; 48 pages; illustrations; photos. "Focus on a special topic each issue, presented from a feminist." Estab. 1977. Circ. 800.
**Needs:** Feminist, humor/satire. Receives 5 unsolicited fiction mss/month. Accepts 1 ms/issue; 3 mss/year. Publishes ms 3-12 months after acceptance. Also publishes short shorts. Occasionally critiques rejected mss. Recommends other markets.
**How to Contact:** Send complete ms with cover letter. Report time varies. SASE for ms. Photocopied submissions and reprints OK. Accepts computer printouts. Sample copy free.
**Payment:** Contributor's copies.
**Terms:** Pays on publication. Publication copyrighted.

**THE CRESCENT REVIEW (II)**, The Crescent Review, Inc., Box 15065, Winston-Salem NC 27113. (919)768-5943. Fiction Editor: Bob Shar. Magazine: 6x9; 112-136 pages; 75 lb Williamsburg Hi-Bulk paper; 65 lb Carnival White cover stock; illustrations on cover only. "A fiction writer's magazine for the literate, college-educated, and young at heart. We don't use essays or reviews and include poetry mainly to fill in gaps. We have a strong bias toward unpublished Southeasterners." Semiannually. Published special fiction issue last year. Estab. 1983. Circ. 300.
**Needs:** Contemporary, erotica, ethnic, experimental, fantasy, humor/satire, literary, mainstream, psychic/supernatural/occult, regional, science fiction, suspense/mystery, and western. No "inspirational, dull, or darkly introspective material." Receives 20 unsolicited mss/month. Accepts 10-12 mss/issue; 20-24 mss/year. Length: 3,000-5,000 words average; 150 words minimum; 8,000 words maximum. Occasionally critiques rejected mss. Recommends other markets.
**How to Contact:** Send complete ms. Reports in 2 months. SASE. Photocopied submissions

OK. Accepts computer printout submissions. Prefers letter-quality. Sample copy $4.
**Payment:** 2 free contributor's copies; $4 charge for extras.
**Terms:** Acquires first North American serial rights.
**Tips:** "We started *The Crescent Review* in 1983 as a vehicle for talented young southeastern writers of short fiction. There seemed to be a great need for a magazine like ours in this part of the country. The quality of some of the submissions we've received bares out this need. We've had stories reprinted in *Best American Short Stories, 1984*, *Harper's* and *Pushcart Prize*." Published 5 new writers within the last year.

**CRITIQUE (IV), Exploring Conspiracy Theories & Metaphysics Publishing** , Critique, Box 11451, Santa Rosa CA 95406. (707)525-9401. Editor: Bob Banner. A journal containing material on the occult, conspiracy, metaphysics, politics, fiction, book reviews, and news analyses, of the global psyche for students and intelligent readers. Semiannually. Estab. 1980. Circ. 3,000.
**Needs:** Contemporary, historical (general), literary, psychic, religious, science fiction, Sufism, gnosticism, and political intrigue. Accepts 2 mss/year of unsolicited fiction. Length: 3,000 words maximum. Occasionally critiques rejected mss.
**How to Contact:** Send complete ms with SASE and short description of manuscript. Photocopied and previously published submissions OK. Accepts computer printout submissions. Reports in 6 months on mss. Publishes ms 4-6 months after acceptance. Sample copy $5. Fiction guidelines free.
**Payment:** $50 maximum and 3 free contributor's copies.
**Terms:** Pays on publication. Buys reprints. Publication copyrighted.
**Tips:** "Send for sample issue to understand what we're publishing." Publishes fiction for variety, "and if it contains some of the themes we focus on it can create a more powerful effect." Published new writers within the last year.

**CROP DUST (I, II)**, Crop Dust Press, Rt. 5, Box 75, Warrenton VA 22186. (703)347-5523. Contact: Editor. Rural and city landscapes for the university and general writing community. Semiannually. Estab. 1979. Circ. 500.
**Needs:** Literary and contemporary, all types of fiction. Accepts 5 mss/issue, 10 mss/year. Receives approximately 10 unsolicited fiction mss/month. Length: 500-5,000 words. Critiques rejected mss "when there is time."
**How to Contact:** Send complete ms. Reports in 2 weeks. Sample copy $3.
**Payment:** 1 free author's copy.
**Terms:** Acquires first North American serial rights which revert to author on publication. Publication copyrighted.
**Tips:** "Read a copy of the magazine before submitting. Send only one story. Short stories fare better with editors in our publishing space."

**‡CROSS TIMBERS REVIEW (II)**, Cisco Junior College, Cisco TX 76437. (817)442-2567. Editor: Monte Lewis. Fiction Editor: Ken Hammes. Magazine: 9½x6; 72 pages average; 65 lb paper; 80 lb cover stock; pen and ink illustrations. Theme is "to serve as a medium through which regional ideas and works may be presented to a broader readership while at the same time not excluding the works of international writers for academic and general audience." Semiannually. Estab. 1983. Circ. 250.
**Needs:** Adventure, ethnic, historical (general), humor/satire, literary, regional, western, southwestern material. Receives 5-10 unsolicited fiction mss/month. Accepts 2-3 mss/issue; 4-6 mss/ year. Does not read mss June/July. Publishes ms 3-6 months after acceptance. Length: 3,000-4,000 words average; 1,000 words minimum; 5,000 words maximum. Critiques rejected mss.
**How to Contact:** Send complete ms with cover letter with name, address. Reports in 6 weeks on queries; 2 months on mss. SASE for ms. Photocopied submissions OK. Accepts computer printouts including dot-matrix. Sample copy $3.
**Payment:** Pays in 3 contributor's copies, $3 charge for extras.

**Terms:** Pays on publication for one-time rights. Sends galleys to author. Publication copyrighted.
**Tips:** "We like stories with *impact*. The story must say something with preciseness and punch. The Southwest has a rich tradition of fiction; we want to encourage writers to keep the tradition alive."

**CROSS-CANADA WRITERS' QUARTERLY (II)**, Box 277, Station F, Toronto, Ontario M4Y 2L7 Canada. Editor-in-Chief: Ted Plantos. Magazine: 8½x11; 32 pages; 70 lb paper; card-coated cover stock; illustrations; photos. "The Canadian literary writer's magazine." Quarterly. Published special fiction issue last year. Estab. 1978. Circ. 2,500.
**Needs:** Literary and regional. "We welcome submissions of fiction from American authors. We offer American as well as Canadian writers the most comprehensive, current literary market listings published in Canada. We keep our readers in touch with the Canadian literary scene and available markets for their work." Receives 6-10 unsolicited fiction mss/month. Accepts 2-4- mss/issue, 10-12 mss/year. Length: 3,000 words maximum. Publishes short shorts. Occasionally critiques rejected mss.
**How to Contact:** Send complete ms with SASE with bio. Photocopied submissions OK. Accepts computer printout submissions. Prefers letter-quality. Reports in 2 weeks on queries; 5 weeks on mss. Publishes ms "up to one year" after acceptance. Sample copy $3.95.
**Payment:** $10/page.
**Terms:** Acquires first rights and one-time rights. Publication copyrighted.
**Tips:** Recommends studying an issue before submitting. Subscriptions: $14 (individuals Canadian); $16 (individuals abroad); $16 (institutions Canadian); $18 (institutions abroad). Quality will be recognized. Published new writers within the last year.

**CROSSCURRENTS (III)**, 2200 Glastonbury Rd., Westlake Village CA 91361. Editor: Linda Brown Michelson. "*Crosscurrents* is a literary magazine offering another corner for today's artistry. We publish short fiction, poetry, graphic arts, and nonfiction. We direct our publication toward an educated audience who appreciate good writing and good art and who enjoy a periodic sampling of current trends in these fields." Quarterly. Estab. 1980. Circ. 3,000.
**Needs:** Most categories except heavy erotica, juvenile and young adult. "Good writing is what we look for and consider first. We want high quality literary fiction." Buys 7-12 mss/issue, 45 mss/year. Approximately 10% of fiction is agented. Length: 6,000 words maximum. Critiques rejected mss "when there is time."
**How to Contact:** Send complete ms with SASE. Reviews material June 1-Nov 30 each year. Accepts computer printout submissions. Prefers letter-quality. Reports in 6 weeks on mss. Publishes ms 4-6 months after acceptance. Sample copy $5.
**Payment:** $35 minimum. Offers 50% kill fee for assigned ms not published.
**Terms:** Pays on publication for first North American serial rights. Publication copyrighted.
**Tips:** "Look at a sample issue to see what we publish. Include a short letter with your manuscript to let us know who you are. If given encouragement, submit three or four times each year, not every week. Good quality photocopies fine, but no simultaneous submissions. Many rejected manuscripts are well done but do not fit our coming issues. Many others, however, are simply not professional."

**THE CROSSTOWN RAG, Bimonthly Newsletter for Advanced & Challenge (Square) Dancers (I, IV)**, 1405 Kahler Ct., San Jose CA 95132. (408)262-6863. Editor-in-Chief: Andrea L. Fuller. "Newsletter for high-level square dancers using articles, humor, occasional fiction, poetry, cartoons, and jokes." Annually. Estab. 1979. Circ. 500.
**Needs:** Fantasy, humor/satire, romance (contemporary), science fiction, and suspense/mystery. "All manuscripts must involve *only* square dancing or dancers." Receives "very few" unsolicited fiction mss/month. Accepts 6 mss/year. Length: 500 words preferred; longer mss considered if it can be serialized. Occasionally critiques rejected mss.
**How to Contact:** Send complete ms with SASE. Accepts computer printout submissions. Prefers letter-quality or dot-matrix. Accepts disc submissions compatible with Apple IIe. Prefers hard

copy on 8½x11 sheet in 2 columns of 3½x9½" (preferred). Simultaneous, photocopied, and previously published submissions OK. Reports in 1 month on mss. Sample copy sent upon request.
**Payment:** $1 per 3½x9½ column (about 250 words) and 1 free contributor's copy.
**Terms:** Pays on publication for one-time rights.
**Tips:** "We're very easy; a good place to learn fiction techniques for the short-short story. Material should be short, concise, loaded with imagery and action."

**CROTON REVIEW (II)**, Croton Council on the Arts, Inc. (non-profit organization), Box 277, Croton on Hudson NY 10520. Editors: Ruth Lisa Schechter and Dan B. Thomas. Magazine: 7x10; 64 pages; "excellent" paper quality; "laminated" cover; illustrations. "An award-winning publication (supported by National Endowment on the Arts grant NYSCA and CAW) based on quality and substance." Publishes contemporary, diverse short prose, poetry, literary essays and translations. Annually. Estab. 1978. Circ. 2,000.
**Needs:** Literary and contemporary. "We are interested in a well-written short-short story of substance and imagination. No trite or hackneyed themes. *CR* reads new material September to January *only*. Approximate length: 8-14 double-spaced pages.
**How to Contact:** Send complete ms with brief biography and SASE. Reports in 8-16 weeks or sooner. Sample copy $4 (add 80¢ postage) or subscription $8 (postpaid); 2 annual issues.
**Payment:** 1 free author's copy; author's payments depend on grant; proviso as to amount.
**Terms:** Publication copyrighted.
**Tips:** "Subscribe to and read the *Croton Review*. Originality evidence of substance, language and craft desirable. Do not take three pages to begin; begin at the beginning; avoid cliché language and themes. Read books; expand vocabulary. Avoid rhetoric and adjectives if possible. Exert clarity; revise."

**C.S.P. WORLD NEWS (II)**, Edition Stencil, Congregation of Saint Paul, Box 2608, Station D, Ottawa, Ontario K1P 5W7 Canada. Editor: Guy F. Claude Hamel. Magazine: 8½x14; 20 pages; bond paper; bond cover stock. Literary journal for general audience. Monthly. Published special fiction issue last year. Estab. 1965. Circ. "varies."
**Needs:** Open to all subjects. Requires magazine subscription of $15.
**How to Contact:** Send complete ms. SASE or IRC. Simultaneous submissions OK. Accepts computer printout submissions. Prefers letter-quality. Sample copy $2 and legal-sized SASE.
**Payment:** Varies.
**Terms:** Acquires first rights. Publication copyrighted.
**Tips:** "Be honest with your readers and be willing to subscribe to the publications you wish to write for." Published new writers within the last year.

**CUMBERLAND JOURNAL (III, IV)**, 175 Berbey Ave., Westerville OH 43081. Contact: Editor. Publishes literary biography and innovative cultural criticism for serious fiction readers, artists and critics. Quarterly. Plans special fiction issue. Estab. 1976. Circ. 400.
**Needs:** Publishes short shorts of "the 3½ minute variety." Length: 1,000-18,000 words. Critiques rejected mss "when there is time."
**How to Contact:** Query or send complete ms. SASE for query, ms and short bio. Reports in 2 weeks. Sample copy $3.
**Payment:** Free author's copies.
**Terms:** Acquires first rights or first North American serial rights. Publication copyrighted.
**Tips:** "Purchase sample copy to see what we publish." Mss are rejected because writers are "unfamiliar with market."

**CUT BANK (II)**, English Department, University of Montana, Missoula MT 59812. Editor-in-Chief: Pamela Uschuk. Magazine: 4x6; 135 pages; high quality paper and cover; b&w illustrations; photos. "Fine writing—poetry, fiction, articles, art, photos, interviews, criticism, reviews, parts of novels, long poems—for anyone interested in the best prose and poetry being written today." Semiannually. Estab. 1973. Circ. 600.

**Needs:** Adventure, contemporary, ethnic, experimental, fantasy, historical, humor/satire, literary, prose poem, translations, and women's. "Only the highest quality will be considered." Receives 40 unsolicited fiction mss/month. Accepts 3-5 mss/issue, 6-10 mss/year. Length: 10,000 words maximum; 4,000 words average. Interested in short shorts less than 2,000 words. Occasionally critiques rejected mss. Does not read mss May-Aug.
**How to Contact:** Send complete ms and brief bio with SASE. Photocopied submissions OK. Accepts computer printout submissions. Prefers letter-quality. Reports in 6-8 weeks on mss. Publishes ms up to 4 months after acceptance. Sample copy $2.
**Payment:** 2 free contributor's copies; regular newsstand price for extras.
**Terms:** Acquires all rights. Publication copyrighted. Rights returned on request.
**Tips:** "*Cutbank* is regularly publishing very high quality fiction by both firmly established and unknown writers. We are most concerned with maintaining and increasing this high level of quality. We receive a surprising number of good stories each month, stories which are easy to read and likable, but which are not as tight or as interesting as they might be. Once you have a pretty good story, don't send it to us—yet. Spend as much time as you can going through line by line, word by word, tightening, sharpening, over and over. Go to extremes. Be a fanatic. *Then*—fire it off to us. Read as a writer. Dissect. It's the only way to learn nuts and bolts. Reading is part of your job not your leisure. Subscribe to as many fiction publishing magazines, as you can afford, both big and small. Know what the masters did but also know what your contemporaries are doing around you. Meet writers and editors. Bother them. Ask them to read and criticize your fiction."

**DAN RIVER ANTHOLOGY (I, II)**, Dan River Press, Box 123, South Thomaston ME 04858. (207)354-6550. Editor: R. S. Danbury III. Book: 5½x8½; 144 pages in 1986, (108 in 1985); 60 lb paper; gloss cover stock; illustrations (as submitted); photos. Annual book. No theme. For general/adult audience. Annually. Estab. 1984. Circ. 500.
**Needs:** Adventure, contemporary, erotica, ethnic, experimental, fantasy, historical (general), horror, humor/satire, literary, mainstream, men's, prose poem, psychic/supernatural/occult, regional, romance (contemporary and historical), science fiction, senior citizen/retirement, suspense/mystery, and western. No "evangelical Christian, pornography or sentimentality." Receives 3-4 unsolicited mss/month. Accepts about 4 mss/year. Reads "mostly in March. The rest of the year we usually don't read them, though mss may be scanned to weed out the amateurish ones." Length: 2,000-2,400 words average; 800 words minumum; 4,000 words maximum.
**How to Contact:** Send complete ms with SASE and $1 (cash) reading fee. Reports in April each year. SASE. Previously published work OK. Accepts computer printout submissions. Prefers letter-quality. Accepts disc submissions if compatible with TI 99/4a, Sanyo 1150 or Compugraphic 7300. Sample copy $9.95 paperback, and $1.25 shipping; $15.95 cloth and $1.25 shipping. Fiction guidelines for #10 SAE.
**Payment:** 10% of all sales attributable to writer's influence: readings, mailings, auto-partys, etc. plus up to 50% discount on copies.
**Terms:** Acquires on publication first rights. Publication copyrighted.
**Tips:** "Make me want to finish the ms. We like fiction and still believe it is important/necessary." Published "quite a few" new writers the last year.

**DARK VISIONS (I)**, Visions Publications, Box 1291, Station B, Ottawa, Ontario K1P 5R3 Canada. Magazine: 8½x5½; 48 pages; white bond paper; Mayfair cover stock; illustrations. Horror, macabre fiction. Some supernatural for horror audience. Published 3 times/year. Plans special fiction issue. Estab. 1984. Circ. 500.
**Needs:** Horror. No explicit sex or violence. Receives 20-30 unsolicited fiction mss/month. Accepts 6-10 mss/issue; 30 mss/year. Publishes ms 3-5 months after acceptance. Agented fiction: 1%. Length: 1,800 words average; 50 words minimum; 3,000 words maximum. Publishes short shorts of 50-500 words. Critiques rejected mss.
**How to Contact:** Send complete ms with cover letter and brief biography. Reports in 4 weeks on queries. SASE for ms. Simultaneous and photocopied submissions OK. Accepts computer printouts including dot-matrix. Sample copy $2.50, 6x9 SAE and 2 Canadian stamps. Fiction guidelines for # SAE and 1 Canadian stamp.

**Payment:** Contributor's copies.
**Terms:** Pays on publication. Acquires one-time rights. Publication copyrighted.
**Tips:** "There are still many markets open to beginners. Many great writers broke into the field by writing for small press publications and then went on to write novels."

**DAY TONIGHT/NIGHT TODAY (II)**, Box 353, Hull MA 02045. (617)925-2860. Editor: S.R. Jade. Magazine: 5½x4¼; 56 pages; 20 lb paper; 120 lb cover stock; b&w illustrations. Magazine of "poetry, fiction, graphics (including cartoons), and essays with a feminist/humanist slant with a sense of humor for a varied readership—probably 75% women because that's who we publish." Seven issues yearly. Published special fiction issue last year; plans another. Estab. 1981. Circ. 350.
**Needs:** Comics, erotica, ethnic, experimental, feminist/lesbian, gay, humor/satire, literary, prose poem, science fiction, serialized/excerpted novel, and women's. "We only publish women. Especially interested in stream-of-consciousness, prose, and free style. No sexism, racism, or pornography." Receives 12-15 unsolicited fiction mss/month. Accepts 0-5 mss/issue; 12-15 mss/year. Publishes short shorts to 7 typewritten, double-spaced pages. Length: 4,000 words maximum; 2,500 words average. Occasionally critiques rejected mss.
**How to Contact:** Send complete ms with SASE. Simultaneous and/or photocopied submissions OK. Accepts computer printout submissions. Reports in 6 weeks on mss. Publishes ms 3-12 months after acceptance. Sample copy for $3.25. Fiction guidelines free for standard SAE and 20¢ postage.
**Payment:** 1 free contributor's copy; $2.50 charge for extras.
**Terms:** Rights revert to author/artist on publication. Publication copyrighted.
**Tips:** "Send several short, strong pieces revolving around being a woman or circumstance special to women/health relationships, economics. Request critique if wanted. No *Reader's Digest* type (no slam intended) stuff—more 'un-cut,' gutsy, real-life published here. Print name on each separate page. Get a sample copy of *DT/NT* before submitting work. Whatever you wish to express, if done well, already has an audience waiting for it. So get to it!" Published new writers within the last year.

**THE DEKALB LITERARY ARTS JOURNAL (II)**, Literary Arts Journal (DLAJ), DeKalb Community College, 555 N. Indian Creek Dr., Clarkston GA 30021. (404)299-4119. Editor: Frances Ellis. Magazine: 6x9; 85 pages; Azalea text 80 lb sunray crystal vellum paper; 10 pt cl5 cover stock. Magazine of original/creative writing: short stories, drama, poetry, black and white visual art, and music for general audience. Estab. 1966. 2 or 3 issues annually. Published special fiction issue last year; plans another.
**Needs:** Humor/satire and literary. No prose over 25 pages. Receives 50 mss/month. Publishes short shorts of 3-10 pages. Accepts 6-10 mss/year. Does not read August-early September.
**How to Contact:** Send complete ms with SASE and brief bio. Reports in 6 months on mss. Only previously un-published submissions OK. Sample copy for $4. Fiction guidelines free with SASE.
**Payment:** Pays 1 contributor's copy; charge for extras: $4 each.
**Terms:** Accepts one-time rights.
**Tips:** Please be willing to revise. "Take a course or read a book on creative writing. Readers still enjoy a good story: characters, motives, action, language." Published new writers within the last year.

**DENVER QUARTERLY (II, III)**, University of Denver, Denver CO 80208. (303)871-2892. Editor: David Milofsky. "We publish fiction, articles and poetry for a generally well-educated audience primarily interested in literature and the literary experience. They read *DQ* to find something a little different from a strictly academic quarterly or a creative writing outlet." Quarterly. Estab. 1966. Circ. 800.
**How to Contact:** Send complete ms with SASE. Do not query. Reports in 1 month on mss. Publishes ms within a year after acceptance. Sample copy $4 with SASE.

**Payment:** Pays $5/page for fiction and $10/page for poetry. 2 free author's copies plus 3 tear sheets.
**Terms:** Acquires first North American serial rights.
**Tips:** "Our readers seem to be enthusiastic about our stories, but we hope to publish somewhat more short fiction than in the recent past, especially new and developing writers, but no novices. We'll be looking for serious, realistic fiction. Nothing so quickly disqualifies a manuscript as sloppy proofreading and mechanics. Also, don't waste time on elaborate cover letters. Some of the best fiction I've read lately came in that form."

**DESCANT (II)**, Department of English, Texas Christian University, Fort Worth TX 76129. (817)921-7240. Editors: Betsy Colquitt and Stanley Traghtenberg. "*Descant* uses fiction, poetry, and essays. No restriction on style, content or theme. It is a little literary magazine, and its readers are those who have interest in such publications." Semiannually. Estab. 1955. Circ. 1,000.
**Needs:** Literary, contemporary, and regional. No genre or category fiction. Receives approximately 50 unsolicited fiction mss each month. Does not read mss in summer. Length: 1,500-5,000 words. Publishes short shorts. Sometimes recommends markets.
**How to Contact:** Send complete ms with SASE. Accepts computer printout submissions. Prefers letter-quality. Reports usually within 6 weeks on ms. Sample copy $2.50.
**Payment:** 4 free author's copies. $2.50 charge/extra copy.
**Terms:** Acquires first North American serial rights. Publication copyrighted.
**Tips:** "Submit good material. Even though a small publication, *Descant* receives many submissions, and acceptances are few compared to the total number of mss received." Mss are rejected because they "are badly written, careless in style and development, shallow in characterization, trite in handling and in conception." We offer a $100 annual prize for fiction—the Frank O'Connor Prize. Award is made to the story considered (by a judge not connected to the magazine) to be the best published in a given volume of the journal." Published new writers within the last year.

**DESCANT (II)**, Box 314, Station P, Toronto, Ontario M5S 2S8 Canada. (416)766-9241. Editor: Karen Mulhallen. High quality poetry and prose for an intelligent audience who wants to see good, new poetry and prose. Published 4 times/year. Published special fiction issue last year; plans another. Estab. 1970. Circ. 1,000.
**Needs:** Literary, contemporary, and translations. "Although most themes are acceptable, all works must have literary merit." Receives 100-200 unsolicited mss/month. Publishes short shorts. Critiques rejected mss "when there is time."
**How to Contact:** Send complete ms with SAE, IRC. Reports in 4 months on mss. Sample copy $6 with 9x11 SAE and IRC (32¢ Canadian postage.)
**Payment:** Pays a modest honorarium and free copies. Extra author's copies at discount.
**Terms:** Varies.
**Tips:** "Edit yourself first. Send your best work. Rewrite your material until you are convinced it is the best that can be done on that theme." Rejects manuscripts because "writer is unfamiliar with magazine or has not mastered his craft." Published new writers within the last year.

**DIMENSION, Contemporary German Arts & Letters**, Box 26673, Austin TX 78755. (512)471-4314. Editor-in-Chief: A. Leslie Willson. Magazine of contemporary (post-1945) German literature *in translation* for scholars, students of literature, general readers. Published 3 times/year. Estab. 1968. Circ. 1,200.
**Needs:** Translations of German fiction since 1945. Literary, gay, feminist. Receives 5 unsolicited fiction mss/month. Accepts 3-5 mss/issue, 12-15 mss/year. Length: 2,000 words minimum; 10,000 words maximum; 4,000 words average. Occasionally critiques rejected mss. Sometimes recommends markets.
**How to Contact:** Send ms of translation with copy of original and SASE. Accepts computer printout submissions. Prefers letter-quality. Accepts disc submissions compatible with Exxon. Prefers hard copy with disc submission. Reports in 2 months on mss. Sample copy $8.
**Payment:** 1 contributor's copy; $6 charge for extra copies of magazine.
**Terms:** Publication retains all rights. Publication copyrighted.

**DOG RIVER REVIEW (II)**, Trout Creek Press, Box 125, Parkdale OR 97041-0125. (503)352-6494. Editor: Laurence F. Hawkins Jr. Magazine: 5½x8; 62 pages; illustrations. Semiannual magazine of poetry, short fiction and art. Estab. 1981. Circ. 300.
**Needs:** Experimental, fantasy, humor (parody)/satire, literary, mainstream, prose poem, psychic/supernatural/occult, and translations. Receives 10-12 unsolicited fiction mss/month. Accepts 3-4 mss/issue; 6-8 mss/year. Approximately 5% of fiction is agented. Length: 3,000 words maximum; 2,500 words average. Recommends other markets.
**How to Contact:** Send complete ms with SASE. Photocopied submissions OK. Reports in 2-3 months on mss. Publishes ms 4-8 months after acceptance. Sample copy (back issue) for $2 postpaid. Fiction guidelines for #10 envelope and 1 first class stamp.
**Payment:** Varied number of contributor's copies.
**Terms:** Acquires first North American serial rights. Sends galleys to author. Publication copyrighted.
**Tips:** "Submit clean copy. Check spelling, punctuation and grammar. Make me think. Everyone loves an entertaining, well-constructed story. Although seemingly impossible—make it new."

**‡DOOR COUNTY ALMANAK (IV)**, The Dragonsbreath Press, 10905 Bay Shore Dr., Sister Bay WI 54234. (414)854-2742. Editor: Fred Johnson. Magazine: 6x9; 224 pages, (issue 2); good paper quality; uncoated cover stock; illustrations; photos. "The major focus is Door County WI and its surrounding areas. Covering the history, recent and distant, of the area and its people, including contemporary profiles of people and businesses. Each issue has a major theme. Also uses poetry and fiction for general audience, mainly aimed at people familiar with the area." Annually. Estab. 1982.
**Needs:** Adventure, contemporary, fantasy, historical (general), humor/satire, literary, regional, suspense/mystery. "Prefer to have the fiction in some way related to the area, at least to the issue's theme." No romance. Receives 10-20 unsolicited fiction mss/month. Buys 1-2 mss/issue. Does not read mss April-September. Length: 4,000 words average; 500 words minimum; 6,000 words maximum.
**How to Contact:** Query first. Reports in 3-4 weeks on queries; 2-3 months on mss. SASE for query and ms. Simultaneous, photocopied submissions and reprints OK. Accepts computer printouts including dot-matrix. Sample copy $5.50 and 7x10 SAE and $1 postage. Fiction guidelines free for #10 SASE and 1 first class stamp.
**Payment:** Pays $10-35 plus contributor's copies.
**Terms:** Pays on publication for first North American serial rights and other rights. Publication copyrighted.
**Tips:** "Query first to find out what coming issue's theme is and what the needs are. We're always looking for nonfiction articles also. Keep in mind this is definitely a regional magazine."

**EARTH'S DAUGHTERS (II), A Feminist Arts Periodical**, Box 41, Central Park Station, Buffalo NY 14215. (716)837-7778. Collective Editorship. Business Manager: Bonnie Johnson. Magazine: size varies; 50 pages. "We publish poetry and short fiction; topics of interest to women; also graphics, art work, and photos." For a general/women/feminist audience. Quarterly. Published special fiction issue last year; plans another. Estab. 1971. Circ. 500.
**Needs:** Adventure, contemporary, erotica, ethnic, experimental, fantasy, feminist/lesbian, humor/satire, literary, prose poem, and women's. "Keep the fiction short." Receives 25-50 unsolicited fiction mss/month. Accepts 2-4 mss/issue; 8-12 mss/year. Length: 400 words minimum; 1,000 words maximum; 800 words average. Occasionally critiques rejected mss. Recommends other markets.
**How to Contact:** Send complete ms. SASE (a must) for query. Simultaneous and photocopied submissions OK. Accepts computer printout submissions. Prefers letter-quality ("must be clearly legible"). Reports in 3 weeks on queries; 3 weeks to 3 months on mss. Publishes ms an average of 6 months after acceptance. Sample copy for $4.
**Payment:** 2 free contributor's copies.
**Terms:** Acquires first rights. Copyright reverts to author upon publication.

**Tips:** Submit "*good*" writing supportive of women. No stories over 1,000 words (we are a small press magazine and are always over the budget). We like to include fiction with our poetry for variety and because we like good fiction." Published "several" new writers within the last year.

**EARTHWISE QUARTERLY (I, II)**, Earthwise Publications, Inc., Box 680536, Miami FL 33168. (305)688-8558. Editor: Barbara Holley. Fiction Editor: Kaye Edwards Carter. "A quarterly journal mainly of poetry and interviews, fiction, articles, etc. We have various quarterly themes, usually announced at the start of the year. We have an eclectic audience of mainly poets, some artists, authors. We aim for quality literature and are attaining a fine reputation. We also publish a quarterly newsletter announcing contests, markets, etc." Quarterly. Estab. 1978. Circ. 500.
**Needs:** Literary, contemporary, psychic/supernatural, regional, science fiction, fantasy, gothic, romance, western, mystery, adventure, humor, and any ethnic. Very interested in translations. Nothing morally or ethically pornographic. Buys 1-2 mss/issue, 4-6 mss/year. Does not read mss June 30-September 5 each year. Buys little, if any, agented fiction. Length: 900-1,200 words. Sample copy newsletter $2. Theme list available for SASE. Publishes ms 3-12 months after acceptance.
**How to Contact:** Query with clips of published work with SASE. Accepts computer printout submissions. Prefers letter-quality. Reports in 3 months on queries and mss. Sample copy $4.
**Payment:** Pays $10+.
**Terms:** Pays on publication for first North American serial rights. Buys reprints if properly credited.
**Tips:** "We like light, amusing or warm stories for *Earthwise*. We much prefer the well done story. Cameos or vignettes are also acceptable. Quality counts here."

**EIDOS: Erotic Entertainment for Women (II IV)**, Brush Hill Press, Inc., Box 96, Boston MA 02137. (617)333-0612. Editor: Brenda L. Tatelbaum. Magazine: 8½x11; 32 pages; 70 lb coated text cover stock; illustrations; photos. Magazine of erotica for women. "Explicit material regarding language and behavior formed in relationships, intimacy, moment of satisfaction—sensual, sexy, honest." For an energetic, well-informed erotica readership of both men and women. Quarterly. Estab. 1984. Circ. 20,000.
**Needs:** Erotica. Humorous or tongue-in-cheek erotic fiction is especially wanted. Accepts 4-6 mss/issue; 16-24 mss/year. Length: 2,000 words average; 500 words minimum; 3,500 words maximum. Occasionally critiques rejected manuscript. Recommends other markets.
**How to Contact:** Send complete ms with SASE "cover letter with history of publication or short bio is welcome." Reports in 2 months. Simultaneous and photocopied submissions OK. Accepts computer printout submissions. Sample copy $5. Fiction guidelines free for business-sized envelope with first class stamp.
**Payment:** Contributor's copies.
**Terms:** Acquires on publication first North American serial rights.
**Tips:** "In erotica there's a demand for honesty and explicitness in writing. Submit manuscript for publication, and if manuscript is returned, request comments from the editor as to why it was not accepted immediately. Revise. Resubmit. Keep asking questions." Published new writers within the last year.

**ELDRITCH TALES (II)**, Yith Press, 1051 Wellington Rd., Lawrence KS 66044. (913)843-4341. Editor-in-Chief: Crispin Burnham. Magazine: 5½x8; 120 pages (average); illustrations; photos. "The magazine concerns horror fiction in the tradition of the old *Weird Tales* magazine. We publish fiction in the tradition of H.P. Lovecraft, Robert Bloch and Stephen King, among others, for fans of this particular genre." Semiannually. Estab. 1975. Circ. 500.
**Needs:** Horror and psychic/supernatural/occult. "No mad slasher stories or similar nonsupernatural horror stories." Receives about 8 unsolicited fiction mss/month. Accepts 12 mss/issue, 24 mss/year. Less than 1% of fiction is agented. Length: 50-100 words minimum; 20,000 words maximum; 10,000 words average. Occasionally critiques rejected mss. Sometimes recommends markets.

**How to Contact:** Send complete ms with SASE and cover letter stating past sales. Photocopied and previously published submissions OK. Accepts computer printout submissions. Prefers letter-quality. Reports in 4 months. Publication could take up to 5 years after acceptance. Sample copy $6.

**Payment:** 1/4¢/word; 1 contributor's copy. $1 minimum payment.

**Terms:** Pays in royalties on publication for first rights. Publication copyrighted.

**Tips:** "Buy a sample copy and read it thoroughly. Most rejects with my magazine are because people have not checked out what an issue is like or what type of stories I accept. Most rejected stories fall into one of two categories: non-horror fantasy (sword & sorcery, high fantasy) or non-supernatural horror (mad slasher stories, 'Halloween Clones,' I call them). When I say that they should read my publication, I'm not whistling Dixie. We hope to up the magazine's frequency to a quarterly. We also plan to be putting out one or two books a year, mostly novels, but short story collections will be considered as well. I feel that there is a market for fiction. Also there are more writers out there that are talented and need a place to appear." Published new writers within the last year.

**EMPIRE (I, IV), The Magazine for Science Fiction Writers**, 1025 55th St., Oakland CA 94608. (203)865-4373. Editor: Millea Kenin. Magazine: 8½x11; 32 pages; 20 lb white offset paper; 60 lb colored offset cover stock; b&w illustrations; b&w photos. "A writers' magazine—we publish articles that assist, inform, and entertain science fiction writers from tyro to professional." Quarterly. Estab. 1974. Circ. 1,500.

**Needs:** Fantasy (occasionally) and science fiction. "Every issue contains a story and three critiques of the story by professional SF writers. This is the *only* use of fiction in *EMPIRE*." Receives 8-10 unsolicited fiction mss/month. Accepts 1 ms/issue, 4 mss/year. Length: 2,000 words minimum; 3,500 words maximum; 3,000 words average. Always briefly critiques rejected mss. Recommends other markets.

**How to Contact:** Send complete ms with SASE and cover letter with "brief publication credits and brief submission history of that story." Photocopied submissions OK, "but must be clean enough to copy again." Accepts computer printout submissions. Letter-quality only. Reports in 2 weeks. Publishes ms 3-12 months after acceptance. Sample copy $2.

**Payment:** 2 free contributor's copies and 1 year subscription. Extra copies by arrangement.

**Terms:** Pays on publication for first English language serial rights. Buys reprints for nonfiction only. Publication copyrighted; story copyrighted in author's name.

**Tips:** "We are looking for stories that have received favorable comments from commercial SF editors without ever quite getting accepted for publication: basically good stories with correctable problems. We use only *one* story per issue *only* to be critiqued. Correct spelling and grammar carefully! We do not change *anything* in fiction mss. Type double-spaced, one side of 8½x11 white paper (no corrasable bond). Enclose SASE! We feel a critique of a piece of fiction is helpful." Published new writers within the last year.

**EPOCH MAGAZINE (II, III)**, 251 Goldwin Smith Hall, Cornell University, Ithaca NY 14853. (607)256-3385. Editor: C.S. Giscombe. Magazine: 6x9; 80-100 pages; good quality paper; good cover stock. "Top level fiction and poetry for people who are interested in and capable of being entertained by good literature." Published 3 times a year. Estab. 1947. Circ. 1,000.

**Needs:** Literary, contemporary, and ethnic. Buys 4-5 mss/issue. Receives approximately 100 unsolicited fiction mss each month. Does not read in summer. Less than 1% of fiction is agented. Length: 10-30 typed, double-spaced pages. Critiques rejected mss "when there is time." Sometimes recommends other markets.

**How to Contact:** Send complete ms with SASE. Accepts computer printout submissions. Prefers letter-quality. No dot-matrix please. Reports in 2-8 weeks on mss (slower response in summer). Publishes ms an average of 3 months after acceptance. Sample copy $3.

**Terms:** Pays on publication for first North American serial rights. Publication copyrighted.

**Tips:** "We notice no trends—quality is quality and we can be optimistic about a writer if he has *vision*. We *strongly suggest* that potential contributors either examine a copy of *Epoch* at the library or purchase one from us before submitting work." Published new writers within the last year.

**EROTIC FICTION QUARTERLY (I, II, IV)**, EFQ Publications, Box 4958, San Francisco CA 94101. Editor: Richard Hiller. Magazine: 5x8, 186 pages; 50 lb offset; 65 lb cover stock. Small literary magazine for thoughtful people interested in a variety of highly original and creative short fiction with sexual themes.
**Needs:** Any style or genre heartfelt, intelligent erotica. (Ethnic, feminist, science fiction, etc.) Also, stories not necessarily erotic whose subject is some aspect of authentic sexual experience. No standard pornography; no "men's" stories; no contrived plots or gimmicks; no broad satire, parody or obscure "literary" writing; no poetry. Length: 500 words minimum; 5,000 words maximum; 1,500 words average. Occasionally critiques rejected ms. "Willing to work with beginners on exceptional mss." Sometimes recommends other markets.
**How to Contact:** Send complete ms only with SASE. Photocopied submissions OK; non-returnable copy also OK with 20¢ SASE for reply. Fiction guidelines free with SASE.
**Payment:** Pays $35 minimum.
**Terms:** Pay on acceptance for all rights. Publication copyrighted.
**Tips:** "I specifically encourage beginners who have something to say regarding sexual attitudes, emotions, roles, etc. Story ideas should come from real life, not media; characters should be real people. There are essentially no restrictions regarding content, style, explicitness, etc.; *originality*, *clarity*, and *integrity* are most important." Published new writers within the last year.

**EVENT (II)**, Douglas College, Box 2503, New Westminster, British Columbia V3L 5B2 Canada. Editor: Dale Zieroth. Fiction Editor: Maurice Hodgson. Managing Editor: Vye Flindall. Magazine: 6x9; 140+ pages; good quality paper; good cover stock; illustrations; photos. Primarily a literary magazine, publishing poetry, fiction, reviews, plays and graphics for creative writers, artists, anyone interested in contemporary literature. Semiannually. Published special fiction issue; plans another. Estab. 1970. Circ. 1,000.
**Needs:** Literary, contemporary, science fiction, fantasy, feminist, adventure, humor, regional, romance. No technically poor or unoriginal pieces. Buys 4-6 mss/issue. Receives approximately 50 unsolicited fiction mss/month. Publishes short shorts at 1,000 words. Length: 4,000 words. Critiques rejected mss "when there is time."
**How to Contact:** Send complete ms with SASE and bio (*must* be Canadian postage or IRC). Accepts computer printout submissions. Prefers letter-quality. Reports in 4 months on mss. Publishes ms an average of 6 months after acceptance. Sample copy $4.
**Payment:** Pays $30 minimum and 1 author's copy.
**Terms:** Pays on publication for first North American serial rights. Publication copyrighted.
**Tips:** "*Read* our magazine first; and read a lot of contemporary literature." Mss are rejected because of "level of maturity." Published new writers within the last year.

**EXIT, A Journal of the Arts**, Rochester Routes/Creative Arts Projects, 193 Inglewood Dr., Rochester NY 14619. (716)328-8818. Editor/Publisher: Frank Judge. "Our magazine has no theme and no particular bias but *quality*; there are some restrictions on length and content, as detailed below. We assume our readership is the 'little magazine' audience; we've had nothing to disprove this assumption so far." Published 3 times/year. Estab. 1976. Circ. 1,000.
**Needs:** Literary, contemporary, science fiction, fantasy, mystery, and translations. "Science fiction, fantasy, and mystery submissions should have a 'literary' slant giving a broader appeal than that of the respective forms; query preferred for these categories." No religious/inspirational, psychic/supernatural, men's, women's, feminist, gay/lesbian, confession, gothic, romance, western, adventure, juvenile, young adult, ethnic, or serialized or condensed novels. Accepts 1-2 mss/issue. Receives 3-5 unsolicited fiction mss each month. Length: 2,000 words maximum. Critiques rejected mss "when there is time."
**How to Contact:** Send query or complete ms with SASE. Accepts computer printout submissions. Accepts disc submissions compatible with Apple IIx. Reports in 3 weeks on queries, 1 month on mss. Publishes ms 6-12 months after acceptance. Sample copy $5.
**Payment:** 2 free author's copies; $2.50 charge for extras.
**Terms:** Pays on publication for first North American serial rights and second serial rights. Publication copyrighted.

**Tips:** Mss are rejected because they are "loaded with adolescent clichés and trite concepts, revel in 'experimental' obscurantising and/or have no sense of plot, liveliness."

**EXPRESSO TILT (II)**, 10B Chatham Lane, Newark DE 19713. (302)737-5852. Editor: Mike Walsh and Leo Peck. Magazine: 11x8; 24-32 pages; medium paper; medium cover stock; illustrations: b&w photos. "Absurdist comedy—fiction, and nonfiction dealing with American trash culture for well-informed/intellectual audience." Semiannually or triannually. Estab. November 1984. Circ. 5,000.
**Needs:** Comics, experimental, fantasy, humor/satire, literary, mainstream, and genre parody. No realistic or sentimental fiction. Receives 10-20 mss each month. Accepts 3-5 mss/issue; 6-15 mss/year. Length: 1,000 words average; 2,000 words maximum. Publishes short shorts. Occasionally comments on rejected ms. Recommends other markets.
**How to Contact:** Query first or send complete ms and cover letter with "info about the author and where he/she heard about *Expresso Tilt.*" Write for submission policies, payment and terms.
**Tips:** "We like fiction and we also write fiction. We feel we have the ability to choose good fiction from bad fiction."

**EXQUISITE CORPSE (III), A Monthly of Books & Ideas**, Culture Shock Foundation, English Dept., L.S.V. Baton Rouge LA 70803. Editor: Andrei Codrescu. Tabloid: 16x16; 24 pages; 60 lb offset paper; illustrations; photos. Tabloid of essays, reviews, polemics, poetry, fiction for literate audience. Monthly. Estab. 1983. Circ. 3,000.
**Needs:** Experimental. Receives 150 unsolicited mss/month. Accepts 1-2 mss/issue; 15 mss/ year. Requires magazine subscription of $15 (12 issues) before reading ms. Length: 1,000 words average; 250 words minimum; 1,000 words maximum.
**How to Contact:** Query first. Reports in 2 weeks on queries and mss. SASE. Simultaneous submissions OK. Accepts computer printout submissions. Requires letter-quality. Accepts disc submissions compatible with Mergenthoyer system. Prefers hard copy with disc submission. Sample copy $2.50.
**Payment:** 5 contributor's copies.
**Terms:** Acquires one-time rights. Publication copyrighted.
**Tips:** "Break the rules. We don't much believe in genre—we like experimental work." Published new writers within the last year.

**‡FAG RAG**, Box 331, Kenmore Station, Boston MA 02215. (617)661-7534. Editor: Collective. Magazine of gay male liberation. Annually. Estab. 1970. Circ. 5,000.
**Needs:** Adventure, comics, confession, erotica, fantasy, gay, historical, men's, prose poem, psychic/supernatural/occult. Receives 5 unsolicited fiction mss/month. Accepts 5 mss/issue. Length: 1-10,000 words average.
**How to Contact:** Query first. Reports in 2 months on queries; 3 months on mss. SASE for query. Photocopied submissions OK. Accepts computer printout submissions. Accepts disc submissions compatible with IBM-PC/Macintosh. Sample copy $5.
**Payment:** Pays in 2 contributor's copies.
**Terms:** Pays on publication for first North American serial rights. Publication copyrighted.
**Tips:** "Read our publication first."

**FANTASY & TERROR, New Series**, Richard Fawcett, Publisher, 61 Teecomwas Dr., Uncasville CT 06382. Editor: Jessica Amanda Salmonson, Box 20610, Seattle WA 98102. Magazine: digest sized; 36 pages; 20 lb paper; 70 lb cover stock; illustrations. Magazine of "macabre-surrealist prose poems á la Baudelaire; traditional ghost stories; fables, parables, idiosyncratic non-commercial fantastic narrative artforms; romanticism for "jaded fantasy readers; aesthetic cynics; dark romantics." Published occasionally. Published special fiction issue last year; plans another. Estab. 1973. Circ. 500.
**Needs:** Fantasy, horror, and macabre surrealism. Length: short-short stories. Reports in 2 weeks on queries; in 4 weeks on mss. SASE for query and ms. Photocopied submissions OK. Prefers let-

ter-quality. Sample copy $2 from publisher's address only. Recommends other markets.
**Payment:** Contributor's copy; 40% discount to contributors only.
**Terms:** Acquires one-time rights on publication. Publication copyrighted.
**Tips:** *"Fantasy and Terror* has nothing to do with popular trends. Writer should have a firm knowledge of surrealist and supernatural fiction; and be a constant reader of same."

**FANTASY BOOK (II)**, Fantasy Book Enterprises, Box 60126, Pasadena CA 91106. Executive Editor: Dennis Mallonee. Editor/Art Director: Nick Smith. Magazine: 8½x11; 64 pages; 40 lb paper; 8-point paper cover stock; illustrations. Magazine of fantasy fiction of all sorts: high fantasy, light fantasy, heroic fantasy, dark fantasy, fairy stories, fables, poems . . . for an older audience, college and up, "though we are not averse to using an occasional piece aimed at the younger reader." Quarterly. Estab. 1981. Circ. 5,000.
**Needs:** Adventure, fantasy, horror, psychic/supernatural, science fiction, and excerpted novel. Receives 80 unsolicited fiction mss/month. Buys 10 mss/issue, 60 mss/year. Approximately 10% of fiction is agented. Length: 2,000 words minimum; 10,000 words maximum; 5,000 words average. Occasionally critiques rejected mss. Recommends other markets.
**How to Contact:** Send complete ms with SASE. Photocopied and previously published submissions OK. Reports in 6 weeks. Publishes ms 6-9 months after acceptance. Sample copy $4; free guidelines with SASE.
**Payment:** 3-5¢/word; 2 free contributor's copies; charge for extras: 45% of cover price.
**Terms:** Pays on "approval of galleys" for first North American serial rights. Copyright notification printed in author's name. Buys reprints.
**Tips:** "The only advice we can give to an author attempting to write for *Fantasy Book* is to tell his story well. We look for strong characterization and a coherent and cohesive plot. We will publish more serialization and more action/adventure stories. We frown upon carelessness and sloppy workmanship. Learn the rules and standards of proper usage of English. *Know* the rules before breaking them. We do want to encourage new writers." Published new writers within the last year.

**FANTASY MACABRE**, , %Richard H. Fawcett, 61 Teecomwas Dr., Uncasville CT 06382. Editor-in-Chief: Richard Fawcett. Fiction Editor: Jessica Amanda Salmonson. Magazine: digest-sized; 60 pages; 20 lb paper; 70 lb cover stock; illustrations. Magazine of "supernatural fiction—short tales of dark fantasy, horror, and ghosts—for devoted readers of dark fantasy and horror." Semiannually. Estab. 1981. Circ. 500.
**Needs:** Horror and literary ghost stories. Receives 2 unsolicited fiction mss/day. Accepts 10 or more per issue, 20 or more per year. Length: no minimum; 3,500 words maximum; 2,000 words average. Publishes short shorts. Recommends other market.
**How to Contact:** Send complete ms with SASE. Reports in 8 weeks. Accepts computer printout submissions. Prefers letter-quality. Sample copy $3.25; free guidelines.
**Payment:** Pays a small cash honorarium and contributor copies; 40% discount for extras.
**Terms:** Pays on publication for first rights. Publication copyrighted.
**Tips:** "I see boring trends of introspective, plodding, dull horror and, conversely, fairly sleazy material horror. This magazine publishes neither sort. The beginning fiction writer should have a wide knowledge of supernatural literature, an ear for tonal quality of his/her own prose, and a gift for suspenseful, well-plotted, well-written horror." Published new writers within the last year.

**FARMER'S MARKET (II IV)**, Midwestern Farmer's Market Inc., Box 1272, Galesburg IL 61401. Fiction Editor: John Hughes. Magazine: 5½x8½; 48-64 pages; 70 lb offset paper; b&w illustrations; b&w photos. Magazine publishing "quality fiction, poetry, nonfiction, plays, etc., with a Midwestern theme and/or sensibility for an adult, literate audience." Semiannually. Estab. 1982. Circ. 500.
**Needs:** Contemporary, feminist, humor/satire, literary, regional, and excerpted novel. "We prefer material of clarity, depth and strength; strong plots, good character development." No "romance, *New Yorker* style, juvenile/teen." Accepts 4-8 mss/year. Occasionally critiques rejected mss. Recommends other markets.

**How to Contact:** Send complete ms with SASE. Reports in 1 month. Photocopied submissions OK. Accepts computer printout submissions. Prefers letter-quality. Publishes ms 2-6 months after acceptance. Sample copy for $3 and 6x9 envelope with 3 first class stamps.
**Payment:** 1 free contributor's copy.
**Terms:** Authors retain rights.
**Tips:** "We're always interested in regional fiction. We have been receiving more and better manuscripts so competition is getting keen. As a literary magazine, we believe fiction to be important both as an artform and as a measure of contemporary culture." Published new writers within the last year.

**FAT TUESDAY (II)**, 808¾ N. Detroit, Los Angeles CA 90046. Editor-in-Chief: F.M. Cotolo. Fiction Editors: B. Lyle Tabor and Thom Savion. Associate Editor: Lionel Stevroid. Journal: 8½x11 or 5x8; 27-36 pages; good to excellent paper; heavy cover stock; b&w illustrations only; photos. "Generally, we are an eclectic journal of fiction, poetry and visual treats. Our debut issue featured fiction by F.M. Cotolo, B. Lyle Tabor, and Dom Cimei, all of which focused on an individualistic nature with fiery elements. We are a literary mardi gras—as the title indicates—and irreverancy is as acceptable to us as profundity as long as there is fire! Our audience is anyone who can praise literature and condemn it at the same time. Anyone too serious about it on either level will not like *Fat Tuesday*." Annually. Plans speical fiction issue. Estab. 1981. Circ. 500.
**Needs:** Comics, erotica, experimental, humor/satire, literary, prose poem, psychic/supernatural/occult, serialized/excerpted novel, and dada. "Although we list categories, we are open to feeling out various fields if they are delivered with the mark of an individual and not just in the format of the particular field. In fiction, we do not appreciate the polished piece which has lost all flair due to the author's concern with form." Receives 10 unsolicited fiction mss/month. Publishes short shorts up to 5 double-spaced typewritten pages maximum. Accepts 4-5 mss/issue, 10-20 mss/year. Length: 1,000 words maximum. Occasionally critiques rejected mss.
**How to Contact:** Send complete ms with SASE. Photocopied submissions OK. Accepts computer printout submissions. Reports in 4 weeks. Publishes ms 3-10 months after acceptance. Sample copy $5.
**Payment:** 1 free contributor's copy.
**Terms:** Pays on publication for one-time rights. Publication copyrighted.
**Tips:** "Retain your enthusiasm. Never write and submit anything without it. Buy an issue and eat it up, page by page. Then, go into your guts and write something. If you're not on fire, we'll tell you so and encourage you to try again. Don't get discouraged. Write looking through your own eyes, and from your own heart. Don't be self-critical when you have something to say that reflects how you feel. Don't think commercial, just think and let the writing happen. Most of all, be aware of life outside of literature, and then let life influence your writing. It is essential that a potential submitter buy a sample issue and experience the 'zine to understand what would work and get a better idea of what we're talking about and help support the continuation of this free form of expression that *FT* calls 'littéraire vérité' and help us exist for it." Published new writers within the last year.

**FEMINIST STUDIES (II)**, Feminist Studies, Inc., c/o Women's Studies Program, University of Maryland, College Park MD 20742. (301)454-2363. Editor: Claire G. Moses. Fiction Editor: Rachel Blau DuPlessis. Business Manager: Lisa M. Laramee. Magazine: 6x9; 200 pages; 50 lb white offset paper; 10 pt cl5 cover stock; photos. Journal of feminist issues. A forum for analysis, debate and exchange. Audience consists of Women's Studies faculty, students, anyone interested in feminist issues and research. Published 3 times/year. Estab. 1972. Circ. 7,000.
**Needs:** Women's, feminist, gay/lesbian, and Third World women's writing. Publishes short shorts of 10-18 manuscript pages.
**How to Contact:** Send complete ms with SASE. Reports in 1-3 months on mss. Publishes ms 1-10 months after acceptance. Free guidelines.
**Terms:** Sends galleys to author. Publication copyrighted.

‡**THE FESSENDEN REVIEW (III)**, The RA Fessenden Educational Fund, Box 7272, San Diego CA 92107. (619)488-4991. Editor: D. Cruickshank. Fiction Editor: L. Deforest. Magazine: 8½x11; 64-72 pages; coated paper; coated cover stock; 20-30 photos. Book review with very few fiction stories for intellectual audience. Quarterly. Plans special fiction issue. Estab. 1975. Circ. 20,000.

**Needs:** Erotica, experimental, gay, humor/satire, psychic/supernatural/occult, observe Nabokov-type stories. "Must be stupendously good." No beginning authors. Receives 5-15 unsolicited fiction mss/month. Accepts 3-4 mss/year. Publishes 3-6 months after acceptance. Reading fee: $25. Length: 5,000 words average; 1,000 words minimum; 20,000 words maximum. Sometimes critiques rejected mss.

**How to Contact:** Send complete ms with cover letter and credentials. SASE for ms. Sample copy $2.50.

**Payment:** Pays $10-250.

**Terms:** Pays on publication. Publication copyrighted.

**Tips:** "Someone should be seeking out the Nabokovs, Dostoevskys and Nathanael Wests of 1990. Write better than anyone else and choose issues and subjects that hurt/wrench/agonize with an overlay of wit and joy. Don't use specious dialogue. And don't be fey or coy."

**FICTION INTERNATIONAL (III)**, English Dept., San Diego State University, San Diego CA 92182. Editors: Harold Jaffe and Larry McCaffery. Serious literary magazine of fiction, extended reviews, essays: 200 pages; illustrations; photos. "Our twin biases are politics and post-modernism." Biannually. Estab. 1973. Circ. 2,500.

**Needs:** Literary, political and innovative forms. Receives approximately 300 unsolicited fiction mss each month. No length limitations but rarely uses manuscripts over 25 pages. Portions of novels acceptable if self-contained enough for independent publication. Unsolicited mss will be considered only from September 1 through December 15 of each year.

**How to Contact:** Send complete ms with SASE. Reports in 1-3 months on mss. For sample copy query Roger Cuniffe, Managing Editor, *Fiction International*, San Diego State University Press, San Diego CA 92182.

**Payment:** Varies.

**Terms:** Pays on publication for first and first North American serial rights. Publication copyrighted.

**Tips:** "Study the magazine. We're highly selective. A difficult market for unsophisticated writers." Published new writers within the year.

‡**FINE MADNESS (II)**, Had We But, Inc., Box 15176, Seattle WA 98115. (206)526-2494. Editors: Kathryn MacDonald, James Snydal, John Marshall, Sean Bentley, Louis Bergsyel. Magazine: 48 pages; light and fairly heavy paper; light and heavy cover stock; illustrations on cover. "We are basically a poetry journal, but are looking at reviews and essays. We want to publish one good story each issue for adults who read and read. Triquarterly. Estab. 1982. Circ. 750.

**Needs:** Adventure, contemporary, historical (general), humor/satire, literary, mainstream. No novel excerpts. Receives 6 unsolicited fiction mss/month. Accepts 1 ms/issue. Publishes 3 months to a year after acceptance. Length: 2,500 words maximum. Critiques rejected ms.

**How to Contact:** Query first; query with published clips; send complete ms with cover letter of previous publications, etc., or submit through agent. Reports in 3 weeks on queries; 3 months on mss. SASE for ms or query. Photocopied submissions OK. Sample copy $2.50. Fiction guidelines free.

**Payment:** Pays in contributor's copies.

**Terms:** Pays on publication. Acquires first North American serial rights and anthology possibilities. Publication copyrighted.

**Tips:** "We receive far too many 'fancy' manuscripts. If the story is good, it *should* be written. Simply do it."

**FICTION NETWORK MAGAZINE (II)**, Fiction Network, Box 5651, San Francisco CA 94101. (415)391-6610. Editor: Jay Schaefer. Managing Editor: Heidi Ellison. Magazine: 8½x11;

48 pages; newsprint paper; 70 lb coated cover stock; illustrations. "Fiction Network distributes short stories to newspapers and regional magazines, and publishes *Fiction Network Magazine*, which circulates new fiction to agents, editors, writers, and others in the publishing and film industries." Biannually. Published special fiction issue; plans another. Estab. 1983. Circ. 6,000.

**Needs:** "All types of stories and subjects are acceptable; novel excerpts will be considered only if they stand alone as stories." No children's or young adult. Receives 500 unsolicited mss/month. Accepts 75 mss/year. Approximately 35% of fiction is agented. Length: 2,500 words average; 5,000 words maximum. Prefers very short stories. Recommends other markets.

**How to Contact:** Send complete ms or submit through agent. Reports in 12 weeks. Publishes ms 6-9 months after acceptance. SASE. "Do not ask us to return submissions from outside US. Do not send a second manuscript until you receive a response to the first." Simultaneous and photocopied submissions OK. Accepts computer printout submissions. Prefers letter-quality. Sample copy $4 US and Canada; $6.50 elsewhere. Fiction guidelines for SASE.

**Payment:** $25 minimum.

**Terms:** Pays on publication. "Fiction Network buys newspaper and magazine rights for one to three years. Each story accepted may appear in several periodicals. Payments from publications that carry the story are divided 50/50 with the author."

**Tips:** Advisory board includes: Ted Solotaroff (editor, Harper & Row, Publishers); John Gregory Dunne; Jane Ciabittari (Editor, the *Dial*; former managing editor, *Redbook*); Alice van Straalen (editor, Quality Paperback Book Club); John Casey; Alan Cheuse; John L'Heureux; and Stephen Minot. Contributors include Alice Adams, Max Apple, Ann Beattie, Andre Dubus, Bobbie Ann Mason, Joyce Carol Oates, Lynne Sharon Schwartz, Marian Thurm, and many previously unpublished writers. Published new writers within the last year.

**FIGHTING WOMAN NEWS (IV)**, Fighting Woman News, Box 1459, Grand Central Station, New York NY 10163. Editor: Valerie Eads. Fiction Editor: Kristen Noakes-Fry. Magazine: 8½x11; 24-36 pages; offset bond paper; self cover stock; illustrations; photos. "Women's martial arts, self-defense, combative sports. Articles, reviews, etc., related to these subjects. Well-educated adult women who are actually involved with martial arts read us because we're there and we're good." Quarterly. Estab. 1975. Circ. 5,600.

**Needs:** Science fiction, fantasy, feminist, adventure, and translations. "No material that shows women as victims, incompetents, stereotypes, or 'fight scenes' written by people who don't know anything about fighting skills." Receives very few unsolicited fiction mss. Length: 2,500 words. Critiques rejected mss "when there is time."

**How to Contact:** Query with clips of published work with SASE. Accepts computer printout submissions. "We must know if it is a simultaneous submission." Reports as soon as possible on queries and mss. Sample copy $3.50. Specify "fiction" when asking for samples. Free guidelines with legal-sized SASE.

**Payment:** Pays author's copies or subscription.

**Terms:** Pays on publication for one-time rights. Publication copyrighted; will print author's copyright if desired.

**Tips:** "It never hurts to read the magazine you want to write for." Mss are rejected because they are "not suitable for our magazine, i.e., submitted to the wrong market by writers who've never read our magazine. Would-be contributors should specify their area of interest when buying samples so we can send a sample with the appropriate material. Not every issue has everything."

**THE FLORIDA REVIEW**, The Island Press/Bahamas International Publishing Co. Ltd., #1 Parliament Square, Box N-1914, Nassau, Bahamas. Editor: Robert Flaum. Magazine of contemporary literature (fiction and nonfiction) with emphasis on the arts, politics, social issues and business for college educated/professional audience. Monthly. Estab. Oct. 1984. Circ. 25,000.

**Needs:** Contemporary, experimental, humor/satire, literary, mainstream, and translations. Must be "very high quality." Receives approximately 50 unsolicited mss/month. Accepts 4-6 mss/issue; 75 mss/year. Length: 1,000-2,500 words average; 3,000 words maximum. Occasionally comments on rejected ms.

**How to Contact:** Send complete ms with SASE. Reports in 3 weeks on mss. Simultaneous, photocopied and previously published submissions OK. Accepts computer printout submissions. Prefers letter-quality. Sample copy with $1 postage.
**Payment:** 2 free contributor's copies.
**Terms:** Acquires one-time rights. Publication copyrighted.
**Tips:** "We see a decline in craftsmanship and quality; we seek to reverse that trend. Have confidence in your ability to mature as a writer."

**FM FIVE (I, II)**, (formerly *Fiction Monthly*), Box 882108, San Francisco CA 94188. Publisher: Dwight Gabbard. Fiction Editor: Stephen Woodhams. Tabloid: 10x15; 16-20 pages; book stock paper; bookstock cover; illustrations; photos. Tabloid of "short shorts, interviews, essays, books reviews." Bimonthly except in summer. Published special fiction issue; plans another. Estab. 1983. Circ. 2,000.
**Needs:** Contemporary. No romantic, escapist, science fiction or fantasy. Receives 100 unsolicited mss/month. Accepts 2 mss/month; 20 mss/year. Length: 500-4,000 words average. Sometimes critiques rejected mss.
**How to Contact:** "Send for guidelines, include 22¢ postage on SASE." Reports in 10 weeks on mss. SASE. Photocopied submissions OK. Accepts computer printout submissions. Prefers letter-quality. Sample copy free.
**Payment:** $5 per page ($35 max) and 5 contributor's copies, and a one year subscription.
**Terms:** Pays on acceptance. Buys first North American serial rights.
**Tips:** "We publish short stories because they have been neglected in other markets and they are the most worthy thing to publish." Published new writers within the last year.

**FOOTSTEPS (II, IV)**, Journal of the Supernatural, Box 75, Round Top NY 12473. (518)699-8968. Editor: Bill Munster. Magazine: 5½x8; 80 pages; standard stock paper; semi-glossy cover stock; b&w illustrations. Magazine of horror short stories and tales of supernatural for general audience. Annually. Published special fiction issue last year; plans another. Estab. 1983. Circ. 500.
**Needs:** Horror and prose poem. No gore. Receives 50-100 mss/month. Accepts 20 mss/year. Length: 3,500 words average; 250 words minimum; 5,000 words maximum.
**How to Contact:** Send complete ms with SASE and cover letter stating previous publications. Reports in 3-4 weeks on mss. Photocopied submissions OK. Accepts computer printout submissions. Sample copy $4. ppd. Fiction guidelines for SAE (legal-sized envelope).
**Payment:** 2 contributor's copy; charge for extras: $4. ppd.
**Terms:** Acquires on publication for first rights. Publication copyrighted.
**Tips:** "In horror, everybody appears to be copying the style of Stephen King—don't, be original. Purchase a copy (supporting a small press magazine is imperative) and study its contents. Always enclose a SASE when writing to editors." Published new writers within the last year.

**‡FOOTWORK (I, II), A Literary Collection of Contemporary Poetry, Short Fiction and Art**, Passaic County Community College, College Blvd., Paterson NJ 07509. (201)684-6555. Editor: Maria Gillan. Fiction Editor: James T. McCartin. Magazine: 8x11; 88 pages; 60 lb paper; 70 lb cover; illustrations; photos. Annually. Plans fiction issue in future.
**Needs:** Contemporary, ethnic, experimental, translations. "We are interested in quality short stories, with no taboos on subject matter." Receives about 20 unsolicited mss/month. Accepts 1 ms/issue. Publishes ms about 6 months after acceptance. Length: 2,500-3,000 words.
**How to Contact:** Query with clips of published work. Reports in 4 weeks on mss. SASE for query and ms. No simultaneous or photocopied submissions or reprints. Accepts computer printouts. No dot-matrix. Sample copy $3.
**Payment:** Pays in contributor's copies. Acquires first North American rights. Publication copyrighted.
**Tips:** We publish fiction because "the short story is—when successful—a major achievement. Because we publish relatively little work, we cannot consider stories which are slight, however charming."

**FORMAT: ART & THE WORLD (II)**, Seven Oaks Press, 405 S. 7th St., St. Charles IL 60174. (312)584-0187. Editor: C.L. Morrison. "Magazine of art, survival information for contemporary artists, essays, interviews, poetry, articles and short fiction with useful information for artists." Quarterly. Estab. 1978. Circ. 1,000.
**Needs:** Survival-oriented; stories related to art, artists, economics or current events. Receives approximately 70 unsolicited fiction mss each month. Length: 1,500 words maximum.
**How to Contact:** Send complete ms with SASE. Reports in 3 weeks on ms. Publishes ms an average of 2 months after acceptance. Sample copy $3.
**Payment:** Pays $5-15; 6 free author's copies.
**Terms:** Pays on publication for simultaneous rights. Publication copyrighted.
**Tips:** "Write honestly about something you know with insight and understanding." Mss are rejected because they are "not original."

**FREEWAY (II)**, Box 632, Glen Ellyn IL 60138. (312)668-6000 (ext. 216). Editor: Cindy Atoji. Magazine: 8½x11; 4 pages; newsprint paper; illustrations; photos. Weekly Sunday school paper "specializing in first-person true stories about how God has worked in teens' lives" for Christian teens ages 15-21. Circ. 70,000.
**Needs:** Comics, humor/satire, allegories, and parables. No historical. No fictional short stories. Receives 100 unsolicited mss/month. Length: 1,000 words average. Occasionally critiques rejected mss. "We use very little fiction, so we're very selective."
**How to Contact:** Send complete ms with SASE. Reports in 1 month. Simultaneous and photocopied submissions OK. Accepts computer printout submissions. Prefers letter-quality. Sample copy or writing guidelines available with SASE. Fiction guidelines free for SASE with 1 first class stamp.
**Terms:** Pays on acceptance for first rights. Publication copyrighted.
**Tips:** "Send us humorous fiction (parables, allegories, etc.) with a clever twist and new insight on Christian principles. Do *not* send us typical teenage short stories." Published new writers within the last year.

**FRONT STREET TROLLEY**, Trolley, Inc., Box 120482, Nashville TN 37212. Contact: Jim Sherraden. "Small magazine: prose, specializing in satire; short stories, any subject, for young to mature adults." Published semiannually. Estab. 1974. Circ. 500.
**Needs:** "We are interested in anything that is well-written." Receives about 20 unsolicited fiction mss/month. Accepts 2-4 mss/issue, 4-8 mss/year. Length: 2,500 words average. Occasionally critiques rejected mss.
**How to Contact:** Send complete ms with SASE. Simultaneous and photocopied submissions OK. Reports in 3 months. Free sample copy for 9x12 SAE and 70¢ postage; free guidelines for SAE and 1 first class stamp.
**Payment:** 2 free contributor's copies; $1 charge for extras.
**Terms:** Acquires one-time rights. Publication copyrighted.
**Tips:** "We are very interested in our stories having a definite beginning, middle and end with congruity and creative language throughout the manuscript."

**FRUITION**, The Fruition Project, Box 872, Santa Cruz CA 95061. (408)429-3020. Editor: C. Olson. Newsletter: 8½x11; 6-12 pages; offset paper; offset cover stock; illustrations; photos. Newsletter promoting "public access to fruit and nut trees and establishing community food tree nurseries in which to grow them. We also publish stories, poetry, and photos." Semiannually. Estab. 1979. Circ. 300.
**Needs:** Contemporary, fantasy, feminist, historical (general), juvenile, prose poem, and regional. "Send it in if you believe in it."Receives 1 unsolicited fiction ms/month. Buys 1 ms/issue; 2 mss/year. Length: 1,500 words maximum; 750-1,000 words average. Critiques rejected ms.
**How to Contact:** Send complete ms with SASE. Simultaneous, photocopied and previously published submissions OK. Accepts computer printout submissions. Prefers letter-quality. Reports in 2-4 weeks on mss. Publishes ms 1-5 months after acceptance. Sample copy $2.

**Payment:** "All payments negotiable."
**Terms:** Pays on publication for first rights. Buys reprints. Publication copyrighted. Published new writers within the last year.

**FUNGI (II)**, Literary Magazine of Fantasy and the Supernatural, Box 8044, Lowell MA 01853. Editor: Pierre Comtois. Magazine: 8½x11; 40-50 pages; good paper; 50 lb cover stock; illustrations. Magazine of nonfiction, articles (analytical), fiction, and poetry for the fantasy and supernatural reader. Quarterly. Published special fiction issue; plans another. Estab. winter, 1984.
**Needs:** Experimental, fantasy, horror, literary, prose poem, and supernatural. No gory, pornographic or banal stuff. Accepts 2 mss/issue; 10 mss/year. Length: 2-5 single-spaced typed pages.
**How to Contact:** Query with clips of published work. Reports in 3 weeks on queries; 3 weeks on manuscripts. SASE for query and ms. Cover letter with background on story, what author is trying to do thematically and stylistically. Simultaneous and photocopied submissions OK. Sample copy for $2.50 and SAE (9x12 envelope and 4 first class stamps). Fiction guidelines free for 1 first class stamp.
**Payment:** Contributor's copies; charge for extras: $2.50/copy.
**Terms:** Acquires on publication for first rights and first reprint rights. Publication copyrighted.
**Tips:** "Read the masters of the genre—Poe, Blackwood, Shelley, Lovecraft, Hodgeson, Stoker, and Smith. A good knowledge of medieval philosophy is a big plus. Write your own stories not your favorite author's." Published new writers within the last year.

**GALACTIC DISCOURSE (I, II)**, Satori Press, 1111 Dartmouth, #214, Claremont CA 91711. (714)621-3112. Editor-in-Chief: Laurie Huff. Magazine: 8½x11; 200 + pages; 20 lb non-gloss paper; 80 lb non-gloss cover stock; illustrations; photos. Magazine of "*Star Trek* fiction (characterization and character interaction are emphasized), poetry, artwork; some visionary/science fiction poetry and art for *Star Trek* fans." *Note:* "This is a 'when there's time' venture!" Published irregularly—annually or once every two years. Plans special fiction issue. Estab. 1977. Circ. 1,000.
**Needs:** Adventure, fantasy, feminist/lesbian, gay, humor/satire, prose poem, psychic/supernatural/occult, science fiction, suspense/mystery, and women's. No pure adventure, x-rated (explicit erotica), or "Mary-Sue." Receives less than 5 unsolicited fiction mss/month. Accepts 8-12 mss/issue. Publishes short shorts under 100 double-spaced pages. Length: 12,000 words maximum; 5,000 words average. "We would consider publishing novellas/novels as a special issue apart from other work." Occasionally critiques rejected mss. Occasionally recommends markets.
**How to Contact:** Query first with SASE and cover letter with description of manuscript(s), including length. Photocopied submissions OK. Accepts computer printout submissions. Accepts disc submissions compatible with Apple II, Franklin, or other compatible system. Prefers hard copy with disc submission. Reports in 6 weeks on queries; 2 months on mss. Publishes ms 6 months-2 years after acceptance. Sample copy "not offered, sorry; send SASE for purchasing info." Fiction guidelines for business-sized SAE and 2 first class stamps.
**Payment:** 1 free contributor's copy; issue price charge for extras.
**Terms:** Pays on publication for second serial rights. Sends galleys to author upon request. Publication copyrighted.
**Tips:** "We are looking for more controversial topics and more humor. Type double-spaced; put your name on your material (and address); enclose return postage (if you want your ms returned) and SASE (for notification); *proofread* your ms." Mss are rejected because they are poorly written, have inappropriate content, and lack (personal) appeal. The new, lower-cost print technologies seem to be spawning more small presses. And many small presses are willing to work with beginning fiction writers. Write the story you'd like to read."

**GAMUT (II), of Culture and Ideas, Artscorp**, 171-238 Davenport Rd., Toronto, Ontario M5R 1J6 Canada. Editors: Haygo Demir and Alfredo Romano. Magazine: 8½x11; 52-60 pages; 80 lb coated paper; heavy coated cover stock; illustrations; photos. Publishing "short fiction, poetry, articles in literature, politics, philosophy, arts, etc., for young adults and adults interested in the literary arts and contemporary ideas." Quarterly. Estab. 1982. Circ. 2,000.

**Needs:** Contemporary, ethnic, experimental, literary, mainstream, prose poem, serialized/excerpted novel, translations, and women's. Receives 1,500 unsolicited mss/year. Accepts 5 mss/issue, 20 mss/year. Length: 2,000 words average; 3,500 words maximum. Occasionally critiques rejected mss. Sometimes recommends other markets.

**How to Contact:** Send complete ms with $1 handling charge, and author's bio. Reports in 2 months. Publishes ms an average of 3 months after acceptance. SAE, IRC. Simultaneous and photocopied submissions OK. Accepts computer printout submissions. Prefers letter-quality. Sample copy $3.

**Payment:** 6 free contributor's copies and subscription to magazine.

**Terms:** Acquires one-time rights. Publication copyrighted.

**Tips:** "Make the stories as tight as possible. The shorter the story, the better. Send manuscripts. They are read carefully. If time permits, comments and suggestions will be made for accepted or rejected manuscripts."

**‡THE GAMUT (II), A Journal of Ideas and Information**, Cleveland State University, 1216 Rhodes Tower, Cleveland State University, Cleveland OH 44115. (216)687-4679. Editor: Louis T. Milic. Managing Editor: Mary Grimm. Magazine: 7x10; 96 pages; 70 lb Patina Matte paper; Patina Matte cover stock; illustrations; photos. *"The Gamut* is a general interest magazine that mainly publishes well-researched, interesting articles; however, we like to publish one or two pieces of fiction per issue, if we find something suitable." For the college-educated audience. Triannually. Estab. 1980. Circ. 1,200.

**Needs:** Contemporary, experimental, feminist, humor/satire, literary, mainstream, regional, translations. "Our only requirement is high quality fiction." No genre fiction, no fiction for specific age groups. Receives 10 unsolicited ms/month. Accepts 1-2 mss/issue; 4-6 mss/year. Publishes usually 3 months, certainly within 1 year after acceptance. Reading fee "only when we have contest, then $2." Length: 3,000 words average; 1,000 words minimum; 6,000 words maximum. Often critiques rejected mss. Recommends other markets.

**How to Contact:** Send complete ms with cover letter. Reports in 1 month on queries; 3 months on mss. SASE for ms. Simultaneous and photocopied submissions OK. Accepts computer printouts. Sample copy $2.50. Fiction guidelines for business size SAE and 1 first class stamp.

**Payment:** Pays $25-150, depending on length; contributor's copies; charge for extras at a reduced rate.

**Terms:** Pays on publication. Acquires first North American serial rights. Publication copyrighted.

**Tips:** "The best advice we have for writers who wish to be published in our magazine is that they should care about the quality of their writing. Further, we are interested in neither stale approaches to fictional situations nor avant-garde experiments that have lost touch with the purpose of literature."

**GARGOYLE MAGAZINE (II)**, Paycock Press, Box 3567, Washington DC 20007. (202)333-1544. Editor: Richard Peabody. Magazine: 4¼x7; 420 pages; standard bulk paper; slick card cover stock; illustrations; photos. Estab. 1976. Published 2 times/year. Published special fiction issue last year; plans another.

**Needs:** Contemporary, literary, experimental, humor/satire, and translations. "We like fiction in the 2-10 typed page range, but often publish much longer works. We generally print 3-6 stories an issue." Approximately 10% of fiction is agented. Read 5,000 stories in six month period for recent *Fiction* issue. "We print 1 out of every 120 stories we read these days." Does not read in August. Critiques rejected mss "when there is time." Recommends markets.

**How to Contact:** Submit complete ms with SASE. Photocopied submissions OK. Accepts computer printout submissions. Prefers letter-quality. Reports in 1-2 months on mss. Publishes ms 6-12 months after acceptance.

**Payment:** Free author's copy. Half the cover price for extras.

**Terms:** Publication copyrighted.

**Tips:** "Small magazines are deluged with mss these days. Writers should keep in mind that rejection doesn't mean a story is bad, only that the magazine editor doesn't want to, or can't, use it. You have to learn to endure. Writers should always be familiar with the market. This means reading all the short stories/fiction you can get your hands on. It is also important to keep up with movements in contemporary fiction. We're interested in printing excerpts from unpublished novels. We're consciously seeking out the new young writers (20 to 30 years old and younger)."

**‡THE GATE (II), Explore the Mysteries**, Box 43518, Richmond Heights OH 44143. Editor: Beth Robbins. Magazine: 8½x11; 20 pages; bond paper; bond cover stock; illustrations. *The Gate* publishes short horror fiction and occult related articles. Book review, illustrations and some poetry also needed for young adult audience. Quarterly. Estab. 1985. Circ. 200.
**Needs:** Horror, psychic/supernatural/occult. No hard core science fiction. Keep the gore, profanity and sex to a minimum. Receives 20-25 unsolicited fiction mss/month. Accepts 3-4 mss/issue; 12-16 mss/year. Publishes ms 2 months after acceptance. Length: 1,500 words average; 300 words minimum; 3,000 words maximum. Publishes short shorts to 800 words. Critiques rejected mss.
**How to Contact:** Send complete ms with cover letter and past published work and a brief outline of what the story is about. Reports in 2 weeks on queries; 2 weeks on mss. SASE for ms. Accepts computer printouts. Sample copy free for 3 first class stamps. Fiction guidelines for #10 SAE and 1 first class stamp.
**Payment:** Pays in contributor's copies.
**Terms:** Pays on publication. Publication copyrighted.
**Tips:** "I can be very optimistic to beginning writers because they're the backbone of all magazines. If editors didn't receive unsolicited manuscripts their magazines would cease to exist."

**GAY CHICAGO MAGAZINE (I, II)**, Ultra Ink, Inc. 1527 N. Wells, Chicago IL 60610. (312)751-0130. Editor: Dan Dileo. Magazine: 5x8; 64-80 pages; newsprint paper; newspaper cover stock; illustrations; photos. Entertainment guide, information for the gay community. Plans special fiction issue.
**Needs:** Erotica, feminist/lesbian, gay, and romance. Receives "a few" unsolicited fiction mss/month. Accepts 10-15 mss/year. Length: 1,000-1,800 words maximum.
**How to Contact:** Send complete ms with SASE. Photocopied submissions OK. Accepts computer printout submissions. Accepts disc submissions compatible with Merganthaler Crtronic 200. Prefers hard copy with disc submission. Reports in 4-6 weeks on mss. Free sample copy for 6x9 envelope and 56¢ postage.
**Payment:** Minimal. 5-10 free contributor's copies; no charge for extras "if within reason."
**Terms:** Acquires one-time rights.
**Tips:** Published new writers within the last year.

**THE GEORGIA REVIEW (II, III)**, The University of Georgia, Athens GA 30602. (404)542-3481. Editor-in-Chief: Stanley W. Lindberg. Assistant Editor: Stephen Corey. Journal: 7x10; 232 pages (average); 50 lb woven old style paper; 80 lb cover stock; illustrations; photos. "*The Georgia Review* is a journal of arts and letters, featuring a blend of the best in contemporary thought and literature—essays, fiction, poetry, graphics, and book reviews—for the intelligent nonspecialist as well as the specialist reader. We seek material that appeals across disciplinary lines by drawing from a wide range of interests." Quarterly. Plans special fiction issue. Estab. 1947. Circ. 4,500.
**Needs:** Experimental and literary. "We're looking for the highest quality fiction—work that is capable of sustaining subsequent readings, not throw-away pulp magazine entertainment. Nothing that fits too easily into a 'category,' e.g., adventure, erotica, ethnic, lesbian, gay, horror, psychic, religious, romance, etc." Receives about 200 unsolicited fiction mss/month. Buys 3-4 mss/issue, 12-15 mss/year. Does not read mss in June, July, or August. Length: open. Occasionally critiques rejected mss.
**How to Contact:** Send complete ms with SASE. Photocopied submissions OK; no multiple submissions. Accepts computer printout submissions. Prefers letter-quality. Reports in 2 months.

Sample copy $3; free guidelines for #10 SAE and 1 first class stamp.

**Payment:** Minimum; $15/printed page; 1 year complimentary subscription; 1 contributor's copy, reduced charge for extras.

**Terms:** Pays on publication for first North American serial rights. Sends galleys to author. Publication copyrighted.

**Tips:** "Obviously the best way to become acquainted with any journal is to look at its recent issues." Published 5 new writers within the last year; over 40 in the last 7 years.

‡**THE GOOFUS OFFICE GAZETTE (I)**, The Goofus Office, 4 Rockland Ave., Nanuet NY 10954. (914)623-6154. Editor: Samuel T. Godfrey. Newsletter: 8½x11; 6 pages; 20 lb offset paper; small illustrations; small photos. "We print mostly humorous short stories, articles concerning music and the arts, silly poetry, tongue twisters, games, trivia, and ficticious news (or humorous reality). Specifically we cater to those with the ability to read printed matter. All others are welcome to just come and watch or provide input." Plans special fiction issue. Estab. 1983. Circ. 300.

**Needs:** Humor/satire; anti-television. "We prefer short, clever, light-hearted humor in reasonably good taste. Shaggy Dog stories and folklore are needed. The feeling is always happy and foolish, good clean fun, balderdash, etc." No violence. No profanity for profanity's sake. No hurtful or distasteful remarks. No heavy, pointed satire. Receives 2 or 3 unsolicited fiction mss/month accepts at least 2 fiction mss/issue. Accepts "countless" fiction mss/year. Publishes ms "next issue unless special interest." Charges reading fee of $1 per 10,000 words. Length: 500 words average; 3 words minimum; 1,000 words maximum. Comments on rejected mss. Recommends other markets.

**How to Contact:** Send complete ms with cover letter and return address, minor biography. Reports in 2 weeks on queries; 1 month on mss. Simultaneous, photocopied and reprint submissions OK. Accepts computer printouts including dot-matrix. Sample copy $1 and #10 SAE with 39¢ postage. Fiction guidelines $1 and #10 SAE with 39¢ postage.

**Payment:** Free subscription to magazine; contributor's copies.

**Terms:** Pays on publication.

**Tips:** "Writers of fiction have the upper hand. They can choose from any cell of the brain to pick their subject matter and present it any way they wish. The reader realizes this and becomes more entertained with the thought. Keep in mind. It's all in your imagination."

**GRAIN (I, II)**, Saskatchewan Writers' Guild, Box 1154, Regina, Saskatchewan S4P 3B4 Canada. Editor: Brenda Riches. Literary magazine: 14cmx21½cm; 64 pages; Chinook offset printing; chrome-coated stock; illustrations; photos sometimes. "Fiction, poetry, songs, drama and essays of the highest quality for people who enjoy high quality writing. Many of our subscribers are writers." No theme. Quarterly. Estab. 1973. Circ. 800.

**Needs:** Contemporary, experimental, literary, mainstream, and prose poem. "No propaganda— only artistic/literary writing." No mss "that stay *within* the limits of conventions such as women's magazine type stories, science fiction, none that push a message." Receives 25-30 unsolicited fiction mss/month. Buys 4-5 mss/issue; 16-20 mss/year. Approximately 1% of fiction agented. Length: "no more than 30 pages." Occasionally critiques rejected ms.

**How to Contact:** Send complete ms with SAE, IRC and brief of one-two sentences. "Let us know if you're just beginning to send out." Photocopied submissions OK. Reports in 3 months on mss. Publishes ms an average of 3 months after acceptance. Sample copy $3.

**Payment:** $35-100; 1 free contributor's copy.

**Terms:** Pays on publication for one-time rights. "We expect acknowledgment if the article is republished elsewhere."

**Tips:** "Attend reputable workshops conducted by practicing writers. Don't submit until a practicing writer of long experience and good judgment feels the work is ready. Don't tell the editor your work is just what the magazine needs. Be professional. *Grain* publishes writing that challenges the traditions of reading and of writing. Our audience responds strongly!" Published new writers within the last year.

**GREAT RIVER REVIEW (II)**, 211 W. 7th, Winona MN 55987. Fiction Editor: Orval A. Lund, Jr. Literary publication of fiction, poetry, art and book reviews. Semiannually. Estab. 1977.
**Needs:** "Quality fiction. No slick or sub-genre fiction." Prints 6-7 stories/issue. Receives approximately 40 unsolicited fiction mss each month. Length: 2,000-10,000 words.
**How to Contact:** Send complete ms with SASE. Accepts computer printout submissions. Publishes ms 3-6 months after acceptance. Sample copy $3.
**Terms:** Photocopied submissions OK. Publication copyrighted.
**Tips:** Priority to Midwestern writers and Midwestern settings. "Address your short story to fiction editor."

**GREEN FEATHER (II)**, Box 2633, Lakewood OH 44107. Editor-in-Chief: Gary S. Skeens. Fiction Editors: Robin Moser and Gary S. Skeens. Magazine: 8½x11; 4-12 pages; 20 lb bond paper; 20 lb bond, almost tabloid type cover stock; illustrations on cover; occasionally on inside cover; inquire first about photo. "A magazine featuring poetry, fiction (short stories and novels), essays, nonfiction coverage of current events and people. This magazine is one dedicated and devoted to the people; to informing, entertaining, perhaps bringing some laughter to the lives that it may touch as well as some thought and quite possibly a few tears, but in the end it is a magazine that wishes to build a family. For a group of people, whether they be artists, writers, poets, or book-keepers, secretaries, teachers, people regardless of their walks of life who know what they want to read." Annually. Plans special fiction issue. Estab. 1978. 1st issue June 1979. Circ. 100-150.
**Needs:** Adventure, contemporary, literary, and western. "No mss of poor taste, thin or no plot, weak characterizations or dialogue." Receives 3-4 unsolicited fiction mss/month. Accepts 2 mss/issue. Length: 1,000-1,500 words average; 500 words minimum; 2,000 words maximum. Occasionally critiques rejected mss. Recommends other markets "when time and schedule permits."
**How to Contact:** Send complete ms with SASE. Photocopied and previously published submissions OK. Reports in 2 months. Sample copy $1; free guidelines with SASE.
**Payment:** 1-3 free contributor's copies.
**Terms:** Pays on publication for first rights, first North American serial rights. Publication copyrighted.
**Tips:** "I look for characterization, plot and dialogue; the writer should be honest, write from the 'gut' and must move me (as editor). Of course, read the magazine. I'm a fiction writer myself. I feel fiction is the medium in which stong commentaries can be made with regard to 'real, everyday living.' Fiction is *not* dead. Never has been. It was just side-tracked for a while. I do, however, prefer shorter fiction—brevity! Brevity, and gut level, real, human writing." Published new writers within the last year.

**THE GREENFIELD REVIEW (II)**, RD 1, Box 80, Greenfield Center NY 12833. (518)584-1728. Editor-in-Chief: Joseph Bruchac. Magazine: 5½x8½; 220 pages; 60 lb paper; illustrations; photos. "Primarily a magazine of poetry but also interested in very short fiction. Special interest in work by Third World writers." For the general literate reader. Published twice yearly. Published special anthology within the last year; plans another. Estab. 1970. Circ. 1,000.
**Needs:** Literary and regional, ethnic. Receives 20-30 unsolicited fiction mss/month. "We do not read manuscripts from June through August." Accepts 2-4 mss/issue, 4-8 mss/year. Length: 500 words minimum; 2,000 words maximum; 1,500 words average. Occasionally recommends other markets.
**How to Contact:** Send complete ms with SASE. Accepts computer printout submissions. Prefers letter-quality. Reports in 1 week on queries; 4 weeks on mss. Publishes ms 2-5 months after acceptance. Sample copy $3.
**Payment:** 1 contributor's copy and $5. 50% discount for extras.
**Terms:** Pays on publication for first North American serial rights. Sends galleys to author. Publication copyrighted.
**Tips:** "We look for prose as finely crafted as a poem, strongly imagistic and clearly written. Avoid overblown accompanying letters. Let the work speak for itself." Rejects mss because "the work may not fit our needs or our interests, which is why it pays people to READ PREVIOUS ISSUES

before submitting to any magazine; and we're often overstocked with material and have no space for even excellent work. We're going to try to publish more short stories in 1987. Read widely, don't rush a story into publication. Know your contemporaries, but even more know your own heart. Remember, many can write good fiction early in their careers but *great* fiction usually only comes with the devotion of years." Published new writers within the last year.

**GREEN'S MAGAZINE,** Green's Educational Publications, Box 3236, Regina, Saskatchewan S4P 3H1 Canada. Editor: David Green. "A family magazine with a carefully balanced array of short fiction and poetry, intended to be exemplary in a variety of high-standard styles for a general audience." Quarterly. Estab. 1972. Circ. 500.
**Needs:** Literary; some psychic/supernatural/occult, and senior citizen/retirement. Accepts 12 mss/issue. Receives approximately 200 unsolicited fiction mss each month. Approximately 1% of fiction is agented. Length: 1,000-2,500 words. Critiques rejected mss "when there is time." Sometimes recommends markets.
**How to Contact:** Send complete ms with SAE, IRC. Reports in 2 months on mss. Publishes ms an average of 6 months after acceptance. Sample copy $3 and free guidelines with legal-sized SAE and IRC.
**Payment:** 2 free author's copies. $3 charge for extras.
**Terms:** Pays on publication for first North American serial rights. Publication copyrighted.
**Tips:** "Study the magazine. Be understanding if we're a bit late (few readers and occasional postal delays). Be aware that editing changes are not made lightly. If major, they will be discussed with the author. We will not consider multiple submissions."

**GREENSBORO REVIEW (II),** University of North Carolina at Greensboro, Dept. of English, Greensboro NC 27412. (919)379-5459. Editor: Lee Zacharias. Fiction Editor: Virginia Dumont. Literary magazine featuring fiction and poetry for readers interested in contemporary literature: 6x9; approximately 100 pages. Semiannually. Circ. 500.
**Needs:** Contemporary and experimental. Accepts 4-8 mss/issue, 8-16 mss/year. Length: 6,000 words maximum.
**How to Contact:** Send complete ms with SASE. Unsolicited manuscripts must arrive by September 15 to be considered for the winter issue and by February 15 to be considered for the summer issue. Manuscripts arriving after those dates may be held for the next consideration.
**Payment:** Pays in contributor's copies.
**Terms:** Acquires first North American serial rights. Byline given. Photocopied submissions OK. Publication copyrighted.
**Tips:** "John Updike selected *two* stories from the *Greensboro Review* for publication in *The Best American Short Stories 1984*." Published beginning writers within the last year.

**GRINNING IDIOT, A Magazine of the Arts (II),** Grinning Idiot Press, Box 1577, Brooklyn NY 11202. Editor: Jerome Weinberger. Magazine: 8½x11; 48 pages; high quality paper; high quality cover stock; illustrations; photos. Annually. Estab. 1982. Circ. 500.
**Needs:** "Class material." Receives "many" unsolicited mss/month. Accepts "a few"/year. Length: open.
**How to Contact:** Send complete ms. Reports in 12 weeks. SASE. Simultaneous and photocopied submissions OK. Accepts computer printout submissions. Accepts disc submissions compatible with Atari. Sample copy $3.
**Payment:** 3 free contributor's copies.
**Terms:** Acquires first rights. Publication copyrighted.
**Tips:** Published new writers within the last year.

‡**GRUE MAGAZINE (IV),** Hell's Kitchen Productions, Box 370, New York NY 10108. Editor: Peggy Nadramia. Magazine: 5½x8½; 64 pages; 18 lb paper; 30 lb glossy cover stock; illustrations; photos. "Quality short fiction centered on horror and dark fantasy—new traditions in the realms of the gothic and the macabre for horror fans well-read in the genre, looking for something

new and different, as well as horror novices looking for a good scare." Quarterly. Plans special fiction issue. Estab. 1985.

**Needs:** Experimental, fantasy, horror, psychic/supernatural/occult. "We'll consider science fiction or 'high' sword-and-sorcery-fantasy *if* it is representative of a crossover into horror/gothic/macabre fiction." Receives 40-50 unsolicited fiction mss/month. Accepts 8 mss/issue; 25-30 mss/year. Publishes ms 6 months after acceptance. Length: 2,500 words average; 6,500 words maximum. Publishes short shorts of 400 words (1 printed page). Critiques rejected ms. Recommends other markets.

**How to Contact:** Send complete ms with cover letter. "I like to hear where the writer heard about *GRUE*, his most recent or prestigious sales, and maybe a word or two about himself." Reports in 3 weeks on queries; 3 weeks on mss. SASE for ms. Photocopied submissions OK. Accepts computer printouts including dot-matrix. Accepts electronic submissions via disc. "I can read a document formatted for the Commodore 64-paperclip word processing program." Sample copy $2.50. Fiction guidelines for business size SAE and 1 first class stamp.

**Payment:** Pays in 2 contributor's copies.

**Terms:** Pays on publication. Acquires first North American serial rights. Publication copyrighted.

**Tips:** "Editors actually vie for the work of the better writers, and if your work is good, you will sell it—you just have to keep sending it out. But out of the 50 mss I read in September, maybe three of them will be by writers who cared enough to make their plots as interesting as possible, their characterizations believable, their settings unique, and who took the time to do the rewrites and polish their prose. Will I be lucky enough to get a great story in my mailbox? Remember that readers of *GRUE* are mainly seasoned horror fans, and *not* interested or excited by a straight vampire, werewolf or ghost story—they'll see all the signs, and guess where you're going long before you get there. Throw a new angle on what you're doing; put it in a new light. How? Well, what scares *you*? What's *your* personal phobia or anxiety? When the writer is genuinely, emotionally involved with his subject matter, and is totally honest with himself and his reader, then we can't help being involved, too, and that's where good writing begins and ends."

**‡HANDICAP NEWS (IV)**, Burns Enterprises, 272 N. 11th Ct., Brighton CO 80601. (303)659-4463. Editor: Phyllis A. Burns. Newsletter: 8½x11; 3 pages; 20 lb paper. "Fiction must deal directly with handicaps, coping, etc. and be written by handicapped people and families." For handicapped people, families, non-profits, hospitals personnel, associations. Monthly. Estab. 1984. Circ. 500.

**Needs:** Confession, contemporary, historical (general), mainstream, religious/inspirational, romance, senior citizen/retirement. "Subject must deal directly with handicapped in the realm of today's and yesterday's society." Publishes ms 3-4 months after acceptance. Length: 500 words average. Sometimes recommends markets.

**How to Contact:** Query first. Reports in 1 month on queries. SASE for query and ms. Simultaneous submissions and reprints OK. Sample copy $1 with 4x9 SAE and 1 first class stamp. Fiction guidelines with sample copy.

**Payment:** Pays in contributor's copies.

**Terms:** Acquires one-time rights.

**Tips:** "Economy in the use of words is necessary in a publication as small as ours. I am trying to get as much information as possible out. Therefore, I cannot afford to print wordy, flowery works. Our policy though is to help the beginning handicapped writer so we will look at them and publish whenever possible."

**HAPPINESS HOLDING TANK (II)**, Stone Press, 9727 SE Reedway, Portland OR 97266. Editor: Albert Drake. Magazine: 8½x11; 30-50 pages; 20 lb bond paper; Bristol cover stock; illustrations, photos sometimes. Primarily a magazine of poetry, articles, reviews, and literary information for poets, students, teachers, other editors and lay people. "I think a good many people read it for the literary information, much of which isn't available elsewhere." Published irregularly. Estab. Oct. 1970. Circ. 300-500.

**Needs:** Literary. "We publish a limited amount of fiction: very short stories, parables, prose poems, fragments, and episodes. Not a good market for traditional fiction." Accepts 4-5 mss/year. Receives very few unsolicited fiction mss each month. Does not read mss in summer. Critiques rejected mss "when there is time."
**How to Contact:** Query. SASE for query, ms. Accepts computer printout submissions. Reports in 1 week on queries, 3 weeks on mss. Publishes ms 3-5 months after acceptance. Sample copy $1 plus 68¢ postage.
**Payment:** 2 free author's copies.
**Terms:** Acquires one-time rights with automatic return of all rights to author.
**Tips:** "Be more careful about what you send out. Rewrite. Tighten. Compress. Read it aloud."

**‡HAUNTS (II), Tales of Unexpected Horror and the Supernatural**, Night Shade Publications, Box 3342, Providence RI 02906. (401)781-9438. Editor: Joseph K. Cherkes. Magazine: 5½; 80-100 pages; 20 lb bond paper; krome-kote cover stock; pen and ink illustrations. "We are committed to publishing only the finest fiction in the genres of horror, fantasy, and the supernatural from both semi-pro and established writers. We are targeted towards the 18-35 age bracket interested in tales of horror and the unknown." Quarterly. Plans special fiction issue. Estab. 1984. Circ. 1,000.
**Needs:** Fantasy, horror, psychic/supernatural/occult. No pure adventure, explicit sex, or blow-by-blow dismemberment. Receives 35-40 unsolicited fiction mss/month. Accepts 6-8 mss/issue; 50-75 mss/year. Publishes ms 6-9 months after acceptance. Length: 3,500 words average; 1,000 words minimum; 10,000 words maximum. Publishes short shorts of not less than 500 words. Critiques rejected mss. Recommends other markets.
**How to Contact:** Query first. Reports in 2-3 weeks on queries; 2-3 months on mss. SASE for query. Photocopied submissions OK. Accepts computer printouts including dot-matrix. Sample copy $2.50 postpaid. Fiction guidelines for #11 SASE and 22¢ postage.
**Payment:** Pays $5-33 (subject to change). Contributor's copies, charge for extras.
**Terms:** Pays on publication. Acquires first North American serial rights. Publication copyrighted.
**Tips:** "Follow writer's guidelines closely. They are a good outline of what your publisher looks for in fiction. If you think you've got the 'perfect' manuscript, go over it again—carefully. Check to make sure you've left no loose ends before sending it out. Keep your writing concise. If your story is rejected, don't give up. Try to see where the story failed. This way you can learn from your mistakes. Remember, success comes to those who persist."

**HAWAII REVIEW (II)**, University of Hawaii Board of Publications, 1733 Donaghho Rd., Co-English Dept., Honolulu HI 96822. (808)948-8548. Editor: Rodney Morales. Fiction Editor: H. Yamada. Magazine: 6x9; 100-150 pages; illustrations; photos. "We publish short stories as well as poetry and reviews by new and experienced writers. Although the *Review* reflects the concerns of writers and artists of Hawaii and the Pacific, its interests are by no means exclusively regional." For residents of Hawaii and non-residents from the continental US and abroad. Semiannually. Published special fiction issue last year; plans another. Estab. 1974. Circ. 3,500.
**Needs:** Contemporary, ethnic, experimental, horror, humor/satire, literary, prose poem, regional, and translations. Receives 5-15 mss/month. Accepts no more than 5 mss/issue; 9 mss/year. Length: 4,000 words average; 1,000 words minimum; 8,000 words maximum. Occasionally critiques mss. Recommends other markets.
**How to Contact:** Send complete manuscript with SASE. Reports in 1-3 months on mss. Photocopied submissions OK. Accepts computer printout submissions. Prefers letter-quality. Sample copy for $3. Fiction guidelines free.
**Payment:** "Varies depending upon funds budgeted." 2 contributor's copies.
**Terms:** Pays on publication for all rights. Sends galleys to author upon request. Publication copyrighted. After publication, copyright reverts to author upon request.
**Tips:** "Good fiction is a *pleasure* to read. Many of our readers and subscribers turn to a story *first*." Published new writers within the last year.

**HELICON NINE (II), The Journal of Women's Arts & Letters**, Box 22412, Kansas City MO 64113. (913)381-6383. Editor-in-Chief: Gloria Vando Hickok. Editor: Ann Slegman. Fiction Editor: Pinky Kase. Magazine: 7x10; 96 pages; illustrations; photos. Magazine publishing "a celebration of women in the arts, past, present and future for women and men interested in women in the arts." Published 3 times/year. Estab. 1979. Circ. 3,500.

**Needs:** Condensed novel, contemporary, ethnic, experimental, fantasy, historical (general), humor/satire, literary, prose poem, translations, women's, and young adult. No "militant feminist tracts." Receives 50-100 unsolicited fiction mss/month. "No set limit" on mss/year. Sometimes recommends other markets.

**How to Contact:** Send complete ms with SASE. Simultaneous and photocopied submissions OK. Reports in 6 weeks on mss. Publishes ms an average of 6 months after acceptance. Sample copy $7.50.

**Payment:** 2 free contributor's copies.

**Terms:** Acquires one-time rights. Publication copyrighted.

**Tips:** Published new writers within the last year.

**HERESIES (I, II, IV): A Feminist Publication on Art & Politics**, Heresies, Box 766, Canal St. Station, New York NY 10013. Magazine: 8½x11; 100 pages; non-coated stock paper; b&w photos. "We are a feminist collective. Each issue is put together by a separate group of women which forms the editorial collective." Nationwide readership gathered from alternative bookshops and women's spaces. Semiannually. Published special fiction last year; plans another. Estab. 1977. Circ. 8,000.

**Needs:** Women's, feminist, and lesbian. Publishes short shorts of 10 typed pages maximum.

**How to Contact:** Query. Reports in 1 month on queries. Free guidelines with SASE.

**Payment:** Small payment post publication and free author's copies.

**Terms:** Publication copyrighted.

**Tips:** "Check back issues for special themes and content. Since each issue has its own guidelines, be specific. We only accept manuscripts directed to special issues which are noted in the back of each publication." Published new writers within the last year.

**HIBISCUS MAGAZINE (I)**, Short Stories, Poetry and Art, Hibiscus Press, Box 22248, Sacramento CA 95822. Editor: Margaret Wensrick. Magazine: 8½x11; 16-24 pages; 50 lb paper; 1 ply vellum cover stock; pen and ink illustrations. Magazine of short stories, poetry, and pen and ink drawings. Estab. 1985. Published 3 times/year. Circ. projected 1,000-2,000 first year.

**Needs:** Adventure, contemporary, fantasy, humor/satire, literary, mainstream, science fiction, suspense/mystery, and western. Receives 300 unsolicited mss/month. Buys 2 mss/issue; 6 mss/year. Length: 1,500-1,800 words average; 1,500 words minimum; 2,500 words maximum.

**How to Contact:** Send complete ms with SASE. Reports in 3-4 weeks on mss. Photocopied submissions OK. Accepts computer printout submissions. Prefers letter-quality. Sample copy $1. Fiction guidelines with SAE (#10 envelope and 1 first class stamp).

**Payment:** $5-25; 2 free copies.

**Terms:** Pays on acceptance for first rights. Publication copyrighted.

**Tips:** "We notice a lack of craftsmanship in today's fiction. Keep writing and submitting. Read magazine so you are familiar with the type of fiction used. Patience and faith required." Published new writers within the last year.

**‡HILL AND HOLLER: Southern Appalachian Mountains**, Seven Buffaloes Press, Box 249, Big Timber MT 59011. Editor: Art Cuelho. Magazine: 5½x8½; 80 pages; 60 lb offset paper; 80 lb cover stock; illustrations; photos rarely. "I use mostly rural Appalachian material: poems and stories. Some folklore and humor. I am interested in heritage, especially in connection with the farm." Annually. Published special fiction issue. Estab. 1983. Circ. 350.

**Needs:** Contemporary, ethnic, humor/satire, literary, regional, rural America farm. "I don't have any prejudices in style, but I don't like sentimental slant. Deep feelings in literature are fine, but they should be portrayed with tact and skill." Receives 10 unsolicited mss/month. Accepts 4-6 mss/issue. Publishes ms 6 months to a year after acceptance. Length: 2,000-3,000 words average. Also publishes short shorts of 500-1,000 words.

**How to Contact:** Query first. Reports in 2 weeks on queries. SASE for query and ms. Accepts computer printouts including dot-matrix. Sample copy $4.

**Payment:** Pays in contributor's copies; charge for extras.

**Terms:** Acquires first North American serial rights "and permission to reprint if my press publishes a special anthology." Send galleys to author sometimes. Publication copyrighted.

**Tips:** "In this Southern Appalachian rural series I can be optimistic about fiction. Appalachians are very responsive to their region's literature. I have taken work by beginners that had not been previously published. There are no real tricks to break into my publication. Art and writing requires a lot of dedication, talent, and hard work. Be sure to send a double space clean manuscript and SASE. I have the only rural press in North America; maybe even in the world. So perhaps we have a bond in common if your roots are rural."

**HOB-NOB (II)**, 715 Dorsea Rd., Lancaster PA 17601. Editor/Publisher: Mildred K. Henderson. Magazine: 8½x11; 56+ pages; 20 lb bond paper; 20 lb (or heavier) cover stock; b&w illustrations; photos. "*Hob-Nob* is a small (one-person operation) amateur publication currently with a literary emphasis in original prose and poetry. This publication is directed toward amateur writers and poets, but many of them would like to be professional. For some, appearance in *Hob-Nob* is simply an opportunity to be published somewhere, while others possibly see it as a springboard to bigger and better things." Semiannually, spring/summer, fall/winter. Estab. 1969. Circ. 300.

**Needs:** Literary, contemporary, religious/inspirational, psychic/supernatural/occult, regional, science fiction, fantasy, romance, mystery, adventure, humor, young adult, senior citizen/retirement, very brief condensed novels, excerpts from novels, and short stories in installments. "Upbeat" subjects are preferred. "No erotica, works with excessive swearing or blatantly sexual words, gross violence, etc." Accepts 25-35 mss/issue. Does not read March 1- September 1, to prevent a backlog, any received before August will be returned, those in August held for later reading. Receives 8-10 unsolicited fiction mss each month. Length: preferably 500-1,500 words (longer if serialized). "May serialize (2 installments) suitable longer stories (up to 3,000-4,000 words)—with permission of author." Critiques rejected mss "when there is time." Sometimes recommends other markets.

**How to Contact:** Send complete ms with SASE. Accepts computer printout submissions. Rejections in 2 weeks. Publishes ms an average of 1 year after acceptance. Sample copy for $2.25 or $2. for a back issue. "No submissions from March 1 September 1, please."

**Payment:** 1 free author's copy first appearance only. $2.25 charge for extras.

**Terms:** Acquires first rights. Occasionally buys reprints. Publication copyrighted.

**Tips:** "Number pages. Include name and address on at least the first page, and name on others. State 'original and unpublished.' I especially appreciate the 'light' touch in both fiction and nonfiction—humor, whimsy, fantasy, etc. Read your work out loud! Get someone else to listen to help you spot inconsistencies, unclear passages, maybe even inappropriate word choices. Bad grammar I can correct myself, but it's best to avoid, unless it is specifically meant to be dialectical. Watch your *tenses*. I prefer consistency here—make it past *or* present, but not *both*, except where obviously needed, as in retellings." My biggest reasons for outright rejection are: OFFENSIVE SUBJECT MATTER or language, excessive length, and generally poor writing. I do sometimes send a story back for a rewrite when it has possibilities but 'problems.' " Readers' choice contest every issue-votes taken on favorite stories and poems. Small prizes. Published new writers within the last year.

**‡HOLIER THAN THOU (IV)**, 11565 Arahwood, N. Hollywood CA 91606. (818)982-1746. Editors: Marty and Robbie Cantor. Amateur magazine: 8½x11; 70-120 pages; mimeo paper; card cover stock; illustrations. "Science fiction fandom—items that tell about fandom or fans preferably 'putrid' in style" for science fiction fans. Published 3 times/yearly. Estab. 1978. Circ. 330.

**Needs:** Humor/satire, SF fandom. Wants nothing long, nothing which doesn't deal with SF fans or SF fandom. Accepts 1-2 fiction mss/year; 6-7 mss/year. Length: 200-500 words average.

**How to Contact:** "Request the magazine—then see if your work fits us." Reports in 4-5 weeks on queries and mss. Photocopied submissions OK. Accepts computer printouts including dot-matrix. Sample copy free or $2. ("Editor's whim on whether it will cost you").
**Payment:** Pays in contributor's copies and the copy of magazine for 2 to 3 issues.
**Terms:** Acquires one-time rights.
**Tips:** "Be a fan first. It's easier to write humorous or satiric fiction about fans and fandom if you are one."

‡HORIZONS SF (IV), University of British Columbia SF Society, Box 75, SUB, Univ. of British Columbia, Vancouver BC V6T 2B5 Canada. Editor: Rod Lohin. Fiction Editor: Michael Dean J., Kyle R. Kirkwood. Magazine: 5½x8½; 40 pages; 20 lb paper; 20 lb cover stock; illustrations. *Horizons SF* is interested in all aspects of speculative fiction. Mostly for the university educated, or heavy reader of the genre who have a good background in literature and science. Semiannually. Plans special fiction issue. Estab. 1979. Circ. 125.
**Needs:** Fantasy, horror, science fiction. The central theme must be SF or fantasy, but a good story dealing in SF humor or SF horror or generally combining any of the above with SF or fantasy is OK. No religious, juvenile, preschool, ethnic, and poetry. Receives 4-5 unsolicited fiction mss/month. Accepts 5-6 mss/issues; 10-15 mss/year. Does not read mss March-April. Publishes ms within 6 months after acceptance. Length: 2,500 average; 5,000 words maximum. Publishes short shorts. Critiques rejected mss. Recommends other markets.
**How to Contact:** Send complete ms with cover letter and short bio of author. Reports on queries in 5-7 weeks. SASE for ms. Photocopied and reprints submissions OK. Accepts computer printout including dot-matrix. Accepts electronic submissions via disc. Disc only for Apple Prodos, preference for Appleworks and Apple writer. "Include hardcopy in case of damage to disc in transit." Sample copy for $1.75, 6x9 SAE and 1 first class stamp. Fiction guidelines free for 8x9 SAE and 1 first class stamp.
**Payment:** Pays in contributor's copies.
**Terms:** Pays on publication. Acquires one-time rights. Publication copyrighted.
**Tips:** "Our readers do not have the time to read novels between classes; short stories allow the reader a break from Quantum Mechanics 208."

THE HORROR SHOW (I), Phantasm Press, 14848 Misty Spring Lane, Oak Run CA 96069. (916)472-3540. Editor: David B. Silva. Magazine: 8½x11; 64-68 pages; 60 lb paper; illustrations; photos. Magazine for "all ages, young and old, who have a spark of dementia that must be satisfied." Quarterly. Estab. 1982. Circ. 2,200.
**Needs:** Horror. No heavy sex or violence. Receives 250 unsolicited mss/month. Buys 20 mss/issue; 80 mss/year. Length: 2,000 words average; 4,000 words maximum. Critiques rejected mss, briefly.
**How to Contact:** Send complete ms with SASE. Reports in 3 weeks. Publishes ms 3-6 months after acceptance. Photocopied submissions OK. Accepts computer printout submissions. Sample copy $4.95. Fiction guidelines for SASE with 1 first class stamp.
**Payment:** ½¢/word and 1 free contributor's copy; $3.95 charge for extras.
**Terms:** Pays on acceptance for first North American serial rights, one-time rights. Sometimes sends galleys to author. Publication copyrighted.
**Tips:** "Please take the time to read an issue of *The Horror Show*. Read as much in the horror field as possible. After that, come up with an idea which is fresh and chilling, wrap it in a unique and fascinating style, and send it my way. Hook me in the first sentence. Don't sink me in background that is not relevant. After finishing a story, put it aside for a week—then rewrite. I'm always looking for new writers with fresh ideas. We publish fiction because there aren't enough markets out there, while the hunger for good short stories is growing in the reading public." Published new writers within the last year.

HOR-TASY (II, IV), Ansuda Publications, Box 158-J, Harris IA 51345. Editor/Publisher: Daniel R. Betz. Magazine: 5½x8½; 72 pages; mimeo paper; index cover stock; illustrations on cover.

"*Hor-Tasy* is bringing back actual *horror* to horror lovers tired of seeing so much science fiction and SF passed off as horror. We're also very much interested in true, poetic pure fantasy." Published special fiction issue; plans another.

**Needs:** Fantasy and horror. "Pure fantasy: Examples are trolls, fairies, and mythology. The horror we're looking for comes from the human mind—the ultimate form of horror. It must sound real—so real that in fact it could very possibly happen at any time and place. We must be able to feel the diseased mind behind the personality. No science fiction in any way, shape, or form. We don't want stories in which the main character spends half his time talking to a shrink. We don't want stories that start out with: 'You're crazy,' said so and so." Accepts 6 mss/issue. Receives 4-8 unsolicited fiction mss each month. Critiques rejected mss "unless it's way off from what we're looking for." Recommends other markets.

**How to Contact:** Query or send complete ms with SASE. Accepts computer printout submissions. Prefers letter-quality. Reports in 1 day for queries. "If not interested (in ms), we return immediately. If interested, we may keep it as long as 6 months." Publishes ms an average of 1 year after acceptance. Sample copy $2.95. Guidelines for legal-sized SASE.

**Payment:** 2 free author's copies. Charge for extras: Cover price less regular discount rates.

**Terms:** Acquires first North American serial rights. Publication copyrighted.

**Tips:** "Most stories rejected are about spooks, monsters, haunted houses, spacemen, etc. Because *Hor-Tasy* is a unique publication, I suggest the potential writer get a sample copy. Only unpublished work will be considered."

‡**HUB RAIL (IV)**, Commonwealth Communications Services, Box 1831, Harrisburg PA 17105. (717)234-5099. Editor: Charlotte Maurer. Magazine: 8½x11; 80-95 pages; heavy paper; illustrations; photos. The magazine is about harness riding. Contributors must be highly familiar with the field. Expert audience. Bimonthly. Estab. 1973. Circ. 5,000.

**Needs:** Nothing not about harness racing. Receives "few" unsolicited fiction mss/month. Accepts 1 or fewer ms/issue. Publishes ms "usually" soon after acceptance. Critiques rejected ms.

**How to Contact:** Send complete ms with cover letter. SASE for ms. Accepts computer printout.

**Terms:** Pays on publication. Acquires all rights. Publication copyrighted.

‡**HURRICANE ALICE (II), A Feminist Review**, Hurricane Alice Foundation, Inc., 207 Lind Hall, 207 Church St. SE, Minneapolis MN 55455. (612)376-7132. Editor: Martha Roth. Newspaper: 11½x16; 12-16 pages; heavy newsprint paper and cover stock; illustrations; photos. Review of the arts and culture. Essays, reviews, fiction graphics for intelligent women and men interested in a feminist perspective. Quarterly. Estab. 1983. Circ. 700.

**Needs:** Feminist. No non-feminist stories. Receives 3-5 unsolicited fiction mss/month. Accepts no more than 1 ms/issue; no more than 4/year. Publishes ms 3-6 months after acceptance. Length: 5,000 words average. Critiques rejected ms.

**How to Contact:** Send complete ms with cover letter. SASE for ms. Photocopied submissions OK. Accepts computer printouts including dot-matrix. Sample copy free.

**Payment:** Pays in contributor's copies.

**Terms:** Acquires all rights unless writer wishes to retain copyright. Publication copyrighted.

**HYSTERIA (IV), A Feminist Magazine**, Little Red Media Foundation, Box 2481, Station B, Kitchener, Ontario N2H 6M3 Canada. (519)576-8094. Editor: Catherine Edwards. Magazine: 8½x11; 28-40 pages; bond book paper; coated cover stock; line illustrations; photos. "A feminist magazine which provides a blend of news, information, and analysis on special and cultural issues to a feminist readership. We publish articles, interviews, essays, bibliographies, fiction, poetry, reviews, and original graphic work by women only." Quarterly. Plans special fiction issue. Estab. 1980. Circ. 1,200.

**Needs:** Comics, erotica, ethnic, experimental, fantasy, feminist/lesbian, gay, psychic/supernatural/occult, regional, and science fiction. "We are interested in most types of fiction, but they must be under 4,500 words, written by women and be of interest to a feminist audience. We are interested in condensed novellas. We are not interested in work by men. Traditional romance is out, too." Receives 12 unsolicited fiction mss/month. Accepts 2 mss/issue; 8 mss/year. Length: 4,500 words maximum; 3,000 words average. "We'll take shorter pieces as well." Occasionally critiques rejected ms on request. Recommends other markets.

**How to Contact:** Send complete ms with SASE. Foreign SASE should have IRC, not foreign stamps. Cover letter stating "why author wants to submit work to a feminist magazine; past published work." Photocopied and previously published submissions OK. Accepts computer printout submissions. Prefers letter-quality. Reports in 2-3 months. Publishes ms an average of 6 months after acceptance. Sample copy and fiction guidelines free.

**Payment:** 1¢ word; 2 free contributor's copy. Charges $2.50 for extras; 40% discount on order of five or more copies.

**Terms:** Pays on publication for first rights. Occasionally buys reprints. Publication copyrighted.

**Tips:** "Our audience tends to like stories which portray women with positive qualities and outlooks. For submissions to a feminist magazine it is important to write from a feminist perspective; it is equally important to avoid turning your story into a political tract. The most common problem we encounter in the short fiction we get is that the writer is trying to cram the complex plotting of a novel into a few pages. Rule of thumb: In short stories, one thing happens. Do not resist suggestions for improvements to a story. Be very careful with details. I frequently stop reading stories that have a lot of grammatical mistakes. As a feminist publication, part of our *raison d' être*, is to provide publishing space for the cultural work of women and to promote a feminist literary sensibility." Published new writers within the last year.

**‡I KNOW YOU KNOW: lesbian views & news (II)**, Jernan Ltd. Inc., Suite 14, 5335 N. Tacoma, Indianapolis IN 46220. (317)252-5381. Editor: Jeri Edwards. Magazine: 8½x11; 48 pages; slick paper and cover; illustrations; photos. "*I Know You Know: lesbian views & news* is a 'lifestyle' magazine for lesbians, published monthly and distributed nationally, predominately by subscription. A four color, semi-gloss magazine, *IKYK* includes regular columns, monthly feature topics, interviews, photography, poetry and short stories" for lesbians. Monthly. Estab. December, 1984. Circ. 10,000.

**Needs:** Feminist, gay, lesbian, women's. "Fiction can be from any category if the story is applicable or of interest to women." No pornography. Receives 3-5 unsolicited fiction mss/month. Accepts 1 ms/issue. Publishes ms 3-6 months after acceptance. Length: 2,000 words average; 1,000 words minimum; 3,000 words maximum.

**How to Contact:** Send complete ms with cover letter saying "we can use your name or if you are using a pseudonym, and a short bio." Reports in 6 weeks on mss. SASE. Simultaneous, photocopied submissions and reprints OK. Accepts computer printouts. No dot-matrix. Sample copy $4.75 (includes mailing package and first class postage). Fiction guidelines free.

**Payment:** Pays in contributor's copies.

**Terms:** Acquires first North American serial rights. Publication copyrighted.

**Tips:** "Send out as much as possible—go for it!"

**IL CAFFÈ (IV), The Italian Experience**, Il Caffè, Suite 3113, 1562 Response Rd., Sacramento CA 95815. (916)927-6368. Editor: R.T. LoVerso. Fiction Editor: Lloyd Bruno. Tabloid: newsprint paper; b&w illustrations and photos. Publishing serialized novels, short stories, interviews, politics, economy, and art for American and Italian-American professional people. Bimonthly. Estab. 1981. Circ. 14,000.

**Needs:** Adventure, comics, condensed novel, confession, contemporary, ethnic, humor/satire, literary, mainstream, prose poem, romance (contemporary, historical, young adult), serialized/excerpted novel, and translations. Receives 5 unsolicited mss/month. Accepts 1-2 mss/issue; 6-12 mss/year. Approximately 20% of fiction is agented. Length: 3,000 words average; 2,000 words minimum; 6,000 words maximum. Also publishes short shorts. Occasionally critiques rejected mss.

**How to Contact:** Send complete ms with SASE. Reports in 1 month. Publishes ms 2-6 months after acceptance. Simultaneous, photocopied and previously published submissions OK. Accepts computer printout submissions. Prefers letter-quality. Free sample copy.

**Payment:** Pays in contributor's copies; $1.25 charge for extras.
**Terms:** Acquires first rights. Buys reprints. Publication copyrighted.
**Tips:** Fiction should reflect "international views." Published new writers within the last year.

‡**ILLUMINATIONS (II), An International Magazine of Contemporary Writing**, The Rathasketz Press, % The University of Maryland-Asian Division, PSC Box 100 APO, San Francisco CA 96328. Editor: Peter McMillan. Magazine: 6½x9; 36-56 pages; 70 lb matt paper; matt cover stock; occasional photos. "To promote the work of new writers by publishing them within the context of more established writers" for readers of serious fiction. Semiannually. Published special fiction issue. Estab. 1982. Circ. 1,000.
**Needs:** Contemporary, erotica, experimental, gay, lesbian, literary, serialized/excerpted novel, translations. "Mainly interested in literary—all other subjects of special interest only if of literary value." Nothing run-of-the-mill; pedestrian; material without formal concerns. Receives a 'dozen' unsolicited fiction mss/month. Buys 2-6 mss/issue; 2-12 mss/year. Don't read in June-July. Publishes ms up to 6 months after acceptance. Reading fee of $15, only if criticism required. Length: under 1,000 words average; 50 words minimum; 5,000 words maximum. Also publishes short shorts of 2-10 pages. Occasionally critiques rejected mss. Recommends other markets.
**How to Contact:** Send complete ms with cover letter with biographical data/age/publications. Reports in 3 months on mss. SASE for ms. No simultaneous or reprinted submissions; photocopied submissions OK. No computer printouts. Sample copy $4. Fiction guidelines for business-size SAE and 1 first class stamp.
**Payment:** Pays $50; "only in exceptional solicited material"; free subscription to magazine; 2 contributor's copies; charge for extras with discount.
**Terms:** Pays on publication. Publication copyrighted.
**Tips:** "We are mostly interested in serious writers—those who are writing by vocation rather than profession. We're not interested in graduate school exercises, but rather prose which embodies a voice which is distinctive. We like prose poetry-modelled after some of the symbolists perhaps. Ramke's prose poems come closest to any contemporary writer's whose prose we admire: the delicate brush store, with sensitive and highly selective sense of details manages to embody, or at least suggest a whole experience. Suggestion, in writing, is perhaps a key for us. We'd much rather have a moment exquisitely suggested than an overly told tale—that's a waste of our time. Writers should be concerned with the music of the prose itself rather recounting incidents."

‡**IMAGE MAGAZINE, A Magazine of the Arts**, Cornerstone Press, Box 28048, St. Louis MO 63119. (314)296-9662. Editor: Anthony J. Summers. Fiction Editor: Jim Finnegan. Magazine. "No set theme. Variety of material is used for each issue. For the educated students, poets, fictioneers, friends of culture." 3 times/year. Estab. 1972. Circ. 600-700.
**Needs:** Literary open. No "romance or religious types mss. Receives 200 + unsolicited mss/ month. Number mss accepted varies." Length: varies. Occasionally comments on rejected ms.
**How to Contact:** Query first. Reports in 2 weeks on queries; 2-6 weeks on mss. SASE for query and ms. Simultaneous submissions, photocopied submissions and previously published work OK. Accepts computer printout submissions. Prefers letter-quality. Sample copy $3. Fiction guidelines free.
**Payment:** Pays $1-100 and contributor's copy; charge for extras: 50% of cover price.
**Terms:** Pays on publication for one-time rights. Other rights negotiable. Publication copyrighted.

**IMPULSE MAGAZINE**, Impulse Publishing Co., Box 370, Station B, Toronto, Ontario M5T 2W2 Canada. (416)368-7511. Editors: Eldon Garnet, Judith Doyle, Carolyn White, Andy Payne and Gerald Owen. "Theme is art and culture with an emphasis on experimental/innovative fiction, interviews, political and cultural analysis, and artwork. Quarterly. Estab. 1971. Circ. 10,000.
**Needs:** "Experimental, innovative writing, feminist, gay, and lesbian. We are also a visual publication and would appreciate any accompanying photos, illustrations, etc. No plays." Accepts 4-

5 mss/issue, 15-20 mss/year. Receives approximately 30 unsolicited fiction mss/month. Length: 250-2,000 words. Critiques rejected mss "when there is time."
**How to Contact:** Send complete ms with SAE and IRCs. Accepts computer printout submissions. Reports in 1 month on mss. Sample copy $4.
**Terms:** Acquires first rights. Publication copyrighted. We have a greater commitment than previously to paying all contributors."
**Tips:** "Keep trying. Avoid too lengthy a manuscript. Most manuscripts are either poorly conceived or simply too conventional in style and content and do not exhibit suitable awareness of the idiosyncracies of *IMPULSE*. We are interested in more experimental pieces of fiction."

**"IN A DIFFERENT REALITY. . ."**, Box 358, Doctors Inlet FL 32030-0358. Editor: Tisha A. Kuntz. Magazine "about human relationships in the most realistic sense—housed in a *Star Trek/* science fiction theme." For "young adults through general public—well-educated readers who appreciate a continuation of the *ST*/SF genre." Quarterly. Estab. summer 1985.
**Needs:** Adventure (theme: *ST*/SF), condensed novel, contemporary, fantasy, humor/satire, mainstream, prose poem, psychic/supernatural/occult, contemporary romance (*must* be well-written), science fiction, serialized/excerpted novel, suspense mystery, in *Star Trek* setting. No "pointless violence to characters; pornography/gay material; romance for its own sake . . ." Expecting 5-7 unsolicited mss/month. Will offer "constructive comments geared to *help* our submitting writers." Will accept ST/SF submissions *ONLY*.
**How to Contact:** Query first. Reports in 4 weeks on queries; 8 weeks on mss. SASE for query and ms. Simultaneous submissions, photocopied submissions, and previously published work OK. Sample copy for cover cost, price pending: plus postage. Fiction guidelines for legal-sized SAE and 40¢ postage.
**Payment:** 1-2 contributor's copies; charge for extras.
**Terms:** Acquires one-time rights on publication. Publication will be copyrighted.
**Tips:** "I see a return to the traditional values: honor, loyalty, relationships—and personal conflicts. Such topics retain literary value regardless . . . Give me a good story that stands alone (without genre entrapments)—and has *human* qualities in addition to good structure and tight editing."

**INDIANA REVIEW (II)**, 316 N. Jordan Ave., Bloomington IN 47405. (812)335-3439. Editor: Pamela Wampler. Associate Editor: Jim Brock. Magazine: 128 pages; illustrations sometimes. "Magazine of contemporary fiction and poetry in which there is a zest for language, some relationship between form and content, and some awareness of the world. For fiction writers/readers, followers of lively contemporary poetry." Triannually. Estab. 1975. Circ. 750 + .
**Needs:** Literary, contemporary, experimental, mainstream, and prose poetry. "We are interested in innovation, logic, unity, a social context, formal experimentation. All genres that meet some of these criteria are welcome." Accepts 6-8 mss/issue. Publishes manuscripts of 1-35 magazine pages.
**How to Contact:** Send complete ms with SASE. Accepts computer printout submissions. Prefers letter-quality. Reports in 3 weeks-3 months. Publishes ms an average of 2-6 months after acceptance. Sample copy $4.
**Payment:** Eligible for prize money.
**Terms:** Acquires North American serial rights. Publication copyrighted.
**Tips:** "Be daring, love the language. Don't imitate anyone. Double space. Never ever send dot-matrix or use italics in typewriters. Strive to send clean copy. Refrain from the chatty cover letter. Send one story at a time (unless they're really short). We are tending toward longer stories, 20,000 words or better." Published "several" new writers within the last year.

**‡INFINITUM (I, II), Science Fiction Fantasy**, Infinitum Press, 5737 Louetta Rd., Spring TX 77379. (713)376-9693. Editor: William H. Doyle. Magazine: 8½x5½; 48 pages; 20 lb bound paper; 67 lb day-glo cover; illustrations. "Interested in all science fiction, particularly 'problem solving' pieces, tightly knit short horror and a variety of fantasy." Semiannually. Plans special fiction issue in future. Estab. fall, 1985. Circ. 400.

**Needs:** Adventure, ethnic, experimental, fantasy, horror, science fiction. No "clichéd SF and horror with nothing new to say or at least a unique way of presenting it." Receives about 30 unsolicited mss/month. Buys 10-12 mss/issue; 20-25 mss/year. Publishes ms 3-6 months generally after acceptance. Length: 3,000 words average; 500 words minimum; 6,000 words maximum. Occasionally critiques rejected mss. Sometimes recommends other markets.

**How to Contact:** Send complete ms with cover letter (thumbnail bio and recent sale). Reports in 1 month on mss. SASE. Photocopied submissions and reprints OK. Accepts computer printouts including dot-matrix. Sample copy $3. Fiction guidelines for #10 SAE and 1 first class stamp.

**Payment:** Pays 1/4¢/word plus contributor's copy; charge for extras.

**Terms:** Pays on publication for first North American serial rights and one-time rights. Publication copyrighted.

**Tips:** "The small press market in SF/fantasy is stale; dare to be different. Build your own world, your own unique setting or situation, and have *something to say* to the reader of your story. Gimmicks and surprise endings are not enough."

‡**INKBLOT**, Inkblot, #11, 439 49th St., Oakland CA 94609. (415)652-7127. Editor: Theo Green. Magazine: 8½x11; 84 pages; 20 lb paper; 67 lb cover stock; illustrations; photos. Experimental/avant-garde excerpts from novels, etc. for "those with a taste for the bizarre." Quarterly. Plans special fiction issue. Estab. 1983. Circ. 1,500.

**Needs:** Erotica, ethnic, experimental, serialized/excerpted novel, suspense/mystery, translations. Receives 10-15 unsolicited fiction mss/month. Accepts 6-8 mss/issue; 20-25 mss/year. Publishes ms 3-6 months after acceptance. Length: 2,000 words average; 500 words minimum; 4,000 words maximum. Publishes short shorts. Recommends other markets.

**How to Contact:** Query with clips of published work or send complete ms with cover letter with brief bio—other publication credits, etc. Reports in 1 week on queries; 4 weeks on mss. SASE for ms and query. Simultaneous, photocopied and reprints submissions OK. Accepts computer printouts including dot-matrix. Sample copy $3. Fiction guidelines for SAE.

**Payment:** Free contributor's copies.

**Terms:** Pays on publication. Publication copyrighted.

**Tips:** "Magazine fiction is used by us mainly to promote our book series, which is expanding. Magazine fiction is essential for someone (the reader) to get a glimpse of an author's work."

**INKY TRAILS PUBLICATIONS (I)**, Box 345, Middleton ID 83644. Editor/Publisher: Pearl Kirk. Magazine consisting of poetry, art, fillers, quotes, fiction and TV or radio scripts: 8½x11; 85 pages or less; 20 lb mimeo paper; soft cover; illustrations of indio ink. Published 3 times/year. Estab. 1967. Circ. 300.

**Needs:** Literary, contemporary, religious/inspirational, psychic/supernatural, fantasy, romance, western, mystery, adventure, humor, preschool, juvenile, young adult, and senior citizen/retirement. "Would like to have themes on senior citizens, horses, family and novels to run in several issues. No filth or four letter words." Plans fiction anthology for the future. Length: 3,500 words maximum. Sometimes recommends markets.

**How to Contact:** Send complete ms with SASE. Reports in 2-4 months. Publishes ms an average of 1 year after acceptance. Sample copy $8.50 with 10x13 SASE plus 70¢ postage. Guidelines for legal-size SASE and 44¢ postage.

**Payment:** "Occasional cash ($15/first, $10/second place) awards. A copy with author's material will be $6, when his/her material is published—or if sending for a sample copy, $7.50." Write for price list for magazines. SASE.

**Terms:** "All rights stay with the writers as long as *Inky Trails* is given credit for first printing." Publication copyrighted.

**Tips:** "Have a title, start with characters and conflict. Let the characters come alive with emotion, and write about something familiar. Solve the problem or conflict. Surprise endings are good. Readers want more short stories. I use all types of good clean material. Awards given at end of year, but recipient must be a subscriber." Write for publishing schedule. "We try to select what we like; and still what the readers will like—and at the same time we're always looking for that something special, a new approach. Non-subscribers material is accepted and published but if there are two submissions of equal quality and suitability, the subscriber will be given the preference."

**INLET (II)**, Virginia Wesleyan College, Norfolk VA 23502. Editor: Joseph Harkey. Magazine: 7x8½; 32-38 pages. "Poetry and short fiction for people of all ages." Annually. Estab. 1970. Circ. 700.
**Needs:** Literary, contemporary, science fiction, fantasy, and humor. "Our main interest is well-written fiction." Accepts 2-5 mss/issue. Receives 10-20 unsolicited fiction mss each month. Does not read in summer. Length: 500-1,500 words but "will consider up to 3,000." Sometimes recommends markets.
**How to Contact:** "Manuscripts are read September through March only." Send complete ms to fiction editor with SASE. Reports in 2 months. Sample copy 75¢. Addressed labels welcomed.
**Payment:** 2 free author's copies. Negotiates charge for extras.
**Terms:** Publication copyrighted.
**Tips:** "Write carefully and present a neatly typed manuscript with SASE. Send an example of your best work; short shorts preferred. Some rejected manuscripts are poorly written. Some are polished and professional but lack imaginative treatments of the problems they raise."

**INTRO (I, II)**, Associated Writing Programs, Old Dominion University, Norfolk VA 23508. (804)440-3840. Annual journal of literary fiction, poetry and drama by university writing students. Annually. Estab. 1968. Circ. 5,000.
**Needs:** "Will consider any genre." Mss read only during March of each year. Accepts 15 mss/issue.
**How to Contact:** Query first for entry requirements with SASE. Photocopied submissions OK. Reports within 2 weeks on queries. Sample copy $4. Fiction guidelines for SASE.
**Payment:** 2 free contributor's copies. 40% discount on extras.
**Terms:** Pays on publication; assignments on work-for-hire basis. Publication copyrighted.

**THE IOWA REVIEW (II)**, University of Iowa, 308 EPB, Iowa City IA 52242. (319)353-6048. Editor: David Hamilton. Magazine: 6x9; 176 pages; first grade offset paper; Carolina CIS-10 pt. cover stock. "Stories, essays, poems for a general readership interested in contemporary literature." Published triannually. Published special fiction issue last year; may plan another. Estab. 1970. Circ. 1,000.
**Needs:** Receives 150-200 unsolicited fiction mss/month. Less than 10% of fiction is agented. Buys 3-5 mss/issue, 12-16 mss/year. Does not read mss in summer.
**How to Contact:** Send complete ms with SASE. "Don't bother with queries." Simultaneous submissions accepted. Photocopied submissions OK. Accepts computer printout submissions. Reports in 3 months on mss. Publishes ms an average of 4-8 months after acceptance. Sample copy $5.
**Payment:** $10/page; 2 free contributor's copies; charge for extras: 30% off cover price.
**Terms:** Pays on publication for first North American serial rights. Hardly ever buys reprints. Publication copyrighted.
**Tips:** Published new writers within the last year.

**IOWA WOMAN**, Iowa Woman Endeavors, Box 680, Iowa City IA 52244. Editor: Valerie Staats. Magazine "dedicated to encouraging and publishing the creation of art by Midwest women." Quarterly. Estab. 1979. Circ. 800 + .
**Needs:** Historical, literary, women's. Receives 5-10 unsolicited mss/month. Accepts 2 mss/issue; 8 mss/year. Length: 5,000 words maximum.
**How to Contact:** Send complete ms. Reports in 3 months. SASE. Sample copy for $3.50 and SAE with 80¢ postage. Fiction guidelines for SAE with 1 first class stamp.
**Payment:** 2 free contributor's copies; $2 charge for extras.
**Terms:** Acquires all rights. Publication copyrighted.

**‡IRON MOUNTAIN: A JOURNAL OF MAGICAL RELIGION (IV)**, Artemisia Press, Box 2282, Boulder CO 80306. (303)939-9067. Editor: Chas S. Clifton. Mountain: 7x8 ½; 52 pages; 50 lb offset paper; cover stock varies; illustrations; photos. "*Iron Mountain* is aimed at an informed and/or scholarly readership interested in magical religion, shamanism, etc. We publish primarily articles, interviews and reviews, plus a *limited* amount of poetry and fiction." Semiannually. Estab. 1984. Circ. 250.

**Needs:** Experimental, psychic/supernatural/occult. Receives 1-2 unsolicited fiction mss/month. Length: 4,000 average. Critiques rejected ms.

**How to Contact:** Send complete ms with cover letter. Reports in 2 weeks on queries; 2 months on mss. SASE for mss. Photocopied and reprint submissions OK. Accepts computer printouts including dot-matrix. Accepts electronic submissions via disc or modem. Please contact editor for specifics. Sample copy $2. Fiction guidelines for #10 SAE and 22¢ postage.

**Payment:** Free subscription to magazine, contributor's copies.

**Terms:** Pays on publication. Acquires first rights. Sends galleys to author. Publication copyrighted.

**JAM TO-DAY (II)**, Jam To-day, Box 249, Northfield VT 05663. Fiction Editor: Judith Stanford. Co-editor: Don Stanford. Magazine: 5½x8½; 80 pages; illustrations; occasionally photos. Forum for serious nonacademic poetry and fiction by unknown and little-known contemporary writers. Annually. Published special fiction issue. Estab. 1973. Circ. 400.

**Needs:** Literary, contemporary, science fiction, and feminist. No light fiction, word-play fiction, highly allusive or allegorical fiction. Buys 2-4 mss/year. Receives approximately 35 unsolicited fiction mss each month. Length: 1,500-7,500. Publishes "good quality short shorts of 300-750 words. Critiques rejected mss "when there is time." Sometimes recommends other markets.

**How to Contact:** Send complete ms with SASE. Accepts computer printout submissions. Prefers letter quality. Reports in 2 months on mss. Publishes ms up to 1 year after acceptance. Sample copy $3.

**Payment:** $5/printed page.

**Terms:** Pays on publication for first rights. Publication copyrighted.

**Tips:** Reasons for rejections: "(1) Poorly conceived: trite, uninteresting, poorly written, too academic; and (2) better suited to another market: well written and holds interest but better suited to mass-market magazine, or extraordinarily obscure but not obviously foolish and ought to go to experimental literary magazine. We wish we could accept more fiction, but space and cost considerations so far forbid it." Published new writers within the last year.

**JAPANOPHILE (IV)**, Box 223, Okemos MI 48864. (517)349-1795. Editor-in-Chief: Earl Snodgrass. Magazine: 8½x5¼; 50 pages; illustrations; photos. Magazine of "articles, photos, poetry, humor, short stories about Japanese culture, not necessarily in Japan, for an adult audience, most with college background; travelers." Published quarterly. Published special fiction issue last year; plans another. Estab. 1974. Circ. 600.

**Needs:** Adventure, historical (general), humor/satire, literary, mainstream, and suspense/mystery. Receives 40-100 unsolicited fiction mss/month. Buys 1 ms/issue, 4 mss/year. Length: 2,000 words minimum; 9,000 words maximum; 4,000 words average. Sometimes recommends other markets.

**How to Contact:** Send complete ms with SASE and cover letter with author bio and information about story. Photocopied and previously published submissions OK. Accepts computer printout submissions. Reports in 2 months on mss. Sample copy $3; free guidelines for large SAE and 1 first class stamp.

**Payment:** $15-50.

**Terms:** Pays on publication for all rights, first North American serial rights or one-time rights (depends on situation). Publication copyrighted.

**Tips:** Short stories usually involve Japanese and 'foreign' (non-Japanese) characters in a way that contributes to understanding of Japanese culture and the Japanese people. However, a *good* story dealing with Japan or Japanese cultural aspects anywhere in the world will be considered even if it does not involve this encounter or meeting of Japanese and foreign characters. Accepted short stories receive $20 on publication plus $100 for the story judged the best. Some stories may also be published in an anthology." Published new writers within the last year.

**JEOPARDY**, Literary Arts Magazine, Western Washington University, HU350, WWU, Bellingham WA 98225. (206)676-3118. Magazine. Theme varies. Material published: fiction, nonfiction, interviews, poetry, photographed artwork for "all inclusive" audience. Annually. Estab. 1965. Circ. 3,000-4,000.
**Needs:** Adventure, confession, contemporary, ethnic, experimental, fantasy, feminist, humor/satire, literary, mainstream, prose poem, regional, contemporary romance, science fiction, and translations. No long stories. Accepts 7-10 mss/year. Charges reading fee of issue price ($2). Length: 4 pages (average 800-1,000 words).
**How to Contact:** Send complete ms. SASE. Simultaneous and previously published submissions OK. Accepts computer printout submissions. Sample copy $2.
**Payment:** $2. "Sometimes *Jeopardy* awards cash prizes or special recognition to winners in various categories."
**Terms:** Publication copyrighted.
**Tips:** "Leave out unnecessary details."

**JEWISH CURRENTS MAGAZINE (IV)**, 22 E. 17th St., New York NY 10003. (212)924-5740. Editor-in-Chief: Morris U. Schappes. Magazine: 5½x8½; 48 pages. "We are a progressive monthly, broad in our interests, printing feature articles on political and cultural aspects of Jewish life in the US and elsewhere, reviews of books and film, poetry and fiction, Yiddish translations; regular columns on Israel, US Jewish community, current events, Jewish Woman Today, secular Jewish life; monthly themes include Holocaust and Resistance, Black-Jewish relations, etc. National audience, some 50-80 years old; many younger; literate and politically left, well educated." Published monthly. Plans special fiction issue. Estab. 1946. Circ. 4,000.
**Needs:** Contemporary, ethnic, feminist, historical (general), humor/satire, literary, senior citizen/retirement, translations, and women's. "We are interested in *authentic* experience and readable prose; Jewish themes; humanistic orientation. No religious, political sectarian; no porn or hard sex, no escapist stuff. Go easy on experimentation, but we're interested." Receives 6-10 unsolicited fiction mss/month. Accepts 0-1 ms/issue, 8-10 mss/year. Length: 1,000 words minimum; 3,000 words maximum; 1,800 words average. Occasionally critiques rejected mss.
**How to Contact:** Send complete ms with SASE. Reports in 2 months on mss. Publishes ms an average of 2 months to 2 years after acceptance. Sample copy $1.25 with SAE and 3 first class stamps.
**Payment:** 1 complimentary one-year subscription; 6 free contributor's copies.
**Terms:** Does not pay. "We readily give reprint permission at no charge." Sends galleys to author. Publication copyrighted.
**Tips:** "Family themes are good, but avoid sentimentality; keep the prose tight, not sprawling; matters of character and moral dilemma, maturing into pain and joy, dealing with Jewish conflicts OK." Published new writers within the last year.

**JOURNAL OF POLYMORPHOUS PERVERSITY (II)**, Wry-Bred Press, Inc., 10 Waterside Plaza, Suite 20-B, New York NY 10010. (212)689-5473. Editor: Glenn Ellenbogen. Magazine: 6¾x10; 24 pages; 60 lb paper; antique india cover stock; illustrations with some articles. "*JPP* is a humorous and satirical journal of psychology, psychiatry, and the closely allied mental health disciplines." For "psychologists, psychiatrists, social workers, psychiatric nurses, *and* the psychologically sophisticated layman." Semiannually. Plans special fiction issue. Estab. January, 1984.
**Needs:** Humor/Satire. "We only consider materials that are 1) FUNNY, 2) relate to psychology *or* behavior." Receives 10 unsolicited mss/month. Accepts 8 mss/issue; 16 mss/year. Length: 1,500 words average; 4,000 words maximum. Comments on rejected ms.
**How to Contact:** Send complete ms *in triplicate*. Reports in 1-3 months on mss. SASE. Simultaneous and photocopied submissions OK. Accepts computer printout submissions. Prefers letter-

quality. Accepts disc submissions compatible with Morrow MD-11. Prefers hard copy with a disc submission. Sample copy $5. Fiction guidelines free for SAE (#10 envelope and 1 first class stamp).

**Payment:** 2 contributor's copies; charge for extras: $5.

**Terms:** Publication copyrighted.

**Tips:** "Take a look at *real* journals of psychology and try to lampoon their *style* as much as their content. Avoid writing in first person; rather use more quasi-scientific style. There are few places to showcase satire of the social sciences, thus we provide one vehicle for injecting a dose of humor into this often too serious area." Most writers published last year were previously unpublished writers.

‡JOURNAL OF REGIONAL CRITICISM (IV), The Surrealist Novel, "Artemis," Arjuna Library Press, 1025 Garner St., Box 18, Colorado Springs CO 80905. Editor: Joseph A. Uphoff, Jr. Pamphlet/pages: size variable; number of pages variable; paper quality variable; Bristol cover stock; b&w illustrations; b&w photos. "Surrealist and dreamlike prose poetry and very short stories to illustrate accompanying mathematical, theoretical material in the fine arts . . . for wide ranging audience, from novice to advanced capability but interested in philosophical sophistication and erudite language . . ." Variable frequency. Plans special fiction issue. Estab. 1979. Presented to singular individuals or organizations.

**Needs:** Adventure, contemporary, ethnic, experimental, fantasy, historical (general), horror, humor/satire, literary, mainstream, psychic/supernatural/occult, regional, religious/inspirational, contemporary romance, science fiction. Nothing other than general audience quality. Receives one or fewer unsolicited fiction ms/month. Accepts 1-5 mss/issue. Publishes mss 1-2 months after acceptance. Agented fiction: 100%. Short stories/long poems. Short short stories preferred. Critiques rejected mss. Recommends other markets.

**How to Contact:** Send complete ms with cover letter. Manuscript will *not* be returned. Cover letter should include goals, behind the scenes explanation, and biographical material or resume. Reports in 2 months on mss. SASE for query. Simultaneous, photocopied and reprint submissions OK. Accepts computer printouts including dot-matrix. Sample copy free if and when available for $1 postage.

**Payment:** By contract after profit, contributor's copies.

**Terms:** Profitable placement. Acquires prototype presentation rights. Publication copyrighted limited edition procedure copyrights.

**Tips:** "Fiction offers an advantage in expressing ideas not reflected through events and documentation. Difficult concepts can be exemplified and experiments engaged in, but, basically, the most beautiful of flowers is the flower of imagination. Our dreams are not rational, but they are beautiful stories. Language need not be colorless! Free expression must nevertheless be socially and psychologically humane and responsible. Irony is dangerous but necessary. Those who do not know what surrealism is are urged to read the surrealist manifestoes of Andre Breton and the literature of H.P. Lovecraft."

JOYFUL NOISE (II, IV), 5500 Monroe Ave., Evansville IN 47715. (812)477-2773. Editor: Brad Chaffin. Magazine: 8½x11; 16 pages; 60 lb paper; 65 lb (color) 80 lb (white) cover stock; cartoons and clip art illustrations; photos. "Inspirational magazine with bits of humor; abundance of love and faith. Uplifting, hopeful materials; literary—for a general audience, but mostly persons with disabilities." Quarterly. Estab. 1980. Circ. 400.

**Needs:** Adventure, comics, historical, literary, prose poem, religious/inspirational, science fiction (moderate), senior citizen/retirement, and suspense/mystery. Accepts original scripts from handicapped *only*. No material "degrading of human kind." Receives 10-15 unsolicited mss/month. Accepts 6-8 mss/issue; 30 mss/year. Length: 350 words minimum; 1,200 words maximum. Occasionally critiques rejected mss.

**How to Contact:** Query first or send complete ms. Reports in 1 month. Publishes ms an average of 3-9 months after acceptance. SASE. Previously published submissions OK. Accepts computer printout submissions. Sample copy $2. Writer's guidelines for 4x9½ SAE and 1 first class stamp.

**Payment:** 2 free contributor's copies; $1 charge for extras.
**Terms:** Acquires first rights or one-time rights. Buys reprints. Publication copyrighted.
**Tips:** "Fiction is another challenge for handicapped writers. Don't take yourself too seriously. Have fun writing. Keep trying to learn to write better." Published new writers within the last year.

**‡JUKEBOX TERRORISTS WITH TYPEWRITERS (II)**, Young Whippersnapper Press, 171 Lincoln Ave., Amherst MA 01002. Editors: Steven Ruhl, Leslie Staub. Magazine: size varies; approximately 40 pages; illustrations; photos. "We publish experimental fiction. Tough, cutting-edge, high energy, avant garde. The magazine concentrates on pop culture and contemporary life." For "anyone with a spirit of adventure." Triquarterly. Estab. summer, 1984. Circ. about 250.
**Needs:** Adventure, condensed novel, confession, contemporary, erotica, ethnic, experimental, fantasy, feminist, gay, horror, humor/satire, lesbian, literary, psychic/supernatural/occult, regional, science fiction, serialized/excerpted novel, suspense/mystery, translations, women's. "We're an international, high-voltage, *xerox* literary/art magazine; we take risks, and we publish the most exciting fiction we receive. People submitting should keep that in mind." No conventional, 'creative-writing workshop,' boring stuff." Accepts 3-4 mss/year. Length: "doesn't matter." Also publishes short shorts. Recommends other markets. Send complete ms with cover letter (some personal info). Reports in 3 months on mss. SASE for ms. Simultaneous, photocopied submissions and reprints OK if acknowledged. Accepts computer printouts including dot-matrix. Sample copy $2 and 11½x14½ SAE and $1 postage.
**Payment:** Pays in contributor's copies.
**Terms:** Acquires one-time rights.
**Tips:** "We're really friendly and accessible to writers who are doing new, innovative work. Just send us some of your recent fiction, and if it knocks us out, no problem—we'll find room for you."

**‡KAIROS (III), A Journal of Contemporary Thought & Criticism**, #3F, Hermes House Press, 127 W. 15th St., New York NY 10011. (212)691-9773. Editors: Alan Mandell, William Rasch. Magazine: 5½x8½; 130 pages; 70 lb paper; 65 lb cover stock; illustrations; photos. "We have attempted to combine literary/artistic work with social and cultural criticism. Thus, *K* includes analytic essays as well as translations, poems, interviews, reviews and we continue to hope—fiction as well. *K* has specific themes that are typically announced in forthcoming notice of each issue." Semiannually. Estab. 1981. Circ. 350.
**Needs:** Experimental, feminist, literary, translations, women's. Receives 3-4 unsolicited fiction mss/month. "We publish every 6 months." Length: 2,500 average. Publishes short shorts. Short short stories would be most appropriate for *K*. (Given size/diversity of work presented, etc.). Critiques rejected mss. Recommends other markets.
**How to Contact:** Query with clips of published work or send complete ms with cover letter. Reports in 6-8 weeks on mss. SASE for query and ms. Photocopied submissions OK. Accepts computer printouts including dot-matrix.
**Payment:** "We provide 3 copies of that issue and extras at discount rate."
**Terms:** Publication copyrighted.
**Tips:** "Short stories serve, for us, as another kind of occasion to present and *diversity* of forms—of expressions—that we seek. We will always be able to include only a very small selection of fiction; but such an inclusion will be important to us."

**KALEIDOSCOPE (II, IV), Literary/Art Magazine**, International Magazine of Literature, Fine Arts, and Disability, 326 Locust St., Akron OH 44302. (216)762-9755, ext. 474, 475. Editor-in-Chief: Darshan Peruse. International Magazine of Literature, Fine Arts and Disability: 8½x11; 45-56 pages; non-coated paper; coated stock; illustrations (all media); photos. Published semiannually. Estab. 1979. Circ. 2,000.
**Needs:** Personal experience, contemporary, experimental, fantasy, feminist, humor/satire, science fiction, serialized/excerpted novel, suspense/mystery. "Writers need not limit themselves to

writing about being disabled. Any quality fiction is acceptable." Receives 20-25 unsolicited fiction mss/month. Accepts 10 mss/issue, 10 mss/year. Approximately 1% of fiction is agented. Length: 3,000 words minimum; 5,000 words maximum. "We accept children's literature as well."

**How to Contact:** Query first or send complete ms and cover letter with author's educational and writing background; if author is disabled, how the disability has influenced the writing. SASE with query, mss. Accepts computer printout submissions. Reports in 2 weeks on queries; 6-8 weeks on mss. Sample copy and guidelines for SAE and 1 first class stamp.

**Payment:** Cash payment on acceptance. 3 free contributor's copies; charge for extras: $4. Also annual cash awards for top submissions.

**Terms:** Pays on acceptance for first rights. Reprints are accepted with credit given to original publication. Publication copyrighted.

**Tips:** "Read the magazine and get fiction guidelines. We publish professional writers and encourage emerging ones. *Kaleidosocope* will consider fiction on the theme of disability by nondisabled writers. We reject manuscripts that convey stereotypes, are not carefully constructed, or don't illuminate that aspect of life which the fiction treats."

**KALLIOPE, A JOURNAL OF WOMEN'S ART (II)**, 3939 Roosevelt Blvd., Jacksonville FL 32205. (904)387-8211. Project Director: Peggy Friedmann. Managing Editor: Sharon Weightman. "A literary and visual arts journal for women, *Kalliope* celebrates women in the arts by publishing their work and by providing a medium of communication through which they may share ideas and opinions." Short stories, poems, plays, essays, criticism, reviews, drawings, and photos. For people interested in visual and verbal art by women. Published 3 times/year. Estab. 1978. Circ. 1,000.

**Needs:** "Literary, contemporary, feminist, regional, science fiction, fantasy, and women's work with a historical perspective, past, present and future." Accepts 2-4 mss/issue. Receives approximately 40-50 unsolicited fiction mss each month. No preferred length—"just short fiction." Critiques rejected mss "when there is time and if requested."

**How to Contact:** Send complete ms with SASE, short biography, and contributor's note. Reports in 2-3 months on ms. Published ms an average of 1-6 months after acceptance. Sample copy $4 for current issue; $2 for issues from '78-'85.

**Payment:** 3 free author's copies. $3.50 charge for extras, discount for large orders.

**Terms:** Acquires first rights. "We accept only unpublished work. Copyright returned to author upon request." Publication copyrighted.

**Tips:** "Read our magazine. The work we consider for publication will be well written and the characters and dialogue will be convincing and have strength and movement. We like a fresh approach and are interested in new or unusual forms. Create characters capable of living, characters we can care about. We would like to publish more work by minority writers." Manuscript is rejected because "1) nothing *happens!*, 2) it is thinly disguised autobiography (richly disguised autobiography is OK), and 3) ending is either too pat or else just trails off. We seem to be getting a good many mss that are well written but should go to *LHJ* or *Redbook*, not a feminist journal. (Vol 4, #2 has four very different prose pieces, so it's a good one for writers to study.)"

**KANSAS QUARTERLY (I, II)**, Kansas Quarterly Association, Denison Hall, Kansas State University, Manhattan KS 66506. (913)532-6716. Editors: Harold Schneider, Ben Nyberg, W.R. Moses, and John Rees. Magazine: 6x9; 104-304 pages; 60 lb offset paper; Frankcote 8 pt. coated (inside white) cover stock; occasionally illustrations; rarely photos. "A literary and cultural arts magazine publishing fiction and poetry. Special material on selected, announced topics in literary criticism, art history, folklore, and regional history. For well-read, general and academic audiences." Quarterly. Published special fiction issue last year; plans another. Estab. 1968. Circ. 1,300.

**Needs:** "We consider most categories as long as the fiction is of sufficient literary quality to merit inclusion, though we have no interest in children's literature. We resist translations and parts of novels, but do not absolutely refuse them." Accepts 25-40 mss/year. Limited reading time in sum-

mer. Approximately 1% of fiction is agented. Length: 350-12,000 words. Sometimes recommends markets.
**How to Contact:** Send complete ms with SASE. Reports in 3 months + on mss. Publishes ms an average of 18-24 months after acceptance. Sample copy $4.
**Payment:** 2 free author's copies and annual awards to the best of the stories published.
**Terms:** Acquires all rights. Sends galleys to author. "We reassign rights on request at time of republication."
**Tips:** "Send story after examining magazine. We are strongly committed to publishing the best fiction available to us. We publish up to 40 stories a year and devote close to half the pages to these stories." Published four new writers within the last year. Sponsors awards: *KQ*/KAC (national); Seaton awards (for Kansas natives or residents). Each offers 4-8 awards from $25-$250.

**KARAMU (II)**, English Dept., Eastern Illinois University, Charleston IL 61920. (217)581-5614. Editor: John Guzlowski. Magazine: 5x8; 60 pages; cover illustrations. "We like fiction that builds around real experiences, real images, and real characters, that shows an awareness of current fiction and the types of experiments that are going on in it, and that avoids abstraction sentimentality, over philosophizing, and fuzzy pontifications." For a literate, college-educated audience. Annually. Estab. 1967. Circ. 600.
**Needs:** Literary, contemporary. Accepts 4-5 mss/issue. Receives approximately 20-30 unsolicited fiction mss each month. Length: 2,000-7,000 words. Critiques rejected mss "when there is time."
**How to Contact:** Send complete ms with SASE. Accepts computer printout submissions. Prefers letter-quality. Reports in 2 months on mss. Publishes ms an average of 1 year after acceptance. Sample copy $1.50.
**Payment:** 1 free author's copy. Half price charge for extras.
**Tips:** "Send for a sample copy, read it, and send a complete ms if your stories seem to match our taste. Please be patient—we sometimes get behind in our reading. Mss submitted between January and June have the best chance. We feel that much of the best writing today is being done in short fiction." Published new writers within the last year.

**THE KINDRED SPIRIT (II)**, Groovy Gray Cat Publications, Rt. 2, Box 111, St. John KS 67576. (316)549-3933. Editor: Michael Hathaway. Tabloid: 10x13; 12 pages; newsprint pager; illustrations; photos. Tabloid of poetry of any style and subject, experimental short stories, black and white photographs and art. Semiannually. Plans special fiction issue. Estab. 1982. Circ. 1,000.
**Needs:** Contemporary, experimental, fantasy, gay, animal/animal rights, humor/satire, lesbian, literary, prose poem, science fiction, and serialized/excerpted novel. Receives approximately 60 unsolicited mss/month. Accepts 3 mss/issue; 6 mss/year. Does not read Dec-Jan. and Aug-Sept. Length: 3,000 words average; 3,500 words maximum.
**How to Contact:** Query first—"describe what you are offering with cover letter of previous publications, if any." Reports in 2 weeks on queries and mss. SASE. Simultaneous, photocopied, and previously published submissions OK. Accepts computer printout submissions. Prefers letter-quality. Sample copy for $1. Fiction guidelines for SAE (business-sized and 1 first class stamp).
**Payment:** 1 contributor's copy; charge for extras: $1.
**Terms:** Acquires one-time rights on publication. Publication coyprighted.
**Tips:** We publish fiction to add variety to our poetry magazine and because our readers like short stories." Published new writers within the last year.

**LABYRIS (I, IV)**, A Feminist Arts Journal, Labyris Press, Box 16102, Lansing MI 48933. (517)339-9572. Editors: Rosa Maria Arenas, Jan Zerfas, Leonora Smith, and Carol Morris. Magazine. "*Labyris* invites contributions of short fiction (under 20 pages double-spaced) by women writers on feminist themes and issues. Interested in experimental work as well." Semiannually. Estab. 1978. Circ. 300.
**Needs:** Experimental, feminist, prose poem, and serialized/excerpted novel. Receives "only a

few—less than 20 mss/month. Accepts 3-4 mss/issue; 8 mss/year. Reading fee only for competitions. Length: open. Occasionally critiques rejected ms.

**How to Contact:** Send complete ms. Query longer fiction; send complete ms of short story. Reports in 2 weeks on queries; 3-6 months on mss. SASE for query and ms. Photocopied submissions OK. Sample copy for $3. ("We pay postage.")

**Terms:** Rights revert to author on publication. Publication copyrighted.

**Tips:** "We receive more poetry submissions than fiction, and would like more fiction submissions. Please revise your work instead of sending us a rough draft. We accept a wide variety of fiction."

**LAKE STREET REVIEW (II)**, Lake Street Review Press, Box 7188, Powderhorn Station, Minneapolis MN 55407. Editor: Kevin FitzPatrick. Magazine:7x8½; 40 pages; good quality paper; good cover stock; illustrations. "A Minneapolis-St. Paul literary magazine which focuses on the work of both developing and experienced writers." Annual. Estab. 1975. Circ. 500.

**Needs:** Literary, contemporary. Accepts 5 mss/issue. Receives approximately 10 unsolicited fiction mss each month. Length 500-4,000 words. Critiques rejected mss "when there is time."

**How to Contact:** Send complete ms with SASE. Accepts computer printout submissions. Prefers letter-quality. Reports: 1 month after 10-1-86 deadline. Sample copy $2.

**Payment:** 1 free author's copy.

**Terms:** Acquires first rights. Publication copyrighted.

**Tips:** "Buy a sample copy and read what we have recently printed." Published new writers within the last year.

**LAPIS (I, IV)**, LAPIS Educational Association, Inc., 1438 Ridge Rd., Homewood IL 60430. (312)957-5856. Editor-in-Chief: Karen Degenhart. Magazine: 5½x8½; 64-80 pages; b&w illustrations. "A professional journal which publishes informative, scholarly articles about Jungian psychology, with related literary criticism, and other psycho/spiritual ideas" for an audience of psychologists, educators and ministers. Published annually. Estab. 1977. Circ. 150.

**Needs:** "We publish little fiction"—only with Jungian or psychological-spiritual slant, rarely over 15 pages. Accepts 3-4 mss/issue (less of fiction). Publishes short shorts under 10 pages. Occasionally critiques rejected mss. "We do publish poetry." Does not read Oct. through June.

**How to Contact:** Query first or send complete ms with SASE and brief bio. Simultaneous and photocopied submissions and previously published work OK. Accepts computer printout submissions. Prefers single spaced, letter-quality. Reports in 3 weeks on queries; "indefinite" on mss. Sample copy $2. Free guidelines with 1 regular SASE.

**Payment:** 3 contributor's copies if person joins for a year for $10.

**Terms:** Acquires one-time rights. Publication copyrighted.

**Tips:** "Query first for manuscripts over 10 pages—be sure to send enough return postage. Also, we publish in summer or fall, send submissions in spring for quicker response." Published new writers within the last year.

**LATIN AMERICAN LITERARY REVIEW (IV)**, Latin American Literary Review, Department of Hispanic Languages and Literatures, 1309 Cathedral of Learning, University of Pittsburgh, Pittsburgh PA 15260. (412)624-5225. Magazine: 6x9; 112-272 pages; 60 lb paper; 90 lb cover stock; occasional photos. "A journal in English devoted to the literature of Latin America and Latin American minorities in the US. Our publication is directed primarily to an audience of young adults and adults with an interest in Latin American literature." Semiannually. Plans special fiction issue. Estab. 1972. Circ. 1,000.

**Needs:** Literary, contemporary, and ethnic (Hispanic, Latin American, chicano). No "themes not pertaining to the focus of our journal." Publishes short shorts. Accepts 3-5 mss/issue. Charges $100 reading fee for books. No preferred length. Critiques rejected mss "when requested."

**How to Contact:** Send complete ms with SASE. Reports in 3 months. Sample copy if requested.

**Terms:** "Rights are relinquished by author upon publication of ms." Sends galleys to author. Publication copyrighted.

**Tips:** "The fiction which appears in the *LALR* is usually translations of works originally written in Spanish by established authors. *LALR* is associated with the Latin American Literary Review Press (Box 8385, Pittsburgh PA 15218) which publishes novels in Spanish and Portuguese and English translations." Published new writers within the last year.

**LAUREL REVIEW (II)**, West Virginia Wesleyan College, Dept. of English, Buckhannon WV 26201. (304)473-8240. Editor: Mark DeFoe. Fiction Readers: Martha Keating, William Trowbridge, and Barbara Tedford. Magazine: 6x9; 80-90 pages; good quality paper; illustrations; photos. "We publish poetry, essays, and fiction of high quality, from the traditional to the avant-garde. We are eclectic, open, and flexible. Good writing is all we seek. We try to encourage writers from Appalachian America, although we publish material from across the country, Canada, and the world." Biannually. Published special fiction issue last year; plans another. Estab. 1960. Circ. 500.
**Needs:** Literary, contemporary, humor, and ethnic (Appalachian). Accepts 2-3 mss/issue, 4-6 mss/year. Receives approximately 12 unsolicited fiction mss each month. Approximately 1% of fiction is agented. Length: 2,000-10,000 words. Critiques rejected mss "when there is time." Recommends other markets.
**How to Contact:** Send complete ms with SASE. Accepts computer printout submissions. Reports in 4 months on mss. "Sometimes slow!" Publishes ms an average of 1-12 months after acceptance. Sample copy $4.
**Payment:** $10 maximum. 2 free author's copies, 1 year free subscription.
**Terms:** Pays on publication for first rights. Publication copyrighted. Copyright reverts to author upon request.
**Tips:** Send $4 for a back copy of the magazine. "Send no long-winded cover letters." Published new writers within the last year.

**LETTERS MAGAZINE**, Maine Writers Workshop and Mainspring Press, Box 905, RFD 1, Stonington ME 04681. (207)367-2484. Editor: Helen Nash. "Accepts only high quality material in all ethical fields of literature." Readership: general public. Quarterly. Estab. 1969. Circ. 6,500.
**Needs:** Literary, short stories, science fiction, poetry, and mystery. "No porno, confessions, etc." Buys 5-10 mss/year. Receives 40-60 unsolicited fiction mss each month. Approximately 10% of fiction is agented. Length: 500-1,000 words. Critiques some of rejected mss "when justified."
**How to Contact:** Query with large SASE US postage or send one chapter with large SASE US postage. "No returns if insufficient postage." Accepts computer printout submissions; letter-quality only. Reports in 1 month on queries. Publishes ms an average of 1 year after acceptance. Free sample copy with SASE US postage. Evaluates full-length mss at usual rate.
**Payment:** Varies. All cash; no copies.
**Terms:** Pays on publication for all rights. Publication copyrighted.

**THE LIMBERLOST REVIEW (II)**, Limberlost Press, Box 1563, Boise ID 83702. (208)344-2120. Editor: Richard Ardinger. A magazine of poetry, fiction, interviews, memoirs. Annually. Published special fiction issue recently. Estab. 1976. Circ. 500.
**Needs:** Contemporary and experimental. Issues of the magazine often devoted to chapbooks. Receives 10-15 unsolicited mss/month. Accepts 1-2 mss/issue. Occasionally comments on rejected ms. Also publishes short shorts.
**How to Contact:** Send complete ms with cover letter and short bio. Reports in 2 months. SASE. Photocopied submissions OK. Accepts computer printout submissions. Prefers letter-quality. Sample copy $5 with SAE.
**Payment:** Contributor's copies; charge for extras: author's discount 20%.
**Terms:** Pays on publication for first rights. Sometimes sends galleys to author to check. Publication copyrighted.

**LIONHEAD PUBLISHING (III)**, Lionhead Publishing/ROAR Recording, 2521 E. Stratford Ct., Shorewood WI 53211. (414)332-7474. Editor: Dr. M.J. Rosenblum. Magazine: size and

page count varies; excellent paper; soft/hard cover stock; illustrations; photos. "Experimental fiction magazine for literary audience. Title varies with each issue." Estab. 1972.
**Needs:** Experimental (only). Receives 2-3 unsolicited fiction mss/month. Number of fiction mss varies with each issue. No preferred word length. Occasionally critiques rejected ms. Recommends other markets.
**How to Contact:** Query first with SASE. Photocopied submissons OK. Accepts computer printout submissions. Prefers letter-quality. Reports in 2 weeks on queries. Publishes ms an average of 2 months after acceptance. Fiction guidelines for SAE.
**Payment:** Free contributor's copies.
**Terms:** Publication copyrighted.

**THE LITERARY REVIEW, An International Journal of Contemporary Writing**, Fairleigh Dickinson University, 285 Madison Ave., Madison NJ 07940. (201)377-4050. Editor-in-Chief: Walter Cummins. Magazine: 9x6; 128 pages; illustrations; photos. "Academic literary magazine specializing in fiction, poetry, criticism, reviews for general readers, professional writers, developing writers, academic and other libraries." Published quarterly. Published special fiction issue; plans another. Estab. 1957. Circ. 1,000.
**Needs:** Works of high literary quality only. Receives 30-40 unsolicited fiction mss/month. Approximately 1-2% of fiction is agented. Accepts 10-12 mss/year. Publishes short shorts of 15-40 pages. Occasionally critiques rejected mss. Sometimes recommends other markets.
**How to Contact:** Send complete ms with SASE. Photocopied submissions OK. Accepts computer printout submissions. Reports in 10 weeks on mss. Publishes ms an average of 6-12 months after acceptance. Sample copy $4.50; free guidelines with SASE.
**Payment:** 2 free contributor's copies; 25% discount for extras.
**Terms:** Pays on publication for first rights. Publication copyrighted.
**Tips:** "Writers we publish are eligible for small annual award. Send in clean copy with adequate margins. Get comments of knowledgeable readers and revise before submitting." Rejects mss because "first, there are more mss submitted than we can possibly print; second, many that come our way are very amateurish in craft: naive stories, thinly disguised autobiography, over-done themes and situations, awkward language and dialogue." Published new writers within the last year. "We pride ourselves on being open to good new authors, and giving fresh reading to everyone."

**LITTLE BALKANS REVIEW (II, IV), A Southeast Kansas Literary & Graphics Quarterly**, Little Balkans Press, Inc., 601 Grandview Heights Terrace, Pittsburg KS 66762. (316)231-1589. Editor: Gene DeGruson. Fiction Editor: Shelby Horn. "Kansas is our theme, historical and contemporary, in poetry, fiction, nonfiction and art." General and academic audience. Quarterly. Estab. 1980. Circ. 1,200.
**Needs:** Adventure, contemporary, ethnic, experimental, fantasy, feminist, gay, historical, horror, humor/satire, lesbian, literary, mainstream, prose poem, psychic/supernatural/occult, regional, science fiction, suspense/mystery, translations, western, women's, and young adult/teen. Receives 200 unsolicited mss each month. Accepts 2 mss/issue; 8 mss/year. Length: 2,500 words average; 200 words minimum; 7,000 words maximum. Occasionally critiques rejected mss.
**How to Contact:** Send complete ms. SASE. Sample copy $2.50.
**Payment:** 3 contributor's copies.
**Terms:** Acquires first rights. Publication copyrighted.
**Tips:** "Write a good introductory letter; we make an attempt to publish half of each issue with 'new' writers."

**THE LIVING COLOR (I), The Magazine of Film and Fiction**, Living Color Productions, 417 Euclid Ave., Elmira NY 14905. Editor: Jack Stevenson. Magazine: 7x8½; pages vary; standard paper; 6016+ cover stock; illustrations; photos. "We print a variety of fiction styles, also articles and interviews concerning underground writers and filmmakers. As such, we have no specific theme." Read by "literates and semi-literates who like things that are free (us); folks who like a cheap laugh without being beat over the head with a message; people who like to look at pictures." Bimonthly. Estab. 1982. Circ. 2,000.

**Needs:** Comics, horror, humor/satire, prose poem; "modern parable and fairy tales. If you consider yourself foremost a 'writer' of the John Updike-Ann Beatty school, you're probably wasting our time. We like Selby, Stiener, Celine, Kafka, Gogol, Burroughs—writers with some sense of humor. No *New Yorker* or *Paris Review* clone stories, no political or feminist material. Absolutely nothing set in Vermont. No 'relationship-awareness' type stuff." Receives 50-100 unsolicited fiction mss/month. Accepts 3-6 mss/issue; 40 mss/year. Occasionally critiques rejected mss. Recommends other markets.

**How to Contact:** Send complete ms with SASE. Simultaneous, photocopied and previously published submissions OK. Reports in 1 month on mss. Sample copy free with 9x12 envelope and 70¢ postage. Fiction guidelines free.

**Payment:** Pays in magazine subscription and free contributor's copies.

**Terms:** Acquires all rights. Publication copyrighted.

**Tips:** "Fiction is such an individual appreciation—much more so than interviews, say, or articles—that overwhelming mass approval is rarely to be expected. Don't waste your time just writing to get printed somewhere—you've got to amuse yourself first, that's most important. Also, don't take an editor's rejection too seriously: Other people's advice is only applicable to a point. You'll never make it following their instructions."

**LONE STAR (II), A Magazine of Humor,** Lone Star Publications of Humor, Suite 103, Box 29000, San Antonio TX 78229. Editor: Lauren Barnett Scharf. "A humor magazine for the general public, comedy connoisseur and professional humorist. Audience: all ages, well-educated, well-read." Published 4-6 times a year. Estab. 1983. Circ. 1,200 +.

**Needs:** Comics and humor/satire. "Do not want to see stories that are three pages long and take three pages before getting to the first laugh." Receives 150-300 unsolicited mss/month. Buys 1-2 mss/issue; 6-12 mss/year. Length: 800 words average; 300 words minimum; 1,000 words maximum. Occasionally critiques rejected mss.

**How to Contact:** "Send SASE for guidelines first"; send complete ms. Reports in 1 month on queries; 2 months on mss. Publishes ms an average of 3 months after acceptance. SASE. Photocopied and "sometimes" previously published submissions OK. Sample copy $3.50 current issues/some back issues available for $1.95. Fiction guidelines for #10 SAE and 1 first class stamp.

**Payment:** $5-20 and 1 free contributor's copy; $3.50 charge for extras.

**Terms:** "Policy is payment on publication, but we try to pay before." Buys first rights, first North American serial rights, one-time rights, some reprints. Publication copyrighted.

**Tips:** "Read the guidelines, read the magazine and don't give up after one rejection. We do publish more humorous fiction now. Although, we publish various styles/subjects, in general, we stay away from anything prevalent in other publications."

**THE LONG STORY (II),** 11 Kingston St., North Andover MA 01845. (617)686-7638. Editor: R. P. Burnham. Fiction Editor: Pat Hennessey. Magazine: 5½x8½; 200 pages, 60 lb paper; 65 lb cover stock; illustrations (b&w graphics). For serious, educated literary people. No science fiction, adventure, romance, etc. "We publish high literary quality of any kind, but especially look for committed fiction; working class settings, left-wing themes, etc." Annually. Published special fiction issue last year. Estab. 1983. Circ. 400.

**Needs:** Contemporary, ethnic, feminist, and literary. Receives 20-30 unsolicited mss/month. Buys 6-7 mss/issue. Length: 8,000 words minimum; 20,000 words maximum. Usually critiques rejected mss. Sometimes recommends other markets.

**How to Contact:** Send complete ms. Reports in 2 + months. Publishs ms an average of 3-12 months after acceptance. SASE. Photocopied submissions OK. Accepts computer printout submissions. Prefers letter-quality. Sample copy for $3 and SAE with 63¢ postage.

**Payment:** Pays $1/page and 2 free contributor's copies; $3 charge for extras.

**Terms:** Pays on publication for first rights. Publication copyrighted.

**Tips:** "Read us first and make sure submitted material is the kind we're interested in. Send clear, legible manuscripts. We publish fiction because we're a literary magazine with an interest and a love for literature. We're not interested in commercial success; rather we want to provide a place for long stories, the *most difficult* literary form to publish in our country."

**LOONFEATHER (II)**, Bemidji Arts Center, 426 Bemidji Ave., Bemidji MN 56601. (218)751-4869. Editor: Betty Rossi and Jeane Sliney. Magazine: 6x9; 32 pages; 50 lb Hammermill Cream woven paper; 65 lb Hammermill Imperial ivory vellum cover stock; illustrations; photos occasionally. A literary journal of short prose, poetry and graphics. Mostly a market for Minnesota, and other Midwest writers. Published 3 times/year. Estab. 1979. Circ. 450.
**Needs:** Literary, contemporary, and regional. Accepts 2 mss/issue, 3-4 mss/year. Length: 600-1,500 words (prefers 1,500).
**How to Contact:** Send complete ms with SASE, and short autobiographical sketch. Reports in 3 months. Sample copy $2.
**Payment:** Free author's copies.
**Terms:** Acquires one-time rights.
**Tips:** "Send carefully crafted and literary fiction. No long mss." Published new writers within the last year.

**LOST AND FOUND TIMES (II)**, Luna Bisonte Prods, 137 Leland Ave., Columbus OH 43214. (614)846-4126. Editor: John M. Bennett. Magazine: 8½x5½; 40 pages; good quality paper; good cover stock; illustrations; photos. Theme: experimental, avant-garde and folk literature, art. Published irregularly. Estab. 1975. Circ. 300.
**Needs:** Literary, contemporary, and experimental. Prefers short pieces. Accepts approximately 2 mss/issue. Sometimes recommends markets.
**How to Contact:** Query with clips of published work. SASE for query, ms. Accepts computer printout submissions. Reports in 1 week on queries, 2 weeks on mss. Sample copy $3.
**Payment:** 1 free author's copy.
**Terms:** Rights revert to authors. Published new writers within the last year.

**THE LOUISVILLE REVIEW**, Louisville Review Corp., English Dept., University of Louisville, Louisville KY 40292. Editor: Sena Naslund. Magazine of quality fiction, both experimental and traditional for university audience. Semiannually. Estab. 1976. Circ. 500.
**Needs:** Experimental, literary, mainstream, and prose poem. No adventure or romance. Receives 75 unsolicited mss/month. Accepts 4-6 mss/issue; 8-10 mss/year. Length: no preference. Occasionally critiques rejected mss.
**How to Contact:** Send complete ms. Reports in varying number of months. SASE. Accepts computer printout submissions; prefers letter quality. Sample copy $3.50.
**Payment:** None.
**Terms:** Publication copyrighted.

**LOVE LETTERS (I)**, Box 11510, Milwaukee WI 53211. Publisher/Editor: Rita Bertolas. Christian/inspirational magazine: 8½x5½; 20 pages; 20 lb white bond paper; Bristol color stock covers; illustrations. Monthly. Estab. 1982. Circ. 300.
**Needs:** Short stories, prose poem, and religious/inspirational. "No short stories longer than 300 words, nothing too religious." Accepts 1-2 mss/issue; 12-18 mss/year. Length: 200 words average.
**How to Contact:** Send complete ms. SASE. Simultaneous, photocopied and previously published submissions OK. Free sample copy.
**Payment:** 2 contributor's copies.
**Tips:** Published new writers within the last year.

**‡MAAT (I, II)**, 1223 South Selva, Dallas TX 75218. (214)324-3093. Editor: Katherine Flanagan. Magazine: 5½x8½; 40-80 pages; 70 lb paper; heavy cover; illustrations; photos on occasion. *Maat* publishes contemporary poetry and some fiction—no restrictions on style or length. "Our audience is mainly composed of writers and poets, students and educators of literature, and those interested in the type of writing being done by today's contemporary writers." Quarterly. Plans special fiction issue. Estab. 1985. Circ. 200.
**Needs:** Adventure, condensed novel, contemporary, erotica, ethnic, experimental, fantasy, feminist, gay, horror, humor/satire, lesbian, literary, mainstream, men's, psychic/supernatural/

occult, science fiction, women's. "We will read any sort of fiction—acceptances are based solely on quality of work." Romance or inspirational manuscripts would have to be vastly different from what is currently seen in other specialty publications. Receives 50-150 unsolicited fiction mss/month. Accepts 0-3 (may expand) mss/issue; 4-12 (this may expand) mss/year. Publishes no longer than 3 months after acceptance. Prefers approximately 1,500 words, but "we will read any length." Always critiques rejected mss. Always recommends other markets.

**How to Contact:** Send complete ms with cover letter. "Should show a bit of personality to make us *want* to read you. Should include a short bio and publication credits." Reports in 1 week on queries; 1 month on mss. SASE for ms. Photocopied and reprints submissions OK. Accepts computer printouts including dot-matrix. Sample copy $3 postage paid, $4 foreign. Fiction guidelines for business size SAE and 22¢ postage.

**Payment:** Contributor's copies; one copy of the issue in which a writer's work appears.

**Terms:** Pays on publication. Prefers first rights, but will buy one-time rights on the basis of work's quality. Sends galleys to author on request.

**Tips:** "One issue each year, our Vernal Equinox issue in late March, is limited to the work of only one writer. Writers may submit manuscripts of 20-25 pages (before illustration, which may be the author's own artwork or we will furnish) in January-February of each year. The manuscript may be fiction, or poetry only, or a mixture of both. Writers should be willing to work closely (through the mail) with our staff, in order to achieve a strong final product. Short fiction is a great part of heritage. We want to reflect the thoughts of our writers, the concerns of our times, through contemporary fiction as well as poetry, etc. Submit often. Do not let rejection discourage you. Pay attention to the outlines of current needs or special themes that you will receive from us when/if we return your submissions. Pay attention to our editorial comments. Send a large selection of work, not just *one* story, etc. Keep trying. Keep trying."

**THE MADISON REVIEW**, Department of English, White Hall, University of Wisconsin, Madison WI 53706. Editor-in-Chief: Sally Weston-DeGraf. Magazine of "fiction and poetry, with special emphasis on literary stories and some emphasis on Midwestern writers." Published semiannually. Estab. 1978. Circ. 500.

**Needs:** Experimental, literary, and prose poem. Receives 20 unsolicited fiction mss/month. Accepts 7-10 mss/issue. Approximately 10% of fiction is agented. Length: 500 words minimum; 7,000 words maximum. Occasionally critiques rejected mss. Sometimes recommends markets.

**How to Contact:** Send complete ms with SASE. Reports in 6 weeks on mss. Publishes ms an average of 1-2 months after acceptance. "We do not report on mss during the summer." Sample copy $2.

**Payment:** 2 free contributor's copies; $2 charge for extras.

**Terms:** Pays on publication for first North American serial rights. Publication copyrighted.

**MAELSTROM REVIEW (III)**, 8 Farm Hill Rd., Cape Elizabeth ME 04107. Editor/Publisher: Leo Mailman. Magazine: 5½x8½; 48-64 pages; offset litho paper; good textured quality cover stock; illustrations; photos. "Poetry, fiction and reviews with contemporary fiction format, but not too experimental, for literary, college-educated, or student readership." Semiannually. "Plans to publish 'book issues' (have done 2) by one or two authors each issue, generally *solicited* by editor—unsolicited authors send $3 for sample followed by submission of sample fiction (under 20 pages of poetry or fiction)." Estab. 1972. Circ. 400-700.

**Needs:** Literary and contemporary. "No highly romantic, gothic, religious, political, or highly experimental material." Accepts 2-3 mss/issue, 5-6 mss/year. Publishes short shorts of 10-15 pages typed double spaced. Receives approximately 5-10 unsolicited fiction mss each month. Requires $3 for sample copy before reading ms. Length: 2,000 words, 10-20 ms pages. Critiques rejected mss "when there is time." Occasionally sends mss on to editors of other publications.

**How to Contact:** Send complete ms with SASE with small paragraph of recent work. Accepts computer printout submissions. Prefers letter-quality. Reports in 2 months on mss. Sample copy $3.

**Payment:** 3-5 free author's copies. Half price charge for extra copies.

**Terms:** Rights revert to author upon publication. Publication copyrighted.
**Tips:** "Buy a sample issue and read the fiction before submitting." Published new writers within the last year.

‡**THE MAGE (I, IV), A Magazine of Science Fiction and Fantasy**, Colgate University Student Association, Hamilton NY 13346. Editor: Jeffrey V. Yule. Magazine: 8½x11; about 50 pages. "Fiction, essays, poetry, artwork and photos within the genre of science fiction and fantasy. Emphasis is on short fiction. We do serialize longer works of exceptional quality. Most of our circulation is to college campuses but is by no means limited to them." Semiannually. Estab. 1984. Circ. 300.
**Needs:** Experimental, fantasy, horror, science fiction, young adult/teen (10-18 years) within SF/fantasy genre. No sword and sorcery adventure or stories based on Dungeons and Dragons and its ilk; no erotica. Receives 8-10 unsolicited fiction mss/month. Accepts 6-10 mss/issue; 12-20 mss/year. Does not read mss June through August. Publishes ms within six weeks after acceptance. Length: 3,500-4,500 words average; 1,000 words minimum. Occasionally critiques rejected mss.
**How to Contact:** Query first or send complete ms with cover letter with list of previous works published. Reports in 2 weeks on queries; 4-6 weeks on mss (report time is longer if submitted just before or during the summer). SASE for ms. Simultaneous, photocopied submissions and reprints OK. Accepts computer printouts including dot-matrix. Sample copy $2 (includes postage).
**Payment:** Pays in contributor's copies.
**Terms:** Acquires first North American serial rights or one-time rights. Sometimes sends galleys to author. Publication copyrighted.
**Tips:** "While we are focusing our magazine on publishing works of beginning writers, we are interested in writers who have practiced enough (even if nothing has been published) to develop a refined writing style. We are interested in presenting good writing first, then good plots and stories. We do publish capsule reviews of new fiction which are less demanding than fiction. Submitting several of these to us will help a new writer develop some recognition of *The Mage* which might help him/her when submitting their first manuscript to us."

**MAGIC CHANGES (II)**, Celestial Otter Press, 8 Huntington Cr., W. #14 Naperville IL 60540. (312)327-5606. Editor: John Sennett. Magazine: 8½x11; 110 pages; 60 lb paper; construction paper cover; illustrations; photos. "Theme: arts renaissance. Material: poetry, songs, fiction, stories, reviews, art, essays, etc. For the entertainment and enlightenment of all ages." Annually. Estab. 1979. Circ. 500.
**Needs:** Literary, psychic/supernatural/occult, science fiction, fantasy, and erotica. "Fiction should have an artistic slant." Accepts 2-3 mss/issue, 8-12 mss/year. Receives approximately 15 unsolicited fiction mss each month. Approximately 30% of fiction is agented. Length: 3,000 words maximum.
**How to Contact:** Send complete ms with SASE. Accepts computer printout submissions. Prefers letter-quality. Accepts disc submissions compatible with Apple. Prefers hard copy with disc submission. Reports in 1 month. Publishes ms an average of 3 months after acceptance. Sample copy $4.
**Payment:** 1-2 free author's copies. $4 charge for extras.
**Terms:** Acquires first North American serial rights. Publication copyrighted.
**Tips:** "Revise your story before you write. Then write an outline. Write well. Rewrite. Read poetry. Read good fiction. Most rejected mss are poorly written and offer dull stories or none at all." Sponsors contest. Offers critiquing service. Published new writers within the last year.

**MAGICAL BLEND**, Box 11303, San Francisco CA 94101. (415)282-9338. Editor: Michael P. Langevin. Fiction Editor: Jerry Snider. Magazine: 8½x11; 80 pages; 60 lb gloss paper; 60 lb gloss cover stock; illustrations; photos. "We believe that people's thoughts create their realities. We publish positive, uplifting material—often visionary—on a variety of themes ranging from mystical/magical/spiritual to the practical for those interested in taking control of their lives, expanding their consciousness, focusing on the positive." Quarterly. Published special fiction issue last year; plans another. Estab. 1980. Circ. 10,000.

**Needs:** Psychic/supernatural/occult, fantasy, and adventure. "We also feature specialized issues, for example: sea mammals and health. No dark or dismal portrayal of life." Accepts 5-7 mss/issue, 20-28 mss/year. Receives approximately 40 unsolicited fiction mss each month. Length: 500-5,000 words. Critiques rejected mss "when there is time." Recommends other markets.

**How to Contact:** Send complete ms with SASE and cover letter "indicating why this story is thought appropriate for Magical Blend." Reports in 5 months on mss. Publishes ms an average of 6-10 months after acceptance. Sample copy $4. Guidelines for legal-size SASE.

**Payment:** 5 free author's copies. $1.75 plus postage and handling for extras.

**Terms:** Acquires first North American serial rights and second serial rights. Buys reprints. Sends galleys to author. Publication copyrighted.

**Tips:** "We like fiction that takes our readers to beautiful worlds and ends happily. Share your fantasies, dreams and stories of magic with us. Cover letters are nice, SASEs are essential. *Believe in yourself*!" Mss are rejected because they are "not well written, not positive or spiritual—too much violence or sex. Write your best original stories. Then take them apart and do them from a different angle. Determine and accept writing as hard work to become good. Have a clear idea where you want to go with your writing and never waver." Published new writers within the last year.

**MALINI (IV), Pan-Asian Journal for the Literati**, Box 195, Claremont CA 91711. Editor: Ms. Chitra Chakraborty. Magazine: 8½x5½; 24-48 pages; 60 lb bond paper; 67 lb bond cover stock; illustrations; photos. "To promote the essence of Pan-Asian cultures (i.e., from India to Japan including some Pacific islands)." Quarterly. Estab. 1981. "Libraries are among our subscribers. Therefore, we have a very large readership."

**Needs:** Ethnic, literary, prose poem, and translations. Accepts 1 ms/issue; 4-8 (approximately)/year. Publishes short shorts. Length: 900 words minimum; 1,200 words maximum. Occasionally critiques rejected mss.

**How to Contact:** Query first with SASE. Reports in 1-5 weeks on queries. Cover letter "with first time submission. No photocopied or simultaneous submissions, please." Sample copy $1.37.

**Payment:** $25-100.

**Terms:** Acquires all rights. Publication copyrighted.

**Tips:** "Write about nothing other than Asian/immigrant experience. References, no more than 7, are welcomed. Italics and footnotes to be avoided as much as possible. Occasionally, previously published work with author/publisher's written permission is accepted. Ethnic folktales and translations of a good story are welcomed. No obscenity or profanity. *Query first*. Study the magazine before submitting your story. And, please, be professional. When we insist on first-time, no photocopied submissions, please don't send us photocopied submissions without any cover letter. Without a moment's delay, we return such submissions."

**‡MANSCAPE**, FirstHand, Inc., 310 Cedar Lane, Teaneck NJ 07666. (201)836-9177. Editor: Jack Veasey. Magazine of "material that will make fetishists smile" for homosexuals. Monthly. Estab. 1984. Circ. 45,000.

**Needs:** Comics, confession, erotica, ethnic, gay. No "florid manuscripts." Receives 25 unsolicited mss/month. Buys 3 mss/issue; 36 mss/year. Length: 1,700 average; 1,500 words minimum; 2,500 words maximum. Occasionally comments on rejected mss.

**How to Contact:** Query first or send complete ms. Reports in 1-2 months on queries. Simultaneous submissions OK. Accepts computer printout submissions. Prefers letter-quality. Sample copy $3.50. Fiction guidelines free.

**Payment:** $25-150.

**Terms:** Pays on acceptance for first rights and other rights. Publication copyrighted.

**THE MASSACHUSETTS REVIEW**, Memorial Hall, University of Massachusetts, Amherst MA 01003. Editors: John Hicks and Mary Heath. Quarterly.

**Needs:** Short stories. Approximately 5% of fiction is agented. Critiques rejected mss "when there is time."
**How to Contact:** Send complete ms. No ms returned without SASE. Reports in 2 months. Publishes ms an average of 6-9 months after acceptance. Sample copy $4.50.
**Payment:** Pays $50 maximum.
**Terms:** Pays on publication for first North American serial rights. Publication copyrighted.
**Tips:** "Shorter rather than longer stories preferred (20-25 pages). There are too many stories about 'relationships,' domestic breakups, etc. Avoid submitting material June to October."

**MATI**, Ommation Press, 5548 N. Sawyer, Chicago IL 60625. Editor: Effie Mihopoulos. "Primarily a poetry magazine but we do occasional special fiction and science fiction issues." Quarterly. Estab. 1975. Circ. 1,000.
**Needs:** Literary, contemporary, science fiction, feminist, translations. No mystery, gothic, western, religious. Receives approximately 10 unsolicited fiction mss each month. Length: 1-2 pages. Occasionally sends mss on to editors of other publications. Sometimes recommends markets.
**How to Contact:** Send complete ms with SASE. Reports in 1 week. Sample copy $1.50 with 9x12 SASE (preferred) plus 80¢ postage.
**Payment:** 1 free author's copy. Special contributor's rates available for extras.
**Terms:** Acquires first North American serial rights. "Rights revert to author but *Mati* retains reprint rights." Publication copyrighted.
**Tips:** "We want to see good quality writing and a neat ms with sufficient return postage; same size return as outside envelope and intelligent cover letter. Editor to be addressed as 'Dear Sir/Ms' instead of 'Dear Sir' when it's a woman editor."

**MEMPHIS STATE REVIEW (II)**, Memphis State University, Dept. of English, Memphis State, Memphis TN 38152. (901)454-2668. Editor: William Page. Magazine: 7½x10; 60 pages. National review of poetry and fiction for university audience and readers of serious poetry and fiction. Semiannually. Estab. 1980. Circ. 2,500.
**Needs:** Contemporary, fantasy, literary, science fiction, short stories, and excerpted novel. Accepts 3-4 mss/issue; 6-8 mss/year. Publishes short shorts. Does not read mss in summer.
**How to Contact:** Send complete ms with SASE and publication background. Accepts disc submissions compatible with CPT 6000, 6100, 8000, 8100. Prefers hard copy with disc submissions. Reports in 3 weeks to 3 months (except in the summer). Publishes ms an average of 18 months after acceptance. Sample copy for $2.
**Payment:** Annual $100 prize for best poem or short story and 2 free contributor's copies. "We pay $50 or more if grant monies are available."
**Terms:** Acquires first North American serial rights. Publication copyrighted.
**Tips:** "Strive to make the story fresh and interesting. Avoid unnecessary length, and proofread with great attention." Published new writers within the last year.

**MENDOCINO REVIEW (II)**, Box 888, Mendocino CA 95460. (707)964-3831. Editor-in-Chief: Camille Ranker. "Journal for art, literature and music, also photography, poetry and short stories." Published annually. Estab. 1972. Circ. 5,000.
**Needs:** Will consider everything including graphics and drawings. No political mss. Receives 50-75 unsolicited fiction mss/month. Accepts varying number of mss/issue. Length: no preferred minimum; 5,000 words maximum.
**How to Contact:** Send complete ms with SASE. Simultaneous and photocopied submissions OK. Accepts computer printout submissions. Prefers letter-quality. Reports in 3 months on mss. Free sample copy and fiction guidelines.
**Payment:** "Payment in copies and dealt with on individual basis."
**Terms:** Pays on publication for one-time rights. Publication copyrighted.
**Tips:** "Submit ms and keep on writing and submitting. Be professional—type, double spaced,

and package your submission as though you value it. The folks that receive it will respect it if you do."

**THE MENOMONIE REVIEW (II)**, English Dept., University of Wisconsin-Stout, Menomonie WI 54751. Editor: William O'Neill. Magazine of stories and poems for a highly literate audience. Annually. Estab. 1982. Circ. 500.
**Needs:** Adventure, contemporary, ethnic, experimental, fantasy, feminist/lesbian, gay, humor/satire, literary, mainstream, men's, prose poem, science fiction, and women's. No sentimental stories. Receives 5 unsolicited fiction mss/month. Accepts 2-3 mss/issue; 2-3 mss/year. Does not read mss April-August. Length: 6,000 words maximum; 2,500 words average. Occasionally critiques rejected mss.
**How to Contact:** Send complete ms with SASE. Reports in 6-10 weeks (if submitted during school year) on mss. Sample copy for $2.
**Payment:** 2 free contributor's copies.
**Terms:** Acquires one-time rights. Publication copyrighted.

**THE MERIDIAN**, Bottom Line Design, Inc., 630 N. College, Ste. 423, Indianapolis IN 46204. (317)638-8228. Magazine. "*The Meridian* presents the unheard-of and too-little-heard-of: words and images which are original and creative and worth experiencing." Audience: 23-47 age group. Monthly. Estab. 1982. Circ. 25,000.
**Needs:** Contemporary, experimental, humor/satire, literary, mainstream, and science fiction. No pornography, religious, romance, confession. Receives 30-50 unsolicited mss/month. Accepts 1-2 mss/issue; 12-14 mss/year. Length: 1,500 words average; 500 words minimum; 2,000 words maximum. Occasionally critiques rejected ms.
**How to Contact:** Send complete ms. Reports in 3-6 weeks. SASE. Simultaneous, photocopied and previously published submissions OK. Accepts computer printout submissions. Prefers letter-quality. Sample copy 50¢ for 8½x11 SAE and 54¢ postage.
**Payment:** Negotiable.
**Terms:** Pays on publication for first North American serial rights. Publication copyrighted. Annual fiction and poetry contest—"subscribe for details."
**Tips:** "Rewrite, rewrite, rewrite. Don't send us first draft."

**‡MERLYN'S PEN (IV), The National Magazine of Student Writing**, Merlyn's Pen, Inc., Box 716, East Greenwich RI 02818. (401)885-5175. Editor: R. Jim Stahl. Magazine: 8½x10⅞; 40 pages; 50 lb (uncoated) paper; 70 lb gloss cover stock; illustrations; photos. Student writing—grades 7 through 10, for english classrooms grades 7 through 10. Bimonthly (Sept.-April). Estab. 1985. Circ. 12,000.
**Needs:** Adventure, experimental, fantasy, historical (general), horror, humor/satire, literary, mainstream, regional, romance, young adult, science fiction, suspense/mystery, western, young adult/teen (13-16). Must be written by students in grades 7-10. Receives 300 unsolicited fiction mss/month. Accepts 50 mss/issue; 250 mss/year. Publishes ms 1-10 months after acceptance. Length: 1,500 words average; 5 words minimum; 5,000 words maximum. Publishes short shorts of 200 words. Responds to rejected mss.
**How to Contact:** Send complete ms with cover letter with name, age, home and school address, home and school telephone number, grade, supervising teacher's name. Reports in 6-8 weeks. SASE for ms. Accepts computer printouts including dot-matrix. Sample copy $3.
**Payment:** Contributor's copy, charge for extras. Each author published receives a free copy of *The Elements of Style*.
**Terms:** Pays on publication for 3-year rights. Publication copyrighted.
**Tips:** "Observe, describe, revise."

**METAMORFOSIS (IV)**, Center for Chicano Studies GN-09, University of Washington, Seattle WA 98195. (206)543-9080. Magazine of "Chicano art and literature." Spanish/English bilingual format for a general audience. Published semiannually. Estab. 1977. Circ. 500.

**Needs:** Condensed novel, ethnic, humor/satire, literary, and prose poem. Receives 5 unsolicited fiction mss/month. Sends mss on to editors of other publications. Sometimes recommends markets.
**How to Contact:** Send complete ms with SASE. Simultaneous and photocopied submissions OK. Accepts computer printout submissions. Prefers letter-quality. Reports in 6 months on mss.
**Payment:** 5 free contributor's copies.
**Terms:** Pays on publication. Publication copyrighted.
**Tips:** "We encourage beginning writers to submit."

‡METROSPHERE (I, II), Literary Magazine, Metropolitan State College, Dept. of English, Box 32, Denver CO 80204. (303)556-3211. Editor: Robert J. Pugel. Magazine: 8½x11; 92 pages; Chambray paper; slick (enamel coated) cover; illustrations; photos. "We try to be a showcase for the literary and artistic talents of new writers with fiction, nonfiction, profiles and interviews, poetry, photos, artwork" for college students/faculty/college-educated readers. Semiannually. Plans special fiction issue. Estab. 1983. Circ. 10,000.
**Needs:** Adventure, confession, contemporary, experimental, fantasy, horror, humor/satire, literary, mainstream, men's, psychic/supernatural/occult, religious/inspirational, contemporary and historical romance, science fiction, suspense/mystery, translations, western, women's. No erotica. Receives 50-75 unsolicited fiction mss/month. Accepts 10 mss/issue; 25 mss/year. Does not read mss in July and August. Publishes ms usually 4 or 5 months after acceptance. Length: 1,500 words average; 100 words minimum; 2,000 words maximum. Occasionally critiques rejected mss. Recommends other markets.
**How to Contact:** Send complete ms with cover letter. Reports in 2 months on mss. SASE for ms. Simultaneous, photocopied submissions and reprints OK. Accepts computer printouts including dot-matrix. Sample copy $1. Fiction guidelines free for #10 SAE and 1 first class stamp.
**Payment:** Pays in contributor's copies.
**Terms:** Acquires one-time rights.
**Tips:** "We're looking for short fiction (2,000 words or less) that moves and touches us, say something in a new, fresh, exciting way. Since the magazine is widely distributed in the 35,000 student Education Center and in Denver Metro area bookstores, our audience is a little more well-read, literate, and discriminating. We use only the best of the heavy, mood stories so that we can 'balance' out each issue. We'd love to see more funny, witty, humorous pieces. Since we're all either writing teachers or writing students, who appreciate and admire creative people, your stories will receive a sympathetic, thorough, and loving study by us."

MICHIGAN QUARTERLY REVIEW, University of Michigan, 3032 Rackham, Ann Arbor MI 48109. Editor: Laurence Goldstein. "An interdisciplinary journal which publishes mainly essays and reviews, with some high-quality fiction and poetry, for an intellectual, widely-read audience." Quarterly. Estab. 1962. Circ. 1,500.
**Needs:** Literary. No "genre" fiction written for a "market." Receives 200 unsolicited fiction mss/month. Buys 2 mss/issue; 8 mss/year. Length: 1,500 words minimum; 7,000 words maximum; 5,000 words average.
**How to Contact:** Send complete ms with SASE. Photocopied submissions OK. Accepts computer printout submissions. Prefers letter quality. Sample copy for $2 and 2 first class stamps.
**Payment:** Pays $8-10/printed page.
**Terms:** Pays on acceptance for first rights. Publication copyrighted. Awards the Laurence Foundation Prize of $500 for best story in *MQR* previous year.
**Tips:** "Read back issues to get a sense of tone; level of writing. *MQR* is very selective; only send the very finest, best-plotted, most-revised fiction."

MID-AMERICAN REVIEW (I, II), Popular Press, Department of English, Bowling Green State University, Bowling Green OH 43403. (419)372-2725. Contact: Robert Early, Editor-in-Chief. Magazine: 5½x8½; 200 pages; 60 lb bond paper; coated, one side cover stock. "We publish serious fiction and poetry, as well as critical studies in modern literature and book reviews."

Published biannually. Plans special fiction issue. Estab. Spring 1981.

**Needs:** Experimental, literary, prose poem, excerpted novel, and translations. Receives about 50 unsolicited fiction mss/month. Buys 5-6 mss/issue. Does not read July, August. Approximately 5% of fiction is agented. Occasionally critiques rejected mss. Sometimes recommends other markets.

**How to Contact:** Send complete ms with SASE. Reports in 2 months. Publishes ms an average of 3 months after acceptance. Sample copy $4.50.

**Payment:** $5/page up to $75; 2 free contributor's copies; $2 charge for extras.

**Terms:** Pays on publication for one-time rights. Publication copyrighted.

**Tips:** "One fiction award yearly, The Sherwood Anderson Short Fiction Prize ($200) for material that has appeared in the magazine. Publishing fiction is our *raison d' être*." Published new writers within the last year.

**MIDCONTINENTAL**, Midcontinental Media Group, #25-221 McDermot, Winnipeg, Manitoba R3C 052 Canada. (204)944-9763. Managing Editor: Marie Medved. Tabloid. "We are an alternative arts publication concentrating most on social issues rather than private obsession. In fiction we are interested in intelligent, modern or post-modern material dealing with contemporary themes." Quarterly. Estab. 1982. Circ. 2,000.

**Needs:** Contemporary, experimental, feminist, gay, humor/satire, lesbian, literary, prose poem, serialized/excerpted novel, and translations. No "sexist, surrealist, or fantasy mss." Buys 2-3 mss/issue; 8-12 mss/year. Length: 2,000 words average; 5,000 words maximum. Occasionally comments on rejected mss.

**How to Contact:** Query first, send complete manuscript, or query with clips of published work. Reports in 2 weeks on queries; 1 month on mss. IRC or SASE for ms. Simultaneous, photocopied, and previously published submissions OK. Accepts computer printout submissions. Prefers letter-quality. Sample copy for $1.50.

**Payment:** Pays $20-100 and 5 contributor's copies.

**Terms:** Pays on publication for first rights.

**Tips:** "We are interested in publishing writers who show awareness of narrative forms."

**‡MIDLAND REVIEW (II), A Journal of Contemporary Lit, Lit. Crit. & Art**, University Printing Services, Oklahoma State University, English Dept., Morrill Hall, Stillwater OK 74078. (405)624-6225 or 624-6138. Editor: Nuala Archer. Fiction Editor: Michael Hartman. Magazine: 5½x8½; 80 pages; 80 lb paper; perfect bond cover stock; illustrations; photos. "A mixed bag of quality work." For "any one who likes to read and for those that wants news that folks in Oklahoma are alive." Annually. Estab. 1985. Circ. 500.

**Needs:** Ethnic, experimental, feminist, gay, historical (general), horror, lesbian, literary, psychic/supernatural/occult, regional, science fiction, translations. Receives 15 unsolicited fiction mss/month. Accepts 4 mss/issue. Publishes ms 3-5 months after acceptance. Length: 4-10 pages double-spaced, typed. Publishes short shorts of 2-4 pages. Critiques rejected mss. Recommends other markets.

**How to Contact:** Send complete manuscript with cover letter. Reports in 6-8 weeks on queries. SASE for ms. Simultaneous and photocopied submissions OK. Accepts computer printouts including dot-matrix. Sample copy for $5 and 6x9 SAE. Fiction guidelines for letter size SAE and 1 first class stamp.

**Payment:** Free contributor's copies.

**Terms:** Pays on publication for first North American serial rights. Publication copyrighted.

**Tips:** "We want to encourage good student stories by giving them an audience with more established writers."

**MIDSTREAM-A MONTHLY JEWISH REVIEW (II, IV)**, The Theodor Herzl Foundation, 515 Park Ave., New York NY 10022. (212)752-0600. Editor: Joel Carmichael. Fiction Editor: Debra Berman. Magazine: 8½x11; 64 pages; 50 lb opaque paper; 65 lb white smooth cover stock. Theme: articles, essays, poetry, and reviews dealing with world and cultural subjects of Jewish in-

terest. "We are aimed at those who wish to keep abreast of developments in world and cultural Jewish affairs. Fiction must have a Jewish slant." Monthly. Estab. 1955. Circ. 15,000.
**Needs:** Literary, religious, and Jewish ethnic. Buys 1 ms/issue. Receives approximately 50 unsolicited fiction mss each month. Approximately 10% of fiction is agented. Length: 2,000-3,000 words.
**How to Contact:** Send complete ms with SASE and cover letter with name, address, credentials, state if manuscript is fiction. Reports in 1 month. Publishes ms an average of 1-2 years after acceptance. Free sample copy.
**Payment:** 5¢ per word and 3 free author's copies.
**Terms:** Pays on publication for first rights. Sends galleys to author. Publication copyrighted.
**Tips:** "Always include a cover letter; state that ms is *fiction*. Always double space." Published new writers within the last year.

**MIDWEST ARTS & LITERATURE**, Sheba Review, Inc., Box 1623, Jefferson City MO 65102. Editor: S.D. Hanson. Tabloid and/or chapbook; varied pages; illustrations; photos. Theme: to promote the arts and literature in the Midwest; poetry; literary and journalistic prose. For those interested in cultural (artistic) concerns. Published irregularly. Published special fiction issue last year; plans another. Estab. 1978.
**Needs:** Literary, contemporary, humor, ethnic, and translations. No pornographic material. Receives approximately 10 unsolicited fiction mss each month. Publishes short shorts. Length varies. Critiques rejected mss "when there is time." Recommends other markets "when time permits."
**How to Contact:** Send complete ms with SASE. Accepts computer printout submissions. Reports in 5 months on mss. Publishes ms an average of 4-6 months after acceptance. *Short* fiction preferred.
**Payment:** Free authors copies and discount subscription to publications.
**Terms:** Acquires one-time rights. Publication copyrighted.
**Tips:** "Review a sample copy prior to submission. We focus on an issue current to social changes per issue, e.g., minority concerns and women's issues. Send clean copy; dark photo copy (if copied) and FAT margins for editorial necessities." Sponsors contests, workshops, and literary advocacy on state/federal levels. Published new writers within the last year.

**‡MILKWEED CHRONICLE JOURNAL**, Milkweed Chronicle/Milkweed Editions, Box 24303, Minneapolis MN 55424. (612)332-3192. Editor: Emile Buchwald, Randall Scholes. Magazine: 10x13; 40-44 pages; good 60 lb offset paper; gloss 80 lb cover stock; graphics; photos. Thematic concerns include 'healing, power, magic' for eclectic, intelligent readers and artists and writers and teachers. Triquarterly. Plans special fiction issue. Estab. 1980. Circ. 1,500.
**Needs:** Contemporary, experimental, fantasy, literary, regional, translations. No pornography, ultra-violent, or jargon-filled political pieces. Receives 50-100 unsolicited fiction mss/month. Accepts 1, sometimes 2 ms/issue; 4-6 mss/year. Publishes ms 3-5 months after acceptance. Agented fiction: 50-70%. Reading fee only for some competitions. Length: 2,500 average; 1,500 words minimum; 5,000 words maximum. Publishes short shorts. Recommends other markets.
**How to Contact:** Send complete ms with cover letter with "a little information, a sense that the writer has *read* the magazine and our books." Reports in 1 month on queries; 2 months on mss. SASE for ms. Simultaneous and photocopied submissions OK. Accepts computer printouts if good quality and readable. Sample copy $4. Fiction guidelines free for SAE and adequate postage.
**Payment:** Pays $50-300; contributor's copies.
**Terms:** Pays on publication for first North American serial rights. Publication copyrighted.
**Tips:** "We are optimistic when we see good work, whoever wrote it, whatever their age."

**MINAS TIRITH EVENING-STAR (II)**, W.W. Publications, Box 277, Union Lake MI 48085. (313)887-4703. Editor: Phillip Helms. Magazine: 8½x11; 25 + pages; typewriter paper; black ink illustrations; photos. Magazine of J.R.R. Tolkien and fantasy—fiction, poetry, reviews, etc. for general audience. Monthly. Published special fiction issue; plans another. Estab. 1967. Circ. 500.

**Needs:** Fantasy and Tolkien. Receives 5 unsolicited mss/month. Accepts 1 ms/issue; 5 mss/year. Length: 1,000-1,200 words preferred; 5,000 words maximum. Also publishes short shorts. Occasionally critiques rejected ms.

**How to Contact:** Send complete ms and bio. Reports in 1 week on queries; 2 weeks on mss. SASE. Photocopied and previously published submissions OK. Accepts computer printout submissions. Prefers letter-quality. Sample copy $1.

**Terms:** Acquires first rights. Publication copyrighted.

**Tips:** Published new writers within the last year.

‡**MIND IN MOTION (II), A Magazine of Poetry and Short Prose**, Mind In Motion Publications, Box 1118, Apple Valley CA 92307. (619)242-2780. Editor: Celeste Goyer. Magazine: 5½x8½; approximately 45 pages; text 70 lb paper; 65 lb cover stock. "No particular theme. All submissions must be articulate, demanding and lucid. For those individuals who would like to see artistic genius reappear on the small press American scene." Quarterly. Estab. 1985. Circ. 250.

**Needs:** Experimental, humor/satire, literary, science fiction. "We believe that enduring art should demand re-reading. We prefer the sweeping, ageless view. We shy away from amateurish, cliched or contemporary topical fiction." Receives 20 unsolicited fiction mss/month. Accepts 6 mss/issue; 25 mss/year. Publishes ms 1 week to 3 months after acceptance. Length: 2,000 words average; 500 words minimum; 3,000 words maximum. Publishes short shorts of 500 words. Critiques rejected mss.

**How to Contact:** Send complete ms with cover letter. Reports in 2-6 weeks. SASE for ms. Simultaneous and photocopied submissions OK. Accepts computer printouts. Sample copy $2.50. Fiction guidelines for business size SAE and 1 stamp.

**Payment:** Charge for extra contributor's copies.

**Terms:** Pays on publication for first North American serial rights. Publication copyrighted.

**Tips:** "There's a lot of perception and art out there: where else could one develop beyond an embroyonic state? There's glory for any writer who has the talent to convey an original vision. We find good short stories to be an irreducible literary phenomenon. If you don't mind a subjective reply, try us."

**MINETTA REVIEW (II)**, New York University, 21 Washington Place, Box 65, New York NY 10003. (212)598-2141. Co-Editors: Soren Ambrose/Jonathan Jackson. Magazine: 5½x8½; Vellum paper and cover; illustrations; photos. "fiction, prose, poetry, criticism, etc., forum for established and beginning writers in the NYU community and the US. We want to provide a balance of various kinds of work." Semiannually. Estab. 1980. Circ. 6,000.

**Needs:** Contemporary, ethnic, experimental, humor/satire, literary, mainstream, men's, prose poem, suspense/mystery, and women's. Receives 100 unsolicited mss/month. Accepts 30 mss/issue. Length: no more than 6,000 words.

**How to Contact:** Send complete ms with short bio. Reports in varying number of months. Publishes ms an average of 2-3 months after acceptance. Do not read mss June-August. SASE. Simultaneous, photocopied and previously published submissions OK. Free sample copy with $1 postage.

**Payment:** None.

**Terms:** Publication copyrighted.

**Tips:** "We plan to publish more short stories. Be neat."

**MIORITA, A JOURNAL OF ROMANIAN STUDIES (IV)**, New Zealand Romanian Cultural Association and the Dept., FLLL, Dewey 482, University of Rochester, Rochester NY 14627. (716)275-4258. Co-Editors: Charla Carlton and Norman Simms. Magazine: 5½x8½; Xerox stock paper; occasionally illustrations. Magazine of "essays, reviews, notes, and translations on all aspects of Romanian history, culture, language and so on" for academic audience. Annually. Estab. 1973. Circ. 100-200.

**Needs:** Ethnic, historical, literary, prose poetry, regional, and translations. "All categories contingent upon relationship to Romania." Receives "handful of mss per year." Accepts "no more

than one per issue." Length: 2,000 words maximum. Occasionally critiques rejected ms.
**How to Contact:** Send complete ms. SASE "preferred." Previously published work OK (depending on quality). Accepts computer printout submissions.
**Payment:** "We do not pay." Publication copyrighted.

**MIRAGE (II, IV)**, Literary Magazine of Cochise College, Douglas Campus and Sierra Vista Campus AZ 85607 and 85635. (602)364-7943. Editor: Linda Meo. Magazine: 32 pages; original illustrations; original photos. Magazine with "material of elegant standard—poetry, fiction and nonfiction for residents of Cochise County primarily, colleges throughout the country." Annually. Estab. 1967. Circ. 2,000.
**Needs:** Historical (local), humor/satire, literary, regional, and western. "Contributions confined to Cochise County, Arizona. No juvenile. Receives 100 mss/year. Accepts 3-4 mss/issue. Length: 700-1,000 words average; 1,000 words maximum. Occasionally critiques rejected mss.
**How to Contact:** Contact faculty advisor. Reports in months on mss. SASE. Simultaneous and photocopied submissions OK. Accepts computer printout submissions. Sample copy with SAE. Free fiction guidelines.
**Payment:** Pays in contributor's copies.
**Terms:** Acquires one-time rights.
**Tips:** "We notice a trend away from realism. We try to publish a wide variety of material in our magazine. If it is of good quality it deserves consideration for our publication." Published new writers within the last year.

**MISSISSIPPI REVIEW**, University of Southern Mississippi, Southern Station, Box 5144, Hattiesburg MS 39406. (601)266-4321. Editor: Frederick Barthelme. Associate Editor: Elizabeth Inness-Brown. Literary publication for those interested in contemporary literature—writers, editors who read to be in touch with current modes. Semiannually. Estab. 1972. Circ. 1,500.
**Needs:** Literary, contemporary, fantasy, humor, translations, experimental, avant-garde, and "art" fiction. No juvenile. Buys varied amount of mss/issue. Does not read mss in summer. Length: 100 pages maximum.
**How to Contact:** Send complete ms with SASE including a short cover letter. Accepts computer printout submissions. Sample copy $4.50.
**Payment:** Honoraria plus 6 free author's copies. Charges cover price for extras.
**Terms:** Pays on publication for first North American serial rights.

**MISSISSIPPI VALLEY REVIEW (III)**, Western Illinois University. Dept. of English, Simpkins Hall, Macomb IL 61455. Editor: Forrest Robinson. Fiction Editor: Loren Logsdon. "A small magazine, *MVR* has won 17 Illinois Arts Council awards in poetry and fiction. We publish stories, poems, and reviews." Biannual. Estab. 1971. Circ. 400.
**Needs:** Literary, contemporary. Does not read mss in summer.
**How to Contact:** Send complete ms with SASE. Reports in 3 months.
**Payment:** 2 free author's copies, plus one copy of the following two numbers.
**Terms:** Individual author retains rights.
**Tips:** "We prefer to receive one story at a time. Getting one's work published has always been difficult. Commitment to one's art, as well as persistence, can sustain." Published new writers within the last year.

**THE MISSOURI REVIEW (II)**, 231 Arts & Science, English Dept., University of Missouri, Columbia MO 65211. (314)882-6421. Editor: Speer Morgan. Theme: fiction, poetry, essays, reviews, interviews. "All with a distinctly contemporary orientation. For writers, academics, others. We present non-established as well as established writers of excellence and offer a forum for modern critical theory. The *Review* frequently runs feature sections or special issues dedicated to particular topics frequently related to fiction." Published 3 times/academic year. Estab. 1977. Circ. 2,000.
**Needs:** Literary, contemporary; open to all categories except juvenile, young adult. Buys 6-8

mss/issue, 18-25 mss/year. Receives approximately 200 unsolicited fiction mss each month. No preferred length. Critiques rejected mss "when there is time."
**How to Contact:** Send complete ms with SASE. Reports in 6 weeks. Sample copy $1.
**Payment:** $5-10/page.
**Terms:** Pays on publication for all rights. Publication copyrighted.
**Tips:** Awards William Peden Prize in fiction; $1,000 to best story published in *Missouri Review* in a given year.

**THE MONTANA REVIEW (II)**, Owl Creek Press, Box 2248, Missoula MT 59806. Editor-in-Chief: Rich Ives. Magazine: 100-150 pages; average paper quality; high quality cover; illustrations rarely; photos cover. For readers of contemporary literature. "We publish only work of literary merit. Any subject, style or approach is acceptable if the result is of lasting literary quality." Published biannually. Estab. 1979. Circ. 1,000.
**Needs:** Contemporary, literary, prose poem, serialized/excerpted novel, and translations. "Genre is irrelevant. Quality of the writing is our only consideration." Receives 20-30 unsolicited fiction mss/month. Accepts 6-10 mss/year. No preferred length. Occasionally critiques rejected mss. Sometimes recommends other markets.
**How to Contact:** Send complete ms with SASE. Simultaneous and photocopied submissions OK if stated. "Work published in magazines may be considered in book form." Accepts computer printout submissions. Prefers letter-quality. Reports in 1 month. Sample copy $5.
**Payment:** 1-year subscription or small cash honorarium; 3 free contributor's copies; $5 charge for extras.
**Terms:** Pays on publication for all rights (books) and first North American serial rights (for magazine stories). Publication copyrighted.
**Tips:** "Seek the advice and assistance of established writers through workshops, conferences and college creative writing programs. We publish *quality* writing and we are dedicated to work in any genre of lasting literary value." Have published many new writers in the last year.

**MOOSEHEAD REVIEW**, Moosehead Press, Box 169, Ayer's Cliff, Quebec, Canada J0B 1C0. (819)838-4801 or (819)842-2835. Editors: Robert Allen, Hugh Dow, Steve Luxton, Jan Draper. "A small literary periodical." Annually. Estab. 1978. Circ. 500.
**Needs:** Literary, science fiction, translations, literary theory. Accepts 2-3 mss/issue, 4-6 mss/year. No preferred length.
**How to Contact:** Send complete ms with SASE. Reports in 6 weeks. Sample copy $4.
**Payment:** 3 free author's copies.
**Terms:** Acquires one-time rights.
**Tips:** "We are a very competitive market. We accept roughly one of every 30 stories submitted. Only top quality fiction is considered, but we do not judge by reputation. A first story has as much chance as a story by a well-known writer."

**‡THE MOUNTAIN LAUREL (II, IV), Monthly Journal of Mountain Life**, Laurel Publications, Inc., Rt. 1, Meadows of Dan VA 24120. (703)593-3613. Editor: Susan Thigpen. Tabloid: 32 pages (average); newsprint paper and cover; illustrations; photos. "People, places and history of Blue Ridge Mountains—shows integrity, dry sense of humor, ingenuity, strength." Family reading for cross section of all age groups. Everyone interested in mountain life and history. Monthly. Estab. 1983. Circ. 20,000.
**Needs:** Historical, humor, regional. No profanity, explicit sex or violence. No mss that are too lengthy, weak story lines filled with philosophy, cruelty, or too descriptive (too many adjectives). Receives 50-100 unsolicited mss/month. Accepts 3-4 mss/issue. Publishes ms "usually in 2-3 months, depends on seasonal nature." Length: 1,000 words average; 2,000 words maximum. Also publishes short shorts. Occasionally critiques rejected mss. Recommends other markets.
**How to Contact:** Send complete ms with cover letter (short sketch about writer). Reports in 2 months on mss. SASE. Simultaneous, photocopied submissions and reprints (if not in market that was very big") OK. Accepts computer printouts including dot-matrix if double spaced. Sample

# Close-up

### Frederick Barthelme
### *Mississippi Review*

In literary circles, Frederick Barthelme is best known as an original gifted novelist and short story writer. He is also the editor of the *Mississippi Review*, the literary magazine to which he has so gracefully transferred and applied his literary talents to make it as unique as one of his contemporary novels.

Before Barthelme assumed the editorship of the University of Southern Mississippi-based publication in 1978, the *Mississippi Review* was already a respected regional publication. "But it didn't offer the range or kind of fiction and poetry that I was raised on," says the editor, referring to the *Paris Review* and *Triquarterly*, whose standards he sought to emulate. The result: Today *MR* has its own identity and personality; it is distributed—and acclaimed—throughout the US. "I'm happy with what has evolved," says Barthelme. "I feel the *Mississippi Review* has become a very interesting magazine with enough diverse material to strike the reader's fancy and distinguish it from the others."

Of the fiction, Barthelme says, "We tend to look at work with catholic eyes—work you might term experimental, maybe *New Yorker*-esque." To broaden the fiction tastes, however, two other editors assist Barthelme—and "if one of us is fond of a story, we will include it," says the editor, lamenting an incident a few years ago when a memorable, "perfectly wonderful story got away" after one rejection.

In his early editing days, Barthelme relied primarily on name writers, like John Hawkes or John Barth, under whom he studied at Johns Hopkins. But now it's about a 50-50 mix of established and beginning authors in the magazine. The editors feel no need to solicit work; fine quality work comes in the mail. There is, as Barthelme says, "a great interest in culture in the South, and the natural by-product is a parallel interest in literature." However, *MR* also draws from equally talented writers all over the country.

Barthelme, a misplaced Texan from a literary family (Houston-based writer Donald Barthelme is his older brother), looks for craft in a good story. "The construction of sentences from the beginning is so important—if they contain all the right things *in* them, as well as all the wrong things *out* of them." Most writers, he concludes from the 100 or so unsolicited manuscripts he receives a week, don't leave out enough, which limits the story. "Learn to edit your own work," says the writer, one of the primary "minimalists" in fiction.

Barthelme, who teaches creative writing and fiction workshops for graduate students, also offers this principal lesson: "Writing is *work*. You write it; then you write it again. You keep your shoulder to the wheel and don't give up." Following his own advice, Barthelme writes every night from 10 to 2 and has produced in a few short years his collection of short stories, *Moon Deluxe*, and two novels, *Second Marriage* and *Tracer*. Both novels have been optioned for films and the author plans to write the screenplays.

Barthelme credits literary magazines for his breakthrough and recognition because they allowed him to see his work in print, work through the changes and eventually find a larger market. Of the future for serious contemporary fiction, he again refers to the litmags. "Our culture demands fiction—and there *will always be* fiction markets."

copy $1 and 9x12 SAE and 2 first class stamps. Publication is best guideline.
**Payment:** Pays in contributor's copies.
**Terms:** Acquires one-time rights. Publication copyrighted.
**Tips:** "Too many writers (including successful established ones) seem to think they have to capture an audience with unnecessary sensationalism. People still like to read a good solid story and a lot of readers are saturated with sex and violence. Forget long descriptive, wordy phrases, concentrate on good solid characters and a tight story line. Don't be afraid to inject emotion and humor. We publish many first stories of beginning writers as well as excerpts from books by well known mountain writers. Keep the story short and believable. We receive too many 'Walked 3 miles to school,' 'Grew everything on the farm.' Use details; avoid generalization. People still like happy endings. They want to be entertained and escape inside their heads. We're looking for the Mark Twain and O'Henry of today."

**MOVING OUT, Feminist Literary & Arts Journal**, Box 21249, Detroit MI 48221. Contact: Editor. Magazine of "material which captures the experience of women for feminists and other humane human beings." Published semiannually. Estab. 1970. Circ. 1,000.
**Needs:** Feminist, lesbian, and senior citizen/retirement. No male chauvinist creations. Accepts about 4-8 mss/issue. Occasionally critiques rejected mss.
**How to Contact:** Send complete ms with SASE. Accepts computer printout submissions. Reports in 6-12 months. Sample copy $3; free guidelines for SASE.
**Payment:** 1 free contributor's copy.
**Terms:** Acquires first rights. Publication copyrighted.
**Tips:** "We like to see work which represents varied experiences of the poor, the handicapped, the minorities, the lonely, as well as other fiction that explores women's esthetics."

**MUNDUS ARTIUM, A Journal of International Literature and Arts**, University of Texas at Dallas, Box 688, Richardson TX 75080. (214)690-2090. Contact: Rainer Schulte. Literary review of nonfiction, poetry, fiction with bilingual format for all levels, "except the scholarly, footnote-starved type." Semiannually. Estab. 1967. Circ. 2,000.
**Needs:** Stories must be experimental and fantasy or translations. Length is open. Critiques rejected mss "when there is time."
**How to Contact:** Send complete ms with SASE. Reports in 3 months. Sample copy $3.50.
**Payment:** Pays $5 minimum.
**Terms:** Pays on publication for all rights. Photocopied submissions OK. Publication copyrighted. Publishing plans are doubtful for 1986. *Query first.*

**MUSCADINE (I)**, 1111 Lincoln Pl., Boulder CO 80302. (303)443-9748. Editor: Lucille Cyphers. Magazine: 8½x11; 24 pages; simple illustrations. "Writers must be over 60 years of age. Everyone enjoys *Muscadine* as a glimpse of oldsters' rich experiences and creativity." Bimonthly. Estab. 1977. Circ. 400.
**Needs:** Literary, contemporary, psychic/supernatural, science fiction, fantasy, men's, women's, western, mystery, adventure, humor, juvenile, and ethnic (all). No horror, erotica, or novels. Receives 4 unsolicited fiction ms each month. Length: 350-1,500 words. Publishes short shorts of 400-600 words. Critiques rejected mss "when there is time."
**How to Contact:** Send complete ms with SASE. Accepts computer printout submissions. Reports in 1 month on mss. Publishes ms an average of 2-12 months after acceptance. Sample copy $1.
**Payment:** 1 free author's copy. $1 charge for extras.
**Terms:** Acquires first rights.
**Tips:** "We give priority to beginners. Try to stay off trite or sentimental themes. Express it your way. It might have the freshness we value—the common touch. The more skilled writers have to compete for space. Brevity is a priority. Mss don't have to be typewritten. We publish fiction to keep a variety of departments, and to encourage more imagination in oldsters."

**MUSICWORKS**, A Quarterly Magazine With Sound, Music Gallery, 1087 Queen St. W., Toronto, Ontario M6J 1H3 Canada. (416)533-0192. Editor: T. Pearson. Tabloid. "Musical innovation in Canada—interviews, articles, scores, visuals, sounds and music on cassette." For musicians, composers, students, artists, administrators, etc. Quarterly. Estab. 1978. Circ. 4,000.
**Needs:** Ethnic, experimental, prose poem, and music-sound. No mainstream, commercial, popular fiction. Accepts less than 1 mss/issue; 1-3 mss/year. Length: 2,000 words average; 5,000 words maximum. Occasionally critiques rejected ms.
**How to Contact:** Send complete ms or query with clips of published work. Reports in 6 weeks. SASE or SAE and IRC for query and ms. Simultaneous, photocopied, and previously published submissions OK. Accepts computer printout submissions. Prefers letter-quality. Sample $2.
**Payment:** Pays $100 maximum and 3 contributor's copies; charge for extras: $1-2.
**Terms:** Buys one-time rights on publication.

**MYSTERY TIME (I), An Anthology of Short Stories**, Box 2377, Coeur d'Alene ID 83814. (208)667-7511. Editor: Linda Hutton. Booklet: 5½x8½; 44 pages; bond paper; illustrations. "Annual collection of short stories with a suspense or mystery theme for mystery buffs." Published special fiction issue last year; plans another. Estab. 1983.
**Needs:** Suspense/mystery only. Receives 10-15 unsolicited fiction mss/month. Acquires 10-12 mss/year. Length: 1,500 words maximum. Occasionally critiques rejected mss. Recommends other markets.
**How to Contact:** Send complete ms with SASE. Simultaneous, photocopied and previously published submissions OK. Accepts computer printout submissions. Prefers letter-quality. Reports in 1 month on mss. Publishes ms an average of 6-8 months after acceptance. Sample copy for $3.50. Fiction guidelines for #10 SAE and 22¢ postage.
**Payment:** 1 free contributor's copy; $5 charge for extras.
**Terms:** Acquires one-time rights. Buys reprints. Publication copyrighted.
**Tips:** "Concentrate on plot! Mysteries with a humorous twist are especially popular. A neatly typed manuscript is always welcome. Study our back issues. Revise and polish till you're blue in the face, then revise again." Published new writers within the last year. Sponsors annual short story contest.

**MYTHELLANY (I), The Fiction Journal of The Mythopoeic Society**, Box 6707, Altadena CA 91001. Editor-in-Chief: Veida Wissler. Magazine for fantasy readers, high school and up. Published annually. Estab. Summer 1981. Circ. 300.
**Needs:** Fantasy, humor/satire, juvenile fantasy, science fiction, young adult fantasy. "Tolkien themes OK, but no re-writes of *Lord of The Rings*. No *Star Wars*, D&D stuff or erotica." Receives about 6 unsolicited fiction mss/month. Accepts 10-15 mss/issue, 10-15 mss/year. Length: 50 words minimum; 10,000 words maximum; 4-5,000 words average. Occasionally critiques rejected mss.
**How to Contact:** Query or send complete ms. with SASE. Photocopied and previously published submissions OK. Reports in 3 weeks on queries; 6 weeks on mss. Sample copy $2; free guidelines with SASE.
**Payment:** 1 free contributor's copy/submission; $2.75 charge for extras.
**Terms:** Pays on publication for one-time rights. Publication copyrighted.
**Tips:** "We are a beginning fiction magazine so new writers are welcome! Please be sure your fantasy story *is* fantasy of the type we like, i.e., 'fairy-tale-like.' Mythical, wondrous."

**NAKED MAN (II)**, c/o Mike Smetzer, Dept. of English, University of Kansas, Lawrence KS 66045. Editor: Mike Smetzer. Magazine: 5½x8½; 48 pages; offset paper; ivory bristol board cover stock; illustrations on cover. "I have eclectic tastes but generally dislike work that is only clever or spontaneous without discipline. Since *Naked Man* reflects my personal interests and tastes, writers should examine a copy before submitting." Published irregularly. Estab. 1982.
**Needs:** Comics, contemporary, experimental, humor/satire, literary, mainstream, prose poem, and regional. Length: no minimum; 15,000 words maximum. Also publishes short shorts. Occa-

sionally critiques rejected ms "as time permits." Publishes ms an average of 6 months after acceptance.
**How to Contact:** Send complete ms with SASE. Photocopied submissions OK. Accepts computer printout submissions. Prefers letter-quality. Sample copy $2.
**Payment:** Pays in 2 contributor's copies.
**Terms:** Acquires first rights. Sends galleys to author. Publication copyrighted.

**THE NANTUCKET REVIEW (II),** Box 1234, Nantucket MA 02554. Co-Editors: Richard Cumbie and Richard Burns. "We are a general literary magazine ascribing to no specific school(s) of literature. We publish primarily fiction (85%) and poetry (15%). Published 3 times/year. Estab. 1974. Circ. 600.
**Needs:** "It's difficult for us to rule out some types of fiction. *The Man From Laramie* and *The Ox-Bow Incident* are both 'western' stories, for example, but stories like the former wouldn't be of much interest to us, while those like the latter would be. We are interested in serious (that is not to say, humorless) fiction." Receives approximately 75 unsolicited fiction mss each month. Length: 1,500-6,000 words. Critiques rejected mss "when there is time."
**How to Contact:** Send complete ms with SASE. Reports in 2-6 months. Publishes ms 3 months-1 year after acceptance. Sample copy $1.50 with 6x9 SAE and 68¢ postage.
**Payment:** $5-$25 and 2 free author's copies.
**Terms:** Pays on publication for first North American serial rights. Publication copyrighted.
**Tips:** "Read an issue of the magazine before submitting fiction to us. It's a constant complaint among editors that they receive many mss totally unsuited to their publications. Any writer serious about his craft and eager to publish can, for $15-$20 (or less, depending on library availability), examine a half-dozen magazines he wishes to try with stories. Be neat. Always, if you feel compelled to do multiple submissions, inform the editor when you submit. Please don't submit stories of more than 6,000 words. Unless you sense that your story is so unusual that we may not be interested, don't query—send us the story, and only one per submission, please."

**NEBO (I), A Literary Journal,** Arkansas Tech University, Dept. of English, Russellville AR 72801. Editor: Laurie A. Williams. Literary, fiction and poetry magazine: 5x8; 60-70 pages. For a general, academic audience. Semiannually. Estab. 1983. Circ. 500.
**Needs:** Experimental, literary, mainstream, prose poem, psychic/supernatural/occult, regional, and science fiction. Receives 20-30 unsolicited fiction mss/month. Acquires 2 mss/issue; 6-10 nss/year. Does not read mss May 31-Aug 1. Length: 3,000 words maximum. Occasionally critiques rejected mss.
**How to Contact:** Send complete ms with SASE and cover letter with bio. Simultaneous and photocopied submissions OK. Accepts computer printout submissions. Prefers letter-quality computer printout. Reports in 12 weeks on mss. Publishes ms an average of 6 months after acceptance. Sample copy for $1.
**Payment:** 2 free contributor's copies.
**Terms:** Acquires one-time rights. "Rarely" buys reprints. Publication copyrighted.
**Tips:** "A writer should carefully edit his short story before submitting it. Write from the heart and put everything on the line. Don't write from a phony or fake perspective. Frankly, many of the manuscripts we receive should be publishable with a little polishing. Manuscripts should *never* be submitted with misspelled words."

**THE NEBRASKA REVIEW (II),** (formerly *Smackwarm* University of Nebraska at Omaha, ASH 212, Omaha NE 68182. (402)554-2771. Editors: Arthur Homer, Richard Duggin. Magazine: 6x9; 64 pages; 60 lb text paper; chrome coat cover stock. "*TNR* attempts to publish the finest available contemporary fiction and poetry for college and literary types." Publishes 2 issues/year. Estab. 1973. Circ. 500.
**Needs:** Contemporary, fantasy, humor/satire, literary, and mainstream. Receives 20 unsolicited fiction mss/month. Accepts 3-5 mss/issue, 8 mss/year. Does not read April 15-August 15. Length: 5,000-6,000 words average.

**How to Contact:** Send complete ms with SASE. Photocopied submissions OK. Reports in 1-2 months. Publishes ms an average of 4-6 months after acceptance. Sample copy $2.50.
**Payment:** 2 free contributor's copies plus 1 year subscription; $2 charge for extras.
**Terms:** Acquires first North American serial rights. Publication copyrighted.
**Tips:** "Don't consider us as the last place to submit your mss. Write 'honest' stories in which the lives of your characters are the primary reason for writing and techniques of craft serve to illuminate, not overshadow, the textures of those lives." Published new writers within the last year.

**NEGATIVE CAPABILITY (II), A Literary Quarterly**, Negative Capability Press, 6116 Timberly Rd. N, Mobile AL 36609. (205)661-9114. Editor-in-Chief: Sue Walker. Fiction Editor: Righter North. Magazine: 5½x8½; 160 pages; 7 lb offset paper; 2 color cover/varnish cover stock; illustrations; photos. Magazine of short fiction, prose poems, poetry, criticism, commentaries, journals and translations for those interested in contemporary trends, innovations in literature. Published quarterly. Plans special fiction issue. Estab. 1981. Circ. 700.
**Needs:** Adventure, contemporary, ethnic, experimental, fantasy, feminist, gothic/historical romance, historical (general), literary, prose poem, psychic/supernatural/occult, regional, romance (contemporary), science fiction, senior citizen/retirement, suspense/mystery, translations, and women's. Accepts 2-3 mss/issue, 6-10 mss/year. Does not read July-Sept. Publishes short shorts. Length: 1,000 words minimum. Sometimes recommends markets.
**How to Contact:** Query or send complete ms. SASE for query, ms. Reports in 2 weeks on queries; 1 month on mss. Publishes ms an average of 6 months after acceptance. Sample copy $3.50; free guidelines for legal-size SAE and 1 first class stamp.
**Payment:** 2 free contributor's copies.
**Terms:** Acquires first rights, first North American serial rights and one-time rights. Sends galleys to author. Publication copyrighted.
**Tips:** "We consider all manuscripts and often offer suggestions for revisions, and work with new authors to encourage and support. We believe fiction answers a certain need that is not filled by poetry or nonfiction." Published new writers within the last year.

**NEW AMERICA (IV)**, % Dept. of American Studies, University of New Mexico, Albuquerque NM 87131. (505)277-3929. Editors are rotating. "A journal of American and Southwestern culture. Our material includes fiction, poetry, photography, and graphic art exploring American and Southwestern culture. Our audience is very diverse. Past themes have been geared toward those interested in SW culture, American studies, chicano literature, Native American literature, photographers, energy buffs, etc. Our aim is to reach a larger audience by having different themes." Semiannually. Estab. 1974. Circ. 1,000.
**Needs:** Literary, contemporary, men's, women's, ethnic (Chicano, Native American), and Southwestern American studies. "We solicit different material for each specific issue." No preferred length.
**How to Contact:** Query first. Each issue has a different and specific theme. SASE for query, ms. Reports in 1 week on queries, 3 months on mss. Sample copy $4.
**Payment:** 1 free author's copy. 40% discount for 10 or more extras.
**Terms:** Buys all rights. Publication copyrighted.
**Tips:** Mss are rejected because "they don't apply to specific theme."

**‡NEW ENGLAND REVIEW AND BREAD LOAF QUARTERLY (III), NER/BLQ**, Kenyon Hill Publications, Box 170, Hanover NY 03755. (603)795-4027. Editors: Sydney Lea, Jim Schley, Maura High. Magazine: 6x9; 140 pages; 70 lb paper; coated cover stock; illustrations; photos. A literary quarterly publishing fiction with a commitment to narrative, poetry which is comprehensible, and penetrating commentary on life and the craft of writing. General readers and professional writers. Quarterly. Estab. 1978. Circ. 2,000.
**Needs:** Literary. Receives 250 unsolicited fiction mss/month. Accepts 5 mss/issue; 20 mss/year. Does not read ms June-August. Publishes ms 3-9 months after acceptance. Agented fiction: less than 5%. Publishes short shorts. Critiques rejected mss.

**How to Contact:** Send complete ms with cover letter with a simple, brief introduction of the writer, and the name of the work(s) enclosed. No long resumes or synopses necessary. Reports in 6-8 weeks on mss. SASE for ms. Photocopied submissions OK. Accepts computer printouts including dot-matrix. Sample copy $5. Fiction guidelines for $4 and business size SAE.
**Payment:** Pays $5 per page; $10 minimum; free subscription to magazine, offprints; contributor's copies; charge for extras.
**Terms:** Pays on publication. Acquires first rights and reprint rights on *NER/BLQ* and Kenyon Hill Publications. Sends galleys to author. Publication copyrighted.
**Tips:** "Read a sample copy before submitting, to get a clear idea of our style and standards."

**NEW ENGLAND SAMPLER (II, IV)**, Seacoast Press, Rt. 1, Box 306, Belfast ME 04915-0306. (207)525-3575. Editor/Publisher: Virginia M. Rimm. "An upbeat family magazine: 5½x8½; 48-56 pages; 50 lb offset white paper; 60 lb offset cream cover; illustrations; photos. Old-time New England values and heritage with strong rural slant. We use historical, biographical and humorous material, interviews, poetry, book reviews, ESP experiences, fiction, off-beat places to visit, etc. Audience is well-educated, over-40 age bracket. We reflect the traditional New England spirit—independent, resourceful, hard-working." Published 9 times/year. Estab. 1980. Circ. 2,000.
**Needs:** Inspirational, historical, psychic/supernatural ("but not too far out"), fantasy, mystery, adventure, humor, regional and outdoor. "New England slant a must! We use only wholesome material suited to a family audience. Inspirational material must be ecumenical in tone, not denominational. Nonfiction or fiction articles on New England heritage and personalities are our greatest need and best chance of breaking in." Accepts 14-18 fiction mss/year. Receives approximately 20-30 unsolicited fiction mss each month. Length: 2,000-3,500 words.
**How to Contact:** Send complete ms and cover letter with brief summation of story idea and bio. Photocopied submissions OK. SASE. "We will no longer return manuscripts sent with insufficient postage, or accept manuscripts mailed to us on which there is postage due." Accepts computer printout submissions. Reports in 2-3 months. Publishes ms an average of 2-4 months after acceptance. Sample copy $1. Free writer's guidelines for SASE. Submit seasonal material 4-5 months in advance.
**Payment:** 1-4 free author's copies; $1 charge for extras.
**Terms:** Acquires one-time rights. Publication copyrighted.
**Tips:** "Send for and study sample copy and free guidelines. Pick a subject with strong New England flavor, write in lively, fast-paced fashion with good plot and characterization. New England settings only. Be fresh and original. We are looking for top quality writing which fits our needs and New England format. We're a young magazine and our entire staff works without pay. To build and grow, we need professional-calibre writing. We hope in time to be able to pay. Because we're small, we're a good place for would-be professionals to break into print. Our annual Creative Writing Contest includes short stories."

**THE NEW KENT QUARTERLY**, Campus Printing, 239 Student Center, Kent State University, Kent OH 44242. Contact: Editor. "The magazine is a creative arts outlet for the university community and other interested artists. We publish poems, prose, and photography for the general public." Biannually. Circ. 300.
**Needs:** Literary. Receives 1-2 unsolicited fiction mss each month. Length: 1,600 words maximum.
**How to Contact:** Send complete ms with SASE. Reports in 1 month. Sample copy $1 with SASE.
**Payment:** Pays in contributor's copies.
**Terms:** Acquires all rights, revert to author 60 days after issue publication. Publication copyrighted.

**NEW LAUREL REVIEW (II)**, 828 Lesseps St., New Orleans LA 70117. (504)947-6001. Editor: Lee M. Grue. Assistant Editor: Celeste Grue. Journal of poetry, fiction, critical articles and reviews. "We have published such nationally known writers as Elton Glaser, Jesse Stuart, H.E. Francis,

Tonita Gardner, Dorothy Stanfill, and Jim Barnes (translations)." Readership: "Literate, adult audiences as well as anyone interested in writing with significance, human interest, vitality, subtlety, etc." Annually. Estab. 1970. Circ. 500.

**Needs:** Literary, contemporary, fantasy, and translations. No "dogmatic, excessively inspirational or political" material. Accepts 1-2 fiction mss/issue. Receives approximately 20 unsolicited fiction mss each month. Length: about 10 printed pages. Critiques rejected mss "when there is time."
**How to Contact:** Send complete ms with SASE. Reports in 3 months. Sample copy $3.
**Payment:** 2 free author's copies.
**Terms:** Acquires first rights. Publication copyrighted.
**Tips:** "Write fresh, alive 'moving' work. Not interested in egocentric work without any importance to others. Be sure to watch simple details such as putting one's name and address on ms and clipping all pages together. Caution: Don't use overfancy or trite language."

**‡NEW LETTERS MAGAZINE (I, II)**, University of Missouri-Kansas City, 5310 Harrison St., Kansas City MO 64110. (816)276-1168. Editor: James McKinley. Magazine: 14 lb cream paper; illustrations. Quarterly. Estab. 1971 (continuation of *University Review* founded 1935). Circ. 2,500.
**Needs:** Contemporary, ethnic, experimental, humor/satire, literary, mainstream, translations. No "bad fiction in any genre." Agented fiction: 10%. Also publishes short shorts. Occasionally critiques rejected mss.
**How to Contact:** Send complete ms with cover letter. Reports in 2 weeks on queries; 4 weeks on mss. SASE for ms. Photocopied submissions OK. Accepts computer printouts.
**Payment:** Honorarium—depends on grant/award money; 5 contributor's copies. Sends galleys to author. "We plan a contest in 1986. One award for a short story; one for poetry."
**Tips:** "Seek publication of representative chapters in high-quality magazines as a way to the book contract."

**NEW MEXICO HUMANITIES REVIEW (II)**, New Mexico Tech, Box A, NMT, Socorro NM 87801. (505)835-5445. Editor: Jerry Bradley. Magazine: 5½x9½; 100 pages; 60 lb lakewood paper; 482 ppi cover stock; illustrations; photos. Review of poetry, essays and prose of Southwest. Readership: academic but not specialized. Published 3 times/year. Estab. 1978. Circ. 700.
**Needs:** Literary, psychic/supernatural/occult, and regional. "No formula." Buys 40-50 mss/year. Receives approximately 20 unsolicited fiction mss each month. Length: 6,000 words maximum. Publishes short shorts. Critiques rejected mss "when there is time." Sometimes recommends markets.
**How to Contact:** Send complete ms with SASE. Accepts computer printout submissions. Prefers letter-quality. Reports in 2 months. Publishes ms an average of 6 months after acceptance. Sample copy $3.
**Payment:** 1 year subscription.
**Terms:** Pays on publication. Sends galleys to author. Publication copyrighted.
**Tips:** Mss are rejected because they are "unimaginative, predictable, and technically flawed. Avoid clichéd and boring situations and predictable characters." Published new writers within the last year.

**‡NEW MOON, A Journal of Science Fiction and Critical Feminism**, SF, Box 1624, Madison WI 53701. (608)251-3854. Editor: Janice Bogstad. "Speculative fiction, fantastic feminist fiction, reviews and criticism of such works in university libraries, feminist and literary collections, womens' studies programs." Semiannually. Estab. 1981. Circ. 450.
**Needs:** Experimental, fantasy, feminist, literary, science fiction, translations, women's. Receives 3-5 unsolicited fiction mss/month. Accepts 2-4 mss/issue; 15 mss/year. Length: 1,000-1,500 word average; 1,000 words minimum; 3,000 words maximum. Occasionally critiques rejected mss.
**How to Contact:** Query first. Reports in 2 months on queries; 4 months on mss. SASE for query and ms. Simultaneous, photocopied submissions, and published work OK. Accepts computer

printout submissions. Prefers letter-quality. Sample copy $3. Fiction guidelines free for business-size SAE and 1 first class stamp.
**Payment:** Pays 1 contributor's copy; 60% cover price charge for extras.
**Terms:** Pays on publication for one-time rights. Publication copyrighted.
**Tips:** "Send clean, clear copy; prefer creativity and innovation."

**NEW OREGON REVIEW (III)**, Transition Publications, 537 NE Lincoln St., Hillsboro OR 97123. (503)640-1375. Editor-in-Chief: Steven Dimeo, Ph.D. Magazine: 5½x8½; 32 pages; 20 lb paper; 40 lb slick cover stock; illustrations; photos. "We seek to publish fiction of lasting literary merit from both unacknowledged and well-established artists who recognize the time-honored values of literary excellence, for the literate who shun the dry self-indulgence of consciously academic fiction in favor of strong, interesting narratives of substance." Published semiannually. Estab. 1981 (*NOR*); 1977 (*Transition*). Circ. 300.
**Needs:** Adventure, contemporary, erotica, fantasy, historical (general), horror, humor/satire, literary, mainstream, men's, psychic/supernatural/occult, science fiction, and suspense/mystery. "We're always looking for the well-integrated tale with thematic depth, skillful characterization, wit, dramatic change, imaginative symbolism, and a strong sense of structure, including an effective narrative hook at the beginning. No self-consciously experimental, moralistic or superficially 'slick' manuscripts." Receives 50 unsolicited fiction mss/month. Buys 3 mss/issue, 6 mss/year. Does not read Jan.-August, or Dec. Approximately 2% of fiction is agented. Length: 3,000 words minimum; 5,000 words maximum. Occasionally critiques rejected mss. Recommends other markets.
**How to Contact:** Send complete ms with SASE. "Manuscripts should also be accompanied by a short bio/bibliographical statement." Simultaneous and photocopied submissions OK. Does not accept computer printout submissions. Reports in 2 months on mss. Publishes ms an average of 6-12 months after acceptance. Sample copy $3 and 5½x8 SAE and 2 first class stamps; free guidelines for 3½x8½ SAE and 1 first class stamp.
**Payment:** $25 flat fee. Charge for extra copies: 1 for $2, 2 for $3.75, 3 for $5, 4 for $6.
**Terms:** Pays on publication for first rights. Publication copyrighted. $100 annual award for best fiction contributors who are also subscribers.
**Tips:** "*Purchase a sample copy of the publication first*. We're always in the market for realistic narratives laced with horror or the fantastic in the manner of Faulkner's 'A Rose for Emily' or Cheever's 'The Enormous Radio.' Stories must involve change or conflict. We prefer fiction of nostalgia and tales of male/female relationships." Published two new writers (one poet, one fiction writer) within the last year.

**NEW ORLEANS REVIEW (II)**, Box 195, Loyola University, New Orleans LA 70118. (504)865-2294. Editor: John Mosier. Magazine: 8½x11; 104 pages; 60 lb Scott offset paper; 12 + King James c/15 cover stock; photos. Publishes poetry, fiction, translations, photographs, nonfiction on literature and film. Readership: those interested in current culture, literature. Published 4 times/year. Estab. 1968. Circ. 2,500.
**Needs:** Literary, contemporary, and translations. No special categories designated. Buys 9-12 mss/year. Length: under 40 pages.
**How to Contact:** Send complete ms with SASE. Accepts computer printout submissions. Accepts disc submissions; inquire about system compatibility. Prefers hard copy with disc submission. Reports in 1 month. Sample copy $7.
**Payment:** "Rates are changing."
**Terms:** Pays on publication for first North American serial rights. Sends galleys to author.

**‡NEW PEOPLE (I)**, The Biracial Society of America, 4817 Winnetka, Houston TX 77021. (713)748-4496. Editor: Ruthie Grant. Magazine: 5x6; 24 pages; 70 lb matte paper; 70 lb matte cover stock; illustrations; photos. "Small literary focusing on fiction, articles and editorial material regarding interracial couples, people from mixed racial backgrounds, race relations in America; including material of interest to any minority or ethnic group in America. For students and college educated adults with a section for children. Quarterly. Published special fiction issue; plans another. Estab. 1984. Circ. 1000 +.

**Needs:** Ethnic, feminist, historical (general), humor/satire, juvenile (5-9 years), literary, women's, young adult/teen (10-18 years). "All material must deal in some way with multi-cultural characters, themes, etc. and reflect sensitivity and insight into the plight of minorities in America or those from the majority who choose to align their sympathies or association with minorities." No stories with exclusive ethnic characters or themes, i.e. white only or black only. No political, religious or self-righteous material. Publishes ms 3-6 months after acceptance. Length: 4,000 average; 2,500 words minimum; 5,000 words maximum. Critiques rejected mss. Recommends other markets.

**How to Contact:** Send complete ms with cover letter with short biography regarding education and previous works. SASE for ms. Simultaneous, photocopied and reprint submissions OK. Accepts computer printouts including dot-matrix. Accepts electronic submissions via disc or modem. Sample copy $2 per issue. Fiction guidelines for legal size envelope and 1 first class stamp.

**Payment:** Free subscription to magazine, contributor's copies.

**Terms:** Pays on publication. Acquires one-time rights. Sends galleys to author. Publication copyrighted.

**Tips:** "We are looking for beginning writers with fresh, uncensored ideas, compelling story lines and open minds."

‡**THE NEW QUARTERLY (IV), New Directions in Canadian Writing**, University of Waterloo, Waterloo, Ontario N2L 3G1 Canada. (519)885-1211. Editors: Linda Kenyon, Kim Jernigan. Fiction Editor: Peter Hinchcliffe. Magazine: 6x9; 100 pages. "*The New Quarterly* explores new directions in Canadian writing. We publish poetry and short fiction by new and published writers from across Canada." For anyone interested in new developments in Canadian writing. Quarterly. Published special fiction issue. Estab. 1981. Circ. 500.

**Needs:** Literary. Receives 20 unsolicited mss/month. Buys 4-5 mss/issue; 20 mss/year. Publishes 4 months after acceptance. Length: 2,500 words average. "Always" critiques rejected mss.

**How to Contact:** Send complete ms with cover letter. Reports in 4 months on mss. SASE or IRC for ms. No simultaneous, photocopied submissions or reprints. Accepts computer printouts. Sample copy $2.50 and 9x6 SAE.

**Payment:** $100 flat rate.

**Terms:** Pays on publication for first North American serial rights. Sends pre-publication galleys to author. Publication copyrighted.

**the new renaissance (II)**, 9 Heath Rd., Arlington MA 02174. Fiction Editors: Louise T. Reynolds and Harry Jackel. Magazine: 6x9; 124-136 pages; 60 lb paper; laminated cover stock; illustrations; photos. "An international magazine of ideas and opinions, with a classicist position in literature and the arts. Publishes a variety of quality fiction, always well crafted, sometimes experimental. For the literate reader. *tnr* is unique among literary magazines for its marriage of the literary and visual arts with political/sociological articles and essays. We publish the beginning as well as the established writer." Biannually. Estab. 1968. Circ. 1,500.

**Needs:** Literary, humor, translations, off-beat, quality fiction and, occasionally, experimental fiction. "We don't want to see heavily plotted stories with one-dimensional characters or academic or obviously 'poetic' writing, fiction, or writing that is self-indulgent. *tnr* is interested in fiction that has something to say, that says it with style or grace and, above all, that speaks in a highly personalized voice." Buys 4-6 mss/issue, 7-12 mss/year. Receives approximately 35-40 unsolicited fiction mss each month. Requires $5.10 for 2 sample back issues or $4.30 for recent issue before reading mss. "We want submissions from January 2- July 2 only." Approximately 8-12% of fiction is agented. Length: 3-36 pages. Comments on rejected mss "when there is time and when we want to encourage the writer or believe we can be helpful." Sometimes recommends other markets.

**How to Contact:** Send complete ms with SASE, of sufficient size for return or IRC. Reluctantly

accepts computer printout submissions but prefers letter-quality. Reports in 4-6 months. Publishes ms an average of 12-18 months after acceptance. Sample copy $5.10 for 2 back issues or $4.30 for recent issue (specify fiction). "Inform us if multiple submission."
**Payment:** $30-75. 1 free author's copy. Query for additional copies.
**Terms:** Pays after publication for all rights. Publication copyrighted.
**Tips:** "We represent one of the best markets for serious fiction writers. We are a biannual (spring and fall) and therefore have limited space available in any one year. We also have a criterion for excellence. But we also publish more variety (of styles, statements, levels of expertise) than most magazines. We're especially interested in writing that holds up to the test of time and repeated reading. Study *tnr* and then send the best manuscript you have on hand; we will read 3 manuscripts if they are 4 pages or less; 2 manuscripts of 9 pages or less; 10 pages or more, send only one ms. Manuscripts are rejected because writers do not study their markets and send out indiscriminately. Fully one-quarter of our rejected manuscripts fall into this category; others are from tyro writers who haven't yet mastered their craft or writers who are not quite honest with themselves or their readers or who haven't fully thought their story through or because writers are careless about language (precision w/language is an excellent trait). Definitive writing should be avoided." Published new writers within the last year.

**THE NEW SOUTHERN LITERARY MESSENGER (II)**, The Airplane Press, 400 S. Laurel St., Richmond VA 23220. (804)780-1244. Magazine: 5x8; 40 pages; medium paper; card stock cover; illustrations; photos on cover only. "We are not regional in viewpoint, but prefer local material." Quarterly. Published special fiction issue last year; plans another. Estab. 1981. Circ. 600+.
**Needs:** Adventure, comics, contemporary, erotica, ethnic, experimental, humor/satire, literary, prose poem, psychic/supernatural, serialized/excerpted novel, and stories set in the outdoors, away from civilization. Wants to see "political satire dealing with specific people or groups—left viewpoint. Good craftsmanship, well-made stories on any subject. No formula stories unless the formula is twisted out of shape." Receives 40-50 unsolicited fiction mss/month. Buys "5 or more" mss/issue. Length: 500 words minimum; 5,000 words maximum; 2,500 words average. Occasionally critiques rejected mss. Occasionally recommends other markets.
**How to Contact:** Send complete ms with SASE and short letter stating where author heard about the magazine. Previously published work OK. Reports in varied number of weeks on mss. Publishes ms an average of 3 months after acceptance. Sample copy $1. Fiction guidelines for business-size SASE.
**Payment:** Pays $5; subscription to magazine; 2 free contributor's copies.
**Terms:** Pays on publication for one-time rights. Buys reprints. Publication copyrighted.
**Tips:** "Send the manuscript with cover letter and sufficient postage on the SASE, making sure the manuscript is neatly typed. I will read it ASAP. Keep extra copies. Find a local small magazine and offer to help the editor. Deal first with small magazines and publishers. Tell me where you heard of *The Messenger* in a short cover letter." Published new writers within the last year.

**NeWEST REVIEW (II)**, Box 394, Sub P.O. 6 Saskatoon, Saskatchewan 57N OWO, Canada. Editor: Paul Denham. Fiction Editor: David Carpenter. Magazine: 20 pages; newsprint paper; illustrations; photos. Tabloid with western Canada regional issues; "fiction, reviews, poetry for middle- to high-brow audience." Monthly September through June. Plans special fiction issue. Estab. 1975. Circ. 600.
**Needs:** Contemporary, ethnic, experimental, fantasy, feminist, gay, historical (general), humor/satire, lesbian, literary, mainstream, science fiction, serialized/excerpted novel, and women's. Receives 10-12 unsolicited mss/month. Buys 1 ms/issue; 10 mss/year. Length: 2,500 words average; 1,500 words minimum; 5,000 words maximum. Recommends other markets.
**How to Contact:** Query first. "We prefer *brief* letters: past publications of fiction and brief instructions from the writers." Reports very prompt on queries and mss. SAE, IRCs or Canadian postage. Photocopied submissions OK. Accepts computer printout submissions. Sample copy $2.
**Payment:** Pays $100 maximum.

**Terms:** Pays on publication for one-time rights. Publication copyrighted.
**Tips:** "We publish 'several' new writers each year. Fiction embodies important truths inaccessible to other kinds of writing. A good short story shows how it *feels* to be someone else. Try to write the story the way the story wants to go. Never strive to sound literary. Plot is two dogs and one bone. Stories can't advance without tension."

**NEXUS (II),** Wright State University, 006 U.C. Wright State University, Dayton OH 45435. (513)873-2031. Editor: Tim Waggoner. Assistant Editor: Vance Wissenger. Magazine: 9x11½; 50 pages; glossy enamel cover stock; illustrations; photos. "We're looking for quality fiction, poetry, essays, and art work from writers—often previously unpublished." Quarterly. Estab. 1966. Circ. 4,000.
**Needs:** Experimental, feminist, gay, lesbian, satire, mainstream, prose poem, translations, science fiction, and fantasy. Receives 20 unsolicited fiction mss/month. Accepts 3-5 mss/issue; 10-15 mss/year. Does not read mss in July-August. Length: 300 words minimum; 3,000 words maximum; 1,500 words average. Short stories should be limited to 20 pages. Occasionally critiques rejected mss.
**How to Contact:** "Send sample of work. SASE. Always include a *brief* cover letter." Simultaneous and photocopied submissions OK. Reports in 6 weeks on mss. Publishes ms an average of 2-6 months after acceptance. Sample copy free with 10x15 SAE and 3 first class stamps. Fiction guidelines free with 10x15 SAE and 3 first class stamps.
**Payment:** 2 free contributor's copies; $1 plus postage charged for extras.
**Terms:** All rights revert to author upon publication. Publication copyrighted.
**Tips:** "Send neat copy. Concise, clear writing. No twisting, confusing plots. Nexus is a university publication and we publish fiction to reflect the types of writing done by the student." Published many new writers within the last year.

**NIGHTSUN,** Department of Philosophy, Frostburg State College, Frostburg MD 21532. Editor-in-Chief: Jorn K. Bramann. Magazine: 5½x8½; 120 pages; acid free paper; varied cover stock; illustrations; photos sometimes. Magazine of "all literary forms and philosophical and literary essays for a literary and/or academic audience." Published annually. Estab. Feb. 1981. Circ. 1,000.
**Needs:** Comics, contemporary, experimental, feminist, prose poem. "We are not dogmatic, but have little interest in science fiction, supernatural, etc." Receives 5 unsolicited fiction mss/month. Accepts 2-7 mss/issue. Does not read mss Jan.-June. Occasionally critiques rejected mss.
**How to Contact:** Send inquiry with SASE. Accepts computer printout submissions. Reporting time "varies." Sample copy $6.80.
**Payment:** Pays in free contributor's copy.
**Terms:** Pays on publication for one-time rights (rights revert to author after publication). Publication copyrighted.
**Tips:** "Try to *say* something. There is too much entertainment writing." Published new writers within the last year.

**NIMROD (II), International Literary Journal**, Arts & Humanities Council of Tulsa, 2210 S. Main, Tulsa OK 74114. Editor-in-Chief: Francine Ringold. Magazine: 9x6; 120-150 pages; illustrations; photos. Magazine for good readers and writers. "We publish 1 thematic issue and 1 open issue (which includes prize winners) each year. Thematic issues—Latin American Voices, A Book of Revelations—have been published. Otherwise, we seek vigorous, imaginative, quality writing." Published semiannually. Estab. 1956. Circ. 1,000 +.
**Needs:** Adventure, contemporary, ethnic, experimental, literary, prose poem, science fiction, and translations. Receives 60 unsolicited fiction mss/month. Accepts 3 mss/issue, 6 mss/year. Length: 6,000 words average. Occasionally critiques rejected mss.
**How to Contact:** Send complete ms with SASE. Photocopied submissions OK. Reports in 3 weeks-3 months. Sample copy $4.50. Send SASE for awards information.
**Payment:** 3 free contributor's copies.
**Terms:** Buys one-time rights. Publication copyrighted.

**Tips:** "Read the magazine. Write well. Be courageous." Published new writers within the last year.

**NIT&WIT (II), Chicago's Literary Arts Magazine**, Box 627, Geneva IL 60134. (312)232-9496. Editor: Harrison McCormick. Magazine: 8½x11; 68 pages (minimum); 60 lb coated paper; 70 lb coated cover stock; illustrations; photos. A literary arts magazine of dance, theater, music, film, fiction, humor, poetry, photography and art. Bimonthly. Published special fiction issue last year; plans another. Estab. 1977. Circ. 10,000. Readership: 110,000.
**Needs:** Humor. Accepts 5-6 mss/issue, 30-40 mss/year. Receives approximately 60 unsolicited fiction mss/month. Approximately 1% of fiction is agented. Length: prefers under 3,000 words. Critiques rejected mss. Frequently recommends markets.
**How to Contact:** Send complete ms with SASE and cover letter with brief bio and published credits. Reports in 2-3 weeks on mss. Publishes ms an average of 0-3 months after acceptance. Sample copy $2. Free guidelines with SASE.
**Payment:** Honorarium plus contributor's copies.
**Terms:** Acquires first rights. Publication copyrighted.
**Tips:** "Review back issues then send us your best appropriate work along with short biographical letter. We prefer 3,000 words or fewer but literary quality is the prime consideration. We are Chicago-based, but have no regional bias."

**NORTH AMERICAN MENTOR MAGAZINE**, John Westburg, 1745 Madison St., Fennimore WI 53809. (608)822-6237. Editor/Publisher: John Westburg. Magazine: 8½x11; 50-80 pages; 50-60 lb offset stock paper; 50 lb (usually) cover stock; illustrations; photos. "We publish short fiction, poetry, essays, including criticism, philosophy, social sciences, humanities in general. We are eclectic, cosmopolitan, and international. Mature readers, most with college education or equivalent. Many are professional writers, professional persons in other fields, including education, law, medicine, religion, engineering, government, military." Quarterly. Open to proposals for special fiction issue. Estab. 1974. Circ. 500 + .
**Needs:** Literary, contemporary, science fiction, and fantasy. "Undesirable fiction would be that which is from the viewpoint of a religious true believer, a political ideologue or person with a loud message or sales pitch. We frown upon raw sex, sensationalism, minority causes, abuse of any race or nation, use of obscenity and vulgarity." Accepts 1-3 mss/issue, 6-8 + mss/year. Receives 250 + unsolicited fiction mss/month. Length: 3,500 words (prefers 1,500). Sometimes recommends other markets.
**How to Contact:** Send complete ms with SASE. Cover letter "not necessary but advisable if letter tells about the author's background." Reports in 6 months. Publishes ms an average of 3-6 months after acceptance. Sample copy $3.
**Payment:** Free author's copies.
**Terms:** Acquires all rights. "We reject manuscripts offering only first North American rights or one-time rights. We must acquire all rights, but we do, upon request, grant permission without charge for publication elsewhere." Publication copyrighted.
**Tips:** "We would consider any kind of fiction that is well-written, well-organized, with a beginning, middle, and ending, good characterization, good description, and reasonable action. We are still looking for a modern Charles Dickens who can combine all those qualities with a keen wit and insight to character. We have yet to find the ideal story, and we are still looking for it, one with clarity, good characterization, description, action, wit, unity, plot, and a good point to it. Modern writers would do well to study the 19th century English short story writers to emulate them in modern or contemporary scenarios. The fiction that writers send to us seems to be a much higher quality of characterization, plot, social and cultural significance, action, etc. than most of what is currently appearing in paperback mass produced and mass marketed books and the popular press." Published new writers within the last year.

**THE NORTH AMERICAN REVIEW**, University of Northern Iowa, Cedar Falls IA 50614. Editor: Robley Wilson, Jr. Theme: quality fiction. Quarterly. Estab. 1815. Circ. 4,100.

**Needs:** "We print quality·fiction of any length and/or subject matter. Excellence is the only criterion." Buys 30-40 mss/year. Does not read fiction between April 1 and January 1. No preferred length.
**How to Contact:** Send complete ms with SASE. Reports in 2-3 months. Sample copy $2.
**Payment:** Approximately $10/printed page. 2 free author's copies. $2 charge for extras.
**Terms:** Pays on acceptance for first North American serial rights.
**Tips:** "We stress literary excellence and read 5,000 manuscripts a year to find an average of 35 stories that we publish. Please *read* the magazine first."

**NORTH COUNTRY ANVIL (II)**, North Country Anvil, Inc. Box 37, Millville MN 55957. (507)798-2366. Editor: Jack Miller. "We publish a variety of material, including articles on lifestyles, social issues, the arts, the environment and fiction. Our audience is made up of people concerned with our themes. Though we include articles from all over the country our readers are mostly in the upper Midwest." Published 4 times/year. Estab. 1972. Circ. 2,000.
**Needs:** Literary, contemporary, historical, humor, regional, and social/political commentary. Accepts 1 ms/issue, 4 mss/year. Receives approximately 10 unsolicited fiction mss each month. Length: 1,000-3,000 words. Critiques rejected mss "when there is time."
**How to Contact:** Send complete ms with SASE. Accepts computer printout submissions. Prefers letter-quality. Reports in 3 months. Sample copy $2.
**Payment:** 3 free author's copies plus 1 year subscription. $2 charge for extras.
**Terms:** Acquires one-time rights. Publication copyrighted.
**Tips:** "Give the reader some new insights and food for thought concerning society or human nature. Address yourself to an intelligent audience, but keep it simple. The *Anvil* likes stories with some social significance or message rather than pure entertainment."

**NORTH DAKOTA QUARTERLY (II)**, University of North Dakota, Box 8237, University Station, Grand Forks ND 58202. (701)777-3321. Editor: Robert W. Lewis. Fiction Editor: Dan Eades. Magazine: 6x9; 200 pages; bond paper; illustrations; photos. Magazine publishing "essays in humanities; some short stories (average 2 per issue); some poetry." University audience. Quarterly. Estab. 1910. Circ. 600.
**Needs:** Contemporary, ethnic, experimental, feminist, historical (general), humor/satire, and literary. Receives 15-20 unsolicited mss/month. Accepts 2 mss/issue; 8 mss/year. Length: 3,000-4,000 words average. Sometimes critiques rejected mss.
**How to Contact:** Send complete ms with SASE. Reports in 3 months. Publishes ms an average of 6-8 months after acceptance. Sample copy $4.
**Payment:** 5 contributor's copies; 20% discount for extras.
**Terms:** Acquires one-time rights. Publication copyrighted.
**Tips:** "Read our recent numbers to see what we're doing. Fiction is an important genre." Published new writers within the last year.

**‡NORTH OF UPSTATE (II, IV)**, Box 220A, R#1, Hammond NY 13646. (315)375-6367. Editor: Maureen Kravac. Fiction Editor: B.J. St. John. Magazine: 7x8½; 45-55 pages; illustrations. "Writers with their roots in the North Country; those having lived in the North Country" for general audience. Quarterly. Plans fiction issue in future. Estab. Oct. 20, 1985. Circ. 500.
**Needs:** Adventure, historical (general), humor/satire, literary, mainstream, men's, regional, senior citizen/retirement, women's, young adult/teen (10-18 years). Receives 20 unsolicited fiction mss/month. Accepts 5 mss/issue. Publishes ms 2-3 months after acceptance. Length: 1,300 words minimum; 2,500 words maximum. Occasionally critiques rejected mss. Recommends other markets.
**How to Contact:** Send complete ms with cover letter. Reports in 6-8 weeks on mss. SASE. Accepts computer printouts including dot-matrix. Sample copy $2. Fiction guidelines free.
**Payment:** Pays in contributor's copies.
**Terms:** Acquires one-time rights. Publication copyrighted.

**NORTH PORTAL (I), Journal of the Joshua Tree Society**, c/o Brice Fialcowitz, 1730 N. Martha Lane, Santa Ana CA 92706. (714)836-1360. Editor: Brice Fialcowitz. Magazine: 5½x9; 44 pages; illustrations; photos. Purpose: "to assist in building a better daily relationship with Christ" for college-educated, religiously-interested audience. Monthly. Estab. 1983. Circ. 500.
**Needs:** Most all subjects with religious slant. Nothing putting down a particular denomination." Will consider Christian erotica if sex is not depicted as demeaning. Receives 1-2 unsolicited fiction mss/month. Accepts 1 ms/issue; 12 mss/year. Publishes short shorts. Length: 500-700 words; "1,000 words if it is excellent. Check with the editor." Always comments on rejected mss. Recommends other markets.
**How to Contact:** Send complete ms with SASE. Reports same day. Photocopied and previously published submissions OK if so advised. Sample copy for 2 first class stamps. Fiction guidelines for legal-sized envelope and 1 first class stamp.
**Payment:** 1 contributor's copy; $1 charge for extras.
**Terms:** Acquires one-time rights on publication.
**Tips:** "Our size and situation make it fairly easy for us to publish beginners. Especially need material on female priests and feminity of God. The editor considers the use of the English language a sacrament—do not abuse it in submissions." Published new writers within the last year.

**NORTHEAST JOURNAL (I, II)**, Box 217, Kingston RI 02881. (401)783-2356. Co-editors: Tina Letcher and Indu Suryanarayan. "A journal concerned with publishing a diverse selection of contemporary literature. The primary focus is on poetry, prose and reviews. Sometimes special issues are published, e.g., women's, Rhode Island poets." Annual. Estab. 1969 (under name of *Harbinger*). Circ. 600.
**Needs:** "Quality." Length: 1,000-3,000 words.
**How to Contact:** Send complete ms with SASE. Reports in 6 months. Sample copy with 10x12 SAE and $1 postage.
**Payment:** 1 free author's copy.

**‡THE NORTHERN NEW ENGLAND REVIEW**, Box 825, Franklin Pierce College, Rindge NH 03461. (603)899-5111. Editor: Michael Terault. Magazine. "The *Review* only publishes material from Northern New England residents (Maine, New Hampshire, and Vermont) or from people with strong ties in the region. We publish quality fiction, poetry, articles, and book reviews. For people who identify with the Northern New England lifestyle. Also, for those who are deeply interested in humanities. A copy is sent to every college library in New England." Annually. Estab. 1973. Circ. 600. brary in New England." Annually. Estab. 1973. Circ. 600.
**Needs:** Confession, contemporary, erotica, ethnic, experimental, fantasy, feminist, historical (general), humor/satire, literary, mainstream, men's, prose, regional, romance, science fiction, translations, women's. "Submissions should have that 'New England' flavor to fit in with the magazine's format. No gay, lesbian fiction and hard-core erotica." Receives 5-10 unsolicited mss/ month. Accepts 3 or 4 mss/issue. Length: 9,000 words average; 5,000 words minimum; 9,000 words maximum. Occasionally comments on rejected mss.
**How to Contact:** Send complete ms. Reports in several weeks on queries; several months on mss. SASE for ms. Photocopied submissions OK. Accepts computer printout submissions. Prefers letter-quality. Sample copy 50¢ and 10x13 SAE with 5 first class stamps.
**Payment:** Pays in 2 contributor's copies; $3.50 charge for extras.
**Terms:** Pays on publication for first rights. Publication copyrighted.
**Tips:** "Today's magazine fiction has more pronounced emphasis on the psychological element, chiefly how man reacts to this confusing, changing world. Characters observe society and then undergo intense self-examination. As long as the submission is well-written and ties in with our

---

 **The double dagger before a listing indicates that the listing is new in this edition. New markets are often the most receptive to freelance contributions.**

northern New England format in a subtle way, we will consider it since a copy of the *Review* is sent to each college library in New England. Submissions dealing with the world of academia will also be considered."

**NORTHWARD JOURNAL (II, IV)**, Penumbra Press, Box 340, Moonbeam, Ontario P0L 1V0 Canada. Editor: John Flood. "A magazine of northern arts which publishes northern (thematically) artwork, poetry, fiction, drama." Quarterly: 8x10; 48 pages; Zephyr Antique said paper; Strathmore cover; illustrations; photos. Estab. 1974. Circ. 2,000.
**Needs:** Literary, ethnic (native peoples). "Note that work must be of the North (Far North)." Buys 6-10 mss/year. Length: 1,500-2,500 words.
**How to Contact:** Send complete ms with biography and SASE (Canadian stamps) or SAE and IRC. Reports in 3 months on mss. Sample copies available. Recommends other markets.
**Payment:** $100 and 1 free author's copy. $5 less 40% discount for extras.
**Terms:** Pays on publication for first North American serial rights.
**Tips:** "Read and know the magazine. Read as much as you write." Published new writers within the year.

**NORTHWEST REVIEW (I, II)**, 369 PLC, University of Oregon, Eugene OR 97403. (503)686-3957. Editor: John Witte. Fiction Editor: Deb Casey. Magazine: 6x9; 180 pages; coated paper; high quality cover stock; illustrations; photos. "A general literary review, featuring poems, stories, essays and reviews, circulated nationally and internationally. For a literate audience in avant-garde as well as traditional literary forms; interested in the important younger writers who have not yet achieved their readership." Published 3 times/year. Estab. 1957. Circ. 1,500.
**Needs:** Literary, contemporary, feminist, translations, and experimental. Accepts 5-10 mss/issue, 20-30 mss/year. Receives approximately 80-100 unsolicited fiction mss each month. Length: "Ms longer than 40 pages is at a disadvantage." Critiques rejected mss "when there is time." Recommends other markets.
**How to Contact:** Send complete ms with SASE. Accepts computer printout submissions. Prefers letter-quality. Reports in 2 months. Sample copy $2.50.
**Payment:** 3 free author's copies. $40% discount.
**Terms:** Acquires first rights. Publication copyrighted.
**Tips:** "Persist. Copy should be clean, double-spaced, with generous margins. Careful proofing for spelling and grammar errors will reduce irksome slowing of editorial process." Mss are rejected because of "weak characters, lack of plot, poor execution." Published new writers within the last year.

**NOSTOC MAGAZINE (II)**, Arts End Books, Box 162, Waban MA 02168. (617)965-2478. Editor: Marshall Brooks. Magazine: size varies; 60 lb book paper; illustrations; photos. Biannually. Estab. 1973. Circ. 500.
**Needs:** "We are open-minded." Receives approximately 15 unsolicited fiction mss each month. Publishes short shorts. Prefers brief word length. Frequently critiques rejected mss and recommends other markets.
**How to Contact:** Query. SASE for ms. Reports in 1 week on queries, 2-3 weeks on mss. Sample copy $2.50.
**Payment:** Free author's copies.
**Terms:** Sends galleys to author. "Copyright; rights revert to author."
**Tips:** "We tend to publish *short* short stories that are precise and lyrical. Recently, we have been publishing *short* short story collections by one author, which are issued as a separate number of the magazine. We are always on the outlook for new material for these small collections. We publish fiction because of the high quality; good writing deserves publication." Published new writers within the last year.

**‡NOTEBOOK: A LITTLE MAGAZINE (II, IV)**, Esoterica Press, Box 26, B43, Los Angeles CA 90026. Editor: Ms. Yoly Zentella. Magazine: 5½x8½; 20-40 pages; bond paper; 90 lb cover stock; illustrations. "We are very interested in receiving intelligently written fiction. Although we have not as yet published any fictional pieces, we are open for submissions as long as they fall into the categories below. *Notebook's* emphasis is on history, culture, literary critique and travel pieces. For ages 25-40 well educated, some academia." Semiannually. Plans special fiction issue. Estab. 1985. Circ. 30.

**Needs:** Ethnic, (focusing especially on Chicano and Latin American pieces), historical (general), humor/satire, literary, regional. "We are planning a special yearly issue that will feature exclusively Chicano and Latin American writers. We are currently accepting manuscripts—fiction and nonfiction." Absolutely no explicit sex or obscenities accepted. Receives approximately 5-6 unsolicited fiction mss/month. Publishes spring and winter. Reading fee $1. Length: 2,000 words average; 2,000 words maximum. Publishes short shorts of 1,500 words. Sometimes critiques rejected mss.

**How to Contact:** Send complete ms with cover letter and (short biography and $1 reading fee) and appropriate size SASE for possible return of ms. Reports in 2 weeks on queries; 2-4 months on mss. SASE for ms. Accepts computer printouts. Sample copy $4. Fiction guidelines for legal size SAE and 1 first class stamp.

**Payment:** 1 free contributor's copy, charges for extras.

**Terms:** Pays 1 copy on publication for first North American serial rights. Publication copyrighted.

**Tips:** "Imagination is a very important part of writing. Fiction exemplifies this as in the short story. Have not published fiction yet due to lack of quality and content."

**NRG**, Skydog Press, 6735 S.E. 78th, Portland OR 97206. Editor: Dan Raphael. Magazine/tabloid: 11x17; 20 pages; electrobrite paper; illustrations; photos. (Varies) for the "educated, creative, curious." Theme is "open-ended, energized, non linear emphasis on language and sounds"; material is "spacial, abstract, experimental." Semiannually. Plans special fiction issue. Estab. 1976. Circ. 400.

**Needs:** Contemporary, experimental, literary, and prose poem. Receives 8 unsolicited mss/month. Accepts 6 mss/issue; 11 mss/year. Length: 2,000 words average; 5,000 words maximum. Occasionally critiques rejected mss.

**How to Contact:** Send complete ms with SASE and cover letter stating where you learned of magazine; 3-5 previous publications (see copy of magazine). Reports in 1 month. Simultaneous and photocopied submissions OK. Accepts computer printout submissions. Publishes ms an average of 1 year after acceptance. Sample copy $1. "Best guideline is sample copy." Fiction guidelines for SASE.

**Payment:** Pays in free contributor's copies only, ½ cover price charge for extras.

**Terms:** Acquires one-time rights.

**Tips:** "I'm trying to get more fiction, but strict in my editorial bias. I don't want it to add up or be purely representational. Energy must abound in the language, or the spaces conjured." Published new writers within the last year.

**THE OHIO JOURNAL (II)**, Department of English, Ohio State University, 164 W. 17th St., Columbus OH 43210. (614)422-4076. Editor: David Citino. Theme: "general interest: fiction, poetry, interviews, book reviews, nonfiction, and photo essays. For an educated audience, knowledgeable in literature and the arts, but not of an academic nature." Biannually. Estab. 1973. Circ. 1,000.

**Needs:** "Any subject." Accepts 2-10 mss/issue. Receives approximately 75 unsolicited fiction mss each month. Does not accept mss in summer. Length: 4,000 words maximum. Critiques rejected mss "when there is time." Sometimes recommends markets.

**How to Contact:** Send complete ms with SASE. Accepts computer printout submissions. Prefers letter-quality. Reports in 2 months. Publishes ms an average of 1-12 months after acceptance. Sample copy $3.

**Payment:** Free author's copies. $3 charge for extras.

**Terms:** "Will reassign rights in exchange for mentioning material first published in *O.J.*" Buys reprints.
**Tips:** Mss are rejected because of "lack of understanding of the short story form, shallow plots, undeveloped characters. Cure: Read as much well-written fiction as possible. Our readers prefer 'psychological' fiction, rather than stories with intricate plots. Each contribution is automatically entered into competition for the annual President's Award of $100 for fiction."

**OHIO RENAISSANCE REVIEW (II)**, Infinity Publications, Box 804, Ironton OH 45638. (614)532-0846. Editor: James R. Pack. Poetry Editor: Ron Houchin. Graphics Editor: Ariyan. Magazine: 7x10; 64 pages; grade 1 offset white paper; color cast cover stock; b&w line art illustrations; b&w photos. Theme: "Material by new and unknown as well as established writers—fiction; experimental, modern, visual poetry; creative photography; surrealistic and visionary art." Readership: Famous people awarded lifetime merit subscriptions for contributions made in the arts, literature, science, etc., that advance new perspectives and promote intellectual renaissance. Quarterly. Plans special fiction issue. Estab. 1984. Circ. 1,000.
**Needs:** Contemporary, psychic/supernatural, science fiction, fantasy, mystery, humor. Accepts 4-6 mss/issue. Length: 500-2,000 words.
**How to Contact:** Send complete ms with SASE and cover letter with bio which includes current activities and publication credits. Reports in 10 weeks. Sample copy $4.
**Payment:** 1 free author's copy, 50% discount for extras; plus $2.50/full printed column; 5¢ a line/partial column.
**Terms:** Acquires first North American serial rights.
**Tips:** "We are looking for writers with 'pizazz and verve' (creative energy and personal integrity), so the clearer and more direct the ms the better. Good English usage is a must. Avoid excessive use of profanities. Be original. Strive for a new perspective. Many of the stories we receive lack a believable plot; in other words the writers neglect to think out their creation and make it concrete. The beginning writers should plan carefully before he writes the first word. Strive to develop a unique personal voice. Avoid falling into the trap of trying to write the way you think you should write." Published new writers within the last year.

**‡THE OHIO REVIEW (II)**, The Ohio Review, Ellis Hall, Ohio University, Athens OH 45701-2979. (614)594-5889. Editor: Wayne Dodd. Magazine: 6x9; 144 pages; Warren Old Style paper; illustrations on cover. "We attempt to publish the best poetry and fiction written today." For all, mainly literary audience. Triannually. Published special fiction issue. Estab. 1971. Circ. 2,000.
**Needs:** Contemporary, experimental, literary. "We lean toward contemporary on all subjects." Receives 150-200 unsolicited fiction mss/month. Accepts 3 mss/issue. Does not read ms June 1-August 31. Publishes ms 6 months after acceptance. Agented fiction: 1%. Critiques rejected mss. Recommends other markets.
**How to Contact:** Query first or send complete ms with cover letter. Reports in 6 weeks on queries; 6 weeks on mss. SASE for query and ms. Photocopied submissions OK. Accepts computer printouts including dot-matrix. Sample copy $4.25. Fiction guidelines free for business size SAE and 1 first class stamp.
**Payment:** Free subscription to magazine, 2 contributor's copies.
**Terms:** Pays on publication for first North American serial rights. Sends galleys to author. Publication copyrighted.
**Tips:** "We feel the short story is an important part of the temporary writing field and value it highly. Read a copy of our publication to see if your fiction is of the same quality. So often people send us work that simply doesn't fit our needs."

**OIKOS (IV), A Journal of Ecology and Community**, 130 Valley Road, Montclair NJ 07042. Editor: Arne Jorgensen. Magazine: 8½x11; 14 pages; illustrations; photos. "*Oikos* exists to present and encourage alternatives to our current society which are sustainable over the long term future. *Oikos* explores visions of the unecological present and possible ecologically sound futures through poetry, short stories and visual art. Through these arts and other writing, *Oikos* will probe the structure of the present unecological world-view and attempt to formulate a new philosophy of humanity and nature." Semiannually. Estab. 1980. Circ. 600.

**Needs:** Comics, experimental, fantasy, humor/satire, prose poem, regional, science fiction, serialized/excerpted novel, and utopian. "No sentimental Bambi-type material, born again, or James Watt inspired eco-fundamentalism. We want to see more mss." Critiques rejected mss "occasionally, when time is plentiful." Occasionally recommends other markets.

**How to Contact:** Send complete ms with SASE. Reports in 2 months. Simultaneous, photocopied and previously published submissions OK. Accepts computer printout submissions. Prefers letter-quality. Current sample $2; past issue $1 sample.

**Payment:** 3 contributor's copies; charge for extras, 2 for $1.50.

**Terms:** Publication copyrighted.

**Tips:** "Order sample copy. Judging from the statement of purpose and other material, send whatever you think will fit in *Oikos*. Send only your best material. Especially like J.G. Ballard for projecting current trends into a future that makes them very obvious. I like his portrayals of ecological disaster for their insights into the mind-set behind ecological ruin. I suggest reading his stories "The Cage of Sand" and "Deep End" to understand the preceding comments. I also like Ursula K. Leguin for imaginative extensions into other times and future places."

**THE OLD RED KIMONO (II)**, Box 1864, Rome GA 30163. (404)295-6312. Editors: Jo Anne Starnes and Johnathan Hershey. Magazine: 7½x10½; 60-70 pages; heavy white stock paper; 10 pt. board cover stock; illustrations; photos. Magazine of short fiction and poetry. Annually. Estab. 1972. Circ. 1,000.

**Needs:** "Quality fiction." Accepts varied number of mss "depending on quality." Does not read June-August. Short fiction only (up to 2,000 words). Prefers short shorts.

**How to Contact:** Send complete ms with SASE. Accepts computer printout submissions. Prefers letter-quality. Reports in 1 month. Sample copy $2.

**Payment:** 2 free contributor's copies.

**Terms:** Acquires first rights. Publication copyrighted.

**Tips:** Published new writers within the last year. "The best thing we can offer a fiction writer is a market for his/her work."

**‡ON THE EDGE (II)**, 32 Churchill Ave., Arlington MA 02174. (617)646-9019. Editor: Cathryn McIntyre. Magazine: 30 average pages; illustrations and photos considered. "Interested in material that deals with contemporary lives, contemporary concerns." Irregular frequency. Estab. 1984.

**Needs:** Contemporary, erotica, experimental, fantasy, feminist, gay, lesbian, literary, mainstream, psychic/supernatural/occult, translations, women's. No sports, western, mystery, romance, etc. Receives 20-30 unsolicited fiction mss/month. Accepts 2-3 mss/issue; up to 6 mss/year. Publishes ms varies (1-6 months) after acceptance. Agented fiction: 2%. Length: 500-2,000 words average. Publishes short shorts. Rarely critiques rejected ms.

**How to Contact:** Send complete ms—cover letter not necessary—sometimes nice if not too long and exhibits some knowledge of *On The Edge* (previous reading). Not to be too full of credits. "I am not that interested in what a writer has published before. I am more interested in what this piece of work is like and what it might offer O.T.E." Reports in 1-8 weeks on queries; 1-8 weeks on mss. SASE for ms. "I may send a response when SASE is not included, but do it regretfully. NO INTERNATIONAL REPLY COUPONS, please. The post office honors them for 22¢ currently, which is not enough. These coupons are not worth it!" Simultaneous and photocopied submissions OK. Accepts computer printouts including dot-matrix. Photocopies and printouts must be readable. Sample copy for $1.50 and 50¢ postage. Fiction guidelines for SASE. Prefers 3x5 card that is self-addressed, stamped, etc.

**Payment:** 2 contributor's copies.

**Terms:** Pays on publication. All rights remain with the authors—no rights purchased. Publication copyrighted.

**Tips:** "I am looking at each submission for the quality of the work, and the subject matter. I am not overly concerned about who the writer is or whether or not he has published before. I prefer not to have any of a writer's 'credits' in front of me as I begin to review his work. Therefore, dislike a cover letter that is packed full of credits. I generally will read the first two sentences that say, 'Hi! Please consider my work . . .' and then go on to the work. It is the subject matter and the point of view that will interest me in a manuscript. Beginners welcome.''

**ORION, A Star Trek Fanzine,** (formerly *Stardate*, Orion Press, c/o Randall Landers, 1529-A Druid Valley Dr., Atlanta GA 30329. (404)325-7261. Editor: Randall Landers. Fiction Editors: Randall Landers, Tim Farley and Linda Marcusky. Magazine of *Star Trek* fiction, nonfiction, poetry, artwork for *Star Trek* fans. Triannually/quarterly. Estab. 1979. Circ. 1,000.
**Needs:** Adventure, comics, erotica, experimental, fantasy, horror, humor/satire, psychic/supernatural/occult, romance (contemporary), science fiction, and suspense/mystery. "No non-*Star Trek* material considered or printed. No homosexual, Kraith, Nu Ormenel, or Kershu." Receives 6-8 unsolicited fiction mss/month. Accepts 4-6 mss/issue, 16-24 mss/year. Length: no preference. Occasionally critiques rejected Star Trek mss "upon request." Sometimes recommends Star Trek markets.
**How to Contact:** Query first. SASE with query, ms. Reports in 3-6 weeks on queries; 3-6 weeks on mss. Publishes ms an average of 3-6 months after acceptance. Simultaneous, photocopied and previously published (after 18 months) submissions OK. Accepts computer printout submissions. Prefers letter-quality. Accepts disc submissions compatible with many formats on 5" disc. Prefers hard copy with disc submission. Sample copy $7.50. Free fiction guidelines with legal-size SAE and 1 first class stamp.
**Payment:** 1 contributor's copy; discount charge for extras.
**Terms:** Acquires one-time rights, not to be reprinted for 6 months after publication in *Orion* press publication. Publication registered with ISSN.
**Tips:** "Be willing to listen to criticism, open-minded to changes, patient for responses. We also publish *Total Entropy*, *Star Trip*, *Regula*, Vol. I and II, *Beyond the Farthest Star* and other publications. Write for information."

**ORO MADRE, Small Press Times,** Glazier Publications, 4429 Gibraltar Dr., Fremont CA 94536. Editor: Loss Glazier. Fiction Editor: Louise Glazier. Magazine. "Material published ranges from contemporary mainstream fiction to experimental. Theme of publication is: new frontiers in writing/richness of human experience/beauty of concisely executed language." Audience: literary, small publishers, universities, experimental writers; creative readers. Quarterly. Estab. 1981. Circ. 500.
**Needs:** "Engaging, cleanly executed fiction that makes a statement, whether experiential (travel, nature, literary) or philosophical (poetic)." Comics, contemporary, erotica, ethnic, experimental, historical (general), humor/satire, literary, mainstream, prose poem, translations. "Style should be unpretentious, crisp; the story cleanly executed. Pieces should be short and direct, unfolding with a snap. Nature pieces, jazz fiction and thought-out surrealism are encouraged. Theme must be strongly expressed." No "self-important, intellectual or 'art for art's sake.' " Receives 30-40 unsolicited mss/month. Accepts 2-3 mss/issue; 8-12 mss/year. Publishes ms 3-6 months after acceptance. Length: 500 words average; 250 words minimum; 1,000 words maximum. Occasionally critiques rejected mss.
**How to Contact:** Query first. SASE. Reports in 2 weeks on queries; 2 months on mss. Sample copy $2.50. Fiction guidelines for #10 SAE and 1 first class stamp.
**Payment:** 1-2 free contributor's copies.
**Terms:** Acquires all rights. Publication copyrighted.
**Tips:** "Keep it short. Make fiction appeal to a wide range of readers (no matter how eclectic the piece): do not tell the story as a simple personal 'cosmic' experience. We encourage beginning fiction writers to submit. We recommend they be willing to: 1) re-write; 2) accept constructive criticism; 3) have something to say and mean what they say; 4) be patient, open-minded and willing to re-examine their work."

**OSIRIS (II),** Box 297, Deerfield MA 01342. Editor: Andrea Moorhead. Fiction Editor: Robert Moorhead. Magazine: 6x9; 32-40 pages; illustrations; photos. "An international journal which prints original texts in English, French, Spanish, and Italian. Material tends to be non-narrative. For an urban intellectual audience. Cuts across cultural boundaries." Semiannually. Estab. 1972. Circ. 1,000.

**Needs:** Literary, contemporary, and experimental fiction in English, Spanish or French. Receives approximately 10 unsolicited fiction mss each month. Length: 1,100-3,000 words. Critiques rejected mss "when there is time." Recommends other markets.

**How to Contact:** Query with SASE and brief bio and publication credits. Accepts computer printout submissions. Reports in 4 weeks. Sample copy $2.

**Payment:** 5 free author's copies. $2 charge for extras.

**Terms:** "Inquire." Publication copyrighted.

**Tips:** "Send piece after piece. Do not be offended by rejection slips." Published new writers within the last year.

**‡OTHER VOICES (II)**, Other Voices, Inc., 820 Ridge Rd., Highland Park IL 60035. (312)831-4684. Editor: Dolores Weinberg. Magazine: 5⅞x9; 168-200 pages; 60 lb paper; coated cover stock; occasional photos. "Original, fresh, diverse stories and novel excerpts" for literate adults. Semiannually. Estab. spring, 1985. Circ. 1,500.

**Needs:** Contemporary, experimental, humor/satire, literary, excerpted novel. No taboos, except ineptitude and murkiness. No fantasy, horror, juvenile, psychic/occult. Receives 30 unsolicited fiction mss/month. Accepts 20-23 mss/issue. Publishes ms sometimes 3-6 months after acceptance. Agented fiction: 50%. Length: 4,000 words average; 1,200 words minimum; 5,000-6,000 words maximum. Also publishes short shorts "if paired together" of 1,000 words. Occasionally critiques rejected mss. Recommends other markets.

**How to Contact:** Send mss with SASE. Cover letter optional, or submit through agent. Reports in 10-12 weeks on mss. SASE. Photocopied submissions OK; no simultaneous submissions or reprints. Accepts computer printouts including dot-matrix. Sample copy $5.70 (includes postage). Fiction guidelines for business-size SAE and 1 first class stamp.

**Payment:** Pays in contributor's copies.

**Terms:** Acquires one-time rights. Publication copyrighted.

**Tips:** "There are so *few* markets for *quality* fiction! We—by publishing 40-45 stories a year—provide new, or established writers a forum for their work. Send us your best voice, your best work, your best best."

**‡OUIJA MADNESS (III)**, Ouija Madness Press, Box 42212, San Francisco CA 94142. Editor: D.A. Smith. Magazine: 8½x11; 90 pages; illustrations; photos. "The wild, the wacky, the insane, contemporary themes appreciated. Make us think." Experimentation and eroticism encouraged; for everyone who thinks. Semiannually. Estab. 1980. Circ. 1,000.

**Needs:** Contemporary, erotica, experimental, gay, horror, humor/satire, lesbian, literary, psychic/supernatural occult, religious/inspirational, science fiction, special interest: sports. No romance, juvenile. Receives 100 unsolicited fiction mss/month; accepts 15 fiction mss/issue. Publishes ms "in a matter of months" after acceptance. Agented fiction: 5%. Length: 5,000 words average. Publishes short stories. Comments on rejected mss. Recommends other markets.

**How to Contact:** Send complete ms with cover letter and SASE. Reports in 2 weeks on queries; 1 month on mss. Simultaneous and photocopied submissions OK. Sample copy $3 with 9x12 SAE and 75¢ postage. Fiction guidelines free for SAE.

**Payment:** Pays $10-100.

**Terms:** Pays on acceptance. Acquires first rights. Publication copyrighted.

**OUTERBRIDGE (II)**, English A-323, The College of Staten Island (CUNY), 715 Ocean Terr., Staten Island NY 10301. (212)390-7654. Editor: Charlotte Alexander. Magazine: 8½x5½; 60 lb white offset paper; 65 lb cover stock. "We are a national literary magazine publishing mostly fiction and poetry. To date, we have had three special focus issues (the 'urban' and the 'rural' experience, 'Southern'), and 2 special 10th anniversary issues. For anyone with enough interest in literature to look for writing of quality and writers on the contemporary scene who deserve attention. There probably is a growing circuit of writers, some academics, reading us by recommendations." Annually. Estab. 1975. Circ. 500-700.

**Needs:** Literary. "No *Reader's Digest* style; that is, very popularly oriented. We like to do an interdisciplinary feature, e.g., literature and music, literature and science. Interested in the experience of war and military." Accepts 8-10 mss/year. Does not read July, August. Publishes short shorts. Length: 10-25 pages. Sometimes recommends other markets.

**How to Contact:** Query. Send complete ms. SASE for query, ms with brief bio. Reports in 2 weeks on queries, 2 months on mss. Sample copy $4 for double annual.

**Payment:** 2 free author's copies. Charges ½ price of current issues for extras to its authors.

**Terms:** Acquires one-time rights. Requests credits for further publication of material used by *OB*.

**Tips:** "Read our publication first. Don't send out blindly; get some idea of what the magazine might want. A *short* personal note with biography is appreciated. Competition is keen. Publishing fiction is how we started, as a literary mag devoted to good stories and poems." Published new writers within the last year.

**OVERTONE SERIES (II), Quarterly**, Overtone Press, 4421 Chestnut St., #3, Philadelphia PA 19104. (215)386-4279. Editor: Beth Brown. Magazine. Quarterly.

**Needs:** Contemporary, erotica, ethnic, experimental, feminist/lesbian, gay, historical, literary, mainstream, prose poem, serialized/excerpted novel, translations, and women's. Receives 5 unsolicited fiction mss/month. Accepts 5 mss/issue; 20 mss/year. Charges $5 for a reading fee. Length: 5,000 words minimum; 20,000 words maximum; 15,000 words average. Occasionally critiques rejected mss.

**How to Contact:** Query or send complete ms with SASE. Simultaneous, photocopied and previously published submissions OK. Reports in 1 month on queries; 6 weeks on mss. Sample copy for $2 with 8½x11 SAE and 75¢ postage. Fiction guidelines free for SASE.

**Payment:** 5 free contributor's copies; $1.50 charge for extras.

**Terms:** Rights revert to author. Publication copyrighted.

**OYEZ REVIEW (I, II)**, 430 S. Michigan Ave., Chicago IL 60605. (312)341-2017. Editor: Helen Forsythe. Magazine: 8½x5½; 91 pages; b&w camera ready illustrations; b&w camera ready photos. Looking for "what is fresh and good" for Chicago audience. Annually. Estab. 1967. Circ. 500.

**Needs:** Contemporary, experimental, feminist, gay, lesbian, literary, prose poem, and regional. No "formula stories, sentimental reminiscences, macho tales of urban violence, etc." Receives 5 unsolicited mss/month. Accepts 2-5 mss/issue. Length: "about 10 pages, double-spaced."

**How to Contact:** Send complete ms with SASE. Reports in 3 months on ms. Photocopied submissions OK. Sample copy $4.

**Payment:** 2 contributor's copies.

**Terms:** Acquires one-time rights on publication. Publication copyrighted.

**Tips:** "*Oyez* encourages imaginative fiction, good diologue, good characterization. Because our magazine is small, and we have more poetry than fiction, we need/want *good*, but short fiction. We are interested in all *writers* (seeing what all writers can do) not just previously published writers."

**PACIFIC REVIEW (II)**, Dept. of English and Comparative Lit., San Diego State University, San Diego CA 92182-0295. Contact: Editor. Magazine: 5½x8½; 50 pages; book stock paper; paper back, extra heavy cover stock; illustrations, photos. "There is no designated theme. We publish high-quality fiction, poetry, and familiar essays: academic work meant for, but not restricted to, an academic audience." Biannually. Estab. 1974. Circ. 1,000.

---

 *When I say 'work' I only mean writing. Everything else is just odd jobs.*

*—Margaret Laurence* 99

**Needs:** "We do not restrict or limit our fiction in any way other than quality. We are interested in all fiction, from the very traditional to the highly experimental. Acceptance is determined by the quality of submissions." Does not read June-August. Publishes short shorts. No preferred length.
**How to Contact:** Send original ms with SASE. Reports in 2-4 months on mss. Sample copy $2.
**Payment:** 2 author's copies.
**Terms:** "First serial rights are *Pacific Review*'s. All other rights revert to author. Copyrighted.
**Tips:** "Send us mss that will trigger paroxysms of glee, fascination, terror, revulsion, transcendence: the point being, we want fiction which produces striking effects. Rattle our sensibilities. Give us language that glows and bleeds and explodes. Most of our published works are fiction and will be so in the future. We continually struggle to help fiction writers reach publication. Above all write a good beginning: one that starts fast, bringing the reader right into the 'world' of the story." Published new writers within the last year.

**PAINTED BRIDE QUARTERLY (II)**, Painted Bride Art Center, 230 Vine St., Philadelphia PA 19106. (215)925-9914. Literary magazine: 6x9; 48-64 pages; illustrations; photos. Quarterly. Estab. 1975. Circ. 500.
**Needs:** Contemporary, ethnic, experimental, feminist, gay, lesbian, literary, prose poem, and translations. Receives 10 unsolicited mss/month. Accepts 2 mss/issue; 8 mss/year. Length: 3,000 words average; 5,000 words maximum. Publishes short shorts. Occasionally critiques rejected ms.
**How to Contact:** Send complete ms. Reports in 3 weeks-3 months. SASE. Accepts computer printout submissions. Prefers letter-quality. Sample copy $3.
**Payment:** 2 contributor's copies.
**Terms:** Acquires first North American serial rights on publication. Publication copyrighted.
**Tips:** "We want quality in whatever—we hold experimental work to as strict standards as anything else. Many of our readers write fiction; most of them enjoy a good reading. We hope to be an outlet for quality. A good story gives, first, enjoyment to the reader. We've seen a good many of them lately. and we've published the best of them." Published new writers within the last year.

**THE PALE FIRE REVIEW**, Arrant Press, 162 Academy Ave., Providence RI 02908. Editors: Catherine Reed and Steven Strang. Magazine of fiction, poetry, satire, parts-of-novels, novellas, plays, nonfiction. Any subject matter, any form, drawings and cartoons. Semiannually. Estab. 1980. Circ. 400.
**Needs:** Contemporary, ethnic, experimental, fantasy, feminist, humor/satire, literary, mainstream, prose poem, psychic/supernatural, science fiction, serialized/excerpted novel, suspense/mystery, and women's. "As far as genre fiction is concerned, we're interested in mss which use the conventions for literary purposes." Receives 50 unsolicited fiction mss/month. Accepts 7-10 mss/issue; 20 mss/year. Length: 3,000-6,000 words average.
**How to Contact:** Send complete ms with SASE. Simultaneous and photocopied submissions OK. Accepts computer printout submissions. Prefers letter-quality. Reports in 2-3 weeks on mss. Sample copy for $5.50.
**Payment:** 1 free contributor's copy; $5.50 charge for extras.
**Terms:** Acquires first North American serial rights. Publication copyrighted.
**Tips:** "Have a concern for quality (style and form as well as content). Avoid careless/indiscriminate obscenity that's meant to be merely attention-getting rather than integral to the work. Avoid polemics. We'd like to see more fiction of all types, but please submit only one story at a time."

**PANDORA (II)**, Empire Books, Box 625, Murray KY 42071-0625. Editor: Jean Lorrah. Fiction Editor: Susan Ross Moore. Magazine: 8½x11; 36 pages; offset paper; heavyweight offset cover stock; illustrations; rarely photos. Magazine for science fiction and fantasy readers. Published 2 times/year. Estab. 1978. Circ. 1,000.
**Needs:** Fantasy, science fiction, and sword and sorcery. "Nothing X-rated. Unless the author created the universe, she/he should not send us stories in that universe." Receives 80 unsolicited fiction mss/month. Buys 5-6 mss/issue, 10-15 mss/year. Length: 200 words minimum; 5,000

words maximum (except controversial stories may be longer); 3,000 words average. Occasionally critiques rejected mss. Recommends other markets.
**How to Contact:** Send complete ms with SASE. Photocopied and previously published submissions, if substantially revised, OK. Accepts computer printout submissions. Prefers letter-quality. Reports in 6 weeks on mss. Publishes ms an average of 3-12 months after acceptance. Sample copy $3.50. Free fiction guidelines with SASE.
**Payment:** 1¢/word and 1 contributor's copy.
**Terms:** Pays on acceptance for first North American serial rights or one-time rights on rewritten previously published mss. Sends galleys to author. Publication copyrighted.
**Tips:** "We try not to use form letters and are willing to help a writer do rewriting if an idea intrigues us. We're interested in both characters and ideas. We like clear images and we particularly appreciate problem-solving stories." Published new writers within the last year.

**PANGLOSS PAPERS,** Pangloss Foundation, Box 18917, Los Angeles CA 90018. Editor: Bard Dahl. Fiction Editor: Al Schoenberg. Magazine of "satire for socially aware book readers." Quarterly. Estab. 1982. Circ. 600.
**Needs:** Experimental, humor/satire, and literary. No religious, slick, or commercial fiction. Receives 12 unsolicited mss/month. Accepts 2-3 mss/issue; 8 mss/year. Length: 3,000-4,000 words average. Occasionally critiques rejected mss.
**How to Contact:** Send complete ms. Reports in 1 month. SASE. Simultaneous, photocopied and previously published submissions OK. Accepts computer printout submissions. Publishes ms an average of 1-3 months after acceptance. Sample copy $2.
**Payment:** 2 free contributor's copies; $1 charge for extras.
**Terms:** Acquires one-time rights.
**Tips:** "Question authority. People seem more aware that every magazine has its own slant and try to target for that."

**PARABOLA (III),** The Society for the Study of Myth and Tradition, 150 5th Ave., New York NY 10011. (212)924-0004. Editor: Lorraine Kisly. Fiction Editor: Jeff Zaleski. "Mythology, folklore, comparative religion—stories, parables, fairytales retold, original fiction, poetry, translations. We have an open cross-cultured, intelligent but not scholarly approach. Audience: educated, professional, informed book readers interested in stories, myths, folklore, psychology, comparative religion and the arts." Quarterly. Estab. 1976. Circ. 16,000.
**Needs:** Literary, contemporary, men's, women's, and translations. No humor, romance, erotica, science fiction, western, inspirational, gothic, or horror. Buys 5 mss/issue. Receives approximately 50 unsolicited fiction mss each month. Approximately 1% of fiction is agented. Length: 1,000-5,000 words.
**How to Contact:** Send complete ms with SASE. Reports in 2 months. Publishes ms an average of 2-3 months after acceptance. Sample copy $5.50. Free guidelines.
**Payment:** $50-200.
**Terms:** Pays on publication for first rights, second serial rights, one-time rights. Occasionally buys reprints. Publication copyrighted.
**Tips:** "Read previous issues to understand our flavor and direction. Most rejected mss are not related to subject matter set forth in guidelines."

**THE PARIS REVIEW (III),** 45-39 171st Place, Flushing NY 11358. (212)539-7085. Editor: George A. Plimpton. Managing Editor: Jeanne McCullock. "Fiction and poetry of superlative quality, whatever the genre, style or mode. Our contributors include the most prominent, as well as little-known and previously unpublished writers. Recent issues have included the work of Raymond Carver, Reinaldo Arenas, Stephen Dixon, James Fetler, Bart Midwood, Helen Chasin, Peter Handke, C.W. Gusewelle, Thom Gunn, Jerome Charyn, Phyllis Janowitz, Andre Dubus, Frank Bidart, Cynthia Koestler, E.L. Doctorow, and Philip Levine. 'The Art of Fiction' interview series includes the most important contemporary writers discussing their own work and the craft of writing in general."

**Needs:** Serious, intense, committed work of boldness and originality, combining excellence of form and content. Buys 2-3 mss/issue. Receives several hundred unsolicited fiction mss each month. No preferred length. Also publishes short shorts. Critiques rejected mss "when there is time." Recommends other markets.

**How to Contact:** Send complete ms with SASE. Accepts computer printout submissions. Prefers letter-quality. Reports in 3 months on ms. Sample copy $6. Submit to *Paris Review*, 541 E. 72nd St., New York NY 10021.

**Payment:** $100-500. 2 free author's copies. Regular charge for extras.

**Terms:** Pays on publication for first North American serial rights. Sends galleys to author. Publication copyrighted.

**Tips:** "Electricity, intensity, the unmistakable roundedness of a fully-realized work of art are what we are seeking. *The Paris Review* has the widest circulation of all the small presses. We are devoted to helping talented, original writers find larger audiences. The Aga Khan Fiction Prize is awarded annually to the best piece of previously unpublished fiction by a relatively unknown writer." Published new writers within the last year.

**PARTISAN REVIEW**, Partisan Review, Inc. (III), 141 Bay State Rd., Boston MA 02215. (617)353-4260. Editor: William Phillips. Executive Editor: Edith Kurzweil. Magazine: 6x9; 160 pages; 40 lb paper; 60 lb cover stock. Theme is of world literature and contemporary culture: fiction, essays and poetry with emphasis on the arts and political and social commentary, for the general intellectual public; scholars. Quarterly. Estab. 1934. Circ. 8,000.

**Needs:** Contemporary, experimental, literary, prose poem, regional, and translations. Receives 50 unsolicited fiction mss/month. Buys 2 mss/issue; 8 mss/year. Length: open. Publishes short shorts.

**How to Contact:** Send complete ms with SASE and cover letter with past credits. Photocopied submissions OK. Accepts computer printout submissions. Prefers letter-quality. Reports in 4 months on mss. Sample copy for $4.50.

**Payment:** Pays $25-200; 1 free contributor's copy.

**Terms:** Pays on publication for first rights. Publication copyrighted.

**PASSAGES NORTH (II)**, Wm. Bonifas Fine Arts Center, Escanaba MI 49829. (906)786-3833. Editor: Elinor Benedict. Tabloid: 13½x11; 24 pages; white uncoated paper; illustrations; photos. "The purpose of *Passages North* is two-fold: To stimulate and recognize writing of high quality in the Northern Michigan and Upper Midwest region and to bring to the same region writing of high quality from other parts of the nation and beyond." Readership: general and literary. Semiannually. Estab. 1979. Circ. 2,000.

**Needs:** Short fiction. "High quality is our aim. Subjects and genre are open. No excerpts of novels, unless they stand alone in a coherent way. No 'pop' or formula stories." Accepts 6-8 mss/year. Length: 300-2,000 words. Critiques rejected mss "when there is time." Occasionally recommends markets.

**How to Contact:** Send complete ms with SASE and brief letter of previous publications, awards, education. Reports in 3 weeks to several months on mss. Publishes ms an average of 3-6 months after acceptance. Sample copy $1.50. Guidelines for legal-size SASE.

**Payment:** 3 free author's copies. $1 charge for extras. Occasional honoraria.

**Terms:** Copyrighted; rights revert to author on publication. Buys reprints only by request of featured writers with interviews.

**Tips:** "Be aware of what is happening in contemporary poetry and fiction. Strive for writing that makes readers see, feel, imagine, and experience. The first page must inspire interest and confidence in what the writer is saying. Don't send mss without extensive crafting and revision. We're not looking for rough work." Published new writers within the last year.

**PASSION FOR INDUSTRY (I, II)**, Box 1252, Athens OH 45701. Editor-in-Chief: Joseph Allgren. Fiction Editor: James Riley. Magazine: 5½x8½; approximately 30-40 pages; "normal" weight paper; heavy cover stock; illustrations. "For intelligent human beings." Semiannually. Estab. 1984.

**Needs:** Adventure, confession, contemporary, erotica, ethnic, experimental, fantasy, feminist, gay, historical, horror, humor/satire, lesbian, literary, prose poem, science fiction, serialized/excerpted novel, suspense/mystery, and translations—"just about anything. We prefer original voices and innovative styles but avoid flashiness for its own sake." Accepts 1-2 mss/issue; 2-4 mss/year. Length: under 5,000 words. Critiques rejected ms "only if we really liked it."
**How to Contact:** Send complete ms. Reports in 3 weeks. SASE. Photocopied submissions OK. Accepts computer printout submissions. Prefers letter-quality. Sample copy $1.50. Fiction guidelines for SASE.
**Payment:** 2 contributor's copies; $1 charge for extras.
**Terms:** Acquires first rights; rights revert to author. Publication copyrighted.
**Tips:** "We are committed to the *word*. We are interested only in writers who want to produce literature; if you are interested in fame, money or groupies, look elsewhere." Published new writers within the year.

**THE PEGASUS REVIEW (I IV)**, Box 134, Flanders NJ 07836. (201)927-0749. Editor: Art Bounds. Magazine: 5½x8½; 6-8 pages; special stock paper; special cover stock; illustrations. "Our magazine is a bimonthly, done entirely in calligraphy, illustrated and each issue is based on a specific theme for an audience appreciative of quality work." Plans special fiction issue. Estab. 1980. Circ. 125.
**Needs:** Humor/satire, literary, prose poem, and religious/inspirational. Themes for 1986-87: January/February, Courage; March/April, dreams; May/June, individualism; July/August, America; September/October, memory; November/December, Christmas. Send "nothing that is in bad taste." Receives 30 unsolicited mss/month. Accepts 6 mss/year. Publishes short shorts 3-3½ pages; 500 words. Occasionally critiques rejected ms. Themes are subject to change throughout the year so query if in doubt. Recommends other markets.
**How to Contact:** Send complete ms. SASE. Cover letter with author's background and full name—no initials. Photocopied submissions OK. Accepts computer printout submissions. Sample copy $1 and SAE. Fiction guidelines for SAE.
**Payment:** 2 contributor's copies.
**Terms:** Acquires one-time rights on publication. Publication copyrighted.
**Tips:** "Study the classics. They achieved that privilege for a reason: durable quality. However, do not overlook our good contemporary writers. Structure, plot and brevity are the things that will catch the reader's eye." Published new writers within the last year.

**PEMBROKE MAGAZINE (I, II)**, Box 60, Pembroke State University, Pembroke NC 28372. (919)521-4214, ext. 433. Editor: Shelby Stephenson. Fiction Editor: Stephen Smith. Magazine: 10x9; 225 pages; illustrations; photos. Magazine of poems and stories plus literary essays. Annually. Estab. 1969. Circ. 500.
**Needs:** Open. Receives 40 unsolicited mss/month. Publishes short shorts. Length: open. Occasionally critiques rejected mss. Recommends other markets.
**How to Contact:** Send complete ms. Reports immediately to 3 months. SASE. Accepts computer printout submissions. Prefers letter-quality. Sample copy $3 and 10x9 SAE.
**Payment:** 1 contributor's copy.
**Terms:** Publication copyrighted.
**Tips:** "Write with an end for *writing*, not publication. The publication, believe it or not, will be—will out—will come about—! *Write* of course, be aware of others' writing mainly—unite." Published new writers within the last year.

**‡PENNSYLVANIA REVIEW**, University of Pittsburgh, 526 C.L./English Dept., Pittsburgh PA 15260. (412)624-0026. Editor: Ellen Darion. Magazine of fiction, poetry, nonfiction, interviews, reviews novel excerpts, long poems for literate audience. Semiannually. Estab. 1985. Circ. 1,000.
**Needs:** Ethnic, experimental, feminist, gay, humor/satire, lesbian, literary, prose poem, regional, translations, women's. "High quality!" Receives 50 unsolicited fiction mss/month. Accepts

3-5 mss/issue; 6-10 mss/year. Length: 5,000 maximum words for prose. Comments on rejected mss "rarely and only if we've had some interest."
**How to Contact:** Send complete ms. Reports in 1 week on queries; 6-8 weeks on ms. SASE for ms. Photocopied submissions OK. Accepts computer printout submissions. Prefers letter-quality. Sample copy $5. Fiction guidelines for #10 SAE and 1 first class stamp.
**Payment:** $5 page/prose; 1 contributor's copy.
**Terms:** Pays on publication for first North American serial rights. Publication copyrighted.
**Tips:** Read sample copy before submitting.

**PERMAFROST (II), A Literary Journal**, Permafrost, c/o University of Alaska, English Dept., Fairbanks AL 99701. (907)474-6452. Editors: R.H. Ober, A. Culhane. Magazine: 5½x8; 90 pages; good quality paper; illustrations; photos. Magazine of "quality, contemporary fiction, poetry, essays for intelligent readers, small press audiences, writers, educators." Published irregularly. Estab. 1976. Circ. 250.
**Needs:** Adventure, contemporary, erotica, ethnic, experimental, fantasy, feminist, gay, historical (general), horror, humor/satire, lesbian, literary, prose poem, psychic/supernatural/occult, science fiction, translations, and western. No "commercial, formula writing." Receives 10-20 unsolicited mss/month. Accepts 5-6 mss/issue; 10-12 mss/year. Does not read in summer. Length: 2,500-5,000 words average; 5,000 words maximum. Also publishes short shorts of 2-10 pages. Occasionally critiques rejected mss.
**How to Contact:** Send complete ms. Reports in 2 months. SASE. Photocopied submissions OK. Accepts computer printout submissions. Prefers letter-quality. Sample copy $5.
**Payment:** Pays in contributor's copies only.
**Terms:** All rights to author. Publication copyrighted.
**Tips:** "Push the boundaries of the art; captivate, educate, enchant us. Pay attention to detail—and to your market. If a publication has a limited number of pages, don't submit long pieces." Published new writers within the last year.

**THE PHOENIX**, Morning Star Press, RFD Haydenville MA 01039. Editor: James Cooney. Theme: "A literary magazine. Subscriptions come from public libraries, universities, colleges, and individuals. Quarterly. Estab. 1938. Letterpress printing; sewn binding; issues of 352 to 384 pages. Sample issue $3. Special rates for those who cannot afford regular rates. Free subscriptions to prison libraries, state hospitals and mental institutions.
**Needs:** Stories, diaries, and serialized novels. No length limitations. Complete contents of each issue covered by the *Arts & Humanities Citation Index*.
**How to Contact:** Send complete ms with SASE. Reports within 1-4 weeks.
**Terms:** Acquires copyright for protection of published materials but arranges permission for author to reprint in collections, anthologies, etc. Publication copyrighted.

**PIEDMONT LITERARY REVIEW (II)**, Piedmont Literary Society, Box 3656, Danville VA 24543. (804)793-0956. Editor: David Craig. "The theme of our publication is human expression through the written word. We publish short stories, essays, and articles. Our publication is directed toward all lovers of literature regardless of their stature in life." Quarterly. Estab. 1976. Circ. 400.
**Needs:** Literary, contemporary, science fiction, fantasy, humor, psychic, and regional. Accepts 8-12 mss/year. Receives approximately 50-100 unsolicited fiction mss each month. Length: 2,000 words maximum. Will exceed maximum if story is of highest quality. Critiques rejected mss "when there is time." Recommends other markets.
**How to Contact:** Send complete ms with SASE. Reports in 3 months on mss. Publishes ms an average of 3-4 months after acceptance. Sample copy $2. Guidelines for legal-size SASE.
**Payment:** 1 free author's copy. $2.50 charge for extras.
**Terms:** Acquires one-time rights. Seldom buys reprints.
**Tips:** "I have none that would guarantee publication. 'Write the truest sentence you know' as Hemingway said. Be honest. Use the tools of fiction. An experience is not a story. To me, characters are what make a story. If I believe the characters, the plot will naturally follow."

**PIG IN A PAMPHLET (II)**, (formerly *Pig in a Poke*), Pig In A Poke Press, 522½ N. Center St., Corry PA 16407-1206. Phone: (814)664-9404. Editor: Harry Calhoun. Magazine: 4¼x5½; 8-12 pages; 40-60 lb paper; varied cover stock; line drawings. "Literary review interested chiefly in emotionally intense but coherent poetry; also takes *very* short fiction/articles. Definitely not sewing-circle stuff, but with wide appeal for a diverse audience." Quarterly. Estab. 1982. Circ. 500.
**Needs:** Contemporary, erotica, experimental, fantasy, humor/satire, prose poem, science fiction. No long fiction, religious themes, children's stories. Receives 50-100 unsolicited mss/month. Accepts 2 mss/issue; 8-10 mss/year. Publishes short shorts of less than 600 words. "I love well-written prose poems." Length: 1,000 words maximum. Occasionally critiques rejected mss. "It pretty much comes with the package—just ask." Frequently recommends other markets.
**How to Contact:** Query first or send complete ms. Reports in 2 weeks. SASE. Simultaneous (if so advised) and photocopied submissions OK; "we prefer unpublished submissions but have taken (and will take) previously published on occasion." Accepts computer printout submissions. Prefers letter-quality. Sample copy $1.00. Fiction guidelines for #10 SAE and 1 first class stamp.
**Payment:** 2 free contributor's copies.
**Terms:** Acquires one-time rights. "All rights revert immediately back to author."
**Tips:** "Read the magazine—it's better than any guidelines I can give you. *Pig* tries to take some of the pomposity out of literary magazine writing—no stuffed shirts, please." Published new writers within the last year.

**PIG IRON (II)**, Pig Iron Press, Box 237, Youngstown OH 44501. (216)744-2258. Editor: Jim Villani. Fiction Editor: Rose Sayre. "Contemporary literature by new and experimental writers. For college-educated young adults." Annually. Estab. 1975. Circ. 1,000.
**Needs:** Literary, psychological, and humor. No mainstream. Buys 1-15 mss/issue; 2-30 mss/year. Receives approximately 50 unsolicited fiction mss each month. Length: 10,000 words maximum.
**How to Contact:** Send complete ms with SASE. Accepts computer printout submissions. Reports in 6 months. Sample copy $2.50.
**Payment:** $2/printed page. 2 free author's copies. $3 charge for extras.
**Terms:** Pays on publication for first North American serial rights.
**Tips:** "Looking for works that do not ignore psychological development in character and plot/action." Mss are rejected because of "lack of new ideas and approaches. Writers need to work out interesting plot/action and setting/set. Send SASE for current themes list. Interested in humorous pieces through July 1986 for special anthology."

**THE PIKESTAFF FORUM (II)**, Box 127, Normal IL 61761. (309)452-4831. Editors: Robert D. Sutherland, James Scrimgeour, James McGowan, and Curtis White. Tabloid: 11½x17½; 40 pages; news print paper; illustrations; photos. "*The Pikestaff Forum* is a general literary magazine publishing poetry, prose fiction, drama. Readership: "General literary with a wide circulation in the small press world. Readers are educated (but not academic) and have a taste for excellent serious fiction." Published irregularly—"whenever we have sufficient quality material to warrant an issue." Estab. 1977. Circ. 1,000.
**Needs:** Literary and contemporary with a continuing need for good short stories or novel excerpts. We welcome traditional and experimental works from established and nonestablished writers. We look for writing that is clear, concise, and to the point; contains vivid imagery and sufficient concrete detail; is grounded in lived human experience; contains memorable characters and situations; and lifts us right out of our chairs. No confessional self-pity or puffery; self-indulgent first or second drafts; sterile intellectual word games or five-finger exercises or slick formula writing, genre-pieces that do not go beyond their form (westerns, mysteries, gothic, horror, science fiction, swords-and-sorcery fantasy), commercially-oriented mass-market stuff, violence for its own sake, or pornography (sexploitation)." Accepts 1-4 mss/issue. Receives approximately 15-20 unsolicited fiction mss each month. Length: from 1 paragraph to 4,000 or 5,000 words. Critiques rejected mss "when there is time."
**How to Contact:** Query. Send complete ms. SASE for query, ms. Accepts computer printout

submissions. Prefers letter-quality. Reports in 3 weeks on queries, 3 months on mss. Publishes ms up to 1 year after acceptance. Sample copy $2.
**Payment:** 3 free author's copies. Cover price less 50% discount for extras.
**Terms:** Acquires first rights. Copyright remains with author. Publication copyrighted.
**Tips:** "We are highly selective, publishing only 3% of the stories that are submitted for consideration. Read other authors with an appreciative and critical eye; don't send out work prematurely; develop keen powers of observation and a good visual memory; get to know your characters thoroughly; don't let others (editors, friends, etc.) define or 'determine' your sense of self-worth; be willing to learn; outgrow self-indulgence. Develop discipline. Show, don't tell; and leave some work for the reader to do. Write for the fun of it (that way there's a sure return for the investment of time and effort). If you're writing serious fiction, don't expect to get rich. If money should come, that's a bonus. Always write to achieve the best quality you can; be honest with yourself, your potential readers, and your story. Learn to become your own best editor: Know when you've done well, and when you haven't done as well as you can. Remember: there's a lot of competition for the available publication slots, and editorial bias is always a factor in what gets accepted for publication. Develop a sense of humor about the enterprise."

**THE PILGRIM WAY (I, IV),** 012 Oak Ave. NE, Box 277, Cass Lake MN 56633. (218)335-6190. Editor: James E. Johnston. Magazine "for ethnic Mayflower Pilgrims and those who confess that there are strangers and Pilgrims on earth." Quarterly. Estab. 1957. Circ. 500.
**Needs:** Historical (general), juvenile, religious/inspirational, preschool, supernatural, regional, romance (young adult), and senior citizen. "Separatist, against religious monopoly, land monopoly, wealth monopoly, abortions, euthanasia, liquor." Length: 500 words minimum; 1,000 words maximum.
**How to Contact:** Query first. Reports in 3 weeks on queries. Sample copy $1.
**Payment:** 25 contributor's copies.
**Terms:** Pays on publication for one-time rights.
**Tips:** "Write about the Pilgrims, past or present with geneological tracings, especially of the Browns. (Editor's mother was a Brown). Also write against stereotyping, abortion, and discriminating against and segregating seniors."

**PINCHPENNY (I),** Pinchpenny Press, 4851 Q St., Sacramento CA 95819. (916)451-3042. Editor: Tom Miner. Magazine for literate general public. "We publish 40-44 pages of hardhitting contemporary poetry. Each issue is planned as a unit, so that it can stand on its own as a collection, yet all issues coalesce into a continuous 'book.' Often issues are arranged around an individual writer or group of writers with interviews, photos, and biographical sketches." Quarterly. Estab. 1979. Circ. 200-300.
**Needs:** Condensed novel, prose poem, and "tiny" stories. "Prose poems are a continuing interest. We do an issue each year devoted to the genre with annotated bibliography, etc. We also do frequent theme issues." Length: usually 100 lines maximum. Occasionally critiques rejected mss.
**How to Contact:** Send complete mss. Reports on rejections in 1 week; all others in 1 month. SASE. Simultaneous and photocopied submissions OK. Sample copy $2.
**Payment:** 1 free contributor's copy/page published.
**Terms:** All rights revert to author. Publication copyrighted.
**Tips:** "We especially welcome new and unknown writers."

**‡THE PIPE SMOKER'S EPHEMERIS (I, II, IV),** The Universal Coterie of Pipe Smokers, 20-37 120 St., College Point NY 11356. Editor: Tom Dunn. Magazine 8½x11; 54-66 pages; offset paper and cover; illustrations; photos. Pipe smoking and tobacco theme for general and professional audience. Irregular quarterly. Estab. 1964.
**Needs:** Historical (general), humor/satire, literary, special interest—pipe smoking-related. Publishes ms up to 1 year after acceptance. Length: 2,500 words average; 5,000 words maximum. Also publishes short shorts. Occasionally critiques rejected mss.
**How to Contact:** Send complete ms with cover letter. Reports in 2 weeks on mss. Simultaneous,

photocopied submissions and reprints OK. Accepts computer printouts including dot-matrix. Sample copy for 8½x11 SAE and 6 first class stamps.
**Terms:** Acquires one-time rights. Publication copyrighted.

**PLAINSWOMAN, INC.**, Plainswoman, Inc., Box 8027, Grand Forks ND 58202. (701)777-8043. Editor: Elizabeth Hampsten. Fiction Editor: Emily Johnson. "A feminist, informational publication which publishes some fiction and poetry." Readership: "Mainly women of the Plains area who want information concerning national and regional women's issues." 10 times/year (February and August excluded). Estab. 1977. Circ. 540.
**Needs:** Feminist and regional. Publishes 1 ms/month.
**How to Contact:** Send complete ms with SASE. Accepts computer printout submissions. Prefers letter-quality. Reports in 2 weeks-3 months. Sample copy $2.
**Terms:** Acquires all rights. Publication copyrighted.
**Tips:** "Rejected manuscripts are sometimes too long, sometimes inappropriate, occasionally not well-crafted."

**‡PLAZA (II), Revista De Literatura**, Plaza Editors, 201 Boylston Hall, Harvard Univ., Cambridge MA 02130. Editor: Erik Canayd, et al. Short story, poetry and criticism *in Spanish* for university, literary and general public. Semiannualy. Estab. 1978. Circ. 350.
**Needs:** Contemporary, ethnic, experimental, literary, regional. Manuscripts in Spanish only. Receives 2 unsolicited fiction mss/month. Accepts 2 mss/issue; 4 mss/year. Does not read ms in summer. Publishes ms 6 months-1 year after acceptance. Length: 10,000 words maximum.
**How to Contact:** Query first or send complete ms with cover letter. SASE for query. No manuscripts returned. Simultaneous, photocopied and reprint submissions OK. Accepts computer printouts including dot-matrix.
**Payment:** Contributor's copies.
**Terms:** Pays on publication for one-time rights. Publication copyrighted.

**PLOUGHSHARES (II)**, Ploughshares, Inc., Dept. M, Box 529, Cambridge MA 02139. (617)926-9875. Editor: DeWitt Henry. "Our theme is new writing (poetry, fiction, criticism) that addresses contemporary adult readers who look to fiction and poetry for help in making sense of themselves and of each other." Quarterly. Estab. 1971. Circ. 4,100.
**Needs:** Literary. "No genre (science fiction, detective, gothic, adventure, etc.), popular formula or commercial fiction whose purpose is to entertain rather than to illuminate." Buys 20 + mss/year. Receives approximately 300-400 unsolicited fiction mss each month. Length: 2,000-6,000 words. Sometimes recommends markets.
**How to Contact:** "Query for best time to submit and examine a sample issue." SASE for query, ms. Reports in 3 weeks on queries, 3 months on mss. Sample copy $5.
**Payment:** $5/page to $50 maximum, plus copies. Offers 50% kill fee for assigned ms not published.
**Terms:** Pays on publication for first North American serial rights. Publication copyrighted.
**Tips:** "Be familiar with our fiction issues, fiction by our writers and by our various editors (e.g., Rosellen Brown, Tim O'Brien, Jay Neugeboren, Jayne Anne Phillips) and more generally acquaint yourself with the best short fiction currently appearing in the literary quarterlies, and the annual prize anthologies (*Pushcart Prize, O'Henry Awards, Best American Short Stories*). Don't, in submitting, look for help in writing. The professional question is: Can you use this, yes or no? Also realistically consider whether the work you are submitting is as good as or better than—in your own opinion—the work appearing in the magazine you're sending to. What is the level of competition? And what is its volume (in our case, we accept about 1 ms in 200). Never send 'blindly' to a magazine, or without carefully weighing your prospect there against those elsewhere. Always keep a copy of work you submit, and if you don't hear back in reasonable time, withdraw your submission and keep it circulating."

**POETRY TODAY (II), The Magazine for Poets**, Spectrum Publishing, Box 20822, Portland OR 97220. (503)231-7628. Editor: Mark Worden. Fiction Editor: Austin Grey. Magazine:

8½x11; 32 pages (average); newsprint paper; self cover stock; illustrations. Magazine publishing "how to" articles for poets. Quarterly. Estab. 1979. Circ. 5,000.
**Needs:** Prose poem. Receives 3-10 unsolicited mss/month. Accepts 1-2 mss/issue. Length: open. Occasionally critiques rejected ms.
**How to Contact:** Send complete ms. Reports in 2 months. Publishes ms an average of 2-3 months after acceptance. SASE. Simultaneous submissions OK. Accepts computer printout submissions. Accepts disc submissions compatible with TRS 80 or AM 5900 or 5810 typesetter. Sample copy $1.50.
**Payment:** ½¢/word.
**Terms:** Pays on publication for one-time rights. Publication copyrighted.

**POOR MAN'S PRESS**, Box 1291, Ottawa, Ontario K1P 5R3 Canada. Editor: B. Brown. Magazine of short stories, poetry and art for general audience. Size 5½x8½; 30-50 pages. "Themes vary each time we publish." Quarterly. Estab. 1983. Circ. 200-500.
**Needs:** Adventure, comics, contemporary, ethnic, experimental, fantasy, historical (general), horror, humor/satire, juvenile, literary, mainstream, men's, preschool, prose poem, psychic/supernatural/occult, religious/inspirational, romance, science fiction, suspense/mystery, western, and young adult/teen. Receives 10-20 unsolicited mss/month. Accepts 5-10 mss/issue/; 20-40 mss/year. Length: 3,500 words average; 5,000 words maximum. Occasionally critiques rejected mss.
**How to Contact:** Send complete ms. Reports in 5 weeks. SAE, IRC. Simultaneous, photocopied and previously published submissions OK. Accepts computer printout submissions. Prefers letter-quality. Sample copy $1.95 and 6x9 SAE with 37¢ Canadian 3rd class postage or IRC. Fiction guidelines for #10 SAE and 37¢ Canadian postage or IRC.
**Payment:** 10% discount subscription to magazine; 2 contributor's copies; $1 and postage charge for extras.
**Terms:** Acquires one-time rights; rights revert back to author. Publication copyrighted.
**Tips:** "Submit and write fiction as much as possible. We're very open to new writers."

**PORTLAND REVIEW**, Portland State University, Box 751, Portland OR 97207. Contact: Editor. Magazine with an eye towards the new and fresh. *PR* is a literary/arts magazine for people who are interested in contemporary writing. Semiannually. Estab. 1955. Circ. 500.
**Needs:** Contemporary, experimental, fantasy, historical, humor/satire, literary, prose poem, psychic/supernatural, science fiction, translations, women's, and young adult. Receives 100 unsolicited fiction mss/month. Accepts 10-15 mss/issue; 20-30 mss/year. Length: 2,000 words average. Occasionally critiques rejected ms.
**How to Contact:** Query first or submit through agent. SASE for query. Photocopied submissions OK. Reports in 3-4 weeks on queries. Publishes ms an average of 3-4 months after acceptance. Sample copy for $2. Fiction guidelines free.
**Payment:** 1 free contributor's copy; 50% discount for extras.
**Terms:** Acquires one-time rights. Publication copyrighted.
**Tips:** "We are generally looking for more short stories dealing with science fiction."

**POTBOILER (I, II)**, Panda Press Publications, Richards Rd., Roberts Creek, British Columbia, V0N 2W0 Canada. (604)885-3985. Editor-in-Chief: L.R. Davidson. Magazine: 8½x11; 64-84 pages; 20 lb bond paper; card cover stock; illustrations; photos. Magazine for science fiction/fantasy and comics fans of all ages. "I publish science fiction, fantasy, horror and unusual mainstream material in prose and graphic form. All manuscripts are illustrated by the best artists I can find. The magazine is intended to be both a literary and visual delight." Published semiannually. Published special fiction issue last year; plans another. Estab. 1980. Circ. 600.
**Needs:** Adventure, comics, erotica, experimental, fantasy, horror, humor/satire, mainstream (unusual), science fiction, and suspense/mystery. "Unusually good juvenile material might be considered. No pretentious material of any sort." Receives 12 unsolicited fiction mss/week. Accepts 10-15 mss/issue; 20-30 mss/year. Length: 600 words minimum; 20,000 words maximum;

4,000-5,000 words average. Publishes short shorts. Occasionally critiques rejected mss. Sometimes recommends other markets.
**How to Contact:** Send complete ms with SASE. Previously published work OK. Accepts computer printout submissions. Prefers letter-quality. Reports in 6 weeks on mss. Publishes ms an average of 4-12 months after acceptance. Sample copy $2. Free fiction guidelines with SAE and International Reply Coupons. "Will accept photocopied manuscripts with a cover letter stating that it is *not* a simultaneous submission . . . It would be nice if the author would include a cover letter, no matter how brief."
**Payment:** 2 free contributor's copies.
**Terms:** Pays on publication for second serial rights and first North American serial rights. Buys reprints. Publication copyrighted.
**Tips:** "Be entertaining and concise. Most fiction manuscripts are not very well written . . . a large majority are not even stories. Learn the basics of fiction mechanics, practice them to a fault, then write your story your own way, keeping the mechanics in the back of your mind in case of need. Be original, but most of all, be yourself!" Published "many" new writers within the last year.

**POTPOURRI LITERARY MAGAZINE (II), Selected Short Stories, Poetry and Art,** Fresno City College, 1101 University Ave., Fresno CA 93741. (209)442-4600. Editor: Sid Harriet. Magazine: 6x9; 60 pages; 60 lb paper; illustrations; photos. Magazine "with emphasis on the short short for college-literary audience." Semiannually. Published special fiction issue last year; plans another. Estab. 1978. Circ. 500.
**Needs:** Contemporary, experimental, literary and short shorts. Accepts 6-10 mss/issue; 12-20 mss/year. Does not read July-August. Length: 500-2,500 words. Occasionally critiques rejected ms. Recommends other markets.
**How to Contact:** Send complete ms with SASE. Reports in 2 months. Simultaneous and photocopied submissions OK. Accepts computer printout submissions. Prefers letter-quality. Sample copy $4.
**Payment:** 3 contributor's copies.
**Terms:** Acquires one-time rights on publication. Publication copyrighted.
**Tips:** "Read Raymond Carver, Mary Robison, and Laura Furman. Make every word count. Rewrite and then rewrite. Fiction is attractive to readers in this market." Published new writers within the last year.

**POULTRY (IV), A Magazine of Voice,** Poultry, Inc., Box 727, Truro MA 02666. Editors: Brendan Galvin and George Garrett. Tabloid of fiction and poetry: 12 pages; newspaper quality; cover photos. Parodies contemporary poems, styles, lit-biz, contribution notes, contests, prizes, etc; for writers and readers of contemporary literature. Semiannually. Estab. 1979. Circ. 1,000.
**Needs:** Humor/satire. "We want fiction that satirizes contemporary writing's foibles, pretensions, politics, etc. No serious fiction." Receives 10-20 unsolicited fiction mss/month. Accepts 3-4 mss/issue; 10 mss/year. Occasionally critiques rejected ms. Publishes short shorts.
**How to Contact:** Send complete ms with SASE. Accepts computer printout submissions. Prefers letter-quality. Reports in 1 month. Sample copy for $1.
**Payment:** 10 free contributor's copies.
**Terms:** Acquires one-time rights.
**Tips:** "Read us; send us parodies of the things in contemporary writing and its scene that bug you the most!"

**PRAIRIE FIRE (II),** Manitoba Writers' Guild, 3rd Floor, 374 Donald St., Winnipeg, Manitoba R3B 2J2 Canada. (204)943-9066. Editor: Andris Taskans. Magazine: 6x9; 96 pages; offset bond paper; sturdy cover stock; illustrations; photos. "Essays, critical reviews, short fiction, and poetry. For writers and readers interested in Canadian/Manitoba literature." Published 4 times/year. Estab. 1978. Circ. 1,000.
**Needs:** Literary, contemporary, experimental. "We will consider work on any topic of artistic

merit, including short chapters from novels-in-progress. We wish to avoid gothic, confession, religious, romance and pornography." Buys 2-3 mss/issue, 8-10 mss/year. Receives 18-20 unsolicited fiction mss each month. Publishes short shorts. Length: 10,000 maximum; no minimum 2,000 words average. Critiques rejected mss "if requested and when there is time." Recommends other market.

**How to Contact:** Send complete ms with SASE and short bio. Reports in 2-3 months.

**Payment:** $30 for the first page, $10 for each additional page. 1 free author's copy. $4 charge for extras.

**Terms:** Buys first-time rights. Rights revert to author on publication. Publication copyrighted.

**Tips:** "Read our publication before submitting. We prefer Manitoba/Canadian material. Most mss are not ready for publication. Be neat, double space. Be the best writer you can be." Published new writers within the last year.

**THE PRAIRIE JOURNAL OF CANADIAN LITERATURE (I, III, IV)**, Prairie Journal Press, Box 997, Station G, Calgary, Alberta, Canada T3A 3G2. Editor: A.E. Burke. Journal: 8½x10; 50-60 pages; white bond paper; regular cover stock; cover illustrations. Journal of creative writing and scholarly essays, reviews for literary audience. Semiannually. Published special fiction issue last year; plans another. Estab. 1983.

**Needs:** Contemporary, literary, regional, excerpted novel. No romance, erotica, pulp. Receives 10-20 unsolicited mss each month. Accepts 1 ms/issue; 2-5 mss/year. Charges reading fee of up to $1/page "if help requested." Suggests sample issue $3 before submitting ms. Length: 2,500 words average; 100 words minimum; 3,000 words maximum. Sometimes critiques rejected ms. Sometimes recommends other markets.

**How to Contact:** Send complete ms. Reports in 1 month. SASE or SAE and IRC. Photocopied submissions OK. Sample copy $3. and SAE with 39¢ postage or IRC with cover letter of past credits . . . a friendly introduction to a new acquaintance. Fiction guidelines for SAE with 32¢ postage or IRC.

**Payment:** Contributor's copies.

**Terms:** Acquires first North American serial rights. In Canada author retains copyright.

**Tips:** Interested in "innovational work of quality. Beginning writers welcome." I have chosen to publish fiction simply because many magazines do not. Those who do in Canada are, for the most part, seeking formulaic writing. There is no point in simply republishing known authors or conventional, predictable plots." Published new writers within the past year.

**PRAIRIE SCHOONER (II)**, University of Nebraska, English Department, 201 Andrews Hall, Lincoln NE 68588. (402)472-1800. Magazine: 9x6; 120 pages; good stock paper; heavy cover stock. A general literary quarterly of stories, poems, essays and reviews for a general educated audience that reads for pleasure. Quarterly. Plans special fiction issue. Estab. 1927. Circ. 2,000.

**Needs:** Good fiction. Accepts 4-5 mss/issue. Receives approximately 200-500 unsolicited fiction mss each month. Length: varies.

**How to Contact:** Send complete ms with SASE and previous publications—where, when. Reports in 2 months.

**Payment:** 2 free author's copies, 10 offprints.

**Terms:** Acquires all rights. Publication copyrighted.

**Tips:** "Read *Prairie Schooner*." Annual prize of $500 for best fiction, $300 for best new writer (poetry or fiction). Published 3 new writers within the last year.

**PRELUDE TO FANTASY (II)**, Hans P. Werner, #103, 3201 Diamond Eight Terrace, Minneapolis MN 55421. Editor: Hans P. Werner. Magazine: 8½x11; 32 pages; 20 lb white paper; 60 lb white cover stock; illustrations. Magazine of primarily "fantasy, horror and terror-oriented fiction, art, and poetry. Mainstream of experimental fiction having this slant is also considered." For "college educated, avid readers of serious, adult fantasy, horror and terror." Irregular, up to once annually. Published special fiction issue; plans another. Estab. 1978. Circ. 100-200.

**Needs:** Adventure, contemporary, experimental, fantasy, horror, literary, mainstream, prose poem, psychic/supernatural/occult, science fiction and suspense/mystery. No children's, comics, erotica, gay, or feminist. Accepts 5-7 mss/issue. Length: 3,000 words average; 1,500 words minimum, 4,500 words maximum. Does not critique rejected ms, but provides limited comments sometimes—especially if asked.

**How to Contact:** Send complete ms with cover letter. Reports in 3 months. SASE. Photocopied submissions OK. Accepts computer printout submissions. No dot-matrix. Accepts disc submissions compatible with Commodore 64 (using Easy Script word processor only). Fiction guidelines for SASE. Issue 3 (24 pages)-$1.50. Issue 4 (32 pages): $2.

**Payment:** 2 contributor's copies; $2 charge for extras. Prizes for best stories: $1 to $3. "Best" is voted by contributors and readers as well as editor.

**Terms:** Acquires first rights on publication. Sends galleys to author. Publication copyrighted.

**Tips:** "Originality, character, mood, plot are essential; no heavy violence or pornography. Send your best—and if not accepted try again. Best 25-50 writers, poets, or artists submitting to an issue receive one free copy if work is not accepted." Published new writers within the last year.

**PRIMAVERA (II, IV)**, University of Chicago, 1212 E. 59th St., Chicago IL 60637. (312)524-1561. Editorial Board. Magazine: 8½x11; 100 pages; 60 lb paper; glossy cover; illustrations; photos. Literature and graphics by women: poetry, short stories, essays, photos, drawings. Readership: "an audience interested in women's ideas and experiences." Annually. Estab. 1975. Circ. 1,000.

**Needs:** Literary, contemporary, science fiction, fantasy, feminist, gay/lesbian, and humor. "We dislike slick stories packaged for more traditional women's magazines." Note: "We publish only work reflecting the experiences of women." Cover letter not necessary. Accepts 6-10 mss/issue. Receives approximately 40 unsolicited fiction mss each month. Length: 25 pages maximum. Critiques rejected mss "when there is time." Often gives suggestions for revisions and invites re-submission of revised ms. Occasionally recommends markets to writers.

**How to Contact:** Send complete ms with SASE. Accepts computer printout submission, "if assured it is not a multiple submission." Prefers letter-quality. Reports in 1 week—5 months on mss. Publishes ms up to 1 year after acceptance. Sample copy $4; $5 for recent issues. Guidelines for legal-size SASE.

**Payment:** 2 free author's copies.

**Terms:** Acquires first rights. Publication copyrighted.

**Tips:** "Read the magazine. We publish a wide variety of stories. We like stories with well developed characters, interesting plots, and convincing dialogue. We like new ideas and techniques." Published new writers within the year.

**PRISM INTERNATIONAL (II)**, E462-1866 Main Mall, University of British Columbia, Vancouver, British Columbia V6T 1W5 Canada. (604)228-2514. Editor: Steve Noyes. Magazine: 6x9; 72-80 pages. "A journal of contemporary writing—fiction, poetry, drama and translation. *Prism's* audience is world-wide, as are our contributors." Readership: "Public and university libraries, individual subscriptions, bookstores—an audience concerned with the contemporary in literature." Published 4 times/year. Estab. 1959. Circ. 1,000.

**Needs:** Literary, contemporary or translations. "Most any category as long as it is *fresh*. No overtly religious, overtly theme-heavy material or anything more message- or category-oriented than self-contained." Buys approximately 50 mss/year. Receives 40 unsolicited fiction mss each month. Length: 5,000 words maximum "though flexible for outstanding work." Publishes short shorts. Critiques rejected mss "when there is time." Occasionally recommends other markets.

**How to Contact:** Send complete ms with SASE or SAE, IRC and cover letter with bio, information and publications list. "Don't explain away your story." US contributors take note: US stamps are not valid in Canada and your ms will not likely be returned if it contains US stamps. Send International Reply Coupons instead." Accepts computer printout submissions. Prefers letter-quality. Reports in 2 months. Sample copy $4.

**Payment:** $25/printed page, 1 free year's subscription.

**Terms:** Pays on publication for first North American serial rights. Publication copyrighted.

**Tips:** "Too many derivative, self-indulgent pieces; sloppy construction and imprecise word usage. There's not enough attention to voice and a beginning and not enough invention. We are committed to publishing outstanding literary work in all genres. Some helpful truisms: 1) Learn from whomever you can, but remember that it's *you* who is writing. Strive to surprise yourself with what you as an individual can write; 2) Rewrite. If you think your prose is flawless you are *wrong*. 3) *Show* us reality, don't *tell* us about it. 4) I'm with Flannery O'Connor; who said, 'Why experiment? Write about what you care about.' "

**PROCESSED WORLD (II)**, #829, 55 Sutter St., San Francisco CA 94104. Editors: Collective. Magazine: 8½x11; 40-48 pages; 20 lb bond; glossy cover stock; illustrations; photos. Magazine about work, office work, computers, and hi-tech (satire). Triannually. May publish special fiction issue. Estab. 1981. Circ. 4,000.
**Needs:** Comics, confession, contemporary, erotica, ethnic, experimental, fantasy, feminist, gay, historical (general), humor/satire, lesbian, literary, prose poem, regional, science fiction, and translations. Accepts 1-2 mss/issue; 3-5 mss/year. Length: 1,250 words average; 100 words minimum; 1,500 words maximum. Occasionally critiques rejected ms.
**How to Contact:** Send complete ms. Reports in 4 months. SASE. Simultaneous and photocopied submissions OK. Accepts computer printout submissions. Prefers letter-quality. Sample copy $2.50 and 9x12 SAE with 5 first class stamps.
**Payment:** Subscription to magazine.
**Terms:** Acquires one-time rights.
**Tips:** "Make it snappy, witty, biting satire, anticapitalist." Published new writers within the last year.

**PROOF ROCK (II), Literary Arts Journal**, Proof Rock Press, Box 607, Halifax VA 24558. Editor: Don R. Conner. Magazine: standard size; 40-60 pages; heavy paper; heavy cover stock; illustrations; photos. "We publish the best of what is submitted in a given period. No taboos if well done." For all segments of the literary readership. Semiannually. Published special fiction issue last year. Estab. 1982. Circ. 300.
**Needs:** Adventure, contemporary, erotica, experimental, fantasy, humor/satire, literary, mainstream, men's, prose poem, psychic/supernatural, romance, translations, and women's. "Excessive sentimentality is frowned upon." Receives 8-10 unsolicited fiction mss/month. Accepts 2-4 mss/issue; 4-8 mss/year. Approximately 1% of fiction is agented. Length: 2,500 words maximum; 2,000 words average. Occasionally critiques rejected ms. Recommends other markets.
**How to Contact:** Send complete ms with SASE. Simultaneous, photocopied and previously published submissions OK. Accepts computer printout submissions. Prefers letter-quality. Reports in 3 months. Publishes ms an average of 1-6 months after acceptance. Sample copy $2.50. Fiction guidelines free with #10 SAE and 1 first class stamp.
**Payment:** 1 free contributor's copy; $2.50 charge for extras.
**Terms:** Acquires one-time rights.
**Tips:** "Our audience is passive. We need something to stir them up. Try to find something new under the sun. Dare to be different but not obtuse. Try something new under the sun without learning the solar system. In other words, be original, but let your originality capture the reader rather than turning him off." Published new writers within the last year.

**PTERANODON MAGAZINE(II)**, Lieb/Schott Publication, Box 229, Bourbonnais IL 60914. Editors: Patricia Lieb and Carol Schott. A literary magazine containing short stories and poetry. Aimed toward poets and writers. Annually. Estab. 1979. Circ. 500.
**Needs:** Literary, contemporary, science fiction, fantasy, gothic, romance, western, mystery, adventure, and humor. Accepts 1-2 mss/issue. Receives 75 unsolicited fiction mss each month. Length: 1,200-5,000 words preferred. Critiques rejected mss "when there is time."
**How to Contact:** Query first with SASE. Reports in 3 weeks. Sample copy $2.50. Free guidelines with SASE.
**Payment:** 1-3 free author's copies. $2.50 charge for extras.
**Terms:** Acquires one-time rights. Publication copyrighted.

**PTOLEMY/THE BROWNS MILLS REVIEW (II)**, Box 908, Browns Mills NJ 08015. Editor-in-Chief: David C. Vajda. Magazine: 8½x5 or 5½x8½; 8-24 pages; good quality paper; illustrations. Published annually. Plans special fiction issue. Estab. 1980. Circ. 250.
**Needs:** Contemporary, erotica, experimental, historical, humor/satire, mainstream, and translations. No "plagiarized material, racist—racism—sexist—per se." Length: 50 words minimum; 10,000 words maximum; 400-2,400 words average. Occasionally critiques rejected mss. Recommends markets.
**How to Contact:** Query first with unpublished samples with SASE. Reports in 1 month on queries; 1 month on mss. Publishes ms an average of 1 year after acceptance.
**Payment:** 5 contributor's copies per page.
**Terms:** Publication copyrighted.
**Tips:** "No previously published material considered."

**THE PUB (I, II)**, Ansuda Publications, Box 158J, Harris IA 51345. Editor/Publisher: Daniel R. Betz. Magazine: 5½x8½; 72 pages; mimeo paper; heavy cover stock; illustrations on cover. "We prefer stories to have some sort of social impact within them, no matter how slight, so our fiction is different from what's published in most magazines. We aren't afraid to be different or publish something that might be objectionable to current thought. *Pub* is directed toward those people, from all walks of life, who are themselves 'different' and unique, who are interested in new ideas and forms of reasoning. Our readers enjoy *Pub* and believe in what we are doing." Published 2 times/year. Estab. 1979. Circ. 350.
**Needs:** Literary, psychic/supernatural/occult, fantasy, horror, mystery, adventure, serialized and condensed novels. "We are looking for honest, straightforward stories. No love stories or stories that ramble on for pages about nothing in particular." Buys reprints. Accepts 4-6 mss/issue. Receives approximately 25-30 unsolicited fiction mss each month. Length: 8,000 words maximum. Sometimes recommends other markets.
**How to Contact:** Send complete ms with SASE. Accepts computer printout submissions. Prefers letter-quality. Reports in 1 month. Publishes ms an average of 6 months after acceptance. Sample copy $2. Guidelines for legal-size SASE.
**Payment:** 2 free author's copies. Cover price less special bulk discount for extras.
**Terms:** Acquires first North American serial rights and second serial rights on reprints. Publication copyrighted.
**Tips:** "Read the magazine—that is *very* important. If you send a story close to what we're looking for, we'll try to help guide you to exactly what we want." We appreciate neat copy, and if photocopies are sent, we like to be able to read all of the story. Fiction seems to work for us—we are a literary magazine and have better luck with fiction than articles or poems." Published new writers within the last year.

**PUERTO DEL SOL (I, II)**, Puerto Del Sol Press, New Mexico State University, Box 3E, Las Cruces NM 88003. (505)646-3931. Editor-in-Chief: Kevin McIlvoy. Poetry Editor: Joe Somoza. Magazine: 6x9; 130 pages; 60 lb paper; 70 lb cover stock; photos sometimes. "We publish quality material from anyone. Poetry, fiction, art, photos, interviews, reviews, parts-of-novels, long-poems, plays." Published semiannually. Estab. 1961. Circ. 1,000.
**Needs:** Contemporary, ethnic, experimental, literary, mainstream, prose poem, excerpted novel, and translations. Receives varied number of unsolicited fiction mss/month. Accepts 4-6 mss/issue; 12-15 mss/year. Does not read mss in July-August. Occasionally critiques rejected ms.
**How to Contact:** Send complete ms with SASE. Simultaneous and photocopied submissions OK. Accepts computer printout submissions. Reports in 3 weeks. Sample copy $3.
**Payment:** 3 contributor's copies.
**Terms:** Pays on publication for one-time rights (reverts to author). Publication copyrighted.
**Tips:** "We are open to all forms of fiction, from the conventional to the wildly experimental, as long as they have integrity and are well-written. Too often we receive very impressively 'polished' mss that will dazzle readers with their sheen but offer no character/reader experience of lasting value." Published "many" new writers within the last year.

**PULPSMITH (II), Anything Goes as Long as It's Good**, The Smith, 5 Beekman St., New York NY 10038. Editor: Harry Smith. Managing Editor: Tom Tolnay. Fiction Editor: Nancy Hallinan. Magazine: 4½x7½; 192 pages (average); 50 lb Groundwood paper; 10 pt/4-color cover stock; illustrations; photos occasionally. "A modern pocket-sized version of pulp-styled pop magazines with a literary bent for people who like to read for entertainment, and with a sense of quality." Published quarterly. Estab. 1981. Circ. 8,000.

**Needs:** Adventure, ghost, fantasy, horror, humor/satire, literary, mainstream, science fiction, suspense/mystery, and western. "Published authors include Jorge Luis Borges, Ernesto Sabato, Manley Wade Wellman, Erica Jong, James T. Farrell, Theodore Sturgeon, and Frank Belknap Long, as well as a host of fine unknowns." No women's/men's mass mag-oriented stories. Receives 200-300 unsolicited fiction mss/month. Buys 15 mss/issue; 60 mss/year. Less than 5% of fiction agented. Length: 12,000 words maximum; 2,500 words average. Sometimes recommends other markets.

**How to Contact:** Send complete ms with SASE. Cover letter with credits and personal background. Simultaneous and photocopied submissions OK. Reports in 8 weeks on mss. Publishes ms an average of 2-18 months after acceptance. Sample copy $2; writer's subscription $7/4 issues.

**Payment:** $35-100 and 2 contributor's copies. $1.50 charge for extras.

**Terms:** Pays on acceptance for first North American serial rights. Rarely buys reprints. Publication copyrighted.

**Tips:** "Read several issues of *Pulpsmith* to get a handle on it. Submit strong writing that avoids clichews—both in language and situation, and which goes beyond the genre in which it functions."

**PURPLE COW "The Newspaper for Teens" (IV)**, Purple Cow, Inc., Suite 107, 1447 Peachtree St., Atlanta GA 30309. (404)872-1927. Editor: Meg Thornton. Tabloid: full page 10x16; 12-16 pages; newspaper paper; illustrations; photos. Tabloid for teens aged 12-18. Monthly. February 1976. Circ. 100,000.

**Needs:** Young adult. Does not read mss in June-Aug. Length: 500 words minimum; 2,000 words maximum. Occasionally critiques rejected ms.

**How to Contact:** Send complete ms with SASE. Simultaneous, photocopied and previously published work OK. Reports in 3-6 weeks on mss. Sample copy for $1 with 10x11 SAE and 42¢ postage.

**Payment:** 5 free contributor's copies; 50¢ charge for extras.

**Terms:** Acquires rights and syndication rights for other *Purple Cow* editions throughout the country. Publication copyrighted.

**Tips:** "Don't write down to teens. No vulgar language or explicit sex." Published new writers within the last year.

**QUARRY (II)**, Quarry Press, Box 1061, Kingston, Ontario K7L 4Y5 Canada. (613)376-3584. Editor-in-Chief: Bob Hilderley. Magazine: 5½x8½; 96 pages; #1 book 120 paper; 160 lb Curtis Tweed cover stock; illustrations. "Quarterly anthology of new Canadian poetry, prose. Also includes graphics, photographs and book reviews. We seek readers interested in vigorous, disciplined, new Canadian writing." Published quarterly. Published special fiction issue; plans another. Estab. 1952. Circ. 1,100.

**Needs:** Experimental, fantasy, literary, science fiction, serialized/excerpted novel, and translations. "We do not want highly derivative or clichéd style." Receives 60-80 unsolicited fiction mss/month. Buys 4-5 mss/issue; 20 mss/year. Does not read in July. Less than 5% of fiction is agented. Publishes short shorts. Length: 3,000 words average. Usually critiques rejected ms. Recommends other markets.

**How to Contact:** Send complete ms with SAE, IRC and brief bio. Photocopied submissions OK. Accepts computer printout submissions. Prefers letter-quality. Publishes ms an average of 3-6 months after acceptance. Sample copy $5 with 4x7 SAE and 41¢ Canadian postage or IRC.

**Payment:** $10/page; 1 year subscription to magazine and 1 contributor's copy.

**Terms:** Pays on publication for first North American serial rights.

**Tips:** "Read previous *Quarry* to see standard we seek. Read Canadian fiction to see Canadian trends. We seek aggressive experimentation which is coupled with competence (form, style) and stimulating subject matter. We also like traditional forms. Our annual prose issue (spring) is always a sellout. Many of our selections have been anthologized. The 'Press' arm of *Quarry* will publish one short story anthology this year . . . we plan more. Don't send US stamps or SASE. Use IRC. Submit with brief bio." Published new writers within the last year.

**QUARRY WEST (II)**, Porter College, UCSC, Santa Cruz CA 95064. (408)429-4645 or 429-2951. Editor: Kenneth Weisner. Fiction Editors: David Lovie, Denny Hoberman. Magazine: 6¾x8¼; 100 pages; 60 lb stock opaque paper; cover stock varies with cover art; illustrations sometimes; photos. Magazine of fiction, poetry, general nonfiction, art, graphics for a general audience. Semiannually. Estab. 1971. Circ. 450.
**Needs:** Accepts 2-5 mss/issue; 4-10 mss/year. Occasionally critiques rejected ms.
**How to Contact:** Send complete ms with SASE. Photocopied submissions OK. Reports in 6 weeks on mss. Publishes ms an average of 1-3 months after acceptance. Sample copy $2.50.
**Payment:** 2 free contributor's copies.
**Terms:** Acquires first North American serial rights. Publication copyrighted.
**Tips:** "We're interested in good writing—we've published first-time writers and experienced professionals—the only criterion is good writing. Don't submit material you are unsure of or perhaps don't like just for the sake of publication—only show your *best* work—read the magazine for a feeling of the kind of fiction we've published. Type double-spaced and legibly."

**QUARTERLY WEST**, University of Utah, 317 Olpin Union, Salt Lake City UT 84112. (801)581-3839. Editor: Christopher Merrill, Ann Snodgrass. Fiction Editor: John Maney. Magazine: 6x9; 148 pages; 60 lb paper; J color cover stock. "We try to publish a variety of fiction by writers from all over the country. Our publication is aimed primarily at an educated audience which is interested in contemporary literature and criticism." Semiannual. Published special fiction issue; plans novella competition 1986-1987. Estab. 1976. Circ. 1,000.
**Needs:** Literary, contemporary, translations. Buys 4-6 mss/issue, 10-12 mss/year. Receives approximately 100 unsolicited fiction mss each month. No preferred length. Critiques rejected mss "when there is time." Recommends other markets.
**How to Contact:** Send complete ms. Cover letters welcome. SASE for ms. Accepts computer printout submissions. Prefers letter-quality. Reports in 2 months; "sooner, if possible."
**Payment:** $25-100.
**Terms:** Pays on publication for first North American serial rights. Publication copyrighted.
**Tips:** "Write a clear and unified story which does not rely on tricks or gimmicks for its effects." Mss are rejected because of "poor style, formula writing, clichés, weak characterization. Don't send more than 2 stories at a time." Published new writers within the last year.

**QUEEN'S QUARTERLY: A Canadian Review (II)**, Queen's Quarterly Committee, John Watson Hall, Queen's University, Kingston, Ontario K7L 3N6 Canada. (613)547-6968. Editors: Dr. Grant Amyot and Mrs. M. Stayer. Magazine: 6x9; 996 pages; 50 lb Zyphyr antique paper; 65 lb Mayfair antique britewhite cover stock; illustrations. "A general interest intellectual review, featuring articles on science, politics, humanities, arts and letters. Extensive book reviews, some poetry and fiction." Published quarterly. Estab. 1893. Circ. 1,600.
**Needs:** Adventure, contemporary, experimental, fantasy, historical (general), humor/satire, literary, mainstream, science fiction, and women's. "Special emphasis on work by Canadian writers." Buys 2 mss/issue; 8 mss/year. Length: 5,000 words maximum. Publishes short shorts up to 25 manuscript pages.
**How to Contact:** "Send complete ms—only one at a time—plus one-paragraph résumé and a brief description of piece submitted with SASE." Photocopied submissions OK if not part of multiple submission. Accepts computer printout submissions. Prefers letter-quality. Reports in 8 weeks. Sample copy $4.50.
**Payment:** $25-150 and 2 contributor's copies. $4 charge for extras.
**Terms:** Pays on publication for first North American serial rights. Sends galleys to author. Publication copyrighted.
**Tips:** Published new writers within the last year.

**QUIXOTE (II)**, Quixote Press, 1810 Marshall, Houston TX 77270. Editor: Morris Edelson. Fiction Editor: Melissa Bondy. Magazine: 4x5 or 8x11; 64-80 pages; high quality paper; heavy cover stock; illustrations; photos. Theme: "anti-capitalist satire, humor, fiction." Readership: "the disaffected, the discontented. Misery loves company." Monthly. Published special fiction last year; plans another. Estab. 1965. Circ. 500.

**Needs:** "Unconventional material." Publishes short shorts. Accepts 20 mss/year. Receives 20-50 unsolicited fiction mss/month. Length: "shortish." Critiques rejected mss "briefly, when there is time."

**How to Contact:** Query. Reports in 2 weeks. Sample copy $2.

**Payment:** 5 free author's copies.

**Terms:** Acquires one-time rights. Publication copyrighted.

**Tips:** "Read our publication. Talk to working class and disenfranchised people. Write about something you care about. We are eclectic but exclude usually the merely clever. We do, however, print the best of what we get, so we often relax from our puritanical leftism." Rejected mss "need integration of action and subjective impression; need point of view consistent with editorial policy of magazine." Published "many" new writers within the last year.

**THE RADDLE MOON (II), an international review**, 9060 Ardmore Dr., Sidney, British Columbia V8L 3S1 Canada. Editor: Susan Clark. Magazine: 6x9; 96 pages; 70 lb Island Hilitz paper; Cornwall CIS cover stock; photos. "An international magazine: we publish translations, essays, poetry, fiction, drama, graphics, photographs" for a literary audience. Semiannually. Estab. 1983. Circ. 600.

**Needs:** Contemporary, erotica, experimental, fantasy, literary, prose poem, and translations. Receives 20-30 unsolicited mss/month. Accepts 2-5 mss/issue; 4-10 mss/year. Length: short. Occasionally critiques rejected mss.

**How to Contact:** Send complete ms. Reports in 2 months. SAE, IRC with biographical information, and statement of contents. Simultaneous and photocopied submissions OK. Accepts computer printout submissions. Prefers letter-quality. Publishes ms usually under 6 months after acceptance. Sample copy $4 with 8x10 SAE and 37¢ IRC. Fiction guidelines for SAE.

**Payment:** $2 charge for extras; one year subscription.

**Terms:** Acquires first Canadian serial rights. Publication copyrighted.

**Tips:** "We get good response to translated prose poetry and short stories. Read the magazine. Submit again if asked to do so on a rejection slip (we mean it). Tell friends and associates about us."

**RAG MAG (I, II)**, Box 12, Goodhue MN 55027. (612)923-4590. Editor: B. Voldseth Allers. Magazine: 60 pages; varied paper quality; illustrations; photos. Magazine for a varied audience. "No theme. We are eager to print poetry and prose and art work. We are open to all styles." Semiannually. Estab. 1982. Circ. 300.

**Needs:** Contemporary, experimental, fantasy, literary, mainstream, prose poem, regional. "Anything well written is a possibility. No extremely violent or pornographic writing." Accepts 1-2 mss/issue. Length: 1,000 words average; 2,200 words maximum. Occasionally critiques rejected ms. Sometimes recommends other markets.

**How to Contact:** Send complete ms. Reports in 2 months. SASE. Simultaneous, photocopied and previously published submissions OK. Accepts computer printout submissions. Prefers letter-quality. Single copy $3.

**Payment:** 1 contributor's copy; $3 charge for extras.

**Terms:** Acquires one-time rights. Publication copyrighted.

**Tips:** "Submit clean copy on regular typing paper (no tissue-thin stuff). We want fresh images, sparse language, words that will lift us out of our chairs. I like the short story form. I think it's powerful and has a definite place in the literary magazine." Published new writers within the last year.

**RaJAH (II), The Rackham Journal of the Arts & Humanities**, University of Michigan, MLB 4024, Ann Arbor MI 48109. Editor: Darcy Engholm. Fiction Editors: Pete Olson, Nash Mayfield, Lynne Huffer, and Allison Bishop-Rein. Magazine: 9x6; 100-130 pages; 60 lb off-white; b&w illustrations; b&w photos. "We publish poetry, short stories, essays and literary translations by new and established authors geared for an educated reading public." Annually. Plans special fiction issue. Estab. 1971. Circ. 500.

**Needs:** Ethnic, experimental, fantasy, feminist, historical, humor/satire, literary, prose poem, science fiction, and translations. Receives 6 unsolicited mss/month. Does not read June-August. Accepts 10 mss/year. Publishes short shorts. Length: 10-20 typed pages, double spaced. Recommends other markets.

**How to Contact:** Send complete ms. Reports in 2 months. SASE with biographical information and reason for sending manuscript *RaJAH*. Photocopied submissions OK. Accepts computer printout submissions. Sample copy $2.50.

**Payment:** 10 contributor's copies; charge for extras.

**Terms:** Publication copyrighted.

**Tips:** "We are especially interested in material focusing on social issues and current culture. We are always on the lookout for manuscripts by unpublished authors. We believe that both fiction and scholarly articles reflect that kind of work being produced by talented young people around the world. *RaJAH* began as a graduate student publication and has since broadened its author base to the public at large. We still publish a great deal of original fiction by unpublished authors."

**RAMBUNCTIOUS REVIEW (II)**, Rambunctious Press, Inc., 1221 W. Pratt Blvd., Chicago IL 60626. (312)338-2439. Editors: Mary Dellutri, Richard Goldman, Beth Hausler, Nancy Lennon. Magazine: 7½x10; 48 pages; b&w illustrations; b&w photos. "Quality literary magazine publishing short dramatic works, poetry and short stories for general audience." Semiannually. Estab. 1984. Circ. 500.

**Needs:** Adventure, confession, contemporary, erotica, ethnic, experimental, feminist, historical, humor/satire, literary, mainstream, prose poem, regional, and contemporary romance. No murder mysteries. Receives 10-20 unsolicited mss/month. Accepts 3 mss/issue; 6 mss/year. Does not read June 1-August 31. Length: 15 page maximum. Publishes short shorts. Occasionally comments on rejected mss.

**How to Contact:** Send complete ms. Reports in 2 months on mss. SASE. Simultaneous and photocopied submissions OK. Accepts computer printout submissions. Prefers letter-quality. Sample copy $3.

**Payment:** 2 contributor's copies.

**Terms:** Acquires first rights. Publication copyrighted.

**Tips:** "We sponsor a yearly fiction contest in the fall. Send SASE for details. Fiction lives—if you can grasp the essentials of fiction, you can recreate a bit of life." Published new writers within the last year.

**THE RAMPANT GUINEA PIG (II), A Magazine of Fantasy & Subcreative Fiction**, 10639 Deveron Dr., Whittier CA 90601. Editor-in-Chief: Mary Ann Hodge. Magazine: 8x11; illustrations. "Though we emphasize fantasy fiction, we also publish some poetry and material relating to the life and works of Donald K. Grundy. Our readers are literate and well read in fantasy. Many have an interest in children's literature." Published annually. Estab. 1978. Circ. 100.

**Needs:** Fantasy, science fantasy, and religious fantasy (Christian or otherwise). "Humorous, satire, parody, and pastiche okay. All stories should be PG rated. No sword and sorcery/barbarian fiction, no *Star Trek* or *Star Wars* stories. I'm particularly looking for mythopoeic and subcreative fantasy, high fantasy, and stories that convey a sense of wonder and the proximity of faerie." Receives 1-3 unsolicited fiction mss/month. Prefers letter-quality or legible dot-matrix. Accepts 2-4 mss/issue; 4-8 mss/year. Length: 8,000 words maximum; 5,000 words average (serials may be longer); also publishes short shorts. Occasionally critiques rejected ms. Sometimes recommends markets.

**How to Contact:** Send complete ms with SASE. Photocopied submissions OK. Accepts computer printout submissions. Accepts disc submissions compatible with Osborne 1. Reports in 4 weeks on mss. Sample copy $2.25. Fiction guidelines with #10 SAE and 1 first class stamp.

**Payment:** 2 contributor's copies. $2.25 charge for extras.

**Terms:** Pays on publication for first North American serial rights. Publication copyrighted.
**Tips:** "Read as much fantasy as you can. Don't write it unless you love it. And read one or more issues of *The Rampant Guinea Pig* before submitting so you'll know the niche we occupy in the genre. At least send for the fiction guidelines. I'm always looking for humorous stories to balance the more serious ones. I think fiction is the highest form of word craft."

**‡REBORN, A Christian SF& F Magazine**, Fandom Unlimited Enterprises, Box 70868, Sunnyvale CA 94086. (415)960-1151. Editor: Randall D. Larson. Magazine. "Fiction, artwork and essays on science fiction, fantasy and horror from from a Biblically Christian point of view. Emphasis is on creativity and art for science fiction and fantasy readers. Irregular, possibly one-shot in 1986. Circ. 1,000. New magazine in preparation.
**Needs:** Fantasy, horror, psychic/supernatural, religious/inspirational, science fiction. "Stories must adhere to Biblical Christian viewpoint, without sermons or mere allegories. Want good *stories* first off." Plans to accept 10-15 fiction mss/issue. Length: 5,000-6,000 words average; 8,000 words maximum. Occasionally critiques rejected ms.
**How to Contact:** Send complete ms. SASE for ms. Photocopied submissions and reprints OK. Reports in 2 weeks on queries; 4-8 weeks on mss. Fiction guidelines for legal-size SAE and 1 first class stamp.
**Payment:** Pays in contributor's copies; charge for extras: 40% of price.
**Terms:** Acquires first rights. Publication copyrighted.
**Tips:** "Have a solid grounding in Christian history and Biblical principles which should *underlie* (not overburden) your fiction. I'm interested in *story*, a tale of fantasy or science fiction or horror with interesting characters, well-told, with an interesting story-line. Biblical emphasis is secondary to this though still required."

**‡RED BASS (I, II)**, Red Bass Productions, Box 10258, Tallahassee FL 32302. (904)222-1318. Editor: Jay Murphy. Fiction Editor: Eugenie Nable. Tabloid: 11x15; 32 pages; 37 lb news print paper; illustrations; photos. "Strongly progressive arts publication—interviews, fiction, poetry, reviews, essays that further social struggle." Quarterly. Estab. 1981. Circ. 3,000.
**Needs:** Contemporary, erotica, experimental, feminist, gay, humor/satire, lesbian, literary, serialized/excerpted novel, translations, women's. "We publish a variety of fiction, but it is all committed to social change in one sense or another." Receives 3-5 unsolicited fiction mss/month. Accepts 1 ms/issue; 4-5 mss/year. Publishes ms time varies after acceptance. Length: 1,000 words average; 500 words minimum; 1,500 words maximum. Also publishes short shorts. Critiques rejected mss. Recommends other markets.
**How to Contact:** Send complete manuscript with cover letter. Reports in 2-3 weeks on queries; 2 months on mss. SASE for ms. Simultaneous submissions OK. Accepts computer printouts including dot-matrix. Sample copy $1.25.
**Payment:** Free contributor's copies.
**Terms:** Pays on publication for first North American serial rights. Publication copyrighted.
**Tips:** "We're in business to publish new work by new writers and we consider fiction important. We appreciate vigorous, innovative work with integrity that also helps further critical understanding and awareness of the surrounding social, cultural, political realities."

**RED CEDAR REVIEW (II)**, Red Cedar Press, Dept. of English, Morrill Hall, Michigan State University, East Lansing MI 48825. (517)355-9656. Editor: Mike Fuller. Magazine: 8½x5½; 90-110 pages; quality illustrations; good photos. Theme: "literary—poetry, fiction, book reviews, one-act plays, interviews, graphics." Biannually. Estab. 1961. Circ. 500.
**Needs:** Literary, feminist, regional, and science fiction. Accepts 3-4 mss/issue, 6-10 mss/year. Does not read mss in summer. Length: 500-7,000 words. Recommends other markets.
**How to Contact:** Send complete ms with SASE. Reports in 2 months on mss. Publishes ms up to 4 months after acceptance. Sample copy $1.
**Payment:** 1 free author's copy. $2.50 charge for extras.
**Terms:** Acquires all rights.

**Tips:** "Read the magazine and good literary fiction. Annual creative writing contest for MSU students only. There are many good writers out there who need a place to publish and we try to provide them with that chance for publication." Published new writers within the last year.

**THE REDNECK REVIEW OF LITERATURE (I, IV)**, Camas Writer's Workshop, Rt. 1, Box 1085, Fairfield ID 83327. (208)764-2536. Editor: Penelope Reedy. Magazine: 8½x11; 75 pages; card stock cover stock; illustrations (sometimes); photos (sometimes). "We consider ourselves an active element in making possible a truly literate West" for an "undefined" audience. Annually. Published special fiction issue last year. Estab. 1975. Circ. 300.

**Needs:** Adventure, contemporary, ethnic, experimental, historical (general), humor/satire, literary, prose poem, regional, and translations. No "formula stuff." Receives 10 "or so" unsolicited mss/month. Accepts 4-5 mss/issue. Does not read in summer. Length: 1,000-2,500 words average. Occasionally comments on rejected mss.

**How to Contact:** Send complete ms. Reports in 3 months. SASE. Photocopied and previously published submissions OK. Accepts computer printout submissions. Prefers letter-quality. Sample copy $4 with SAE and 75¢ postage.

**Payment:** 2 contributor's copies.

**Terms:** Acquires one-time rights on publication. Publication copyrighted.

**Tips:** "We publish fiction because there is no market for what we (editors) personally want to say." Published new writers within the last year.

**REFLECT (II)**, 3306 Argonne Ave., Norfolk VA 23509. (804)857-1097. Editor: W.S. Kennedy. Magazine: 5½x8½; 38 pages; cover and cartoon illustrations. "A magazine of thought-inspiring fiction, articles, poetry. *Reflect*'s editorial policy and direction suggests the question: 'Did you ever think of that, or look at it that way?' Following the truth where it may lead takes us into diverse fields including science, philosophy, the occult. In addition, we use cartoons and regular columns on antiques/collectibles. So audience is literate but diverse." Published quarterly. Estab. 1979.

**Needs:** Adventure, comics, contemporary, ethnic, experimental, fantasy, historical (general), humor/satire, literary, men's, psychic/supernatural/occult, science fiction, senior citizen/retirement, and women's. "As to style, we are using prose and poetry representative of the newly-emerging back-to-beauty euphonic movement (Spiral Mode)." Accepts 3 or 4 mss/issue; 12 to 16 mss/year. Length: 500 words minimum; 2,500 words maximum; 1,000 words average. Occasionally critiques rejected mss. Recommends other markets.

**How to Contact:** Send complete ms with SASE. Reports in 4 weeks on mss. Publishes ms an average of 3 months after acceptance. Sample copy $1. Free fiction guidelines with SAE and 1 first class stamp.

**Payment:** 1 contributor's copy. $1 charge for extras.

**Terms:** Pays on publication for first rights.

**Tips:** "Ideally, writers should study several issues of the magazine before submitting. I am using mainly Spiral fiction (and poetry) in promotion of the 1980's trend in literature exemplified by the Spiral Back-to-Beauty Movement . . . See a copy of *REFLECT* for the four rules of the new art form of Spiral Fiction." Published new writers within the last year.

**REVIEW, LATIN AMERICAN LITERATURE AND ART**, Center for Inter-American Relations/Americas Society, 680 Park Ave., New York NY 10021. (212)249-8950. Editor: Alfred Mac Adam. Magazine of Latin American fiction, poetry and essays in translation for academic, corporate and general audience. Biannually.

**Needs:** Literary. No political or sociological mss. Receives 5 unsolicited mss/month. Buys 8 mss/issue; 16 mss/year. Length: 1,500-2,000 words average. Occasionally critiques rejected mss.

**How to Contact:** Query first or send complete ms. Reports in several months. Previously published submissions OK if original was published in Spanish. Sample copy free.

**Payment:** $50-200, and 2-3 contributor's copies.

**Terms:** Pays on publication. Publication copyrighted.

**Tips:** "We are always looking for good translators."

**RFD (I)**, Rt. 1, Box 127 E, Bakersville NC 28705. Contact: Fiction Editor. Magazine: 8½x11; average 68 pages; 50 lb paper; 65 lb cover stock; illustrations; photos. "Published by and for gay men who share a country or rural consciousness. We seek fiction, poetry and articles dealing with gay men living in a non-urban environment. Gay men read the magazine mainly for contact with other gay men in the country and relief from a feeling of isolation." Quarterly. Plans special fiction issue. Estab. 1974. Circ. 2,000.

**Needs:** Gay, adventure. "No sexist or racist material or anything not dealing with gay men or a non-urban consciousness." Receives 1 unsolicited fiction ms each month. Critiques rejected mss "when there is time." Sometimes recommends other markets.

**How to Contact:** Send complete ms with SASE. Accepts computer printout submissions. Reports in 3 months on mss. Publishes ms generally in 3-6 months. Sample copy $4.25. Free guidelines.

**Payment:** 2 free author's copies. $2 charge for extras.

**Terms:** Acquires simultaneous rights.

**Tips:** "Write for guidelines or read some back issues." Most mss are rejected because of "inappropriate subject matter." Published new writers within the last year.

**RHINO (II)**, The Poetry Forum, 3915 Foster, Evanston IL 60203. Editor-in-Chief: Laurie Buehler. Magazine: 5½x8; 80 pages, "best" quality paper; 65 lb Tuscan cover stock; cover illustrations only. "Exists for writers of short prose and poetry—for new writers whose eyes and ears for language are becoming practiced, and whose approaches to it are individualistic. Aimed toward the poetically inclined." Annually. Estab. 1976. Circ. 500.

**Needs:** "Short prose (sometimes referred to as prose poems—approx. 200 to 500 words). We aim for artistic writing; we also accept the well-written piece of wide or general appeal." Receives approximately 4 unsolicited fiction mss each month. "We 'read' mss between March 1-May 31." Length: 200-750 words. Critiques rejected mss "when there is time." Sometimes recommends other markets.

**How to Contact:** Send complete ms with cover letter with credits and SASE. Accepts computer printout submissions. Reports in 6 weeks on mss. Recommends other markets. Sample copy $3.

**Payment:** 1 free author's copy.

**Terms:** Acquires one-time rights. Publication copyrighted.

**Tips:** "We recommend you know how to construct a variety of idiomatic English sentences; take as fresh an approach as possible toward the chosen subject; and take time to polish the ms for its keenest effect." Mss are rejected because they are "either too grim or too sentimental. We like strong writing—human warmth, humor, originality, beauty! Our publication appears the first week in October of each year." Published new writers within the last year.

**‡RIGHT HERE (I, II), The Hometown Magazine**, Right Here Publications, Box 1014, Huntington IN 46750. (219)356-4223. Editor: E.J. Carroll. Magazine: 8½x11; 40 pages; illustrations; photos. General family magazine for Indiana readers of all ages but primarily 40-plus. Bimonthly. Estab. 1984. Circ. 2,000.

**Needs:** Humor, juvenile (5-9 years), mainstream, religious/inspirational, senior citizen, suspense/mystery, women's. Wholesome fiction for adults and juveniles. Maximum for juveniles 1,000 words. Accepts 1 ms/issue; 6 mss/year. Publishes ms 4-6 months after acceptance. Length: 2,000 average; 800 words minimum; 2,500 words maximum. Publishes short shorts of 800-1,000 words. Sometimes critiques rejected mss. Sometimes recommends other markets.

**How to Contact:** Send complete ms with cover letter. Reports in 1 month on queries; 2-3 months on mss. SASE for ms. Simultaneous, photocopied and reprint submissions OK. Accepts computer printouts. Sample copy $1.25. Fiction guidelines for business size SAE and 1 first class stamp.

**Payment:** Pays $5-20, contributor's copies.

**Terms:** Pays on publication. Acquires one-time rights. Publication copyrighted.

**RIPPLES MAGAZINE** 1426 Las Vegas Dr., Ann Arbor MI 48103. Editor: Karen M. Schaefer. Short story and poetry magazine.

**Needs:** Literary. Occasionally comments on a rejected ms.
**How to Contact:** Send complete ms. Reports in 1 week on ms. SASE. Simultaneous submissions OK. Accepts computer printout submissions. Prefers letter-quality.
**Payment:** Pays in contributor's copies.

**RIVER CITY REVIEW (II)**, River City Review Press, Inc., Box 34275, Louisville KY 40232. Editors: Richard L. Neumayer and Alan Naslund. Magazine: 8½x11; 40 pages; b&w illustrations; photos. "Small literary magazine publishing short fiction, poetry, some drama, and original art" for "readers of quality writing." Semiannually (fall/spring). Plans special fiction issue. Estab. 1982. Circ. 500.
**Needs:** Adventure, contemporary, ethnic, experimental, fantasy, horror, humor/satire, literary, mainstream, men's, regional, science fiction, suspense/mystery, and western. "We want the best, *original* and *imaginative*." Receives 15-20 unsolicited mss/month. Accepts 6-10 mss/issue; 12-20 mss/year. Length: 2,500-5,000 words average. Publishes short shorts. Occasionally comments on rejected mss.
**How to Contact:** Send complete ms and biographical material suitable for a contributor's note. Reports in 3 weeks-2 months. SASE. Photocopied submissions OK. Accepts computer printout submissions. Prefers letter-quality. Sample copy $3.50; fiction guidelines for SASE.
**Payment:** 1 contributor's copy; 40% discount ($2.10) charge for extras.
**Terms:** Acquires first North American serial rights on publication. Publication copyrighted.
**Tips:** "We want to see originality, seriousness of purpose, and artistic integrity. We love literature and wish to help keep it alive. Stick with what you know. Keep it clear and simple as much as possible. Don't forget you are telling a story; readers will look elsewhere for philosophy of moralizing. The first paragraph is crucial. A bad one often gets a story rejected without further consideration."

**‡RIVERSIDE QUARTERLY (I, II)**, Box 833-044, Richardson TX 75083. Editor: Leland Sapiro. Fiction Editor: Redd Boggs. "We print criticism, reviews, fiction, interviews, poetry, and graphics of the type that commercial science-fiction magazines find unacceptable. While the emphasis is on literary criticism, we try to print at least one story per issue." Quarterly. Magazine: 8½x5½; 64 pages; illustrations; occasional photos. Estab. 1964. Circ. 1,100.
**Needs:** Specific dislikes are space-war stories, media-derived science-fiction, and allegories in science-fictional form (e.g., a future society in which only women are bosses or Caucasians are the objects of racial prejudice). Preferred length is under 3,500 words, although longer stories are sometimes accepted. Publishes short shorts.
**How to Contact:** Send mss with SASE to fiction editor, Redd Boggs, Box 1111, Berkeley CA 94701. Photocopied submissions OK. Sample copies $1.25. "No fiction guidelines offered, since we believe a contributor can best determine the type of material we print by examining a few copies of the magazine."
**Payment:** 4 free contributor's copies.
**Terms:** All rights released to contributors.
**Tips:** "Ours is the most critical audience anywhere: consequently our editors are the most critical anywhere. Would-be contributors are urged to read a copy of the magazine—obtainable at any major public or college library—before sending in any mss."

**ROADWERK (II, IV), A Journal of Travel Art**, On the Move Press, 655 Oakland Ave., Oakland CA 94611. (415)653-5251. Editor: James F. Prchlik. Magazine: 36 pages; 60 lb paper; 10 pt. crome coated cover stock; illustrations; photos. "Travel related art (prose to collage to poetry and photography) for alternative travelers (i.e., low budget 'vagabonds')." Quarterly. Estab. 1982. Circ. 500.
**Needs:** Adventure, comics, ethnic, historical (general), humor/satire, excerpted novel, translations. Must be travel related. Receives 10-15 unsolicited mss/month. Accepts 3-5 mss/issue; 10-15 mss/year. Approximately 5-10% of fiction is agented. Length: 500 words average; 150 words minimum; 1,000 words maximum. Occasionally critiques rejected ms.

**How to Contact:** Send complete ms. Reports in 1 month. SASE. Simultaneous, photocopied and previously published submissions OK. Accepts computer printout submissions. Publishes ms 3-6 months after acceptance. Sample copy for $2.50 and 9x10 SAE with 37¢ postage. Fiction guidelines for legal size SAE and 1 first class stamp.
**Payment:** $25 maximum; 2 contributor's copies.
**Terms:** Pays on publication for first rights. Sends galleys to author. Publication copyrighted.
**Tips:** Read and edit your work at least 3 times and then have someone else do it. Fiction is sometimes the most authentic vision of reality." Published new writers within the last year.

**ROAR (IV), A Journal and Tapebook of Experimental Writing and Reading**, Lionhead Publishing, 2521 E. Stratford Court, Shorewood WI 53211. (414)332-7474. Editor: Dr. M. J. Rosenblum. Experimental magazine/tapebook for college readers, professional writers. "We are interested in content and form that further literature in this century." Estab. 1979. Circ. minimal.
**Needs:** Literary. "We are not interested in traditional works." Receives 2-3 unsolicited mss/month. Length: no limits. Occasionally critiques rejected mss.
**How to Contact:** No unsolicited manuscripts. Query first and include standard information. Reports in 1 week. Publishes ms an average of 2 months after acceptance. SASE. Photocopied submissions OK. Accepts computer printout submissions.
**Payment:** 2 free contributor's copies; charge for extras.
**Terms:** Acquires variable rights. Publication copyrighted.
**Tips:** "We are nonprofit; that is, any money made goes into publishing younger, innovative authors."

**ROOM OF ONE'S OWN (II)**, Growing Room Collective, Box 46160, Station G, Vancouver, British Columbia V6R 4G5 Canada. Editors: Gayla Reid, Jean Wilson, Pat Robertson, Jeannie Wexler, Mary Schendlinger, and Eleanor Wachtel. Magazine: 5½x8¼; 92 pages; bond paper; bond cover stock; illustrations; photos. Feminist literary: fiction, poetry, criticism, reviews. Readership: general, nonscholarly. Quarterly. Published special fiction issue last year; plans another. Estab. 1975. Circ. 1,200.
**Needs:** Literary, women's, feminist, and lesbian. No "sexist or macho material." Buys 6 mss/issue. Receives approximately 40 unsolicited fiction mss each month. Approximately 2% of fiction is agented. Length: 3,000 words preferred. "No critiques except under unusual circumstances."
**How to Contact:** Send complete ms with SASE or SAE and IRC. Reports in 3 months. Publishes ms an average of 1-3 months after acceptance. Sample copy $2.75 with SASE or SAE, IRC.
**Payment:** $50 plus 2 free author's copies. $2 charge for extras.
**Terms:** Pays on publication for first rights. Publication copyrighted.
**Tips:** "Write well and unpretentiously." Mss are rejected because they are "unimaginative." Published new writers within the last year.

**‡THE ROUND TABLE (II), A Journal of Poetry and Fiction**, 206 Sherman St., Wayne NE 68787. Editor: Alan & Barbara Lupack. Magazine: 6x9; 40-48 pages. "We publish serious poetry and fiction." Semiannually, (1 fiction and 1 poetry issue). Estab. 1984. Circ. 150.
**Needs:** Experimental, literary, mainstream. "The quality of the fiction is the most important criterion. We would consider work in other categories if it were especially well written." Accepts 7-10 mss/year. Does not read ms September 1-April 30. Publishes ms never more than 5 months after acceptance. Publishes short shorts.
**How to Contact:** Send complete ms with cover letter. Reports usually in 1 month, but stories under consideration may be held longer. SASE for ms. Simultaneous submissions OK—if notified immediately upon acceptance elsewhere; photocopied submissions OK. Sample copy $3 (specify fiction issue). Fiction guidelines for 1 first class stamp.
**Payment:** 2 contributor's copies, $3 charge for extras.
**Terms:** Pays on publication.

**Tips:** "Each fiction issue has a featured writer. All submissions are considered, but those submitting more than one story have a better chance at being featured."

**RUBICON (II)**, McGill University, 853 Sherbrooke St. W., Montreal, Quebec H3A 2T6 Canada. (514)286-0652. Editor: Peter O'Brien. Magazine: 5x8; 200-230 pages; high quality paper; illustrations; photos. Magazine of contemporary fiction, poetry, interviews, book reviews, and art for a creative/academic audience. Semiannually. Published special fiction issue. Estab. 1983. Circ. 750.
**Needs:** Contemporary, experimental, literary, prose poem, and translations. Receives 10 unsolicited mss/month. Accepts 3 mss/issue; 6 mss/year. Length: 5,000 words average. Usually comments on rejected mss. Occasionally recommends other markets.
**How to Contact:** Send complete ms with SASE or SAE and IRC and short bio note; previous publications, if any. Reports in 3 months. Photocopied submissions OK. Accepts computer printout submissions. Prefers letter-quality. Sample copy $4 with SAE. Fiction guidelines for SAE.
**Payment:** $5 per page, 2 contributor's copies; $4 charge for extras.
**Terms:** Acquires first North American serial rights on publication. Publication copyrighted.
**Tips:** "Write about what is essential to you, what you *must* say. If you are writing mainly for the sake of publication don't bother; have friends etc. read stories first before they go out to journals, find the flaws, write draft after draft. A good short story should take a month, NOT an afternoon." Published new writers within the last year.

**ST. ANDREWS REVIEW(II)**, St. Andrews Presbyterian College, Laurinburg NC 28352. (919)276-3652. Editor: Jack Roper. Fiction Editor: Roberta Rankin. General literary magazine for literary and fine arts audience. Semiannually. Estab. 1970. Circ. 1,000.
**Needs:** Condensed novel, contemporary, experimental, fantasy, historical (general), humor/satire, literary, mainstream, and prose poem. Receives 25 unsolicited mss/month. Accepts 2-6 mss/ issue; 5-12 mss/year.
**How to Contact:** Send complete ms. Reports in 2 months. SASE. Simultaneous and photocopied submissions OK. Accepts computer printout submissions. Prefers letter-quality. Sample copy $5 with legal-size SAE and 3 first class stamps.
**Payment:** 2 contributor's copies.
**Terms:** Publication copyrighted.

**SALOME: A LITERARY DANCE MAGAZINE (IV)**, Ommation Press, 5548 N. Sawyer, Chicago IL 60625. Editor: Effie Mihopoulos. "*Salome* tries to bring together all the arts with a prime focus on literature and dance for all those interested in the arts." Quarterly. Estab. 1976. Circ. 1,000.
**Needs:** Literary, contemporary, science fiction, fantasy, women's, feminist, gothic, romance, mystery, adventure, humor, serialized novels, prose poems, translations. "We seek mss relating to the dance. The theme doesn't have to be specifically about dance (one of the characters can be a dancer or choreographer; one of the characters might have a friend who is, etc.) but there must be some sort of dance relation. We seek dance-related fiction of all kinds and lengths, including prose poems." Accepts 40 mss/year. Receives approximately 25 unsolicited fiction mss each month. No preferred length. Sends mss on to editors of other publications. Recommends markets.
**How to Contact:** Send complete ms with SASE. Reports in 1 month. Sample copy $4. 9x12 SASE with 80¢ postage preferred.
**Payment:** 1 free author's copy. Contributor's rates for extras upon request.
**Terms:** Acquires first North American serial rights. "Rights revert to author but we retain reprint rights." Publication copyrighted.
**Tips:** "Write a well-written story or prose poem relating to dance." Rejected mss are "usually badly written—improve style, grammar, etc.—too often writers send out mss before they're ready. See a sample copy. Specify fiction interest."

**SAMISDAT (II)**, Box 129, Richford VT 05476. Editor: Merritt Clifton. Magazine: 8½x5½; 52-82 pages; standard bond paper; Vellum bristol cover stock; illustrations; photos. "*Samisdat* creates the culture of the future. Our stories, poems, and essays discuss the gradual but inevitable and necessary trend toward self-reliance, conservation, live-and-let-live politics, and Transcendentalist philosophy. We're outlaws and activists who direct our publication to reading eco-freaks, war-resisters, back-to-the-earthers, unschoolers, atheists, anarchists, libertarians—individualists who extend a willing hand from choice, not because Big Brother says so. They read us because we live out the beliefs we espouse and set a good, honest example of the possibilities." Published irregularly. Estab. 1973. Circ. 300-500.

**Needs:** Literary, contemporary, psychic/supernatural, science fiction, feminist, gay/lesbian, erotica, gothic, regional, western, and humor. "We don't use anything belonging to narrow genre confines. Our most frequent fiction contributors write war stories, gothics, outdoor stories, contemporary, psychic, and religious/inspirational—but the common denominator is that we all write about life, for the living, for those of us daring to choose our own destinies. No material modeled after anything seen in slicks or on bestseller lists. We'll consider anything genuine." Accepts 3-10 mss/issue, 15-50 mss/year. Receives approximately 100-300 unsolicited fiction mss each month. Approximately 1% of fiction is agented. Length: 1,500-5,000 words. Critiques rejected mss "when there is time."

**How to Contact:** Send complete ms with SASE. Reports in 3 weeks. Publishes ms an average of 2-3 months after acceptance. Sample copy $2.50.

**Payment:** 2 free author's copies. Cover price less discount for extras.

**Terms:** Acquires first rights, one-time rights. Buys reprints if out of print elsewhere. Publication copyrighted.

**Tips:** "Read *Samisdat* first. If you belong here, you'll know it instinctively. Be willing to rewrite and rethink. We prefer short manuscripts. Anything over 3,000 words is usually padded and verbose. We will reprint submissions if so designated. We work hard to help writers and expect writers to work equally hard toward helping themselves. Write the way marathoners train—for love of it, not the hope of 'success.' A few achieve 'success', but only a few, even at the top level of ability, and it's as much luck as anything else which few do 'succeed' at the right time and place to make a living at it."

**SAN JOSE STUDIES (II)**, San Jose State University Foundation, 125 S. 7th St., San Jose CA 95152. Editor: Selma Burkom. "A journal for the general, educated reader. Covers a wide variety of materials: fiction, poetry, interviews, interdisciplinary essays. Aimed toward the college-educated common reader with an interest in the broad scope of materials." Triannually. Estab. 1975. Circ. 500.

**Needs:** Literary, contemporary, men's, women's, humor, ethnic (black/Jewish, etc.), lesbian, gay, feminist, and regional. Accepts 1-2 mss/issue, 3-6 mss/year. Receives approximately 25 unsolicited fiction mss each month. Length: 2,500-5,000 + words. Critiques rejected mss "when there is time." Sometimes recommends markets.

**How to Contact:** Send complete ms with SASE. Accepts computer printout submissions. Prefers letter-quality. Reports in 2 months. Publishes ms an average of 6-12 months after acceptance.

**Payment:** 2 free author's copies.

**Terms:** Acquires first rights. Sends galleys to author. Publication copyrighted.

**Tips:** "Manuscripts read 'blind.' Name should appear *only* on cover sheet. We seldom print beginning writers of fiction." Annual $100 award for best story, essay or poem.

**SANDS (I, II), A Literary Review**, 17302 Club Hill Dr., Dallas TX 75248. (214)931-0190. Editors: Joyce Meier, Bob Loftus, Susan Charles Baugh. Magazine: 5½x8½; 100 + pages; line drawings. Magazine of short fiction, poetry, reviews, essays and art work. Published annually. Estab. 1979. Circ. 500.

**Needs:** Contemporary, fantasy, literary, mainstream, prose poem, psychic/supernatural/occult, regional, and translations. "We have no restrictions, really, but the writing must be of fine quality with emphasis on excellent use of the English language. No porno, lesbian or gay. Receives 15-20 unsolicited fiction mss/month. Accepts 6-10 mss/issue. Does not read Oct. through January. Publishes short shorts under 1,000 words. Length: 4,000 words maximum with some exceptions. Occasionally critiques rejected ms. Recommends other markets.

**How to Contact:** Send complete ms with SASE. Simultaneous and photocopied submissions OK. Accepts computer printout submissions. Letter quality, please. Reports in 3 months on mss. Sample copy $3.
**Payment:** 1 contributor's copy.
**Terms:** Acquires first rights. Publication copyrighted.
**Tips:** "Send us a ms with a clear story, specific details, fine language and interesting narrative and we will seriously consider it. We are committed to publishing short fiction because we feel the markets are too limited. We consider the short story an important *literary* tradition of American writing; it is the responsibility of small presses and literary magazines to keep the medium alive. We are getting better quality submissions now—we spend a lot of time with beginning writers to help them improve writing, whether we publish the story or not—most have been published in recommended markets." Published seven new writers within the last year.

**SCANDINAVIAN REVIEW (IV)**, American-Scandinavian Foundation, 127 E. 73rd St., New York NY 10021. (212)879-9779. Editor: Patricia McFate. Magazine of literature translated from Nordic languages and articles on art, politics, economics exploring contemporary Scandinavia. Quarterly. Estab. 1913. Circ. 5,000.
**Needs:** Literary, translations of Danish, Finnish, Icelandic, Norwegian or Swedish literature of authors born after 1880. These submissions are for the ASF Translation Prize.
**How to Contact:** Query first. Entries consist of 4 copies of the translation, including title page and a table of contents for proposed book, one copy of work in original language, and a letter signed by the author. Mss must be typed and double spaced.
**Payment:** $1,000 award.
**Terms:** Pays on publication for one-time rights. Publication copyrighted.

**‡SCRIVENER (II), Creative Journal**, 853 Sherbrooke St. W., Montreal, Quebec H3A 2T6 Canada. Editor: Andrew Burgess. Fiction Editor: Scott Hollinder. Magazine: 21.5 cm.x27.8 cm., 40 pages; glossy paper; illustrations; b&w photos. "*Scrivener* is a creative journal publishing fiction, poetry, graphics, photography, reviews, interviews and scholarly articles. We publish the best of new and established writers. We examine how current trends in North American writing are rooted in multimedia creative directions; our audience is mostly scholarly and in the writing field." Semiannually. Estab. 1980. Circ. 1,250.
**Needs:** Literature. Receives 20 unsolicited mss/month. Buys 5 mss/issue; 10 mss/year. Does not read mss in summer. Publishes ms up to 6 months after acceptance. Length: 10 pages maximum. Occasionally publishes short shorts. Occasionally critiques rejected mss. Recommends other markets.
**How to Contact:** Query first. Order sample copy ($2); send complete ms with cover letter with "artistic statements; where we can reach you; biographical data; education; previous publications." Reports in 6 months on queries and mss. SASE/IRC but not required "if you send $2 (Canadian) for sample copy." Simultaneous, photocopied submissions, and reprints OK. Accepts computer printouts including dot-matrix. Sample copy $2 (Canadian). Fiction guidelines for SAE/IRC.
**Payment:** Pays $3-25; contributor's copies and charges for extras.
**Terms:** Pays on publication.
**Tips:** "Send us your best stuff."

**SECOND COMING (III)**, Second Coming, Inc., Box 31249, San Francisco CA 94131. Editor/Publisher: A.D. Winans. "An international literary journal. Publishes only first class prose and fiction from professional writers for a literary audience." Biannual. Estab. 1971. Circ. 1,000.
**Needs:** Literary, science fiction, humor. "We do not buy the common or trite story outlines and first person confessional stories seen elsewhere." Accepts 2-6 mss/issue. Receives approximately 50-100 unsolicited fiction mss each month. Length: 1,500-3,500 (prefers 3,000) words. Not accepting new material until 1-1-86.
**How to Contact:** Query. Send complete ms. SASE for query, ms. Reports in 1 month. Sample copy $4.

**Payment:** Free author's copies. Occasionally pays $25 on publication.
**Terms:** Acquires first rights. Publication copyrighted.
**Tips:** "Be previously published in other literary journals before contacting us. We are a small publishing house, but our reputation is world-wide and we have published some of the best writers practicing their trade today. Current fall '85 fiction issue ($5) excellent example of what we're looking for."

**SECURITY CHECK (I, II, IV)**, c/o C. Atkinson, 2017 Kentucky Ave., Ft. Wayne IN 46805. (219)424-7816. Editor: Joy Baker. Fiction Editor: Carolyn Atkinson. Magazine. "This publication is genre-related. *Very* specifically, it deals with the character of Pavel Chekov of the *Star Trek* genre for anyone who enjoys *Star Trek* fiction in general, and Pavel Chekov in particular." Annually. Estab. 1980. Circ. 500 + .
**Needs:** Adventure, condensed novel, contemporary, fantasy, humor/satire, prose poem, psychic/supernatural/occult, contemporary romance, science fiction, serialized/excerpted novel, and suspense/mystery. No "blatant pornography; violence without cause; gay material." Receives approximately 5 unsolicited mss/month. Accepts 5-8 mss/issue; 5-8 mss/year. Length: varies. Comments on rejected ms only on request.
**How to Contact:** Query first. Reports in 2 weeks on queries; 2 months on mss. SASE. Simultaneous and photocopied submissions OK. Accepts computer printout submissions. Prefers letter-quality. Sample copy $8 (125 pages average, offset method).
**Payment:** 1 contributor's copy; regular copy price of $8 for extras.
**Terms:** Acquires one-time rights on publication. Publication copyrighted.
**Tips:** "We see less romance-oriented fiction as well as a resurgence of action/adventure submissions. Offer us something *different*—a different aspect of Chekov's personality, interests, personal life."

**SEEMS (II)**, Lakeland College, Sheboygan WI 53081. (414)565-3871. Editor: Karl Elder. Magazine: 8½x7; number of pages varies. "We publish fiction and poetry for an audience which tends to be highly literate. People read the publication, I suspect, for the sake of reading it." Published irregularly. Estab. 1971. Circ. 250.
**Needs:** Literary. Accepts 6-8 mss/issue. Receives approximately 10 unsolicited fiction mss each month. Length: 5,000 words maximum. Also publishes short shorts. Critiques rejected mss "when there is time."
**How to Contact:** Send complete ms with SASE. Accepts computer printout submissions. Prefers letter-quality. Reports in 2 months on mss. Publishes ms an average of 1-2 years after acceptance. Sample copy $3.
**Payment:** 1 free author's copy; $3 charge for extras.
**Terms:** Rights revert to author. Publication copyrighted.
**Tips:** "Read the magazine in order to help determine the taste of the editor." Mss are rejected because of "lack of economical expression, or saying with many words what could be said in only a few. Good fiction contains all of the essential elements of poetry; study poetry and apply those elements to fiction."

**SENIOR SCRIBES (II)**, 1200 S. Courthouse Rd., Arlington VA 22204. Editor: Pauline W. Reiher. Magazine: 16 pages, is "to encourage older people to write for publication" for senior citizen audience. Monthly. Estab. 1980. Circ. 350.
**Needs:** "We use very little fiction."
**Payment:** Contributor's copies.
**Tips:** "We publish articles and poems, mainly nostalgia." Published "many" new writers within the last year.

**SEQUOIA, Stanford Literary Magazine**, Storke Publications Bldg., Stanford CA 94305. "Publishes poetry, prose, fiction, interviews with selected authors, b&w photography and artwork; 90% freelance; student writing welcome. *Sequoia* prints fiction and poetry to be read by those outside as well as within the Stanford community. Many of our readers are authors themselves; others are interested in our magazine because of the well-known writers and interviewees featured in past issues." Published 3 times/year. Estab. 1956. Circ. 100.

**Needs:** "Literary excellence is the primary criterion. We'll consider anything but prefer literary, contemporary, men's, women's, ethnic, translations, and satire." Length: 8,000 words or 20 pp. maximum.

**How to Contact:** Send complete ms with SASE. Reports in 3 months "during academic year." Sample copy $1.

**Payment:** 1-2 free author's copies. Contributor's rates on request.

**Terms:** Acquires all rights.

**Tips:** "Be persistent. Don't allow your fiction to rely on shock value. Don't submit to a student-run publication during the summer; we generally close down then."

**THE SEWANEE REVIEW (III)**, University of the South, Sewanee TN 37375. (615)598-1245. Editor: George Core. Magazine: 6x9; 192 pages. "A literary quarterly, publishing original fiction, poetry, essays on literary and related subjects, book reviews and book notices for well-educated readers who appreciate good American and English literature." Quarterly. Estab. 1892. Circ. 3,500.

**Needs:** "Literary, contemporary. No translations, juvenile, gay/lesbian, erotica." Buys 10-15 mss/year. Receives approximately 100 unsolicited fiction mss each month. Length: 6,000-7,500 words. Critiques rejected mss "when there is time." Sometimes recommends markets.

**How to Contact:** Send complete ms with SASE with cover letter stating previous publications, if any. Accepts computer printout submissions. Reports in 1 month on mss. Sample copy $4.75.

**Payment:** $10-12/printed page. 2 free author's copies. $2.25 charge for extras.

**Terms:** Pays on publication for first North American serial rights and second serial rights by agreement. Publication copyrighted.

**Tips:** "Send only one story at a time, with a serious and sensible cover letter. We think fiction is of greater general interest than any other literary mode." Published new writers within the last year.

**SEZ/A MULTI-RACIAL JOURNAL OF POETRY & PEOPLE'S CULTURE (IV)**, Shadow Press, USA, Box 8803, Minneapolis MN 55408. (612)822-3488. Editor/Publisher: Jim Dochniak. Magazine: 8½x11; 72 pages; high grade matt paper; glossy cover stock; illustrations; photos. "Minnesota's only multicultural literary magazine. It places special emphasis on supporting writing which is class-conscious, deals with current social concerns, and, in some way, helps readers focus on building a new human culture. Publishes poetry, journal/diary excerpts, reportage, interviews, articles dealing with current social/cultural concerns and reviews, in addition to fiction. *Sez* is geared toward readers who may not necessarily read or appreciate academic, obscure, or self-indulgent art-for-art's-sake journals. Our audience, therefore, is one which believes that art is for humanity's sake, an audience which reads clear, understandable writing that is meaningful to their lives." Published irregularly. Plans special fiction issue. Estab. 1978. Circ. 1,500.

**Needs:** Literary, contemporary, men's, women's, feminist, gay/lesbian, ethnic (all), folklore, regional, reportage, and political. "We favor first-person, subjective narrative in any form. No material that is self-indulgent, cynical, racist, elitist, sexist or otherwise degrading." Accepts 2-10 mss/issue. Receives approximately 10 unsolicited fiction mss each month. Requires $3.50 for sample copy or $7 for subscription before reading ms. Does not read mss June 1- Oct. 10. Length: 250-2,500 words. Critiques rejected mss "on request." Sometimes recommends markets.

**How to Contact:** "Request sample copy with query." SASE for query, ms. A brief, non-academic bio and notes on what inspired the particular material sent. Reports in 1 month on queries, up to 6 months on mss.

**Payment:** Free author's copies. Cover price less 50% discount for extras.

**Terms:** Acquires one-time rights. Publication copyrighted.

**Tips:** "Study sample issues; query with list of possible writing ideas or projects. Quality is very important. We favor writers and writing from and about the upper Midwest region and writing from Third World writers. Issues are often focused on a particular theme and, therefore, writers should inquire before sending. Work and re-work your material. Most of what we receive is well-conceived, but only about half executed. Also, it helps immensely to 'study' the trends in fiction today and to read many many small press publications and books. Too many young writers today are trying to sound more intelligent than they really are; write about what you *know*, and write well about it—that makes the best story."

**‡SF INTERNATIONAL (II), Science Fiction from Around the World**, Andromeda Press, 99 Teardrop Ct., Newbury Park CA 91320. (805)498-9151. Editor: William H. Wheeler. Magazine: 8½x5½; 100 pages; 60 lb book paper; 65 lb cover stock; illustrations: b&w line. "Science fiction stories—short-short to about 10,000 words, occasionally novellas. Published in English from previously published or unpublished English or other language original for mature teens to adults. Bimonthly. Estab. 1985.
**Needs:** Some fantasy, science fiction. "Manuscripts accepted from US and foreign authors in English, French, Spanish, German, Italian, Portuguese, and Dutch. Other languages send an editable English translation plus the original language ms for reference." No nuclear holocaust or crazed robots. Receives 7 or 8 unsolicited mss/month. Accepts average 10 mss depending on lengths of selected mss; maybe 60/year. Publishes ms a few months after acceptance. Agented fiction maybe 20%. Length: 2,500 average; 1,000 words minimum; 10,000 words maximum. Publishes short shorts.
**How to Contact:** Send complete ms with cover letter. Reports in 1-2 months on mss. SASE for ms. Simultaneous, photocopied and reprint submissions OK. Accepts computer printouts including dot-matrix, "but we don't like them." Sample copy $2.50. Fiction guidelines for #10 SAE and 1 first class stamp.
**Payment:** Pays .01-.02/word.
**Terms:** Pays on acceptance for first North American serial for English originals, first English language for non-English originals. Publication copyrighted.
**Tips:** "Stories must get our interest in the first few paragraphs and hold it. Action is important, go easy on philosophical discourses. First-person fiction is very hard to do well. Be consistent in format details like captialization and hyphens in compound words, and please spell correctly."

**SHENANDOAH: THE WASHINGTON AND LEE UNIVERSITY REVIEW (II)**, Box 722, Lexington VA 24450. (703)463-8765. Editor: James Boatwright. Poetry Editor: Richard Howard. Magazine: 6x9; 100-120 pages. "We are a quarterly literary review publishing fiction, poetry, essays, and reviews." Published special fiction issue last year. Estab. 1950. Circ. 1,000.
**Needs:** Quality fiction.
**How to Contact:** Send complete ms with SASE. Sends galleys to author.
**Payment:** "By arrangement." One-year subscription. 2 free author's copies. $1.25 charge for extras.

**SHMATE, A Journal of Progressive Jewish Thought**, Box 4228, Berkeley CA 94704. Editor: Steve Fankuchen. Magazine "providing a forum for un-, mis- and under-represented social, political, and literary ideas and activities for Jews and non-Jews interested in issues of mutual concern and/or primary importance to Jews." Bimonthly. Estab. 1982. Circ. 3,500.
**Needs:** Comics, ethnic, experimental, fantasy, feminist, gay, historical (general), humor/satire, lesbian, literary, mainstream, men's, preschool, religious/inspirational, science fiction, senior citizen/retirement, translations, women's, young adult/teen, political, social. Receives 8 unsolicited mss/month. Accepts 2 mss/issue; 12 mss/year. Length: 1,500 words average. Sometimes critiques rejected mss.
**How to Contact:** Send complete ms. Reports in varying number of weeks. SASE. Simultaneous, photocopied and previously published submissions OK. Accepts computer printout submissions. Prefers letter-quality. Sample copy $3.
**Payment:** Pays in contributor's copies.
**Terms:** Acquires "all rights legally, but informal mutual rights." Publication copyrighted.
**Tips:** "Read the magazine."

**SIBYL-CHILD: A Woman's Arts and Culture Journal (II)** ,Sibyl-Child Press, Box 1773, Hyattsville MD 20788. (301)949-6267. Editors: Nancy Prothro, Saundra Maley. Magazine for "mostly women, but anyone who is interested in good literature for and about women." Semiannually. Estab. 1974. Circ. 200.
**Needs:** "Open to all categories." Receives 10 unsolicited fiction mss/month. Length: 500 words minimum, 2,500 words maximum, 2,000 words average. Occasionally critiques rejected mss.
**How to Contact:** Send complete ms with SASE. Send query with SASE. Photocopied submissions OK. Reports in 2 months on mss. Sample copy $2 and 5 first class stamps.
**Payment:** 3 free contributor's copies; $2 charge for extras.
**Terms:** Acquires one-time rights. Publication copyrighted.
**Tips:** "Proficiency in the use of the English language is obligatory. We are often republished."

**SIDEWINDER (II)**, College of the Mainland, 8001 Palmer Highway, Texas City TX 77591. (409)938-1211, ext. 313 or 223. Editor: Brett Jarrett. Fiction Editor: Thomas Carter. Magazine of contemporary fiction and poetry for adult, general audience. Biannually. Estab. 1983.
**Needs:** Contemporary, ethnic, experimental, literary and prose poem. No genre or formula stories. Receives variable number of mss/month. Accepts approximately 5 mss/issue; approximately 10 mss/year. Length: open. Sometimes critiques rejected ms.
**How to Contact:** Send complete ms. Reports in 2 months. SASE. Simultaneous and photocopied submissions OK. Sample copy $3. Fiction guidelines for SAE and 1 first class stamp.
**Payment:** 2 contributor's copies; $2 charge for extras.
**Terms:** Acquires first North American serial rights. Publication copyrighted.

**SIGN OF THE TIMES (II), A Chronicle of Decadence in the Atomic Age**, Studio 403 Corp., Box 6464, Portland OR 97228-6464. (206)784-8999. Editor: Mark Souder. Tabloid: 20 pages; book paper; 120 lb cover stock; illustrations; photos. "Decadence in all form, forms for those seeking literary amusement." Semiannually. Published special fiction issue last year; plans another. Estab. 1980. Circ. 750.
**Needs:** Comics, erotica, experimental, gay, lesbian, and men's. No religious or western manuscripts. Receives 3 unsolicited mss/month. Buys 6 mss/issue; 12 mss/year. Length: 5,000 words average; 500 words minimum, 7,500 words maximum. Publishes short shorts. Occasionally comments on rejected ms. Recommends other markets.
**How to Contact:** Send complete ms. Reports in 6 weeks on mss. SASE with bio. Photocopied submissions OK. Accepts computer printout submissions. Prefers letter-quality. Sample copy $2.50. Fiction guidelines for #10 SASE.
**Payment:** $0-20, subscription to magazine, 2 contributor's copies; 2 times cover price charge for extras.
**Terms:** Pays on publication for first rights plus anthology in the future. Publication copyrighted.
**Tips:** "Write what you know and feel. We publish fiction because many magazines do not." Published new writers within the last year.

**SIGNALS (II)**, Alpha Epsilon Rho, The National Broadcasting Society, USC College of Journalism, University of South Carolina, Columbia SC 29208. (803)777-6783. Executive Secretary: Dr. Richard Uray. "Geared to articles, mainly nonfiction, about the radio-TV film business, industry, personalities; for university students majoring in broadcasting and professionals employed in radio-TV-film." Monthly (Sept.-May). Estab. 1977. Circ. 2,000.
**Needs:** Men's, women's, and humor. "We are not really seeking fiction pieces as much as in-depth nonfiction related to the communications industry." Receives approximately 4-5 unsolicited fiction mss each month. Critiques rejected mss "when there is time."
**How to Contact:** Query. SASE for query, ms. Reports in 3 weeks on queries, 2 weeks on mss. Sample copy with 9x14 SAE plus 50¢ postage.
**Payment:** 2 free author's copies. $2 charge for extras.
**Terms:** Acquires first rights.

**SILVERFISH REVIEW (IV)**, Silverfish Press, Box 3541, Eugene OR 97403. (503)342-2344. Editor: Rodger Moody. High quality literary material for a general audience. Published 3 times/ year. Estab. 1979. Circ. 500.
**Needs:** Literary. Accepts 1-2 mss/issue.
**How to Contact:** Send complete ms with SASE. Reports in 1 month on mss. Sample copy $2 with SAE and 80¢ for postage.
**Payment:** 3 free author's copies.
**Terms:** Pays on publication; rights revert to author.
**Tips:** "We publish primarily poetry; we will, however, publish good quality fiction."

**SING HEAVENLY MUSE! (II)**, Sing Heavenly Muse, Box 13299, Minneapolis MN 55414. (612)822-8713. Editor: Sue Ann Martinson. Magazine: 6x9; 125 pages; 55 lb acid-free paper; 10 pt. glossy cover stock; illustrations; photos. Women's poetry, prose and artwork. Semiannually. Published special fiction issue. Estab. 1977.
**Needs:** Literary, contemporary, fantasy, women's, feminist, mystery, humor, and ethnic minority. Receives approximately 30 unsolicited fiction mss each month. "Accepts ms for consideration only in April and September." Publishes short shorts. Recommends other markets.
**How to Contact:** Cover letter with "brief writing background and publications." Accepts computer printout submissions. Reports in 1-3 months on queries and mss. Publishes ms an average of 6 months after acceptance. Sample copy $3.50.
**Payment:** Honorarium; 2 free copies.
**Terms:** Pays on publication for first rights. Publication copyrighted.
**Tips:** "As part of our editorial policy, we include all types of women's creative writing fiction, poetry, creative essay." Published new writers within the last year.

**SKYLARK (I)**, 2233 171st St., Hammond IN 46323. (219)844-0520, ext. 372. Contact: Editor. Magazine: 8½x11; 120 pages; illustrations; photos. Fine arts magazine—short stories, poems and graphics for adults and children. Annually. Plans special fiction issue. Estab. 1971. Circ. 500.
**Needs:** Contemporary, ethnic, experimental, fantasy, feminist, historical (general), horror, humor/satire, juvenile, literary, mainstream, prose poem, psychic/supernatural/occult, regional, science fiction, serialized/excerpted novel, suspense/mystery, and western. Receives 20 mss/ month. Accepts 6-7 mss/issue. Length: 1-20 double-spaced pages.
**How to Contact:** Send complete ms. Photocopied submissions OK. Accepts computer printout submissions. Prefers letter-quality. Sample copy $4 and 9x12 SAE.
**Payment:** 2 contributor's copies.
**Terms:** Acquires first rights. Publication copyrighted. Copyright reverts to author.
**Tips:** 1986 issue—special section written by Vietnam Veterans (poetry, prose, graphics). "Encourage submissions from children 6-18. The goal of *Skylark* is to encourage *Creativity* and give beginning authors the opportunity of being published." Published new writers within the last year.

**SLIPSTREAM (II)**, Slipstream Publications, Box 2071, New Market Station, Niagara Falls NY 14301. (716)282-2616. Editor: Dan Sicoli. Fiction Editors: R. Borgatti and D. Sicoli. Magazine: 8½x7; 60-80 pages; glossy cover stock; illustrations; photos. "We use poetry and short fiction with a contemporary urban feel." Estab. 1981. Circ. 400.
**Needs:** Contemporary, erotica, ethnic, experimental, fantasy, feminist, gay, humor/satire, lesbian, literary, mainstream, prose poem, and science fiction. No religious, juvenile, young adult, or romance. Receives 40-50 unsolicited mss/month. Accepts 2-5 mss/issue; 5-7 mss/year. Publishes short shorts. Rarely critiques rejected ms. Recommends other markets.
**How to Contact:** Send complete ms. Reports in 3 months. SASE. Accepts computer printout submissions. Sample copy $3. Fiction guidelines for business-size SASE.
**Payment:** 1 contributor's copy; discount for extras. "Hopefully there soon may be a cash payment—pending NYSCA grant."
**Terms:** Acquires one-time rights on publication. Publication copyrighted.

**Tips:**"Writing should be honest, fresh; develop your own style. Check out a sample issue first. Don't write for the sake of writing, write from the gut as if it were a biological need. Write from experience and mean what you say, but say it in the fewest number of words." A special erotica/porn theme issue is planned for 1986.

**THE SMALL POND MAGAZINE,** Box 664, Stratford CT 06497. (203)378-4066. Editor: Napoleon St. Cyr. Magazine: 5½x8½; 42 pages; 60 lb offset paper; 65 lb cover stock; illustrations (art). "Features contemporary poetry, the salt of the earth, peppered with short prose pieces of various kinds. The college educated and erudite read it for good poetry, prose and pleasure." Triannually. Estab. 1964. Circ. 300.
**Needs:** "Rarely use science fiction or formula stories you'd find in *Cosmo*, *Redbook*, *Ladies Home Journal*, etc." Buys 10-12 mss/year. Longer response time in July and August. Receives approximately 50 unsolicited fiction mss each month. Approximately 1% of fiction is agented. Length: 200-2,500 words. Critiques rejected mss "when there is time." Sometimes recommends other markets.
**How to Contact:** Send complete ms with SASE and short VITA; publishing credits. Accepts computer printout submissions. Prefers letter-quality. Reports in 2 weeks-1 month. Publishes ms an average of 2-12 months after acceptance. Sample copy $2.50.
**Payment:** 2 free author's copies. $2/copy charge for extras.
**Terms:** Pays on publication for all rights. Publication copyrighted.
**Tips:** "Send for a sample copy first. All mss must be typed. Name and address and story title on front page, name of story on succeeding pages." Mss are rejected because of "tired plots and poor grammar; also over-long—2,500 maximum." Published new writers within the last year.

**SNAPDRAGON (II),** English Dept., University of Idaho, Moscow ID 83843. (208)885-6937. Editors: Gail Eckwright, Margaret Snyder and Tina Foriyes. "Poems, artwork, photos and stories are the types of material published for a largely local, Northwest community and university students." Biannually. Estab. 1977. Circ. 200.
**Needs:** Literary, contemporary, and regional. "We will consider whatever we see. Accepts 2 or 3 mss/issue, 5 mss/year. Receives approximately 2-3 unsolicited fiction mss each month. Length: 200-5,000 words.
**How to Contact:** Send complete ms with SASE. Accepts computer printout submissions. Prefers letter-quality. Reporting time varies on mss; if sent in September or early March there is a rapid response. Publishes ms an average of 2-3 months after acceptance. Sample copy $2 and 80¢ for postage.
**Payment:** Free author's copy, occasionally small cash payments.
**Terms:** One-time rights. Publication copyrighted.
**Tips:** "Be honest, proofread your work, don't overwrite. Write a sound conventional story (without clichés) before you try experimental modes. Proofread! Mss are rejected because "they lack sophistication in the development of character and of a recognizable style. In general, the writer simply hasn't the maturity of style."

**SNOWY EGRET,** 205 S. Ninth St., Williamsburg KY 40269. (606)549-0850. Editor: Humphrey A. Olsen. Fiction Editor: Alan Seaburg. Natural history and material related to natural history. Semipopular. Semiannually. Estab. 1922. Circ. 400.
**Needs:** Literary, regional, and translations, stories that are natural history related. Buys 1-2 mss/issue, 3-4 mss/year. Length: 0-10,000 words. Critiques rejected mss "when there is time." Sometimes recommends markets.
**How to Contact:** Send complete ms with SASE. Accepts computer printout submissions. Reports in 2 months on mss. Sample copy $2.
**Payment:** Pays $2/magazine page. Free author's copy. $1.50 per copy up to 5 extra.
**Terms:** Pays on publication for first North American serial rights. Publication copyrighted.
**Tips:** "Write the kind of fiction we are looking for. Be sure material is related to natural history and has the element of surprise."

**SOJOURNER, A Women's Forum (II)**, 143 Albany St., Cambridge MA 02139. (617)661-3567. Editor-in-Chief: Shane Snowdon. Magazine: 11x17; 44 pages; newsprint paper and cover stock; illustrations; photos. "Feminist journal publishing interviews, nonfiction features, news, viewpoints, poetry, reviews (music, cinema, books) and fiction for women." Published monthly. Published special fiction issue last year. Estab. 1975. Circ. 45,000.
**Needs:** Contemporary, ethnic, experimental, fantasy, feminist, lesbian, humor/satire, literary, prose poem, and women's. Receives 20 unsolicited fiction mss/month. Accepts 10 mss/year. Approximately 10% of fiction is agented. Length: 1,000 words minimum; 4,000 words maximum; 2,500 words average. Recommends other markets.
**How to Contact:** Send complete ms with SASE and cover letter with previous publications; current works. Photocopied submissions OK. Publishes ms an average of 1-2 months after acceptance. Sample copy $1.75 with 10x13 SAE and 86¢ postage. Free fiction guidelines with SASE.
**Payment:** Subscription to magazine and 2 contributor's copies. No extra charge up to 5; $1 charge each thereafter.
**Terms:** First rights only. Sends galleys to author. Publication copyrighted.
**Tips:** "Pay attention to appearance of manuscript. Very difficult to wade through sloppily presented fiction, however good. Do write a cover letter. If not cute; can't hurt and may help. Mention previous publication(s)." Published new writers within the last year.

**‡SONOMA MANDALA (II)**, Dept. of English, Sonoma State University, 1801 E. Cotati Ave., Rohnert Park CA 94928. Editor: Sonoma Mandala. Magazine: 8½x7; varied pages; bond paper; card cover stock; some illustrations; some photos. 'We have no static thematic preference. We publish several short pieces (up to 2,500 words) of fiction in each issue." For campus community of a small liberal arts college and the surrounding rural/residential area. Annually. Estab. 1972. Circ. 500-1,000.
**Needs:** Contemporary, ethnic, experimental, fantasy, feminist, gay, humor/satire, lesbian, literary, mainstream, men's, translations, women's, western regional. Receives 10-15 unsolicited fiction mss/month. Accepts 3-5 mss/issue. Does not read ms January to September. Publishes 9-12 months after acceptance. Length: 1,000 average; 2,500 words maximum. Publishes short shorts.
**How to Contact:** Send complete ms with cover letter. Reports in 1-3 months. SASE for ms. Photocopied submissions OK. Accepts dot-matrix computer printouts. Sample copy $3 (if available) and 8½x11 SAE.
**Payment:** 2 contributor's copies.
**Terms:** Pays on publication for one-time rights, revert to author upon publication.

**SONORA REVIEW (II)**, University of Arizona, Department of English, Tucson AZ 85721. (602)621-1836. Editors: Scott Wigton and Antonya Nelson. Fiction Editor: Peter Turchi. Magazine: 9x6; 120 pages; 16 lb paper; 20 lb cover stock; rarely illustrations; photos. *The Sonora Review* publishes short fiction and poetry of high literary quality. Semiannually. Published special fiction issue; plans another. Estab. 1980. Circ. 500-700.
**Needs:** Literary. "We are open to a wide range of stories with accessibility and vitality being important in any case. We're not interested in genre fiction, formula work." Buys 4-6 mss/issue. Approximately 10% of fiction is agented. Length: open, though prefers work under 25 pages. Sometimes recommends other markets.
**How to Contact:** Send complete ms with SASE. Cover letter with previous publications. Accepts computer printout submissions. Prefers letter-quality. Reports in 2 months on mss. Publishes ms an average of 2-6 months after acceptance. Sample copy $3.
**Payment:** 3 free author's copies. $2 charge for extras. Annual cash prizes.
**Terms:** Acquires first North American serial rights.
**Tips:** "All mss are read carefully, and we try to make brief comments if time permits. Our hope is that an author will keep us interested in his or her treatment of a subject by using fresh details and writing with an authority that is absorbing." Mss are rejected because "1) we only have space for 6-8 manuscripts out of several hundred submissions annually, and 2) most of the manuscripts we receive have some merit but are not of publishable quality. It would be helpful to receive a cover letter with all manuscripts." Published new writers within the last year.

**SOUNDINGS EAST (II)**, English Dept., Salem State College, Salem MA 01970. (617)745-0556, Ext. 2333. Advisory Editor: Claire Keyes. Magazine: 5½x8½; 64 pages; illustrations; photos. "No theme necessarily. Mainly a college audience, but we also distribute to libraries throughout the country." Biannually. Estab. 1973. Circ. 2,000.
**Needs:** Literary and contemporary. No juvenile. Publishes 4-5 stories/issue. Receives 30 unsolicited fiction mss each month. Does not read April-August. Publishes short shorts of 12-15 typed, manuscript pages. Length: 2,500-10,000 words. "We are open to short pieces as well as to long works." Critiques rejected mss "when there is time." Recommends other markets.
**How to Contact:** Send complete ms with SASE only between September and March. Accepts computer printout submissions. Prefers letter-quality. Reports in 2 months on mss. Sample copy $2.
**Payment:** 2 free author's copies.
**Terms:** All publication rights revert to authors.
**Tips:** "The writer should read a few of our issues to get a sense of the range of fiction we publish. The mss should be clean—that is, clearly typed with no hand-written revisions. We seek authors with an original point of view." Published new writers within the last year.

**SOUTH CAROLINA REVIEW**, Clemson University, Clemson SC 29631. (803)656-3229. Editors: R.J. Calhoun, Frank Day, and Carol Johnston. Managing Editor: Martin V. Jacobi. Magazine: 6x9; 132 pages; 60 lb cream white vellum paper; 65 lb cream white vellum cover stock; rarely illustrations; rarely photos. Semiannually. Estab. 1967. Circ. 700.
**Needs:** Literary, contemporary, humor and ethnic. Receives approximately 50-60 unsolicited fiction mss each month. Does not read mss June-August. Critiques rejected mss "when there is time."
**How to Contact:** Send complete ms with SASE. Accepts computer printout submissions. Reports in 2 months on mss. Sample copy $3.
**Payment:** Pays in contributor's copies.
**Terms:** Publication copyrighted.
**Tips:** Mss are rejected because of "poorly structured stories, or stories without vividness or intensity. The most celebrated function of a little magazine, is to take a chance on writers not yet able to get into the larger magazines . . . . the little magazine can encourage promising writers at a time when encouragement is vitally needed. (We also publish 'name' writers, like Joyce Carol Oates, Stephen Dixon, George Garrett.) Read the masters extensively. Write and write more, with a *schedule*. Listen to editorial advice when offered. Don't get discouraged with rejections. Read what writers say about writing (e.g. The Paris Interviews with Geo. Plimpton, gen. ed.; Welty's *One Writer's Beginnings*, etc. Take courses in writing and listen to, even if you do not follow, the advice." Published new writers within the last year.

**SOUTH DAKOTA REVIEW (II)**, University of South Dakota, Box 111, University Exchange, Vermillion SD 57069. (605)677-5966. Editor: John R. Milton. Magazine: 6x9; 100 + pages; book paper; glossy cover stock; illustrations sometimes; photos on cover. Literary magazine for university and college audiences and their equivalent. Emphasis is often on the West and its writers, but will accept mss from anywhere. Issues are generally fiction and poetry with some literary essays. Specific needs vary according to budget and other conditions. Quarterly. Estab. 1963. Circ. 500.
**Needs:** Literary, contemporary, ethnic, experimental, excerpted novel, regional, and translations. "We like very well-written stories. Contemporary western American setting appeals, but not necessary. No formula stories, sports, or adolescent 'I' narrator." Receives 30 unsolicited fiction mss/month. Accepts about 8-12 mss/year more or less. Assistant editor needs mss in June-July, sometimes August. Approximately 5% of fiction is agented. Publishes short shorts of 5 pages double-spaced typescript. Length: 3,000 words minimum; 6,000 words maximum. Sometimes recommends markets.
**How to Contact:** Send complete ms with SASE. Photocopied submissions OK. Reports in 1 month. Publishes ms an average of 1-6 months after acceptance. Sample copy $3.
**Payment:** 2-4 free author's copies depending on length of ms. $2 charge for extras.

**Terms:** Acquires first rights and second serial rights. Publication copyrighted.

**Tips:** $100 to best story published in the magazine every year or every other year. Rejects mss because of "careless writing; often careless typing; stories too personal ('I' confessional), adolescent; working-manuscript, not polished; subject matter that editor finds trivial. We are trying to use more fiction and more variety. We would like to see more sophisticated stories." Published new writers the last year.

**SOUTHERN HUMANITIES REVIEW (II)**, Auburn University, 9088 Haley Center, Auburn University AL 36849. Co-Editors: Thomas L. Wright and Dan R. Latimer. Magazine: trim 6x9; i-iv- + 96 pages; 60 lb neutral PH, natural paper, 65 lb natural PH med; coated cover stock; occasional illustrations; occasional photos. "We publish essays, poetry, fiction, and reviews. Our fiction has ranged from very traditional in form and content to very experimental. Literate, college-educated audience. We hope they read our journal for both enlightenment and pleasure." Quarterly. Estab. 1967. Circ. 800.

**Needs:** Serious fiction, fantasy, feminist, humor, psychic/supernatural/occult, and regional. Receives approximately 8-10 unsolicited fiction mss each month. Accepts and prints 1-2 mss/issue, 4-6 mss/year. Slower reading time in summer. Length: 3,500-5,000 words. Critiques rejected mss "when there is time." Recommends other markets.

**How to Contact:** Send complete ms with SASE and cover letter with an explanation of topic chosen—special, certain book, etc., a little about author if they have never submitted. Accepts computer printout submissions. Prefers letter-quality. Reports in 90 days. Sample copy $4. Charge for extras $4.

**Payment:** 1 complete copy, plus 10-15 offprints; $3 charge for extras.

**Terms:** Pays on publication for first rights. Sends galleys to author. Publication copyrighted.

**Tips:** "Send us the ms with SASE. If we like it, we'll take it or we'll recommend changes. If we don't like it, we'll send it back as promptly as possible. Read the journal. Send a typewritten, clean copy carefully proofread. We also award annually the Hoepfner Prize of $100 for the best published essay or short story of the year. Let someone you respect the opinion of read your story and give you an honest appraisal. Rewrite, if necessary, to get the most from your story." Published new writers within the last year.

**THE SOUTHERN REVIEW (II)**, Louisiana State University, 43 Allen Hall, Baton Rouge LA 70803. (504)388-5108. Editors: James Olney and Lewis P. Simpson. Magazine: 10x6¾; 240 pages; 50 lb Warren's Oldstyle paper; 65 lb #1 grade cover stock; occasional photos. A literary quarterly publishing critical essays, poetry and fiction for the highly intellectual audience. Quarterly. Published special fiction issue. Estab. 1935. Circ. 3,000.

**Needs:** Literary and contemporary. "We emphasize style and substantial content. No mystery, fantasy or religious mss." Buys 3-4 mss/issue. Receives approximately 100 unsolicited fiction mss each month. Approximately 17% of fiction is agented. Length: 2,000-10,000 words. Sometimes recommends markets.

**How to Contact:** Send complete ms with SASE. Accepts computer printout submissions. Prefers letter-quality. Reports in 2 months on mss. Publishes ms an average of 1-2 years after acceptance. Sample copy $5.

**Payment:** Pays $12/printed page. 2 free author's copies.

**Terms:** Pays on publication for first North American serial rights. "We transfer copyright to author on request." Sends galleys to author. Publication copyrighted.

**Tips:** "Develop a careful style with characters in depth." Sponsors annual contest for best collection of short stories published during the calendar year. Published new writers within the last year.

**SOUTHWEST REVIEW (II)**, Box 4374, Southern Methodist University, Dallas TX 75275. (214)373-7440. Editor: Willard Spiegelman. Magazine: 6x9; 145 pages. "The majority of our readers are college-educated adults, who wish to stay abreast of the latest and best in contemporary fiction, poetry, literary criticism, and books in all but the most specialized disciplines." Quarterly. Estab. 1915. Circ. 1,350.

**Needs:** "High literary quality; no specific requirements as to subject matter, but cannot use sentimental, religious, western, poor science fiction, pornographic, true confession, mystery, juvenile, or serialized or condensed novels." Receives approximately 85 unsolicited fiction mss each month. Length: prefers 3,000-5,000 words. Occasionally critiques rejected mss. Sometimes recommends markets.

**How to Contact:** Send complete ms with SASE. Accepts computer printout submissions. Prefers letter-quality. Reports in 3 months on mss. Publishes ms 6-12 months after acceptance. Sample copy $3. Free guidelines with SASE.

**Payment:** Pays ½¢/word, plus 3 free author's copies.

**Terms:** Pays on publication for first North American serial rights. Sends galleys to author. Publication copyrighted.

**Tips:** "We have become less regional. A lot of time would be saved for us and for the writer if he looked at a copy of the *Southwest Review* before submitting." Published new writers within the last year.

**SOU'WESTER (II)**, English Dept., Southern Illinois University-Edwardsville, Edwardsville IL 62026. (618)692-2289. Editor-in-Chief: Dickie A. Spurgeon. Magazine: 6x9; 88 pages; 60 lb cover stock. General magazine of poetry and fiction (to 10,000 words). Published 3 times/year. Estab. 1960. Circ. 300.

**Needs:** Contemporary, erotica, ethnic, experimental, fantasy, feminist/lesbian, gay, literary, mainstream, regional, and translations. Receives 40-50 unsolicited fiction mss/month. Accepts 3 mss/issue, 9 mss/year. Publishes short shorts. Length: 5,000 words minimum; 10,000 words maximum. Occasionally critiques rejected mss.

**How to Contact:** Send complete ms with SASE. Simultaneous and photocopied submissions OK. Accepts computer printout submissions. Reports in 1 month. Publishes ms an average of 2 months after acceptance. Sample copy $1.50.

**Payment:** 2 contributor's copies. $1.50 charge for extras.

**Terms:** Acquires all rights. Publication copyrighted.

**Tips:** "I like reading fiction. The editor's job wouldn't be as much fun if all submissions were poetry. Send just one story at a time. Keep sending them. We have at times rejected half a dozen stories by an author before accepting one." Published new writers within the last year.

**SOVEREIGN GOLD LITERARY MAGAZINE (I)**, Box 1631, Iowa City IA 52244. (319)354-1191. Executive Editor: Gary J. King. Magazine. "Positive for America." Readership: all ages. Triquarterly. Estab. 1973. Circ. 750. "Publication is worldwide, will be published in 5 booklets. All fiction in *Fiction Parade*."

**Needs:** Adventure, historical, juvenile, literary, preschool, prose poem, religious/inspirational, science fiction ("not too futuristic, down-to-earth"), and senior citizen/retirement. "We want fiction with positive theme and good moral message—no off-beat or sex. We would like to see science fiction and senior citizen/retirement material. No bad language or sex." Receives 25-75 unsolicited mss/month. Accepts 25-50 mss/year. Length: 500-2,500 words average; 5,000 words maximum "for the present, but will read longer." Usually critiques rejected mss.

**How to Contact:** Query or send complete ms. Reports in 1 week. SASE. No simultaneous submissions. Accepts computer printout submissions. Prefers letter-quality. Publishes ms an average of 3-4 months after acceptance. Sample copy $4 with 6x9 SAE. Fiction guidelines free; SASE.

**Payment:** 1 contributor's copy.

**Terms:** Acquires first rights. Buys reprints "if excellent and after query." Publication copyrighted. Write for award program guidelines.

**Tips:** Writers, unpublished or professional, can be published in *Sovereign Gold*. We will publish 50-170 mss in 1986.

**SPACE AND TIME (IV)**, 138 W. 70th St., New York NY 10023. Editor-in-Chief: Gordon Linzner. Magazine: 8½x5½; 120 pages; 20 lb paper; index cover stock; illustrations. Magazine of "fantasy fiction of all types and sub-genres (including science fiction)—the less categorizable,

the better. *S&T* tends to feature new writers and odd pieces for which there are few if any other markets. Some poetry. *S&T* attracts readers who cannot get enough of this material or who want something new and different. Because it is small, *S&T* can take chances on stories that are either too traditional or too experimental, and prides itself on its variety of styles and story types. Also well illustrated." Published semiannually. Published special fiction issue; plans another. Estab. 1966. Circ. 400.
**Needs:** Adventure, fantasy, horror, humor/satire, psychic/supernatural/occult, and science fiction. "Actually, will consider almost any type of fiction as long as it has a fantastic slant. No media clones—no tales involving characters/situations that are not your creation (*Star Trek*, et al) except for certain types of satire. No stories based on Von Daniken, etc., type cults." Receives 75-100 unsolicited fiction mss/month. Accepts 12 mss/issue, 24 mss/year. Length: 15,000 words maximum. Occasionally critiques rejected mss. Sometimes recommends markets.
**How to Contact:** Send complete ms with SASE. Photocopied submissions OK. Accepts computer printout submissions. Prefers letter-quality. Reports in 8 weeks. Publishes ms an average of 1-2 years after acceptance. Sample copy $4.
**Payment:** 1/4¢/word and 2 contributor's copies. Charges cover price less 40% contributor discount for extras.
**Terms:** Pays on acceptance for first North American serial rights. Publication copyrighted.
**Tips:** "Keep writing and learning your craft. Don't telephone us—this is a very small, part-time press." Published "several" new writers within the last year.

**THE SPIRIT THAT MOVES US** , The Spirit That Moves Us Press, Inc., Box 1585, Iowa City IA 52244. (319)338-7502. Editor: Morty Sklar. Publishes fiction, poetry, essays and artwork. "We want feeling and imagination, work coming from the human experience." Semiannually. Estab. 1975. Circ. 1,500-2,000.
**Needs:** Literary and contemporary, men's, women's, feminist, gay/lesbian, humor, ethnic, and translations. No sensational. Buys 1-2 mss/issue and 25 mss for special fiction issues. Receives approximately 50 unsolicited fiction mss each month. Length: 7,000 words maximum. Critiques rejected mss "when there is time. We published a special fiction issue in 1985. Please. Send SASE to find out what our needs are."
**How to Contact:** Send SASE for theme and plans. Accepts computer printout submissions. Prefers letter-quality. Reports in 1 week-1 month on mss. Publishes ms an average of 6 months after acceptance. Sample copy $5 for *Here's the Story* (all fiction issue); $4 for *The Spirit That Moves Us Reader* (7th anniversary anthology).
**Payment:** Free cloth and paper copy, 40% discount for extras; 25% on all other publications.
**Terms:** Pays on publication for first rights. Buys reprints for anthology issue. Publication copyrighted.
**Tips:** "Query for theme with SASE. We're small but good and well-reviewed. Send the work you love best. Write from yourself and not from what you feel is the fashion or what the editor wants. This editor wants what you want if it has heart, guts, imagination and skill. Aside from the obvious reason for rejection, poor writing, the main reason for rejection is lack of human concerns or moral conviction . . . that is, the writer seems to be concerned with style more than content. Read a copy of the magazine you'll be submitting work to. Don't rely on your writing for money unless you're in it for the money. Have time to write, as much time as you can get (be anti-social if necessary). We have published a 504-page volume of fiction, poetry, essays and graphics entitled *Editor's Choice: Literature & Graphics From The US Small Press, 1965-1977*. *Editor's Choice II* will be published in 1986. In 1986 we're publishing only poetry. Send SASE in 1987 for fiction needs then," (covering the period from 1978-1983). Selections are made from nominations by editors of other magazines and presses."

**SPITBALL (I)** ,1721 Scott Blvd., Covington KY 41011. Editor: Mike Shannon. Magazine: 8½x5½; 40+ pages; 20 lb white paper; 65-67 lb cover stock; illustrations; rarely photos. Magazine publishing "fiction and poetry about *baseball* exclusively for an educated, literary segment of the baseball fan population." Quarterly. Estab. 1981. Circ. 500.

**Needs:** Confession, contemporary, experimental, historical, literary, mainstream, and suspense. "Our only requirement concerning the type of fiction written is that the story be *primarily* about baseball." Receives "25 or so" unsolicited fiction mss/year. Accepts 3-4 mss/year, "7-8 if we would receive that many publishable manuscripts." Length: No limit. The longer it is, the better it has to be. "Almost always critiques" rejected mss; "sometimes at length."

**How to Contact:** Send complete ms with SASE and cover letter with brief bio about author. Simultaneous, photocopied and previously published submissions OK. Reports in 1 month on mss. Publishes ms an average of less than 3 months after acceptance. Sample copy $2.

**Payment:** "No monetary payment at present. We may offer nominal payment in the near future." 2 free contributor's copies per issue in which work appears.

**Terms:** Acquires first North American serial rights. Buys reprints "if the work is good enough and it hasn't had major exposure already." Publication copyrighted. "We sponsor an annual fiction contest. We award baseball-related merchandise prizes to winners."

**Tips:** "Our audience is mostly college educated and knowledgeable about baseball. The stories we have published so far have been very well written and displayed a firm grasp of the baseball world and its people. In short, audience response has been great because the stories are simply good as stories. Thus, mere use of baseball as subject is no guarantee of acceptance. We need many submissions. Unlike many literary magazines, we have no backlog of accepted material. Thus, we can publish good stories almost immediately. Submit, get our feed-back and keep trying. Consult Charles Einsteins' *Fireside Books of Baseball*, *Baseball Diamonds* (ed. by Kerrane and Grossinger), *Fielder's Choice* (ed. by Jerome Holtzman), and *The Thrill of the Grass* by W.P. Kinsella, as a start. Also read sample *Spitballs*. Fiction is a natural genre for our exclusive subject, baseball. There are great opportunities for writing in certain areas of fiction, baseball being one of them. Baseball has become the 'in' spectator sport among intelectuals, the general media, and the 'Yuppie' crowd. Consequently, as subject matter for adult fiction it has gained a much wider acceptance than it once enjoyed." Published new writers within the last year.

**‡SQUARE ONE (I, II), A Magazine of Fiction**, Square One Publications, Union Box 102; UW-Milwaukee, Milwaukee WI 53201. Editors: William D. Gagliani, Dennis K. Michel. Magazine: 8½x11; 70-85 pages; 20 lb white bond paper; 70 lb colored cover stock; illustrations; pen and ink drawings or any black on white. "There is no specific theme at *Square One*, but we publish only fiction and illustrations. Aimed at a general literate audience—people who *enjoy* reading fiction." Annually (currently). Estab. 1984. Circ. 250.

**Needs:** Open to categories. "We like exciting stories in which things happen and characters *exist*." Receives 10-12 unsolicited fiction mss/month. Accepts 6-12 mss/issue, depending on lengths; 6-12 mss/year. Publishes ms generally 2-9 months after acceptance. Length: 3,000 words average; 7,500 words maximum. Publishes short shorts. "It is editorial policy to comment on at least 85% of submissions rejected."

**How to Contact:** Send complete ms with cover letter. Cover letter is optional. Reports in 2-9 months on mss. SASE for ms. Simultaneous (if so labeled), photocopied and reprint submissions OK. Accepts computer printouts including dot-matrix if legible. Accepts electronic submissions via disc or modem. "We can *only* accept DS/DD disks—system is Kaypro 2X (CP/M), Wordstar." Sample copy $2.50, 9x12 SAE and 7 first class stamps. Fiction guidelines for #10 SAE and 1 first class stamp.

**Payment:** Two contributor's copies.

**Terms:** Pays on publication for one-time rights. Publication copyrighted.

**Tips:** "We like to see new writers in *Square One*, writers that (we hope) will go on to publish in the paying markets. We also like to see established writers—people who are interested in expanding the field of fiction and don't care whether they are paid to do so or not. *Square One* is not a journal for beginners, despite what the name may imply. Rather, it refers to the back to basics approach that we take—fiction must first and foremost be compelling. We want to see stories that elicit a response from the reader. We will give slight preference to Wisconsin writers, but will gladly consider submissions from anywhere."

**THE SQUATCHBERRY JOURNAL, Northern Ontario's Journal of Arts, Letters, and Local History**, Box 205, Geraldton, Ontario, Canada P0T 1M0. (807)854-1184. Editor: Edgar J. Lavoie. Magazine featuring writers and artists who portray Northern Ontario in fact or fiction, prose or poetry for general audience. Semiannually. Estab. 1975. Circ. 1,200.
**Needs:** Adventure, ethnic, historical, humor/satire, literary, prose poem, regional, senior citizen/retirement. Must be set in Northern Ontario. Accepts 12 mss/issue; 24 mss/year. Length: 1,000 words average; 1,500 words maximum. Sometimes critiques rejected mss "if asked."
**How to Contact:** Send complete ms. Reports in varying number of weeks. SAE, IRC. Simultaneous and photocopied submissions OK. Accepts computer printout submissions. Sample copy $2.50. Fiction guidelines for $2 postage (IRC).
**Payment:** Contributor's copies.
**Terms:** Acquires one-time rights. Publication copyrighted.

**STAR-WEB PAPER**, All This & Less Publishers, Box 40029, Berkeley CA 94704. Editor: Thomas Michael Fisher. Magazine of "20th-century consciousness, all types of material" for "enlightened doers of the literate world." Annually. Estab. 1974.
**Needs:** No category limitations. Open to all subjects. Receives 10 unsolicited mss/month. Accepts 30 mss/issue; 30 mss/year. Occasionally critiques rejected mss upon request. Send $3 for detailed response, $3 for reading fee.
**How to Contact:** Send mss with appropriate fees and SASE. Accepts computer printout submissions. Reports in 1 month. Sample copy $5 postpaid.
**Payment:** Pays in 2 contributor's copies.
**Terms:** Copyrighted in name of authors.
**Tips:** "We look for language craft, not necessarily experimental. A 'story plot; is not enough—how conciousness moves, how syllables juxtapose. Check out past issues, literally, from a library or from us. Read Pound, Olsen, Williams."

**STONE SOUP, The Magazine by Children (I)**, Children's Art Foundation, Box 83, Santa Cruz CA 95063. (408)426-5557. Editor: Gerry Mandel. Magazine: 6x8¾; 48 pages; high quality paper; Wausau text cover stock; illustrations; photos. Theme: stories, poems, book reviews, and art by children up to age 13. Readership: children, librarians, educators. Published 5 times/year. Published special fiction issue last year. Estab. 1973. Circ. 10,000.
**Needs:** Serious writing by children on themes based on their own experiences. No clichés, no formulas, no writing exercises; original work only. Accepts approx. 15 mss/issue. Receives approximately 500 unsolicited fiction mss each month. Length: 150-2,500 words. Critiques rejected mss upon request.
**How to Contact:** Send complete ms with SASE. Accepts computer printout submissions. Prefers letter-quality. Reports in 2 months on mss. Publishes ms an average of 1-6 months after acceptance. Sample copy $3.50. Free guidelines with SASE.
**Payment:** 2 free author's copies. $1.75 charge for extras.
**Terms:** Acquires all rights. Publication copyrighted.
**Tips:** Mss are rejected because they are "derivatives of movies, TV, comic books; or classroom assignments or other formulas." Published new writers within the last year.

**STORY QUARTERLY (II)**, Story Quarterly, Inc., Box 1416, Northbrook IL 60065. (312)835-4168. Co-Editors: Anne Brashler and Diane Williams. Magazine: approximately 6x9; 130 pages; good quality paper; illustrations; photos. A magazine devoted to the short story and committed to a full range of styles and forms. Also features interviews with writers. Readership: "literate readers and writers of short fiction who read us for our quality and variety." Published irregularly. Estab. 1975. Circ. 3,000.
**Needs:** Literary, contemporary, women's, humor, and self-contained novel excerpts. "No slick women's magazine material with contrived endings. No science fiction, religious, psychic, horror, romantic, juvenile, or young adult material." Accepts 12-15 mss/issue, 20-30 mss/year. Re-

ceives 200 unsolicited fiction mss each month. Approximately 1% of fiction is agented. Length: 5,000 words maximum. Critiques rejected mss "when there is time." Sometimes recommends markets.

**How to Contact:** Send complete ms with SASE and brief cover letter with latest published credits. Accepts computer printout submissions. Reports in 3 months on mss. Publishes ms an average of 6-12 months after acceptance. Sample copy $4.

**Payment:** 3 free author's copies.

**Terms:** Acquires one-time rights. Copyright reverts to author after publication. Publication copyrighted.

**Tips:** "Have sensibility, a mastery of language and technique, relationships, and a non-imitative, fresh voice." Mss are rejected because of "clumsy prose; lack of story. Send clean copy and one story at a time (no more than 30 pages). The competition is tough. It helps to: 1. Send a clean copy 2. Polish your work—we receive many poorly-constructed, poorly thought-out stories. 3. Send new, fresh, ideas—well-written, of course." Published "about 5" new writers within the last year.

‡**STREAMLINES, Minnesota Journal of Creative Writing,** *Mike McConray* Midwest Writers Group, 207 Church St. SE, Minneapolis MN 55455. Fiction Editor: Connie Greenberg. Magazine: 11x7½; variable number of pages; illustrations; photos. "No partiuclar theme. Various types of material published for general and literary audience." Estab. 1978. Circ. 1,000.

**Needs:** Published fiction anthology. Confession, contemporary, ethnic, experimental, fantasy, historical (general), humor/satire, literary, men's, regional, science fiction, women's. Receives 10 unsolicited mss/month. Accepts 50-100 mss/year. Publishes ms 1-3 months after acceptance. Length: 6-14 pages double-spaced. Occasionally critiques rejected mss.

**How to Contact:** Send complete ms with cover letter with brief biography. Reports in 1-2 months on mss. SASE. Simultaneous and photocopied submissions OK. Accepts computer printouts including dot-matrix. Sample copy $2 and 9x13 SASE. Fiction guidelines $2 and 9x13 SASE.

**Payment:** Pays in contributor's copies.

**Terms:** Acquires other rights. Publication copyrighted.

**Tips:** "Submit original, fresh prose in a polished form (type quality and stock)."

**STREET MAGAZINE,** Street Press, Box 555, Port Jefferson NY 11777. Editor: Graham Everett. Thematic. Quarterly (pending). Estab. 1973. Circ 750.

**Needs:** Adventure, condensed novel, contemporary, ethnic, experimental, fantasy, historical (general), horror, psychic/supernatural, serialized/excerpted novel, and suspense/mystery. "Stories should be short, tight, precise—as much as needed." Receives "not enough" unsolicited fiction mss/month. Buys various number mss/year. Length: 10 pp. double spaced average. Occasionally critiques rejected mss.

**How to Contact:** Query first with sample and SASE. Photocopied submissions OK. Accepts computer printout submissions. Prefers letter-quality. Reports in 2 months on queries. Sample copy $3.

**Payment:** $0-100; contributor's copies; 60% of list price charge for extras.

**Terms:** Publication copyrighted.

**Tips:** "Often positive/often downright hostile" response to stories. "No schools-of-thought stylists unless it's strong satire. Don't expect a thing."

**STROKER MAGAZINE (II),** 129 2nd Ave. +3, New York NY 10003. Editor: Irving Stettner. Magazine: 5½x8½; average 52 pages; medium paper; 80 lb good cover stock; illustrations; photos. "An Un-literary literary review interested in sincerity, verve, anger, humor and beauty. For an intelligent audience—non-academic, non-media dazed in the US and throughout the world." Published 3-4 times/year. Estab. 1974, 31 issues to date. Circ. 600.

**Needs:** Literary, contemporary. No academic material. Length: "3-5 pages preferred but not essential."

**How to Contact:** Send complete ms with SASE. Reports in 6 weeks. Sample copy $2.50.
**Payment:** 2 free author's copies. $1 charge for extras.
**Terms:** Acquires one-time rights.
**Tips:** "We are interested in fiction. Be sure your name and address are on the manuscript."
Published new writers within the last year.

**STUDIA MYSTICA (II)** ,The Foundation, California State University, 6000 J St., Sacramento
CA 95819. (916)454-6444. Editor: Mary E. Giles. Magazine: 5½x8½; 80 pages; glossy cover
stock; illustrations; photos. Magazine featuring "mystical experience for an artistic, scholarly, religious audience." Quarterly. Estab. 1978. Circ. 400.
**Needs:** Literary and religious/inspirational. No occult stories. Receives 4 unsolicited fiction
mss/month. Accepts 2 mss/year. Publishes short shorts of 3-5 pages. Length: 3,500 words minimum. Occasionally critiques rejected mss. Sometimes recommends other markets.
**How to Contact:** Send complete ms with SASE. Cover letter with author bio; places of publication. Simultaneous submissions OK. Reports in 1 month on mss. Publishes ms an average of 12-
16 months after acceptance. Sample copy $4.
**Terms:** Acquires first rights. Publication copyrighted. Sends galleys to author.
**Tips:** "Read the journal ahead of time so that we do not receive stories whose themes are not appropriate to our concerns. Our concern is with the expression of mystical experience through all
the arts. Although poetry is the literary form preferred by mystics, some do turn to fiction."
Published new writers within the last year. "We don't care about the 'track record' of a writer so
much as the quality of the writing and whether it expresses mystical (not occult) experience."

**THE SUN (II)**, The Sun Publishing Company, Inc., 412 W. Rosemary St., Chapel Hill NC
27514. (919)942-5282. Editor: Sy Safransky. Magazine: 8½x11; 40 pages; offset paper; glossy
cover stock; illustrations; photos. *"The Sun* is a magazine of ideas. We publish all kinds of writing—fiction, articles, poetry. Our only criteria are that the writing make sense and enrich our common space. We direct *The Sun* toward interests which move us, and we trust our readers will respond." Monthly. Published special fiction issue. Estab. 1974. Circ. 10,000.
**Needs:** Open to all fiction. Accepts 1 ms/issue. Receives approximately 30 unsolicited fiction
mss each month. Length: 5,000 words maximum.
**How to Contact:** Send complete ms with SASE. Reports in 1 month. Publishes ms an average of
1-3 months after acceptance. Sample copy $3.
**Payment:** 2 free author's copies and a complimentary subscription.
**Terms:** Acquires one-time rights. Publishes reprints. Publication copyrighted.
**Tips:** "Nothing's necessarily 'wrong' with most rejected mss—just not what we're looking for.
Helpful to read magazine first." Published new writers within the last year.

**SUN DOG (II)**, English Department, 4th Floor Williams, Florida State University, Tallahassee
FL 32306. (904)644-1248. Editors: Robyn Allers. Magazine: 85-100 pages; illustrations; photos.
Published biannually. Estab. 1979. Circ. 2,000.
**Needs:** "We want stories which are well written, beautifully written, with striking images, incidents, and characters. We are interested more in quality than in style or genre." Accepts 20 mss/
year. Publishes short shorts. Receives approximately 60 unsolicited fiction mss each month. Critiques rejected mss "when there is time." Occasionally recommends other markets.
**How to Contact:** Send complete ms with SASE. Typed, double-spaced, on good bond. Clean
photocopy acceptable. "Short bio or cover letter would be appreciated." Publishes ms an average
of 2-6 months after acceptance.
**Payment:** 3 free author's copies. $2 charge for extras. When funds are available, *Sun Dog*
awards $100 to the outstanding story in each issue as picked by an independent judge.
**Terms:** Acquires first North American serial rights which then revert to author. Publication copyrighted.
**Tips:** "There is a market for fiction. Short story collections seem to be resurging, so fictionists
can take heart. Everyone was a beginner at one time." Published new writers within the last year.

**SUNRUST (I, II, IV)**, Dawn Valley Press, Box 58, New Wilmington PA 16142. (412)946-2948 or (412)946-7352. Editors: Nancy E. James and Keith D. Rowland. Magazine: 5½x8½; 72 pages; 70-80 lb paper; regular heavy paper cover stock; featured artist/photographer in each issue. "*Sunrust* is a magazine of poetry, fiction, and art about rural life, nature, memories, and small communities. It is read by people of all ages who are interested in the 'simple' life. Stories relate an everyday problem and its solution, fanciful recollections of the past, or a realistic narrative of an important incident in a character's life." Semiannually. Estab. 1983. Circ. 400.

**Needs:** Humor/satire, literary, mainstream, and regional. No erotica, experimental, feminist, or gay. Receives 10-20 unsolicited mss/month. Accepts 3-5 mss/issue; 6-10 mss/year. Does not read August-October; February-April. Publishes short shorts. Length: 2,000 words maximum.

**How to Contact:** Send complete ms. SASE. Photocopied submissions OK. Accepts computer printout submissions. Prefers letter-quality. Sample copy $3. Fiction guidelines for business-size SASE.

**Payment:** 2 contributor's copies; $3.50 charge for extras; possible discounts on multiple orders.

**Terms:** Acquires one-time rights on publication. Publication copyrighted.

**Tips:** Published new writers within the last year.

**‡SWIFT KICK (II)**, 1711 Amherst St., Buffalo NY 14214. (716)837-7778. Robin Kay Willoughby. Magazine: size, number of pages, paper quality, cover stock varies; illustrations; photos, b&w line art, xerographs. Specializes in unusual formats, hard-to-classify works, visual poetry, found art, etc. for pataphysical, rarified audience. Published special fiction issue; plans another. Estab. 1981. Circ. 100.

**Needs:** Open. "If it doesn't seem to fit a regular category, it's probably what we'd like!" No boring, slipshod, everyday stuff like in mass-market magazines. Receives 5 unsolicited fiction mss/month. Accepts 1-2 mss/issue. Does not read just before Christmas. Publishes ms depending on finances (6 months-1 year) after acceptance. Publishes short shorts of 1,000 words (or 1 picture). Recommends other markets.

**How to Contact:** Query first for longer works or send complete ms with cover letter with short work. Reports in 2-12 months, varies, depending on amounts received. SASE ("or include reply card with OK to toss enclosed work.") Simultaneous and photocopied submissions OK. Reprints of astoundingly good work (out of print). Accepts computer printouts including dot-matrix. Sample copy for $4, and 73¢ postage.

**Payment:** Contributor's copies, (½ cover price) charge for extras.

**Terms:** CC on publication for one-time rights. Reverts to artists/authors. Sometimes sends galleys to author. Publication copyrighted.

**Tips:** "We always get less fiction than poetry—if a story is good, it has a good chance of publication in little mags. Editorially, I'm a snob, so don't write like anyone else; be *so* literate your writing transcends literature and (almost) literacy."

**‡TALES AS LIKE AS NOT . . . (II)**, Second Unit Productions, 2939 San Antonio Dr., Walnut Creek CA 94598. Editor: Dale Hoover. Magazine: 8½x11; 50 pages; stock paper; 60 lb cover; computer illustrations. Anthology-type, using SF, fantasy, horror and mystery *only*. No fillers. Pure fiction. Quarterly.

**Needs:** Fantasy, horror, science fiction, suspense/mystery. Receives 300 unsolicited fiction mss/month. Accepts 10 mss/issue; Publishes ms 3 months-1 year after acceptance. Length: 3,000 words average; 500 words minimum; 4,000 words maximum. Occasionally critiques rejected mss. Recommends other markets.

**How to Contact:** Send complete ms with cover letter. Queries are a waste of time and rarely answered. Reports in 1-6 months on mss. SASE for mss. Photocopied submissions OK. Accepts computer printouts including dot-matrix. Sample copy $4 and 9x12 SAE and 4 first class stamps. Fiction guidelines for legal-size SAE and 1 first class stamp.

**Payment:** Pays in contributor's copies; charge for extras.

**Terms:** Acquires one-time rights. Sends pre-publication galleys to author "depending on editorial changes made." Publication copyrighted.

**Tips:** "Write from the heart and don't try to impress anyone. Short stories are becoming a lost art, little more than a stepping stone to the success of the novelist. As S. King says, 'A story is like a swift kiss in the dark.' I like being kissed swiftly. And effectively. As an editor, it is not my responsibility to tell a writer what is wrong with his work. We each learn from our own suffering, and become proficient in recognizing lessons from suggestive response. Even a form rejection slip tells you something about your work. I do not spoon-feed my submitters. They would never learn that way."

**TELESCOPE (II)**, The Galileo Press, 15201 Wheeler Lane, Sparks MD 21152. (301)771-4544. Contact: Editor-in-Chief: Jack Stephens; Julie Wendell. Magazine: 6x9; 120 + pages; 50 lb acid free paper; 80 lb coated cover stock; illustrations; photos. "*Telescope* is a review of literature. Poetry, criticism, fiction, interviews, and more can be found within. For the literate, sensitive, interested in what's new and progressive in literature." Published 3 times/year. Estab. 1981. Circ. 750.
**Needs:** Contemporary, ethnic, experimental, literary, prose poem, translations. "By 'literary' we mean anything well written, with a meshing of content *and* form, style, etc." Receives 100 unsolicited fiction mss/month. Buys 1-4 mss/issue. Publishes short shorts. Length: no preference. Occasionally critiques rejected mss. Recommends other markets.
**How to Contact:** Send complete ms with SASE. Reports in 1-2 months on mss. Sample copy $2.
**Payment:** $6/page and 2 contributor's copies.
**Terms:** Pays for first North American serial rights. Reverts to author upon publication. Sends galleys to author. Publication copyrighted.
**Tips:** "Check a sample copy first. Our aim is to be as inclusive and balanced as the quality of submissions permits. Published new writers within the last year.

**TELEWOMAN (II), A Women's Newsletter**, Telewoman, Inc., Box 2306, Pleasant Hill CA 94523. (415)465-0069. Editor: Anne J. D'Arcy. Newsletter: 8½x11; 16 pages; illustrations; photos. Newsletter's theme is "networking; emphasis is on literature, art, photography" for lesbian readership. Monthly. Estab. 1978. Circ. 500.
**Needs:** Feminist, lesbian, literary, prose poem, and women's. No erotica, mainstream romance. Receives 16-18 unsolicited mss/month. Accepts 2-6 short stories/year. Length: 1,000-1,500 words average; 2,000 words maximum. Usually critiques rejected mss. Recommends other markets.
**How to Contact:** Send complete ms and cover letter with bio. Reports in 2 weeks. SASE. Photocopied and previously published submissions OK. Accepts computer printout submissions. Prefers letter-quality. Publishes ms an average of 1-12 months after acceptance. Sample copy $2 and #10 SAE and 2 first class stamps.
**Payment:** 2 free contributor's copies; $2 charge for extras.
**Terms:** Acquires one-time rights.
**Tips:** Will publish "more in-depth inverviews, more poetry, and more fiction (expanded issues)." Published new writers within the last year.

**TEMPEST (I, II)**, Earthwise Publications, Inc., Box 680536, Miami FL 33168. (305)688-8558. Editor: Barbara Holley. Fiction Editor: Kaye Edwards Carter. A journal with avant-garde theme. Biannually. Estab. 1979. Circ. 300.
**Needs:** Human interest and environmental. Theme list on request. No pornography or confessional submissions.
**How to Contact:** Query with clips of published work. SASE for query, ms. Accepts computer printout submissions. "No mss from June 30-Sept. 15, please." Reports in 30-60 days. Publishes ms an average of 6-24 months after acceptance. Sample copy $5.
**Payment:** $20 up.
**Terms:** Pays on publication for first North American serial rights. Buys reprints "if complete credit given."

**Tips:** "We use two or more pieces per issue and are hoping to increase. Name and address on each page of ms, please. We will accept simultaneous submissions but be sure the print is clear."

**THE TEXAS REVIEW (II)**, Sam Houston State University Press, Huntsville TX 77341. (713)294-1423. Editor: Paul Ruffin. Magazine: 6x9; 148-190 pages; best quality paper; 70 lb cover stock; illustrations; photos. "We publish top quality poetry, fiction, articles, interviews, and reviews for a general audience." Semiannually. Estab. 1976. Circ. 700.
**Needs:** Literary and contemporary. "We are eager enough to consider fiction of quality, no matter what its theme or subject matter. No juvenile fiction." Accepts 4 mss/issue. Receives approximately 40-60 unsolicited fiction mss each month. Length: 500-10,000 words. Critiques rejected mss "when there is time." Recommends other markets.
**How to Contact:** Send complete ms with SASE. Reports in 3 months on mss. Sample copy $2.
**Payment:** Free author's copies plus one year subscription.
**Terms:** Acquires all rights. Sends galleys to author. Publication copyrighted.
**Tips:** "We publish few new writers due to increased manuscript flow."

**THE THREEPENNY REVIEW (II)**, Box 9131, Berkeley CA 94709. (415)849-4545. Editor: Wendy Lesser. Tabloid: 11x17; 28 pages; electrobrite paper; white book stock cover stock; original graphic illustrations; photos. Publishes "literature and performing arts reviews, essays, fiction, poetry, and other reviews for a wide-ranging audience including anyone interested in the arts." Quarterly. Estab. winter/spring 1980. Circ. 8,000.
**Needs:** Short fiction. Accepts 1 ms/issue; 4 mss/year. Receives approximately 20-30 unsolicited fiction mss each month. Publishes short shorts. Length: 3,000-5,000 words. Recommends other markets.
**How to Contact:** Query. SASE for query, ms with a cover letter "showing evidence of familiarity with publication; prior credits." Accepts computer printout submissions—letter-quality only. Reports in 2 weeks on queries, 2 months on mss. Sample copy $2 with 9x12 SAE and $1 postage. Guidelines for legal-size SASE.
**Payment:** Cash payment of $25-50 (depending on availability of funds).
**Terms:** Acquires first rights. Sends galleys to author. Publication copyrighted.
**Tips:** "We receive approximately 100 times as many stories as we can publish in a given quarter. Also, most of the stories we receive are either stylistically experimental without having any interesting plot or characters, or naively sentimental." Published new writers within the last year.

**THRESHOLD OF FANTASY (II), A Magazine of Fantastic Literature**, Fandom Unlimited Enterprises, Box 70868, Sunnyvale CA 94086. (415)960-1151. Editor: Randall D. Larson. Magazine: 8½x11; 30-40 pages; 60 lb bond stock; card stock cover; illustrations. Magazine of original short fiction (fantasy, science fiction and horror) and interviews for active SF and fantasy fans. Semiannually. Estab. 1982. Circ. 1,000.
**Needs:** Fantasy, horror, humor/satire, and science fiction. No "rehashes of familiar plots or themes (unless featuring a twist)." Receives 50 unsolicited fiction mss/month. Accepts 10-15 mss/issue. Length: 8,000 words maximum; 4,000 words average. Occasionally critiques rejected mss. "We prefer a strong sense of *story*; tales of adventure, of fear, of human growth; peopled with realistic characters and a strong involving narrative."
**How to Contact:** Send complete ms with SASE. Photocopied submissions OK. Accepts computer printout submissions. Reports in 4-6 weeks on mss. Publishes ms up to 2 years after acceptance. Sample copy $3.50. Fiction guidelines free with letter-size SASE.
**Payment:** ⅕ (one-fifth of a cent/per word) and contributor's copy.
**Terms:** Acquires first North American serial or one-time rights. Publication copyrighted.
**Tips:** Readers are "enthusiastic, with constructive criticism. Submit ms in clean, standard professional format. Include name, address and word count on first page. Submit ms. Flat or folded only once if possible." Published new writers within the last year.

**TIME TO PAUSE (I)**, Inky Trails, Box 345, Middleton ID 83644. Editor: Pearl Kirk. A review of prose and poetry: 8½x11; 85 pages or fewer; 20 lb paper, mimeo; soft cover; illustrations with indio ink. Biannually (Jan. and May). Plans special fiction in future. Estab. 1970. Circ. 150.

**Needs:** Literary, contemporary, religious/inspirational, psychic/supernatural, fantasy, romance, western, mystery, adventure, humor, preschool, juvenile, young adult, senior citizen/retirement, and novels. No horror, gay/lesbian, erotica, profanity. Accepts 5-8 mss/year in *Time to Pause* and *Inky Trails*. Receives approximately 10 unsolicited fiction mss each month. Length: 5,500 words maximum. Publishes short shorts 500-1,000 words. Sometimes recommends markets.

**How to Contact:** Send complete ms with SASE. Reports in 2-4 months. Publishes ms an average of 6 months after acceptance. Sample copy $7.50 plus postage. Guidelines for legal-sized SASE with 44¢ postage. "Do not send mss in July, August, September. For these months send mss at least 4 months ahead."

**Payment:** Author's copy $5.50. Send for fees on publication. Occasional cash awards. "No free copies unless given by editor through contest."

**Terms:** All rights stay with the writer as long as *Time to Pause* is given credit for 1st printing. Fiction contest each year; cash awards.

**Tips:** "We plan to maybe stay with fiction in *Time to Pause*; serials interest me. Put return postage in small envelope or loose as we may want to send more information/copy of magazine special. Put your postage stamps on/or between 2 heavy cardboards or a plastic covering—do not paste on a large envelope. If we accept your material we can use postage to let you know. Send a regular envelope for acceptance notification. We ask that you buy the one copy in which you will appear."

**TIMEWARP (I)**, Box 1291, Station B, Ottawa, Ontario K1P 5R3 Canada. Editor: Bruce Brown. Magazine: 8½x5½; 48 pages; white bond paper; mayfair cover stock; b&w illustrations. Magazine of science fiction short stories for "SF-oriented audience from youth to old age." Quarterly. Published special fiction issue; plans another. Estab. July 1985. Circ. 500.

**Needs:** Experimental, fantasy, horror, psychic/supernatural/occult, science fiction, and suspense/mystery. No extreme sex or violence. Receives about 30 unsolicited mss/month. Accepts 5-10 mss/issue; 30-40 mss/year. Publishes short shorts. Length: 3,000 words average; 50 words minimum; 5,000 words maximum. Occasionally critiques rejected ms. Occasionally recommends other markets.

**How to Contact:** Send complete ms and brief (50 words) bio. Reports in 3 weeks. SAE, IRC. Simultaneous, photocopied, and previously published submissions OK. Accepts computer printout submissions. Prefers letter-quality. Sample copy $2.50. Fiction guidelines with SAE (#10) and 37¢ Canadian postage or IRC.

**Payment:** 2 contributor's copies. "We offer 10% discount on subscriptions; extra copies also of work published."

**Terms:** Pays on publication for rights that revert back to author upon publication.

**Tips:** Write "tight, fast-moving stories—shorter lengths. It is the basis of the magazine and part of our philosophy to help promote and develop new talent and keep this art form thriving. Read excellent stories by your favorite authors. Notice how beginnings, conflict, character, plot and endings are written. Study these uses. Write everyday. Study current trends by reading fiction magazines." Published new writers within the last year.

**TOUCHSTONE (II), New Age Journal**, Box 42331, Houston TX 77042. Fiction Editor: Kathy Williams. Magazine: 8½x5½; 36 pages; 20 lb paper; chrome cover stock; illustrations; photos, both camera-ready. "We publish poetry, short stories, articles, and reviews. We reach a liberal, well-educated audience." Quarterly. Estab. 1976. Circ. 1,000.

**Needs:** Contemporary, experimental, historical (general), humor/satire, literary, minority viewpoints, mainstream, prose poem, and translations. "No moralizing." Receives 24 unsolicited fiction mss/month. Accepts 2 mss/issue, 8 mss/year. Length: 750 words minimum, 3,000 words maximum, 1,500 words average. Occasionally critiques rejected mss. Charges $8.50 (one-year subscription) for critique.

**How to Contact:** Send complete ms with SASE. Photocopied submissions OK. Accepts computer printout submissions. Prefers letter-quality. Reports in 6 weeks. Sample copy $3. Fiction guidelines for legal-size SAE and 1 first class stamp.

**Payment:** 1 free contributor's copy; $2.50 charge for extras.

**Terms:** Acquires first rights. Publication copyrighted.
**Tips:** "Innovative form and experimental styles preferred. We are committed to publishing the work that commercial presses no longer touch." Pubished 6 new writers within the last year.

**TOYON (II)**, Humboldt State University, English Dept., Arcata CA 95521. (707)826-3758. Co-editors: Laurel Tueling and Michelle Kagan. *"Toyon* is the literary journal for Humboldt State University. We publish poetry and short fiction, both student works and those of the general public." Annually. Estab. 1954. Circ. 1,000.
**Needs:** Open. "Anything original and short enough for our publication." Receives 75 unsolicited mss/year. Accepts 36 pages of fiction/year. Length: 1,000-1,500 words average.
**How to Contact:** Send complete ms. Submission deadline February 15 for annual issue. Reports 4-8 weeks after final deadline (Feb. 15). SASE. Accepts computer printout submissions. Sample copy $2 and 8x10 SAE with 5 first class stamps.
**Payment:** Contributor's copy. "The Ray Carver Short Story Contest, a national competition, pays $250 first prize. Deadline: December 1.
**Terms:** Acquires first rights. Publication copyrighted.
**Tips:**"Submit your best to us and you may see it published. Also, submit for the Ray Carver Award."

**TRANSLATION (IV)**, The Translation Center, Columbia University, 307A Mathematics Bldg., New York NY 10027. (212)280-2305. Executive Director: Diane G.H. Cook. Magazine: 6x9; 200-300 pages; coated cover stock; photos. Semiannually. Estab. 1973. Circ. 1,500.
**Needs:** Literary translations only. Accepts varying number of mss/year. Receives approximately 20-30 unsolicited fiction mss each month. Length: very short or excerpts; not in excess of 15 mss pages. Critiques rejected mss "rarely because of time involved."
**How to Contact:** Send complete translation ms accompanied by original language text, 5-line autobiography, 5-line author's biography and SASE. Must have letter of intent to publish from the publisher. Copyright clearance must have been obtained. Reports in 3-6 months on mss. Single copy $8. Subscription $15.
**Payment:** 2 complimentary translator copies.
**Terms:** Acquires first North American serial rights. Publication copyrighted.
**Tips:** "We are particularly interested in translations from the lesser-known languages. Annual awards of $1,000 for outstanding translation of a substantial part of a book-length literary work. Write for description and application for awards program."

**TRIQUARTERLY**, Northwestern University, 1735 Benson Ave., Evanston IL 60201. (312)491-3490. Fiction Editors: Reginald Gibbons and Susan Hahn. Magazine: 6x9; 250-600 pages; fine paper; heavy cover stock; illustration; photos. "A general literary quarterly especially devoted to fiction. We publish short stories, novellas, or excerpts from novels, by American and foreign writers. Genre or style is not a primary consideration. We aim for the general but serious and sophisticated reader. Many of our readers are also writers." Published 3 times/year. Published special fiction issue. Estab. 1964. Circ. 5,000.
**Needs:** Literary, contemporary, and translations. "No prejudices or preconceptions against anything *except* genre fiction (sci fi, romances, etc.)." Buys 15 mss/issue, 45 mss/year. Receives approximately 500 unsolicited fiction mss each month. Publishes short shorts. Does not read June 1-Sept. 30. Approximately 10% of fiction is agented. Length: no requirement.
**How to Contact:** Send complete ms with SASE. Reports in 8-10 weeks on mss. Publishes ms an average of 6-12 months after acceptance. Sample copy $3.
**Payment:** $100-500, 2 free author's copies. Cover price less 40% discount for extras.
**Terms:** Pays on publication for first North American serial rights. Sends galleys to author. Publication copyrighted.
**Tips:** "Read a few recent copies of the magazine to become familiar with the kinds of fiction we publish. Fiction is the essential American literary genre, and there are many wonderful stories." Published new writers within the last year.

**‡TV-TS TAPESTRY JOURNAL (II)**, Tiffany Club, Inc., Box 19, Wayland MA 01778. (617)358-5575. Editor: Merissa S. Lynn. Magazine: 11x8½; 130 pages; coated paper; 80 lb coated cover; illustrations; photos. "Transvestism/transsexualism fiction, nonfiction (how-to, biography, etc.), editorial and opinion, etc. For *all* persons interested in transvestism and transsexualism." Quarterly. Estab. 1978. Circ. 3,000.

**Needs:** Condensed novel, contemporary, fantasy, historical (general), humor/satire, contemporary and historical romance, TVism and TSism psychology. True-to-life, tasteful, non-sexual, positive stories. "No unbelievable fantasy, fetishistic, negative work." Receives 2-5 unsolicited fiction mss/month. Accepts 1-2 mss/issue; 4-8 mss/year. Length: 3,000 words average; 2,000 words minimum; 5,000 words maximum. Also publishes short shorts. Occasionally critiques rejected mss. Recommends other markets.

**How to Contact:** Send complete ms with cover letter. SASE. Simultaneous, photocopied submissions and reprints OK. Accepts computer printouts including dot-matrix. Accepts electronic submissions via disc only, IBM compatible, MS DOS 1.1 and 2.1. Sample copy $5.

**Payment:** Pays in contributor's copies.

**Terms:** Publication copyrighted.

**Tips:** "We are more interested in what the writer has to say than the quality of the writing. If the writer has a valuable message to our readers, we will help the writer with editing and rewriting. *Tapestry* is a non-profit tax exempt journal designed to provide education and support. Submitted items should be positive and informative."

**‡TWISTED (II)**, 6331 N. Lakewood Ave., Chicago IL 60660. (312)761-7812. Editor: Christine Hoard. Magazine: 8½x11; average around 60-70 pages; 20 lb paper; 60 lb card cover; illustrations. "Emphasis on contemporary horror and fantasy, anything on the dark side of reality." For readers of horror, "weird," fantasy, etc. Semiannually. Estab. April 1985. Circ. 200.

**Needs:** Fantasy, horror, psychic/supernatural/occult, science fiction. "No hard science fiction, no sword and sorcery. Graphic horror or sex scenes OK if tastefully done. Sexist-racist writing turns me off." Receives 5-20 unsolicited fiction mss/month. Accepts 10 mss/issue. "Prefer not to read ms in early summer, early winter. Publishes ms 2 months to 1 year after acceptance. Length: 2,000 words average; 500 words minimum; 5,000 words maximum. Also publishes short shorts of 300-600 words. Sometimes critiques rejected ms. Sometimes recommends other markets.

**How to Contact:** Query first. Reports in 2 weeks on queries; 2-4 weeks on mss. SASE for query and ms. Photocopied submissions OK. Accepts computer printouts including dot-matrix. Sample copy $4 ("Includes postage. We provide envelopes.") Fiction guidelines for SAE, regular size SAE and 1 first class stamp.

**Payment:** Pays in contributor's copies ("as of now").

**Terms:** Acquires first North American serial rights.

**Tips:** "I think beginners should look to small press as a place to refine skills. There's a lot of talent working in smaller press magazines. New writers should try to be original and avoid re-hashing formula stories. I cannot respond to unsolicited mss without proper SASE."

**‡UNCLE (I), The Magazine for Those Who Have Given Up**, Heart's Desire Press, R.R. #4, Box 798, Springfield MO 65802. Editor: John Mort. Magazine: 5x8; 60-90 pages; 60 lb paper; 80 lb cover stock; illustrations. Humor publication for literary audience. Semiannually. Estab. 1981. Circ. 250.

**Needs:** Adventure, contemporary, experimental, fantasy, horror, humor/satire, literary, mainstream, men's, psychic/supernatural/occult, regional Ozarks, science fiction, suspense/mystery, western. "Any category, but in some cases only as parody. These listed we'd at least consider as serious material." Not interested in outright porn or romance. Receives 20-30 unsolicited fiction mss/month. Accepts 5-10 mss/issue; 10-20 mss/year. Publishes ms 3 or 8 months maximum after acceptance. Agented fiction: 5%. Publishes short shorts. "I think of them as prose poems: 250 words." Critiques rejected mss. Recommends other markets.

**How to Contact:** Send complete ms with cover letter. Reports in 2 months on mss. SASE for ms. Simultaneous, photocopied and reprint submissions OK. Accepts computer printouts including

dot-matrix. Sample coy $2.50 without SAE; $2 with SAE.
**Payment:** Free contributor's copies.
**Terms:** Pays on publication for one-time rights. Sends galleys to authors. Publication copyrighted.
**Tips:** "You'll publish if you keep at it and you have even a little talent, but making any real money is almost impossible, and getting into major magazines is about as likely as winning a lottery. In the end you should think in terms of books, where the short story collection has actually made a comeback. Be funny and write well, though without inhibition—which does not mean your subject is necessarily sex or that you have axes to grind; it means you're willing to confront sacred cows no matter who's calling them sacred."

**UNICORN QUARTERLY (II)**, Loyola College, 4501 N. Charles St., Baltimore MD 21210. (301)323-1010. Editor-in-Chief: Thomas G. Paravati. Magazine of poetry, short fiction, photography, and drawings for the college community. Quarterly. Estab. 1972. Circ. 1,500.
**Needs:** Contemporary, fantasy, humor/satire, short stories, photography and drawing. Receives 50 unsolicited fiction mss/month. Accepts 4 mss/issue, 10 mss/year. Approximately 20% of fiction is agented. Length: 900 words minimum; 3,000 words maximum; 2,100 words average.
**Terms:** Acquires all rights.
**Editor's note:** As we go to press *Unicorn Quarterly* has changed its name to *The Garland*.

**U.S. 1 WORKSHEETS (II)**, U.S. 1 Poets Cooperative, 21 Lake Dr., Roosevelt NJ 08555. Rotating Editors. "We publish poetry and prose of many styles for anyone interested in contemporary fiction and poetry." Biannually. Estab. 1971. Circ. 1,000.
**Needs:** Literary and contemporary. "We're interested in good, traditional, plotted fiction as well as experimental work. Genre or topic is subordinate to craft." Length: approximately 2,500-6,000 words. Critiques rejected mss "when there is time."
**How to Contact:** Send complete ms with SASE. Reports in up to 6 months on mss. Publishes ms an average of 2-3 months after acceptance. Sample copy $2.50 with 8x11 SAE and postage for 4-ounce 1st class mail. "A query as to when we will next be doing an issue would save writer's time in getting a report."
**Payment:** 2 free author's copies; ½ cover price charge for extras. Publication copyrighted.
**Tips:** "I think we might best be described as a publication that wants to avoid labels and stereotypes; we seek instead good writing. Write carefully, rather than in over-enthusiastic haste. Tell a good story. Most of the manuscripts we reject have craft flaws including grammatical and spelling errors. We desire style and sophistication in craft beyond what we find in many mss. The author should demonstrate conviction in the characters. Compelling characterization and plot are important. We encourage you to send for a sample copy of our magazine before submitting ms."

**UNIVERSITY OF PORTLAND REVIEW (II)**, University of Portland, 5000 N. Willamette Blvd., Portland OR 97203. (503)283-7144. Editor-in-Chief: Thompson M. Faller. Magazine: 8x5; 40-55 pages. Magazine for the college-educated layman of liberal arts background. "Its purpose is to comment on the human condition and to present information in different fields with relevance to the contemporary scene." Published semiannually. Established 1948. Circ. 1,000.
**Needs:** "Only fiction that makes a significant statement about the contemporary scene will be employed." Receives 4 unsolicited mss/month. Accepts 2-3 mss/issue, 4-6 mss/year. Length: 1,500 words minimum; 3,500 words maximum; 2,000 words average. Recommends other markets.
**How to Contact:** Send complete ms with SASE. Reports in 3 weeks on queries; 6 months on mss. Publishes ms up to 1 year after acceptance. Sample copy 50¢.
**Payment:** 5 contributor's copies. 50¢ charge for extras.
**Terms:** Pays on publication for all rights. Publication copyrighted.
**Tips:** "Send manuscript in line with guidelines." Published new writers within the last year.

**UNIVERSITY OF WINDSOR REVIEW**, University of Windsor, Windsor, Ontario N9B 3P4 Canada. Editor: E. McNamara. Fiction Editor: Alistair MacLeod. Biannually. Estab. 1965. **Needs:** Literary, contemporary. Buys 4-8 mss/year. Receives 4-8 unsolicited fiction mss each month. Length: No requirement.
**How to Contact:** Send complete ms with SAE, IRC. Reports in 6 weeks.
**Payment:** $25 Canadian funds.
**Terms:** Publication copyrighted.

**UNKNOWNS (I, II)**, (formerly *Beginnings*), Abni Publications, Suite 1, 1900 Century Blvd., Atlanta GA 30345. (404)636-3145. Publisher: Julia B. Davidson. Editor: Christine Puckett. Magazine: 11x8; 70-100 pages; good quality paper; excellent cover stock; few illustrations. Quarterly collection of short fiction and poems. Estab. 1973. Circ. 500.
**Needs:** Short fiction and poems that combine simplicity and beauty of language with dramatizations of ageless truth. "Please write for an audience whose tastes are traditional and for whose reading time there is much competition." Length: 2,700-2,800 words. Recommends other markets.
**How to Contact:** Send complete ms with SASE. Reports as soon as possible. Publishes ms an average of 1 year after acceptance. Sample copy $4; postage $1.
**Payment:** 1 contributor's copy.
**Terms:** Pays on publication for first rights (all rights revert to author). Publication copyrighted.
**Tips:** "Become craftsmen in private before trying to become artists in public. Learn all you can about publishing in general. Write for the enjoyment and benefit of readers, and think about how your work can affect civilization."

**UNMUZZLED OX**, Unmuzzled Ox Foundation Ltd., 105 Hudson St., New York NY 10013. Editor: Michael Andre. Magazine about life for an intelligent audience. Quarterly. Estab. 1971. Circ. 10,000.
**Needs:** Comics, contemporary, literary, prose poem, and translations. No commercial material. Receives 10-15 unsolicited mss/month. Buys 1-5 mss/issue. Requires magazine subscription of $20 before reading ms. Occasionally critiques rejected mss.
**How to Contact:** "Cover letter is significant." Reports in 1 month. SASE. Sample copy $7.50.
**Payment:** Varies.
**Terms:** Publication copyrighted.

**THE UNSPEAKABLE VISIONS OF THE INDIVIDUAL (III, IV)**, Box 439, California PA 15419. (412)938-8956. Editors: Arthur and Kit Knight. Magazine. Beat generation-oriented for "well educated—above average literacy." Annually. Estab. 1971. Circ. 2,000.
**Needs:** Confession, contemporary, erotica, literary, prose poem, excerpted novel. Autobiographical fiction, i.e., Jack Kerouac. Receives 10-15 unsolicited mss/month. Buys 2 mss/issue. Length: 2,000-3,000 words average. Occasionally comments on rejected ms.
**How to Contact:** Send complete ms. Reports in 3 months maximum. SASE. Photocopied submissions OK. Accepts computer printout submissions. Sample copy $3.
**Payment:** 2 copies plus $10.
**Terms:** Pays on publication for first rights. Publication copyrighted.
**Tips:** "See a sample copy."

**UROBOROS (I, II)**, Allegany Mountain Press, 111 N. 10th St., Olean NY 14760. (716)372-0935. Fiction Editor: Ford F. Ruggieri. "Fiction dealing with current mythological motifs, dreams, folklore, psychological insights, history of consciousness, etc. for those interested in these topics." Published irregularly. Estab. 1973. Circ. 500.
**Needs:** Literary, erotica, humor, and experimental. "No formula hackwork." Accepts 4-6 mss/year. Receives approximately 30 unsolicited fiction mss each month. Length: No requirement. Critiques rejected mss "when there is time."
**How to Contact:** Send complete ms with SASE. Reports in 2 months on mss. Sample copy $2.

**Payment:** Free author's copies. Cover price less 50% discount for extras.
**Terms:** Acquires first rights and one-time rights. Rights revert to author. Publication copyrighted.
**Tips:** "Be familiar with a magazine before sending mss (saves time and money in the long run)."

**VALLEY GRAPEVINE (II)**, Seven Buffaloes Press, Box 249, Big Timber MT 59011. Editor/Publisher: Art Cuelho. Theme: "Poems, stories, history, folklore, photographs, ink drawings, or anything native to the Great Central Valley of California which includes the San Joaquin and Sacramento Valleys. Focus is on land and people and the oilfields, farms, orchards, Okies, small town life, hobos." Readership: "Rural and small town audience, the common man with a rural background, salt-of-the-earth. The working man reads *Valley Grapevine* because it's his personal history recorded." Annually. Estab. 1978. Circ. 500.
**Needs:** Literary, contemporary, western, and ethnic (Okie, Arkie). No academic, religious (unless natural to theme), gay/lesbian, or supernatural material. Receives approximately 10-15 unsolicited fiction mss each month. Length: 2,500-10,000 (prefers 5,000) words.
**How to Contact:** Query. SASE for query, ms. Reports in 1 week. Sample copy available to writers for $4.
**Payment:** 1-2 author's copies.
**Terms:** Acquires first North American serial rights. Returns rights to author after publication, but reserves the right to reprint in an anthology or any future special collection of Seven Buffaloes Press. Publication copyrighted.
**Tips:** "Buy a copy to get a feel of the professional quality of the writing. Know the theme of a particular issue. Some contributors have 30 years experience as writers; most 15 years. Age does not matter; quality does."

**‡THE VILLAGE IDIOT (II), an irregular periodical**, Mother of Ashes Press, Box 135, Harrison ID 83833. Magazine: 6⅝x10; 32 pages; newsprint paper; 40 lb coated text cover stock; illustrations; photos. *The Village Idiot* publishes poetry, pictures, and stories. Well-written stories are preferred, but that criteria can be overlooked if the fiction "breathes." For literate audience. Irregularly. Estab. 1970. Circ. 100.
**Needs:** Adventure, confession, contemporary, erotica, ethnic, experimental, fantasy, feminist, gay, historical (general), horror, humor/satire, lesbian, literary, mainstream, men's, contemporary romance, historical romance, young adult romance, science fiction, senior citizen/retirement, suspense/mystery, translations, western, women's, young adult/teen (10-18 years). "Subject matter is not so important as style. The magazine has a bias in favor of a literal method of story telling; no stream-of-consciousness and none of this writing that seems to work at obscuring the story's action and/or intent. Most important is that the fiction 'breathe.'" No novels, preteen, occult, religious, stream-of-consciousness. Publishes ms up to 1 year after acceptance. Length: 2,000-3,000 words average; 100 words minimum; 5,000 words maximum. Publishes short shorts of 250 words. Critiques rejected mss.
**How to Contact:** Send a complete ms with SASE. Reports 3 months maximum. Photocopied submissions OK. Accepts computer printouts including dot-matrix. Sample copy $3.50.
**Payment:** Pays 1¢/word minimum (for 1st use), and contributor's copies (2 if the second one is requested).
**Terms:** Pays on publication for one-time rights (copyright for author). Publication coyrighted.
**Tips:** "I am not receiving many fiction manuscripts. What I have received and the stories I read in other publications are, for the most part, adequate though I have not seen anything first rate in awhile. The beginning fiction writer eager to break into *The Village Idiot* should submit a well-crafted story, cleanly typed and without obvious grammartical or spelling errors."

**THE VILLAGER (II)**, The Bronxville Women's Club, 135 Midland Ave., Bronxville NY 10708. (914)337-5252. Editor: Amy Murphy. Magazine: 7½x10; 28-40 pages; photos. "Literary magazine—fiction, nonfiction, poetry, articles on current affairs—for families in area." Published monthly (October through June only). Estab. 1928. Circ. 750.

**Needs:** Adventure, historical (general), humor/satire, literary, and suspense/mystery. Length: 800 words minimum; 2,000 words maximum.
**How to Contact:** Send complete ms with SASE. Accepts computer printout submissions. Prefers letter quality. Publishes ms an average of 2-9 months after acceptance. Sample copy $1.
**Payment:** 1 contributor's copy.
**Terms:** Acquires first rights. Publication copyrighted.
**Tips:** If it is seasonal, submit *several* months ahead. "We are a literary publication. If the story is *good* we accept it!"

**VINTAGE '45 (II), A Uniquely Supportive Quarterly Journal for Women**, Box 266, Orinda CA 94563. (415)254-7266. Editor: Susan L. Aglietti. Magazine: 5½x8½; 28 pages; non-glossy paper; occasionally illustrations. "Essentially an informative, supportive publication, stressing opportunities for individual growth. Limited creative writing section." For "active, introspective women born in the years 1928-48 who have outgrown traditional women's publications." Quarterly. Published special fiction issue last year; plans another. Estab. 1983.
**Needs:** Women's. Does not want to see "anything not clearly related to the needs and lives of midlife women." Written entirely by women. Receives very few unsolicited mss/month. Accepts very few mss/year. Length: 1,000-1,500 words average; 1,500 words maximum. Usually comments on rejected ms. Sometimes recommends other markets.
**How to Contact:** Query first. An introduction to the author, how she happened to write this specific piece, how she heard of *Vintage '45*. Reports in 2-4 weeks on queries; 6 weeks on mss. SASE. Photocopied submissions OK. Accepts computer printout submissions. Prefers letter-quality. Sample copy $2.50. Writer's guidelines for SASE.
**Payment:** One year's subscription to magazine; $1.75 charge for extra copies.
**Terms:** Publication copyrighted.
**Tips:** "I encourage new writers as long as they become familiar with my publication and address the specific needs of my target readership. I publish material on certain themes directly related to midlife women. These themes may be expressed through nonfiction, fiction or poetry according to the skills and inspiration of the individual author. Publishing various kinds of writing lends interest and diversity to the magazine."

**VINTAGE NORTHWEST (I, II)**, Northshore Senior Center (Sponsor), Box 193, Bothell WA 98011. (206)487-1201. Editors: Volunteer Committee. Magazine: 7x8½; 60 pages; illustrations. "We are a senior literary magazine, published by and for seniors. All work done by volunteers except printing." For "all ages who are interested in our seniors' experiences." Semiannually. Estab. 1980. Circ. 500.
**Needs:** Adventure, comedy, condensed novel (1,000 words maximum), fantasy, humor/satire, prose poem, inspirational, historical, senior citizen/retirement, suspense/mystery. No religious or political mss. Receives 2-3 unsolicited mss/month. Accepts 2 mss/issue. Length: 1,000 words maximum. Occasionally critiques rejected ms.
**How to Contact:** Send complete ms. SASE. Simultaneous, photocopied and previously published submissions OK. Accepts computer printout submissions. Sample copy for $1.85. Fiction guidelines with SASE.
**Payment:** None.
**Terms:** Publication copyrighted.
**Tips:** "Our only requirement is that the author be over 50 when submission is written." Published new writers within the last year.

**VIRGINIA QUARTERLY REVIEW (III)**, 1 W. Range, Charlottesville VA 22903. (804)924-3124. Editor: Staige Blackford. "A national magazine of literature and discussion. A lay, intellectual audience, people who are not out-and-out scholars but who are interested in ideas and literature." Quarterly. Estab. 1925. Circ. 4,500.
**Needs:** Literary, contemporary, men's, women's, feminist, romance, adventure, humor, ethnic, serialized novels (excerpts), and translations. "No gay/lesbian or pornography." Buys 3 mss/issue, 20 mss/year. Length: 3,000-7,000 words.

**How to Contact:** Query or send complete ms. SASE for query, ms. Reports in 2 weeks on queries, 2 months on mss. Sample copy $3.
**Payment:** $10/printed page.
**Terms:** Pays on publication for all rights. "Will transfer upon request."
**Tips:** "Because of the competition it's difficult for a nonpublished writer to break in." Emily Clark Balch Award for best published short story of the year.

**WASCANA REVIEW (II)**, University of Regina, Regina, Saskatchewan, Canada. Editor: Joan Givner. Theme: "literary criticism, fiction, poetry for readers of serious fiction." Semiannually. Estab. 1966. Circ. 500.
**Needs:** Literary and humor. Buys 6 mss/year. Receives approximately 20 unsolicited fiction mss/month. Approximately 5% of fiction is agented. Length: no requirement. Occasionally recommends other markets.
**How to Contact:** Send complete ms with SASE. Accepts computer printout submissions. Prefers letter-quality. Reports in 2 months on mss. Publishes ms an average of 1 year after acceptance. Sample copy $2.50. Free guidelines with SAE, IRC.
**Payment:** $3/page for prose; $10/page for poetry. 2 free author's copies.
**Terms:** Pays on publication for all rights. Publication copyrighted.
**Tips:** "Stories are often technically incompetent or deal with trite subjects. Usually stories are longer than necessary, by about one-third. Be more ruthless in cutting back on unnecessary verbiage."

**WASHINGTON REVIEW**, Friends of the Washington Review of the Arts, Box 50132, Washington DC 20004. (202)638-0515. Fiction Editor: Roz Kuehn. "We publish fiction, poetry, articles and reviews on all areas of the arts. We have a particular interest in the interrelationships of the arts and emphasize the cultural life of the DC area." Readership: "Artists, writers and those interested in cultural life in this area." Bimonthly. Estab. 1975. Circ. 10,000.
**Needs:** Literary. Buys 1-2 mss/issue. Receives approximately 50-100 unsolicited fiction mss each month. Length: Prefers 2,000 words or less. Critiques rejected mss "when there is time."
**How to Contact:** Send complete ms with SASE. Reports in 2 months. Publishes ms an average of 6 months after acceptance. Sample copy for tabloid-sized SASE.
**Payment:** Author's copies plus small payment whenever possible.
**Terms:** Pays on publication for first North American serial rights. Publication copyrighted.
**Tips:** "Read our publication. Occasionally we have an all fiction issue." Mss are rejected because of "incorrect length, insufficient quality. Most manuscripts we receive are not of the literary quality we seek."

**WAVES (II)**, 79 Denham Dr., Richmond Hill, Ontario, L4C 6H9 Canada. (416)889-6703. Fiction Editor: Bernice Lever. Magazine: 5x8; 100-140 pages; 70 lb offset paper; 12 pt. cover stock; b&w illustrations; few photos. "A college literary journal, printing poems, short stories, reviews with graphics by international artists and writers." Readership: English teachers, writers and fans of quality literature. Published 3 times/year. Estab. 1972. Circ. 1,100.
**Needs:** Literary, contemporary, regional, supernatural, fantasy, horror, gothic, romance, mystery, adventure, humor, ethnic, and translations. Also interested in "sample chapters of novels. Type of submission is not important—style and quality are. No dull plots, careless writing, cardboard characters, lecturing dialogues, stupid themes, boring clichés, etc." Accepts 3-6 mss/issue, 20 mss/year. Receives approximately 40 unsolicited fiction mss each month. Length: 1,000-5,000 words. Also publishes short shorts. Critiques rejected mss "if requested and time permits." Recommends other markets.
**How to Contact:** Send complete ms with SASE or SAE and IRC. Accepts computer printout submissions. Prefers letter-quality. Reports in 2 months on mss. Sample back issue copy $2.
**Payment:** $6.50/page; 1 free author's copy; $2 charge for extras.
**Terms:** Buys first North American serial rights. Publication copyrighted.
**Tips:** "Read *Waves* in a library or buy a sample. Look at many literary and commercial maga-

zines. Spend time being creative with the writing and inventive with language. Know contemporary writing. Develop your own voice. Note: Canadian banks now charge $1 to cash foreign checks. So send postal order. Published new writers within the last year.

**WEBSTER REVIEW (II)**, Webster University, Webster Groves MO 63119. Editor/Publisher: Nancy Schapiro. Magazine: 5½x8½; 104 pages; 60 lb white paper; 10 pt. C15 black ink varnish cover stock; illustrations, photos on cover only. "We have no specific theme. We're interested in quality contemporary fiction and in translations of international fiction." Readership: Writers, students, teachers and anyone interested in contemporary international fiction. Semiannually. Estab. 1974. Circ. 1,500.
**Needs:** Literary, contemporary stories, translations, prose poems, and excerpted novels. "Not interested in popular (i.e., nonserious) work." No pornographic, sentimental, or *Star Wars*-type science fiction. Accepts 4 mss/issue, 8 mss/year. Receives approximately 40 unsolicited fiction mss each month. Publishes short shorts. No preferred length. Critiques rejected mss "when there is time."
**How to Contact:** Send complete ms with SASE. Simultaneous and photocopied submissions OK. Accepts computer printout submissions. Prefers letter-quality. Reports in 1 month. Free sample copy.
**Payment:** 2 free author's copies. No charge for extras.
**Terms:** Acquires first rights. Publication copyrighted.
**Tips:** "The competition is stiff so a writer should master his craft before attempting to publish. Don't send us unsuitable work (amateurish, slick, pop or sentimental stuff). Include SASE for report on work even if you don't want work returned—and a *big* enough envelope if you do. The short story seems to me to be the most exciting form of writing being done." Published new writers within the last year.

**WEIRDBOOK (II)**, Box 149, Amherst Branch, Buffalo NY 14226. Editor: W. Paul Ganley. Magazine: 8½x11; 68 pages; self cover stock; illustrations. "Latter day 'pulp magazine' along the lines of the old pulp magazine *Weird Tales*. We tend to use established writers. We look for an audience of fairly literate people who like good writing and good characterization in their fantasy and horror fiction, but are tired of the clichés in the field." Annually. Estab. 1968. Circ. 900.
**Needs:** Psychic/supernatural, fantasy, horror, and gothic (not modern). No psychological horror; mystery fiction; physical horror (blood); traditional ghost stories (unless original theme); science fiction; swords and sorcery without a supernatural element; or reincarnation stories that conclude with 'And the doctor patted him on . . . THE END!' " Buys 8-12 mss/issue. Length: 15,000+ words maximum. Sometimes recommends markets. Currently overstocked.
**How to Contact:** Send complete ms with SASE. Reports in 3 months on mss. Sample copy $5.75. Guidelines for legal-sized SASE.
**Payment:** 1¢ word minimum, and 1 free author's copy.
**Terms:** Pays on publication ("part acceptance only for solicited mss") for first North American serial rights plus right to reprint the entire issue.
**Tips:** "Read a copy and then some of the best anthologies in the field (such as Daw's 'Best Horror of the Year,' Arkham House anthologies, etc.) Occasionally we keep mss longer than planned. When sending a SASE marked 'book rate' (or anything not first class) the writer should add 'Forwarding Postage Guaranteed.' "

**WEST BRANCH (II)**, Dept. of English, Bucknell University, Lewisburg PA 17837. Editors: K. Patten and R. Taylor. Magazine: 5½x8½; 96-120 pages; good quality paper; illustrations; photos. Theme: Fiction and poetry. Readership: "Readers of contemporary literature." Biannually. Estab. 1977. Circ. 600.
**Needs:** Literary, contemporary, and translations. No science fiction. Accepts 3-6 mss/issue. No preferred length.
**How to Contact:** Send complete ms with SASE. Reports in 6 weeks on mss. Sample copy $2.
**Payment:** 2 free author's copies and one-year subscription; cover price less 20% discount charge for extras.

**Terms:** Acquires first rights. Publication copyrighted.
**Tips:** "Narrative art fulfills a basic human need—our dreams attest to this—and storytelling is therefore a high calling in any age. Find your own voice and vision. Make a story that speaks to your own mysteries. Cultivate simplicity in form, complexity in Theme. Look and listen through your characters." Published new writers within the last year.

**WEST COAST REVIEW (II),** A Quarterly Magazine of the Arts, West Coast Review Publishing Society, c/o English Dept., Simon Fraser University, Burnaby, British Columbia V5A 1S6 Canada. (604)291-4287. Magazine: 20cm.x20cm.; 70 pages; illustrations; photos. Magazine focusing on "contemporary poetry, short fiction, drama, music, graphics, photography and reviews of books for persons interested in the contemporary arts." Quarterly. Published special fiction issue. Estab. 1966. Circ. 500.
**Needs:** Contemporary, experimental, literary, prose poem, serialized/excerpted novel (possibly), and translations (possible if translator arranges for all necessary permissions). Receives 10-20 unsolicited fiction mss/month. Accepts 1-2 ms/issue, 3-8 mss/year. Less than 10% of fiction is agented. Length: 250 words minimum, 3,000 words maximum.
**How to Contact:** Send complete ms with SAE, IRC. "Photocopies acceptable with assurances that they are not under consideration elsewhere." Accepts computer printout submissions. Prefers letter-quality. Include a short biographical note. Reports "generally" in 2 weeks-2 months on mss. Publishes ms an average of 1-12 months after acceptance. Sample copy $3.50 (in Canada) and $4 (outside Canada) with 8x11 SAE and 50¢ postage (IRC).
**Payment:** $50 maximum; 3 free contributor's copies; $2.50 charge for extras.
**Terms:** Pays on acceptance for first rights. Publication copyrighted.
**Tips:** "Read several issues of the *Review* before submitting. Send standard, professional submissions. We have published new writers within the last year."

**WESTERN HUMANITIES REVIEW (III),** University of Utah, Salt Lake City UT 84112. (801)581-7438. Editor: Jack Garlington. Managing Editors: Nancy Roberts and Robert Shapard. Magazine: 6½x10; 96 pages; 12 pt. chrome, oneside coated paper; 60 lb coated cover stock; illustrations. "Articles on various aspects of the humanities: fiction, poetry, book and film reviews." Readership: Highly educated. Quarterly. Estab. 1947. Circ. about 1,200.
**Needs:** Literary, contemporary, humor, ethnic (all), serialized and condensed novels, and translations. Buys 2-3 mss/issue; 8-12 mss/year. Receives approximately 60 unsolicited fiction mss each month. Length: no requirement. Occasionally critiques rejected ms.
**How to Contact:** Send complete ms with SASE. Accepts computer printout submissions. Prefers letter-quality. Reports in 1 month on mss. Sends galleys to author. Publishes ms an average of 6 months after acceptance. Sample copy $4.
**Payment:** $150 maximum.
**Terms:** Pays on acceptance for all rights. Publication copyrighted.
**Tips:** "Read an issue and see what we like. Wait a while before making the first submission—until you are sure you have mastered your technique." Mss rejected because of "poor style, overworked themes." Published new writers within the last year.

**WESTWIND (II), UCLA's Journal of the Arts,** Division of Honors, A311 Murphy Hall, UCLA, Los Angeles CA 90024. (213)825-8607. Editor: Erik Bucy. Magazine: 8x12; 75 pages; glossy paper; illustrations; photos. Magazine of local and student art and literary work for a general audience; geared toward UCLA campus. Plans special fiction issue. Estab. 1956. Circ. 3,000.
**Needs:** Contemporary, experimental, literary, prose poem, regional, serialized/excerpted novel, and translations. Must be local/student work. No mainstream. Receives approximately 20 mss/month. Length: open. Publishes short shorts of 2-3 double-spaced typed pages. Occasionally comments on rejected ms. Recommends other markets.
**How to Contact:** Send complete ms. SASE. Simultaneous submissions "maybe"; photocopied submissions OK. Accepts computer printout submissions. Sample copy $4 and SAE (8x11).
**Payment:** Contributor's copies; "no charge for extras but need SASE."
**Terms:** Publication copyrighted.

**Tips:** "We feel that our readers, being students primarily, need a break from actual and realistic events and goings on. They need a bit of fantasy and imagination to relieve them. One cannot stress the importance of creativity, and imagination in today's society. Fiction is always wanted, always needed, and always welcome." Published new writers within the last year.

**WHETSTONE (II)**,University of Lethbridge, English Dept., Lethbridge, Alberta T1K 3M4 Canada. (403)329-2365. Contact: Editor. Magazine: approximately 6x9; 35 pages; superbond paper; pen or pencil sketch illustrations, photos. Magazine publishing "poetry, prose, drama, prints, photographs, and occasional music compositions for a university audience." Semiannually. Published special fiction issue. Estab. 1971. Circ. 100.
**Needs:** Experimental, literary, and mainstream. Receives 1 unsolicited fiction ms/month. Accepts 1 ms/issue, 3 mss/year. Does not read in summer. Length: 12 double-spaced pages maximum. Recommends other markets.
**How to Contact:** Send complete ms with SAE, IRC and cover letter with author's background and experience. Simultaneous and photocopied submissions OK. Accepts computer printout submissions. Prefers letter-quality. Reports in 3 months on mss. Publishes ms an average of 3-4 months after acceptance. Sample copy 50¢ and 10½x7½ or larger SAE and 2 Canadian first class stamps or IRCs.
**Payment:** 1 free contributor's copy.
**Terms:** Acquires no rights. Publication copyrighted.
**Tips:** "We seek good writing. Avoid moralizing." Published new writers within the last year.

**WHISKEY ISLAND MAGAZINE (I, II)**, Cleveland State University, University Center 7, Cleveland OH 44115. (216)687-2056. Contact: Fiction Editor. Magazine with no specific theme of fiction, poetry, photography. For college/liberal/humanist/literary audience. Semiannually. Estab. 1978. Circ. 2,500.
**Needs:** Confession, contemporary, erotica, ethnic, experimental, fantasy, humor/satire, literary, mainstream, prose poem, psychic/supernatural/occult, science fiction, suspense/mystery, and translations. "Nothing by a member of any right-wing group." Receives 20-35 unsolicited fiction mss/month. Acquires 4-8 mss/issue. Approximately 5% of fiction is agented. Length: 5,000 words maximum; 2,000-3,000 words average.
**How to Contact:** Send complete ms with SASE. Simultaneous, photocopied and previously published submissions OK. Reports in 4 months on mss. Publishes ms an average of 2-3 months after acceptance. Sample copy free.
**Payment:** 2 free contributor's copies.
**Terms:** Acquires one-time rights. Publication copyrighted.
**Tips:** Recommends a "professional presentation of ms with a *brief* bio."

**‡WHISPERING WIND MAGAZINE (I, II, IV), American Indian: Past & Present**, Louisiana Indian Heritage Association, Inc., 8009 Wales St., New Orleans LA 70126. (504)241-5866. Editor: Jack B. Heriard. Magazine: 8½x11; 32 pages; 60 lb paper; 70 lb cover stock; b&w illustrations; b&w photos. "American Indian theme; material culture, illustrated craft articles. Articles are welcome that reflect our American Indian culture, both past and present." Audience: 52% Indian, 12# years of age. Bimonthly. Estab. 1967. Circ. 4,000.
**Needs:** Special interest: American Indian. "Fiction must be American Indian related (theme) and yet historically accurate. Accuracy must also include material culture. Stories must not be stereotyped." Publishes ms up to one year after acceptance. Length: 2,500 words average. Publishes short shorts. Critiques rejected mss. Recommends other markets.
**How to Contact:** Send complete ms with cover letter with reasons for submissions. Illustration requirements. Reports in 3 months on queries. SASE for ms. Simultaneous submissions OK. Accepts computer printouts including dot-matrix. Sample copy $2.50. Fiction guidelines free.
**Payment:** Free subscription to magazine, contributor's copies (6), charge for extras.
**Terms:** Pays on publication for first rights. Publication copyrighted.
**Tips:** "There is a need for quality fiction about the American Indian. We have published two sto-

ries in the past, both received well by our readership. The story must be accurate in every detail, i.e. tribal location, dress, material culture, historical perspectives, except that of the characters and basic storyline. Although fiction, it will be better received if the story is believable. Do not stereotype the characters."

**‡THE JAMES WHITE REVIEW (II, IV), A Gay Men's Literary Quarterly**, The James White Review Association, 3356 Traffic Station, Minneapolis MN 55403. (612)291-2913. Editor: Collective (5). Tabloid: 26x17; 16 pages; illustrations; photos. "We publish work by *male* gay writers—any subject for primarily gay and/or gay sensitive audience." Quarterly. Estab. 1983. Circ. 2,000.

**Needs:** Contemporary, experimental, gay, humor/satire, literary, men's, translations. No pornographic. Receives 15 unsolicited fiction mss/month. Accepts 4 mss/issue; 16 mss/year. Publishes ms 3 months or sooner after acceptance. Agented fiction: 1%. Length: 22 pages, double spaced. Critiques rejected mss. Recommends other markets "when we can."

**How to Contact:** Send complete ms with cover letter with short bio, exactly what is enclosed. SASE. Reports in 2-3 months. SASE for ms. Photocopied submissions OK. Sample copy $2. Fiction guidelines $1.

**Payment:** 3 contributor's copies.

**Terms:** Acquires one-time rights; return to author. Publication copyrighted.

**WHITE WALLS, A Magazine of Writings by Artists**, White Walls, Inc., Box 8204, Chicago IL 60680. Editor: Buzz Spector. Magazine. "Texts by visual artists (i.e., painters, sculptors, photographers, graphic artists), with accompanying images." For "artists, critics, museum professionals, and others interested in contemporary art." Published three times/year. Estab. 1978. Circ. 650.

**Needs:** Experimental. Authors should be practicing visual artists. Occasionally critiques rejected ms.

**How to Contact:** Send ms accompanied by slides or photographs of artwork, plus résumé. Reports in 3 weeks. SASE. Photocopied submissions OK. Accepts computer printout submissions. Prefers letter-quality. Sample copy for $4.

**Payment:** Pays $2.50/page ($10 minimum) and 5 contributor's copies; 40% discount from cover price for extras.

**Terms:** Pays on publication for all rights. Publication copyrighted.

**‡THE WIDENER REVIEW (II)**, Widener University, 14th and Chestnut Sts., Chester PA 19013. (215)499-4266. Editor; Michael Clark. Magazine: 5¼x8½; 120 pages; Fiction, poetry, book reviews for general audience. Annually. Estab. 1984. Circ. 250.

**Needs:** Contemporary, experimental, literary, mainstream, regional, serialized/excerpted novel. Receives 20 unsolicited mss/month. Publishes 4-5 mss/issue. Does not read mss in summer. Publishes ms 3-9 months after acceptance. Length: 1,000 words minimum; 5,000 words maximum. Occasionally critiques rejected mss.

**How to Contact:** Send complete ms with cover letter. Reports in 3 months on mss. SASE for ms. No simultaneous or photocopied submissions or reprints. Accepts computer printouts including dot-matrix. Sample copy $3. Fiction guidelines for business-size SAE and 1 first class stamp.

**Payment:** Pays in contributor's copies; charge for extras. Acquires all rights. Publication copyrighted.

**THE WILLIAM AND MARY REVIEW (II)**, College of William and Mary, Williamsburg VA 23185. (804)253-4862. Editors change annually. Magazine: 80 pages; illustrations; photos. "We publish quality fiction, poetry, essays and art. Our audience is primarily undergraduate and professional." Semiannually. Estab. 1962. Circ. 2,800.

**Needs:** Literary, contemporary, and humor. Accepts 7 mss/issue, 14 mss/year. Receives approximately 50 unsolicited fiction mss each month. Length: 5,000 words maximum. Critiques always. Recommends other markets.

**How to Contact:** Send complete ms with SASE and cover letter with name, address, and phone number. Reports in 2 months. Do not submit in June, July or August. Sample copy $3.
**Payment:** 5 free author's copies and $50 for first place in each category.
**Terms:** Acquires first rights. Publication copyrighted.
**Tips:** "We want original, well-written stories. Staff requests names be attached separately to anonymous works. Page allotment to fiction will rise in relation to quality fiction received. Include a cover letter to editor with biographical information and social security number. 2nd prize 1985 for literary magazine in Society for Collegiate Journalists." Published new writers within the last year.

**WIND MAGAZINE (I, II)**, Rt. 1, Box 809K, Pikeville KY 41501. (606)631-1129. Editor: Quentin R. Howard. "Literary journal with stories, poems, book reviews from the small presses and some university presses. Readership is students, literary people, professors, housewives and others." Triannually. Estab. 1971. Circ. 500.
**Needs:** Literary and regional. "No restriction on form, content or subject." Accepts 4 mss/issue. Receives approximately 450 unsolicited fiction mss each month. Length: No requirement. Critiques rejected mss "when there is time."
**How to Contact:** Send complete ms with SASE. Photocopied submissions OK. Accepts computer printout submissions. Prefers letter-quality. Reports in 1 month. Publishes ms an average of 1 year after acceptance. Sample copy $2.
**Payment:** Free author's copies. $1.25 charge for extras.
**Terms:** Acquires first rights. Publication copyrighted.
**Tips:** "We're constantly looking for beginning fiction writers. Diversity is one of our major editorial goals. We have published since 1971 approximately 80 beginners in fiction; 45 are publishing regularly today in many magazines. No multiple submissions please. We have no taboos, but set our own standards on reading each ms."

**WIND ROW (I, II)**, English Department, Washington State University, Pullman WA 99164-5020. (509)335-2581. Editor: Alex Kuo. Magazine: 8x10; 64 + pages; bonded exc. paper; glossy cover stock; illustrations; photos. Semiannually. Circ. 1,500.
**Needs:** Condensed novel, contemporary, experimental, literary, prose poem, science fiction, and translations. Receives 50 unsolicited mss/month. Publishes short shorts. Accepts 3-5 mss/issue. Occasionally critiques rejected ms. Recommends other markets.
**How to Contact:** Send complete ms. Reports in 2 months on ms. SASE. Simultaneous and photocopied submissions OK. Accepts computer printout submissions. Prefers letter-quality. Sample copy $5.
**Payment:** 2 contributor's copies.
**Terms:** Acquires first rights on publication. Publication copyrighted.
**Tips:** Published new writers within the last year.

**WISCONSIN ACADEMY REVIEW (II)**, Wisconsin Academy of Sciences, Arts & Letters, 1922 University Ave., Madison WI 53705. (608)263-1692. Editor-in-Chief: Patricia Powell. Magazine: 8½x11; 64-80 pages; 75 lb coated 2 sides paper; coated cover stock; illustrations; photos. "The *Review* reflects the focus of the sponsoring institution with its editorial emphasis on Wisconsin's intellectual, cultural, social, and physical environment. It features short fiction, poetry, essays, and Wisconsin-related book reviews for well-educated, well-traveled people interested in furthering regional arts and literature and disseminating information about sciences." Published quarterly. Published special fiction issue last year; plans another. Estab. 1954. Circ. 2,000.
**Needs:** Experimental, historical (general), humor/satire, literary, mainstream, prose poem, science fiction, suspense/mystery, and women's. "Author must have lived or be living in Wisconsin or fiction must be set in Wisconsin." Receives 5-6 unsolicited fiction mss/month. Buys 1-2 mss/issue; 8-10 mss/year. Length: 1,000 words minimum; 4,000 words maximum; 3,000 words average.

**How to Contact:** Send complete ms with SASE and author's connection to Wisconsin, the prerequisite. Photocopied submissions OK. Accepts computer printout submissions. Prefers letter-quality. Publishes ms an average of 6 months after acceptance. Sample copy $2. Fiction guidelines with SAE and 1 first class stamp.
**Payment:** 5 contributor's copies.
**Terms:** Pays on publication for first rights. Publication copyrighted.
**Tips:** Published new writers within the last year.

**WISCONSIN REVIEW (II)**, Box 158, Radford Hall, University of Wisconsin, Oshkosh WI 54901. (414)424-2267. Editor: Patricia Haebig and Debbie Guenther. Magazine: 8½x11; 32-48 pages; illustrations. Literary of prose and poetry. Triquarterly. Estab. 1966. Circ. 2,000.
**Needs:** Literary and experimental. "We look for strong characterization, fresh situations and clipped, hammering dialogue." Receives 30 unsolicited fiction mss each month. Does not read in summer. Publishes short shorts. Length: up to 5,000 words. Critiques rejected mss "when there is time." Occasionally recommends other markets.
**How to Contact:** Send complete ms with SASE and cover letter with background on ms. "We distrust copies and computer printout." Reports in 1-6 months. Publishes ms an average of 1-2 months after acceptance. Sample copy $1.50.
**Payment:** Pays in contributor's copies.
**Terms:** Acquires first rights. Publication copyrighted.
**Tips:** "Length is the major problem with rejected mss. Due to space limitations, shorter pieces are best." Published new writers within the last year.

**‡WITT REVIEW (II), The Wittenberg Review of Literature and Art**, Wittenberg Student Government Association, Box 720, Springfield OH 45501. (513)325-3075. Editor: Candice J. Floyd. Magazine: 8½x11; 56-72 pages; coated offset paper; linen-look cover stock; illustrations; photos. "We strive to explore the spectrum of creativity with works which demonstrate discipline in thought and language—this includes high-quality poetry, fiction, plays, art, and photography. Our publication is accessible to curious adults, especially college-educated ones, since we are a college-funded and staffed magazine." Annually. Estab. 1975. Circ. 500.
**Needs:** "Mainly poetry with two or three high-quality fiction pieces—competiton is fierce." Contemporary, experimental, historical, literary, regional, translations. "A warning about any eroticism: there must be a visible reason for it: We don't go for erotica for its own sake. Our audience is fairly conservative. No romance, juvenile, anything that does not fit in with our serious endeavor to publish lasting *literature*." Receives 20-30 unsolicited fiction mss/month. Accepts 2-3 mss/issue; 2-3 mss/year. Does not read ms in summer. Publishes ms 3-4 months after acceptance. Length: 3,000; 2,500 words minimum; 4,500 words maximum. Publishes short shorts under 10 typewritten pages.
**How to Contact:** Send complete ms with cover letter. A short biographical note including previous publications, professional work, and avocational interests for use in our contributor's notes. Reports in 10 weeks. SASE for ms. Simultaneous and photocopied submissions OK. Accepts computer printouts. Sample copy $3.50. Fiction guidelines for legal size SAE and 1 first class stamp.
**Payment:** Contributor's copies, charge for extras.
**Terms:** Pays on publication. Rights reserved for authors. Publication copyrighted.
**Tips:** "From what I see from my mailbox, everyone wants to be a fiction writer. When I read manuscripts, I'm not looking for a quick fiction fix, but for an individual voice who knows the literary

**The double dagger before a listing indicates that the listing is new in this edition. New markets are often the most receptive to freelance contributions.**

score because s/he has a lot of reading in her/his background, not only modern literature, but also literature from other centuries and cultures. We do publish primarily poetry, which is the condensed product of thought and emotion. By publishing fiction, we seek a balance with the rational mind which expands upon an idea, as in fiction, and with the subconscious mind which makes quick associations, as in good poetry. Send us a manuscript after looking through a copy of the magazine; you'll know whether or not to try us."

‡WOMAN OF POWER (I), A Journal of Feminism, Spirituality and Politics, Woman of Power, Inc., Box 827-02238, Cambridge MA 02238. (617)491-6204. Editor: Char McKee. Magazine: 8½x11; 96 pages; 60 lb offset paper; 60 lb wt. coated cover; illustrations; photos. "Each issue has a theme. For instance, issue #4, Summer/Fall '86 will be 'Woman of Color/A Celebration of Power.' Winter/Spring '87 will be 'Healing.' These will be followed semiannually by 'International Woman' and 'Revisioning the Dark,' then 'Nature.' Our magazine is read by women in the peace camps, living on Lesbian lands, in Europe, India, Japan and is used in feminist study courses." Semiannually. Estab. summer 1984. Circ. 10,000 copies printed; estimated readership 50,000.
**Needs:** Ethnic, experimental, fantasy, feminist, gay, humor/satire, lesbian, translations. "We are very interested in publishing fiction by *women only*, from anywhere in the world but it should have a feminist/spiritual perspective and has the best chance of publication *when related to the theme* of that issue. We receive very little fiction of any kind so if the material is right for us, it stands a good chance of being published." Accepts 2-3 fiction mss/issue; 4-6 mss/year. Publishes ms 1-2 months after acceptance. Length: 2,000 words average; 200 words minimum; 3,500 words maximum. 4,000 words with no illustrations "but we prefer to illustrate. We often use *very* short pieces (200-300 words)—myths, fairy tales." Occasionally critiques rejected mss.
**How to Contact:** Query with clips of published work. Send complete ms with cover letter and 2 copies. "A bio note is helpful later if the work is published; phone number." Reports in 6 months on queries. SASE for query and ms. "Prefers no simultaneous submissions and we don't usually print already published work. Photocopied submissions OK. Accepts computer printouts including dot-matrix. Sample copy $5. Fiction guidelines for SAE.
**Payments:** Pays in contributor's copies.
**Terms:** Acquires all rights which revert to author. Publication copyrighted.
**Tips:** "It is imperative that women read our magazine before submitting. We have a very *specific* focus which is related to womens spirituality and is best understood by studying the past three issues. We print high quality photographs and artwork by women. In addition, we are very interested in fiction and poetry (which seems a good deal easier to come by!) Also, although we like shorter pieces, we like to see characters who *do* something, have relationships, exist in an environment etc. In other words, something *happens*."

WORKING CLASSICS (I), Red Wheelbarrow Press, 298 Ninth Ave., San Francisco CA 94118. (415)387-3412. Editor: David Joseph. Magazine: 8½x7; 44 pages; 70 lb cover stock; illustrations; photos. Magazine of "creative work, fiction, nonfiction, poetry, interviews, reviews, comics, by and for working people—especially the organized, trade unionists (both rank and file and leadership), artists, leftists, progressives." Semiannually. Plans special fiction issue. Estab. 1982. Circ. 500.
**Needs:** Comics, contemporary, ethnic, experimental, feminist, gay, historical, humor/satire, lesbian, literary, prose poem, and regional. No psychic/supernatural/occult, religious/inspirational. Receives 12 unsolicited mss/month. Accepts 2 mss/issue; 4 mss/year. Length: 2,400 words average; 250 words minimum; 18,000 words maximum. Occasionally critiques rejected mss. Recommends other markets.
**How to Contact:** Send complete ms. "We're interested in the concrete process involved in your actual conditions. We like to know why you believe your story is for our audience of working people and working writers." Reports in 3 months. SASE. Simultaneous, photocopied and previously published submissions OK. Accepts computer printout submissions. Prefers letter-quality. Accepts disc submissions compatible with IBM Displaywriter. Prefers hard copy with disc submis-

sion. Sample copy with #75 SAE and 71¢ postage.
**Payment:** 1 free contributor's copy; 40¢ charge for extras.
**Terms:** Acquires one-time rights. Publication copyrighted.
**Tips:** "Character is central. Know who the story is about and who it's for. From that the style and substance develop. Show your sympathy and understanding for the specific situations and concerns of working people. We focus on working people's creative concerns. We find one major form these take is the story." Published 2 new writers within the last year.

**‡WORLDS OF WONDER (I), New Writings in Imaginative Fiction**, Quixsilver Press, Box 7635, Baltimore MD 21207. Editor: Bob Medcalf, Jr. Magazine: 5½x8½; 24 pages; offset paper; vellum cover stock; illustrations. Short shorts on imaginative themes and treatment for well-read readers of imaginative fiction. Annually. Plans special fiction issue. Estab. 1986. Circ. 100.
**Needs:** Adventure, experimental, fantasy, horror, psychic/supernatural/occult, science fiction. Short shorts only. Nothing over 2,500 words. Receives 10 unsolicited ficiton mss/month. Accepts 12 mss/issue; 12 mss/year. Publishes ms 1 year after acceptance. Charges reading fee of $2. Length: 600 words; 100 words minimum; 2,500 words maximum. Publishes short shorts of 600 words. Critiques rejected mss. Recommends other markets.
**How to Contact:** Send complete ms with cover letter with brief publication highlights, reading interests in the field of imaginative fiction. Reports in 2 months. SASE for ms. Simultaneous, photocopied and reprint submissions OK. Accepts computer printouts including dot-matrix. Sample copy $3. Fiction guidelines $1.
**Payment:** Free subscription to magazine, contributor's copies, charge for extras.
**Terms:** Pays on publication for one-time rights. Publication copyrighted.
**Tips:** "The beginning fiction writer can fulfill the journeyman requirements in the small press magazines if he/she dilligently searches out editors willing to work with him/her on his/her beginning work. Supporting the publictions that serve him or her—through subscriptions and reading fees is a requirement of this process. Send your best work. Be eager and willing to revise or rewrite new work guided by comments. Submit to other suggested markets."

**STEPHEN WRIGHT'S MYSTERY NOTEBOOK (II, IV)**, Box 1341, F.D.R. Station, New York NY 10150. Editor: Stephen Wright. Journal and Newsletter: 8½x11; 10-12 pages; photocopied; self-cover; illustrations sometimes. "Mystery books, news, information; reviews and essays. Separate section covers books of merit that are not mysteries." For mystery readers and writers. Quarterly. Estab. 1984. Circ. less than 1,000.
**Needs:** Excerpted novel (suspense/mystery). Receives few unsolicited mss. Length: brief. Short shorts considered. Occasionally comments on rejected ms.
**How to Contact:** Query first or query with clips of published work (preferably on mystery). Reports in 2 weeks on queries; 3 weeks on mss. SASE for ms. Photocopied and previously published submissions OK (if query first). Accepts computer printout submissions on Editor's approval. Prefers letter-quality. Sample copy $3.
**Payment:** None. "If author is a regular contributor, he or she will receive complimentary subscription. Usually contributor receives copy of the issue in which contribution appears."
**Terms:** Publication copyrighted.
**Tips:** "The quality mystery magazines use all kinds of stories in various settings. This is also true of mystery books except that clever spy stories are now much in demand. Mystery fiction books have increased in demand—*but* the competetion is more keen than ever. So only those with real talent *and* a good knowledge of mystery writing craft have any chance for publication."

**WRIT MAGAZINE (II)**, 2 Sussex Ave., Toronto, Ontario, Canada M5S 1J5. Editor: Roger Greenwald. Assoc. Editor: Richard M. Lush. Magazine: 6x9; 96 pages; Zephyr laid paper; fine art etching cover stock; cover illustrations. "Literary magazine for literate readers interested in the work of new writers." Annually. Published special fiction issue last year; plans another. Estab. 1970. Circ. 700.

**Needs:** Literary, short stories, short shorts, parts of novels, translations. No other categories. Accepts 10-15 mss/year. Does not read mss in summer. Length: 300-20,000 words. Critiques rejected mss "when there is time. Sometimes recommends other markets."

**How to Contact:** Send complete ms with SASE and brief biographical note on author and/or translator, and a phone number. Accepts computer printout submissions if letter quality. Reports in 6 weeks. Sample copy $5.

**Payment:** 2 free author's copies. Negotiates charge for extras.

**Terms:** Acquires first North American serial rights. Copyright reverts to author.

**WRITERS' FORUM (I, II)**, University of Colorado at Colorado Springs, Colorado Springs CO 80933-7150. Editor: Dr. Alex Blackburn. "Ten to fifteen short stories or self-contained novel excerpts published once a year along with 25-35 poems. Highest literary quality only: mainstream, avant-garde, with preference to western themes. For small press enthusiasts, teachers and students of creative writing, commercial agents/publishers, university libraries and departments interested in contemporary American literature." Vol. 11 (1985) highlights Nobel Prize nominee Frank Walters. Annually. Estab. 1974. Circ. 1,000.

**Needs:** Literary, contemporary, ethnic (Native American, chicano, not excluding others), and regional (West). No "sentimental, over-plotted, pornographic, anecdotal, polemical, trendy, disguised autobiographical, fantasy (sexual, extra-terrestrial), pseudo-philosophical, passionless, placeless, undramatized, etc. material." Accepts 10-15 mss/issue. Receives approximately 40 unsolicited fiction mss each month and will publish new as well as experienced authors. Length: 1,500-10,000. Critiques rejected mss "when there is time and perceived merit."

**How to Contact:** Send complete ms and letter with brief bio and relevant career information with SASE. Accepts computer printout submissions. Prefers letter-quality. Reports in 3-5 weeks on mss. Publishes mss an average of 6 months after acceptance. Sample back copy $5.95 to FWM readers. Current copy $8.95.

**Payment:** 1 free author's copy. Cover price less 25% discount for extras.

**Terms:** Acquires one-time rights. Rights revert to author. Publication copyrighted.

**Tips:** "Read our publication. Be prepared for constructive criticism. We especially seek submissions that show immersion in place (trans-Mississippi West) and development of credible characters. Turned of by slick 'decadent' New York-ish content. Probably the TV-influenced fiction is the most quickly rejected. Our format—a 5½x8½ professionally edited and printed paperback book—lends credibility to authors published in our imprint." Funded by grants from National Endowment for the Arts, Coordinating Council for Literary Magazines, University of Colorado, McGraw Hill, and others.

**WRITER'S GAZETTE NEWSLETTER (I, II)**, Trouvere Company, Rt. 2, Box 290, Eclectic AL 36024. Editor: Brenda Williamson. Newsletter: 8½x11; 30-40 pages; 20 lb bond paper; index cover stock; illustrations; photos sometimes. For writers, by writers, about writing. Monthly. Plans special fiction issue in future. Estab. 1983.

**Needs:** Adventure, contemporary, fantasy, gothic/historical romance, horror, humor/satire, literary, mainstream, prose poem, psychic/supernatural, religious/inspirational, contemporary romance, science fiction, suspense/mystery, and western. Wants to see a "definite story—ficticious." Buys 50 mss/year. Length: 300 words minimum; 2,000 words maximum; 800 words average.

**How to Contact:** Send complete ms with SASE. Simultaneous, photocopied and reprint submissions OK. Reports in 4-8 weeks on ms. Sample copy $2.50 with #10 SAE and 1 first class stamp. Fiction guidelines for 50¢ with #10 SAE and 1 first class stamp.

**Payment:** Pays $6-40; contributor's copy $2.50.

**Terms:** Pays on publication for first, second or one time rights. Publication copyrighted.

**Tips:** Be "creative and unique." Published beginning writers within the last year.

**WRITERS WEST (II), By and for Professional Writers**, Box 16097, San Diego CA 92116-0097. (619)278-6108. Editor: Doug Emry. Magazine: 8½x11; 16+ pages; coated cover stock;

b&w photos. "Articles of interest to working writers, profiles of professional organizations, quality short stories and poetry" for professional writers and authors. Bimonthly. Published special fiction issue last year. Estab. 1982. Circ. 2,500.

**Needs:** Open. "Prefer non-writing stories." Receives 15-25 unsolicited mss/month. Accepts 1 ms/issue; 6 mss/year. Length: 2,000 words average; 2,500 words maximum. Occasionally comments on rejected ms. Sometimes recommends other markets.

**How to Contact:** Send complete ms. Reports in 10 days on ms. SASE. Simultaneous and photocopied submissions OK. Accepts computer printout submissions. Prefers letter-quality. Sample copy $2. Fiction guidelines for SASE.

**Payment:** "Token" payment and 3 contributor's copies.

**Terms:** Pays on publication for first North American serial rights. Publication copyrighted.

**Tips:** "Stories should have a beginning, middle and end, and endeavor to make a point, however subtle. Not interested in seeing esoteric 'philosophies,' stories on the travails of 'the writing life,' or slice-of-life vignettes." Published new writers within the last year.

**XAVIER REVIEW (I, II)**, Xavier University, Box 110C, New Orleans LA 70125. (504)486-7411, ext. 481. Editor: Thomas Bonner Jr. Magazine of "poetry/fiction/nonfiction/reviews (contemporary literature) for professional writers/libraries/colleges/universities." Published semiannually. Estab. 1980. Circ. 500.

**Needs:** Contemporary, ethnic, experimental, fantasy, historical (general), literary, Latin-American, prose poem, Southern, religious, serialized/excerpted novel, translations, and women's. Receives 30 unsolicited fiction mss/month. Buys 2 mss/issue; 4 mss/year. Length: 10-15 pages. Occasionally critiques rejected mss.

**How to Contact:** Send complete ms or query with clips of published work. SASE with ms, query. Sample copy $3.

**Payment:** 2 contributor's copies.

**Terms:** Pays on publication. Publication copyrighted.

**X-IT (II), Arts and Provocative Journalism**, Image Design Ltd., Box 102, St. Johns, Newfoundland A1C 5H5 Canada. (709)753-8802. Editor: Ken J. Harvey. Fiction Editor: Allela English. Magazine. Triannually. Estab. 1984. Circ. 3,000.

**Needs:** Contemporary, erotica, experimental, humor/satire, mainstream, and prose poem. Receives approximately 40 unsolicited mss/month. Buys 3-4 mss/issue; 9-12 mss/year. Length: 1,000 words minimum; 4,000 words maximum. Occasionally comments on rejected ms.

**How to Contact:** Send complete ms. Reports in 3-4 weeks on mss. SASE or SAE and IRC. Simultaneous and photocopied submissions OK. Accepts computer printout submissions. Sample copy $3.

**Payment:** Pays $5-50; $10 subscription to magazine; 2 contributor's copies; 50% of cover price charge for extras.

**Terms:** Pays on publication for first rights and first North American serial rights. Publication copyrighted.

**Tips:** "Send personal letter with submissions. Submissions without cover letter give an uncaring impression."

**THE YALE LITERARY MAGAZINE (II)**, American Literary Society, Inc., Box 243A, Yale Station, New Haven CT 06520. (203)436-4946. Editor-in-Chief: Andrei Navrozov. Magazine: 8½x11; 100 pages; dull-coated 70 lb paper; gloss 80 lb cover stock; illustrations; photos. "The paper we print on is guaranteed to endure for centuries, and we seek to publish and reproduce what will last at least as long. The content of America's oldest review, enhanced and augmented by its appearance, attracted an exceptional audience, comprised of some of the most influential men in the United States, in the very first year of national publication." Quarterly. Estab. 1821. Circ. 10,000.

**Needs:** Translations and memoirs. "*No* Barth, Doctorow, (John) Irving, Styron, Kosinski, Talese, Roth, Capote, Updike, Mailer, Gardner, Oates—and certainly not those who sound like

338 Fiction Writer's Market

them. We are sure you will understand." Receives 50 unsolicited fiction mss/month. Buys 1-3 mss/issue; 3-10 mss/year. Length: 600 words minimum; 3,000 words maximum. Occasionally critiques rejected ms. Sometimes recommends other markets.
**How to Contact:** Send complete ms with SASE, cover letter with author's views on life and literature. Simultaneous, photocopied and previously published submissions OK. Reports in 3 months on mss. Sample copy $6 with 9x12 SAE.
**Payment:** $25-1,000.
**Terms:** Pays on publication for all rights, first rights, or first North American serial rights; makes assignments on work-for-hire basis. Sends galleys to author. Publication copyrighted.
**Tips:** "We do not make formalized distinctions between 'fiction' and 'non fiction' at all; we seek talent, which always transcends such distinctions. The status of fiction today is not an issue that can be discussed separately from such broader issues as the State of American Intellectual Life or the relationship between cultural freedom and democracy. The goal is to increase creative freedom by fragmenting and broadening our cultural establishment. Read Shakespeare rather than D.M. Thomas. Listen to faint voices. And do not write unless you have something to say."

**THE YALE REVIEW (II)**, Yale University Press, 1902A Yale Station, New Haven CT 06520. (203)436-8307. Editor: Kai T. Erikson. Associate Editor: Penelope Laurans. Managing Editor: Wendy Wipprecht. "A general interest quarterly; publishes literary criticism, original fiction and poetry, cultural commentary, book reviews for an educated, informed, general audience." Quarterly. Estab. 1911. Circ. 6,000.
**Needs:** Literary and contemporary. Buys 4-8 mss/year. Less than 1% of fiction is agented. Length: 3,000-5,000 words.
**How to Contact:** Send complete ms with SASE. Reports in 2 months. Publishes ms up to 1 year after acceptance. Sample copy $6.
**Payment:** Approximately $100. 1 free author's copy; $2.50 charge for extras.
**Terms:** Makes assignments on a work-for-hire basis. Pays on publication for first North American serial rights.

**YELLOW SILK (II, IV): Journal of Erotic Arts**, Verygraphics, Box 6374, Albany CA 94706. Editor/Publisher: Lily Pond. Magazine: 8½x11; 52 pages; Electrobrite paper; glossy cover stock; illustrations; photos. "We are interested in nonpornographic erotica: joyous, mad; musical, elegant, passionate and beautiful. 'All persuasions; no brutality' is our editorial policy. Literary excellence is a priority; innovative forms are welcomed, as well as traditional ones." Published quarterly. May publish special fiction issue in future. Estab. 1981. Circ. 10,000.
**Needs:** Comics, erotica, ethnic, experimental, fantasy, feminist/lesbian, gay, humor/satire, literary, prose poem, science fiction, and translations. No "blow-by-blow" descriptions; no hackneyed writing except when used for satirical purposes. Nothing containing brutality. Buys 4-5 mss/issue; 16-20 mss/year. Length: no preference. Occasionally critiques rejected ms.
**How to Contact:** Send complete ms with SASE and include short, *personal* bio notes. No prepublished material. No simultaneous submissions. Name, address, and phone number on each page. Photocopied submissions OK. Accepts computer printout submissions. Prefers letter-quality. Reports in 6-8 weeks on mss. Publishes ms up to 2 years after acceptance. Sample copy $3.50.
**Payment:** 3 contributor's copies plus $10 per prose item.
**Terms:** Pays on publication for all periodical and anthology rights for one year following publication at which time they revert back to author and non-exclusive reprint and anthology rights for the duration of the copyright. Publication copyrighted.
**Tips:** "Read, read, read! Including our magazine—plus Nabokov and Nin, and Rimbaud, Virginia Woolf, William Kotzwinkle, James Joyce. Then send in your story! Trust that the magazine/editor will not rip you off—they don't. As they say, 'find your own voice,' then trust it. Most manuscripts I reject appear to be written by people without great amounts of writing experience. It takes years (frequently) to develop your work to publishable quality; it can take many re-writes on each individual piece. I also see many approaches to sexuality (for my magazine) that are trite and not fresh. The use of language is not original, and the people do not seem real. However, the gems

come too, and what a wonderful moment that is." Holds a fiction contest yearly. $200 for the best story that has been published in the magazine during the year. Submit to magazine, not contest. Enclose SASE. Published new writers within the last year.

**YESTERDAY'S MAGAZETTE (I)**, "Everyone Has a Yesterday," Independent Publishing Co., Box 15126, Sarasota FL 34277. Editor: Ned Burke. Tabloid: 10x14; 12-20 pages; newsprint paper; illustrations; photos. Nostalgia for senior citizens, nostalgia buffs, antique dealers, etc. Monthly. Estab. 1973. Circ. 6,500.
**Needs:** Historical, humor/satire, prose poem, religious/inspirational. No contemporary pieces; prepare settings between 1900-1950. Receives 20-30 unsolicited fiction mss/month. Accepts 2 fiction mss/issue; 15-20 mss/year. Publishes short shorts of 250-500 words. Length: 500 words minimum; 1,500 words maximum; 750-1,000 words average. Occasionally critiques rejected mss. Recommends other markets.
**How to Contact:** Send complete ms with SASE and "background info on writer; even photo." Simultaneous, photocopied and previously published submissions OK. Reports in 2-3 weeks on mss. Sample copy $1. Fiction guidelines free with # SASE.
**Payment:** 2 free contributor's copies; 50¢ charge for extras.
**Terms:** Acquires all rights. Publication copyrighted.
**Tips:** "Stories should be of a 'general interest' so most readers can identify with writer's message." *YM* "best" stories chosen at year's end. $25 award offered. "Take a 'memory' and relate it in a simple and interesting style. Nothing fancy here. Edit out all unnecessary adjectives. Keep it brief and to the point. Use 'conversational' tone in story. Forget style; just tell the story in your own words." Published new writers within the last year.

**ZEPHYR**, Great South Bay Poetry Co-op, Box 216, Station H, Central Islip NY 11722. Magazine. "*Zephyr* mainly concentrates on poetry but does use some *short* fiction as well as essays and other prose pieces. The magazine is aimed at an audience of all ages and educational and environmental background interested in poetry and all aspects of the poetic art." Annually. Estab. 1980. Circ. 500.
**Needs:** Experimental, fantasy, feminist, historical (general), humor/satire, literary, mainstream, prose poem, science fiction, suspense/mystery, and women's. No pornographic or violent material, no sexism or racism. Accepts 2-3 mss/issue. Length: 1,500 words average; 2,100 words maximum. Occasionally critiques rejected mss.
**How to Contact:** Send complete ms. Reports in 9 months. SASE. Simultaneous, photocopied and previously published submissions OK. Accepts computer printout submissions. Sample copy for $4 and 5x7 envelope with 75¢ postage. Fiction guidelines for #10 SASE.
**Payment:** 2 free contributor's copies; $4 charge for extras.
**Terms:** Acquires one-time rights. Publication copyrighted.
**Tips:** "Imitate the writing masters' skills, but not their outdated prejudicial attitudes."

**ZÖNE (II), A Feminist Journal for Women and Men**, Zöne Press, Box 85, Cambridge MA 02141. (617)492-0526. Editor: Richard Waring. Fiction Editor: Robert Cataldo. Magazine: 6x9; 132 pages; 60 lb high quality paper; 10 lb glossy cover stock; illustrations; photos. Magazine's theme is "new forms of femininity and masculinity; ethnic, philosophical mix; gay/straight; feminism in translation." Audience: "politically/sexually aware; feminists—both women and men; seriously popular literature addicts." Published irregularly. Estab. 1983. Circ. approximately 1,000.
**Needs:** Contemporary, ethnic, experimental, feminist, gay, historical, lesbian, literary, men's, prose poem, science fiction, translations, women's, veteran's, handicapped. "Nothing meant for the more commercial outlets." Receives 10 unsolicited mss/month. Length: 2,500 words or under average; 500 words minimum; 3,000 words maximum. Rarely accepts above 10 pages. Occasionally critiques rejected mss.
**How to Contact:** Query first or send complete ms. "Unless author knows our theme, query is best initial contact." Reports in 1 week on queries; 3 months on mss. SASE. Photocopied submis-

sions OK. Accepts computer printout submissions. Prefers letter-quality. Accepts disc submissions compatible with Compugraphic. Prefers hard copy with disc submission. Sample copy $5. Fiction guidelines for legal size SAE and 1 first class stamp.

**Payment:** 2 contributor's copies.

**Terms:** Acquires one-time rights. Publication copyrighted.

**Tips:** "Be language conscious. Make it new. Don't posture, simply record what you think and feel." Published new writers within the last year.

**‡ZYZZYVA (II), The Last Word: West Coast Writers and Artists**, Zyzzyva, Inc., 55 Sutter St., San Francisco CA 94104. (415)387-8389. Editor: Howard Junker. Magazine: 6x9; 152 pages; Starwhite Vicksburg smooth paper; illustrations; photos. "Literate" magazine. Quarterly. Estab. spring, 1985. Circ. 2,500.

**Needs:** Contemporary, experimental, literary. Receives 200 unsolicited mss/month. Buys 5 fiction mss/issue; 20 mss/year. Agented fiction: 20%. Length: varies.

**How to Contact:** Send complete ms with cover letter. Reports in 2 weeks on mss. SASE. No simultaneous or photocopied submissions or reprints. Accepts computer printouts including dot-matrix. Accepts electronic submissions via disc or modem. Sample copy $6. Fiction guidelines on masthead page.

**Payment:** Pays $25-100 and free subscription for one year.

**Terms:** Pays on acceptance for first North American serial rights. Publication copyrighted.

---

# Foreign literary/little magazines

The following is a list of foreign literary/little magazines, those journals or quarterlies published in countries other than the US or Canada which accept or buy short fiction in English.

Before sending a manuscript overseas, we recommend that you query the magazine first for their needs and interests in short stories and their submission requirements. All foreign correspondence must include international reply coupons (IRCs) to ensure an answer to your query or the return of your manuscript. (See Manuscript Mechanics.)

**AQUARIUS**, Aquarium Ltd., Flat 3, 114 Sutherland Ave., London W9 England. 01-286-3317. Editor-in-Chief: Eddie S. Linden. Magazine for a literary audience. Humor/satire, literary, prose poem, and serialized/excerpted novel.

**BROADSHEET**, Broadsheet Collective, Box 5799, Wellesley St., Auckland, New Zealand. 794-751AUCK. Editor: Sanda Coney. Feminist magazine of news, reviews, interviews, fiction, and poetry for people interested in feminism.

**BUSY BEES' NEWS**, People's Dispensary for Sick Animals, PDSA House, South St. Dorking, Surrey, England RH4 2LB. 888219. Editor-in-Chief: R.I. Cookson. "Magazine for children up to 11 years old interested in animals; stories, puzzles, things to do, cartoons, jokes, features, etc. on animals."

**CHANDRABHAGA**, A Magazine of New Writing, The Chandrabhaga Society, Tinkonia Bagicha, Cuttack, Orissa, India 753 001. 20-566. Editor: Jayanta Mahapatra. Magazine of "poetry mainly, fiction, essays on poetry/fiction, with a bias on Indian poetry for university English departments, poets, writers and discriminating readers."

**CHAPMAN**, 35 E. Claremont St., Edinburgh EH7 4HT Scotland. 031-556-5863. Editor: Joy Hendry. Scottish literary magazine.

**COMPASS POETRY & PROSE**, Compass, Box 51, Burwood, NSW 2134 Australia. (02)560-8729. Editor: Chris Mansell. Literary quarterly.

**DARK HORIZONS**, British Fantasy Society, c/o 194 Station Rd., Kings Heath, Birmingham B14 7TE England. Editor: Dave Sutton. Magazine of dark fantasy, heroic fantasy, film fantasy, fact, and fiction for fantasy fans.

**EQUOFINALITY**, 87 Lansdowne Rd., Worcester WR3 8LJ, England. Rod Mengham, John Wilkinson. Poetry, fiction, criticism, long-poems.

**FANTASY TALES**, A Magazine of the Weird and Unusual, 194 Station Rd., Kings Heath, Birmingham B14 7TE England. Editor-in-Chief: Stephen Jones. Fiction Editor: David Sutton. "A magazine of entertaining stories and verse which visually is a tribute to the pulps. We publish a wide range of themes in the fantasy genre for both devotees of fantasy and more general readers."

**FORESIGHT**, 44 Brockhurst Rd., Hodge Hill, Birmingham B36 8JB. England. (021)783-0587. Editor: John Barklam. Fiction Editor: Judy Barklam. Magazine with "new age material, world peace, psychic phenomena, research, occultism, spiritualism, mysticism, UFO's, philosophy, etc." Needs: Psychic/supernatural/occult.

**FRANK**, An International Journal of Contemporary Writing and Art, 6 rue Monge, 75005 Paris France. Editor: David Applefield; or Mixed General Delivery APO New York 09777. "Eclectic, serious fiction—all styles, voices, and translations, novel extracts" for literary international audience.

**GLOBAL TAPESTRY JOURNAL**, BB Books, 1 Spring Bank, Longsight Rd., Salesbury, Blackburn, Lancashire BB1 9EU England. 0254-49128. Editor: Dave Cunliffe. "Post-underground with avant-garde, experimental, alternative, counterculture, psychedelic, mystical, anarchist, etc., fiction used for a bohemian and counter culture."

**GRANTA**, Granta, 44a Hobson St., Cambridge CB1 1NL England. Editor: Bill Buford. US office: 13 White St., West New York NY 10018 USA. Editor: Jonahan Levi. "Paperback magazine (250-320 pp.) publishing fiction and cultural and political journalism: fiction (including novellas and works-in progress), essays, political analysis, journalism, etc."

**HECATE**, A Women's Interdisciplinary Journal, Hecate Press, Box 99, St. Lucia, Queensland 4067, Australia. Editor: Carole Ferrier. Magazine of "material relating to women, particularly that which employs a feminist, marxist or other radical methodology to focus on the position of women in relation to patriarchy and capitalism in any given area."

**HOWL'T**, Bactrianus Enterprises, Solliveien 37, 1370 Asker, Norway. Editor: Ragnar F. Lie. Magazine for "Elfquest" fans.

**IMPEGNO 80**, Sicilian Antigruppo/Cross-Cultural Communications, Villa Schammachanat, Via Agrentaria Km 4, Tcapani, Sicily, Italy 91026. Editor: Nat Scammacca.

**INDIAN LITERATURE**, Indian Academy of Letters, 35 Feroze Shah Road, New Delhi, 110001 India. Tel. 388667. Editor: Keshav Malik. Magazine of fiction, poetry, novelettes, critical literary essays for a select audience.

**INS & OUTS**, A Magazine of Awareness, Ins & Outs Press, Box 3759, Amsterdam, Holland 276868. Tel. (020)27-6868. Editor: Edward Woods. "An eclectic magazine. Only criterion is quality. All subjects and styles considered. Erotica especially welcome. For lovers of language in its most meaningful form as well as incorrigible word addicts who can't resist a good read."

**INTERZONE**, Ground Zero Productions, 21 The Village Street, Leeds, England LS4 2PR. Editors: Simon Ounsley and David Pringle. Science fiction and fantasy magazine.

**IRON MAGAZINE**, Iron Press, 5 Marden Ter., Cullercoats, North Shields, Tyne & Wear NE30 4PD UK. (091)531901. Editor: Peter Mortimer. "Literary magazine of contemporary fiction, poetry, articles and graphics."

**JENNINGS**, Jennings Magazine Limited, 336 Westbourne Park Rd, London W11 1EQ. (01)221-5914. "Each issue contains a £300 short story competition; an intimate interview with an established author; outlets for new and not so new writers, poets, illustrators; features, reviews, literary crossword."

**JOE SOAP'S CANOE**, 90 Ranelagh Road, Felixstowe, Suffolk IP11 7HY, England, Martin Stannard. Poetry, fiction, articles, art, photos, interviews, reviews, parts-of-novels, long-poems, plays.

**KADATH**, Weird and Fantasy Fiction, Kadath Press, Corso Aurelio Saffi 5/9, 16128 Genova, Italy. Editor: Francesco Cova. Magazine of "original stories in English-weird and fantasy fiction—for fans and collectors of weird and fantasy fiction."

**LINQ**, Literature in North Queensland, English Language and Literature Association, English Dept. James Cook University of North Queensland, Townsville, 4811 Australia. Editor: Elizabeth Perkins. Magazine of articles, stories, poems, reveries on literature, history for academic and general audience.

**LUDDS MILL**, Eight Miles High, Home Entertainment, 44 Spa Croft Rd., Teall St., Ossett, W. Yorkshire WF5, 0HE, UK. Wakefield 275814. Editor: Andrew Darlington. "Alternative culture in the Bohemian tradition, experimental but accessible, direct, exciting, 'beat,' 'hipster,' 'punk,' etc. Aimed at late-teens, twenties, plus anyone with a mental orientation open to 'alternative' culture. Dada, surrealism, anarchist-left, pre-raphaelite, 60s underground, beat generation, etc."

**MATILDA-LITERARY & ARTS MAGAZINE**, Matilda Publications, 7 Mountfield St., Brunswick 3056, Victoria, Australia. Magazine for housewives, poets, writers, academics, students, unemployed, and those seeking alternatives to TV. Needs: Adventure, comics, contemporary, fantasy, humor/satire, literary, mainstream, psychic/supernatural/occult, regional, romance (contemporary and young adult), senior citizen/retirement, and women's.

**THE MOORLANDS REVIEW**, The Moorlands Press, 11 Novi Lane, Leek, Staffs, ST13, 6NS England. Editor: J.C.R. Green. Magazine of poetry, short fiction and artwork. "We publish short, innovative fiction, of any style, as long as it is well-written."

**THE NEPEAN REVIEW**, An Australian Magazine of the Arts, The Firebird Press, Box 10, Kingswood, N.S.W. 2750 Australia. Tel. (04)736-0344. Editor: Phillip Kay. Magazine of the arts for literary groups, artists, academics, students.

**NEW EDINBURGH REVIEW, EUSPB**, 1 Buccleuch Pl., Edinburgh EH8 Scotland. (031)667-5718. Editor: Allan Massie. Features, fiction, poetry, reviews for general readership.

**ORBIS**, An International Quarterly of Poetry and Prose. 199 The Long Shoot. Nuneaton, Warwickshire CV11 6JQ England. Tel. (0203)327440. Editor: Mike Shields. Quarterly magazine covering literature in English and other languages. "We are looking for short (1,200) pieces of original and interesting work: prose poems, mood pieces, short stories, etc."

**PACIFIC QUARTERLY MOANA**, A Multi-Cultural and Multi-lingual Review, Outrigger Publishers, Box 13-049, Hamilton, New Zealand. Editor-in-Chief: Norman Simms. "We alternate general and special issues; mostly concerned with interaction of multicultural and multilingual societies, particularly in the Asia-Pacific rim countries, for intelligent, imaginative readers with cosmopolitan tastes."

**PARIS EXILES**, 118 rue Vieille du Temple, 75003 Paris, France. Editor: John Strand. Poetry, fiction.

**PROSPICE**, Johnston Green Publishing (UK) Ltd., Box 1, Portree Isle of Skye, Scotland IV51 9BT. Telephone: National (047)852 257, International (44)47852257. Editors: J.C.R. Green & Roger Elkin. Literary.

**QUADRANT**, Box C344, Clarence Street, P.O. Sydney 2000. New South Wales, Australia. "A monthly journal of high literary and intellectual standing published by the Australian Association for Cultural Freedom, for serious writers only."

**SEPIA**, Poetry & Prose Magazine, Kawabata Press, Knill Cross House, Higher Anderton Rd., Millbrook, Nr Torpoint, Cornwall, England. Editor-in-Chief: Collin David Webb. Magazine for those interested in modern un-clichéd work.

**SMOKE**, Windows Project, 22 Roseheath Dr., Halewood, Liverpool L26 9UH, England. Contact: Dave Ward. Magazine of poetry, fiction, art, long-poems, collages, concrete art, photos, cartoons.

**SPHINX: WOMEN'S INTERNATIONAL LITERARY/ART REVIEW**, 175 avenue Ledru Rollin, 75011 Paris, France. Editor: Carol Pratl.

**START**, The Scribery, Waterhouses, STOKE-ON-TRENT, Staffs. ST ART, United Kingdom, Waterhouses (053 86) 567. 1978. Editor: Charles Mansfield. Poetry, fiction, articles, art, photos, cartoons, interviews, satire, criticism, reviews, music, letters, news items, nonfiction.

**THE STONY THURSDAY BOOK**, 128 Sycamore Ave., Rath bhan, Limerick, Republic of Ireland. Editor-in-Chief: John Liddy. "Literary magazine prose, story, poetry, review, illustration."

**STRIDE**, Stride Publications, 80 Lord Street, Crewe, Cheshire CW2 7DL, England. Contact: Rupert Loydell, Graham Palmer. Poetry, fiction, articles, art, interviews, criticism, reviews, music, long-poems, collages, concrete art.

**TEARS IN THE FENCE**, 12 Hod View, Stourpane, Nr. Blandford Forum, Doset DT11 8TN, United Kingdom. Contact: David Caddy. A magazine of poetry, fiction and graphics, "blended with a conservation section to develop the concepts of ecology and conservation beyond their present narrow usage".

**TOGETHER**, For All concerned with Christian Education, General Synod Board of Education, Church House, Dean's Yard, London, England SW1P 3NZ. Editor-in-Chief: Mrs. P. Egan. Magazine of forward-looking Christian education for children under 12. Short stories, plays, services, projects, etc. Also songs, cards, occasional poems. Readers are primary school and Sunday school teachers, clergy.

**2PLUS2**, Mylabris Press, Case Postale 171, 1018 Lausanne, Switzerland. Editor: James Gill.

**WESTERLY**, C/o University of Western Australia, Nedlands, W.A. 6009 Australia. A quarterly of articles of the literary, academic and critical kind plus short stories of a literary or experimental type.

**WORDS-The New Literary Forum**, 7 Palehouse Common, Uckfield, East Sussex TN22 5QY Great Britain. Editor: Phillip Vine. "Publication of reviews and articles, although some poetry, fiction and drama is used."

**WORDS AND VISIONS**, Arts Showcase, Words & Visions Publications, Box 545, Norwood, Adelaide 5067 South Australia. Editor/Publisher: Adam Dutkiewicz. Magazine "to showcase work by and talk to artists-with an Australian/South Australian emphasis."

**ZELOT**, Solliveien 37, 1370 Asker, Norway. Editor: Ragnar F. Lie. Magazine. Fantasy, humor/satire, and science fiction.

*There is no way that writers can be tamed and rendered civilized. Or even cured. In a household with more than one person, of which one is a writer, the only solution known to science is to provide the patient with an isolation room, where he can endure the acute stages in private, and where food can be poked in to him with a stick. Because, if you disturb the patient at such times, he may break into tears or become violent. Or he may not hear you at all . . . and, if you shake him at this stage, he bites.*
—*Robert A. Heinlein, from* **The Cat Who Walks Through Walls**

# Commercial periodicals

Short fiction continues to enjoy a resurgence; or "renaissance"; or, as experts like to term the recent interest in short stories, an "acknowledgment." Such interest may in part be a result of *Esquire*'s successful and acclaimed first all-fiction issue, a "smashing literary success," in August, 1984. The summer reading issue ranked right up there with one or two other *Esquire* topsellers, prompting the editors to declare it an annual event. *Redbook* and *Cosmopolitan* also publish a summer reading issue. In 1985, in addition to the annual short story contests sponsored by commercial magazines (e.g., *Ms, Twilight Zone, Mademoiselle, Redbook, Seventeen, Writer's Digest*), *Playboy* sponsored a college short story contest and *Ladies' Home Journal* (with co-sponsor Doubleday) ran a one-time competition—The Barbara Taylor Bradford *LHJ* Short Story contest with the top prize of $10,000.

In the fall of 1985, new and revised TV shows—*Amazing Stories, Alfred Hitchcock Presents* and *Twilight Zone*—helped increase the viewer/reader awareness of the related publications, and the public has responded positively to both magazines and TV. In addition, expansion in short fiction is evident in other areas. The best fiction from *Esquire* is now available on cassette; many more anthologies (genre, special interest) came out in 1985 along with the usual award-winning stories (*Best American Short Stories, Prize Stories: The O'Henry Awards*, etc.). *New Black Mask*, a bookazine and the revival of the 1920 pulp magazine of the Dashiell Hammett and Erle Stanley Gardner era, features the best mystery and contemporary detective fiction in anthology form. And short fiction continues to appear in the newspapers via the PEN Syndicated Fiction Project (see Contests and Awards) and the Publishers Syndication International. Short fiction is also making a small comeback in the Sunday magazine sections of newspapers, like *Washington Post Magazine* and *Northeast*.

## Broad base

Still, many more magazines do not publish fiction than do. Compare the 3,000 plus publications (fiction and nonfiction) in *Writer's Market* to the 800 periodicals (all fiction), in *Fiction Writer's Market*. But many commercial magazines have been steadfast in maintaining their fiction. *Harper's* has published short stories for years—"out of tradition." *The New Yorker* publishes about 100 stories a year. Even *GQ*, *Vanity Fair*, *Connoisseur* and *Rolling Stone* have carried fiction, and although it is usually agented material by established writers, the publishing of any fiction is an affidavit of its viability.

The majority of magazines state they depend on freelancers—even the *New Yorker*. Granted, the competition is very keen—about 300 unsolicited manuscripts arrive each week, but fiction editor Charles McGrath states that in an earlier study of published authors, 17 were unknowns. "We welcome stories from writers," he says. "If we spot talent, even if that story is not right for us, we encourage the writer to try again."

Women's magazines consistently offer a challenge to freelancers. But first they stress, although they all address women, there are differences between the magazines, and occasional editorial changes, which the writer needs to observe. For example, both *Woman's Day* and *Family Circle* are now directed to younger readers, as a result of an editorial rehaul. Each woman's magazine has its own demographics, format, interests, and its focus is reflected in the fiction. On the other hand, there is such a thing as being too specific. "Don't try to impress us that your story was written *just* for *Redbook*," says Kathryne Sagan, fiction editor. It's important to write what you *want* to write or it will show; that is, you must strike a careful balance between *your* interest in the story and the *needs* of the magazine.

There are noticeable basic trends in women's fiction as a result of society's influence. The era of the Happy Homemaker is over; women are involved in careers and families and are not only busier, their life experience is broader. Stories must demonstrate the diversity. Because of the harried lifestyles, women have little time to read. Thus most women's magazines request shorter—and livelier—pieces. Readers *do* enjoy the stories, the surveys tell the editors, even if advertisers and editorial content don't allow a lot of space for fiction.

The strongest subject in any women's magazine, including the fiction, is relationships. Stories for the most part are realistic and portray complex characters. Compare the protagonists in, for example, *Mademoiselle* (target age: 18-34) versus a story in *Redbook* or even *The New Yorker*. The stories in *Mademoiselle* tend to reflect youthful optimism, protagonists who dream large dreams. Those characters in magazines for older or more mature adults tend to be more realistic and represent individuals who may retreat from life and its challenges. Thus, the writer can conclude that the age of the magazine audience does make a difference in the tone or focus of the story.

Genre magazines rely on freelancers and often provide a launch pad for the bigger commercial markets. Two genre magazines, however, are broadening their subject bases in an effort to lure those who are not genre readers. *Rod Serling's Twilight Zone's* editor, Michael Blaine, is looking for quality prose to attract more readers beyond the hardcore science fiction fans. *Night Cry*, basically a horror magazine, accepts related subjects—adventure, SF, occult. "Just scare me," challenges editor Alan Rodgers.

## Fiction's mother

In the religious markets—and there are many (see Category Index)—the competition is less keen. Generally the fiction is not always the best, the editors report, which leaves great opportunity for creative, quality religious and inspirational writers. Children's magazines are tough to break into, the editors acknowledge, because too many writers think children's storywriting is easier. Quite the contrary—and what editors see are stories that are too long, too sweet and too sentimental.

Publishing a short story in a special interest or regional magazine may be easier for a beginner because of less competition. The assignment, however, is a difficult one: writing a story related to a special theme, such as for *Outlaw Bikers*'s hardcore Harley Davidson devotees, or a story involving lefties for *Lefthander*—both new markets this year. The subjects are necessarily limiting. But most hobbies and segments of the population are represented in magazine form—including dark fantasy, single life, animal health technology, Jewish culture, martial arts, handicapped, black romance plus many other even more obscure subjects. There are also religious magazines for all faiths and children's magazines for every age. It's likely one or more areas may strike your story fancy. There are also the fanzines and the semi-prozines, genre publications, which thrive on beginning storytellers. They are a useful, practical and sometimes financially rewarding avenue to learn your craft and establish your credibility.

Nearly 50 additional commercial magazines listed with us this year in *Fiction Writer's Market*. In an era of how-to, service magazines, editors see the benefit of balancing their hard-sell message with a little fiction. Reader surveys tell editors their readers enjoy this "satisfying form of entertainment." Bonni Price, fiction editor of *Seventeen*, speaks in general for magazine fiction editors: "We believe good fiction can move the reader toward thoughtful examination of his/her own life as well as the lives of others, providing a fuller appreciation of what it means to be human."

Editors also declare their genuine obligation to writers to provide publishing space. "After all," says one editor, "magazines are the mother of American fiction." Price also states *Seventeen*'s strong commitment to publish the work of new writers, as does *Redbook*, which presented the work of seven first-timers in 1985. *Ladies' Home Journal* believes there's talent to be discovered, hence their short story contest.

# Find your match

What makes the difference between a selling and a nonselling writer? The professional manner of submission, the appropriateness of subject matter for that particular magazine and the excellence of literary skills. The latter can be summed up by Gail Godwin, who used the following as her editorial guideline in her selection of stories for *Best American Short Stories of 1985*: "Tell me something I *need* to know—about art, about the world, about human behavior, about myself."

The editors allay a writer's fears saying that in a manuscript "a typo really can't do you in." But professionalism in presenting your manuscript *is* important, all the editors stress. Too long a cover letter, or stating that this is your first effort, or that you need the money, make an undesirable first impression. And editors have long memories about writers who do not include a self-addressed, stamped envelope (SASE) of the proper size and with the correct postage, or an international reply coupon (IRC).

Finding the appropriate market begins here. Start first with the Category Index in the back or read through the listings that follow. When you think you've matched your story to a potential market, *read the listing carefully*. Check the needs (interests in stories) and the submission requirements to establish if the magazine accepts fiction from writers at your level. If you're a beginner or an unpublished writer, it's a safer bet to send a story to magazines with (I) after the title, like *Aim*, *Jive* or *Gentleman's Companion*. If you're an established writer or a beginner with a quality story, you can approach those markets marked with (II). Magazines with (III) are for the pros, writers with agents and exceptional beginners—*The New Yorker*, *Atlantic Monthly*, *Harper's*, etc. The publications with (IV) are specialized by subject and region; send your related story to that special magazine.

Before you submit your manuscript, it's important to know as much as possible about the publication your story may appear in. It's best to buy a sample copy off the newsstands, send for one through the mail or check your library or bookstore. If a copy is not available, read the listing again for the description of the magazine: its size, number of pages, quality of paper and cover, appearance of illustrations and photos. Check the established date also. The newer the magazine, the greater the risk that the magazine's publishing life may be a short one.

Although short stories are an established part of many magazines' formats, there are those like *Chicago* Magazine, whose editor this year lamented having to curtail fiction to allow more space for articles about the city. Alas, fiction may often be the first thing bumped. But to help offset these deletions in the short fiction market, we suggest you try another approach: Query a magazine of your particular interest, one that doesn't generally carry fiction, and suggest a story related to that magazine. Such a unique idea may be just what the editor needs for the next issue.

As a short story writer, consider it your own responsibility to help keep this vital medium going. Buy the magazines that publish fiction, and if you particularly enjoy a story, write a letter to the editor to tell him/her just that. Your support helps keep fiction not just alive—but thriving.

**ACTION**, Dept. of Christian Education, Free Methodist Headquarters, 901 College Ave., Winona Lake IN 46590. (219)267-7161. Editor: Vera Bethel. Sunday school take-home paper for children in grades 4-5-6. Weekly. Estab. 1970. Circ. 35,000.
**Needs:** Juvenile. "We buy fiction involving kids aged 9-12 in school and play situations wherein some conflict must be solved in a manner suggesting positive attitudes and growth." No talking animals, Biblical background, or informational articles parading as fiction. Buys 1 ms/issue, 52 mss/year. Receives approximately 100 unsolicited fiction mss each month. Length: 1,000 words.
**How to Contact:** Send complete ms with SASE. Reports in 1 month on mss. Free sample copy, free fiction guidelines with 6x9 SASE.
**Payment:** $25; 2 free author's copies. 10¢ charge for extra.
**Terms:** Pays on publication for simultaneous, first, second serial (reprint), and one-time rights.
**Tips:** Rejects mss because of "predictable, yet unbelievable (unreal) characters."

**AFFAIRE DE COEUR (II), Leading Publication for Romance Readers and Writers**, Affaire de Coeur, Inc., 5660 Roosevelt Place, Fremont CA 94538. (415)656-4804. Publisher: Barbara N. Keenan. Editor: Beth Rowe. Magazine: 8x11½; 24 pages; illustrations; photos. Theme: The Romance Genre—book reviews, author/agent profiles; publishing tips and trends; articles geared to the romance writer and reader. Monthly. Estab. 1981. Circ. 8,000.
**Needs:** Gothic/historical and contemporary romance. Romantic short story only 1,000 to 3,000 words. Receives variable number of unsolicited fiction mss/month. Buys 1 ms/issue; 12 mss/year. Charges reading fee of $15-25/ms—novel length.
**How to Contact:** Query first with SASE (with background of author; previous short stories sold). Simultaneous, photocopied and previously published submissions (with appropriate permissions) OK. Accepts computer printout submissions. Prefers letter-quality. Reports in 4 months on queries. Sample copy $2. Subscription $18/year.
**Payment:** Pays $15-25.
**Terms:** Pays on publication for first North American rights only. Publication copyrighted.
**Tips:** "Think of creative ways of dealing with the romantic fiction genre. Avoid the blatantly graphic—our publication is dedicated to building a credibility of respect and professionalism in the romantic genre." Published new writers within the last year.

**AIM MAGAZINE (I, II)**, 7308 S. Eberhart Ave., Chicago IL 60619. (312)874-6184. Editor: Ruth Apilado. Fiction Editor: Mark Boone. Newspaper: 8½x11; 48 pages; slick paper; photos and illustrations. "Material of social significance: down-to-earth gut. Personal experience, inspirational." For "high school, college, and general public." Quarterly. Published special fiction issue

last year; plans another. Estab. 1973. Circ. 10,000.
**Needs:** Open. No "religious mss. Receives 25 unsolicited mss/month. Buys 15 mss/issue; 60 mss/year. Length: 800-1,000 words average. Publishes short shorts. Sometimes comments on rejected mss.
**How to Contact:** Send complete ms. SASE. Simultaneous submissions OK. Accepts computer printout submissions. Sample copy for $2.50 with SAE (8x11½) and 65¢ postage. Fiction guidelines for regular envelope and 1 first class stamp.
**Payment:** Pays $15-25.
**Terms:** Pays on publication for first rights.
**Tips:** "Search for those in your community who are making unselfish contributions to their community and write about them. Write from the heart. We encourage writers, and have published new writers within the last year."

**ALASKA OUTDOORS (II, IV)**, Box 82222, Fairbanks AK 99708, (907)455-6691. Contact: Chris Batin. Magazine: 8½x11; 80-120 pages; 60 lb paper; 70 lb cover stock; 3-8 illustrations; 28 color photos. "The only magazine dealing exclusively in outdoor recreation in Alaska," directed to "the avid outdoorsman interested in Alaska." Bimonthly. Estab. 1978. Circ. 70,000.
**Needs:** Adventure, humor/satire. "Setting must be Alaska; no Canada or Northwestern material." Buys 2 mss/issue, 15 mss/year. Length: 600 words minimum; 2,000 words maximum; 1,400 words average. Occasionally critiques rejected mss. Recommends other markets.
**How to Contact:** Query first with synopsis of story. SASE. Reports in 2 weeks on queries, 3 weeks on mss. Sample copy $2. Free fiction guidelines for SAE and 1 first class stamp.
**Payment:** $100-200.
**Terms:** Pays on acceptance for first North American serial rights. Publication copyrighted.
**Tips:** "Read the publication first. Keep to humor/satire. 20% of the manuscripts we purchase fall in this category. Experience in the outdoor sports is helpful." Published new writers within the last year.

**ALFRED HITCHCOCK'S MYSTERY MAGAZINE (I, II)**, Davis Publications, Inc., 380 Lexington Ave., New York NY 10017. (212)557-9100. Editor: Cathleen Jordan. Mystery fiction magazine: 5¼x7⅜; 160 pages; 29 lb newsprint paper; 75 lb machine-/coated cover stock; illustrations; photos. Published 13 times/year. Published special fiction issue last year; plans another. Estab. 1956. Circ. 200,000.
**Needs:** Mystery and detection. No horror or sensationalism. Number of mss/issue varies with length of mss. Length: up to 14,000 words. Also publishes short shorts.
**How to Contact:** Send complete ms and SASE. Accepts computer printout submissions. Reports in 2 months. Free guideline sheet for SASE.
**Payment:** 5¢/word on acceptance.
**Tips:** Published new writers within the last year.

**ALIVE! for Young Teens (II)**, Christian Board of Publication, Box 179, St. Louis MO 63166. (314)371-6900. Editor: Michael Dixon. Magazine: 8x11; 32 pages; rough paper; slick cover stock; illustrations; photos. *Alive!* is a leisure reading magazine for junior high youth (ages 12-15) in several major Protestant denominations. "We are one of the few magazines to slant toward the specific needs and interests of this age group, and we encourage youth participation in its creation." Monthly. Estab. 1969. Circ. 20,000.
**Needs:** Religious/inspirational, adventure, humor, young adult, and ethnic. "Please deal with concerns and situations peculiar to the age group of *Alive!* readers. Stories about children or older youth have little chance of acceptance. Religious stories shouldn't be 'preachy' or with obvious moral." Buys 2-3 mss/issue. Receives approximately 50 unsolicited fiction mss/month. Length: 500-1,200 words.
**How to Contact:** Send complete ms with SASE. Accepts computer printout submissions. Prefers letter-quality. Reports in 3 weeks on ms. Publishes ms 10-24 months after acceptance. Sample copy $1. Free guidelines for legal-sized SASE.

**Payment:** 3¢/word. Free author's copy. $1 charge for extras.
**Terms:** Pays on publication for simultaneous and one-time rights. Buys reprints. Publication copyrighted.
**Tips:** "Keep your audience in mind—know what would interest junior high youth. We return many well-written manuscripts that are too 'childish' or oriented around older teen interests. We are very strict on maximum length of stories. Include an honest word count." Published new writers within the last year.

**alive now! (I, II)**, The Upper Room, Box 189, Nashville TN 37202. (615)327-2700. Editor: Mary R. Coffman. Magazine of devotional writing and visuals for young adults. Bimonthly. Estab. 1971. Circ. 75,000.
**Needs:** Religious/inspirational. Buys 4 mss/issue; 12 mss/year. Length: 10 words minimum; 300 words maximum.
**How to Contact:** Send complete mss with SASE. Photocopied and previously published submissions OK. Accepts computer printout submissions. Prefers letter-quality. Reports in 4 weeks on mss. Sample copy free. Fiction guidelines free.
**Payment:** Pays $5-25; 12 contributor's copies.
**Terms:** Pays on publication for first rights, one-time rights, newspaper and periodical rights. Occasionally buys reprints. Publication copyrighted.

**ALOHA, The Magazine of Hawaii and the Pacific (IV)**, Davick Publishing Co., 828 Fort St. Mall, Honolulu HI 96816. (808)523-9871. Editor: Rita Ariyoshi. Magazine about the 50th state. Upscale demographics. Bimonthly. Estab. 1979. Circ. 85,000.
**Needs:** "Only fiction that illuminates the Hawaiian experience. No stories about tourists in Waikiki or beachboys or contrived pidgin dialogue." Receives 3-4 unsolicited mss/month. Length: 2,500 words average.
**How to Contact:** Send complete ms. Reports in 2 months. Publishes ms up to 1 year after acceptance. SASE. Photocopied submissions OK. Accepts computer printout submissions. Letter-quality only. Sample copy $2.50.
**Payment:** 10¢/word minimum.
**Terms:** Pays on publication for all rights. Publication copyrighted.
**Tips:** "Submit only fiction that is truly local in character. Do not try to write anything about Hawaii if you have not experienced this culturally different part of America."

**AMAZING SCIENCE FICTION STORIES (II)**, TSR, Inc., Box 110, Lake Geneva WI 53147. (414)248-8044. Editor: George H. Scithers. Magazine: digest-sized $5^3/_{16}x7^5/_8$; 164 pages; 5 pt Dombook paper; 9 pt federal cover stock; illustrations; rarely photos. Magazine of science fiction and fantasy fiction stories for adults and young adults. Bimonthly. Published special fiction issue last year; plans another. Estab. 1926. Circ. 10,000.
**Needs:** Adventure, fantasy, humor/satire, science fiction, and serialized/excerpted novel. No "stories that are boring and do not hold interest or manuscripts typed with worn-out ribbons." Receives 500 unsolicited fiction mss/month. Buys 8 mss/issue; 48 mss/year. Approximately 5% of ficiton is agented. Length: 300 words minimum; 20,000 words maximum. Publishes short shorts of 300 words. Occasionally critiques rejected ms.
**How to Contact:** Cover letter with short plot synopsis, estimated word length, SASE. Send complete ms with SASE. Photocopied submissions OK. Accepts computer printout submissions. Prefers letter-quality. Reports in 1 month on mss. Publishes ms 6-18 months after acceptance. Sample copy $2.50. Fiction guidelines $2.
**Payment:** Pays 4-6¢/word.
**Terms:** Pays on acceptance for first North American serial rights. Sends galleys to author. Publication copyrighted.
**Tips:** "*Read* this or other science fiction magazines and our book *On Writing Science Fiction*. Know proper ms format—it is hard to take seriously a really sloppy ms. Despite our culture's emphasis on the visual media, we are searching for good escapist literature (especially in heroic fanta-

sy) and for promising but realistic views of the future (especially in SF). Research the market so that we don't get rehashes of trite themes or of other authors' works." Published new writers within the last year.

**AMERICAN DANE (IV)**, The Danish Brotherhood in America, 3717 Harney, Box 31748, Omaha NE 68131. (402)341-5049. Editor: Pamela K. Dorau. Magazine: 8¼x11; 20-28 pages; 40 lb paper; slick cover stock; illustrations; photos. "Official monthly publication of The Danish Brotherhood in America, a nationwide fraternal benefit organization of approximately 10,000 members. *The American Dane* seeks ethnic poetry, prose, puzzles, children's stories and photographs geared toward a conservative, family-oriented Danish-American audience." Published special fiction issue last year; plans another. Estab. 1916. Circ. 9,300.

**Needs:** Adventure, ethnic, historical, juvenile (5-9 years), suspense/mystery, and young adult/teen (10-18 years). Material submitted without a Danish ethnic interest will be rejected, as will material the editor feels is in poor taste morally, politically, religiously, or literarily. Buys 12 mss/year. Does not read January, July, October or December. Length: 1,000 words average; 1,500 words maximum. Publishes short shorts.

**How to Contact:** Query first. SASE for query and ms. Sample copy for $1. Fiction guidelines free for any SAE and 1 first class stamp.

**Payment:** Pays $15-50.

**Terms:** Pays on publication for first rights. Sends galleys to author.

**Tips:** Published new writers within the last year.

**THE AMERICAN NEWSPAPER CARRIER (II)**, Box 15300, Winston-Salem NC 27113. (919)725-3400. Editor: Marilyn H. Rollins. "A motivational newsletter publishing upbeat articles—mystery, humor, adventure and inspirational material for newspaper carriers (younger teenagers, male and female)." Monthly. Estab. 1927.

**Needs:** Adventure, comics, humor/satire, inspirational, suspense/mystery, and young adult/teen. No erotica, fantasy, feminist, gay, juvenile, lesbian, preschool, psychic/supernatural, or serialized/excerpted novel. Receives approximately 12 unsolicited mss/month. Buys 1 ms/issue; 12 mss/year. "About all" of fiction is agented. Length: approximately 1,000 words average; 800 words minimum; 1,200 words maximum. Publishes short shorts of 1,000 words. Rarely critiques rejected mss.

**How to Contact:** Send complete ms. Reports in 1 month. Publishes ms 3-6 months after acceptance. SASE. Accepts computer printout submissions. Free sample copy and fiction guidelines with #10 SAE and 1 first class stamp for each.

**Payment:** $25 maximum.

**Terms:** Pays on acceptance for all rights.

**Tips:** "We prefer that stories concern or refer to newspaper carriers. Well-written upbeat stories—happy and humorous—are rare indeed." Published new writers within the last year.

**AMERICAN SQUAREDANCE (IV)**, Burdick Enterprises, Box 488, Huron OH 44839. (419)433-2188. Editors: Stan and Cathie Burdick. Magazine: 5x8½; 100 pages; 50 lb offset paper; glossy, 60 lb cover stock; illustrations; photos. Magazine about square dancing. Monthly. Estab. 1945. Circ. 13,000.

**Needs:** Adventure, fantasy, historical, humor/satire, romance, science fiction, and western. Must have square dance theme. Buys 2 + mss/year. Length: 2,500 words average. Publishes short shorts of 1,000 words.

**How to Contact:** Send complete ms with SASE and cover letter with bio. Reports in 2 weeks on queries. Publishes ms within 6 months after acceptance. Free sample copy. Free fiction guidelines.

**Payment:** Pays $1/column inch minimum; free magazine subscription or free contributor's copies.

**Terms:** Pays on publication for all rights. Publication copyrighted.

**AMÉRICAS (IV)**, Organization of American States, Washington DC 20006. Editor: Enrique Durand. Managing Editor: A.R. Williams. Magazine: 64 pages; 50 lb glossy paper; heavy glossy cover stock; b&w illustrations; photos. Magazine of cultural articles on Latin America and the Caribbean for a general audience. Bimonthly. Estab. 1949. Circ. 75,000.

**Needs:** Latin American and Caribbean themes. "We publish one short story per issue, for a total of six per year. These are winners of our short story contest, announced in January/February issue. New guidelines to appear in January/February issue for contest." Publishes short shorts 1,000 to 1,700 words.

**How to Contact:** Cover letter with previous short story sales. Enter short story contest.

**Payment:** $100-500; 4 contributor's copies; no charge for extras up to 20 copies; $2.50/copy if more than 20 requested.

**Terms:** Acquires one-time rights.

**Tips:** "As an official publication of the OAS, we cover hemisphere culture." Published new writers within the last year.

**ANALOG SCIENCE FICTION/SCIENCE FACT (II)**, Davis Publications, Inc., 380 Lexington Ave., New York NY 10017. (212)557-9100. Editor: Stanley Schmidt. Magazine: $7\frac{3}{8}x5\frac{3}{16}$; 192 pages; illustrations (drawings); photos. "Well-written science fiction based on speculative ideas and fact articles on topics on the present and future frontiers of research. Our readership includes intelligent laymen and/or those professionally active in science and technology." Thirteen times yearly. Published special fiction issue. Estab. 1930. Circ. 110,000.

**Needs:** Science fiction and serialized novels. "No stories which are not truly science fiction in the sense of having a plausible speculative idea *integral to the story*." Buys 4-8 mss/issue. Receives 300-500 unsolicited fiction mss/month. Publishes short shorts. Approximately 30% of fiction is agented. Length: 2,000-80,000 words. Critiques rejected mss "when there is time." Sometimes recommends other markets.

**How to Contact:** Send complete ms with SASE. Cover letter with "anything that I need to know before reading the story, e.g. that it's a rewrite I suggested or that it incorporates copyrighted material. Otherwise, no cover letter is needed." Query with SASE only on serials. Accepts computer printout submissions. Prefers letter-quality. Reports in 3 weeks on both query and ms. Free guidelines with SASE.

**Payment:** 4¢-8¢/word.

**Terms:** Pays on acceptance for first North American serial rights and nonexclusive foreign rights. Sends galleys to author. Publication copyrighted.

**Tips:** Mss are rejected because of "inaccurate science; poor plotting, characterization, or writing in general. We literally only have room for 1-2% of what we get. Many stories are rejected not because of anything conspicuously *wrong*, but because they lack anything sufficiently *special*. What we buy must stand out from the crowd." Published new writers last year.

**ARARAT**, Armenian General Benevolent Union of America, 585 Saddle River Rd., Saddle Brook NJ 07682. (201)797-7600. Editor: Leo Hamalian. Readership consists of people interested in Armenian background, culture and history. Quarterly. Estab. 1960. Circ. 2,000.

**Needs:** Armenian ethnic. Prefers Armenian written. Buys 1-2 mss/issue.

**How to Contact:** Query with SASE. Reports in 1 month on query, 3 months on ms. Free guidelines with SASE.

**Payment:** $10-75 plus 2 free author's copies.

**Terms:** Pays on publication.

**‡THE ARCTOPHILE (IV)**, Bear-in-Mind, Inc., 20 Beharrel St., Concord MA 01742. (617)369-1167. Editor: Fran Lewis. Fiction Editor: Sharon Burns. Newsletter: 4 pages; 60 lb uncoated; illustrations; photos. Devoted to the Teddy Bear collector for adults. Quarterly. Estab. 1982.

**Needs:** Fantasy, humor/satire, literary, religious/inspirational, young adult/teen (10-18 years). "The Teddy collector loves nostalgia and poignancy as well as 'cute' stories." Buys 1-2 fiction mss/issue; 5-10 mss/year. Publishes ms 2 months after acceptance. Length: 500 words average; 200 words minimum.

**How to Contact:** Send complete ms with cover letter with name, address, and a bio sketch. Reports in 4-6 weeks on ms. SASE for ms. Simultaneous, photocopied submissions and reprints OK. Accepts computer printouts. Sample copy for SAE and 1 first class stamp. Fiction guidelines for SAE and 1 first class stamp.
**Payment:** $15-40.
**Terms:** Pays on publication for one-time rights. Publication copyrighted.
**Tips:** "The bear collector loves stories about teddies. Write tongue-in-cheek, heart warming or poignant stories."

**‡ART TIMES (II), Cultural & Creative News of the Catskill & Mid-Hudson Region**, CSS Publications, Inc., Box 730, Mount Marion NY 12456. (914)246-5170. Editor: Raymond J. Steiner. Magazine: 12x15; 20 pages; 30" Jet quality paper and cover; illustrations; photos. "We are an 'arts' magazine covering all disciplines. Fiction and poetry of all types accepted—literary excellence sole criterion." For "over 40, affluent, arts-conscious, largely distributed through art galleries, select restaurants and resorts throughout Manhattan, Ulster, Greene & Dutchess counties in upstate New York." Monthly. Estab. August 1984. Circ. 15,000.
**Needs:** Adventure, contemporary, ethnic, experimental, fantasy, feminist, gay, historical, humor/satire, lesbian, literary, mainstream, science fiction, women's. Mainly interested in literary quality. No excessive violence or sex. No violent, sexist erotic, juvenile, romance, politically biased, etc. Receives 4-5 unsolicited mss/month. Buys 1 ms/issue; 12 mss/year. Publishes 6 months after acceptance. Length: 1,500 words average. Critiques rejected mss. Recommends other markets. Send complete ms with cover letter including "some biography and past credits and why *Art Times* was chosen." Reports in 4 weeks on mss. SASE for ms. Simultaneous and photocopied submissions OK. No computer printouts. Sample copy $1.50.
**Payment:** $15 only and contributor's copies.
**Terms:** Pays on publication for one-time rights.
**Tips:** "We are not generally a publication for fiction—we are primarily a magazine which showcases the arts. As editors and as a writer, however, I feel an obligation to allow for space which will include good fiction. I receive a great many submissions of poetry and short stories but do not publish many because few are professionally presented nor written. A writer who does not take the time to proofread, to correct misspellings, does not deserve my time to read the submission. I would like to see more good, solid, short stories."

**‡THE ASSOCIATE REFORMED PRESBYTERIAN MAGAZINE (I, II)**, The Associate Reformed Presbyterian, Inc., 1 Cleveland St., Greenville SC 29601. (803)232-8297. Editor: Ben Johnston. Magazine: 8½x11; 32-48 pages; 50 lb offset paper; illustrations; photos. "We are the official magazine of our denomination. Articles generally relate to activities within the denomination—conferences, department work, etc., with a few special articles that would be of interest to readers. Christian adults, primarily. We are including fiction short stories, resulting from our annual writers' contest, in order to gain the interest of children. Monthly. Estab. 1976. Circ. 5,900.
**Needs:** Adventure, contemporary, juvenile, religious/inspirational, suspense/mystery, young adult/teen. "Stories may or may not have direct religious references, but all should portray Christian values. No retelling of Bible stories or 'talking animal' stories. Stories for youth should deal with resolving real issues for young people without moralizing or being preachy." Receives 3-5 unsolicited fiction mss/month. Buys 1 ms/some months; 6-8 mss/year. Publishes ms within 1 year after acceptance. Length: 300-750 (children); 1,250 words maximum (youth). Sometimes critiques rejected mss. Occasionally recommends other markets.
**How to Contact:** Query first. Reports in 6 weeks on queries and mss. Simultaneous submissions OK. Sample copy $1; fiction guidelines for #10 SAE and 1 first class stamp.
**Payment:** Pays $20-50 and contributor's copies.
**Terms:** Buys first rights.
**Tips:** "Contests are announced in our publication. Write to inquire when another contest will be held, and receive a copy of the contest rules."

**ATLANTIC MONTHLY**, 8 Arlington St., Boston MA 02116. (617)536-9500. Editor: William Whitworth. Senior Editor: Michael Curtis. General magazine for the college educated with broad cultural interests. Monthly. Estab. 1857. Circ. 440,000.
**Needs:** Literary and contemporary. "Seeks fiction that is clear, tightly written with strong sense of 'story' and well-defined characters." Buys 2 mss/issue. Receives approximately 1,000 unsolicited fiction mss each month. Length: 4,000-6,000 words.
**How to Contact:** Send complete ms with SASE. Accepts computer printout submissions. Prefers letter-quality. Reports in 2 months on mss.
**Payment:** $2,000 and beyond.
**Terms:** Pays on acceptance for first and first North American serial rights. Publication copyrighted.
**Tips:** "Read magazine with great care and write well."

**THE AUGUSTA SPECTATOR (II)**, FKB Enterprises, Box 3168, Augusta GA 30904. (404)733-1476. Publisher/Editor: Faith B. Bertsche. Magazine: 8½x11; 48 pages; illustrations; photos. Regional publication, modern in outlook; short stories, poems, articles for upper-income marrieds; average age 45. Published every 4 months. Estab. 1980. Circ. 5,000.
**Needs:** Literary, contemporary, romance, mystery, adventure, regional, and humor. No explicit sex or violence. Buys 1-2 mss/issue. Receives approximately 12 unsolicited fiction mss each month. Publishes short shorts up to 2,000 words. Critiques rejected mss "when there is time."
**How to Contact:** Cover letter with short bio. Query with SASE. Accepts computer printout submissions. Prefers letter-quality. Reports in 2 months. Publishes ms 3-4 months after acceptance. Free guidelines with SASE. Sample magazine $1.
**Payment:** $25; 2 copies of issue.
**Terms:** Pays on publication for first rights. Publication copyrighted.
**Tips:** Mss are rejected because they "ramble—no story." Will not read handwritten stories. "We receive *many* scripts 3-5,000 words which are returned unread. 2,000 words maximum. Fiction holds our readership." Published new writers within the last year.

**BAKERSFIELD LIFESTYLE MAGAZINE (II)**, American Lifestyle Communications Inc., 123 Truxtun Ave., Bakersfield CA 93301. Editor: Steve Walsh. Magazine: 8½x11; 64-112 pages; slick paper; slick cover stock; illustrations; photos. City magazine for general audience. Monthly. Estab. 1981.
**Needs:** Condensed novel, science fiction, senior citizen/retirement, and suspense/mystery. Receives 25-30 unsolicited mss/month. Buys 1-2 mss/issue. Length: 1,000-1,500 words average. Occasionally comments on rejected mss.
**How to Contact:** Send complete ms. SASE and cover letter with summary of story. Simultaneous, photocopied and previously published submissions OK. Accepts computer printout submissions. Prefers letter-quality. Sample copy for $5.
**Payment:** Pays $10+.
**Terms:** Pays on publication. Publication copyrighted.
**Tips:** "Although many publishers have decided to make their publication a widely targeted and specialized one, I feel that magazines are the mother of American fiction and therefore have a responsibility to continue publishing fiction in some capacity. Know the beginning and ending of your story before you start, and slant the location and characters of your story to the special interest of the publication you are trying to sell." Published new writers within the last year.

**BALTIMORE JEWISH TIMES (II, IV)**, 2104 N. Charles St., Baltimore MD 21218. (301)752-3504. Magazine with subjects of interest to Jewish readers. Weekly. Estab. 1918. Circ. 19,000.
**Needs:** Contemporary Jewish themes only. Receives 7-10 unsolicited fiction mss/month. Buys 5-6 mss/year. Length: 1,500 words minimum; 3,500 words maximum (or 6-15 typed pages). Occasionally critiques rejected mss.
**How to Contact:** Send complete ms. Simultaneous, photocopied and previously published submissions OK "on occasion." Accepts computer printout submissions. Prefers letter-quality. Re-

ports in 2 months on mss. Sample copy $1 and legal-size envelope.
**Payment:** Pays $35-100.
**Terms:** Pays on publication. Publication copyrighted.

**‡BANFF LIFE (IV), Art, Leisure, and Thought in Canada's West**, Box 2380, Banff, Alberta T0L 0C0 Canada. (403)762-3156. Magazine: 8x10; 74 pages; illustrations; photos. "*Banff Life* covers a wide range of topics, from arts to leisure, sports, environment and political issues pertaining to Canada's west. Readers of all ages interested in understanding this area of the world, and most specifically the Rocky Mountains and Banff National Park. Often travellers." Quarterly. Plans special issue in future. Estab. 1983. Circ. 60,000.
**Needs:** Adventure, historical (general), humor/satire, literary, regional, western. Receives 6 unsolicited mss/month. Buys 1-2 mss/issue. Publishes ms 3-9 months after acceptnace. Length: 1,000-2,000 words average; 200 words minimum; 2,500 words maximum. Publishes short shorts of 200-2,000 words. Recommends other markets.
**How to Contact:** Send complete ms with cover letter. Reports in 2 months on mss. SASE for ms. Accepts computer printouts including dot-matrix. Accepts electronic submissions via disc or modem. Sample copy $2. Fiction guidelines free.
**Payment:** Pays $10-400.
**Terms:** Pays on publication for first North American serial rights.

**BAY & DELTA YACHTSMAN (II, IV)**, Recreation Publications, Alameda Marina, 2019 Clement Ave., Alameda CA 94501. (415)865-7500. Editor: Dave Preston. Tabloid for upper-middle to upper income audience. Monthly. Estab. 1966. Circ. 30,000.
**Needs:** Adventure, comics, condensed novel, fantasy, historical, humor/satire, literary, psychic/supernatural/occult, romance (historical), science fiction, senior citizen/retirement, and suspense/mystery. "We look for stories relevant to power and sail boats over 30'; a Northern California slant or tie is important. No heavy dialogue, youth-oriented fiction." Receives 12 + unsolicited mss/month. Buys 2-3 mss/issue; 32 mss/year. Length: 2,500-3,000 words; 2,000 words minimum; 4,000 words maximum.
**How to Contact:** Send complete ms. Reports in 3 weeks. SASE. Accepts computer printout submissions. Prefers letter-quality. Free sample copy.
**Payment:** Open.
**Terms:** Pays on publication for one-time rights. Publication copyrighted.
**Tips:** "Our readers prefer fun-to-read material."

**BIKE REPORT (II, IV)**, Bikecentennial, Box 8308, Missoula MT 59807. (406)721-1776. Editor: Daniel D'Ambrosio. Magazine on bicycle touring: 8½x11; 24 pages; coated paper; 70 lb cover stock. Bimonthly. Special fiction issue last year. Estab. 1974. Circ. 18,000.
**Needs:** Adventure, fantasy, historical (general), humor/satire, regional, senior citizen/retirement, and suspense/mystery with a bicycling theme. Buys variable number mss/year. Length: 2,000 words average; 200 words minimum; 2,500 words maximum. Publishes short shorts of 1,200 words. Occasionally comments on a rejected ms.
**How to Contact:** Send complete ms with SASE. Reports in 6 weeks on mss. Photocopied and previously published submissions OK. Accepts computer printout submissions. Prefers letter-quality. Accepts disc submissions compatible with Morrow CP/M. Prefers hard copy with disc submission. Sample copy free for 9x12 SAE and $1 postage. Fiction guidelines free for business-size SAE and 1 first class stamp.
**Payment:** Pays $25-65.
**Terms:** Pays on publication for first North American serial rights. Publication copyrighted.
**Tips:** "Fiction sets us apart from other cycling mags." Published new writers within the last year.

**BIRD TALK**, Fancy Publications, Box 6050, Mission Viejo CA 92690. (714)240-6001. Editor-in-Chief: Linda W. Lewis. General pet bird magazine, consumer oriented, "for cage bird owners." Bimonthly. Circ. 55,000.

**Needs:** Pet bird-centered theme. Buys 8 mss/year. Length: 3,000 words maximum.
**How to Contact:** Query first or send complete ms. SASE always. Photocopied submissions OK. Reports in 2 weeks on queries, 2 months on mss. Sample copy $3. Free writer's guidelines with SASE.
**Terms:** Buys one-time rights. Publication copyrighted.

‡**BORDERLAND (IV), Dark Fantasy**, Artimus Publications, 7305 Woodbine Ave., Suite 517, Markham, Ontario L3R 3V7 Canada. Fiction Editor: R.S. Hadji. Magazine: 8½x11; 40 pages; newsprint; coated cover stock; illustrations; photos. Dark fantasy and horror. Quarterly. Estab. 1984. Circ. 400.
**Needs:** Fantasy, horror, psychic/supernatural/occult. "No sword and sorcery or cute fantasy." Reviews 5-10 unsolicited mss/month. Buys 4-6 mss/issue; 16-24/year. Publishes ms usually within 9 months after acceptance. Agented fiction 10%. Length: 3,500 words average; 500 words minimum; 5,000 words maximum. Publishes short shorts. Occasionally critiques rejected mss. Recommends other markets.
**How to Contact:** Send complete ms with cover letter (with bio). Reports in 4 months. SASE for ms. Simultaneous and photocopied submissions OK. Accepts computer printouts including dot-matrix. Sample copy $2.50 (US). Fiction guidelines free.
**Payment:** Pays 1½-3¢/word.
**Terms:** Pays on acceptance or publication (50/50) for first North American serial rights. Publication copyrighted.
**Tips:** "The market is very thin, especially in our field. There are not enough magazines on the market devoted to quality dark fantasy. We decided to help fill that void. In our first two issues we have published some beginning writers."

**BOYS' LIFE (III), For All Boys**, Boy Scouts of America, Magazine Division, 1325 Walnut Hill Lane, Irving TX 75062. (214)659-2000. Editor: Robert E. Hood. Fiction Editor: William E. Butterworth IV. Magazine: 8x11; 68 pages; slick cover stock; illustrations; photos. "*Boys' Life* covers Boy Scout activities and general interest subjects for ages 8 to 18, Boy Scouts, Cub Scouts and others of that age group." Monthly. Estab. 1911. Circ. 1,500,000.
**Needs:** Adventure, contemporary, humor/satire, science fiction, suspense/mystery, western, young adult, and sports. "We publish short stories aimed at a young adult audience and frequently written from the viewpoint of a 10- to 16-year-old boy protagonist." Receives approximately 100 unsolicited mss/month. Buys 12-18 mss/year. Length: 1,000 words minimum; 3,000 words maximum; 2,500 words average. "Very rarely" critiques rejected ms.
**How to Contact:** Cover letter with qualifications to write story. Send complete ms with SASE. "We'd much rather see manuscripts than queries." Simultaneous and photocopied submissions OK. Accepts dot-matrix printout submissions; prefers letter-quality. Reports in 2 weeks on mss. For sample copy "check your local library."
**Payment:** Pays $350 and up, "depending on an author's reputation." Offers 50% kill fee.
**Terms:** Pays on acceptance for one-time rights. Publication copyrighted.
**Tips:** "We tend to use many of the same authors repeatedly because their characters, themes, etc., develop a following among our readers. Fiction is *not* easy. Take a little longer and write it a little shorter, and keep it simple."

**BREAD (II)**, Church of the Nazarene, 6401 The Paseo, Kansas City MO 64131. (816)333-7000. Editor: Gary Sivewright. Magazine: 8½x11; 34 pages; illustrations; photos. Christian leisure reading magazine for junior and senior high students. Monthly.
**Needs:** Adventure and how-to stories on Christian living. Themes should be school and church oriented. Adventure stories wanted, but without sermonizing. Buys 25 mss/year. Does not read in summer. Publishes short shorts of 300-500 words.
**How to Contact:** Send complete ms with SASE. Reports in 6 weeks on mss. Free sample copy and guidelines.
**Payment:** Pays 3½¢/word for first rights and 3¢/word for second rights.

**Terms:** Pays on acceptance for first rights and sometimes second serial rights. Accepts simultaneous submissions. Byline given.
**Tips:** "Our readers clamor for the fiction." Published new writers last year.

**‡BUF (II)**, G&S Publications, Inc., 1472 Broadway, New York NY 10036. (212)840-7224. Editor: Will Martin. Magazine devoted and flattering to attractive heavy women. Bimonthly. Estab. 1961. Circ. 100,000.
**Needs:** Erotica, humor/satire, men's. No pornographic (explicit, graphic description of sex acts) or violence. Receives 50 unsolicited mss/month. Buys 12-20 mss/issue. Publishes ms 6 months after acceptance. Length: 2,500 words average. Also publishes short shorts of "several hundred words or so." Occasionally critiques rejected mss.
**How to Contact:** Query with clips of published work or send complete ms with cover letter. Reports in 2 months on queries; 3 months on mss. SASE for ms. Photocopied submissions OK. Accepts computer printouts. No dot-matrix. Sample copy $3.95. Fiction guidelines free.
**Payment:** Pays $40-100.
**Terms:** Pays on assignment for all rights. Publication copyrighted.
**Tips:** "The writer should know his market and submit material that fits our format."

**BUFFALO SPREE MAGAZINE (II, IV)**, Spree Publishing Co., Inc., 4511 Harlem Rd., Buffalo NY 14226. (716)839-3405. Editor: Johanna V. Shotell. Fiction Editor: Gary L. Goss. "City magazine for professional, educated and above-average income people." Quarterly. Estab. 1967. Circ. 21,000.
**Needs:** Literary, contemporary, men's, women's, feminist, mystery, adventure, humor, and ethnic. No pornographic or religious. Buys 1 ms/issue, 4 mss/year. Length: 1,500 words maximum.
**How to Contact:** Send complete ms with SASE. Reports within 1 week to 2 months on ms. Sample copy for $1.50 with 9x12 SASE and $1.50 postage.
**Payment:** $50-125; 1 free author's copy.
**Terms:** Pays on publication for first rights.

**CAMPUS LIFE MAGAZINE (II)**, Christianity Today, Inc., 465 Gundersen Drive, Carol Stream IL 60188. (312)260-6200. Senior Editor: Gregg Lewis. Magazine: 8¼x11¼; 100 pages; 4-color and b&w illustrations; 4-color and b&w photos. "General interest magazine with a religious twist. Not limited strictly to Christian content. Articles on mopeds and forgiveness, videogames and divorce, Frisbees and self-worth, etc., for high school and college age readers." Monthly. Plans special fiction issue. Estab. 1942. Circ. 200,000.
**Needs:** Condensed novel, fantasy, humor/satire, prose poem, science fiction, serialized/excerpted novel, and young adult. Prefers "realistic situations. We are a Christian magazine but are *not* interested in sappy, formulaic, sentimentally religious stories. We *are* interested in well-crafted stories that portray life realistically, stories high school and college youth relate to. Nothing contradictory of Christian values. If you don't understand our market and style, don't submit." Receives 30 unsolicited fiction mss/month. Buys 10 mss/year. Reading, response time slower in summer. Length: 1,000-3,000 words average, "possibly longer." Publishes short shorts.
**How to Contact:** Query with clips of published work and SASE. Simultaneous, photocopied and previously published submissions OK. Reports in 4-6 weeks on queries. Sample copy $2 and 9½x11 envelope.
**Payment:** Pays $250-400, "generally"; 2 contributor's copies.
**Terms:** Pays on acceptance for one-time rights.
**Tips:** "A good realistic story generally captures high readership in *Campus Life*. Read the magazine—understand our purpose, style, and stance. Perfect your craft. Ask us for sample copy with fiction story. Fiction communicates to our reader. We want to encourage fiction writers who have something to say to or about young people without getting propogandistic." Published new writers within the last year.

**CAPPER'S WEEKLY (II)**, Stauffer Communications, Inc., 616 Jefferson, Topeka KS 66607. (913)295-1108. Editor: Dorothy Harvey. Magazine: 20-40 pages; newsprint paper; newsprint cover stock. A "clean, uplifting and nonsensational newspaper for families from children to grandparents." Biweekly. Estab. 1879. Circ. 400,000.
**Needs:** Serialized novels. "We only accept novel-length stories for serialization. No fiction containing violence or obscenity." Buys 2-3 stories/year. Receives 2-3 unsolicited fiction mss each month. Sometimes recommends other markets.
**How to Contact:** Send complete ms with SASE. Reports in 5-6 months on ms. Sample copy 55¢.
**Payment:** $150-200 for one-time serialization. Free author's copies (1-2 copies as needed for copyright).
**Terms:** Pays on acceptance for second serial (reprint) rights and one-time rights.
**Tips:** "Most rejections are because we try to avoid obscenity in language, explicit sex, bloody violence, or lack of morality. And sometimes the stories are poorly written."

**CAT FANCY (IV)**, Fancy Publications, Box 6050, Mission Viejo CA 92690. (714)240-6001. Editor-in-Chief: Linda W. Lewis. General cat and kitten magazine, consumer oriented for "cat and kitten lovers." Published monthly. Circ. 150,000.
**Needs:** Cat-related themes only. Receives approximately 60 unsolicited fiction mss/month. Accepts 12 mss/year. Approximately 20% of fiction agented. Length: 3,000 words maximum. Sometimes recommends other markets.
**How to Contact:** Send complete ms with SASE. Simultaneous and photocopied submissions OK. Reports in 6 weeks. Publishes ms 2-10 weeks after acceptance. Sample copy $2.50. Free fiction guidelines with SASE.
**Payment:** 3¢/word and 2 contributor's copies. $2.50 charge for extras.
**Terms:** Rarely buys reprints. Publication copyrighted.
**Tips:** "Stories should focus on a cat or cats, not just be about people who happen to have a cat. We will be going to a larger book and will be looking for more fiction."

**‡CATHOLIC FORESTER (II)**, Catholic Order of Foresters, 425 W. Shuman Blvd., Naperville IL 60566. (312)983-4920. Editor: Barbara Cunningham. Magazine: 8¼x10¾; 32 pages; 45 lb paper and cover stock; illustrations; photos. "No special theme but we want interesting, lively stories and articles. No true confessions type, no dumb romances. People who have not bothered to study the art of writing need not apply." For middle class, family-type audience. Bimonthly. Estab. 1984. Circ. 160,000.
**Needs:** Adventure, contemporary, ethnic, feminist, humor/satire, mainstream, men's, regional, senior citizen/retirement, suspense/mystery, women's. Receives 200 unsolicited fiction mss/month. Buys approximately 4 mss/issue; 25 mss/year. "Publication may be immediate or not for 4-5 months." Agented fiction: 5%. Length: 2,000 words average; 3,000 words maximum. Also publishes short stories. Occasionally critiques rejected mss. Sometimes recommends other markets.
**How to Contact:** Send complete ms. "Cover letters do not help—manuscripts stand or fall on their own merit. I do not accept queries anymore—too many problems in authors misunderstanding 'speculation.' " SASE for ms. Simultaneous, photocopied submissions and reprints OK. No computer printouts. Sample copy for 8½x11 SAE and 56¢ postage. Fiction guidelines for #10 SAE and 1 first class stamp.
**Payment:** Pays 5-10¢/word ("our pay is very flexible"); and 2 contributor's copies.
**Terms:** Pays on acceptance for one-time rights. Publication copyrighted.
**Tips:** "I think good magazine fiction is coming back. People want to be entertained, touched, informed. Beginning writers, if they have studied their craft (and write and rewrite) have an excellent chance. But far too many don't seem to bother. They don't seem to have an idea in the world what good writing really is. Also, they should have something to say and give us an idea of what that will be early in the story—make a point. Be specific but not PURPLE. We haven't received a good short story in months. And we really are looking. Our readers enjoy fiction but I'm not going

to use substandard writing. We want something meaty. And neatness counts. We don't have a lot of free time. When we receive a messy or hard-to-read manuscript, or one on which the author has had second thoughts or has done final editing, we don't even read it. That tells us the author either doesn't know or doesn't care about being professional, and his writing, unless he is unusually talented, will reflect that."

**CAVALIER MAGAZINE (II)**, Dugent Publishing Corp., 2355 Salzedo St., Coral Gables FL 33134. (305)443-2378. Editor: Douglas Allen. Fiction Editor: M. DeWalt. Magazine: 8½x11; 103 pages; 60 lb paper; laminated cover stock; illustrations; photos. Sexually-oriented, sophisticated magazine for single men aged 18-35. Published special fiction issue last year; plans another. Monthly. Estab. 1952. Circ. 250,000.
**Needs:** Adventure, horror, men's, and erotica. No material on children, religious subjects or anything that might be libelous. Buys 3 mss/issue. Receives approximately 200 unsolicited fiction mss each month. Length: 1,500-3,000 words. Critiques rejected mss "when there is time." Sometimes recommends other markets.
**How to Contact:** Send complete ms with SASE. Accepts computer printout submissions. Prefers letter-quality. Reports in 3 weeks on mss. Sample copy for $3. Free fiction guidelines with SASE.
**Payment:** $200-300. Offers 50% kill fee for assigned mss not published.
**Terms:** Pays on publication for first North American serial rights. Publication copyrighted.
**Tips:** Mss are rejected because writers "either don't know our market or the manuscripts are too long or too short. Length and erotic content are crucial (erotica in *every* story). Fiction is often much sexier and more imaginative than photos. Rejections are a result of unrelated subject matter, sloppy manuscripts, carbon copies or trite, tired subjects. All writers should ask for our guidelines first before submitting. They are detailed and helpful." Occasionally sponsors contests . . . watch publication. Published new writers within the last year.

**CHATELAINE**, Maclean Hunter Limited, 777 Bay St., Toronto M5W 1A7 Canada. (416)596-5000. Editor: Mildred Istona. Fiction Editor: Barbara West. "This is a magazine for Canadian women. We present articles, fiction, service material, news and reviews relevant to their lives. Because Canada's population is relatively small we do not concentrate on a specific part of the market but address ourselves to all Canadian women, including homemakers, career women, married, single, etc." Monthly. Estab. 1928. Circ. 1,100,000.
**Needs:** Contemporary, romance, mystery, adventure, and humor. Length: 3,000-3,500 words.
**How to Contact:** Send complete ms with SAE and IRC. Reports in 4 weeks on ms. Free fiction guidelines with SAE, IRC.
**Payment:** $1,500 in Canadian currency. 1 free author's copy. $1.50 (Canadian) per extra copy.
**Terms:** Pays on acceptance for first North American serial rights in English and French. Publication copyrighted.
**Tips:** "We're looking for good, human interest stories in which women play the leading parts, or at least share center stage with men. We are primarily interested in Canadian stories, particularly those about contemporary relationships. Stories that are too explicit sexually don't work for us, nor do avant-garde pieces, nor nostalgic reminiscences. Drug taking, four-letter words are not for us, nor do old-fashioned-type 'women's stories' appeal." Mss are rejected because they are the "wrong type of stories for this magazine; also because of poor writing, poor structure, hackneyed subject. Not many writers can produce the kind of story—fast-moving, involving, readable—that we are looking for. We're looking for *good, popular* fiction. What we tend to receive is either too literary or incompetent."

**CHESAPEAKE BAY MAGAZINE (II, IV)**, Chesapeake Bay Communications, Inc., 1819 Bay Ridge Ave., Annapolis MD 21403. (301)263-2662. Editor: Betty Rigoli. Magazine: 8½x11; 80 pages; coated stock paper; coated cover stock; illustrations; photos. "*Chesapeake Bay Magazine* is a regional publication for those who enjoy reading about the Bay and its tributaries. Most of our articles are boating-related. Our readers are yachtsmen, boating families, fishermen, ecologists, anyone who is part of Chesapeake Bay life." Monthly. Estab. 1971. Circ. 18,500.

**Needs:** Fantasy, mystery, adventure, humor, and historical. "Any fiction piece *must* concern the Chesapeake Bay. Only stories done by authors who are familiar with the area are accepted. No general type stories with the Chesapeake Bay superimposed in an attempt to make a sale." Buys 1 ms/issue, 8 mss/year. Receives approximately 3 unsolicited fiction mss each month. Length: 1,250-3,000 words. Publishes short shorts. Critiques rejected mss "when there is time." Recommends other markets.

**How to Contact:** "Cover letter with bio information to indicate familiarity with our publication. "Query or send ms. SASE always. Reports in 1 month on queries, 2 months on mss. Publishes ms an average of 12-14 months after acceptance. Sample copy $2. Free fiction guidelines with SASE.

**Payment:** $60-85. 2 free author's copies.

**Terms:** Pays on publication for all rights or first North American serial rights. Publication copyrighted.

**Tips:** "Make sure you have knowledge of the area. Send only material that is related to our market. All manuscripts must be typed, double-spaced, in duplicate. Our readers are interested in any and all material about the Chesapeake Bay area. Thus we use a limited amount of fiction as well as factual material." Published new writers within the last year.

**CHICKADEE (II), The Magazine for Young Children from Owl**, Young Naturalist Foundation, 59 Front St. E, Toronto, Ontario M5E 1B3 Canada. (416)364-3333. Editor: Janis Nostbakken. Magazine: 8½x11¾; 32 pages. "*Chickadee* is created to give children under nine a lively, fun-filled look at the world around them. Each issue has a mix of activities, puzzles, games and read-aloud stories." Monthly except July and August. Estab. 1979. Circ. 85,000.

**Needs:** Juvenile. No fantasy, religious or anthropomorphic material. Receives a varied amount of unsolicited fiction mss/month. Buys 1 ms/issue; 10 mss/year. Length: 200 words minimum; 800 words maximum; 500 words average. Recommends other markets.

**How to Contact:** Send complete ms with SASE. Reports in 8 weeks. Publishes ms an average of 1 year after acceptance. Sample copy for $1.50 for 8x11 SAE and IRCs. Free fiction guidelines for SAE, IRC.

**Payment:** Pays $25-350; 1 free contributor's copy; $1.25 charge for extras.

**Terms:** Pays on publication for all rights. Occasionally buys reprints. Publication copyrighted.

**Tips:** "We are looking for shorter stories that contain a puzzle, mystery, twist, or tie-in to a puzzle that follows on the next spread. Read back issues and review editorial guidelines. Avoid writing 'down' to children. Know the interests of your readers. Thoroughly research subject matter." Published new writers in the last year.

**CHILDREN'S DIGEST**, Children's Better Health Institute, 1100 Waterway Blvd., Box 567, Indianapolis IN 46206. Editor: Elizabeth A. Rinck. Magazine with special emphasis on health, nutrition, exercise, and safety for 8-10 year olds.

**Needs:** "Realistic stories, short plays, adventure, and mysteries. Humorous stories are highly desirable. We especially need stories that *subtly* encourage readers to develop better health or safety habits. Stories should not exceed 1,800 words." Receives 40-50 unsolicited fiction mss each month.

**How to Contact:** Send complete ms with SASE. Sample copy 75¢. Queries not needed. Reports in 10 weeks. Free guidelines with SASE.

**Payment:** Pays approximately 6¢/word with 2 free author's copies.

**Terms:** Pays on publication for all rights. Publication copyrighted.

**Tips:** "We try to present our health-related material in a positive—not a negative—light, and we try to incorporate humor and a light approach wherever possible without minimizing the seriousness of what we are saying. Fiction stories that deal with a health theme need not have health as the primary subject but should include it in some way in the course of events. Most rejected health-related manuscripts are too preachy or they lack substance. Although we emphasize the development of better health habits, we want our stories to be exciting and interesting as well as educational. Simultaneous submissions are not accepted."

**CHILDREN'S PLAYMATE**, The Benjamin Franklin Literary & Medical Society, Inc., 1100 Waterway Blvd., Box 567, Indianapolis IN 46206. (317)636-8881. Editor: Elizabeth A. Rinck. Juvenile magazine for children ages 5-7 years.
**Needs:** Juvenile with special emphasis on health, nutrition, safety, and exercise. No adult or adolescent fiction. Receives approximately 150 unsolicited fiction mss each month. Length: 700 words or less. Indicate word count on material.
**How to Contact:** Send complete ms with SASE. Accepts computer printout submissions. Prefers letter-quality. Reports in 8-10 weeks.
**Payment:** Approximately 6¢/word.
**Terms:** Pays on publication for all rights. Publication copyrighted.
**Tips:** "Stories should be kept simple and entertaining. Study past issues of the magazine—be aware of vocabulary limitations of the readers. Stories or articles must be interesting for the target age of the readers." Rejects mss because "we receive thousands of manuscripts every year and have space to publish only about 30 stories a year."

**CHRISTIAN ADVENTURER (IV)**, Messenger Publishing House, Box 850, Joplin MO 64802. (417)624-7050. Editor-in-Chief: Dr. Roy M. Chappell. Fiction Editor: Rosmarie Foreman. Magazine: 8 pages; clip art. "Religious-oriented teen magazine." Weekly. Circ. 2,500.
**Needs:** Adventure, historical (general), religious/inspirational, suspense/mystery, and young adult. *All* material must be religious oriented. Receives approximately 100 unsolicited fiction mss/month. Does not read Feb.-Mar.; May-June; Aug.-Sept; Nov.-Dec. Buys 13 mss/issue, 52 mss/year. Length: 1,500 words minimum; 1,750 words maximum; 1,600 words average. Occasionally critiques rejected mss.
**How to Contact:** Send complete ms with SASE. Simultaneous and photocopied submissions and previously published work OK. Reports in 2 weeks on mss. Sample copy 50¢ or standard-sized SAE and 1 first class stamp. Fiction guidelines for 50¢ or standard-sized SAE and 1 first class stamp.
**Payment:** 1½¢/word and 2 contributor's copies.
**Terms:** Pays on publication for simultaneous rights. Publication copyrighted.
**Tips:** "When writing for a specific magazine, be sure and read their *Guidelines*. Only send your manuscripts that meet their *Guidelines*!" Published "several" new writers within the last year.

**CHRISTIAN HOME (II)**, The Upper Room, Box 189, 1908 Grand Ave., Nashville TN 37202. (615)327-2700. Editor: David Bradley. Magazine: 8½x11; 64 pages; coated paper; coated cover stock; illustrations; photos. Magazine of family/parenting/marriage for adults. Quarterly. Estab. 1897. Circ. 40,000.
**Needs:** Contemporary, ethnic, juvenile (5-9 years), and religious/inspirational. Receives 80 unsolicited mss/month. Buys 20 mss/issue. Length: 1,400 words average; 600 words minimum; 1,500 words maximum. Publishes short shorts from 100 to 600 words.
**How to Contact:** Send complete manuscript with SASE. Reports in 3 months on mss. Simultaneous submissions OK. Sample copy free for 8½x11 SAE and 3 first class stamps.
**Payment:** Pays 7¢ a word and 1 contributor's copy.
**Terms:** Pays on acceptance for all rights and one-time rights.
**Tips:** "We tend to use fiction that focuses on any number of family relationships or issues that show family, sibling, spouse, or peer interaction." Published new writers within the last year.

**CHRISTIAN LIFE (IV)**, Christian Life Missions, 396 E. St. Charles, Wheaton IL 60188. (312)653-4200. Editor-in-Chief: Robert Walker. *Christian Life* magazine is read by the leadership group in religious circles. Surveys show that 40.3 percent have attended college; 14.3 percent have gone on to graduate school. Therefore, copy for *Christian Life* should be bright, contemporary and significant. It also should be highly readable to attract the prospective buyer who sees it on a newsstand." Monthly. Estab. 1945. Circ. approximately 100,000.
**Needs:** Adventure, religious/inspirational, and women's. "All fiction must have a strong spiritual emphasis." Occasionally critiques rejected mss.

**How to Contact:** Send complete ms with SASE. Free sample copy.
**Payment:** $50-125.
**Terms:** Pays on publication for all rights, "but usually are happy to let second rights revert to author upon request." Publication copyrighted.
**Tips:** "Fiction must be top quality. Obvious solutions, pat endings, stilted dialogue, and unreal characters too often make stories unacceptable. We are looking for tightly written short stories of approximately 1000 words, and also longer stories (up to 2,500 words) with a strong interwoven spiritual emphasis—not preachy. We especially need seasonal stories—Easter, Thanksgiving, Christmas, etc."

**CHRISTIAN LIVING FOR SENIOR HIGHS (IV)**, David C. Cook Publishing Co., 850 N. Grove, Elgin IL 60120. (312)741-2400. Editor: Anne E. Dinnan. A take-home Sunday school paper: 8½x11; 4 pages; Penegra paper and cover; full color illustrations and photos. For senior high classes. Weekly.
**Needs:** "Each piece must present some aspect of the Christian life without being preachy. No closing sermons and no pat answers. Any topic appropriate to senior high is acceptable." Buys 16-20 mss/year. Length: 900-1,200 words.
**How to Contact:** Send complete ms with SASE. Cover letter with brief bio and religious credentials. Reports in 2 months on mss. Phone queries OK. Free guidelines with SASE.
**Payment:** Pays $80-100.
**Terms:** Pays on acceptance for all rights.
**Tips:** "Get to know as much as possible about today's senior high-age student. Write from a firm evangelical conviction. We encourage teens to write to us." Rejects mss because "many are contrived and shallow; they are written to make a moralistic or spiritual point. Writer should write a good story and let publisher decide what it might illustrate rather than writing toward a moral." Published new writers within the year.

**THE CHURCH MUSICIAN (IV)**, The Sunday School Board of the Southern Baptist Convention, 127 9th Ave. N., Nashville TN 37234. (615)251-2961. Editor: William M. Anderson Jr. "*The Church Musician* is for church music leaders in local churches—music directors, pastors, organists, pianists, choir coordinators, and members of music councils and/or other planning committees or groups. Music leaders read the magazine for spiritual enrichment, testimonials, human interest stories and other materials related to music programs in local churches." Monthly. Estab. 1950. Circ. 20,000
**Needs:** Categories related toward church music. Receives 1-2 unsolicited fiction mss each month. Length: 750-2,000 words.
**How to Contact:** Send complete ms with SAE. Reports in 2 months on ms. Free sample copy with SAE and 30¢ postage. No simultaneous submissions.
**Payment:** Maximum 4¢ per word.
**Terms:** Pays on acceptance for all rights. Publication copyrighted.
**Tips:** "Avoid mushy sentiment when writing. It must be believable and, of course, practical." Many mss are rejected because they are "too long, too general, too sweet and sentimental, shallow."

**‡CITY PAPER (II)**, City Paper, Inc., 2612 N. Charles St., Baltimore MD 21218. (301)889-6600. Editor: Russ Smith. Fiction Editor: Richard Rabicoff. Tabloid: 64 pages; newsprint paper; illustrations; photos. "Alternative newspaper, like *Village Voice*, serving Balto metro area." For 18-44 year-old educated audience. Weekly. Plans fiction issue in future. Estab. 1977. Circ. 70,000.
**Needs:** Adventure, confession, ethnic, experimental, historical, humor/satire, literary, mainstream. No inspirational, ideological, romance, pornography. Receives 10 unsolicited fiction mss/month. Buys ms every other issue. Publishes 4-8 weeks after acceptance. Length: 500 words minimum. Occasionally critiques rejected mss.
**How to Contact:** Send complete ms with cover letter with basic bio. Reports in 4-6 weeks. SASE. Accepts computer printouts. Sample copy for SAE and $2 postage.

**Payment:** Pays $25-100 and contributor's copies.
**Terms:** Pays on publication for first rights. Publication copyrighted.

**CLUBHOUSE (II)**, Your Story Hour, Box 15, Berrien Springs MI 49103. (616)471-3701. Editor-in-Chief: Elaine Meseraull. Magazine: 6x9; 32 pages; 60 lb offset paper; self cover stock; illustrations and some photos. "A Christian magazine designed to help young people feel good about themselves. Our primary goal is to let them know there is a God and that He loves kids. Stories are non-moralistic in tone and full of adventure." Readers are "children between the ages of 9-13. (Program your stories for the 12-13 year-olds.) Primary audience—kids without church affiliation." Published 10 times/year. Plans special fiction issue. Estab. 1982. Circ. 17,000.
**Needs:** Adventure, contemporary, ethnic, historical (general), juvenile, religious/inspirational, suspense/mystery, and western. No science fiction, fantasy or anything which does not uphold high morals. Receives 200 ƒ unsolicited fiction mss/month. Buys 5 mss/issue, 50 mss/year. Reads mss in April-May only. Length: 650-850 words and 1,000-1,200 words (2 different story lengths in magazine). Recommends other markets. Occasionally critiques rejected mss.
**How to Contact:** Send complete ms with cover letter with bio, title of manuscript, very short synopsis. SASE always. Simultaneous and photocopied submissions and previously published work OK. Accepts computer printout submissions. Prefers letter-quality. Reports in 4 weeks on queries and mss. Publishes ms 6-18 months after acceptance. Free sample copy with 6½x9½ SAE and 3 first class stamps. Free fiction guidelines with business-sized SAE and 1 first class stamp.
**Payment:** Pays $30-35 and 2 contributor's copies.
**Terms:** Pays on acceptance for simultaneous rights, first rights and second serial rights. Buys reprints. Publication copyrighted.
**Tips:** "Especially interested in stories in which children are responsible, heroic, kind, etc., not stories in which children are pushed into admitting that a parent, sibling, friend, etc., was right all along. I want upbeat, fun, exciting stories. Do not mention church, Sunday School, etc., just because this is a Christian magazine. General tone of the magazine is warmth, not criticism. Remember that a story should follow a plot sequence and be properly wrapped up at the end. Most stories I reject involve kids who have regrettable turns of behavior which they finally change, appeal to a too-young age group, are preachy, are the wrong length or lack sparkle. Fiction can be more exact than truths, because details can be fashioned to complete the plot which might by necessity be omitted if the account were strictly factual." Published new writers within the last year.

**COBBLESTONE (IV)**, Cobblestone Publishing, Inc., 20 Grove St., Peterborough NH 03458. Editor-in-Chief: Carolyn P. Yoder. History magazine for children (ages 8-14): 7x9; 48 pages; 4-color covers; illustrations; b&w photos. Monthly with a national distribution.
**Needs:** Adventures, historical, regional and biographical fiction, reminiscences, plays, and retold folk tales. Must relate to month's theme. Length: 500-1,200 words. Publishes short shorts of 750-1,000 words.
**How to Contact:** Simultaneous and previously published submissions OK. Accepts computer printout submissions. Publishes ms an average of 6 weeks after acceptance. Sample copy $2.95. Free guidelines with SASE.
**Payment:** Pays up to 15¢/word.
**Terms:** Pays on publication. Buys all rights. Buys reprints. Makes work-for-hire assignments.
**Tips:** "Request an editorial guideline sheet that explains the upcoming issue themes and gives query deadlines. Prefer queries to unsolicited manuscripts." Rejects mss because "it appears that many writers do not obtain our guidelines before submitting fiction. In addition, we receive much fiction that is predictable and *too* juvenile for our readers. We publish fiction (usually one story per issue) as it pertains to the issue's theme. Fiction offers diverstiy, especially to a history magazine. Write as much as possible. Don't give up. Be true to your own style, don't try to write like other writers. Look to other writers for inspiration." Published new writers in the last year.

**CORVETTE FEVER MAGAZINE (IV)**, Prospect Publishing Co., Inc., Box 55532, Ft. Washington MD 20744. (301)839-2221. Editor-in-Chief: Patricia E. Stivers. "General magazine: 8½x11; 72 pages; coated paper; +60 coated cover stock; illustrations; photos. About Corvettes covering history of the car, restorations, stock and customizing, how-to articles on maintenance and repair, and coverage of the Corvette culture that surrounds the car. Corvette owners mainly are 25 to 45 years of age with incomes ranging from $25,000-$55,000 average. Majority are male. All have a keen loyalty in the Corvette." Bimonthly. Estab. 1978. Circ. 35,000.

**Needs:** Adventure, fantasy, and humor/satire. "Must deal with Corvettes." Receives 2-3 unsolicited fiction mss/month. Accepts 1 ms/issue, 6-8 mss/year. Length: 800-1,200 words. Occasionally critiques rejected mss, "but not extensively."

**How to Contact:** Send complete ms with SASE. Photocopied submissions OK. Reports in 8 weeks. Sample copy $2. Free fiction guidelines with SASE.

**Payment:** 10¢/word.

**Terms:** Pays on publication (within 60 days) for first rights and second serial rights (second rights can be nonexclusive). Publication copyrighted.

**Tips:** Likes to see "good humor or satire that laughs with the Corvette owner but not at him." Published new writers within the last year.

**COSMOPOLITAN MAGAZINE (III)**, The Hearst Corp., 224 W. 57th St., New York NY 10019. (212)262-5700. Editor: Helen Gurley Brown. Fiction Editor: Betty Kelly. Associate Fiction Editor: Miranda Cowley. Most stories include male-female relationships, traditional plots, characterizations. Single career women (ages 18-34). Monthly. Circ. just under 3 million.

**Needs:** Contemporary, women's, romance, mystery, and adventure. "Stories should include a romantic relationship and usually a female protagonist. The characters should be in their 20s or 30s (i.e., same ages as our readers). No highly experimental pieces. Upbeat endings." Buys 1 short story plus a novel or book excerpt/issue. Approximately 98% of fiction is agented. Length: short shorts (1,500 words); longer (2,000-4,000 words). Occasionally recommends other markets.

**How to Contact:** Send complete ms with SASE. Accepts computer printout submissions. Free guidelines with legal-sized SASE. Publishes ms 6-18 months after acceptance.

**Payment:** Pays $750-2,000.

**Terms:** Pays on acceptance for first North American serial rights. Buys reprints.

**Tips:** "It is rare that unsolicited mss are accepted. We tend to use agented, professional writers. The majority of unsolicited short stories we receive are inappropriate for *Cosmo* in terms of characters used and situations presented, or they just are not well written. Research the magazine you are submitting to."

**CRICKET MAGAZINE (II)**, Open Court Publishing Co., Box 100, La Salle IL 61301. (815)224-6666. Editor: Marianne Carus. Magazine: 7x9; 64 pages; groundwood paper; +1 enamel cover stock; illustrations; photos. Magazine for children, ages 6-12. Monthly. Estab. 1973. Circ. 150,000.

**Needs:** Juvenile, including literary, contemporary, science fiction, historic fiction, fantasy, western, mystery, adventure, humor, ethnic, and translations. No adult articles. Buys 10-12 mss/year. Receives approximately 500 unsolicited fiction mss each month. Approximately 1-2% of fiction is agented. Length: 500-1,500 words. Recommends other markets.

**How to Contact:** Do not query first. Send complete ms with SASE. Reports in 2 months on mss. Publishes ms 6-24 months after acceptance. Sample copy $2. Free guidelines with SASE.

**Payment:** Up to 25¢/word; 2 free author's copies. $1 charge for extras.

**Terms:** Pays on publication for first North American serial rights and one-time rights. Sends edited mss. Buys reprints. Publication copyrighted.

**Tips:** "Do not write *down* to children. Write about subjects you are familiar with which have been well researched. Children *need* fiction and fantasy." Published new writers within the last year. Sponsors contests for children, ages 6-12.

**CRUSADER MAGAZINE (II)**, Calvinist Cadet Corps, Box 7244, Grand Rapids MI 49510. (616)241-5616. Editor: G. Richard Broene. Magazine: 8½x11; 24 pages; 50 lb white paper; 50 lb white cover stock; illustrations; photos. Magazine to help boys ages 9-14 discover how God is at

work in their lives and in the world around them. 7 issues/year. Estab. 1958. Circ. 14,000.
**Needs:** Adventure, comics, confession, ethnic, juvenile, religious/inspirational, and science fiction. Receives 80 unsolicited fiction mss/month. Buys 3 mss/issue; 21 mss/year. Length: 800 words minimum; 1,500 words maximum; 1,200 words average. Publishes short shorts.
**How to Contact:** Send complete ms with SASE with cover letter with theme of story. Simultaneous, photocopied, and previously published submissions OK. Accepts computer printout submissions. Prefers letter-quality. Reports in 3 weeks on mss. Publishes ms 4-11 months after acceptance. Free sample copy. Free fiction guidelines with #10 SAE and 1 first class stamp.
**Payment:** Pays 2-5¢/word; 1 free contributor's copy.
**Terms:** Pays on acceptance for one-time rights. Buys reprints.
**Tips:** "On a cover sheet list the point your story is trying to make. Our magazine has a theme for each issue, and we try to fit the fiction to the theme." Published new writers within the last year.

**CURRENTS (II, IV), Voice of the National Organization for River Sports**, National Organization for River Sports, 314 N. 20th St., Colorado Springs CO 80904. (303)473-2466. Editor: Eric Leaper. Magazine: Standard size; 24-32 pages; bookstock paper; bookstock cover; illustrations; b&w photos. Magazine of kayaking and rafting—news, events, techniques, features—for kayakers and rafters. Monthly. Estab. 1979. Circ. 6,000.
**Needs:** Adventure, historical, literary, prose poem, psychic/supernatural, and science fiction. No cliché accounts of "killer rivers" and "violent rapids." Buys 2 mss/year. Length: 1,500 words minimum; 5,000 words maximum; 2,500 words average. Publishes short shorts 1 or 2 pages double spaced. Recommends other markets. Occasionally critiques rejected mss.
**How to Contact:** Cover letter stating when ms was written and background on author. Query first. Simultaneous, photocopied, and previously published submissions OK; "just tell us who else is getting it." Accepts computer printout submissions. Prefers letter-quality. Reports in 2 weeks on queries. Publishes ms 3-12 months after acceptance. Sample copy for $1 including postage. Free fiction guidelines for #10 SAE and 1 first class stamp.
**Payment:** Pays $25-250; subscription to the magazine; 3 free contributor's copies; postage charged for extras. Offers kill fee of 25%.
**Terms:** Pays on acceptance for first North American serial rights. Sometimes sends galleys to author. Publication copyrighted.
**Tips:** "Submissions are usually inappropriate for our audience. Read a sample copy of our publication first to see if our readers would be interested in your idea. Send us a sample page to see if we're even on the same wave length. We will continue to look at fiction because our readers enjoy a change of pace from our technical pieces." Published new writers within the last year.

**DAUGHTERS OF SARAH (II)**, 2716 W. Cortland, Chicago IL 60647. (312)252-3344. Editor: Reta Finger. Magazine: 8½x11; 40 pages; illustrations and photos. "Christian feminist publication dealing with Christian theology, history, women and social issues from a feminist point of view." Bimonthly. Estab. 1974. Circ. 3,600.
**Needs:** Historical, religious/inspirational, feminist, and women's. "No subjects unrelated to feminism from Christian viewpoint." Receives 4-8 unsolicited fiction mss/month. Buys 2-3 mss/year. Length: 1,500 words maximum. Publishes short shorts. Occasionally critiques rejected mss "if related and close to acceptance."
**How to Contact:** Cover letter stating why ms was written; biography on author. Query first with description of ms and SASE. Simultaneous, photocopied, and previously published submissions OK "but won't pay." Accepts computer printout submissions. Prefers letter-quality. Reports in 2 weeks on queries. Publishes ms 3-12 months after acceptance. Sample copy for $1.25.
**Payment:** Pays $15/printed page; 3 free contributor's copies. Offers kill fee of one-half stated fee.
**Terms:** Pays upon acceptance for first North American serial or one-time rights.
**Tips:** "Many stories are not to the point of our magazine. Be more discerning as to the purpose of our magazine. We like a variety but publish less fiction than we'd like to because it seems much harder to write. Our stories must be from both a Christian and feminist perspective and be authentic and realistic; must *show* rather than *tell*." Published new writers within the last year.

**DELTA SCENE MAGAZINE (IV)**, Delta State University, Box B3, Delta State University, Cleveland MS 38733. (601)846-4710. Editor-in-Chief: Curt Lamar. Magazine: 8½x11; 32 pages; excellent cover stock; illustrations; photos. Magazine for college graduates. Quarterly. Estab. 1973. Circ. 2,500.
**Needs:** Adventure, gothic/historical romance, historical (general), humor/satire, literary, regional, and suspense/mystery. "Stories are about or set in the Mississippi Delta. We accept manuscripts of quality material." Receives approximately 4 unsolicited fiction mss/month. Buys 1-2 mss/issue, 4-8 mss/year. Length: 1,000 words minimum; 2,000 words maximum; 1,500 words average. Publishes short shorts.
**How to Contact:** Send complete ms with SASE and cover letter with address. Simultaneous submissions OK. Reports in 3 months. Publishes ms up to 2 years after acceptance. Sample copy $1.50. Free fiction guidelines with SASE.
**Payment:** $15-20 and 3 contributor's copies.
**Terms:** Pays on publication for one-time rights. Publication copyrighted.
**Tips:** Published new writers within the last year.

**DIALOGUE (IV), The Magazine for the Visually Impaired**, Dialogue Publications, Inc., 3100 Oak Park Ave., Berwyn IL 60402. (312)749-1908. Editor-in-Chief: Nolan Crabb. Fiction Editor: Bonnie Miller. Magazine: 8x11; 200 large print pages; standard paper and stock; illustrations and photos rare. Recorded, Braille, and large print magazine of general interest for visually impaired adults. Quarterly. Estab. 1962. Circ. 40,000.
**Needs:** Adventure, contemporary, humor/satire, men's, psychic/supernatural, suspense/mystery, western, and women's. "*Dialogue*'s contributors are themselves visually handicapped. Graphic sex or violence is out, as is religious material or portrayals of blind characters as helpless or pathetic." Receives approximately 20 unsolicited fiction mss/month. Buys 3-4 mss/issue, 10-12 mss/year. No fixed length requirements, but short pieces 2,000 words (3-6 typed pages) strongly preferred. Occasionally critiques rejected mss. Sometimes recommends other markets.
**How to Contact:** Cover letter stating visual impairment status. Send complete ms with SASE. Simultaneous and photocopied submissions OK. Accepts computer printout submissions. Prefers letter-quality. Reports in 6-8 weeks. Publishes ms an average of 6 months after acceptance. Sample copy free to visually impaired prospective contributors. Free fiction guidelines with SASE.
**Payment:** $50 maximum and 1 contributor's copy.
**Terms:** Pays on acceptance for first North American serial rights. Publication copyrighted.
**Tips:** "Study back issues; write a believable story with a beginning, a middle and an end. Use dialogue to keep the action moving. Don't get cute or experimental. Don't take constructive criticism the wrong way—we're all the great unsung American novelist. If you can supplement yourself with nonfiction work, the market is easier, more lucrative and is good for your portfolio and your self esteem." Published new writers within the last year.

**DISCOVERIES (II)**, Nazarene Publishing House, 6401 The Paseo, Kansas City MO 64131. (816)333-7000. Editor: Libby Huffman. *Discoveries* is a Sunday School story paper for children ages 8-11: 8½x11; 8 pages; 2 illustrations/issue; full color photo. Stories should be character building and teach Christian truths. The audience is composed of children who attend Sunday school in the Church of the Nazarene. The paper is for leisure reading. Weekly. Estab. 1976. Circ. 75,000.
**Needs:** Religious/inspirational, mystery, adventure, and juvenile. Fiction must appeal to children ages 8-11. In a survey of our readership they listed mystery as the favorite type of fiction. No erotica, horror, gay/lesbian, fantasy, confession, gothic, etc. Buys 1-2 mss/issue, 75-104 mss/year. Receives 400 unsolicited fiction mss each month. Length: 800-1,000 words.
**How to Contact:** Send complete ms with SASE. Reports in 2-3 weeks. Publishes ms 6-24 months after acceptance. Free sample copy with SAE plus postage. Free fiction guidelines with SASE.
**Payment:** 3.5¢/word up to $35; 2¢ per word for second rights. Offers 100% kill fee for assigned mss not published.

**Terms:** Pays on acceptance for first rights or whatever is offered. Buys reprints. Publication copyrighted.

**Tips:** "Writers should contact our office for the brochure describing our publication's needs. Stories which fit our requirements should then be submitted for consideration. Fiction should be action-oriented with a strong beginning and ending. Christian teaching should be implicit and not added on at the end of the manuscript. It must correlate with the purposes of one of our Sunday school lessons for it to be purchased and used. Most of the stories published in *Discoveries* are fiction; we are always looking for talented authors of short stories for children that teach Christian principles. Manuscripts that show merit may be purchased and edited as much as necessary to adjust them to fit the purposes of the story paper." Published new writers within the year.

**DOG FANCY,** Fancy Publications, Box 6050, Mission Viejo CA 92690. (714)240-6001. Editor-in-Chief: Linda W. Lewis. General dog and puppy magazine, consumer oriented, "for dog and puppy lovers." Monthly. Circ. 75,000.

**Needs:** Dog-centered theme. Receives approximately 40 unsolicited fiction mss/month. Buys 12 mss/year. Length: 3,000 words maximum.

**How to Contact:** Query first or send complete ms. SASE always. Simultaneous and photocopied submissions OK. Reports in 1 week on queries, 2 months on mss. Publishes ms an average of 6 months after acceptance. Sample copy $2.50. Free fiction guidelines with SASE.

**Payment:** 3¢/word and 2 contributor's copies. $2.50 charge for extras.

**Terms:** Publication copyrighted. Buys reprints.

**Tips:** "Must be about dogs (and people), candid; first person is preferable. Include *brief* cover letter. Write to style of publication so that no re-write is necessary."

**DRAGON MAGAZINE (IV), The Monthly Adventure Role-Playing Aid**, Dragon Publishing, Box 110, Lake Geneva WI 53147. (414)248-8044. Editor: Kim Mohan. Magazine: 8½x11; 96 pages; 50 penn. plus paper; 80 lb northcote cover stock; illustrations; rarely photos. "*Dragon* contains primarily nonfiction—articles and essays on various aspects of the hobby of fantasy and science fiction role-playing games. Fiction is used occasionally if the story has relevance to fantasy and science fiction or fantasy and science fiction gaming. Readers are mature teens and young adults; over half our readers are under 18 years of age." Monthly. Estab. 1976. Circ. 120,000.

**Needs:** "It's not essential for a fiction writer to be involved or familiar with role-playing games, but it helps. The gaming approach to fantasy and science fiction is somewhat different than the so-called 'traditional' fantasy and science fiction genres." Receives 50-60 unsolicited fiction mss/month. Buys 4-6 mss/year. Approximately 5% of fiction is agented. Length: 1,500 words minimum; 10,000 words maximum; 3,000-4,000 words average. Occasionally critiques rejected mss.

**How to Contact:** Cover letter with short plot synopsis, estimated word length, SASE. Query with clips of published work with SASE. Photocopied submissions OK. Accepts computer printout submissions. Prefers letter-quality. Reports in 2-3 weeks on queries. Publishes ms 6-12 months after acceptance. Sample copy for $4.50. Free fiction guidelines for 9" wide SAE and 1 first class stamp.

**Payment:** Pays 3-5¢/word; 1 free contributor's copy; $2 charge for extras. Offers kill fee of 25%.

**Terms:** Pays on publication (or by prior arrangement, in advance) for all or first rights. Publication copyrighted.

**Tips:** "Know the basic principles of fantasy and science fiction role-playing games to develop a feel for the specific sort of fantasy and science fiction we're interested in. Fiction is a nice complement to our gaming articles." Published new writers within the last year.

**EASYRIDERS MAGAZINE, Entertainment for Adult Riders**, Box 52, Malibu CA 90265. (213)889-8740. Editor: Lou Kimzey. Magazine: 8½x10⅞; 118 pages; 50 lb coated paper; 70 lb coated cover stock; illustrations; photos. Men's magazine with bike-related material: how-to's, travel, new equipment information, and fiction for adult men who own or desire to own expensive custom motorcycles, and rugged individualists who own and enjoy their choppers and the good times derived from them. Monthly. Circ. 488,000.

**Needs:** Men's and adventure. Only interested in hard-hitting rugged fiction. Should be bike-oriented, but doesn't have to dwell on the fact. Length: 3,000-5,000 words. Publishes short shorts to 1,500 words.

**How to Contact:** Send complete ms with SASE. Reports in 3 weeks on mss. Sample copy $2.95.

**Payment:** Pays 10-15¢/word; payment depends on quality, length and use in magazine.

**Terms:** Pays on acceptance for first rights. Sends galleys to author on paperback books.

**Tips:** "Gut level language accepted; dope or sex scenes OK but are not to be graphically described. As long as the material is directly aimed at our macho intelligent male audience, there should be no great problem breaking into our magazine. Before submitting material, however, we strongly recommend that the writer observe our requirements and study a sample copy." Published new writers within the last year.

**‡ECLIPSE COMICS (I, II)**, Box 199, Guerneville CA 95446. (707)869-9401. Editor: Catherine Yronwode. Comic books. "Adventure and super-heroic serial comics; will select promising concepts for development into full script submissions." For discriminating comic book fans. "We publish as many adventure and super-heroic series as our schedule permits." Circ. 35,000-85,000.

**Needs:** Adventure, fantasy, horror, humor/satire, psychic/supernatural occult, romance, science fiction, suspense/mystery, western. Special needs: moody, romantic, character-oriented pieces with overtones of humanism, morality, political, opinion, philosophical speculation, and/or social commentary. No sexually explicit material. Buys 150 mss (mostly from established comic writers). Publishes ms 1 month after acceptance. Length: 8-11 pages.

**How to Contact:** Query with published clips or send sample science fiction, horror script, or plot synopsis. Reports in 1 month on mss. SASE for query and ms. Simultaneous submissions (also queries), and photocopied submissions OK. Accepts computer printouts. Sample copy $1.50. Fiction guidelines for business-size SAE and 1 first class stamp.

**Payment:** Pays $30/page.

**Terms:** Pays on acceptance for first North American serial rights and second serial reprint rights; exclusive rights to sell material to South American or European markets (with additional payments).

**Tips:** "85% of the stories in these anthologies have downbeat twist endings of the kind popularized O. Henry and the EC comic books of the 1950s. The other 15% start off in that mold but lead to an unexpected upbeat resolution."

**ELLERY QUEEN'S MYSTERY MAGAZINE (II)**, Davis Publications, Inc., 380 Lexington Ave., New York NY 10017. (212)557-9100. Editor: Eleanor Sullivan. Magazine: digest sized; 160 pages. Magazine for lovers of mystery fiction. Published 13 times/year. Published special fiction issue; plans another. Estab. 1941. Circ. 350,000.

**Needs:** "We accept only mystery, crime, and detective fiction." Buys 10-15 mss/issue. Receives approximately 300 unsolicited fiction mss each month. Approximately 50% of fiction is agented. Length: up to 9,000 words. Critiques rejected mss "only when a story might be a possibility for us if revised." Sometimes recommends other markets.

**How to Contact:** Send complete ms with SASE. Cover letter with publishing credits and brief biographical sketch. Reports in 1 month or sooner on mss. Publishes ms 6-12 months after acceptance. Free fiction guidelines with SASE.

**Payment:** 3¢ per word and up.

**Terms:** Pays on acceptance for first North American serial rights. Occasionally buys reprints. Publication copyrighted.

**Tips:** "Read the magazine; know what we publish. Originality of a writer's work and an awareness of what has been published help. We have Department of First Stories and usually publish at least one first story an issue—i.e., the author's first published fiction. No magazine can begin to publish the huge number of manuscripts submitted to them. We select stories that are fresh and of the kind our readers have expressed a liking for." Published new writers within the last year.

**ESPIONAGE MAGAZINE (II)**, Leo 11 Publications, Ltd., Box 1184, Teaneck NJ 07666. (201)836-9177. Editor: Jackie Lewis. Digest-sized: 164 pages; good newsprint paper; illustrations, photos. Magazine totally devoted to espionage stories. Stories of international intrigue, suspense, blackmail, confused loyalties, deception and other things "immoral." Bimonthly. Special fiction issue planned. Estab. 1984.
**Needs:** Essentially mystery and adventure, confession, contemporary, ethnic, fantasy, historical (general), humor/satire, mainstream, psychic/supernatural/occult, contemporary romance, science fiction, suspense/mystery, and western, "as long as spies are prominently involved." Offbeat spy stories accepted. No "gratuitous sex, horror, or gore." Receives 50 unsolicited fiction mss each month. Buys about 13 mss/issue; 75 mss/year. Length: 1,000 words minimum; 6,000 words maximum. Publishes short shorts. Occasionally comments on rejected ms. Recommends other markets.
**How to Contact:** Cover letter with bio info, reprint or origianl work, etc. Send complete ms with SASE or submit through agent. "Don't query." Reports in 4-6 weeks on mss. Photocopied and acknowledged previously published submissions OK. Accepts computer printout submissions; letter-quality only. Sample copy for $2.50. Fiction guidelines free for #10 SASE. No multiple or simultaneous submissions.
**Payment:** Pays 3-8¢/word.
**Terms:** Pays on publication for first and other rights. Publication copyrighted.
**Tips:** "Excellent cross-over for mystery and science fiction writers." Published new writers within the last year.

**ESQUIRE (III)**, Esquire Associates, 2 Park Ave., New York City NY 10016. (212)561-8100. Editor-in-Chief: Phillip Moffitt. Fiction Editor: Rust Hills. Assistant Fiction Editor: Jean-Christope Castelli. Male-oriented magazine with good modern American writing for young professional men ages 25-40. Estab. 1933.
**Needs:** Literary, contemporary, and short stories. No erotica, horror, religious, detective or science fiction. Approximately 50% of fiction is agented. Length: 2,500-5,000 words.
**How to Contact:** Send complete ms with SASE. Accepts computer printout submissions. Reports in 1 month on mss. Publishes ms up to 1 year after acceptance.
**Payment:** Varies.
**Terms:** Pays on acceptance for varied rights.
**Tips:** "Send a clearly typed, proofread story with a plain straightforward cover letter. Don't summarize or characterize the story. Let it speak for itself. Never send a query for fiction manuscripts."

**ESSENCE (II)**, 1500 Broadway, New York NY 10036. (212)730-4260. Editor: Susan L. Taylor. Fiction Editor: Cheryl Everette. General interest magazine with historical, how-to, humor, fashion, career, food, interior design, financial, health, education, beauty, and travel subjects for black women. Monthly. Estab. 1970. Circ. 950,000.
**Needs:** Romance, adventure, humor, fantasy, feminist, experimental, and condensed and serialized novels. Buys 3 mss/year. Length: 1,500-2,000 words.
**How to Contact:** Send complete ms with SASE. Typed and double-spaced. Reports in 3 months on mss. Sample copy $1.50. Free guidelines with query.
**Payment:** Pay varies.
**Terms:** Pays on acceptance. 25% kill fee and byline given. Buys second serial rights for serialized novels.
**Tips:** "We're looking for fiction that teaches and inspires—stories about contemporary black people, the challenges they face, their joys and sorrows."

**EVANGEL**, Dept. of Christian Education, Free Methodist Headquarters, 901 College Ave., Winona Lake IN 46590. (219)267-7161. Editor: Vera Bethel. Sunday School take-home paper for distribution to young adults who attend church. Fiction involves young couples and singles coping with everyday crises, making decisions that show growth; ages 25-35. Weekly. Estab. 1896. Circ. 35,000.

**Needs:** Religious/inspirational. "No fiction without any semblance of Christian message or where the message clobbers the reader." Buys 1 ms/issue, 52 mss/year. Receives approximately 75 unsolicited fiction mss each month. Length: 1,000-1,200 words.

**How to Contact:** Send complete ms with SASE. Reports in 1 month on ms. Free sample copy and free fiction guidelines with 6x9 SASE.

**Payment:** $35; 2 free author's copies. 10¢ charge for each extra.

**Terms:** Pays on publication for simultaneous, first, second serial (reprint), first North American serial, and one-time rights.

**Tips:** "Choose a contemporary situation or conflict and create a good mix for the characters (not all-good or all-bad heroes and villains). Don't spell out everything in detail; let the reader fill in some blanks in the story. Keep him guessing." Rejects mss because of "unbelievable characters and predictable events in the story."

**EXPLORER MAGAZINE,** Flory Publishing Co., Box 210, Notre Dame IN 46556. (219)277-3465. Editor: Ray Flory. Magazine with "basically an inspirational theme including love stories in good taste." Christian writing audience. Semiannually. Estab. 1960. Circ. 200 + .

**Needs:** Literary, mainstream, prose poem, religious/inspirational, romance (contemporary, historical, young adult), and science fiction. No pornography. Buys 2-3 mss/issue; 5 mss/year. Length: 600 words average; 300 words minimum; 900 words maximum. Occasionally critiques rejected mss.

**How to Contact:** Send complete ms with SASE. Reports in 1 week. Publishes ms up to 2 years after acceptance. Photocopied submissions OK. Sample copy $1. Fiction guidelines for SAE and 1 first class stamp.

**Payment:** Up to $10 and 1 free contributor's copy; $1.50 charge for extras.

**Terms:** Cash prizes of $10, $7, $6 and $5 based on subscribers' votes. A plaque is also awarded to first place winner.

**Tips:** "See a copy of magazine first; have a good story to tell—in *good* taste! Most fiction sent in is too *long*!"

**‡FAITH FOR THE FAMILY (IV),** Bob Jones University, 1700 Wade Hampton Blvd., Greenville SC 29614. (803)242-1500, ext. 4200. Editor: Dr. Bob Jones, Jr. Magazine: 8½x11; 32 pages. "Reports, practical nonfiction, sermons, articles on issues of interest to Fundamentalist Christians. Fiction for youth, teens, or adults for Conservative Prostestants." 10 times/year. Estab. 1973.

**Needs:** Religious/inspirational. "For serious consideration, all fiction must have a Christian emphasis. No Biblical fiction." Receives 20 unsolicited mss/month (average). Buys 2 mss/issue; 20/year. Ms published "at least 3 months" after acceptance. Length: 1,200 average; 1,000 words minimum; 1,500 words maximum. Occasionally critiques rejected ms. Recommends other markets.

**How to Contact:** Send complete ms with cover letter (with bio info). Reports on ms in 3-4 weeks. SASE for the ms. Accepts computer printouts including dot-matrix. Sample copy and fiction guidelines free.

**Payment:** Pays .03¢/word and contributor's copies.

**Terms:** Pays on acceptance for all rights. Publication copyrighted.

**Tips:** "Thoroughly study back issues to learn our editorial viewpoints on various matters of importance to Christians."

**FAMILY CIRCLE (III),** Family Circle, 488 Madison Ave., New York NY 10022. Editor: Gay Bryant. Fiction Editor: Jamie Raab. Magazine: 8x11; average 190 pages; coated 40 lb sheet paper; 60 lb free sheet cover stock; illustrations; photos. Service magazine with emphasis on how-to articles: food, crafts, decorating, fitness and beauty, childcare, career, and consumer advice. "Our

# Close-up

### Jamie Raab
*Family Circle*

Jamie Raab is always looking for new writers, so she reads all the time—even in the morning before work while she's waiting for her swimming lane at the Y. Raab carries the same energy into the spacious modern office on Madison Avenue where she is fiction editor for *Family Circle*.

"I read everything with great enthusiasm," she says undaunted by the 400 manuscripts she must tackle each month. Raab accepted the *FC* job in late 1984 determined to bring more fiction to the magazine's readers. But even with the support of editor Gay Bryant, the campaign has not gone as swimmingly as hoped, admits fiction's "unsinkable" champion. Today there are more and better quality stories, she reports, so quality is not the issue. The greatest barrier is space in the magazine, most of which is reserved for food, craft and service articles and advertising.

Convinced that readers want "a respite from the practical to offset the hardcore how-to material," Raab surveyed readers to find out if they want fiction in *Family Circle*. Yes indeed, they responded by the hundreds, they enjoy reading fiction very much—at odd moments during the day, or maybe they'll save it for later in the evening, like dessert.

The interest in fiction is there; space is not. The answer to break in is *brevity*. "The shorter the story is, the more likely it is to get in the magazine," Raab says with encouragement. Three thousand words is tops, but if a very long story of merit comes in, she may ask for a rewrite. *FC* fiction has also included two-part novel excerpts, and Raab is contemplating serials, but she aims for at least one story in each issue every three weeks (17 per year).

To the beginning writer, Raab a freelance writer herself, offers this additional advice: A writer will do herself (95% of *FC* writers are women) a service to become familiar with the entire magazine and its demographics. *Family Circle* with its recent changes attracts younger readers than a few years ago; thus the protagonists (women *and* men) are generally in their 30s and 40s. People stories have the strongest appeal to the editor (hence, the readers)—family women and men dealing with the problems we all confront in marriage, careers, and children. And the stories lean to a folksy theme to which readers relate more easily than, say, stories of the rich and famous.

"We don't want formless fiction," Raab reports. She recommends some structure and resolution but a happy ending is not necessary, and at the same time mood pieces or character sketches do not work well. Certain themes lack freshness and are done to death—including death, which as a subject is a "downer." But some element of romance might be "magic," and "we'd love a strong humor story," she says.

Maybe one out of 100 stories published in *Family Circle* comes from slush; agented work by established writers fares better—simply because of the writing quality. Why so few from new writers? Because they're poorly written, with surprising amateurish mistakes: "The grammar is incorrect or the sentences just may not make any sense."

Sometimes, Raab says with regret, the fiction is "bumped" from the *FC* lineup; the fiction editor reacts very personally, like a protective mother. "I would like to encourage writers because *I* am encouraged by what I see. But it's a tough market." What may *help* make your story stand out, says the empathetic editor, is a very short cover letter with pertinent publishing or personal data.

readers are primarily women ages 30-50, whose interests reflect their varied roles as wives, mothers, homemakers, working women and concerned citizens." Published every 3 weeks. Estab. 1932. Circ. 8 million.

**Needs:** Well-plotted stories of strong human interest, with identifiable characters and situations. "We are looking for nonformula short fiction that deals with family relationships, love and romance, life choices, personal conflict and resolution, and mysteries. *Family Circle* is not an appropriate vehicle for experimental prose or unrelievedly depressing subjects." Length: 1,000-3000 words, but longer mss will be considered. Publishes short shorts 1,500 words or less. Recommends other markets. Receives approximately 400 mss/month. Publishes fewer than 1 mss/issue; 10-15 a year. "Of the stories we accept, the large majority are agented (90%), though new writing talent is certainly encouraged. We also serialize and condense novels."

**How to Contact:** Cover letter with biographical material relevant to author's writing career. Send complete ms with SASE. Seasonal material should be submitted at least 6 months prior to appropriate issue. Reports in 4-6 weeks. Publishes ms 6-18 months after acceptance. Mss will be critiqued only if story is a strong possibility with recommended revisions. Free guidelines with SASE.

**Payment:** Pays varied rate. Sometimes sends galleys to author.

**Terms:** Pays on acceptance for varied rights. "Might" buy reprints. Publication copyrighted.

**Tips:** "We have a strong commitment to short stories. More consideration will be given to the genre, with an emphasis on stories that have carefully structured plots and family-oriented themes. Our readers tell us that they prefer stories about 'ordinary' people to those about the rich and famous. We publish fiction for several reasons: because many of our readers have indicated that they enjoy reading fiction in women's magazines; because entertainment is needed, even in a service magazine; because there are so many fine writers who deserve to be published in a magazine that has a huge readership and that pays fairly; because I love fiction and want to see the fine tradition of short stories preserved in *all* publications." Published new writers within the last year.

**FAMILY MAGAZINE (II), The Magazine for Military Wives,** Box 4993, Walnut Creek CA 94596. (415)284-9093. Editor: Mary Jane Ryan. Magazine: 80 pages; glossy paper; 80 lb glossy cover stock; illustrations; photos. Magazine with stories of interest to military wives. Audience: high school-educated women. Published 10 times/year. Estab. 1958. Circ. 525,000 worldwide.

**Needs:** Contemporary, mainstream, and women's. Receives 100 unsolicited mss/month. Buys 3-5 mss/year. Length: 1,000-3,000 words. Also publishes short shorts.

**How to Contact:** Send complete ms. Reports in 2 months. SASE. Simultaneous and photocopied submissions OK. Accepts computer printout submissions. Prefers letter-quality. Publishes ms an average of 1 year after acceptance. Sample copy $1.25. Fiction guidelines for SASE.

**Payment:** Pays $75-300; 1 contributor's copy; $1.25 charge for extras.

**Terms:** Pays on publication for first rights. Publication copyrighted.

**Tips:** "Good quality still jumps out as a pearl among swine." Published new writers within the last year.

**‡FESTIVALS (IV),** (formerly *Family Festivals*), Resource Publications, Inc., #290, 160 E. Virginia St., San Jose CA 95112. (408)286-8505. Editor: Sam Mackintosh. Magazine: 8½x11; 32 pages; matte 50 lb paper; self-cover; illustrations. "*Festivals* promotes the recovery of the experience of the sacred through family and small-group ritual. We publish stories, legends, tales that connect readers to seasons, earth, assorted spiritual traditions." Bimonthly. Estab. 1981. Circ. 9,000.

**Needs:** Ethnic, religious (not inspirational). Receives 5 unsolicited fiction mss/month. Buys 1 ms/issue. Publishes ms 1 year after acceptance.

**How to Contact:** Query first. Reports in 1 month on queries; 3 months on mss. SASE for ms. Photocopied submissions OK. Accepts computer printouts including dot-matrix. Sample copy $2.75 and 8½x11 SAE with 3 first class stamps. Fiction guidelines free for # SAE and 1 first class stamp.

**Payment:** $50 maximum and contributor's copies.

**Terms:** Pays on publication for all rights. Publication copyrighted.

‡**FIGHTING STARS NINJA (II, IV)**, Rainbow Publications, 1813 Victory Place, Burbank CA 91504. (818)843-4444. Editor: Dave Cater. Magazine: 68 pages; illustrations. *"Fighting Stars Ninja* is a martial arts magazine specializing in the art of ninjutsu. We accept only fiction pieces with an aspect of the ninja warrior tradition, although it need not be historical in nature." Audience geared toward the study of ninjutsu. Bimonthly. Plans special fiction issue in future. Estab. 1973. Circ. 75,000.

**Needs:** Adventure, fantasy, historical, women's, young adult/teen (10-18 years). "As long as its foundation includes the study of ninjutsu, we're open to a myriad of categories." No erotica, and anything else that does not pertain to our focus." Receives 5-10 unsolicited mss/month. Buys 1 ms/issue; 6 mss/year. Length: 1,500-2,000 words average; 1,500 words minimum; 2,500 words maximum. Occasionally critiques rejected mss. Recommends other markets.

**How to Contact:** Query first. Reports in 2-4 weeks on queries and mss. SASE for query and ms. Simultaneous and photocopied submissions OK. Accepts computer printouts including dot-matrix. Sample copy $1.75. Fiction guidelines free.

**Payment:** Pays $50-125.

**Terms:** Pays on publication for first North American serial rights. Publication copyrighted.

**Tips:** "Fiction can be sold to smaller magazines as long as the focus is clear, the characters developed and the storyline strong. It's a matter of finding the right market. As a martial arts magazine, we run quite a few 'hard' stories dealing with weapons, techniques or tradition. Fiction not only gives the reader a break, but also provides a change in terms of what issues can be addressed and how they can be presented. Do your homework. The majority of our readers know ninjutus inside out. And they'll spot someone who has not taken the trouble to learn the language and terminology of the art. Also, the story has to be believable."

**FIRST HAND (II, IV), Experiences for Loving Men**, First Hand Ltd., 310 Cedar Lane, Teaneck NJ 07666. (201)836-9177. Editor: Jack Veasey. "Magazine's theme is that gay sex and gay lifestyles are ultimately rewarding." Readership: homosexual men plus bisexuals. Monthly. Estab. 1980. Circ. 60,000.

**Needs:** Comics, erotica, ethnic, gay, and serialized/excerpted novel. "No material that is anti-woman, or contains beastiality." Receives 20 unsolicited mss/month. Buys 7 mss/issue; 84 mss/year. Length: 1,800 words average; 1,600 words minimum; 2,200 words maximum. Occasionally critiques rejected mss.

**How to Contact:** Query first or send complete ms. Reports in 3 weeks. SASE. Accepts computer printout submissions. Prefers letter-quality. Publishes ms 4-12 months after acceptance. Sample copy $3. Free fiction guidelines.

**Payment:** $100 and 1 free contributor's copy. ($150 for all rights.)

**Terms:** Pays one month after acceptance for one-time rights. Buys reprints. Publication copyrighted.

**Tips:** "Base your articles on true experiences; write in first person. Hand in a professional manuscript. Use a dictionary."

‡**FLING (II)**, Relim Publishing Co., Inc., 550 Miller Ave., Mill Valley CA 94941. (415)383-5464. Editor: Arv Miller. Magazine: 8½x11; 80 pages; slick paper and cover; 4 illustrations; 70 photos. "Sex-type publication for young males 18-34, who like photos of very busty young models. They also like to read sex-type stories of bosomy heroines"; for "blue-collar" audience. Bimonthly. Estab. 1957. Circ. 100,000.

**Needs:** Erotica, fantasy, men's. "Much of the text material in *Fling* deals with sex in combination of busty females." No historicals, mysteries, westerns, plotless stories. Receives 2 dozen unsolicited mss/month. Buys 2-3 mss/issue; 12-15 mss/year. Publishes 2-12 months after acceptance. Length: 4,000 average; 2,000 words maximum. Occasionally critiques rejected mss.

**How to Contact:** Send complete ms with cover letter. Reports in 2 weeks. SASE for ms. Accepts computer printouts including dot-matrix. Accepts electronic submissions via disc or modem. Sample copy $4. Fiction guidelines for SAE and 22¢ postage.

**Payment:** Pays $135-200.

**Terms:** Pays on acceptance for first rights. Publication copyrighted.
**Tips:** "Read a copy of *Fling*, plus study the fiction requirement sheet. Fiction gives *Fling* a special department we feel is necessary. There is a new aspect of sensuality that can be explored by readers. Know exactly what *Fling* wants in the way of story. Or, in some cases, query editor about story ideas. *Fling* has very specific requirements in fiction that must be clearly understood by potential author. While the men's sophisticate market is big, *Fling* needs stories that are tailor-made, not the usual 'sex-mag' submissions. Most authors forget *Fling* needs a lot of emphasis on descriptions of female characters, particularly 'big-bosom' descriptions."

**THE FLYFISHER (IV)**, Federation of Flyfishers, 1387 Cambridge Dr., Idaho Falls ID 83401. (208)523-7300. Editor: Dennis Bitton. Magazine for fly fishermen. "We only publish material directly related to fly fishing." Quarterly. Estab. 1967. Circ. 10,000.
**Needs:** Fiction related to fly fishing only. Accepts 1 ms/issue, 4 mss/year. Length: 1,000 words minimum; 2,500 words maximum; 2,000 words average (preferred).
**How to Contact:** Query first with SASE. Reports in 4 weeks on queries and mss. Sample copy $3 with 9x12 SAE and 10 first class stamps. Free fiction guidelines with legal-sized SAE and 1 first class stamp.
**Payment:** $50-175.
**Terms:** Pays on publication for first North American serial rights and one-time rights. Publication copyrighted.
**Tips:** "See a current issue of the magazine."

**FRIDAY OF THE JEWISH EXPONENT, A Forum of Literature and Opinion**, Federation of Jewish Agencies, 226 S. 16th St., Philadelphia PA 19102. (215)893-5745. Editor-in-Chief: Jane Biberman. Newspaper for the Jewish community of Philadelphia. "We publish short fiction and articles on Jewish themes." Monthly. Circ. 85,000.
**Needs:** Condensed novel, confession, contemporary, ethnic, historical (general), humor/satire, literary, prose poem, religious/inspirational, and translations. Receives approximately 20 unsolicited fiction mss/month. Accepts 1-2 mss/issue, 12-16 mss/year. Length: 1,000-2,000 words preferred; 5,000 words maximum. Occasionally critiques rejected mss. Sometimes recommends other markets.
**How to Contact:** Send complete ms with SASE. Photocopied submissions OK. Reports in 3 weeks.
**Payment:** $50-250 and 2 contributor's copies. Offers 25% kill fee for assigned ms not published.
**Terms:** Pays on publication for first rights. Publication copyrighted.
**Tips:** Rejects mss because they are "poorly written, cliché-ridden."

**THE FRIEND (II)**, Church of Jesus Christ of Latter-Day Saints, 50 E. North Temple, Salt Lake City UT 84150. (801)531-2210. Managing Editor: Vivian Paulsen. Children's magazine directed toward ages 12 and under. Monthly. Estab. 1971. Circ. 210,000.
**Needs:** Literary, contemporary, inspirational, adventure, humor, prose, preschool, and juvenile. Buys 8-10 mss/issue. Length: Prefers 800-1,200 words; accepts up to 2,000.
**How to Contact:** Send complete ms with SASE. Accepts computer printout submissions. Prefers letter-quality. Accepts disc submissions compatible with Wang. Prefers hard copy with disc submission. Reports in 2 months on ms. Free sample copy and guidelines.
**Payment:** 8¢ and up per word.
**Terms:** Pays on acceptance for all rights unless otherwise specified. Publication copyrighted.
**Tips:** Mss are rejected because of "poor writing, wrong market."

**GAMBLING TIMES MAGAZINE**, The Player's Guide and Newsmagazine, Gambling Times Inc., 1018 N. Cole Ave., Hollywood CA 90038. (213)466-5261. Editor: Len Miller. Fiction Editor: Ms. Terri Hartman. Magazine with articles on games of chance for people who bet on sports, racing, casino games. Monthly. Estab. 1977. Circ. 110,000.
**Needs:** Contemporary, humor/satire, suspense/mystery, and stories related to gambling. "Write

for instructions on manuscript preparation. No stories in the 'gambler wins big and dies' formula. Receives 20 unsolicited mss/month. Buys 9 mss/year. Length: 2,500 words average. Occasionally comments on rejected ms.

**How to Contact:** Query first. SASE for ms.

**Payment:** $100-150.

**Terms:** Pays on publication for first North American serial rights. Publication copyrighted.

**GEM (II)**, G&S Publications, Inc., 1472 Broadway, New York NY 10036. (212)840-7224. Editor: Will Martin. Men's sophisticate magazine: 8x11; 64 pages; "good" quality paper; illustrations; photos. Estab. 1961. Circ. 100,000.

**Needs:** Erotica (but not pornography), humor/satire, and men's. Receives 50 unsolicited fiction mss/month. Buys 3-4 mss/month; 35-40 mss/year. Length: 1,000 words minimum; 2,500 words maximum; 2,000 words average. Occasionally critiques rejected mss.

**How to Contact:** Send complete ms with SASE. No simultaneous submissions; photocopied submissions OK. Sample copy for $3.95.

**Payment:** Pays $40 (for short-shorts, 400-500 words) to $100; 1 free contributor's copy if requested.

**Terms:** Payment is usually on assignment to a specific issue for all rights. Publication copyrighted.

**Tips:** Also publishes "*Buf*, which caters to men with a preference for attractive, plump and heavy women, with copy slanted in that direction—factual or fiction. We do not use explicit, graphic descriptions of sex acts and we've just about had it with violence. Humor, satire and spoofs of sexual subjects that other magazines treat seriously are welcome. Stories written for *Buf* should be flattering to attractive heavy women."

**‡THE GEM (II)**, Churches of God, General Conference, Box 926, Findlay OH 45839. (419)424-1961. Editor: Marilyn Rayle Kern. Magazine: 6x9; 8 pages; 50 lb uncoated paper; illustrations (clipper art). "True-to-life stories of healed relationships and growing maturity in the Christian faith for senior high students through senior citizens who attend Churches of God, General Conference Sunday Schools." Weekly. Estab. 1865. Circ. 7,700.

**Needs:** Adventure, feminist, humor, mainstream, men's, religious/inspirational, senior citizen/retirement, women's. Nothing that denies or ridicules standard Christian values. Receives 30 unsolicited fiction mss/month. Buys 1 ms every 2-3 issue; 20-25 mss/year. Publishes ms 4-12 months after submission. Length: 1,500 words average; 1,000 words minimum; 1,700 words maximum.

**How to Contact:** Send complete ms with cover letter ("letter not essential, unless there is information about author's background which enhances story's credibility or verifies details as being authentic"). Reports in 6 months on mss. SASE for ms. Simultaneous, photocopied submissions and reprints OK. Accepts computer printouts including dot-matrix if "correspondence quality." Can use Kaypro 2 or 4 disks written with Perfect Writer, Wordstar, or NewWord, or Victor 900 disks written with Victor Writer or Benchmark. Sample copy free with 4x9 SAE and 1 first class stamp. Fiction guidelines for "one 4x9 SAE will accomodate guidelines plus one sample copy for one stamp. If more than one sample copy is desired along with the guidelines, will need 2 oz. postage."

**Payment:** Pays $10-15 and contributor's copies. Charge for extras (postage for mailing more than one).

**Terms:** Pays on publication for one-time rights.

**Tips:** "Competition at the mediocre level is fierce. There is a dearth of well-written, relevant fiction which wrestles with real problems involving Christian values applied to the crisis times and 'passages' of life. Humor which puts the daily grind into a fresh perspective which promises hope for survival is also in short supply. Write from your own experience. Avoid religious jargon and stereotypes. Conclusion must be believable in terms of the story—don't force a 'Christian' ending. Avoid simplistic solutions to complex problems. Reader should care enough about the characters and be interested enough in the plot to keep reading when story is 'continued on page 6.' Listen to the story-telling art of Garrison Keillor on 'Prairie Home Companion' National Public Radio program. Feel how very particular experiences of small town life in Minnesota become universal with which people everywhere can identify."

**GENESIS MAGAZINE**, Cycle Guide Publications, Inc., 770 Lexington Ave., New York NY 10021. (212)486-8430. Editor: J.J. Kelleher. Fiction Editor: Norman Kelley. "Men's sophisticate magazine." Monthly. Estab. 1973. Circ. 300,000.
**Needs:** Erotica, fantasy, and men's. Receives 15 unsolicited mss/month. Buys 20 mss/year. Approximately 10% of fiction is agented. Length: 3,500 words average.
**How to Contact:** Query first or send complete ms. Reports in 1 month. Publishes ms 3-6 months after acceptance. Simultaneous and photocopied submissions OK. Accepts computer printout submissions. Prefers letter-quality.
**Payment:** Pays $500 and up.
**Terms:** Pays 30 days after acceptance for variable rights. Publication copyrighted.
**Tips:** "We're ready for anything—mystery, action/adventure, fantasy/science fiction—so long as it has some erotic content. Otherwise: Surprise us, and you'll probably make a sale. READ THE BOOK! It also helps to study the *Elements of Style*, and the basics of proper manuscript preparation. Without these, you've got three strikes against you; and around here, your sloppy manuscript may not even get read."

**GENT (II)**, Dugent Publishing Corp., Suite 204, 2355 Salzedo St., Coral Gables FL 33134. (305)443-2378. Editor: John C. Fox. "Men's magazine designed to have erotic appeal for the reader. Our publications are directed to a male audience, but we do have a certain percentage of female readers. For the most part, our audience is interested in erotically stimulating material, but not exclusively." Monthly. Estab. 1959. Circ. 175,000.
**Needs:** Contemporary, psychic/supernatural, science fiction, horror, men's, erotica, mystery, adventure, and humor. *Gent* specializes in D-Cup cheesecake, and fiction should be slanted accordingly. "Most of the fiction published includes several sex scenes. No fiction that concerns children, religious subjects, or anything that might be libelous." Buys 3 mss/issue, 36 mss/year. Receives approximately 30-50 unsolicited fiction mss/month. Approximately 10% of fiction is agented. Length: 2,000-3,500 words. Critiques rejected mss "when there is time."
**How to Contact:** Send complete ms with SASE. Reports in 1 month on mss. Publishes ms an average of 6 weeks after acceptance. Sample copy $4.50. Free fiction guidelines with legal-sized SASE.
**Payment:** $125-175. Free author's copy.
**Terms:** Pays on publication for first North American serial rights. Publication copyrighted.
**Tips:** "Since *Gent* magazine is the 'Home of the D-Cups,' stories and articles containing either characters or themes with a major emphasis on large breasts will have the best chance for consideration. Study a sample copy first." Mss are rejected because "there are not enough or ineffective erotic sequences, plot is not plausible, wrong length, or not slanted specifically for us."

**‡GENTLEMAN'S COMPANION (I)**, Gentleman's Companion, Inc., #2305, 450 7th Ave., New York NY 10001. (212)564-0112. Editor: Jeff Goodman. Magazine: 8½x11; 96 pages; 50 lb coated paper; 80 lb cover stock; illustrations; photos. Men's magazine, sexually oriented material of a heavily erotic nature, geared to young heterosexual males for men 18 + . Monthly. Published special fiction issue. Estab. 1976. Circ. 175,000.
**Needs:** Erotica, fantasy, men's. No non-erotic fiction. Receives 50 unsolicited fiction mss/month; accepts 50 fiction mss/issue. Publishes ms 6 weeks to 6 months after acceptance. Length: 2,500 words average; 1,750 words minimum; 3,000 words maximum.
**How to Contact:** Send complete ms with cover letter. SASE. Reports in 4 weeks on queries. Accepts computer printouts including dot-matrix. Accepts electronic submissions via disc or modem for IBM PC ASCII or PFS Files, others query. Sample copy $3.95 and 8½x11 SAE with 2 first class stamps. Fiction guidelines for $3.95 and 8½x11 SAE with 2 first class stamps.
**Terms:** Pays on publication. Acquires all rights. Publication copyrighted.

**GEORGIA JOURNAL (II)**, Agee Publishers, Inc., Box 526, Athens GA 30603. (404)548-5269. Editor: Jane Agee. Fiction Editor: Hugh Agee. Magazine: 8½x11; 40-48 pages; 60 lb enamel cover stock; illustrations and photos. "A regional magazine with articles on Georgia—homes, cooking, profiles, history, sports, poetry, and fiction. Although most of our readers are over 35, we are in a number of school libraries around the state." Bimonthly. Estab. 1980. Circ. 5,000.

**Needs:** "We won't publish anything risque, violent, or highly controversial." Receives 10-15 unsolicited mss/month. Buys 3-5 mss/year. Length: 1,500-2,000 words. Occasionally critiques rejected mss.

**How to Contact:** Send complete ms. Reports in 6 weeks. SASE. Photocopied submissions OK. Publishes ms 3-6 months after acceptance. Sample copy $3.

**Payment:** Pays $25.

**Terms:** Pays on acceptance for first rights. Publication copyrighted.

**Tips:** "We see all too many sentimental reminiscences thinly disguised as fiction. We are always ready to see a quality piece of fiction about the South. A good short story is a pleasure to read. We also like to encourage unpublished writers who show promise." Published new writers within the last year.

**‡GLAD (IV), The Christian Humor Magazine**, Word-Centered Productions, Inc., 421 W. High St., Box 11, St. Marys OH 45885. (419)394-3238. Editor: M. Taylor Overbey. Magazine: 8¼x10½; 32 pages; newsprint; glossy cover; illustrations; photos. Christian humor—satirical and humorous articles designed to teach a point in a funny way for general Christians. Bimonthly. Estab. 1982. Circ. 2,000.

**Needs:** Fantasy, humor/satire, science fiction. "All articles should have a Biblical theme, and a specific point to make about it." Receives 3-4 unsolicited mss/month. Buys 1-4 mss/issue. Publishes ms 1-3 months after acceptance. Length: 400 words average; 50 words minimum; 400 words maximum. Occasionally critiques rejected ms. Recommends other markets.

**How to Contact:** Query first or send complete ms. Reports in 6 weeks on queries and ms. SASE for ms. Photocopied submissions OK. Accepts computer printouts including dot-matrix. Sample copy $2. Fiction guidelines free.

**Payment:** Pays $10-50; charge for extra copies.

**Terms:** Pays on publication for all rights. Publication copyrighted.

**Tips:** "Read several copies to begin to get a feel for what we want. Many times I get contributions from people who have never seen our publication. Sending mss out in this manner is like going on a blind date: You think you know what you're getting into, but 9 times out of 10 your 'guess' is wrong. Same with 'blind submissions'! We have a *Mad* magazine-type format. Fiction is really all that fits in our magazine."

**GOLF JOURNAL (II)**, United States Golf Assoc., Golf House, Far Hills NJ 07931. (201)234-2300. Editor: Robert Sommers. Managing Editor: George Eberl. Magazine: 36-40 pages; good paper; self cover stock; illustrations and photos. "The magazine's subject is golf—its history, lore, rules, equipment, and general information. The focus is on amateur golf and those things applying to the millions of American golfers. Our audience is generally professional, highly literate, and knowledgeable; presumably they read *Golf Journal* because of an interest in the game, its traditions, and its noncommercial aspects." Published 8 times/year. Estab. 1949. Circ. 140,000.

**Needs:** Humor. "Fiction is very limited. *Golf Journal* has had an occasional humorous story, topical in nature. Generally speaking, short stories are not used. Golf jokes will not be used." Buys 10-12 mss/year. Length: 1,000-2,000 words. Recommends other markets. Critiques rejected mss "when there is time."

**How to Contact:** Send complete ms with SASE. Reports in 2 months on mss. Free sample copy with SASE.

**Payment:** $300-500. 1-10 free author's copies.

**Terms:** Pays on acceptance. Publication copyrighted.

**Tips:** "Know your subject (golf); edit your copy thoroughly; familiarize yourself first with the publication." Rejects mss because "fiction usually does not serve the function of *Golf Journal*, which, as the official magazine of the United States Golf Association, deals chiefly with nonfiction subjects. We publish fiction because, when it's properly done, it's entertaining, and we like to entertain our readers. We seldom see a well done piece of fiction in our field, however, although we must admit our field is restricted." Published new writers within the last year.

**GOOD HOUSEKEEPING**, 959 Eighth Ave., New York NY 10019. Editor: John Mack Carter. Fiction Editor: Naome Lewis. Homemaking magazine of informational articles, how-to's for homemakers of all ages. Monthly. Circ. 13 million.
**Needs:** Contemporary, women's, gothic, romance, and mother-child stories. Buys 2 short stories/issue. Approximately 75% of fiction is agented. Length: 1,000-4,000 words.
**How to Contact:** Query or send complete ms. SASE always. Accepts computer printout submissions. Prefers letter-quality. Reports in 1 month on both queries and mss. Publishes ms an average of 6 months after acceptance.
**Payment:** Pays standard magazine rates.
**Terms:** Pays on acceptance for periodical publishing rights, second serial, and first North American serial rights.

**‡GOOD NEWS, ETC. (IV)**, Good News Publishers, Inc., Box 2017, Carlsbad CA 92008. (619)434-6397. Editor; Rick Monroe. Tabloid: 24 pages; newsprint paper; illustrations; photos. "Good news about Christian ministry, life, business, etc., mostly news style for locals and Christians mostly in Northern San Diego county." Monthly. Estab. 1984. Circ. 20,000.
**Needs:** Christian. No "stories without Jesus or Christian victory." Receives 3 unsolicited mss/month. Buys 0-1 ms/issue; 6-20 mss/year. Publishes ms 1-2 months or sooner after acceptance. Length: 300-700 words average; 50 words minimum; 1,000 words maximum.
**How to Contact:** Query first. Reports in 2 months on queries and mss. Simultaneous, photocopied submissions and reprints OK. Accepts computer printouts including dot-matrix. Accepts electronic submissions via ACSI. Sample copy for 10x12 SAE and 3 first class stamps. Fiction guidelines for #10 SAE and 1 first class stamp.
**Payment:** Pays $10 maximum, free subscription to magazine and contributor's copies.
**Terms:** Pays on publication.
**Tips:** "News is one primary intent, but some first person work—if it's short and of interest—*especially* from a writer who lives in this area—will be considered."

**GOSPEL CARRIER (IV)**, Messenger Publishing House, Box 50, Joplin MO 64802. (417)624-7050. Editor-in-Chief: Dr. Roy M. Chappell. Fiction Editor: Rosmarie Foreman. Magazine: 8 pages; clip art. Magazine for adults—all material religious oriented. Weekly. Circ. 2,500.
**Needs:** Adventure, historical (general), religious/inspirational, suspense/mystery, and young adult. "All material must be religious oriented." Receives approximately 100 unsolicited fiction mss/month. Does not read Feb-Mar; May-June; Aug-Sept; Nov-Dec. Length: 1,500 words minimum; 1,750 words maximum; 1,600 words average. Occasionally critiques rejected mss.
**How to Contact:** Send complete ms with SASE. Simultaneous, photocopied, and previously published submissions OK. Reports in 2 weeks on mss. Sample copy 50¢ or free with standard-sized SAE and 1 first class stamp. Fiction guidelines 50¢ or free with standard-size SASE.
**Payment:** 1½¢/word and 2 contributor's copies.
**Terms:** Pays on publication for simultaneous rights. Publication copyrighted.
**Tips:** Published "several" new writers within the last year.

**GULFSHORE LIFE (I, IV)**, Gulfshore Publishing Co., Inc., 3620 Tamiami Trail N., Naples FL 33940. (813)262-6425. Editor: Anita Atherton. Lifestyle magazine about people, sports, homes, boats, business, features of interest to winter residents, and year-round residents of and visitors to Southwest Florida. Published October through August. Estab. 1970. Circ. 18,000.
**Needs:** Articles must have Southwest Florida setting.
**How to Contact:** Send complete ms with SASE. Photocopied and simultaneous submissions OK. Accepts computer printout submissions. Prefers letter-quality.

**Terms:** Pays on publication for one-time rights. Byline given. Publication copyrighted.
**Tips:** Mss are rejected because of "inappropriate subject matter."

**HADASSAH MAGAZINE (II)**, 50 W. 58th St., New York NY 10019. Executive Editor: Alan M. Tigay. Senior Editor: Roselyn Bell. General interest magazine: 8½x11; 64-80 pages; coated and uncoated paper; slick, medium weight coated cover; illustrations; photos. Primarily concerned with Israel, the American Jewish community and American current affairs. Monthly except combined June/July and August/September issues. Circ. 375,000.
**Needs:** Ethnic (Jewish). Receives 20-25 unsolicited fiction mss each month. Length: 3,000 words maximum. Also publishes short shorts 1,500-2,000 words.
**How to Contact:** Send complete ms with SASE. Accepts computer printout submissions. Reports in 6 weeks on mss.
**Payment:** Pays $300 minimum. Offers $100 kill fee for assigned mss not published.
**Terms:** Pays on publication for US publication rights. Publication copyrighted.
**Tips:** "We get too many 'I Remember Mama' stories. Write a good short story with strong plot showing positive Jewish values." Mss are rejected because they are "too long, not an appropriate theme for magazine, not well written, or not written for a 'family' audience." Occasionally sponsors contests. Published new writers within the year.

**HANG GLIDING MAGAZINE (I, IV)**, US Hang Gliding Association, Box 66306, Los Angeles CA 90066. (213)390-3065. Editor-in-Chief: Gil Dodgen. Magazine for hang glider pilots. Publishes stories, technical articles, competition reports, and features about hang gliding. Monthly. Estab. 1971. Circ. approximately 9,000.
**Needs:** Adventure, comics, experimental, fantasy, historical (general), horror, humor/satire, science fiction, and suspense/mystery. "Fiction must relate strongly to the sport of hang gliding." Occasionally critiques rejected mss.
**How to Contact:** Query, query with clips of published work, or send complete ms. SASE always. Reports in 1 month on queries and mss. Free sample copy for 8½x11 SAE and $1.07 postage.
**Payment:** "Negotiable—varies with the quality of the work and our needs at the time." Up to 4 free contributor's copies.
**Terms:** Pays on publication for all rights (usually). Publication copyrighted.
**Tips:** "Learn to hang glide, read the magazine. No erotica."

**HARPER'S MAGAZINE (II, III)**, 2 Park Ave., Room 1809, New York NY 10016. (212)481-5251. Editor: Lewis H. Lapham. Magazine: 8x10¾; 80 pages; illustrations. Magazine for well-educated, widely read and socially concerned college-aged and older, those active in political and community affairs. Monthly. Circ. 152,000.
**Needs:** Contemporary and humor. Stories on contemporary life and its problems. Receives approximately 300 unsolicited fiction mss/month. Length: 1,000-5,000 words. Also publishes short shorts.
**How to Contact:** Query through agent. Reports in 6 weeks on queries.
**Payment:** Pays $500-1,000. Negotiable kill fee and byline given.
**Terms:** Pays on acceptance for rights though they vary on each author and material. Sends galleys to author. Publication copyrighted.
**Tips:** Mss are rejected because of "poor writing and petty concerns—often they are too long (over 25 pages)." Buys very little fiction but *Harper's* has published short stories traditionally. Published new writers within the last year.

**HARVEY FOR LOVING PEOPLE**, Harvey Shapiro Inc., Suite 2305, 450 7th Ave., New York NY 10001. (212)564-0112. Editor: Harvey Shapiro. Managing Editor: Jack Sharp. Magazine dedicated to the enrichment of loving relationships between couples, offering sexually informative material in graphically erotic manner about swingers' lifestyles. "Our readership consists of people interested in highly informative sex-related information." Monthly. Estab. 1979. Circ. 200,000.

**Needs:** Lesbian and heterosexual erotica. No material accepted that is not sexually oriented. Buys 2-3 mss/issue. Length: 1,000-2,000 words.
**How to Contact:** Send mss with SASE. Reports in 1 month.
**Payment:** $50-200.
**Terms:** Pays on publication for all rights.
**Tips:** Send SASE. "We reserve the right to edit."

**HI-CALL (II)**, Gospel Publishing House, 1445 Boonville Ave., Springfield MO 65802. (417)862-2781. Editor: Jennifer J. Eller. Take-home Sunday school paper for teenagers (ages 12-17). Weekly. Estab. 1954. Circ. 120,000.
**Needs:** Religious/inspirational, romance, western, mystery/suspense, adventure, humor, and young adult, with a strong but not preachy Biblical emphasis. Receives approximately 100 unsolicited fiction mss/month. Length: up to 1,800 words.
**How to Contact:** Send complete ms with SASE. Simultaneous and previously published submissions OK. Accepts computer printout submissions. Prefers letter-quality. Reports in 3 weeks on mss. Free sample copy and guidelines.
**Payment:** Pays 2-3¢/word. Offers 100% kill fee for assigned mss not published.
**Terms:** Pays on acceptance for one-time rights.
**Tips:** "Most manuscripts are rejected because of shallow characters, shallow or predictable plots, and/or a lack of spiritual emphasis."

**HIGH ADVENTURE (II)**, General Council Assemblies of God (Gospel Publishing Co.), 1445 Boonville, Springfield MO 65802. (417)862-2781, ext. 1497. Editor-in-Chief: Johnnie Barnes. Magazine: 8⁵/₁₆x11¹/₈; 16 pages; lancer paper; self cover stock; illustrations; photos. Magazine for adolescent boys. "Designed to provide boys with worthwhile, enjoyable, leisure reading; to challenge them in narrative form to higher ideals and greater spiritual dedication; and to perpetuate the spirit of the Royal Rangers program through stories, ideas and illustrations." Quarterly. Published special fiction issue; plans another. Estab. 1971. Circ. 70,000.
**Needs:** Adventure, historical (general), religious/inspirational, suspense/mystery, and western. Length: 1,200 words minimum. Publishes short shorts to 1,000 words. Occasionally critiques rejected mss.
**How to Contact:** Send ms with SASE. Include social security number. Simultaneous, photocopied, and previously published submissions OK. Reports in 6 weeks on mss. Free sample copy; free fiction guidelines for 9x12 SASE.
**Payment:** 2¢/word (base) and 3 contributor's copies.
**Terms:** Pays on acceptance for first rights and one-time rights. Publication copyrighted.
**Tips:** "Read the magazine; know the readership; give attention to writing style; be accurate." Published new writers within the last year.

**HIGHLIGHTS FOR CHILDREN**, 803 Church St., Honesdale PA 18431. (717)253-1080. Editor-in-Chief: Walter Barbe. Address fiction to: Kent L. Brown, Jr., Editor. Magazines: 8¹/₂x11; 40 pages; newsprint paper; coated cover stock; illustrations; photos. Published 11 times/year. Circ. 1.9 million.
**Needs:** Juvenile (ages 2-12). Unusual, wholesome stories appealing to both girls and boys; stories with strong emotional appeal, vivid, full of action. "Begin with action rather than description, have strong plot, believable setting, suspense from start to finish." Length: 900 words maximum. "We also need easy stories for very young readers (500 words)." No war, crime, or violence. Buys 6-7 mss/issue. Receives 500-600 unsolicited fiction mss/month. Also publishes short shorts of 200-250 words for the 3-4 year old child. Critiques rejected mss occasionally, "especially when editors see strong possibilities in story."
**How to Contact:** Send complete ms with SASE and include a rough word count and cover letter "with any previous acceptances by our magazine; any other published work anywhere." Accepts computer printout submissions. Prefers letter-quality. Reports in 2 months on mss. Publishes ms an average of 3 years after acceptance. Free guidelines with SASE.
**Payment:** Pays about 10¢ per word.

**Terms:** Pays on acceptance for all rights. Sends galleys to author. Publication copyrighted.
**Tips:** "We accept a story on its merit whether written by an unpublished or an experienced writer. Mss are rejected because of poor writing, lack of plot, trite or worn-out plot, or poor characterization. Children *like* stories and learn about life from stories. Children learn to become lifelong fiction readers by enjoying stories." Published new writers within the last year. Sponsors occasional contests. Write for information. Include a rough word count.

**HIS MAGAZINE (II)**, Inter-Varsity Christian Fellowship, 5206 Main St., Downers Grove IL 60515. (312)964-5700. Magazine: 32 pages; 60 lb matte paper; 100 lb cover stock; illustrations; photos. "Magazine of Christians on campus; helping students integrate faith and campus life. First person; allegories." Published monthly during the school year. Estab. 1941. Circ. 24,000.
**Needs:** Young adult. "General fiction—we're looking for well-developed stories that reflect (even subtly reflect) a Biblical Christian viewpoint." Receives 15 unsolicited fiction mss/month. Buys 7 mss/year. Length: 200 words minimum; 2,000 words maximum; 1,500 words average. Publishes short shorts.
**How to Contact:** Cover letter with author's back ground (college) and background relating to story. Send complete ms with SASE. Previously published submissions (if identified as such) OK. Accepts computer printout submissions. Prefers letter-quality. Reports in 3 months. Publishes ms 6-12 months after acceptance. Free sample copy for 9x12 SAE and 1 first class stamp.
**Payment:** Pays $35-100; 2 free contributor's copies. Sometimes sends galleys to author.
**Terms:** Pays on acceptance for first rights. Buys reprints "if identifed as such." Publication copyrighted.
**Tips:** "Fiction is one of the best forms available to convey truths—people are naturally drawn into stories. Fiction is perhaps our best mirror of real life. Please include vivid details that will make me feel like I'm there—and that will make me *care* about your character." Published new writers within the last year.

**HOME LIFE (I)**, The Sunday School Board of the Southern Baptist Convention, 127 9th Ave. N., Nashville TN 37234. (615)251-2271. Editor: Reuben Herring. A Christian family magazine: 8⅛x10⅞; 66 pages; coated paper; separate cover stock; illustrations; photos. "Top priorities are strengthening and enriching marriage; parenthood; family concerns and problems; and spiritual and personal growth. Most of our readers are married couples and parents between the ages of 25-50. They read it out of denominational loyalty and desire for Christian growth and discipleship." Monthly. Estab. 1947. Circ. 800,000.
**Needs:** Contemporary, religious/inspirational, humor, and young adult. "We do not want distasteful, risque or raunchy fiction. Nor should it be too fanciful or far-fetched." Buys 1-2 mss/issue, 12-24 mss/year. Receives approximately 800 unsolicited fiction mss/month. Critiques rejected mss "when there is time." Less than 1% of fiction is agented. Length: 750-2,500 words. Publishes short shorts of 500 + words. Recommends other markets.
**How to Contact:** Query or send complete ms. SASE always. Accepts computer printout submissions. Prefers letter-quality. Reports in 2 weeks on queries, 4 weeks on mss. Publishes ms 12-20 months after acceptance. Free sample copy with 9x11½ SAE and 70¢ postage. Free fiction guidelines with SASE.
**Payment:** Up to 4¢/word for unsolicited mss. 3 free author's copies.
**Terms:** Pays on acceptance for all rights, first rights, and first North American serial rights. Rarely buys reprints. Publication copyrighted.
**Tips:** "We publish fiction to communicate Christian values." Published new writers within the last year.

**HORSE ILLUSTRATED**, Fancy Publications, Box 6050, Mission Viejo CA 92690. (714)240-6001. Editor: Jill-Marie Jones. "General all-breed horse magazine for horse lovers of all ages but mainly young women riding for show and pleasure. All material is centered around horses; both English and Western riding styles are profiled." Monthly. Estab. 1982. Circ. 60,000.
**Needs:** Adventure, comics, juvenile, suspense/mystery, western, and young adult/teen. "Must

concern horses. Liberal—nothing unsuitable to a younger audience." Receives 3-5 unsolicited mss/month. Buys 5-6 mss/year. Length: 1,500-2,000 words average; 1,000 words minimum; 2,500 words maximum. Occasionally critiques rejected mss.

**How to Contact:** Query first or send complete ms. Reports in 2 weeks on queries; 6 weeks on mss. SASE. Photocopied submissions OK. Accepts computer printout submissions. Prefers letter-quality. Publishes ms 4-6 months after acceptance. Sample copy $3. Free fiction guidelines. SASE.

**Payment:** $50-150; 2 contributor's copies; $2 charge for extras ("free if request is for a reasonable number of copies").

**Terms:** Pays on publication for first North American serial rights. Publication copyrighted.

**Tips:** "Write about young girls and their horses. It must be a believable, interesting story that they can identify with."

**HUMPTY DUMPTY'S MAGAZINE (II)**, Children's Better Health Institute, Benjamin Franklin Literary & Medical Society, Inc., 1100 Waterway Blvd., Box 567, Indianapolis IN 46206. Editor: Christine French Clark. Children's magazine stressing health, nutrition, hygiene, exercise, and safety for children ages 4-6. Monthly, except bimonthly February-March, April-May, June-July and August-September.

**Needs:** Juvenile health-related material and material of a more general nature. No inanimate talking objects. Rhyming stories should flow easily with no contrived rhymes. Buys 1-3 mss/issue. Receives 250-300 unsolicited fiction mss/month. Length: 600 words maximum.

**How to Contact:** Send complete ms with SASE. Reports in 8-10 weeks. Sample copy 75¢. Editorial guidelines with SASE. No queries.

**Payment:** Pays 6¢/word for stories plus 2 author's copies.

**Terms:** Pays on publication for all rights. Publication copyrighted.

**Tips:** "In contemporary stories, characters should be up-to-date, with realistic dialogue. We're looking for health-related stories with unusual twists or surprise endings. We want to avoid stories and poems that 'preach.' We try to present the health material in a positive way, utilizing a light humorous approach wherever possible." Most rejected mss "are unsuitable for the 4-6 age range, using too difficult vocabulary and situations unfamiliar to young children. Stories should not exceed 600 words." Also, "authors do not study *current* issues of our magazine. They don't know their market." Published new writers within the last year.

**IDEALS MAGAZINE (II)**, Ideals Publishing Corp., Nelson Place at Elm Hill Pike, Nashville TN 37214 (615)889-9000. Director of Publishing: Patricia Pingry. Magazine: 8½x11; 80 pages; uncoated paper; illustrations; photos. *Ideals* is a family-oriented magazine with issues corresponding to seasons and based on traditional values. Published 8 times a year. Estab. 1944. Circ. 700,000.

**Needs:** Religious/inspirational, women's, humor, juvenile, seasonal/holidays, and nostalgia. No lewd or risque fiction. Buys 4-5 mss/issue, 40 mss/year. Publishes short shorts of less than 850 words.

**How to Contact:** Send complete ms with SASE and cover letter with name, address, social security number, and short description of ms. Reports in 2 months on mss. Free sample copy with 8½x11 SASE and $1.35 postage.

**Payment:** Varies.

**Terms:** Pays on publication for one-time rights.

**Tips:** "We publish fiction that is appropriate to the theme of the issue, well-written and appropriate to our audience. Say *only* what you want your reader to see (e.g. 'Her hair was still wet' not 'Her hair was not dry.') Make sure your manuscript is as clean and stylistically correct as possible." Published new writers within the last year.

**IN TOUCH (II, IV)**, Wesleyan Publishing House, Box 2000, Marion IN 46952. (317)674-3301. Editor: Jim Watkins. Magazine: 8½x11; 32-40 pages; offset paper and cover stock; illustrations; photos. Publication for teens, ages 13-18. Weekly.

**Needs:** *True* experiences and Christian testimonies told in fiction style, humorous fiction and C.S. Lewis-type allegories. Receives 100 unsolicited fiction mss/month. Does not read mss in summer. Length: 500-1,500 words.

**How to Contact:** Send complete ms with SASE. "Queries are not encouraged." Accepts computer printout submissions. Prefers letter-quality. Reports in 1-3 weeks on mss. Publishes ms 6-9 months after acceptance.

**Payment:** Pays 3¢/word. 2¢/word on reprints.

**Terms:** Pays on acceptance. Byline given and brief autobiographical sketch. Buys reprints.

**Tips:** "Send SASE for writer's guide before submitting. We are only using true events written in fiction style, humor and allegories. Most religious fiction is unrealistic." Published new writers within the last year.

**INDIAN LIFE MAGAZINE (IV)**, Intertribal Christian Communications, Box 3765, Station B, Winnipeg, Manitoba RAW 3R6 Canada. (204)949-9452. Editor: George McPeek. Magazine: 8½x11; 16 pages; newsprint paper; newsprint cover stock; illustrations; photos. A nondenominational Christian magazine written and read mostly by North American Indians. Bimonthly. Estab. 1979. Circ. 12,000.

**Needs:** Adventure, confession, ethnic (Indian), historical (general), juvenile, men's, religious/inspiration, women's, and young adult/teen. Receives 2-3 unsolicited mss/month. Buys 1 ms/issue; 4-5 mss/year. Length: 1,000-1,200 words average. Publishes short shorts of 600-900 words. Occasionally comments on rejected mss.

**How to Contact:** Query first, send complete manuscript (with cover letter; bio and published clips), or query with clips of published work. Reports in 1 month on queries; in 2 months on mss. IRC or SASE ("US stamps no good up here"). Accepts computer printout submissions. Prefers letter-quality. Sample copy free for 8½x11 SAE and IRCs or *Canadian* stamps only. Fiction guidelines free for business-sized SAE and Canadian postage or IRC only.

**Payment:** 2-4¢/word and 5 contributor's copies; 50¢ charge for extras.

**Terms:** Pays on publication for first rights. Publication copyrighted.

**Tips:** "Keep it simple with an Indian viewpoint at about an 8th grade reading level. Read story outloud. Have someone else read it to you. If it doesn't come across smoothly and naturally, it needs work." Published new writers within the last year.

**INSIDE (II), The Magazine of the Jewish Exponent**, Jewish Federation, 226 S. 16th St., Philadelphia PA 19102. (215)893-5700. Editor-in-Chief: Jane Biberman. Magazine: 175-225 pages; illustrations; photos. Aimed at middle- and upper-middle-class audience, Jewish-oriented articles and fiction. Quarterly. Estab. 1980. Circ. 85,000.

**Needs:** Contemporary, ethnic, humor/satire, literary, and translations. No erotica. Receives approximately 10 unsolicited fiction mss/month. Buys 1-2 mss/issue, 4-8 mss/year. Length: 1,500 words minimum; 4,000 words maximum; 2,500 words average. Also publishes short shorts. Occasionally critiques rejected mss.

**How to Contact:** Send complete ms with SASE. Simultaneous and photocopied submissions OK. Sample copy $3 with 8x10 SAE. Free fiction guidelines with SASE.

**Payment:** $100-400.

**Terms:** Pays on publication for first rights. Sometimes buys reprints. Sends galleys to author. Publication copyrighted.

**Tips:** "We're looking for original, avant-garde, stylish writing. First person reminiscences are usually boring." Published new writers within the last year.

**INSIDE KUNG FU, The Ultimate in Martial Arts Coverage (II, IV)**, Unique Publications, 4201 Vanowen Pl., Burbank CA 91505. (818)845-2656. Editorial Director: Russel Maynard. Magazine of martial arts history, technique, philosophy, theory, training methods, and self defense (especially Chinese arts). Audience: mostly men, sports-oriented, ages 18-35. Monthly. Estab. 1973. Circ. 130,000.

**Needs:** "Want Chinese-flavored fiction, rather than Japanese (as in *Shogun*, etc.). No movie

plots, please. We do not accept mundane, personal, diary-type writing." Receives 2 unsolicited fiction mss/month. Buys 1 ms/issue, 10 mss/year. Length: 1,000 words minimum; 4,000 words maximum; 2,000 words average, photographs with text expected. Usually critiques rejected mss.
**How to Contact:** Send complete ms with SASE. Accepts computer printout submissions. Prefers letter-quality. Reports in 4-6 weeks on mss. Publishes ms 3-9 months after acceptance. Sample copy $2.
**Payment:** $75-250 and 2 contributor's copies.
**Terms:** Pays on publication for first North American serial rights. Publication copyrighted.
**Tips:** "We encourage manuscript submissions and will give personal attention to each."

**INSIDE RUNNING AND FITNESS (II, IV), The Tabloid Magazine That Runs Texas,** (formerly *Inside Running*), 9514 Bristlebrook, Houston TX 77083. (713)498-3208. Publisher/Editor: Joanne Schmidt. Specialized tabloid for Texas joggers/runners—novice to marathoner, bicycling, aerobics and general fitness. Monthly. Estab. 1977. Circ. 10,000; overall readers 25,000.
**Needs:** Historical (general), humor/satire, literary, and serialized/excerpted books on running and general fitness. "Nothing sexually explicit—we're family-oriented." Texas-oriented mss preferred. Buys 1 ms/issue. Length: 1,000 words minimum; 2,000 words maximum. Occasionally critiques rejected mss.
**How to Contact:** Send complete ms with SASE. Simultaneous, photocopied, and previously published submissions OK. Reports in 4 weeks on mss. Sample copy $2. Free fiction guidelines with SASE.
**Payment:** $25-75.
**Terms:** Pays on acceptance for one-time rights. Publication copyrighted.
**Tips:** "Know running basics and keep story clean. Avoid typical race experience (first marathon, etc.)."

**INSIGHT (II)**, Young Calvinist Federation, Box 7244, Grand Rapids MI 49510. (616)241-5616. Editor: John Knight. Fiction Editor: Martha Kalk. Magazine: 8½x11; 32 pages; 60 lb coated paper; 80 lb coated cover stock; illustrations; photos. "*Insight* magazine is designed to help young people recognize Christ as Lord, and to prepare them to serve Him always and everywhere. Our readership is made up of young people 15 to 21 years of age in American and Canadian urban and rural areas." Published 10 times per year. Estab. 1919. Circ. 19,000.
**Needs:** Literary, contemporary, religious/inspirational, and young adult/teen. Buys 3 mss/issue; 30 mss/year. Length: 900-2,000 words. Publishes short shorts 800-2,000 words. Recommends other markets.
**How to Contact:** Send complete ms with SAE. Reports in 1 month on mss. Publishes ms 2-12 months after acceptance. Free sample copy with 9x12 SAE and 50¢ postage. Free fiction guidelines with legal-sized SASE.
**Payment:** $35-100.
**Terms:** Pays on publication for simultaneous, first, second serial (reprint), and one-time rights. Publication copyrighted.
**Tips:** "Short stories should lead our readers into a better understanding of how their Christian beliefs apply to their daily lives. The events and the characters must be lively, and so must the dialogue. Anything unrealistic or overly sentimental cannot be used. We still prefer stories that feature older teens or young adults. Canadian settings are as important to us as regional US locations. Minority fiction is welcome. We feel fiction communicates ideas at feeling level, ideal for our 16-20 age group. Write good opening paragraphs with sufficient tension, or hint at conflict, to tease the reader to go on." Published new writers within the last year.

**‡INTIMACY (I, II), The Black Romance Magazine**, Lexington Library, 355 Lexington Ave., New York NY 10017. (212)391-1400. Editor: Judy Andrews. Magazine of black romance stories for women between the ages of 18-45. Monthly. Circ. 70,000.
**Needs:** Ethnic, contemporary romance. Receives 30-40 unsolicited mss/month. Buys 6 mss/is-

# Close-up

**Christine French Clark**
*Jack and Jill, Humpty Dumpty*

It's a hot day in late September at the editorial offices of the Children's Better Health Institute in Indianapolis and editor Christine Clark is checking the paste-up copy of a short story about snowmen for the February issue of *Jack and Jill*. "We plan our Christmas issue in July," says Clark, pointing out a problem she encounters with authors: They simply are not aware of the six to eight month lead time.

Such editorial policy is not just for *Jack and Jill* (for ages 6-8), but also for *Humpty Dumpty* (4-6 years), the other magazine Clark edits, plus the five other children's publications based there. They are: *Turtle* (2-5 years); *Children's Playmate* (5-7 years); *Child Life* (7-9 years); *Children's Digest* (8-10 years); and *Medical Detective* (10-12 years). The seven magazines from one office provide graduated reading for children from crib to junior high age.

Thus from one address 52 issues go out each year. Translated into story markets that's about 32 each for *HD* and *J&J*, or more than 200 short stories a year for all the publications. Although occasionally stories are staff-written to fill a hole in a special issue, the senior editor *relies* on freelancers. Also to a writer's advantage, the four editors (Clark plus Beth Wood Thomas, Steve Charles, and Elizabeth Rinck) work together, exchanging ideas and manuscripts, especially if a story seems inappropriate for their particular readers.

But the assignment is a tough one. Children's stories are more difficult to write than adult fiction. "The shorter the story, the harder it is to write," says Clark. The writing must be tight, succinct, yet full of action—preferably in only 1,200 words (1,800 tops) for *Jack & Jill*; 600 words work for *Humpty Dumpty*. Also a young reader needs a "hook" to draw him into the story; otherwise "you've lost him."

Stories published by the Health Institute have a health orientation. But that doesn't mean a preachy tone or a sledge-hammer message. Kids respond to subtle suggestions. All stories don't have to be health-related, Clark explains. "Some are just pure fun."

That means fun for adults, too. If *they* like it, it's a good indication children will also. What the editors *don't* like in stories is violence. No guns unless it's an historical war story. Also avoid sex stereotypes (fewer than half of American mothers stay at home), and slang—unless it's natural—can date a story or confine it geographically.

Kids today aren't all that different, but they are more sophisticated, and it's important to stay current. Certain anachronistic expressions indicate that writers are not quite in touch. Passé expressions are "blackboard," "schoolhouse," even "card catalog," which in today's schools is usually a computer center.

"Right away, you can tell from the manuscript if the author has children, works with or knows children well." Clark speaks from her own experience as a freelance children's writer, a Sunday School teacher, scout leader and stepmother of an 11-year-old. "One of our best authors is a junior high teacher," she says. "His dialogue is funny and right on the mark."

The editors seek freelancers who *like* to write for children—and not those who want to make money or find a "home" for their writing school assignments, many of which have the same themes and titles and end up on these editors' desks. Although the staffs are small and the editors work hard, Clark urges writers to submit more stories. "We'd rather have many that we can choose from."

sue; 72 mss/year. Length: 2,000-3,000 words average. Occasionally critiques rejected mss. Appeals highly to black and beginning unpublished writers.
**How to Contact:** Query first or send complete ms. Reports in 2 weeks on queries; 3-4 weeks on mss. SASE for ms. Simultaneous and photocopied submissions OK. Accepts computer printout submissions. Prefers letter-quality. Sample copy and fiction guidelines free.
**Payment:** Pays $45-100.
**Terms:** Pays on acceptance for first rights. Publication copyrighted.

**ISAAC ASIMOV'S SCIENCE FICTION MAGAZINE (II)**, Davis Publications, Inc., 380 Lexington Ave., New York NY 10017. Editor: Gardner Dozois. Magazine: 5³/₁₆x7³/₈, (trim size); 192 pages; 29 lb news paper; 70 lb to 8 pt CIS cover stock; illustrations; photos. Magazine consists of science fiction and fantasy stories for adults and young adults. 13 issues a year. Estab. 1977. Circ. 120,000.
**Needs:** Science fiction and fantasy. No horror or psychic/supernatural. Buys 10 mss/issue. Publishes short shorts. Receives approximately 800 unsolicited fiction mss each month. Approximately 50% of fiction is agented. Length: up to 20,000 words. Critiques rejected mss "when there is time." Sometimes recommends other markets.
**How to Contact:** Send complete ms with SASE. Photocopied submissions OK. Accepts computer printout submissions. Strongly prefers letter-quality. Reports in 4-8 weeks on mss. Publishes ms 6-12 months after acceptance. Free fiction guidelines with legal-size SASE. Sample copy $2.
**Payment:** 6¢/word for stories up to 7,500 words long, 4¢/word for stories over 12,500 long, $450 for stories between those limits.
**Terms:** Pays on acceptance for first North American serial rights plus specified foreign rights, as explained in contract. Very rarely buys reprints. Sends galleys to author. Publication copyrighted.
**Tips:** We are "looking for character stories rather than those emphasizing technology or science. New writers will do best with a story under 10,000 words. Every new science fiction or fantasy film seems to 'inspire' writers—and this is not a desirable trend. We consider every submission. We published several first stories last year—two of these authors were nominated for major awards. Be sure to be familiar with our magazine and the type of story we like; workshops and lots of practice help."

**JACK AND JILL**, The Benjamin Franklin Literary & Medical Society, Inc., 1100 Waterway Blvd., Box 567, Indianapolis IN 46206. (317)636-8881. Editor: Christine French Clark. Children's magazine of articles, stories and activities many with a health, safety, exercise or nutritional-oriented theme, ages 6-8 years. Monthly except February/March, April/May, June/July, August/September. Estab. 1938.
**Needs:** Science fiction, mystery, sports, adventure, historical fiction and humor. Health-related stories with a subtle lesson. No religious subjects. Length: 500-1,500 words.
**How to Contact:** Send complete ms with SASE. Reports in 10 weeks on mss. Sample copy 75¢. Free fiction guidelines with SASE.
**Payment:** 4¢/word.
**Terms:** Pays on publication for all rights.
**Tips:** "Try to present health material in a positive—not a negative—light. Use humor and a light approach wherever possible without minimizing the seriousness of the subject."

**THE JEWISH MONTHLY**, B'nai B'rith International, 1640 Rhode Island Ave. NW, Washington DC 20036. (202)857-6645. Editor: Marc Silver. Jewish general interest magazine that publishes occasional short stories; journalistic articles (political, cultural, sociological), and book reviews. Family audience. Monthly. Estab. 1886. Circ. 200,000.
**Needs:** Ethnic, historical, humor, literary, and religious. Receives 2 unsolicited mss/month. Buys 2 mss/year. Length: 3,000 words average; 1,000 words minimum; 5,000 words maximum. Occasionally critiques rejected mss.
**How to Contact:** Send complete ms. Reports in 1 month. Publishes ms 3-9 months after acceptance. SASE. Photocopied submissions OK. Sample copy $1.

**Payment:** 10-20¢/word; 2 contributor's copies.
**Terms:** Pays on publication for first North American serial rights. Publication copyrighted.

**JIVE (I, II)**, Lexington Library, 355 Lexington Ave., New York NY 10017. (212)391-1400. Senior Editor: Judy Andrews. Magazine: 76 pages; photos on cover, inside. Confession magazine with Black male and female perspectives on romance and relationships in the 80s, for women between the ages of 18-35 (black). Buys 6 mss/issue, as well as special features, on fashion and beauty.
**Needs:** Confession. "No unrealistic, Black stereotypes, untimely stories." Length: 3,000 words minimum; 5,000 words maximum. Critiques rejected mss. Recommends other markets.
**How to Contact:** Send complete ms with SASE "with a cover letter with writer's background, interests, hobbies, why they're interested in our magazine, and a synopsis of their manuscript." Reports in 4 weeks on mss. Free sample copy; fiction guidelines with SASE.
**Payment:** $75-250; subscription to magazine and 1 contributor's copy. $1.50 charge for extras.
**Terms:** Pays on publication for one-time rights and assignments on work-for-hire basis. Publication copyrighted.
**Tips:** "Be enthusiastic, creative, and send material that reflects black relationships with realistic and pleasant endings. We appreciate that there are a number of talented writers struggling for work. We feel that our magazines give them an opportunity to get published, get paid and improve their writing skills. We also give writers advice on ways of improving their grammar, vocabulary, sentence structure, etc. We try to encourage writers to be accurate, professional, and serious about their work." Also publishes *Intimacy*.

**JUNIOR TRAILS (I, II)**, Gospel Publishing House, 1445 Boonville Ave., Springfield MO 65802. (417)862-2781. Editor: Charles Ford. Elementary Editor: John Maempa. Magazine: 8½x11; 4 pages; 36 lb coated offset paper; coat and matte cover stock; art illustrations; photos. A Sunday School take-home paper of nature articles and fictional stories that apply Christian principles to everyday living for 9-12 year old children. Weekly. Estab. 1920. Circ. 85,000.
**Needs:** Contemporary, religious/inspirational, and juvenile. Adventure stories are welcome. No Biblical fiction or science fiction. Buys 2 mss/issue. Publishes short shorts. Length: 1,000-1,800 words.
**How to Contact:** Send complete ms with SASE. Accepts computer printout submissions. Reports 4-6 weeks on mss. Free sample copy and guidelines.
**Payment:** 2½-3¢/word. 3 free author's copies.
**Terms:** Pays on acceptance for first rights.
**Tips:** "Know the age level and direct stories relevant to that age group. Since junior-age children (grades 5&6) enjoy action, fiction provides a vehicle for communicating moral/spiritual principles in a dramatic framework. Fiction, if well done, can be a powerful tool for relating Christian principles. It must, however, be realistic and believable in its development." Published new writers within the last year.

**LADIES' HOME JOURNAL (III)**, (Published by Family Media, Inc.), 3 Park Ave., New York NY 10016. Editor-in-Chief: Myrna Blyth. Fiction/Books Editor: Mary Lou Mullen. Magazine: 190 pages; 34-38 lb coated paper; 65 lb coated cover; illustrations and photos.
**Needs:** Book mss and short stories, *accepted only through an agent*. Return of unsolicited material cannot be guaranteed. Publishes short shorts of 5,000 words approximately.
**How to Contact:** Cover letter with ms (credits). Publishes ms 4-12 months after acceptance.
**Terms:** Rarely buys reprints.
**Tips:** "Our readers like stories, especially those that have emotional impact. We are using fiction every month, whether it's an excerpt from a novel or a short story. Stories about relationships between people—husband/wife—mother/son—seem to be subjects that can be explored effectively in short stories. Our reader's mail and surveys attest to this fact that readers enjoy our fiction. Fiction today is stronger than ever. Beginners can be optimistic; if they have talent, I do believe that talent will be discovered." Published new writers within the last year.

**LEATHERNECK (II, IV)**, Magazine of the Marines, Marine Corps Association, Box 1775, Quantico VA 22134. (703)640-6161. Editor: William Z. H. White. Magazine with "features and photographs of interest to Marines, past and present, as well as their families." Estab. 1916. Circ. 92,000.
**Needs:** Adventure, cartoons, historical, humor/satire, men's, prose poem, and inspirational. "Stories must relate to Marines or their families. Receives 3-4 unsolicited mss/month. Buys 6 mss/year. Length: 1,000 words average. Occasionally comments on a rejected ms.
**How to Contact:** Send complete manuscript. Reports in 1 month on mss. SASE. Photocopied submissions OK. Sample copy for $1 and SAE. Fiction guidelines free for 10x12 SAE.
**Payment:** Pays $50/printed page.
**Terms:** Pays on acceptance for all rights. Publication copyrighted.
**Tips:** Best to query first.

**‡LEFTHANDER MAGAZINE (IV)**, Lefthanders International, Box 8249, Topeka KS 66608. (913)234-2177. Editor: Susan Menendez. Magazine: 32 pages; 70 lb gloss paper and cover; illustrations; photos. "We accept fiction for juvenile insert, ages 7-13, which has some connection to lefthanders." Bimonthly. Estab. 1975. Circ. 14,500.
**Needs:** Young adult/teen (10-18 years); special interest: lefthandedness. Buys 3 fiction mss/year. Publishes ms 2 months after acceptance. Length: 750-1,000 words average. Occasionally critiques rejected mss.
**How to Contact:** Query first. Reports in 3 weeks on queries; 3 weeks on mss. SASE for query and ms. Accepts computer printouts including dot-matrix. Sample copy $2. Fiction guidelines free for business size SAE and 1 first class stamp.
**Payment:** Pays $40-75.
**Terms:** Pays on publication for all rights. Publication copyrighted.

**LIGHTED PATHWAY (II)**, Church of God Publishing House (Pathway Press), 922 Montgomery Ave., Cleveland TN 37311. (615)476-4512. Editor: Marcus V. Hand. Magazine: 8½x11; 28 pages; b&w photos. Christian, evangelical, youth inspiration magazine (ages 15-25) with at least two fiction short stories per issue. Monthly. Estab. 1929. Circ. 26,000.
**Needs:** Adventure, contemporary, feminist, historical (general), humor/satire, juvenile, religious/inspirational, and young adult. "Real life problems, no profanity." Receives 1-24 unsolicited fiction mss/month. Buys 2 (minimum) mss/issue; 24 (minimum) mss/year. Length: 800-1,600 words preferred; 2,000 words maximum. Occasionally critiques rejected mss.
**How to Contact:** Query first or send complete ms. SASE always. Simultaneous and previously published submissions OK sometimes. Accepts computer printout submissions. Prefers letter-quality. Reports in 3 weeks on queries and mss. Free sample copy with SAE and free fiction guidelines with SASE.
**Payment:** 2-4¢/word; 3 contributor's copies. 75¢ charge for extras.
**Terms:** Pays on acceptance for first North American serial rights and one-time rights. Publication copyrighted.
**Tips:** "Study a sample. Make story exciting."

**LIGUORIAN (I, II, IV)**, "A Leading Catholic Magazine", Liguori Publications, 1 Liguori Dr., Liguori MO 63057. (314)464-2500. Editor-in-Chief: Norman J. Muckerman, CSS.R. Managing Editor: Francine M. O'Connor. Magazine: 5x8½; 64 pages. "*Liguorian* is a Catholic magazine aimed at helping our readers to live a full Christian life. We publish articles for families, young people, children, religious and singles—all with the same aim." Monthly. Estab. 1913. Circ. 500,000.
**Needs:** Religious/inspirational, young adult, and senior citizen/retirement (with moral Christian thrust). "Stories submitted to *Liguorian* must have as their goal the lifting up of the reader to a higher Christian view of values and goals. We are not interested in contemporary works that lack purpose or are of questionable moral value." Receives approximately 25 unsolicited fiction mss/month. Buys 4-5 mss/year. Length: 1,500-2,000 words preferred. Also publishes short shorts. Occasionally critiques rejected mss "if we feel the author is capable of giving us something we

need even though this story did not suit us." Occasionally recommends other markets.

**How to Contact:** Send complete ms with SASE. Accepts computer printout submissions. Prefers letter-quality. Accepts disc submissions compatible with TRS-80 Model III. Prefers hard copy with disc submission. Reports in 6 weeks on mss. Free sample copy and fiction guidelines.

**Payment:** 7-10¢/word and 6 contributor's copies. Offers 50% kill fee for assigned mss not published.

**Terms:** Pays on acceptance for all rights. Publication copyrighted.

**Tips:** "First read several issues containing short stories. We look for originality and creative input in each story we read. Since most editors must wade through mounds of manuscripts each month, consideration for the editor requires that the market be studied, the manuscript be carefully presented, and polished before submitting. Our publication uses only one story a month. Compare this with the 25 or more we receive over the transom each month. Also, many fiction mss are written without a specific goal or thrust, i.e., an interesting incident that goes nowhere is *not a story*. We believe fiction is a highly effective mode for transmitting the Christian message and also provides a good balance in an unusually heavy issue." Published new writers within the last year.

**LIVE,** The Gospel Publishing House, 1445 Boonville, Springfield MO 65802. Editor: Kenneth D. Barney. A Sunday School take-home paper for adults containing articles and stories of believable characters working out their problems according to Bible principles. Weekly. Circ. 200,000.

**Needs:** Religious/inspirational. No controversial stories about such subjects as race, feminism, war, or capital punishment. Buys 2 mss/issue. Length: 1,000-2,000 words.

**How to Contact:** Send complete ms with SASE. Reports in 6 weeks on mss. Free sample copy only with SASE. Free fiction guidelines only with SASE.

**Payment:** 3¢/word (first rights); 2¢/word (second rights).

**Terms:** Pays on acceptance for one-time rights.

**LIVING MESSAGE (II),** The Anglican Church of Canada, Box 820, Petrolia, Ontario N0N Canada 1R0. (519)882-2497. Editor: Rita Baker. "*Living Message* calls forth from its readers a Christian response to family and social concerns. Encourages and aids the ministry of clergy and lay people. Especially interested in human rights. Our readers are committed Christians, especially of the Anglican Church (Episcopal). Readers want to know about Anglican work in all areas of the world. They want to know how they can minister to people in local communities." Monthly except July and August. Estab. 1889. Circ. 10,000.

**Needs:** Literary, contemporary, and humor. "We do not require religious/inspirational stories. No sentimental writing; no moralizing please!" Buys 1 ms/issue. Receives approximately 10 unsolicited fiction mss/month. Length: 1,000-1,500 words. Critiques rejected mss "when there is time."

**How to Contact:** Send complete ms with SAE and IRC (not US stamps). Reports in 1 month on ms. Publishes ms 3-6 months after acceptance. Free sample copy.

**Payment:** $20-30; 2 free author's copies; extras are free on request.

**Terms:** Pays on acceptance for second serial (reprint) and first North American serial rights. Buys reprints. Publication copyrighted.

**Tips:** "Don't write long letters to the editor. Make sure you study the market; read the whole magazine, not just the fiction. We receive very few good stories. If you can write simply, with insight and sensitivity, let us see your work. If it's done well, fiction can be highly effective in informing and helping the reader to understand and respond to an issue—to know what it feels like to be a certain person in a certain situation. Stories do not have to be overly 'religious' to reflect the truth about God's children." Mss are rejected because they are "too long or there is too much moralizing. We want to publish stories of high quality, but we are unable to pay adequate rates for these. Therefore, we probably do not attract highly skilled writers. However, we sometimes 'discover' a beginning writer who has potential."

**LIVING WITH TEENAGERS (II),** Baptist Sunday School Board, 127 9th Ave. North, Nashville TN 37234. (615)251-2273. Editor: Jimmy Hester. Magazine: 8x11; 52 pages; illustrations; photos. Magazine especially designed "to enrich the parent-teen relationship with reading material from a Christian perspective" for Southern Baptist parents of teenagers. Quarterly. Estab. 1978. Circ. 35,000.

**Needs:** Religious/inspirational and parent-teen relationships. Nothing not related to parent-teen relationships or from a Christian perspective. Buys 2 mss/issue. Receives approximately 50 unsolicited fiction mss/month. Length: 600-1,200 words (short shorts).

**How to Contact:** Cover letter with reason for writing article; credentials for writing. Query with clips of published work or send complete ms. SASE always. Reports in 2 months on both queries and mss. Free sample copy with 9x12 SAE and proper postage.

**Payment:** 5¢/published word. 3 free author's copies.

**Terms:** Pays on acceptance for all and first rights. Publication copyrighted.

**Tips:** Mss are rejected most often because "subject is inappropriate, the events and characters are unrealistic. Sometimes a fictitious story can communicate a principle in the parent-youth relationship quite well." Published new writers within the last year.

**LOLLIPOPS, LADYBUGS AND LUCKY STARS (II)**, Good Apple, Inc., Box 299, Carthage IL 62321. (217)357-3981. Editor: Cindy Stansbery. Newspaper: 11x16; 32 pages; illustrations. "Preschool-2nd grade publication for teachers and their students. All educational material. Short stories, poems, activities, math, gameboards." 5 times/year. Estab. 1980. Circ. 12,000.

**Needs:** Preschool (0-4 years). "Include a story that has educational value to it. No rabbit stories!" Receives 30-40 unsolicited mss/month. Fiction mss vary per issue. Publishes ms within 1 or 1½ years after acceptance. Length: 900 words average; 500 words minimum; 1,800 words maximum. Occasionally critiques rejected mss. Recommends other markets.

**How to Contact:** Query first or write for guidelines and a free sample copy. Reports in 1 week on queries; 2 weeks on mss. SASE for ms. Simultaneous submissions OK. Accepts computer printouts including dot-matrix. Sample copy for 9½x12½ SAE. Fiction guidelines free.

**Payment:** Depends on story.

**Terms:** Pays on publication for all rights. Publication copyrighted.

**Tips:** "*Lollipops, Ladybugs and Lucky Stars* has found that, even though it's educational, children love stories!"

**THE LOOKOUT (II)**, Standard Publishing, 8121 Hamilton Ave., Cincinnati OH 45231. (513)931-4050. Editor: Mark A. Taylor. Magazine: 8½x11; 16 pages; newsprint paper; newsprint cover stock; illustrations; photos. Inspirational/motivational publication "for Christian adults who need to be informed, to get tips for building Christian marriages and families, to find help in living a Christian life in a secular world." Weekly. Estab. 1894. Circ. 160,000 + .

**Needs:** Religious/inspirational, men's, women's, and young adults. No predictable, preachy material. Taboos are blatant sex, swear words, and drinking alcohol. Buys 1 ms/issue. Length: 1,200-2,000 words.

**How to Contact:** Send complete ms with SASE. Accepts computer printout submissions. Prefers letter-quality. Reports in 2 months on ms. Publishes ms 2-12 months after acceptance. Sample copy 50¢. Free guidelines with legal-sized SASE.

**Payment:** 4-5¢/word for first rights. 4¢/word for other rights. Free author's copies.

**Terms:** Pays on acceptance for simultaneous, first, second serial (reprint), first North American serial, and one-time rights. Buys reprints.

**Tips:** "No queries please. Send us a believable story which is inspirational and helpful but down to earth." Published new writers within the last year.

**LOS ANGELES READER (IV)**, 8471 Melrose Ave., Los Angeles CA 90069. (213)655-8810. Editor: Dan Barton. Newspaper: 8½x14; 50 pages newspaper paper; newspaper cover stock; illustrations; photos. Newspaper of features and reviews with emphasis on Los Angeles themes/subjects. "We publish little fiction (3-4 per year); may be experimental but not off-the-wall. Readers are young (ages 20-40), well educated, affluent, sophisticated." Weekly. Estab. 1978. Circ. 82,000.

**Needs:** Receives less that 12 unsolicited fiction mss/month. Buys 3-4 mss/year. Length: 1,000 words minimum; 4,000 words maximum; 1,500 words average. Publishes short shorts to 1,000 words. Occasionally critiques rejected mss.
**How to Contact:** Cover letter with name, address, social security number. Send complete ms with SASE. Photocopied submissions OK. Accepts computer printout submissions. Prefers letter-quality. Reports in 2 months on mss. Free sample copy for 9x12 SAE and $1.25 postage. Free fiction guidelines for business-sized SAE and 20¢ postage.
**Payment:** Pays $50-200; 2 free contributor's copies; $1 charge for extras.
**Terms:** Pays on publication for first North American serial rights. Publication copyrighted.
**Tips:** "Stories should have LA setting or theme (with rare exceptions). Resist the urge to submit satires/parodies/jokes/dream stories."

**THE LUTHERAN JOURNAL**, Outlook Publications, Inc., 7317 Cahill Rd., Minneapolis MN 55435. (612)941-6830. Editor: Rev. A.U. Deye. A family magazine to provide wholesome and inspirational reading material for the enjoyment and enrichment of Lutherans. Quarterly. Estab. 1936. Circ. 136,000.
**Needs:** Literary, contemporary, religious/inspirational, romance (historical), men's, senior citizen/retirement, women's, and young adult. Must be appropriate for distribution in the churches. Buys 2-4 mss/issue. Length: 1,000-2,500 words.
**How to Contact:** Send complete ms with SASE. Accepts computer printout submissions. Free sample copy with SASE (52¢ postage).
**Payment:** $10-25. 6 free author's copies.
**Terms:** Pays on publication for all and first rights.

**LUTHERAN WOMEN (II)**, Lutheran Church Women, 2900 Queen Ln., Philadelphia PA 19129. (215)438-2200. Editor-in-Chief: Ms. Terry Schutz. Magazine: 7x10; 32 pages; 50 lb paper and cover; illustrations; photos. Articles and fiction addressing issues and concerns of Christian women today "who are more interested in insightful formulations of questions than in pat answers." Published 10 times/year. Estab. 1962. Circ. 35,000.
**Needs:** "We look for stories showing growth of character and understanding. Explicitly Christian or religious themes are not essential. We do not want to see anything sentimental, what is usually thought of as 'inspirational.' " Receives approximately 50 unsolicited fiction mss/month. Buys 1 ms/issue, 10 mss/year. Length: 500 words minimum; 2,500 words maximum.
**How to Contact:** Send complete ms with SASE. Simultaneous, photocopied, and previously published submissions OK. Reports in 12 weeks on mss. Free fiction guidelines with SASE. Sample copy for 75¢.
**Payment:** $20-50 and 2 contributor's copies. 75¢ charge for extras.
**Terms:** Pays on publication for simultaneous and one-time rights. Publication copyrighted.
**Tips:** "Become familiar with our magazine and with basic rules of fiction; be credible, don't be solemn, don't be afraid of the ordinary, write well. We reject mss because they are not appropriate for our audience or purpose. Best come from writers who are familiar with what we do."

**‡MAD (IV)**, EC Creations, 485 Madison Ave., New York NY 10022. (212)752-7685. Editor: John Ficarra/Nick Meglin. Magazine: 48 pages; illustrations; occasional photos. "Although we are a 'fiction' magazine we never publish straight prose pieces. *MAD* is a visual magazine and writers should submit art notes accompanying their submissions. *MAD* appeals to an extremely wide audience, especially young people." Published every 6 weeks. Estab. 1952. Circ. "around one million."
**Needs:** Humor/satire. Write for specific needs. Nothing "bland." Receives "lots" unsolicited mss each month. Buys "lots" mss/issue. Publishes ms 4-12 months after acceptance.
**How to Contact:** Query first. SASE. Fiction guidelines for SAE.
**Payment:** Pays $300-550/MAD page.
**Terms:** Pays on acceptance for all rights. Publication copyrighted.
**Tips:** "Write on anything or everything that catches your fancy and is funny. Especially prized are

articles on current hot trends (topics might be rock videos, computers, etc.). Send us a paragraph or two explaining the premise of your article with 3 or 4 examples of how you intend to carry it through, describing the action and visual content of each example. Rough sketches are welcomed but not necessary. Remember! No straight text pieces! MAD is a visual magazine! You can include more than one idea in a submission. Each is judged on its own merit, have fun! Don't be afraid to be stupid and don't self-edit yourself because *you* don't think it's what *you* think *we're* looking for. Sometimes *we* don't know what we're looking for until we see it! Make us earn our money as editors.''

**MADEMOISELLE MAGAZINE**, Condé Nast Publications, Inc., 350 Madison Ave., New York NY 10017. (212)880-8690. Editor: Amy Levin. Fiction Editor: Eileen Schnurr. Fashion magazine for women from ages 18-34 with articles of interest to women; beauty and health tips, features, home and food, fiction. Audience interested in self-improvement, curious about trends, interested in updating lifestyle and pursuing a career. Monthly. Estab. 1935. Circ. 1 million.
**Needs:** Literary, contemporary, men's, women's, and very occasionally excerpts from novels. Buys 1 ms/issue, 12/year. Length:7-25 pages.
**How to Contact:** Send complete ms with SASE. Reports in 8 weeks. Publishes ms up to a year after acceptance. Free fiction guidelines with SASE.
**Payment:** $1,000 minimum for short shorts; $1,500 for short stories.
**Terms:** Pays on acceptance for first North American serial rights. Occasionally buys reprints.
**Tips:** "We want stories that have appeal for young single women, and we continue in the *Mademoiselle* tradition of publishing fiction of literary quality. Be sure to see the listing in Contest and Awards section for guidelines for *Mademoiselle's* Fiction Writers Contest.''

‡**THE MAGAZINE FOR CHRISTIAN YOUTH! (II)**, The United Methodist Publishing House, Box 801, Nashville TN 37202. (615)749-6432. Editor: S.D. Fowler. Magazine: 8½x11; 48 pages; illustrations; photos. "The purpose of *Youth*! is to help teenagers live out the Christian faith in contemporary culture. Includes subject matter relevant to teens; focus is on the individual rather than youth groups for junior and senior high. Monthly. Estab. 1985.
**Needs:** Adventure, contemporary, ethnic, fantasy, humor/satire, mainstream, religious/inspirational, young adult romance, science fiction, young adult/teen (10-18 years). "No mss that *preach* at readers, rather make them think, discover for themselves. Don't want sex-role or racial stereotype, or stereotypes of teenage 'pretty people.' '' Receives 100-150 unsolicited mss/month. Buys 2-3 mss/issue; 40 mss/year. Publishes ms 6-12 months after acceptance. Length: 2,000-2,500 words. Publishes short shorts, 700-2,500 words.
**How to Contact:** Send complete ms with cover letter (with writer's experience). Reports in 2 months. SASE for ms. Simultaneous and photocopied submissions OK. Accepts computer printouts including dot-matrix. Sample copy and fiction guidelines free for legal sized SASE.
**Payment:** Pays .04/word and contributor's copies.
**Terms:** Pays on acceptance for first rights. Publication copyrighted.
**Tips:** "We want stories that involve the reader's mind and feelings. Simplistic situations and sentimental resolutions do not help Christian youth deal with their world. Some stories, if written well, can involve teenage readers in the language, names, and events of the past. Fables and fantasy are often strengthened by such language. However, contemporary stories must include characters that talk like contemporary young people. This does not mean a heavy use of slang. We are delighted when we discover a surprise twist, a lovable and laughable character, a simple clever use of words, or a real faith experience. We treasure creativity in use of words, a story line, and format.''

**MAINE LIFE (I)**, Atlantic Publishing Group, 8 St., Pierce St., Lewiston ME 04240. (207)782-5952. Editor: Timothy E. Rice. Magazine: 8x10¾; 80-96 pages; glossy stock paper; varied cover stock; illustrations; photos. "Theme is found in the title of our magazine—'*Maine Life*, past, present and future. The people and places of Maine emphasize the contemporary.' Our readers are people who love Maine and its unique environment, what it was like and especially what it is like now." Published 6 times/year. Estab. 1945. Circ. 30,000.

**Needs:** "Upbeat or innovative material that will capture the interest of a young, professional readership welcome." Buys 1-2 mss/year. Receives 2-3 unsolicited fiction mss each month. Publishes short shorts. Length: 1,000-4,000 words. Critiques rejected mss "when there is time." Sometimes recommends other markets.

**How to Contact:** Send complete ms with SASE with cover letter of "why the writer feels the story pertains to our magazine." Reports ASAP. Free sample copy with SASE, from Atlantic Publishing Group, Inc.

**Payment:** 7¢/word; 2 free author's copies.

**Terms:** Pays on publication for first rights.

**Tips:** "I'm a fiction fan and will publish material in the future if I feel it's appropriate. I believe an interest in good fiction is common to the readers of most leisure-type magazines, and more outlets for writers are needed. Discard pretension. Write as you would speak. Write from personal experience, using people you've actually known or met as characters. If writing comes hard, begin by writing anything at all, then revise." Published new writers within the last year.

**MATURE LIVING (II)**, Sunday School Board of the Southern Baptist Conv., MSN 140, 127 Ninth Ave. N., Nashville TN 37234. (615)251-2191. Editor: Jack Gulledge. Fiction Editor: Zada Malugen. Magazine: 8½x11; 48 pages; non-glare paper; slick cover stock; illustrations; photos. "Our magazine is Christian in content and the material required is what would appeal to 60 + age group (mainly Southern Baptists): inspirational, instructional, nostalgic, humorous. Our magazine is distributed mainly through churches (especially Southern Baptist churches) that buy the magazine in bulk and distribute it to members in this age group." Monthly. Estab. 1977. Circ. 306,000.

**Needs:** Contemporary, religious/inspirational, humor, and senior citizen/retirement. Avoid all types of pornography, drugs, liquor, horror, science fiction, and stories demeaning to the elderly. Buys 1 ms/issue. Length: 425-1,475 words (prefers 900).

**How to Contact:** Send complete ms with SASE. Reports in 6 weeks on mss. Publishes ms an average of 1 year after acceptance. Sample copy $1. Free guidelines with SASE.

**Payment:** $21-73; 3 free author's copies. 75¢ charge for extras.

**Terms:** Pays on acceptance for all and first rights 15% less. Rarely buys reprints. Publication copyrighted.

**Tips:** Mss are rejected because they are too long or subject matter unsuitable. "Our reader seem to enjoy an occasional short piece of fiction. It must be believable, however, and present senior adults in a favorable light." Published new writers within the last year.

**MATURE YEARS (II, IV)**, United Methodist Publishing House, 201 Eighth Ave. S., Nashville TN 37202. (615)749-6438. Editor: Daisy D. Warren. Magazine helps persons in and nearing retirement to appropriate the resources of the Christian faith as they seek to face the problems and opportunities related to aging. Quarterly. Estab. 1953.

**Needs:** Religious/inspirational, nostalgia. "We don't want anything poking fun at old age, saccharine stories or anything not for older adults." Buys 3-4 mss/issue, 12-16 mss/year. Needs at least one unsolicited fiction ms each month. Length: 1,000-1,800 words.

**How to Contact:** Send complete ms with SASE. Reports in 2 months on mss. Usually publishes ms 12-18 months after acceptance. Free sample copy with 10½x11 SAE and 67¢ postage.

**Payment:** 4¢/word.

**Terms:** Pays on acceptance for all and first rights. Publication copyrighted.

**Tips:** "We need more *good* short stories, settings clearly described, characterization ample, and main point clear. Should be rich and meaty, containing older characters readers can identify with, inspiring people to lead happier, more interesting, more meaningful lives. Stories rejected most often because they are too superficial and so simple that they insult the imagination. Make every word count."

**McCALL'S (I, II)**, The McCall's Publishing Co., 230 Park Ave., New York NY 10169. (212)551-9500. Editor: Elizabeth Sloan. Fiction Editor: Helen DelMonte. General women's magazine for "adult women of considerable literary sensibility who are interested in every facet of family life as well as the world around them." Monthly. Estab. 1876. Circ. 5,000,000.

**Needs:** Literary, contemporary, humor, love, and family stories. "No vague mood pieces; character sketches that aren't real stories; slick, formula stories; stories that are heavily contrived; depressing stories that offer no redeeming catharsis; stories that have no discernible point." Buys approximately 16 mss/year. Receives approximately 1,000 unsolicited fiction mss/month. Length: 1,800-4,000 words. Critiques rejected mss "if story is a strong possibility for purchase but in need of revision."

**How to Contact:** Send complete ms with SASE. Reports in 1-2 months on ms. Free guidelines with SASE.

**Payment:** $1,500-3,000.

**Terms:** Pays on acceptance for first North American serial rights. Publication copyrighted.

**MEDICAL DETECTIVE (II)**, Children's Better Health Institute, Benjamin Franklin Literary and Medical Society, 1100 Waterway Blvd., Box 567, Indianapolis IN 46206. (317)636-8881. Executive Editor: Beth Wood Thomas. Fiction Editor: Stephen D. Charles. "*Medical Detective* contains stories and articles dealing with advancements in medical technology, factual stories of famous medical investigations, and medical mysteries. Recent topics included the eradication of smallpox, discovery of polio vaccine, use of lasers in eye surgery, and how wild plants saved the Pilgrims from malnourishment, Center for Disease Control investigation of bubonic plague in New Mexico. Introduces early teens and adults to the 'mysterious' aspects of health and illness." Quarterly. Estab. 1981.

**Needs:** Fictional medical mysteries with factual basis. Receives 12-15 unsolicited fiction mss/month. Buys 4-6 mss/month; 16-24 mss/year. Length: 500 words minimum; 1,500 words maximum; 1,000 words average. Occasionally critiques rejected mss.

**How to Contact:** Send complete ms with SASE. Photocopied submissions OK. Accepts computer printout submissions. Prefers letter-quality. Reports in 6-10 weeks on mss. Publishes ms an average of 1 year after acceptance. Sample copy for 75¢.

**Payment:** Pays 6¢/word minimum; 2 free contributor's copies.

**Terms:** Pays on publication for all rights. Publication copyrighted.

**Tips:** "Send for the editorial requirements and copy(ies) of the magazine. Write on a subject you can handle."

**MESSENGER OF THE SACRED HEART (II)**, Apostleship of Prayer, 661 Greenwood Ave., Toronto, Ontario M4J 4B3 Canada. (416)466-1195. Editor: Rev. F.J. Power, S.J. Fiction Editor: Mary Pujolas. Magazine: 7x10; 24 pages; coated paper; selfcover; illustrations; photos. Magazine for Canadian and US Catholics who are interested in the Apostleship of Prayer as a way to lead a Christian life. Monthly. Estab. 1891. Circ. 16,000.

**Needs:** Religious/inspirational, psychic/supernatural, science fiction, romance, western, mystery, adventure, and humor. No gay/lesbian, erotica, confession, or feminist stories. Buys 1 ms/issue. Length: 1,500 words. Recommends other markets.

**How to Contact:** Send complete ms with SAE or IRC. Reports in 1 month on mss. Sample copy $1.

**Payment:** 2¢/word. 3 free author's copies.

**Terms:** Pays on acceptance for first North American serial rights. Rarely buys reprints.

**Tips:** "Use a dictionary to ensure words are used correctly. Develop a plot that does not peter out but reaches a climax. Do not preach but get the message across through plot and characters. A light touch and a sense of humor help."

**‡MICHIGAN (IV), The Magazine of the Detroit News**, The Evening News Association, *(The Detroit News)*, 615 W. Lafayette, Detroit MI 48231. (313)222-2620. Editor: Lisa K. Velders. Magazine: 10¾x12; number of pages varies; illustrations; photos. Michigan authors or themes for broad audience. Weekly. Plans special fiction issue in future.

**Needs:** Adventure, condensed novel, contemporary, historical, horror, humor/satire, literary, mainstream, regional, science fiction, serialized/excerpted novel, suspense/mystery. Receives "dozen" unsolicited mss/month. Buys dozen mss/year. Agented fiction 20%. Length: 2,500 words average; 3,000 words maximum. Also publishes short shorts. Occasionally critiques rejected mss.

**How to Contact:** Send complete ms with cover letter. Reports in 2-4 weeks on mss. Simultaneous, photocopied submissions and reprints OK. Accepts computer printouts including dot-matrix. Sample copy 75¢ with SAE. Fiction guidelines free.

**Payment:** Pays $200-500.

**Terms:** Pays on publication for first rights. Sends pre-publication galleys to authors. Publication copyrighted.

**Tips:** "I think short stories are making a comeback in Sunday magazines."

**‡MILWAUKEE MAGAZINE (II)**, Quad/Graphics, 312 E. Buffalo St., Milwaukee WI 53202. (414)273-1101. Editor: Charles Sykes. Fiction Editor: Judith Woodburn. Magazine: 8x11; 150-250 pages; glossy cover stock; illustrations; photos. "Regional material/issues related to Milwaukee business, arts, entertainment and personalities" for median age; education and income. Monthly. Circ. 40,000.

**Needs:** Contemporary, feminist, literary, mainstream, regional. "We prefer (strongly) to use Wisconsin writers, and we do not publish fiction regularly." No overt romances, no thinly-veiled historical treatises, no quaint reminiscences. Busy 1-2 fiction mss/year. Publishes ms 2-3 months after acceptance. Length: 5,000 words. Very rarely critiques rejected ms.

**How to Contact:** Send complete ms with cover letter. SASE for ms. Simultaneous and photocopied submissions OK. Accepts computer printouts including dot-matrix. Sample copy $2.25.

**Payment:** Pays $200-300.

**Terms:** Pays on publication for one-time rights. Sends galleys to authors. Publication copyrighted.

**Tips:** Check August issue of each year for contest details.

**MODERN LITURGY**, Resource Publications, Inc., Suite 290, 160 E. Virginia St., San Jose CA 95112. Fiction Editor: Ken Guentert. Magazine for religious leaders, artists, teachers, and worship leaders using "themes from the field of liturgy, the seasons, scripture—especially contemporary parables, and imaginative pieces which express contemporary theology well." Monthly. Estab. 1973. Circ. 15,000.

**Needs:** Religious. Receives 4-6 unsolicited fiction mss/month. Buys 1 ms/issue; 9 mss/year. Length: 500 words minimum; 2,000 words maximum; 1,000 words average. Occasionally critiques rejected mss. Sometimes recommends other markets.

**How to Contact:** Query first with SASE. Reports in 6 weeks on queries and mss. Sample copy $4.

**Payment:** 3¢/word-$30 and 2 contributor's copies.

**Terms:** Pays after publication for all rights. Publication copyrighted.

**Tips:** "Read several copies of published issues, and try to prepare something that the readers will find practical use for in worship or in religious education." Mss are rejected because most "are not appropriate to the readership or to the thematic content plan of our issues. Submit a schedule of personal appearances, lectures, workshops, talks, conferences, that you plan to give in coming months."

**MOMENT MAGAZINE (III, IV)**, Jewish Educational Ventures, 462 Boylston St., Boston MA 02116. (617)536-6252. Editor-in-Chief: Leonard Fein. Managing Editor: Nechama Katz. Magazine: 7¾x10⅞; 64 pages; 45 lb coated paper; 80 lb cover stock; photos. Modern, historical magazine publishing material on intellectual, cultural, and political issues of interest to the Jewish community. Audience is college-educated, liberal, concerned with Jewish affairs. Monthly. Estab. 1975. Circ. 30,000.

**Needs:** Contemporary, ethnic, historical, religious, excerpted novel, and translations. "All fiction should have Jewish content. No sentimental stories about 'Grandma' etc. Do not encourage

Holocaust themes." Receives 60-80 unsolicited fiction mss/month. Buys 0-1 ms/issue, 2-3 mss/year. Length: 1,500 words minimum; 6,000 words maximum; 3,000 words average. Publishes short shorts. Occasionally recommends other markets.
**How to Contact:** Cover letter with bio. Query first or send complete ms. SASE always. Photocopied submissions OK. No multiple submissions. Accepts computer printout submissions. Prefers letter-quality. Reports in 4 weeks on queries; 1-2 months on mss. Publishes ms 1-12 months after acceptance. Sample copy $3.50. Free fiction guidelines for business-sized SAE and 1 first class stamp.
**Payment:** Varies.
**Terms:** Pays on publication for first rights. Publication copyrighted.
**Tips:** "We caution against over-sentimentalized writing which we get way too much of all the time. Query first is helpful, reading stories we've published a must." Published new writers within the last year.

**MOTORCYCLIST**, Petersen Publishing Co., 8490 Sunset Blvd., Los Angeles CA 90069. (213)657-5100. Editor: Art Friedman. Magazine about "motorcycles, tests, product evaluations, and news articles for the 18-35 + aged motorcycle enthusiasts (street bikes only). Monthly. Estab. 1927. Circ. 230,000.
**Needs:** Adventure, horror, humor/satire, literary, and science fiction. Receives 6-8 unsolicited mss/month. Buys 0-1 mss/issue; 2-3 mss/year. Length: 1,000 words average. Nonfiction required with good photos.
**How to Contact:** Send complete ms with SASE. Reports on mss in 2-4 months. No simultaneous or photocopied submissions. Accepts computer printout submissions. Guidelines free.
**Payment:** $25-50.
**Terms:** Pays on publication for all rights. Publication copyrighted.

**MS MAGAZINE (II)**, 119 W. 40th St., New York NY 10018. (212)719-9800. Contact: Fiction Editor. Consciousness-raising magazine for "feminists of all ages," those committed to exploring new lifestyles and changing roles in society. Monthly. Published special fiction issue last year; plans another. Estab. 1972. Circ. 500,000.
**Needs:** All kinds of fiction. Buys 1 ms/issue. Receives approximately 300-400 unsolicited fiction mss/month. Length: 500-3,000 words. Also publishes short shorts to 12 typed pages. Recommends other markets.
**How to Contact:** Mark envelope "Fiction. Must query fiction. It's very difficult to get a manuscript accepted."
**Payment:** Varies. Offers kill fee for assigned mss not published.
**Terms:** Pays on acceptance for first North American serial rights. Publication copyrighted.
**Tips:** "We seek good writing. With the addition of so many new voices the nature of fiction can't help but change for the better, we believe. The market is tough but quality and persevereance usually pay off. Published new writers within the last year. Sponsors college fiction contest.

**MY FRIEND (II), A Magazine for Children**, Daughters of St. Paul, 50 St. Paul's Ave., Boston MA 02130. (617)522-8911. Editor: Sister Mary Anne. Magazine: 7¼x10; 32 pages; smooth, non-glossy paper; smooth, non-glossy cover stock; illustrations; photos. Magazine of "religious truths and positive values for children in a format which is enjoyable and attractive. Each issue contains Bible stories, lives of saints and famous people, short stories, science corner, contests, projects, etc." Monthly during school year (September-June). Estab. 1979. Circ. 16,000.
**Needs:** Juvenile, prose poem, religious/inspirational. Receives 4-5 unsolicited fiction mss/month. Accepts 1-2 mss/issue; 10-20 mss/year. Length: 500 words minimum; 700 words maximum; 600 words average.
**How to Contact:** Send complete ms with SASE. Simultaneous, photocopied, and previously published submissions OK. Accepts computer printout submissions. Reports in 4-8 weeks on mss. Publishes ms an average of 1 year after acceptance. Free sample copy for 8x10 SAE and 60¢ postage.

**Payment:** 6 free contributor's copies.
**Tips:** "We prefer child-centered stories in a real-world setting which teach positive values. Children enjoy fiction. They can relate to the characters and learn lessons that they might not derive from a more 'preachy' article. Generally, we accept only stories that teach wholesome, positive values." Published new writers within the last year.

**NASSAU, City Review for The Bahamas' Capital**, Bahamas International Publishing Co., Ltd., Box N-1914, Nassau, Bahamas. (809)322-1149. Editor: Paul Drake. Fiction Editor: Barbara Solomon. Magazine with five or six short stories each issue for literate audience in a sophisticated resort area. Monthly. Estab. 1983. Circ. 50,000.
**Needs:** Contemporary, literary, mainstream, serialized/excerpted novel, suspense/mystery, and "stories on island themes." Receives 20-30 unsolicited mss/month. Buys 5-6 mss/issue. Length: 1,500-3,000 words.
**How to Contact:** Send complete ms with SASE. Reports in 2 weeks. Simultaneous, photocopied and previously published submissions OK. Sample copy $3. Fiction guidelines for SAE and 2 first class stamps.
**Payment:** $25-100.
**Terms:** Pays on publication for one-time rights. Publication copyrighted.

**NATIONAL RACQUETBALL MAGAZINE (IV)**, Publication Management, 4350 Di Paola Center Dearlove Rd., Glenview IL 60025. (312)699-1706. Editor: Jason Holloman. Magazine with news, current events, and fitness dealing with the sport of racquetball. Monthly. Estab. 1981. Circ. 40,000.
**Needs:** Call editor *before* submitting ms. "We take *very* little fiction."
**How to Contact:** Send complete ms with SASE. Photocopied submissions OK with SASE.
**Payment:** Pays $50-300.
**Terms:** Pays on publication for all rights. Publication copyrighted.

**NEW AGE JOURNAL**, Rising Star Associates, 342 Western Ave., Brighton MA 02135. (617)787-2005. Editor: Marc Barasch. Fiction Editor: Patsy Vigderman. Magazine for "highly educated, socially conscious individuals interested in self-development and human awareness." Monthly. Estab. 1974. Circ. 70,000.
**Needs:** Contemporary. *Very* infrequently publishes fiction, and then only absolutely first-rate material (i.e., *New Yorker*, *Esquire*, etc.). Receives 150 unsolicited mss/month. Accepts 0-1 ms/issue; 1-3 mss/year. Approximately 75% of fiction is agented. Length: 1,200 words minimum; 4,000 words maximum. Occasionally critiques rejected mss.
**How to Contact:** Query first (with clips if possible), send complete ms, or submit through agent. Reports in 6 weeks on queries; 2 months on mss. SASE. Photocopied and previously published submissions OK. Accepts computer printout submissions. Prefers letter-quality. Writer's guidelines for #10 SAE and 1 first class stamp.
**Payment:** 10-20¢/word and 2 free contributor's copies; cover cost charge for extras.
**Terms:** Pays on publication for first North American serial rights and one-time rights. Very occasionally buys reprints. Publication copyrighted.
**Tips:** "Submit beautiful, extraordinary material."

**NEW ALASKAN (IV)**, R.W. Pickrell Agency, Rt. 1, Box 677, Ketchikan AK 99901. (907)247-2490. Tabloid sized; 24-32 pages; newsprint paper; newsprint cover stock; illustrations; photos. Magazine with both fiction and nonfiction dealing with the history and lifestyle of Southeast Alaska. Monthly. Published special fiction issue last year; plans another. Estab. 1964. Circ. 6,000.
**Needs:** Adventure, humor, preschool, regional, and senior citizen/retirement. "We accept only stories dealing with Southeast Alaska." Buys 12 mss/year. Publishes short shorts. Approximately 100% of fiction is agented. Length: 1,000-5,000 words.
**How to Contact:** Send complete ms with SASE. Reports in 4 months on mss. Sample copy $1.50 with 8x13 or larger SAE with 66¢ postage.

**Payment:** 1½¢/word.
**Terms:** Pays on publication for first, second serial (reprint), and one-time rights. Buys reprints.
**Tips:** "We publish fiction to diversify editorial material." Published new writers within the last year.

**NEW BEDFORD (II, IV), The Magazine of Southeastern New England**, New Bedford Magazine, Inc., 488 Pleasant St., New Bedford MA 02740. (617)992-6682. Editor: Ms. Dee Giles Forsythe. Magazine: 8½x11; 56-80 pages; 60 lb glossy paper; 80 lb glossy cover stock; illustrations and photos. "Reflecting the life, past and present, etc., of the New Bedford/Fall River area and surrounding southeastern Massachusetts/Rhode Island towns" for a general readership. Published five times a year. Published special fiction issue last year; plans another. Estab. 1981. Circ. 7,000.
**Needs:** Receives 3-8 unsolicited mss/month. Buys 1-2 mss/issue. Length: up to 3,000 words. Publishes short shorts.
**How to Contact:** Send complete ms with SASE. Reports in 5 weeks. Photocopied and previously published submissions OK. Accepts computer printout submissions. Prefers letter-quality. Publishes ms an average of 3-8 months after acceptance. Sample copy for $1.25 or 9x12 SAE with 5 first class stamps. Fiction guidelines for #10 SASE.
**Payment:** 30 days from on-newsstand date. Pays $50 minimum; 1 contributor's copy; $1.25 charge for extras.
**Terms:** Pays during publication period for one-time rights. Publication copyrighted.
**Tips:** "Write a great story with a good hook, interesting characters; type neatly, double-spaced and send SASE." Published new writers within the last year.

**‡NEW BLACK MASK (II)**, Harcourt Brace Jovanovich, Bruccoli Clark Inc., 2006 Sumter St., Columbia SC 29201. Bookazine: 5¼x8; 225 pages; book quality paper; photos on back cover. "Best mystery fiction we can get" for literate audience. Quarterly. Estab. 1985.
**Needs:** Suspense/mystery (mystery, detective, suspense, cops and robbers, crime, thriller, espionage). Buys 8-10 mss/issue. Publishes ms 3-6 months after acceptance. Agented fiction 50%. Length: 3,000-5,000 words. Publishes short shorts. Occasionally critiques rejected mss.
**How to Contact:** Send complete ms with cover letter (with curriculum vitae) or submit through agent. Reports in 2 weeks on queries; 1 month on mss. SASE for ms. Photocopied submissions OK. Accepts computer printouts including dot-matrix.
**Payment:** Pays up to 10¢/word.
**Terms:** Pays on publication for first world rights in NBM. Sends pre-publication galleys to the author. Publication copyrighted.
**Tips:** "The *New Black Mask* will publish the best of contemporary detective fiction, with detective stories as well as mystery, suspense, thriller, and spy fiction by the leading American, British, and European writers. Its predecessor was the original *Black Mask*, founded in 1920 by H.L. Mencken and George Jean Nathan, the premier pulp magazine of its time."

**NEW ENGLAND SENIOR CITIZEN/SENIOR AMERICAN NEWS (II)**, Prime National Publishing Corp., 470 Boston Post Rd., Weston MA 02193. (617)899-2702. Editor-in-Chief: Eileen DeVito. Tabloid: 10x16; 16-24 pages; newsprint paper; illustrations; photos. Tabloid newspaper for senior citizens. "We publish articles of particular interest to seniors." Monthly. Estab. 1970.
**Needs:** Adventure, comics, contemporary, ethnic, historical (general), humor/satire, mainstream, suspense/mystery, and western. Receives about 15-20 unsolicited fiction mss/month. Buys 1 ms/issue; 12 mss/year. Length: 1,500 words minimum; 2,000 words maximum.
**How to Contact:** Send complete ms with SASE. Simultaneous, photocopied, and previously published submissions OK. Accepts computer printout submissions. Prefers letter-quality. Reports in 6 months on mss. Sample copy 50¢.
**Payment:** $25-100.
**Terms:** Pays on publication for all rights. Publication copyrighted.

**Tips:** Mss rejected because "we have limited space for fiction." Published new writers within the last year.

**‡NEW METHODS (IV), The Journal of Animal Health Technology**, Box 22605, San Francisco CA 94122. (415)664-3469. Editor: Ronald S. Lippert, Aht. Newsletter ("could become magazine again"): 8½x11; 4 pages and up; 60 lb paper; self cover; illustrations; photos. Network service in the animal field educating services for mostly professionals in the animal field; e.g. animal health technicians. Monthly. Estab. 1976. Circ. 5,608.
**Needs:** Adventure, condensed novel, contemporary, experimental, historical, mainstream, regional, science fiction, western, animals. No stories unrelated to animals. Receives 4 unsolicited fiction mss/month. Buys one ms/issue; 12 mss/year. Length: open. "Rarely" publishes short shorts. Occasionally critiques rejected mss. Recommends other markets.
**How to Contact:** Query first with theme, length, expected time of completion, photos/illustrations, if any, biographical sketch of author, all necessary credits or send complete ms. Report times varies. SASE for query and ms. Simultaneous and photocopied submissions OK. Accepts printouts including dot-matrix. Sample copy $3.60 and #10 SAE and 2 first class stamps. Fiction guidelines free for #10 SAE and 2 first class stamps.
**Payment:** Varies.
**Terms:** Pays on publication for one-time rights. Publication copyrighted.
**Tips:** Contests: theme changes but is generally the biggest topics of the year in the animal field. "Emotion, personal experience—make the person feel it. We are growing."

**NEW YORK ACTION, PHILADELPHIA ACTION (II)**, P/S Inc., Suite 144, 1601 Easton Road, Willow Grove PA 19090. (215)572-6969. Editor: Bob Rose. Fiction Editor: George Finster. Tabloid: 48 pages; newsprint paper; newsprint cover stock; illustrations; photos. "Our publications are for adults interested in the erotic pleasures. Besides covering the entire commercial sex entertainment industry, we print the unique and the unusual in erotic fiction." Monthly. Estab. 1979. Circ. 10,000.
**Needs:** Erotica, fantasy, humor/satire, men's, science fiction, and women's (erotic). "No stories in which one character (or more) is not having fun. No stories about children." Receives 20-30 unsolicited mss/month. Buys 1-2 mss/issue; 12-15 mss/year. Length: 2,500-3,000 words average; "we occasionally accept longer pieces when needed." Occasionally critiques rejected mss. Recommends other markets.
**How to Contact:** Query first or send complete ms. Reports in 1 month on queries; 2 months on mss. SASE. Simultaneous and photocopied submissions OK. Accepts computer printout submissions. Prefers letter-quality. Accepts disc submissions compatible with Comp/Set 3500. Prefers hard copy with disc submission "until writer is established with us." Publishes ms 1-2 months after acceptance. Sample copy $1 and 9x12 SASE. Fiction guidelines for #10 SASE.
**Payment:** $50-200; subscription to magazine; 1 contributor's copy; $1 plus postage for extras.
**Terms:** Pays on publication for first North American serial rights and "rights to reprint only in our own publications. Publication date and date check will be issued are included with letter of acceptance." Publications copyrighted.
**Tips:** "Prepare your manuscript professionally. Don't send stories *not* conforming to our guidelines. Get guidelines *before* submitting material." Published new writers within the last year.

**THE NEW YORKER (III)**, The New Yorker, Inc., 25 W. 43rd St., New York NY 10036. (212)840-3800. Editor: William Shawn. A quality magazine of interesting, well-written stories, articles, essays, and poems for a literate audience. Weekly. Estab. 1925.
**Needs:** Publishes 2 mss/issue.
**How to Contact:** Send complete ms with SASE. Reports in 6-8 weeks on mss.
**Payment:** Varies.
**Terms:** Pays on acceptance.
**Tips:** "Be lively, original, not overly literary. Write what you want to write, not what you think the editor would like."

**‡NIGHT CRY (II)**, Montcalm Publishing, 800 2nd Ave., New York NY 10017. Editor: Alan Rodgers. Magazine: digest-sized; 196 pages; newsprint paper; slick cover stock; illustrations. "We're a horror magazine, but we try not to let that back us into a corner: The only things a *Night City* story has to be are good and frightening. Our audience is an ordinary, mass-market—one that likes being scared." Quarterly. Estab. 1984. Circ. 30,000.

**Needs:** Adventure, condensed novel, contemporary, fantasy, horror, literary, mainstream, men's, psychic/supernatural/occult, science fiction, serialized/excerpted novel, suspense/mystery, translations, women's. No whimsy; no world fantasy. Receives 500 unsolicited mss/month. Buys 15-20 mss/issue; 60-80 mss/year. Publishes ms 3-10 months after acceptance. Agented fiction 5-10%. Length: 3,000-4,000 words average; 300 words minimum; no maximum word limit. Publishes short shorts over 300 words. Occasionally critiques rejected mss. Recommends other markets.

**How to Contact:** Send complete ms with cover letter. Reports in 2½ months. SASE for ms. Simultaneous, photocopied submissions OK. Accepts computer printouts; no dot-matrix. Sample copy for $3.50. Fiction guidelines for #10 SAE and 1 first class stamp.

**Payment:** Pays 5-7¢/word and contributor's copies; charge for extras.

**Terms:** Payment is one half on acceptance and one half on publication for one-time rights. Sends galleys to author. Publication copyrighted.

**Tips:** "While there is a market for short fiction, it's a flooded one. A young writer has to have an incredible amount of talent and persistence to break through, even at a magazine like *Night Cry*, where sometimes as many as half of the stories in a given issue come from first-timers. Fiction is *Night Cry*'s blood and bone. Our readers come to us for stories, and they complain when they feel they haven't had enough."

**‡NOAH'S ARK (II, IV), A Newspaper for Jewish Children**, 7726 Portal, Houston TX 77071. (713)774-5235 or 729-6221. Editors: Debbie Israel Dubin and Linda Freedman Block. Tabloid: 4 pages; newsprint paper; illustrations; photos. "All material must be on some Jewish theme. Seasonal material relating to Jewish holidays is used as well as articles and stories relating to Jewish culture (charity, Soviet Jewry, ecology), etc" for Jewish children, ages 6-12. Monthly Sept.-June. Estab. 1979. Circ. 450,000.

**Needs:** Juvenile (5-9 years); religious/inspirational; young adult/teen (10-12 years); ages 6-12 Jewish children. "Newspaper is not only included as a supplement to numerous Jewish newspapers, and sent to individual subscribers but is also distributed in bulk quantities to religious schools; therefore all stories and articles should have educational value as well as being entertaining and interesting to children." Receives 2 unsolicited mss/month. Buys "few mss but we'd probably use more if more were submitted." Length: 750 words maximum.

**How to Contact:** Send complete ms with cover letter with SASE. "The cover letter is not necessary; the submission will be accepted or rejected on its own merits." Simultaneous, photocopied submissions and reprints OK. Accepts computer printouts including dot-matrix. Sample copy 50¢ with #10 envelope and 1 first class stamp. "The best guideline is a copy of our publication."

**Payment:** Varies; contributor's copies.

**Terms:** Pays on acceptance for one-time rights. Publication copyrighted.

**Tips:** "Our newspaper was created by two writers looking for a place to have our work published. It has grown in only 8 years to nearly 1½ million readers throughout the world. Beginners with determination can accomplish the impossible."

**THE NORTH AMERICAN VOICE OF FATIMA (II)**, Barumbite Fathers, 1023 Swan Rd., Youngstown NY 14174-0167. (716)754-7489. Editor: Steven M. Grancini. Magazine of Christian ideas for adults. Bimonthly. Estab. 1961. Circ. 3,000.

**Needs:** Religious/inspirational. Length: 1,000 words average.

**How to Contact:** Send complete ms with SASE. Reports in 1 month on mss. Sample copy free.

**Payment:** 2¢/word.

**Terms:** Pays on acceptance for first rights.

‡**NORTHCOAST VIEW (II)**, Blarney Publishing, Box 1374, Eureka CA 95502. (707)443-4887. Editors: Scott K. Ryan and Damon Maguire. Magazine; 8½x11; 48 pages; electrabrite, 32 lb paper and cover; illustrations; photos. "Entertainment, recreation, arts and news magazine but open to all kinds of fiction." For Humboldt county, ages 18-45 and others. Monthly. Plans anthology in future. Estab. 1982. Circ. 20,000.
**Needs:** Open to most subjects. Adventure, condensed novel, contemporary, erotica, ethnic, experimental, fantasy, historical (general), horror, humor/satire, literary, psychic/supernatural occult, regional, science fiction, suspense/mystery, translations. No romances. Receives 30-50 unsolicited mss/month. Buys 1-2 mss/issue; 12-20 mss/year. Publishes ms 1-3 months after acceptance. Length: 2,500 words average; 250 words minimum; 5,000 words maximum.
**How to Contact:** Send complete ms with cover letter (background info or bio if published). Reports in 3-6 months on mss. SASE. Simultaneous, photocopied submissions and reprints (sometimes) OK. Accepts computer printouts. No dot-matrix. Sample copy $1. Fiction guidelines for #10 SAE and 1 first class stamp.
**Payment:** Pays $5-150.
**Terms:** Pays on publication for all rights. Publication copyrighted.

**NORTHEAST, the Sunday Magazine of the Hartford Courant**, 285 Broad St., Hartford CT 06115. (203)241-3700. Editor: Lary Bloom. Magazine: 11½x10; 32-100 pages; illustrations; photos. "A regional (New England, specifically Connecticut) magazine, we publish stories of varied subjects of interest to our Connecticut audience" for a general audience. Weekly. Published special fiction issue last year. Estab. 1981. Circ. 300,000.
**Needs:** Contemporary and regional. No children's stories or stories with distinct setting outside Connecticut. Receives 60 unsolicited mss/month. Buys 1 ms/issue. Publishes short shorts. Length: 750 words minimum; 4,500 words maximum.
**How to Contact:** Send complete ms with SASE. Reports in 3 weeks. Simultaneous and photocopied submissions OK. No reprints or previously published work. Accepts computer printout submissions. Prefers letter-quality. Free sample copy and fiction guidelines with 12x10 or larger SASE.
**Payment:** $250-600.
**Terms:** Pays on acceptance for one-time rights. Publication copyrighted.
**Tips:** "We are committed to providing a vehicle for quality stories." Published new writers within the last year.

**NUGGET (II)**, Dugent Publishing Corp., Suite 204, 2355 Salzedo St., Coral Gables FL 33134. (305)443-2378. Editor: John C. Fox. A newsstand magazine designed to have erotic appeal for a fetish-oriented audience. Bimonthly. Estab. 1956. Circ. 100,000.
**Needs:** Contemporary, psychic/supernatural, science fiction, horror, men's, erotica, mystery, adventure, and humor. Offbeat, fetish-oriented material should encompass a variety of subjects. Most of fiction includes several sex scenes. No fiction that concerns children or religious subjects. Buys 3 mss/issue. Approximately 5% of fiction is agented. Length: 2,000-3,500 words.
**How to Contact:** Send complete ms with SASE. Reports in 1 month on ms. Sample copy $4.50. Free guidelines with legal-sized SASE.
**Payment:** $125-150. Free author's copy.
**Terms:** Pays on publication for first rights.
**Tips:** "Keep in mind the nature of the publication which is fetish erotica. Subject matter can vary, but we prefer fetish themes."

‡**OCEAN SPORTS INTERNATIONAL (II, IV)**, 6-A Hangar Way, Watsonville CA 95076. (408)724-7474. Editor; Joe Grassadonia. Fiction Editor: George Fuller. Magazine: 8½x11; 96 pages; glossy paper and cover; illustrations; color/b&w photos. Articles on ocean sports of all kinds for ocean people and general audience. Quarterly. Estab. 1981. Circ. 40,000.
**Needs:** Adventure, historical (general), humor/satire, literary, special interest: water related. No

experimental. "We are just starting to consider fiction. Plans to buy 1 ms/issue. Publishes 3-6 months after acceptance. Length: 2,000 words average; 1,000 words minimum; 4,000 words maximum. Occasionally comments on rejected mss if requested. Recommends other markets if requested.

**How to Contact:** Query first or send complete ms with cover letter with SASE. Reports in 2 weeks on mss. SASE for query and ms. Simultaneous, photocopied submissions and reprints OK with rights obtained. Accepts computer printouts including dot-matrix if readable. Sample copy $3. Fiction guidelines for #10 SAE and 1 first class stamp.

**Payment:** Pays 7-10¢/word, plus contributor's copies; $2 charge for extras.

**Terms:** Pays on publication for first rights. Publication copyrighted.

**Tips:** "There are many markets open to the right *kind* of fiction. Particularly fiction of specific readership; shorts, regional, parent/children, etc. A good query letter helps. Remember that we're looking for stories on ocean sports, and stories on relationships with the ocean/water. Remember also that editors have little time, so if you call or write, be prepared, conscious of time, and specific."

**OMNI (II, III, IV)**, Penthouse International, 1965 Broadway, New York NY 10023. Fiction Editor: Ellen Datlow. Magazine: 8½x11; 114-134 pages; 40-50 lb stock paper; 100 lb Mead off cover stock; illustrations; photos. Magazine of science and science fiction with an interest in near future; stories of what science holds, what life and lifestyles will be like in areas affected by science for a young, bright and well-educated audience between ages 18-45. Monthly. Estab. 1978. Circ. 1,000,000.

**Needs:** Science fiction, contemporary, fantasy, and technological horror. No sword and sorcery or space opera. Buys 48 mss/year. Receives approximately 400 unsolicited fiction mss/month. Approximately 5% of fiction is agented. Length: 2,000 words minimum, 12,000 words maximum. Critiques rejected mss that interest me "when there is time." Sometimes recommends other markets.

**How to Contact:** Send complete ms with SASE. Accepts computer printout submissions. Prefers letter-quality. Reports within 3 weeks on mss. Publishes ms 3-24 months after acceptance. Free guidelines with legal-sized SASE.

**Payment:** Pays $1,250-2,000; 1 free author's copy.

**Terms:** Pays on acceptance for first North American serial rights with exclusive worldwide English language periodical rights and nonexclusive anthology rights. Publication copyrighted.

**Tips:** "Buy a copy and study our magazine. We are not the same as other science fiction magazines. Beginning writers should read a lot of the best science fiction short stories today. We are looking for strongly, well-written stories dealing with the next 100 years. Don't give up on a market just because you've been rejected several times. If you're good, you'll get published eventually. Don't ever call an editor on the phone and ask why he/she rejected a story. You'll either find out in a personal rejection letter (which means the editor liked it or thought enough of your writing to comment) or you won't find out at all (most likely the editor won't remember a form-rejected story)." Mss are rejected because "they rehash old ideas, are poorly written or are trite." Published new writers within the last year.

**ON THE LINE (II)**, Mennonite Publishing House, 616 Walnut Ave., Scottdale PA 15683-1999. (412)887-8500. Editor: Virginia A. Hostetler. Magazine: 7x10; 8 pages; illustrations; cover photos. "A religious take-home paper with the goal of helping children grow in their understanding and appreciation of God, the created world, themselves, and other people." For children ages 10-14. Weekly. Estab. 1970. Circ. 11,000.

**Needs:** Adventure and religious/inspirational for older children and young teens (10-14 years). Receives 50-100 unsolicited mss/month. Buys 1 ms/issue; 52 mss/year. Length: 750-1,000 words.

**How to Contact:** Send complete ms. Reports in 1 month. SASE. Simultaneous, photocopied, and previously published work OK. Accepts computer printout submissions. Prefers letter-quality. Sample copy and fiction guidelines free.

**Payment:** Pays on acceptance for one-time rights. Publication copyrighted.
**Tips:** "Write and write some more before submitting. We believe in the power of story to entertain, inspire and challenge the reader to new growth. Know children, the readers of our publication, their thoughts, feelings and interests. Be realistic with characters and events in the fiction. Stories do not need to be true, but need to *feel* true."

**‡ORANGE COAST MAGAZINE (II, IV), The Magazine of Orange County**, O.C.N.L., Suite E, 18200 W. McDurmott St., Irvine CA 92714. (714)660-8622. Editor: Katherine Tomlinson. Fiction Editor: John Morell. Magazine: 8½x11; 250-450 pages; slick high-quality paper; glossy cover stock; illustrations; photos. "We are a regional monthly presenting ourselves as *the* source of information about Orange County." For educated, affluent, involved audience. Monthly. Estab. 1960. Circ. 30,000.
**Needs:** Contemporary, experimental, humor/satire, mainstream, regional, serialized/excerpted novel, suspense/mystery. No pornography, ethnic, humor, little magazine submissions, romance novellas, O. Henry endings, children's stories. Receives 25-30 unsolicited fiction mss/month. Buys 2 mss/year. Publishes ms as soon as possible after acceptance. Length: 2,000 words average; 1,500 words minimum; 3,000 words maximum. Occasionally critiques rejected mss. Recommends other markets.
**How to Contact:** Send complete ms with cover letter with name, address, phone number, social security number. "NO, NO phone queries—they make us very cranky." Reports in 1 month on mss. Photocopied submissions OK. Accepts computer printouts. Accepts electronic submissions via disc or modem if Compaq compatability. Sample copy $5. Fiction guidelines free for letter-size SAE and 1 first class stamp.
**Payment:** Pays $100-150; contributor's copies—"we send tears as a matter of course."
**Terms:** Pays on acceptance for first North American serial rights. Sends pre-publication galleys to author "if time permits." Publication copyrighted.
**Tips:** "I read a lot of magazines and it seems that there's a lot of razzle-dazzle passing itself off as serious fiction. A writer who can *tell a story*, whether straightforwardly or in a wildly imaginative new way, shouldn't have any trouble. Unfortunately, much of the ficiton is poorly written (Are there other editors out there tired of seeing a lot written as 'alot'?), badly plotted and unstructured. I have no patience with semi-articulate autobiography masquerading as fiction."

**THE OTHER SIDE (III)**, Jubilee, Inc., Box 3948, Fredericksburg VA 22402. (703)371-7416. Editor: Mark Olson. Fiction Editor: Joseph Comanda. Magazine of justice rooted in discipleship for Christians with a strong interest in peace, social and economic justice. Monthly. Estab. 1965. Circ. 15,000.
**Needs:** Contemporary, ethnic, experimental, fantasy, feminist, humor/satire, literary, mainstream, and suspense/mystery. Receives 30 unsolicited fiction mss/month. Buys 6 mss/year. Length: 1,000 words minimum; 6,000 words maximum; 3,000 words average.
**How to Contact:** Send complete ms with SASE. Photocopied submissions OK. Accepts computer printout submissions. Accepts disc submissions compatible with Northstar, Osborne or IBM PC. Reports in 6-8 weeks on mss. Publishes ms 3-9 months after acceptance. Sample copy for $2.50.
**Payment:** Pays $50-250; free subscription to magazine; 5 free contributor's copies.
**Terms:** Pays on acceptance for all or first rights; assignments on work-for-hire basis. Publication copyrighted.

**OUI MAGAZINE (II)**, 6th Floor, 300 W. 43rd St., New York NY 10036. Editor: Barry Janoff. Magazine: 8x11; 112 pages; illustrations; photos. Magazine for college-age males and older. Monthly. Estab. 1972. Circ. 1 million.
**Needs:** Contemporary, fantasy, lesbian, men's, mystery, and humor. Buys 1 ms/issue; 12 mss/year. Receives 200-300 unsolicited fiction mss/month. Length: 1,500-3,000 words.
**How to Contact:** Cover letter with author background, previous publications, etc. Send complete ms with SASE. Accepts computer printout submissions. Prefers letter-quality. Reports in 6-to-8 weeks on mss.

**Payment:** Pays $250 and up.
**Terms:** Pays on publication for first rights. Publication copyrighted.
**Tips:** "Many mss are rejected because writers have not studied the market or the magazine. We want writers to take chances and offer us something out of the ordinary. Look at several recent issues to see what direction our fiction is headed." Published new writers within the last year.

**OUR FAMILY (II, IV)**, Oblate Fathers of St. Mary's Province, Box 249, Battleford, Saskatchewan S0M 0E0 Canada. (306)937-7344. Fiction Editor: John Patrick Gillese, 10450-144 St., Edmonton AB T5N-2V4 Canada. Magazine: 8½x11; 40 pages; illustrations; photos. Magazine primarily for Catholic families who want information, inspiration and encouragement in Christian living. Monthly. Estab. 1949. Circ. 16,452.
**Needs:** Religious/inspirational and senior citizen/retirement. "The material we use must have Christian content and values. No science fiction or adult sex stories." Buys 3 mss/month. Length: 1,000-3,000 words. Recommends other markets.
**How to Contact:** Send complete ms with SAE and IRC or personal check and cover letter with author's credits and credentials. (US stamps cannot be used in Canada.) Accepts computer printout submissions. Prefers letter-quality. Reports in 4 weeks after receipt of the ms. Publishes ms 4-6 months after acceptance. Sample copy $1.50. Free Fiction Requirement Guide with SAE and 39¢ for postage.
**Payment:** 7-10¢/word for original ms. Lesser payment for reprint. 2-4 free author's copies. $1 charge for extras.
**Terms:** Pays on acceptance for simultaneous, second serial (reprint), and first North American serial rights. Buys reprints.
**Tips:** "Base your story on an actual Christian experience, a personal experience or one you have come to know. We reject a good number of stories simply because they have no Christian dimension. Obtain our guide and study it to understand the policy we follow consistently." Published new writers within the last year.

**‡OUTLAW BIKER (II, IV)**, Outlaw Biker Enterprises, 450 Seventh Ave., New York NY 10001. (212)564-0112. Editor: Dian Hansen. Fiction Editor: Chris Brewer. Magazine: 8½x11; 96 pages; 50 lb color paper; 80 lb cover stock; illustrations; photos. Hard-core Harley Davidson bikers for biker and tattoo enthusiasts. Published 9 times/year. Plans special fiction issue. Estab. 1984. Circ. 200,000.
**Needs:** Adventure, men's, special interest: bikers. Receives 40 unsolicited mss/month. Accepts 3 fiction mss/issue. Publishes ms 4 months after acceptance. Length: 1,000 words minimum; 3,000 words maximum. Critiques rejected mss.
**How to Contact:** Send complete ms with cover letter. SASE very important. Reports on queries in 1 month. Simultaneous, photocopied and reprint submissions OK. Sample copy $3.50.
**Payment:** Pays $50-300.
**Terms:** Pays on publication. Acquires all rights. Publication copyrighted.

**PENNSYLVANIA SPORTSMAN (II)**, Northwoods Publications, Inc., Box 5196, Harrisburg PA 17110. (717)233-4797. Editor: Lou Hoffman. Magazine for field sports audience: 8/1/2x11; 96 pages; 30 lb coated paper; 70 lb cover stock; illustrations; photos. Estab. 1959. Circ. 52,000.
**Needs:** Hunting- and fishing-related stories. Receives 6 unsolicited mss/month. Buys 1-2 mss/issue; 6-14 mss/year. Length: 1,000-1,200 words average. Occasionally critiques rejected mss.
**How to Contact:** Query first. Reports in 2 months on queries. SASE. Simultaneous submissions OK "if not within our audience." Accepts computer printout submissions. Prefers letter-quality. Does not read mss summer or winter. Sample copy $1 with 9x12 SAE and $1.25 postage.
**Payment:** $30-75.
**Terms:** Pays on publication for all rights. Publication copyrighted.
**Tips:** Published new writers within the year.

**‡PENNYWHISTLE PRESS (II)**, Gannett Co., Inc., Box 500-P, Washington DC 20006. Editor: Anita Sama. Magazine: tabloid size; 8 pages; newsprint paper; illustrations; photos. Education

and information for children ages 6-12. Weekly. Estab. 1981. Circ. 2.5 million.
**Needs:** Juvenile (5-9 years), young adult/teen (10-18 years). No talking animals, poorly spelled, and unprofessional mss. Receives "hundreds" of unsolicited fiction mss/month. Accepts 20 mss/year. Publishes ms 6 months after acceptance. Length: 450 words for 5-7 year olds; 850 words for older children.
**How to Contact:** Send complete ms with cover letter with SASE. *No* queries. No simultaneous submissions accepted. Sample copy 75¢.
**Payment:** Varies.
**Terms:** Pays on publication.

**PENTHOUSE**, Penthouse International, Ltd., 1965 Broadway, New York NY 10023. (212)496-6100. Fiction Editor: Kathryn Green. A men's entertainment magazine featuring high quality sophisticated articles of interest to men between the ages of 18-34. Exposés, humor, profiles and interviews. Monthly. Estab. 1965. Circ. 5,350,000.
**Needs:** Contemporary, psychic/supernatural/occult, science fiction, horror, men's, erotica, western, adventure, and first serial excerpts from novels. No stories with women's point of view, plotless sexual encounters or extreme avant-garde fiction. Buys 12 mss/year. Receives approximately 400 unsolicited fiction mss/month. Length: 3,000-6,000 words.
**How to Contact:** Send ms with SASE. Reports in 1 month on mss.
**Terms:** Pays on acceptance for exclusive first English language rights and sometimes world rights. Publication copyrighted.
**Tips:** "Send us well-written stories, neatly typed and of interest to our audience. We are always looking for new fiction talent." Many mss are rejected because they are "not right for our audience; characters are not fully developed; they are too short."

**PILLOW TALK (II)**, 801 2nd Ave., New York NY 10017. Editor: Brian Riley. Magazine: digest-sized; 130 pages; illustrations; photos. Bimonthly letters digest magazine filled cover-to-cover with *scorching* sexual experiences.
**Needs:** "We are in need of approximately 40 short letters per issue in length of no more than four manuscript pages, and five long letters in length of approximately 10 manuscript pages. We also buy confession/how-to/advice pieces written in a serious nonfiction style, though, for the most part, these pieces are fictitious." Recommends other markets.
**How to Contact:** In general, "we assign the majority of the material to established writers, but often we receive excellent unsolicited material, and encourage unsolicited mss."
**Terms:** *Pillow Talk* pays $5 per page for short sexperience letters, and $75 for long ten-page letters. Pays on publication.
**Tips:** *Pillow Talk*'s format has recently changed with new editorial and management policies. "We need extremely hot erotic fiction and sexperiences that deals with exceedingly vivid sexual activity. We are primarily a fantasy magazine." Published new writers within the last year. Writing adult erotica is a fine way for a writer to break in. "We may not be *The New Yorker*, but we pay. Avoid overwriting and keep the story titillating throughout."

**PIONEER WOMAN, Magazine of Pioneer Women/Na'amat, The Women's Labor Zionist Organization of America**, Pioneer Women/Na'amat, 200 Madison Ave., New York NY 10016. (212)725-8010. Editor: Judith A. Sokoloff. Magazine covering a wide variety of subjects of interest to the Jewish community—including political and social issues, arts, profiles; many articles about Israel; and women's issues. Fiction must have a Jewish theme. Readers are the American Jewish community. Published 5 times/year. Estab. 1926. Circ. 30,000.
**Needs:** Contemporary, literary, feminist, and women's. Receives 10 unsolicited fiction mss/month. Buys 3-5 fiction mss/year. Length: 1,500 words minimum; 3,000 words maximum. Also buys nonfiction.
**How to Contact:** Query first or send complete ms with SASE. Photocopied submissions OK. Accepts computer printout submissions. Prefers letter-quality. Reports in 3 months on mss. Free sample copy for 9x11½ SAE and 71¢ postage.
**Payment:** Pays 8¢/word; 2 free contributor's copies. Offers kill fee of 25%.

**Terms:** Pays on publication for first and first North American serial rights; assignments on work-for-hire basis.
**Tips:** Submit "good writing. No maudlin nostalgia or romance; no hackneyed Jewish humor and no poetry."

**PLAYBOY MAGAZINE (III)**, Playboy Enterprises, Inc., 919 N. Michigan Ave., Chicago IL 60611. (312)751-8000. Editorial Director: Arthur Kretchmer. Fiction Editor: Alice K. Turner. Magazine: 8½x11; 250 pages; glossy cover stock; illustrations; photos. Entertainment magazine for a male audience. Plans special fiction issue. Monthly. Estab. 1953. Circ. 4,250,342.
**Needs:** Literary, contemporary, science fiction, fantasy, horror, men's, western, mystery, adventure, and humor. No pornography or fiction geared to a female audience. Buys 1-3 mss/issue; 25 mss/year. Receives approximately 1,200 unsolicited fiction mss each month. Length: 1,000-10,000 (average 6,000) words. Also publishes short shorts of 1,200 words. Critiques rejected mss "when there is time." Recommends other markets "sometimes."
**How to Contact:** Send complete ms with SASE and cover letter with prior publication information. Reports in 6 weeks on mss. Free guidelines with SASE.
**Payment:** $2,000 minimum; $1,000 minimum for short-shorts.
**Terms:** Pays on acceptance for all rights. Publication copyrighted.
**Tips:** "Writers should take a close look at *Playboy* to see the kind and quality of fiction we publish." Published new writers within the last year.

**PLAYERS MAGAZINE (I, II)**, Players International Publications, 8060 Melrose Ave., Los Angeles CA 90046. (213)653-8060. Editor: Joseph Nazel. Associate Editor: Leslie Gersicoff. The "basic black" *Playboy* magazine with profiles, reviews, sports, travel, and general interest for the black male. Monthly. Estab. 1973. Circ. 202,000.
**Needs:** Science fiction, fantasy, erotica, adventure, historical, humor, and experimental. "No crime or prison-type stories. We get 'tons' of those." Receives approximately 50 unsolicited fiction mss/month. Length: 1,000-4,000 words. Also publishes short shorts. Critiques rejected mss "when there is time." Sometimes sends mss to editors of other publications.
**How to Contact:** Send complete ms with SASE. Reports in 3-4 weeks.
**Payment:** Pays 10¢/word maximum.
**Terms:** Pays on publication for one-time use. Publication copyrighted.
**Tips:** "We want to see stories that are light-hearted and positive." Many mss are "poorly written, not for our market. Our market is select. Our readers are interested in fiction composed of black characters and situations—reality-based." Published new writers within the last year.

**PLAYGIRL MAGAZINE (III)**, Ritter/Geller Communications, Inc., 3420 Ocean Park Blvd., Santa Monica CA 90405. (213)450-0900. Editor-in-Chief: Thomasine E. Lewis. Fiction Editor: Mary Ellen Strote. Magazine: 8x10; 120 pages; 40 lb paper; 60 lb cover stock; illustrations; photos. Magazine for today's young women ages 18-40, average age 26, featuring entertainment, fiction, beauty and fashion, current events, sex, and health. Monthly. Published special fiction issue last year; plans another. Estab. 1973. Circ. 800,000.
**Needs:** Feminist, romance (contemporary), excerpted novel, and women's. "No gay, juvenile, murder, mystery, graphic sex." Receives approximately 200 unsolicited fiction mss/month. Buys 1-2 mss/issue. Approximately 40% of fiction is agented. Length: 1,000 words minimum; 5,000 words maximum; 3,500 words average. Publishes short shorts. Occasionally critiques rejected mss.
**How to Contact:** Send complete ms with SASE. Simultaneous, photocopied, and previously published submissions OK. Accepts computer printout submissions. Prefers letter-quality. Reports in 4-6 weeks on mss. Publishes ms an average of 3-6 months after acceptance. Sample copy from Customer Service Department; $5 includes postage and handling.
**Payment:** $500 minimum and 1-2 contributor's copies.
**Terms:** Pays on acceptance for one-time magazine rights in the English language. Occasionally buys reprints. Publication copyrighted.

**Tips:** "Know your market. We find fiction is essential in women's entertainment." Published new writers within the last year.

**POCKETS (II), Devotional Magazine for Children**, The Upper Room, 1908 Grand Ave., Box 189, Nashville TN 37202. (615)327-2700. Editor-in-Chief: Willie S. Teague. Magazine: 7x9; 32 pages; 50 lb white econowrite paper; 80 lb white coated, heavy cover stock; illustrations; photos. Magazine for children ages 6-12, with articles specifically geared for ages 8 to 11. "The magazine offers stories, activities, prayers, poems—all geared to giving children a better understanding of themselves as children of God. Much of the material will not be overtly religious but will deal with situations, special seasons and holidays, and ecological concerns from a Christian perspective. The overall goal is to build into a child's daily life a need for a devotional aspect." Published monthly except for January. Estab. 1981. Estimated Circ. 80,000.
**Needs:** Adventure, contemporary, ethnic, fantasy, historical (general), juvenile, religious/inspirational, and suspense/mystery. "All submissions, whatever the genre, should address the broad theme of the magazine. Each issue will be built around several themes with material which can be used by children in a variety of ways. Scripture stories, fiction, poetry, prayers, art, graphics, puzzles, and activities will all be included. Submissions do not need to be overtly religious. They should help children experience a Christian lifestyle that is not always a neatly wrapped moral package, but is open to the continuing revelation of God's will. Seasonal material, both secular and liturgical, is desired. No violence, horror, sexual, and racial stereotyping or fiction containing heavy moralizing." Receives approximately 60 unsolicited fiction mss/month. Buys 1-2 mss/issue; 11-22 mss/year. Publishes short shorts. A peace with justice theme will run throughout the magazine. Approximately 50% of fiction is agented. Length: 600 words minimum; 1,500 words maximum; 1,200 words average.
**How to Contact:** Send complete ms with SASE. Photocopied and previously published submissions OK, but no simultaneous submissions. Accepts computer printout submissions. Reports in 2 months on mss. Publishes ms 12-18 months after acceptance. Sample copy $1.25. Free fiction guidelines and themes with SASE.
**Payment:** 7¢/word and up and 2-5 contributor's copies. $1.25 charge for extras; 65¢ each for 10 or more.
**Terms:** Pays on acceptance for first North American serial rights. Buys reprints.
**Tips:** "Do not write *down* to children." Rejects mss because "we receive far more submissions than we can use. If all were of high quality, we still would purchase only a few. The most common problems are overworked story line and flat, unrealistic characters. Most stories simply do not 'ring true', and children know that." Published new writers within the last year.

**‡THE POWER EXCHANGE, A Newsleather for Women on the Sexual Fringe (I)**, Box 527, Richmond Hill NY 11415. Editor: Pat Califia. Magazine: 8½x11; 40 pages; bond quality paper; glossy cover stock; illustrations; b&w photos. "My newsleather is a networking magazine for women interested in woman-to-woman S/M. I publish fiction and nonfiction of interest to that readership." For lesbian or bisexual women involved with S/M. Published irregularly. Estab. 1984.
**Needs:** Confession, erotica, fantasy, feminist, gay, horror, humor/satire, lesbian, psychic/supernatural, regional, contemporary romance, science fiction, suspense/mystery, women's. "I prefer short fiction which depicts mutually consenting, lesbian S/M. Other than that, the writer has a free hand with setting, genre, etc." Nothing anti-porn or anti-sex. Receives 12 unsolicited fiction mss/month. Accepts 3 fiction mss/issue. Length: "Can't accept anything over 10 double-spaced pages." Always critiques on rejected mss. Recommends other markets.
**How to Contact:** Send complete ms with cover letter. Reports in 3 weeks on queries and mss. SASE for ms. Accepts computer printouts including dot-matrix. Accepts electronic submissions via disc or modem. "I have a Kaypro-II (CP/M). Modem runs at 300 baud. But I can convert a disc from IBM or compatibles." Fiction guidelines for #10 SAE and 1 first class stamp.
**Payment:** Free subscription to magazine and contributor's copies.
**Terms:** Acquires one-time rights. Publication copyrighted.

**Tips:** "Many of my readers are women who have literally no contact with other women who share their sexuality. The fiction serves as fantasy fuel and a goal to contact others, be less isolated. Porn is precious. Women need more of it, not less. Write me a letter and send me something short and hot, and my gratitude will be boundless. I don't pay anything but I am willing to do a lot of work with revisions, editing, etc. I don't think there are enough women writing sexually explicit material and I foster that whenever I can."

**‡PREVIEWS MAGAZINE (II), A Community Magazine,** Santa Monica Bay Printing & Publishing Co., #245, 919 Santa Monica Blvd., Santa Monica CA 90401. (213)458-3376. Editor: Jan Loomis. Magazine: 8½x11; 32-64 pages; glossy 50 lb paper and cover; illustrations; photos. "Local editorial pertinent to the upscale areas of West Los Angeles." For "average income over $60,000, college educated, literate." Monthly.
**Needs:** Adventure, fantasy, historical (general), humor/satire, literary, science fiction. No pornography, voyeurism/blood and gore. Receives 2-3 unsolicited fiction mss/issue. Buys 4-6 mss/year plus 2-3 at Christmas. Publishes ms 3-6 months after acceptance. Length: 1,000-1,500 words average; 800 words minimum; 2,000 words maximum. Also publishes short shorts of 500-800 words.
**How to Contact:** Send complete ms with cover (background on writer). Reports in 6 weeks on mss. SASE. Accepts computer printout, including dot-matrix. Accepts electronic submissions via disc or modem. IBM PC/Hayes Modem in office. Can also interface with typesetting service. Sample copy free. Fiction guidelines free.
**Payment:** Pays $100-300 and contributor's copies.
**Terms:** Pays on publication for all rights and first North American serial rights. Publication copyrighted.
**Tips:** "Written fiction, especially well written short stories with punch, are well received by the public. We are particularly interested in Christmas stories."

**PRIME TIMES (II),** National Association for Retired Credit Union People, Inc., (NARCUP), Editorial Offices: Suite 120, 2802 International Ln., Madison WI 53704. Associate Managing Editor: Joan Donovan. Magazine: medium sized; 40 pages; illustrations; photos. Editorial slant is toward redefining midlife and retirement lifestyle and promoting a dynamic vision of the prime-life years. Each edition revolves loosely around a theme—for example, stress management and preventive health help, second careers, unique problems of the midlife or "bridge" generation. The short story may sketch relational conflicts and resolutions between prime-life men and women, or with their children, parents, etc., or place them in situations that try their spirits and revalidate them. Fiction that is not targeted to this group but of excellent quality and broad general appeal is also very welcome. Staff will review adventure, ethnic, science fiction, fantasy, mainstream and humorous fiction as well. No sentimental romances or nostalgia pieces, please. Quarterly. Published special fiction issue last year, plans another. Estab. 1979. Circ. 65,000.
**Needs:** Literary, contemporary, romance, adventure, humor, ethnic. Buys 1 ms/issue, 4 mss/year. Approximately 10% of fiction is agented. Length: 2,500-5,000 words. Shorter lengths preferred.
**How to Contact:** Send complete ms. SASE always. Accepts computer printout submissions. Prefers letter-quality. Reports in 4-6 weeks on queries and mss. Publishes ms 6-12 months after acceptance. Free sample copy with 9x12 SASE (5 first class stamps). Free guidelines with SASE.
**Payment:** $150-750. 3 free author's copies; $1 charge for each extra.
**Terms:** $250-750 for fiction entries. Pays on publication for first North American serial rights and for second serial (reprint).
**Tips:** "Readers favor the short stories we've featured on positive human relationships. We like to include a short story in each publication. It may be up to 5,000 words in length. We are very happy to feature second-serial work as long as it hasn't appeared in another *national* 'maturity market' publication."

**‡PRO-CLAIMER (I, II), A Posact Publication for Christian Teenagers,** Box 1948, Rocky Mount NC 27801. (919)977-9977. Editor: Jess Snow. Fiction Editor: Linda Gillian. Newspaper: 11¼x17½; 4 pages; 60 lb offset white paper; 60 lb offset white cover stock; illustrations; photos. *"Pro-Claimer* is designed to help Christian teenagers 12-18 years old, in their day-by-day living and also provide some entertainment. Monthly October through June. Estab. 1982. Circ. under 5,000.

**Needs:** Adventure, historical (general), religious/inspirational, young adult/teen (12-18 years). "Every story should have a theme or purpose that's useful to a Christian teenager." Nothing that doesn't have to do with teens. Receives approximately 10-15 unsolicited mss/month. Buys 1 ms/ issue; 9 issues/year. Does not read June-August. Publishes ms 1-2 months after acceptance. Length: 1,000 words average; 400 words minimum; 1,200 words maximum. Occasionally critiques rejected mss.

**How to Contact:** Send complete ms, query letter not necessary. Reports in 1-2 months. SASE for ms. Reprints OK. Accepts computer printouts including dot-matrix. Sample copy free. Fiction guidelines free.

**Payment:** Pays $20-25 and contributor's copies.

**Terms:** Pays on acceptance for first rights, first North American rights and one-time rihts. Publication copyrighted.

**Tips:** "A beginning writer who wants to make a significant contribution to the religious market should work toward applying basic techniques for good writing. Then he or she would probably excel. Be familiar with our Biblically-conservative philosophy and know what interests and concerns Christian teenagers. It also helps to be more interested in communicating Biblical principals via *quality* fiction than in receiving a large check. We treasure such writers and look forward to a day when we can pay more."

**‡PUBLISHERS SYNDICATION INTERNATIONAL (II)**, 1377 K St. NW, Suite 856, Washington DC 20005. Editor: A.P. Samuels. Romances and mysteries for general audience.

**Needs:** Romance, suspense/mystery. No other genre. Buys 60 mss/year. Length: 6,000 words minimum; prefers 6,000-30,000 words.

**How to Contact:** Send complete ms with cover letter. Reports in 6 weeks. SASE for ms. Accepts computer printouts including dot-matrix. "We can accept electronic submissions in 8 or 16 bit at 1200 band with prior written permission. Fiction guidelines free.

**Payment:** Pays 1-2¢/word.

**Terms:** Pays on acceptance for first North American serial rights. Publication copyrighted.

**Tips:** "PSI will be offering a completely new market to writers."

**PURPOSE (II)**, Mennonite Publishing House, 616 Walnut Ave., Scottdale PA 15683-1999. (412)887-8500. Editor: James E. Horsch. Magazine: 5¼x8¼; 8 pages; illustrations; photos. Magazine discipleship—how to be a faithful Christian in the midst of tough everday life complexities. Use story form to present models and examples for Christians interested in exploring faithful discipleship." Weekly. Estab. 1969. Circ. 18,000.

**Needs:** Historical, men's, religious/inspirational, and women's. No militaristic/narrow patriotism or racism. Receives 100 unsolicited mss/month. Buys 3 mss/issue; 40 mss/year. Publishes short shorts. Length: 800 words average; 350 words minimum; 1,200 words maximum. Occasionally comments on rejected ms.

**How to Contact:** Prefer full manuscript. Will respond to query. Reports in 4 weeks on queries; 6 weeks on mss. Simultaneous, photocopied, and previously published work OK. Accepts computer printout submissions. Prefers letter-quality. Sample copy free with SASE (6x9 and 2 first class stamps). Fiction guidelines free with sample copy only.

**Payment:** Up to 5¢/word and 2 contributor's copies.

**Terms:** Pays on acceptance for one-time rights. Publication copyrighted.

**Tips:** Many stories are "situational—how to respond to dilemmas. Write crisp, action moving, personal style, focused upon an individual or a group of people. The story form is an excellent literary device to use in exploring discipleship issues. We have many issues to explore. Each writer brings a unique solution. Let's hear them. The first two paragraphs are crucial in establishing the mood/issue to be resolved in the story. Work hard on this." Published new writers within the last year.

**QUEEN OF ALL HEARTS (II), Queen Magazine**, Montfort Missionaries, 26 S. Saxon Ave., Bay Shore NY 11706. (516)665-0726. Editor-in-Chief: James McMillan, S.M.M. Managing Editor: Roger M. Charest, S.M.M. Magazine: 10¾x7¾; 48 pages; self cover stock; illustrations; photos. Magazine of "stories, articles and features on the Mother of God by explaining the Scriptural basis and traditional teaching of Catholic Church concerning the Mother of Jesus, her influence in fields of history, literature, art, music, poetry, etc." Bimonthly. Estab. 1950. Circ. 7,000.
**Needs:** Religious/inspirational. "No mss not about Our Lady, the Mother of God, the Mother of Jesus." Receives 3 unsolicited fiction mss/month. Buys 3-4 mss/issue; 24 mss/year. Length: 1,500-2,000 words. Sometimes recommends other markets.
**How to Contact:** Send complete ms with SASE. Photocopied submissions OK. Reports in 1 month on mss. Publishes ms 6-12 months after acceptance. Sample copy $1.75 with 9x12 SAE.
**Payment:** Varies. 6 free contributor's copies.
**Terms:** Pays on acceptance.
**Tips:** "We are publishing stories with a Marian theme." Published new writers within the last year.

**R-A-D-A-R (II)**, Standard Publishing, 8121 Hamilton Ave., Cincinnati OH 45231. (513)931-4050. Editor: Margaret Williams. Paper: 12 pages; newspaper print; illustrations; a few photos. "*R-A-D-A-R* is a take-home paper, distributed in Sunday school classes for children in grades 3-6. The stories and other features reinforce the Bible lesson taught in class. Boys and girls who attend Sunday school make up the audience. The fiction stories, Bible picture stories, and other special features appeal to their interests." Weekly. Estab. 1877.
**Needs:** Fiction—The hero of the story should be an 11- or 12-year-old in a situation involving one or more of the following: mystery, animals (preferably horses or dogs), sports, adventure, school, travel, relationships with parents, friends, and others. Stories should have believable plots and be wholesome, Christian character-building, but not "preachy." Receives approximately 150 unsolicited fiction mss/month. Length: 900-1,100 words. Publishes short shorts of 500-1,000 words.
**How to Contact:** Send complete ms with SASE. Accepts computer printout submissions. Prefers letter-quality. Reports in 4-6 weeks. Free sample copy and guidelines.
**Payment:** 2-3¢ a word. Free author's copy.
**Terms:** Pays on acceptance for first and second serial (reprint) rights. Publication copyrighted.
**Tips:** "Send for sample copy, guidesheet, and theme list. Study them carefully and follow instructions." Mss are rejected because "they are too lengthy, have fuzzy plots, poorly-constructed sentences, or are in poor taste for Christian lifestyle." Published new writers within the last year."

**RANGER RICK'S NATURE MAGAZINE (II)**, National Wildlife Federation, 1412 16th St. NW, Washington DC 20036. (703)790-4217. Editor: Trudy Farrand. Fiction Editor: Lee Stowell Cullen. Magazine; 8x10; 48 pages; glossy paper; 60 lb cover stock; illustrations; photos. "*Ranger Rick* emphasizes conservation and the enjoyment of nature through full-color photos and art, fiction and nonfiction articles, games and puzzles, and special columns. Our audience ranges in ages from 4-12, with the greatest number in the 7 to 10 group. We aim for a fourth grade reading level. They read for fun and information." Monthly. Estab. 1967. Circ. 700,000.
**Needs:** Science fiction, fantasy, mystery, adventure, and humor. "Any kind of interesting stories for kids about nature and related subjects. Science fiction that carries a conservation message is always needed, as are adventure stories involving kids with nature or the outdoors. Moralistic 'lessons' taught children by parents or teachers are not accepted. Human qualities are attributed to animals only in our regular feature, 'Adventures of Ranger Rick.' " Receives 10-12 unsolicited fiction mss each month. Buys 1 ms/issue; 12 mss/year. Length: 900 words maximum. Critiques rejected mss "when there is time."
**How to Contact:** Query with sample lead and any clips of published work with SASE. Does not accept computer printout submissions. Letter-quality only. Reports in 2 weeks on queries, 2 months on mss. Publishes ms 8-12 months after acceptance, but sometimes longer. Free sample copy. Free guidelines with legal-sized SASE.

**Payment:** $400 maximum/full-length ms.

**Terms:** Pays on acceptance for all rights. Very rarely buys reprints. Sends galleys to author. Publication copyrighted.

**Tips:** "Read past issues to learn preferred style and approach; write naturally with no affectation; keep reader in mind at all times without being condescending." Mss are rejected because they are "contrived and/or condescending—often overwritten. Some mss are anthropomorphic, others are above our readers' level. We find that fiction stories help children understand the natural world and the environmental problems it faces. Beginning writers have an equal chance with established authors *provided* the quality is there."

**READ (II)**, Field Publications, 245 Long Hill Rd., Middletown CT 06457. (203)347-7251. Senior Editor: Edwin A. Hoey. Magazine: digest size; 32 pages; newsprint paper and cover stock; illustrations; photos. "*Read* is a bimonthly magazine for young people in junior high schools. Each issue includes a play and a short story." For junior high/middle school students. Estab. 1951.

**Needs:** Adventure, fantasy, science fiction, suspense/mystery, and young adult. No historical, religious or animal fiction. Receives 45-50 unsolicited fiction mss/month. Accepts 5 mss/year. Length: 1,000 words minimum; 4,000 words maximum. Publishes short shorts.

**How to Contact:** Send complete ms with SASE. Simultaneous, photocopied, and previously published submissions OK. Reports in 8 weeks on mss. Free sample copy for 7x9 SAE. Free fiction guidelines for 8½x4 SAE.

**Terms:** Acquires all or one-time rights. Publication copyrighted.

**‡RECONSTRUCTIONIST (II)**, Federation of Reconstructionist Congregations & Havurot, 270 W. 89th St., New York NY 10024. (212)496-2960. Editor: Jacob Staub. Magazine: 8½x11; 32 pages; illustrations; photos. Review of Jewish culture—essays, fiction, poetry of Jewish interest for American Jews. Published 8 times/year. Estab. 1935. Circ. 8,500.

**Needs:** Ethnic. Receives 2 unsolicited mss/month; buys 3-4 mss/year. Publishes ms 1-2 years after acceptance. Length: 2,500 words average; 3,000 words maximum. Publishes short shorts. Recommends other markets.

**How to Contact:** Send complete ms with cover letter. Reports in 6-8 weeks. SASE for mss. Photocopied submissions OK. Accepts computer printouts including dot-matrix. Sample copy free.

**Payment:** Pays $25-36 and contributor's copies.

**Terms:** Pays on publication for first rights. Publication copyrighted.

**REDBOOK (I)**, The Hearst Corporation, 224 W. 57th St., New York NY 10019. (212)262-8284. Editor: Annette Capone. Fiction Editor: Kathyrne V. Sagan. *Redbook*'s readership consists primarily of young American women 25-44 years of age, most married, some single, many mothers of young children, many working outside the home. *Redbook* readers are well-educated, progressive in their attitudes toward the roles and opportunities open to them as women and concerned with larger social issues as well as with their homes, their personal relationships and their health and appearance." Monthly. Publishes special fiction issue each August. Estab. 1903. Circ. 4,100,000.

**Needs:** "*Redbook* takes fiction very seriously, which may be why *Redbook* is one of the few magazines to win the National Magazine Award for fiction *twice*. We publish three or four fiction pieces in every issue (except in August, when our special fiction issue features five or six stories); these can be short stories, novel excerpts or condensations. We are looking for fiction that will appeal to active, thinking, contemporary women. Stories need not be about women exclusively; we also look for fiction reflecting the broad range of human experience. We are interested in new voices and buy around a quarter of what we publish each year from our unsolicited submissions. But standards are high; stories must be fresh, felt and intelligent; no straight formula fiction, surprise endings, highly oblique or symbolic stories without conclusions, please." Receives approximately 2,000 unsolicited fiction mss each month. Length: 15-20 manuscript pages for short stories, 5-10 pages for short shorts. Sometimes recommends other markets.

**How to Contact:** Send complete ms with large SASE. No queries, please. Reports in 10-12

weeks. Free guidelines for submission available on request with SASE.
**Terms:** Pays on acceptance. Buys first North American serial rights. Publication copyrighted.
**Tips:** "Short short stories are always in demand. We wish we saw more of the following: intelligently humorous stories (not anecdotes); stories about women in situations other than the home, in jobs other than the traditionally female ones, in relationships with persons other than family, mates or lovers. But do remember our readership is primarily women between 25-45 and so stories about young, single lifestyle are not really appropriate. Submit seasonal material at least nine months before the appropriate issue." Sponsors Short Story Contest for unpublished writers 18 years of age and up. "We announce contest and publish rules in the magazine. See March issue of *Redbook* for complete rules." Published 7 new writers last year.

**‡REFORM JUDAISM (II)**, Union of American Hebrew Congregations, 838 5th Ave., New York NY 10021. (212)249-0100, ext. 400. Editor: Steven Schnur. Fiction Editor: Aron Hirt-Manheimer. Magazine: 8½x11; 32 pages; illustrations; photos. "In-depth analysis of events and issues of interest to Reform Jews throughout the World." For "members of Reform Jewish congregations and others interested in Judaism generally and Reform Judaism in particular." Quarterly. Estab. 1972. Circ. 280,000.
**Needs:** Contemporary, ethnic, gay, humor/satire, literary, religious. Receives 30 unsolicited mss/month. Buys ¼ received. Publishes ms 3 months after acceptance. Length: 1,500 words average; 750 words minimum; 2,500 words maximum. Sometimes recommends other markets.
**How to Contact:** Send complete ms with cover letter. Reports in 2 weeks on queries; 3 weeks on mss. SASE for queries and ms. Accepts computer printouts. Sample copy and fiction guidelines free.
**Payment:** Pays $50-300 (10¢/word).
**Terms:** Pays on publication for first North American serial rights. Sends pre-publication galleys to author. Publication copyrighted.

**‡RELIX MAGAZINE (II, IV), Music for the Mind**, Relix, Inc., Box 94, Brooklyn NY 11229. (718)258-0009. Editor: Toni A. Brown. Magazine: 8x12; 36 pages; 100 lb coated cover stock. "Music—rock, blues, psychedelic, reggae, country-rock, bluegrass; non-commercial music—*60's related themes especially*; for holdovers from the 60's, aging hippies, youths looking to relive that era—mostly fans of the good ol' Grateful Dead. Bimonthly. Plans special issue in future. Estab. 1974. Circ. 15,000.
**Needs:** Fantasy, humor/satire, science fiction. Mostly interested in science fiction-related rock stories. Receives 3-5 unsolicited mss/month. Length: 1,500 words average; 1,200 words minimum; 1,700 words maximum. Publishes short shorts of 250-500 words. Occasionally critiques rejected mss. Recommends other markets.
**How to Contact:** Send complete ms with cover letter. Reports in 2 months. SASE for ms. Simultaneous and photocopied submissions OK. Accepts computer printouts including dot-matrix. Sample copy for $2. Fiction guidelines free.
**Payment:** Pays $1.50/column inch and contributor's copies.
**Terms:** Pays on publication for all rights. Publication copyrighted.
**Tips:** "*Relix* is open to new writers. Though our format can't always include fiction material, I have been compiling material for a book that we hope to publish. The strongest themes included will be rock/science fiction-fantasy. We are always looking for *fresh* writers. We can't always use the material, but I love to read it! Some incredible work has passed across my desk. I have recommended other publications for potential interest in material we can't use."

**ROAD KING MAGAZINE (II)**, William A. Coop, Inc., Box 250, Park Forest IL 60466. (312)481-9240. Magazine: 5¾x8; 48-88 pages; 55 lb enamel paper; 55 lb enamel cover stock; illustrations; photos. "Quarterly leisure-reading magazine for long-haul, over-the-road professional truckers. Contains short articles, short fiction, some product news, games, puzzles, and industry news. Truck drivers read it while eating, fueling, during layovers and at other similar times while they are enroute."

**Needs:** Science fiction, fantasy, men's, western, mystery, adventure, and humor. "Remember that our magazine gets into the home and that some truckers tend to be Bible belt types. No erotica or violence." Buys 1 ms/issue; 4 mss/year. Receives 200 unsolicited fiction mss each year. Length: 1,200 words.

**How to Contact:** Send complete ms with SASE. Reports in 3-6 months on mss. Publishes ms 1-2 months after acceptance. Sample copy with 6x9 SAE with 71¢ postage.

**Payment:** $400 maximum.

**Terms:** Pays on acceptance for all rights. Publication copyrighted.

**Tips:** "Don't phone. Don't send mss by registered or insured mail or they will be returned unopened by post office. Don't try to get us involved in lengthy correspondence. Be patient. We have a small staff and we are slow." Mss are rejected because "most don't fit our format . . . they are too long; they do not have enough knowledge of trucking; there is too much violence; they are not really short stories, nothing happens. Our readers like fiction. We are a leisure reading publication with a wide variety of themes and articles in each issue. Truckers can read our bit over coffee in the washroom, etc., then save the rest of the magazine for the next stop." Published new writers within the last year.

**ST. ANTHONY MESSENGER (II)**, St. Anthony Messenger, 1615 Republic St., Cincinnati OH 45210. Editor: Norman Perry, O.F.M. Magazine: 10¾x8; 56 pages; illustrations; photos. "*St. Anthony Messenger* is a Catholic family magazine which aims to help its readers lead more fully human and Christian lives. We publish articles which report on a changing church and world, opinion pieces written from the perspective of Christian faith and values, personality profiles, and fiction which entertains and informs." Monthly. Estab. 1893. Circ. 360,000.

**Needs:** Contemporary, religious/inspirational, romance, and senior citizen/retirement. "We do not want mawkishly sentimental or preachy fiction. Stories are most often rejected for poor plotting and characterization; bad dialogue—listen to how people talk; inadequate motivation. Many stories say nothing, are 'happenings' rather than stories." No fetal journals, no rewritten Bible stories. Receives 50-60 unsolicited fiction mss/month. Buys 1 ms/issue; 12 mss/year. Length: 2,500-3,000 words. Critiques rejected mss "when there is time." Sometimes recommends other markets.

**How to Contact:** Send complete ms with SASE. Accepts computer printout submissions. Prefers letter-quality. Reports in 6 weeks on mss. Publishes ms up to 1 year after acceptance. Free sample copy and guideline with legal-sized SASE.

**Payment:** 12¢/word maximum; 2 free author's copies; $1 charge for extras.

**Terms:** Pays on acceptance for first North American serial rights. Publication copyrighted.

**Tips:** "We publish one story a month and we get 500 or 600 a year. Stick to published word length. Read guidelines and look at back issues to see what we *do* publish. Plots and characters have to be real. Too many offer simplistic 'solutions' or answers. Fiction entertains but can also convey a point in a very telling way just as the Bible uses stories to teach." Published new writers within the last year.

**ST. JOSEPH'S MESSENGER AND ADVOCATE OF THE BLIND (II)**, Sisters of St. Joseph of Peace, 541 Pavonia Ave., Jersey City NJ 07306. (201)798-4141. Magazine: 11x14; 16 pages; illustrations; photos. For Catholics generally but not exclusively. Theme is "religious—relevant—real." Quarterly. Estab. 1903. Circ. 35,000.

**Needs:** Contemporary, humor/satire, mainstream, religious/inspirational, romance, and senior citizen/retirement. Receives 30-40 unsolicited fiction mss/month. Buys 3 mss/issue; 20 mss/year. Length: 800 words minimum; 1,800 words maximum; 1,500 words average. Occasionally critiques rejected mss.

**How to Contact:** Send complete ms with SASE. Simultaneous, photocopied, and previously published submissions OK. Publishes ms an average of 1 year after acceptance. Free sample copy with legal-sized SAE and 1 first class stamp. Free fiction guidelines with SASE.

**Payment:** $10-25 and 2 contributor's copies.

**Terms:** Pays on acceptance for one-time rights. Buys reprints.

**Tips:** Rejects mss because of "vague focus or theme. Have a story in mind as you write. *Do not preach*—the story will tell the message. Keep the ending from being too obvious. Fiction is the greatest area of interest to our particular reading public." Published new writers within the last year.

**SAN GABRIEL VALLEY MAGAZINE (IV)**, Miller Books, 2908 W. Valley Blvd., Alhambra CA 91803. (213)284-7607. Editor: Joseph Miller. Magazine: 5¼x7¼; 48 pages; #60 book paper; vellum Bristol cover stock; illustrations; photos. "Regional magazine for the Valley featuring local entertainment, dining, sports and events. We also carry articles about successful people from the area. For upper-middle class people who enjoy going out a lot." Bimonthly. Published special fiction issue last year; plans another. Estab. 1976. Circ. 3,000.
**Needs:** Contemporary, inspirational, psychic/supernatural/occult, western, adventure, and humor. No articles on sex or ERA. Receives approximately 10 unsolicited fiction mss/month. Buys 2 mss/issue; 20 mss/year. Length: 500-2,500 words. Also publishes short shorts. Recommends other markets.
**How to Contact:** Send complete ms with SASE. Accepts computer printout submissions. Reports in 2 weeks on mss. Sample copy $1 with 9x12 SASE.
**Payment:** 5¢/word; 2 free author's copies.
**Terms:** Payment on acceptance for one-time rights. Publication copyrighted.
**Tips:** "Write a good story with positive attitudes." Mss are rejected because "they do not relate to our region or readers." Published new writers within the last year.

**SATURDAY EVENING POST (I, II)**, Benjamin Franklin Literary and Medical Society, 1100 Waterway Blvd., Indianapolis IN 46202. (317)636-8881. Editor: Dr. Cory Servaas, M.D. Senior Editor: Ted Kreiter. Magazine with articles on general interest, health care, personalities, book reviews and games for conservative middle age, middle income, college-educated audience. Published 9 times/year. Estab. 1728. Circ. 700,000.
**Needs:** Religious/inspirational, science fiction, gothic, romance, western, mystery, adventure, and humor. No explicit sex, profanity, perversion, ethnic humor or anti-traditional family life. Buys 3-4 mss/issue. Length: average of 2,500 words.
**How to Contact:** Send complete ms with SASE. Reports in 1-8 weeks.
**Payment:** Pays average of $250.
**Terms:** Pays on publication for all rights.
**Tips:** "We want positive stories about romance, family and love, people winning out in the end. Humor has a better chance. Keep it simple."

**‡SCORE (IV), Canada's Golf Magazine**, Canadian Controlled Media Communications (CCMC), 287 MacPherson Ave., Toronto, Ontario M4V 1A4 Canada. (416)928-2909. Managing Editor: Lisa A. Leighton. Magazine: 8½x10⅞; 48-80 pages; 70 lb coated stock and cover; b&w and color illustrations; b&w and color photos. "Golf: players, events, travel (as golf destinations), equipment, technical, instruction, humor, fiction, etc." For "over 25, upper income, socially active, those usually belonging to private or semi-private golf clubs." Published 7 times/year. Estab. 1981. Circ. 171,000 +.
**Needs:** Special interest—golf related. No adventure or science fiction. Receives approximately 8 unsolicited fiction mss/month. Buys 0-2 mss/issue; between 4 and 9 mss/year, "depending on their calibre and our editorial needs." Publishes mss 1½-6 months after acceptance. Length: 800-1,500 words average; 1,700 words maximum. Also publishes short shorts of 250-450 words. Occasionally critiques rejected mss. Recommends other markets.
**How to Contact:** Query with clips of published work or send complete ms with cover letter with "resume, published references, full name, address, phone number, reasons why writer wishes to work with *Score*, and some indication writer is familiar with magazine." Reports in 1 month on queries and mss. SASE for query and ms. Simultaneous submissions OK. Accepts computer printouts. No dot-matrix. Sample copy for $2 and 9x12 SAE and 65¢ postage. Fiction guidelines for business size SAE and 65¢ postage.

**Payment:** Pays $125-300 (CDN).
**Terms:** Pays on publication for all rights. Publication copyrighted.
**Tips:** "*Score* is a special interest and a consumer magazine, and North American consumers are better educated and more discriminatory than ever. So writers of fiction must have a solid foundation in researching their subjects (as far as possible) in order to make it *good* fiction rather than just fantasy. Writers wishing to work for *Score* must have a background in the game of golf, whether they write technical material or fiction. Writing is also obviously very competitive, so writers just breaking in will have to not only show their knowledge, they will have to have a firm fluency in the basics of presentations: grammar, usage, spelling, typing, etc. and introductory letters. You have only one chance to make a first impression, and that's quite often what catches the editor's eye, or sends the query into limbo. Golf lends itself to various facets of fiction writing. It also breaks up what can become an annoying continuum of technical/instructional material. Decide exactly what you want to write before you contact us. If you have a half-baked idea we are not going to finish it for you. Make us aware that you have taken the trouble to familiarize yourself with *Score* before you write to us, and present yourself well."

**‡SCREW MAGAZINE (II), The Sex Review**, Milky Way Productions, Box 432, Old Chelsea Station, New York NY 10011. (212)989-8001. Editor: Al Goldstein. Fiction Editor: Manny Neuhaus. Tabloid: 56 pages; pulp paper; 2-color pulp cover stock; illustrations; photos. Humor, sex, satire, parody, first-person erotica stories for adult males. Weekly. Estab. 1968. Circ. 150,000.
**Needs:** Confession, erotica, ethnic, experimental, feminist, gay, humor/satire, lesbian, men's. Nothing non-sexual. Receives 5-15 unsolicited fiction mss/month. Buys 1-3 mss/issue. Publishes ms 1-6 months after acceptance. Length: 1,300 words average; 1,000 words minimum; 2,500 words maximum. Occasionally critiques rejected mss. Recommends other markets.
**How to Contact:** Send complete ms with cover letter. Reports in 1-2 months. Photocopied submissions OK. Accepts computer printouts including dot-matrix. Sample copy and fiction guidelines free.
**Payment:** Pays $40-150; contributor's copies.
**Terms:** Pays on publication for all rights. Publication copyrighted.

**SECRETS (I)**, Macfadden Women's Group, 215 Lexington Ave., New York NY 10016. (212)340-7500. Editor: Jean Press Silberg. Confession magazine for blue-collar women with families; ages 18-35. Monthly. Estab. 1936.
**Needs:** Women's interest pieces, based on true incidents or situations. Themes heavy on romance and family; involving family, marriage, work; should be relevant to readers' lives. First person narrator may be male or female. Buys 10-12 mss/issue; 150 mss/year. Occasionally critiques rejected mss when they "may be usable, if reworked." Length: 1,500-10,000 words. Some 10,000-word "novelettes."
**How to Contact:** Send complete ms with SASE. Reports in 2 months on mss. No photocopied or simultaneous submissions. Seasonal stories should be submitted 4-5 months in advance.
**Payment:** 3¢/word.
**Terms:** Pays on publication for all rights. Publication copyrighted.
**Tips:** Mss are rejected because of "lack of familiarity with our needs and our style. Suggest close examination of magazine, and understanding of our readers. Stories must be written in first person."

**SEEK (II)**, Standard Publishing, 8121 Hamilton Ave., Cincinnati OH 45231. Editor: Eileen H. Wilmoth. Magazine: 8½x5½; 8 pages; newsprint paper; art and photos in each issue. "Inspirational stories of faith-in-action for Christian young adults; a Sunday School take-home paper." Weekly. Published special fiction issue last year; plans another. Estab. 1970. Circ. 75,000.
**Needs:** Religious/inspirational. Buys 100 mss/year. Length: 500-1,200 words. Recommends other markets.
**How to Contact:** Send complete ms with SASE. Accepts computer printout submissions. Pre-

fers letter-quality. Reports in 2 weeks on mss. Publishes ms an average of 1 year after acceptance. Free sample copy and guidelines.

**Payment:** 2½-3¢/word.

**Terms:** Pays on acceptance. Buys reprints.

**Tips:** "Write a credible story with Christian slant—no preachments; avoid overworked themes such as joy in suffering, generation gaps, etc. Most mss are rejected by us because of irrelevant topic or message; unrealistic story; or poor character and/or plot development. We use fiction stories that are believable." Published new writers within the last year.

**ROD SERLING'S THE TWILIGHT ZONE MAGAZINE (I)**, TZ Publications, 800 Second Ave., New York NY 10017. Editor: Michael Blaine. "A magazine devoted to imaginative and speculative fiction. We're always on the lookout for originality, strong writing, and a fresh viewpoint." Bimonthly. Estab. 1981. Circ. 150,000.

**Needs:** Experimental, fantasy, horror, science fiction and surrealism, and psychic/supernatural. "Characterizations are important. No sword-and-sorcery, or imaginary world fantasy." Receives 500 unsolicited fiction mss/month. Buys 8-10 mss/issue. Approximately 25% of fiction is agented. Length: short-short to 6,000 words. Seldom critiques rejected mss.

**How to Contact:** Send complete ms with SASE. No queries please. Simultaneous and photocopied submissions OK. Reports in 4-6 months on mss. Publishes ms 2-12 months after acceptance. Free fiction guidelines for legal-sized SAE and 22¢ postage.

**Payment:** Pays $150-800; 2 free contributor's copies. Buys reprints "only in exceptional cases."

**Terms:** Pays one-half on acceptance and one-half on publication. Publication copyrighted.

**Tips:** "The number of submissions seems to be increasing each year—which is a sad comment on the small size of the market. As is probably inevitable in the supernatural horror genre, we tend to get the same two dozen or so plots over and over."

**SEVENTEEN (II)**, Triangle Communications, 850 3rd Ave., New York NY 10022. (212)759-8100. Editor-in-Chief: Midge Richardson. Managing Editor: Joan Downs. Editor: Sarah Crichton. Fiction Editor: Bonni Price. Magazine: 8½x11; 125-400 pages; 40 lb coated paper; 80 lb coated cover stock; illustrations; photos. A service magazine with fashion, beauty care, pertinent topics such as trends in dating, attitudes, experiences and concerns during the teenage years. Monthly. Estab. 1944. Circ. 1.7 million.

**Needs:** High-quality fiction on topics of interest to teenage girls. The editors look for fresh themes and well-paced plots. Buys 1 ms/issue. Receives 200-300 unsolicited fiction mss/month. Approximately 50% of fiction is agented. Length: approximately 1,500-3,000 words. Also publishes short shorts.

**How to Contact:** Send complete ms with SASE and cover letter with relevant credits. Reports in 2 months on mss. Free guidelines with SASE.

**Payment:** Pays $700-1,000.

**Terms:** Pays on acceptance for one-time rights. Publication copyrighted.

**Tips:** "Adult writers underestimate the intelligence and sophistication of today's teenage reader; plots are either worn out or sloppily constructed, with too little character development. *Seventeen* remains open to the surprise of the new voices. Our commitment to publishing the work of new writers remains strong; we continue to read every submission we receive. We believe that good fiction can move the reader toward thoughtful examination of her own life as well as the lives of others—providing her ultimately with a fuller appreciation of what it means to be human.' Published new writers within the last year. Sponsors annual fiction contest. Rules are announced each year in April issue.

**‡SHINING STAR (II), Practical Teaching Magazine for Christian Educators and Parents**, Good Apple, Box 299, Carthage IL 62321. (800)435-7234. Editor: Becky Daniel. Magazine: 8½x11; 96 pages; illustrations. "Biblical stories only for teachers and parents of children K-8th graders." Quarterly. Estab. 1982. Circ. 10,000.

# Close-up

### Bonni Price
### *Seventeen* Magazine

"This really is a dream job," says Bonni Price, fiction editor for *Seventeen*. "It's exciting to work with the pros, and especially to discover new writers"—and certainly not impossible. Sylvia Plath and Meg Wolitzer got their literary boost after winning *Seventeen*'s annual short story contest. So did Lorrie Moore *(Self-Help)* in 1976 and recently Paul Leslie, Moore's student at the University of Wisconsin.

In 1984, *Seventeen* won the National Magazine Award for fiction, edging out such heady competitors as *Harper's, Redbook, The New Yorker*, and *Chicago* Magazine. "We publish quality fiction," Price says—"stories that are as much about the human condition as well as they are about being a teenager. We assume our readers can appreciate good writing."

Essentially *Seventeen*'s pitch is toward the 16-17 year-old girl although readers range from 12-20; a good story should have something for everybody. Deciding on their story each month is a matter of "gut feeling . . ." says the fiction editor. "It's a visceral sense, a physical response when something is good or when we find something that moves us."

"Us" refers to the several editors who read a story and to the editor-in-chief, Midge Richardson, who gives the final nod. The fiction department staff? "I'm it," says Price, who oversees the monthly fiction production, edits the article and monthly advice column and heads the short story contest, now co-sponsored with Dell with larger cash awards.

Bonni Price began her publishing career at *Redbook* several years ago in the fiction department. She loves to read, she says—and there's plenty; about 3,000 unsolicited manuscripts a year, or 250 or so a month. One-third of the published stories come out of slush; the rest are via agents. "We read them all," she insists. But not all of everything. Of course, the physical details—the manuscript's appearance and preparation—do not make or break a story, but an unprofessional look is too often telltale, she finds. A poorly-prepared story folded into a too-small business-size envelope *suggests* that "the writer doesn't care enough about the manuscript to make it presentable. Why then should we care?" The most successful stories usually arrive neatly-typed and flat in a manila envelope.

The common pitfall of the rejected story at *Seventeen* is the author's tendency to moralize, to try to teach teenagers something. There are also the here-we-go-again-teen themes: the fat girl with the gorgeous friend; the overwhelming crush on the high school hunk; the sainted grandmother; etc. "We're looking for a fresh and clearly written story that tells our readers something they don't already know." The same subjects *will* surface frequently because they are vital in a teen's life, but, Price adds, "we hope they'll be treated with a new angle to make them publishable."

Delicate topics such as abortion and homosexuality are acceptable only if handled well. Today's kids are more aware. Life today *is* more complex and presents more options than 10 or 15 years ago, but the essential difficulties of adolescence endure. *Seventeen* has historically helped ease teen traumas subtly through its fiction.

Price also excerpts chapters of serious, solid young adult books, like *A Little Love*, by Virginia Hamilton, for example. But generally the preference is for the 6-15 manuscript page-story. "We're a wide-open market," Price says, and then adds, as if to offer a challenge, "I think there are very good writers out there who are not sending in submissions; they're putting them away in their desk drawers."

**Needs:** Biblical only! No Biblical settings. Receives 30 unsolicited mss/month. Buys 3 mss/issue; 12 mss/year. Publishes ms 9-12 months after acceptance. Length: 500-1,000 words. Publishes short shorts. Recommends other markets.
**How to Contact:** Send complete ms with cover letter. Reports in 4 weeks. SASE for ms. Simultaneous and photocopied submissions OK. Accepts computer printouts including dot-matrix. Sample copy $1. Fiction guidelines free.
**Payment:** Pays $20-50 and contributor's copies.
**Terms:** Pays on publication for all rights. Publication copyrighted.
**Tips:** "Know the scriptures and be a teacher or person that has worked with young children."

**THE SINGLE PARENT (I, IV), Journal of Parents Without Partners**, Parents Without Partners, Inc., Suite 1008, 7910 Woodmont Ave., Bethesda MD 20814. (301)654-8850. Editor: Donna Duvall. Magazine: 8½x11; 48 pages; 40 lb glossy paper; 60 lb cover stock; illustrations; photos. Publication for divorced, separated, widowed or never-married parents and their children. Published 6 times/year. Estab. 1965. Circ. 205,000.
**Needs:** Short stories for *children only*, not adults. Stories should deal with issues that children from one-parent families might face. Buys 1 ms/issue. Length: 1,000 words maximum. Publishes short shorts. Sometimes recommends other markets.
**How to Contact:** Query letter before sending manuscript. Send complete ms with SASE (10x10 manila envelope; 50¢ postage). Reports within 6 weeks.
**Payment:** Pays up to $50; 2 free contributor's copies.
**Terms:** Pays on publication.
**Tips:** "A children's page is a new addition to the magazine. Would prefer stories short enough to fit on one page. Upbeat, problem-solving themes preferred." Published new writers within the last year.

**‡SINGLELIFE MAGAZINE (II)**, Single Life Enterprises, Inc., 606 W. Wisconsin Ave., Suite 706, Milwaukee WI 53202. (414)271-9700. Editor: Leifa Butrick. Magazine: 8x11; 82 pages; slick paper; illustrations; photos. "Issues to do with being single for readers from 25-50 age group." Primarily a nonfiction magazine. Bimonthly. Estab. 1982. Circ. 25,000.
**Needs:** Humor/satire, literary, contemporary romance. Receives 20 unsolicited mss/month. "We have only published 2 stories (fictional items) in 3 years." Publishes 2-4 months after acceptance. Length: 1,000 words minimum; 2,500 words maximum. Also publishes short shorts. Occasionally critiques rejected mss.
**How to Contact:** Send complete ms with cover letter. Reports in 1-4 weeks, "depends on production schedule." SASE for ms. Simultaneous, photocopied and reprint submissions OK. Accepts computer printouts including dot-matrix. Accepts electronic submissions via disc or modem. Sample copy $2.50. Fiction guidelines for SAE and 1 first class stamp.
**Payment:** Pays $50 and contributor's copies.
**Terms:** Pays on publication for one-time rights. Publication copyrighted.
**Tips:** "Present us with good characters. Please, no stories that take place in bars."

**‡SOUTHERN EXPOSURE (IV)**, Institute for Southern Studies, Box 531, Durham NC 27702. (919)688-8167. Contact: Editor. Magazine: 8½x11; Carolina Bond paper; illustrations. Regional magazine of politics and culture. Bimonthly. Estab. 1973. Circ. 5,000.
**Needs:** Contemporary, ethnic, experimental, feminist, gay, historical, lesbian, regional. No non-political or non-southern mss. Buys 6 fiction mss/year. Agented fiction: 5%. Publishes short shorts. Rarely critiques rejected mss.
**How to Contact:** Query first. Reports in 3 weeks on queries; 2 months on mss. SASE for ms. Simultaneous and photocopied submissions and reprints OK. Accepts computer printouts including dot-matrix. Fiction guidelines for SAE and 1 first class stamp.
**Payment:** $50-200; contributor's copies.
**Terms:** Sends galleys to author.

**‡SPORTS AFIELD (II, IV)**, Hearst Magazine, 250 W. 55th St., New York 10019. (212)262-8835. Editor: Tom Paugh. Magazine: 11x8; 128 pages minimum; "the best paper"; 70 lb cover stock; illustrations; photos. "This is an outdoor magazine: hunting, fishing, camping, boating, conservation, etc." for upscale, adult males. Monthly. Estab. 1887. Circ. 542,000.
**Needs:** Adventure, humor/satire (if outdoors), special interest—hunting and fishing. No old-fashioned me-and-Joe yarns. Receives 20 unsolicited mss/month. Buys a few mss each year. Publishes ms up to 2 years after acceptance. Agented fiction: 5%. Length: 2,500 words average. Also publishes short shorts of 200-250 words.
**How to Contact:** Query first. Reports in 4 weeks on queries and mss. SASE for query. Accepts computer printouts including dot-matrix. Sample copy $1.95.
**Payment:** Pays $700.
**Terms:** Pays on acceptance for first rights. Publication copyrighted.
**Tips:** "Fiction is a very tough market—and not just in the outdoor field."

**STAG MAGAZINE**, 888 7th Ave., New York NY 10106. (212)541-7100. Editor-in-Chief: Bill Bottiggi. Slick men's sex magazine, mostly photos, also humor, interviews. Readers are blue collar men ages 20-45. Monthly. Estab. 1951. Circ. 125,000.
**Needs:** Adventure, contemporary, erotica, humor/satire, and men's. Do not send "boring manuscript; has to have more than just sex." Receives approximately 15 unsolicited fiction mss/month. Buys 1 ms/issue; 12 mss/year. Length: 2,000 words minimum; 3,000 words maximum; 2,500 words average.
**How to Contact:** Query with clips of published work with SASE. Photocopied submissions OK. Reports in 6 weeks. Free sample copy with SAE.
**Payment:** $200-400.
**Tips:** Rejects mss because "the stories are unimaginative or not geared to reader interests."

**‡STANDARD (II, IV)**, Nazarene International Headquarters, 6401 The Paseo, Kansas City MO 64131. (816)333-7000. Editor: Sheila Boggess. Magazine: 8½x11; 8 pages; illustrations; photos. Inspirational/leisure reading for adults. Weekly. Estab. 1936. Circ. 177,000.
**Needs:** Religious/inspirational. Receives 80-100 unsolicited fiction mss/month. Accepts 2 mss/issue; 100 mss/year. Publishes ms 9-24 months after acceptance. Length: 1,000 words average; 300 words minimum; 1,500 words maximum. Also publishes short shorts of 300-350 words.
**How to Contact:** Send complete ms with cover letter (short 1-2 paragraphs telling of submission; include name, address, phone number). Reports in 3-4 weeks on mss. SASE. Simultaneous, photocopied submissions and reprints OK but will pay only reprint rates. Accepts computer printouts. Sample copy for SAE and 1 first class stamp. Fiction guidelines for SAE and 1 first class stamp.
**Payment:** Pays 2¢/word (reprint) or 3.5¢/word; contributor's copies; charge for extras.
**Terms:** Pays on acceptance for one-time rights. Publication copyrighted.
**Tips:** "Too much is superficial; containing the same story lines. Give me something original, humorous, yet helpful."

**‡STARWIND (I, II)**, Starwind Press, Box 98, Ripley OH 45167. (513)392-4549. Editor: David F. Powell. Magazine: 8½x11; 64 pages; 60 lb offset paper; 60 lb offset cover stock; b&w illustrations; line shots photos. "Science fiction and fantasy for young adults (teen 25 or so) with interest in science, technology, science fiction and fantasy." Quarterly. Plans special issue in future. Estab. 1974. Circ. 2,000.
**Needs:** Fantasy, humor/satire, science fiction. "We like SF that shows hope for the future and protagonists who interact with their environment rather than let themselves be manipulated by it." No horror, pastiches of other authors, stories, featuring characters created by others (i.e. Captain Kirk and crew, Dr. Who, etc.). Receives 50 + unsolicited mss/month. Buys 4-6 mss/issue; 16-24 mss/year. Publishes between 4 months-2 years after acceptance. Length: 3,000-8,000 words average; 2,000 words minimum; 10,000 words maximum. Occasionally critiques rejected mss.
**How to Contact:** Send complete ms with cover letter. Reports in 6-8 weeks. SASE for ms. Pho-

tocopied submissions OK. Accepts computer printouts including dot-matrix. Accepts electronic submissions via disc or modem for the IBM PC or PC compatible; MacIntosh; word processors: Multimate, Word Star, MacWrite, or ASCII. Sample copy $2.50. Fiction guidelines free for legal-size SAE and 1 first class stamp.

**Payment:** Pays .01-.04/word and contributor's copies.

**Terms:** Pays 25% on acceptance; 75% on publication. "25% payment is kill fee if we decide not to publish story." Rights negotiable. Sends galleys to the author. Publication copyrighted.

**Tips:** "I certainly think a beginning writer can be successful if he/she studies the publication *before* submitting, and matches the submission with the magazine's needs. As a science fiction publication, short stories are essential. We also publish nonfiction which complements the science fiction. Get our guidelines and study them *before* submitting. Don't submit something *way over* or *way under* our word length requirements. Take our needs into account—the types of stories we look for, etc. Be understanding of editors; they can get swamped very easily, *especially* if there's only one editor handling all submissions. With many small magazines, editors have other full time jobs. Be professional. Type your manuscript on typing paper, with a minimum of erasures, and editorial notes. Don't write a synopsis of your story in your cover letter—the story should be able to stand on its own."

**STORIES (II)**, 14 Beacon St., Boston MA 02108. Editor-in-Chief: Amy R. Kaufman. "*Stories* is a short story magazine that publishes short fiction exclusively. It is designed to encourage the writing of stories that evoke an emotional response." Quarterly. Estab. 1982.

**Needs:** Contemporary, ethnic, historical (general), humor/satire, and literary. "Translations and sharply perceptive humor interest us; romance, mystery, fantasy, science fiction, and political pieces generally do not. We will not exclude any story on the basis of genre; we wish only that the piece be the best of its genre." Buys 5-6 mss/issue. Length: 750 words minimum; 13,000 words maximum; 4,000-7,000 words average. "Editor will make every effort to assist in revising stories she feels have merit."

**How to Contact:** Send complete ms with SASE. Do not use certified mail. Photocopies preferred. Simultaneous submissions OK "if marked as such." Reports in 8-10 weeks on mss. Free fiction guidelines with SASE.

**Payment:** $150 average.

**Terms:** Pays within 7 days of publication for first North American serial rights.

**Tips:** "Simplicity is achieved after a struggle, and universality is possible only to a degree, but we feel that these are the qualities most likely to evoke readers' sympathy and concern. Timelessness is another ideal we pursue, by avoiding language and subjects that are fashionable. Most writers submit half-finished work—they haven't taken themselves seriously enough. Study Strunk & White's *Elements of Style*, and emulate your favorite authors. You can't aim too high."

**STORY FRIENDS (II)**, Mennonite Publishing House, 616 Walnut Ave., Scottdale PA 15683. (412)887-8500. Editor: Marjorie Waybill. Sunday school publication which portrays Jesus as a friend and helper. Nonfiction and fiction for children 4-9 years of age. Weekly.

**Needs:** Juvenile. Stories of everyday experiences at home, in church, in school or at play, which provide models of Christian values. Length: 300-800 words.

**How to Contact:** Send complete ms with SASE. Seasonal or holiday material should be submitted six months in advance. Free sample copy.

**Payment:** Pays 3-5¢/word.

**Terms:** Pays on acceptance for rights. Buys reprints. Not copyrighted. Byline given.

**Tips:** "It is important to include relationships, patterns of forgiveness, respect, honesty, trust and caring. Prefer exciting yet plausible short stories which offer different settings, introduce children to wide ranges of friends and demonstrate joys, fears, temptations and successes of the readers."

**STRAIGHT (II)**, Standard Publishing Co., 8121 Hamilton Ave., Cincinnati OH 45231. (513)931-4050. Editor: Dawn Brettschneider. Publication helping and encouraging teens to live a victorious, fulfilling Christian life. Distributed through churches and some private subscriptions.

Magazine: 6½x7½; 12 pages; newsprint paper and cover; illustrations (color); photos. Quarterly in weekly parts. Estab. 1951. Circ. 100,000.

**Needs:** Contemporary, religious/inspirational, romance, mystery, adventure, and humor—all with Christian emphasis. "Stories dealing with teens and teen life, with a positive message or theme. Topics that interest teenagers include school, family life, recreation, friends, church, part-time jobs, dating, and music. Main character should be a 15- or 16-year old boy or girl, a Christian and regular church goer, who faces situations using Bible principles." Buys 1-2 mss/issue; 75-100 mss/year. Receives approximately 100 unsolicited fiction mss/month. Less than 1% of fiction is agented. Length: 800-1,200 words. Recommends other markets.

**How to Contact:** Send complete ms with SASE with cover letter (experience with teens). Accepts computer printout submissions. Reports in 6 weeks on mss. Publishes ms an average of 1 year after acceptance. Free sample copy and guidelines with SASE.

**Payment:** 2-3½¢/word.

**Terms:** Pays on acceptance for first and one-time rights. Buys reprints. Publication copyrighted.

**Tips:** "Get to know us before submitting, through guidelines and sample issues. It's a good idea to give the editor an 'out' for changing stories—from a boy character to a girl, from an in-school story to one that can be adapted to summertime. A writer must know what today's teens are like, and what kinds of conflicts they experience. There's always room for another good fiction writer. Don't try to accomplish too much. In 1,000 words you can't create total characters; they will tend to be 'flatter' than if you could flesh them up a bit. If your character is dealing with the problem of prejudice, don't also deal with his/her fights with sister, desire for a bicycle, or anything else that is not absolutely essential to the reader's understanding of the major conflict." Published both teen and adult new writers last year.

**THE STUDENT (I, II), A Christian Collegiate Magazine**, National Student Ministries of the Baptist Sunday School Board, 127 Ninth Ave., North, Nashville TN 37234. (615)251-2783. Magazine: 8¼x11; 50 pages; uncoated paper; coated cover stock; illustrations; photos. Magazine for Christians and nonChristians about life and work with Christian students on campus and related articles on living in dorm setting, dating life, mission activities, Bible study, and church ministry to students. Monthly. Estab. 1929. Circ. 22,000.

**Needs:** Adventure, humor, comics, confession, contemporary, ethnic, and religious/inspirational. Does not want to see mss "without purpose or without moral tone." Receives approximately 25 unsolicited fiction mss/month. Buys 1-2 mss/issue; 12-24 mss/year. Length: 300 words minimum (or less, depending on treatment); 1,000 words maximum; 750 words average.

**How to Contact:** Cover letter with bio and description of published works. Query first with SASE. Simultaneous, photocopied, and previously published submissions OK. Reports in 3 weeks on queries; 6 weeks on mss. Sample copy 61¢. Free fiction guidelines with SASE.

**Payment:** 4¢/word and 3 contributor's copies.

**Terms:** Pays on publication for all rights, first rights, one-time rights, and assignments for work-for-hire basis. Publication copyrighted.

**Tips:** "Fit writing to format and concept of the piece. View many issues of the magazine before you write. Our readers demand fiction which conveys our message in an interesting way." Published approximately 10 new writers within the last year.

**STUDENT LAWYER (II, IV)**, American Bar Assoc., 750 N. Lake Shore Dr., Chicago IL 60611. (312)988-6048. Editor: Lizanne Poppens. Associate editor: Sarah Hoban. "Magazine for law students as part of their Law Student Division/ABA membership. Features legal aspects, trends in the law, social/legal issues, and lawyer profiles. Monthly (September-May). Circ. 40,000.

**Needs:** "All stories have to have a legal/law/lawyer/law school element to them. No science fiction." Buys 1 full-length or 2-3 short humorous pieces/year. Length: 1,000-3,000 words. Sometimes recommends other markets.

**How to Contact:** Send complete ms with SASE. Accepts computer printout submissions. Reports in 1 month on mss. Publishes ms 1-6 months after acceptance. Sample copy $2, contact Order Fulfillment at above address.

**Payment:** $75-500.
**Terms:** Pays on acceptance for first rights. Buys very few reprints.
**Tips:** Rejects mss because "usually, the stories are of mediocre quality. Because we favor nonfiction pieces, the fiction we do publish has to be outstanding or at least very original."

**SUNDAY DIGEST (II)**, David C. Cook Publishing Co., 850 N. Grove Ave., Elgin IL 60120. (312)741-2400. Editor: Judy C. Couchman. Magazine: 5½x8½; 104 pages; 50 lb penegra paper; 50 lb penegra cover stock; illustrations-suede offset; photos. A take-home paper distributed weekly to adults in Sunday schools. "We are a nondenominational, Christian magazine. We tell stories that inspire by showing how faith relates to everyday living." Quarterly.
**Needs:** Religious/inspirational. Only accepts Christian themes. Receives approximately 25 unsolicited fiction mss/month. Less than 1% of fiction is agented. Length: 500-1,500 words.
**How to Contact:** Send complete ms with SASE. Cover letter with short bio and brief idea of story enclosed. Reports in 6-8 weeks on mss. Publishes ms 9-12 months after acceptance. Free sample copy with 6x9 SAE and 40¢ postage.
**Payment:** 10¢ word.
**Terms:** Pays on acceptance for first North American serial rights. Publication copyrighted.
**Tips:** "Write believable fiction with an implicit—not tacked-on or phony—Christian emphasis. Much fiction we see is simplistic, overly sentimental, with undefined characters or poorly developed plots." Published new writers within the last year.

**SUNSHINE MAGAZINE (I)**, Henrichs Publications, Box 40, Litchfield IL 62056. Magazine: 5¼x7¼; 48 pages; matte paper; matte cover stock; illustrations. "Family publication with inspirational short stories generally based on true life experiences. Humorous at times and uplifting. *Sunshine* is also produced in large print format. Audience ranges in age from preschool through the 90s. Stories are brief and inspiring and can be read quickly." Monthly. Estab. 1924. Circ. 100,000.
**Needs:** Literary, inspirational, men's, women's, humor, juvenile, and senior citizen/retirement. No religious subjects dealing with heavily depressing material, sex or violence. Receives 300-400 unsolicited fiction mss/month. Buys 8-11 mss/issue. Length: 500-1,000 words. Publishes short shorts. Recommends other markets.
**How to Contact:** Send complete ms with SASE and cover letter with name, date, type of submission, payment required, rights available. Accepts computer printout submissions. Prefers letter-quality. Reports in 2 months on mss. Publishes ms an average of 1 year after acceptance. Sample copy 50¢. Free guidelines with legal-sized SASE.
**Payment:** $10-100. Free author's copy. 40¢ charge for extra copy.
**Terms:** Pays on acceptance for first North American serial rights. Publication copyrighted.
**Tips:** Many mss are rejected because "they are sloppily prepared, too long, and about unsuitable subjects. Writers should send for our guidelines and a sample copy. Only a dozen or so stories can appear each month, and over 350 are received. Fiction fulfills the message we are trying to get across to our readers." Published new writers within the last year.

**SURFING MAGAZINE (IV)**, Western Empire, Box 3010, San Clemente CA 92672. (714)492-7873. Editor: David Gilovich. Magazine: 8x11; 112 pages; 50 lb free sheet paper; 70 lb cover stock; photos. Magazine covering "all aspects of the sport of surfing for young, active surfing enthusiasts." Monthly. Estab. 1964. Circ. 80,000.
**Needs:** Surfing-related fiction. Receives 2 unsolicited mss/month. Buys 3 mss/year. Length: 2,000-3,000 words average. Occasionally critiques rejected mss. Also publishes short shorts.
**How to Contact:** Cover letter with background on surfing. Query first. Reports in 2 weeks.

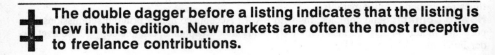

**The double dagger before a listing indicates that the listing is new in this edition. New markets are often the most receptive to freelance contributions.**

SASE. Photocopied submissions OK. Accepts computer printout submissions. Prefers letter-quality. Free sample copy and fiction guidelines.
**Payment:** 10-15¢/word.
**Terms:** Pays on publication for one-time rights. Publication copyrighted.
**Tips:** "Establish yourself as a *Surfing* general contributor before tackling fiction."

**THE SURGICAL TECHNOLOGIST (IV)**, Association of Surgical Technologists, Inc., Caller E, Littleton CO 80120. (303)978-9010. Editor: Michelle Armstrong. Magazine of surgery, operating room and hospital environment for surgical technologists—ages 20-50, predominantly female. Bimonthly. Estab. 1969. Circ. 11,000.
**Needs:** Subject matter must primarily focus on medical, surgical issues of technical and/or socio-economic relations. Length: 3,000 words minimum; 5,000 words maximum. Occasionally critiques rejected mss.
**How to Contact:** Send complete ms with SASE. Simultaneous submissions OK. Reports in 1 month on mss.
**Terms:** Pays on acceptance for all rights. Publication copyrighted.
**Tips:** "Stories must be about operating, surgical techniques, surgical fields, or microbiology."

**SWANK MAGAZINE (II, IV)**, Swank Corp., 888 7th Ave., New York NY 10106. Editor: Eve Ziegler. Magazine: full size; 98 pages; good paper; coated stock; illustrations; photos. "Men's sophisticate format. Sexually-oriented material. Presumably our reader is after erotic material." Monthly. Estab. 1952. Circ. 350,000.
**Needs:** High-caliber erotica. Fiction always has an erotic theme; writers should try to avoid the clichés of the genre. Buys 1 ms/issue, 12 mss/year. Receives approximately 30 unsolicited fiction mss each month. Length: 1,500-2,500 words.
**How to Contact:** Send complete ms with SASE. Accepts computer printout submissions. Prefers letter-quality. Reports in 6 weeks on mss. Sample copy $3.50 with SASE.
**Payment:** $250-400. Offers 25% kill fee for assigned ms not published.
**Terms:** Buys first North American serial rights. Publication copyrighted.
**Tips:** "Research the men's magazine market." Mss are rejected because of "lame storylines, poor execution. Stories are usually either all plot and no sex or all sex and no plot. We need a mixture of tight plot and hot sex. Please have a story to tell. Too much fiction has no story or substance. Be creative, but be literate." Published new writers within the year.

**'TEEN MAGAZINE (II)**, Petersen Publishing Co., 8490 Sunset Blvd., Los Angeles CA 90069. Editor: Roxanne Camron. Managing Editor: Lori Shaw-Cohen. Magazine: 100 + pages; illustrations; photos. "The magazine contains fashion, beauty, and features for the young teenage girl. The median age of our readers is 16. Our success stems from our dealing with relevant issues teens face, printing recent entertainment news and showing the latest fashions and beauty looks." Monthly. Estab. 1957. Circ. 1 million.
**Needs:** Romance, mystery, humor, and young adult. Every story, whether romance, mystery, humor, etc., must be aimed for teenage girls. The protagonist should be a teenager, preferably female. No experimental, science fiction, fantasy or horror. Buys 1 ms/issue; 12 mss/year. Publishes short shorts. Length: 2,500-4,000 words.
**How to Contact:** Send complete ms with SASE. Reports in 2 months on mss. Publishes ms 3-5 months after acceptance. Free guidelines with SASE.
**Payment:** Pays $100.
**Terms:** Pays on acceptance for all rights.
**Tips:** "Try to find themes that suit the modern teen. We need innovative ways of looking at the age-old problems of young love, parental pressures, making friends, being left out, etc. Mss must be typed neatly and double spaced. Handwritten mss will not be read." Send ms to fiction editor. Published new writers within the last year.

**TEENAGE MAGAZINE (I, II, IV)**, The Magazine for Young Adults, Highwire Associates, 217 Jackson St., Box 948, Lowell MA 01853. (617)458-6416. Editor: Andrew Calkins. "*TeenAge* is a general interest, news, and humor magazine, for and by literate high school students." Monthly. Estab. 1981. Circ. 180,000.

**Needs:** Adventure, contemporary, ethnic, experimental, horror, humor/satire, literary, mainstream, men's, psychic/supernatural, romance (young adult), suspense/mystery, women's, and young adult. "*TeenAge* is most interested in fiction written by high school and college students, or fiction that is geared to the interests of that audience. No poetry, inspirational pieces, moralistic tales or erotica." Receives approximately 40 unsolicited fiction mss/month. Buys 0-1 ms/month; 5-10 mss/year. Length: 1,000 words minimum; 2,000 words maximum; 1,500 words average. Occasionally critiques rejected mss written by student.

**How to Contact:** Send complete ms with SASE. Photocopied submissions OK. Accepts computer printout submissions. Reports in 6 weeks on mss. Publishes ms 2-6 months after acceptance. Sample copy $2.50. Free fiction guidelines.

**Payment:** Pays $400 maximum. Offers kill fee of 25%.

**Terms:** Pays on publication for first rights. Publication copyrighted.

**Tips:** "We expect more fiction this year—same sort. Teenage-written or of interest to teenagers."

**TEENS TODAY (II)**, Church of the Nazarene, 6401 The Paseo, Kansas City MO 64131. (816)333-7000. Editor: Gary Sivewright. Sunday school take-home paper: 8½x11; 8 pages; illustrations; photos. For junior and senior high students involved with the Church of the Nazarene who find it interesting and helpful to their areas of life. Weekly. Circ. 60,000.

**Needs:** Contemporary, religious/inspirational, romance, humor, juvenile, young adult, and ethnic. "Nothing that puts teens down or condemns lifestyle not in keeping with the denomination's beliefs and standards." Buys 1-2 mss/issue. Length: 1,200-1,500 words. Does not read mss in summer.

**How to Contact:** Send complete ms with SASE. Reports in 6 weeks on mss. Publishes ms 8-10 months after acceptance. Free sample copy and guidelines with SASE.

**Payment:** Pays 3½¢/word and 3¢/word on second reprint.

**Terms:** Pays on acceptance for first and second serial rights. Buys reprints.

**Tips:** "Study sample copies. Don't be too juvenile. Target on a higher quality of writing than what we are presently receiving and publishing." Published new writers within the last year.

**‡TIGER BEAT (II)**, Edrei Communications, 105 Union Ave., Cresskill NJ 07626. (201)569-5055. Editor: Diane Umansky. Magazine: 72-80 pages; illustrations; photos. Entertainment, service, fiction for teenage girls. Monthly. Estab. 1965. Circ. 400,000.

**Needs:** Humor/satire, young adult romance, young adult/teen (10-18 years). "Interested in lively, fast-paced fiction with a romantic edge or focus on the entertainment or beauty industry." Receives 5-10 mss/month. Buys 1 ms/issue. Agented fiction "almost none." Length: 2,000 words average; 1,000 words minimum; 3,000 words maximum. Also publishes short shorts.

**How to Contact:** Query with clips of published work or send complete ms with cover letter. SASE for ms. Simultaneous, photocopied submissions and reprints OK. Sample copy $1.75.

**Payment:** Pays $100-200 and contributor's copies.

**Terms:** Pays on publication for first North American serial rights. Publication copyrighted.

**TODAY'S CHRISTIAN WOMAN** , 2029 P St., NW, Washington DC 20036. Editor-in-Chief: Dale Hanson Bourke. Magazine: 8½x11; 96-128 pages. "*TCW* is a magazine for Christian women of all ages, single and married, homemakers and career women. It includes a variety of articles on topics ranging from self-help to fiction, cooking to careers." Bimonthly. Estab. 1978. Circ. 175,000.

**Needs:** Contemporary, literary, religious/inspirational, and women's. "No manuscript not women-oriented with a redemptive tone. Buys 1 ms/issue; 6 mss/year. Length: 1,000 words minimum; 4,000 words maximum. Also publishes short shorts.

**How to Contact:** Cover letter with credits. Send complete manuscript.

**Payment:** 10¢/word and 1 contributor's copy.

**Terms:** Pays on acceptance for first rights. Publication copyrighted.

**Tips:** Published new writers within the last year.

**TORCH ROMANCES (I)**, Quest Publications, Inc., Box 3307, McLean VA 22103. (703)734-5700. Editor: Elizabeth Brandon-Brown. Digest sized; 148 pages; high quality coated paper; 100 lb coated cover stock; cover illustrations; photos. Magazine of "contemporary romantic fiction in the sensual category for women who enjoy romance." Monthly. Published special fiction issue last year; plans another. Estab. 1983. Circ. 100,000.
**Needs:** Contemporary romance. Receives 30 unsolicited mss/month. Buys 6 mss/year. Approximately 30 unsolicited mss/month. Buys 6 mss/year. Approximately 30% of fiction is agented. Length: 54,000 words average; 52,000 words minimum; 54,000 words maximum. Also printing romantic suspense/adventure short stories of 6,000-8,000 words.
**How to Contact:** Send complete ms or first three chapters and an outline and cover letter with past credits in fiction or nonfiction. Reports in 3 months. SASE. Photocopied submissions OK. Accepts computer printout submissions. Prefers letter-quality. Publishes ms usually within 6 months. Sample copy $2.25. Fiction guidelines for legal-sized SASE and 1 first class stamp.
**Payment:** Royalty plus advance or outright payment.
**Terms:** Pays on publication. Publication copyrighted.
**Tips:** "The main theme of our magazine is fiction—contemporary romance novels and short stories." Published new writers within the last year.

**TOUCH (II)**, Calvinettes, Box 7259, Grand Rapids MI 49510. (616)241-5616. Editor: Joanne Ilbrink. Magazine: 8½x11; 24 pages; 50 lb paper; 50 lb cover stock; illustrations; photos. "Our purpose is to lead girls into a living relationship with Jesus Christ. Puzzles, poetry, crafts, stories, articles, and club input for girls ages 9-14." Monthly.
**Needs:** Adventure, ethnic, juvenile, and religious/inspirational. "Articles must help girls discover how God is at work in their world and the world around them." Receives 50 unsolicited fiction mss/month. Buys 3 mss/issue; 30 mss/year. Usually does not read during February, March, September and October. Length: 900 words minimum; 1,200 words maximum; 1,000 words average. Occasionally critiques rejected mss.
**How to Contact:** Send complete ms with 8x10 SASE. Prefers no cover letter. Simultaneous, photocopied, and previously published submissions OK. Reports in 4 weeks on mss. Free sample copy for 8x10 SASE. Free fiction guidelines.
**Payment:** Pays 2¢/word-$35.
**Terms:** Pays on acceptance for simultaneous, first, or second serial rights.
**Tips:** "Write for guidelines and theme update and submit manuscripts in advance of deadline. In fiction often the truths we choose to convey can be done with short stories." Published new writers within the last year.

**TRAILER BOATS MAGAZINE (II, IV)**, Poole Publications Inc., 16427 S. Avalon, Box 2307, Gardena CA 90248. Editor-in-Chief: Jim Youngs. Magazine: 80 + pages; high paper quality; 80 lb cover stock. "Our magazine covers boats of 26 feet and shorter, (trailerable size limits), and related activities; skiing, fishing, cruising, travel, racing, etc. We publish how-to articles on boat and trailer maintenance, travel, skiing, boat tests, and evaluations of new products." Audience: owners and prospective owners of trailerable size boats. Monthly. Estab. 1971. Circ. 80,000.
**Needs:** Adventure, contemporary, fantasy, humor/satire, science fiction, and suspense/mystery. "Must meet general guidelines of the magazine regarding boats and related activities." Receives very few unsolicited fiction mss/month. Buys 1-3 mss/year. Length: 200 words minimum; 1,000 words maximum. Publishes short shorts of 500 words. Occasionally critiques rejected mss. Sometimes recommends other markets.
**How to Contact:** Query first with SASE. Accepts computer printout submissions. Prefers letter-quality. Reports in 4 weeks on queries; 4-6 weeks on mss. Publishes ms 1-6 months after acceptance. Free general guidelines. Sample copy $1.50.
**Payment:** 7-10¢/word.
**Terms:** Pays on publication for all rights. Publication copyrighted.
**Tips:** "In our case, knowing the audience is of prime importance. Our readership and experience with fiction is limited. We are a consumer magazine with an audience of dedicated boaters. My

suggestion is to know the audience and write for it specifically." Published new writers within the last year.

**TURTLE MAGAZINE (I, II)**, Children's Better Health Institute, Benjamin Franklin Literary & Medical Society, Inc., 1100 Waterway Blvd., Box 567, Indianapolis IN 46206. Editorial Director: Beth Wood Thomas. Magazine of picture stories and articles for preschool children 2-5 years old.

**Needs:** Juvenile (preschool). Receives approximately 75 unsolicited fiction mss/month. Length: 8-24 lines for picture stories; 500 words for bedtime or naptime stories. Special emphasis on health, nutrition, exercise, and safety. Also has need for humorous and anthropomorphic animal stories.

**How to Contact:** Send complete ms with SASE. Reports in 8-10 weeks on mss. No queries. Send SASE for Editorial Guidelines. Sample copy, 75¢.

**Payment:** 6¢/word (approximate). Payment varies for poetry and activities.

**Terms:** Pays on publication for all rights. Publication copyrighted.

**Tips:** "Keep it simple and easy to read. Vocabulary must be below first grade level. Be familiar with past issues of the magazine. Mss should be checked thoroughly before submission for misspelled words, errors in grammar, and suitability of subject matter and vocabulary for the preschooler."

**VIRTUE, The Christian Woman's Journal (II)**, Virtue Ministries, Inc., Box 850, Sisters OR 97759. (503)549-8261. Managing Editor: Becky Durost. Magazine: 8⅛x10⅞ 80 pages; illustrations; photos. Christian women's magazine featuring food, fashion, family, etc., aimed primarily at homemakers—"real women with everyday problems, etc." Published 10 times/year. Estab. 1978. Circ. 125,000.

**Needs:** Condensed novel, contemporary, humor/satire, religious/inspirational, romance, serialized/excerpted novel, and women's. "Must have Christian slant." Buys 1-2 mss/issue; 10 mss/year (maximum). Publishes short shorts. Length: 1,200 words minimum; 2,500 words maximum; 2,000 words average. Sometimes recommends other markets.

**How to Contact:** Query with SASE. Cover letter with educational and professional background. Will only respond *after* query. Accepts computer printout submissions. Prefers letter-quality. Reports in 4 weeks on query, 6-8 weeks on ms. Sample copy $3 with 9x13 SAE and 90¢ postage. Free fiction guidelines with SASE.

**Payment:** 10¢/published word.

**Terms:** Pays on publication for first rights or reprint rights. Publication copyrighted.

**Tips:** "Send us descriptive, colorful writing with good style. *Please*—no simplistic, unrealistic pat endings. There are three main reasons *Virtue* rejects fiction: 1) The stories are not believable, 2) writing is dull, and 3) the story does not convey a Christian message." Published new writers within the last year.

**VISTA (II, IV)**, Wesleyan Publishing House, Box 2000, Marion IN 46952. Managing Editor: Christina G. Lamb. Magazine: 8¼x10¾; 8 pages; 60 lb white paper; 60 lb cover stock; illustrations; photos. Publication of the Wesleyan Church for adults. Weekly. Circ. 56,000.

**Needs:** First-person fiction, humor. "Humor is an excellent way to convey spiritual instruction in palatable form (500-800 words). True stories (first-person or "as told to")—1,000-1,500 words. Receives 200-300 unsolicited fiction mss each month.

**How to Contact:** Send complete ms with SASE. Reports in 6-8 weeks.

**Payment:** Pays 2½-3¢/word. Offers kill fee for assigned mss not published.

**Terms:** "Not copyrighted. Along with mss for first use, we also accept simultaneous submissions, second rights and reprint rights. It is the writer's obligation to secure clearance from original publisher."

**Tips:** "Stories should have definite Christian emphasis and character-building values without being preachy. Setting, plot and action should be *realistic*, and not like 'soap operas.' Realistic fiction is an excellent way to promote spiritual instruction and Christian virtues." Published new writers within the last year.

**‡THE WASHINGTON POST MAGAZINE (III)**, The Washington Post, 1150 15th St. NW, Washington DC 20071. (202)334-7585. Editor: Stephen Petranek. Fiction Editor: Jeanne Mc-Manus. Magazine: Pages vary weekly. General interest. Weekly. Estab. 1978. Circ. 1,000,000.
**Needs:** Contemporary, historical (general), humor/satire, literary. Receives 10 unsolicited mss/ month. Buys 4 mss/year. Does not read September-May. Publishes ms 3 months after acceptance. Length: 4,000 words. Also publishes short shorts.
**How to Contact:** Send complete ms with cover letter. Reports in 8-10 weeks on mss. SASE for ms. Photocopied submissions OK. Accepts computer printouts.
**Terms:** Pays on acceptance for first North American serial rights. Publication copyrighted.

**THE WASHINGTONIAN (IV)**, Washington Magazine Co., Suite 200, 1828 L St. NW, Washington DC 20036. (202)296-3600. Editor: John A. Limpert. General interest, regional magazine. Monthly. Estab. 1965. Circ. 135,795.
**Needs:** Short pieces, must be set in Washington. Receives 8-10 unsolicited fiction mss/month. Buys 3 fiction mss/year. Length: 1,000 words minimum; 5,000 words maximum. Occasionally critiques rejected mss.
**How to Contact:** Send complete ms with SASE. Simultaneous and photocopied submissions OK. Reports in 2 months on mss.
**Payment:** $100-1,000. Negotiates kill fee for assigned mss not published.
**Terms:** Pays ⅓ on acceptance, ⅔ on publication for first North American rights. Publication copyrighted.

**WESTERN PEOPLE (II)**, Western Producer Publications, Box 2500, Saskatoon, Saskatchewan S7K 2C4 Canada. (306)665-3500. Editor/Publisher: R.H.D. Phillips. Managing Editor: Mary Gilchrist. Magazine: 8½x11; 16 pages; newsprint paper; newsprint cover stock; illustrations; photos. "*Western People* is for and about Western Canadians, a supplement of the region's foremost weekly agricultural newspaper. Includes fiction, nonfiction (contemporary and history) and poetry. Readership is mainly rural and Western Canadian." Weekly. Publihsed special fiction issue last year; plans another. Estab. 1978. Circ. 142,407.
**Needs:** Contemporary, adventure, humor, and serialized novels. Buys 50 mss/year. Publishes short shorts. Length: 750-2,500 words (unless for serialization).
**How to Contact:** Send complete ms with SAE, IRC. Reports in 3 weeks on mss. Free sample copy with 9x12 SAE, IRC. Free general guidelines with legal-sized SAE, IRC.
**Payment:** $150 maximum (more for serials).
**Terms:** Pays on acceptance for first and first North American serial rights.
**Tips:** "The story should be lively, not long, related in some way to the experience of rural Western Canadians. We believe our readers enjoy a good story, particularly when it has some relevance to their own lives. Although most of the stories in Western people are nonfictional, we offer variety to our readers, including fiction and poetry. Write about what might happen, not what did happen. We find that beginning writers try to fictionalize actual events with a result that is neither fish nor fowl." Published new writers within the last year.

**THE WISCONSIN RESTAURATEUR**, Published: Wisconsin Restaurant Association, 122 W. Washington, Madison WI 53703. (608)251-3663. Editor: Jan LaRue. Magazine: 8½x11; 80 pages; 80 lb enamel cover stock; illustrations; photos. Published for foodservice operators in the state of Wisconsin and for suppliers of those operations. Theme is the promotion, protection and improvement of the foodservice industry for foodservice students, operators and suppliers. Monthly except November/December combined. Estab. 1933. Circ. 3,600.
**Needs:** Literary, contemporary, feminist, science fiction, men's, regional, women's, western, mystery, adventure, humor, juvenile, and young adult. "Only exceptional fiction material used. No stories accepted that put down persons in the foodservice business or poke fun at any group of people. No off-color material. No religious, no political." Buys 1-2 mss/issue, 12-24 mss/year. Receives 15-20 unsolicited fiction mss/month. Length: 500-2,500 words. Critiques rejected mss "when there is time."

**How to Contact:** Send complete ms with SASE. Accepts computer printout submissions. Reports in 4 weeks on mss. Free sample copy with 8½x11 SASE. Free guidelines with SASE.
**Payment:** $2.50-20. Free author's copy. 50¢ charge for extra copy.
**Terms:** Pays on acceptance for first and first North American serial rights. Publication copyrighted.
**Tips:** "Make sure there is some kind of lesson to be learned, a humorous aspect, or some kind of moral to your story." Mss are rejected because they are not written for the restaurateur/reader. Published new writers within the last year.

**WOMAN'S DAY (II)**, CBS Publications, 1515 Broadway, New York NY 10036. (212)719-6250. Editor-in-Chief: Ellen R. Levine. Fiction Editor: Eileen Herbert Jordan. A strong service magazine geared to women, with a wide variety of well-written subjects (foods, crafts, beauty, medical, etc.). Publishes 15 issues/year. Estab. 1939. Circ. 7½ million; readership 17 million.
**Needs:** Literary, contemporary, religious/inspirational, fantasy, women's, feminist, humor, and juvenile of high quality. No violence, crime or totally male-oriented stories. Approximately 50% of fiction is agented.
**How to Contact:** Send complete ms with SASE. Free guidelines with SASE.
**Payment:** Pays top rates.
**Terms:** Pays on acceptance. Occasionally buys reprints.
**Tips:** "Read the magazine and keep trying."

**WOMAN'S WORLD (II), The Woman's Weekly**, Heinrich Bauer, N.A., 177 N. Dean St., Englewood NJ 07631. (201)569-0006. Editor-in-Chief: Dennis Neeld. Fiction Editor: Elinor Nauen. Magazine: 9x11⅜; 56 pages; super calendar paper and cover stock; illustrations; photos. Service magazine for women, lower to middle income, ages 18-80. Includes both career and family oriented stories. Weekly. Estab. 1981.
**Needs:** Mainstream romance (contemporary), suspense/mystery. "No science fiction, graphic language, explicit sex, gruesome or grotesque stories." Receives 500-600 unsolicited fiction mss/month. Buys 2 mss/issue; 104 mss/year. Approximately 10-20% of fiction is agented. Length: 4,500 words for short stories; 1,500 words for mini-mysteries. Occasionally critiques rejected mss.
**How to Contact:** Send complete ms with SASE. Simultaneous and photocopied submissions OK. Reports in 1-2 months on mss. Publishes ms an average of 4 months after acceptance. Free fiction guidelines with SASE.
**Payment:** $500-1,000.
**Terms:** Pays on acceptance for first North American serial rights. Publication copyrighted.
**Tips:** "Read several issues and send for guidelines first before submitting stories. Our prime interest is stories with a romance theme and positive resolution." Most rejected mss "fail to follow guidelines." Published new writers within the last year.

**WONDER TIME (II)**, Beacon Hill, Press of Kansas City, 6401 Paseo, Kansas City MO 64131. (816)333-7000. Editor: Evelyn Beals. Magazine: 8¼x11; 4 pages; self cover stock; illustrations; photos. Hand-out story paper published through the Church of the Nazarene Sunday school; stories should follow outline of Sunday school lesson for 6-7 year olds. Weekly. Circ. 45,000.
**Needs:** Religious/inspirational and juvenile. Stories must have controlled vocabulary and be easy to read. No fairy tales or science fiction. Buys 1 ms/issue. Receives 50-75 unsolicited fiction mss/month. Approximately 25% of fiction is agented. Length: 300-550 words. Also publishes short shorts. Recommends other markets.
**How to Contact:** Send complete ms with SASE. Reports in 6 weeks on mss. Publishes ms an average of 1 year after acceptance. Free sample copy and curriculum guide with SASE.
**Payment:** Pays 3½¢/word.
**Terms:** Pays on acceptance for first rights. Buys reprints. Publication copyrighted.
**Tips:** "Control vocabulary. Study children to know what children are interested in; stories should deal with children's problems of today and must be tastefully handled." Mss may be rejected be-

cause they "do not correlate with the Sunday school lessons." Published new writers within the last year.

**WORKING FOR BOYS (II)**, Xaverian Brothers, Box A, Danvers MA 01923. (617)774-2664. Editor: Bro. Alphonsus Dwyer. "We publish articles of human interest, nature, biography, travel, religion, how-to, sports, etc., for elementary school children and their parents." Published 3 times/year. Estab. 1884. Circ. 15,000.
**Needs:** Literary, religious/inspirational, adventure, humor, juvenile, and senior citizen/retirement. Buys 25 mss/year. Receives approximately 10 unsolicited fiction mss/month. Length: 800-1,200 words.
**How to Contact:** Query or send complete ms. SASE always. Reports in 2 weeks on queries and mss. Free sample copy. Free guidelines with SASE.
**Payment:** 4¢/word.
**Terms:** Pays on acceptance.

**WORKING MOTHER (II, IV)**, McCall's Publishing Co., 230 Park Ave., New York NY 10169. (212)551-9412. Editor: Vivian Cadden. Magazine: 8½x11; 120 pages; illustrations; photos. For working mothers. Monthly. Estab. 1978. Circ. 500,000.
**Needs:** Contemporary, women's, and juvenile. Length: 2,500-3,000 words. Publishes short shorts. Critiques rejected mss "when there is time." Sometimes recommends other markets.
**How to Contact:** Cover letter with address, telephone number, social security number. Send complete ms with SASE. Accepts computer printout submissions. Reports in 6 weeks. Sample copy $2.
**Payment:** Average $500. Offers 20% kill fee for assigned mss not published.
**Terms:** Pays on acceptance for all rights. Publication copyrighted.
**Tips:** "The stories we like most feature a working mother as the central character. We like fiction. We give advice to working mothers but we also want them to laugh, to connect with other women and to simply have a good read when they pick up the magazine." Published new writers within the last year.

**WYOMING RURAL ELECTRIC NEWS (WREN) (II)**, Wyoming Rural Electric Association, Suite 101, 340 W. B St., Casper WY 82601. (307)234-6152. Editor: Gale Eisenhauer. Magazine: 8½x11; 20-24 pages; 50 lb paper; 70 lb cover stock; illustrations; photos. Magazine for Wyoming people who use rural electric power. Publishes a variety of material: features on Western people, places, historicals, short fiction and some poetry; energy and conservation material pertinent to readers. Monthly. Published special fiction issue last year; plans another. Circ. 38,500.
**Needs:** Adventure, ethnic, historical (general), humor/satire, literary, men's, regional, romance (historical), senior citizen/retirement, western, women's, and energy. "Fiction must appeal in one form or another to our audience of rural Wyomingites." Receives approximately 6 unsolicited fiction mss/month. Buys 1 ms/issue (maximum); approximately 11 mss/year. Length: 750 words minimum; 2,000 words maximum; 1,600 words average. Occasionally critiques rejected mss.
**How to Contact:** Send complete ms with SASE. Simultaneous and photocopied submissions OK. "We prefer not to use previously published work but will if it is exactly something we are looking for." Accepts computer printout submissions. Prefers letter-quality. Reports in 8 weeks on mss. Publishes ms 2-4 months after acceptance. Free sample copy with 8½x11 SASE and 37¢ postage. Free fiction guidelines with SASE.
**Payment:** Pays $10-25, "with a possibility of higher pay in special circumstances."
**Terms:** Pays on publication for first rights or one-time rights. Rarely buys reprints.
**Tips:** "We are publishing fewer short stories, less fiction—more features." Published new writers within the last year.

**YANKEE MAGAZINE (II, III)**, Yankee, Inc., Dublin NH 03444. Editor: Judson D. Hale. Fiction Editor: Edie Clark. Magazine: 6x9; 300 + pages; glossy paper; 4-color glossy cover stock; illustrations; 4-color photos. Entertaining and informative New England regional of current issues, people, history, antiques, crafts for general reading audience. Monthly. Published special fiction issue last year. "We will be publishing a collection of *Yankee* fiction this spring." Estab. 1935. Circ. 1,000,000.

**Needs:** Literary. Fiction is to be set in New England or compatible with the area. No religious/inspirational, formula fiction or stereotypical dialect, novels or novellas. Buys 1 ms/issue; 12 mss/year. Length: 2,000-4,000 words. Publishes short shorts up to 1,500 words. Recommends other markets.

**How to Contact:** Send complete ms with SASE and previous publications. Reports in 3-6 weeks on mss.

**Payment:** $750.

**Terms:** Pays on acceptance; rights negotiable. Sends galleys to author.

**Tips:** "Read previous ten stories in *Yankee* for style and content. Fiction must be realistic and reflect life as it is—complexities and ambiguities inherent. Our fiction adds to the 'complete menu'—the magazine includes many categories—humor, profiles, straight journalism, essays, etc.—and our readers tell us: They like our fiction. Listen to the advice of any editor who takes the time to write a personal letter. Go to workshops; get advice and other readings before sending story out cold." Fiction prize of $600 awarded to best story published each year.

**YOUNG AMBASSADOR (II)**, Good News Broadcasting Co., Box 82808, Lincoln NE 68501. (402)474-4567. Managing Editor: Nancy Bayne. Magazine: 8½x11; 64 pages; illustrations; photos. "It's designed to aid the spiritual growth of young teen Christian readers by presenting Biblical principles." 11 issues/year. Special fiction issue planned. Estab. 1946. Circ. 80,000.

**Needs:** Religious/inspirational, regional, romance, adventure, fantasy, and science fiction. "Stories must be grounded in Biblical Christianity and should feature teens in the 14-17 year range." Buys 3-4 mss/issue; 35-40 mss/year. Receives 50-60 unsolicited fiction mss/month. Length: up to 2,500 words. Also publishes short shorts to 1,800 words. Critiques rejected mss "when there is time."

**How to Contact:** Send complete ms with SASE. Accepts computer printout submissions. Prefers letter-quality. Reports in 2 months. Publishes ms 6-24 months after acceptance. Free sample copy and guidelines for 9x12 SASE.

**Payment:** 4-7¢/word for unassigned fiction. More for assignments. 3¢/word for reprints.

**Terms:** Pays on acceptance for first or reprint rights. Buys reprints. Publication copyrighted.

**Tips:** "The most common problem is that writers don't understand the limitations of stories under 2,500 words and try to cram a 6,000-word plot into 2,000 words at the expense of characterization, pacing, and mood. We feel that fiction communicates well to our teenage readers. They consistently rank fiction as their favorite part of the magazine. We get hundreds of stories on 'big issues' (death, drugs, etc). Choose less dramatic subjects, that are important to teenagers and give us a new storyline that has a Biblical emphasis, but isn't preachy." Published new writers within the last year. Teen fiction writers under age 20 may enter annual contest.

**YOUNG AMERICAN (II)**, America's Newsmagazine for Kids, Box 12409, Portland OR 97212. (503)230-1895. Managing Editor: Kristina T. Linden. Magazine: 10½x13; 16-32 pages; newsprint paper; newsprint cover stock; illustrations; photos. "Our focus is on children, and they are taken seriously. Articles are intended to inform and entertain. We are particularly interested in stories about newsworthy kids." Monthly. Plans special fiction issue. Estab. 1983. Circ. 125,000.

**Needs:** Short (1,000 words) fiction pieces—fantasy, humor, mystery. "We hope to use longer pieces which can be serialized as we become more frequent." Receives more than 50 mss/month. Buys 4-6 mss/issue; 60 mss/year. Length: Up to 1,000 words. Recommends other markets.

**How to Contact:** Queries, clips; cover letters not necessary. Finished work encouraged. Reports within 4 months. SASE with mss. Sample copy available for 50¢. Guidelines available with SASE.

**Payment:** Pays 7¢/word.

**Terms:** Pays on publication for first North American rights. Publication copyrighted.

**Tips:** "Speak to the kids, not down to them."

**THE YOUNG CRUSADER**, National Woman's Christian Temperance Union, 1730 Chicago Ave., Evanston IL 60201. (312)864-1396. Editor-in-Chief: Mrs. Kermit S. Edgar. Managing Editor: Michael C. Vitucci. Character building material showing high morals and sound values; inspirational, informational nature articles and stories for the 6-12 year olds. Monthly. Estab. 1887. Circ. 10,000.
**Needs:** Juvenile. Stories should be naturally written pieces, not saccharine or preachy. Buys 3-4 mss/issue; 60 mss/year. Length: 600-800 words.
**How to Contact:** Send complete ms with SASE. Reports in 6 months or longer on mss. Free sample copy with SASE.
**Payment:** Pays ½¢/word and free author's copy.
**Terms:** Pays on publication. "If I like the story and use it, I'm very lenient and allow the author to use it elsewhere."

**YOUNG JUDAEAN (IV)**, Hadassah Zionist Youth Commission, 50 W. 58th St., New York NY 10019. (212)355-7900, ext. 452. Editor: Mordecai Newman. Magazine. "*Young Judaean* is for members of the Young Judaea Zionist youth movement, ages 9-12." Published 7 times/year. Circ. 4,000.
**Needs:** Children's fiction including adventure, ethnic, fantasy, historical, humor/satire, juvenile, prose poem, religious, science fiction, suspense/mystery, and translations. "All stories must have Jewish relevance." Receives 3-4 unsolicited fiction mss/month. Buys 1 ms/issue; 7 mss/year. Length: 500 words minimum; 1,500 words maximum; 1,000 words average.
**How to Contact:** Send complete ms with SASE. Simultaneous, photocopied, and previously published submissions OK. Reports in 3 months on mss. Sample copy for 75¢. Free fiction guidelines.
**Payment:** Pays $20-50; 2 free contributor's copies; 75¢ charge for extras.
**Terms:** Pays on publication. Publication copyrighted.
**Tips:** "Stories must be of Jewish interest—lively and accessible to children without being condescending."

**YM (II)**, (formerly *Young Miss*), Gruner and Jahr USA, Inc., 685 3rd Ave., New York NY 10017. Editor: Phyllis Schneider. Magazine: 8½x11; 84-116 pages; glossy coated stock; 70 lb cover stock; illustrations; photos, (not on fiction). Magazine for teenage girls (ages 12-19). Published 10 times/year.
**Needs:** Stories addressing young women's concerns in the areas of family, friendship, school, emotional growth, social issues, love, etc. "We're looking for complexity, a contemporary tone, originality of style, and fully-drawn characters. The protagonist may be female or male." Buys 1-2 mss/issue. Receives hundreds of unsolicited fiction mss/month. Approximately 30% of fiction is agented. Length: 2,500-3,500 words. Sometimes recommends other markets.
**How to Contact:** Send complete ms with SASE to Deborah Purcell, Articles/Fiction Editor. Cover letter with list of previous publications. Reports in 6-8 weeks on mss. Sample copy $2 with free writer's guidelines.
**Payment:** $350 and up; 2 free author's copies.
**Terms:** Pays on acceptance for first rights. Publication copyrighted.
**Tips:** Mss are rejected because of "awkward style, trite themes, undeveloped plots, and weak characterizations. Poor understanding of teen behavior and concerns—resulting in outdated dialogue and themes. Our readers—12 to 19—enjoy fiction; also, we feel that fiction is an important part of a general 'lifestyle' magazine." Published new writers within the last year.

---

 *Those who dream by day are cognizant of many things which escape those who dream only by night.*

*—Edgar Allan Poe*

# Foreign commercial periodicals

The following commercial magazines located in the United Kingdom, Europe, India, Japan, Australia and South Africa, are paying markets for short fiction in English. Query first for fiction needs and submission requirements and always include proper return postage (IRCs—see Manuscript Mechanics).

**AUSTRALIAN VIDEO AND COMMUNICATIONS**, General Magazine Company Pty., Ltd., 9 Paran Place, Glen Iris, Victoria 3146 Australia. (03)25-6456. Editor: Geoffrey M. Gold. Monthly magazine covering home video and telecommunications.

**DISCOVERY**, Emphasis (Hong Kong) Limited, 10/F Wilson House, 19-27 Wyndham St., Hong Kong. (5)215392. Editor: Dereck A C Davies. Monthly magazine on travel.

**ENCOUNTER**, Encounter, Ltd., 59 St. Martin's Lane, London WC2N 4JS England. Tel. (01)836-4194. Editor: M.J. Lasky. A monthly review of current affairs, literature and the arts for a mainly professional and academic audience.

**FAIR LADY**, National Magazine, Box 1802, Cape Town 8000, South Africa. Tel. (021)25-48-78. Editor: Dene Smuts. "Women's glossy magazine with regular fashion features, beauty, cooking, teen and young world section, competitions, fiction, book reviews, interviews (especially celebrity, serious articles in general on self-help, health, and current affairs for a very broad spectrum of population, including men."

**FAMILY RADIO & TV MAGAZINE**, Republican Press (PTY) Ltd., Box 32083 Mobeni Durban 4060 South Africa. (031)422041. Editor: Mike Fisher. Family magazine concentrating on TV and film stars for a middle income group with a bias toward married women.

**LIVING & LOVING**, The Magazine That Cares, Republican Press (PTY) Ltd., Box 32083 Mobeni, Durban 4060 South Africa. Tel. 422041. Editor: June Vigor. Magazine for parents dealing mainly with pregnancy, baby care, family and marriage advice, and health.

**MY WEEKLY**, The Magazine for Women Everywhere, D.C. Thomson & Co., Ltd., 80 Kingsway East, Dundee, Scotland. Editor: Stewart D. Brown. Magazine whose theme is to entertain women of all ages.

**OVERSEAS! The Leisure Time Magazine for the Military Man in Europe**, Military Consumer Today. Inc., 17 Bismarckstrasse. 6900 Heidelberg, West Germany 06221-2543 1/32/33. Editor: Charles L. Kaufman. "*Overseas!* is aimed at the U.S. military in Europe. It is the leading men's military lifestyle magazine slanted towards life in Europe, specifically directed to males ages 18-35."

**R&R ENTERTAINMENT DIGEST**, R&R Werbe GmbH, 17 Bismarckstrasse, 6900 Heidelberg, W. Germany, 06221-25431/32/33. Editor: Mrs. Tory Billard. Monthly entertainment guide for military and government employees and their families stationed in Europe "specializing in travel in Europe, audio/video/photo information, music, and the homemaker scene."

**SIMPLY LIVING**, Otter Publications Pty/Ltd., 53 Sydney Road, Manly, N.S.W. 2095, Australia. (02)977-8566. Editor: Mr. Pip Wilson. Quarterly magazine covering the environment and anti-nuclear, spiritual and natural health topics.

# Small press

For years the small press has taken on the responsibility of keeping alive noncommercial books—the good, serious, literary "books that won't sell." Indeed the small press owes much of its own success to the commercial publishers' "Fahrenheit 451 attitude," their resistance to publish literary fiction and nonfiction unless the author is well known and highly regarded.

Small press editors have moved in and neatly filled this vacated territory left by the commercial presses. Energetic and visionary, partisan and passionate in their interests, these editors start their presses because they are disgruntled by the commercial publishing powers that be—or won't be. What the small presses also share is their philosophy to be anti-trend, anti-corporation and independent. They choose a special subject or segment of the population and cultivate its isolated, often small audience.

Although still in use today, the term "small press" is not entirely accurate; it is, in fact, anachronistic. Currently there are about 14,000 small presses in the US, Canada and abroad (according to R.R. Bowker). They are a sizable and recognizably growing force publishing all types of books. "Small press" is also pejorative, as the term implies that editors are still producing amateurish and unprofessional books. Quite the contrary. Small presses publish books that are beautifully-bound and printed—even collector items. The days of the mimeographed, stapled home product are long gone.

What generally remains "small," however, is the budget. Even the most successful small press is not financially equipped to compete with the commercial publishers on the same grand scale in royalties, advertising or promotion. But because of the increased professionalism and literary quality, national attention *is* now possible. More book reviewers in major publications accept small press books for reviews. Promotion, advertising and distribution, once an almost insurmountable problem for these cottage industries, are available via the special companies designed for those purposes or through grants from the NEA (National Endowment for the Arts). More and more major commercial presses are taking on the distribution for small press books. Also as a result of the proliferation nationally of small presses, there are now small press literary centers throughout the country for greater reader accessibility.

## Pressed for success

The increasing growth in the number of new small presses (about 200 a month) is inspiring and invigorating. Thanks to more astute business practices and computer technology, small presses are now more stable, stay in business longer, and their books remain in print longer. It's a quiet phenomenon extolled by editors throughout the publishing world plus authors like James Michener, who published two books with the small press, and Jayne Anne Phillips. Phillips, novelist and short story writer (*Black Tickets*, *Dream Machines*), acknowledges her literary boost via the small press and her continued loyalty and interest: "I think it's important for those who have been helped early on with the small press to publish with them." According to Frank Conroy, director of NEA's Literary Program, the small press offers more than just an alternative to big publishers—small presses are the mainstream. More than 90% of the "significant" fiction is currently published by small presses and literary magazines.

The independent press is also a key source for reprints. For example, Ballantine paid $150,000 for *Raney*, the first novel by Clyde Edgerton, published originally by Algonquin Books. And bestselling . . .*And Ladies of the Club*, by Helen Hooven Santmyer was first published by Ohio State University Press. Some small publishers, especially university presses, prefer to keep their own successful book and reprint it themselves—to control the quality it might not receive with a larger publisher.

A cohesive and unified industry the small presses are not. They are disparate and diverse in subject and interests and they are geographically spread all over the country, as opposed to the majority of commercial publishers based primarily in New York and Boston. The titles of the small presses often define not only their philosophy, but their location, too, indicating what kinds of authors they are seeking. Overlook Press, a successful independent publisher in New York, capitalizes nicely on rejections or literary leftovers from their commercial neighbors. Banned Books suggests its spirit, and presses like Down East and New England Press indicate the area where they prefer their authors to live or set their stories.

## New territory

The future is an especially strong one for regional publishing, an industry fueled by the regional/area book fairs and conferences held more and more frequently in sections in the US and Canada. The submission requirements for authors state any special focus: For instance, if you live in Brooklyn, New York or have a book by, for, or about people or places in Brooklyn, you should submit your manuscript to Somrie Press. For an Ohio-based novel there's Vimach Associates; for a novel set in Florida, try Pineapple Press; and if you have a novel about New York State, there's the Empire State imprint for Library Research Projects.

Many small presses are purely literary in their interests and publish only general, serious quality, noncategory fiction and nonfiction. The majority of small presses we have listed in *Fiction Writer's Market*, however, specialize in a particular subject or publish for one segment of the audience or location. They may tackle issue-oriented themes that only interest a small readership, such as Third World topics or minority political and social issues. Or a press may center its sole publishing interest on an obscure subject like homesteading, survivalism, adoption, infertility, bilingual children's stories, juvenile Judaica, etc. As an example, the editor of Cave Books challenges writers to write a novel involving the Carlsbad Caverns or Mammoth Cave.

A small press may also be formed around an entire genre: science fiction, fantasy, translations, young adult, preschool/juvenile. Thus with such variance, there should be a publisher for *every* writer—but the research for the right match will—and should—be an extensive one.

Small presses not only take risks on their subject matter, that is, publishing mostly noncommercial titles, but they also employ what commercial presses would define as a noncommercial format—novellas, short story collections, first novels, and most often paperbacks of all sizes. Paycock Press and The Spirit That Moves Us Press publish anthologies with special themes during the year, as do other presses periodically. And SOS Publications has charted new publishing territory with their newly-devised Mini-bound series, four category novels a month. The rack-size hardcover format is a departure from the norm; Mini-bound is for collectors. Cherryable Brothers, a new press, began with a goal to publish new hardcover fiction. Other presses begin with innovative, artistic objectives: to produce beautifully bound, graphically original books, often handmade, which will last. "It doesn't cost any more to put out a handsome book," one editor maintains. The range in appearance from press to press varies, but more and more booksellers, including the large bookstore chains, acknowledge the great improvement in small press books.

## Coming to terms

The small controlled size of an independent press is the writer's great advantage, in most cases. Contrary to what you can usually expect with a large commercial publisher, you may be invited, even encouraged to participate in the editing and production of your book. Small press editors regard the author/editor relationship as a vital nurturing process, and they are very conscientious about the responsibility, per the comment by the editor of Prairie Publishing: "We work with all the devotion and intensity of a Max Perkins or Charles Scribner." An intimate and complementary partnership, it's much like a marriage, says the editor of Somrie Press, "with a lot of give and go." Especially so if you live near the press or work with a cooperative publisher which may require your involvement in the publishing process.

Long before the editor-author merger can begin, you must search for the best press to represent your work. Because of the vast diversity of small presses—in size, subject, location, policy, and quality of books—you should expect to spend time in your research learning as much as possible about the publisher *before* you send off your manuscript or query.

A good starting point is the category index in the back of this book—find a press whose needs and expectations match your story. Then find the listing(s) and read each one *entirely*. Editors admonish us here saying, "Your readers are *not* reading the listing carefully and are sending us very inappropriate material." It's a common complaint—which sometimes leads to an irate editor withdrawing his/her listing from our book. To find out how receptive an editor will be to your material, check the ranking (I, II, III, IV) after the title. Most small presses are (I) and (II) or (IV) and eager for unknowns and quality beginners or specialists in their subject or location.

Your next assignment is to study the books published by the press you're interested in. Go to the bookstore, send for a sample copy of a novel, or at least write for a catalog or booklist. Read also the description of the books in the listing (type of paper and printing, number of copies per print run, etc.).

Once you've decided on which press to pursue, read again the submission requirements—they are as individualized and unique as the press itself. Honor their requests and understand they mean what they say: "Manuscripts sent without a query will be burned," (In Between Books). Occasionally you may be required to pay a fee or join an association before you submit your story or even after it is accepted.

Small presses universally agree on the importance of the return postage policy. Either nonprofit or very low budget, these little businesses cannot afford the extra financial burden of returning a manuscript. Without the proper SASE or IRC for a query or manuscript, you probably will not receive a response or see your manuscript again.

Once your manuscript has been accepted and before you reach a publishing agreement or sign a contract, it's important to become familiar with the terms: Some presses pay royalties. Others offer only contributor's copies, and occasionally there may be partial subsidy wherein you, the author, are expected to pay a fee—and sometimes it is sizable. Or there may be a vanity arrangement, in which you would pay for the entire production. Before you commit yourself, be very careful to understand the terms involved.

## Career ahead

Also ask how the press is funded—by grants, awards, donations or by smart business practices. Ascertain the age of the press and if the publishing is consistent—and not just when funds allow. It's also important to inquire about the promotion and distribution policies because you don't want your novels to end up in a warehouse. Not infrequently, as a representative of the press, you may be expected to participate in the promotion of the book. In short, know exactly what you are getting into in your publishing commitment in order to avoid "surprises" and disappointments later.

If you do publish with a small press, you can—and should—expect the same professionalism you would with a larger publisher. Your publishing arrangement should be the most ethical and rewarding one you can find. But it's also important to be realistic. Small press editors relate unfortunate stories dealing with authors with illusions of fame and fortune. Accept the publication of your book for what it is: an opportunity to see your book successfully in print, an endorsement that you are now a published writer with a career ahead.

The greatest opportunity with the small press is for the quality writer, the first novelist or unknown writer of short stories or novellas. The editors seek, even encourage, nonestablished writers with talent and enjoy discovering and promoting their "find."

To find the most appropriate market for your story, read on:

**ACHERON PRESS (I, II)**, Bear Creek at the Kettle, Friendsville MD 21531. Fiction Editor: Robert E. Pletta. Estab. 1981. Publishes paperpack originals. Plans 1 first novel this year. Averages 7 total titles, 1 fiction title each year. Occasionally critiques mss for $60, less for short pieces.
**Needs:** Adventure, comics, contemporary, experimental, juvenile (historical), literary, suspense/mystery, young adult (problem novels) and especially academic. Recently published: *Masked Avenger*, by Doug DeMars; and *Knife Gift*, by Kevin Schlegle.
**How to Contact:** Query first or submit outline/synopsis and sample chapters. SASE always. Photocopied submissions OK. Reports "as promptly as possible, but sometimes at irregular intervals because of frequent traveling." Closed June-September.
**Terms:** Negotiable. Free book catalog.
**Tips:** "Form: Have a story (plot) and/or wit. Content: a serious problem, not just 'a good story.' "

**ADLER PUBLISHING COMPANY (II)**, Box 9342, Rochester NY 14604. (716)377-5804. Imprints include Nightsun Books. Publisher: Jeanette Axelrod. Estab. 1983. Small independent publisher with plans to expand. Publishes paperback originals and reprints. No first novels this year. Averages 7 total titles, 3-5 fiction titles each year. Average first novel print order 1,000 copies. Occasionally critiques rejected ms.
**Needs:** General fiction, especially translations. "No romances please!" Recently published *Another Story*, by Brian Swann (novella); and *Uprising in East Germany and Other Stories*, by Jochen Ziem (short story translations).

**How to Contact:** Accepts unsolicited mss. Submit outline/synopsis and sample chapters with SASE. Reports in 3-6 months. Simultaneous and photocopied submissions OK. Accepts computer printout submissions; prefers letter-quality. Disc submissions OK with Xerox 820. Prefers hard copy with disc submission. Publishes ms an average of 1 year after acceptance.
**Terms:** "All terms subject to negotiation individually. No vanity publishing."
**Tips:** "All publications are in quality trade paperback format. Also interested in excellent quality scholarly works in the fields of philosophy and the humanities and translations."

‡**ADVOCACY PRESS (IV)**, Box 236, Santa Barbara CA 93102. Publisher: Mindy Bingham. Estab. 1983. Small publisher with 2-4 titles/year; gross 1985-86 $400,000. Hardcover originals and paperback originals. Books: perfect smythe sewn binding; illustrations; average print order: 20,000 copies; first novel print order: 10,000. Plans 2 first novels this year. Averages 2-4 total titles/year; 2 fiction titles/year.
**Needs:** Juvenile (5-9 years); preschool/picture book. Wants only feminist/nontraditional messages to boys or girls—picture books. Recently published *Father Gander Nursery Rhymes*, by Dr. Doug Harch (picture book); *Minou*, by Mindy Bingham (picture book).
**How to Contact:** No unsolicited mss; will not return them. Submit outline/synopsis with SASE. Reports in 6 weeks on queries. Simultaneous submissions OK. No photocopies. Accepts computer printouts including dot-matrix.
**Terms:** Pays in royalties of 5% minimum; 10% maximum. Sends pre-publication galleys to the author. Books catalog free on request.
**Tips:** "We are looking for fictional stories for children 4-8 years old that give messages of self sufficency for little girls; little boys can nurture and little girls can be anything they want to be, etc. Looking for talented writers/artists."

**AEGINA PRESS (I, II)**, 4937 Humphrey Rd., Huntington WV 25704. Fiction Editor: Ira Herman. Estab. 1983. Small independent publisher with plans to expand. Publishes paperback originals and reprints. Books: 60 lb library weight paper; photo offset printing; perfect binding; illustrations; average print order; 500-1,000; first novel print order: 500-1,000. Plans 5 first novels this year. Averages 10-12 total titles each year. Average first novel print order 1,000 copies. Often critiques rejected ms.
**Needs:** Adventure, contemporary, ethnic, experimental, faction, fantasy, feminist, gay, historical (strong emphasis), horror, humor/satire, juvenile (will consider all types), literary (strong emphasis), mainstream, regional (strong emphasis), religious/inspirational, historical romance, science fiction, short story collections, translations (emphasis on, especially literary and historical), women's, and young adult/teen (fantasy/science fiction, historical, problem novels). "Novels in all categories will be considered for this year. Special needs include literary or historical fiction, or other fiction that might serve as supplementary reading in higher education classrooms." Recently published *The Horror of Hoard's Creek*, by Kenneth Winslett (mystery).
**How to Contact:** Accepts unsolicited mss. "All of our books begin as unsolicited manuscripts." Query or submit outline/synopsis and 3 sample chapters or complete ms. "We like to see the complete manuscript, but we will consider queries and partials as well." SASE for query, ms. Reports in 1 week on queries; 1 month on mss. Simultaneous and photocopied submissions OK. Accepts computer printout submissions; prefers letter-quality.
**Terms:** Pays negotiable royalty. Sends galleys to author. Individual payment arranged on each project; depends upon subject and author. Subsidy publishes 50% of titles.
**Tips:** "Study the market for which you are writing. Compare your work with examples of the genre in bookstores. We have nearly doubled our fiction output over last year. We publish paperbacks only because fewer book buyers want to pay high hardcover prices. We have published first novelists in 1985 and will do so again in 1986. If you have no luck with the large commercial presses, try the smaller independents."

**AGAPÉ (II)**, Subsidiary includes Cypress Books, 921 3rd St., Franklin LA 70538. (318)828-4170. Fiction Editors: Bernard Broussard and Ray Broussard. Estab. 1980. Publishes hardcover and paperback originals. Plans 2 first novels this year. Averages 8-10 total titles, 3-4 fiction titles each year. Occasionally critiques rejected mss.

**Needs:** Adventure, contemporary, juvenile, historical, religious/inspirational, and women's. No erotica or fantasy. Recently published *A Cajun Reunion*, by Ray Broussard (historical); and *Blood at the Roots*, by Bernard Broussard (historical).

**How to Contact:** Query first with outline, synopsis and 2-3 sample chapters. Simultaneous submissions OK. Reports in 1 month on mss.

**Terms:** Pays in royalties. Subsidy publishes "3-4 books/year."

**Tips:** "We publish books dealing with (1) love of neighbor as the touchstone of morality, (2) works showing how there is mystery present in all our human relationships, and (3) works promoting international peace, interracial and social justice, human liberation, creative love, and the celebration of life and creation-centered spirituality."

**AKIBA PRESS**, Box 13086, Oakland CA 94661. (415)339-1283. Fiction Editor: Sheila Baker. Estab. 1978. Publishes hardcover and paperback originals and paperback reprints. Plans 2 first novels this year. Averages 2-3 total titles, 1 fiction title each year. Occasionally critiques rejected mss.

**Needs:** Ethnic (Jewish), historical (general), psychic/supernatural, and young adult (historical). No erotic or gothic romances.

**How to Contact:** Query first with SASE, then submit outline/synopsis and 3 sample chapters with SASE. Simultaneous and photocopied submissions OK. Reports in 2 weeks on queries; 8 weeks on mss. Publishes ms 12-18 months after acceptance.

**Terms:** Pays in royalties of 10% minimum, 12% maximum. Free book catalog on request.

**Tips:** "We want only first class fiction and feel people are becoming more responsive."

**ALLEGANY MOUNTAIN PRESS (I, II)**, 111 N. 10th St., Olean NY 14760. (716)372-0935. Imprints include Uroboros Books. Editorial Director: Ford F. Ruggieri. Estab. 1972. Publishes hardcover and paperback originals. Encourages new writers. Sometimes comments on rejected mss.

**Needs:** Literary, experimental, erotica, and humor/satire. "We want to see fiction with a serious literary intent. Though we are interested in books that will sell, we are not interested in 'bestsellers' if it means pandering to bad taste. Previously we have only published poetry in book form, mainly because we haven't received the kind of ms we'd like to publish in the novel."

**How to Contact:** Submit outline/synopsis with 2-3 sample chapters. No simultaneous submissions; photocopied submissions OK. Reports in 6 weeks on mss.

**Terms:** Pays in 50 author's copies and 10-15% royalties. Book catalog for 6x9 SASE plus 62¢ postage.

**Tips:** "Study the market you're aiming for and look to the people who have written the best things in that field as a guide. We are looking for work that is innovative in form and content. Don't waste your time or money sending us pop or hack-type fiction. We will only consider work that we believe will have a significant cultural impact."

**ALYSON PUBLICATIONS, INC. (II)**, 40 Plympton St., Boston MA 02118. (617)542-5679. Subsidiary includes Carrier Pigeon Distributors. Fiction Editor: Sasha Alyson. Estab. 1977. Medium-sized publisher specializing in lesbian- and gay-related material. Publishes paperback originals and reprints. Books: paper and printing varies; trade paper, perfect bound binding; average print order: 8,000; first novel print order: 6,000. Plans 4 first novels this year. Averages 15 total titles, 8 fiction titles each year. Average first novel print order 6,000 copies.

**Needs:** "We are interested in all categories; *all* materials must be geared toward lesbian and/or gay readers." Recently published *Between Friends*, by Gillian E. Hanscombe (lesbian); and *China House*, by Vince Lardo (gay male romance/gothic).

**How to Contact:** Query first with SASE. Reports in 3 weeks on queries; 2 months on mss. Photocopied submissions OK but not preferable. Prefers letter-quality.

**Terms:** "We prefer to discuss terms with the author." Sends galleys to author. Book catalog for SAE and 37¢ postage.

**Tips:** Encourages first novelists and published new writers last year.

**‡AND BOOKS (II)**, 702 S. Michigan, South Bend, IN 46618. Editorial Director: Janos Szebedinsky. Estab. 1977. Publishes paperback originals. Number of titles: 15 in 1985. Occasionally comments on rejected mss. Occasionally recommends other markets.
**Needs:** Occasional translations. "No romance, please."
**How to Contact:** Prefers submission of outline/synopsis and sample chapters with 9x12 or larger SASE, before complete ms. Simultaneous and photocopied submissions OK. Reports in 6 weeks on mss.
**Terms:** Pays 5-10% royalties. Book catalog for legal-sized SASE plus appropriate postage.
**Tips:** "Send mss that will sell. Consider your market and how it will be reached. We sell mainly through book stores and are a general reading market. We do not read or publish fiction."

**ANDREW MOUNTAIN PRESS**, Box 14353, Hartford CT 06114. Editor: Candace Catlin Hall. Estab. 1979. Publishes paperback originals. Averages 3 total titles, 1 fiction title each year. Occasionally critiques rejected mss.
**Needs:** Juvenile (picture book). "We don't want to see anything except children's picture books." Recently published: *The Yellow Thread Cat* (children's picture book).
**How to Contact:** Accepts unsolicited mss. Submit complete ms with SASE. Simultaneous and photocopied submissions OK. Accepts computer printout submissions. Reports in 2 months on mss. Publishes ms under 6 months after acceptance.
**Terms:** Pays in author's copies.
**Tips:** "We like to publish people who have not appeared in book form. We specialize in 'first' children's books. They should not be moralistic—update your style. Don't send anything but picture book ideas."

**ANDROGYNE**, 930 Shields St., San Francisco CA 94132. (415)586-2697. Contact: Ken Weichel. Estab. 1971. "Independent press working within the cultural coincidence of San Francisco." Publishes books and a periodical, *Androgyne*. Publishes paperback originals. Averages 3 total titles, 1 fiction title each year. Average first novel print order 500 copies.
**Needs:** Contemporary, experimental, and literary.
**How to Contact:** Does not accept unsolicited mss. Query. Reports in 1 month on queries; 2 months on mss. Simultaneous and photocopied submissions OK. Accepts computer printout submissions; prefers letter-quality.
**Terms:** Pays in author's copies (10%). See magazine for writer's guidelines. Free book catalog.

**‡ANDROMEDA PRESS (II)**, Subsidiary of W.H. Wheeler Associates, 99 Teardrop Ct., Newbury Park CA 91330. (805)498-9151. Imprint includes *SF International* (Magazine). Publisher/Editor: William H. Wheeler. Estab. 1984. One-person operation at present. Publishes hardcover originals. Books: 50-60 lb offset book, acid-free paper; offset printing; cloth, sewn signature binding; average print order: 2,000; first novel print order: 2,000. Plans 2 first novels this year. Critiques on rejected ms.
**Needs:** Some science fiction, fantasy, SF short story collections, SF translations. Needs for novels include science fiction only. Recently published *The Labyrinth*, by Daniel Dickinson (science fiction).
**How to Contact:** Accepts unsolicited mss. Submit complete ms with cover letter. SASE. Reports in 1-2 months on mss. Simultaneous and photocopied submissions OK. Accepts letter-quality computer printouts.
**Terms:** Pays in royalties of 15% minimum; 15% maximum. Sends galleys to author. Writer's guidelines free for #10 SAE and 1 first class stamp.
**Tips:** Encourages first novelists. "As a 'miniature' press, probably all our novels by US/Canadian or other English-language authors will be first novels. If we have a hit, we may well lose the author to a larger and better-heeled publishing house." In regard to the author—editor relationship, "we feel almost everyone's writing can benefit from a little fine-tuning here and there. But it *is* the author's book and we won't make changes without the author's consent. On the other hand, if we feel something in an otherwise good book is really bad, and the author won't change, we probably

won't publish it. Old-fashioned virtues like proper spelling and punctuation are still important. And don't confuse the reader—you may know who's doing what to whom, but make sure the reader does too. Especially important in dialogue.''

**ANNICK PRESS LTD. (IV)**, 5519 Yonge St., Willowdale, Ontario M2N 5S3 Canada. (416)221-4802. Publisher of children's books only. Publishes hardcover and paperback originals. Books: 1 lb offset paper; fullcolor offset printing; perfect and library binding; full-color illustrations; average print order: 9,000; first novel print order: 7,000. Plans 3 first picture books this year. Averages approximately 20 titles each year, all fiction. Average first picture book print order 2,000 cloth, 8,000 paper copies. Occasionally critiques rejected ms.
**Needs:** Juvenile (easy-to-read, contemporary), and preschool/picture book.
**How to Contact:** "Annick Press publishes only work by Canadian citizens or residents." Does not accept unsolicited mss. Query with SASE. Free book catalog.
**Terms:** Sends galleys to author.
**Tips:** "Publishing more fiction this year, because our company is growing. But our publishing program is currently full."

**ANSUDA PUBLICATIONS (II)**, Box 158J, Harris IA 51345. Fiction Editor: Daniel Betz. Estab. 1978. One-man operation on part-time basis, "planning to someday expand into a full-time business." Publishes paperback originals. Books: mimeo paper; mimeo printing; index stock covers with square spine binding illustrations on cover; average print order varies; first novel print order varies. Plans 1-2 first novels this year. Averages 3-5 total titles, 1 fiction title each year. Occasionally critiques rejected mss.
**Needs:** Fantasy, horror, literary, mainstream, psychic/supernatural, short story collections, and suspense/mystery. "Interested mostly in fantasy, horror, psychic and supernatural. No romance, juvenile, experimental, translations, or science fiction." Recently published: *Hor-Tasy*, edited by Daniel Betz (anthology of horror and fantasy stories).
**How to Contact:** Query first or submit outline/synopsis and 1-2 sample chapters. SASE always. Photocopied submissions OK. Accepts computer printout submissions. Prefers letter-quality. Reports in 1 day on queries, 1-4 weeks on mss. Publishes ms an average of 1 year after acceptance.
**Terms:** Pays in royalties by arrangement and 2 author's copies. Writer's guidelines and book catalog for #10 SASE. Sample copy $2.95.
**Tips:** "We appreciate neat copy. If photocopies are sent, we like to be able to read dark letters and to read all of the story. We try to work closely with the author through the period from first submission to publication."

**APPLEZABA PRESS**, Box 4134, Long Beach CA 90804. Editorial Director: Shelley Hellen. Estab. 1977. "We are a family-operated publishing house, working on a part-time basis. We plan to expand over the years." Publishes paperback originals. Averages 1 fiction title each year.
**Needs:** Contemporary, literary, experimental, faction, feminist, gay, lesbian, fantasy, humor/satire, translations, and short story collections. No gothic, romance, confession, inspirational, satirical, black humor or slapstick. Recently published: *The Historical Document*, by Nichola Manning (experimental).
**How to Contact:** Accepts unsolicited mss. Submit complete ms with SASE. No simultaneous submissions; photocopied submissions OK. Accepts computer printout submissions. Prefers letter-quality. Reports in 2 months. Publishes ms 2-3 years after acceptance.
**Terms:** Pays in author's copies and 8-15% royalties; no advance. Free book catalog.
**Tips:** "Write legibly. Cover letter with previous publications, etc. is OK. Each book, first or twentieth, has to stand on its own. If a first-time novelist has had shorter works published in magazines, it makes it somewhat easier for us to market the book. We publish only book-length material."

**ARIADNE PRESS (I)**, 4817 Tallahassee Ave., Rockville MD 20853. (301)949-2514. President: Carol F. Hoover. Estab. 1976. Publishes hardcover originals. "Primarily interested in first novels, new writers."

**Needs:** Contemporary, literary, adventure, mystery, spy, historical, war, women's, feminist, and humor/satire. No juvenile or science fiction. "No short stories, only novels." Recently published: *Lead Me to the Exit*, by Ellen Moore (a woman's changing role); *The Rudelstein Affair*, by Michael Marsh (cloak-and-dagger spoof); and *The Lattice*, by Henry Alley (mainstream literary).

**How to Contact:** Accepts unsolicited mss. Query with SASE. Simultaneous and photocopied submissions OK. Reports in 2 weeks on queries, 2 months on mss. Publishes ms 6-12 months after acceptance.

**Terms:** Pays 10% in royalties; no advance.

**Tips:** "Try major publishers first. This is a shoestring operation, producing some 900 copies/book. Our aim is to publish first-rate, readable fiction which has not been accepted by major markets. It helps if the writer has the capacity and energy to publicize his own book and/or assist with distribution. We do receive quite a few manuscripts with a writing style of good quality. But the problem of organizing a plot which expresses the book's major themes through its characters, who develop the logic of their own actions, has usually not been solved."

**ARSENAL PULP PRESS (I)**, Suite 202, 986 Homer St., Vancouver, British Columbia V6B 2W7 Canada. (604)687-4233. Imprints include Tillacum Library, Pulp Press, Arsenal Editions. Editor: C. Wharton. Estab. 1972. Small, co-operative publisher. Publishes hardcover and paperback originals. Books: 60 lb deluxe book paper; offset printing; perfect binding; occasional illustrations; average print order: 1,000; first novel print order: 500-1,000. Plans 1 first novel this year. Averages 8 total titles, 3 fiction titles each year. Average first novel print order 1,000-2,000 copies. Occasionally critiques rejected ms.

**Needs:** Contemporary, experimental, feminist, gay, lesbian, literary, short story collections, translations, and women's. "We are an open-minded organization always on the lookout for new, fresh works." No romance, supernatural/occult, or religious. Recently published *Still*, by Nichol (contemporary); *The Promise*, by W. Campbell (short stories); and *This Guest of Summer*, by J. Doran (contemporary), and *Nothing So Natural*, by J. Curry (contemporary).

**How to Contact:** Accepts unsolicited mss. Submit outline/synopsis and sample chapters or complete ms with SASE or SAE and IRC. Simultaneous and photocopied submissions OK. Accepts computer printout submissions; prefers letter-quality.

**Terms:** Pays in royalties of 10% minimum, 15% maximum; offers $30 average advance. Sends galleys to author. Subsidy publishes. "Approximately 20-30% of our titles are funded or partially funded by grants."

**Tips:** "Publishing of first novels depends entirely on quality of work." Publishing "more fiction this year as an objective, being a literary house." Published new novelists last year. "We have a 3-day novel contest, held annually on Labor Day weekend, and actively encourages new writers."

**‡AYA PRESS (I, II)**, Box 1153, Station F, Toronto, Ontario M4Y 1T0 Canada. Imprints include Pencil Books. Publisher: Beverly Daurio. Fiction Editor: Heather Hallard. Estab. 1978. Samll independent publisher. Publishes hardcover and paperback originals. Books: high quality/often zephyr laid paper; quality press printing; perfect binding; illustrations; average print order: 500-1,500 copies; first novel print order: 500 copies. Publishes 6 total titles/year; 1-4 fiction titles/year. Occasionally critiques ms "but only if requested; fee for market advice, exacting critique."

**Needs:** Contemporary, erotica, ethnic, experimental, feminist, humor/satire, literary, mainstream, short story collections, translations. Needs "compact, accessible but very intelligent style, daring in the intellectual sense." No romance or any other genre work. Recently published *Penumbra*, by Susan Kerslake (esoteric); *Shoes and Shirt: Stories for Pedestrians*, by Geoff Hancock, Ed. (short story collection); and *The Mikveh Man*, by Sharon Drache (short stories).

**How to Contact:** Accepts unsolicited mss. Submit complete ms with cover letter. SASE. Agented fiction 5%. Reports in 2 months. No simultaneous submissions; photocopied submissions OK. Accepts computer printouts; no dot-matrix.

**Terms:** Pays in royalties of 10%; advance is negotiable; in author's copies of 10% of print run. "*Aya Press* does not subsidy publish. Our subsidiary, Pencil Books, does only subsidy work. Arrangements with the author are negotiated—services offered include complete editorial guidance, design, promotion advice, market analysis, and everything else to make beautiful finished books." Book catalog free on request.

**Tips:** Plans to publish more fiction. "We encourage first novelists, especially if the possibility of a sale of paperback rights exists. Be professional. Learn your market (publisher's needs) so your work reaches those who want to see it. Listen carefully to criticism, regardless of how painful it is, and keep writing."

**BAKER STREET PRODUCTIONS LTD. (II)**, 502 Range St., Box 3610, Mankato MN 56001. (507)625-2482. Contact: Karyne Jacobsen. Estab. 1981. Independent publisher and producer with plans to expand. Publishes hardcover originals. Books: coated stock paper; library bound sewn printing; sewn binding; illustrations; average print order: 2,500. Plans 4-6 first novels this year. Averages 5 total titles each year.

**Needs:** Juvenile (easy-to-read, sports, contemporary). "Publishing schedule filled through 1986." Recently published *I'm Afraid of the Dark* and *Homesick*, by Neese (values clarification).

**How to Contact:** Accepts unsolicited mss. Query with SASE. Reports in 2 weeks on queries; 6 weeks on mss. No simultaneous submissions; photocopied submissions OK. Accepts computer printout submissions. Disc submissions OK with Apple II. Prefers hard copy with disc submission. Sends galleys to author.

**Tips:** Trends include "books with a message or lesson to be learned." Encourages new writers and published previously unpublished writers within the year.

**BALANCE BEAM PRESS, INC. (II)**, 12711 Stoneridge Rd., Dayton MN 55327. (612)427-3168. President/Fiction Editor: Mary Ellis Peterson. Estab. 1982. One-woman operation on part-time basis. Publishes paperback originals. Books: paper varies; letter press printing; perfect binding; b&w illustrations; average print order: 250; first novel print order: 250. "Current plans include only short stories; these could change." Averages 2 total titles each year—currently only anthologies. Occasionally critiques rejected mss; query first. No fiction was published in 1985.

**Needs:** "Currently publishing work dealing with alternatives to nuclear/militaristic society/future. I am planning an anthology of student writing, poetry, short stories, humor, fantasy, science fiction, etc., dealing with fears and concerns, but more important, with possible alternatives and solutions. Also interested in new age fiction."

**How to Contact:** Query first with SASE. Reports in 1 month. Simultaneous and photocopied submissions OK. Accepts computer printout submissions.

**Terms:** Pays in royalties of 10% minimum "or may cost share with larger percentage of net profits going to author." Sends galleys to author. Book catalog for #10 SASE.

**Tips:** Fiction published only in paperback. Recent trends include "nuclear concerns, children, one title dealing with adoption of disabled and multiracial children. I am very excited about bringing out the work of new authors. We regard the author/editor relationship as a team. Keep trying and be flexible. Be aware of necessity of assisting in marketing."

**‡BANK STREET PRESS**, 24 Bank St., New York NY 10014. (212)255-0692. Publisher: Mary Bertschmann. Estab. 1985. Small independent publisher with plans to expand. Publishes hardcover and paperback originals. Books: Spring Hill offset white paper; printing varies; perfect binding; illustrations; average print order: 500-1,000; first novel print order: 700. Plans 1 first novel this year. Averages 4 total titles/year; 2 fiction titles/year.

**Needs:** Only aesthetically oriented books.

**How to Contact:** Query first in writing. SASE for query. No agents. Reports in 3 weeks on queries; 6 weeks on mss.

**Terms:** To be determined eventually. Sends galleys to author.

**Tips:** Encourages first novelist and published new writers last year.

**‡BANNED BOOKS (I, II)**, Subsidiary of Edward Williams Publishing Co., Box 33280—#231, Austin TX 78764. Imprints include Banned Books and Mirage Books. Senior Editor: Tom Hayes. Estab. 1985. Small press with plans to expand. Publishes hardcover originals and paperback originals. Books: 60 lb book paper; sheet-fed and web offset printing; edition and perfect binding; illustrations; average print order: 1,000-5,000 (1st run); first novel print order: 1,000-5,000. Plans 5 first novels this year. Averages 5 total titles, 4 fiction titles each year. Critiques or comments on rejected ms.

**Needs:** Gay, lesbian. Needs for novels include almost anything of interest to the gay market. Nothing pornographic, violence or sex for its own sake. Recently published *Fairy Tales Mother Never Told You*, by Benjamin Eakin (humor).

**How to Contact:** Accepts unsolicited mss. SASE. Query first. Reports in 1 week on queries; 4-6 weeks on mss. Simultaneous and photocopied submissions OK—only very good copies. Accepts computer printouts.

**Terms:** Pays in royalties of 10% minimum; 15% maximum; 10 author's copies. Sends galleys to author. Writer's guidelines free for #SAE and 1 first class stamp.

**Tips:** "We intend to do a great deal of fiction. Many of these will be paperback originals. We encourage first novelists. Our first book is by an unpublished author."

**‡BARRINGTON PRESS (II)**, Subsidiary of Ben Martin Publishing Group, Inc., 175 Calle Magdalena, Encinitas CA 92024. (619)942-9470. Estab. 1983. Small, independent publisher with plans to expand. Publishes hardcover and paperback originals. Books: 60 lb offset paper; offset printing; perfectbound only; average print order: 15,000; first novel print order "depends on deal, we coop much with majors." Plans 4 first novels this year. Averages 7 total titles/year; 4 novels/year. Occasionally critiques rejected mss.

**Needs:** Contemporary, literary, mainstream, suspense/mystery. "Needs novels which reflect some social commentary; criminal justice principally." No juvenile, gothic, historical. Recently published *Sleeping Neighbors*, by William Hester (contemporary action); and *No Chance*, by David Westheimer (crime).

**How to Contact:** No unsolicited mss. Query first. SASE. Agented fiction 50%. Reports in 3 weeks on queries; 2 months on mss. Simultaneous and photocopied submissions OK. No computer printouts.

**Terms:** Pays in royalties of 8% minimum; 15% maximum; $700 advance; advance is negotiable. Sends galleys to author. Book catalog for #10 SASE.

**Tips:** "We see growing interest in rapid social changes that we try and reflect in fiction form. We are not super-liberals, but sustain great concern in the emergence of 'police states'; too many laws, and the meddling of police, prosecutors, attorneys, etc. into social concerns and private matters."

**BILINGUAL REVIEW PRESS**, Box M, Campus Post Office, SUNY-Binghamton, Binghamton NY 13901. (607)724-9495. Editor: Gary Keller. Estab. 1974. Publishes hardcover and paperback originals. Plans 4 first novels this year. Averages 15 total titles, 10 fiction titles each year. Publishes also in Spanish. Occasionally critiques rejected mss.

**Needs:** Ethnic, historical, literary, short story collections, and translations. US Hispanic themes only. "We will publish up to 12-15 good novels per year on US Hispanic life if the material is available." Recently published: *Inheritance of Strangers*, by Nash Candelaria (third novel in a trilogy of historical novels about New Mexico; and *The Plum Plum Pickers*, by Raymond Barrio (new edition of a "classic" Chicano novel about Migrant workers, first self-published in 1968).

**How to Contact:** Query first with SASE. Simultaneous and high-quality photocopied submissions OK. Reports in 1 month on queries. Publishes ms an average of 1 year after acceptance.

**Terms:** Pays in standard royalty of 10% with an average of $300 advance. Must return advance if book is not completed or is unacceptable. Subsidy publishes less than 10% of total books. "We occasionally subsidy publish a scholarly book. We never subsidy publish fiction, poetry or any books in the trade market." Free book catalog.

**Tips:** "A strong market is developing for US Hispanic fiction. Double space all manuscripts! Send original plus 1 copy or 2 high quality copies."

**BINFORD & MORT PUBLISHING (IV)**, 1202 NW 17th Ave., Portland OR 97209. (503)221-0866. Imprints include Metropolitan Press. Assistant Editor: P.L. Cardenier. Estab. 1891. Small regional publisher. Publishes hardcover and paperback originals and reprints. Averages 24 total titles, 0-1 fiction title each year. Average first novel print order 5,000 copies.

**Needs:** Historical, juvenile (historical), regional, western, young adult/teen (historical). "Must be strongly laced with historical background.'

**How to Contact:** Accepts unsolicited mss. Query with SASE. Reports in 1 month on queries; 4 months on mss. Simultaneous and photocopied submissions OK. Accepts computer printout submissions; prefers letter-quality. Disc submissions OK; inquire for compatibility. Prefers hard copy with disc submission.

**Terms:** Pays in royalties of 5% minimum, 10% maximum. Sends galleys to author. Individual arrangement with author depending on book. Free book catalog.

**Tips:** "Trends include regional historic fiction. Limited acceptance for first novels. Seek out a publisher that is definitely interested in your subject matter and its marketability."

**BKMK PRESS (I, II)**, UMKC, 107 Cockefair Hall, 5100 Rockhill Rd., Kansas City MO 64110. (816)276-1305. Editor-in-Chief: Dan Jaffe. Assistant Editor: Pat Nuyett. Estab. 1971. Publishes paperback originals. Books: standard paper; offset printing; perfect and case bound binding; average print order: 1,000; first novel print order: 1,000. Averages 6 total titles; 1 fiction title each year.

**Needs:** Contemporary, ethnic, experimental, historical, literary, and translations. "We are new to fiction publishing but we plan to print one collection or anthology of short stories per year."

**How to Contact:** Query first with SASE. Reports in 3-4 weeks on queries.

**Terms:** Pays in royalties (approximately 10%, adjustable by contract). Sends galleys to author Free book catalog.

**Tips:** "We are new to fiction publishing and encourage first novelists. We regard the author/editor relationship as tough and friendly."

**‡BLACKBERRY (IV)**, Box 687, South Harpswell ME 04079. (207)833-6051. Contact: Gary Lawless. Estab. 1974. One person small press publisher—35 titles to date. Publishes paperback originals and reprints. Books: offset printing. Plans 1 first novel this year. Averages 5-8 titles/year. Occasionally critiques rejected mss.

**Needs:** Ethnic, feminist, gay, lesbian, literary, translations.

**How to Contact:** Accepts unsolicited mss. Query first. SASE for query and ms. Reports in 1 week on queries and mss. Simultaneous and photocopied submissions OK. Accepts computer printouts. No dot-matrix.

**Terms:** Pays in royalties of 10% minimum and 10 author's copies. Money depends on grant/ award money. Sends galleys to author. Book catalog free on request.

**BLIND BEGGAR PRESS**, Box 437, Bronx NY 10467. Imprints include LampLight Editions. Fiction Editors: Gary Johnston, C.D. Grant. Estab. 1975. Small press with plans to expand. Publishes paperback originals. Plans to publish first novels "dependent upon budget." Averages 2-3 total titles each year; "no fiction titles thus far." Average first novel print order 2,000 copies. Occasionally critiques rejected ms.

**Needs:** Ethnic (Third World), experimental, juvenile (animal, easy-to-read, fantasy, historical), preschool/picture book, short story collections, translations, women's, and young adult/teen (historical).

**How to Contact:** Accepts unsolicited mss. Query first with SASE. Reports in 1 month on queries; 2 months on mss. Simultaneous and photocopied submissions OK. Publishes ms 6-12 months after acceptance.

**Terms:** Pays in author's copies (10-15% of run). "If author wishes to pay all or part of production costs, we work out individual arrangements directly." Book catalog free on request.

**Tips:** Recent trends include ethnic historical (biographies, political history, etc.). In first novels interested in high quality, relevancy to Third World readers. "Within two years we plan to publish children's books, short stories and *maybe* a small novel."

**BOGUS BOOKS (II)**, #10A, 120 W. 97th St., New York NY 10025. Imprints include *bogus review*. Fiction Editors: Jay Goldberg and Kirk McElhearn. Estab. 1982. Small independent press: two-man operation on part-time basis. Publishes paperback originals. Books: 20 lb white raw stock paper; offset, photocopying printing; saddle wire binding; b&w illustrations; some photos; average print order: 300; first novel print order: 300. Averages 2 total titles, 1 fiction title each year. Average first novel print order 300 + copies.
**Needs:** Contemporary, experimental, fantasy, humor/satire, literary, science fiction, short story collections, and translations. Needs for novels include contemporary and experimental, but are open. Book catalog for SASE.
**Tips:** "Young, experimental, promising, (leaning to fantasy)" are trends in recent fiction lists. "We encourage the publishing of first novels; however, in the past we have worked out a deal with our writers to split the fees on an indiviudal basis. Don't let anything stop, or get in the way of your desire to write; however, if you are distracted easily, make sure you have another source of income/support." Write for submission policies and terms.

**BOOK PUBLISHERS INC. (II)**, (formerly Mariner Publishing Company, Inc.) 5700 Mariner St., Suite 601, Box 21492, Tampa FL 33622. (813)876-1521. President: M.N. Manougian. Fiction Editor: J.M. Manougian. Estab. 1979. Small press with plans to expand. Publishes hardcover and paperback originals. Plans 4 first novels this year. Average first novel print order 5,000 copies. Occasionally critiques rejected mss.
**Needs:** Adventure, contemporary, historical, literary, mainstream, romance (historical, contemporary), and women's. No juvenile.
**How to Contact:** Submit outline/synopsis and 4 sample chapters. Reports in 5 weeks. Simultaneous and photocopied submissions OK. Accepts computer printout submissions.
**Terms:** Pays in royalties; author's copies; advance negotiable. Subsidy publishes 25% of books/year. Writer's guidelines for SASE.

**BOOKMAKERS (IV)**, (formerly Northwest Matrix Bookmakers), #3, 385 E. 11th Eugene OR 97401. (503)343-7449. Publisher: Charlotte Mills. Estab. 1975. "Bookmakers is a small publishing and publishing consultant firm. We distribute 5 feminist books. We publish 5-10 books for self-publishers, offering editing, design, production and marketing services. We also publish conference proceedings." Publishes paperback originals. Books: Hi-bulk, acid free paper; web printing; perfect or case binding; illustrations; average print order: 1,000; first novel print order: 1,000. Averages 5-10 total titles each year. "Evaluations average 3 typed pages, include recommendations for publishers, agents and/or budget for self-publication."
**Needs:** Self-publishers: local and regional authors. Considers exceptional feminist fiction mss.
**How to Contact:** Send ms for evaluation and/or bid.
**Terms:** "We provide complete publishing service, which includes editorial evaluations; editing, design, production and marketing for authors, especially authors of local and regional books and authors who publish gift books for friends and family. Provide low-cost short runs of 25-250-500 copies and longer runs of 1,000-5,000. Editorial evaluations: $100. Book bids: $50 which is credited to total production cost if author decides to publish. Author bears entire cost of book. We keep per book cost low so author has chance to earn reasonable return on cover price. Author pays 50% on signing publishing agreement; 25% after proofing and paste-up; 25% on delivery of books. Marketing agreement—similar payment plan." Sends galleys to author.

**BOOKS FOR ALL TIMES, INC.**, Box 2, Alexandria VA 22313. Publisher/Editor: Joe David. Estab. 1981. One-man operation. Publishes hardcover and paperback originals. "No plans for new writers at present." Averages 1 fiction title to date. Occasionally critiques rejected mss.
**Needs:** Contemporary, literary, and short story collections. "No novels at the moment; hopeful, though, of someday soon publishing a collection of quality short stories. No popular fiction or material easily published by the major or minor houses specializing in mindless entertainment. Only interested in stories of the Victor Hugo or Sinclair Lewis quality." Recently published: *The Fire Within*, by Joe David (literary).

**How to Contact:** Query first with SASE. Simultaneous and photocopied submission OK. Reports in 1 month on queries.
**Terms:** Pays negotiable advance. "Publishing/payment arrangement will depend on plans for the book." Book catalog free on request.
**Tips:** Interested in "controversial, honest books which satisfy the reader's curiosity to know."

**BOOKWRIGHTS (II)**, (formerly Laranmark Press), BookWrights, Inc., 220 Main St., Box 253, Neshkoro WI 54960. (414)293-4377. Imprints include Unicorn-Star Press. President: Larry D. Names. Estab. 1980. Independent publisher with plans to expand. Publishes hardcover and paperback originals and paperback reprints. Plans 5 first novels this year. Averages 5 total titles, 4 fiction titles each year. Occasionally critiques rejected mss.
**Needs:** Adventure, contemporary, ethnic, fantasy, historical, humor/satire, psychic/supernatural/occult, regional, romance (historical, contemporary), suspense/mystery, war, western, and women's. "We like fast-paced books that are well-plotted. We are especially interested in psychic novels and spy-adventure." No literary, short story collections, young adult, erotica or experimental. Recently published: *When Spirits Walked*, by Chris Gentry (psychic-mystery); *The Summers of the Ferris Wheel*, by James V. McMakin; and *Ever Watchful, Ever Present* by Leda Indio and Staara (psychic-mystery).
**How to Contact:** Query first with SASE. Reports in 2 weeks on queries; 2 months on mss. Photocopied submissions preferred. Accepts computer printout submissions. Prefers letter-quality. Accepts disc submissions compatible with IBM system. Prefers hard copy with disc submission.
**Terms:** Pays in royalties of 8% minimum; 15% maximum. Possible advance. Writer's guidelines for SASE with 2 first class stamps. Free book catalog.
**Tips:** "We enjoy publishing good novels by new authors."

**BROKEN WHISKER STUDIO (I, II)**, Box 1303, Chicago IL 60690. Editorial Director: Joan H. Lee. Estab. 1976. Publishes paperback originals. Books: paper varies with project; offset, some letter press printing; perfect, some hand-sewn signatures binding; average print order: 300-1,000. Encourages new writers.
**Needs:** Contemporary literary, and experimental.
**How to Contact:** Submit complete ms or first 10 pages of fiction with SASE. Photocopied submissions OK. Reports in 1 month on mss. Publishes ms 6-12 months after acceptance.
**Terms:** Pays in author's copies and royalties. Sends galleys to author. "We use a negotiable contract." No advances.
**Tips:** "We publish *short* fiction of no more than 150 pages. Novellas, short stories, poetry, juveniles. We use art work. Interested in material for chapbooks, broadsides, and poemcards. We are publishing more fiction, less poetry. Poetry increasingly difficult to sell. We look for very promising new writers, have published more firsts than work by established authors. We look for stories that we will want to read again and again, that are honest in content and style. Authors we like pay

*Talk was, for John O'Hara, the beginning of many of his stories. Often he would sit at his typewriter and start by thinking of a couple of faces he had seen. He would put them together in a restaurant or on an airplane, and they would begin to talk. 'I let them do small talk for a page or two,' said O'Hara, 'and pretty soon they begin to come to life. They do so entirely through dialogue. I start by knowing nothing about them except what I remember of their faces. But as they chatter away, one of them, and then the other, will say something that is so revealing that I recognize the signs of created characters. From then on it is a question of how deeply I want to interest myself in the characters.*
—*Frank MacShane on John O'Hara*

careful attention to character, dialogue, atmosphere, action, and purpose. Strong writing, not slick, interests us, and we welcome new authors. We have no restrictions on theme or subject. Send the best presentation you can and stay with it. Find the right publisher; it may be a long almost heartbreaking search. Specifically, gather as much *information* as you can about placing your manuscript. Good luck."

**BRUNSWICK PUBLISHING COMPANY (II)**, Box 555, Lawrenceville VA 23868. (804)848-3865. Editor/Publisher: M.S. Raymond. Estab. 1978. Small independent publisher—expanding. Publishes hardcover and paperback originals and reprints. Books: 70 lb offset paper; offset printing; perfect or hardbound binding; illustrations; first novel print order: 500. Plans 5-6 first novels this year. Averages 30 total titles; 8-10 fiction titles each year. Critiques rejected ms for $150 and up depending on length.

**Needs:** Adventure, autobiographies, biographies, contemporary, ethnic, experimental, faction, fantasy, feminist, historical, humor/satire, juvenile, literary, mainstream, psychic/supernatural/occult, regional, religious/inspirational, romance, science fiction, short story collections, suspense/mystery, translations, war, western, women's, and young adult/teen. Recently published *In The Shadow of a God*, by Susan Spitzer (historical novel re. Alexander The Great); and *Cain's Descendants*, by V.H. McCaskill (autobiographical novel).

**How to Contact:** Accepts unsolicited mss. Query or submit complete ms with SASE. Reports in 2 weeks on queries; 3 weeks on mss. Simultaneous and photocopied submissions OK. Accepts computer printout submissions.

**Terms:** Cooperative publishing arrangement; costs shared, usually 80% author/20% publisher; individual arrangements with author; 50 author's copies. Sends galleys to author. Writer's guidelines and book catalog for SASE.

**Tips:** "We encourage first novelists and published new writers last year."

**CARNIVAL ENTERPRISES**, Box 19087, Minneapolis MN 55419. (612)823-7216. Editorial Consultants: Jay E. Johnson and Gregory N. Lee. Estab. 1981. Number of titles: 30-45 trade editions in 1984-85 (Carnival Press Books imprint for Raintree Publishers Group and other publishers); many book titles and audio visual projects planned for 1986 with a variety of publishing and toy firms. Encourages new writers. "*Not* a publishing company; a production or design firm for books. Carnival solicits mss and contacts writers whose resumés are on file, and presents projects and stories to publishers and retail firms coupled with the work of prominent juvenile illustrators."

**Needs:** Author resumés for Carnival's permanent files, along with short samples of writing in the juvenile fiction area. "No adult or adolescent fiction." Recently created *Ceremony—In the Circle of Life*, by White Deer of Autumn (a "Notable Children's Trade Book in the Field of Social Studies"); *Mother Told Me So*, by Carol A. Marron (an IRA-CBC "Children's Choice" winner for 1983); Ringling Bros. Series of titles for Little, Brown and Company; *Angel Child, Dragon Child*, by Maria Surat (a "Reading Rainbow" review selection).

**How to Contact:** Send cover letter and résumé, plus samples of work for permanent files. "Carnival often solicits work for its clients from authors on file. No unsolicited mss, please!"

**Terms:** "Varies from client to client; flat fees usually for toy company accounts, advance and royalty for publishing accounts."

**Tips:** "The talent has to be there, plus an understanding of the marketplace and the audience."

**CARPENTER PRESS (I, II)**, Rt. 4, Pomeroy OH 45769. Editorial Director: Robert Fox. Estab. 1973. One-man operation on part-time basis with plans to expand. Publishes paperback originals. Books: alkaline paper; offset printing; perfect or saddle stapled binding; illustrations sometimes; average print order: 500-2,500; first novel print order: 1,000.

**Needs:** Contemporary, literary, experimental, science fiction, and fantasy. "Literary rather than genre science fiction and fantasy." Recently published *Song for Three Voices*, by Curt Johnson (novel); and the 10th anniversary first novel contest winner, *The Three-Week Trance Diet*, by Jane Piirto. "Do not plan to publish more than one books/year including chapbooks, and this depends upon funding, which is erratic. Contemplating future competitions in the novel and short story."

**How to Contact:** Accepts unsolicited mss. Query. SASE. Simultaneous and photocopied submissions OK. Accepts computer printout submissions. Prefers letter-quality. Reports promptly.
**Terms:** Pays in author's copies or 10% royalties. "Terms vary according to contract." No cash advance. Free book catalog.
**Tips:** "Don't try to impress us with whom you've studied or where you've published. Read as much as you can so you're not unwittingly repeating what's already been done. I look for freshness and originality rather than superlative technique. I wouldn't say that I favor experimental over traditional writing. Rather, I'm interested in seeing how recent experimentation is tying tradition to the future and to the work of writers in other countries. In the next few years, I see an increase in the publishing of small press fiction and an increase in sales, because of greater awareness by the reading public. Our books should be read before submitting. We encourage first novelists, and plan a 10th anniversary edition."

**‡CAVE BOOKS (IV)**, Subsidiary of Cave Research Foundation, 756 Harvard Ave., St. Louis MO 63130. (314)862-7646. Editor: Richard A. Watson. Estab. 1957. Small press. Publishes hardcover originals and reprints and paperback originals and reprints. Books: acid free paper; various methods printing; sewn in signatures binding; illustrations; average print order: 1,500; first novel print order: 1,500. Averages 4 total titles. Number of fiction titles vary each year. Critiques or comments on rejected ms.
**Needs:** Adventure (cave exploration). Needs any novel with caves as central theme.
**How to Contact:** Accepts unsolicited mss. Submit complete ms with cover letter. Reports in 1 week on queries; 1 month on mss. Simultaneous and photocopied submissions OK. Accepts computer printouts.
**Terms:** Pays in royalties of 10% minimum; 10% maximum. Sends galleys to author. Book catalog free on request.
**Tips:** Encourages first novelists. "We would very much like to publish some fiction, but although we've put notices here and there, we get no submissions. Why doesn't someone write a historical novel about Mammoth Cave, Carlsbad Caverns, . . .?"

**THE CENTER FOR STUDY OF MULTIPLE BIRTH (II, IV)**, 333 E. Superior St., Suite 476, Chicago IL 60611. (312)266-9093. Executive Director: Donald Keith. Estab. 1977. Publishes hardcover and paperback originals and reprints. Encourages new writers. Sometimes comments on rejected mss.
**Needs:** "Will only consider mss related to twins, triplets or other multiples. Do not send anything that is not related. None will be returned or acknowledged. We sell fictional books on our subject through our bookstore." Recent titles include *The Twins Strike Back*, by V. Flournoy; and *The Triplets*, (for children).
**How to Contact:** Query with SASE. Simultaneous and photocopied submissions OK. Reports in 6 weeks.
**Terms:** Pays 4-6% royalties; no advance. Book catalog for legal-sized SASE.
**Tips:** "Do not send unless it has been queried first. Do not query unless it's about our subject! Do your homework. Edit the work before you send it out. Send neat and readable material. Unsolicited mss in other fields will be disposed of and unanswered."

**CHALLENGE PRESS**, 1107 Lexington Ave., Dayton OH 45407. (513)275-6879. Imprint includes *Confrontation/CHANGE Review*. Editor: F.M. Finney. Estab. 1976. Publishes hardcover originals and reprints. Number of titles: 1 in 1983; plans 3 in 1985.
**Needs:** Literary, mystery, historical, and ethnic (black). "No historical-Southern fiction." Recently published *Papa Babe Stamp Collective*, by Gladys T. Turner.
**How to Contact:** Query with SASE. Simultaneous and photocopied submissions OK. Reports in 2 weeks on queries, 6 weeks on mss. Will not accept unsolicited mss until mid-1986.
**Terms:** Pays 15-40% royalties and by outright purchase of $1,000 maximum; no advance. Book catalog for 7x10 SASE.
**Tips:** "We are a small operation; therefore do not expect a 'quick' reply. We are reasonable and encourage simultaneous submissions."

‡**CHELSEA GREEN (I, II)**, Box 283, Chelsea VT 05038. (802)685-3108. Editor: Ian Baldwin Jr. Estab. 1984. Small independent publisher with about 6 titles per year and may grow to a dozen—not more. Some fiction—prefer regionally-focused fiction, especially rural-strong sense of place. Publishes hardcover originals and reprints and paperback originals and reprints. Books: acid free paper; photo comp printing; sewn and perfect binding; illustrations; average print order: 5,000; first novel print order: 2,500-5,000. Plans 1 first novel this year. Averages 6 total titles, 1 or 2 fiction titles each year. Critiques or comments on rejected ms.

**Needs:** Contemporary, historical, humor/satire, literary, regional, translations. "We are looking for a translation of first rate novelist (like Giono) or regional novel or novellas." No highly experimental. Recently published *In a Pig's Eye*, by Karl Schwenke (regional/humor); *The Man Who Planted Trees*, by Jean Giono (regional/short story/novella).

**How to Contact:** Accepts unsolicited mss. Query first. Submit outline/synopsis and 2 sample chapters. Reports in 2-3 weeks on queries; 2-3 months on mss. Simultaneous and photocopied submissions OK. Accepts computer printouts including dot-matrix. Accepts electronic submissions via disc or modem, for Macintosh. Query first.

**Terms:** Pays in royalties of net contract with royalty tied to sales; pays advance of not more than $500-2,500 range, negotiable; does not always give advances. Sends galleys to author. Book catalog free on request.

**Tips:** Encourages first novelists.

‡**CHERRYABLE BROTHERS (I, II)**, 130 7th St., Suite 448, Garden City NY 11530. (516)486-5090. Editorial Director: William Jabanoski. Estab. 1984. Small independent hardcover and paperback publisher specializing in the publication of novels and short story collections. Publishes hardcover originals and paperback originals. Books: 50 lb natural paper; letterpress printing; hardcover-high grade cloth; softcover-Kromlite binding; "rarely" illustrations; average print order: 500-2,000; first novel print order: 500-2,000. Plans 4 first novels this year. Averages 4 total titles, 4 fiction titles each year. Critiques on rejected ms for $50—only if specifically requested by author.

**Needs:** Adventure, contemporary, erotica, ethnic, experimental, fantasy, feminist, gay, historical, horror, humor/satire, juvenile (5-9 yrs.; including: animal, easy-to-read, fantasy, historical, sports, spy/adventure, contemporary), lesbian, literary, mainstream, psychic/supernatural/occult, regional, romance (contemporary, historical), science fiction, short story collections, suspense/mystery, western, women's, young adult/teen (10-18 years; including: easy-to-read, fantasy/science fiction, historical, problem novels, romance, sports, spy/adventure). Recently published *The Narrow Edge*, by Bernard Lyons (psychological thriller praised by authors Jeffrey Archer and Terence Jelly); and *The Millennium Compact*, by Robert Whitebrook (spy/adventure with anti-arms race message).

**How to Contact:** Accepts unsolicited mss. Submit complete ms with cover letter. Agented fiction: 25%. Reports in 4 weeks. Simultaneous and photocopied submissions OK. Accepts computer printouts including dot-matrix.

**Terms:** Pays in royalties of 10% minimum; 18% maximum. Sends galleys to author. "Approximately half of our titles are subsidized by the author. We offer this arrangement only when we feel the work in question merits publication, but its market is too questionable for us to commit a considerable sum of our limited capital to this end. In these cases, we ask the author to cover the cost of the first printing of the work in exchange for a 40% share of the retail price of the book on each copy sold. As with all our titles, we place a considerable amount of marketing and publicity behind our subsidized books. Further printings, if the first sells, are done at our expense. We are not a 'vanity' press, as we only accept books on a subsidized basis which meet our standards and stand, in our opinion, a reasonable chance of making money on the open market." Writer's guidelines free for standard #10 SASE and 1 first class stamp. Book catalog for #10 SAE and 44¢ postage and 2 first class stamps.

**Tips:** "Cherryable Brothers was established as a press with the main goal of publishing new fiction. As such, we publish fiction almost exclusively, although we may occasionally publish a title outside this form. We tend to publish hardcovers, due to the fact that the hardcover bookbuying market, although not always easy to reach itself, is more open, as a rule, than the paperback market. We strongly encourage first time novelists. To this point, our catalog is currently made up entirely of first time novelists. Our most recent title, *The Narrow Edge*, is by first time novelist Bernard Lyons. Be original. Many manuscripts lack the originality we seek, even when the writer has practiced his craft (in terms of style) well."

**COLUMBIA PUBLISHING COMPANY, INC. (I)**, Frenchtown NJ 08825. (201)996-2141. President: Bernard Rabb. Estab. 1971. "A small press devoted to quality books and book production." Publishes hardcover and paperback originals. Plans 1 first novel this year. Averages 6 total titles, 3 fiction titles each year. Average first novel print order 2,000 copies. Occasionally critiques rejected mss.
**Needs:** No genre or popular fiction. Recently published *Cousin Drewey*, by Sinclair; and *Odyssey of Revenge*, by Diamond (novels).
**How to Contact:** Accepts unsolicited mss. Submit complete ms with SASE. Reports in 6 months. Simultaneous and photocopied submissions OK. Accepts computer printout submissions; prefers letter-quality. Publishes ms an average of 1 year after acceptance.
**Terms:** Pays in royalties of 10% minimum; 15% maximum. Advance is negotiable. No subsidy publications.
**Tips:** Planning more fiction—mysteries, alternative life-styles. "I would very much like to publish more first novels if I could find worthy titles and find them economically feasible."

**‡COMMONERS' PUBLISHING SOCIETY, INC.**, Subsidiary of Cheriton Graphics Systems, Ltd., 432 Rideau St., Ottawa K1N 5Z1 Canada. Editorial contact person: Glenn Cheriton. Fiction Editor: Lucille Shaw. Publishes hardcover originals and paperback originals. Books: 140M Oxford antique book paper; offset printing; perfect binding; illustrations; average print order: 1,000-2,500; first novel print order: 1,000-2,500. Plans 2 or 3 first novels this year. Averages 12 total titles, 5-6 fiction titles each year. Critiques or comments on rejected ms; charge depends on ms (negotiable).
**Needs:** Contemporary, ethnic, experimental, fantasy, historical, humor/satire, literary, mainstream, regional, science fiction. No poorly-written fiction.
**How to Contact:** Accepts unsolicited mss. SASE; IRC. Submit complete ms with cover letter. Reports in 2 weeks on queries; 6-8 weeks on mss. Simultaneous and photocopied submissions OK. Accepts electronic submissions via disc or modem for 1200 Baud Gandolf/Xon Xoff/Pre-circyrc.
**Terms:** Pays in royalties of 10% minimum; advance is negotiable. Sends galleys to author. Subsidy publishes 40% of books. Writer's guidelines free for #10 SAE and 37¢ (Canadian). Book catalog for #10 SAE and Canadian postage.
**Tips:** Encourages first novelists.

**‡CONFLUENCE PRESS INC. (I, II, III)**, Spalding Hall, Lewis-Clark State College, Lewiston ID 83501. (208)799-2336. Imprints include Blue Moon Press. Fiction Editor: James R. Hepworth. Estab. 1976. Small trade publisher. Publishes hardcover originals and reprints; paperback originals and reprints. Books: photo offset printing; Smythe sewn binding; average print order: 2,000-5,000 copies. Averages 10 total titles/year. Critiques on rejected ms for $25/hour.
**Needs:** Contemporary, historical, literary, mainstream, short story collections, translations. "Our needs favor serious fiction, 1 novel and 1 short fiction collection a year, with preference going to work set in the contemporary western United States." Recently published *Decoys and Other Stories*, by Ken Smith (short fiction collection); *With the Indians in the Rockies*, by J.W. Schultz (historical); and *Quest of the Fishdog Skin*, by J.W. Schultz (historical).
**How to Contact:** Accepts unsolicited mss. Query first. SASE for query and ms. Agented fiction 50%. Reports in 6-8 weeks on queries and mss. Simultaneous and photocopied submissions OK. Accepts computer printouts. No dot-matrix.
**Terms:** Pays in royalties of 10% minimum; 15% maximum; advance is negotiable; payment depends on grant/award money. Sends galleys to author. Book catalog for 6x9 SASE.

**Tips:** Published new writers this year. "We are publishing because we finally have good distribution. Have confidence, patience, and persistence. If you must compete, compete with Joyce, Faulkner, Hemingway, not contemporaries. Concentrate, as they did, on fundamentals: craft, character, point of view. An enlargement of a writer comes about more often than not from an enlargement of self and materials, from perspective. Literary fashion is just that. In fiction, we like story, just as in music we like rhythm. Belief is more important to a story than understanding."

**COUNCIL FOR INDIAN EDUCATION (I)**, 517 Rimrock Rd., Billings MT 59102. (406)252-7451. Editor: Hap Gilliland. Estab. 1963. Small, non-profit organization publishing Native American materials for schools. Publishes hardcover and paperback originals. Books: offset printing; perfect bound or saddle stitched binding; b&w illustrations; average print order; 1,500; first novel print order: 1,500. Plans 4 first novels this year. Averages 6 total titles, 5 fiction titles each year. Usually critiques rejected ms.
**Needs:** Adventure, ethnic, historical, juvenile (historical, adventure and others), preschool/picture book, regional, western, young adult/teen (easy-to-read, and historical). Especially needs "short novels, and short stories accurately portraying American Indian life past or present—fast moving with high interest." No sex emphasis. Recently published *Quest for Courage*, by Stormy Rodolph (junior novel).
**How to Contact:** Accepts unsolicited mss. Submit complete ms with SASE. Reports in 3 months. Simultaneous and photocopied submissions OK. Accepts computer printout submissions.
**Terms:** 10% of wholesale price or 1½¢/word. Sends galleys to author. Free writer's guidelines and book catalog.
**Tips:** Mostly publishes original fiction in paperbacks. "Be sure material is culturally authentic and good for the self-concept of the group about whom it is written. We encourage first novelists and published new writers last year."

**COYOTE LOVE PRESS (II)**, 27 Deering St., Portland ME 04101. (207)774-8451. Managing Editor: George B. Benington. Estab. 1982. "Small press which publishes when there is money enough and work worth publishing: one-man basement handpress and offset." Publishes hardcover and paperback originals. Books: highest quality paper; illustrations. Averages 4 total titles, 2 fiction titles each year.
**Needs:** Contemporary, experimental, literary, and short story collections. No "romance, light, or trashy fiction." Recently published *Three American One-Act Monologues*, by Dan Domench (short stories); and *The Wild Man*, by Martin Steingesser.
**How to Contact:** Query first with SASE. Reports in 3 weeks on queries; 6 weeks on mss. Simultaneous and photocopied submissions OK.
**Terms:** Pays 10% of press run; honorarium depends on grant/award money.

**CREATIVE ARTS BOOK COMPANY**, 833 Bancroft Way, Berkeley CA 94710. (415)848-4777. Imprints include Donald S. Ellis, Black Lizard. Editors: Pennfield Jansen, Barry Gifford. Estab. 1976. Small press specializing in *serious* fiction and literary nonfiction, how-to titles, some cookbooks and health titles. Publishes hardcover originals and paperback originals and reprints. Plans 2 first novels this year. Averages 15 total titles-5 fiction titles each year. Average first novel print order 3,500 copies.
**Needs:** "Serious fiction of any category, also unusual and high-quality mystery and suspense." No "romance, frivolity, hogwash." Recently published *Against the Current: As I remember F. Scott Fitzgerald*, by Francis Kroll Ring; and *Californians: Searching for the Golden State*, by James D. Houston.
**How to Contact:** Submit outline/synopsis and 1 sample chapter with SASE. Reports in 6 weeks. No simultaneous submissions; photocopied submissions OK. Accepts computer printout submissions; prefers letter-quality.
**Terms:** Pays in royalties, offers advance. Free book catalog.

‡**CREATIVE CONCERN PUBLICATIONS (I)**, Box 5284, Lake Worth FL 33466. (305)433-5735. Publisher: Dr. Richard G. Hughes. Fiction Editor: Mrs. Gloria Thomas. Estab. 1980. Two-person operation on part-time basis. Publishes paperback originals and reprints. Books: printing offset; perfect binding; average print order: 500; first novel print order: 500. Plans 1 first novel this year. Averages 2 total titles, 1 fiction title each year. Critiques or comments on rejected ms for $100.

**Needs:** Contemporary, erotica, juvenile (5-9 yrs; animal, easy-to-read, fantasy), contemporary, preschool/picture book, contemporary romance, young adult/teen (10-18 years; easy-to-read, fantasy/science fiction, historical, problem novels, romance, sports, spy/adventure). No X-rated/gothic fiction. Recently published *Palm Beach: The Novel*, by R. Glynne Hughes (romance).

**How to Contact:** Accepts unsolicited mss. Query first. Reports in 3 months on queries; 5 months on mss. No simultaneous submissions; photocopied submissions OK.

**Terms:** "We do not pay." Sends galleys to author. Subsidy publishes 100%. Down payment upon approval. Total costs of publishing paid by author.

**Tips:** Fiction books have increased in 1984. Encourages first novelists.

**CREATIVE WITH WORDS PUBLICATIONS (II, III)**, Box 223226, Carmel CA 93922. Editor-in-Chief: Brigitta Geltrich. Estab. 1975. Two-woman operation on part-time basis. Books: bond and stock paper; mimeographed printing; saddle stitch binding; illustrations; average print order: varies. Publishes paperback originals. Publishes anthologies of new and established writers. Averages 3-4 anthologies each year. Critiques rejected mss; $10 for short stories; $20 for longer stories, folklore items.

**Needs:** Humor/satire, juvenile (animal, easy-to-read, fantasy), and short story collections. "Editorial needs center on folkloristic items (according to themes): tall tales and such for biannual anthologies." Needs short stories appealing to children; "tales" of folklore nature, appealing to all ages, poetry and prose written by children. Prose not to exceed 900 words.

**How to Contact:** Accepts unsolicited mss. Query first; submit complete ms with SASE. Photocopied submissions OK. Accepts computer printout submissions. Prefers letter-quality. Reports in 1 month on queries; 2 months on mss. Publishes ms 1-6 months after acceptance.

**Terms:** Pays in 20% reduced author copies. Writer's guidelines and catalog sheet (2 oz.) for SASE.

**Tips:** "Our fiction appeals to general public: children-senior citizens. Query with SASE; request guidelines; follow guidelines and rules of *Creative With Words* publications and not those the writer feels we should have. We only consider fiction along the lines of folklore genres. Work hard; research well; do quality work; make effective use of the language; use both sides of brain, particularly the right side."

**CREATIVITY UNLIMITED PRESS (II)**, 30819 Casilina, Rancho Palos Verdes CA 90274. 377-7908. Contact: Rochelle Stockwell. Estab. 1980. One-person operation with plans to expand. Publishes paperback originals. Books: perfect binding; illustrations; average print order: 1,000. Averages 1 title (fiction) each year. Average first novel print order 1,000 copies.

**Needs:** Recently published *Insides Out*, by Shelley Stockwell (plain talk poetry).

**Tips:** Write for more information.

**CROISSANT & COMPANY (IV)**, Box 282, Athens OH 45701. (614)593-3008. Editor/Publisher: Duane Schneider. One-man operation. Publishes hardcover originals. Books: Warren olde style paper; offset printing; hardcover binding; illustrations sometimes; average print order: 300-500. Averages 2 total titles. Occasionally critiques rejected ms.

**Needs:** "We would consider reprinting a significant out of print work." Recently published *Southern Delight*; and *Forever and the Earth*.

**How to Contact:** Very rarely accepts unsolicited mss. Query with SASE. Reports in 1 week. Simultaneous and photocopied submissions OK. Accepts computer printout submissions.

**Terms:** Pays in variable number of author's copies; honorarium; negotiates advance. Sends galleys to author. Does not usually subsidy publish.

**CROSS-CULTURAL COMMUNICATIONS (IV)**, 239 Wynsum Ave., Merrick NY 11566. (516)868-5635. Editorial Director: Stanley H. Barkan. Estab. 1971. "Small/alternative literary arts publisher focusing on the traditionally neglected languages and cultures in bilingual and multimedia format." Publishes chapbooks, magazines, anthologies, novels, audio cassettes (talking books) and video cassettes (video books, video mags); hardcover and paperback originals. Number of titles: 83; 1 bilingual chapbook, 6 stories in translations (Israel, Sicily and Macedonia), 1 anthology.
**Needs:** Contemporary, literary, experimental, ethnic, humor/satire, juvenile and young adult folktales, and translations. "Main interests: bilingual short stories and children's folktales, parts of novels of authors of other cultures, translations; some American fiction. No fiction that is not directed toward other cultures. For an annual anthology of authors writing in other languages (primarily), we will be seeking very short stories with original-language copy (other than Latin script should be print quality 10/12) on good paper. Title: *Cross Cultural Review Anthology: International Fiction 1*. In 1986, we expect to extend our *CCR* series to include 10 fiction issues: *Five Contemporary* (Dutch, Swedish, Yiddish, Norwegian, Danish, Yugoslav, Sicilian, Greek, Israeli, etc.) *Fiction Writers*." Recently published *New Worlds from the Lowlands*, edited by Manuel van Loggem; forthcoming: *No Telephone to Heaven*, by Joseph Bruchac (novel about Native American in Ghana); and *Bye-Bye America*, by Nat Scammacca (stories of a Siculo-American during and after World War II, in India and Sicily).
**How to Contact:** Accepts unsolicited mss. Query with SASE with 63¢ postage to include book catalog. "Note: Original language ms should accompany translations." Simultaneous and photocopied submissions "of good quality" OK. Accepts computer printout submissions. Prefers letter-quality. Reports in 1 month.
**Terms:** Pays "sometimes" 10-25% in royalties and "occasionally" by outright purchase, in author's copies—"10% of run for chapbook series," and "by arrangement for other publications." No advance.
**Tips:** "Write because you want to or you must; satisfy yourself. If you've done the best then you've succeeded. You will find a publisher and an audience eventually. Generally, we have a greater interest in nonfiction-novels and translations. Short stories and excerpts from novels written in one of the traditional neglected languages are preferred—with the original version (i.e., bilingual). Our kinderbook series will soon be in production with a similar bilingual emphasis, especially for folktales, fairy tales, and fables."

**THE CROSSING PRESS (II)**, Box 640, Trumansburg NY 14886. Editor: Elaine Gill. Editor, Gay Literature and Literature: John Gill. Editor, Feminist: Kate Dunn. Publishes paperback and hardcover originals. Books: 50-55 lb offset paper; offset printing; perfect and hardbound binding; illustrations sometimes; average print order: 3,500-5,000; first novel print order: 1,500-3,000. Estab. 1966.
**Needs:** Literary, contemporary, women's, feminist, gay/lesbian.
**How to Contact:** Query with SASE.
**Terms:** Standard royalty contracts.
**Tips:** "We are publishing more fiction and more paperbacks, and published new writers last year. Keep writing. Don't submit first work before showing to very critical friends. Do the necessary research in library, to see which publisher would possibly be interested in your work."

**CUBE PUBLICATIONS INC.**, 1 Buena Vista Rd., Port Jefferson NY 11777. (516)331-4990. President: George L. Manthe. Fiction Editor: Katherine B. Glean. Estab. 1982. "Two-man operation planning expansion in a limited variety of publications, casebound and paperback." Publishes hardcover and paperback originals. Plans 1 first novel this year. Averages 4 total titles; 1 fiction title each year. Average first novel print order 1,000 copies. Critiques rejected mss.
**Needs:** Humor/satire, short story collections, and women's. Needs for novels include "humor/satire—human interest/political."
**How to Contact:** Query first or submit outline/synopsis and sample chapters with SASE. Reports in 3 weeks on queries; 1 month on mss. Simultaneous and "legible" photocopied submis-

sions OK. Accepts computer printout submissions. Prefers letter-quality. Publishes ms 9-12 months after acceptance.

**Terms:** To be determined. "Individual arrangements are currently used, but we intend to form contractual agreements (standardized type)."

**CURBSTONE PRESS (III)**, 321 Jackson St., Willimantic CT 06226. Imprints include Augustinus/Curbstone. Co-Directors: Judy Doyle, Alexander Taylor. Estab. 1975. Number of titles: 7 in 1984. Average first novel print order 2,000 copies. Editions published simultaneously in paperback and hardcover.

**Needs:** Contemporary, literary, fiction of social significance, faction, historical, women's, feminist, gay, lesbian, ethnic, and translations. Recently published *The Pillows*, by Benny Andersen (Danish-short stories); *Anna (I) Anna*, by Klaus Rifbjerg (Danish-novel); and *Beasts*, by Harold Jaffe (short story collection).

**How to Contact:** Prefers contact through agent; accepts unsolicited mss from writers who have published widely in magazines and literary journals or submit outline/synopsis and sample chapters with SASE. Simultaneous submissions allowable; clear photocopied submissions OK. Accepts letter-quality computer printout submissions. Allow up to 6 months for reports on mss.

**Terms:** Royalty payment of 10% of net; no advance. Free book catalog.

**Tips:** "We are looking for good first novels by serious writers. Our authors have usually established a reputation in magazines. We are especially interested in socially engaged work or works expressing the struggle for equality and human rights. We also publish translations of contemporary world authors."

**DAN RIVER PRESS (I, II)**, Box 123, South Thomaston ME 04858. (207)354-6550. Editor-in-Chief: Richard S. Danbury III. Estab. 1972. Small independent publisher. Publishes hardcover and paperback originals. Books: quality book paper; offset printing; paperback and hardcover binding; illustrations sometimes; average print order: 1,000. Plans 2-3 first novels this year. Buys juvenile mss with illustrations. Averages 8-10 total titles, 4-5 fiction titles each year. Average first novel print order 1,000 copies.

**Needs:** Will consider most categories. No feminist, gay, lesbian, religious/inspirational or translations. Accepts short stories from freelancers. Recently published *Days before the Tube*, by A. M. Munoz (Americana/collection of related stories).

**How to Contact:** Accepts unsolicited mss. Submit outline/synopsis and sample chapters. Reports in 2 months. Simultaneous submissions OK; no photocopied submissions (unless on plain bond paper). Accepts computer printout submissions. Publishes ms 2-12 months after acceptance.

**Terms:** Pays in royalties of 5% minimum; 25% maximum. Sends galleys to author. Advance varies. "We do consider subsidy publishing books of exceptional merit with little or no commercial appeal." Book catalog for 7x10 SASE.

**Tips:** Publishes less fiction than in the past. "We encourage first novelists."

**‡JOHN DANIEL, PUBLISHER (I, II)**, Box 21922, Santa Barbara CA 93121. (805)962-1780. Imprint includes Fithian Press. Fiction Editor: John Daniel. Estab. 1980/reestablished 1985. Small publisher with plans to expand. Publishes paperback originals. Books: 55-65 lb book text paper; offset printing; perfect bound paperbacks; illustrations sometimes; average print order: 1,000; first novel print order: 1,000. Plans 2 first novels this year. Averages 4-5 total titles, 3-4 fiction titles each year. Critiques on rejected ms.

**Needs:** "I'm open to all subjects (including nonfiction)." Literary, mainstream, short story collections. No pornographic, exploitive, illegal, or badly written fiction. Recently published *In the Time of the Russias*, by Stella Zamvil (Jewish short stories); and *Brief Cherishing*, by Hildegarde Flanner (memoirs).

**How to Contact:** Accepts unsolicited mss. Query first. SASE. Submit outline/synopsis and 2 sample chapters. Reports in 3 weeks on queries; 6 weeks on mss. Simultaneous and photocopied submissions OK. Accepts computer printouts including dot-matrix.

**Terms:** Pays in royalties of 10% of net minimum. Sends galleys to author. Subsidy publishes with

the Fithian Press imprint. Arrangements vary to suit the project. "John Daniel Publisher, is a regular, royalty-paying publisher. Fithian Press is a cooperative publisher—the author generally pays production costs and receives a large royalty; but the arrangement is tailor-made for each project."
**Tips:** Encourages first novelists. "As an acquiring editor, I would never sign a book unless I were willing to publish it in its present state. Once the book is signed, though, I, as a developmental editor, would do hard labor to make the book everything it could become. Read a lot, write a lot, and stay in contact with other artists so you won't burn out from this, the loneliest profession in the world."

**‡DAWNWOOD PRESS (III, IV)**, Suite 2650, Two Park Ave., New York NY 10016. (212)532-7160. President: Kathryn Drayton. Fiction Editor: John Welch. Estab. 1984. Publishes hardcover originals. Books: 50 lb Lakewood-white paper; offset litho printing; adhesive case bind, kivar 5 cloth, 088" over binded board; average print order: 2,500. Averages 1 fiction title each year.
**Needs:** Contemporary. "Our needs are taken care of for the next 2 years." No experimental. Recently published *Condemned*, by Paul Kuttner (post-Holocaust (WWII) pub. 1984; *Absolute Proof*, by Paul Kuttner (1985; geo-political espionage novel); *The Iron Virgin*, by Paul Kuttner (humorous novel about life in the U.S.) pub 1986.
**How to Contact:** Does not accept unsolicited mss. Submit through agent only. Agented fiction: 100%. Reports in 2 weeks on queries; 2 weeks on mss. Simultaneous and photocopied submissions OK.
**Terms:** Advance negotiable. Sends galleys to author.

**DE YOUNG PRESS (I)**, Box 7252, Spencer IA 51301. Fiction Editor: Garry De Young. Estab. 1964. Indpendent publisher. Publishes hardcover and paperback originals and reprints. Books: Depends on arrangement with author; letter press, offset press, handset printing; staple, hard back binding, depending on size of book and other variables; photos, b&w drawings; "we also do art work"; average print order: 2,000 copies; first novel print order: 1,000 copies. Plans to publish first novel(s) this year, number depends on length of book and number of copies. Averages 2 total titles each year. Occasionally critiques rejected ms (depending on workload) for $100 nonrefundable charge.
**Needs:** "We are seeking writings which reinforce marriage. No pornography accepted—all other categories considered for review." Recently published *Quest for Justice—Systemic Discrimination in Iowa*, by Garry De Young.
**How to Contact:** Accepts unsolicited mss; "not returnable due to expense and workload; do not send original copy." Query with SASE. Reports in 6 months depending on workload. Simultaneous and photocopied submissions OK. Accepts computer printout submissions; prefers letterquality.
**Terms:** Pays in author's copies; number negotiable. "We subsidy publish. We require a $100 nonrefundable fee to review the manuscript. If accepted we then open negotiations with the author. All costs are 50% deposit with placement of order and the remainder to be COD, or net 30 after approval of credit application."
**Tips:** "Try to write short stories because they will cost less to get published. Remember that small publishers work on a shoestring and absorb many expenses which large publishers charge for." Recognize the problems a publisher has timewise, that he cannot possibly be expected to read a manuscript and provide a critique without compensation. Many manuscripts are in poor format, are often hardly readable and need a great deal of revision, all of which takes time and experience.

**DIMENSIONIST PRESS/VIDEO (IV)**, 5931 Stanton Ave., Highland CA 92346. (714)882-5708. Editor: Arnold Arias. Estab. 1978. Publishes paperback originals.
**Needs:** Literary, experimental, psychic/supernatural, science fiction, and fantasy.
**How to Contact:** Query and send complete ms with SASE. Simultaneous and photocopied submissions OK. Reports in 1 month on queries and mss.
**Terms:** Negotiates terms with author. No advance.
**Tips:** "Dimensionist Press represents a new movement in the arts, *Dimensionism*. A Dimen-

sionist strives to evoke or describe a visionary-mystical experience or future world or extra-dimensional realm in art, music, or literature."

**DOUBLE M PRESS (II)**, 16455 Tuba St., Sepulveda CA 91343. (818)360-3166. Publisher: Charlotte M. Stein. Estab. 1975. Small independent press with plans to expand. Publishes hardcover and trade paperback originals. Buys juvenile mss with illustrations. Buys 25% agented fiction. Average first novel print order 2,000 copies. Occasionally critiques rejected ms for $50.
**Needs:** Contemporary, fantasy, feminist, historical, juvenile (fantasy, historical, contemporary), preschool, inspirational, and young adult (fantasy, historical, problem novels). "We are interested in work that deals with the problems of growth and solving contemporary situations in a 'healthful' manner." No degradation, violence, or exploitation of the characters.
**How to Contact:** Accepts unsolicited mss. Query first with outline/synopsis and 2 sample chapters. Reports in 2 weeks on queries; 2 months, if possible, on mss. Photocopied submissions OK. Publishes ms usually within 1 year after acceptance.
**Terms:** Pays in royalties of 7% minimum. "We do not pay advances." Subsidy publishing by individual arrangement with author depending on the book, etc.
**Tips:** "Don't send letters asking how to write, or how to submit manuscripts, or the format. Find out from library books etc. Work at your craft to make it as good as you can."

**‡DOWN EAST BOOKS (IV)**, Subsidiary of Down East Enterprise, Inc., Box 679, Camden ME 04843. Contact: Karin Womer. Estab. 1954. Small publisher concentrating exclusively on regional titles. "We are *considering* branching out into fiction but to date have published nonfiction." Publishes hardcover originals and paperback originals and reprints. Averages 14 total titles, 1 or 2 juvenile fiction titles each year. Sometimes critiques or comments on rejected ms.
**Needs:** Regional. "We are interested in seeing good, creative books with a Maine *theme*, not *just* stories with a Maine setting that could equally well have been set in Indiana or New Mexico."
**How to Contact:** Accepts unsolicited mss. SASE. Submit outline/synopsis and 3 sample chapters. SASE. Reports in 2 weeks on queries; 6 weeks on mss. Simultaneous submissions OK. Accepts computer printouts including some, not all, dot-matrix. Depends on quality.
**Terms:** Pays in royalties of 7% minimum; 15% maximum; advance negotiable. Sends galleys to author. Book catalog free on request.
**Tips:** "Except for a handful of reprints, and juvenile titles, we have not in the past published fiction. We are looking at fiction manuscripts now, though, and may start a new line of Maine novels in the future."

**THE DRAGONSBREATH PRESS (IV)**, 10905 Bay Shore Dr., Sister Bay WI 54234. Editor: Fred Johnson. Estab. 1973. One-man operation on part-time basis. Publishes paperback and hardback originals in small editions as handmade books. Books: varied paper; letterpress printing hand binding; illustrations.
**Needs:** Contemporary, literary, experimental, erotica, science fiction, fantasy, and humor/satire. "NO NOVELS, but rather single short stories."
**How to Contact:** "We are not currently accepting any unsolicited mss." Query and when requested send complete ms with SASE. Simultaneous and photocopied submissions OK. Accepts computer printout submissions. Prefers letter-quality. Reports in 1 month on queries, 2 months on mss. "Always include a cover letter and SASE."
**Terms:** Negotiates terms. No advance. "Since we are a small press, we prefer to work cooperatively, sharing the work and expenses between the author and the press. We are not a 'vanity press'."
**Tips:** "This is a small press working with the book as an art form producing handmade limited-edition books combining original artwork with original writing. Since we work with hand-set type and have limited time and money we prefer shorter writing suited to handwork and illustrating. We are not a typical publishing house; books would have limited distribution, mainly to art and book collectors. We are now also looking for regional (Wisconsin) writing for a yearly regional magazine the press has begun publishing entitled *The Door County Alamanak*. Always include cover letter with brief description of story."

**THE ECCO PRESS**, 18 W. 30th St., New York NY 10001. (212)685-8240. Associate Editor: Megan Ratner. Editor: Daniel Halpern. Estab. 1970. Small publisher. Publishes hardcover and paperback originals and reprints. Averages 25 total titles, 10 fiction titles each year. Average first novel print order 3,000 copies. Occasionally critiques rejected mss.
**Needs:** Literary and short story collections. "We can publish possibly one or two novels a year." No science fiction, romantic novels, western (cowboy). Recently published: *The Barracks Thief*, by Tobias Wolff (novel); *The Orchard Keeper*, by Cormac McCarthy (fiction reprint); *Sing Me No Love Songs I'll Say You No Prayers*, by Leon Rooke (short story collection).
**How to Contact:** Accepts unsolicited mss. Query first especially on novels with SASE. Photocopied submissions OK. Accepts computer printout submissions. Prefers letter-quality. Reports in 1 week on queries; 6-8 weeks on mss.
**Terms:** Pays in royalties of 5% minimum, 10% maximum; advance is negotiable. Writer's guidelines for SASE. Book catalog free on request.
**Tips:** "We are always interested in first novels and feel it's important that they be brought to the attention of the reading public."

**‡ERESPIN PRESS (II)**, 929 E. 50th, Austin TX 78751. Editorial Contact: Carol Kent. Fiction Editor: D.L. Kent. Estab. 1980. A private press interested in publishing miniature books, poetry broadsides, short stories in small editions. Books: mould-made or handmade paper; letterpress only printing; binding done in-house; various; illustrations as appropriate; average print order: limited editions (150-200 copies). Averages 3 total titles, 2-3 fiction titles each year. Critiques or comments on rejected ms.
**Needs:** Faction, fantasy, historical, humor/satire, literary, psychic/supernatural/occult, science fiction, translations, western. No full-length novels. Short stories are welcome of whatever variety. No novels. Recently published *To Cairo Came a Certain Man*, by Shirbini (multiple satire); *The White Goddess*, by Sharp (poem broadside); *Strong-in-Right-is-Ra*, by Kent (historical essay).
**How to Contact:** Accepts unsolicited mss. Submit outline/synopsis and sample chapters. Reports in 1 week on queries; 2 weeks on mss. Simultaneous and photocopied submissions OK "if we are notified."
**Terms:** Pays in author's copies (half). Sends galleys to author. Book catalog for SASE.
**Tips:** "If you like what you have written, and if I do, it is ready to publish."

**EXILE PRESS**, Box 1768, Novato CA 94948. (415)883-2132. Editor/Publisher: Dr. L. W. Hedley. Estab. 1984. Small independent publisher. Publishes paperback originals and reprints. Plans 2 first novellas this year plus books of short stories. Averages 4-5 titles each year, all fiction. Average first novella print order 500-1,000 copies. Occasionally critiques rejected ms.
**Needs:** Novellas and collections of short stories. Contemporary, experimental, satire, and literary. No "religious, academic kitsch, westerns, gothic, science fiction, pornography, or political propaganda. Recently published *Monkey*, by Rod Moore (novella); *Fiction '85; The Way Things Are*, by Phillip Corwin (stories); *Imaginary People & Other Strangers*, by Layle Silbert (stories); and *XYZ & Other Stories*, by Leslie Woolf Hedley.
**How to Contact:** Accepts unsolicited mss. Submit complete ms with SASE. Does not work through agents. Reports in 2 months. Simultaneous and photocopied submissions OK. Accepts computer printout submissions. Prefers letter-quality. Highly selective.
**Terms:** Pays in 12 or more author's copies. "The number of copies to author depends on size of book and of the edition." Free book catalog.
**Tips:** "*Innovative* is the key word."

**‡EXPOSITION PRESS OF FLORIDA, INC. (I)**, 1701 Blount Rd., Pompano Beach FL 33069. Contact: Edward Uhlam. Estab. 1936. Subsidy/trade book publisher. Publishes hardcover originals and reprints, paperback originals and reprints. Books: average print order: 5,000 copies; first novel print order: 3,000-5,000 copies. Plans 6-10 first novels this year. Averages 180 total titles/year; 40 fiction titles/year. Occasionally critiques rejected mss.

**Needs:** Open to all categories. "Needs novels with specialized audience appeal." No hard porno.
**How to Contact:** Accepts unsolicited mss. Query first. Agented fiction 10%. Reports in 2 weeks on queries; 1 month on mss. Simultaneous and photocopied submissions OK. Accepts computer printouts including dot-matrix. Accepts almost all electronic submissions via disc or modem.
**Terms:** Subsidy publishes books. "Can only publish books on cooperative basis." Terms negotiable. Writer's guidelines free for SASE or IRC. Book catalog free for SASE or IRC.
**Tips:** Frequently encourages and publishes first novelists.

**FICTION COLLECTIVE INC. (I, II)**, %Department of English, Brooklyn College, Brooklyn NY 11210. (718)780-5547. Co-Directors: Mark Leyner and Curtis White. Estab. 1974. "The Fiction Collective is an expanding cooperative of 36 writers dedicated to the publication of quality fiction. We publish hardcover and paperback originals. We encourage new writers of contemporary and experimental fiction. The Collective is primarily interested in new fiction and all that term implies." Average first novel print order: 2,000-2,500 copies.
**Needs:** Contemporary, literary, and experimental. Recently published: *Plane Geometry*, by R. M. Berry; *Heroes and Villains*, by Jerry Bumpus; and *The Endless Short Story*, by Ronald Sukenick.
**How to Contact:** Accepts unsolicited mss "only if we have first responded in the affirmative to an author's query." Query with SASE. Photocopied submissions OK. Reports in 1 month on queries, 5 months on mss. Send queries to Fiction Collective Manuscript Central, Dept. of English, Illinois State University, Normal, Illinois 61761. Publishes ms 9-12 months after acceptance.
**Terms:** Pays 10% royalties plus 50 copies of the book (upon publication) after production costs have been met. "The Collective is a nonprofit writers' cooperative. The Collective makes editorial decisions. Books are published with assistance from NEA and NYSCA. If a manuscript is accepted for publication, then the author shares in editorial decisions." No advance. Free book catalog.
**Tips:** "Manuscripts are chosen for publication wholly on the basis of artistic merit, free of commercial considerations, tending toward innovative fiction. Since commercial publishers are often not willing to take the risk of publishing first novels regardless of their quality, this is one area to which the Collective is committed. Query first, rather than sending manuscripts without having first queried us. Once a book has been accepted, it is much easier to promote the book if the author provides us with information that can be used for publicity and is generally cooperative and interested in helping to promote his or her book."

**‡FIREBRAND BOOKS (II)**, 141 The Commons, Ithaca NY 14850. (607)272-0000. Contact: Nancy K. Bereano. Estab. 1985. Publishes quality trade paperback originals and reprints. Plans 2 first novels in 1986. Averages 6 total titles each year.
**Needs:** Feminist, lesbian.
**How to Contact:** Accepts unsolicited mss. Submit outline/synopsis and sample chapters or send complete ms with cover letter. SASE. Reports in 2 weeks on queries; 2 months on mss. Simultaneous and photocopied submissions OK with notification. Accepts computer printouts.
**Terms:** Pays in royalties.

**THE FIRST EAST COAST THEATRE AND PUBLISHING COMPANY, INC. (I, II)**, Box A244, Village Station, New York NY 10014. (718)296-1979. Fiction Editor: Karen Corinne Boccio. Estab. 1979. "Small but expanding press with staff always available. Work primarily with poetry and fiction." Publishes hardcover and paperback originals and reprints. Books: heavy bonded paper; negatives printing; perfect binding; average print order: 1,000; first novel print order: 1,000. Plans 2 first novels this year. Averages 2-3 total titles, 1-2 fiction titles each year. "Very frequently" critiques rejected ms.
**Needs:** Contemporary, experimental, literary, regional, and short story collections. No fads, romance, "non-serious" work. Recently published: *A Matter of Honor*, By Charles F. Powers (per-

# Close-up

### Mark Leyner
### Fiction Collective

A few years ago as a student at Brandeis University, Mark Leyner read several books published by the Fiction Collective. He was so excited by the fiction that, after completing a teaching fellowship at the University of Colorado, he decided to submit his own work. The match was a perfect one; his short story collection, *I Smell Esther Williams*, was published—and acclaimed by major reviewers. Said one, "Leyner defuses language's banality and reshapes our lingos into verbal pyrotechnics." His is not an average narrative style, nor is the Collective a conventional contemporary press.

Leyner joined the Collective; today he is a director, one of its most active participants, and the spokesperson. "The Fiction Collective offers one of the fairest selection processes an author can get," says Leyner. "We provide an outlet for writers that are adventurous, controversial, and unique." The group of editors that has evolved from its original corps of founders makes decisions solely on the merit or the excitement of the authors' work, and the choices are never commercially oriented. In 12 years of publishing, FC books have received numerous awards; they are used in fiction classes; and its early writers, like Russell Banks, for example, have gone on to major publishers.

"It's just the beginning," says Leyner. "We expect to be around a very long time." Which means continued long, hard hours for the working board of editors—Leyner, Ron Sukenich, Peter Spielberg, and Curtis White. A significant part of Leyner's week is devoted to work on the Collective, selection of manuscripts, the editing, the production of the four to five titles a year, plus the contest book co-sponsored by Illinois State University—a labor of love; none of the editors is paid. There's also Leyner's own writing, his current work on his second short story collection, *My Cousin, My Gastroenterologist*. To support his artistic habits, Leyner freelances two to three days a week as an advertising copywriter, the most lucrative and expeditious employment he has found that is related to his writing interests.

Leyner admits to being "driven" in his work, but acknowledges that he hasn't had to "struggle" in the young writer's sense; publication came immediately. Still the writer/editor is empathetic and offers similar hope for beginning writers of serious fiction. "We read manuscripts by any author with the kind of adventurous book the commercial industry won't publish," Leyner states. But because of its standards, there is a heavy rejection rate.

It's important to query the office first about the publishing schedule to prevent tying up your manuscript if the publishing lineup is full. If the timing allows and the editors like the author's idea and style, they will ask to see the manuscript. No synopsis or outline. "We're interested in the text and style," says Leyner.

Once the Collective accepts a book, the production is completely funded by the group, with help from NEA grants and other awards. Money from sales goes directly back into the publishing of more books, and the Collective has recently initiated author royalties.

Although the Fiction Collective depends on author participation in the production process, location of the writer is not a factor. There are writers from all over the US—and of all ages. "We encourage the widest possible range of people, all generations, in fact. And we'd like to see more work by Asian, black, and Hispanic writers." In short the Collective publishes the unusual books most people *won't* want to read. That still leaves a considerable readership, and says Leyner, "We plan to let them know there's marvelous work available."

sonal experience of Vietnam war done as fiction).

**How to Contact:** Accepts unsolicited mss. Query or submit outline/synopsis and 3 sample chapters with SASE. Reports in 2 weeks on queries; 1 month on mss. Simultaneous and photocopied submissions OK "if clear copies." Accepts computer printout submissions. Prefers letter-quality.

**Terms:** Pays in royalties of 10% minimum; author also receives copies per contract. Sends galleys to author. Free writer's guidelines and book catalog. "We do matching grants for lectures and readings by state sponsored programs."

**Tips:** Trends include "portrayal of contemporary lifestyles in literate and intelligent fashion. We are interested in promoting serious material; that is, fiction written in a strong, individual style, demonstrating a unique and new voice. Author must work with us and be open to legitimate editing and promotion work. Send clearly thought-out synopsis and work—small number of sample chapters first. As far as material is concerned, proofread work; read contemporary works to know what's happening. Publishing 1-2 fiction titles in hardcover each year. We encourage first novelists. Have perseverance and a good presentation. Adhere to publishers' guidelines. Send SASE, decently done sample and concise bios/info. Avoid juvenile, trendy and long-winded inquiries. We've heard it all . . . just show good work."

**FJORD PRESS (III)**, Box 16501, Seattle WA 98116. (206)625-9363. Editor: Steven T. Murray. Estab. 1981. Imprints include Fjord International Suspense. Small independent publisher. Books: acid-free 50-60 lb paper; offset printing; Smythe and callbound binding; b&w illustrations; average print order: 2,000-5,000; first novel print order: 2,000 Publishes paperback and clothbound originals and reprints. Averages 3 total titles, 3 fiction titles each year.

**Needs:** Contemporary, literary, regional (West Coast), suspense/mystery, and women's—*translations and ethnic American* material. Interested in "translations of modern or contemporary European fiction that has not previously been done in English, and original ethnic American fiction." Recently published *Stolen Spring*, by Hans Scherfig; and *The First Polka*, by Horst Bienek.

**How to Contact:** Query first with SASE. Photocopied submissions OK. Reports in 1 week on queries; 3 months on mss. Publishes ms 12-24 months after acceptance.

**Terms:** Pays in royalties of 1% minimum, 7.5% maximum (for public domain works) and author's copies. Sends galleys to author. Must return advance if book is not completed or is unacceptable. "We try to arrange a suitable mixture of advance/royalties/copies with translators. Advances are small." Book list for legal-size SASE with 22¢ postage.

**Tips:** "We specialize in translations of literature from Europe and plan to do regional/ethnic American fiction and suspense as well. Query with SASE should include plot summary and a few sample pages if desired. We do not respond to queries without SASE." Published more fiction; fewer hardcover. "We employ old-fashioned editing here—we suggest changes. More interested in suspense, thrillers—no murder mysteries, please. Read a lot and soak up good writing style and organization. Don't submit anything that isn't as good as what's being published in your genre."

**FOLDER EDITIONS**, 103-26 68th Rd., Forest Hills NY 11375. (781)275-3839. Chief Editor: Daisy Aldan. Estab. 1953. Small press publisher of poetry, poetic drama, poetry translations, and original fiction. Publishes hardcover and paperback originals. Averages 1 title/year, fiction or poetry. Average first novel print order 1,000 copies. Occasionally critiques rejected ms.

**Needs:** Literary and translations. No science, mystery or erotica. Recently published *Vigil*, by Stewart Easton (literary philosophical); *Visiting Mists*, by Angeln Ray.

**How to Contact:** Does not accept unsolicited mss. Query. SASE for query, ms. Reports in 2 weeks on queries and mss. Simultaneous submissions OK. Accepts computer printout submissions.

**Terms:** Pays in royalties of 15% maximum; sometimes honorarium; 10 author's copies. Occasionally subsidy publishes by individual arrangement with author.

**Tips:** "First novels must represent the highest literary standards. Hopefully, the reading public will grow tired of the present plethora of violence, pornography and mediocrity in fiction. Remain faithful to the Word. Keep your integrity. Do not compromise for material gains."

**FROG IN THE WELL (I, II, IV)**, 25 A Buena Vista Terrace, San Francisco CA 94117. (415)431-2113. Fiction Editor: Susan Hester. Estab. 1980. One-woman operation. Publishes paperback originals. Books: 50 lb off-white paper; web/offset printing; perfect binding; illustrations; average print order: 2,500; first novel print run: 2,500. Averages 2-3 total titles, 1-3 fiction titles each year. Occasionally critiques rejected mss.
**Needs:** Feminist, lesbian, regional, short story collections (about women), and women's.
**How to Contact:** Submit outline/synopsis and 3 sample chapters with SASE. Simultaneous (if noted) and photocopied submissions OK. Accepts computer printout submissions. Reports in 2-3 months on mss.
**Terms:** Pays in royalties (varies); 12 author's copies. Sends galleys to author. Free book catalog on request.
**Tips:** "Write well—write from personal experience. Develop your own style. We like to publish first novels by serious writers. We consider our publishing house a place for writers to publish works which may not be placed elsewhere. Publishing more paperback fiction this year because the market demands it. We regard the author/editor relationship as very important—should be very open with each other. Go out and meet people in the book world—it's not so much good working as who you know, and do readings/events. Get known in your community—build a following."

**GALLOPADE: CAROLE MARSH BOOKS (I, II)**, (formerly Gallopade), GPO Bath NC 27808. (919)923-4291. Imprint includes The Gallopade Press. Fiction Editor: Carole Marsh. Estab. 1979. Medium size publisher; handles *all* operations including printing and binding. Publishes paperback originals. Plans 24 first novels 1986. Averages 24 fiction titles each year. Occasionally critiques rejected mss at no charge, but offers service for $25-45, depending on length.
**Needs:** Adventure, contemporary, fantasy, historical, humor/satire, juvenile, literary, preschool/picture book, psychic/supernatural/occult, regional, religious/inspirational, short story collections, and young adult/teen. "We are open to new opportunities for novels." Recently published *The Fortune* and *North Carolina Silly Trivia Book*, by Carole Marsh.
**How to Contact:** Query first. SASE. Reports in 1-2 weeks on queries. Accepts computer printout submissions. Prefers letter-quality.
**Terms:** Pays in royalties of 10% "of what we take in"; 12 author's copies. Authors can purchase books at 33% discount. Mainly subsidy publishes; negotiates with each author. Book catalog for 5x7 SASE with 50¢ postage.
**Tips:** Trends include fiction of regional interest; juvenile original paperbacks. "We are open and receptive to first novels."

**GAY PRESSES OF NEW YORK (IV)**, Box 294, New York NY 10014. (212)255-4713 or 691-9066. Co-Publishers: Terry Helbing, Larry Mitchell, and Felice Picano. Publishes paperback originals. Plans 2 first novels this year. Averages 5 total fiction titles each year.
**Needs:** Feminist/lesbian, gay, and literary. Recently published *Ambidextrous*, by Felice Ricano (novel); *Mad to Be Saved*, by Kevin Esser (novel); and *Standing By*, by Terry Miller (novel).
**How to Contact:** Query first; submit outline/synopsis and sample chapters. Simultaneous and photocopied submissions OK. Reports in 3 weeks on queries.
**Terms:** Pays in royalties of 6% minimum, 10% maximum. Book catalog free on request.

**GAY SUNSHINE PRESS (IV)**, Box 40397, San Francisco CA 94140. (415)824-3184. Editor: Winston Leyland. Estab. 1970. Publishes hardcover and paperback originals. Books: natural paper; perfectbound binding; illustrations; average print order: 5,000-10,000; first novel: 5,000-10,000. Number of titles: 9 in 1983; 11 in 1984, 10 in 1985.
**Needs:** Literary, experimental and translations—all gay material only. "We desire fiction on gay themes of *high* literary quality and prefer writers who have already had work published in literary magazines." Recently published *My Deep Dark Pain Is Love: Latin American Gay Fiction*.
**How to Contact:** "Do not send an unsolicited manuscript." Query letter with SASE. Reports in 3 weeks on queries, 2 months on mss.

**Terms:** Negotiates terms with author. Sends galleys to author. Royalties or outright purchase.
**Tips:** "We continue to be interested in receiving queries from authors who have manuscripts of high literary quality. We feel it is important that an author know exactly what to expect from our press (promotion, distribution etc.) before a contract is signed. Before submitting a query or manuscript to a particular press, obtain critical feedback from knowledgeable people on your manuscript, e.g. a friend who teaches college English. If you alienate a publisher by submitting a manuscript shoddily prepared/typed, or one needing very extensive re-writing, you may well not get a second chance with that press."

**GRAPHIC IMAGE PUBLICATIONS (II, III)**, Box 1740, La Jolla CA 92038. Managing Editor: Susan Ross. Small independent publisher that is expanding. Estab. 1981. Publishes paperback originals. Books: newsprint paper; web printing; perfect bound binding; line art in texts; average print order: 20,000; first novel print order: 5,000. Plans 2-3 first novels this year. Averages 4-5 total titles, all fiction novels.
**Needs:** Contemporary romance. Would like to see settings of exotic travel locals, history of area required.
**How to Contact:** Query first; submit outline/synopsis and 3-4 sample chapters with SASE. Simultaneous and photocopied submissions OK. Accepts computer printout submissions. Prefers letter-quality. Reports in 6-8 weeks on queries; 12-14 weeks on mss.
**Terms:** Pays in royalties of 5% minimum; 15% maximum; negotiates advance; or outright purchase. Sends galleys to author. "Would consider subsidy publishing if the author has experience and background to make it worthwhile." Inquire to subsidy editor department. Writer's guidelines $1. "No stamps, please."
**Tips:** "Be confident of your work and be aggressive when looking for a publisher (send queries). We don't accept unsolicited material. Publishing more paperbacks-cost effective. We encourage first novelists-looking for quality writers of romance novels that feature exotic settings of travel and knowledge of area. Query first with sample type written chapters and final chapter and a brief history of 'you' the writer."

**GRAYWOLF PRESS (III)**, Box 142, Port Townsend WA 98368. (206)385-1160. Publisher: Scott Walker. Estab. 1974. Growing small press, nonprofit corporation. Publishes hardcover and paperback originals and paperback reprints. Books: acid-free quality paper; offset printing; hardcover and soft binding; illustrations occasionally; average print order: 3,000-10,000; first novel print order: 2,000-3,000. Averages 12-16 total titles, 6-8 fiction titles each year. Occasionally critiques rejected ms.
**Needs:** Literary, and short story collections. Recently published *A Pagan Place*, by Edna O'Brien; *The Pegnitz Junction*, by Mavis Gallant; and *Stringer*, by Ward Just (literary).
**How to Contact:** Query with SASE. Reports in 2 weeks. Simultaneous and photocopied submissions OK.
**Terms:** Pays in royalties of 7½% minimum, 10% maximum; negotiates advance and number of author's copies. Sends galleys to author. Writer's guidelines for SASE. Free book catalog.
**Tips:** "We are publishing more and encourage first novelists."

**GRIFFON HOUSE PUBLICATIONS**, Box 81, Whitestone NY 11357. (212)767-8380. President: Frank D. Grande. Estab. 1976. Small press. Publishes paperback originals and reprints.
**Needs:** Contemporary, literary, experimental, ethnic (open), translations, reprints, and multinational theory.
**How to Contact:** Query with SASE. No simultaneous submissions; photocopied submissions OK. Accepts computer printout submissions. Reports in 1 month on queries, 6 weeks on mss.
**Terms:** Pays in 6 free author's copies. No advance.

**GUERNICA EDITIONS (IV)**, Box 633, Station N.D.G., Montreal, Quebec H4A 3R1 Canada. Imprint includes *Vice Versa*. President: Antonio D'Alfonso. Fiction Editor: Umberto Claudio. Estab. 1978. Publishes hardcover and paperback originals and reprints. Books: offset printing; sewn

# Close-up

### Scott Walker
### Graywolf Press

In 1975 Scott Walker founded Graywolf Press in Oregon. In Cincinnati, Ohio, that same year, the Elliston Book Award was created. The first Elliston Book Award was given to Graywolf's first trade book, a collection of Tess Gallagher's poetry called *Instructions to the Double*. Graywolf's second trade book, *Inner Weather* by Denis Johnson was named runner-up.

Praises for Graywolf didn't begin nor have they ended with the Elliston Book Award. Graywolf had a brief stint as a fine printer before turning to trade book publishing and received design awards and encouragements. *Esquire* saluted Scott Walker in its 1985 Register as one of those under 40 years of age who is changing the nation in the category of Arts & Letters. Also in 1985, the National Endowment for the Arts selected Graywolf to publish its 20th anniversary commemorative anthology, which featured 35 writers.

With reputation preceding it, Graywolf enjoys the confidence of writers. Says Walker, "Authors have been very good about assisting on the selection of cover art. [In the] design, printing, and production of a book authors generally trust us."

Walker's attitude toward beginning writers might seem that of a parent offering guidance. "I try to encourage writers to wait. Hold off on publication until they can put out a really first-rate work." He considers a writer's reputation as well as his own: "Too many writers are so anxious to get their first book in print. Talented writers may put a book out that gets fairly good reviews and sells fairly well, but they put a D-level book out."

Walker, a graduate of the University of Oregon, began Graywolf as a part-time venture in his Port Townsend backyard. Today, in the St. Paul, Minnesota headquarters, Walker—along with a managing editor, production and design director, sales director, accountant, and two interns—works on the business of publishing 12 to 16 books a year. Besides poetry, Graywolf handles short fiction (perhaps most well-known is the *Graywolf Annual*), and re-

photo by Sandy May

prints. According to Walker, Graywolf's products are a "mixed bag of high literary quality."

Walker feels this is the age of the small press. Small presses are publishing what large commercial houses can't afford. Walker theorizes the reasons for larger presses cutting back: Corporations buying up major publishing houses want to take fewer risks and produce only maximum profit-making books; inflation has raised publishing costs, forcing cutbacks; the IRS now taxing books that publishers stock in their warehouses. Because Graywolf's selection of books proved to be noncommercial, it was declared nonprofit and tax exempt.

Walker's hope is that now small presses in general start thinking nationally in their distribution and promotion—"striving for a balance in their publishing programs. Most small presses are interested in the editorial aspect first and they never quite get around to promotion, marketing, or distribution." Walker is assisting with a future project to create a distribution company, called Consortium, for literary presses.

Walker also has some future plans for Graywolf Press. He may try to expand his yearly output to 20 books. This increase could mean more space and staff as well, so Walker is looking at the possibility of moving to downtown St. Paul to accommodate.

*—Katherine Jobst*

binding; average print order: 1,000. Occasionally comments on rejected mss.

**Needs:** Contemporary, literary, romance, confession, women's, feminist, gay/lesbian, erotica, psychic/supernatural/occult, religious/inspirational, humor/satire, juvenile, young adult, and translations. Does not read mss September-March.

**How to Contact:** Query with SASE or SAE and IRC. No simultaneous submissions; photocopied submissions OK. Accepts computer printout submissions. Accepts disc submissions compatible with Apple II. Reports in 2 weeks on queries; 6 weeks on mss.

**Terms:** No advance. Sends galleys to author. Free book catalog with SASE.

**Tips:** "Have perseverance, intelligence, courage. *Guernica* was established for writers who know the value of their work." Publishing more fiction and more hardcovers this year. "The editor is like a film-editor, without whom there can never be a book. There are publishers for every writer. It is the writer's task to find his publisher. Useless to submit to publishers you know nothing of. Don't expect strangers to offer you paradise or cash. Every pleasure is paid for through the patience of friendship."

**MAX HARDY—PUBLISHER (IV)**, Box 28219, Las Vegas NV 89126-2219. (702)368-0379. Contact: Max Hardy. Estab. 1976. Publishes paperback originals. Books: offset printing; perfect binding; illustrations; average print order: 2-3,000; first novel print order: 3,000. Averages 6 total titles each year. Occasionally critiques rejected ms.

**Needs:** Publishes fiction on bridge only. Recently published *The Mexican Contract*: by Allan De Serpa (novel); and *Everything's Jake with Me*, by Don Von Elsner (anthology).

**How to Contact:** Accepts unsolicited mss. Submit complete ms. Simultaneous and photocopied submissions OK.

**Terms:** Pays in royalties of 10% maximum. "Author pays all expenses; receives 80% of all returns until he recovers 150%—then revert to royalties." Free book catalog.

**Tips:** "We encourage first novelists. Of our 30 + titles we have 5 novels and 2 anthologies."

**HERITAGE PRESS (II, IV)**, Box 18625, Baltimore MD 21216. (301)383-9330. President: Wilbert L. Walker. Estab. 1979. One-man operation, full-time basis; uses contractual staff as needed. Publishes hardcover originals. Books: 60 lb white offset paper; offset printing; sewn hardcover binding; average print order: 2,000; first novel print order: 1,000. Averages 2 total titles, 1-2 fiction titles each year.

**Needs:** Ethnic (black). Interested in "fiction that presents a balanced portrayal of the black experience in America, from the black perspective. No fiction not dealing with blacks, or that which views blacks as inferior. Recently published *Stalemate at Panmunjon* (the Korean War), and *Servants of All*, by Wilbert L. Walker.

**How to Contact:** Does not accept unsolicited mss. Query first with SASE. Simultaneous and photocopied submissions OK. Reports in 2 weeks on queries, 2 months on mss. Publishes ms an average of 9 months after acceptance.

**Terms:** Must return advance if book is not completed or is unacceptable. "We plan to subsidy publish only those works that meet our standards for approval. No more than 1 or 2 a year. Payment for publication is based on individual arrangement with author." Book catalog free on request.

**Tips:** "Write what you know about. No one else can know and feel what it is like to be black in America better than one who has experienced our dichotomy on race." Would like to see new ideas with broad appeal. "First novels must contain previously unexplored areas on the black experience in America. We regard the author/editor relationship as open, one of mutual respect. Editor has final decision, but listens to author's views."

**HERMES HOUSE PRESS (I, II)**, Apt. 3F, 127 W. 15th St., New York NY 10011. (212)691-9773. Imprints include translations. Director: Reuben Mandelbrat. Estab. 1980. Small press, few-person operation. Publishes paperback originals and reprints. Books: 70 lb paper; offset printing; paper binding; illustrations; average print order: 500; first novel print order: 500. Plans 1-2 first novels this year. Averages 2 total titles, 1-2 fiction titles each year. Generally critiques rejected mss.

**Needs:** Contemporary, experimental, feminist, literary, short story collections, novellas and translations. No sexist, erotica, horror. Recently published *Three Stories*, by R.V. Cassill (short stories) and *The Deadly Swarm & Other Stories*, by LaVerne Harrell Clark.
**How to Contact:** Query first or submit outline/synopsis and 3 sample chapters with SASE. Reports in 3 weeks on queries; 2 months on mss. Simultaneous and photocopied submissions OK. Accepts computer printout submissions. Prefers letter-quality. Publishes ms within 6 months after acceptance.
**Terms:** Pays in author's copies plus percentage above costs. Sends galleys to author.
**Tips:** Encourages first novelists. "We regard the author/editor relationship as open communication/free dialogue. Be persistent."

**HICKMAN SYSTEMS (IV)**, New Age Books, 4 Woodland Lane, Kirksville MO 63501. Contact: Irene Hickman. Estab. 1983. Small independent press. Publishes hardcover and paperback originals; hardcover and paperback reprints. Average print order: 2,000-3,000 copies; first novel print order: 2,000 copies. No first novel planned yet for 1986. Averages 2 titles/year. Occasionally comments on rejected ms.
**Needs:** Psychic/supernatural, inspirational, special interest: new age, hypnotherapy, reincarnation. No ethnic, horror, science fiction. Recently published *Free Spirit*, by Antoinette May (historical with reincarnation theme).
**How to Contact:** Accepts unsolicited mss. Query. SASE for query and ms. Reports in 4 weeks on queries; 6 weeks on mss. Simultaneous and photocopied submissions OK. No dot-matrix. Accepts computer printouts.
**Terms:** Pays in royalties of 10%; advance is negotiable. Sends galleys to author. Book list free on request.
**Tips:** "Editor/author partnership is for the purpose of producing the best book possible. I edit very carefully and submit all editorial changes to the author for approval. Keep writing and writing and writing."

**LAWRENCE HILL & CO., INC.**, 520 Riverside Ave., Westport CT 06880. (203)226-9392. Publisher: Lawrence Hill. Estab. 1973. Publishes hardcover and paperback originals and reprints. Averages 12-15 total titles, 2-3 fiction titles each year. Buys 90% agented fiction. Occasionally critiques rejected mss.
**Needs:** Literary and translations. No genres (in general): romance, science fiction (in particular). Recently published *To the Honorable Miss S . . .*, by B. Traven (short stories); *Chirundu*, by E. Mphaele (African-anglophone); and *King Albert*, by F. Bebey (African-francophone in translations).
**How to Contact:** Query first with SASE. Reports in 2 weeks on queries. Publishes ms 6-18 months after acceptance.
**Terms:** Pays in royalties. Book catalog for #10 SASE.
**Tips:** "Provide the editor with an impeccably clean copy! We are a small publishing house with an overworked and understaffed situation."

**H.W.H. CREATIVE PRODUCTIONS, INC.**, 87-53 167th St., Jamaica NY 11432. (718)297-2208. Imprints include Phase One Graphic. Contact: Maxine Bayliss. Estab. 1972. Small to mid-size independent publisher with plans to expand; 7-person operation, part- and full-time, fiction and nonfiction lines. Publishes paperback originals. Plans 2-4 first nonfiction/fiction books this year. Averages 3 total titles each year. Average first nonfiction/fiction book print order 3,000-5,000 copies. Occasionally critiques rejected ms.
**Needs:** Fantasy, humor/satire, contemporary romance, science fiction, and young adult/teen (fantasy/science fiction, problem novels). No terrorism. Recently published *Black Collections*, by Charles Frazier; and *Native New Yorkers*, by Fern Hoffer.
**How to Contact:** Does not accept unsolicited mss. Submit outline/synopsis or 2 sample chapters with SASE. Reports in 3 months. Photocopied submissions OK. Accepts computer printout outline/synopsis; letter quality. Disc submissions OK with IBM Displaywriter. Hard copy with disc submission.

**Terms:** Pays in royalties of 10% minimum, 15% maximum; 30 author's copies; offers $300 average advance.
**Tips:** "First nonfiction/fiction books must be exciting and commercial."

**ILLUMINATIONS PRESS (II, IV)**, 2110 9th St., Apt. B, Berkeley CA 94710. (415)849-2102. Publisher: N. Moser. Estab. 1965. One-man operation with plans for possible expansion in 1985-86. Publishes paperback originals occasionally. Books: regular stock paper; offset printing; perfect (side) binding for some, stapling for others; illustrations; average print order: 400-800; first novel print order: 400-500. Encourages new writers. Sometimes comments on rejected mss.
**Needs:** Contemporary, literary, experimental, regional (possibly), and humor/satire. Recently published *El Grito del Norte and Other Stories*, by N. Moser.
**How to Contact:** Query with SASE. Simultaneous and photocopied submissions OK. Accepts computer printout submissions. Reports in 1 month on queries, 6 months on mss. Publishes ms from 1-2 years after acceptance.
**Terms:** Pays in 1 or more author's copies usually. Sometimes sends galleys to author. No advance. Most recent arrangements "have been made on a share-costs 50-50 basis or something similar. This would be the only way I could do a first novel for the next year or two, probably." Free book catalog with $1.95 postage.
**Tips:** "Keep language simple. Don't try to change the world in fiction. Write what you know and feel for sure. Avoid excessively complicated language or poor characterizations. I think there will be a return to clarity and the narrative. Be sure to query first, prior to sending a fiction ms. Publishing more fiction because my magazine *Illuminations* folded. Initiated new 1980s book series."

**IN BETWEEN BOOKS**, Box T, Sausalito CA 94965. (415)331-2423. Contact: Karla Andersdatter. Estab. 1973. Publishes paperback originals, children's fantasy and adult poetry.
**Needs:** Open to children's subjects if queried first. Recently published *Marissa The Tooth Fairy*, by Karla Andersdatter (children's fantasy), and *Follow the Blue Butterfly*.
**How to Contact:** Query with SASE. No simultaneous submissions. Photocopied submissions OK. Reports in 6 weeks on queries. "Manuscripts sent without query will be burned!"
**Terms:** After first printing, pays 10% in royalties. Negotiable author's copies. No advance. Free book catalog.
**Tips:** "Golden Books have taken over. Commercialism is rampant and boring. I like quality and a fresh, unique style. Write on two levels so adults get the 'message' too. Read at least 1,000 children's stories, before you write your own."

**INTERTEXT (II)**, 2633 E. 17th Ave., Anchorage AK 99508. Imprints include Santa Amaro Books. Editor: Sharon Ann Jaeger. Estab. 1982. Independent publisher. Publishes hardcover and paperback originals. Books: PH-neutral paper; offset printing; Smyth-sewn and perfectbound binding for books; Chapbooks usually hand-sewn; illustrations sometimes-occasionally do 4-color covers; average print order: 500-1,000; first novel print order: 1,000-2,000. "We publish writers of excellence only, whether novices or veterans. No novels planned for this year. We might publish a fiction (short story) chapbook, but no novels yet." Averages 1-3 titles each year. Occasionally critiques rejected ms.
**Needs:** Literary, short story collections, and translations. "We are presently concentrating on poetry, translations, and literary criticism, together with selected (and solicited) titles in the fine arts."
**How to Contact:** Query with SASE. Reports in 1 month on queries; 6 months on mss. Simultaneous queries and photocopied submissions OK.
**Terms:** Pays in author's copies (10% of print run). Sends galleys to author. Writer's guidelines for SASE. Free book catalog.
**Tips:** "A novel would have to be very extraordinary indeed—truly compelling, with exquisite craftsmanship and a powerful and poetic style—for us to get into this field. Get a variety of experience. Learn about people. Don't be (or at least sound) self-centered. Revise, revise, revise. We encourage first novelists if they are really good. Relationship with author/editor varies with individual. Our selections reflect a careful but eclectic choice. Leave no stone unturned."

**‡INVERTED-A, INC. (II)**, 401 Forrest Hill, Grand Prairie TX 75051. (214)264-0066. Editors: Amnon Katz or Aya Katz. Estab. 1977. A small press which evolved from publishing technical manuals for other products. "Publishing is a small part of our business." Publishes paperback originals. Books: bond paper; offset printing; illustrations; average print order: 250; first novel print order: 250. Publishes 4 total titles/year; 2 fiction titles/year. Comments on rejected mss.
**Needs:** "We are interested in justice, freedom, individual rights and free enterprise." Recently published *The Few Who Count*, by Aya Katz (novel); and *Damned in Hell*, by A.A. Wilson (novella).
**How to Contact:** Submit complete ms with cover letter. SASE. Reports in 6 weeks on queries; 3 months on mss. Simultaneous and photocopied submissions OK. Accepts computer printouts including dot-matrix. Accepts electronic submissions via disc or modem for IBM and Apple Disketts.
**Terms:** We do not pay with few exceptions. Sends galleys to author. Book catalog for 6.5x9 SAE and 1 first class stamp.

**JELM MOUNTAIN PUBLISHING (II)**, Box 338, Main & Montgomery Sts., Markleeville CA 96120. Includes Jelm Mountain Press. Editors: Jean Jones and Richard Close. Estab. 1976. Small independent publisher; two persons full time. Publishes paperback originals, some hardcovers. Number of titles: 4 in 1985. Encourages new writers. Buys juvenile mss with illustrations, but does not publish preschool books. Occasionally comments on rejected ms; "charges only when critique or comment is requested by author." Fee variable.
**Needs:** Prefers historical, fantasy, psychic/supernatural/occult, and regional (West). Recently published *The Stone and the Candle*, by Joseph Digrande; and *Wyoming Sun*, by Edward Bryant (science fiction fantasy).
**How to Contact:** Accepts unsolicited mss. Query and submit outline/synopsis and sample chapters with SASE. Simultaneous and photocopied submissions OK. Accepts computer printout submissions. Prefers letter-quality. Accepts disc submissions compatible with IBM Personal XT/CPM. Prefers hard copy with disc submissions. Reports in 3 weeks on queries, 6 weeks on mss. Publishes ms an average of 1 year after acceptance.
**Terms:** No advance. Subsidy publishes 50% of total books; ⅓ up front. Free book catalog with SASE or 50¢ postage.
**Tips:** "We prefer an up-beat approach—meeting life's challenges! We major in regional materials with historical authenticity. Our press is small enough to give writers, especially novices, a lot of attention, but we hope they are willing to pay for extra services." In first novels looks for "offbeat and experimental forms, but the message should be clearly optimistic—no end-of-the-world doom and gloom, solutions to life in a new world."

**‡KAR-BEN COPIES, INC. (II)**, 6800 Tildenwood La., Rockville MD 20852. (301)984-8733. President: Judye Groner. Estab. 1974. Small publisher specializing in juvenile Judaica. Publishes hardcover originals and paperback originals. Averages 8-10 total titles, 6-8 fiction titles each year. Critiques or comments on rejected ms.
**Needs:** Juvenile (5-9 years) (easy-to-read, historical). Recently published *The Passover Parrot*, by E. Zusman; *The Secret Spinner*, by H. Cushnir; *Butchers & Bakers, Rabbis & Kings*, by J. Greene.
**How to Contact:** Accepts unsolicited mss. SASE. Submit outline/synopsis and sample chapters or complete ms with cover letter. SASE. Reports in 1 week on queries; 4 weeks on mss. Simultaneous and photocopied submissions OK. Accepts computer printouts including dot-matrix.
**Terms:** Pays in royalties of 5% minimum; 10% maximum; average advance: $500; 12 author's copies. Sends galleys to author. Writer's guidelines free for SASE. Book catalog free on request.

**MICHAEL KESEND PUBLISHING, LTD. (II)**, 1025 5th Ave., New York NY 10028. (212)249-5150. Imprints include Kesendart Co. Inc. President: Michael Kesend. Estab. 1979. Midsize independent publisher. Publishes hardcover and paperback originals and reprints. Books: 50-60 lb paper; offset printing; Smythe sewn or perfect bound binding; illustrations; average print order: 2,500-5m; first novel print order: 1,500-2,500. Plans 2 first novels each year. Averages 4 total titles each year, all fiction. Occasionally critiques rejected ms, "but sparingly; $100 for 100-200 pages."

**Needs:** Erotica, historical, literary, mainstream, suspense/mystery, translations, and young adult/teen.

**How to Contact:** Does not accept unsolicited mss. Query or submit outline/synopsis and 2-3 sample chapters with SASE. Reports in 1 month. No simultaneous submissions; photocopied submissions OK. Accepts computer printout submissions; prefers letter-quality.

**Terms:** Negotiates advance. Free book catalog.

**Tips:** "We must be careful in choosing a first novel, but we are open to it. Publishing less fiction due to smaller sales. We encourage first novelists and published new writers last year. There should be a willingness between author/editor. To change or revise if they should agree on it."

**KINDRED JOY PUBLICATIONS (IV)**, 554 W. 4th, Coquille OR 97423. Publisher: Marilee Miller. Estab. 1983. "One-person operation on part-time basis but with high hopes of expanding as soon as time, energy, and *money* permit." Publishes paperback originals. Books: offset or computer printed; perfect (paper) binding; average first novel print order: 1,000 copies.

**Needs:** At present only subsidy publishing available. "Favorite subjects: Christian books, Pacific Northwest; but would look at other topics. No vulgarity or violence merely for shock value. The needs of Kindred Joy are somewhat specialized. In general, Christian or 'wholesome secular' *only*."

**How to Contact:** Query first. SASE.

**Terms:** "Writers pay for printing and typesetting costs and the cost of printing a flyer or the like for advertising purposes. Fees for critiques would be based on actual work done. I would also like to assist teams of one experienced writer working with others who have 'local' expertise: i.e., local history themes, ideas for Christian living, other. But at this time I could only do this under two conditions: that the individual (or library, museum or group) provide their own funding; and that they set up their own group and supervise it. But I could provide coordination and editorial assistance of a limited nature."

**Tips:** "We are not publishing fiction at the moment because it is harder to market. But since we would be able to publish outside authors only by subsidy, we'll look at anything of quality."

**‡KITCHEN TABLE: WOMEN OF COLOR PRESS (I, II, IV)**, Box 2753, New York NY 10185. (212)308-5389. Administrative Coordinator: Betty Powell. Estab. 1981. "Independent press with several paid employees, very good distribution." Publishes paperback originals. Books: 50 lb stock paper; offset/web press printing; perfect binding/glued not sewn; some graphic elements/designs b&w; average print order: 6,500; first novel print order: 2,000-3,000. Averages 2 total titles each year; 1 fiction title every two years. Occasionally critiques rejected ms.

**Needs:** Ethnic, feminist, lesbian, literary, short story collections. Needs for novels include novels by women of color authors that reflect in some way the experiences of women of color. "We are looking for high quality, politically conscious writing and would particularly like to hear from American Indian women fiction writers." Recently published *Cuentos: Stories by Latinas*, edited by Alma Gómez, Cherríe Moraga, & Mariana Romo-Carmona (short story anthology with selections in both English and Spanish).

**How to Contact:** Accepts unsolicited mss. Query first. Submit outline/synopsis and 3 sample chapters. SASE. Reports in 4 weeks on queries; 6 months on mss. Simultaneous and photocopied submissions OK.

**Terms:** Pays in royalties of 8% minimum; 10% maximum and 5 author's coies. Sends galleys to author. Book catalog for #10 SASE and 2 first class stamps.

**Tips:** "A number of contributors to our three anthologies, some of whom are fiction writers, have not been published previously. We encourage first novelists."

**‡KNIGHTS PRESS (II)**, Box 454, Pound Ridge NY 10576. (203)322-7381. Publisher: Elizabeth G. Gershman. Estab. 1983. Small press publishing only gay male fiction. Publishes paperback originals. Books: variable paper; variable printing; perfect binding; average print order: 8,000; first novel print order: 8,000. Plans 6 first novels this year. Averages 12 total titles, 12 fiction titles each year.

**Needs:** Adventure, contemporary, ethnic, fantasy, gay, historical, horror, humor/satire, literary, psychic/supernatural/occult, romance, science fiction, suspense/mystery, war, western. "Fiction must have a gay theme (not lesbian or non-gay). We publish on merit, not category." No erotica, short stories. Recently published *American Lives*, by Ron Denby, (political thriller); *Fete*, by Daniel McVay (family life); and *Portrait In Murder & Gay Colors*, by H. Paul Jeffers (murder mystery).

**How to Contact:** Accepts unsolicited mss. Query first. SASE. Submit outline/synopsis and sample chapters. SASE. Agented fiction: 25%. Reports in 3 weeks on queries; 3 months on mss. No simultaneous submissions. Photocopied submissions OK. Accepts computer printouts including dot-matrix.

**Terms:** Pays in royalties of 10% minimum; average advance: $500. Sends galleys to author. Writer's guidelines free for #10 SASE and 1 first class stamp. Book catalog free on request.

**Tips:** "We encourage first novelists and published new writers last year. Consider that a book costs money to buy and to produce. Would *you* spend your money for your submission? Would you spend thousands of dollars to produce it? If you wouldn't, neither would the book buyer or the publisher."

**LACE PUBLICATIONS INC. (IV)**, Box 10037, Denver CO 80210-0037. (303)778-7702. Fiction Editor: Miss Artemis OakGrove. Estab. 1983. Two-woman operation. Publishes paperback originals. Book: white offset paper; web or caweron belt printing; b&w line illustrations; average print order: 2,000; first novel print order: 100-200. Plans 3 + first novels this year, 7 total titles, all fiction.

**Needs:** Lesbian. Sub-categories include adventure, erotica, fantasy, humor/satire, romance (historical, contemporary), science fiction, suspense/mystery, translations, and western. "We are looking for fiction with strong Lesbian main characters. The plots must center around their lives and struggles. We are always looking for well thought-out fiction with *strong* sexual content for our Lady Winston Series." No political stories. Forthcoming titles: *Just Hold Me*, by Linda Parks; and *Daughters of Khaton*, by Ani Meril.

**How to Contact:** Accepts unsolicited mss. Query first; submit outline/synopsis and 4 sample chapters; or submit complete ms. SASE for query and ms. Reports in 1 month on queries; 2 months on mss. Simultaneous (please advise) and photocopied submissions OK. Accepts computer printout submissions. Prefers letter-quality.

**Terms:** Pays in royalties of 15% after recovery; and 10 author's copies. Send galleys to author. Book store discount 40%. Query for writer's guidelines and book list.

**Tips:** "Within the context of Lesbian fiction, we look for characters that are real and that our readers can relate to; solid entertainment that doesn't question the issue of preference or the reader's lifestyle, but dignifies it. I like our readers to be able to say 'I've felt like that,' or 'I know that person.' We like the freshness that comes with a first novel. If it's well written and has promise, we are willing to work with the author to improve it. We take into consideration the novelist's personality and needs. We try to maintain a 'personal' business relationship where possible. Learn to write! Have your work critiqued by a professional in her field. Don't ever give up trying to find a publisher. Don't stop learning how to improve your skills."

**LAPIS EDUCATIONAL ASSOCIATION, INC. (II, IV)**, 1438 Ridge Rd., Homewood IL 60430. Editor and Director: Karen Degenhart. Estab. 1977. One-person operation on part-time basis; nonprofit organization's annual journal is main publication. Journal: regular paper; offset printing; staple binding; b&w illustrations; average print order: 100-200.

**Needs:** Contemporary, literary, religious/inspirational, psychology; some feminist, alternative lifestyles; and psychic/supernatural/occult with psychological slant. "Jungian psychology and informed Christianity-related topics are the focus." Rarely publishes fiction; some poetry. Also, contemporary issues in ministry.

**How to Contact:** Accepts unsolicited mss. Query. SASE for query, ms. Simultaneous and photocopied submissions OK. Accepts computer printout submissions. Reports in 2 weeks on queries, "indefinite" on mss.

**Terms:** "We do not pay. Authors must be fee-paying members of this association to be published but may join after submitting ms. Members pay a $10 yearly fee (and receive 3 copies of the issue they are published in) if they are selected to be published. Don't have to join to submit ms." No advance.

**Tips:** "The few fiction titles we've published are about psychological and spiritual life journeys. We do not publish any novels. We regard the author/editor relationship as a personal friendship and creative endeavor."

**‡LAUGHING WATERS PRESS (IV)**, 1416 Euclid Ave., Boulder CO 80302. (303)443-7489. Editor: Gary Erb. Estab. 1980. One person part-time operation. Publishes paperback originals. Books: bond paper; offset printing; perfect binding; line drawings; average print order: 300 copies. Averages 1 title/year. "We include fiction in anthologies." Occasionally critiques rejected mss.

**Needs:** Contemporary, ethnic, faction, fantasy, literary, war. "No fiction that does not deal with peace."

**How to Contact:** Accepts unsolicited mss. Query first or submit complete ms with cover leter. SASE for query and ms. Reports in 1 week on queries; 3 weeks on mss. Simultaneous and photocopied submissions OK. Accepts computer printouts including dot-matrix.

**Terms:** Authors are paid in 10 author's copies. Writer's guidelines free for SASE and 1 first class stamp.

**LIBRARY RESEARCH ASSOCIATES, INC.**, RD. 5, Box 41, Dunderberg Rd., Monroe NY 10950. Imprints include Lloyd-Simone Publishing Co. Editorial Director: Matilda A. Gocek. Estab. 1968. Publishes hardcover and paperback originals. Books: 50 lb paper; narrow web offset printing; perfect bound hard cover binding; b&w half-tones, line drawings; average print order: 5,000; first novel print order: 3,500. Encourages new writers.

**Needs:** Historical romance, psychic/supernatural/occult, and mysteries. Recently published *Immortal Spirit*, by Bill Bodell; and *Rock on the Hudson*, by John Van de Water; and *Caroline Oxbow's American Bonaparte*, by Ethel Comins.

**How to Contact:** Accepts unsolicited mss. Submit outline/synopsis and sample chapters with SASE. No simultaneous submissions; photocopied submissions OK. Accepts computer printout submissions. Prefers letter-quality. Reports in 10 weeks. Publishes ms from 8-10 months after acceptance.

**Terms:** Pays in royalties; no advance. Sends galleys to author. Book catalog for legal-sized SASE.

**Tips:** "There is a gradual return to a good story line less dependent upon violence and explicit sex. I am looking to develop our line Empire State Fiction. Fictionalized biographies based on fact would be welcomed, particularly of women in New York, any period. Prepare clean, doublespaced manuscripts—one-page outline or abstract is most helpful. I want to develop *new authors* so I work willingly with them. Publishing more fiction and more hard covers this year because of a new line we developed called Empire State Fiction—hardcovers only aimed at public libraries and schools. We published two new writers last year. Make an effort to understand the economic risk assumed by a small press and do not make demands *after contract* that cannot be met."

**LINTEL (II)**, Box 8609, Roanoke VA 24014. Editorial Director: Walter James Miller. Estab. 1977. Two-person organization on part-time basis. Books: 90% opaque paper; photo offset printing; perfect binding; illustrations; average print order: 1,000; first novel print order: 1,250. Publishes hardcover and paperback originals. Occasionally comments on rejected mss.

**Needs:** Experimental, short fiction, feminist, gay, lesbian, psychic/supernatural/occult, and regional. Recently published *The Mountain*, by Rebecca Rass (experimental/fantasy).

**How to Contact:** Accepts unsolicited mss. Query with SASE. Simultaneous and photocopied

submissions OK. Accepts computer printout submissions. Prefers letter-quality. Reports in 1 month on queries, 8 weeks on mss. Publishes ms from 6-8 months after acceptance.
**Terms:** Negotiated. No advance. Sends galleys to author. Free book catalog.
**Tips:** *Lintel* is devoted to the kinds of literary art that will never make The Literary Guild or even the Book-of-the-Month Club; literature concerned with the advancement of literary art. We still look for the innovative work ignored by the commercial presses. We consider any ms on its merits alone. We encourage first novelists. The novelist invents, the editor appreciates. Be innovative, advance the *art* of fiction, but still keep in mind the need to reach reader's aspirations as well as your own."

**LION ENTERPRISES**, 8608 Old Dominion Ct., Indianapolis IN 46231. (219)369-9498. President: Judith Ellen Villegas. Fiction Editor: Robert Villegas. Estab. 1974. Publishes paperback originals and reprints. Averages 3 total titles, 2 fiction titles each year. Average first novel print order 1,000 copies. Sometimes critiques rejected ms.
**Needs:** Adventure, ethnic, science fiction, suspense/mystery. Needs for novels include: "unique, un-rehashed plots; positive heroes who have high values and who win. We will look at all types of fiction except left-liberal orientation."
**How to Contact:** Accepts unsolicited mss. Query first or submit outline/synopsis and sample chapters with SASE. Reports in 2 weeks on queries; 1 month on mss. Simultaneous and photocopied submissions OK. Accepts computer printout submissions. Disc submissions OK with Commodore 64/Word Pro 3. Prefers hard copy with a disc submission.
**Terms:** Pays in royalties of 10%. "We will handle book publishing for authors or groups 50% down, 50% with delivery of books."
**Tips:** "If a first novel is good, we'll take a good look. We're not afraid to be first."

**LITTLE BALKANS PRESS, INC. (III)**, 601 Grandview Heights Terrace, Pittsburg KS 66762. Managing Editor; Gene DeGruson. Fiction Editor: Shelby P. Horn. Estab. 1980. Five-person operation on a part-time basis. Occasionally critiques rejected ms.
**Needs:** Contemporary, ethnic, experimental, fantasy, historical, humor/satire, literary, mainstream, science fiction, and women's.
**How to Contact:** Accepts unsolicited mss. Query first. Reports in 2 weeks on queries; 6 weeks on mss. Photocopied submissions OK.
**Terms:** Pays in 3 author's copies.
**Tips:** "Two-thirds of book is text; 1/3 is art/graphics. Stories should be imaginative and fun to read."

**LOLLIPOP POWER, INC. (IV)**, Box 1171, Chapel Hill NC 27514. (919)929-4857. Manuscript editor: Tonie Goldstein. Estab. 1970. A women's collective publishing feminist, multiracial children's books. Publishes paperback originals. Buys juvenile mss with illustrations. Averages 1 title (fiction) each year. Average first book print order 2,500 copies. Occasionally critiques rejected ms.
**Needs:** Juvenile. "We are currently seeking stories which deal directly with issues of sex-role or race stereotyping or which provide strong female role models."
**How to Contact:** Query first with SASE. Reports in 2 weeks on queries; 6 weeks on mss. Simultaneous and photocopied submissions OK. Publishes ms from 6-12 months after acceptance.
**Terms:** Pays in 10 author's copies. "We pay $300 honorarium per book split between author and illustrator." Must return advance if book is not completed or is unacceptable. Writer's guidelines and book catalog for SASE.
**Tips:** "We are seeking stories about divorce and child sexual abuse."

**LONGHORN BOOKS (I, II, IV)**, The Seymour Rossel Co., Inc., 44 Dunbow Dr., Chappaqua NY 10514. (914)238-8954. President: Seymour Rossel. Estab. 1981. Small, independent publishing house. Publishes hardcover and paperback originals and paperback reprints. Encourages new writers. Averages 4 total titles, 2 fiction titles each year. Average first novel print order 3,000 copies. Occasionally critiques rejected mss.

**Needs:** Adventure, historical, humor/satire, juvenile (historical, adventure), preschool/picture book, regional (Southwest and/or Texas), short story collections, western, and young adult (historical, adventure). "All must be aimed at Southwest and/or Texas." Needs for novels include "historical fiction for adults and young adults on Texas and Southwest themes." No romance, science fiction, horror, gothics.

**How to Contact:** Accepts unsolicited mss with SASE. Query first or submit outline/synopsis and 1-2 sample chapters with SASE. Report in 2 weeks on queries; 6 weeks on mss. Photocopied submissions OK. Accepts computer printout submissions. Prefers letter-quality.

**Terms:** Royalties negotiable. Advance is more for agented ms.

**Tips:** "We are eager to publish first novels or short story collections for regional consumption."

**LOS TRES OSOS/Ltd. Enterprises (IV)**, Subsidiary of Walnut Press, 6036 N. 10th Way, Phoenix AZ 85014. (602)265-7765. Director: Janny Davis. Estab. 1978. Publishes paperback originals. First novels are not encouraged. Averages 4 total titles, 4 fiction titles each year.

**Needs:** Juvenile, K-4 (easy-to-read, picture book, bilingual).

**How to Contact:** Query first. Simultaneous submissions OK. Reports in 1 month on queries.

**Terms:** Negotiates for outright purchase by individual arrangement with author depending on book.

**Tips:** "Know your readers. Try your stories out on children first. Many writers are not in tune with today's readers, vocabulary, interests, sense of humor. Often too condescending. Learn as much as you can about the publishing industry through your library and wirters clubs."

**LOW-TECH PRESS (II)**, 30-73 47th St., Long Island City NY 11103. (212)721-0946. Publisher: Ron Kolm. Estab. 1981. Publishes paperback originals. Books: 50 lb opaque paper; offset printing; perfect, saddle-stitched binding; illustrations; average print order 500. "We publish new writers, but only in anthologies—no novels planned in the future." Averages 2 total titles each year. Occasionally critiques rejected mss "if the ms is good."

**Needs:** Contemporary, experimental, satire, literary, mainstream, and short story collections.

**How to Contact:** Does not accept unsolicited manuscripts. Query first with SASE. Reports in 1 week on queries. Publishes ms up to 1 year after acceptance.

**Terms:** Pays in author's copies (depending on size of printing).

**Tips:** "We're trying to emphasize a new-wave quality. We really only publish short pieces, and I know most of the people we publish personally."

**MAINE WRITERS WORKSHOP**, Box 905, R.F.D, Stonington ME 04681. (207)367-2484. Editor: H. Nash. Midsize independent publisher. Publishes hardcover and paperback originals. Plans 1 first novel this year. Averages 3 total titles, 1 fiction title each year. Average first novel print order 5,000 copies. Always critiques good rejected ms; sometimes charges for more than 1 sample chapter. Query first on complete book.

**Needs:** Contemporary, faction, historical, literary, and science fiction. Recently published *Born to Die*, by H.G. Woods.

**How to Contact:** Accepts unsolicited mss with large SASE. Submit outline/synopsis and first, middle and last chapters; complete ms on request. Reports in 1 month. No simultaneous submissions; legible photocopied submissions OK. Accepts computer printout submissions (no dot-matrix); prefers letter-quality.

**Terms:** Pays in royalties of 10% minimum, 15% maximum; seldom an honorarium but always cash, not copies, for all rights. Writer's guidelines for SASE.

**Tips:** "We encourage first novels."

**MAINESPRING PRESS (I, II) of Maine Writers Workshop**, Imprint includes *Letters* Magazine, Box RDI 905, Stonington ME 04681. (207)367-2484. Fiction Editor: Helen Nash. Estab. 1969. Independent publisher. Books: 50-60 lb paper; photo offset computerized printing; perfect binding; illustrations; average print order: 1,000-5,000; first novel print order: 1,000. Contributors include: R. Buckminster Fuller, E.B. White, Jack Matthews, Carlos Baker, Kay Boyle,

George Garrett, William Meredith, Richard Eberhart, etc. Averages 3 fiction titles each year. Buys 10% of agented fiction.

**Needs:** Adventure, contemporary, faction, historical, humor/satire, literary, science fiction, and young adult (fantasy/science fiction, historical). No pornography, non-ethic, confessions.

**How to Contact:** Accepts unsolicited ms for review. Query first with SASE US postage or submit 25 pages with large SASE US postage. Reports in 1 week on queries. Publishes ms an average of 1 year after acceptance.

**Terms:** Pays in royalties of 10% minimum, 15% maximum; cash only, no author's copies. Sends galleys to author. Free sample copy with large SASE, US postage.

**Tips:** "Write endlessly, then rework. Publishing more fiction this year. We encourage first novelists and published new writers last year."

**MAIZE PRESS (I, IV)**, Box 8251, San Diego CA 92102. (714)455-1128. Managing Editor: Xelina. Estab. 1971. Publishes paperback originals and reprints. Books: coated 101 pt covers-60 lb text paper; offset printing; illustrations on cover only; average print order: 1,000; first novel print order: 1,000. Plans 2 first novels this year. Averages 4 total titles, 1-2 fiction titles each year. Occasionally critiques rejected mss.

**Needs:** Erotica, ethnic, experimental, juvenile (contemporary), literary, women's. No science fiction. Recently published: *Old Faces and New Wine*, by Alejandro Morales (fiction); *Cronicas Diagolicas*, Jorge Ulica, edited by Juan Rodriquez (prose collection); *Watching Teresa Die*, by Herbert Espinoza (short story collection).

**How to Contact:** Query first or submit complete ms with SASE. Photocopied submissions OK. Reports in 3 weeks on queries; 3 months on mss.

**Terms:** Pays in author's copies. Sends galleys to author. Writer's guidelines free.

**Tips:** "Social realism is essential. We regard the author/editor relationship as open—the novelist should be able to feel completely confident that the editor is being honest and forward. Remain optimistic and if you feel positive about the work, follow through with it until publication. Always query the publisher first so as not to waste time and postage and don't always take criticism too hard—but try to work with it."

**‡MANIC D PRESS**, 1853 Stockton, San Francisco CA 94133. (415)788-6459. Editor/Publisher: Jennifer Joseph. Estab. 1984. Small-time effort to bring new writers into print. Publishes paperback originals. Books: varied paper; offset printing; varied binding; illustrations; average print order: 500. Plans 1 first novel this year. Averages 4 total titles, number fiction titles vary each year. Occasionally critiques rejected ms.

**Needs:** Contemporary, experimental, literary, translations, women's. "We are looking for well-written fiction that confronts modern America." No romance, war, sports.

**How to Contact:** Accepts unsolicited mss. Submit outline/synopsis and 1 sample chapter. SASE. Reports in 4 weeks on queries; 6-8 weeks on mss. Simultaneous and photocopied submissions OK. Accepts computer printouts including dot-matrix.

**Terms:** Pays in author's copies. Amount varies. Sends galleys to author. Writer's guidelines free for #10 SASE and 22¢ postage. Book catalog for #10 SASE and 22¢ postage.

**Tips:** "We have plans to increase our production, and are especially interested in first novelists."

**METIS PRESS, INC. (IV)**, Box 25187, Chicago IL 60625. Editorial Director: Chris Johnson. Estab. 1976. Small collective of volunteers, part time. Publishers and printers of paperback originals, member of the Alliance of Lesbian and Feminist Printers. Books: 50 lb offset paper; offset printing; perfectbound binding; line-art illustrations sometimes; average print order: 2,000; first novel print order: 2,000. Number of titles: 6 in 1984. Encourages new writers.

**Needs:** Women's, feminist, and lesbian. Especially needs novels with lesbian content. Recently published *Bernice: A Comedy in Letters*, by Georgia Jo Ressmeyer; and *The Secret Witch*, by Linda J. Stem (children's).

**How to Contact:** Query or "enclose a synopsis with short section of work; this is preferred to entire manuscript. We'll inquire further if interested." SASE with query, ms. Publishes ms 12-18 months after acceptance.

**Terms:** Pays in royalties, by outright purchase and in author's copies; no advance. Sends galleys to author. Free book catalog.
**Tips:** Noticeable trends include "short stories, new writers, Midwest voice and humor. All fiction we publish is original; unknown writers. We publish first novels not over 250 pages in print with lesbian content. We have to reject most. We are publishing more fiction and more paperbacks this year. We encourage first novels and published new writers last year."

**MICAH PUBLICATIONS (II)**, 255 Humphrey St., Marblehead MA 01945. (617)631-7601. Imprints include Echad, A Whole Global Anthology Series. Literary and General Editor: Roberta Kalechofsky. Estab. 1975. Publishes paperback originals and reprints. Books: 55 lb opaque paper; offset printing; paper binding, hardcover for scholarly works; illustrations; average print order: 1,000; first novel print order: 400-500. Averages 3 total titles each year. Occasionally critiques rejected mss.
**Needs:** Historical (specific), literary, religious, short story collections, and translations. Recently published: *Encounters with Israeli Authors*, by Esther Fuchs; and *Kaputt*, by Curzio Malaparte.
**How to Contact:** Submit outline/synopsis and sample chapters (about 40 pages) with SASE. Simultaneous and photocopied submissions OK. Reports in 3 months on mss.
**Terms:** Pays in royalties of 50% minimum and 15 author's copies. Sends galleys to author if requested. "Our arrangements are flexible and subject to specific requirements of each book or what kind of cooperation the author can make towards advertising, printing (production) or distributing his/her work. We do not accept money or subsidies of any kind, but we will accept work—for instance, if the author can typeset his ms or do art work for it, and we fully expect him or her to undertake a portion of the work in trying to sell, advertise or promote the book—in return for which our royalties are high." Book catalog free on request.
**Tips:** "Practice a sterner discipline in fighting the market mentality, the illusions of quick fame—and the corrupting need for media publicity. We are publishing less fiction because of uninteresting submissions and slick magazines. We definitely encourage first novelists. Our greatest problem in dealing with new writers, is that they have illusions about fame and publishing, which are hard to eradicate. I think that writers should do hard research in publishing and consider publishing their own novels or works of poetry. With computers and new printing technology, any writer can publish his or her own work."

**‡MILKWEED EDITORS**, Box 24303, Minneapolis MN 55424. (612)332-3192. Editor: Emilee Buchwald. Estab. 1980—*Milkweek Chronicle*/1984—*Milkweek Editors*. Small press with emphasis on literary and visual arts work. Publishes hardcover and paperback originals. Books: book text quality—acid free paper; offset printing; perfect or hardcover binding; illustrations in all books; average print order: 2,000 copies; first novel print order depends on book. Averages 5 total titles/year. Number of fiction titles "depends on mss."
**Needs:** Contemporary, experimental, literary. Looking for excellent writing. No romance, mysteries, science fiction. Recently published *Backbone*, by Carol Bly (short stories).
**How to Contact:** Accepts unsolicited mss. Submit outline/synopsis and 2 sample chapters. SASE for query and mss. Reports in 3 weeks on queries; 2 months on mss. Simultaneous and photocopied submissions OK. Accepts computer printouts. No dot-matrix.
**Terms:** Authors are paid in royalties of 10% minimum; 20% maximum; advance is negotiable; 10 author's copies. Sends galleys to author. Book catalog for SASE or IRC and 2 first class stamps.
**Tips:** "Read good contemporary fiction; find your own voice."

**‡MILLERS RIVER PUBLISHING CO. (I, IV)**, Box 159, Athol MA 01331. Owner: Allen Young. One person operation on part-time basis; New England regional interest. Publishes paperback originals. Books: Glatfelter 60 lb paper; offset printing; perfect binding; illustrations; average print order: 2,000; first novel print order: 1,000. Averages 2 total titles, 1 fiction title each year. Critiques or comments on rejected ms.
**Needs:** Regional (New England setting). Recently published *EZ*, by William H. Walker (Americana folklore).

**How to Contact:** Accepts unsolicited mss. SASE. Query first. Submit outline/synopsis and 2 sample chapters. SASE. Reports in 4 weeks on queries; 4 weeks on mss. Simultaneous and photocopied submissions OK. Accepts computer printouts including dot-matrix.
**Terms:** Pays in royalties of 5% minimum; 10% maximum; average advance: $300; advance is negotiagle. Sends galleys to author. Subsidy—will consider and negotiate. Book catalog for #10 SASE and 39¢ postage.
**Tips:** Encourages first novelists.

**MINA PRESS (II)**, Box 854, Sebastopol CA 95472. (707)829-0854. Fiction Editors: Mei Nakano, Adam David Miller. Estab. 1982. Three-person part-time operation. Publishes hardcover and paperback originals. Books: offset printing; paper binding; average print order; 2,000; first novel print order: 2,500. Plans 3 first novels this year. Averages 1-5 total titles each year. Occasionally critiques rejected ms.
**Needs:** Ethnic, feminist, gay, juvenile (contemporary), lesbian, science fiction, and easy-to-read (teen). "No works that glorify war; no gratuitous violence; nothing racist, sexist, ageist." Recently published: *Riko Rabbit*, by Mei Nakano (folk children's); and *Is a Mountain Just a Rock*, by Gregory Uba (early teen initiation).
**How to Contact:** Accepts unsolicited mss. Submit complete ms with SASE. Reports in 3 months. Simultaneous and photocopied submissions OK. Accepts computer printout submissions; prefers letter-quality. Disc submissions OK with HP 125. Prefers hard copy with disc submission.
**Terms:** Pays in royalties of 10% maximum; 10 author's copies; no advance. Sends galleys to author. Writer's guidelines and book catalog for SASE.
**Tips:** "Publishing first novels is our mission, more or less. Published less last year because of cash flow problems. We encourage new novelists. We regard the author/editor relationship as one of close collaboration on all aspects/phases of publications." Determine your market and send ms to publisher who most fits it.

**MOGUL BOOKS AND FILMWORKS**, Box 2773, Pittsburgh PA 15230. (412)461-0705. Contact: Vincent Risoli. Small publishing and film production company. Estab. 1982. Publishes hardcover originals. Averages 1-2 total titles each year.
**Needs:** Gay and lesbian. Recently published: *Devil in Disguise*, by Vinnie Robinson (fiction with gay theme).
**How to Contact:** Query first. Reports in 2 weeks on queries; 4-6 weeks on mss. Photocopied submissions OK.

**MOLE PUBLISHING CO. (IV)**, Rt. 1, Box 618, Bonners Ferry ID 83805. (208)267-7349. President: Mike Oehler. Estab. 1978. Publishes hardcover and paperback originals. "We would be willing to publish new writers. Averages 1-2 titles each year. Occasionally critiques rejected mss.
**Needs:** Experimental and literary. "We are looking only for novels specifically dealing with the 'back to the land movement.' Homesteading, redneck vs. long-hair conflict, environmental decay, homesteaders vs. authorities, survivalists, etc. This is a field which we believe has not been covered."
**How to Contact:** Submit outline/synopsis and 2 sample chapters with SASE. Simultaneous and photocopied submissions OK. Reports in 2 months on mss.
**Terms:** Negotiable. Self-publishers with plans to expand.

**MORGAN PRESS (I, II)**, 1819 N. Oakland Ave., Milwaukee WI 53202. (414)272-3256. Imprint includes *Hey Lady*, a poetry magazine. President: Edwin Burton. Estab. 1967. Two-man, full-time operation. Publishes hardcover and paperback originals. Averages 6-7 total titles, 1-3 fiction titles each year.
**Needs:** Contemporary, experimental, literary, mainstream, and short story collections. "There is very little we are dead-set against."

**How to Contact:** Accepts unsolicited mss. Submit complete ms with SASE. Reports in 2 weeks. Simultaneous and photocopied submissions OK. Accepts computer printout submissions. Prefers letter-quality.
**Terms:** Pays in author's copies. Book catalog free on request.
**Tips:** "We'd like to do more fiction."

**MOSAIC PRESS (II, IV), Fine Miniature Books**, 358 Oliver Rd., Cincinnati OH 45215. (513)761-5977. Publisher: Miriam Irwin. Estab. 1977. Publishes hardcover originals in miniature format. Books: acid-free archival paper; litho or letter press printing; hardbound, cloth, leather or half-leather binding; illustrations; average print order: 2,000. Plans to publish 4 new authors this year. Averages 15-20 total titles, 2 fiction titles each year. Occasionally buys juvenile mss with or without illustrations. Sometimes critiques rejected mss.
**Needs:** Comics, historical, humor/satire, juvenile (animal, historical, picture book, sports), literary, regional, religious/inspirational, romance, and young adult (historical, sports). "Our books are short (3,500 words maximum). No fantasy, science fiction or occult." Recently published: *Healing and Belief*, by Norman Cousins.
**How to Contact:** Accepts unsolicited mss. Query first or submit complete ms. SASE always. Simultaneous and photocopied submissions OK. Accepts computer printout submissions. Reports in 2 weeks on queries; 2 weeks on mss. Publishes ms an average of 2 years after acceptance.
**Terms:** Pays in outright purchase of $50 and 5 author's copies. "We also do subsidy publishing of private editions. Negotiable arrangements." Book catalog $3.
**Tips:** "We want a good topic, beautifully written, in very few words; no full-length novel submissions. Regarding the author/editor relationship, the writer should trust editor; editor should trust designer." Read the publisher's stated purpose more carefully.

**MOSAIC PRESS (II)**, Box 1032, Oakville, Ontario, Canada L6J 5E9. (416)825-2130. Contact: Editorial Director. Estab. 1975. Publishes hardcover and paperback originals. Number of titles: 4 in 1984; 4 in 1985. Recently published *Fool*, by Leon Whiteson; and *Cracked Wheat*, by Hugh Cook.
**Needs:** Literary only.
**How to Contact:** Query with SAE and IRC. No simultaneous submissions; photocopied submissions OK. Reports in 2 weeks on queries, 3-6 months on mss.
**Terms:** Pays 10% royalties; no advance. Free book catalog.

**MOTHEROOT PUBLICATIONS (II)**, Box 8306, Pittsburgh PA 15218. Fiction Editor: Sonya Jones. Estab. 1977. Small feminist independent press on part-time basis. Publishes paperback originals. Averages 1 title each year—fiction. Average first novel print order 5,000 copies. Occasionally critiques rejected ms.
**Needs:** Feminist, lesbian, and women's. No pornography or traditional romance.
**How to Contact:** Query with SASE. Reports in 2 weeks. Simultaneous and photocopied submissions OK. Accepts computer printout submissions; prefers letter-quality.
**Terms:** Pays in royalties of 25% maximum; 10 author's copies.

**MTM PUBLISHING CO. (II)**, Box 245, Washougal WA 98671. (206)254-9467. MTM Fiction Editor: S. Taylor Moore. Estab. 1974. Independent publisher with plans to expand. Publishes hardcover and paperback originals. Books: 20 lb and up paper; photo offset printing; perfect binding; illustrations; average print order: 5,000; first novel print order: 1,000. Plans 3 novels this year. Averages 1-3 total titles each year; varying number of fiction titles. Occasionally critiques rejected ms.
**Needs:** "MTM needs young adult/teen, juvenile (animal, easy-to-read), political satire, science fiction, suspense/mystery, and fantasy.
**How to Contact:** Accepts unsolicited mss. Query or submit outline/synopsis and 1 sample chapter with SASE. Reports in 1 month on queries and mss. Simultaneous and photocopied submissions OK. Accepts computer printout submissions. Prefers letter-quality. Disc submissions OK with Kaypro 2 or 4 system.

**Terms:** Individually arranged. Pays in negotiable number of author's copies; depends on award money. Sometimes subsidy publishes ("if agreed upon in advance"); depends on marketability of book. Writer's guidelines for SASE.

**Tips:** "Send your best query letter and SASE if you really want to put your best foot forward. Don't send anything registered if you want it read. Trust is a two-way street. We are publishing more fiction, more hardcovers and more paperbacks. We encourage first novelists and have published new writers within the last year."

**THE NAIAD PRESS, INC. (I, IV)**, Box 10543, Tallahassee FL 32302. (904)539-9322. Imprints include Pagoda Publications and Volute Books. Editorial Director: Barbara Grier. Estab. 1973. Books: 50 lb offset paper; (Webb) photo offset printing; perfect binding; illustrations seldom; average print order: 12,000; first novel print order: 12,000.

**Needs:** Feminist and lesbian. Recently published *Horizon of the Heart*, by Shelly Smith; *An Emergence of Green*, by Katherine V. Forrest; and *Lesbian Nuns*, edited by Rosemary Curb and Nancy Manahan.

**How to Contact:** Query. SASE for query, ms. No simultaneous submissions; photocopied submissions OK "but we prefer original mss." Reports in 1 week on queries, 2 months on mss. Publishes ms 6-8 months after acceptance.

**Terms:** Pays 15% royalties; no advance. Book catalog for legal-sized SASE.

**Tips:** "We publish lesbian/feminist fiction primarily and prefer honest work (i.e., positive, upbeat lesbian characters). Lesbian content must be accurate . . . a lot of earlier lesbian novels were less than honest. No breast beating or complaining." New imprint will publish reprints and original fiction. "Our fiction titles are becoming increasingly *genre* fiction which we encourage. Original fiction in paperback is our main field and its popularity increases. First novels are where the world is . . . really. We publish 10 books a year. Don't be a smart aleck. Send a simple letter, who, what, why, where, when, about yourself and a single page with at most 2 paragraphs precisly of your BOOK . . . not how good but WHAT IT IS ABOUT. How many double spaced typed pages? Include a self-addressed stamped envelope . . . remember that no editor has time to waste, and the more accurate your self-description is, the more chance you have of getting a reader who will READ your book. Include telephone numbers, day and evening if possible . . . make it VERY easy for the editor to deal with you."

**NERVE PRESS**, 1048 Canyon Blvd., North Vancouver, British Columbia V79 2K4 Canada. (604)986-3843. Fiction Editor: Claudia Cornwall. Estab. 1982. One-man operation on part-time basis. Publishes paperback originals. Plans 1-2 first novels this year. Averages 1-2 total titles each year. Average first novel print order 2,000 copies. Occasionally critiques rejected ms.

**Needs:** Juvenile (spy/adventure, contemporary), science fiction, and young adult/teen (fantasy/science fiction, spy/adventure). Novel needs include science, speculative fiction for juveniles or adults. No Harlequin or erotic. Recently published: *Print-Outs—the Adventures of a Rebel Computer*, by Claudia Cornwall (juvenile science fiction).

**How to Contact:** Accepts unsolicited mss. Query or submit outline/synopsis and 1 sample chapter with SASE. Reports in 1 month on queries; 3 months on mss. Simultaneous and photocopied submissions OK. Accepts computer printout submissions. Prefers letter-quality.

**Terms:** Pays in royalties of 10% minimum, 15% maximum; advance is more for agented ms.

**NEW BEDFORD PRESS**, Subsidiary of Anacre Industries, Inc., 5800 W. Century Blvd., Division 91502, Los Angeles CA 90009. (213)837-2961. Editorial Director: Saul Burnstein. Fiction Editor: Mary Bloom. Estab. 1978. Midsize publisher. Publishes hardcover originals. Books: paper varies; offset priting; spindle and Smyth sewn binding; average print order 5,000 copies; first novel print order 5,000 copies. Plans 2 first novels this year. Buys 2% agented fiction. Averages 3 total titles, 3 fiction titles each year. Average first novel print order 5,000 hardcover. Occasionally critiques rejected ms.

**Needs:** Adventure, contemporary, faction. "We want to see novels with good characterizations, good universal plots that the average reader could identify with. We welcome first novels." No

westerns, science fiction, gothic, war or feminist. Recently published *559 to Damascus*, by Jefferson (political suspense).
**How to Contact:** Query first with SASE. All unsolicited manuscripts are returned unopened. Simultaneous and photocopied submissions OK. Accepts computer printout submissions. Prefers letter-quality. Reports in 3 weeks on queries, 1 month on mss. Publishes ms an average of 1 year after acceptance.
**Terms:** Pays in royalties of 7% minimum, 15% maximum; $2,500-3,500 in advance.
**Tips:** "We have success with fiction that can be easily adapted to film and television. The worldwide audience always identifies with a good, solid story. We encourage first novelists but their material must meet our rather strict and narrow guidelines for fiction. Mainly we are looking for highly exploited contemporary action/adventure material with political yet universal themes. We want to exploit the film and television markets and to do so one must have material that can be easily adaptable. Check out all of the best films ever seen: You'll find they had excellent stories with good crisp dialogue, well flushed out characters with universally understandable themes. Controversy, polemics and allegories are always good. But controversy must always be rooted in reality—not contrived. Try to avoid issue-oriented themes that would only appeal to small readership audience. We want to publish books the entire world will read and understand—not just the local sewing society."

**NEW RIVERS PRESS**, 1602 Selby Ave., St. Paul MN 55104. Editorial Director: C.W. Truesdale. Fiction Editors: C.W. Truesdale and Roger Blakely. Estab. 1968. Number of fiction titles: 2 in 1984.
**Needs:** Contemporary, literary, experimental, historical (especially personal), and translations. "No popular fantasy/romance. Nothing pious, polemical (unless very good other redeeming qualities). We are interested in only quality literature and always have been (though our concentration in the past has been poetry)."
**How to Contact:** Query. SASE for query, ms. Photocopied submissions OK. Reports in 1 month on queries, within 2 months of query approval on mss.
**Terms:** Pays in 100 author's copies; no advance. Free book catalog.
**Tips:** "We are not really concerned with trends. We read for quality, which experience has taught can be very eclectic and can come sometimes from out of nowhere. We are interested in publishing short fiction (as well as poetry and translations) because it is and has been a great American indigenous form and is almost completely ignored by the commercial houses. Find a *real* subject, something that belongs to you and not what you think or surmise that you should be doing by current standards and fads." Sponsors Minnesota Voices Project.

**NEW SEED PRESS (II, IV)**, Box 9488, Berkeley CA 94709. (415)540-7576. Editor: Helen Chetin. Estab. 1971. Publishes paperback originals in Spanish/English and Chinese/English, and only English. Books: 70 lb paper; typeset printing; saddle-stitched binding; b&w line art or line and wash; average print order: 2,000-3,000. Encourages new writers. Comments on rejected mss.
**Needs:** Feminist, ethnic, regional, juvenile (historical, contemporary), and young adult (historical, problem novels, easy-to-read teen). "No adult fiction that is not appropriate for children." Recently published *Angel Island Prisoner 1922*, by Helen Chetin (bilingual book in Chinese and English).
**How to Contact:** Accepts unsolicited mss. Query or submit complete ms. SASE always. Simultaneous and photocopied submissions OK. Accepts computer printout submissions. Reports in 2 weeks on queries, 1 month on mss.
**Terms:** Pays in royalties and by outright purchase. Sends galleys to author. Book catalog legal-sized SASE.
**Tips:** "As we are a feminist collective, we discourage writers from sending us 'apolitical animal-type stories' whose intent is to avoid rather than confront issues. We publish children's books free from stereotyping with content that is relative to today's happenings, stories with active female characters who take responsibility for their lives, stories that challenge assumptions about the inferiority of women and Third World peoples." Rejects mss that are "trite or trivial."

‡**NIGHT TREE PRESS (IV)**, 414 W. Thomas St., Rome NY 13440. (315)337-4142. Publisher: Gregg Fedchack. Estab. 1985. "New, extremely small press; one-person full-time, another part-time." Paperback originals. Books: 60 lb paper; typeset printing; perfect bound softcover; regional photographs; average print order: 1,000 copies; first novel print order: (est) 500 copies. Plans 1-2 first novels this year. Averages 1-2 total titles/year.
**Needs:** Adventure, historical, humor/satire, literary, regional, short story collections. "Within each category, fiction *must* be strictly regional in nature; the far north country of New York (Adirondacks, St. Lawrence River, etc.)" Needs "traditional, conservative fiction based upon a first-hand knowledge of the North Country of New York State, a very traditional, conservative area."
**How to Contact:** Query first. SASE. Reports in 1-2 weeks. Simultaneous and photocopied submissions OK. Accepts computer printouts including dot-matrix.
**Terms:** Pays in authors copies; 10% of total press run and/or individual author negotiations. Sends galleys to author. Book catalog free on request.
**Tips:** "We are looking for first novels by serious, professional authors who can bring the experience of our region to life. Night Tree wants to be their first break. We decided to begin with paperbacks because of their increasing acceptance as a legitimate, reviewable format. A small run of hardcovers with 'permanent paper' for esthetic, historic, and library trade purposes is still our eventual goal on each project. We haven't published any fiction yet, but we *prefer* first novelists to established ones. If the very small presses can't be a first time fiction writer's home, then we have little reason to exist. Read. Know classical fiction, the historical roots of your trade. You have to be able to place your novel in a time perspective. Read modern fiction but don't model your work after another author or book. Be professional in your submissions. And—surprise!—watch TV to see what's 'in' or exciting in the world today. Television, as a fast medium, can teach the 'slow' writer a lot if viewed critically and not passively."

**NORTH POINT PRESS (III)**, Box 6275, Albany CA 94706. (415)527-6260. Editor-in-Chief: Jack Shoemaker. Editor: Thomas Christensen. Editorial Assistant: Kathleen Moses. Estab. 1980. Publishes hardcover and paperback originals and reprints. Books: acid-free paper; sewn binding; illustrations; average print order: 5,000; first novel print order: 5,000. Averages 24 total titles, 6 fiction titles each year. Buys 50% agented fiction.
**Needs:** Contemporary, experimental, literary, short story collections, and translations. Especially needs serious and experimental. No "genre" fiction written for a "market." Recently published *A Servant's Tale*, by Paula Fox; *Son of the Morning Star*, by Evan S. Connell; and *The Mind of Clover*, by Robert Aitken. Chances for fiction not good.
**How to Contact:** Query first with SASE. Photocopied submissions OK. Reports in 2 months on queries; 6 months on mss. Publishes ms 8-36 months after acceptance.
**Terms:** Royalty payment varies; advance negotiable. Sends galleys to author. Must return advance if book is not completed or is unacceptable.
**Tips:** "Chances for acceptance of fiction here continue to diminish. We receive about 2,000 submissions a year, few appropriate for our publishing program. No block letter computer printouts. Type. We encourage first novels and published new writers last year."

**OMMATION PRESS (II, IV)**, 5548 N. Sawyer, Chicago IL 60625. Imprints include *Mati Magazine*, *Ditto Rations Chapbook Series*, *Offset Offshoot Series*, *Salome: A Literary Dance Magazine*, *Dialogues on Dance Series*, Editorial Director: E. Mihopoulos. Estab. 1975. Number of book titles: 2 in 1981; 10 in 1982. Encourages new writers. Rarely comments on rejected mss.
**Needs:** Contemporary, literary, experimental, feminist, prose poetry. "For *Salome: A Literary Dance Magazine* Dialogues on Dance Series, dance-related fiction; for *Mati's* Offset Offshoot Series, poetry mss that include prose poems." Recently published *Songs for Isadora*, by Linda W. Wagner; *The Dancer's Muse*, by Karren L. Alenier.
**How to Contact:** Submit complete ms with SASE. Simultaneous, if so indicated, and photocopied submissions OK. Reports in 1 month.
**Terms:** Pays in 50 author's copies (and $100 honorarium if grant money available). Book catalog for legal-sized SASE.

**ON THE MOVE PRESS (II, IV)**, 655 Oakland Ave., Oakland CA 94611. (415)653-5251. Editor/Publisher: James F. Prchlik. Estab. 1980. One-man operation on part-time basis. Publishes paperback originals. Books: 60 lb paper: offset printing; saddle stitch binding; illustrations; average print order: 500. Averages 4 total titles, "each issue has some fiction." Occasionally critiques rejected mss.
**Needs:** Adventure, ethnic, historical, literary, and translations. Accepts short stories for text. *Travel-related* fiction or journal.
**How to Contact:** Reports in 2 weeks on queries, 1 month on mss. Simultaneous and photocopied submissions OK. Publishes ms about 2 months after acceptance.
**Terms:** Pays in 2 author's copies; "also profit sharing, but there's not much profit." Sends galleys to author. Free book catalog.
**Tips:** The author/editor relationship: Shaman/patient: "We want to exorcise the 'bad' spirits."

**THE OVERLOOK PRESS**, 12 W. 21st St., New York NY 10010. (212)675-0585. Estab. 1972. Small-staffed, full-time operation. Publishes hardcover and paperback originals and reprints. Plans 2 first novels this year. Averages 20 total titles; 7 fiction titles each year. Occasionally critiques rejected mss.
**Needs:** Adventure, contemporary, ethnic, experimental, fantasy, historical, humor/satire, juvenile (fantasy, historical, sports, contemporary), literary, psychic/supernatural/occult, science fiction, translations. No romance or horror. Recently published *The Last Days of Alfred Hitchcock*, by David Freeman; *The Emperor's Tomb*, by Joseph Roth; and *Up the Financial Ladder in a Downwardly Mobile Society*, by Dallas Whitney.
**How to Contact:** Query first or submit outline/synopsis and 3 sample chapters with SASE. Allow up to 6 months for reports on queries and mss. Simultaneous and photocopied submissions OK.
**Terms:** Vary.

**OWL CREEK PRESS (II)**, Box 2248, Missoula MT 59806. (206)633-5929. Subsidiary includes *The Montana Review*. Editor: Rich Ives. Estab. 1979. Small independent literary publisher with plans to expand. Publishes hardcover and paperback originals. Books: photo offset printing; sewn or perfect binding; illustrations sometimes; average print order: 1,000; first novel print order: 1,000. Plans 3-4 short fiction collections/novels in next year or two. Averages 7 total titles, 0-3 fiction titles each year. Occasionally critiques rejected ms.
**Needs:** Contemporary, literary, short story collections, and translations. "Literary quality is our only criteria." No formula fiction.
**How to Contact:** Accepts unsolicited mss. "We recommend purchase of sample issue ($3 back issue, $5 current) of *The Montana Review* to determine our interests." Submit outline/synopsis and 1-3 sample chapters with SASE. Reports in 2 months. Simultaneous (if stated) and photocopied submissions OK. Accepts computer printout submissions (if clear copy). Publishes ms 3-18 months after acceptance.
**Terms:** Payment depends on grant/award money. Possible payment in royalties of 10% minimum, 20% maximum; author's copies, 10% of run minimum. Book catalog for SASE.
**Tips:** "We are expanding in all areas. The number of fiction titles in the next 2-3 years will depend on grants, sales, and the quality of submissions. We ignore trends. Subject is irrelevant. Our *only* criterion is quality of the writing itself. Write what interests and challenges you, ignore market trends. Never alter your best goals and the direction of your abilities to suit a market, but try to learn from the advice of experienced editors and writers about your craft."

**PACIFIC ARTS AND LETTERS**, Subsidiaries include *Alps Monthly*, Peace & Pieces Books, Box 99394, San Francisco CA 94109. (415)771-3431. Fiction Editor: Rev. Maurice Custodio. Estab. 1970. Nonprofit independent literary arts press. Publishes hardcover and paperback originals and paperback reprints. Established writers only. Averages 2-4 total titles, 1 fiction title each year.
**Needs:** Humor/satire and literary. Needs "short novels/novellas in sharp social satire style. For a

tax-deductible contribution of $150 we mention fiction authors and books on our TV program in San Francisco and our video programs at the PAL Small Press Bookfairs. SASE required for application and information." Recently published *Today's Outstanding Writers*, by Richard Morris, et. al.; and *The 69 Days of Easter*, by Todd S.J. Lawson (humor/satire).

**How to Contact:** Query first with SASE. "Unsolicited manuscripts and manuscripts by non-*Alps Monthly* subscribers will not be accepted since we cannot handle the volume with our limited staff." Photocopied submissions OK. Accepts computer printout submissions. Prefers letter-quality. Reports in 3 weeks on queries.

**Terms:** Pays honorarium ("we are nonprofit"). Note: Authors must be *Alps Monthly* subscribers to submit manuscripts. Subscriptions are: $28/year individual and small presses; $48 for libraries and institutions; $75 corporations and businesses (all tax-deductible). "Under exceptional circumstances and for $25,000-75,000 tax-deductible donation fee, we will publish and promote 5,000 to 20,000 copies of a fiction book by well-known public figure or movie star. Individual arrangement with author." Writer's guidelines for SAE and 3 first class stamps. Book catalog for SAE and 3 first class stamps.

**Tips:** "Fiction is in danger of existential death; the emergence of the marriage of nonfiction and fiction in creative writing may save it." Publishes more original fiction in paperback "especially in our short fiction anthologies."

**PADRE PRODUCTIONS (II)**, Box 1275, San Luis Obispo CA 93406. (805)543-5404. Imprints include Bear Flag Books, Channel X series, The Press of MacDonald and Reénecke. Editor/Publisher: Lachlan P. MacDonald. Fiction Editor: Mack Sullivan. Estab. 1974. Small independent publisher. Publishes hardcover and paperback originals and paperback reprints. Books: 60 lb book paper; offset printing; hardcover and perfect binding; average print order: 3,000; first novel print order: 3,000. Plans 1 novel per year. Averages 8-12 total titles, 1 fiction title each year. Buys 5% agented fiction. Occasionally critiques rejected ms.

**Needs:** Contemporary, fantasy, literary, regional, science fiction, and short story collections. "Overstocked on juveniles." Accepts short stories for Channel X anthology. Juveniles must run 160 pages, for 8-14 year-old readers, both male and female protagonists. No romances or westerns. Recently published *Chrona*, by Aaron Carob (fantasy); and *Joel in Tananar*, by Robert M. Walton (juvenile fantasy). Accepts unsolicited mss. Query first with SASE. Reports in 1 month. Simultaneous and photocopied submissions OK. Accepts computer printout submissions. Prefers letter-quality. Publishes ms 1-4 years after acceptance.

**Terms:** Pays in royalties of 6% minimum; 12% maximum. Sends galleys to author. Advance is negotiable. No subsidy publishing; "we package and produce books for self-publishers and small publishers, however." Writer's guidelines and book catalog free for #10 SASE.

**Tips:** "California-based historical fiction welcome." Published less fiction this year. "We encourage first novelists and published new writers last year. Try 40 or 50 publishers with summary and sample chapter."

**PANJANDRUM BOOKS (II, III)**, Imprint includes Panjandrum Press, Inc., 5428 Hermitage Ave., North Hollywood CA 91607. (213)477-8771. Editor: Dennis Koran. Estab. 1971. Publishes paperback originals. Averages 5-6 total titles, 1-2 fiction titles each year. Buys 10% agented fiction. Occasionally critiques rejected mss.

**Needs:** Experimental, literary, and translations. "We are *highly* selective." Recently published *Fighting Men*, by Willard Manus (contemporary war novel with social message); and *Alfred Jarry: The Man with the Axe*, by Nigey Lennon (biography with novelette).

**How to Contact:** Query first with return postcard or SASE for reply. Photocopied submissions OK. Reports in 4 weeks on queries, 6-8 weeks on mss. No mss will be returned or answered without SASE. Publishes ms an average of 18 months after acceptance.

**Terms:** Pays in royalties of 6% minimum, 10% maximum; 10 author's copies. Book catalog for 6x9 SAE and 2 first class stamps.

‡**PAPIER-MACHE PRESS (II)**, 34 Malaga Pl. E., Manhattan Beach CA 90266. (213)545-3812. Editor/Publisher: Sandra Martz. Estab. 1984. One person operation on a part-time basis. Publishes paperback originals. Books: 50-60 lb offset paper; perfect binding; occasional illustrations; average print order: 500-1,000 copies. Publishes 1-2 total titles/year; 1-2 fiction titles/year. Comments on rejected mss.
**Needs:** Contemporary, experimental, feminist, short story collections, women's.
**How to Contact:** Query first. SASE. Reports in 4 weeks on queries; 3 months on mss. Simultaneous and photocopied submissions OK. Accepts computer printouts including dot-matrix.
**Terms:** Honorarium—depending on circumstances. Pays 1-2 author's copies. Some potential for co-publishing with authors.

**PARKHURST PRESS (IV)**, Box 143, Laguna Beach CA 92652. (714)494-3092. Editor: Lynne Thorpe. Estab. 1981. Independent, part-time publisher with plans to expand. Publishes paperback originals. Books: offset printing; perfect binding; average print and first novel order 2,500 copies. Plans for first novels very limited this year. Averages 1 total title, 1 fiction title each year.
**Needs:** Fantasy, feminist, and humor/satire. Recently published *Alida*—, by Edna MacBrayne (erotic).
**How to Contact:** Query first with SASE. All unsolicited manuscripts are returned unopened. Photocopied submissions OK. Accepts computer printout submissions. Prefers letter-quality. Reports in 2 weeks on queries; 4 weeks on mss.
**Terms:** Negotiates author's copies and royalties. Prefers individual arrangement with author. "Cooperative or collective would be considered."
**Tips:** "Read, write, study, follow your instincts, and produce well crafted work. We foresee a growing demand for and support of publishers who produce quality work that is relevant, entertaining, and thought-provoking." Noticeable trends include "changing the mythology about women. First novels have to be exceptionally well written and relevant to our purpose."

**PASCAL PUBLISHERS**, 21 Sunnyside Ave., Wellesley MA 02181. (617)235-4278. Contact: J. Greene. Estab. 1980. One-man operation. Publishes paperback originals. Averages 1-2 total titles, 1-2 fiction titles each year. Average first novel print order 1,000 copies first run. Occasionally critiques rejected mss.
**Needs:** Juvenile (historical, picture book, Jewish topics). Needs story books with Jewish content for young readers. No adult material. Recently published *The Hanukah Tooth*, by Jacqueline Greene (picture book); and *A Classroom Hanukah* (story/project book).
**How to Contact:** Accepts unsolicited mss. Submit complete ms with SASE. Simultaneous and photocopied submissions OK. Accepts computer printout submissions. Prefers letter-quality. Reports in 3 weeks on queries.
**Terms:** Pays in royalties or in outright purchase. "We would consider joint venture with author under special circumstances." Book catalog free on request.
**Tips:** "We welcome first novel submissions that fit our publishing focus."

**PATH PRESS, INC. (II)**, Suite 1040, 53 W. Jackson, Chicago IL 60604. (312)663-0167. Editorial Director: Herman C. Gilbert. "Small independent publisher which specializes in books by, for and about Black Americans and Third World Peoples." Averages 8 total titles, 4 fiction titles each year. Occasionally critiques rejected ms.
**Needs:** Ethnic, historical, sports, and short story collections. Needs for novels include "black or minority-oriented novels of any genre, style or subject." Recently published *The Negotiations*, by Herman Cromwell Gilbert (political—"a novel of tomorrow"); and *American Diary: A Personal History of the Black Press*, by Enoch P. Waters (autobiographical).
**How to Contact:** Accepts unsolicited mss. Query first or submit outline/synopsis and 5 sample chapters with SASE. Reports in 1 month on queries; 2 months on mss. Simultaneous and photocopied submissions OK. Accepts computer printout submissions.
**Terms:** Pays in royalties of 10% minimum; 15% maximum. No advance.

**PAYCOCK PRESS (II)**, Box 3567, Washington DC 20007. Imprint includes *Gargoyle Magazine*. Editor/Publisher: Richard Peabody, Jr. Estab. 1976. Small independent publisher with international distribution. Publishes paperback originals and reprints. Books: regular stock paper offset printing; perfect bound binding; illustrations sometimes; average print order: 1,000; first novel print order: 1,000. Number of titles: 2 in 1983; 2 in 1984, 1 planned for 1985. Encourages new writers. Occasionally comments on rejected mss.
**Needs:** Contemporary, literary, experimental, humor/satire, and translations. "No tedious AWP resume-conscious writing or NEA-funded minimalism. We'd be interested in a good first novel that deals with the musical changes of the past few years." Recently published *The Love Letter Hack*, by Michael Brondoli (contemporary/literary); *Natural History*, by George Myers, Jr. (poems and stories); and *Fiction/84* (anthology).
**How to Contact:** Accepts unsolicited mss. Query with SASE. No simultaneous submissions; photocopied submissions OK. Accepts computer printout submissions. Prefers letter-quality. Reports in 1 week on queries, 1 month on mss.
**Terms:** Pays in author's copies 10% of print run plus 50% of all sales "after/if we break even on book." Sends galleys to author. No advance.
**Tips:** "Keep trying. Many good writers simply quit. Many mediocre writers keep writing, eventually get published, and become better writers. If the big magazines won't publish you, try the small magazines, try the local newspaper. Always read your fiction aloud. If you think something is *silly*, no doubt we'd be embarrassed too. Write the kind of stories you'd like to read and can't seem to find. We are more concerned with *how* a novelist says what he/she says, than with *what* he/she says. We are more interested in *right now* than in books about the 50's, 60's, 70's, etc. We are publishing more in anthology format, and encourage first novelists. We regard the author/editor relationship as important. Trust is everything."

**PEACHTREE PUBLISHERS, LTD. (II)**, 494 Armour Circle NE, Atlanta GA 30324. (404)876-8761. Executive Editor: Chuck Perry. Estab. 1977. Small, independent publisher specializing in general interest publications, particularly of Southern origin. Publishes hardcover and paperback originals and hardcover reprints. Plans 2 first novels this year. Averages 16 total titles, 3 fiction titles each year. Average first novel print order 10,000-15,000 copies.
**Needs:** Contemporary, literary, mainstream, regional, and short story collections. "We are primarily seeking Southern fiction: Southern themes, characters, and/or locales." No science fiction/fantasy, children's/young adult, horror, religious, romance, or mystery/suspense. Recently published: *The El Cholo Feeling Passes*, by Fredrick Barton (mainstream); *Elvis is Dead and I Don't Feel So Good Myself*, by Lewis Grizzard (humor); and *The Whisper of the River*, by Ferrol Sams (mainstream).
**How to Contact:** Accepts unsolicited mss. Query, submit outline/synopsis and 50 pages, or submit complete ms with SASE. Reports in 1 month on queries; 3 months on mss. Simultaneous and photocopied submissions OK. Accepts computer printout submissions. Prefers letter-quality.
**Terms:** Pays in royalties. Sends galleys to author. Free writer's guidelines and book catalog.
**Tips:** "We encourage original efforts in first novels." Published new writers last year.

**THE PEPPERMINT PRESS LTD. (I, II)**, R.R. 1, Cavan, Ontario L0A 1C0 Canada. (705)944-8977. Imprints include Aura Publications. Contact: Richard Miller. Estab. 1973. Small press producing hand-made books in small quantities. Publishes hardcover originals. Books: often hand-made, neutral pH; letter press printing; binding by hand; wood engravings, etching, etc., average print order: 250. Averages 1 total title (fiction) each year.
**Needs:** Erotica, humor, juvenile, preschool/picture book, regional (southern Ontario), science fiction, short story collections, and young adult/teen. "I would like to publish 1 or 2 quality children's book per year. As they will be made with care they will be expensive. Selection is entirely at the publisher's whim so stories must be special. No poorly written or cute fiction (i.e., no duckies or bunnies).
**How to Contact:** Accepts unsolicited mss. Query or submit outline/synopsis and sample chapters with SASE or SAE and IRC. "Manuscript will not be returned without international postage

or Canadian stamps." Simultaneous submissions OK. Submit only photocopies, not originals.
**Terms:** Pays in royalties and author's copies; offers advance. Sends galleys to author to check.
**Tips:** "Every novelist was a first novelist." Published unpublished writers within the year.

**‡PERFECTION FORM COMPANY (IV)**, 8350 Hickman, Suite 15, Des Moines IA 50322. (515)278-0133. Young Adult Editor: Beth Obermiller. Estab. 1926. Small educational publisher. Publishes paperback originals. Books: 50 lb white offset paper; web offset printing; perfect binding; illustrations sometimes; average print order: 5,000; first novel print order: 2,500. Plans 6 first novels this year. Averages 10 total titles, 10 fiction titles each year. Critiques or comments on rejected ms.
**Needs:** Young adult/teen (12-18 years) (easy-to-read, fantasy/science fiction, problem novels, romance, sports, spy/adventure). No stories with adult protagonists, graphic violence or sex; religious or heavily moralistic books. Recently published *The Last Gralok*, by Laurel McKeever (science fiction/fantasy); *Last Chance Haul*, by Don Snyder (adventure); *Dream Killer*, by Claire Stewart (personal conflict).
**How to Contact:** Accepts unsolicited mss. Submit complete ms with cover letter. SASE. Agented fiction: 5%. Reports in 2 weeks on queries; 6 weeks on mss. Simultaneous and photocopied submissions OK. Accepts computer printouts including dot-matrix.
**Terms:** Pays in royalties of 8% minimum; 10% maximum; average advance: $500; and 5 author's copies. Writer's guidelines free for 4½x9½ SASE and 1 first class stamp.
**Tips:** Encourages first novelists and published new writers last year.

**‡THE PERIGEE PRESS (II)**, Box 639, Walpole NH 03608. (603)756-3084. Publisher: Frank T. Moss. Estab. 1985. Publishes hardcover and paperback originals. Plans 1 first novel this year.
**Needs:** Adventure, mainstream, suspense/mystery. Needs nautical adventure stories. Recently published *Bluefin*, by Frank T. Moss (nautical adventure).
**How to Contact:** Does not accept unsolicited mss; returns mss. Query first or submit outline/synopsis and 2-3 sample chapters. SASE for query and ms. Reports in 3 weeks on queries; 6 weeks on mss.
**Terms:** Individual arrangement with author depending on the book.
**Tips:** "Know your subject. Tell it so the experts won't pick you apart, but so any non-expert can understand and enjoy it."

**PERIVALE PRESS (I)**, 13830 Erwin St., Van Nuys CA 91401. (818)785-4671. President: Lawrence P. Spingarn. Estab. 1968. One-man midsize operation, part time. Books: 50-60 lb cover paper; offset printing; perfect paper bound binding; illustrations on cover only; average print order: 1,200; first novel print order: 500. Buys 5% agented fiction. Encourages new writers. Occasionally comments on rejected mss.
**Needs:** Contemporary, mainstream, literary, experimental, women's, ethnic (any), erotica, regional (West), and translations. Accepts short stories from freelancers. No adventure, mystery, spy, historical, war, gothic, romance, confession, gay/lesbian, psychic, religious, science fiction, horror or juvenile. Novellas up to 100 pp. in typescript; no limitation on genres or styles. Publishes one per year. Recently published *Rice Powder*, by Sergio Galindo (novella of Mexico); *Mountainhouse*, by Pat McDermid; and *Foolscape*, by Richard Collins.
**How to Contact:** Does not accept unsolicited mss. Query with SASE. Simultaneous and photocopied submissions OK. Reports in 6 weeks on queries, 8 weeks on mss. Publishes ms 6-12 months after acceptance.
**Terms:** Pays 10-12½% in royalties. Sends galleys to author. No advance. Subsidy publishes 20% of total books. Author pays cost of printing and gets contract which stipulates that this amount, usually about $1,800, will be returned from sales within 2 years. Free book catalog with SASE and 22¢ postage. Writer's guidelines free for SASE and 1 first class stamp.
**Tips:** "Place stories first, even in literary magazines, before submitting ms to publisher. Novels should appeal to a college-educated audience. We foresee the publication of more serious novels of a less sensational kind in the next few years. On translated work, get clearance from original

publisher before submitting. Writer should consider a subsidy plan whereby his investment is returned through sales; he should also agree to making personal appearances (lectures, TV shows, etc.) if we offer contract." Publishing more original fiction in paperback "particularly novellas if subsidized by author under returnable arrangement. We want first novels but author must promote his/her work via readings, appearances, etc. to overcome problem of being unknown."

**PERSEVERANCE PRESS (I, II, IV)**, Box 384, Menlo Park CA 94026. Editor: Meredith Phillips. Estab. 1979. One-person press publishing only mysteries. Publishes paperback originals. Books: 55 lb paper; offset litho printing; perfect binding; average print order: 1,500; first novel print order: 1,000. Plans 1 to 4 first novels this year. Averages 2-3 total titles each year, all fiction. Always critiques rejected ms.
**Needs:** "Mysteries only, of the old-fashioned sort: whodunits, puzzlers, 'village cozies,' suspense thrillers, etc., with no gratuitous violence, excessive gore, or exploitive sex." No romance, horror, occult. Recently published *To Prove a Villain*, by Guy Townsend and *Play Melancholy Baby*, by John Daniel.
**How to Contact:** Accepts unsolicited mss "reluctantly." Submit outline/synopsis and 3 sample chapters with SASE. Reports in 1 month. Simultaneous and photocopied submissions OK.
**Terms:** Pays in royalties of 10% (net receipts); 20 author's copies. Sends galleys to author. Writer's guidelines for SASE.
**Tips:** "We are delighted to find new novelists. We ask for revisions if necessary, and do as much substantive editorial work as required—working with the author till it's right. The quality of material is rising and we are publishing more. We regard the author/editor relationship as open, honest, co-operative, professional."

**‡PERSPECTIVES PRESS (IV)**, 905 W. Wildwood Ave., Fort Wayne IN 46807. (219)456-8411. Publisher: Pat Johnston. Estab. 1981. Small operation expanding to become *the* publisher of fiction and nonfiction materials related to adoption and infertility. Publishes hardcover originals and paperback originals. Books: offset printing; smyth sewn cloth, perfect bound, and saddle stitched binding; average print order: 5,000. Plans 1 first novel this year. Averages 2-6 total titles, 1 fiction title each year. Critiques or comments on rejected mss.
**Needs:** Submissions for adults or children but must have adoption or infertility as the theme.
**How to Contact:** Query first. SASE. Reports in 2 weeks on queries; 4 weeks on mss. Simultaneous and photocopied submissions OK. Accepts computer printouts.
**Terms:** Pays in royalties of 5% minimum; 15% maximum. Advance negotiable. Sends galleys to author. Book catalog for #10 SAE and 39¢ postage.
**Tips:** "We are publishing more fiction, more hardcover because libraries want them. We encourage first novelists and have just published a juvenile piece from a first time author, but we are primarily a nonfiction press on infertility and adoption."

**PIKESTAFF PUBLICATIONS, INC. (I, II)**, Box 127, Normal IL 61761. (309)452-4831. Imprints include The Pikestaff Press: Pikestaff Fiction Chapbooks; *The Pikestaff Forum*, general literary magazine. Editorial Directors: Robert D. Sutherland and James R. Scrimgeour. Estab. 1977. Small independent publisher with plans to expand gradually. Publishes hardcover and paperback originals. Books: paper varies; offset printing; b&w illustrations; average print orders varies. Encourages new writers. One of the purposes of the press is to encourage new talent." Occasionally comments on rejected mss.
**Needs:** Contemporary, literary, and experimental. "No slick formula writing written with an eye to the commercial mass market or pure entertainment that does not provide insights into the human condition. Not interested in heroic fantasy (dungeons & dragons, swords & sorcery); science-fiction of the space-opera variety; westerns; mysteries; love-romance; gothic adventure; or pornography (sexploitation)."
**How to Contact:** Query or submit outline/synopsis and sample chapters (1-2 chapters). SASE always. "Anyone may inquire; affirmative responses may submit ms." No simultaneous or photocopied submissions. Accepts computer printout submissions. Prefers letter-quality. Reports in 1

month on queries, 3 months on mss. Publishes ms within 1 year after acceptance.

**Terms:** Negotiates terms with author. Sends galleys to author.

**Tips:** "Develop your craft. Have fictional characters we can really *care* about; we are tired of disembodied characters wandering about in their heads unable to relate to other people or the world about them. Avoid too much TELLING; let the reader participate by leaving something for him or her to do. Yet avoid vagueness, opaqueness, personal or 'private' symbolisms and allusions. Here we regard the relationship between the novelist and editor as a cooperative relationship—we are colleagues in getting the book out. The novelist has an obligation to do the best self-editing job of which he or she is capable; novelists should not rely on editors to make their books presentable. Don't give up easily; understand your reasons for wanting the novel published (personal satisfaction? money? fame? to 'prove' something? to 'be a novelist'? etc.) Ask yourself honestly, Should it be published? What can it provide for a reader that makes it worth part of that reader's *lifetime* to read? Be prepared for shocks and disappointments; study contracts carefully and retain as many rights and as much control over the book's appearance as possible. Be prepared to learn how to be your own best promoter and publicist."

**PINEAPPLE PRESS (II),** Box 314, Englewood FL 33533. (813)475-2238. Executive Editor: June Cussen. Estab. 1982. Small independent trade publisher. Publishes hardcover and paperback originals and paperback reprints. Books: book quality paper; offset printing; Smythe sewn hardcover perfect bound paperback binding; illustrations occasionally; average print order: 5,000; first novel print order: 2,000-5,000. Averages 6-10 total titles each year. Occasionally critiques rejected ms.

**Needs:** Contemporary, experimental, historical, environmental, regional, and young adult/teen. Recently published *Saint*, by Christine Bell (an extraordinary first novel).

**How to Contact:** Prefers query sometime or synopsis with sample chapters and SASE. Submit complete ms with SASE. Reports in 6 weeks. Simultaneous and photocopied submissions OK. Accepts computer printout submissions. Prefers letter-quality.

**Terms:** Pays in royalties of 7½% minimum; 15% maximum. Sends galleys to author. Advance is negotiable. "Basically, it is an individual agreement with each author depending on the book." Book catalog sent if label and 39¢ stamp enclosed.

**Tips:** "We have only just begun publishing fiction. Quality first novels will be published in both Florida regional books and general trade fiction and nonfiction." We published new writers last year. We regard the author/editor relationship as a trusting relationship with communication open both ways." Learn all you can about the publishing process and about how to promote your book once it is published."

**POET GALLEY PRESS,** Box 1206, New York City NY 09221. Editor: E.J. Paulos. Estab. 1970. Publishes paperback originals. Number of titles: 5 in 1980; 7 in 1981. Encourages new writers. We publish mainly poetry." Sometimes comments on rejected mss.

**Needs:** Contemporary, literary and experimental. No poorly written, poorly plotted stories. Specializes in works of American authors living outside continental United States. "Right now—over committed on novels, especially with current market."

**How to Contact:** Query with SASE. Simultaneous and photocopied submissions OK. Reports in 6 weeks on queries and mss. Publishes ms 6 months after acceptance.

**Terms:** Pays in royalties. No advance.

**PORCUPINE'S QUILL, INC. (III),** 68 Main St., Erin, Ontario, N0B 1T0 Canada. (519)833-9158 and (816)454-2001. Contact: Ann Reatherford. Estab. 1974. Small press. Publishes hardcover and paperback originals and occasional paperback reprints. Books: 70 lb Zephyr antique paper; offset on Heidelberg Kord 64 printing; paper, occasional hand hardcover binding; illustrations; average print order: 750; first novel print order: 750. Averages 7 total titles, 3 fiction titles each year.

**Needs:** Contemporary, fantasy, historical, literary, and young adult/teen (historical). Recently published *Jewels*, by David Carpenter.

**How to Contact:** Accepts unsolicited mss. Query. Reports in 2 weeks. Simultaneous and photocopied submissions OK. Accepts computer printout submissions.
**Terms:** Pays in royalties of 5% minimum; 10% maximum; 10 author's copies. Sends galleys to author. Free book catalog.
**Tips:** "We are publishing more fiction and published new writers last year."

**THE PRAIRIE PUBLISHING COMPANY**, Box 264, Station C, Winnipeg, Manitoba R3M 3S7 Canada. (204)885-6496. Publisher: Ralph Watkins. Estab. 1969. Buys juvenile mss with illustrations.
**How to Contact:** Query with SASE or SAE, IRC. No simultaneous submissions; photocopied submissions OK. Reports in 1 month on queries, 6 weeks on mss. Publishes ms 4-6 months after acceptance.
**Terms:** Pays 10% in royalties. No advance. Free book catalog.
**Tips:** "We work on a manuscript with the intensity of a Max Perkins of Charles Scribner's Sons of New York. A clean, well-prepared manuscript can go a long way toward making an editor's job easier. On the other hand, the author should not attempt to anticipate the format of the book, which is a decision for the publisher to make. Do not be discouraged by rejections."

**PROPER TALES PRESS**, Box 789, Station F, Toronto, Ontario M4Y 2N7 Canada. Editor: Stuart Ross. Imprints include Weeping Monk Editions, Cops Going For Doughnuts Editions. Estab. 1979. "Small press publisher of the bizarre." Publishes paperback originals. Averages 6 total titles, 2-3 fiction titles each year. Average first novel print order 500 copies. Occasionally critiques rejected ms.
**Needs:** Experimental, horror, short story collections, and suspense/mystery. Novel needs include: surrealist, absurdist, fringe. "The key word is 'bizarre.' " No religious or romance.
**How to Contact:** Accepts unsolicited mss. Submit complete ms with SASE or SAE and IRC. Reports in 3 months. Publishes ms 6-18 months after acceptance. Photocopied submissions OK.
**Terms:** Pays in author's copies (10% of print run). Writer's guidelines for 6x9 SAE and 2 first class stamps (Canadian postage or IRC). Book catalog for 6x9 SAE with 2 first class stamps (Canadian postage or IRC).
**Tips:** "Whether it's a first novel or a 712th, if I like it, I'll publish it if possible. Enclose a short bio and return envelope with *Canadian* postage or IRC; send a few bucks to see sample books we've done."

**‡PULP PRESS BOOK PUBLISHER (I)**, Subsidiary of Arsenal Pulp Press Book Publishers, Ltd., 202-986 Homer St., Vancouver, British Columbia V6B 2W7 Canada. (604)687-4233. Imprints include Tillacum Library, Arsenal Editions. Editor: S. Gunner. Estab. 1972. Small, literary-based co-operative. Paperback originals. Books: deluxe book 60 lb paper; offset printing; perfect binding; illustrations "sometimes"; average print order: 1,500; first novel print order: 1,000 copies. Plans 1 first novel this year. Averages 5 total titles/year. Occasionally comments on rejected mss.
**Needs:** Ethnic, experimental, feminist, gay, literary, mainstream, regional, short story collections, women's. "Always open to new authors and subjects." No romance, western, science fiction, horror. Recently published *Nothing So Natural*, by Jim Curry (novel); *This West of Summer*, by Jeff Boran (novel); and *New: West Coast Fiction*, by various authors (anthology).
**How to Contact:** Accepts unsolicited mss. Query first. SASE, IRC for query and mss. Agented fiction: less than 25%. Reports in 4 weeks on queries; 3 months on mss. Simultaneous and photocopied submissions OK. Accepts computer printouts including dot-matrix.
**Terms:** Pays in royalties of 10% minimum; 15% maximum and $50 average advance. Sends galleys to author. "95% of our titles are subsidized, either pre- or post-production." Book catalog for 9x12 SAE and IRC for US.
**Tips:** "There is a 3-day novel contest, held annually on Labor Day weekend for best novel written in 72-hour period wins publication following year. Write for more details (SASE, SVP)."

**QUALITY PUBLICATIONS, INC. (II)**, Box 2633, Lakewood OH 44107, Executive Editor: Gary S. Skeens. Estab. 1978. Publishes paperback originals. Books: 60 lb bond paper; offset, typeset printing; perfect bound, saddle stitched binding; illustrations on cover; average print order: 250-500 (can be up to 1,000); first novel print order: 500. Averages 6 total titles, 3 fiction titles each year. Occasionally critiques rejected mss.
**Needs:** Adventure, contemporary, faction, historical, short story collections, and western. No mss of low quality, pornography, lack of characterization, plot, etc. Recently published *Days of Darkness*, by Lawrence Harvey; *In Light's Delay*, by Ron Terpening; and *Grover*, by William Bruton.
**How to Contact:** Query first; submit outline/synopsis and 4 sample chapters with SASE. Simultaneous and photocopied submissions OK. Reports in 2 weeks on queries, 6 weeks on mss.
**Terms:** Pays in royalties of 10% minimum, 20% maximum. Sends galleys to author on individual basis. Payment "depends on the book; discussion with individual authors." Writer's guidelines free. Book catalog free on request.
**Tips:** "Be honest. Have good characterization, plot, write from the gut and make the reader feel . . . I mean, really feel. Most of all, *write*. Considering queries write for guidelines and or catalog 60¢. We have novels scheduled from unpublished fiction writers. Remain undaunted. Never take a rejection as a rejection but as a stepping stone to that one publisher who will say, yes! Never fear to take risks."

**QUINTESSENCE PUBLICATIONS (III)**, 356 Bunker Hill Mine Rd., Amador City CA 95601. (209)267-5470. Publisher: Marlan Beilke. Estab. 1976. Letterpress printer/publisher. Publishes hardcover and paperback originals. Books: Mohawk letterpress paper; high-quality letter press printing; Smythe sewn binding; line drawing illustrations; average print order: 1,500; first novel print order: 500. "Might" buy juvenile mss with illustrations.
**Needs:** Literary and regional. "We prefer work of a *literary* quality."
**How to Contact:** Query with SASE. Simultaneous and photocopied submissions OK. Reports in 2 weeks on queries, 1 month on mss. Publishes ms an average of 2 years after acceptance.
**Terms:** Open to negotiation. Sends galleys to author.
**Tips:** "We print/publish strictly letterpress editions—handset and linotype typography exclusively. We have the largest linotype facility in California."

**R&M PUBLISHING COMPANY, INC. (I)**, Box 1276, Holly Hill SC 20959. President: Mack B. Morant. Books: 60 lb white paper; perfect binding; b&w illustrations, color cover; average print order: 1,000-2,000. Estab. 1978. Number of titles: 2 in 1985. 2 planned for 1986.
**Needs:** Mystery, confession, women's, feminist, ethnic, psychic/supernatural, religious/inspirational. Accepts short stories from freelancers.
**How to Contact:** Query or submit ms. SASE always. Simultaneous and photocopied submissions OK. Reports in 1 month on queries, 8 weeks on mss.
**Terms:** "We will work things out with the author if we like the work." Sends galleys to author. No advance. Free book catalog.
**Tips:** "Write what you feel, and read everything available to stay in touch with the most recent trends or societal fads. We encourage first novelists."

**RANGER ASSOCIATES, INC. (II)**, 600 Washington Court, Guilderland NY 12084. (518)456-6401. Director of Publications: Sharon M. Lane. Estab. 1979. Small press with plans to expand; presently considers approximately 50 submissions per year, selecting 4-5 for publication. Publishes hardcover and paperback originals and reprints. Books: 50 lb paper; offset printing; perfect binding; illustrations; average print order: 5,000; first novel print order: 3,000. Plans 3-4 first novels this year. Averages 5 total titles, 1 fiction title each year. Usually critiques rejected ms.
**Needs:** Adventure, historical, and war. Accepts short stories from freelancers. Novel needs include military historical. No erotica. Recently published *Goodness Gracious*, by Harry Levitt (juvenile); *The Pestilence Plot*, by Betty Patterson (adventure/terrorism); and *A Special Breed of Man*, by Ed Edell (Vietnam war).

**How to Contact:** Query with SASE. Reports in 6 weeks on queries; 2-3 months on mss. Simultaneous and photocopied submissions OK. Accepts computer printout submissions. Prefers letter-quality. Disc submissions OK with Radio Shack Model 1. Prefers hard copy with disc submissions.

**Terms:** Individual arrangements with authors. Sends galleys to author. Pays in royalties of 5% minimum, 7% maximum; 25 author's copies; honorarium. Subsidy arrangement: copyright to author; author agrees to market book; author receives proportion of books related to subsidy, e.g., if author subsidizes at 50% of manufacturing costs, author receives 50% of books. Book catalog for SASE.

**Tips:** "Rewrite, review, rewrite. Let someone you dislike read your manuscript; rewrite once more before submitting. Will publish first novels if good enough. Novelist must be willing to promote his/her own work in every way possible. Small presses cannot afford to publish without *very* active author promotions."

**RDC PRESS (II)**, Box 5005, Red Deer, Alberta T4N 5H5 Canada. (403)342-3304. Editor: Dennis Johnson. Estab. 1972. Small institutionally affiliated publisher of poetry, short story collections and anthologies, biography, children's pictorial literature and drama. Publishes paperback and hardcover originals. Books: offset and quality stock paper; offset printing; softcover, some hard cover binding; illustrations; average print order: 500-3,000 copies. Averages 3-4 titles per year.

**Needs:** Quality children's stories and drama, queries for illustrations, short story collections.

**How to Contact:** Accepts unsolicited mss, but submit outline/synopsis with sample chapters with SASE or SAE and IRC. Reports in 3 months. Simultaneous and photocopied submissions OK. Publishes ms 1 year after acceptance.

**Terms:** Pays royalties of 7-12% depending on genre. Sends galleys to author. Advance is negotiable. Book catalog for SASE or SAE and IRC.

**Tips:** "Enclose publishing credits in submission, and offer concrete proposal for promoting a title." Published more fiction and more hardcovers last year."

**REALITIES LIBRARY (II)**, #76, 2745 Monterey Highway, San Jose CA 95111. (408)578-3546. Editor: Rick Soos. Estab. 1972. One-man operation on part-time basis. Publishes paperback originals. Plans 1 first novel this year. Averages 15 total titles, 1-2 fiction titles each year. Average first novel print order 2,000 copies. Occasionally critiques rejected ms.

**Needs:** Experimental and literary. "We need authors with novel approach to novel." Recently published *A Chimney Sweep Comes Clean*, by Chandler Brossard ("strange" novel).

**How to Contact:** Accepts unsolicited mss. Query or submit outline/synopsis and 1 sample chapter with SASE. Reports in 1 week on queries; 1 month on mss. Simultaneous and photocopied submissions OK. Accepts computer printout submissions. Prefers letter-quality.

**Terms:** Pays in royalties of 15% minimum or author's copies: 15% of press run (300). "Individual arrangement, if necessary." Writer's guidelines and book catalog for SASE.

**Tips:** "There is no 'average' reader, so write what's important, not what's watered for the masses. I'm personally looking more diligently at humor/satire."

**ROSSEL BOOKS (I, II, IV)**, 44 Dunbow Dr., Chappaqua NY 10514. (914)238-8954. President: Seymour Rossel. Estab. 1981. Small, specialized publishing firm serving the Jewish marketplace. Publishes hardcover and paperback originals and paperback reprints. Averages 5 total titles, 1 fiction title each year. Average first novel print order 2,500 copies. Occasionally critiques rejected mss.

**Needs:** Jewish, juvenile (easy-to-read, historical, picture book, spy/adventure, contemporary), and young adult (easy-to-read, fantasy/science fiction, historical, problem novels, spy/adventure). "We seek fiction manuscripts for young adults and juveniles only; must have Judaic content, since we specialize in Jewish publishing." No adult fiction.

**How to Contact:** Accepts unsolicited mss. Query first; submit outline-synopsis and 2 sample chapters with SASE. Simultaneous and photocopied submissions OK. Accepts computer printout

submissions. Prefers letter-quality. Reports in 2 weeks on queries; 1 month on mss. Publishes ms 12-18 months after acceptance.
**Terms:** Pays in negotiable royalties; negotiates advance. Book catalog for #10 SASE and 37¢ postage.
**Tips:** "As our list increases, we hope to expand our publishing of original fiction. We read all queries carefully!"

**ST. LUKE'S PRESS, INC. (II)**, Suite 401, Mid-Memphis Tower, 1407 Union, Memphis TN 38104. Consulting Editor: Dr. Robert Easson. Senior Editor: Phyllis Tickle. Editor: Dr. Kay Easson. Estab. 1975. Midsize independent publisher. Publishes hardcover and paperback originals. Books: offset printing; cloth binding; illustrations sometimes; average print order: 5,000; first novel print order: 5,000. Averages 10 total titles each year. Rarely critiques rejected mss.
**Needs:** "Open"
**How to Contact:** Accepts unsolicited mss. Submit outline/synopsis and 3 sample chapters with SASE. Simultaneous and photocopied submissions OK. Accepts computer printout submissions. Reports in 4-6 weeks on mss.
**Terms:** Pays "according to circumstances. Sends galleys to author. Individual arrangements with author depending on book, etc." Free book catalog on request.
**Tips:** "We like first novels if the author is Southern and has another manuscript or two in hand. We are publishing more fiction and more hardcovers. Published new writers last year."

**SALT LICK PRESS (I)**, 1804 E. 38½ St., Austin TX 78722. Imprint includes Lucky Heart Books. Publisher/Editor: James Haining. Estab. 1969. Publishes paperback originals. Books: bond paper; offset printing; saddle stitch, perfect bound, hand sewn binding; illustrations; average print order: 500; first novel print order: 500. Encourages new writers. Occasionally comments on rejected mss.
**Needs:** Contemporary, literary, experimental, women's, feminist, gay/lesbian, ethnic, erotica, psychic/supernatural, science fiction, fantasy, horror, humor/satire, and translations. Recently published *Next Services*, by Michalea Moore; *Happy Hour*, by R. Zielienski; and *Wrecking the Cactus*, by M. Cadnum .
**How to Contact:** Submit complete ms with SASE. No simultaneous submissions, photocopied submissions OK. Reports in 4-6 weeks on mss.
**Terms:** Pays in author's copies; no advance. Sends galleys to author.
**Tips:** "We are publishing more paperbacks than last year."

**SAMISDAT (II)**, Box 129, Richford VT 05476. Imprint includes *Samisdat Magazine*. Editor/Publisher: Merritt Clifton. Estab. 1973. Publishes paperback originals. Books: standard bond paper; offset printing; saddle-stitch or square back binding; illustrations sometimes; average print order: 300-500. Encourages new writers. "Over 60% of our titles are first books—about 1 first novel per year." Occasionally comments on rejected mss.
**Needs:** Literary, feminist, gay, lesbian, and regional. Recently published *Somebody's Brother*, by Carla Eugster (novel); *A Baseball Classic*, by Merritt Clifton (novel); and *Decade*, by Geoff Geiger (2 stories, several poems).
**How to Contact:** Query or submit complete ms. SASE always. Reports in 1 week on queries, time varies on mss.
**Terms:** No advance. Free book catalog with SASE. "Our author payments for books are a paradox: At this writing, we've published over 190 titles over the past 11 years, about 85% of which have earned the authors a profit. On the other hand, we've relatively seldom issued royalty checks—maybe 15 or 20 in all this time, and all for small amounts. We're also paradoxical in our modus operandi: Authors cover our cash expenses (this comes to about a third of the total publishing cost—we're supplying equipment and labor) in exchange for half of the press run, but we make no money from authors, and if we don't promote a book successfully, we still lose." Publishes ms from 2-6 months after acceptance.
**Tips:** "We do not wish to see *any* book-length ms submissions from anyone who has not already

either published in our quarterly magazine, *Samisdat*, or at least subscribed for about a year to find out who we are and what we're doing. We are not a 'market' engaged in handling books as commodities and are equipped to read only about one novel submission per month over and above our magazine submission load." Submissions are getting much slicker, with a lot less guts to them. This is precisely the opposite of what we're after. Our regular magazine contributors are providing all the book-length material we can handle right now. Read the magazine. Submit stories or poems or chapters to it. When familiar with us, and our subscribers, query about an appropriate book ms. We don't publish books except as special issues of the magazine, and blind submissions stand absolutely no chance of acceptance at all."

**SAN DIEGO PUBLISHING COMPANY**, Box 9222, San Diego CA 92109-0060. (619)698-5105. Editor-in-Chief/Fiction Editor: T.L. Thomson. Estab. 1980. Small press/self-publishing publisher. Two-man operation; subcontracts all book manufacturing. Publishes hardcover and paperback originals. Plans 4 first novels this year. Averages 4 total titles each year. Average first novel print order 3,000-10,000 copies. $40 quotation research fee; "refundable if author publishes with us."
**Needs:** "We consider all categories." Recently published *Laughing & Griping with the 97th Seabees*, by Rocky DeLaurentis (humor); and *Constitutional Convention—A Compelling Case for Enactment of Fair Enterprise Economics*.
**How to Contact:** Accepts unsolicited ms (must be accompanied by $40 quotation research fee). Send complete ms ("must be perfectly clean ms ready for production"). Reports in 2 weeks. Simultaneous and photocopied submissions OK. Accepts computer printout submissions. Prefers letter quality.
**Terms:** Author pays for publication. Sends galleys to author. "Author keeps all profits, rights, and books manufactured. We publish using author's money. The rest is all the author's property."
**Tips:** "We are not a subsidy publisher, vantage press, or royalty publisher. We take ms and return manufactured books to the author. We bill author *at cost* for printing and composition. We negotiate with author for cost of our services, which can be as little as $500. We thoroughly edit all stages of production, help with design, work closely with author, advise on marketing and sales. We require ½ of cost upon delivery of ms for production (composition stage) and balance of cost prior to printing and after review by author of camera-ready copy." Also, "we will ghost-write or rewrite any book for negotiated fee. Publisher offers 25 years of writing and publishing experience."

**SCHOOL OF LIVING PRESS (II)**, RD. 7, Box 388, York PA 17402. (717)755-2666. Editor: Mildred J. Loomis. Estab. 1936. Publishes paperback originals.
**Needs:** "We work only with titles that either fictionally or nonfictionally deal with human, decentralist social change. Recently published *Alternative Americas*.
**How to Contact:** Simultaneous and photocopied submissions OK. Reports in 1 week on queries, 1 month on mss.
**Terms:** Pays in 5 author's copies; no advance. Free brochure with SASE.
**Tips:** "We see a larger public interest in social change. Keep at it. Be clear, brief and illustrate with specifics. Avoid long treatises; be sure of researched facts."

**SEA FOG PRESS, INC. (II)**, Box 210056, San Francisco CA 94121-0056. (415)221-8527. President: Rose Evans. Estab. 1984. Small one-person press. Publishes hardcover and paperback originals. Occasionally critiques rejected ms.
**Needs:** Contemporary, ethnic, feminist, juvenile (animal, historical, contemporary), religious/inspirational, translations, war (anti-war theme), women's, and young adult/teen (historical, problem novels). "We are mainly interested in books that promote reverence for life, including animal welfare, animal rights, disabled achievement and disabled rights, social justice, peace, and reverence for human life." Recently published *The Whale's Tale*, by Deborah Evans Smith (children's).
**How to Contact:** Accepts unsolicited mss. Query first or submit outline/synopsis and 3 sample chapters with SASE. Reports in 2 weeks on queries. Simultaneous and photocopied submissions

OK. Accepts computer printout submissions. Prefers letter-quality.
**Terms:** Negotiates royalties and advance. Free writer's guidelines and book catalog.
**Tips:** "We are willing to publish a first novel if we like the manuscript."

**‡SECOND CHANCE PRESS AND THE PERMANENT PRESS (II)**, R.D.#2 Noyac Rd., Sag Harbor NY 11963. (516)725-1101. Editor: Judith Shepard. Estab. 1977. Small, independent publishers. Publishes hardcover originals. Books: average print order: 3,000; first novel print order: 3,000. Plans to publish 3 first novels this year. Averages 12 total titles; 8 fiction titles each year.
**Needs:** Adventure, contemporary, experimental, literary, mainstream, supsense/mystery. "I like novels that have a unique point of view and have a high quality of writing." No gothic, romance, horror, science fiction, pulp. Recently published *The Last Skiff*, by Donald Wetzel; and *The Zeal of the Convert*, by Bruce Wilkinson.
**How to Contact:** Query first. SASE. Agented fiction: 5%. Reports in 2 weeks on queries; 2 months on mss. Simultaneous and photocopied submissions OK. Accepts computer printouts.
**Terms:** Pays in royalties of 10% minimum; 15% maximum of net sales. Advance to $1,000. Sends galleys to author. Book catalog for $1.25.
**Tips:** Encourages first novelists.

**SECOND COMING PRESS (III)**, Box 31249, San Francisco CA 94131. (415)647-3679. Imprint includes Second Coming. Editor/Publisher: A.D. Winans. Estab. 1972. Publishes hardcover and paperback originals. Plans 1 first novel this year. Averages 3-4 total titles. Occasionally critiques rejected mss.
**Needs:** Contemporary, humor/satire, literary, science fiction, and short story collections. Recently published: *Skinny Dynamite*, by Jack Micheline (short story collection).
**How to Contact:** Accepts queries in spring and fall only. "Send sample chapter with outline." Simultaneous and photocopied submissions OK. Reports in 1-3 months on mss.
**Terms:** Pays in author's copies (10% print run). Book catalog available.

**SEVEN BUFFALOES PRESS (II)**, Box 249, Big Timber MT 59011. Editor/Publisher: Art Cuelho. Estab. 1975. Publishes paperback originals. Averages 4-5 total titles each year.
**Needs:** Contemporary, short story collections, "rural, American Hobo, Okies, American Indian, Southern Appalachia, Arkansas, and the Ozarks. Wants farm and ranch based stories. Recently published *Rig Nine*, by William Rintoul (collection of oilfield short stories).
**How to Contact:** Query first with SASE. Photocopied submissions OK. Reports in 1 week on queries; 2 weeks on mss.
**Terms:** Pays in royalties of 10% minimum, 15% on second edition or in author's copies (10% of edition). No advance. Free writer's guidelines and book catalog for SASE.
**Tips:** "There's too much influence from TV and Hollywood; media writing I call it. We need to get back to the people; to those who built and are still building this nation with sweat, blood, and brains. More people are into it for the money; instead of for the good writing that is still to be cranked out by isolated writers. Remember, I was a writer for 20 years before I became a publisher."

**SHAMELESS HUSSY PRESS (IV)**, Box 3092, Berkeley CA 94703. (415)547-1062. Publisher: Alta. Estab. 1969. Book: 50 lb white paper; offset printing; perfect bound binding; illustrations; average print order: 1,000-3,000; first novel print order: 1,000-3,000.
**Needs:** Contemporary, literary, experimental, spy, historical, women's, feminist, ethnic, fantasy, humor/satire, juvenile, and young adult. Accepts short stories for text. "Our specialty is women's and feminist." Recently published *The Wise Queen*, by K. Simon (children's fiction).
**How to Contact:** Submit outline/synopsis and sample chapters. SASE for query and ms. Simultaneous and photocopied submissions OK. Reports in 6 months. Publishes ms 2-4 years after acceptance.
**Terms:** Pays in author's copies; no advance. Free book catalog.
**Tips:** "We are publishing less—2-3 books a year rather than 3-4. We encourage first novelists."

**THE SMITH (II)**, 5 Beekman St., New York NY 10038. Editor: Harry Smith. Managing Editor: Tom Tolnay. Estab. 1964. Publishes paperback originals. Books: 50 lb bookmark stock paper; offset printing; perfect bound binding; illustrations sometimes; average print order: 1,500; first novel print order: 1,500.
**Needs:** Fiction, poetry with Literary merit. "Only two titles per year currently. Very little market." Recently published *Hearing Out*, by James T. Farrell; and *Traffic*, by Tom Smith.
**How to Contact:** Submit short outline and/or single chapter with SASE.
**Terms:** Pays by outright purchase of $500-1,000; no advance. Free book catalog.
**Tips:** Books published are by writers already published in *Pulpsmith* magazine.

**SOMRIE PRESS (I)**, Ryder Street Station, Box 328, Brooklyn NY 11234. Publisher/Editor: Robert A. Frauenglas. Estab. 1979. One-person operation on part-time basis with plans to expand. Publishes paperback originals. Books: paper varies; offset printing; perfect bound binding; 1-2 photos, b&w line illustrations; average print order: 500; first novel print order: 500. Encourages new writers. Averages one total title (fiction) each year. Rarely critiques rejected ms.
**Needs:** Adventure, contemporary, erotica, ethnic (Jewish), experimental, fantasy, historical, humor/satire, literary, regional (Brooklyn), and short story collections. "Novel needs depend upon our finances. We are attempting to grow. We are looking for books by and for and about the people and places in Brooklyn, NY. No genre or overtly religious."
**How to Contact:** Accepts unsolicited mss. Query first with SASE. Reports in 2 weeks on queries. Simultaneous and photocopied submissions OK. Accepts computer printout submissions. Prefers letter-quality.
**Terms:** Depends on grant/award money. Sends galleys to author. "We have done cooperative publishing with the author. If I like the book, but don't have the money to publish, I might make an individual arrangement with the author."
**Tips:** Encourages first novelists. "We regard author/editor relationships like a marriage with lots of give and go."

**‡SPACE AND TIME (IV)**, 138 W. 70th St. (4-B), New York NY 10023-4432. Book Editor: Jani Anderson. Estab. 1966—book line 1984. Two-person operation on part-time basis. Publishes paperback originals. Books: 50 lb Lakewood white 512PPi paper; offset Litho printing; perfect binding; illustrations on cover only; average print order: 1,000; first novel print order: 1,000. Averages 1-2 total titles; 1-2 fiction titles each year. Critiques or comments on rejected ms.
**Needs:** Fantasy, horror, psychic/supernatural/occult, science fiction. Wants to see cross-genre material, such as horror-western, sf-mystery, occult-spy adventure, etc. "Our 1986 line is set, but we're looking at proposals for 1987 publication." Does not want anything *without* some element of fantasy or sf (or at least the 'feel' of same). Recently published *The Steel Eye*, by Chet Gottfried (sf-mystery); *The Spy Who Drank Blook*, by Gordon Linzner (occult-spy-sf); *Bringing Down the Moon*, by Jani Anderson (anthology-fantasy-horror).
**How to Contact:** Accepts unsolicited mss. Query first or submit outline/synopsis and 2 sample chapters. Reports in 4-6 weeks on queries; 3-4 months on mss. Simultaneous and photocopied submissions OK. Prefer photocopies.
**Terms:** Pays in royalties of 10% based on cover price and print run, within 60 days of publication (additional royalties, if going back to press). Average advance $100, negotiable. Sends galleys to author. Book catalog free on request.
**Tips:** "We encourage first novelists, and published new writers last year."

**SPINSTERS INK PUBLISHING CO. (II)**, Box 410687, San Francisco CA 94141. (415)647-9360. Editor: Sherilyn Thomas. Estab. 1978. Moderate size women's publishing company growing steadily. Publishes paperback originals and reprints. Books: 55 lb acid free natural paper; photo offset printing; perfect binding; illustrations when appropriate; average print order: 3,000. Plans 3 first novels this year. Averages 6 total titles, 3-5 fiction titles each year. Occasionally critiques rejected ms.
**Needs:** Feminist, lesbian, and women's. Wants "full-length quality fiction—thoroughly revised novels which display deep characterization, theme and style. We *only* consider books by women.

No books by men, or books with sexist, racist, or ageist content." Recently published *The Woman Who Owned the Shadows*, by Paula Gunn Allen (native-American); and *Winter Passage*, by Judith McDaniel (traditional).

**How to Contact:** Accepts unsolicited mss. Query or submit outline/synopsis and 3 sample chapters with SASE. Reports in 4 weeks on queries; 2 months on mss. No simultaneous submissions without specific permission; photocopied submissions OK. Accepts computer printout submissions. Prefers letter-quality. Disc submissions OK with Morrow Designs MDII system. Prefers hard copy with disc submission.

**Terms:** Pays in royalties of 8% minimum, 12% maximum (after 5,000) plus 25 author's copies; unlimited extra copies at 50% discount. Free book catalog.

**Tips:** "Our recent titles are primarily feminist and/or lesbian. We are interested in first novels, provided they are not early drafts and that the author is open to significant editorial input. Our press is in a period of rapid growth and will be publishing more titles and more novels steadily each year. We published new writers last year. We regard the author/editor relationship as interactive and complementary."

**SPIRITUAL FICTION® PUBLICATIONS (II, IV)**, Subsidiary of: Garber Communications, Inc., 5 Garber Hill Rd., Blauvelt NY 10913. (914)359-9292. Editor-in-Chief: Bernard J. Garber. Fiction Editor: Patricia Abrams. Midsize publisher. Averages 4-5 titles each year. Average first novel print order 5,000 copies paperback; 1,000 copies cloth.

**Needs:** Psychic/supernatural/occult, historical, religious/inspirational, and science. No science fiction. Recently published or reprinted: *Zanoni: A Rosicrucian Tale*, by Edward Bulwer-Lytton; *A Romance of Two Worlds*, by Marie Corelli; and *Seraphita* by Balzac.

**How to Contact:** Accepts unsolicited mss. Query first or send 2-3 page outline, plus 10-15 pages of sample chapter. SASE with query, ms. Photocopied submissions OK. Reports in 2 weeks on queries; 2 months on mss. Publishes ms 6-12 months after acceptance.

**Terms:** Must return advance if book is not completed or is not acceptable.

**Tips:** "Read what we have published. We accept first novels if they are good."

**‡STAR BOOKS, INC. (IV)**, 408 Pearson St., Wilson NC 27893. (919)237-1591. President: Irene Burk Harrell. Estab. 1983. "One-person operation expecting to become BIG." Publishes paperback originals and reprints. Books: quality paperback paper; offset printing; perfect binding; illustrations sometimes; average print order: 1,000-10,000. "Expect to publish first novel in 1986." Critiques on rejected ms for $25 minimum, $1 per page.

**Needs:** Juvenile (5-9 years; religious), religious/inspirational, Christian "romance." Needs for novels include Christian themes, also Christian romances. No mss without a Christian emphasis.

**How to Contact:** Accepts unsolicited ms. Submit complete ms with cover letter. SASE. Reports in 4 weeks on queries; 3 months on ms. Photocopied submissions OK. Accepts computer printouts.

**Terms:** Pays in royalties of 8% minimum; 15% maximum and 20 author's copies. Sends galleys to author. Author has helped with production cost financing on two of our three major books out so far. Next book financed by publisher. "As a new company we are feeling our way along here and expect to be financing books ourselves on a regular basis before the end of the next year." Individual arrangements vary. Book catalog for #10 SASE and 39¢ postage.

**Tips:** "We do expect to be publishing fiction before the end of 1986. We encourage first novelists."

**STATION HILL PRESS (II, III)**, Barrytown NY 12507. (914)758-5840. Imprints include Open Book and Cordella, Artext, Clinamen Studies, and Contemporary Artists Series. Publishers: George Quasha and Susan Quasha. Estab. 1978. Publishes paperback and cloth originals. Averages 10-15 total titles, 5-7 fiction titles each year.

**Needs:** Contemporary, experimental, literary, translations, and new age. "We are interested in 2-3 short- to medium-length novels, novella, or short story collections by gifted writers." Recently published *When the Time Comes* and *Vicious Circles*, by Maurice Blanchot (novellas); *Violence*

*and Defiance*, by Herbert Lust (first novel experimental); and *The Scorpions*, by Robert Kelly (experimental).
**How to Contact:** Query first with SASE before sending ms. Reports in 4-6 weeks on queries; 4 months on mss.
**Terms:** Pays in author's copies (10% of print run) or by standard royalty, depending on the nature of the material. Occasional subsidy publishing. "Co-venture arrangements are possible with higher royalty." Book catalog free on request.

**STEELDRAGON PRESS (III)**, Box 7253, Powderhorn Station, Minneapolis MN 55407. (612)721-6076. Fiction Editors: Will Shetterly and Emma Bull. Estab. 1984. Publishes hardcover and paperback originals and reprints. Books: acid-free paper; offset printing; Smythe sewn binding; illustrations; average print order: 1,000. "It is extremely unlikely that we would publish a new writer." Critiques rejected ms if requested.
**Needs:** Fantasy. No horror or sword-and-sorcery. Recently published *To Reign in Hell*, by Steven Brust; and *The Time of the Warlock*, by Larry Niven.
**How to Contact:** Accepts unsolicited mss. Query first or submit outline/synopsis and 1-3 sample chapters with SASE. Reports in 1 month on queries; 3 months on mss. Simultaneous and photocopied submissions OK. Accepts computer printout submissions. Prefers letter-quality.
**Terms:** Pays in royalties of 8% minimum, 10% maximum; negotiates advance. Sends galleys to author. Writer's guidelines and book catalog for SASE.
**Tips:** "The author/editor relationship is a supportive one that requires tolerance on both sides; after all, both are after the same thing; the best possible book. Study your craft. Write often. Submit constantly."

**STILL POINT PRESS (II)**, 4222 Willow Grove Rd., Dallas TX 75220. (214)352-8282. Editor/Publisher: Charlotte T. Whaley. Estab. 1984. Small independent publisher, producing a few books each year. Publishes hardcover originals. Books: acid-free Warrens olde style, 60 lb paper; letterpress, offset, photocomposition printing; cloth (Roxite B grade) case binding; photos, engravings, drawings; average print order: 1,000 trade editions; 300 limited editions.
**Needs:** Literary and short story collections. Novels in late 1986. "We are interested in publishing in the future an annual collection of short fiction, to be called the *Still Point Stories*."
**How to Contact:** Does not accept unsolicited mss. Query with SASE. Reports in 3 weeks on queries. Simultaneous and photocopied submissions OK. Accepts computer printout submissions. Prefers letter-quality.
**Terms:** Individual arrangement with author, depending on the book. Sends galleys to author. Pays in royalties of 10% minimum, 15% maximum; 6 author's copies; contingent advance.
**Tips:** "In late 1986 we will consider first novels of high merit by competent writers of serious literature. Query. We regard author/editor relationships a friendly, collaborative effort."

**STILLPOINT PUBLISHING**, Box 640, Walpole NH 03608. (603)756-3508. Imprints include Angelfood Books. Executive Editor: Caroline M. Myss. Estab. 1983. Midsize publisher in the field of human consciousness. Publishes hardcover and paperback originals and reprints. Averages 10-12 total titles, 2-4 fiction titles each year. Average first novel print order 4,000-7,500 copies.
**Needs:** Fantasy, juvenile (easy-to-read, fantasy), psychology/new age physics, spirituality, channelled material and religious/inspirational. Novel needs include "adult and children's books which promote a greater understanding of oneself and the world. We only want fantasy, consciousness fiction." Recently published *Butterfly*, by John M. Beach (fiction/consciousnes).
**How to Contact:** Accepts unsolicited mss. Submit complete ms with SASE. Reports in 2

---

 **The double dagger before a listing indicates that the listing is new in this edition. New markets are often the most receptive to freelance contributions.**

months. Simultaneous and photocopied submissions OK. Accepts computer printout submissions. Prefers letter-quality. Disc submissions OK with Altos 515, Spellbinder system.
**Terms:** Pays in graduated royalties, 7½-15% on net; no advance. Book catalog free.
**Tips:** "Realizing first novels take more time to develop, we balance them with others. We publish nonfiction predominantly—fiction where it falls into our field."

**STORY PRESS (II)**, Box 10040, Chicago IL 60610. (312)442-7295. Editor: Richard Meade. Editorial Director: David Meade. Estab. 1978. Publishes hardcover and paperback originals. Books: 60 lb offset paper; offset printing; perfect and casebound binding; illustrations; average print order: 1,000; first novel print order: 1,000. Encourages new writers. Occasionally comments on rejected mss.
**Needs:** Contemporary, literary, women's, and ethnic. "We are a literary press and are not interested in most kinds of popular fiction. We publish fiction, photography, guide books. We also are interested in talented illustrators." Recently published *Crimes of Passion*, by David Jauss; *Squid Soup*, by Michael Mooney (short fiction); and *August Heat*, by Richard Dokey (short stories).
**How to Contact:** Query with SASE. Simultaneous and photocopied submissions OK. Reports in 2 weeks on queries, 3 months on mss.
**Terms:** Pays in author's copies (10% of press run); no advance. Sends galleys to author. Writer's guidelines for SASE. Free book catalog. Publishes ms an average of 9 months after acceptance.
**Tips:** "We notice movement toward interior landscapes away from fiction with a clear narrative line. In the next few years we foresee fewer outlets for literary fiction, especially short stories. We try to keep open an outlet for serious short fiction, promoting our titles extensively. We are currently undergoing a shift toward work which supports feminist issues. Publishing less fiction this year because we have moved into other areas of interest. We regard the author/editor relationship as crucial. The editor must work to aid the writer in creating the best work, without violating the spirit of the text. Write a good query letter. Have a good book. Submit to the right publisher."

**STUDIA HISPANICA EDITORS (IV)**, Box 7304, UT Station, Austin TX 78713. Attention: Luis Ramos-Garcia. (512)471-9113 (request to speak to Dave Oliphant). Imprints include Prickly Pear Press. Fiction Editor: Dave Oliphant. Estab. 1978. Small independent publisher (a group operation on part-time basis). Publishes paperback originals. Books: 60-70 lb off-white paper; offset printing; perfect binding; illustrations; average print order: 500-1,000. Averages 2 total titles, 1 fiction title each year.
**Needs:** Contemporary, ethnic, literary, regional, short story collections and translations. Especially needs regional novels and novel translations. No horror or science fiction. Recently published *Tales from Austin* and *A South American Trilogy*, edited by L.A.R.G.; and *From the Threshold: Contemporary Peruvian Fiction in Translation* (short stories).
**How to Contact:** Does not accept unsolicited mss. Query with SASE. Reports in 3 weeks. No simultaneous submissions; photocopied submissions OK. Accepts computer printout submissions. Prefers letter-quality.
**Terms:** "Author pays for all expenses except salaries, design (inside and cover). We keep 25% of published books and deliver the rest to author(s). 50% of all expenses should be paid in advance and 50% upon notice of release." Sends galleys to author. Book flyers for SASE.
**Tips:** "Our recent title lists are moving towards Texas and Latin American fiction—more regional (southwest) and international interest."

**SUCCESS PUBLICATIONS**, Box 3931, Regina, Saskatchewan S4T 3N9 Canada. (306)522-2459. President: Helen Stec. Estab. 1983. One-person operation on part-time basis. Publishes hardcover and paperback originals. Occasionally critiques rejected ms.
**Needs:** Ethnic, experimental, faction, fantasy, horror, and literary.
**How to Contact:** Does not accept unsolicited mss. Submit outline/synopsis and 3 sample chapters with SASE or SAE and IRC. Reports in 2 months on queries. Simultaneous and photocopied submissions OK. Accepts computer printout submissions. Prefers letter-quality.
**Terms:** "We subsidy publish. Author is actually publisher. We arrange for the printing, marketing and distribution of books."
**Tips:** "Essentially a how-to publisher with interest in fiction."

**SUN & MOON PRESS (III)**, 6363 Wilshire Blvd., Suite 115, Los Angeles CA 90048. (213)653-6711. Imprints include New American Fiction series. Subsidiary of the Contemporary Arts Educational Project, Inc. Editor-in-Chief: Douglas Messerli. Estab. 1979. Publishes hardcover and paperback originals and reprints. Books: acid-free high quality paper; offset printing; perfect and Smythe sewn binding; average print order: 3,000; first novel print order: 1,500. Averages 15 total titles, 10 fiction titles each year. Occasionally critiques "if quality ms."
**Needs:** Contemporary, experimental, literary, mainstream, short story collections, translations, and women's. Recently published *New Jerusalem*, by Len Jenkin; *The Contemporary American Fiction*, edited by Douglas Messerli; and *The Relation of My Imprisonment*, by Russell Banks.
**How to Contact:** Submit complete ms with SASE. Photocopied submissions OK. Reports in 3 months on mss.
**Terms:** Pays in royalties of 10%. Sends galleys to author. Book catalog for 39¢ postage.
**Tips:** Publishing more fiction in paper and cloth; have new line, New American Fiction Series. Published new writers last year.

**SUNSTONE PRESS (II)**, Box 2321, Santa Fe NM 87504-2321. (505)988-4418. President: James C. Smith Jr. Estab. 1971. Midsize publisher. Publishes hardcover and paperback originals. Plans 2 first novels this year. Averages 8-12 total titles; 3-4 fiction titles each year. "Sometimes" buys juvenile mss with illustrations. Average first novel print order 2,000 copies.
**Needs:** Juvenile and young adult (historical). "We have a Southwestern theme emphasis." Recently published *Ways of Indian Magic*, by Teresa Van Etten (Indian theme); *Walks Two Worlds*, by Robert B. Fox (Indian theme); and *Curandero*, by Jose Ortiz y Pino (Spanish historical).
**How to Contact:** Accepts unsolicited mss. Submit outline/synopsis and 2 sample chapters with SASE. Reports in 6 weeks. Simultaneous and photocopied submissions OK. Accepts computer printout submissions. Prefers letter-quality. Publishes ms 9-12 months after acceptance.
**Terms:** Pays in royalties, 10% maximum.
**Tips:** "Don't send complete manuscript unless requested to do so. We encourage first novelists."

**‡SWAMP PRESS**, 323 Pelham Rd., Amherst MA 01002. Chief Editor: Ed Rayher. Estab. 1977. One-person part-time. Publishes hardcover and originals and paperback originals. Books: hardcover/mouldmade paper; letterpress printing; hard/soft binding; illustrations; average print order: 200 softcovers, 100 hardbound. Averages 3 total titles, 1 fiction title each year. Critiques or comments on rejected ms.
**Needs:** Experimental, literary, short story collections, translations. Recently published *Thus May be Figured in Numberless Ways*, by Bonie Gordon (short-story narrative).
**How to Contact:** Accepts unsolicited mss. SASE. Query first or submit outline/synopsis and 1 or 2 sample chapters or complete ms with cover letter. SASE. Reports in 2 months on queries; 2 months on mss. Simultaneous and photocopied submissions OK. Accepts computer printouts including dot-matrix.
**Terms:** Pays in author's copies 10% of run, depending on grant/award money. Individual arrangement with author. Sends galleys to author. Writer's guidelines free for SASE and 1 first class stamp. Book catalog free on request.
**Tips:** Encourages first novelists.

**TEAL PRESS**, Box 4346, Portsmouth NH 03801. (603)431-2319. Editor: Robert Jebb. Estab. 1983. Small press publishing 3-4 titles per year. Publishes hardcover and paperback originals. Average first novel print order 500 hardcover, 1,000 paperback copies.
**Needs:** Contemporary and literary. Especially needs "serious novels that deal with the diversity, complexity of our age." Recently published *Heirs of a Mongrel*, by Richard B. Davidson.
**How to Contact:** Accepts unsolicited mss. Submit outline/synopsis and sample chapters or complete ms with SASE. Reports in 1 month on mss. Simultaneous and photocopied submissions OK.
**Terms:** Pays in royalties of 10% minimum.
**Tips:** "Will consider first novel if author is willing to work with small press editor. We are seeking

manuscripts that do not pander to mass market and best seller mentality. Make sure manuscript is clean copy, free of grammatical and other errors and that it has been edited as many times as necessary for author's full confidence in his own work."

**THIRD WORLD PRESS**, 7524 S. Cottage Grove Ave., Chicago IL 60619. (312)651-0700. Assistant Editor: Rose L. Blouin. Estab. 1967. Small independent publisher with plans to expand. Publishes hardcover and paperback originals. Plans 2 first novels this year. Averages 10 total titles, 3 fiction titles each year. Average first novel print order 15,000 copies.

**Needs:** Ethnic, historical, juvenile (animal, easy-to-read, fantasy, historical, contemporary), preschool/picture book, science fiction, short story collections, and young adult/teen (easy-to-read/teen, fantasy/science fiction, historical). "We primarily publish nonfiction, but will consider fiction by and about Blacks."

**How to Contact:** Accepts unsolicited mss. Query or submit outline/synopsis and 1 sample chapter with SASE. Reports in 3 weeks on queries; 2 months on mss. Simultaneous and photocopied submissions OK. Accepts computer printout submissions. Prefers letter-quality.

**Terms:** Individual arrangement with author depending on the book, etc.

**THISTLEDOWN PRESS (LITERARY PUBLISHER) (II)**, 668 E. Place, Saskatoon, Saskatchewan S7J 2Z5 Canada. Editor-in-Chief: Mr. P. O'Rourke. Estab. 1975. Publishes hardcover and paperback originals. Books: quality stock paper; offset printing; Smythe-sewn binding; occasionally illustrations. Occasionally critiques rejected mss.

**Needs:** Literary. Fiction needs (limited.) "We *only* want to see Canadian-authored submissions."

**How to Contact:** Accepts unsolicited mss. Query first with SASE. Photocopied submissions OK. Reports in 2 months on queries.

**Terms:** Pays in royalties of 10% maximum. Sends galleys to author. Free writer's guidelines and book catalog.

**Tips:** To date, has published 3 collections of short stories—Canadian authored. Publishing more fiction in both hardcover and paperback. "We always encourage first novelists. We regard the author/editor relationships as cooperative/sensitive. Be persistent."

**THREE TREES PRESS**, 2 Silver Ave., Toronto, Ontario M6R 3A4 Canada. (416)534-4456. Publisher: W. Horak. Estab. 1976. Small independent publisher with plans to expand. Publishes paperback and hardcover originals. Averages 9 fiction titles each year. "Sometimes" buys juvenile mss with illustrations. Buys less than 5% agented fiction. Average first novel print order 2,000-3,000 quality paperback plus 10-20% hardcover-type paperback copies.

**Needs:** Juvenile (fantasy, picture book, contemporary), and young adult (fantasy). Canadian authors only.

**How to Contact:** Accepts unsolicited mss. Submit outline/synopsis and sample chapters with SASE or SAE and IRC. Reports in 2 months on mss. Photocopied submissions OK. No multiple submissions.

**Terms:** Pays in royalties of 10% maximum. Writer's guidelines and book catalog for SASE or SAE and IRC. Publishes ms 12-24 months after acceptance.

**Tips:** "Only Canadian citizens or residents need apply. Stress on flair and imagination. Read other Three Trees books before submitting. We mainly need text for picture books."

**THRESHOLD BOOKS (IV)**, RD 3, Box 208, Dusty Ridge Rd., Putney VT 05346. (802)387-4586. Director: Edmund Helminski. Fiction Editor: Camille Helminski. Estab. 1981. Small independent publisher with plans for gradual expansion. Publishes paperback originals. Books: 60 lb natural paper; offset litho printing; sew-wrap binding; average print order: 2,500; first novel print order; 2,000. Plans 1 first novel this year. Averages 2-3 total titles, 1 fiction title each year. Occasionally critiques rejected ms.

**Needs:** Literary and translations. "We are interested in fiction based on Islamic, Third World or oriental subjects." Recently published *I Come From Behind KAF Mountain*, by Murat Yagan (autobiographical).

**How to Contact:** Accepts unsolicited mss. Query first, submit outline/synopsis and sample chapters or complete ms with SASE. Reports in 3 weeks on queries; 5 weeks on mss. Simultaneous and photocopied submissions OK. Accepts computer printout submissions. Prefers letter-quality. Publishes ms an average of 18 months after acceptance.
**Terms:** Pays in royalties of 10% of net. Sometimes sends galleys to author. Book catalog free on request.
**Tips:** "We are still small and publishing little fiction." Published "less fiction, more paperbacks due to our particular area of concentration and our size."

**TIDE BOOK PUBLISHING COMPANY**, Box 101, York Harbor ME 03911. Subsidiary of Tide Media. President: Rose Safran. Estab. 1979. Independent, small publisher. Publishes paperback originals. Averages 1 title each year. Occasionally critiques rejected mss.
**Needs:** Contemporary, contemporary romance, feminist, historical, humor/satire, literary, mainstream, regional, and women's. Needs women's novels with a social service thrust; contemporary. No gothic, trash.
**How to Contact:** Query first; submit outline synopsis and 1-2 sample chapters with SASE. Simultaneous submissions OK. Accepts computer printout submissions. Prefers letter-quality. Reports in 1 month on queries and mss.
**Terms:** Pays in 100 author's copies. Considering cost plus subsidy arrangements—will advertise.

**‡THE TRANSLATION CENTER (II)**, 307A Mathematics, Columbia U., New York NY 10027. (212)280-2305. Managing Editor: Diane G.H. Cook. Editors: Frank MacShane, William Jay Smith, Lane Dunlop. Estab. 1974. Publishes paperback originals. Averages 2 total titles/year.
**Needs:** Translations.
**How to Contact:** Accepts unsolicited ms. Submit complete ms with cover letter and SASE. Photocopied submissions OK. Accepts computer printouts including dot-matrix.
**Terms:** Pays in 3 author's copies. Writer's guidelines free for #10 SAE and 1 first class stamp. Book catalog free for #10 SAE and 1 first class stamp.

**TREE FROG PRESS (II)**, 10144-89 St., Edmonton, Alberta T5H 1P7 Canada. (403)429-1947. Fiction Editor: Allan Shute. Estab. 1971. "Small press intent on publishing good literature for kids." Publishes paperback originals. Averages 4 total titles (fiction) each year. Average first novel print order 1,500 copies. Occasionally critiques rejected ms "if time, and ms will benefit from the time thus spent."
**Needs:** Juvenile (animal, easy-to-read, fantasy, historical, sports, spy/adventure, contemporary), and young adult/teen (easy-to-read, fantasy/science fiction, historical, problem novels, sports, spy/adventure). "We do not accept anthropomorphic works generally—those that turn animals into semi-humans." Recently published *Prophecy of Tau Ridoo*, by Welwyn Katz (fantasy); *Comet's Tale*, by Sue Ann Alderson (fantasy); and *Beyond His Balloon*, by The Children of La Loche & Friends (English and Chipewyan counting book).
**How to Contact:** Accepts unsolicited mss. "We will review *only* manuscripts by Canadian authors." Preference: Alberta authors. Submit complete ms with SASE (Canadian stamps). Reports in 2 months. Simultaneous submissions OK. "We prefer to see photocopies, not originals." Welcomes computer printout submissions. Prefers letter-quality.
**Terms:** Pays in royalties; author's copies. Sends galleys to author. Writer's guidelines for SASE (Canadian stamps) with 35¢ postage. Book catalog for SASE with 35¢ postage.
**Tips:** "We prefer children's books written from a child's viewpoint." Publishes more fiction than in the past (new computer typesetter—easier, faster storage). "We have and continue to publish a variety of first and subsequent novels. A first novel receives no special treatment or consideration. We want a fresh idea touched with a sense of magic and groomed so well that the grooming does not show."

**TRES AMIGOS PUBLICATIONS**, 26325 Carmelo, Carmel CA 93923. (408)625-1579. Publisher: Richard Tevis. "Small staff, large expectations." Publishes hardcover and paperback originals. Will consider first novels. Estab. 1983.

**Needs:** Adventure, contemporary, faction, fantasy, historical, humor/satire, literary, and mainstream. "We are interested only in work of exceptional literary merit." Occasionally critiques rejected mss.
**How to Contact:** Accepts unsolicited mss. Query with SASE. Reports in 2 weeks.
**Terms:** Individual agreement with author depending on the book.

**TRIPLE 'P' PUBLICATIONS INTERNATIONAL (II)**, Box 1321, Kendall Square, Cambridge MA 02142. (617)437-1856. Subsidiaries include *Persuasion Magazine* and *The Kiosk Newsletter*. Editorial Manager: Eugene FPC de Mesne. Fiction Editor: Monica Selwyn-Jones. Estab. 1974. Independent publisher with expansion plans. Publishes hardcover and paperback originals. Books: Velum/mottled paper (depending on type of book published); offset printing from print-set mock-ups; hardbound binding (unless paperback when card stock is used); illustrations infrequently; average print and first novel order 250 copies (first ed.) Plans 2 first novels this year. Average 3-4 total titles, 3-4 fiction titles each year. Buys 60% agented fiction.
**Needs:** Adventure, fantasy, horror, historical, historical romance, literary, psychic/supernatural/occult, regional ("must be solid entertainment"), science fiction, short story collections; feminist, gay, and lesbian ("if done subtly with emphasis on plot"). Needs "the unusual, bizarre, suspense story, with definable characters, and tight plots, set in different periods of history. No melodramas. We do *not* want fiction that conforms to life, but rather, fiction that gives the reader an unusual view of human struggle and coping with situations that arise. No pat solutions or trite romance mush will be considered. Also, no religion or political harangues, please." Recently published *Kingdom of Ants* (man versus religion, politics and society), *The Tea Rose* (exposé about momism), and *Animal, Animal* (the inner self), all written by Julian Ocean.
**How to Contact:** Query to editorial manager with SASE, brief outline, business-like letter only. Simultaneous and photocopied submissions OK. Accepts computer printout submissions. Prefers letter-quality. Reports in 4-6 weeks on queries. Publishes ms an average of 6 months after acceptance.
**Terms:** Negotiates advance. Sends galleys to author to check.
**Tips:** "Fiction is our mainstay." Wants to see "unusual slants on the human experience, with well-developed characters the reader can identify with, and plots that are not only believable but remain with the reader long after he has finished the story. Each book is treated as a separate entity. We have found flexibility is most advantageous. Books of any subject *must* be individual and stand out. First novels must be *unusual*, interesting to the general reader, and have sales prospects and potential. Always write a very good, biting, query letter. Above all, have something to write about—something that will interest others."

**TURNSTONE PRESS**, 6th Floor, 99 King St., Winnipeg, Manitoba R3B 1H7 Canada. (204)947-1555. Estab. 1976. Publishes paperback originals. Averages 8 total titles. Occasionally critiques rejected ms.
**Needs:** Experimental and literary. "We have just started to consider and publish fiction, and will be doing only 2-3 a year. Interested in new work exploring new narrative/fiction forms."
**How to Contact:** Query first with SASE or SAE and IRC. Photocopied submissions OK. Reports in 1 month on queries; 2-4 months on mss.
**Terms:** "Like most Canadian literary presses, we depend heavily on government grants which are not available for books by nonCanadians." Pays in royalties of 10%; 10 (complimentary) author's copies. Book catalog free on request.

**22 PRESS (I, II)**, Box 6236, Wilmington DE 19804. (302)655-3223. Publishers: Terry Persun and Jean Persun. Estab. 1979. Three-man operation on part-time basis. Publishes paperback originals. Plans 1-2 first novels this year. Occasionally critiques rejected ms.
**Needs:** Contemporary, experimental, fantasy, literary, science fiction, short story collections, suspense/mystery. "We published *Goblets* poetry magazine for several years. No books have been printed to date, but we are reading. We do have two mss in house which we expect to have completed for an '86 deadline."

**How to Contact:** Accepts unsolicited mss. Query first or submit outline/synopsis and 3 sample chapters with SASE. Reports in 3 weeks on queries; 2 months on mss. Photocopied submissions OK. Accepts computer printout submissions. Publishes ms an average of 1 year after acceptance.
**Terms:** "Totally negotiable." Sends galleys to author.
**Tips:** "We encourage first novelists. Send whatever is requested to all those houses that take simultaneous submissions. Keep records of where the work is, and when (or if) all the copies return rejected, hit everyone else one at a time."

**ULTRAMARINE PUBLISHING CO., INC. (III)**, Box 303, Hastings-on-the-Hudson NY 10706. (914)478-2522. Publisher: Christopher P. Stephens. Estab. 1973. Small publisher. "We have 150 titles in print. We also distribute for authors where a major publisher has dropped a title." Encourages new writers. Averages 15 total titles, 12 fiction titles each year. Buys 90% agented fiction. Occasionally critiques rejected ms.
**Needs:** Experimental, fantasy, mainstream, science fiction, and short story collections. No romance, westerns, mysteries.
**How to Contact:** Accepts unsolicited mss. Submit outline/synopsis and 2 sample chapters with SASE. Prefers agented ms. Reports in 6 weeks. Photocopied submissions OK. Accepts computer printout submissions. Publishes ms an average of 8 months after acceptance.
**Terms:** Pays in royalties of 10% minimum; advance is negotiable. Sends galleys to author. Free book catalog.
**Tips:** "We encourage first novelists."

**UNDERWOOD/MILLER (III)**, 651 Chestnut St., Columbia PA 17512. (717)684-7335. Imprints include Underwood/Miller and Branoywyne Books. Publisher: Chuck Miller. Estab. 1976. Publishes hardcover originals and reprints. Books: acid free paper; offset printing; Smythe sewn, full cloth, binding; illustrations; average print order 1,000. Averages 12 total titles, 10 fiction titles each year.
**Needs:** Open.
**How to Contact:** Query first with SASE. Simultaneous and photocopied submissions OK. Reports on queries in 1 month.
**Terms:** Pays in royalties of 10% minimum; negotiable advance. Sometimes sends galleys to author. Book catalog free on request.

**UNIQUE GRAPHICS (I, II)**, 1025 55th St., Oakland CA 94608. (415)655-3024. Subsidiaries include Owlflight Books and *Empire*. Editor: Millea Kenin. Estab. 1981. Small magazine publisher expanding into small trade paperback lines. Publishes paperback originals. Books: 20 lb paper; offset printing; perfect binding (trade paperback); b&w illustrations; color on cover; average print order: 1,500. Averages 2 total titles, 1 fiction title each year. Buys juvenile and adult mss with or without illustrations. No novels. Occasionally critiques rejected ms.
**Needs:** Experimental (if also fantasy), fantasy, science fiction, and short story collections. "We are only interested in novellas or short story collections. We are particularly interested in fiction, 10,000-40,000 words." No mss longer than 40,000 words. Science fiction or fantasy only.
**How to Contact:** Query first. Reports in 3 weeks on queries; acknowledgement of ms in 3 weeks, decision in 3 months. Simultaneous and photocopied submissions OK. Accepts computer printout submissions. Letter-quality only. Publishes ms an average of 1 year after acceptance.
**Terms:** Negotiable for anthologies. Sends galleys to author. Cooperative publishing by individual arrangement (cost and profit sharing) for one-author books. Writers guidelines for #10 SASE with 37¢ postage. Book catalog free on request.
**Tips:** Forthcoming titles: offbeat fantasy and science fiction. "We're just starting to publish fiction because we want to get things in print that don't fit a periodical format. We publish individual-author fiction only in formats for which commercial markets do not exist—short story collections or midlength individual works. We don't plan to publish novels."

**UNIVERSITY EDITIONS (I, II)**, 4937 Humphrey Rd., Huntington WV 25704. Imprints include Aegina Press. Publisher: Ira Herman. Estab. 1983. Independent publisher presently expanding. Publishes paperback originals and reprints. Books: 50 lb library-weight paper; litho offset printing; perfect binding; illustrations; average print order: 500-1,000; first novel print order: 500-1,000. Plans 5 first novels this year. "We strongly encourage new writers." Averages 10-12 total titles, approximately 2-3 fiction titles each year. Often critiques rejected ms.

**Needs:** Adventure, contemporary, ethnic, experimental, faction, fantasy, feminist, gay, historical, horror, humor/satire, juvenile (all types), literary, mainstream, regional, science fiction, short story collections, translations, war, and women's. "Historical, literary, regional and translation fiction are our main areas of emphasis." Recently published *The Wicks and the Wacks*, by Louis Reed (children's).

**How to Contact:** Accepts unsolicited mss. "We depend upon manuscripts that arrive unsolicited." Query or submit outline/synopsis and 3 or more sample chapters or complete ms. "We prefer to see entire manuscripts; we will consider queries and partials as well." SASE for queries, mss. Reports in 1 week on queries; 1 month on mss. Simultaneous and photocopied submissions OK. Accepts computer printout submissions. Prefers letter-quality.

**Terms:** Payment, in royalties, is negotiated individually for each book. Sends galleys to author. Depends upon author and subject. Subsidy publishes 50% of titles.

**Tips:** "We attempt to encourage and establish new authors. Editorial tastes in fiction are eclectic. We try to be open to any type of fiction that is well written. We are publishing more fiction now that the very large publishers are getting harder to break into. We publish perfect-bound paperbacks, in order to keep books affordable. We have published more than one first novelist in the past year and hope to publish more in 1986."

**THE UNIVERSITY OF ARKANSAS PRESS (II)**, Fayetteville AR 72701. (501)575-3246. Director: Miller Williams. Estab. 1980. Small university press. Publishes hardcover and paperback originals. Averages 10 total titles, 1 short fiction title each year. Average print order 500 cloth and 1,500 paper copies.

**Needs:** Literary, mainstream, regional, short story collections, and translations. Recently published *Oxbridge Blues*, by Frederic Raphael (short fiction).

**How to Contact:** Accepts unsolicited mss. Query first with SASE. Simultaneous and photocopied submissions OK "if very clean." Accepts computer printout submissions. No dot-matrix. Reports in 2 weeks on queries. Publishes ms an average of 1 year after acceptance.

**Terms:** Pays in royalties of 10%; 10 author's copies. Writer's guidelines and book catalog free for 9x12 SASE.

**Tips:** "We are looking for short fiction written with energy. Clarity and economy. Apart from this, we have no predisposition concerning style or subject matter. The University of Arkansas Press does not respond to queries or proposals not accompanied by SASE."

**UNIVERSITY OF ILLINOIS PRESS (I)**, 54 E. Gregory, Champaign IL 61820. (217)333-0950. Fiction Editor: Ann Lowry Weir. Estab. 1918. Not-for-profit university press. Publishes clothbound originals. Books: acid free paper; cloth binding; average print order: 1,500-2,000. Number of titles: 4 per year. Encourages new writers who have journal publications. Occasionally comments on rejected mss.

**Needs:** Contemporary, literary, and experimental. "No novels." Recently published *Honeymoon*, by Merrill Joan Gerber; *Tentacles of Unreason*, by Joan Givner; *The Christmas Wife* by Helen Norris; *Getting to Know the Weather*, by Pamela Painter.

**How to Contact:** Accepts unsolicited mss. Query or submit complete ms. SASE for query, ms. Simultaneous and photocopied submissions OK. Accepts computer printout submissions. Reports in 1 week on queries, 2-4 months on mss.

**Terms:** Pays 7½% net of all copies sold. No advance. Free book catalog.

**Tips:** "We do not publish novels, and we have no outlet for individual short stories. We publish collections of short fiction by authors who've usually established their credentials by being accepted for publication in periodicals, generally literary periodicals. But some recently published books are by authors who have had no previous book publications."

**SHERRY URIE (II, IV),** Barton VT 05822. Editorial Director and Fiction Editor: Sherry Urie. Estab. 1974. Small independent publisher with plans to expand. Publishes paperback originals and reprints. Books: standard paper; offset printing; paper binding; illustrations; average print order: 2,000. Occasionally comments on rejected mss.
**Needs:** Contemporary, literary, mystery, historical, regional, women's, and religious/inspirational. "New England settings. We will consider all types of fiction." Recently published *Green Mountain Farm*, by Elliott Merrick (Vermont adventures).
**How to Contact:** Accepts unsolicited mss. Submit complete ms with SASE. Simultaneous and photocopied submissions OK. Accepts computer printout submissions. Reports in 1 month on mss. Publishes ms 6-12 months after acceptance.
**Terms:** Pays by individual arrangement; no advance. "Would consider subsidy publishing by individual arrangement." Book catalog for $1.
**Tips:** "We will consider original fiction, but our emphasis is on paperback reprints. We are interested in promoting good writing and will accept new work as our limited finances permit. Individual treatment is important between the author/editor."

**VÉHICULE PRESS (IV),** Box 125, Place du Parc Station, Montreal, Quebec H2W 2M9 Canada. Imprints include Signal Editions for poetry. Publisher/Editor: Simon Dardick. Estab. 1973. Small publisher of scholarly, literary and general culture books. Publishes hardcover and paperback originals. Books: lb offset paper; offset printing; perfect binding; average print order: 1,000-2,000. Averages 7 total titles. Published first collection of short stories in 1984. Second collection: 1985.
**Needs:** Short story collections, translations, and women's—"by Canadian residents only." No romance or formula writing. "We do not accept novels at this point." Fiction published to date has included: *Fatal Recurrences: New Fiction in English From Montreal*, edited by Hugh Hood and Peter O'Brien; and *The Bequest*, by Jerry Wexler (short stories).
**How to Contact:** Accepts unsolicited mss. Query first; SASE or SAE and IRC ("no US stamps, please"). Reports in 2 weeks on queries, 2 months on mss.
**Terms:** Pays in royalties of 10% minimum, 15% maximum; "depends on press run and sales. Sends galleys to author. Translators of fiction can receive Canada Council funding which publisher applies for. Some Council money is also available for assistance to writers for specific projects." Free book catalog.
**Tips:** "Our only fiction titles at this point are short story collections. Quality in almost any style is acceptable. No novels."

**‡VIMACH ASSOCIATES (IV),** 3039 Indianola Ave., Columbus OH 43202. (614)262-0471. Editorial Editors: Christine Schnitzer or Mark Doersam. Estab. 1983. Regionally based subsidy publisher interested in local works. Publishes hardcover originals and paperback originals. Books: 60 lb offset paper; offset printing; case, perfect, saddle-stitched binding; illustrations; average print order: 500-1,000; first novel print order: 500. Plans 5 first novels this year. Averages 15 total titles each year. Critiques or comments on rejected ms for $50.
**Needs:** Adventure, fantasy, gay, historical, humor/satire, juvenile (5-9 years old; fantasy, historical, spy/adventure), lesbian, literary, short story collections, suspense/mystery, war, western, young adult/teen (historical, sports, spy/adventure). Needs for novels include: children's, Ohio based, mystery. Recently published *The Big Buckeye*, by Edward Fisher (Ohio interest); *The Magic Moccasins*, by Jane Barks Ross (Ohio history).
**How to Contact:** Accepts unsolicited mss. Query first. SASE. Reports in 1 month on queries; 1 month on mss. Simultaneous and photocopied submissions OK. Accepts computer printouts including dot-matrix. Accepts electronic submissions via 5¼" disk.
**Terms:** Pays in royalties of 40% minimum; 70% maximum and 50-100 author's copies. Sends galleys to author. All books are subsidy published. Arrangements 70% of sales on first printing. *Vimach* pays for second printing and royalties drop to 50% until initial investment is recovered, then royalty payment is set at 40%.
**Tips:** "We have established ourselves as publishers of the Ohio regional area." Encourages first novelists and published new writers last year.

**WARLORDS AND WIZARDS PUBLICATIONS (I, II)**, 1909 Ferndale, Box 15, Canton OH 44709. (216)453-5832. Publisher: Andrew A. Berger. Estab. 1984. One-man operation on part-time basis with plans to expand. Publishes paperback originals. Book: photocopy print; illustrations; average print order: 500-1,000; novel print order 500. Plans 3 first novels this year. Averages 2-4 titles each year, all fiction. Occasionally critiques rejected mss.

**Needs:** Experimental, fantasy, juvenile (fantasy), psychic/supernatural/occult, science fiction, short story collections, and young adult/teen (fantasy/science fiction). Accepts short stories for texts. "I am looking for short stories in the genre of science-fantasy, barbaric fiction and sword and sorcery only. All stories must be fresh and experimental." Recently published *Warlords & Wizards, Vol. I & II*, by Andrew A. Berger (science-fantasy).

**How to Contact:** Accepts unsolicited mss. Submit complete ms with SASE. Reports in 6 weeks. Simultaneous and photocopied submissions OK. Accepts computer printout submissions.

**Terms:** Pays in 2 author's copies. Sends galleys to author. "I am a self-publisher with plans to expand. I am willing to make individual arrangements with authors depending on the book."

**Tips:** "Be bold. Never be afraid of trying new ideas. Always submit a perfect manuscript and keep on writing. I am in the process of expanding and plan to publish more fiction. I do encourage first novelists. I believe the editor should work closely with his novelist on problems within his novel."

**‡WATERFRONT PRESS (IV)**, 52 Maple Ave., Maplewood NJ 07040. (201)762-1565. President: Kal Wagenheim. Estab. 1982. Two persons, active part-time small press. Hardcover originals and reprints; paperback originals and reprints. Books: standard trade and textbook formats, illustrations occasionally; average print order: 1,000-1,500; first novel print order: 500-1,000. Averages 4 total titles/year; 1 or 2 fiction titles/year. Occasionally critiques rejected mss.

**Needs:** Ethnic, translations. "Our main focus is Puerto Rico and Hispanics in the US. We may consider other Caribbean nations." Recently published *The Labyrinth*, by Enrique A. Laguerre (translation from Spanish of book first published 1959); and *La Charca*, by Manvel Zeno-Gandia (translation from Spanish of 19th century novel).

**How to Contact:** Does not accept unsolicited mss. Query first or submit outline/synopsis and sample chapters. SASE for query and ms. Reports in 1 month on queries; 2 months on mss. Simultaneous and photocopied submissions OK. Accepts computer printouts including dot-matrix if legible.

**Terms:** Pays in royalties of 10% minimum; 15% maximum; $250-500 advance; advance is negotiable. Sends galleys to author. "On a few occasions, with books of great merit, we have co-published with author, who provided part of costs (in cases where our budget did not permit us to proceed quickly with the project)."

**Tips:** "We will endorse or support grant applicants made by writers to foundations, if we believe the work has merit."

**JOHN WESTBURG (I, II)**, 1745 Madison St., Fennimore WI 53809. (608)822-6237. Subsidiaries include Westburg Associates Publishers, John Westburg and Associates, and *The North American Mentor Magazine*. Editorial Director: John Westburg. Estab. 1964. Sometimes publishes in French, Spanish and German. Books: paper varies; offset printing; binding varies; illustrations; average print order: 300-500; first novel print order: varies.

**Needs:** Contemporary, literary, experimental, adventure, historical, western, war, science fiction, fantasy, and humor/satire. "We desire writing that is in good taste, for mature readers of above average education. Short stories should have action, plot, significance, depth of thought and should be elevating rather than depressing; tragedy is welcome provided there is a true tragic flaw in the protagonist; character should be depicted in the action rather than by description. Sustained wit without sarcasm or humiliation would be welcome. Propaganda pieces, whether racial, religious, or political, are not wanted. No vulgarity, no obscenity, no blasphemy, no pornography, no 'ethnic' whatsoever that debases any nationality or race, no anti-Caucasian racism, no religious works presenting ideas of 'true' believers, no ugliness or shoddiness in human behavior, no vilification, etc. The only fiction stories that we published last year were short fiction stories in the *North American Mentor Magazine*.

**How to Contact:** Submit complete ms with SASE. "Post office will not accept prepaid postage by metered machines. Must include return postage." Reports in 3-6 months. Publishes ms 3-6 months after acceptance.
**Terms:** Pays in 1 author's copy; no advance. Book catalog for SASE.
**Tips:** "Be sure to read your ms carefully again and again before you put it in the mail. Good writing does require rereading, rewriting, and revision after revision to put it in finest order. *The North American Mentor Magazine* is a noncommercial literary and humanities quarterly supported entirely by subsidies and subscriptions and donations. We have limited record-keeping facilities. Therefore, owing to the complexity of the new copyright laws, we must obtain all rights to the work we publish in order to keep the record-keeping categories to a bare minimum. However, we readily give permission to the author to publish elsewhere any of his work that we publish. We encourage first novelists and published new writers last year. If the author is not able to handle the self-publishing aspects, then he might think about sharing the costs of productions and marketing with the publisher, for many publishers are, like us, unwilling to speculate large sums on new and inexperienced writers, without this kind of cooperation."

**GEORGE WHITTELL MEMORIAL PRESS (I, II)**, 3722 South Ave., Youngstown OH 44502. (216)783-0645. Managing Editor: Sherri Zander. Estab. 1982. Publishes paperback originals. Plans 1 first novel this year. Averages 1 title each year. Buys juvenile mss with illustrations. Occasionally critiques rejected mss.
**Needs:** Fantasy, juvenile (animal, fantasy), short story collections, and young adult/teen (fantasy). "We publish primarily children's books though we are open to manuscripts aimed at a general audience. Manuscripts must be of high literary quality. However, subject matter is limited to animals, nature study, ecology and the interrelationship and interdependence of all life." Recently published *If You Have a Duck . . .*, by Jean McClure Kelty.
**How to Contact:** Accepts unsolicited mss. Query first. SASE for query, ms. Reports in 3 months on queries; 6 months on mss. Photocopied submissions OK. Publishes ms 1-2 years after acceptance.
**Terms:** Pays in author's copies. Free writer's guidelines.
**Tips:** "We are open to new writers. See *If You Have a Duck . . .* as a sample of the attitudes which are necessary for publication. We regard the author/editor relationship as a close one. Put the polish and style into the work itself. Omit the fancy cover letters that tell what you are going to do."

**WILSON BROTHERS PUBLICATIONS (I)**, Box 712, Yakima WA 98907. (509)457-8275. Editorial Director: Robert S. Wilson. Estab. 1978. One-man operation on part-time basis. Publishes paperback originals. Books: 20 lb sulfite bond paper; typescript by offset printing; hand stapled binding; b&w illustrations; average print order: 500. "We are an extremely small firm. We have published a series entitled *Trolley Trails Through the West* and a travelog entitled *Rambling Through British Columbia*. We also offer custom publishing for other authors, any type of work whether fiction or nonfiction on a limited basis. Thus far our production in that line has been nonfiction. We produce only soft cover books, usually 8½x11 though can also produce 5½x8½. Our services include editing, production of the book, and advice to the author about advertising and marketing. We do not buy mss for our own use. Author *pays entire cost* of production and books are his when completed, shipped to destination of his choice."
**How to Contact:** Accepts unsolicited mss. Query or submit complete ms. SASE for query, ms. No simultaneous submissions; photocopied submissions OK. Reports in 1 week on queries, 2 weeks (usually) on mss. Publishes ms 2-3 months after acceptance.
**Terms:** ½ when contract signed, balance when books ready for shipment; author pays freight. Sends proofs to author.
**Tips:** "Try some established royalty publishers first; employ book producers as last resort; stay away from vanity publisher houses; latter are long on promises and short on performance."

**WIM PUBLICATIONS (II)**, Box 367, College Corner OH 45003. (513)523-5994. Editorial Director: SDiane Bogus. Contact: Daisy M. De Oca, Associate Editor, Marketing and Promotions. Estab. 1979. Publishes paperback originals and hardcover. Books: 60 lb White Gebhast; off-set printing; perfect binding; up to 10 illustrations.

**Needs:** Feminist and gay/lesbian. No abstract experimentational or plotless work. Recently published *Sapphire's Sampler*. by SDiane Bogus.

**How to Contact:** Query with SASE. Simultaneous and photocopied submissions OK. Reports in 1-6 weeks.

**Terms:** "We do not pay royalties on books. We are a small press which likes its authors to help with promotion of books." Sends galleys to author. Author receives ½ of press run. Free book catalog.

**Tips:** "Trust that there *is* a publisher for your work. Work at getting better. Associate with writers. Read. Operate professionally. Women's work is greatly in demand. Do not believe publishers, agents, or informed friends when they tell you your novel is no good or weak or needs improvements, not if you have revised many times over, followed basic rules of composition and you feel you are in the stream of literary times past or present (popular or academic). If *you believe* in your work that's enough. Stein says classics are discovered when everyone stops looking at what they're looking at to suddenly see what's been there all the time. We will be publishing more fiction, a new direction for press. We want to diversify."

**WINGBOW PRESS,** 2929 5th St., Berkeley CA 94710. (415)549-3030. Editor: Randy Fingland. Estab. 1971. Small independent publisher. Publishes hardcover originals (occasionally) and paperback originals and reprints. Averages 2-3 total titles, 1-2 fiction titles each year. Critiques rejected mss if requested.

**Needs:** Contemporary, feminist, literary, psychic/supernatural/occult, regional (West Coast), women's, and experimental. Novel needs: "One that sells well enough to break even—good, strong, well-written in any genre, style or subject." No romance. Recently published *That Back Road In*, by John Brandi.

**How to Contact:** Accepts unsolicited mss. Query first with SASE before sending complete ms. Reports in 6 weeks. Simultaneous and photocopied submissions OK. Accepts computer printout submissions. Prefers letter-quality. Accepts disc submissions compatible with Epson. Prefers hard copy with disc submission.

**Terms:** Pays in royalties of 7.5% minimum; 10% maximum; $250 average advance. Book catalog free on request.

**Tips:** Publishes less fiction than in the past "because of marketplace."

**WOMEN'S PRESS (I, II, IV),** 229 College St., Toronto, Ontario M5T 1R4 Canada. (416)598-0082. Estab. 1972. Publishes paperback originals. Book: web coat paper; web printing; perfect binding; average print order: 3,000; first novel print order: 3,000. Plans 1 first novel this year. Averages 5 total titles, 1 fiction title each year. Sometimes "briefly" critiques rejected ms.

**Needs:** Contemporary, experimental, feminist, historical, juvenile and adolescent (fantasy, historical, contemporary), lesbian, literary, preschool/picture book, short story collections, women's, and young adult/teen (problem novels). Nothing sexist, pornographic. Recently published *Quilt*, by Donna Smyth (realistic feminist); *Baker's Dozen: Stories by Women* (short story collection); and *Good Morning Franny, Good Night Franny* (32-page picture book).

**How to Contact:** Submit complete ms with SAE and "Canadian NB. stamps or a cheque. We give preference to writers who are Canadian citizens or landed immigrants." Reports in 3 months. Simultaneous or photocopied submissions OK. Accepts computer printout submissions. Prefers letter-quality.

**Terms:** Pays in royalties of 7% minimum; 10% maximum. Sends galleys to author. Advance is negotiable. Free book catalog.

**Tips:** "We have so far published three novels and a collection of short stories. Our three adult novels have all been first novels. A translated work of fiction from Quebec was published in 1985 and we plan more lesbian fiction and a collection of short fiction. We encourage first novelists. We edit very carefully. We can sometimes suggest alternative publishers."

**WOODSONG GRAPHICS INC. (II),** Box 238, New Hope PA 18938. (215)794-8321. Editor: Ellen Bordner. Estab. 1977. "Small publishing firm dedicated to printing quality books and marketing them creatively." Publishes paperback and hardcover originals. Books: standard or coated stock paper; photo offset printing; GBC or standard binding; illustrations; average print order: 5,000; first novel print order; 5,000. Averages 6-8 total titles each year. "Sometimes" buys juvenile mss with illustrations. Occasionally critiques rejected mss.

**Needs:** Adventure, contemporary, gothic/historical and contemporary romance, historical (general), humor/satire, juvenile (animal, easy-to-read, fantasy, historical, picture book, spy/adventure, contemporary), literary, mainstream, psychic/supernatural/occult, science fiction, suspense/mystery, war, western, women's, and young adult (easy-to-read/teen, fantasy/science fiction, historical, problem novels, spy/adventure). No deviant sex of any kind or pornography.

**How to Contact:** Accepts unsolicited mss. Query first or submit complete ms. SASE always. Simultaneous and photocopied submissions OK. Accepts computer printout submissions. Prefers letter-quality. Reports in 3 weeks on queries, longer on mss. "We do everything possible to get replies out promptly, but do read everything we're sent . . . and that takes time." Publishes ms 6-12 months after acceptance.

**Terms:** Pays in royalties; negotiates advance. Sends galleys to author. "Arrangements will depend totally on the author and manuscript."

**Tips:** "If first novels are good, we have no problem with them, and we're always happy to look. Along with queries, send at least a few pages of actual ms text, since quality of writing is more important than topic where fiction is concerned. If you believe in what you've written, stick with it. There is so much good material that we must reject simply because we can't afford to do everything . . . others must have the same problem, and it's a matter of being on the right desk on the right day to finally succeed."

**WORD BEAT PRESS**, Box 10509, Tallahassee FL 32302. Editor: Allen Woodman. Estab. 1982. Publishes trade paperback originals. Publishes four short story anthologies, collections, or novellas a year.

**Needs:** Short story collections and novellas. "We plan on publishing a series of tradesize fiction collections. We have also recently published an anthology that contains stories by Raymond Carver, Joy Williams, Tobias Wolff, Jayne Anne Phillips, and others. Barbara Milton recently won a Pushcart Prize with one of our books."

**How to Contact:** Query first with SASE. Photocopied submissions OK. Reports in 3 months on queries.

**Terms:** Pays in royalties of 6-10%; advance of $100 average; 10 author's copies. "We are interested in short story collections of 40 to 90 typed, double-spaced manuscript pages. Most mss will be selected from the yearly competition; Past judges have included George Plimpton, Janet Burroway, Eve Shelnutt. 1986 judge will be Joy Williams. Book catalog for SASE. Offers Word Beat Press Fiction Book Award.

**STEPHEN WRIGHT PRESS (I, II)**, Box 1341, F.D.R. Station, New York NY 10150. Publisher/Editor: Stephen Wright. Estab. 1978. Printing and publishing service: fiction and nonfiction; books and pamphlets. Publishes hardcover and paperback originals and hardcover and paperback reprints. Books: standard paper; latest method printing; hard or soft cover binding; average print order; 500-1,000; first novel print order; 500-1,000.

**Needs:** "We consider all genres, styles and subjects. No pornography for its own sake; anti-people (against ethnic and religious groups, etc.); illiterate manuscripts."

**How to Contact:** Query first; then submit complete ms with SASE. Reports in 2 weeks on queries; 1 month on mss. Photocopied submissions OK. "The standard way is to submit manuscript (original *or* copy). Other submissions acceptable if there is special reason for them, and with permission of the Stephen Wright Press." Publishes ms 6-12 months after acceptance.

**Terms:** "Our press depends wholly on the author's payment of subsidy. Sends galleys to author. Usual arrangement is ½ payment at the time of signing agreement, and ½ payment upon furnishing of proofs or other evidence that the production of book or pamphlet has begun. Please note that every author who takes advantage of the Stephen Wright Press printing and publishing services is entitled to a complimentary letter of suggestions on what we believe is a good way to gain promotion and distribution of the author's book. It is understood, however, that the author must *request* such letters."

**Tips:** "Romantic and mystery/suspense fiction—in every category for each genre—are on the rise in titles and number of sales. These are both specialized fields, so in addition to the novelist's skill, he or she must also have a wide knowledge in either genre. The 'secret' is to write *every* day, evening or weekend. If you can discover what you *should be* writing—or what you write best because of the kind of person you are, as well as your interests—you are ahead of the writing game. Editor should be sympathetic—and so should the author!''

**W.W. PUBLICATIONS (I, II)**, Subsidiary of A.T.S., Box 277, Union Lake MI 48085. (313)887-4703. Imprints include *Minas Tirith Evening Star*. Editor: Phillip Helms. Estab. 1967. One-man operation on part-time basis. Publishes paperback originals and reprints. Books: typing paper; offset printing; staples binding; black ink illustrations; average print order: 500 +; first novel print order: 500. Averages 1 title (fiction) each year. Occasionally critiques rejected ms.
**Needs:** Fantasy, science fiction, and young adult/teen (fantasy/science fiction). Novel needs: "Tolkien-related mainly, some fantasy."
**How to Contact:** Accepts unsolicited mss. Submit complete ms with SASE. Reports in 2 weeks. No simultaneous submissions; photocopied submissions OK. Accepts computer printout submissions. Prefers letter-quality.
**Terms:** Individual arrangement with author depending on book, etc.; 5 author's copies. Free book catalog.
**Tips:** "We are publishing more fiction and more paperbacks. The author/editor relationship: a friend and helper."

**YITH PRESS (II)**, 1051 Wellington Rd., Lawrence KS 66044. (913)843-4341. Subsidiary: *Eldritch Tales Magazine*. Editor/Publisher: Crispin Burnham. Estab. 1984. One-man operation on part-time basis. Publishes paperback originals and reprints. Books: offset printing; perfect bound binding; illustrations; average print order: 900-1,000. Averages 1-2 titles each year. Average first novel print order 500-1,000 (depending pre-publication orders). Occasionally critiques rejected ms.
**Needs:** Fantasy and horror. Accepts short stories for collections only. Novels needs include "anything in the supernatural horror category." No "mad slasher or sword and sorcery."
**How to Contact:** Accepts unsolicited mss. Submit complete ms with SASE. Reports in 2 months. Simultaneous and photocopied submissions OK. Accepts computer printout submissions. Prefers letter-quality. Disc submissions OK with Apple IIc system.
**Terms:** Individual arrangement with author depending on the book. Sends galleys to author. Pays in royalties of 25% minimum; 35% maximum.
**Tips:** "Be original, don't try to be the next Lovecraft or Stephen King. We hope to have our first book out in 1986. Currently, I plan to publish one or two books/year, along with *Eldritch Tales*. The author/editor relationship should be give and take on both sides. I will try *not* to rewrite the author's work. If I feel that it needs some changes then I'll suggest them to the author."

**YORK PRESS**, Box 1172, Fredericton, New Brunswick E3B 5C8 Canada. (506)458-8748. Editorial Director: Dr. S. Elkhadem. Estab. 1975. Midsize independent publisher with plans to expand. Publishes hardcover and paperback originals. Publishes in English exclusively. Number of titles: 35 in 1985. Average first novel print order 1,000 copies.
**Needs:** Contemporary, experimental, and translations by established writers. "No mss written mainly for entertainment, i.e., those without literary or artistic merit." Recently published *Modern Egyptian Short Stories* and *Three Contemporary Egyptian Novels*, translated and edited by Saad El-Gabalawy; and Michel Butor's *Description of San Marco*, translated by Barbara Mason..
**How to Contact:** Accepts unsolicited mss, "although an initial query is appreciated." Query with SASE or SAE and IRC. No simultaneous submissions; photocopied submissions OK. Reports in 1 week on queries, 1 month on mss.
**Terms:** Pays 5-10% in royalties; no advance. Free book catalog.
**Tips:** "We are devoted to the promotion of scholarly publications; areas of special interest include general and comparative literature, literary criticism, and creative writing of an experimental nature."

**ZEPHYR PRESS (II)**, 13 Robinson St., Somerville MA 02145. Subsidiary of Aspect, Inc. Editors: Ed Hogan, Miriam Sagar, Leora Zeitlin. Estab. 1980. Small press, with part-time staff of 3. Publishes hardcover and paperback originals. Books: acid free paper; offset printing; sewn binding; illustrations sometimes; average print order: 1000-1,500; first novel print order: 1,000. Averages 2 total titles, 0-2 fiction titles each year. $12 reading fee for all mss submitted; written critique with all responses.

**Needs:** Contemporary, ethnic, experimental, feminist/lesbian, gay, historical, humor/satire, literary, mainstream, regional, science fiction, short story collections, and women's. "We in general seek fiction or short stories by younger or less-established writers, a continuation of our interests as editors of the now defunct *Aspect* magazine." Recently published *Two Novels*, by Philip Whalen.

**How to Contact:** Accepts unsolicited mss. Query first with SASE recommended. Accepts computer printout submissions. Prefers letter-quality. Reports in 2-4 weeks on queries.

**Terms:** Pays in author's copies of 10% of print (1st edition); 20% royalties on publisher's net (subsequent editions, if any). Sends galleys to author by arrangement. "There can be some flexibility of terms, based on mutual arrangements, if desired by author and publisher." Book catalog for SAE and 1 first class stamp.

**Tips:** "Get lots of feedback in a constructive atmosphere (writing classes, formal or informal workshops or writers' groups) before deciding your ms has reached publishability. We are especially interested in first novels. We encourage first novelists if they truly feel they are ready. We regard the author/editor relationship as one of close cooperation, from editing through promotion."

---

# Foreign small presses

The following small presses, represented in countries other than the US and Canada, accept fiction—novels, novelettes, novellas, or short story collections. They usually do not pay. Query first for subject needs and interests and submission requirements, and always include proper return postage to ensure a response or the return of the manuscript. (See Manuscript Mechanics.)

**BRAN'S HEAD**, 45 Milk St., Frome, Somerset, England BA11 3DB. Editor: Grahaeme Barrasford Young. One-man operation on full-time basis. Publishes paperback originals.

**CHAPMAN**, 35 E. Claremont St., Edinburgh EH7 4HT Scotland. Imprints include Lothlorien. Editorial Director: Joy M. Hendry. One-woman operation on part-time basis. Contemporary, literary, and experimental.

**EASTERN CARIBBEAN INSTITUTE (ECI) (IV)**, Box 1338, Frederiksted, Virgin Islands 00840. (809)772-1011. Editor/President: S.B. Jones-Hendrickson, PhD. Estab. 1982. Small press with plans to expand. Publishes hardcover originals and paperback originals. Regional. Needs for novels include Caribbean issues and setting. No religious.

**EXPANDED MEDIA EDITIONS**, Box 190136, 5300 Bonn, West Germany. Tel. 0228-229583. Fiction Editor: Paciao. One-woman operation on full-time basis. Contemporary, experimental, and literary.

**GOLD ATHENA PRESS**, GPO Box 252W, Melbourne, Victoria, Australia 3001. "Arts and humanities, especially literature, philosophy, and theoretical physchology."

**HEMKUNT**, Publishers Pvt. Ltd., 1/E-15 Patel Rd., New Delhi, India 110008. Tel. (011)584174. Managing Director: Bhagat Singh.

**KAWABATA PRESS**, Knill Crass House, HR Anderton Rd., Millbrook, NR Torpoint, Cornwall, England. Fiction Editor: C. Webb. One-man operation on part-time basis.

**MATILDA PUBLICATIONS**, 7 Mountfield St., Brunswick, Victoria, Australia 3056. (03)386-5604. Publisher/Editor: Mr. Fonda Zenofon. "Small-size independent publisher and printer to the arts." Short stories. Contemporary, experimental, literary, mainstream, and short story collections.

**PRESSED CURTAINS**, 4 Bower St., Maidstone, Kent ME16 8SD England. Tel. (0622)63681. Subsidiary includes *Curtains* Magazine. Editor: Paul Buck. One-man operation, part-time. Contemporary, erotica, experimental, feminist, gay, lesbian, literary, and translations.

**SYNERGETIC PRESS**, 24 Gloucester St., London WCI 3AL, England, (01)242-7367. Contact: Tango Parrish Snyder, Kathy Dyer. Poetry, fiction, art, cartoons, long-poems, plays, nonfiction.

**TOKYO ENGLISH LITERATURE SOCIETY (TELS)**, TELS "Tomeoki," Koishikawa Post Office Bunkyo-Ru, 112, Japan. Tel. (03)312-0481. Coordinator: Thomas Ainlay Jr. Small, independent, nonprofit organization.

*The changes from first draft to last draft are enormous. The first drafts of my novels run to as many as 1,500 pages. When I start my first revision, I will often throw out 200 or 300 pages at a time. When I have finished going through the entire book again, I return to page one and start the process all over. I spend up to a year and a half revising my novels and will do as many as a dozen revisions. Be careful not to fall into the trap of impatience. When you have worked on a manuscript for a long time, it is natural to want to get it out to a publisher as quickly as possible. But if that book is not as good as you know how to make it, then you are doing yourself a disservice, for it is the first impression that will determine whether anyone is interested in publishing it.*
—*Sidney Sheldon*

# Commercial publishers

Commercial publishing has never been a static industry, but in 1985 it was unusually "nervous," even volatile. Publishing houses continued to merge; conglomerates took over smaller companies; independent presses and imprints declared bankruptcy or were dissolved; and new lines sprang up—much like a game of monopoly. Meanwhile publishers and editors played musical chairs within their divisions or hopscotched from company to company. Regardless of the changes, commercial publishing recovered from the recession of a few years ago to enjoy a reasonably successful year.

On the fiction front, hardcover sales were soaring with a 73% increase over 1984. Although fiction sales were up 12%, the paperback industry suffered a decline, proving contrary to predictions years ago that paperback publishing is cost effective. Even paperback houses like Avon began publishing in hardcover.

The usual familiar names dominated the bestseller lists: Sidney Sheldon, Danielle Steel, Stephen King, and at year's end, blockbusters like Michener's *Texas*, Jean Auel's *The Mammoth Hunters*, and Garrison Keillor's *Lake Woebegone Days* broke records with their "megaprintings." Crown Publishers, for example, printed over one million hardcover copies of Auel's book (which if stacked would be 29 miles high). In late 1985 James Clavell's new novel was auctioned at a beginning price of $3 million, for a bigger-than-ever final sale at $5 million.

The year ended on a note of optimism with publishers anticipating a steady rise in sales (and associated products) in the next few years, thanks primarily to the baby-boomers and their soon-to-be-reading offspring. Which is not to say business is better than ever. In 1985 there were fewer books published than in 1984, mainly because of the reduced space available for books. Bookstores now sell video tapes, games, magazines and audio cassettes—books on tape, a new aspect of the industry which is expected to take off. Also, the midlist books, the novels and nonfiction books that receive little advertising and promotion, suffer because of the predominant focus on the top books that bring in the money. Publishers are paying less for midlist books. And there are also fewer money auctions for reprints because more hardcover houses are keeping their better books to reprint themselves.

# Woman's work

Although there were not as many first novels as 1984 (the average is about 225), last year was blessed with "remarkable" fine first fiction by a "crop of emerging writers," according to a major reviewer. Several nonfiction writers published first novels (e.g. Carl Sagan, *Contact*), but the greatest publishing story comes out of Texas. Random House, which had not pursued an unknown author of commercial fiction in years, paid a $350,000 advance to Southern writer Karleen Koen for her historical novel, *Through a Glass Darkly* (sold by an agent she pursued after reading a *Writer's Digest* article on agents). Shortly thereafter, Bantam Books topped that sum with a $1 million advance (for hardcover and paperback rights) to Sally Beauman for *Destiny*. (Technically Beauman is not a first novelist; she has published romances, paperback, under the name of Vanessa James.) There were other success stories: Carolyn Chute catapulted from poverty to literary and financial success with *The Beans of Egypt, Maine*; 21-year-old Bret Easton Ellis published *Less Than Zero*, a highly acclaimed first novel about adolescence; Mary Monroe, after 80 rejections in six years, published *The Upper Room*, recently reprinted in paperback; and *Hunt for Red October*, by Tom Clancy was an unqualified success, a first novel published by the Naval Institute Press (and a book President Reagan particularly enjoyed).

Such successes and outstanding advances are usually the stuff of fiction itself. Generally a first novel advance is $7,500, somewhat higher than a decade ago, according to Peter Skolnik of Sanford J. Greenburger Literary Agency, probably because the majority of houses are publishing less fiction altogether. The fierce competition is for authors who show signs of being a Judith Krantz or Sidney Sheldon, writers whose talent editors believe they can build on. "What we want is an exceptionally good novel, fresh and practically earth-shattering," says an E.P. Dutton editor. A tall assignment for the writer in a tight industry.

The blockbuster craze hasn't hurt serious fiction, editors maintain; in fact, the successful novels help finance the unadvertised books that usually do not sell well or make money. The number of literary novels, noticeably reduced in the last 15 years, remains steady, now that the small press is the acknowledged publisher of the majority of serious fiction. Often, however, the publishing of a second novel (noncommercial) is harder to publish, if the first doesn't sell well. Computerized sales statistics are unforgiving, regardless of a writer's talent. The alternative within the commercial press might be to heed the advice of an editor at Zebra: "Put away your literary ideas and be commercial."

Most commercial publishers are not exclusively bound to popular fiction. Aware of the importance and the tradition of perpetuating good literature, many publishers have instituted imprints to recognize serious fiction and/or introduce new writers. Obelisk (Dutton), Washington Square Press (Pocket Books), Signet (NAL), and others, reprint books of literary merit. Random House's Aventura, Avon's Bard and Ballantine's Available Press publish translations of Third World or Latin American writers; the Gold Medal imprint publishes original fiction in paperbacks; and Vintage Contemporaries has experimented successfully with Jay McInerney's *Bright Light, Big City* in trade paperback.

Publishing short story collections with the commercial press is not an impossibility, as often thought; today it is just less difficult. The turning point in acceptability was in 1978 with *Stories of John Cheever* and it was reemphasized recently by the surge of interest in magazine short fiction. Raymond Carver and others have helped establish the short story as an important medium, and there has been steady interest by isolated major publishers in collections. A few even reached bestseller status. Generally, however, collections are only by established and acclaimed novelists or writers with a firm track record in the best literary and commercial magazines, but even then most sales are modest. Particularly evident this year are women writers—Grace Paley, Mary Morris, Mavis Gallant, Hortense Calisher, Bobbie Ann Mason, Elizabeth Tallent. There are also men like Tobias Wolff, Mark Strand and André Dubus. Last year Scribners published an anthology, *20 Under 30*, of stories by young writers. A medium the very commercial publishers won't touch, short story collections are firm, charted territory for many of the best literary writers today, and some have declared it their *only* medium.

## Baby book boomlet

The smaller regional commercial publishers are challenging the attitude that New York is the only reputable publishing center in the US. There are recognized regional publishing areas in the US and Canada, usually surrounding college writing programs, but the New York houses have also picked up on the regional interest. Obvious talent continues to come from the South; and noteworthy authors like Lee Smith, George Garrett, Bobbie Ann Mason and Louise Shivers are just a few who write stories reflecting their southern roots and culture. Presses in the Northeast, the Southwest, Northern California and the Northwest and other regions produce native writers of national reputation. With effective promotion and distribution from the regional presses, these fine writers are not being labeled or limited by their addresses.

Genre publishers and imprints remain the most active fiction publishers and the area most responsive to newcomers. In the last few years there has been an explosion of genre paperbacks from specialized publishers. They may lack the prestige of the literary novels and the impact of blockbusters, but they are not the financial risk of a hardcover first novel and cost less to produce.

In every genre it's quite naturally the best reader of that subject that makes the best writer. As a genre novelist you will be expected to have the subject expertise plus a quality, readable style. Therefore it's imperative to read a broad selection of the category, know what's been done, and study the structure of the novels from several category publishers. Even *within* a specialty house there may be a wide spectrum of subject interests, due to the expanded definitions of the genre itself and its evolution in the last few years. Most recently there is a blending of the subject into mainstream writing. Knowledge *about* the market is required before you seek a publisher.

In juvenile and preschool writing, the demographics—that is, the number of reading age children—determine much of the production of children's books. Currently the babyboomers are creating a boom in baby books; as conscientious parents they insist their children be exposed to books at crib age. The market for older children is "lighter," however, due to budget cuts in schools and libraries.

Critics eschew the quality of new children's titles today; they lack depth, they say. But surveys show girls enjoy lighter subjects (mysteries, fairy tales and romances) and boys are drawn to comics, space and sports stories. Juvenile multiple series attract youngsters of all ages (Choose Your Own Adventure, Which Way Adventure, etc.); they also sell better and are more economical to publish than single publications. Publishers are also reprinting and updating the old traditional stories with new illustrations and graphics, which reduces the freelancer's opportunities. Still, publishers like Bantam, for example, maintain they expect growth, diversity and more innovative publishing projects in the late '80s.

## Murder they wrote

An area of certain growth in both juvenile and young adult fiction is in the genre or special format series, the highly successful concept that booksellers applaud. Most major houses have created series for the young adult/teen market, the 10-16 age group, usually girls. To name a few, there are Mirrors, Two Hearts, Pacer, and Zodiac Club from Putnam. Laurel Leaf (Dell) publishes Seniors, Twilight, Young Romances. Scholastic has Sunfire and Cheerleaders; Bantam produces the very popular Sweet Valley High and Sweet Dreams; and Avon has just begun a series for young girl athletes, Going For It.

Teen romance sells best; 19 of the 20 books on a recent B. Dalton YA Bestseller List were romances. "Squeaky clean," they are the equivalent of French fries. "Girls are just gobbling them up," says one bookseller. Single authors write various series; other series beg for original quality writers. Study the displays in the bookstore; then read the publishers' listings for submission requirements or query the editor for specific information.

In the romance industry in general (excepting teen romance), the thrill is gone; the business has leveled off. There are fewer new category lines, and those remaining have expanded and improved in quality (see Silhouette close-up). Category romances are still popular, but less structured and formulaic and more similar to a mainstream romance. The audience is more selective now and prefers less predictability. Thus there is greater interest in single women's novels, a trend major publishers have picked up on. Avon, Ballantine, Dell, Leisure, Warner and Zebra all include an expanded women's fiction department.

Interest in the inspirational romances has cooled with the major publishers. But more religious publishers (Bethany, Tyndale, Word Book, Zondervan) are publishing "romances without the blush" (prairie, frontier romances; contemporary romances), acknowledging fiction as an effective method to convey the Christian message. Romantic intrigue still captures a healthy readership. Check the bookstores for the most prominently displayed romance lines which are usually the most successful/profitable.

Mystery is the most enduring genre and the number one reading entertainment, *Newsweek* and surveys declared last year. A hot market, mysteries continue to sell very well; sales have quintupled since 1976. Prime time TV shows like "Murder She Wrote" have generated recent interest in the genre, as have its byproducts: mystery bookstores, mystery weekends and cruises, courses and seminars.

Along with its success and evolution, the sub-genres have broadened, and readers are no longer segregated by sex. The good writers attract men *and* women; stereotypes are breaking down and women are more prominent as readers, writers and protagonists—in all colors and from all regions. The only area where women seem to have made no impact is the suspense novel.

Frequently on the bestseller lists, mystery is a genre that attracts quality, "some of the strongest writing in the country," according to Otto Penzler, publisher of the Mysterious Press (see close-up). "There has never been a time when more first rate books have been written in this area," he says. Readers expect more today than just a good puzzle; quality writing is important, too. Each year 600 mystery books are published, but competition is heavy. In addition, advances are only modest; somewhere between romance and science fiction.

## Authentic action

Science fiction and fantasy are the fastest growing areas of fiction; sales have risen steadily at category and mainstream level. Top writers are commanding large sums and new writers are sparked by respectable advances. According to Lou Aronica, editor of

Bantam's new Spectra line, the interest and expansion (and even a greater legitimacy of the genre) are due to the recent popular science fiction films and movie tie-ins and TV shows. They have brought the hardcore SF of a few years ago to a mainstream, more accessible level. The better, more expanded lines attract the established quality writers, and the result is a broader readership.

Once heavily masculine, now SF is 50-50. The old fashioned, it's-a-man's world, hardcover genre is also "soft," with the introduction of more women writers who develop their characters and give special attention to detail. The new publishers who entered this burgeoning field in 1985 have created the possibility of a glut, however. But for now there are unlimited challenges for the talented, innovative SF and fantasy writer, say the editors, particularly those with publishing credits in genre magazine and "zines." Publication is possible—if you do your homework (science), know the field thoroughly, know what has been published and what the publishers are looking for.

A genre that has enjoyed a recent comeback is the western, thanks largely to Louis L'Amour. Again, women writers have entered the field, younger authors, too. They are blending serious history and research with more realistic, good writing to eliminate the longtime grade-B movie, mindless pulp image. Frontier characters are still self-reliant and noble, of course, but today's hero may have problems with his love life, etc. The black-white hat stereotypes are fading also, as is the interest in adult westerns, all sex and violence. Western fans are hungry for authentic books about the West.

Men's action/adventure novels and series have experienced changes. Editors today expect material with more than blood and guts: "It's high adventure with a difference." Sales are up; imprint editors are soliciting manuscripts. "We're buying for a more upscale market," says a series editor. Mark Howell of Harlequin's Gold Eagle says they are going after the nontraditional readers, looking for male-oriented novels with lots of action, books that also cross over into female readership. In general, single and multiple author series are thriving, and novels on Vietnam continue to sell—if authentic.

## Support system

Despite encouragement from responsive genre and mainstream editors who work with the anticipation that the next manuscript or query will produce a great, talented novelist, the odds are still decidedly against the many thousands of hopefuls. Editors are very discouraged, they tell us, at the volume of inferior material. As Melissa Ann Singer of Berkley Publishing Group says, "The slush just gets slushier, and the gems are rarer."

To be a fine writer takes years and years of devoted effort, an apprenticeship that may last a lifetime, editors say over and over. "Too many writers believe the ability to read is license to write. *Be realistic*," says Hy Steirman, chairman of Richardson and Steirman. All editors echo the sentiment.

Accept the fact, also, that marketing your manuscript will demand as much patience and energy as writing. It is—should be—time consuming to research the appropriate publisher for your book. Study the current novels in the bookstores, and libraries, and read and learn about the publishing industry and its trends and current interests.

As a member of the writing community, consider the importance of active participation and support. To illustrate: At a writers' conference, Barbara Grossman, senior editor of Crown Publishers, explaining why there is not more first fiction, asked her audience how many writers had bought a first novel during the year. Five raised their hands. "That's why," she said. "And three of you are lying."

Support your colleagues; buy a first novel or many; and invest in your writing future—which may begin with the list that follows.

**ABINGDON PRESS (III)**, The United Methodist Publishing House, 201 8th Ave. S, Nashville TN 37202. (615)749-6450. Subsidiaries include Festival Books. Vice President: Ronald P. Patterson. Estab. 1789. Large religious publisher. Publishes hardcover and paperback originals and paperback reprints. Averages 100-120 total titles each year. Buys 1% agented fiction. "We publish no fiction for adults, only 1 or 2 children's books annually."
**Needs:** Religious/Bible stories for children.
**How to Contact:** Submit outline/synopsis and 2-3 sample chapters with SASE. Accepts unsolicited mss. Reports in 2 weeks. Photocopied submissions OK. Accepts computer printout submissions. Prefers letter-quality. Publishes ms 1-2 years after acceptance.
**Terms:** Pays in royalties of 2.5% minimum; 15% maximum; average advance $500.

**ACADEMY CHICAGO PUBLISHERS (I, II)**, 425 N. Michigan Ave., Chicago IL 60611. Imprints carrying fiction include Cassandra Editions and Academy Mystery. Editor: Anita Miller. Estab. 1975. Midsize independent publisher. Publishes hardcover originals and paperback reprints. Books: 55 lb. Glatfelter; mostly sheet fed; perfect, sometimes Smyth-sewn for hardcovers; b&w illustrations; average print order for paperback 5,000, for hardcover 1,500-3,000. Published 35 in 1985. Encourages new writers. Published 1 first novel in 1982; published 3 first novels in 1985; will publish at least 2 first novels in 1986. Buys 20% agented fiction for reprints only. Average first novel print order 5,000 copies paper, 3,000 copies hardbound. Occasionally comments on rejected mss.
**Needs:** Mystery, historical, feminist, and translations. No experimental, religious, romance, or children's. "Mysteries interest us especially." Recently published *One for the Money*, by Dick Belsky; and *Aunt Ellen Stories*, by Kenan Heise.
**How to Contact:** Accepts unsolicited mss. Query and submit first three chapters with SASE. No simultaneous submissions; photocopied submissions OK. Reports in 2 weeks on queries, 6 weeks on mss. "*No* micro-dot printer. Manuscripts without envelopes will be discarded. *Mailers* are a *must*." Publishes ms an average of 1 year after acceptance.
**Terms:** Pays 7-15% in royalties; no advance. Sends galleys to author.
**Tips:** "We are growing and publishing more of everything. We try to publish one first novel every season. The relationship between novelist and editor should be close; the manuscript is gone over line by line, word by word. An aspiring novelist should submit manuscripts directly to publishers and avoid agents. If the big houses turn it down there are many smaller independent presses which will read everything that comes in a bound manuscript. We do not like to receive postage and label *without* a mailing envelope—it prejudices us against the work from the outset."

**ACCENT BOOKS (II)**, A Division of Accent Publications, Box 15337, Denver CO 80215. (303)988-5300. Imprint includes Frontier Romance Series. Managing Editor: Mary B. Nelson. Estab. 1975. Growing midsize independent publisher of Christian books. Publishes paperback and some hardcover originals. Plans 3 first novels this year. Books: type of paper varies; established book printers; binding varies but usually perfect with some special comb., misc.; average print order varies; first novel print order 5,000-7,500. Averages 12-24 total titles, 5-8 fiction titles this year. Occasionally critiques rejected ms.
**Needs:** "Only Christian books in these categories: contemporary, inspirational, mystery/romance, Biblical fiction, inspirational frontier romance, contemporary suspense/mystery, and young adult/teen (easy-to-read, fantasy/science fiction/allegory, historical, problem novels, romance, spy/adventure). We will look at any Christian novel on these topics. All must have strong, evangelical, Christian storylines showing how Christ makes a difference in a person's life." Recently published *In the House of the Enemy*, by Bea Carlton (inspirational contemporary mystery/romance); *Montana Bride*, by Linda Boorman (frontier romance).; *In Search of Perlas Grandes* by Timothy C. Davis (youth fiction/allegory); *The Man Who Would Kill God*, by David Welty (suspense/mystery).
**How to Contact:** Does not accept unsolicited mss. Submit outline/synopsis and 3-4 sample chapters with SASE. Reports in 8 weeks on queries, 90 days on mss. Simultaneous submissions and clear photocopied submissions accepted. Accepts computer printout submissions if letter-quality.

**Terms:** Pays in royalties of 5% minimum, 10% maximum; 10 author's copies. Sends galleys to author. Writer's guidelines for SASE; book catalog for 9x12 SASE.

**Tips:** "We are looking for fiction with a solid evangelical message written with an evident command of plot and character development. We encourage and accept new writers. We're looking for quality writers. We like a personal, privileged and pleasant relationship with authors. We foresee conservative, planned growth in both fiction and nonfiction in a wider number of subject areas."

**ACE CHARTER BOOKS**, Berkley Publishing Group, 200 Madison Ave., New York NY 10016. (212)686-9820. Estab. 1977. Publishes paperback originals and reprints. Number of titles: 75 in 1986. See Berkley Publishing Group.

**ALCHEMY BOOKS**, Suite 531, 685 Market St., San Francisco CA 94105. (415)777-2197. President/Editor-in-Chief: Kenneth Park Cameron. Submissions Editor: Graham Phillips. Estab. 1975. Publishes hardcover and paperback originals. Total number of titles: 40 titles in 1986 (projection).

**Needs:** Contemporary, literary, science fiction, political, historical, humor/satire, fantasy, easy-to-read, animal, and children's. "Alchemy Books is looking for current subjects which relate to today's concerns. Thoughtful and important books with emotional content; also those which are just for fun. We are willing to consider any type or style of work providing that it is genuinely good. We are especially interested in developing a line of quality science fiction and fantasy titles." Recently published *Flossie the Christmas Mermaid*, by Flossie Langdon; *The Crooked Side of Hell*, by Coralia Nelson (novel about terrorism in El Salvador); and *Lost Summers*, by Lorraine Foster.

**How to Contact:** "We prefer to receive completed manuscripts along with a return mailer. Query letters are acceptable, as are photocopied and simultaneous submissions. Our report time is 6-8 months."

**Terms:** Regular royalty schedule. No advance.

**Tips:** "We are not limited to fiction or nonfiction, poetry or prose. However, we are seeking thought provoking works dealing with human realities. This does not confine us to somber philosophical creations; we appreciate humor, satire, and the fantastic. Our program calls on the author to participate fully and vigorously in the promotion of his work. We are still interested in developing our science fiction line."

**APPLE BOOKS, Scholastic, Inc.**, 730 Broadway, New York NY 10003. (212)505-3000. Senior Editor: Brenda Bowen. Children's imprint. See Scholastic, Inc.

**Needs:** "Apple books are generally contemporary. There are no restrictions as to length or subject matter, but all Apple Books are geared toward the capacities and interests of 8-12 year olds." Recently published *The Cybil War*, by Byars; and *The Computer That Said Steal Me*, by Levy.

**How to Contact:** Accepts unsolicited mss. Submit outline/synopsis and 3 sample chapters. Reports in 2 weeks on queries; 6 weeks on mss. Single submissions only. Accepts computer printout submissions. Prefers letter-quality.

**Terms:** Pays in royalties.

**APPLE-WOOD BOOKS, INC.**, Box 2870, Cambridge MA 02139. (617)923-9337. Editorial Director: Phil Zuckerman. Estab. 1976. Publishes paperback reprints. Plans 50 reprints for 1986.

**ARBOR HOUSE PUBLISHING COMPANY**, 235 E. 45th St., New York NY 10017. Imprints include Timbre Books, Belvedere Books, and Arbor House Library of Contemporary Americana. Editor-in-Chief: Ann Harris. Publisher: Eden Collinsworth. Estab. 1969. Publishes hardcover originals and Timbre trade paperbacks. Wide range of subjects, now in science fiction.

**Needs:** Subjects open. Recently published *Glitz*, by Elmore Leonard; *Stone 588*, by Gerald A. Browne; and *Murder at the FBI*, by Margaret Truman.

**How to Contact:** Submit through agent. No unsolicited mss. Simultaneous and photocopied submissions OK (but does not prefer them).

**Terms:** Pays in negotiable royalties; offers advance. Free book catalog.

**ARCHWAY PAPERBACKS**, 1230 Avenue of the Americas, New York NY 10020. (212)246-2121. Subsidiary of Pocket Books. Imprints include Which Way Adventure Stories (for ages 8-12); Follow Your Heart Romances (for girls 11 and up); and Which Way Secret Door Books (for ages 6-8). Publishes paperback originals.
**Needs:** Young adult (girls' novels, suspense/adventure, adventure). Recently published Which Way series; Follow Your Heart romances.
**How to Contact:** Submit query first; SASE "mandatory."
**Tips:** "Look at previously published novels in Archway series."

**THE ATLANTIC MONTHLY PRESS**, 8 Arlington St., Boston MA 02116. (617)536-9500. Children's Books Editor: Melanie Kroupa. Executive Editor: Upton Birnie Brady. Publishes hardcover and quality paperback originals. Number of titles: 16 in 1982; 11 in 1983. "Sometimes" buys juvenile mss with illustrations.
**Needs:** General fiction, juvenile: sports, animal, mystery/adventure, realistic contemporary fiction, picture books, and easy-to-read. Very interested in first novels.
**How to Contact:** Submit complete ms or submit through agent (but not necessary) with SASE. No simultaneous submissions; photocopied submissions OK.
**Terms:** Pays variable advances and royalties.
**Tips:** "Books for young adults should show superior story telling with strong characterization and convincing action and plot development."

**AUGSBURG PUBLISHING HOUSE**, Box 1209, Minneapolis MN 55440. (612)330-3432. Editor: Roland Seboldt. Estab. 1850. Publishes paperback originals.
**Needs:** Religious/inspirational short stories for young readers (grades 8-12); for young teens ages 12-14, youth ages 14-17, adults. Recently published *Who Am I Lord*, by Betty Steele Everett (short story devotions for girls); *How Do I Make Up My Mind Lord*, by Robert Kelly (short story devotions for boys); and *A Triangle Has Four Sides*, by Phyllis Reynolds Naylor (short stories for teenagers).
**How to Contact:** Query or submit complete ms or submit outline/synopsis and sample chapters with SASE. Simultaneous and photocopied submissions OK. Reports in 6 weeks on queries.
**Terms:** Pays 10% in royalties and offers $500 advance. Free book catalog with SASE.
**Tips:** "We are looking for short stories with life-related problems and Christian themes."

**AVALON BOOKS (II, IV)**, 401 Lafayette St., New York NY 10003. Imprint of Thomas Bouregy & Co., Inc. Small category line. Editor: Rita Brenig. Publishes hardcover originals. Books; average print order: 3,000; average first novel print order: 3,000. Number of titles: 60 in 1985; 60 planned for 1986. Buys 2% agented fiction. Recently published *The Love Match*, by Hope Goodwin (romance); *The Deadly Circle*, by Juanita Tyree Osborne (gothic); and *Vendetta!*, by Terrell L. Bowers (western).
**Needs:** "We want well-plotted, fast-moving romances, gothics, westerns, and nurse romances, all of about 50,000 words."
**How to Contact:** Accepts unsolicited mss. Send one-page outline with SASE or submit complete ms with ms-sized SASE. Do not telephone. Reports in 15 weeks on mss. Publishes ms "a few months" after acceptance.
**Terms:** Offers $400 advance which is applied against sales of the first 3,500 copies of the book.
**Tips:** "We like the writers to focus on the plot, drama, and characters, not the background. We consider first novels and novelists new to this company; if they fit our specific category needs, we print them. We have a *very* small staff so our relationship with the author is not as close as we like."

**AVON BOOKS (II)**, The Hearst Corporation, 1790 Broadway, New York NY 10019. (212)399-4500. Imprints include Avon, Bard, Camelot, Discus, and Flare. Estab. 1941. Large paperback publisher. Publishes paperback originals and reprints. Averages 160 titles a year.
**Needs:** Men's, adventure, fantasy, historical, romance, mainstream, occult/ horror, science fiction, women's contemporary, medical thrillers, suspense/mystery, intrigue, war, western, and

young adult/teen (young adult romance, sports, spy/adventure). No poetry, short story collections, religious, limited literary, or esoteric nonfiction. Recently published *Come Love a Stranger*, by Kathleen E. Woodiwiss (historical romance); and *Stick*, by Elmore Leonard (mystery/suspense).
**How to Contact:** Query letters only. SASE to insure response.
**Terms:** Vary. Book catalog for SASE. Offers Flare Novel competition.
**Tips:** Trends include historical and contemporary romances, occult/horror and thrillers. "We encourage first novelists."

**BAEN BOOKS (II)**, 260 5th Ave., New York NY 10001. (212)947-8244. Baen Science Fiction, Baen Fantasy, Baen High Tech. Senior Editor: Elizabeth Mitchell. Estab. 1983. Independent publisher; books are distributed by Simon & Schuster. Publishes hardcover and paperback originals and paperback reprints. Plans 6-10 first novels this year. Averages 65 total titles, 55 fiction titles each year. Occasionally critiques rejected mss.
**Needs:** Fantasy and science fiction. Interested in science fiction novels (generally "hard" science fiction) and fantasy novels that "are *not* rewrites of last year's bestsellers." Recently published *Killer Station*, by Martin Caidin (science fiction); and *The Frankenstein Papers*, by Fred Saberhagen (science fiction); *The Forty-Minute War*, by Janet and Chris Morris (science fiction).
**How to Contact:** Accepts unsolicited mss. Submit outline/synopsis and 3 sample chapters with SASE. Reports in 3 weeks on queries; 6 weeks on mss. Will consider simultaneous submissions, "but not as seriously as exclusives." Accepts letter-quality computer printout submissions.
**Terms:** Pays in royalties; offers advance. Sends galleys to author. Writer's guidelines for SASE.
**Tips:** "We are publishing more—our line is healthy and growing. We encourage first novelists. We like to maintain long term relationships with authors."

**BALLANTINE BOOKS**, 201 E. 50th St., New York NY 10022. Subsidiary of Random House. Senior Editor: Pamela Strickler. Publishes paperback originals (general fiction, mass-market and trade paperback). Averages over 120 total titles each year.
**Needs:** Major historical fiction, war, gothic/historical, and women's contemporary. The above categories can be submitted unsolicited to Pamela Strickler; others to the house must be agented.
**How to Contact:** Submit outline/synopsis and complete ms or at least 100 pages with SASE. Photocopied submissions OK. Reports in 2 months on queries; 4-5 months on mss.
**Terms:** Pays in royalties and advance.

**BALLANTINE/EPIPHANY BOOKS (II)**, 201 E. 50 St., New York NY 10022. (212)572-2473. Subsidiary of Random House. Publicist: Toni Simmons. Fiction Editors: Michelle Rapkin and Toni Simmons. Estab. 1983. Imprint includes Ballantine/Epiphany Hardcover. Publishes hardcover and paperback originals and paperback reprints. Books: offset printing; average print order: 30,000. Averages 12 total titles, 20% fiction titles each year. Average first novel print order 30,000 copies. Occasionally critiques rejected mss.
**Needs:** Religious/inspirational. "Novels must have inspirational qualities of a Christian nature." No Christian romances. Recently published *Search for Sanity*, by Pat Assimakopoulas; and *By God, You Can Do It*, by Robert Kirkley.
**How to Contact:** Query; submit outline/synopsis, 3 sample chapters, and SASE. Reports in 4-6 weeks on queries and mss. Simultaneous and photocopied submissions OK. Accepts computer printout submissions; prefers letter-quality.
**Terms:** Offers negotiable advance. Sends galleys to author. Writer's guidelines for legal-sized SASE. Book catalog for 9x12 SAE and 40¢ postage.
**Tips:** "We are eager to see fictional pieces containing inspirational elements—Christian works that would also appeal to the non-Christian, not overly religious. We encourage first novelists."

**BANTAM BOOKS, INC. (II)**, 666 5th Ave., New York NY 10103. (212)765-6500. Imprints include Skylark, New Age, Loveswept, Windstone, Sweet Dreams, Sweet Valley High, Spectra, and Starfire. Estab. 1945. Complete publishing: hard-cover, trade, mass market. Number of titles: Plans 600 for 1985.

**Needs:** Contemporary, literary, adventure, mystery, spy, historical, western, war, gothic, romance, women's, feminist, gay/lesbian, ethnic, psychic/supernatural, religious/inspirational, science fiction, fantasy, horror, humor/satire, and young adult. Recently published *The Clash*, by Erich Segal; and *The Postman*, by David Brin.

**How to Contact:** Submit through agent. No unsolicited material accepted. Simultaneous and photocopied submissions OK. Reports on queries as soon as possible.

**Terms:** Individually negotiated; offers advance.

**BEAUFORT BOOKS, INC. (III)**, 9 E. 40th St., New York NY 10016. (212)685-8588. Estab. 1980. Midsize independent publisher with plans to expand. Publishes hardcover and trade paperback originals. Number of titles: 65 in 1982. Buys 90% agented fiction. Average first novel print order 3,500 copies. Occasionally comments on rejected mss.

**Needs:** Contemporary, and spy/adventure. Recently published *Deathwatch*, by Elleston Trenor; and *A Book of Pot-Pourri*, by Gail Duff.

**How to Contact:** Accepts unsolicited mss. Submit complete ms with SASE. No simultaneous submissions; photocopied submissions OK. Reports in 6 weeks on mss. Publishes ms an average of 1 year after acceptance.

**Terms:** Royalties vary with individual; advance also varies with each author. Sends galleys to author.

**Tips:** "Previously published, please—newspaper and magazine experience counts. Our fiction list is geared toward libraries and trade."

**THE BERKLEY PUBLISHING GROUP (III)**, Putnam's Publishing Group, 200 Madison Ave., New York NY 10016. (212)686-9020. Imprints include Berkley, Jove, Ace Science Fiction, Charter, Tempo, Second Chance at Love, and To Have & To Hold. Editorial Director: Roger Cooper. Editor-in-Chief: Nancy Coffey. Large publisher owned by MCA, Inc. Publishes paperback originals and reprints. Averages approximately 1,000 total titles, 75% fiction titles each year. Occasionally critiques rejected mss.

**Needs:** Contemporary, fantasy, horror, mainstream, psychic/supernatural/occult, romance, science fiction, and war. Novel needs include: suspense, historical romances, espionage, and contemporary romances. Recently published . . . *And Ladies of the Club*, by Helen Hooven Santmyer; *The Hunt for Red October*, by Tom Clancy; *Tapestry of Dreams*, by Roberta Gellis.

**How to Contact:** No unsolicited mss. "We prefer material presented through agent." Reports in 3 weeks on queries; 3 months on mss. Photocopied submissions OK.

**Terms:** Pays in royalties of 4% minimum; 10% maximum; 20-100 author's copies; or individual arrangement with author dependent on the book. Sends galleys to author. Writer's guidelines for Second Chance at Love for #10 SASE.

**Tips:** "We encourage first novelists; and we feel the author-editor relationship is crucial to the success of the novel."

**BERKLEY/ACE SCIENCE FICTION (II)**, Berkley Publishing Group, 200 Madison Ave., New York NY 10016. Imprints include Berkley, Jove, Ace, Charter, Tempo, and Second Chance at Love. Editor-in-Chief: Susan Allison. Estab. 1948. Publishes paperback originals and reprints. Number of titles: 15/month. Buys 85-95% agented fiction.

**Needs:** Science fiction and fantasy. No other genre accepted. No short stories. Recently published *Icehenge*, by Kim Stanley Robinson; *Demon*, by John Varley; and *The Infinity Concerto*, by Greg Bear.

**How to Contact:** Submit outline/synopsis and 3 sample chapters with SASE. No simultaneous submissions; photocopied submissions OK. Reports in 2 months minimum on mss. "Queries answered immediately if SASE enclosed." Publishes ms an average of 18 months after acceptance.

**Terms:** Standard for the field. Sends galleys to author.

**Tips:** "Good science fiction and fantasy are almost always written by people who have read and

# Close-up

### Lou Aronica
### Spectra (Bantam)

photo by Susan Oristaglio

"Science fiction is probably the fastest growing area of fiction, now that romance has started to slow down," says Lou Aronica, senior editor and publishing director of Bantam's new Spectra line. Aronica then qualifies his statement, adding that Spectra is *not* a category line. It publishes science fiction and fantasy plus related genres, including surrealism and magic realism: *imaginative fiction*, that is, the kind of fiction South American novelists are known for. Spectra, says its editor, is the first real home for all novels of the fantastic.

Spectra is Lou Aronica's baby; it's a concept he developed working for Bantam in another department. To prepare for its launch in June 1985, Aronica talked with SF and fantasy fans at conventions and booksellers all over the country to find out their reading interests. The result is a broad range of Spectra titles that continues to "deepen its audience and break down barriers," for those who think SF is all ray guns and bug-eyed monsters. It's also for those who say they don't like the genre but enjoyed *1984* or *Brave New World* and don't recognize they are reading science fiction. Aronica's mission is to raise the level of writing while maintaining credibility and greater accessibility.

How to account for SF's recent expansion and increased "respectability"? The popularity of big movies—*E.T.*, *Star Wars*, etc.—helped jolt the genre out of its slump. In addition, longtime favorites (like Asimov, Heinlein, Clarke and Herbert) produced new bestsellers and thus raised the consciousness of the general reader. Also there's more attention today to the characters and their human concerns—even if set 3,000 years from now—thanks in part to the advent of more women writers, about 40% of Spectra's authors. In SF's expanded form there's more room to express oneself—and better writers are attracted to this type of fiction.

Established writers like Ursula K. Le Guin, Norman Spinrad and Samuel Delany publish at Spectra, but so do beginning talented authors. If the editor sees a manuscript with potential, he calls in the author to get a sense of ideas, his/her likely pace, and what he/she wants to write. "We don't take anybody we don't plan to develop a publishing program around," says the editor. Aronica responds first to the quality of writing and also looks for "the writer who can develop his characters quickly and write a good story with a sense of scope or size to it."

Aronica's interest in imaginative fiction goes back to his early teens when he was "turned on" by the mind-expanding possibilities of Ray Bradbury and Arthur Clarke, who demonstrated that "ability to ignore convention and go way beyond these four walls." Aronica is a writer himself, but not of SF—"there's not enough distance" as editor of Spectra—but he admits to several stories "cooking on the back burner."

"There's a lot of opportunity in this field now," Aronica says of his first priority. The busy editor, ably assisted by Senior Editor, Shawna McCarthy and Editor Lisa Novak who help him choose and edit the four to six titles a month, advises the beginning writer to follow his own example: "Go to conventions, meet SF writers." Also get involved in the field, join a local SF writers' club for the community support. And *read*. See what's happening in the publishing industry; subscribe to *Locus* or *SF Chronicle*. Most important, says the editor: "Don't write because it's a hot subject or market. Tastes change. Write what you really care about and want to say."

loved a lot of it. We are looking for knowledgeable science or magic, as well as sympathetic characters with recognizable motivation. We need less fantasy and more science fiction. In science fiction, we are looking for solid, well-plotted SF: good action adventure, well-researched hard science with good characterization, and books that emphasize characterization without sacrificing plot. In fantasy, again, we are looking for all types of work, from high fantasy to sword and sorcery." Submit fantasy and science fiction to Susan Allison, Ginjer Buchanan, Beth Fleisher, and Susan Stone.

**BETHANY HOUSE PUBLISHERS (II)**, 6820 Auto Club Rd., Minneapolis MN 55438. (612)829-2500. Imprints include Heartsong Books, Springflower Books, Prairie Love Stories. The Stonewyck Trilogy, The Straight Trilogy, George MacDonald Classics, Canada West, The Love Comes Softly Series. Editor: Carol Johnson. Assistant Editor: Nathan Unseth. Estab. 1956. Mid-size independent religious publisher with plans to expand; publishing in a variety of categories from theological to fiction. Publishes paperback and hardcover originals. Books: type of paper varies; offset printing; average print order: 20,000; first novel print order average: 15,000. Number of fiction titles: 11 in 1984; 12 in 1985. Average first novel print order 20,000 copies.

**Needs:** Religious/inspirational, adventure, mystery, regional, romance (historical and young adult), gothic, and juvenile. Recently published *When Comes the Spring*, by Janette Oke (prairie romance); and *The Wishing Star*, by Marian Wells (historical).

**How to Contact:** Query or submit outline/synopsis and 2-3 sample chapters with SASE. Simultaneous and photocopied submissions OK. Accepts computer printout submissions. Prefers letter-quality. Reports in 1 month on queries, 6 weeks on mss. Publishes ms an average of 1 year after acceptance.

**Terms:** Pays in royalties. Sends galleys to author. Free book catalog and fiction guidelines with 8½x11 SASE.

**Tips:** "Prairie romances are *very* strong in our line; next are gothic romances, then young adult contemporary romances. We look at everything that is submitted; a first novel has a good chance with us if it meets our criteria. We do *not* recommend an agent—this puts an unnecessary barrier up between publisher and author (chances for misunderstanding, mistrust). Send queries and proposals around till you have raised some interest; work with the editor to fit it to a publisher's needs."

**JOHN F. BLAIR, PUBLISHER (I, II, IV)**, 1406 Plaza Dr., Winston-Salem NC 27103. (919)768-1374. Editor: Gail Lathey Warner. Editor-in-Chief: John F. Blair. Estab. 1954. Small independent publisher. Publishes hardcover and paperback originals. Books: acid free paper; offset printing; casebound or softbound; illustrations; average print order 3,500-5,000. Number of titles: 5 in 1985. Encourages new writers. Occasionally comments on rejected mss.

**Needs:** Contemporary, literary, ethnic and regional. Generally prefers regional material dealing with southeastern US. No confessions or erotica. "We do not limit our consideration of manuscripts to those representing specific genres or styles. Our primary concern is that anything we publish be of high literary quality." Recently published *More Tales of the South Carolina Low Country*, by Nancy Rhyne (regional folklore); and *Southern Dreams and Trojan Women*, by Leo Snow (novel).

**How to Contact:** Query or submit through agent with SASE. Simultaneous and photocopied submissions OK. Accepts computer printout submissions. Prefers letter-quality. Reports in 1 month on queries, 3 months on mss. Publishes ms 1-2 years after acceptance.

**Terms:** Pays 10% standard royalties, 7% on paperback royalties. Royalties can go as high as 15% by special arrangement. Sends galleys to author. Must return advance if book is not completed or is not acceptable. Free book catalog.

**Tips:** "We are not interested in books for the very young. Currently we are saturated with historical and juvenile novels. We are primarily interested in serious adult novels of high literary quality. They are usually regional—*Southern* literature with a—tie-in to North Carolina or Southeastern US. We will continue to publish first novels of high quality, but we are not publishing as many as we would like because of economic considerations. Enclose a cover letter and outline with the manuscript. Write us for a catalog first. Our line is so limited that an author could tell almost with a glance whether a manuscript might interest us. New authors should submit their manuscripts to a small house that accepts novels similar to this rather than the large houses that will throw them at the bottom of the 'slush pile.' "

**BLUEJAY BOOKS (III)**, Suite 306, 1123 Broadway, New York NY 10010. (212)206-1538. Publisher: James Frenkel. Estab. 1983. Full-scale trade science fiction and fantasy publisher. Publishes hardcover and paperback originals and reprints. Plans 5-6 first novels this year. Averages 36 total titles, 34 fiction titles each year.
**Needs:** Fantasy, feminist, science fiction, American mysteries, and young adult/teen (fantasy/science fiction). Interested in "science fiction and fantasy—strong novels, adult and young adult." Recently published *Eon*, by Greg Bear; *The Isle of Glass*, by Judith Tarr; and *Embrace the Woolff*, by Benjamin M. Schutz.
**How to Contact:** Submit outline/synopsis and 4 sample chapters or complete ms with SASE. Reports in 4 months. Photocopied submissions OK. Accepts computer printout submissions. Prefers letter-quality.
**Terms:** Royalties vary; advance is negotiable. Book catalog for 10x13 SASE with 63¢ postage.

**BOOKCRAFT, INC.**, 1848 W. 2300 South, Salt Lake City UT 84119. (801)972-6180. Editor: George Bickerstaff. Publishes hardcover originals. Books: #60 stock paper; sheet-fed press; hardcover; average print order: 4,000-5,000; 2,000 reprint. Number of titles: 30 in 1985. Encourages new writers. "We are always open for creative, fresh ideas."
**Needs:** Contemporary, historical, western, romance, women's and religious/inspirational. Recently published *Two Women, Two Worlds*, by Melinda Jennings; *Love and the Mountain*, by Gordon T. Allred; and *Circle of Fire*, by Herbert Harker.
**How to Contact:** Query or submit outline/synopsis and sample chapters with SASE. No simultaneous submissions; photocopied submissions OK. Reports in 2 months on both queries and mss.
**Terms:** Pays royalties; no advance. Sends galleys to author. Free book catalog.
**Tips:** "Read our fiction. Our market is the membership of The Church of Jesus Christ of Latter-Day Saints (Mormons), and all stories must be related to the background, doctrines or practices of that church. No preaching, but tone should be fresh, positive, and motivational. No anti-Mormon works. We encourage first novelists. Copy of information for authors supplied on request."

**BOREALIS PRESS (IV)**, 9 Ashburn Dr., Ottawa, Ontario K2E 6N4 Canada. Imprint includes *Journal of Canadian Poetry*. Editor: Frank Tierney. Fiction Editor: Glenn Clever. Estab. 1970. Publishes hardcover and paperback originals and reprints. Books: standard book quality paper; offset printing; perfect and cloth binding; average print order: 1,000. Buys juvenile mss with b&w illustrations. Average number of titles: 8.
**Needs:** Contemporary, literary, adventure, historical, juvenile and young adult. "Must have a Canadian content or author; otherwise query first." Accepts short stories. Recently published: *Tale Spinner in a Spruce Tipi*, by Evalyn Gantreau (Cree Indian tales); *Trouble with Heroes*, by Guy Vanderhaeghe (short stories); and *Dry Waters*, by Robert Stead (novel).
**How to Contact:** Submit complete ms with SASE (Canadian postage) or IRCs. No simultaneous submissions; photocopied submissions OK. Reports in 2 weeks on queries, 3-4 months on mss. Publishes ms 1-2 years after acceptance.
**Terms:** Pays 10% in royalties and 3 free author's copies; no advance. Sends galleys to author. Free book catalog with SASE or IRC.
**Tips:** "Have your work professionally edited. We generally publish only material with a Canadian content or by a Canadian writer. We are publishing more short story collections than in the past."

**BRADBURY PRESS, INC. (I, II)**, Affiliate of Macmillan, Inc., 866 3rd Ave., New York NY 10022. (212)702-9809. Editor: Norma Jean Sawicki and Richard Jackson. Publishes juvenile hardcover originals. Books: excellent quality paper printing and binding; full color or black-and-

white illustrations—depends on what the book needs. Number of titles: 24 in 1984, 40 in 1985. Encourages new writers. Seldom comments on rejected mss.
**Needs:** Juvenile and young adult: contemporary, adventure, science fiction, romance (realistic), and humor/satire. "*Very* interested in picture books, especially preschool and nonfiction for *young* children." No fantasy or religious material. Recently published *The Pain and the Great One*, by J. Blume; and *One-Eyed Cat*, by P. Fox; and *Pig William*, by Arlene Dubanevich.
**How to Contact:** Query first on novels. Send complete picture book ms with SASE. No simultaneous submissions; photocopied submissions OK. Reports in 3 months on mss.
**Terms:** Pays 10% or 5% to author and 5% to artist on retail price; advance negotiable. "We simply like good stories that are well-crafted. Be a good storyteller; write well."

**BRANDEN PUBLISHING COMPANY INC.(I, II)**, I.P.L. Dante University of America Press, 17 Station St., Box 843, Brookline Village MA 02147. (617)734-2045. Imprint includes Popular Technology. President: Adolph Caso. Estab. 1903. Small independent publishing company with plans to expand nationally and internationally. Publishes hardcover and paperback originals and reprints. Books: 55-60 lb paper; WEB or equivalent printing; paper or cloth binding; drawings or photographs; average print order: 5,000, average first novel print order: 3,000. Plans 1-4 first novels this year. Averages 20 total titles, 5 fiction titles each year. Average first novel print order 3,000 copies.
**Needs:** Contemporary, ethnic, juvenile (historical), religious/inspirational, historical romance, short story collections and translations. No pornography. Recently published *Erebus-Child of Chaos*, by Sam Saladino and *Merger-Takeover Conspiracy*, by David Thomsen.
**How to Contact:** Does not accept unsolicited mss. Query with SASE. Reports in 2 weeks. No simultaneous submissions. Prefers computer printout submissions.
**Terms:** Pays in royalties of 10% minimum; 15% maximum; 10 author's copies. Sends galleys to author. Book catalog for SASE.
**Tips:** "First novels have to be very good and should have a message. We are publishing more fiction hardcover because of greater profits and movie possibilities. We like an extremely close relationship with the author."

**GEORGE BRAZILLER, INC. (III)**, One Park Ave., New York NY 10016. (212)889-0909. Estab. 1955. Publishes hardcover originals and paperback reprints. Books: cloth binding; illustrations sometimes; average print order 4,000, average first novel print order: 3,000. Buys 40% agented fiction. Averages 25 total titles, 6 fiction titles each year. Occasionally critiques rejected mss.
**Needs:** Experimental, feminist, literary, short story collections and translations. Recently published *Flying to Nowhere*, by John Fuller (literary); *Cal*, by Bernard MacLaverty (literary); and *Marbot*, by Wolfgang Hildesheimer (literary).
**How to Contact:** Query first with SASE. Photocopied submissions OK. Reports in 2 weeks on queries. Publishes ms an average of 1 year after acceptance.
**Terms:** Negotiates advance. Must return advance if book is not completed or is not acceptable. Sends galleys to author. Free book catalog on request with over-sized SASE.
**Tips:** "We are publishing less fiction, more paperbacks."

‡**BRIDGE PUBLISHING, INC. (IV)**, 2500 Hamilton Blvd., South Plainfield NJ 07080. (201)754-0745. Imprints include Logos, Haven, Open Scroll. Assistant Editor: Robert Oliver. Estab. 1981. Midsize independent publisher of Christian literature. Publishes paperback originals and paperback reprints. Books: 55 lb natural paper; web or belt printing; binding paper, perfect bound; sometimes line drawings or half-tones; average print order: 7,500; first novel print order: 5,000. Plans 2 first novels this year. Averages 20 total titles/year. Critiques rejected ms for $30. Average 2 novels/year.
**Needs:** Religious/inspirational. Looking for good Christian fiction, including juvenile and young adult. No "stories that insist on one denominational viewpoint that must be accepted by the reader." Recently published *Kingsword*, by Jim Fitzgerald (quarterly comic book featuring continuing stories).

**How to Contact:** Accepts unsolicited mss. Submit complete ms with cover letter. SASE. Reports in 3 months. Simultaneous or photocopied submissions OK. Accepts computer printouts including dot-matrix.

**Terms:** Pays in royalties of 6% minimum; 10% maximum. Sends galleys to author. Subsidy publishes. "Author pays for typesetting, proofreading, cover art, printing and manufacturing. Author owns books, which are stored in our warehouse. No charge for storage. We pay author 35% of retail on copies we sell. Book is listed on our order forms and in our catalog." Writer's guidelines free for #10 SASE and 1 first class stamp.

**Tips:** "We encourage first novelists. One currently under contract. The editor's job here is to make sure the author is communicating ideas clearly and to make sure the writing is suited to our market. Conforming the writing to our house style helps us achieve consistency and minimize errors in editing, typesetting and proofreading. Major changes are worked out to satisfaction of author and editor." Subject matter should be timely or timeless. Use enough detail and dialogue to make the events and people seem real.

**BROADMAN PRESS (II)**, 127 9th Ave. N., Nashville TN 37234. (615)251-2433. Editorial Director: Harold S. Smith. Religious publisher associated with the Southern Baptist Conference. Publishes hardcover and paperback originals. Books: offset or Cameron stock; offset Cameron belt; perfect Smyth sewn binding; illustrations possible; average print order: depends on forecast. Average number of titles: 5.

**Needs:** Adventure, historical, religious/inspirational, humor/satire, juvenile, and young adult. Will accept no other genre. Recently published: *Like a Promise*, by Phyllis C. Gobbell (adult); *Decision at Brushy Creek*, by Ruby C. Tolliver (juvenile/youth); and *The Dream Lives On*, by Muriel F. Blackwell (juvenile/youth).

**How to Contact:** Query but decision is not made until ms is revised. No simultaneous submissions; photocopied submissions OK. Reports in 2 months on queries and mss.

**Terms:** Pays 10% in royalties; no advance. Sends galleys to author if requested.

**Tips:** "We publish very few fiction works, but we encourage first novelists. We encourage a close working relationship with the author to develop the best possible product."

**‡CAEDMON (II)**, 1995 Broadway, New York NY 10023. (212)580-3400. Associate Editor: John Wynne. Fiction Editor: Linda Morgenstern. Estab. Caedmon 1952; Caedmon Books 1983. Publishes paperback originals. Books: matte paper; offset printing; paperback (perfect) binding; four color illustrations; average print order: 7,500-10,000 copies; first novel print order: 7,500 copies. Occasionally critiques rejected mss.

**Needs:** Juvenile (5-9 yrs.)—including animal, easy-to-read, fantasy, historical, sports, spy/adventure, contemporary), preschool/picture book. Needs read-alongs (pre-K-grade six only). No young adult. Recently published *The Tree That Cried*, by Doris Schwerin (picture book); *So Many Raccoons*, by Jan Wahl (picture book); and *The Bat Family*, by Bryon Preiss (ages 5-8).

**How to Contact:** Accepts unsolicited mss. SASE. Submit complete ms with cover letter. Agented fiction 75%. Reports in 3 months. Simultaneous and photocopied submissions OK. Accepts computer printouts including dot-matrix.

**Terms:** Sends galleys to author. Payment is individual arrangement with author depending on the book. Book catalog free on request.

**Tips:** "We are publishing more paperbacks because our publishing program is directly linked to our recording program." Encourages first novelists. Write what really interests you, not what you think will sell."

**CAMELOT BOOKS (I, II)**, Children's book imprint of Avon Books. 1790 Broadway, New York NY 10019. (212)399-1384. Senior Editor, Books for Young Readers: Ellen Krieger. Estab. 1967. Mass market publisher. Publishes paperback originals and reprints. Buys juvenile mss with illustrations.

**Needs:** Juvenile and young adult: contemporary, adventure, mystery, animal, fantasy/science fiction and humor. No historical. Recently published *Howliday Inn*, by James Howe; and *Rainbow Kid*, by Jeanne Betancourt.

**How to Contact:** Accepts unsolicited mss. Submit outline and sample chapters with SASE. Simultaneous and photocopied submissions OK. Accepts computer printout submissions. Prefers letter-quality. Reports in 8 weeks on mss.

**Terms:** Pays 6-8% royalty: advance average $7,000. Sends galleys to author.

**Tips:** Considers first novels. "We are primarily interested in young adult fiction about contemporary teenagers."

**CAROLRHODA BOOKS, INC. (II)**, Lerner Publications Co., 241 1st Ave. N, Minneapolis MN 55401. (612)332-3344. Editorial Director: Beverly Charette. Estab. 1969. Midsize children's hardcover publisher. Publishes hardcover originals. Books: Vellum or matte paper depending on type of illustration; web printing; reinforced school and library binding; illustrations every spread; average print order: 5,000 copies; first novel print order: 5,000. Plans 1-2 first novels this year. Buys 10% agented fiction. Averages 25-35 total titles, 3-4 fiction titles, not counting picture books, each year. Average first novel print order 5,000 copies.

**Needs:** Juvenile (easy-to-read, historical, spy/adventure, contemporary, humor, biography, nature-oriented nonfiction), and young adult/teen (fantasy/science fiction, mysteries, historical for 10-13 year olds). Needs include novels for ages 7-10 and 10-13; no problem novels. Recently published *Keep the Lights Burning Abbie*, by Peter and Connie Roop (historical easy-to-read); and *Bunnies and Their Hobbies*, by Nancy Carlson (humorous easy-to-read).

**How to Contact:** Accepts unsolicited mss. Submit outline/synopsis and 3 sample chapters for nonfiction, complete ms for fiction, both with SASE. Reports in 1 month on queries; 3 months on mss. Simultaneous and photocopied submissions OK. Accepts computer printout submissions if close to letter-quality. Publishes ms an average of 1 year after acceptance. Sends galleys to author.

**Terms:** Variable. Individual arrangement with author depending on the book. Writer's guidelines for 9½x4 SASE with 22, postage. Free book catalog on request.

**Tips:** Publishes very few single-title picture books. "Our emphasis is on quality rather than trend. Submissions are improving in quality, but we're still not getting publishable novels for 7-10- and 10-13 year-olds. Be sure *not* to send us adult material, problem novels, or forget an SASE. Make sure easy-to-read material is short, no more than 10-15 double-spaced typewritten pages, and indeed easy to read. Research your appropriate market carefully to avoid wasted effort. Write what you want to write or that which is begging to come out of you onto paper, not what you will sell in a particular market. Marketing of your manuscript comes after the creation, not before. Expect a slower response between April and August."

**CARROLL & GRAF PUBLISHERS, INC. (III)**, 260 5th Ave., New York NY 10001. (212)889-8772. Contact: Editor. Estab. 1983. Publishes hardcover and paperback originals and paperback reprints. Plans 5 first novels this year. Averages 60 total titles, 45 fiction titles each year. Average first novel print order 10,000 copies. Occasionally critiques rejected mss.

**Needs:** Adventure, contemporary, erotica, experimental, fantasy, literary, mainstream, suspense/mystery, and war. No romance.

**How to Contact:** Does not accept unsolicited mss. Query first or submit outline/synopsis and sample chapters. SASE for query, ms. Reports in 2 weeks. Photocopied submissions OK. Accepts computer printout submissions. Prefers letter-quality.

**Terms:** Pays in royalties of 6% minimum; 12½% maximum; advance negotiable. Sends galleys to author. Free book catalog on request.

**Tips:** Publishes more fiction than in the past. Encourages first novels.

**CHARLES RIVER BOOKS**, 1 Thompson Sq., Charlestown MA 02129. Senior Editor: B. Comjean. Editorial Director: Robert Kent. Estab. 1978. Publishes hardcover and paperback originals and hardcover reprints. Number of titles: 12 in 1983; 12 planned in 1984.

**Needs:** Open to all categories. Recently published *Sweet Wild World*, by William White; *Rustler on the Beach*, by Frank Mulville; and *The Child Snatchers*, by Bobbi Lawrence and Olivia Taylor-Young.

**How to Contact:** Query. Simultaneous and photocopied submissions OK. Reports in 6 weeks.

**Terms:** Pays 7½-12% royalties; "modest" advance. Book catalog for 8½x11 SASE.

**CHILDRENS PRESS (II)**, Division of Regensteiner Publishing Enterprises, Inc., 1224 W. Van Buren, Chicago IL 60607. (312)666-4200. Editorial Director: Fran Dyra. Estab. 1946. Publishes hardcover originals. Plans 6 first novels this year. Averages 125-150 total titles, 40 fiction titles each year.
**Needs:** Juvenile (easy-to-read, picture books, biographies (historical and contemporary) for middle and junior high grades. Recently published *Hans Christian Andersen*, (people of distinction); Miracle of Genetics, (intermediate level); *Picture Stories Biographies*, (intermediate level).
**How to Contact:** Query first if long ms (more than 5 ms pages or series idea); submit outline/ synopsis and sample chapters or complete ms with SASE. Simultaneous submissions and photo-copied submissions OK. Do not send original artwork. Reports in 3 months.
**Terms:** Pays occasionally in royalties of 5% minimum; negotiates advance. Generally pays in outright purchase of $500 minimum; 6 author's copies. Occasionally subsidy publishes; offers 25% subsidiary rights. Free writer's guidelines; free book catalog on request.
**Tips:** "Have patience and determination. Know the market needs of publisher by looking in public library and seeing what types of product publisher distributes."

**THE CHILD'S WORLD, INC. (II)**, Box 989, Elgin IL 60120. (312)741-7591. President: Jane Buerger. Estab. 1968. Publishes hardcover and paperback originals. Number of titles: approximately 50/year.
**Needs:** Supplemental books for school and library market. Juvenile: concept books, sports, animal, spy/adventure, historical, fantasy/science fiction and easy-to-read. "All of our titles are for the juvenile market. Most are only 32 pages." Recently published *Holiday Series*, by various authors; *Word Bird, My Number Books—First Steps to Math*, by Jane Moncure; and *Double Rhyme*, by Dick Punnett.
**How to Contact:** Submit complete ms with SASE. Simultaneous and photocopied submissions OK. Reports in 4 months on queries.
**Terms:** Pays by outright purchase of $400-$700; no advance. Free book catalog.
**Tips:** "Avoid sending material for high school and adult age groups."

**CITADEL PRESS (II)**, Lyle Stuart Inc., 120 Enterprise Ave., Secaucus NJ 07094. (201)866-4199. Vice President: Allan J. Wilson. Estab. 1942. Publishes hardcover and paperback originals and paperback reprints. Averages 65 total titles, 8-10 fiction titles each year. Occasionally critiques rejected mss.
**Needs:** No religious, romantic, or detective. Recently published *Howard Hughes in Hollywood*, by Tony Thomas; *Woody Allen: His Films and Career*, by Douglas Brody; and *Naked in the Streets*, by James Rush.
**How to Contact:** Accepts unsolicited mss. Query first with SASE. Reports in 6 weeks on queries; 2 months on mss. Simultaneous and photocopied submissions OK.
**Terms:** Pays in royalties of 10% minimum; 15% maximum; 12-25 author's copies. Advance is more for agented ms; depends on grant/award money.

**CLARION BOOKS, TICKNOR & FIELDS: A Houghton Mifflin Company (II)**, 52 Vanderbilt Ave., New York NY 10017. (212)972-1190. Editor/Publisher: James C. Giblin. Estab. 1965 "as the children's book division of Seabury Press; 1979 as a new children's book imprint of Houghton Mifflin Company." Midsize children's book imprint of a major publishing company. Publishes hardcover originals and paperback reprints from its own backlist. Number of titles: 31 in 1984; 33 in 1985. Encourages new writers. Published 2 first novels in 1985. Buys 10-15% agented fiction. Comments on rejected mss "only if we're encouraging a revision."
**Needs:** Juvenile and young adult: adventure, suspense, and humorous contemporary stories for ages 8-12 and 10-14; "fresh, personal stories that capture our attention, and that we think young readers would enjoy." Recently published *One Order to Go*, by Mel Glenn (contemporary young adult novel); *Patrick's Dinosaurs*, by Carol Carrick (picture book adventure); and *Annabelle Starr, E.S.P.*, by Lila Perl (school and family story). Especially interested in humorous stories for ages 8 to 12.

**How to Contact:** Accepts unsolicited mss. Query on mss of more than 50 pages. SASE for query, ms. Reluctantly considers simultaneous submissions; photocopied submissions OK. Accepts computer printout submissions. Reports in 2 weeks on queries, 8 weeks on mss. Publishes ms 12-18 months after acceptance.

**Terms:** Pays 5% royalties on picture books; 10% on older books; offers $1,500-$2,000 advances. Must return advance if book is not completed or is not acceptable. Free book catalog.

**Tips:** "I really believe that the best novels come out of the author's self-knowledge of his or her own experience and background. Don't send us imitations of other writers' successes. We're always open to first novelists in the hope that they'll become regular contributors to our list. We've noticed a return to lighter stories from the heavier problem novels of recent years. Attend a writer's workshop or critique group in order to study the structure of successful novels."

**COLUMBIA PUBLISHING COMPANY, INC.**, Frenchtown NJ 08825. (201)996-2141. President: Bernard Rabb. Estab. 1971. Small independent publisher. Publishes hardcover originals.

**Needs:** Literary, experimental, gay, historical, regional, and translations.

**How to Contact:** Accepts unsolicited mss. Submit complete ms with SASE. Simultaneous and photocopied submissions OK. Accepts computer printout submissions. Prefers letter-quality. Accepts disc submissions with IBM-PC. Prefers hard copy with disc submissions. Reports in 6 months.

**Terms:** Pays in royalties; offers advance.

**Tips:** "Thoughtful writers, serious writers, and writers with vision, sensitivity, and style are always welcome. If the writer thinks his work will be a blockbuster bestseller and will be a movie at MGM, chances are the work is not for us. But if the work is intended for the smaller audience of literate readers, then we would like to consider it for publication."

**CONCORDIA PUBLISHING HOUSE (II)**, 3558 S. Jefferson Ave., St. Louis MO 63118. (314)664-7000. Imprints include Arch Books. Contact: Children's Books Dept. Estab. 1869. Average 30 titles/year. Encourages new writers. Rarely comments on rejected mss.

**Needs:** Religious/inspirational fiction "is all that we will consider." Recently published *Numbers . . ., Colors . . ., Shapes . . ., and Sizes in God's World*, by Beverly Beckmann; *You Are Special to Jesus*, by Annetta Dellinger (children's); and *Sarah's Story*, by Lillian Cantleberry (the story of Abraham through the eyes of his wife; adult).

**How to Contact:** Query or submit outline/synopsis. SASE for query, ms. Simultaneous and photocopied submissions OK. Reports in 2 weeks on queries, 6-12 weeks on mss.

**Terms:** Pays 5-10% in royalties and 6 author's copies.

**Tips:** "We publish very little *adult* fiction. Except for a few series which are well established, we are cutting back on fiction. Our market looks to us for a different kind of book. Need in the marketplace: well-written book with *series* potential, like Haley Adventure stories. We prefer to do our own art."

**DAVID C. COOK PUBLISHING COMPANY**, 850 N. Grove, Elgin IL 60120. (312)741-2400. Imprint: Chariot Books. Managing Editor: Catherine L. Davis. Estab. 1875. Publishes hardcover and paperback originals. Number of fiction titles: 35-40 juvenile. Encourages new writers.

**Needs:** No adult. Religious/inspirational, juvenile and young adult: sports, animal, spy/adventure, historical, Biblical, fantasy/science fiction, picture book, and easy-to-read. Recently published *The Forbidden Door*, by Jeanne K. Norweb; *Don't Cry for Anna*, by Mary E. Erickson, and *Sixteen and Away from Home*, by Arleta Richardson.

**How to Contact:** Query with SASE. All unsolicited mss are returned unopened. Simultaneous and photocopied submissions OK. Accepts computer printout submissions. Reports in 3 months on queries.

**Terms:** Pays 5-10% on an escalating clause ("depending on whether it is trade, mass market or cloth") in royalties and 10 author's copies; offers advance. Free writer's guidelines with SASE.

**Tips:** Chariot Books includes Making Choices books, which are reader participation novels.

**CROSSWAY BOOKS (II)**, Division of Good News Publishers, 9825 W. Roosevelt Rd., Westchester IL 60153. (312)345-7474. Editorial Director: Jan P. Dennis. Estab. 1938. Midsize independent religious publisher with plans to expand. Publishes hardcover and paperback originals. Book: illustrations sometimes; average print order 3,000-5,000. Plans 4 first novels this year. Buys 50% agented fiction. Averages 25 total titles, 4-5 fiction titles each year.
**Needs:** Contemporary, adventure fantasy, juvenile (fantasy, animal), literary, religious/inspirational, science fiction, short story collections, and young adult (fantasy/science fiction). "All fiction published by Crossway Books must be written from the perspective of historic orthodox Christianity. It need not be *explicitly* Christian, but it must understand and view the world through Christian principle. For example, our book *Alpha Centauri* takes place in a pre-Christian era, but Christian themes (e.g., sin, forgiveness, sacrifice, redemption) are present. We will publish as many novels in the next two or so years as we can find, as long as they meet these criteria. We are *eager* to discover and nurture Christian novelists." No sentimental, didactic, "inspirational" religious fiction; heavy-handed allegorical or derivative (of C.S. Lewis or J.R.R. Tolkien) fantasy; Biblical or "end times" fiction. Recently published *Dragon King Trilogy* and Empyrion: Search for Fierra, by Stephen R. Lawhead.
**How to Contact:** Accepts unsolicited mss. Submit complete ms with SASE; also accepts phone calls. Accepts computer printout submissions. Prefers letter-quality. Reports in 3 weeks to 4 months on mss. Publishes ms 1-2 years after acceptance.
**Terms:** Pays in royalties and negotiates advance. Free book catalog on request.
**Tips:** "Christian novelists—you must get your writing *up to standard*. The major reason novels informed by a Christian perspective do not have more presence in the market is because they are inferior. Sad but true. I believe Crossway can successfully publish and market *quality* Christian novelists. Also read John Gardner's *On Moral Fiction*. The market for fantasy/science fiction continues to expand (and genre fiction in general). There are more attempts lately at Christian science fiction and fantasy, though they generally fail from didacticism or from being overly derivative."

**T.Y. CROWELL JUNIOR BOOKS (II)**, 10 E. 53rd St., New York NY 10022. (212)207-7044. Recently published *Snail Saves the Day*, by John Stadler (ages 4-8); and *Lights! Camera! Action!: How a Movie is Made*, by Gail Gibbons (ages 6-9). See: Harper & Row Junior Books Group.

**CROWN PUBLISHERS, INC.**, 225 Park Ave. S., New York NY 10003. (212)254-1600. Imprints include Harmony Books, Clarkson N. Potter, Inc. Sr. Editor: Barbara Grossman. Managing Editor: Laurie Stark. Estab. 1933. Large independent publisher of fiction and nonfiction. Publishes hardcover and paperback originals and reprints. Plans 4 first novels this year. Averages 250 total titles, 26 fiction titles each year. Average first novel print order: 15,000 copies. Occasionally critiques rejected mss.
**Needs:** Adventure, contemporary, historical, horror, humor/satire, literary, mainstream, romance (historical, contemporary), science fiction, war, women's, juvenile and young adult (fiction for ages 8-12, young adult, picture books). Needs for novels: genre. Recently published *The Mammoth Hunters*, by Jean M. Auel; *Easy in the Islands*; by Bob Shacochis (short stories).
**How to Contact:** Query first or submit outline/synopsis and 3 sample chapters; send complete ms for picture books; other complete mss are returned unread. SASE. Reports in 3-4 months. Photocopied submissions OK; no simultaneous submissions for children's books.
**Terms:** Pays advance against royalty; terms vary and are negotiated per book. Book catalog for SASE.

**‡DAHLSTROM & COMPANY, INC. (I)**, 76 Prospect St., Farnklin MA 02038. (617)528-1043. Imprints include Study Buddy Books, Life Line Books. Senior Editor: Harry Dahlstrom. Estab. 1979. Small independent publisher serving school, library and professional markets. Publishes paperback originals. Books: 60 lb white offset paper; offset printing; perfect bound binding; pen & ink photography; average print order: 5,000-10,000; first novel print order: 5,000. Plans 5-10 first novels this year. Averages 30 total titles, 5 fiction titles each year. Critiques or comments on rejected ms.

**Needs:** Adventure, contemporary, ethnic, historical, juvenile (5-9; easy-to-read, contemporary), young adult/teen (10-18 years; easy-to-read, problem novels). Accepts short stories for texts. Would like to do anthology of stories on teen problems. Need situation novels for teenagers—prejudice, drugs, handicaps, etc. Must be high interest, easy to read and offer solutions. No mystery, occult or erotica.

**How to Contact:** Accepts unsolicited mss. Submit complete ms with cover letter. SASE. Reports in 1 month. Simultaneous and photocopied submissions OK. Accepts computer printouts.

**Terms:** Pays in royalties of 8% minimum; 15% maximum; advance is negotiable. Sends galleys to author. Writer's guidelines free for #10 SASE and 1 first class stamp. Book listing for #10 SASE and 2 first class stamps.

**Tips:** "We want to build and nurture a group of authors who can recommend new ideas and also handle assignment work. We are expanding into school and library markets. Important—author must be able to take advice and make changes without being insulted."

**DAW BOOKS, INC. (II, IV)**, 1633 Broadway, New York NY 10019. Imprint includes DAW Books. Editor-in-Chief: Betsy Wollheim. Senior Editor: Sheila Gilbert. Estab. 1971. Publishes paperback originals, hardcover reprints and hardcover originals. Books: illustrations sometimes; average print and first novel order vary widely. May publish as many as 4 first novels a year. Averages 60 total titles, 60 fiction titles each year. Occasionally critiques rejected mss.

**Needs:** Fantasy and science fiction only.

**How to Contact:** Submit complete ms with SASE. Reports in 8-12 weeks on mss.

**Terms:** Pays an advance against royalties. Sends galleys to author (if there is time).

**Tips:** "We strongly encourage new writers. This year we have published first novels by Tad Williams, Terry Adams, Linda Steele, and John Steakley and are working with three more now. We like a close and friendly relationship with authors. We are publishing more fantasy than previously, but we are looking for more *serious* fantasy and science fiction. To unpublished authors, try to make an educated submission and don't give up."

**DELACORTE JUVENILE (III, IV)**, 1 Dag Hammarskjold Plaza, New York NY 10017. See Dell Publishing Co., Inc. "We prefer query letters with detailed synopses of novel length contemporary fiction only. No picture books." For ages 6 and up. "Will regrettably, no longer consider unsolicited material at this time." Annual contest for the Delacorte Prize for outstanding Delacorte Young Adults First Novel. Query for deadline dates in 1986.

**Tips:** Send queries addressed to BVYR, Delacorte Juvenile, 1 Dag Hammarskjold Plaza, New York NY 10017.

**DELACORTE PRESS**, 1 Dag Hammarskjold Plaza, New York NY 10017. See Dell Publishing Co., Inc.

**‡DELACORTE PRESS BOOKS FOR YOUNG READERS (II, III)**, Subsidiary of Doubleday, 245 E. 47 St., New York NY 10028. Editor: Bebe Willoughby. Mid-size independent publisher with plans to expand. Publishes hardcover originals and paperback originals and reprints. Plans 2 first titles this year. Averages 30 total titles, 30 fiction titles each year. Critiques or comments on rejected ms.

**Needs:** Fantasy, juvenile (5-9 years including: animal, easy-to-read, fantasy, historical, sports, spy/adventure, contemporary), young adult (10-18 years including easy-to-read, fantasy/science fiction, historical, problem novels, romance, sports, spy/adventure). No romance of the formula type. Recently published *Catch Me, I'm Falling in Love*, by Mary Anderson (fiction); *Traveler by Night*, by Vivian Alcock (middle grade); and *Walk Through Cold Fire*, by Cin-Forshay-Humsford (YA).

**How to Contact:** Submit compelte outline/synopsis and 3 sample chpaters. Agented fiction: 80%. Reports on ms in 1 month. Photocopied submissions OK. Accepts electronic submissions via disc or modem.

**Terms:** Pays in royalties; advance: $5,000 average amount for beginner; advance is negotiable. Sends galleys to author. Book catalog free on request.

**Tips:** "We are publishing more fiction than in the past. The market is good. We encourage first novelists and published new writers last year."

**DELL PUBLISHING CO., INC. (III)**, 1 Dag Hammarskjold Plaza, New York NY 10017. Imprints include Candlelight Ecstasy and Ecstasy Supreme Romances, Delacorte Press, Delacorte Juvenile, Delta, Dell, Laurel, Laurel-Leaf, Yearling, and Purse. Estab. 1922. Publishes hardcover and paperback originals and paperback reprints.
**Needs:** See below for individual imprint requirements.
**How to Contact:** General guidelines for unagented submissions. Reports in 3 months. Photocopied and simultaneous submissions OK. Please adhere strictly to the following procedures: 1. Send *only* a 4-page synopsis or outline with a cover letter stating previous work published or relevant experience. Enclose SASE. 2. *Do not* send ms, sample chapters or artwork. 3. *Do not* register, certify or insure your letter. Dell is comprised of several imprints, each with its own editorial department. Please review carefully the following information and direct your submissions to the appropriate department. Your envelope must be marked: Attention: (One of the following names of imprints), Editorial Department—Proposal.
DELACORTE: Publishes in hardcover; looks for top-notch commercial fiction; historical romance. Recently published *Galapagos*, by Kurt Vonnegut; and *Secrets*, by Danielle Steel. 25 titles/year.
DELTA: Publishes in trade paperback; rarely publishes original fiction; looks for useful, substantial guides (nonfiction). 5-10 titles/year.
DELL: Publishes mass-market paperbacks; rarely publishes original nonfiction; looks for family sagas, historical romances, sexy modern romances, adventure and suspense thrillers, psychic/supernatural, horror, and war novels. Especially interested in submissions for Candlelight Ecstasy Romances. Not currently publishing original mysteries, westerns, or science fiction. 450 titles/year.
DELACORTE JUVENILE: Publishes in hardcover for children and young adults, grades K-12. 25 titles/year. "We prefer complete mss for fiction."
LAUREL-LEAF: Publishes originals and reprints in paperback for young adults, grades 7-12. 60 titles/year.
YEARLING: Publishes originals and reprints in paperback for children, grades K-6. 48 titles/year.
**Terms:** Pays 6-15% in royalties; offers advance. Sends galleys to author. Book catalog for 8½x11 SASE plus $1.30 postage (Attention: Customer Service).
**Tips:** "Don't get your hopes up. Query first only with 4-page synopsis plus SASE. Study the paperback racks in your local drugstore. We encourage first novelists. We also encourage all authors to seek agents."

**DELTA PRESS**, 1 Dag Hammarskjold Plaza, New York NY 10017. See Dell Publishing Co., Inc.

**DEMBNER BOOKS (II)**, Division of Red Dembner Enterprises, 80 8th Ave., New York NY 10011. Editor: S. Arthur Dembner. Fiction Editor: Therese Eiben. Publishes hardcover originals. Books: quality consignment stock paper; sheet and Web printing; hardcover binding; illustrations rarely; average print order: 5,000-10,000; first novel print order: 3,000-5,000. Encourages new writers.
**Needs:** Contemporary, adventure, mystery/suspense, and historical. "We are prepared to publish a limited number of well-written, nonsensational works of fiction." Recently published *Let Sleeping Dogs Lie*, by John Riggs; *Requiem for a River Rat*, by Neal Ekker.
**How to Contact:** Submit outline/synopsis and sample chapters with SASE. Simultaneous and photocopied submissions OK.
**Terms:** Offers negotiable advance. Sends galleys to author.
**Tips:** Encourages first novelists. Mystery is big these days. Recently we did a novel about whitewater rafting, which seems to have a growing following. Have patience and forbearance. Those

who make it big on first novel are a very not-so-select few. The randomness of publishing success stories is one of the hardest things about being a writer (and editor, I must add)."

**DENLINGER'S PUBLISHERS LTD (II)**, Box 76, Fairfax VA 22030. (703)631-1500. Publisher: W.W. Denlinger. Estab. 1926. Publishes hardcover and paperback originals. Books: 50 lb offset paper; Web-belt across; paper and hard binding; line drawing sometimes; average print order: 3,000 to 5,000. Averages 12-20 total titles, 3-5 fiction titles each year.
**Needs:** Historical. Especially interested in Southern historical novels.
**How to Contact:** Does not accept unsolicited mss. Query with outline/synopsis, and 1 sample chapter and SASE. Reports in 2 weeks on queries; 6 weeks on mss. Simultaneous and photocopied submissions OK. Accepts computer printout submissions.
**Terms:** Pays in royalties of 10% mimimum; 15% maximum; 6 author's copies. Sends galleys to author.

**DODD, MEAD & COMPANY, INC.**, 79 Madison Ave., New York NY 10016. (212)685-6464. Fiction Editors: Jerry Gross, Allen Klots, Margaret Norton, and Cynthia Vartan. Estab. 1839. Publishes hardcover and paperback originals and reprints. Number of titles: averages 200.
**Needs:** High quality mysteries and romantic novels of suspense.
**How to Contact:** Query or submit outline/synopsis and sample chapters. SASE for queries. "Reluctantly" considers simultaneous submissions. Photocopied submissions OK. Reports in 1 month to 6 months.
**Terms:** Pays in royalties; offers advance. Free book catalog with SASE.

**DORCHESTER PUBLISHING CO., INC. (II)**, Leisure Books, Suite 900, 6 E. 39th St., New York NY 10016. (212)725-8811. Imprint includes Leisure Books. Editorial Director: Jane Thornton. Estab. 1982. Publisher of mass market paperbacks. Publishes paperback originals and reprints. Books: photo offset printing; average print order varies. Receptive to first novels. Averages 120 total titles, 115 fiction titles each year. Buys 10% agented fiction.
**Needs:** Contemporary, historical, war, horror, psychic/supernatural/occult, mystery (60,000 words), romance (historical, minimum length 100,000 words;) and women's, minimum length 100,000 words. "At present, Dorchester is looking for historical romance, contemporary women's novel (*not* sweet romance), horror and occult." No juvenile, science fiction, gothic, or romantic suspense. Recently published *Fangs*, by Richard Forsythe (occult); *Ashes and Ecstasy*, by Catherine Hart (historical romance); and *Disposable People*, by Marshall Goldberg, M.D. and Kenneth Kay (novel).
**How to Contact:** Query first or submit outline/synopsis and 3 sample chapters with SASE. No unsolicited mss. "*Nothing* will be returned without SASE." Reports in 3-6 weeks on queries; 2 months on mss. Simultaneous and photocopied submissions OK. Accepts computer printout submissions. Letter-quality only. Publishes ms usually within 2 years after acceptance.
**Terms:** Pays in royalties of 4% minimum, 8% maximum; also outright sale, no royalties; advance is negotiable. Must return advance (minus 10% which author retains) if book is not completed or is unacceptable. Sends galleys to author.
**Tips:** "We are concentrating more heavily on horror/occult and historical romance. *Learn to spell*! Learn the difference between *its* and *it's*. And most important, don't get discouraged by all those rejection slips—if you're any good, you'll get published sooner or later. We encourage first novelists. Our relationship with authors is 'a limited partnership with limitless possibilities.' "

**DOUBLEDAY AND CO., INC.**, 245 Park Ave., New York NY 10167. Editorial Director: Patrick Filley. Estab. 1897. Publishes hardcover originals.
**Needs:** Will consider fiction for mystery/suspense, science fiction and romance imprints. Send copy of complete ms (60,000-80,000 words) to Crime Club Editor, Science Fiction Editor or Starlight Romance Editor as appropriate. Sufficient postage for return via fourth class mail must accompany ms.
**How to Contact:** Publisher advises a copy be retained. Reports in "up to 3 months."
**Terms:** Pays in royalties; offers advance.

# Close-up

### Patrick Filley
### Doubleday

photo by Alex Gotfryd

At 5 p.m. just as most everyone is leaving Doubleday's Park Avenue complex, Patrick Filley is getting his second wind for an evening of catch-up work. In this fast-paced industry for book editors like Filley, it's not unusual to put in a 12-hour day—and then go home and read.

Two years ago, Filley proved you can go home again, returning to Doubleday where he started in 1972, after interim terms at New York Times Books and Macmillan. His re appearance was just prior to the 1985 shake-down and restructuring of the editorial division, one of the 15 companies in Doubleday's big "family" (including rock radio stations, bookstores, printing plants, direct mail houses and the Mets ballclub). The result: Editorial staffs were trimmed; the historic Dial imprint was discontinued; submission policies were updated; and Filley settled into his position as Vice President and Executive Editor.

Despite the changes, the total title list remains around 400—and the editor maintains, Doubleday is buying more literary fiction, at least five to six first novels a year. For now, however, general freelance submissions are *not* invited. But the editors encourage submissions for their genre series, which comprise about 75 books a year. To submit a manuscript, it's important to address the appropriate editor: Veronica Mixon (romance); Patrick Lo Brutto (westerns, science fiction); and Michele Tempestra (mysteries, crime).

For their general and mainstream books, the DD editors actively pursue and woo writers. "We don't wait for an author or agent to send us a manuscript; we go after it," says Filley. Author "shopping" sometimes begins at writers' programs and conferences around the country, a ploy Filley believes "may pay off two to three years down the line." Timing is crucial in this industry; therefore editors must be business-oriented and sensitive to the market. But most important is "editorial passion," says the exec. editor. "Our editors really have to *care* about a book, fight for it, and want to work on it"; trends are not the decisive factor.

Of course, every house is looking for the blockbuster, currently a club of 20 or so "bankable" authors who write on the bestselling subjects: horror in the Stephen King vein; Follett and Maclean mystery/thriller/crime/suspense types; sagas in exotic settings; get-behind-the-scenes professional stories (Robin Cook, Arthur Hailey); and modern women's novels á la Krantz and Steel. An area evolved from paperbacks, women's novels can be an author's transition to hardcover, a profitable format for fiction lately.

According to Filley, a successful writer work is both credible and accessible. The reader must be able to get into a book easily—and stay. How? "With a good beginning, a clear, original style, believable dialogue, and craft—without the pretensions. My real concern for all books is *craft*," he says.

Also advises Filley, be realistic. Don't rely on the concept of the benevolent publisher; this is a dog-eat-dog business. Also don't expect individual correspondence or a prompt response from a company where the annual volume of submissions would strip a small forest.

Keep on top of the market; *read* current novels and publications about the industry. There's nothing a writer can change in this "bizarre" business, Filley explains. But the more you learn and understand subliminally about writing and publishing, the more publishable your manuscript will be.

**Tips:** "Your letter of inquiry should be addressed to Editorial Department. First sentence should tell us whether the book is a novel, mystery or whatever and what the book's about in a clear and straightforward description. Summarize plot and background and give a sketch of major characters. If you have already been published, give us details at the end of your letter along with credentials or experience that qualify you to write your book."

**DOUBLEDAY CANADA**, 105 Bond St., Toronto, Ontario M5B 1Y3 Canada. (416)977-7891. Senior Editor: Denise Schon. Submissions should be sent Attn: Trade Editorial Dept. Publishes hardcover and trade paperback originals and reprints. Number of titles: 14 in 1983. Buys 50% agented fiction. Average first novel print order 5,000 copies.
**Needs:** Contemporary, literary, faction, adventure, mystery, spy, and historical. "Encourage Canadian content or Canadian writers." Recently published *Smith and Other Events*, by Paul St. Pierre; *Me Too*, by Donald Jack; and *Home Game*, by Paul Quarrington.
**How to Contact:** Submit outline/synopsis, brief character sketches, and 2-3 chapters along with brief biography. Photocopied submissions OK. Replies in 2 months. Publishes ms an average of 1 year after acceptance.
**Terms:** Pays in royalties; offers advance. Must return advance if book is not completed or is not acceptable. Free book catalog.
**Tips:** "It helps if the author tells who his potential market is. We will consider first novels, but would only publish if considered outstanding."

**DOUGLAS & McINTYRE**, 1615 Venables St., Vancouver, British Columbia V5L 2H1 Canada. (604)254-7191. Imprints include Groundwood Books (juvenile). Estab. 1972. Large independent publisher, expanding. Publishes hardcover and paperback originals and reprints. Averages approximately 30 titles each year. Plans first novel average print order 3,000 copies. Occasionally critiques rejected mss.
**Needs:** Contemporary, ethnic, experimental, feminist, gay, historical, juvenile (contemporary), lesbian, literary, short story collections, translations, women's, and young adult/teen (problem novels). "We are introducing our fiction list in fall 1986, but are now considering manuscripts. Interested only in literary work; no conventional, mass-market type materials, no romance. We will begin with 5 to 6 books each season. We prefer Canadian authors."
**How to Contact:** Accepts unsolicited mss. Submit outline/synopsis and at least 3 sample chapters, or complete ms, with SAE, IRC to Shaun Oakey, Manuscript Editor. Reports in 2 months. No simultaneous submissions; photocopied submissions OK. Accepts computer printout submissions; prefers letter-quality. Disc submissions OK with MICOM system. Prefers hard copy with disc submission.
**Terms:** Pays in royalty of 8% minimum; 15% maximum; 6 author's copies. Offers negotiable advance; $500 average. Free book catalog.

**E.P. DUTTON (II)**, 2 Park Ave., New York NY 10016. Division Of New American Library. Imprints include Dial Books for Young Readers, Pied Piper Books, Easy-to-Read Books, Very First Books, Unicorn Paperbacks, Lodestar Books, and Obelisk. Editor-in-Chief: William Whitehead. Juvenile: Ann Durrell. Artbook Editor: Cy Nelson. Publishes hardcover and paperback reprints in the Obelisk line. Books: illustrations sometimes. Encourages new writers.
**Needs:** Contemporary, experimental, humor/satire, literary, juvenile, suspense/mystery, war, women's, young adult, and translations. No gothics, historicals, romance, or poetry. Recently published *Crampton Hodnet*, by Barbara Pym; *Caracole*, by Edmund White; and *Midair*, by Frank Conroy.
**How to Contact:** Does not accept unsolicited mss. Writers may send a query letter. Reports in 8 weeks on queries. SASE required for response.
**Terms:** Rates vary individually; offers advance. Sends galleys to author.
**Tips:** "Do not overlook literary magazines and journals. They are often receptive and have more time to supply feedback. Literary agents are very helpful. What we and the public want is the exceptionally good first novel. We work closely with the author."

**EAKIN PUBLICATIONS (II)**, Box 23066, Austin TX 78735. (512)756-6911. Imprint includes Nortex. Editor: Edwin M. Eakin. Estab. 1978. Publishes hardcover and paperback originals. Books: woven old style (acid free); offset printing; case binding; illustrations; average print order 2,000; first novel print order 5,000. Averages 40 total titles each year.
**Needs:** Juvenile. Specifically needs historical fiction for school market, juveniles set in Texas for Texas gradeschoolers. Recently published *Paradise Called Texas*, by Janice Shefelman; *Girl of the Alamo*, by Rita Kerr; and *Where the Pirates Are*, by Tom Townsend.
**How to Contact:** First send query or submit outline/synopsis and sample chapters. Simultaneous and photocopied submissions OK. Accepts computer printout submissions. Prefers letter quality. Reports in 3 months on queries.
**Terms:** Pays 10-15% in royalties; no advance. Free book catalog on request.
**Tips:** Juvenile fiction only with strong Texas theme.

**PAUL S. ERIKSSON, PUBLISHER**, 208 Battell Bldg., Middlebury VT 05753. (802)388-7303. Editor: Paul S. Eriksson. Estab. 1960. Publishes hardcover and paperback originals.
**Needs:** Mainstream. Recently published *The Headmaster's Papers*, by Richard A. Hawley.
**How to Contact:** Submit outline/synopsis and sample chapters. No simultaneous submissions; photocopied submissions OK. Publishes ms an average of 6 months after acceptance.
**Terms:** Pays 10-15% in royalties; advance offered if necessary. Free book catalog.
**Tips:** "Our taste runs to serious fiction."

**FARRAR, STRAUS & GIROUX (II, IV)**, 19 Union Sq. W., New York NY 10003. Imprints include Hill & Wang. Children's Books Editor-in-Chief: Stephen Roxburgh. Number of titles: 25 planned for 1985 (3 first novels), 30 planned for 1986. Buys juvenile mss with illustrations. Buys 50% agented fiction.
**Needs:** Juvenile and young adult. Recently published *The Boy Soloman, the Rusty Nail*, by Roald Dahl; *Sir Cedric*, by William Steig.
**How to Contact:** Submit outline/synopsis and 3 sample chapters. No simultaneous submissions; photocopied submissions OK. Reports in 1 month on queries, 8 weeks on mss. Publishes ms 12-18 months after acceptance.
**Terms:** Pays in royalties; offers advance. Free book catalog with SASE.
**Tips:** "Study our list before sending something inappropriate."

**FAWCETT (I, II, III)**, Division of Random House/Ballantine, 201 E. 50th St., New York NY 10022. (212)572-2477. Imprints include Crest, Gold Medal, Columbine, and Juniper. Senior Editor: Barbara Dicks. Editor-in-Chief: Leona Nevler. Estab. 1955. Major publisher of mass market and trade paperbacks. Publishes paperback originals and reprints. Prints 160 titles annually. Encourages new writers. "Always looking for *great* first novels."
**Needs:** Historical, suspense, occult, men's adventure, mysteries, and particularly women's. Recently published *The First Directive*, by Joseph McMarra; *So Grand*, by Cynthia Logan; and *Laurel World*, by Marcella Thum.
**How to Contact:** Query with SASE. Send outline and sample chapters for adult mass market. If ms is requested, simultaneous and photocopied submissions OK. Accepts computer printout submissions. Prefers letter-quality. Reports in 1 month on queries; 3 months on mss.
**Terms:** Pays usual advance and royalties.
**Tips:** "Gold Medal list consists of 5 original paperbacks per month—usually 4 are novels."

---

 *The writer is a spiritual anarchist. He is discontented with everything and everybody. The writer is everybody's best friend and only true enemy—the good and great enemy. He neither walks with the multitude nor cheers with them.*

*—William Saroyan*

**FLARE BOOKS (I, II)**, Young Adult Book Imprint of Avon Books, 1790 Broadway, New York NY 10019. (212)399-1384. Senior Editor, Books for Young Readers: Ellen Krieger. Publishes paperback originals and reprints. Averages 36 total titles each year.
**Needs:** Contemporary, experimental, humor, mainstream, mystery, and suspense for readers ages 12-20. "We prefer manuscripts about contemporary children." Recently published *President's Daughter*, by Ellen Emerson White; and *Downtown*, by Norma Fox Mazer; and *The Death Ticket*, by Jay Bennett.
**How to Contact:** Submit entire ms or outline and sample chapters, with SASE. Simultaneous and photocopied submissions OK. Reports in 8-10 weeks on queries and mss.
**Terms:** Pays a 6-8% royalty; advance averages $2,000. Sends galleys to authors.
**Tips:** "We consider first novels."

**BERNARD GEIS ASSOCIATES, INC. (III)**, 128 E. 56th St., New York NY 10022. (212)752-1975. Editorial Director: Alice Baer. Estab. 1958. Publishes hardcover and paperback originals, Plans 5-10 first novels this year. Averages 12-15 total titles, 10 fiction titles each year.
**Needs:** Adventure, contemporary, faction, horror, literary, mainstream, psychic/supernatural, and suspense/mystery. Recently published *Dancehall*, by Bernard Conners; *Lord of the Dance*, by Andrew Greeley; and *Talbot Odyssey*, by Nelson DeMille.
**How to Contact:** Submit outline/synopsis and 3 sample chapters. Photocopied submissions OK. Reports in approximately 4 weeks on queries; 6 weeks on mss.
**Terms:** Sends galleys to author.

**GEMSTONE BOOKS (II)**, Imprint of Dillon Press, 242 Portland Ave. S., Minneapolis MN 55415. (612)333-2691. Fiction Editor: Ann-Louise Taylor. Estab. 1966. "Dillon Press is a children's book publisher, specializing in educational books for schools and libraries." Publishes hardcover and paperback originals and reprints. Books: type of paper varies; offset lithography; Smyth sewn binding; illustrations; average print order: 5,000. Averages 30 total titles, 10 fiction titles each year. Averages first novel print order 5,000 copies. Occasionally comments on rejected ms.
**Needs:** Juvenile (7-9 years), fantasy, adventure, contemporary, suspense/mystery; and (10-14 years) fantasy/science fiction, problem novels, adventure, mystery and sports novels for girls. No romance.
**How to Contact:** Accepts unsolicited mss. Submit complete ms with SASE. Reports in 6 weeks. Simultaneous and photocopied submissions OK. Accepts computer submissions. Prefers letter-quality.
**Terms:** Individual arrangement with author. "We pay both in royalties and straight fees, sometimes with an advance. Payment is negotiable." Sends galleys to author. Book catalog for 9x12 SASE with 54¢ postage.
**Tips:** "We welcome unpublished writers and give their work serious consideration. Our primary responsibility and loyalty is to the author's book, so our relationship with the author is our number one consideration."

**DAVID R. GODINE, PUBLISHER, INC. (I, II)**, 306 Dartmouth St., Boston MA 02116. (617)536-0761. Imprint includes Nonpareil Books (trade paperbacks). President: David R. Godine. Editorial Director: William B. Goodman. Manuscript Submissions: Deanne Smeltzer. Juve-

---

 The double dagger before a listing indicates that the listing is new in this edition. New markets are often the most receptive to freelance contributions.

nile Ms Submissions: Jill Smilow. Estab. 1970. Books: acid free paper; sewn binding; illustrations; average print order: 4,000-5,000; first novel print order: 3,500-6,500. Small independent publisher (10-person staff). Publishes hardcover and paperback originals and reprints. Number of titles: 45 in 1985. Distributed by Harper & Row. Average first novel print order: 4,000-5,000 copies. Encourages new writers. Comments on rejected mss "if of particular interest."
**Needs:** Contemporary, literary, mystery, historical, ethnic, humor/satire, and juvenile. Recently published *All Set About With Fever Trees*, by Pam Durban; *A Leak in the Heart*, by Fay Moskowitz; and *Upon Some Midnights Clear*, by K.C. Constantine.
**How to Contact:** Accepts unsolicited mss with self-addressed, stamped book envelope. Query with outline synopsis. Simultaneous and photocopied submissions OK. Accepts computer printout submissions; letter-quality only.
**Terms:** Standard royalties; offers advance. Sends galleys to author. Free book catalog.
**Tips:** Published new writers within the last year.

**GOSPEL LIGHT PUBLICATIONS (II, III, IV)**, 2300 Knoll Dr., Ventura CA 93003. (805)644-9721. Subsidiaries include Regal Books and Vision House. Imprint includes Galaxy Books. Senior Editor: Earl O. Rowe. Estab. 1933. Midsize religious publisher. Publishes hardcover and paperback originals. Averages 40 total titles each year. Buys 1-2% agented fiction. Average first print order 10,000 copies. Occasionally critiques rejected mss.
**Needs:** Juvenile (adventure, contemporary), adult religious/inspirational, and young adult (problem novels, adventure). "No charismatic, prophetic/end times, or anything promoting loose morals (no explicit sex, etc.)." Recently published *StarLife*, by Lynda Rutledge Stephens (teen and adult); *Before the Dawn Wind Rises*, by Lurie B. Clifford (adult fiction); *Enjoying Good Books* (8 book series); *Little Fish Books About Bible Animals*, (8 book series for 4-8 year olds).
**How to Contact:** Query first with SASE. Simultaneous and photocopied submissions OK. Accepts computer printout submissions. Prefers letter-quality. Synopsis or outline with 2-3 example chapters. Publishes ms 12-18 months after acceptance. Reports in 4 weeks on queries.
**Terms:** Pays in royalties of 10% maximum; 10 author's copies. Must return advance if book is not completed or is not acceptable. Free writer's guidelines for #10 SASE; book catalog for 9x12 SAE and 2 first class stamps.

**GREEN TIGER PRESS (II, IV)**, 1061 India St., San Diego CA 92101. Imprint: Star & Elephant. Editor-in-Chief: Harold Darling. Editor: Joseph M. Cahn. Estab. 1971. Publishes hardcover and paperback originals and reprints. Number of titles: 6 in 1985; 12 in 1986. Buys 10% agented fiction. Encourages new writers.
**Needs:** Specific interest in imaginative fiction for children lending itself to illustration. "We are publishers of illustrated picture books. Our work tends to be imaginative or lyrical in flavor, somewhat anachronistic in sentiment, and solidly visual in focus."
**How to Contact:** Query or submit complete ms or outline/synopsis and sample chapters with SASE or submit through agent. Simultaneous and photocopied submissions OK. Reports in 4 weeks on queries, 3-4 months on mss. Publishes ms 12-18 months after acceptance.
**Terms:** A variety of arrangements is possible depending upon the capacity in which a given work is used; offers advance. Free Star and Elephant Catalogue with 5x9 SAE and 44¢ postage.
**Tips:** "In the last year we have scaled down the number of new books we publish and have instead been concentrating on reprints. We are gradually expanding the scope of what we publish and are publishing more European books. Read voraciously. Even bad books can provide much by way of negative example." The types of manuscripts published are determined by "our inner beliefs and needs matched with our understanding of the curiosity and hungers of the reading public."

**GREENLEAF CLASSICS, INC. (II, IV)**, Box 20194, San Diego CA 92120. Editorial Director: Douglas Saito. Managing Editor: Ralph Vaughan. Estab. 1961. Publishes paperback originals. Prints 450 new titles annually. "We usually publish a dozen or more first novels a year."
**Needs:** Erotica. No science fiction, fantasy, mysteries, satire, memoirs, period pieces, gay fiction or occult themes.

**How to Contact:** Query (requesting guidelines) or submit complete ms with SASE. No simultaneous, computer or photocopied submissions. Reports in 1 week on queries, 1 month on mss.
**Tips:** "Our needs are very specific, and the average writer will not know those needs without receiving our guidelines. Don't waste time submitting until you've received them." Send SASE for writer's guidelines.

**GREENWILLOW BOOKS (II)**, Division of Wm. Morrow & Co., 105 Madison Ave., New York NY 10016. (212)889-3050. Editor-in-Chief: Susan Hirschman. Estab. 1975. Publishes hardcover originals. Books: illustrations. Number of titles: 60 annually.
**Needs:** Juvenile and young adult: easy-to-read, sports, animal, spy/adventure, historical, and fantasy/science fiction. Primarily picture books, easy readers, and some young-adult novels. Recently published *Whiskers and Rhymes*, by Arnold Lobel (picture alphabet book); *The Nature of the Beast*, by Janni Hawker (a first novel); and *The Hero and the Crown*, by Robin McKinley.
**Needs:** Juvenile and young adult: easy-to-read, sports, animal, spy/adventure, historical, and fantasy/science fiction. Primarily picture books, easy readers, and some young-adult novels. Recently published *Whiskers and Rhymes*, by Arnold Lobel (picture alphabet book); *The Nature of the Beast*, by Janni Hawker (a first novel); and *The Hero and the Crown*, by Robin McKinley (fantasy).
**How to Contact:** Accepts unsolicited mss. Submit complete ms or outline/synopsis and 2-3 sample chapters or submit through agent with SASE. No simultaneous submissions; photocopied submissions OK. Accepts computer printout submissions. Prefers letter-quality. Reports in 2 weeks on queries, 6 weeks on mss.
**Terms:** Royalty and advance. Sends galleys to author. Free book catalog.
**Tips:** Encourages first novelists.

**GROSSET & DUNLAP, INC. A Division of the Putnam Young Readers Group (III)**, 51 Madison Ave., New York NY 10010. Editor-in-Chief: Bernette Ford.
**Needs:** Juvenile, preschool/picture book. Queries only. "Include such details as length and intended age group and any other information that you think will help us to understand the nature of your material. Be sure to enclose a stamped, self-addressed envelope for our reply. We can no longer review manuscripts that we have not asked to see, and they will be returned unread."

**HARCOURT BRACE JOVANOVICH (III)**, 1250 6th Ave., San Diego CA 92101. Imprints include Voyager Paperbacks and Gulliver Books. Manager: Maria Modugno. Editor: Bonnie Ingbe. Associate Editor: Susan Tehrani. Publishes hardcover originals and reprints. Number of titles: 35-40 per year, including several first novels. Actively seeking new writers. Sometimes comments on rejected ms "if it shows real promise on the part of the author."
**Needs:** "We are looking for honestly approached and thoughtfully written mss with high appeal for children and young adults: contemporary fiction, animals, spy-adventure, fantasy/science fiction, easy-to-read, and humor. We are especially looking for board books and other material with potential for bookstore sales." Recently published *The Worry Week*, by Anne Lindbergh; *A Solitary Secret*, by Patricia Hermes; and *The Napping House*, by Audrey Wood, illustrated by Don Wood.
**How to Contact:** Submit complete ms for picture books and outline/synopsis or (2-4) sample chapters for novels. No phone calls. No simultaneous submissions; photocopied submissions OK. Send SASE. Please do not send original art; photocopies preferred. Reports in 2 weeks on queries; 6-8 weeks on mss.
**Terms:** Varies according to individual book. Send for free catalog.
**Tips:** "We are enlarging our lists in all categories and we do encourage first novelists."

**HARLEQUIN ENTERPRISES, LTD. (II)**, 225 Duncan Mill Rd., Don Mills, Ontario M3B 3K9 Canada. (416)445-5860. Imprints include Harlequin Romances, Harlequin Presents, Harlequin American Romances, Gold Eagle, Superromances, Temptation, Intrigue, Regency, Silhouettes and Gothic and Worldwide Library. Editorial Director: Star Helmer. Estab. 1949. Publishes pa-

perback originals and reprints. Number of titles: averages 350/year. Buys 80% agented fiction.
**Needs:** Romance and heroic adventure. Accepts short stories for texts. Will accept nothing that is not related to the desired categories.
**How to Contact:** Send outline and first 50 pages (2 or 3 chapters) or submit through agent with IRC and SASE (Canadian). Absolutely no simultaneous submissions; photocopied submissions OK. Reports in 1 month on queries; 2 months on mss. Publishes ms 12-18 months after acceptance.
**Terms:** Offers royalties, advance. Must return advance if book is not completed or is unacceptable. Sends galleys to author.
**Tips:** "The quickest route to success is to follow directions for submissions: query first. We encourage first novelists. Before sending a manuscript, read as many Harlequin titles as you can get your hands on. It's very important to study the style and do your homework first." Authors may send manuscript for Romances and Presents to Maryan Gibson, senior editor; Super romances: Laurie Bauman, senior editor; Temptations: Margaret Carney, senior editor, to the Canada address. American Romances, Debra Matteucci, senior editor; Intrigue, Gothic, and Regency, Reva Kindser, editor, Harlequin Books, 300 E. 42 Street, 6th Floor, New York, NY 10017. Silhouette submissions should also be sent to the New York office. Gold Eagle query letters should be addressed to Mark Howell, editorial director, at the Canada address. The relationship between the novelist and editor regarded highly and treated with professionalism."

**HARMONY BOOKS (II, III)**, Division of Crown Publishers, 1 Park Ave., New York NY 10016. (212)532-9200. Assistant Editor: Owen O'Donnell. Publishes hardcover and paperback originals. Number of titles: 10 in 1986. Buys "usually all" agented fiction.
**Needs:** Contemporary and literary. Recently published *Sea Star*; and *Singapore, A Novel of the Bronx*.
**How to Contact:** Query with SASE. Simultaneous and photocopied submissions OK. Reports in 2 months on query. Publishes ms 10-12 months after acceptance.
**Terms:** Terms vary and are negotiated individually. Must return advance if book is not completed or is unacceptable.
**Tips:** "Be sure and send query letter first. Do not send complete mss; we return them."

**HARPER & ROW JUNIOR BOOKS GROUP (II)**, 10 E. 53rd St., New York NY 10022. (212)207-7044. Imprints include Harper & Row Junior Books, including Charlotte Zolotow Books; T.Y. Crowell, and Lippincott Junior Books. Publisher: Elizabeth Gordon. Editors: Charlotte Zolotow, Nina Ignatowicz, Marilyn Kriney, Barbara Fenton, Laura Geringer, Robert O. Warren and Antonia Markiet. Publishes hardcover originals and paperback reprints. Number of titles: *Harper—Cloth*: 73 in 1984, 66 in 1985; *Harper—Trophy* (paperback): 38 in 1984, 55 in 1985; *Crowell*: 26 in 1984, 32 in 1985; *Lippincott*: 17 in 1984; 14 in 1985. First novel print order: 4,000 copies.
**Needs:** Picture books, easy-to-read, middle-grade, teen-age and young adult novels; fiction, fantasy, animal, sports, spy/adventure, historical, science fiction, problem novels, and contemporary. Recently published *George Shrinks*, by William Joyce (ages 3-7); *Sarah, Plain and Tall*, by Patricia MacLachlan (ages 8-10); and *Amy's Eyes*, by Richard Kennedy, pictures by Richard Egielski (all ages).
**How to Contact:** Query; submit complete ms; submit outline/synopsis and sample chapters; submit through agent. SASE for query, ms. Please identify simultaneous submissions; photocopied submissions OK. Reports in 2-3 months.
**Terms:** Average 10% in royalties. Royalties on picture books shared with illustrators. Offers advance. Book catalog for self-addressed label.
**Tips:** "Write from your own experience and the child you once were. Read widely in the field of adult and children's literature. Realize that writing for children is a difficult challenge. Read other young adult novelists as well as adult novelists. Pay attention to styles, approaches, topics. Be willing to rewrite, perhaps many times. We have no rules for subject matter, length or vocabulary but look instead for ideas that are fresh and imaginative. Good writing that involves the reader in a

story or subject that has appeal for young readers is also essential. One submission is considered by the four imprints.''

**HARPER & ROW PUBLISHERS, INC. (III)**, 10 E. 53rd St., New York NY 10022. (212)207-7000. Publisher/Editorial Director: Edward L. Burlingame. Managing Editor: Katharine Kirkland. Estab. 1817. Publishes hardcover originals. Planned 6-8 first novels for 1985.
**Needs:** Harper & Row will review only mss and proposals submitted by agents or those works submitted upon recommendation of someone known by one of Harper's editors. Recently published *Him With His Foot in His Mouth*, by Saul Bellow; *The Unbearable Lightness of Being*, by Milan Kundera; and *Almost Paradise*, by Susan Isaacs.

**HARVEST HOUSE PUBLISHERS (IV)**, 1075 Arrowsmith, Eugene OR 97402. (503)343-0123. Editor: Eileen L. Mason. Estab. 1974. Midsize independent publisher with plans to expand. Publishes hardcover and paperback originals. Books: Mandoprint paper; Web press; perfect binding; average print order 10,000-30,000; first novel print order: 10,000. Plans 3 first novels this year. Averages 45-50 total titles, 8 fiction titles each year.
**Needs:** Historical, romance (historical, mystery), and women's. Recently published *Love Leads Home*, by June Masters Bacher (pioneer romance); *Sweetbriar*, by Brenda Wilbee (pioneer romance); and *Mist Over Morrs Bay*, by Caroll Gifte Page and Doris Fell (mystery romance).
**How to Contact:** Accepts unsolicited mss. Submit outline/synopsis and 3 sample chapters with SASE. Reports in 1 month. Simultaneous and photocopied submissions OK.
**Terms:** Pays in royalties of 8% minimum. Sends galleys to author. Writer's guidelines for SASE. Book catalog for 8½x11 SASE.
**Tips:** "Our goal is to provide light, entertaining reading that will encourage the faith of the readers and turn their attention to Jesus Christ as the answer to the problems and questions of life. The focus of the story, however, is the romantic relationship, and the spiritual dimension should be a natural outgrowth of the plot." Interested in first novels "if the material is of exceptional quality."

**HERALD PRESS (II)**, Division of Mennonite Publishing House, 616 Walnut Ave., Scottdale PA 15683. (412)887-8500. Editor: Paul M. Schrock. Denominational publisher with full line of religious books. Publishes hardcover and paperback originals. Books: acid free paper; offset printing; squareback adhesive bound paperback; illustrations in juveniles; average print order: 5,000; first novel print order 3,500. Number of fiction titles: 4-6 per year.
**Needs:** Religious/inspirational, juvenile, and young adult. Recently published *The Weight*, by Joel Kauffmann (young adult); *For Conscience's Sake*, by Solomon Stucky (historical); and *Mystery of the Missing Stallions*, by Ruth Nulton Moore (juvenile).
**How to Contact:** Accepts unsolicited mss. Query or submit outline/synopsis and 2 sample chapters with SASE. No simultaneous submissions; photocopied submissions OK. Accepts computer printout submissions. Prefers letter-quality. Accepts disc submissions compatible with CP/M. Prefers hard copy with disc submissions. Reports in 2 weeks on queries, 6 weeks on mss.
**Terms:** Pays 10-15% in royalties; 12 free author's copies; no advance. Sends galleys to author. Book catalog 50¢.
**Tips** "We are happy to respond to book proposals from Christian authors of adult and juvenile fiction. We like to reflect a Christian response to social issues such as world hunger and peacemaking." First novels "no problem if the quality is excellent." Usually publishes original fiction in trade paperback rather than hardcover. Published new authors last year.

**HOLIDAY HOUSE, INC.(I, II)**, 18 E. 53rd St., New York NY 10022. (212)688-0085. Editor: Margery Cuyler. Estab. 1935. Small independent publisher. Books: paper quality depends on age level of reader; high quality printing; occasionally reinforced binding; illustrations sometimes; average print order: 7,500; first novel print order: depends on novel. Books: paper quality depends on age level of reader; high quality printing occasionally reinforced binding; illustrations sometimes; average print order: 7,500; first novel print order depends on novel. Publishes hardcover originals and paperbacks. Number of titles: 35 in 1984; 35 hardcovers in 1985; 5 paperbacks in 1985. Encourages new writers.

**Needs:** Contemporary, literary, adventure, science fiction, humor, and animal stories. Recently published *Stage Fright*, by Ann M. Martin; *Christina's Ghost*, by Betty Ren Wright (mystery); and *Judge Benjamin: The Superdog Surprise*, by Judith Whitelock McInerney (humor). "We're not in a position to be too encouraging, as our list is tight, but we're always open to good 'family' novels and humor."

**How to Contact:** Query first on picture books or submit outline/synopsis and 3 sample chapters. Simultaneous and photocopied submissions OK as long a covering letter mentions that other publishers are looking at the same material. Accepts computer printout submissions. Prefers letter-quality. Reports in 1 week on queries, 1 month on mss.

**Terms:** Advance and royalties are flexible, depending upon whether the book is illustrated. Sends galleys to author.

**Tips:** "This appears to be a decade in which publishers are interested in reviving the type of good, solid story that was popular in the '50s. Certainly there's a trend toward humor, formula series, science fiction, romance, biographies and historical novels. Problem-type novels and romances seem to be on the wane. We are always open to well-written manuscripts, whether by a published or nonpublished author. Submit only one project at a time." Published new writers within the last year.

**HOLLOWAY HOUSE PUBLISHING**, 8060 Melrose, Los Angeles CA 90046. (213)653-8060. Editor: Peter Z. Stone. Associate Editor: Leslie Spencer. Estab. 1961. Midsize independent publisher. Publishes paperback originals and reprints. Number of titles: averages 36/year.

**Needs:** Contemporary, adventure, ethnic, sports and biographies, gaming and gambling books, historical and saga-type romance (contemporary and young adult). No computer books. Manuscripts should not be less than 220 pages, double-spaced." Recently published *Hot Snake Nights*, by Romare Duke; and *Bound by Blood*, by Charles R. Goodman.

**How to Contact:** Query with SASE. Simultaneous and photocopied submissions OK, only excellent copies. Reports in 2 weeks on queries, 6 weeks on mss.

**Terms:** Pays standard rate on royalties; offers advance. Free book catalog with business-sized SASE.

**Tips:** "Too many writers assume that because they have worked on a book, someone should read it. Follow guidelines; query letters are usually uninformative, necessitating a letter to query the 'author's query.' A query letter should contain information enough to intrigue the editor. Query letters reading . . . 'and I'd appreciate your reading my book,' with no description, direction or outline are most often ignored. A manuscript will be reviewed upon arrival. If it is unacceptable for any of the above reasons, it will be returned promptly. We welcome first novels and the opportunity to develop beginning writers. Unless you are famous, we're not interested in your life story. We've also started a 'soap-opera' series."

‡**HOLT, RINEHART & WINSTON (II)**, 521 5th Ave., New York NY 10175. (212)599-7600. Imprint includes Owl (paper). Publishes hardcover originals and reprints and paperback originals and reprints. Averages 50-60 total titles, ¼ to ⅓ of total is fiction each year.

**Needs:** Adventure, contemporary, erotica, ethnic, fantasy, feminist, gay, historical, humor/satire, juvenile (5-9 years, including animal, easy-to-read, fantasy, historial, sports, spy/adventure, contemporary), literary, mainstream, psychic/supernatural occult, romance (contemporary, historical), suspense/mystery, translations, war, western, young adult/teen (10-18 years including easy-to-read, fantasy/science fiction, historical, problem novels, romance, sports, spy/adventure). Recently published *Queen of Hearts*, by Dan McCall (contemporary); *Lord, Do You Remember Me*, by Julius Lester (issue-related); and *Here Be Dragons*, by Sharon Penman (historical).

**How to Contact:** Agented fiction 100%.

**Terms:** Pays in royalties of 10% minimum; 15% maximum; advance. Sends galleys to author. Book catalog free on request.

**Tips:** "We encourage first novelists and published new writers last year."

**HOUGHTON MIFFLIN COMPANY (III)**, 2 Park St., Boston MA 02108. (617)725-5000. Subsidiary includes Ticknor and Fields Inc. Managing Editor: Linda Glick Conway. Publishes hardcover and paperback originals and paperback reprints. Averages 150 (includes childrens) total titles, 45 fiction titles each year. Buys 70-80% agented fiction.
**Needs:** Adventure, contemporary, fantasy, contemporary romance, historical, literary, mainstream, science fiction, suspense/mystery, war, and women's. No religious, gothic, occult or westerns. Recently published *Honorable Men*, by Louis Auchincloss; *A Life of Her Own*, by Mave Braudel; and *The Immigrant's Daughter*, by Harvard Fast.
**How to Contact:** Query first; submit outline/synopsis and 3 sample chapters with SASE. Simultaneous and photocopied submissions OK but no dot-matrix. Reports in 1 month on queries; 2 months on mss. Publishes ms an average of 1 year after acceptance.
**Terms:** Pays in royalties on sliding scale of 10-12-15%; pays advance. Must return advance if book is not completed or is unacceptable.

**IDEALS PUBLISHING CORP.**, Nelson Place at Elm Hill Pike, Nashville TN 37214. VP Editorial: Patricia Pingry. Estab. 1944. Number of titles: 22 in 1985.
**Needs:** Juvenile: easy-to-read. No adult fiction or any other subjects or categories.
**How to Contact:** Submit complete ms with SASE. No simultaneous submissions; photocopied submissions OK. Reports in 6 weeks on mss.
**Terms:** Varies; offers variable advance.
**Tips:** "Know the publisher's books before submitting."

**INDIANA UNIVERSITY PRESS (I, II)**, 10th and Morton Sts., Bloomington IN 47405. (812)337-4203. Director: John Gallman. Estab. 1950. Publishes hardcover and paperback originals and reprints. "Little by little publishing more original fiction. We hope to do 3-5 novels per year." First novel print order 2,000.
**Needs:** "Serious, quality, novel-length fiction. We hope to establish ourselves as a major publisher of important fiction by American writers, the kinds of books which will not readily be taken by large publishers because they do not look toward a specific audience or necessarily offer the right kind of 'entertainment.' The word *serious* implies an effort on the part of the writer to offer insights about character, society, the structure of thought, the nature of the universe. We will not be disappointed if our books are also entertaining, and we are not looking for any particular style or approach: narrative stories are welcome, as are complex constructions in the manner of Thomas Pynchon or John Barth. There is no particular criterion with regard to length. We want our books to be distinctive, distinguished, special. And we would prefer works that are unself-conscious about either self or art." Recently published *Twofold Vibration*, by Raymond Federman; and *Oxherding Tale*, by Charles Johnson.
**How to Contact:** Query first describing ms. "The next step in consideration would be to see a sample chapter. As the third step, we would ask to see the entire work." All unsolicited mss are returned unopened. No simultaneous submissions; photocopied submissions OK. Reports in 2 weeks on queries.
**Terms:** Pays 6-10% of list price in royalties; occasional small advance. Sends galleys to author. Some subsidy publishing (waiver of royalties or nonrefundable cash grant). Free writer's guidelines and book catalog for SASE.
**Tips:** "We absolutely do not want simultaneous submissions. Follow guidelines. We encourage first novelists. Remember 1) you are writing for readers; 2) the novel is a commercial art form; and 3) don't get dicouraged too easily."

**THE INTERNATIONAL UNIVERSITY PRESS (I)**, Subsidiary of The International University Foundation, 1301 S. Noland Rd., Independence MO 64055. (816)461-3633. Fiction Editor: Israel Abundis. Estab. 1973. Midsize academic press that does some fiction and poetry publishing. Publishes hardcover and paperback originals. Books: 40 lb paper; litho printing; paper binding; illustrations. Plans 25 first novels this year. Averages 100 total titles; 40 fiction titles each year. Occasionally critiques rejected mss.

**Needs:** Adventure, contemporary, historical, humor/satire, literary, mainstream, psychic/supernatural/occult, religious/inspirational, romance (historical, contemporary), science fiction, short story collections, suspense/mystery, and translations. Accepts short stories. No erotica or horror. Recently published *Ensnared*, by Loretta Sallman Jackson (mystery); *Riverbend*, by Vickie May (western); and *The Demon Fire*, Marilyn Meredith (mystery).

**How to Contact:** Query or submit outline/synopsis and 4 sample chapters with SASE. Reports in 6 weeks on queries, 4 months on ms. Simultaneous and photocopied submissions OK. Accepts computer printout submissions. Prefers letter-quality.

**Terms:** Pays in royalties of 10% minimum; 35% maximum; 6 author's copies. Sends galleys to author. "A $10 per page proofreading and copysetting cost is requested in some instances, especially for poetry works and first fiction efforts. Our contract terms are designed to meet the special demands of each writer and manuscript." Writer's guidelines for SAE and 1 first class stamp. Book catalog for SAE and 2 first class stamps.

**Tips:** "We plan to greatly expand our list of titles, and this will include many types of fiction. We like the opportunities afforded by working with writers trying to break into print for the first time. We published 15 new writers last year. We are publishing more fiction and more paperbacks"

**ALFRED A. KNOPF**, 201 E. 50th St., New York NY 10022. Senior Editor: Ashbel Green. Estab. 1915. Publishes hardcover originals. Number of titles: 40 in 1983. Buys 75% agented fiction.

**Needs:** Contemporary, literary, mystery, and spy. No western, gothic, romance, erotica, religious, or science fiction. Recently published *The Accidental Tourist*, by Anne Tyler, *The Red Fox*, by Anthony Hyde; and *The Nuclear Age*, by Tim O'Brien.

**How to Contact:** Submit complete ms with SASE. Simultaneous and photocopied submissions OK. Reports in 1 month on mss. Publishes ms an average of 1 year after acceptance.

**Terms:** Pays 10-15% in royalties; offers advance. Must return advance if book is not completed or is unacceptable.

**Tips:** Publishes book length fiction of literary merit by known and unknown writers. "Don't submit manuscripts with matrix type."

**KNOPF BOOKS FOR YOUNG READERS (II)**, 201 E. 50th St., New York NY 10022. Subsidiary of Random House, Inc. Editor-in-Chief: Janet Schulman. Publishes hardcover originals. Averages 50 total titles, approximately 20 fiction titles each year.

**Needs:** "High-quality" adventure, contemporary, humor, and juvenile. "Young adult novels, picture books, middle group novels." Recently published *Beyond the Chocolate War*, by Robert Cormier (young adult novel): *Gorilla*, by Anthony Browne (picture book); and *Blackberries in the Dark*, by Mavis Jukes (middle group).

 *Many of my characters live what might be called boring and dreary lives. In a short story you can appreciate their frustration, but it might be difficult to live with them for a whole novel. You can get through a story before you get uncomfortable. Small things—the attention to detail—can keep you going.*

*—Bobbie Ann Mason*

**How to Contact:** Query with outline/synopsis and 2 sample chapters with SASE. Simultaneous and photocopied submissions OK. Reports in 6-8 weeks on mss.
**Terms:** Sends galleys to author.

**LARKSDALE (I, II)**, 133 S. Heights Blvd., Houston TX 77007. (713)869-9092. Imprints include Linolean Press (Religious), Lindahl Press (General), Harle House (Mass Market). Publisher: James F. Goodman. Editor-in-Chief: Frances Burke Goodman. Estab. 1978. Medium-size independent general trade publisher. "We have national distribution and are not interested in a regional market." Publishes hardcover and paperback originals. Books: 20 lb opaque paper; sheet fed press; ACL binding; illustrations; average print order 6,000. Number of titles: 20 in 1984. Average first novel print order 6,000 copies.
**Needs:** No special categories desired. Recently published *In the Line of Duty*, by Louis Rigler and Judyth Rigler; *The Temptation*, by Jack Coombe.
**How to Contact:** Accepts unsolicited mss. Query or submit complete ms to James F. Goodman, Publisher. SASE for query, ms. Photocopied and simultaneous submissions OK, if so indicated. Accepts computer printout submissions. Prefers letter-quality. Reports in 1-2 months on queries, 4 months on mss. "Mss SASE *must* include container."
**Terms:** Pays in royalties; no advance. Sends galleys to author.
**Tips:** "We are primarily interested in novels with a purpose, a philosophy, and a moral position; hero/heroine type books—positive, uplifting, no smut. Offensive language, illicit sex, immoral conduct by hero or heroine are out. Letter of transmittal must tell us what it's about and the purpose of the book, and include author's bio. We welcome first novels. Poetry accepted. No queries until completion of manuscript."

**LIBRA PUBLISHERS, INC. (II)**, Suite 207, 4901 Morena Blvd., San Diego CA 92117. (619)273-1500. President: William Kroll. Estab. 1960. Publishes hardcover originals. Books: 60 lb offset paper; offset printing; Smyth sewn binding; illustrations occasionally; average print order: 3,000; first novel print order: 500-3,000. Buys juvenile mss with illustrations. Buys 10% agented fiction. Number of titles: 6 planned for 1985.
**Needs:** All categories considered. Recently published *Please Stand By—Your Mother's Missing*, by Tallman & Gilsenan (satire of women's movements); *Billie Is Black*, by S. Forman (adventures of black slave escapees in Old West); and *The Gentle Losers*, by F. Gerber (WWII experiences of Dutch under German occupation).
**How to Contact:** Prefers submission of complete ms but queries OK. SASE for query, ms. Simultaneous and photocopied submissions OK. Accepts computer printout submissions. Prefers letter-quality. Reports in 1 week on queries, 2 weeks on mss. Publishes ms 8-12 months after acceptance.
**Terms:** Pays 10-15% in royalties; no advance. Sends galleys to author. Also subsidy publishes. Free book catalog.
**Tips:** "Have persistence. With a limited budget for fiction, we have to be very selective with first novels. We prefer finished copy rather than drafts."

**LIBRARY OF CRIME CLASSICS**, Subsidiary of International Polygonics, Ltd., Madison Square, Box 1563, New York NY 10159. (212)683-2916. Editor-in-Chief: B.N. Hare. Estab. 1969. Small publisher specializing in mysteries. Publishes hardcover and paperback originals and paperback reprints. Averages 20 fiction titles each year.
**Needs:** Mystery only. "We *prefer* classic whodunits. We have no interest in action-adventure or gothic." Recently published *Banshee*, by Margaret Millar; *Death Turns the Tables*, by John Dickson Carr; and *Cat and Mouse*, by Christianna Brand (mysteries).
**How to Contact:** Query. Reports in 3 weeks. "We do not accept unsolicited manuscripts." Photocopied submissions OK. Accepts computer printout submissions; letter-quality only.
**Terms:** Pays in royalties; offers negotiable advance. Free book catalog.
**Tips:** Will consider first novels.

**THE LINDEN PRESS (I, II, III)**, Subsidiary of Simon & Schuster, 1230 Avenue of the Americas, New York NY 10020. (212)245-6400. Fiction Editors: Allen Peacock and Joni Evans. Estab. 1979. Small imprint publishing commercial fiction and nonfiction and literary fiction. Publishes hardcover and paperback originals. Plans 1-2 first novels this year. Averages 15-20 total titles, approximately 6 fiction titles each year. Average first novel print order 7,500-10,000 copies. Occasionally critiques rejected ms.

**Needs:** Adventure, contemporary, fantasy, feminist, historical, literary, mainstream, suspense/mystery. No westerns or pulp romance. Recently published *First Among Equals*, by Jeffrey Archer (commercial); *The Sicilian*, by Maria Puzo (commercial); and *Short History of a Small Place*, by T.R. Pearson (first novel/Southern).

**How to Contact:** Accepts unsolicited mss. Submit outline/synopsis and 3 sample chapters with SASE. Reports in 2 months. Simultaneous and photocopied submissions OK. Accepts computer printout submissions; prefers letter-quality.

**Terms:** Pays in royalties of 10% minimum, 15% maximum; offers negotiable advance. Book catalog for SASE.

**Tips:** "Get an agent."

**LIPPINCOTT JUNIOR BOOKS (II)**, 10 E. 53rd St., New York NY 10022. (212)207-7044. Recently published *More Short Scary Stories to Tell in the Dark* by Alvin Schwartz, pictures by Stephen Gammell. (ages 9-12); and *Devil's Race*, a Lippincott page-Turner by Avi (ages 12 and up). See Harper & Row Junior Books Group.

**‡LITTLE, BROWN AND COMPANY, INC. (II, III)**, 34 Beacon St., Boston MA. (617)227-0730. Imprints include Little, Brown, New York Graphic Society. Medium-size house. Publishes hardcover and paperback originals. Averages 100-125 total titles/year. Number of fiction titles varies. Occasionally critiques rejected mss.

**Needs:** Open. No science fiction. Recently published *Inside, Outside*, by Herman Wouk; *A Maggot*, by John Fowles; and *Victory Over Spain*, by Ellen Gilchrist (stories).

**How to Contact:** Does not accept unsolicited mss. Query first; "we accept submissions from authors who have published before, in book form, magazines, newspapers, or journals. No submissions from unpublished writers." Reports in 4-6 months on queries. Simultaneous and photocopied submissions OK (prefers copies). Accepts computer printouts.

**Terms:** "We publish on a royalty basis, with advance." Writer's guidelines free. Book catalog for SASE.

**Tips:** Published new writers in last year.

**LITTLE, BROWN & CO. Children's Books (II)**, 34 Beacon St., Boston MA 02106. Editorial Department, Trade Division; Children's Book: John G. Keller, Publisher. Books: 70 lb paper; sheet fed printing; illustrations. Sometimes buys juvenile mss with illustrations "if by professional artist." Buys 60% agented fiction.

**Needs:** Middle grade fiction, and young juvenile. Publishes ms 1-2 years after acceptance.

**How to Contact:** Will accept unsolicited mss but prefers a query letter.

**Terms:** Pays on royalty basis. Must return advance if book is not completed or is unacceptable. Sends galleys to author.

**Tips:** "There is a need for quality nonfiction for beginning readers. Young adult 'problem' novels are no longer in vogue, but there is now a dearth of good fiction for that age group. We are looking for young children's (ages 3-5) books that might be adapted to unusual toy/book formats. We encourage first novelists."

**LODESTAR BOOKS (II, III)**, A Division of E.P. Dutton, 2 Park Ave., New York NY 10016. (212)725-1818. Imprints include E.P. Dutton Children's Books; Dial Books for Young Readers, and E.P. Dutton adult trade. Editorial Director: Virginia Buckley. Associate Editor: Rosemary Brosnan. Young adult and middle-age imprint of juvenile department of trade publisher bought by New American Library in 1985. Publishes hardcover fiction for young adults, ages 12-17, ages

10-14, ages 8-12. Books: 50 or 55 lb antique cream paper; offset printing; hardcover binding; illustrations sometimes; average print order: 5,000-6,000; first novel print order 5,000. No picture books. Number of titles: approximately 20 annually, 10-12 fiction titles annually. Buys 80% agented fiction.

**Needs:** Contemporary, humorous, and mystery/supernatural for ages 8-12. Adventure, juvenile (fantasy, sports, spy/adventure, contemporary), and young adult (contemporary, humorous, sports, spy/adventure). Recently published *Come Sing, Jimmy Jo*, by Katherine Paterson (young adult novel); *The Glitch* by Ronald Kidd (humor, computer fantasy); and *Chip Mitchell: The Case of the Chocolate-Covered Bugs*, by Fred D'Ignazio (humor, computers).

**How to Contact:** Query first or submit complete ms with SASE. Simultaneous and photocopied submissions OK. Accepts computer printout submissions. Prefers letter-quality. Reports in 3 months. Publishes ms an average of 1 year after acceptance.

**Terms:** Pays 7½-10% in royalties; offers negotiable advance. Sends galleys to author. Free book catalog.

**Tips:** "Know the market, read other juvenile books, polish your manuscript. We are looking for more fiction for the younger age group (8-10) and are finding that humorous, contemporary novels, and family relationships are popular. We are also finding that shorter books do better. We are publishing less fiction and family relationships in young adult hardcover. We encourage first novelists."

**‡LOUISIANA STATE UNIVERSITY PRESS (II)**, French House, Baton Rouge LA 70893. (504)388-6294. Executive Editor: Ms. Beverly Jarrett. Fiction Editor: Martha Hall. Estab. 1935. University press—medium size (50-60 books per year). Publishes hardcover originals. Average print order: 1,500-2,500; first novel print order: 2,000. Averages 50 total titles/year; 4 fiction titles/year.

**Needs:** Contemporary, literary, mainstream, short story collections. No science fiction and/or juvenile material. Recently published *I Am One of You Forever*, by Fred Chappell; and *Cousins to the Kudzu*, by Bill Doxey.

**How to Contact:** Does not accept unsolicited mss. Query first. Reports in 2-3 months on queries and mss. Simultaneous and photocopied submissions OK. No computer printouts.

**Terms:** Pays in royalties. Sends pre-publication galleys to the author. Royalty paid on copies sold; percentage varies.

**Tips:** Encourages first novelists.

**LOVESWEPT (I, II)**, Bantam Books, 666 5th Ave., New York NY 10103. (212)765-6500. Subsidiaries include Seal Books (Canada) and Transworld/Corgi (UK). Editorial Assistant: Susann Koenig. Assistant Editor: Elizabeth Barrett. Senior Editor: Alicia Condon. Estab. 1982 (imprint). Publishes paperback originals. Plans several first novels this year. Averages 48 total titles each year. Occasionally critiques rejected mss.

**Needs:** Contemporary romance. "Contemporary romance, highly sensual, believable primary characters, fresh and vibrant approaches to plot. No gothics, regencies, or suspense. Check with editorial assistant for trend-setting titles recommended by the editors."

**How to Contact:** Query with SASE; no unsolicited ms.

**Terms:** Pays in royalties of 6%; negotiates advance.

**Tips:** "Use and/or devise new twists and approaches to the genre and be highly creative and sensual."

**McCLELLAND AND STEWART-BANTAM LIMITED (I, II)**, #601, 60 St. Clair Ave. E, Toronto, Ontario, Canada M4T 1N5. (416)922-4970. Publisher Janet Turnbull. Estab. 1977. Canada's largest mass market paperback publisher. Publishes paperback originals and reprints. Aver-

 **The double dagger before a listing indicates that the listing is new in this edition. New markets are often the most receptive to freelance contributions.**

ages about 40 total titles, about 30 fiction titles each year.
**Needs:** Adventure, contemporary, historical, horror, mainstream, suspense/mystery, women's. Needs for novels: "fiction that will appeal to mass market and to a Canadian readership." Recently published *Mecca*, by William Deverell (thriller); *Berlin Solstice*, by Sylvia Fraser; and *Dreamland*, by Garfield Reeves-Stevens (horror).
**How to Contact:** Accepts unsolicited mss. Submit outline/synopsis and 4 sample chapters. Reports in 2 months. Simultaneous and photocopied submissions OK. Accepts computer printout submissions. Prefers letter quality.
**Terms:** Pays in royalties; advance.
**Tips:** Publishes work by Canadian citizens or landed immigrants only.

**MARGARET K. McELDERRY BOOKS/ATHENEUM PUBLISHERS (II)**, 115 5th Ave., New York NY 10003. (212)614-1355. Publisher: Margaret K. McElderry. Division Estab. 1971; now owned by Macmillan Publishing. Midsize independent publisher. Publishes hardcover originals and paperback editions of some titles in Aladdin Books. Number of titles: 29 in 1982; 28 in 1983; 20 in 1984; 26 in 1985. Buys juvenile and YA mss. Buys small percentage of agented books. Average first novel print order 7,500 copies.
**Needs:** All categories for juvenile and young adult: picture books, contemporary, literary, experimental, adventure, mystery, science fiction, and fantasy. "We will consider any category. Results depend on the quality of the imagination and the writing." Recently published *The Changeover*, by Margaret Mahy (supernatural); and *A Place to Come Back to*, by Nancy Bond.
**How to Contact:** Accepts unsolicited mss. Query or submit complete ms. SASE for query, ms. Simultaneous submissions OK only if so indicated (and preferably *not*); no photocopied submissions unless clear and clean. Accepts computer printout submissions. Prefers letter-quality. Reports in 2 weeks on queries, 6-8 weeks on mss. Publishes ms an average of 1 year after acceptance.
**Terms:** Pays in royalties; offers advance. Free book catalog.
**Tips:** "Fantasy, the supernatural, and science fiction are much in demand; also picture books that are original and unusual. We publish only a few contemporary problem novels for young readers, and only when outstanding."

**MACMILLAN CHILDREN'S BOOKS**, MacMillan Publishing Co., 866 Third Ave., New York NY 10022. (212)702-4299. Imprints include Four Winds Press, Alladin Books, and Collier Books. Estab. 1919. Large children's trade list which has been expanding. Publishes hardcover originals and paperback reprints.
**Needs:** Juvenile submissions.
**How to Contact:** Accepts unsolicited mss. Send complete ms with SASE. Reports in 6-8 weeks. No simultaneous submissions; photocopied submissions OK. Accepts computer printout submissions. Prefers letter-quality.
**Terms:** Pays in royalties; negotiates advance. Free book catalog.

**MACMILLAN OF CANADA (III)**, A Division of Canada Publishing Corporation, Suite 685, 146 Front Street West, Toronto, Ontario M5J 1G2 Canada. (416)597-1060. Publisher: Douglas M. Gibson. Editorial Director: Anne Holloway. Publishes in English exclusively. Estab. 1905. Major Canadian trade publisher. Publishes hardcover and quality paperback originals and reprints. Books: perfect hardcover binding; average print order: 5,000; first novel print order 3,000. Number of titles: 42 in 1984. Buys 30% agented fiction. Average first novel print order 3,000 copies. Comments on rejected mss "only if there is considerable merit." Do not publish genre or category fiction or for non-adult market.
**Needs:** Quality fiction for discriminating market, preferably with Canadian theme, setting or author. Recently published *My Present Age*, by Guy Vanderhaeghe (author of Governor-Generals Award winning collection of short stories, *Man Descending); Our Lady of the Snows*, by Morley Callaghan; and *PQ: René Levesque and the Parti Quebécois in Power*, by Graham Fraser.
**How to Contact:** Accepts unsolicited mss only with first 3 chapters, a brief outline and a resume. SASE for return of ms. Note: Canadian postage only. Simultaneous and photocopied sub-

missions acceptable. Accepts computer printout submissions. Prefers letter-quality. Replies within 12 months. Publishes ms 6-18 months after acceptance.

**Terms:** Negotiable. Must return advance if book is not completed or is not acceptable, "unless other arrangements are made." Sends galleys to author.

**Tips:** Will publish "between five and ten novels yearly." Looks for "literary quality; Canadian content. First novels must be of outstanding literary quality by a *Canadian* author."

**MACMILLAN PUBLISHING CO., INC. (III)**, 866 3rd Ave., New York NY 10022. (212)702-2000. Imprints include Collier Books, The Free Press, Bradbury, and Schimer. Publishes hardcover originals and hardcover and paperback reprints. Recently published *The Secret Lives of Marilyn Monroe*, by Anthony Summers; *My Father and I*, by Camelia Sadat.

**How to Contact:** Query, submit outline/synopsis and sample chapters or submit through agent. Photocopied submissions OK. Reports in 6 weeks.

**Terms:** Pays in royalties; offers advance. Free book catalog.

**MARVEL COMICS (II, IV)**, 387 Park Ave. S, New York NY 10016. (212)576-9200. Imprints include Marvel, Epic Star Comics, and Marvel Books. Vice President/Editor-in-Chief: James Shooter. Estab. 1939. Largest comic book publisher in the world. Publishes comic books, magazines, graphic novels, and storybooks. Encourages new writers. Averages 600-800 total titles (fiction) each year. Buys romance, juvenile mss with illustrations.

**Needs:** Adventure, fantasy, horror, humor/satire, psychic/supernatural/occult, science fiction, romance, juvenile, western, and young adult/teen (fantasy/science fiction, spy/adventure). No non-comics.

**How to Contact:** Accepts unsolicited mss. Submit short outline/synopsis with SASE. Photocopied submissions preferred. Reports in 6 months. Publishes ms from 6 months to 6 years after acceptance.

**Terms:** "Payments, royalties, incentives, and benefits vary with format and type of work." Pays on acceptance.

**Tips:** "Now publishing comics and humor for young children."

**‡MERCURY HOUSE (II)**, Box 640, Forest Knolls, CA 94933. (415)488-4005. Executive Editor: Alev Lytle. Publisher: William Brinton. Fiction Editor: Editorial Board of 7. Estab. 1983. Small, independent publisher which publishes quality fiction and nonficiton. Publishes hardcover originals and reprints and paperback originals (trade size only) and reprints. Average print order: 5,000; first novel print order: 5,000. Plans 3 first novels this year. Averages 12 total titles, 10 fiction titles each year.

**Needs:** Contemporary, experimental, literary and translations. Quality fiction only—expansion into foreign translations. Recently published *Personality Surgeon*, by Colin Wilson (mystery); *Lovers & Fugitives*, by Gabriella Mautner (historical); *The Maiden Ape*, by Robert Brancatelli (literary).

**How to Contact:** Query first. SASE. Submit complete ms with cover letter. SASE. Agented fiction 100%. Reports in 2 weeks on queries; 8 weeks on mss.

**Terms:** Pays royalties of 15% minimum; 35% maximum; 10 author's copies. Sends galleys to author. Individual arrangement with author depending on book. Book catalog for 9x12 SASE and $2 postage.

**Tips:** "We are expanding, and encourage gifted novelists with unique voices."

**MILLER BOOKS (II)**, 2908 W. Valley Blvd., Alhambra CA 91803. (213)284-7607. Imprint includes San Gabriel Valley Magazine. Editorial Director: Joseph Miller. Estab. 1962. Midsize publisher. Publishes hardcover originals and paperbacks. Buys juvenile mss with illustrations. Encourages new writers.

**Needs:** Considers all categories except erotica and religious. Especially needs western, regional, and political novels. Accepts short stories for texts. Recently published *Every Feeling Is Desire*, by James J. Smith, M.D.

**How to Contact:** Accepts unsolicited mss. Submit complete ms. SASE for query, ms. Simultaneous and photocopied submissions OK. Accepts computer printout submissions. Prefers letter-quality. Reports in 2 weeks on mss. Publishes ms 6-12 months after acceptance.
**Terms:** Pays 10-15% royalties; no advance. Sends galleys to author. "Private books paid by author." Subsidy publishes "private books—mostly about families or poetry." Free book catalog.
**Tips:** "Write something original that is not about someone of stature. Do not send good reporting; this should be sent to our magazine. Write positive, not depressing or negative, stories. Have a little humor in fiction. We are publishing more paperbacks than in the past."

**WILLIAM MORROW AND COMPANY, INC. (II)**, 105 Madison Ave., New York NY 10016. Imprints include Beech Tree Books, Quill, Perigord, Greenwillow Books, Lothrop, Lee & Shepard and Fielding Publications (travel books), and Morrow Junior Books. Publisher, Morrow Adult: Sherry W. Arden. Publisher, Quill: Alison Brown Cerier; Beech Tree: James D. Landis. Estab. 1926. Plans to publish approximately 350 total hardcover and paperback editions in 1985, of which approximately one fourth will be fiction.
**Needs:** "Morrow accepts only the highest quality submissions" in contemporary, literary, experimental, adventure, mystery, spy, historical, war, romance, women's, feminist, gay/lesbian, science fiction, horror, humor/satire, and translations. Juvenile and young adult divisions are separate. Recently published *The Cider House Rules*, by John Irving; and *If Tomorrow Comes*, by Sidney Sheldon.
**How to Contact:** Submit through agent. All unsolicited mss are returned unopened. "We will only accept queries, proposals, or mss when submitted through a literary agent." Simultaneous and photocopied submissions OK. Accepts computer printout submissions. Prefers letter-quality. Reports in 2-3 months.
**Terms:** Pays in royalties; offers advance. Sends galleys to author. Free book catalog.
**Tips:** "The Morrow divisions of Morrow Junior Books, Greenwillow Books, and Lothrop, Lee and Shepard handle juvenile books. We do 5-10 first novels every year and about ¼ titles are fiction. Having an agent helps to find a publisher."

**MOTT MEDIA, INC., PUBLISHERS (I, II)**, 1000 East Huron St., Milford MI 48042. (313)685-8773. Imprint includes Mott Media and The Crystal Collection. Senior Editor: Leonard George Goss. Estab. 1974. Publishes hardcover and paperback originals and paperback reprints. Plans 2-3 first novels this year. Averages 25 total titles each year. Critiques rejected mss.
**Needs:** Juvenile (fantasy, historical), religious/inspirational, and women's. Especially needs religious, historical Biblical characters, futuristic narrative. First fiction title was published in spring/summer 1983, *The Christmas Duck*, by Ken Gire. Several more planned in near future.
**How to Contact:** Submit outline/synopsis with 3 sample chapters. Simultaneous and photocopied submissions OK. Reports in 3 weeks on queries.
**Terms:** Pays in royalties of 7% minimum, 15% maximum. Free book catalog on request.
**Tips:** "Fiction must demonstrate the highest standards of literary excellence and have a Christian perspective, though not necessarily an overt moral or crisis decision. Imaginative fiction with the qualities of classical fantasy or true myth should be along the lines of J.R.R. Tolkien, C.S. Lewis, or Charles Williams."

**THE MYSTERIOUS PRESS (III)**, 129 W. 56th St., New York NY 10019. (212)765-0923. Imprints include Penzler Books. Publisher: Otto Penzler. Fiction Editor: Michael Seidman and Sara Ann Freed. Estab. 1976. Small independent publisher, publishing only mystery and suspense fiction. Publishes hardcover originals and paperback reprints. Books: hardcover (some Smyth sewn) and paperback binding; illustrations rarely. Averages 32-36 fiction titles each year. Average first novel print order 5,000 copies. Critiques "only those rejected writers we wish particularly to encourage."
**Needs:** Suspense/mystery. Recently published *High Adventure*, by Donald E. Westlake (caper); *The Man From Internal Affairs*, by Nat Hentoff (procedural); and *Roses are Dead*, by Loren D. Estleman (suspense).

**How to Contact:** Prefers agented material. Query or submit outline/synopsis and 3 sample chapters with SASE. Reports in 6-8 weeks on queries, 8-12 weeks on mss. Simultaneous and photocopied submissions OK "if they are clear and clean." Accepts computer printout submissions; prefers letter-quality only ("dot-matrix will be returned, unread.").

**Terms:** Pays in royalties of 10% minimum; offers negotiable advance. Sends galleys to author. Buys hard and softcover rights. Book catalog for SASE.

**Tips:** "We have a strong belief in the everlasting interest in and strength of mystery fiction. Don't talk about writing, do it. Don't ride bandwagons, create them. Our philosophy about publishing first novels is the same as our philosophy about publishing: the cream rises to the top. We are looking for writers with whom we can have a long term relationship. *I, Anna*, by Elsa Lewin is a first novel published this year. The writer functions, really, as a god, creating a universe, populating it, and controlling the destinies of his/her characters. A good editor is an angel, assisting according to the writer's needs. My job is to see to it that the writer writes the best book he/she is capable of, *not* to have the writer write *my* book. Don't worry, publishing will catch up to you; the cycles continue as they always have. If your work is good, keep it circulating and begin the next one, and keep the faith."

**NATIONAL LITERARY GUILD (II)**, Subsidiary of Authors Unlimited, #204, 210 N. Pass Ave., Burbank CA 91505. (818)845-2687. Fiction Editor: John Rappaport, Cooperative, Trade and Variety. Estab. 1982. Complete publishing services from typing ms to completed book; independent publisher with plans to expand. Publishes hardcover and paperback originals. Books: 60 lb paper; offset printing; soft and hardcover; illustrations; average print order: 2,000. Averages 50-60 total titles, 35-40 fiction titles each year. Average first novel print order 2,000 copies. Critiques rejected ms for a fee depending on the length of ms; $250 average fee.

**Needs:** Adventure, contemporary, gay, juvenile (fantasy), religious/inspirational, and spy/adventure. No excessive, explicit sex or lewd illustrations (no pornography). Recently published *Sambos'*, by Charles Bernstein (mystery); *Courthouse*, by Glen Stadler (political); and *Beach Hotels*, by Jack White.

**How to Contact:** Accepts unsolicited mss. Submit complete ms with SASE. Reports in 2 weeks. Simultaneous and photocopied submissions OK. Accepts computer printout submissions; prefers letter-quality.

**Terms:** Cooperative and individual arrangement with author depending on book, etc. Sends galleys to author. "We are cooperative publishers for unpublished authors. They pay approximately 40-50% and we pay balance if the manuscript is accepted by our editors." Writer's guidelines for 6x9 SASE and 80¢ postage. Book catalog for 8x11 SASE and 95¢ postage.

**Tips:** "Be sure manuscript is in proper form before submitting it. The editors return it unread if it isn't in accepted form. We are publishing less fiction and less hardcover. We encourage first novelists."

**NAVAL INSTITUTE PRESS (II, IV)**, Book publishing arm of US Naval Institute, Annapolis MD 21402. Fiction Editor: Deborah Guberti. Estab. 1873. Nonprofit publisher with area of concentration in naval and maritime subjects. Publishes hardcover originals. Plans 1 first novel this year. Averages 25 total titles, 1 fiction title each year. Average first novel print order 15,000 copies.

**Needs:** Adventure (naval and maritime), historical (naval), and war (naval aspects). "We are looking for exceptional novels written on a naval or maritime theme." Recently published *Hunt for Red October*, by T. Clancy (naval adventure, contemporary).

**How to Contact:** Accepts unsolicited mss. Submit outline/synopsis and 2 sample chapters. Reports in 6 weeks. Simultaneous and photocopied submissions OK. Accepts computer printout submissions; prefers letter-quality.

**Terms:** Pays in royalties of 14% of net sales minimum; 21% maximum; 6 author's copies; offers negotiable advance. Sends galleys to author. Free writer's guidelines and book catalog.

**Tips:** "Fiction must be on a naval or maritime theme and *exceptionally well written*. We published a first novel, *The Hunt for Red October*, in 1985."

# Close-up

### Otto Penzler
### Mysterious Press

As one looks around the quaint two-story Mysterious Bookshop in midtown Manhattan, completely lined from floor to ceiling with mystery books (every available kind in or out of print), it's no mystery as to what Otto Penzler's interest—passion—is. Penzler owns the specialty bookstore, where his inner-sanctum office also houses probably the most extensive collection of first edition mysteries in the world. He is also publisher of the Mysterious Press, based upstairs.

Recent surveys show mysteries today are the number one genre. "Finally the public is coming to its senses. But I've *never* seen a period when people were *not* interested in mysteries," says the expert, hooked on the subject since his introduction to Sherlock Holmes as a child. Penzler admits a particular surge of interest in the genre in the last few years, however, during which time his seven-year-old shop has flourished.

Actually, explains Penzler, the mystery category has expanded. It is much more mainstream and includes thrillers, crime detection, espionage, psychological and romantic intrigue. Penzler also reports a return to the pure detective story which was so popular in "the golden years" between the World Wars, i.e., Agatha Christie, Ellery Queen, Dashiell Hammett, Raymond Chandler. Fine writers like Norman Mailer, Michael Malone, Sidney Sheldon and Andrew Greeley, have successfully used the mystery form. "It's the dramatic event that is so important in fiction writing," says Penzler, "and there's little more dramatic than murder."

Ten years ago, Penzler began the Mysterious Press to publish better quality hardcover books for mystery lovers and collectors—a project unheard of in the predominantly paperback genre. Even though he publishes about 50 mysteries a year, more than most US publishers, Penzler considers his press a small independent commercial publishing house. Still growing and establishing his reputation—but with consistent Edgar Award nominees each year—he seeks tested, more seasoned authors.

Thus the Mysterious Press is not for a beginner unless he/she has an exceptional manuscript and is represented by an agent. Once his line is more established, the publisher states he would like to pursue quality first-timers.

However, Penzler maintains, there *is* hope out there. With 600 mysteries published each year it's easier to break into publishing with a mystery than any other genre. The publisher, also the editor of the quarterly *Armchair Detective* and the author of 20-some books about mysteries, *knows* that it is a very difficult kind of book to write. In fact, many fine writers are incapable of writing a mystery because there *has* to be a beginning, middle and end. Today's readers demand more than a good puzzle so there must be more literary form and contain the same qualities as a good mainstream novel.

Of course, every good editor wants to publish great writers. How to connect with those editors? Penzler suggests: Study the greats in mystery, beginning with Sherlock Holmes' books. "Read them again and again—you get so much more as you mature." Join the Mystery Writers of America—"There you'll see your problems aren't yours alone; you'll enjoy the camaraderie and profit from the practical advice." Most important, understand that there's no mysterious formula for success. Otto Penzler says simply, "Hone your craft."

**NEW AMERICAN LIBRARY (III)**, 1633 Broadway, New York NY 10019. (212)397-8000. Imprints include Signet, Mentor, Signet Classic, Plume, Plume Fiction, DAW, Meridian, Signet Vista, and E.P. Dutton. Hardcover. Queries Editor: Ms. Pat Taylor. Estab. 1948. Publishes hardcover and paperback originals and paperback reprints. Number of titles: 690 in 1984.
**Needs:** Contemporary, adventure, mystery, spy, historical, war, romance (historical, young adult), gay, confession, women's, psychic/supernatural/occult, science fiction, horror, regency romance, and series. No short stories or poetry. Recently published *Pet Sematary*, by Stephen King; *On Wings of Eagles*, by Ken Follett; and *Parachutes and Kisses*, by Erica Jong.
**How to Contact:** Queries accepted with SASE. Submit complete ms or outline/synopsis and sample chapters with SASE *only* through agent. Simultaneous and photocopied submissions OK. Accepts computer printout submissions. Prefers letter-quality. Reports in 3 months.
**Terms:** Pays in royalties and author's copies; offers advance. Sends galleys to author. Free book catalog.
**Tips:** "We publish many first novels both *as* originals and reprints. Yes, we encourage first novels, agented manuscripts only."

**W.W. NORTON & COMPANY, INC.**, 500 5th Ave., New York NY 10110. (212)354-5500. For unsolicited mss contact: Hilary Hinzmann. Estab. 1924. Midsize independent publisher of trade-books and college textbooks. Publishes hardcover originals. Occasionally comments on rejected mss.
**Needs:** Contemporary, adventure, mystery, spy, historical, western, war, women's, feminist, humor/satire, and translations. No occult, science fiction, religious, gothic, romances, experimental, confession, erotica, psychic/supernatural, fantasy, horror, juvenile or young adult. Recently published *The Magnificent Spinster*, by May Sarton (contemporary); *Field of Blood*, by Gerald Seymour (suspense); and *American Falls*, by John Calvin Batchelor (historical).
**How to Contact:** Submit outline/synopsis and sample chapters. Simultaneous and photocopied submissions OK. Accepts computer printout submissions. Prefers letter-quality. Reports in 4-6 weeks on queries and mss. Return of material not guaranteed unless return postage is enclosed.
**Terms:** Graduated royalty scale starting at 7½% or 10% of net invoice price, in addition to 25 author's copies; offers advance. Free book catalog.
**Tips:** "We will occasionally encourage writers of promise whom we do not immediately publish. We are principally interested in the literary quality of fiction manuscripts. A familiarity with our current list of titles will give you an idea of what we're looking for. Chances are, if your book is good and you have no agent you will eventually succeed; but the road to success will be easier and shorter if you have an agent backing the book. We encourage the submission of first novels."

**OAK TREE PUBLICATIONS, INC. (IV)**, 9601 Aero Dr., San Diego CA 92123. (619)560-3200. Editor: Beth Ingram. Publishes hardcover and paperback originals. Books: 80 lb-100 lb matte finish text paper; offset web printing; case and saddle stitch binding; 4-color and ink illustrations; average print order: 5,000-10,000. Encourages new writers. Rarely comments on rejected mss.
**Needs:** Young children. To read or be read to. Picture books OK. "Prefer story with positive values." Recently published *Make Believe and Me Series*, by Barbara Alexander.
**How to Contact:** Query or submit complete ms with SASE. Simultaneous and photocopied submissions OK.
**Terms:** Offers variable advance. Sends galleys to author. Free book catalog with 9x12 SASE.
**Tips:** "We look for a well-written story with new subject slant. Generally prefer not to pay large advance, especially for first-time author. We would like books that either parents or children will relate to. We are publishing more children's picture books in a variety of styles."

**ODDO PUBLISHING CO. (II)**, Beauregard Blvd., Box 68, Fayetteville GA 30214. (404)461-7627. Imprint includes Read: Read, Explore, and Develop. Managing Editor: Charles W. Oddo. Midsize independent publisher with plans to expand. Publishes hardcover and paperback originals. Books: 80# matte coated paper; hard cover binding; illustrations; color; average print order

5,000; first novel print order 3,000. Would consider buying juvenile mss with illustrations. Prefers not to work with agents.

**Needs:** Short children's supplementary readers. Recently published *Bobby Bear and The Friendly Ghost*, by Marilue; and *Bobby Bear and The Band*, by Judy Saul.

**How to Contact:** Accepts unsolicited mss. Submit complete ms with SASE. Reports in 3-4 months on mss.

**Terms:** Pays in royalties for special mss only. "We judge all manuscripts independently and pay by outright purchase accordingly." Send 50¢ for book catalog and postage cost.

**Tips:** "Manuscripts must be easy to read, general with current themes. Must be easily coordinated to illustrations. No stories of grandmother long ago, no romance, permissive or immoral words or statements. We encourage first novelists. We are publishing more hardcover books."

**PARKER BROTHERS CHILDREN'S BOOKS**, 50 Dunham Rd., Beverly MA 01915. (617)927-7600. Subsidiary of General Mills. Contact: Jack McMahon. Estab. 1883. Publishes hardcover originals.

**Needs:** Juvenile (animal, easy-to-read, picture book). "We want to see ideas for themes/characters around which we can build a series of books in different formats."

**How to Contact:** Simultaneous and photocopied submissions OK with SASE. Reports within 6 weeks on mss.

**PELICAN PUBLISHING COMPANY (II)**, Box 189, 1101 Monroe St., Gretna LA 70053. Assistant Editor: Karen Leathem. Editorial Director: James Calhoun. Estab. 1928. Publishes hardcover reprints and originals. Books: hardcover and paperback binding; illustrations sometimes. Number of titles: 31 in 1985. Buys juvenile mss with illustrations. Comments on rejected mss "infrequently."

**Needs:** Contemporary, literary, historical, war, ethnic, religious/inspirational, humor/satire, juvenile, and young adult. No sex, violence, romance fiction, or science fiction.

**How to Contact:** Prefers query. May submit complete ms or outline/synopsis and 3-5 sample chapters with SASE. No simultaneous submissions; photocopied submissions only. Reports in 2 weeks on queries; varies on mss. Publishes ms 12-18 months after acceptance.

**Terms:** Pays 10% in royalties; 10 free author's copies; advance only under special conditions. Sends galleys to author. Free list of titles with SASE.

**Tips:** "We would like to see more regional fiction. We are publishing less fiction; it's difficult to sell unknown authors these days. We encourage first novelists."

**PHILOMEL BOOKS (III)**, 51 Madison Ave., New York NY 10010. (212)689-9200. Subsidiary of The Putnam Publishing Group. Editor: Ann Beneduce. Publishes hardcover originals and paperback reprints. Averages 20 total titles each year. "Critiques only if we feel there is some reason to from our point of view."

**Needs:** Juvenile (animal, easy-to-read, historical, picture book, contemporary), and young adult (contemporary, historical, psychological, and problem novels). "We are not closed to any kind of subject matter, but it must be very well written, with interesting and credible characterizations."

**How to Contact:** Query first with SASE. Photocopied submissions OK. Accepts computer printout submissions. Prefers letter-quality. Reports in 2 weeks on queries; 6 weeks on mss.

**Terms:** Payment "arrangement varies." Sends galleys to author.

**Tips:** "Philomel is devoted to children's and young adult books. We do fiction and nonfiction, picturebooks and some paperbacks. All are high quality and suited mainly for the bookstore market. Our new books are also definitely 'up market.' We are quite filled for some time to come, so cannot be too encouraging about new projects, but our door is never entirely closed. If they are good enough for Philomel, we publish first novels, but we publish mostly established authors. Do not send unsolicited manuscripts. Don't send 'blind' query letters."

**POCKET BOOKS (III)**, Division of Simon & Schuster, 1230 Avenue of the Americas, New York NY 10020. (212)246-2121. Imprints include Washington Square Press, Poseidon, and Star Trek. Vice

President/Editorial Director: William Grose. Publishes paperback originals and reprints. Number of titles: averages 300/year. Buys juvenile mss with illustrations. Buys 90% agented fiction.

**Needs:** Contemporary, literary, faction, adventure, mystery, spy, historical, western, gothic, romance, women's, feminist, ethnic, erotica, psychic/supernatural, fantasy, horror, and humor/satire.

**How to Contact:** Query with SASE. Reports in 6 months on queries only. Publishes ms 12-18 months after acceptance.

**Terms:** Pays in royalties; by outright purchase; and offers advance. Must return advance if book is not completed or is not acceptable. Free book catalog.

**POINT BOOKS**, Scholastic, Inc., 730 Broadway, New York NY 10003. Senior Editor: Brenda Bowen. Young adult imprint. See Scholastic, Inc.

**POSEIDON PRESS**, 1230 Avenue of the Americas, New York NY 10020. (212)246-2121. Distributed by Simon & Schuster. Publisher: Ann E. Patty. Estab. 1981. Hardcover. Averages 10-12 total titles, 6-8 fiction titles (2 first novels) each year. Does "not critique rejected ms by unsolicited authors unless work merits it."

**Needs:** General fiction and nonfiction, contemporary, and literary.

**How to Contact:** Submit outline/synopsis and 1 sample chapter (small, no more than 30 pages). Photocopied submissions OK. Reports in 2 months.

**Terms:** Payment varies, discussed according to content of book.

**CLARKSON N. POTTER, INC.**, 1 Park Ave., New York NY 10016. (212)532-9200. Distributed by Crown Publishers, Inc. Vice President Editorial Director: Carol Southern. Managing Director: Michael Fragnito.

**Needs:** Contemporary, literary, adventure, historical, juvenile, women's, and humor/satire. No lurid romance.

**How to Contact:** Prefers submissions through an agent. Simultaneous and photocopied submissions OK. Accepts computer printout submissions.

**Terms:** Pays 8-12% in royalties on hardcover; 6-7½% in royalties on paperback; offers $3,500 up in advance.

**PRENTICE-HALL (II, III)**, Children's Book Division, Englewood Cliffs NJ 07632. Editor-in-Chief: Barbara Francis. Publishes hardcover originals and paperback reprints. Books: offset printing; illustrations sometimes. Number of titles: averages 30 children's hardcover books and 15 children's reprint paperbacks/year. Encourages new writers. Occasionally comments on rejected mss.

**Needs:** Juvenile, picture books, humor, mystery, non-gimmicky science fiction, and imaginative nonfiction. Recently published *Bear's Bargain*, by Frank Asch (picture book); *Dinosaurs That Swam and Flew*, by David Knight, illustrations by Lee Ames. *Joey Runs Away*, by Jack Kent, (picture book).

**How to Contact:** Query first. Submit outline/synopsis and sample chapters ("if multi-published author with established reputation") or complete ms ("if new unpublished writer") with SASE. Simultaneous and photocopied submissions OK. Reports in 4 weeks on queries, 6-8 weeks on mss.

**Terms:** Pays in royalties; offers average advance. Sends galleys to author. Free book catalog with SASE.

**Tips:** "New emphasis on first-rate fiction for 8-12 and 10 up age group. Will continue with high caliber picture books. Also interested in easy-to-read and good historical fiction."

**‡PRESIDIO PRESS (IV)**, 31 Pamaron Way, Novato CA 94947. (415)883-1373. Editor: Adele Horwitz, Joan Griffin. Estab. 1976. Small independent general trade—specialist in military. Publishes hardcover originals. Plans 1 first novel this year. Averages 15 total titles each year. Critiques or comments on rejected ms.

**Needs:** Historical with military background, war.
**How to Contact:** Accepts unsolicited mss. Query first or submit 4 sample chapters. SASE. Reports in 2 weeks on queries; 3 months on mss. Simultaneous and photocopied submissions OK. Accepts computer printouts.
**Terms:** Pays in royalties of 15% minimum; advance: $1,000 average. Sends galleys to author. Book catalog free on request.
**Tips:** "Think twice before entering any highly competitive genre; don't imitate; do your best."

**PRESS GANG PUBLISHERS (IV)**, 603 Powell St., Vancouver, British Columbia, Canada V6A 1H2. (604)253-1224. Estab. 1972. Publishes hardcover and paperback originals. Books: 60 lb book stock paper; offset printing; perfect binding; illustrations; average print order; 1,000-3,000. Number of titles: 1 in 1985; 2 in 1984. Sometimes comments on rejected ms.
**Needs:** Non-sexist children's books; novels for adolescents or adults, with a feminist perspective. Recently published *Common Ground; Stories by Women*, (anthology).
**How to Contact:** Query if in doubt, submit complete ms or submit outline/synopsis and sample chapters with SAE and IRC. Simultaneous and photocopied submissions OK (but we must be told). Reports in 3 weeks on queries, 3 months on mss.
**Terms:** Pays 5-10% in royalties. Terms vary and are negotiated individually. No advance. Free book catalog.
**Tips:** We seek to produce books for as general an audience as possible, but with a particular focus on feminist and lesbian material. We give priority to Canadian authors. Sexist or racist material not considered. We are publishing less fiction but encourage first novelists."

**‡PRICE/STERN/SLOAN PUBLISHING INC. (II)**, Subsidiaries are Wonder Books, Troubador, Serendipity, Doodle Art, 410 N. La Cienega Blvd., Los Angeles CA 90048. (213)657-6100. Contact: Editorial Dept. Estab. 1962. Midsize independent, expanding. Publishes hardcover originals and paperback originals and reprints. Books: perfect bound, saddle stitched binding; illustrations. Averages 100 total titles each year.
**Needs:** Humor/satire, juvenile (animal, series, easy-to-read, fantasy). No adult fiction. Recently published *Little Choo-Choo*, (pop-up/storybook); *Glitterby Baby*, by S. Cosgrove (juvenile); and *Jingle Bear*, by S. Cosgrove (juvenile).
**How to Contact:** Accepts unsolicited mss. Query first. SASE. Submit outline/synopsis and sample chapters or send complete ms with cover letter. SASE required. Reports in 1-2 months on queries; 2-3 months on mss. Simultaneous and photocopied submissions OK. Accepts computer printouts including dot-matrix.
**Terms:** Terms vary. Writer's guidleines free for SASE and 1 first class stamp.

**‡PROMISE ROMANCES (II)**, Subsidiary of Thomas Nelson Publishers, Box 141000, Nashville TN 37214. (615)889-9000. Managing Editor: Etta Wilson. For Biblical fiction contact: Larry Weeden. Estab. 1984. Contemporary inspirational category romance series from large Christian publisher. Publishes paperback originals. Books: cameron belt printing and binding; average print order: 20,000. Publishes 24 romance titles per year. Critiques on rejected ms.
**Needs:** Juvenile (animal, easy-to-read), religious, romance (contemporary). Needs for novels include Biblical novels, contemporary romances. Recently published *No Limits on Love*, by Patricia Dunaway (light romance); *The Scarlet Cord*, by Mary Ellen Keith (Biblical fiction); and *Destination Unknown*, by Elee Landress (light romance).
**How to Contact:** Accepts unsolicited mss. SASE. Submit outline/synopsis and 3 sample chapters. SASE. Reports in 2 weeks on queries; 3 months on mss. Simultaneous and photocopied submissions OK. Accepts computer printouts. Accepts electronic submissions via disc or modem for the IBM or Apple.
**Terms:** Pays in royalties, negotiable; advance negotiable, 10-25 author's copies. Sends galleys to author. Writer's guidelines free.
**Tips:** "We are seeking writers who can give fresh treatment to traditional values in well-crafted fiction. Read everything you can—from the classics to current ficiton." Published new writers within the last year.

**G.P. PUTNAM'S SONS (III)**, The Putnam Publishing Group, 200 Madison Ave., New York NY 10016. (212)576-8900. Imprints include Perigee, Philomel, Platt and Munk, Coward McCann, Grosset and Dunlap Pacer. Publishes hardcover originals.
**Needs:** Recently published *Skeleton Crew*, by Stephen King; *Elvis and Me*, by Priscilla Presley; and *The Fourth Deadly Sin*, by Lawrence Sanders.
**How to Contact:** Does not accept unsolicited mss.

**‡QUARTET BOOKS LTD. (IV)**, Subsidiary of Quartet Books, Inc., #2005, 215 Park Ave. S., New York NY 10003. (212)254-2277. Imprints include Robin Clark, Quartet Encounters, Women's Press, Quartet Qrime. Editor: Catherine Norden. Midsize independent subsidiary of U.K. Co. Publishes hardcover originals and reprints and paperback originals and reprints. Plans 1 first novel this year. Averages 30 titles, 10 fiction titles each year. Critiques or comments on rejected ms "very briefly."
**Needs:** Faction, feminist, historical, humor/satire, literary, short story collections, translations, women's. Emphasis on translations, literary, women's, historical. No romance, science fiction, westerns, horror, juvenile. Recently published *Elizabeth & Alexandra*, by Anthony Lambton (historical); *Ask for the Uncalled*, by Maximov (translations); *After the Divorce*, by De Ledda (translations); *The Nets*, by Kanelli (women's).
**How to Contact:** Accepts unsolicited mss. Query first. SASE. Submit outline/synopsis and 2 sample chapters. SASE. Reports in 4 weeks on queries; 2 months on mss. Simultaneous and photocopied submissions OK.
**Terms:** Vary. Sends galleys to author if in U.K. Book catalog free on request.
**Tips:** "We have more established fiction, especially in translation, cloth and paperback. Our fiction is generally selected to fit a series such as Quartet Encounters (20th century literature in translation) or Quartet Quire."

**RANDOM HOUSE, INC.**, 201 E. 50th St., New York NY 10022. (212)751-2600. Imprints include Pantheon Books, Vintage Books and Knopf. Publishes hardcover and paperback originals. Number of titles: averages 80/year. Encourages new writers. Rarely comments on rejected mss.
**Needs:** Adventure, contemporary, historical, literary, mainstream, short story collections, suspense/mystery, and women's. "We publish fiction of the highest standards." Authors include James Michener, Robert Ludlum, Mary Gordon.
**How to Contact:** Query with SASE. Simultaneous and photocopied submissions OK. Reports in 4-6 weeks on queries, 2 months on mss.
**Terms:** Payment as per standard minimum book contracts. Free writer's guidelines.

**RANDOM HOUSE, INC./Juvenile Division (III)**, 201 E. 50th St., New York NY 10022. (212)751-2600. Imprints include Happy House, Knopf, and Pantheon. Managing Editor: Penny Seiden. "Large mass market *juvenile* publisher (division of a multi-faceted publishing house)— many licensed characters." Publishes hardcover and paperback originals. Books: various kinds of paper, binding and printing; color illustrations. Number of titles: 190 in 1984; 220 in 1985.
**Needs:** Juvenile.
**How to Contact:** "At present, we are only reviewing mss from published authors and agents." Publishes ms 12-18 months after acceptance.
**Terms:** Sends galleys to author on longer books.
**Tips:** "Usually most of work is generated in-house, or freelancers are commissioned for flat fee. No first novels (or any novels) published in several years. Most of our books still feature licensed characters."

**RESOURCE PUBLICATIONS, INC. (I, IV)**, Suite 290, 160 E. Virginia St., San Jose CA 95112. (408)286-8505. Book Editor: Kenneth Guentert. Richardson. Estab. 1973. "Independent book and magazine publisher focusing on the liturgical and religious arts." Publishes paperback originals. Plans 1 first novel this year. Averages 10-12 total titles, 2-3 fiction titles each year.
**Needs:** Story collections for the religious education market. "Novels dealing with contemporary

religious issues would be considered. Rarely handle clearly evangelical pieces." Recently published *In Season and Out*, by Bruce Clanton (short stories); *Joanna, the Pope*, by Daniel Tanger (historical); and *One Perfect Lover*, by Matthew Ignoffo (Biblical).
**How to Contact:** Query first or submit outline/synopsis and 1 sample chapter with SASE. Reports in 2 weeks on queries; 6 weeks on mss. Photocopied submissions OK "If specified as *not* simultaneous." Accepts computer printout submissions. Prefers letter-quality. Accepts disc submissions compatible with CP/M, IBM system. Prefers hard copy with disc submissions.
**Terms:** Pays in royalties of 8% minimum, 10% maximum; 10 author's copies. "We do not subsidy publish. We do require that the author purchase a minimum number of copies of the first press run.

**RICHARDSON & STEIRMAN (I, II)**, 300 Central Park W., New York NY 10024. (212)724-3148. President: Stewart Richardson. Fiction Editors: Hy Steirman and Stewart Richardson. Estab. 1984. Publishes hardcover originals and paperback reprints (trade). Books: offset printing; average first novel print order: 5,000-10,000 copies. Plans 5 first novels this year; 25 total titles, 5-6 fiction titles. Occasionally critiques rejected ms "if author has talent."
**Needs:** Adventure suspense novels. No domestic novels or partial mss.
**How to Contact:** Accepts unsolicited mss. Query. Reports in 2 weeks on queries; 1 month on mss. No simultaneous submissions. Computer printout submissions OK. Prefers letter-quality. Disc submissions OK with IBM. Sends galleys to author.
**Terms:** Pays in royalties of 10% minimum, 15% maximum; advance is more for agented ms. Book catalog for $1.
**Tips:** "Every writer has to begin with a first novel. We are interested in real talent, with writing that creates a world in which characters live—atmosphere and originality. What makes novels work is the growth, decline, triumph, or *change* in characters you care about. The autobiographical novel doesn't work unless the author sees his fictional creation from a distance, so to speak. We will publish books of quality in adventure, suspense, in the sense of Hammond Innes, Helen Mac-Innes, Graham Greene's 'entertainments,' and writers who can tell a story like the late Desmond Bagley and the live John Gardner (now 007's creator.) We are also interested in 'scenario' fiction. We will be publishing one by Drew Middleton, Military Correspondent of *The New York Times*. We don't have the facilities to handle a lot of unsolicited manuscripts. But we prefer a query with a description or a synopsis of a work of fiction envisioned to be at least 75,000 words long. Submissions will be read within four weeks."

**RIVERRUN PRESS, INC.(III)**, Subsidiary of John Calder (Publishers) Ltd., 1170 Broadway, New York NY 10001. (212)889-6850. President: J. Calder. Estab. 1978. Publishes hardcover and paperback originals and reprints. Books: quality paper; cloth or paper binding; illustrations sometimes; average print order 4,000; first novel print order 3,000. Plans 3 first novels this year. Averages 50 total titles, 20 fiction titles each year. Average first novel print order 4,000 copies. Occasionally critiques rejected mss.
**Needs:** Contemporary, experimental, literary, short story collections, and translations. No unliterary fiction.
**How to Contact:** Accepts unsolicited mss. Submit complete ms with SASE.
**Terms:** Pays in royalties of 7½% minimum; 10% maximum; 10 author's copies; negotiable advance, $1,000 average. Sends galleys to authors. Free book catalog on request.
**Tips:** "We are publishing less fiction, more paperbacks."

**‡ROUNDTABLE PUBLISHING, INC. (II)**, 933 Pico Blvd., Santa Monica CA 90405. (213)450-9777. Editor: Shirley Pescia. Estab. 1976. "Midsize independent publisher of mainly nonfiction, Hollywood stories, some fiction and children's books." Publishes hardcover originals. Books: quality paper; offset printing; average print order: 5,000 copies. Plans 4-6 first novels this year. Averages 8-12 total titles/year. Occasionally critiques rejected mss.
**Needs:** Adventure, contemporary, fantasy, humor/satire, juvenile (animal, easy-to-read, fantasy, historical, sports, spy/adventure, contemporary), mainstream, preschool/picture book, sus-

pense/mystery. Would like more humor. Recently published *Seldom Sung Songs*, by Ray Locke; and *The Olympian*, by Peter Dixon (mainstream).

**How to Contact:** Accepts unsolicited mss. Submit outline/synopsis and 2-3 sample chapters. SASE for ms. Agented fiction: 25%. Reports in 3-4 months on mss. Simultaneous submissions and photocopied submissions OK. Accepts computer printouts. Prefers letter-quality.

**Terms:** Pays in royalties. Sends galleys to the author. Individual arrangement with author. Book catalog for SASE or IRC.

**ST. MARTIN'S PRESS**, 175 5th Ave., New York NY 10010. (212)674-5151. Imprint includes Joan Kahn Imprint. President: Thomas J. McCormack. Publishes hardcover and paperback originals.

**Needs:** Contemporary, literary, experimental, faction, adventure, mystery, spy, historical, war, gothic, romance, confession, women's, feminist, gay, lesbian, ethnic, erotica, psychic/supernatural, religious/inspirational, science fiction, fantasy, horror, and humor/satire. No plays, children's literature or short fiction. Recently published *Death in Berlin*, by M.M. Kaye; *Betsey Brown*, by Ntozaki Shange; and *The Fallen Angels*, by Susannah Kells.

**How to Contact:** Query or submit complete ms with SASE. Simultaneous (if declared as such) and photocopied submissions OK. Reports in 2-3 weeks on queries, 4-6 weeks on mss.

**Terms:** Pays standard advance and royalties.

**SCHOLASTIC**, Scholastic, Inc., 730 Broadway, New York NY 10003. Senior Editor for Romance Books: Ann Reit. Publishes a variety of books (paperback originals and reprints) for children and young adults, under the following imprints:

POINT BOOKS: Senior Editor: Brenda Bowen. Estab. 1984. A paperback line of young adult fiction for readers aged 12-up. Not restricted as to length, setting, or subject matter. Most Point novels have contemporary settings, and take as their central characters young adults between the ages of 13-20. No romances. Include SASE.

APPLE BOOKS: Senior Editor: Brenda Bowen. Estab. 1981. A paperback line of juvenile fiction for readers aged 8-11. Not restricted to setting or subject matter, but most Apples are "slim novels" (between 128-200 pages), and all are geared to the capabilities and interests of readers 8-12 years old. Single submissions only. Include SASE.

Scholastic also publishes original paperback books for its school book clubs.

TAB BOOK CLUB (TEEN AGE BOOK CLUB) (Grades 7-12) Contact: Greg Holch.

**How to Contact:** Query first or submit outline/synopsis and 3 sample chapters with SASE. Simultaneous and photocopied submissions OK. Accepts computer printout submissions.

**CHARLES SCRIBNER'S SONS (II)**, 115 5th Ave., New York NY 10003. President and Publisher: Mildred Marmur. Fiction Editors: Laurie G. Schieffelin, Susanne Kirk, Michael Pietsch, Betsy Rapoport. Estab. 1846. Publishes hardcover originals and paperback reprints of its own titles. Number of titles: over 50 in 1985. Does not comment on rejected ms.

**Needs:** Contemporary, adventure, mystery, spy, women's, feminist, horror, humor/satire, juvenile and young adult.

**How to Contact:** Submit outline/synopsis and sample chapter with SASE or submit through agent. "Go to writing workshops. Most important, *find* an agent." Reports in 2 months on queries. Does not accept unsolicited mss, only queries.

**Terms:** Pays in royalties; offers advance. Sends galleys to author.

**Tips:** Two literary prizes offered.

**CHARLES SCRIBNER'S SONS, BOOKS FOR YOUNG READERS**, Division of Macmillan Publishing Co., 115 Fifth Ave., New York NY 10017. (212)613-1300. Director: Clare Costello. Managing Editor: David Toberisky. Publishes hardcover originals. Averages 20-25 total titles, 8-13 fiction titles each year. Critiques some rejected mss.

**Needs:** Juvenile (animal, easy-to-read, fantasy, historical, picture book, sports, spy/adventure, contemporary, ethnic, science fiction), and young adult (fantasy/science fiction, romance, historical, problem novels, sports, spy/adventure). Recently published *The Giver*, by Lynn Hall (young adult contemporary fiction); *How Do You Know It's True?*, by David and Marymae Klein (young adult nonfiction); and *Welcome to Grossville*, by Alice Fleming (intermediate contemporary fiction).

**How to Contact:** Submit complete ms with SASE. Simultaneous and photocopied submissions OK. Reports in 6-8 weeks on mss.

**Terms:** Free book catalog free on request. Sends galleys to author.

**Tips:** "Stories about contemporary children, their problems and experiences are doing well for us in today's market. We encourage first novelists."

**SEAL BOOKS, McCLELLAND AND STEWART-BANTAM LTD.**, 60 St. Clair Ave. E., #601, Toronto, Ontario M4T 1N5 Canada. (416)922-4970. Publisher: Janet Turnbull. Estab. 1977. Mass market publisher. Publishes paperback originals and reprints. Plans 5 first novels this year. Averages 40 titles, 30 fiction titles each year. Buys 10% agented fiction. Average first novel print order approximately 15,000 copies.

**Needs:** Adventure, contemporary, historical (general), horror, mainstream, regional, suspense/ mystery, and war. Wants to see novels by Canadian authors suitable for the mass market. Nothing highly experimental. Recently published *An American Spy Story*, by David Gurr (thriller); *Dreamland*, by Garfield Reeves-Stevens (horror); and *My Present Age*, by Guy Vanderhaeghe (contemporary fiction).

**How to Contact:** Accepts unsolicited mss. Query first; submit outline/synopsis and 3-4 sample chapters or complete ms if available. Simultaneous and photocopied submissions OK. Accepts computer printout submissions. Prefers letter-quality. Reports in 2 weeks on queries; 6 weeks on mss. Publishes ms an average of 1 year after acceptance.

**Terms:** Pays in royalties; offers advance.

**Tips:** "First novel has to be pretty outstanding and show a writer with potential before we can take it on." Sponsors Seal Books First Novel Award, annual competition.

**SECOND CHANCE AT LOVE (II)**, 200 Madison Ave., New York NY 10016. (212)686-9820. Subsidiary of Berkley Publishing Group. Senior Editor: Ellen Edwards. Estab. 1981. Commercial category line. Publishes paperback originals. Plans "many" first novels. Publishes 72 Second Chance at Love titles each year. Open to unagented mss/writers.

**Needs:** Second Chance at Love: contemporary romance. No gothic, suspense, mystery or historicals. Recently published *Pink Satin*, by Jeanne Grant; *Siren's Song*, by Linda Barlow; *Forbidden Dream* by Karen Keast; and *For Love of Mike*, by Courtney Ryan.

**How to Contact:** Accepts unsolicited mss. Submit outline/synopsis and 3 sample chapters if published romance writer or complete ms if unpublished with SASE. Photocopied submissions OK. Accepts computer printout submissions. Prefers letter-quality. Reports in 1 month on queries; 2 months on mss. Publishes ms 7-24 months after acceptance.

**Terms:** Advance against royalties. Sends galleys to author. Free writer's guidelines with SASE.

**Tips:** "Study the books published in our line along with our guidelines and *target* submissions to our needs. We are willing to publish first novels that are of high quality."

**SHARON PUBLICATIONS INC. (II)**, Subsidiary of Edrei Communications Corp., 105 Union Ave., Cresskill NJ 07626. (201)568-8800. Editor: Mary J. Edrei. Estab. 1976. Publishes hardcover and paperback originals and reprints. Books: various kinds of paper; offset printing; hard cover, paperback saddle stitch binding; illustrations sometimes; average print order: 30,000. Averages 150 total titiles, 24 fiction titles each year. Average first novel print order 30,000 copies.

**Needs:** Adventure, contemporary, fantasy, humor/satire, juvenile (animal, easy-to-read, fantasy, sports, spy/adventure, contemporary), preschool/picture book, romance (historical, contemporary), science fiction, short story collections, suspense/mystery, women's, and young adult/ teen. Accepts short stories for texts for teens only.

**Terms:** Free book catalog.

**Tips:** "Our recent titles include teen-oriented, children's, and entertainment field." Write for information on terms and submission policies.

**SIERRA CLUB BOOKS**, 2034 Fillmore St., San Francisco CA 94115. (415)931-7950. Subsidiary includes Sierra Club. Editor-in-Chief: D. Moses. Estab. 1892. Midsize independent publisher. Publishes hardcover and paperback originals and paperback reprints. Averages 15-20 titles, 1-2 fiction titles each year.
**Needs:** Contemporary (conservation, environment).
**How to Contact:** Accepts unsolicited mss. Query only with SASE. "We publish virtually no fiction. We will only deal with queries; we are not staffed to deal with mss." Simultaneous and photocopied submissions OK. Accepts computer printout submissions. Prefers letter-quality. Reports in 6 weeks on queries.
**Terms:** Pays in royalties. Free book catalog for SASE.
**Tips:** "Only rarely do we publish fiction. We will consider novels on their quality and on the basis of their relevance to our organization's environmentalist aims."

**SIGNET (III)**, 1633 Broadway, New York NY 10019. (212)397-8000. Imprints include Plume Books and New American Library, Inc. Submissions Editor: Ms. Pat Taylor. Estab. 1948. Publishes hardcover and paperback originals and paperback reprints. Encourages new writers. Averages 120 + fiction titles each year. Occasionally critiques rejected mss.
**Needs:** Gay, horror, psychic/supernatural/occult, women's, historical romance, regancy romace and young adult (romance and problem novels). "We are not particularly keen to receive unsolicited regular original novels at this time." No literary novels or any type not suited to mass market paperback distribution.
**How to Contact:** Query first with SASE; submit outline through agent. Simultaneous and photocopied submissions OK. Accepts computer printout submissions. Prefers letter-quality. Reports in 3 weeks on queries; 8-10 weeks on mss, agent sent only.
**Terms:** Royalties "vary according to author's experience and previous credits. Our advances and royalties are in line with the major established paperback houses." Free writer's guidelines. Free book catalog on request.
**Tips:** "Study the books which are being published, the authors who are most successful, and get a true picture of the marketplace. An agent is a big help. Horror novels, children in jeopardy, hard-hitting novels of contemporary life, novels which could lend themselves to series are doing well in today's market. We notice that authors are not writing with as much care. Style is lacking. Subject matter is too familiar and plots often confusing."

**SILHOUETTE BOOKS (II, IV)**, 6th Floor, 300 E. 42nd St., New York NY 10017. (212)682-6080. Imprints include Silhouette Romances, First Love from Silhouette, Silhouette Special Edition, Silhouette Desire, Silhouette Intimate Moments, and Silhouette Inspirations. Editorial Director: Karen Solem. Senior Editor: Alicia Condon. Senior Editor: Mary Clare Kersten. Senior Editor: Leslie J. Wainger. Senior Editor: Isabel Swift. Assistant Editors: Phyliss Leskowitz, Jerri Smith. Associate Editor: Lucia Macro. First Love from Silhouette: Senior Editors: Nancy Jackson, Roz Noonan. Estab. 1979. Publishes paperback originals. Buys 90% agented fiction. Number of titles: 334 in 1985. Occasionally comments on rejected mss.
**Needs:** Contemporary romance, adult and young adult. No historical. Recently published *Night Moves*, by Heather Graham Pozzessere; *Summer Deserts*, by Nora Roberts; and *Love by Proxy*, by Diana Palmer.
**How to Contact:** Submit query letter. No unsolicited or simultaneous submissions; photocopied submissions OK. Accepts computer printout submissions. Prefers letter-quality. Publishes ms from 9-24 months after acceptance.
**Terms:** Pays in royalties; offers advance (negotiation on an individual basis). Must return advance if book is not completed or is unacceptable.
**Tips:** "Study our published books before submitting to make sure that the submission is a potential Silhouette."

**SIMON & PIERRE PUBLISHING COMPANY LIMITED (II)**, Box 280, Adelaide St. Postal Stn., Toronto, Ontario M5C 2J4 Canada. Imprint includes Bastet Books, Canplay Series, Canadi-

# Close-up

### Karen Solem
### Silhouette Books

Karen Solem would reject a story about a pretty college graduate who left her midwest college for the Big Apple to become in a few years editorial director of a large publishing company. It's been done. Solem is living proof.

Solem's six-year tenure at Silhouette Books has been less than romantic, however; it's been long hard work. But tremendously satisfying, she says, to participate in the successful development of a company that today commands 30% of the romance market. Silhouette tapped into the romance revolution just as the industry was about to take off—a Cinderella story in itself. The editorial director began with a skeletal crew of five editors. Today a staff of 18 produces 28 contemporary novels a month—from Silhouette Romances, Special Editions, Desires, Intimate Moments, and First Love.

Harlequin bought Silhouette Books in the spring of 1984, but the two companies remain editorially independent. Solem oversees the monthly production of all Silhouette books from the acquisition and developmental stage to their final book form. The editor of each series is responsible for the authors and books in that line, plus any writer that she began to work with. Such flexibility allows the "honored relationship" between author and editor that Silhouette feels is so vital.

Silhouette's original series continue, but "we're always looking for new ideas," says Solem, who heads the ambitious project launched last fall—the Choice Readers Service, a book club of all types of women's fiction. Solem explains that although the romance industry is not growing as fast now, there is still expansion possible within certain lines. Special Edition romances are now longer and there's greater attention to detail, for instance. And there's renewed interest in the "sweeter" stories in the Romance series and continued desire for sexier stories (Desire, Intimate Moments). In general, Solem says, romances are more realistic with believable resolutions. The result is a greater variety of improved quality novels which attract better writers—who frequently return to categories even after "breaking out."

Breaking in is quite possible, insists Karen Solem. "The doors are generally open, and you don't need an agent." Because the staff could not contend with the overwhelming volume of unsolicited manuscripts, Silhouette now requires a letter with a short synopsis, and if possible the name of the line and/or editor on the envelope. If the series editor sees potential, she will ask for sample chapters.

Be familiar with *all* the Silhouette lines, Solem stresses. "The biggest problem we encounter is the lack of awareness about the kind of books we publish." Each series is different. Before submitting a query, read a broad range of romances, at least two from each line. Find the series that is best for you and then read 10 or 15 within that line. And write romances *only* if you sincerely enjoy them. "If you don't write the kind of story you believe in," says Solem, "we'll pick up on it, and our readers will, too."

In communication with their readers, the editors discovered that "women wanted more," so, Solem says, "we just looked at life around us." Thus today's heroines are more "reflective of our real lives"—women from diverse backgrounds with career and educational interests. There are no longer rigid guidelines for writers. "Just write a solid romance," is Solem's now-general instruction. "A really good writer can make her own rules, enhance and expand on them. But you *must* give your story emotional impact. Touch your reader some way—make her laugh, or make her cry."

an Theatre History Series, The Canadian Dramatist, and Drama for Life. Editor: Marian M. Wilson. Estab. 1972. Publishes hardcover and paperback originals. Books: 55 lb hi bulk Web printing; perfect binding; line drawing illustrations; average print order 2,000. Number of titles: averages 6/year.

**Needs:** Contemporary, literary, adventure, mystery, spy, historical, humor/satire, juvenile, young adult, and translations. No romance, erotica, horror, science fiction, or poetry. Recently published *In Bed with Sherlock Holmes*, by Christopher Redmond; and *Kate Rice, Prospector*, by Helen Duncan.

**How to Contact:** Query or submit complete ms or submit outline/synopsis and sample chapter or submit through agent with SASE (Canadian stamps), IRC. Simultaneous and photocopied submissions OK. Reports in 1 month on queries, 4 months on mss.

**Terms:** Pays in royalties; no advance. Sends galleys to author. Free book catalog.

**Tips:** "We prefer Canadian authors. Include with submissions: professional resumé listing previous publications, detailed outline of proposed work and sample chapters. We publish novelists who are good at proofing themselves and not afraid of being involved in their own marketing, but the fiction must be based on a current topics or themes."

**SIMON & SCHUSTER**, 1230 Avenue of the Americas, New York NY 10020. Imprints include Pocket Books, Linden Press.

**Needs:** General adult fiction, mostly commercial fiction.

**How to Contact:** Agented material preferred. Queries/mss may be routed to other editors in the publishing group.

**GIBBS M. SMITH, INC. (II)**, Box 667, Layton UT 84041. (801)544-9800. Imprint includes Peregrine Smith Books. Fiction Editor: James Thomas. Estab. 1970. Publishes hardcover and paperback originals. Books: average print order 5,000. Number of titles: 22 in 1985.

**Needs:** Contemporary and literary. No children's, historical, western, young adult or romance categories. Recently published *The Hunting Years*, by David Kranes (novel).

**How to Contact:** Send entire ms with SASE. Reports in 2-4 months. Substantial advance for right book.

**Terms:** Negotiable royalties. Sends galleys to author. Free book catalog with 6x9 SASE.

**Tips:** Mss rejected because "they are not literary enough, too common or mainstream. We encourage first novelists but they should have short story publication credentials. In trying to get published, take advantage of who you know and try, try, try."

**‡PEREGRINE SMITH BOOKS (I, II)**, Subsidiary of Bibbs M. Smith, Inc., Box 667, Layton UT 84041. (801)544-9800. Fiction Editor: James Thomas. Estab. 1968. "Midsize independent publisher, presently doing 30 titles/year, and plans to expand." Hardcover originals and reprints and paperback originals and reprints. Books: varied paper, printing and binding; illustrations sometimes; average print order: 3,000; first novel print order: 2,500. Plans 4 first novels this year. Averages 30 total titles/year. Publishes 6 fiction titles/year. Occasionally critiques rejected mss.

**Needs:** Contemporary, experimental, literary, mainstream, short story collections, translations. "Sometimes publishes short stories for textbooks. In the fall of '86, we are publishing an anthology of very short stories entitled *Blasters: American Shorts*. Any writer is free to submit to it. We will publish approximately four *literary* novels per year for the next two years." No adventure, romance, western, etc. Recently published *The Hunting Years*, by David Kranes (literary); and *The Western Shore*, by Clarkson Crane (literary).

**How to Contact:** Accepts unsolicited mss. Submit complete ms with cover letter. SASE for query and ms. Agented fiction 40%. Reports in 3 weeks on queries; 2-4 months on mss. Simultaneous and photocopied submissions OK. Accepts computer printouts including dot-matrix.

**Terms:** Pays in royalties of 10% minimum; 15% maximum; $2,500 advance. Sends galleys to the author. Subsidy publishes 15% "(grants and awards are best form of subsidy—author subsidies are frowned upon, though sometimes considered.)" Writers guidelines free. Book catalog free on request.

# Close-up

### Michael Korda
### Simon & Schuster

photo by Milton H. Greene

Check a bestseller list any week for Simon & Schuster titles (or books from their imprints: Linden Press, Summit Books, Archway, Pocket Books, Poseidon, Touchstone) and it's apparent that Simon & Schuster specializes in commercial books. At one point a couple of years ago, the 61-year-old publishing house boasted 9 of the 36 bestsellers listed. "Commercial," of course, includes fiction—40% of the conglomerate's total output, states Michael Korda, the editor-in-chief/senior vice president and the one responsible for bringing in six of the nine bestsellers that successful week.

"I look for books that are *readable*, not trendy," says Korda. Some subjects or categories, of course, work better at certain times than others. No advertising can make a reader buy a book if it's not a good one, maintains the editor. "We don't tell our authors what to write about nor our editors what to publish. We publish what is available—and has good market potential." Which means few if any short story collections.

Despite the ever-present rumor in publishing, Korda insists that fiction is selling better than ever, first novels included. But it's a successful first novel by nonfiction bestselling Carl Sagan or a commercial novel like *Lucky*, by Jackie Collins that allows S&S to publish, as many as six lesser-known first novelists each season. Even though first novels are "financial risks" they are, however, the acknowledged life blood of the industry. "After all," says Korda, "*Scruples* and *Valley of the Dolls* were first novels."

Korda says in a year he sees probably 5,000 to 6,000 proposals, queries, and manuscripts, including those submitted by agents or recommended to him by friends. The S&S policy is *not* to accept unsolicited manuscripts, but the V.P. says they read everything, mainly "out of fear actually that something will come in that we want."

Unfortunately only about five percent warrant another look. Page one of a proposal or manuscript too often determines its own dismal fate because of "telltale, glaring errors." Not one to mince words, Michael Korda says, "A high percentage of what Simon & Schuster editors see from the slush pile is basically illiterate."

They also see too many imitations of Sidney Sheldon or Danielle Steel. And Korda eschews authors who write on word processors with cheap printers—"Life is too short to read dot-matrix." The keys to publishing a manuscript at S&S: originality, quality and professional manuscript preparation.

Korda, considered one of the most meticulous trade editors in publishing, elects to line edit certain writers' manuscripts—and he's even been known to write an ending on occasion for a book by one of his authors with writer's block. His long day religiously begins at 5:30 a.m. when he works on his own fiction, nonfiction books and essays. He is the author of *Queenie*, the bestselling thinly-disguised, fictionalized biography of his aunt (by marriage), Merle Oberon. Work, he admits, is his addiction, but writing and editing *are* compatible. "I like balance," says this high-energy editor/writer. "I think I'd be bored if I just wrote. I need some involvement beyond the world of writing"—such as the eight-week author tour he made for *Queenie* in early 1985.

Korda bases much of his unerring instinct for sniffing out bestsellers on his formula for a book's success, which he also tells his salespeople: "If you can't describe a book in one or two pithy sentences that would make you or my mother want to read it, then of course, you can't sell it." That goes for potential authors, too.

**SOS PUBLICATIONS (II)**, Subsidiary of Bradley Products, Inc., 4223 W. Jefferson Blvd., Los Angeles CA 90016. (213)730-1815. Publisher: Sean Paul Bradley. Estab. 1979. Publishes Minibound 4½x6¾ (hardcover) as part of Private Library Collection. Books: 50 lb Glatfelter Tustin G 50 paper. Publishes 48 fiction titles each year, one per category a month.
**Needs:** Adventure, mainstream, romance (historical, contemporary), suspense/mystery.
**How to Contact:** Accepts unsolicited mss. Submit short synopsis and complete ms with SASE which will enclose mss. Reports in 3-4 months. Simultaneous and photocopied submissions OK.
**Terms:** Pays in royalties. Sends galleys to author. Writer's guidelines for SASE.
**Tips:** "We welcome new writers. Queries without SASE will go unanswered. Published more fiction and more hardcovers last year. We also published new writers last year."

**‡SPECTRA BOOKS (II, IV)**, Subsidiary of Bantam Books, 666 5th Ave., New York NY 10103. (212)765-6500. Senior Editor and Publishing Director: Lou Aronica. Senior Editor: Shawna McCarthy; Editor: Lisa Novak. Estab. 1985. Large science fiction, fantasy and imaginative fiction line. Publishes hardcover originals and paperback originals and reprints. Plans to publish 2-3 first novels this year. Averages 72 total titles, 72 fiction titles each year.
**Needs:** Fantasy, literary, science fiction, young adult/teen (fantasy/science fiction). Needs for novels include novels that attempt to broaden the traditional range of science fiction and fantasy. Strong emphasis on characterization. Especially well written traditional science fiction and fantasy will be considered. No fiction that doesn't have at least some element of speculation or the fantastic. Recently published *Child of Fortune*, by Norman Spinrad (science fiction); *The Dream Years*, by Lisa Goldstein (fantasy); *The Postman*, by David Brin (science fiction).
**How to Contact:** Accepts unsolicited mss. Query first. SASE. Agented fiction 90%. Reports in 3-4 weeks on queries; 6-8 weeks on mss. Photocopied submissions OK. Accepts computer printouts including dot-matrix, "only very dark and very readable ones."
**Terms:** Pays in royalties; advance; advance is negotiable. Sends galleys to author.
**Tips:** "We are always looking for first novelists. We published two first novels over the last 12 months, though both writers had previously published short fiction. Don't pay much attention to current trends, just write what really comes from the heart. We work very closely with our writers on both development of his/her fiction and long-term career goals."

**STANDARD PUBLISHING (IV)**, 8121 Hamilton Ave., Cincinnati OH 45231. (513)931-4050. Director: Marjorie Miller. Estab. 1866. Independent religious publisher. Publishes hardcover and paperback originals and reprints. Number of titles: averages 18/year. Rarely buys juvenile mss with illustrations. Occasionally comments on rejected mss.
**Needs:** Religious/inspirational and easy-to-read. "Should have some relation to moral values or Biblical concepts and principles." Recently published *Marty's Secret*, by Jerry Jenkins; *Boy Friend*, by Jane Sorenson; and *Upside-down Eddie*, by Daniel Schantz (all are for children).
**How to Contact:** Accepts unsolicited mss. Query or submit outline/synopsis and 2-3 sample chapters with SASE. Simultaneous and photocopied submissions OK. Accepts computer printout submissions. Prefers letter-quality. Reports in 2 months on queries, 12 weeks on mss. Publishes ms 12-24 months after acceptance.
**Terms:** Pays varied royalties and by outright purchase; offers varied advance. Sends galleys to author. Free catalog with SASE.
**Tips:** Publishes fiction with "strong moral and ethical implications." First novels "should be appropriate, fitting into new or existing series. We're dealing more with issues."

**STEIN AND DAY PUBLISHERS**, Scarborough House, Briarcliff Manor NY 10510. (914)762-2151. Imprints include Stein and Day Paperbacks and Scarborough Books. President: Sol Stein. Vice President/Editor: Patricia Day. Vice President and Executive Editor: Benton M. Arnovitz. Estab. 1962. Small independent publisher. Publishes fiction for the general reader. Buys 95% agented fiction.
**Needs:** Fiction. No westerns or romance. Recently published *The Therapy of Avram Blok*, by Simon Louvish; *The Worm in the Rose*, by Tom Stacey; and *Cozumel*, by E. Howard Hunt.

**How to Contact:** *Must* send query letter first with SASE; no unsolicited mss. Reports as soon as possible. Publishes ms from 9 months on after acceptance.
**Terms:** Standard. Must return advance if book is not completed or is unacceptable.
**Tips:** "We try for an intelligent up-market readership and enjoy working with established writers."

**STEMMER HOUSE PUBLISHERS, INC. (II),** 2627 Caves Rd., Owings Mills MD 21117. (301)363-3690. Imprint includes International Design Library, Victoria and Albert Museum Introductions to the Decorative Arts. Editor: Barbara Holdridge. Independent publishing house. Publishes hardcover and paperback originals and reprints. Books: acid free paper; offset printing; Smyth sewn binding; illustrations occasionally; average print order 5,000; first novel print order 3,000-4,000. Number of titles: averages 1/year. Encourages new writers.
**Needs:** Contemporary, literary, historical, war, ethnic, regional, juvenile, and young adult. No fantasy, detective or science fiction. Recently published *Paradise*, by Dikkon Eberhart (6th century A.D.); *The Fringe of Heaven*, by Margaret Sutherland (contemporary); and *Naked in Deccan*, by Venkatesh Kulkarni (contemporary).
**How to Contact:** Accepts unsolicited mss. Query or submit complete ms or outline/synopsis and 3 sample chapters or submit through agent (not necessary) with SASE. Simultaneous and photocopied submissions OK if well reproduced. Reports in 2 weeks on queries, 6 weeks on mss depending on backlog. Publishes ms 1-2 years after acceptance.
**Terms:** Pays 5-10% in royalties; offers small advance upon publication. Sends galleys to author. Free book catalog.
**Tips:** "Trend today seems to be less literate work. Write to be read 50 years from today. Don't tell us how good the novel is. Perfect your grammar and spelling. Most writers seem to have read the latest paperback and swear to write something 'just as good'—but it's most often not even as competent." Interested in "literary quality rather than trendy or genre material. We plan to continue trying to find worthwhile fiction, including first novels, on a longterm basis. Send a cogent query letter, not coy, not a teaser, not selfpitying. Perfection in spelling and grammar. Crisp, mostly unblemished typing, with good margins."

**SWEET DREAMS,** Cloverdale Press, 133 5th Ave., New York NY 10003. (212)420-1555. Editor: Apple Ives. Estab. 1981. Book packager. Publishes paperback originals.
**Needs:** Young adult romance. Recently published *The Great Boy Chase*, by Janet Quin-Harkin; *Kiss and Tell*, by Shannon Blair; and *Two's a Crowd*, by Diana Gregory.
**How to Contact:** Query first with SASE. Simultaneous and photocopied submissions OK. Accepts computer printout submissions. Prefers letter quality. Reports in 1 month on queries; 2 months on mss.
**Terms:** Negotiated. Free writer's guidelines for SASE.
**Tips:** Interested in "contemporary fiction with realistic protagonists and situations. We do publish first novels."

**TAB BOOKS CLUB (TEEN AGE BOOK CLUB),** Scholastic Inc., 730 Broadway, New York NY 10003. Contact: Gret Holch. See Scholastic Inc.

**TEXAS MONTHLY PRESS (II),** Box 1569, Austin TX 78767. (512)476-7085. Subsidiary of Mediatex, Inc. Managing Editor: Anne Norman. Director and Editor-in-Chief: Scott Lubeck. Estab. 1978. "Regional publisher with a strong identification with *Texas Monthly* magazine." Publishes hardcover and paperback originals and reprints (60,000 word minimum). Plans 3 first novels this year. Averages 22 total titles, 2-3 fiction titles ("would like more") each year. Buys 10% agented fiction. Occasionally critiques rejected mss.
**Needs:** Contemporary, ethnic, faction, historical, humor/satire, literary, mainstream, suspense/mystery, and western. "Books must reflect some facet of life in Texas or the Southwest. A southwestern setting alone is not enough—must be intrinsically regional. We hope to publish at least two original works of fiction each year." No experimental, gothic, historical romance, or short

stories. Recently published *Deerinwater*, by Jan Reid; *A Flatland Fable*, by Joe Commer; and *Strange Sunlight*, by Peter LaSalle (the seamy side of life in the sunbelt).

**How to Contact:** Query first; submit outline/synopsis and 3 sample chapters with SASE. Simultaneous and photocopied submissions OK. Accepts computer printout submissions. Prefers letter-quality. Accepts disc submissions compatible with Osborne, Lanier, Xerox, IBM. Prefers hard copy with disc submissions. Reports in 2 weeks on queries; 1 month on mss. Publishes ms 12-18 months after acceptance.

**Terms:** Pays in royalties on net. Negotiates advance. Must return advance if book is not completed or is unacceptable. Free book catalog on request.

**Tips:** "We are making a concerted effort to find more quality fiction. It is our goal to offer writers of fiction a publishing option outside of New York." Noticeable trends include suspense, mystery, detective (regional). "We consider first novels."

**THORNDIKE PRESS (IV)**, One Mile Rd., Thorndike ME 04986. (207)948-2962. Senior Editor: Timothy A. Loeb. Estab. 1977. Midsize independent publisher with plans to expand. Publishes hardcover and paperback originals and reprints. Books: acid free paper; offset printing; Smyth sewn and perfect bindings; illustrations. Number of titles: 140 total in 1985. Buys 10% of agented fiction. Occasionally comments briefly on rejected mss.

**Needs:** Humor/satire, quality fiction, regional history and lifestyle (New England or Eastern), nature and outdoors. "We are not publishing children's fiction or young adult material, nor are we interested in books out of the mainstream, such as feminist or gay, for example." Recently published *Polly Hill*, by Clifford S. Reynolds; *Beer and Skittles*, by B.J. Morrison (mystery); and *Stories Told in the Kitchen*, by Kendall Morse (humor).

**How to Contact:** Query or submit outline/synopsis and 3-4 sample chapters with SASE. Simultaneous and photocopied submissions OK. Accepts computer printout submissions. Prefers letter-quality. Accepts disc submissions compatible with IBM PC. Reports in 3 weeks on queries, 2 months on mss. Publishes ms 1-2 years after acceptance.

**Terms:** Pays 5-10% in royalties; by outright purchase $1,000-2,500; offers $500-4,000 advance. Must return advance if book is not completed or is unacceptable. Sends galleys to author. Free book catalog.

**Tips:** "We *are* emphasising New England regional fiction, but this does *not* mean just nostalgia; we will consider mysteries and literate fiction, provided it has a New England setting. A little research beforehand will pay dividends in time and money saved." Most over-the-transom material is "best labeled mass market and is not of interest to us. We look for quality fiction of high literary value, plus regional fiction/mysteries. We are excited about publishing quality work—whether it's a *first* novel or the hundredth."

**THREE CONTINENTS PRESS (II)**, 1346 Connecticut Ave. N.W., Washington DC 20036. (202)457-0288. Fiction Editor: Donald Herdeck. Estab. 1973. Small independent publisher with expanding list. Publishes hardcover and paperback originals and reprints. Books: paper and printing vary; library binding; illustrations; average print order: 1,000-1,500; first novel print order 1,000. Plans first novels. Averages 15 total titles, 6-8 fiction titles each year. Average first novel print order 1,000 copies. Occasionally critiques ("a few sentences") rejected ms.

**Needs:** "We publish original fiction only by writers from Africa, the Caribbean, the Middle East, Asia, and the Pacific. No fiction by writers from North America or Western Europe." Recently published *The Web: Stories by Argentine Women*, by Lewald, ed. (short stories); *Mother Comes of Age*, by Driss Chraibi (translation); and *Tales from Cameroon*, by Rene Philombe (collected stories).

**How to Contact:** Query with outline/synopsis and sample pages and SAE, IRC. Reports in 1 month on queries; 2 months on mss. Simultaneous and photocopied submissions OK. Computer printout submissions OK.

**Terms:** "We are not a subsidy publisher, but do a few specialized titles a year with subsidy. In those cases we accept grants or institutional subventions. Foundation or institution receives 20-30 copies of book and at times royalty on first printing. We pay royalties twice yearly (against advance) as a percentage of net paid receipts. Royalties of 5% minimum, 10% maximum; 10 author's copies; offers negotiable advance, $300 average. Depends on grant/award money. Sends galleys to author. Free book catalog.

**Tips:** "We are publishing more paperbacks if book is expected to be frequently adapted for university text use. We encourage first novelists. We publish fiction by non-Western authors only."

**TICKNOR & FIELDS (I, II)**, Affiliate of Houghton-Mifflin, 52 Vanderbilt Ave., New York NY 10017. (212)687-8996. Editor: Katrina Kennison. Estab. 1979. Publishes hardcover originals.

**Needs:** Open to all categories but only to "the best there is. We are very fussy."

**How to Contact:** No unsolicited mss accepted. No simultaneous submissions (unless very special); photocopied submissions OK. Reports in 8 weeks on ms.

**Terms:** Pays standard amount of royalties. Offers advance depending on the book. Free book catalog with SASE and first class stamps.

**TOR BOOKS (II)**, 49 W. 24th St., New York NY 10010. Managing Editor: Nancy Weisenfeld. Editorial Director: Harriet McDougal. Science Fiction Editor: Beth Meacham. Estab. 1980. Publishes paperback originals and reprints. Books: 5 point Dombook paper; offset printing; Bursel and perfect binding; few illustrations. Averages 120 total titles, 120 fiction titles each year. Buys 75% agented fiction.

**Needs:** Adventure, fantasy, horror, mainstream, science fiction, suspense, and young adult (fantasy/science fiction). Recently published *Spy in Winter*, by Michael Hasting (suspense); *Cander*, by Graham Masterson (fiction); and *Race Against Time*, by Piers Anthony (science fiction).

**How to Contact:** Agented mss preferred. Photocopied submissions OK. Publishes ms a maximum of 18 months after acceptance.

**Terms:** Pays in royalties and advance. Must return advance if book is not completed or is unacceptable. Sends galleys to author. Free book catalog on request.

**Tips:** "We have expanded the number of titles per year; we have launched a hardcover list distributed by St. Martin's Press." Encourages first novelists.

**TSR, INC. (II)**, Box 756, Lake Geneva WI 53147. (414)248-3625. Managing Editor, Books: Jean Blashfield Black. Imprints include Dragon Publishing, SPI, Endless Quest, Advanced Dungeons and Dragons® Gamebooks, (formerly called Super Endless Quest® Gamebooks), Amazing® Stories Books, One-On-One® Adventure Gamebooks. Estab. 1974. Game and book operation, including *Dungeons & Dragons* role-playing game. Publishes paperback originals. Books: standard paperback; offset printing; perfect binding; illustrations, usually (b&w). Plans 6 first novels this year. Averages 35-45 titles each year, all fiction. Average first novel print order 75,000 copies. Occasionally critiques rejected ms "if it looks retrievable."

**Needs:** Adventure, fantasy, horror, juvenile (easy-to read, fantasy, spy/adventure), psychic/supernatural/occult, science fiction, suspense/mystery, and young adult/teen (fantasy/science fiction, mystery, spy/adventure). "Primarily we need adept writers who can respond quickly to need for interactive fiction. Most of our books relate to TSR's games, especially *Dungeons & Dragons*, and *Star Frontiers*. Our original series is *Endless Quest*, all books still selling. In addition, we need authors for lightly interactive novels that take advantage of Steven Spielberg's *Amazing Stories* TV anthology. No general mainstream novels; all straight novels must relate specifically to our games." Recently published *Dragonlance Chronicles*, by Weis and Hickman (fantasy trilogy); *The 4-D Funhouse*, by Clayton Emery and Earl Weyenberg; and *The Soulforge*, by Terry Philips.

**How to Contact:** Accepts unsolicited mss. Submit outline/synopsis and 30 pages with SASE. Reports in 3 months. No simultaneous submissions. "Most of our books are very closely tied to our other products." Accepts computer printout submissions; prefers letter-quality.

**Terms:** Pays flat fee in some series; royalties of 5-7% percent of net in other series. Sometimes sends galleys to author. Offers advance. Free writer's guidelines.

**Tips:** "Unpublished writers should submit elaborate outlines and strong samples. First books are fine if writer is willing to work to produce what we need. We are interested primarily in fantasy."

**TYNDALE HOUSE PUBLISHERS (II, IV)**, 336 Gundersen Dr., Wheaton IL 60187. (312)668-8300. Editor-in-Chief: Dr. Wendell C. Hawley. Estab. 1960. Privately owned religious press. Publishes hardcover and paperback originals and paperback reprints. Plans 6 first novels this year. Averages 87 total titles, 15-20 fiction titles each year. Average first novel print order 5,000-10,000 copies.
**Needs:** Religious/inspirational.
**How to Contact:** Accepts unsolicited mss. Submit complete ms. Reports in variable number of weeks. Simultaneous and photocopied submissions OK. Publishes ms an average of 1 year after acceptance.
**Terms:** Pays in royalties of 10% minimum; negotiable advance. Must return advance if book is not completed or is unacceptable. Sends galleys to author. Free writer's guidelines. Free book catalog on request.
**Tips:** "We are publishing less fiction."

**UNIVERSITY OF GEORGIA PRESS**, Terrell Hall, Athens GA 30602. (404)542-2830. Flannery O'Connor Short Fiction Award Editor: Charles East. Estab. 1938. Midsize university press with editorial program focusing on scholarly nonfiction. Publishes hardcover and paperback originals and reprints.
**Needs:** Short story collections. No novellas or novels. Recently published *Rough Translations*, by Molly Giles; and *Living With Snakes*, by Daniel Curley; (all short story collections).
**How to Contact:** Short story collections are considered only in conjunction with the Flannery O'Connor award competition. Next submission period is June 1-July 31, 1985. *Manuscripts cannot be accepted at any other time. Competition information for SASE.*
**Terms:** The Flannery O'Connor Award carries a $500 cash award plus standard royalties. Free book catalog.

**UNIVERSITY OF MISSOURI PRESS**, 200 Lewis Hall, Columbia MO 65211. (314)882-7641. Associate Director: Susan McGregor Denny. Publishes hardcover and paperback originals. Number of titles: averages 2-3/year.
**Needs:** Contemporary, literary, adventure, war, feminist, ethnic, and humor/satire. No novels.
**How to Contact:** No simultaneous submissions; photocopied submissions OK. Submissions accepted February and March of odd-numbered years only. Send SASE for rules in fall of even-numbered years. Publishes ms 6-18 months after acceptance.
**Terms:** Competition for publication only. Free book catalog.
**Tips:** "Publishes short fiction in Breakthrough Series, not to exceed 35,000 words."

**VANGUARD PRESS, INC. (II)**, 424 Madison Ave., New York NY 10017. (212)753-3906. Editor: Bernice Woll. Estab. 1926. Publishes hardcover originals. Number of titles: averages 15-20/year.
**Needs:** Contemporary, literary, adventure, mystery, spy, war, humor/satire, juvenile, and young adult. Recently published *Father Dowling Mysteries*, by Ralph McInerny; *Iwo Jima*, by Bill Rose; and *Go, Go, Said the Bird*, by Anne Nall Stallworth.
**How to Contact:** Query or submit outline/synopsis and 3 sample chapters with SASE. Advise if simultaneous submissions; photocopied submissions OK. Reports in 3-4 weeks on queries, 8-12 weeks on mss.
**Terms:** Pays in royalties; offers advance, amount depending on book. Sends galleys to author.

**VESTA PUBLICATIONS, LTD. (II)**, Box 1641, Cornwall, Ontario K6H 5V6 Canada. (613)932-2135. Editor: Stephen Gill. Estab. 1974. Midsize publisher with plans to expand. Publishes hardcover and paperback originals. Books: Bond paper; offset printing; paperback and sewn hard cover binding; illustrations; average print order: 1,200; first novel print order: 1,000. Plans 7 first novels this year. Averages 18 total titles, 5 fiction titles each year. Negotiable charge for critiquing rejected ms.
**Needs:** Adventure, contemporary, ethnic, experimental, faction, fantasy, feminist, historical,

humor/satire, juvenile, literary, mainstream, preschool/picture book, psychic/supernatural/occult, regional, religious/inspirational, romance, science fiction, short story collections, suspense/mystery, translations, war, women's, and young adult/teen. Recently published *Sodom in Her Heart*, by Donna Nevling (religious); *The Blessings of a Bird*, by Stephen Gill (juvenile); and *Whistle Stop and Other Stories*, by Odrach.

**How to Contact:** Accepts unsolicited mss. Submit complete ms with SASE or SAE and IRC. Reports in 1 month. Simultaneous and photocopied submissions OK. Accepts computer printout submissions. Disc submissions OK with CPM/Kaypro 2 system.

**Terms:** Pays in royalties of 10% minimum. Sends galleys to author. "For the first novel we usually ask the author from outside of Canada to pay half of our printing cost. Free book catalog.

**Tips:** "We published new writers last year. Don't be discouraged; keep trying."

**VIKING PENGUIN, INC. (III)**, 40 W. 23rd St., New York NY 10010. Imprints include Viking (hardcover adult and juvenile) and Penguin Books (trade paperback). Estab. 1925. Number of fiction titles: averages 100/year.

**Needs:** Open.

**How to Contact:** Submissions accepted only through agent or through intermediary to specific editor. No unsolicited query letters, proposals or manuscripts.

**Terms:** Amount and type of advance payment and royalty scale depend on the individual situation.

**WALKER AND COMPANY (II)**, 720 5th Ave., New York NY 10019. Imprint includes Walker Educational Book Co. (WEBCO). Editorial Director: Richard K. Winslow. Editors: Ruth Cavin, Judy Sullivan. Midsize independent publisher with plans to expand. Publishes hardcover and paperback originals and reprints. Number of titles: averages 250/year. Buys 50% agented fiction. Occasionally comments on rejected mss.

**Needs:** Nonfiction, mystery (classic crime "whodunits"), romance (regency and romantic suspense), quality male adventure, western, and literary fiction. Recently published *Medical Mayhem*, by David T. Nash, M.D., and *Stepkids*, by Ann Tetzoff and Carolyn McClenahan.

**How to Contact:** Submit complete ms. Photocopied submissions OK, "but must notify if multiple submissions." Accepts computer printout submissions; must be letter-quality. Reports in 1-2 months on queries, 6-8 weeks on mss. Publishes ms an average of 1 year after acceptance.

**Terms:** Negotiable (usually advance against royalty). Must return advance if book is not completed or is unacceptable.

**Tips:** "Manuscripts should be sophisticated. As for mysteries, we prefer the conventional whodunit, the English type of police procedure or 'country house' kind of murder mystery, as opposed to violent, overtly sexual, tough novels. We are always looking for well-written western novels. While we publish some of the traditional 'revenge' westerns, we like to publish historical 'explorations' about any aspect of the West."

**WANDERER BOOKS (III)**, Imprint of Simon & Schuster, 1230 Avenue of the Americas, New York NY 10020. (212)245-6400. Editorial Director: Grace Clarke. Estab. 1978. Trade and mass market juvenile list for 8-14 year olds. Publishes paperback originals. Averages 60 total titles, 10 fiction titles each year.

**Needs:** Juvenile (8-14 years). All categories. Recently published Nancy Drew, Hardy Boys, and Bobbsey Twins titles.

**How to Contact:** Query first with SASE. Reports in 3 weeks. Photocopied submissions OK. Accepts computer printout submissions. Prefers letter-quality. Publishes ms 8-18 months after acceptance.

**Terms:** Free writer's guidelines for SASE. Must return advance if book is not completed or is unacceptable.

**Tips:** "Know the marketplace, the competition, try to understand who buys books and why. No matter how wonderful an author's idea seems, if we can't sell it we don't publish it."

**WARNER BOOKS (II)**, 666 5th Ave., New York NY 10103. Editor-in-Chief: Bernard W. Shir-Cliff. Estab. 1970. Publishes hardcover and paperback originals. Number of titles: averages 225/year.
**Needs:** "Buys mss on individual merit, not by category; wants to see all categories." Recently published *Angels of September*, by Andrew Greeley; *Fit for Life*, by Harvey and Marilyn Diamond; and *Word of Honor*, by Nelson De Miller.
**How to Contact:** Query with detailed letter or detailed outline, enough for editor to tell quickly if book is in area desired; also include writing credentials. Simultaneous and photocopied submissions OK. Reports in 1 day to 5 weeks on queries.
**Terms:** Pays 6-10% in royalties; offers advance. Free book catalog with standard SASE.
**Tips:** "We want to see strong contemporary fiction."

**WESTERN PUBLISHING COMPANY, INC.**, 850 3rd Ave., New York NY 10022. (212)753-8500. Imprint includes Golden Books. Juvenile Editor-in-Chief: Rosanna Hansen. Estab. 1907. High-volume mass market and trade publisher. Publishes hardcover and paperback originals. Number of titles: averages 120/year. Buys 20-30% agented fiction.
**Needs:** Juvenile: adventure, mystery, humor, sports, animal, easy-to-read picture books, and "a few" nonfiction. Recently published *Cheltenham's Party*, by Jan Wahl illustrated by Lucinda McQueen (Little Golden Book edition); *I Had a Bad Dream*, by Linda Hayward illustrated by Eugenie (Learn about Living book), and *Suppertime for Freda Fuzzypaws*, by Cyndy Szekeres.
**How to Contact:** Send a query letter with a description of the story and SASE. Unsolicited mss are returned unread. Publishes ms an average of 1 year after acceptance.
**Terms:** Pays by outright purchase or royalty.
**Tips:** "Read our books to see what we do. Call for appointment if you do illustrations, to show your work. Do not send illustrations. Illustrations are not necessary; if your book is what we are looking for, we can use one of our artists."

**‡ALBERT WHITMAN & COMPANY (II)**, 5747 W. Howard, Niles IL 60648. (312)647-1358. Senior Editor: Ann Fay. Associate Editor: Abby Levine. Editor-in-Chief: Kathleen Tucker. Estab. 1919. Small independent juvenile publisher. Publishes hardcover originals. Books: paper varies; printing varies; library binding; "Most of our books are illustrated"; average print order: 7,500. Average 20-26 total titles/year. Number fiction titles varies.
**Needs:** Juvenile (3-12 years including easy-to-read, fantasy, historical, adventure, contemporary, mysteries, picture-book stories, teen). "A few of our novels appeal to teen readers as well as middle-grade and junior-high school children." Wants to see novels for middle-grade readers. Recently published *Casey the Nomad*, by Susan Sussman (contemporary); *When the Dolls Woke*, by Marjorie Stover (fantasy); and *Dead Man in Catfish Bay*, by Mary Blount Christian (mystery).
**How to Contact:** Accepts unsolicited mss. Submit outline/synopsis and 1-3 sample chapters; complete ms for picture books. SASE. "Half or more fiction is not agented." Reports in 3 weeks on queries; 8 weeks on mss. Simultaneous and photocopied submissions OK. ("We prefer to be told.") Accepts computer printouts including dot-matrix.
**Terms:** Payment varies depending on a variety of factors. Royalties, advance; number of author's copies varies. Some flat fees. Sends galleys to author. Writer's guidelines free for SASE. Book catalog for 9x12 SASE and 69¢ postage.
**Tips:** Encourages first novelists. Published new writers in the last year.

**WINSTON-DEREK PUBLISHERS (I, II)**, Box 90883, Nashville TN 37209. (615)356-7384, 329-1319. Imprints include Scythe Books. Senior Editor: Marjorie Staton. Estab. 1978. Midsize publisher. Publishes hardcover and paperback originals and reprints. Books: 60 lb old Warren style paper; printing varies; perfect and/or sewn binding; illustrations sometimes; average print order 3,000-5,000 copies; first novel print order 2,000 copies. Plans 3 first novels this year. Averages 35-50 total titles, 10-12 fiction titles each year; "90% of material is from freelance writers; each year we add 15 more titles."
**Needs:** Gothic, historical, juvenile (historical), psychic, religious/inspirational, and young adult

(easy-to-read, historical, romance) and programmed reading material for middle and high school students. "Must be 50,000 words or less. Novels strong with human interest. Characters overcoming a weakness or working through a difficulty. Prefer plots related to a historical event but not necessary. No science fiction, explicit eroticism, minorities in conflict without working out a solution to the problem. Down play on religious ideal and values." Recently published *With Wings of an Eagle*, by James H. Goodman; *The Banana Horse*, by Velma Armstrong; *The Good Judge*, by Jim Lynch.

**How to Contact:** Submit outline/synopsis and 3-4 sample chapters with SASE. Simultaneous and photocopied submissions OK. Accepts computer printout submissions. Prefers letter-quality. Reports in 4-6 weeks on queries; 6-8 weeks on mss. Must query first. Do not send complete ms.

**Terms:** Pays in royalties of 10% minimum, 15% maximum; negotiates advance. Book catalog on request for $1 postage.

**Tips:** "Stay in the mainstream of writing. The public is reading serene and contemplative literature. Problem solving is salable." Published new writers within the last year.

‡**WORD BOOKS (II, IV),** Subsidiary of Word Publishing (American Broadcasting Company), 4800 West Waco Dr., Waco TX 76796. (817)772-7650. Editor, Special Projects: Anne Christian Buchanan. Estab. 1967. Publishes hardcover originals. Books: standard trade book weight—varies from book to book; photo offset or Cameron (letterpress using polymer plates) printing; usually perfect bound binding; average print order: 15,000; first novel print order: 15,000. Plans 2-3 first novels this year. Averages 50 total titles, 2-6 fiction titles each year. Critiques or comments on rejected ms (depending on time available and quality of writing).

**Needs:** Adventure, fantasy, literary, religious/inspirational, romance (contemporary, historical), suspense/mystery, western, women's. "We are specifically not doing a romance 'line' or other genre 'line,' but we are open to good quality fiction that would appeal to our general audience—the 'evangelical' religious market. This would mean books with a Christian theme integral to the story, not 'tacked on.' Largest audience probably female. We do look at Biblical fiction. We do not do well with futuristic-type fantasies, those with a 'down' or negative message, those written to a largely male audience. Also, we are not prepared to deal with mass-produced romance-line titles." Recently produced *Stone of Help*, by Robin Hardy (historical romance/fantasy—Christian); *A Light in Babylon: A Novel About the Life of Daniel*, by Carol Carlson (Biblical fiction); *The Cocooning*, by Sue Ann Kautz (general fiction/fantasy).

**How to Contact:** Accepts unsolicited mss on a limited basis. SASE. Submit outline/synopsis and 2-3 sample chapters. SASE. Agented fiction 50%. Reports in 2-4 months on queries however, "we will acknowledge receipt in 1-2 weeks;" 2-4 months on mss. Simultaneous and good quality photocopies OK. Accepts computer printouts including dot-matrix of high quality.

**Terms:** Pays in royalties (negotiated); advance is negotiated; 6 author's copies. Sends galleys to author. Writer's guidelines free for regular business letter SASE and 5 first class stamps. Book catalog for 9x12 SASE and 1 first class stamp.

**Tips:** "We are currently making plans to expand our fiction on a limited basis (perhaps 6 books a year), although specific plans will depend on market—we will never be *first* a fiction publisher. We are looking for good 'reads' that appeal to our general audience but are written with integrity. A certain percentage of our offerings each year will be books by authors established in our market, although we are open to new authors on a limited basis. In the past two years we have published one or two unpublished fiction writers and will probably continue to do this again on a limited basis. The editor must realize she has the author's 'lifeblood' in her hands; the writer must realize that there will be things about the book she can't see because of being too close to it. In our market, there are often certain elements such as language, situations, that must be negotiated for acceptability. Author must realize this and be willing to work with us."

**YEARLING (II, III),** 1 Dag Hammarskjold Plaza, New York NY 10017. (212)605-3500. See Dell Publishing Co., Inc. Publishes originals and reprints for children grades K-6. Most interested in humorous upbeat novels, mysteries, and family stories. 42 titles a year. "Will, regrettably, no longer consider unsolicited material at this time."

**Terms:** Sends galleys to author.
**Tips:** Encourages first novelists and more fiction.

**ZEBRA BOOKS (II)**, 475 Park Ave. S, New York NY 10016. (212)889-2299. President: Roberta Grossman. Editorial Director: Leslie Gelbman. Estab. 1975. Publishes hardcover reprints and paperback originals. Number of titles: 200 planned for 1986. Averages 200 total titles/year.
**Needs:** Contemporary, adventure, English-style mysteries, historical, war, Vietnam novels, gothic, saga, romance, thrillers and horror. No science fiction. Recently published *Stolen Ecstasy*, by Janelle Taylor; *Savage Kiss*, by Sylvia F. Sommerfield; and *Iacocca*, by David Adodaher.
**How to Contact:** Query or submit complete ms or outline/synopsis and sample chapters with SASE. Simultaneous and photocopied submissions OK. Address women's mss to Leslie Gelbman and male adventure mss to Wally Exman. Reports in 3-5 months on queries and mss.
**Terms:** Pays royalties and advances. Free book catalog.
**Tips:** "Put aside your literary ideals, be commercial. We like big contemporary women's fiction; glitzy career novels, espionage, and horrors. Work fast and on assignment. Keep your cover letter simple and to the point. Too many times, 'cutesy' letters about category or content turn us off some fine mss. More involved family and historical sagas. But please do research. We buy many unsolicited manuscripts, but we're slow readers. Have patience." Encourages first novelists.

**CHARLOTTE ZOLOTOW BOOKS (II)**, 10 E. 53rd St., New York NY 10022. (212)207-7044. "Editor works mainly with authors she has edited over the years." See Harper & Row Junior Books Group.

**ZONDERVAN**, 1415 Lake Dr. SE, Grand Rapids MI 49505. (616)698-6900. Imprints include Pyranee Books, Zondervan Books, Judith Markham Books, Lamplighter Books, Daybreak Books, Franc Ashbury, Academic Books, Ministry Resources Library. Contact: Review Editor. Estab. 1931. Large evangelical Christian publishing house. Publishes hardcover and paperback originals and reprints. Plans 2 first novels this year. Averages 120 total titles, 3 fiction titles each year. Average first novel 7,500 copies.
**Needs:** Contemporary, fantasy, historical, literary, mainstream, religious/inspirational, and women's. No prophecy novels.
**How to Contact:** Accepts unsolicited mss. Query or submit outline/synopsis and 2 sample chapters. Reports in 2 weeks on queries; 2 months on mss. Simultaneous and photocopied submissions OK. Accepts computer printout submissions.
**Terms:** "The author receives a percentage of the retail price of each copy sold (usually 10%). Free writer's guidelines.

---

# Foreign commercial publishers

Commercial publishers are often interested in fiction submissions from Americans and Canadians. Query the press of your choice first for a catalog or their guidelines to be sure your manuscript is appropriate for their needs. And always include the proper postage (IRCs) with any foreign correspondence to ensure a response or the return of your manuscript. (See Manuscript Mechanics.)

**ANDERSON PRESS LTD**, 19-21 Conway St., London W1P 6B5, England. Tel. (01)388-7601. Editor: Audrey Adams. Publishes hardcover originals.

**ANGUS & ROBERTSON UK LTD.**, Bay Books, 16 Golden Sq., London England W1. (01)437-9602. Marketing Manager: Murray Mahon. "Small UK publisher with some indepen-

dent publishing and acting as marketing/scouting office for major Australian publishing house."
Australian adventure, ethnic, feminist, gay, juvenile (sports, spy/adventure, contemporary), lesbian, psychic/supernatural/occult, film, theatre, health, language/linguistics, and humor.

**ACQUILA PUBLISHING COMPANY**, Johnston Green Publishing (U.K.) Box 1, Portree. Isle of Skye IV51 9BT Scotland. Sligachan 257. Managing Director/Editor: J.C.R. Green. "Small specialist (alternative or 'fringe') publisher of poetry, fiction, etc." Needs for novels include "good quality fiction, modern in style, but readable and entertaining. No pulp, no way-out either. Any subject at all, any reasonable style, but must be well written."

**BAHAMAS INTERNATIONAL PUBLISHING COMPANY LTD.**, Box N-1914, Nassau, Bahamas. (809)322-1149. Fiction Editor: Paul Drake. Publishes quality paperback originals. Contemporary, literary, and mainstream.

**THE BLACKSTAFF PRESS**, 3 Galway Park, Dundonald BT 160AN N. Ireland. Editor: Kerry Campbell. Midsize, independent publisher, wide range of subjects. Publishes hardcover and paperback originals and reprints. Contemporary, ethnic (Irish), feminist, historical, humor/satire, literary, short story collections, and women's-Irish interest.

**MARION BOYARS PUBLISHERS INC.**, Box 223, Canal Street Station, New York NY 10013. Send all mss and mail to 18 Brewer St., London, England W1R 4AS. Fiction Editor: Marion Boyars. "Compact independent publisher."

**J.M. DENT & SONS LTD.**, Aldine House, 33 Welbeck St., London W1M 8LX, England. Tel. (01)486-7233. Fiction Editor: Robyn Sisman. Publishes hardcover and paperback originals and reprints.

**GRAFTON BOOKS**, A Division of Collins Publishing Corp., 8 Grafton St., London W1X 3LA England. (01)493-7070. Editorial Directors: John Boothe, Nick Austin. Publishes hardcover and paperback originals and paperback reprints. Adventure, contemporary, erotica, faction, fantasy, historical, horror, psychic/supernatural/occult, science fiction, and war.

**ROBERT HALE LIMITED**, Clerkenwell House, 45/47 Clerkenwell Green, London EC1R 0HT England. Managing Director: John Hale. Chief Editor: Carmel Elwell. Publishes hardcover and trade paperback originals and hardcover reprints. Adventure, gothic, historical, mainstream, mystery, romance, suspense and western.

**JOHNSTON GREEN PUBLISHING (UK) LIMITED**, Box 1, Portree, Isle of Skye, 1V51 9BT Scotland. Imprints include Aquila Publishing. Managing Director: JCR Green. Publishes hardcover and paperback originals. Contemporary, literary, experimental, adventure, mystery, spy, historical, erotica, psychic/supernatural, science fiction, fantasy, horror, humor/satire, translations, and short stories.

**ANNE JOHNSTON/THE MOORLANDS PRESS**, 11 Novi Lane, Leek, Staffordshire ST13 6NS England. Editor: J.C.R. Green. Publishes hardcover and paperback originals and reprints. Contemporary, erotica, experimental, faction, fantasy, literary, mainstream, psychic/supernatural, science fiction short story collections, translations.

**MICHAEL JOSEPH LTD.**, Subsidiary of Thomson Books Ltd., 44 Bedford Square, London WC1 3DP, England. (01)323-3200. Contact: Fiction Editor. Midsize general publisher of adult fiction and nonfiction. Publishes hardcover originals and "a few trade paperback originals and reprints, not mass market." Adventure, contemporary, fantasy, feminist, historical, horror, humor/satire, literary, mainstream, psychic/supernatural/occult, regional, romance, (historical, contemporary), science fiction, short story collections, suspense/mystery, war, and women's.

**O'BRIEN PRESS**, 20 Victoria Rd., Dublin 14, Ireland. Tel. (01)-979598. Fiction Editor: Peter Fallon. Publishes hardcover and paperback originals and reprints. Contemporary, literary, translations from Irish.

**PRICE MILBURN AND CO. LTD.**, Private Bag, Petone, New Zealand, Tel. (04)687179. Subsidiary of Education House Ltd. Editor: Beverly Price. Publishes hardcover and paperback originals and reprints. Juvenile (animal, easy-to-read, historical, picture book, contemporary), young adult (easy-to-read, historical, problem novels, spy/adventure).

**SPHERE BOOKS**, 30/32 Gray's Inn Rd., London WC1X 8JL, England. Tel. (01)405-2087; (01)405-6683 or (01)242-4562. Editorial Director: Ms. Chris Holifield. Publishes paperback originals and reprints. General mass market genre fiction.

**WOLFHOUND PRESS**, 68 Mountjoy Sq., Dublin, Ireland. Tel. (01)740354. Publisher: Seamus Cashman. Publishes hardcover and paperback originals and reprints.

> " All I needed was a steady table and a typewriter . . . a marble topped bedroom washstand table made a good place; the dining room table between meals was also suitable.
> —Agatha Christie "

# Contests and awards

Convinced that there are yet undiscovered and unrecognized writers of great talent, the *Ladies' Home Journal* co-sponsored with Doubleday the Barbara Taylor Bradford *LHJ* Short Story Contest in the fall of 1985. Prizes for the one-time contest were an unprecedented $5,000 and $10,000 for an unpublished and published winner respectively. "We wanted to encourage not only beginning writers but those who have already published," says Bradford. "They, too, dream of becoming successful novelists, with that dream perhaps a little closer on the horizon, but still elusive."

Winning—or sometimes even just entering—a contest may help make those dreams less elusive. There are other benefits as well. As coordinators of other contests declare, they give recognition and attention to excellence and achievement of younger or less established creative writers. They also offer incentive to continue writing, and even support fiction writers when the economics of publishing make writing more difficult. In addition, winning helps ease the writer's search for the publisher of the next novel or short story, it brings new names to the attention of agents and editors. Very basically, and most important for beginners, an award allows a "closet writer" to say quite legitimately, "I am a writer."

Fiction contests and awards are as diverse and specialized as the magazines, publishing houses and associations that sponsor them. With representation locally, regionally, nationally and internationally, there are contests, for example, for novelists in Maine and for children's writers in California. Most every genre or subject offers some kind of competition: mystery, romance, science fiction, western, erotica, as well as Judaism, baseball, or parody—on every level of writing. In other words there's a contest for every fiction writer—regardless of sex, age, location, nationality, subject, achievement level.

To assist you in your contest search, we have marked those 30-plus *new* listings with a dagger (‡). We have also asked the sponsoring publishers and organizations to rank their competition according to the writing level of achievement they are seeking. If you are an unestablished or unknown writer of short stories or novels, it's wise to approach those contests marked with a (I). As a more seasoned, published writer of short or long fiction, you can compete in contests ranked with (II). The ranking (III) is for contests requiring published submissions—by nomination only—of the best short stories and novels of the current year, or those fellowships requiring lengthy credits and applications.

Finding the most appropriate contest for your work demands as much research as for publishing your fiction in a magazine or with a publishing house. Check the listings that follow for eligibility requirements—age, area, subject, story length, entry fee, etc. If the information is not complete, send for the contest rules.

**AGA KHAN PRIZE,** *Paris Review,* 541 E. 72nd St., New York NY 10021. Contact: George Plimpton, editor. Annual award. To promote younger and lesser known writers. Unpublished submissions with SASE. Deadline entry: May 1 to June 1. Award judged by the editors. Award: $1,000. Unpublished short story (1,000-10,000 words). Translations acceptable but should be accompanied by a copy of the original text. Contest/award rules and entry forms available with SASE.

**AIM MAGAZINE SHORT STORY CONTEST (I, II),** Box 20554, Chicago IL 60619. (312)874-6184. Contact: Ruth Apilado and Mark Boone, publisher and fiction editor. Estab. 1984. Contest likely to be offered annually when money is available. "To encourage and reward good writing in the short story form. The contest is particularly for new writers." Unpublished submissions. Award: $100 plus publication in fall issue. "Judged by *AIM*'s editorial staff." Deadline: June 30, 1986. Contest rules for SASE. "We're looking for compelling, well-written stories with lasting social significance."

**ALBERTA NEW NOVELIST COMPETITION (II),** Alberta Culture in cooperation with Irwin Publishing Co. Inc. of Toronto, 12th Floor, CN Tower, Edmonton, Alberta T5J 0K5 Canada. Contact: Ruth B. Fraser, director. Biannual award. To encourage the development of fiction writers living in the province of Alberta. The competition is open to any writer who has never before had a novel published and who is a resident of the province of Alberta. Deadline entry for both: Dec. 31. No SASE is necessary. Brochures and further information available. Award: Novel: $4,000; of this, $2,500 is an outright award given by Alberta Culture and $1,500 is an advance against royalties given by Irwin Publishing Co. Inc. Novel length may range from 60,000-100,000 words.

**THE ALBERTA SHORT STORY COMPETITION (II),** Alberta Culture in cooperation with *Edmonton* and *Calgary* magazines and ACCESS-CKUA Radio, 12th Floor, CN Tower, Edmonton, Alberta T5J 0K5 Canada. Contact: Ruth B. Fraser, director. Estab. 1983. Annual award. "The competition is designed to encourage short story writers living in Alberta and to provide a drawing card for Alberta magazines." Unpublished, original submissions no longer than 3,000 words. Deadline: December 31. The competition is for resident Alberta writers only. The competition brochure will be sent upon request. Award: $2,000 first prize; $1,500 second prize, $1,200 third prize; up to ten $100 honorable mentions; publication of winning entries in *Edmonton* and *Calgary* magazines, and broadcasting of winning stories on ACCESS-CKUA Radio.

**THE ALBERTA WRITING FOR YOUNG PEOPLE COMPETITION (II),** Alberta Culture in cooperation with Irwin Publishing Co. Inc., 12th Floor, CN Tower, Edmonton, Alberta T5J 0K5 Canada. Contact: Ruth B. Fraser, director. Biannual award. The competition is designed to direct Alberta's writers to the challenging world of writing for juveniles. Unpublished submissions. Deadline entry: Dec. 31. The competition brochure and/or further information will be sent, upon request. Award: There is a $3,000 prize; an outright award of $2,000 from Alberta Culture and a $1,000 advance against royalties from Irwin Publishing Co. Inc. "We have 2 categories: book mss for young adults (up to age 16) averaging 40,000 words in length; and book mss suitable for younger readers (8-12 years) running between 12,000 and 20,000 words."

**THE NELSON ALGREN AWARD (II),** *Chicago Tribune,* 435 N. Michigan Ave., Chicago IL 60611. (312)222-3232. Contact: Nadia Cowen. Formerly sponsored by *Chicago Magazine.* Annual award. To recognize an outstanding, unpublished short story, maximum 10,000 words. Unpublished submissions by American writers. Awards: $5,000 first prize, three runners-up receive $1,000 awards. Publication of four winning stories in the *Chicago Tribune.* Deadline: Entries are accepted from October 15th-February 1. No entry fee. A poster bearing the rules of the contest will be sent to writers who inquire.

**‡ALLEGHENY REVIEW AWARDS (I),** Box 32, Allegheny College, Meadville PA 16335. Contact: Thomas J. Stout, senior editor. Annually. Short stories unpublished. US undergraduate students. Deadline: January 31. SASE for rules.

*AMELIA MAGAZINE* AWARDS (II), The Reed Smith Fiction Prize; The Willie Lee Martin Short Story Award; The Cassie Wade Short Fiction Award; The Patrick T. Bradshaw Book-Length Fiction Award, 329 "E" St., Bakersfield CA 93303. (805)323-4064. Contact: Frederick A. Raborg, Jr., editor. Estab. 1984. Annually. "To publish the finest fiction possible and reward the writer; to allow good writers to earn some money in small press publication. *AMELIA* strives to fill that gap between major circulation magazines and quality university journals." Unpublished submissions. Length: The Reed Smith—3,500-5,000 words; The Willie Lee—3,500-5,000 words, The Cassie Wade—3,500 words. Occasional shorts to 2,000 words. Award:"Each prize consists of $200 plus publication and five contributor's copies of issue containing winner's work. The Reed Smith Fiction Prize offers two additional awards and publication at *AMELIA*'s standard fiction honorarium of $35; Bradshaw Book Award $300 plus publication. Deadline: The Reed Smith Prize—September 1; The Willie Lee—March 1; The Cassie Wade—June 1. Entry fee: $5. Bradshaw Award fee: $10. Contest rules for SASE. Looking for "high quality work equal to finest fiction being published today."

**THE AMERICAN BOOK AWARDS (TABA) (III)**, Association of American Publishers, 1 Park Ave., New York NY 10016. Annual award. To honor distinguished literary achievement in three categories including fiction. Books published Nov. 1 through Oct. 31. Deadline is July 31. Awards judged by panels. November ceremony. Award: $10,000 award and a Louise Nevelson sculpture to each winner. $1,000 to two runners-up in each category. Selections are submitted by publishers only. A $100 fee is required for entry. Read *Publishers Weekly* for additional information.

**SHERWOOD ANDERSON SHORT FICTION PRIZE (II)**, *Mid-American Review*, Dept. of English, Bowling Green State University, Bowling Green OH 43403. (419)372-2725. Contact: Robert Early, editor. Annual award. "To encourage the writer of quality short fiction." Unpublished material. Award: $200. No deadline. No entry fee. "Winners are selected from stories published by the magazine, so submission for publication is the first step."

*ANTIETAM REVIEW* LITERARY AWARD (II), *Antietam Review*, Room 215, 33 W. Washington St., Hagerstown MD 21740. (301)791-3125. Contact: Ann B. Knox, editor. Estab. 1984. Annual award. To encourage and give recognition to excellence in short fiction. Open to writers from Maryland, Pennsylvania, Virginia, West Virginia, and Washington DC. "We consider only previously unpublished work. We read manuscripts between Oct. 1 and March 1." Award: $200 and the story is printed as lead in the magazine. "We consider all fiction mss sent to *Antietam Review* as entries for the prize. We look for well-crafted, serious literary prose fiction under 5,000 words.

**ARIZONA AUTHORS' ASSOCIATION (II)**, Annual Literary Contest, Box 10492, Phoenix AZ 85064. (602)952-0163. Contact: Margaret De Mente, executive secretary. Estab. 1982. Annually. "To encourage AAA members and all other writers in the country to discipline themselves to write regularly, steadily for competition and publication." Unpublished submissions. Award: "Cash prizes totalling $1,000 for winners and honorable mentions in short stories, essays, and poetry. Winning entries are published in the *Arizona Literary Magazine*." Deadline: July 29. Entry fee: $6 for essays and short stories. Contest rules for SASE. Looking for "strong concept; good, effective writing, with emphasis on the subject/story instead of technical skill."

*ARIZONA QUARTERLY* BEST SHORT STORY (I, II), University of Arizona, Tuscon AZ 85721. (602)621-6396. Contact: Albert Gegenheimer, editor. Annual award. To recognize the best short story published in *Arizona Quarterly* from the past year as chosen by the editorial board. Award: Bound copy of the year's volume and appropriate certificate.

**ASF TRANSLATION PRIZE (I, IV)**, American-Scandinavian Foundation, 127 E. 73rd St., New York NY 10021. Contact: Charles Doane, editorial assistant. Estab. 1980. Annual award. Competition includes submissions of poetry, drama, literary prose, and fiction translations. To encourage the translation and publication of the best of contemporary Scandinavian poetry and fiction and to make it available to a wider American audience. Previously published in the original Scandinavian language. No previously translated publication. Original authors should have been born within past 100 years. Deadline entry: June 1. Competition rules and entry forms available with SASE. Award: $1,000 and publication in *Scandinavian Review*.

**THE ATHENAEUM LITERARY AWARD (III, IV)**, The Athenaeum of Philadelphia, 219 S. 6th St., Philadelphia PA 19106. Contact: Literary Award Committee. Annual award. To recognize and encourage outstanding literary achievement in Philadelphia and its vicinity. Must be previously published submissions from the preceding year. Deadline entry: December. Nominations shall be made in writing to the Literary Award Committee by the author, the publisher, or a member of the Athenaeum accompanied by a copy of the book. Award judged by committee appointed by Board of Directors. Award: A bronze medal bearing the name of the award, the seal of the Athenaeum, the title of the book, the name of the author, and the year. The Athenaeum Literary Award is granted for a work of general literature, not exclusively for fiction. Juvenile fiction is not included.

*AURA* **CREATIVE WRITING**, *AURA* Literary/Arts Review, 117 Campbell Hall, University Station, Birmingham AL 35294. (205)934-3216. Contact: Andrea Mathews, editor. Annual award. "To encourage creative writing by the students of our University and to award them the opportunity to see their work in print." Unpublished submissions and essays. Award: Cash awards in three categories, one of which is short fiction. First, second and third places awarded (money depends on what is available)." Deadline varies. "Sometimes we run the contest in the spring, then the next year in the fall, and the reverse." No entry fee. "The entries are restricted to the students at our University. Notices are posted, and given to the writing teachers." Length isn't as important as quality of work.

**AWP AWARD SERIES IN SHORT FICTION**, The Associated Writing Programs, c/o Old Dominion University, Norfolk VA 23508. Annual award. The AWP Award Series was established in cooperation with several university presses in order to make quality short fiction available to a wide audience. Unpublished submissions. Deadline entry: December 31. Awards judged by distinguished writers in each genre. Contest/award rules and entry forms available with SASE. Award: The winning manuscript in short fiction is published by the University of Missouri Press. Carries a $1,000 honorarium. $10 submission fee with ms.

**AWP AWARD SERIES IN THE NOVEL**, The Associated Writing Programs, c/o Old Dominion University, Norfolk VA 23508. Annual award. The AWP Award Series was established in cooperation with several university presses in order to publish and make fine fiction available to a wide audience. Unpublished submissions in book form. Deadline entry: December 31. Awards judged by distinguished writers in each genre. Contest/award rules and entry forms available with SASE. Award: The winning novel ms is published by the State University of New York Press. Carries a $1,000 honorarium. In addition, AWP tries to place mss of finalists (from 3-8 in each genre) with participating presses. $10 submission fee with ms.

**EMILY CLARK BALCH AWARDS**, *The Virginia Quarterly Review*, 1 West Range, Charlottesville VA 22903. Contact: Staige D. Blackford, editor. Annual award. To recognize distinguished short fiction by American writers. Stories published in *The Virginia Quarterly Review* during the calendar year. No unsolicited stories considered. Submit a story to *VQR* for consideration. Award: $500.

**IRMA SIMONTON BLACK CHILDREN'S BOOK AWARD (III)**, Bank Street College, 610 W. 112th St., New York NY 10025. (212)663-7200, ext. 254. Contact: Williams Hooks, publications director. Annual award. "To honor the young children's book published in the preceeding year judged the most outstanding in text as well as in art." Previously published submissions.

"Must be published the year preceeding the May award." Award: Press luncheon at Harvard Club, a scroll, and seals by Maurice Sendak for attaching to award book's run. Entry deadline: January 15. No entry fee. "Write to address above. Usually publishers submit books they want considered, but individuals can too. No entries are returned."

**BOOKS IN CANADA AWARD FOR FIRST NOVELS**, Books in Canada, 366 Adelaide St. E, Toronto, Ontario, Canada M5A 3X9. (416)363-5426. Contact: Michael Smith, editor. Annual award. "To promote and recognize Canadian writing." Published submissions from the previous calendar year. Award: $1,000. No entry fee. Submissions are made by publishers. Contest is restricted to first novels in English published in Canada in the previous calendar year.

**BOSTON GLOBE-HORN BOOK AWARDS**, *Boston Globe* Newspaper, *Horn Book* Magazine, Promotion Department, 135 Morrissey Blvd., Boston MA 02107. Contact: Stephanie Loer, children's book editor. Annual award. "To honor most outstanding children's fiction, illustration and nonfiction books published within the US." Previously published material from July 1-June 30 of following year. Submit by April 1. Award: $500 first prize in each category; silver plate for the 3 honor books in each category. Entry deadline: April 1. No entry fee. Entry forms or rules for SASE.

**BULWER-LYTTON FICTION CONTEST (I)**, San Jose State University, Washington Square, San Jose CA 95192. (408)277-3363. Contact: Scott Rice, award director, editor. Estab. 1983. Annual award. "To involve more people in literary activities; especially to foster parody and the joys of active word-play as the means promoting a concern for language." Unpublished submissions. Award: " The overall winner of the adult (masters) division will receive an Apple Macintosh 512K computer. Category winners and dishonorable mentions will receive handsome (well, almost) genuine simulated parchment certificates." Deadline: April 15. Contest rules for SASE. "We sponsor a parody contest, asking entrants to compose the worst of all possible opening sentences to hypothetical novels (judged by category).

**JOHN W. CAMPBELL AWARD (III, IV)**, World Science Fiction Convention, c/o Howard DeVore, 4705 Weddel St., Dearborn Heights MI 48125. To award the best new writer in science fiction. Previously published submissions in the field of science fiction or fantasy. Award: Associated with the Hugo Science Fiction Achievement Awards. Members of the World Science Fiction Convention *nominate* contestants by ballot. Writers may not nominate their own work.

**CANADA COUNCIL GOVERNOR GENERAL'S LITERARY AWARDS**, Canada Council, Box 1047, 255 Albert St., Ottawa, Ontario K1P 5V8 Canada. Contact: writing and publication section. Eight annual awards. "To honor the Canadian writers of 4 English-language and 4 French-language works published during the preceding year. Awards are given in the fields of fiction, nonfiction, poetry, and drama." All Canadian books in these 4 categories published in the preceding year are considered. No entry forms are required. Award: $5,000 each award. Canadian authors only.

**CANADIAN AUTHORS ASSOCIATION LITERARY AWARD (FICTION) (III, IV)**, Canadian Authors Association, 24 Ryerson Ave., Toronto, Ontario, Canada M5T 2P3. (416)364-4203. Contact: G. Sumodi, Executive Director. Annual award. "To honor writing that achieves literary excellence without sacrificing popular appeal." Submissions must be published during the previous calendar year. Award: $5,000 plus silver medal. Entry deadline: December 31 of calendar year. No entry fee. Entry forms or rules for SASE. Restricted to a full-length novel. Author must be Canadian or Canadian-landed immigrant. CAA also sponsors the Air Canada Award.

**CANADIAN FICTION MAGAZINE CONTRIBUTOR'S PRIZE**, *Canadian Fiction Magazine*, Box 946, Station F, Toronto, Ontario M4Y 2N9 Canada. Contact: Geoffrey Hancock, editor-in-chief. Annual award. To celebrate the best story published in either French or English during the preceding year. Contributors must reside in Canada or be Canadians living abroad. Unpublished submissions only. All manuscripts published in *CFM* are eligible. Deadline: August 15. Award: $250, public announcement, photograph. "Looking for contemporary creative writing of the highest possible literary standards."

**CANADIAN LIBRARY ASSOCIATION BOOK OF THE YEAR FOR CHILDREN AWARD (III, IV)**, 151 Sparks St., Ottawa, Ontario, Canada K1P 5E3. Annual award. "To encourage the writing and publishing of children's books in Canada." Published submissions during the calendar year preceding the announcement of the award. Award: Specially designed and engraved medals presented at annual banquet.

**‡RAYMOND CARVER SHORT STORY CONTEST (I, II)**, Dept. of English, Humboldt State University, Arcata CA 95521. Contact: Jeanne M. Whitmer, coordinator. Annually. Short stories, unpublished. For authors living in United States only. Deadline: December 1. Entry fee $5. SASE for rules/entry form.

**CCL STUDENT WRITING CONTEST (I)**, Conference on Christianity and Literature, Department of English, Baylor University, Waco TX 76798. (817)755-1768. Contact: James Barcus, editor. Annual award. "To recognize excellence in undergraduate writing." Unpublished submissions. Award: $75, $50, and $25 awarded in book certificates. Entry deadline: March 1. Looking for "excellence in artistic achievement and reflection of writer's Christian premises."

**CENTER FOR THE STUDY OF CHRISTIAN VALUES IN LITERATURE WRITING CONTEST (II, IV)**, 3134 JKHB, Brigham Young University, Provo UT 84602. (801)378-2304. Contact: Jay Fox, center director and editor of journal *Literature and Belief*. Annual award. "To encourage the writing of quality literature that represents affirmative values and themes." Unpublished submissions. Personal essay, critical essay, poetry, and short story. Awards: Fiction and essay—1st $150; 2nd $100. Poetry—1st $100; 2nd $75; both are student and non-student divisions. Entry deadline: May 15. No entry fee. Entry forms or rules for SASE. "The Center is interested in literature that achieves a meaningful blend of artistic form and moral content. Entries that represent religious values in the Judeo-Christian tradition are especially encouraged."

**‡THE CHATTAHOOCHEE PRIZE (II)**, *The Chattahoochee Review*, 2101 Womack Rd., Dunwoody GA 30338. (404)393-3300. Contact: Lamar York, editor. Annually. Short stories. "Prize winner is selected from contributions throughout the year to the *Chattahoochee Review*." Must be published in the *Review* during the year. No entry fee.

**CHILD STUDY CHILDREN'S BOOK AWARD (III)**, Child Study Children's Book Award, Committee at Bank St. College, 610 W. 112th St., New York NY 10025. Contact: Anita Wilkes Dore, Committee Chair. Annual award. "To honor a book for children or young people which deals realistically with problems in their world. It may concern universal, personal or emotional problems." Only books sent by publishers for review are considered. No personal submissions. Books must be published within current calendar year. Award: Certificate. Cash prize.

**THE CHRISTOPHER AWARD (III)**, The Christophers, 12 E. 48th St., New York NY 10017. Contact: Ms. Peggy Flanagan, awards coordinator. Annual award. "To encourage creative people to continue to produce works which 'affirm the highest values of the human spirit' in adult and children's books." Published submissions only. "Award judged by a grass roots panel and a final panel of experts. Juvenile works are 'children tested.' " Award: Bronze medallion. Examples of books awarded: *Dear Mr. Henshaw*, by Beverly Cleary (ages 8-10); *Sign of the Beaver* by Elizabeth George Speare (ages 10-12).

**CLEVELAND MAGAZINE FICTION CONTEST (IV)**, *Cleveland Magazine*, 1621 Euclid Ave., Cleveland OH 44115. Contact: Frank Bentayou, managing editor. Annual award. Unpublished submissions only. Award judged by editorial staff. Deadline entry: September 30. Awards: $350 and publication usually in December. "Story must be set in Greater Cleveland and contain a little of the true flavor of the area. The short story is not to exceed 10,000 words."

‡*COLUMBIA MAGAZINE* EDITOR'S AWARDS (I, II), *Columbia; a Magazine of Poetry and Prose*, Writing Division, 404 Dodge Hall, Columbia University NY 10027. Contact: Fiction Editors. Annually. Short stories and sections of novels, unpublished. Deadline: March 1. Entry fee $5, made payable to *Columbia Magazine*. SASE for rules/entry forms. "Submissions can be no more than 25 pages; include SASE; award is publication and $450."

**COMMONWEALTH CLUB OF CALIFORNIA (III, IV)**, California Book Awards, 681 Market St., San Francisco CA 94105. (415)362-4903. Contact: Michael J. Brassington, executive director. Annually. "To encourage California writers and honor literary merit." Submissions previously published during the year of the particular contest. Three copies of book required. Awards: Gold and silver medals. Deadline: January 31. Contest rules for SASE. "Either an author or publisher may enter a book."

**CONNECTICUT WRITERS LEAGUE ANNUAL WRITING CONTEST (II)**, Box 10536, West Hartford CT 06110. Contact: Betty Hoffman, editor. Estab. 1982. Annual award. "To encourage writing. Winners are published in the annual publication, *The Connecticut Writer*, produced by the Connecticut Writers League." Unpublished submissions. Award: "1985 prizes were $50 for 1st place in poetry and fiction; 2nd place, $25 each in above categories. A contest committee screens the manuscripts; final selections are made by judges outside the Connecticut Writers League. Interested persons should send for guidelines with SASE in the early spring. Entry fee: $2.

**DEEP SOUTH WRITERS CONFERENCE ANNUAL COMPETITION (I, II)**, DSWC Inc., English Dept., University of Southwestern Louisiana, Box 44691, Lafayette LA 70504. (318)231-6908. Contact: Herb Fackler, director. Annual award. "To encourage aspiring, unpublished writers." Unpublished submissions. Award: Certificate and cash. Contest rules for SASE. Deadline: July 15.

**DELACORTE PRESS ANNUAL PRIZE FOR AN OUTSTANDING FIRST YOUNG ADULT NOVEL (II)**, Delacorte Press, Department BFYR (Books for Young Readers), 1 Dag Hammarskjold Plaza, New York NY 10017. (212)605-3000. Contact: George Nicholson, editor-in-chief, BFYR. Estab. 1983. Annual award. "To encourage the writing of contemporary young adult fiction and publish first novelists." Unpublished submissions; fiction with a contemporary setting in the United States or Canada that will be suitable for ages 12-18. Award: Contract for publication of book; $1,000 cash prize and a $4,000 advance against royalties. Deadline: December 31. Contest rules for SASE.

‡**JOHN DOS PASSOS PRIZE FOR LITERATURE (III)**, Longwood College, Farmville VA 23901. (804)392-9356. Contact: W.C. Woods, director. Annually. Short stories, novels, novellas, short story collections, previously published. Established major writers by nomination only. SASE for rules/entry forms.

‡**DOUBLEDAY/COLUMBIA FELLOWSHIP (II, IV)**, Doubleday & Co./Columbia University, Doubleday & Co., 245 Park Ave., New York NY 10167. (212)953-4995. Contact: Anne Hukill Yeager, associate editor. Award offered "when submission warrants it." Novels, novellas, unpublished or previously published. Requirements: Author must live close enough to New York City to attend class at Columbia. Must have a novel finished or almost finished to submit. Deadline: rolling admissions. SASE for rules/application. "Winner of award receives tuition for one semester of novel-writing class at Columbia University."

**EDITORS FICTION AWARD (II)**, (formerly Carlos Fuentes Fiction Award), *Columbia: A Magazine of Poetry & Prose*, 404 Dodge, Columbia University, New York NY 10027. Contact: Rick Moody or Chris Newbound, fiction editors. Annual award. "To recognize and promote talented writing." Unpublished submissions only. Deadline: March 15. Rules for SASE. Award: $450 and publication in magazine.

**EDMONTON JOURNAL'S LITERARY AWARDS**, *Edmonton Journal*, Box 2421, Edmonton, Alberta T5J 2S6 Canada. (403)429-5100. Contact: D. Skijlsky, assistant promotions manager, community relations dept. Annual award. "To recognize novice writers in our circulation area; promote writing and reading; establish good-will in the community." Unpublished submissions. Award: $1,600 total; $400 in each category—short fiction, fiction for juvenile audience, short poetry and long poetry. Deadline: April 30.

**ROBERT L. FISH MEMORIAL AWARD (I, III)**, Mystery Writers of America, 150 Fifth Ave., New York NY 10011. (212)255-7005. Estab. 1984. Annually. "To encourage new writers in the mystery/detective/suspense short story—and, subsequently, larger work in the genre." Previously published submissions published the year prior to the award. Award: $500. Judged by the MWA committee for best short story of the year in the mystery genre. Deadline: December. Looking for "a story with a crime that is central to the plot that is well written and distinctive."

**DOROTHY CANFIELD FISHER AWARD**, Vermont Congress of Parents and Teachers and Vermont Department of Libraries, 131 Main St., Montpelier VT 05602. Contact: Sylvia La Combe, Chairperson. Annual award. "To encourage Vermont school children to become enthusiastic and discriminating readers and to honor the memory of one of Vermont's most distinguished and beloved literary figures." Publishers send the committee review copies of books to consider. Only books of the current publishing year can be considered for next year's award. Master list of titles is drawn up in late February or March each year. Children vote each year in the spring and the award is given before the school year ends. Illuminated scroll. Submissions must be "written by living American authors, be suitable for children in grades 4-8, and have literary merit. Can be nonfiction also."

**FOSTER CITY ANNUAL WRITERS CONTEST (II)**, Foster City Committee for the Arts, 650 Shell Blvd., Foster City CA 94404. Contact: Ted Lance, contest chairman. Annually. "To foster and encourage aspiring writers." Unpublished submissions. Award: 1st prize in each of four categories $200. Ribbons for two honorable mentions in each category. "Contest begins in late March or April and usually closes in July. Dates are announced." Entry fee: $5. Contest rules for SASE. Looking for short stories (fiction, children's stories); 3,000 words maximum.

**GENERAL ELECTRIC FOUNDATION AWARDS FOR YOUNGER WRITERS (IV)**, General Electric Foundation and Coordinating Council of Literary Magazines, 666 Broadway, New York NY 10012. (212)614-6550. Contact: James Gwynne, program director. Estab. 1982. Annual award. "To recognize excellence in younger and less established creative writers and to support the literary magazines that publish their work. Only literary magazine editors may nominate writers." Previously published submissions published the two years preceding the award. Award: "Up to six prizes of $5,000 each will be offered to the best writers of fiction, literary essays, and poetry published in literary magazines. No more than 3 prizes given in any one category."

**GOLDEN HEART AWARD (I, IV)**, Romance Writers of America, Suite 207, 5206 F.M. 1960 West, Houston TX 77069. (713)440-6885. Contact: Patricia Hudgins, executive secretary. Annual award. "To give recognition and attention to the unpublished writer of romance." Unpublished submissions. Partial ms at preliminary competition is a proposal form of first three chapters plus any other with a love scene and a synopsis (limit of 10 pages on synopsis). Author must be unsold in romance genre. Requires multiple copies for judging. Award: Golden heart with a 14 kt. gold necklace. Request brochure for rules with SASE to RWA. Entry fee and form must be submitted by November 30; manuscript postmarked between December 30 and January 15.

**GOLDEN KITE (III)**, Society of Children's Book Writers, Box 296, Mar Vista Station, Los Angeles CA 90066. Contact: Sue Alexander, chairperson. Annual award. "To recognize outstanding works of fiction, nonfiction and picture-illustration for children created by members of the Society of Children's Book Writers and published in the award year." Published submissions during January-December of publication year. Deadline entry: December 15. Rules for SASE. Award: Statuette and plaque. Looking for quality material for children. Individual "must be member of the SCBW to submit books."

**GOLDEN MEDALLION (II, III)**, Romance Writers of America, Suite 207, 5206 FM 1960 West, Houston TX 77069. (713)440-6885. Contact: Patricia Hudgins, executive secretary. Estab. 1982. Annual award. "To recognize best of works published the preceding year in romantic fiction in several categories." Previously published submissions. "1984 awards were for works published in 1983." Award: "A specially designed plaque with medallion and etched plate." Deadline: Jan. 15. Request brochure with rules with SASE. Looking for "the best representatives of published works—in each category of romantic fiction (contemporary sensual, contemporary traditional, young adult, regency, mainstream historical, single title release contemporary, and inspirational). Entry fee and form deadline is November 30. Multiple copies of books must be submitted with postmark between December 30 and January 15.

**‡THE GREAT CANADIAN NOVELLA COMPETITION (II, IV)**, Pottersfield Press, RR 2, Porters Lake, Nova Scotia B0J 2S0 Canada. Contact: Lesley Choyce, editor. Annually. Novella, unpublished. Requirements: all ages; "author must be Canadian citizen, Canadian born or living in Canada and have created a novella that is any genre or subject." Entry fee: $5 check, international postage coupons or stamps. SASE, IRC for rules/entry form. "$200 cash award advance plus contract to publish with national distribution. Royalties: 10% list."

**GREAT LAKES COLLEGES ASSOCIATION NEW WRITERS AWARD IN FICTION (I, IV)**, Great Lakes Colleges Association, Suite 240, 220 Collingwood, Ann Arbor MI 48103. (313)761-4833. Contact: James W. Cook, director, Department of English, Albion College, Albion MI 49224. Annually. "To encourage excellence in literature and creative writing and expose authors and their works to students and faculty at the 12 liberal arts colleges which comprise the association." 4 copies of published books or galleys from fall and spring publishers' lists. Publishers may submit one work of fiction and one volume of poetry. Award: A tour of a number of the GLCA schools with honoraria at each participating school of at least $150 plus travel expenses and hospitality. Deadline: February 28. Contest rules for SASE.

**GREAT LAKES COLLEGES ASSOCIATION NEW WRITERS AWARDS (III)**, Great Lakes Colleges Association, Albion College, Albion MI 49224. Contact: James W. Cook, director. Annual award. "To recognize good young writers, promote and encourage interest in good literature." Submissions previously published "during the year preceding each year's February 28 deadline for entry, or the following spring." Award judged by critics and writers in residence at Great Lakes Colleges Association colleges and universities. Entry form or rules for SASE. Award: "Invited tour of up to 12 Great Lakes Colleges (usually 7 or 8) with honoraria and expenses paid. Entries in fiction (there is also a poetry section) must be novels or volumes of short stories already published, and must be submitted (four copies) *by publishers only*—but this may include privately published books."

**GREAT PLAINS STORY TELLING & POETRY READING CONTEST (I, II)**, 106 Navajo, Council Bluffs IA 51501. (712)366-1136. Contact: Robert Everhart, director. Estab. 1976. Annual award. "To provide an outlet for writers to present not only their works, but also to provide a large audience for their presentation live by the writer." Previously published or unpublished submissions. Award: 1st prize $50; 2nd prize $25; 3rd prize $15; 4th prize $10; and 5th prize $5. Entry deadline: day of contest, which takes place over Labor Day Weekend. Entry fee: $5. Entry forms or rules for SASE.

**THE GREENSBORO REVIEW LITERARY AWARDS (II)**, Dept. of English, UNC-Greensboro, Greensboro NC 27412. (919)379-5459. Contact: Lee Zacharias, editor. Annually. Unpublished submissions. Award: $250. Deadline: September 15. Contest rules for SASE.

**‡HACKNEY LITERARY AWARDS (I)**, Birmingham Southern College, Box A-3, Birmingham AL 35254. (205)226-4921. Contact: Sharon Brackner. Annually. Short stories, unpublished. Deadline: December 30. No entry fee. Rules/entry form for SASE.

**‡JAMES B. HALL SHORT FICTION COMPETITION (I)**, Jazz Press, Box 2409, Dept. F, Aptos CA 95001. (408)662-0259. Contact: George Fuller, publisher. Annually. Short stories, unpublished; 5,000 words or fewer. Deadline: December 15. Entry fee $5. Rules/entry forms for SASE. Prizes: $200 1st; $75 2nd; $25 3rd.

**DRUE HEINZ LITERATURE PRIZE (II)**, The Howard Heinz Endowment and the University of Pittsburgh Press, University of Pittsburgh Press, 127 North Bellefield Ave., Pittsburgh PA 15260. (412)624-4110. Annual award. "To support the writer of short fiction at a time when the economics of commercial publishing make it more and more difficult for the serious literary artists working in the short story and novella to find publication." Manuscripts must be unpublished in book form. The award is open to writers who have published a book-length collection of fiction or a minimum of three short stories or novellas in commercial magazines or literary journals of national distribution. Award: $7,500 and publication by the University of Pittsburgh Press. Request complete rules of the competition before submitting a manuscript. Entry deadline: August 31. Submissions will be received only during the months of July and August.

**ERNEST HEMINGWAY FOUNDATION AWARD (III)**, PEN American Center, 47 5th Ave., New York NY 10003. Contact: John Morrone, coordinator of programs. Annual award. "To give beginning writers recognition and encouragement and to stimulate interest in first novels among publishers and readers." Submissions previously published during calendar year under consideration. Deadline entry: December 31. Entry form or rules for SASE. Award: $7,500. "The Ernest Hemingway Foundation Award is given to an American author of the best first-published booklength work of fiction published by an established publishing house in the US each calendar year."

**HIGHLIGHTS FOR CHILDREN (IV)**, 803 Church St., Honesdale PA 18431. Contact: Constance McAllister, senior editor. "To honor quality stories (previously unpublished) for young readers." Stories/two age categories/for beginning readers (to age 8) 600 words maximum; for more advanced readers (ages 9 to 12) 900 words maximum. No minimum word length. No entry form necessary. To be submitted by March 31 to "Fiction Contest" at address above. Award: $300. No violence or crime. Non-winning entries returned after deadline if SASE. Write for information.

**THEODORE CHRISTIAN HOEPFNER AWARD (II)**, *Southern Humanities Review*, 9088 Haley Center, Auburn University AL 36849. Contact: Thomas L. Wright or Dan R. Latimer, co-editors. Annual award. "To award the authors of the best essay, the best short story, and the best poem published in *SHR* each year." Unpublished submissions to the magazine only. Award judged by editorial staff. Award: $100 for the best short story. Only published work in the current volume (4 issues) will be judged.

**HOHENBERG AWARD (I, II)**, *Memphis State Review*, Dept. of English, Memphis State University, Memphis TN 38152. (901)454-2668. Contact: William Page, editor. Estab. 1982. Annual award. "To encourage writing of outstanding merit." Unpublished submissions. Award: $100. Judged by a review panel. No entry fee. For entry submit fiction for publication in *Memphis State Review*.

**‡HOUGHTON MIFFLIN LITERARY FELLOWSHIP (III)**, Houghton Mifflin Company, 2 Park St., Boston MA 02108. (617)725-5923. Contact: Amy Parelman, administrative secretary. Awarded "when a worthy submission is received." To recognize promising American authors early in their career. Nonfiction or novel, unpublished. $10,000; $2,500 outright, $7,500 advance against royalties. SASE for rules/entry forms.

**THE 'HUGO' AWARD (Science Fiction Achievement Award) (III, IV)**, The World Science Fiction Convention, c/o Howard DeVore, 4705 Weddel St., Dearborn Heights MI 48125. Temporary; address changes each year. "To recognize the best writing in various categories related to science fiction and fantasy." The award is voted on by ballot by the members of the World Science Fiction Convention from previously published material of professional publications. Writers may not nominate their own work. Award: Metal spaceship 15 inches high. "Winning the award almost always results in reprints of the original material and increased payment. Winning a 'Hugo' in the novel category frequently results in additional payment of $10,000-$20,000 from future publishers."

**INDIANA REVIEW FICTION AWARD**, *Indiana Review*, 316 N. Jordan, Bloomington IN 47405. (812)335-3439. Contact: Jim Brock, editor. Annual award. "To encourage, locate and publish stories that are moving, interesting or innovative in conception, and to reward outstanding literary writers with publication and a small sum." All fiction published in *Indiana Review* will automatically be considered for the award, which will carry a cash value of ($300, $150, and $50.) Looking for "quality of language, command of voice, ability to move the reader *fairly*, awareness of a world outside the living room, innovation in technique: all these things in harmony."

**INKY TRAILS FICTION OF THE YEAR AWARD (I)**, Inky Trails Publications, Box 345, Middleton ID 83644. Contact: Pearl L. Kirk, editor/publisher. Annual award. "To help a new writer get started, and to reach the better publications." Unpublished submissions only. "If used for magazine we will use those published. If ms is published we give credit for first printing." Deadline: February 15. Entry form or rules for SASE. Entry fee $5 for adults; $2.50 for ages 15 to 19. Award: $15 and $10. "Any subject except science fiction, horror and sexual natures. Keep it clean. For under 14 years: romance, war, love, history, personal, western, mystery, adventure, humor, juvenile, young adult, religion. Please specify if adult or teen."

**INTERNATIONAL IMITATION HEMINGWAY COMPETITION (I)**, Harry's Bar & American Grill, 2020 Avenue of the Stars, Los Angeles CA 90067. (213)417-3038. Contact: Mark S. Grody, chairman, Grody/Tellem Communications, Inc., Suite 200, 9100 S. Sepulveda Blvd., Los Angeles CA 90045. Annual award. "To select the best entry under the guideline: one really good page of really 'bad' Hemingway; i.e., select the best 'Imitation Hemingway' entry." Unpublished submissions. Award: "Dinner for two at Harry's Bar & American Grill in Florence, Italy plus the round-trip plane fare for two. If the winner is from Europe, he/she comes to Los Angeles." Judged by "a distinguished panel of literary/Hemingway experts; panel may change annually. Entry deadline: February 15. No entry fee. Send SASE for official entry blank to Harry's Bar & American Grill, 2020 Avenue of the Stars, Los Angeles, CA 90067; or, enter on a plain piece of paper." Looking for "great imitation. Some entries will be funny; the best entries will be *very* funny. All entries must mention Harry's—nicely."

**‡INTERNATIONAL JANUSZ KORCZAK LITERARY COMPETITION (III, IV)**, International Center for Holocaust Studies Anti-Defamation League of B'nai B'rith, 823 United Nations Plaza, New York NY 10017. (212)490-2525. Contact: Dr. Dennis B. Klein, director. Annually. Novels, novellas, translations, short story collections. "Books for or about children which best reflect the humanitarianism and leadership of Janusz Korczak, a Jewish and Polish physician, educator, and author." Deadline: January. SASE for rules/entry form.

**INTERNATIONAL READING ASSOCIATION CHILDREN'S BOOK AWARD (II, III),** IRA/Institute for Reading Research, 800 Barksdale Rd., Box 8139, Newark DE 19711. (302)731-1600. Contact: Professor Arlene Pillar, 67 Forester St., Long Beach NY 11561. Annual award. "To encourage an author who shows unusual promise in the field of children's books. The award is given for an author's first or second book." Previously published submissions. Submissions must be published during the calendar year prior to the year in which the award is given. Award: $1,000 stipend. Entry deadline: December 1. No entry fee. Contest/award rules and awards flyer for SASE. To enter the contest, the author or publisher should send seven copies of the book to above address.

**IOWA ARTS COUNCIL LITERARY AWARDS (II, IV),** Iowa Arts Council, State Capital Complex, Des Moines IA 50319. (515)281-4451. Contact: Marilyn Parks, grants officer. Estab. 1984. Annually. "To give exposure to Iowa's fine poets and fiction writers." Unpublished submissions by legal residents of Iowa. Award: 1st prize, $1,000; 2nd prize, $500. Deadline: last working day in July. Contest rules for SASE.

**IOWA SCHOOL OF LETTERS AWARD FOR SHORT FICTION (II),** Iowa Writers' Workshop, Iowa School of Letters/English-Philosophy Building/The University of Iowa, Iowa City IA 52242. Contact: Connie Brothers. Annual award. To encourage writers in short fiction. Deadline entry: September 30. Entries must be at least 150 pages, typewritten, and submitted between August 1 and September 30. Rules for SASE. Award: "$1,000 plus publication of the winning collection by University of Iowa Press the following fall, and a visit to the University of Iowa Campus to be honored at a reception. Iowa Writers' Workshop does initial screening of entries; finalists (about 5) sent to a judge for final selection. A different well-known writer is chosen each year as judge."

**JOSEPH HENRY JACKSON AWARD (II, IV),** The San Francisco Foundation, 8th Floor, 500 Washington St., San Francisco CA 94111. Contact: Adrienne Krug, assistant coordinator. Annual award. "To award the author of an unpublished, work-in-progress of fiction (novel or short stories), nonfiction, or poetry." Unpublished submissions only. Applicant must be resident of Northern California or Nevada for 3 consecutive years immediately prior to the date for which submission is being made. Age of applicant must be 20 through 35. Deadline entry: January 15. Entry form and rules available in November for SASE. Award: $2,000 and award certificate.

***JAPANOPHILE* SHORT STORY CONTEST (II, IV),** *Japanophile*, Box 223, Okemos MI 48864. (517)349-1795. Contact: Earl R. Snodgrass, editor. Estab. 1982. Annually. "To encourage quality writing on Japan-America understanding." Prefers unpublished submissions. Stories involve Japanese and non-Japanese characters. Award: $100 plus possible publication. Deadline: Dec. 31. Entry fee: $5. Contest rules for SASE.

**JESSE H. JONES AWARD (III, IV),** Texas Institute of Letters, Box 8594, Waco TX 76714-8594. Contact: J. Edward Weems, secretary/treasurer. Annual award. "To recognize the best work of fiction by a Texan or about Texas." Award judged by a jury of Texas Institute of Letters members for novel and short story. Entry form or rules for SASE. Deadline: Jan. 15.

**‡JUBILEE SHORT FICTION AWARD (I),** *The Other Side* magazine, 300 W. Apsley St., Philadelphia PA 19144. (215)849-2178. Contact: Mark Olson, editor. Annually. Short stories, unpublished, suitable for publication in *The Other Side*. Deadline: May 15, 1986. $3 plus SASE for rules/entry forms (includes sample copy of *The Other Side* with a copy of the winning 1985 story). Rules appear in the sample copy).

# Close-up

### Pamela Painter
### New England Writers' Conference

It was Flannery O'Connor who said, "The only way to learn to write short stories is to write them—and then discover what you've done." The "discovery" might begin at a writers' conference.

Participants at the annual New England Writers' Conference at Simmons College in Boston bring their stories to Pamela Painter's fiction workshop every summer. Class members help each other discover/uncover the problems in their work by critiquing the story which is read aloud by the author.

This "oral editing process" starts right with the first few sentences or paragraphs of the story. "Beginnings are absolutely crucial," says Painter. "Once the first pages are up to standard"—the voice of authority is established; the characters are delineated; the active verbs replace weak adverbs and storyline begins to work; etc.—"then the rest of the story rises to that occasion, too."

After a sometimes grueling workshop session, Painter's students cringe at the homework, hard exercises they critique the next day in class. But via such direct application, "they're able to bring fresh criticism to fresh work," says the writing teacher, "see the process of rewriting as we sit there, and even see their own work transformed." Such energy begets better writing—and students find significant advances *can* be made in the five-day session.

It's a mistake for any writer to attend a writing conference expecting praise and recognition for his/her work, says Painter. Also if a writer is too sensitive and finds it too difficult to take criticism, then it's counterproductive. In order to benefit from the conference experience—and investment—the participant should be open-minded, willing to work hard and motivated into improving and readying his/her manuscript for publication. Youth is not a factor for success, she stresses; in fact life experience is a benefit to a "mature" writer. (And older writers are more open-minded than younger writers.)

A conference's great advantage is having

photo by Lilian Kemp

a manuscript looked at by editors, teachers, agents. Their suggestions can save a lot of rewriting time. At the New England Writers' Conference, for instance, the participant expects the one-on-one experience, when the instructor sits down with the writer to dissect the short story or novel.

An especially happy by-product of a conference is the writer-camaraderie, the unique sense of community and support. Painter urges her writers to share their manuscripts, and for those geographically-isolated writers, she even passes out address lists for correspondence and manuscript-exchange, just as Gail Godwin and John Irving did for many years.

Writer-contact is *vital*, for all levels of writing experience, Pamela Painter tells her conference and Harvard extension short story classes. As the author of many short stories; a recent short story collection, *Getting to Know the Weather*, and another in progress; and one of the founders of Chicago's *Story Quarterly*, Painter regularly attends a local workshop to discuss her *own* work and get the feedback so necessary for her writing growth and direction.

After a conference, Pamela Painter advises joining a writers' group to keep the momentum, motivation—and the faith. Or form your own group once you're back home. And then quoting Mark Twain, the writing teacher gives the most important—and toughest—advice a writer will ever get: "Writing is 10 percent talent, and 90 percent applying the seat of your pants to the seat of your chair."

**JANET HEIDINGER KAFKA PRIZE IN FICTION BY AMERICAN WOMEN (IV)**, University of Rochester: Annual Writers Workshop & Department of English, University College, University of Rochester, Rochester NY 14627. Contact: Ms. Patty Miller. Annual award. "The prize will be awarded (no more than once a year) to a woman citizen of the US who has written the best book-length published work of prose fiction, whether novel, short stories, or experimental writing." Previously published material during the calendar year in which it is submitted. Deadline entry: December 31. Entry forms are distributed to publishers. "Works written primarily for children and vanity house publication will not be considered. Mss must be submitted by the publishers."

**KANSAS QUARTERLY/KANSAS ARTS COMMISSION AWARDS (II)**, *Kansas Quarterly*, 122 Denison Hall, Kansas State University, Manhattan KS 66506. Contact: Editors. Annual awards. "To reward and recognize the best fiction published in *Kansas Quarterly* during the year from authors anywhere in the US or abroad. Anyone who submits unpublished material which is then accepted for publication becomes eligible for the awards." No deadline; material simply may be submitted for consideration at any time. To submit fiction for consideration, send it in with SASE. Award: Recognition and monetary sums of $300, $200, $100, $50. Ours are not 'contests'; they are monetary awards and recognition given by persons of national literary stature."

**ROBERT F. KENNEDY BOOK AWARDS (III)**, 1031 31st St., NW, Washington DC 20007. (202)628-1300. Contact: Ms. Caroline Croft. Endowed by Arthur Schlesinger, Jr., from proceeds of his biography, *Robert Kennedy and His Times*. Annual award. "To award the author of a book which most faithfully and forcefully reflects Robert Kennedy's purposes." Previously published submissions during the calendar year. Deadline: January 10. The 5th Annual RFK Book Awards contest was judged by Dr. Kenneth Clark, Gloria Emerson, Dr. William Emerson and Dr. Walter Lord (for books published in 1984). Award: $2,500 cash prize is awarded in the spring. Looking for "a work of literary merit in fact or fiction that shows compassion for the poor or powerless or those suffering from injustice."

‡**LAKES & PRAIRIE PRESS AWARD (I)**, *Milkweed Chronicle*, Box 24303, Minneapolis MN 55242. (612)332-3192. Contact: Deborah Keenan, general manager. Annually. Award: $350 and publication of ms. Short stories, novellas, unpublished. Deadline: October 1, 1986. SASE for rules/entry form.

‡**LAWRENCE FELLOWSHIP (II, III)**, University of New Mexico, University of New Mexico, Dept. of English Language and Literature, Albuquerque NM 87131. (505)277-6347. Contact: Prof. Lee Bartlett, chairperson. Annually. Fellowship; unpublished or previously published fiction, facts, drama. (June-August residency, $700 stipend). Deadline: January 31. $5 processing fee. Write for rules, application form.

‡**THE LAWRENCE FOUNDATION AWARD (II)**, *Prairie Schooner*, University of Nebraska, Lincoln NE 68588. (402)472-1830. Contact: Hugh Luke, editor. Annually. "The award is given to the author of the best short story published in *Prairie Schooner* during the preceding year." Award $500. "Only short fiction published in *Prairie Schooner* is eligible for consideration."

‡**LAWRENCE FOUNDATION PRIZE (II)**, *Michigan Quarterly Review*, 3032 Rackham Bldg., Ann Arbor MI 48109. (312)764-9265. Contact: Laurence Goldstein, editor. Annually. Award: $500. Short stories, previously published in *MQR* previous year.

**LOS ANGELES TIMES BOOK PRIZES (III)**, *L.A. Times*, Book Review, Times Mirror Square, Los Angeles CA 90053. (213)972-7777. Contact: Jack Miles, book editor. Annual award. "To recognize finest books published each year." Previously published submissions between September 1 to September 1. Award: $1,000 cash prize plus a handmade, leather-bound version of the winning book. Entry is by nomination by 80 reviewers; publishers only. No entry fee.

**LOUISIANA LITERARY AWARD (IV)**, Louisiana Library Association (LLA), Box 131, Baton Rouge LA 70821. (504)342-4928. Contact: Chair, Louisiana Literary Award Committee. Annual award. "To promote interest in books related to Louisiana and to encourage their production." Submissions are to be previously published during the calendar year prior to presentation of the award. (The award is presented in March or April.) Award: Bronze medallion and $250. Entry deadline: publication by December 31. No entry fee. "All Louisiana-related books which committee members can locate are considered, whether submitted or not. Interested parties may correspond with the committee chair at the address above. All books considered *must* be on subject(s) related to Louisiana. Each year, there may be a fiction *and/or* nonfiction award. Most often, however, there is only one award recipient, and he or she is the author of a work of nonfiction."

**MADEMOISELLE FICTION WRITERS COMPETITION (II)**, *Mademoiselle Magazine*, 350 Madison Ave., New York NY 10017. Send entries to Fiction Writers Contest. Each entry must be accompanied by self-addressed stamped envelope, the entry coupon or a 3x5 card with name, age, home address. Award: 1st prize: $1,000 plus publication (at regular purchase rate) of winning story in a future issue of *Mademoiselle*; 2nd prize: $500 cash prize. Open to all short story writers 18-30, who have not been published in a magazine with a circulation over 25,000. Entries will not be returned unless accompanied by SASE. "Agents have contacted us about winners."

**‡MAINE NOVEL AWARD (II, IV)**, The Dog Ear Press, Box 143, S. Harpswell ME 04079. (207)729-7791. Contact: Mark Melnicove, publisher. Annually. Novels, unpublished. Requirements: Open to both Maine residents and non-residents; novel must be set in Maine. Deadline: January 15, 1987. Writers must request guidelines before submitting.

**MASSACHUSETTS ARTISTS FELLOWSHIP (II, IV)**, Artists Foundation—Artists Fellowship Program, 110 Broad St., Boston MA 02110. (617)482-8100. Contact: Lucine Folgueras or Paula Marshall. Annual award. "To encourage artists to live and work in Massachusetts." Massachusetts residents 18 years of age or older are eligible to apply as long as resident is not enrolled as a student. Application form and two typed copies of writing sample (separately bound) must be received at the Foundation offices by 5:00 pm, October 1. Publication is not necessary, but any published work must be submitted in typewritten form. Entry forms available upon request. Award: $7,500 for winners; $500 for finalists. "Looking for artistic excellence. Work is judged anonymously by a panel of professional working writers who live outside Massachusetts."

**THE MCCLELLAND AND STEWART AWARDS FOR FICTION**, National Magazine Awards Foundation, Suite 501, 44 Eglinton Ave. W., Toronto, Ontario M4R 1A1 Canada. (416)488-6578. Annual award. "To honor excellence in Canadian magazine writing." Submissions must be previously published work appearing in the calendar year previous to that in which the award is issued." Award: 1st $1,000 and 2nd $500. Entry deadline: Early January—exact day differs slightly from year to year. Entry fee: $25. Entry forms or rules for SASE. "This contest is open only to Canadian citizens or landed immigrants whose work has appeared in Canadian magazines."

**THE JOHN H. MCGINNIS MEMORIAL AWARD (II)**, *Southwest Review*, Box 4374, Southern Methodist University, Dallas TX 75275. Contact: Betsey McDougall, managing editor. Biannual award. (One year for fiction and the next for nonfiction). Publication in the *Southwest Review* within a two-year period prior to the announcement of the award. Award: $1,000, given each year for material—alternately fiction and nonfiction—that has been published in the *Southwest Review* in the previous two years. Stories are not submitted directly for the award, but simply for publication in the magazine.

**MCKENDREE WRITERS' ASSOCIATION WRITING CONTEST (I)**, McKendree Writers' Association, East 30, Lot 32, Glen Carbon IL 62034. Contact: Karin Bracken, conference director. Annual award. "To encourage literary excellence." Unpublished submissions. Award: First place, $25; second place, $15; third place, $10. Honorable mentions when appropriate. Deadline: March or early April. "The Association sponsors an annual writing conference each spring. The winners are announced at the conference." Entry fee: $3. In addition, contestant must be a member of the organization. Contest rules for SASE. "Do not request rules before January 1." Looking for "fiction of any genre."

**THE VICKY METCALF BODY OF WORK AWARD (III, IV)**, Canadian Authors Association, 24 Ryerson Ave., Toronto, Ontario M5T 2P3 Canada. (416)364-4203. Contact: Ginny Sumodi, executive director. Annual award. "The prize is given solely to stimulate writing for children, written by Canadians, for a *number* of strictly children's books—fiction, nonfiction or even picture books. No set formula." Previously published submissions. "No limitation on when the first ones were published." Minimum of 4 published works. Award: $2,000 for a body of work inspirational to Canadian youth. Entry deadline: December 31. No entry fee. "Nominations may be made by any individual or association by letter *in triplicate* listing the published works of the nominee and providing biographical information. The books are usually considered in regard to their inspirational value for children. Entry forms or rules for SASE.

**VICKY METCALF SHORT STORY AWARD (III, IV)**, Canadian Authors Association, 24 Ryerson Ave., Toronto, Ontario M5T 2P3 Canada. (416)364-4203. Contact: Ginny Sumodi, executive director. "To encourage Canadian writing for children (open only to Canadian citizens)." Submissions must be previously published during previous calendar year in Canadian children's magazine or anthology. Award: $1,000 (Canadian). Entry deadline: December 31. No entry fee. Entry forms or rules for SASE. Looking for "books with originality, literary quality for ages 7-17."

**MINNESOTA VOICES PROJECT (IV)**, New Rivers Press, 1602 Selby Ave., St. Paul MN 55104. Contact: C.W. Truesdale, editor/publisher. Annual award. "To foster and encourage new and emerging regional writers of short fiction, novellas, personal essays, and poetry." Requires bibliography of previous publications and residency statement. Awards: $500 to each author published in the series plus "a generous royalty agreement if book goes into second printing." Entry deadline: April 1. No entry fee. SASE for guidelines. Send two copies of each manuscript of 125-200 pages; restricted to writers from Minnesota, Wisconsin, North and South Dakota and Iowa.

**‡MOJAVE STUDIOS WRITING AWARDS (I)**, *Newstories* Magazine/Mojave Studios, Box 1349, Lucerne Valley CA 92356. (619)248-6074. Contact: Mark James Miller, Director. Biannually. Short stories, unpublished. Deadline: January 1 and July 1. Entry fee $5. Rules/entry form for SASE..

*MS* **MAGAZINE COLLEGE FICTION CONTEST**, Ms. Foundation, 119 W. 40th St., New York NY 10018. Contact: College Fiction Editor. Award: Electronic typewriter plus publication in annual college issue (October). Contest announced annually in March or April issue. Full or part-time students of all ages enrolled in a degree course are eligible.

**MYTHOPOEIC FANTASY AWARD (IV)**, The Mythopoeic Society, Box 6707, Altadena CA 91001. Contact: Christine S. Lowentrout, award chairman. Annual award. "To present a literary award to a fantasy writer for a work of outstanding quality in the spirit of the Inklings." Previously published submissions from the year prior. Award: Trophy of a lion, special honors at the annual Mythopoeic Conference; letters of honorable mention to runners-up. Many publishers note the award on book jacket. Nominated and judged by a committee of society members. Entry deadline: February 20. No entry fee. Entry forms or rules for SASE. Write to Correspondence Secretary: Christine S. Lowentrout, 1017 Seal Way, Seal Beach CA 90740. Looking for the best fantasy fiction of the year. "This is an honorary award, similar to the 'Hugo' award for Best Science Fiction book of the year."

**NATIONAL JEWISH BOOK AWARDS**, JWB Jewish Book Council, 15 E. 26th St., New York NY 10010. Contact: Ruth Frank, director. Annual award. "To promote greater awareness of Jewish-American literary creativity." Previously published submissions in English only by a US or Canadian author/translator. Submissions must be during the calendar year. Award judged by authors/scholars. Award: $500 to the author/translator plus citation to publisher. Awards include National Jewish Book Award—Children's Literature, William (Zev) Frank Memorial Award (for the author of a children's book on a Jewish theme); National Jewish Book—Children's Picture Book, Marcia and Louis Posner Award (for the author and illustrator of a children's book on a Jewish theme in which the illustrations are an intrinsic part of the text); National Jewish Book Award—Fiction, William and Janice Epstein Award (for the author of a book of fiction of Jewish interest, either a novel or a collection of short stories); and National Jewish Book Award—Yiddish Literature, The Workmen's Circle Award (for the author of a book of literary merit in the Yiddish language in fiction, poetry, essays and memoirs).

**NATIONAL WRITERS CLUB ANNUAL BOOK CONTEST (II)**, National Writers Club, 1450 S. Havana, Aurora CO 80012. (303)751-7844. Contact: Donald E. Bower, director. Annual award. To encourage and recognize writing by freelancers in the field of the novel. Unpublished submissions. Entry deadline: July 20. Award judged by successful writers. Contest/award rules and entry forms available with SASE. Charges $20 for entry fee. Award: $1,000 in prizes; $400 first prize.

**NATIONAL WRITERS CLUB ANNUAL SHORT STORY CONTEST (II)**, National Writers Club, 1450 S. Havana, Aurora CO 80012. (303)751-7844. Contact: Donald E. Bower, director. Annual award. To encourage and recognize writing by freelancers in the short story field. Unpublished submissions. Award judged by professional writers. Write for entry form and rule sheet. Charges $10 for entry fee.

**‡NEBULA AWARDS (III, IV)**, Science Fiction Writers of America, Box H, Wharton NJ 07885. Contact: Peter D. Pautz, executive secretary. Annually. Short stories, novels, novellas, novellettes, previously published. SF/fantasy only. "No submissions; nominees upon recommendation of members only." Deadline: December 31. "Works are nominated throughout the year by active members of the SFWA."

**THE NENE AWARD (IV)**, Hawaii Association of School Librarians and Children's and Youth Section, Hawaii Library Association, Hongwanji Mission School, 1728 Pali Highway, Honolulu HI 96813. Contact: Mrs. Betty Arakaki, chairperson (chairperson changes annually). Annual award. "To help the children of Hawaii become acquainted with the best contemporary writers of fiction for children; to become aware of the qualities that make a good book; to choose the best rather than the mediocre; and to honor an author whose book has been enjoyed by the children of Hawaii." Award: Koa plaque. Judged by the children of Hawaii. No entry fee.

**NEUSTADT INTERNATIONAL PRIZE FOR LITERATURE (III, IV)**, *World Literature Today*, 110 Monnet Hall, University of Oklahoma, Norman OK 73019. Contact: Dr. Ivar Ivask, director. Biennial award. To recognize distinguished and continuing achievement in fiction, poetry, or drama. Awards: $25,000, an eagle feather cast in silver, an award certificate and a special issue of *WLT*. "We are looking for outstanding accomplishment in world literature. The Neustadt Prize is not open to application. Nominations are made only by members of the international jury, which changes for each award. Jury meetings are held in February of even-numbered years. Unsolicited manuscripts, whether published or unpublished, cannot be considered.

***NEW ENGLAND SAMPLER* CREATIVE WRITING CONTEST (II, IV)**, *New England Sampler*, Box 306, Belfast ME 04915-0306. (207)525-3575. Contact: Virginia M. Rimm, editor/publisher. Annual awards in fiction, poetry, and nonfiction. "To promote quality writing for the family market, superior writing with strong human interest, reflecting traditional New England values of hard work, integrity, independence, self reliance and resourcefulness." Unpublished submissions. Award: 1st prize, $100; 2nd, $50; 3rd, $25. Deadline: June 15. Entry fee: $3 per entry. Contest rules and entry form for SASE. Looking for "depth; literary quality, style, originality. New England setting required. Open to all writers. Winning entries are published in the New England Sampler."

**NEW JERSEY AUTHOR AWARDS (III, IV)**, NJIT Alumni Association, New Jersey Institute of Technology, 323 High St., Newark NJ 07102. (201)889-7336. Contact: Dr. Herman A. Estrin, professor of English-Emeritus. Annual award. "To recognize New Jersey writers." Previously published submissions. Award: Citation inscribed with the author's name and his work. Author is an invited guest at the Authors Luncheon. Entry deadline: February. No entry fee. Entry forms or rules for SASE.

*NEW OREGON REVIEW* **SHORT STORY CONTEST FOR BEST SHORT STORY OF THE YEAR (II)**, Transition Publications, 537 N.E. Lincoln St., Hillsboro OR 97124. (503)640-1375. Contact: Steven Dimeo, Ph.D., editor. Estab. 1984. Annual award. "To honor excellent fiction." Unpublished submissions. Award: $100. Deadline: October 31. Entry fee: the price of a one-year subscription to the magazine—$4.50. Contest rules for SASE. "We're looking for literary fiction that deals meaningfully with male/female relationships.

**JOHN NEWBERY AWARD (III)**, American Library Association (ALA) Awards and Citations Program, Association for Library Service to Children, 50 E. Huron St., Chicago IL 60611. Annual award. Entry restricted to US citizen-resident. Only books for children published during the preceding year are eligible. Award: Medal.

**THE JULIAN OCEAN LITERATURE AWARD (II)**, Triple "P" Publications International, Box 1321, Kendall Square, Cambridge MA 02142. (617)437-1856. Contact: Eugene F.P.C. de Mesne, editorial manager. Annual award, named after Julian Ocean, publisher, author, poet, critic, book designer and artist. "To further new talent; to promote art and publishing; to give incentive to artists and writers who would like to compete for an award; to give fiction a broader scope and presentation." Unpublished submissions. Award: $20 prize money and a large certificate, plus recognition via National Writers Club, COSMEP Newsletter and Support Services Newsletter (winners announced in these publications). Entry deadline: December 31. Entry fee: $1. SASE is a *must* for entry forms; rules sent on request. "No taboos. Only requirement for entry is excellence and professionalism in presentation, development and theme. New writers are encouraged to submit."

**THE FLANNERY O'CONNOR AWARD FOR SHORT FICTION (II)**, The University of Georgia Press, Terrell Hall, Athens GA 30602. (404)542-2830. Contact: award coordinator. Annual award. "To recognize outstanding collections of short fiction. Published and unpublished authors are welcome." Award: $500 and publication by the University of Georgia Press. Deadline: June 1-July 31. "Manuscripts cannot be accepted at any other time." Entry fee: $10. Contest rules for SASE.

**FRANK O'CONNOR FICTION AWARD (II)**, *Descant*, Department of English, Texas Christian University, Fort Worth TX 76129. (817)921-7240. Contact: Betsy Colquitt or Stan Trachtenberg, editors. Estab. 1979 with *Descant*; earlier awarded through *Quartet*. Annual award. To honor achievement in short fiction. Submissions must be published in the magazine during its current volume. Award: $250 prize. No entry fee. "About 12 to 15 stories are published annually in *Descant*. Winning story is selected from this group."

**THE SCOTT O'DELL AWARD FOR HISTORICAL FICTION (III, IV)**, Scott O'Dell (personal donation), c/o Houghton Mifflin, 2 Park St., Boston MA 02108. (617)725-5000. Contact: Mrs. Zena Sutherland, professor, 1100 E. 57th St., Chicago IL 60637. Annual award. "To encourage the writing of good historical fiction about the New World (Canada, South and Central America, and the United States) for children and young people." Previously American published submissions during the year preceding that year in which the award is given. To be written in English by a US citizen set in New World (Canada, Central or South America and the US). Award: $5,000. Entry deadline: December 31. Entry forms or rules for SASE. Looking for "accuracy in historical details, and all the standard literary criteria for excellence: style, setting, characterization, etc."

**OHIOANA BOOK AWARD (III, IV)**, Ohioana Library Association, 1105 Ohio Departments Bldg., 65 S. Front St., Columbus OH 43215. Contact: James P. Barry, director. Annual award (only if the judges believe a book of sufficiently high quality has been submitted). To bring recognition to outstanding books by Ohioans or about Ohio. "Books to be submitted on or before publication date, in two copies. Each spring a jury considers all books received since the previous jury. Award judged by a jury, selected each year from librarians, book reviewers, and other knowledgeable people. No entry forms, etc., are needed. We will be glad to answer letters asking specific questions." Award: Certificate and medal. "Books must be by an Ohioan (defined as a person born in Ohio or who has lived there for a total of at least 5 years), or about Ohio or the state's people. The submission must be of high quality."

**THE OKANAGAN SHORT FICTION AWARD (II, IV)**, *Canadian Author & Bookman*, 24 Ryerson Ave., Toronto, Ontario M5T 2P3 Canada. Contact: Geoff Hancock, fiction editor. Award offered 4 times a year. To present good fiction "in which the writing surpasses all else" to an appreciative literary readership, and in turn help Canadian writers retain an interest in good fiction. Unpublished submissions. Entries are invited in each issue of our quarterly *CA&B*. Sample copy $3.50; guideline printed in the magazine. "Our award regulations stipulate that writers must be Canadian, stories must not have been previously published, and be under 3,500 words. Mss should be typed double-spaced on 8½x11 bond. SASE requested. Award: $125 to each author whose story is accepted for publication. Looking for superior writing ability, stories with good plot, movement, dialogue and characterization.

**MINDY GATES O'MARY SCHOLARSHIP (I)**, California Press Women, Southern District, 4461 Moraga Ave., San Diego CA 92117. (619)272-8503, 272-1714. Contact: Vicki Porter Adams, president. Estab. 1983. Annual award. "To give beginning writers recognition and an impetus to continue writing." Unpublished submissions. Age limit—30 years and under. Award: Cash prizes for grand prize winner (overall). Amount depends on interest earned on trust fund set up by parents of Mindy Gates O'Mary. Deadline: Dec. 31. Entry fee: presently $4 for first entry; $3 for each subsequent entry. Contest rules for SASE. Looking for surprise plots and endings.

**PACIFIC NORTHWEST WRITERS CONFERENCE**, 1811 NE 199th St., Seattle WA 98155. (206)364-1293. Contact: Margaret McGee. Annual award. "To encourage writers." Unpublished submissions. Award: $250 first prize; $150 second prize; $100 third prize. Entry deadline: April 15. Entry fee: $5 (plus $12 regular, or $5 senior citizen—62 or over, and students membership dues). Entry forms or rules for SASE. Looking for "adult short fiction (not to exceed 4,000 words, may be any type; short story, confession, etc.); juvenile short story (not to exceed 1,500 words); novel (one chapter and synopsis required, total not to exceed 7,000 words); nonfiction book, juvenile novel same rules as for novel. Grand prize for best manuscript selected from all contests, $300."

**WILLIAM PEDEN PRIZE IN FICTION (II)**, *The Missouri Review*, 231 Arts & Sciences, University of Missouri, Columbia MO 65211. (314)882-2339. Contact: Speer Morgan, editor. Annual award. "To honor the best short story published in *The Missouri Review* each year." Previously published in *The Missouri Review*. Submissions are to be previously published in the volume year for which the prize is awarded. Award: $1,000 cash. No deadline entry or entry fee. No rules; all fiction published in *MR* automatically become contestants.

**THE PEN/FAULKNER AWARD (II, III)**, c/o The Folger Shakespeare Library, 201 E. Capitol St. SE, Washington DC 20003. Attention: Katharine Zadravec, PEN/Faulkner coordinator. Annual award. "To award the most distinguished book-length work of fiction published by an American writer." Published submissions only. Publishers submit four copies of eligible titles published the preceding year. No juvenile. Authors must be American citizens or permanent residents of the US. Book award judged by three writers chosen by the Trustees of the Award. Award: $5,000 for winner; $1,000 for nominees.

**PEN/SOUTHWEST HOUSTON DISCOVERY AWARDS (IV)**, PEN Friends of Houston, Dept. of English, University of Houston, Houston TX 77004. Annual award. "To encourage and support new literary talent in the Houston area." Unpublished submissions. "Applicants must have been residents of the Houston metro area for at least 6 months and may not have had work published in book form." Award: $1,000. Deadline: January 15. No entry fee. Send 20-30 pages of prose (double-spaced) in English. Mss are not returned.

**PEN SYNDICATED FICTION PROJECT (II)**, Box 6303, Washington, DC 20015. (301)229-0933. Contact: Richard Harteis, director. Estab. 1982. Ongoing award. "To select short stories which will then be syndicated to newspapers across the US for possible publication." Unpublished submissions of one or more stories whose total word count is not to exceed 3,000 words. Award: "A cash award for each story selected and the possibility of publication in newspapers. Each time the story is published in a newspaper the author receives an additional payment. Stories best suited are straight narratives not longer than 3,000 words."

**MAXWELL PERKINS PRIZE**, Charles Scribner's Sons, 115 5th Ave., New York NY 10003. (212)614-1300. "To find talented writers never before published and encourage beginning authors. Given to a first work of fiction about the American experience." Unpublished submissions. Write Scribner's for submission requirements.

**JAMES D. PHELAN AWARD (II,IV)**, The San Francisco Foundation, 8th Floor, 500 Washington St., San Francisco CA 94111. Contact: Andrienne Krug, assistant coordinator. Annual award. To award the author of an unpublished work-in-progress of fiction, (novel or short story), nonfictional prose, poetry or drama. Unpublished submissions. Applicant must have been born in the state of California and be 20-35 years old. Entry deadline: January 15. Contest/award rules and entry forms available from above address after November 1. Award: $2,000 and a certificate.

**‡PLAINSWOMAN FICTION CONTEST (I)**, Box 8027, Grand Forks ND 58202. (701)777-8043. Contact: Emily Johnson, fiction editor. Annually. Short stories, unpublished, on active women, humor, conflict, friendship, etc." 4,000 word limit; 1 story only. Deadline: March 15, 1986. Sample issue for $2. SASE for rules/entry form.

**EDGAR ALLAN POE AWARDS (III, IV)**, Mystery Writers of America, Inc., 150 5th Ave., New York NY 10011. Annual award. To enhance the prestige of the mystery. Previously published submissions in the calendar year. Entry deadline: December 31. Each award committee operates differently. Contact above address for specifics. Award: Ceramic bust of Poe. Awards for best mystery novel, best first novel, best softcover original novel, best short story, best juvenile novel, best screenplay, best television feature, and best episode in a series.

**KATHERINE ANNE PORTER PRIZE FOR FICTION (II)**, *Nimrod*, Arts and Humanities Council, 2210 S. Main St., Tulsa OK 74114. (918)584-3333. Francine Ringold, editor. Annual award. Accepts mss for consideration beginning December 1. Deadline for submissions, April 1, 1986. Award: $1,000 first prize and $500 second prize. Winning entries will be published in the Fall/Winter 1986 issue of *Nimrod*. Winners will be brought to Tulsa for a reading and the presentation of the prize. Only one submission per author (2 photocopies). No minimum length; 7,500 words maximum. No previously published works, works accepted for publication or dual submissions are eligible. *Nimrod* requires first refusal rights on all submissions. *Nimrod* editors read each manuscript and a final judge chooses from the 20 selected finalists. In the past, fiction judges have included: Ishmael Read, Charles Johnson, R.V. Cassill, Richard Howard, and Paul West. Author's name must not appear on the manuscript. Submission should be accompanied by a cover sheet containing the title of the work and the author's name and address. The title of the work, however, should also appear on the first page of the manuscript. "CONTEST ENTRY" should be clearly indicated on both the outer envelope and the cover sheet. Manuscripts should be typed and fiction manuscripts should be double-spaced. All entries not officially accepted for publication will be released to their authors within six weeks after the contest results are announced. Manuscripts will not be returned. Send SASE for further information. Entry fee: $5 "for which you will receive a copy of *Nimrod*. Entry fee is waived for *Nimrod* subscribers. Subscription: $10/year."

**THE *PRESENT TENSE*/JOEL H. CAVIOR LITERARY AWARD (II, IV)**, *Present Tense Magazine*, 165 E. 56th St., New York NY 10022. (212)751-4000. Contact: Murray Polner, editor. Annual award. "To encourage the flourishing of Jewish literary and intellectual life by stimulating the writing of significant, serious works with Jewish themes." Submissions are to be previously published during the year immediately preceding the granting of awards. Award: $500 bond for 5-8 categories, one of which is for fiction. Entry deadline: December 9. No entry fee. Nominations may only be made by the publisher.

**‡*PRISM* INTERNATIONAL SHORT FICTION CONTEST (I)**, PRISM International, Dept. of Creative Writing, University of British Columbia, E455-1866 Main Mall, Vancouver, British Columbia V6T 1W5 Canada. (604)228-2514. Contact: Managing Editor. "We hope to offer contest annually." Short stories, unpublished. Deadline: November 30, 1986. Entry fee $15 for first story. SASE for rules/entry forms.

**‡*PRISM* WRITING COMPETITION (I)**, *Prism Magazine*, 2868 Rockefeller Center Station, New York NY 10185. (212)795-8381. Contact: Diana Phillips, director. Annually. Short stories, unpublished. Deadline: April 15. Entry fee $3. SASE for rules/entry forms.

**PRIZE STORIES: THE O. HENRY AWARDS (III)**, Doubleday & Company, Inc., 245 Park Avenue, New York NY 10167. Contact: Sally Arteseros, senior editor. Annual award. To honor the memory of O. Henry with a sampling of outstanding short stories and to make these stories better known to the public. These awards are published by Doubleday every spring. Previously published submissions. "All selections are made by the editor of the volume, William Abrahams. No stories may be submitted."

**PULITZER PRIZE IN FICTION (III)**, Columbia University, Graduate School of Journalism, 702 Journalism Bldg., New York NY 10027. Contact: Robert C. Christopher. Annual award. For distinguished fiction published in book form during the year by an American author, preferably dealing with American life. 4 copies of the book, entry form, biography and photo of author and $20 handling fee. Open to American authors. Deadline entry: November 1. Award: $1,000.

**‡PULP PRESS INTERNATIONAL, 3 DAY NOVEL-WRITING COMPETITION (II)**, Arsenal Pulp Press, 202-986 Homer St., Vancouver, British Columbia V6B 2W7 Canada. (604)687-4233. Contact: Frances Eger, promotions director. Annually. Novels, unpublished. "Novel must be written during the 3 days of the Labor Day weekend." Deadline: last week before Labor Day. IRC, SASE for rules/entry forms.

**PUSHCART PRIZE (III)**, Pushcart Press, Box 380, Wainscott NY 11975. Contact: Bill Henderson, editor. Annual award. To publish and recognize the best of small press literary work. Previously published submissions; books or short stories on any subject or short self-contained sections. Must have been published during the current calendar year. Deadline: Oct. 15. Nomination by small press publishers/editors only. Award: Publication in *Pushcart Prize: Best of the Small Presses* plus $100 to lead story.

**SIR WALTER RALEIGH AWARD (IV)**, North Carolina Literary and Historical Association, 109 E. Jones St., Raleigh NC 27611. (919)733-7305. Contact: Becky Myer, assistant secretary-treasurer. Annual award. To stimulate among the people of the state an interest in their own literature. Previously published submissions only by North Carolina authors. It must be an original work published during the 12 months ending June 30 of the year for which the award is given. Entry Deadline: July 15. Contest/award rules and entry forms available with SASE. Award: Statuette of Sir Walter Raleigh.

**‡RAMBUNCTIOUS REVIEW, ANNUAL FICTION CONTEST (I)**, 1221 W. Pratt, Chicago IL 60626. (312)338-2439. Contact: Nancy Lennon, co-editor. Annually. Short stories. Requirements: Typed, double-spaced, maximum 15 pages. SASE for deadline rules/entry forms.

**REDBOOK SHORT STORY CONTEST (I, II)**, *Redbook*, 224 W. 57th St., New York NY 10019. (212)262-5690. Contact: Kathyrne Sagan or Susan Spano, fiction editors. Annual award. "To reward the achievements of unpublished short story writers and to acquaint them with the most effective ways to submit their work professionally." Unpublished submissions. Open to men and women 18 years and over. See March 1986 *Redbook* for complete rules. Award: 1st prize: $1,000, plus $1,000 for publication in *Redbook* Magazine; 2nd prize: $500; 3rd prize: $300. Entry deadline: May 31, 1986. No entry fee.

**REGINA MEDAL AWARD (III)**, Catholic Library Association, 461 W. Lancaster Ave., Haverford PA 19041. Contact: Matthew R. Wilt, executive director. Annual award. To honor a distinguished contribution to children's literature. Award: Silver medal. Award given during Easter week. Selection by a special committee; nominees are suggested by the Catholic Library Association Membership.

**HAROLD U. RIBALOW PRIZE, (III, IV)** *Hadassah Magazine*, 50 W. 58th St., New York NY 10019. (212)355-7900. Contact: Alan M. Tigay, Executive Editor. Estab. 1983. Annually. "To award a book of fiction on a Jewish theme. Harold U. Ribalow was a noted writer and editor who devoted his time to the discovery and encouragement of young Jewish writers." Book on a Jewish theme published the year preceding the award. Award: $500 and excerpt of book in *Hadassah Magazine*. Deadline: Dec. 31.

**SAN JOSE STUDIES BEST STORY AWARD (II)**, Bill Casey Memorial Fund, 125 S. 7th St., San Jose CA 95192. Contact: Fauñeil J. Riñn. To recognize the author of the best story (or essay or poem) appearing in a previous volume of *San Jose Studies*. Award: $100. Winning author to receive a year's complimentary subscription to the journal.

**‡CARL SANDBURG AWARDS (III)**, Friends of the Chicago Public Library, 78 E. Washington, Chicago IL 60602. (312)269-2922. Annually. To honor excellency in Chicago area authors (including 6 counties). Material previously published during the preceding year June 1, 1984-June 1, 1985. Cash honorarium for each separate category. Deadline: June 1. Rules: write or call (312)269-2922.

**SCHOLASTIC WRITING AWARDS (II, IV)**, Scholastic Inc., 730 Broadway, New York NY 10003. (212)505-3000. Contact: Scholastic Writing Awards. Annual award. To provide opportunity for the best student writing to be seen and judged for students in grades 7-12. Unpublished submissions. Award: Cash prizes and certificates of merit, Smith-Corona typewriters, scholarships. Information available between October 1 and January 1. Send postcard and specify rule book needed (writing).

**SCIENCE FICTION/FANTASY SHORT STORY CONTEST**, Science Fiction Writers of Earth, Box 12293, Fort Worth TX 76116. (817)451-8674. Contact: Gilbert Gordon Reis, administrator (SFWoE). Annual award. "To promote the art of science fiction/fantasy short story writing." Unpublished submissions by unpublished authors. Award: 1st prize, $100; 2nd prize, $50; and 3rd prize, $25. "A nominating committee (from SFWoE members) will select the best stories. A panel of independent judges (from science fiction editors and authors) determines the winner from the nominated stories." Entry deadline: Each October 30th contest closes; winners awarded in January of the following year. Entry fee: $5; $2 for second entry ($5 includes a year's membership in SFWoE). Entry forms/rules for business-size SASE. Looking for "well-written science fiction or fantasy from 2,000 to 7,500 words."

**SCRIBNER CRIME NOVEL AWARD**, Charles Scribner's Sons, 115 5th Ave., New York NY 10017. (212)614-1300. "To find talented writers never before published and encourage beginning authors." Award given to a first mystery. Unpublished submissions. Award: $7,500—$5,000 as an advance against royalties; $2,500 advertising guarantee. Entry deadline: December 31. No entry fee. "Ms must be of classic detection, historical reconstructions, fictionalized 'true crime,' espionage, police procedurals, private-eye. No supernatural, pastiche, or parody of an established character in fiction." SASW for return of ms.

**SEAL BOOKS FIRST NOVEL COMPETITION (II, IV)**, Seal Books, Suite 601, 60 St. Clair Ave. E., Toronto, Ontario M4T 1N5 Canada. Contact: Editor. Unpublished submissions. Entry deadline: December 31. Contest/award rules and entry forms available with SASE. Applicant must be either a Canadian citizen or a Canadian-landed immigrant. Award: $50,000 which is a nonreturnable advance against earnings plus a contract with Seal Books (the mass market imprint of McClelland & Stewart-Bantam Ltd.) that will guarantee publication of novel first in hardbound edition, then as paperback. Mss to be not less than 60,000 words. Must be double-spaced on white paper, submitted in English under author's own name.

**THE SEATON AWARDS (II, IV)**, *Kansas Quarterly*, 122 Denison Hall, Kansas State University, KS 66506. Contact: Editors. Annual awards. To reward and recognize the best fiction published in *KQ* during the year from authors native to or resident in Kansas. Submissions must be unpublished. Anyone who submits unpublished material which is then accepted for publication becomes eligible for the awards. Seaton Awards are specifically for Kansas natives or Kansas residents. No deadline. Material simply may be submitted for consideration at any time with SASE. Award: Recognition and monetary sums of $200, $150, $100 and $50. "Ours are not contests. We give monetary awards and recognition by Kansas writers with national literary stature."

**ROD SERLING'S *THE TWILIGHT ZONE* MAGAZINE'S ANNUAL SHORT STORY CONTEST (I, II)**, Department 15, 800 Second Ave., New York NY 10017. Contact: Alan Rodgers, associate editor. Annual award. "Our annual short story contest is dedicated to the memory of Rod Serling, whose professional career was launched when he became a prizewinner in a nationwide writing contest." Unpublished submissions. Award: First prize, $500; second $300; third $200. All prizewinning stories will be published in *The Twilight Zone* Magazine. Deadline: September 1985. Contest rules for SASE. Looking for "stories about the intrusion of the unnatural or unearthly into ordinary American settings by writers who have never published fiction professionally."

**SEVENTEEN MAGAZINE/ DELL FICTION CONTEST(I,IV)**, *Seventeen Magazine*, 850 3rd Ave., New York NY 10022. Contact: Bonni Price. To honor best short fiction by a teenage writer. Rules are found in the October issue. Contest for 13-19 year olds. Submissions judged by a panel of *Seventeen*'s editors. Award: $2,000 first prize; $1,200 second prize; $700 third prize; Prizes of books valued at $50 to 6 honorable mentions.

**CHARLIE MAY SIMON BOOK AWARD (III, IV)**, Arkansas Department of Education, Elementary School Council, State Education Building, Capitol Mall, Division of Instruction, Room 301B, Little Rock AR 72201. (501)371-1861. Contact: Bill W. Heinley, coordinator of elementary education. Annual award. "To encourage reading by children in quality children's literature."

Previously published submissions. Award: Medallion. No entry fee. "The committee doesn't accept requests from authors. They will look at booklists of books produced during the previous year and check recommendations from the following sources; *Booklist, Bulletin of the Center for Children's Books, Children's Catalog, Elementary School Library Collection, Hornbook, Library of Congress Children's Books, School Library Journal.*"

*SONORA REVIEW* FICTION CONTEST (II), Dept. of English, ML445, University of Arizona, Tucson AZ 85721. (602)621-1836. Contact: Antonya Nelson, editor. Annual award. "To encourage and support quality short fiction." Unpublished submissions. Award: $100 first prize, plus publication in *Sonora*; $50 second prize, plus publication in *Sonora*. "We accept manuscripts all year." Contest rules for SASE.

*SOUTHERN REVIEW*/LOUISIANA STATE UNIVERSITY ANNUAL SHORT FICTION AWARD (I), *Southern Review*, 43 Allen Hall, Louisiana State University, Baton Rouge LA 70803. (504)388-5108. Contact: editors, *Southern Review*. Annual award. "To encourage publication of good fiction." First collection of short stories by American writer appearing during calendar year. Award: $500 to author. Possible campus reading. Deadline a month after close of each calendar year. The book of short stories must be published by an American publisher. Two copies to be submitted by publisher. Looking for "style, sense of craft, plot, in-depth characters."

‡*SOVEREIGN GOLD* ANNUAL FICTION SELECTION AWARD (I), Box 1631, Iowa City IA 52244. (319)354-1191. Contact: director, awards program. Annually. Short stories, unpublished. Requirements: 500-5,000 words; subject inspirational, uplifting, of good moral theme. Deadline: December 21, 1986. Entry fee $5. SASE for rules. "This annual award program will select the ten best short stories in 1986 and publish them in a booklet form with each of the ten winners to receive a copy as their prize."

ANNUAL *SPITBALL* FICTION CONTEST (I), *Spitball* Poetry Magazine, 1721 Scott Blvd., Covington KY 41011. (606)261-3024. Contact: Mike Shannon, editor. Annual award. "To attract high quality baseball fiction to publish in our magazine." Previously unpublished submissions. Award: Publishing in *Spitball*, copies of issue story appears in, and merchandise prizes (baseball-related). Entry deadline: June 25. No entry fee. "Our only rule is that a SASE must be included in order for the manuscript (or a reply) to be returned. We have no preference in style, as long as subject is baseball. (Reading our fiction issue would probably help the writer unfamiliar with baseball fiction.)"

SPUR AWARD CONTEST, Western Writers of America, Fairgrounds 1753 Victoria, Sheridan WY 82801. Contact: Barb Ketcham, secretary-treasurer. Annual award. To encourage excellence in western writing. Previously published submissions. Entries are accepted only from the current calendar year for each year's award; that is, books can only be entered in the year they are published. Entry deadline: December 31. Award judged by a panel of experienced authors appointed by the current Spur Awards Chairman. Contest/award rules and entry forms available with SASE. Award: A wooden plaque shaped like a W with a bronze spur attached. "No money is awarded in Spur categories; however, a special $500 Medicine Pipe Bearer Award, funded by a WWA member, is offered in the Best First Western Novel competition. First novels may be entered in both Spur and Medicine Pipe Bearer competition. Books must be of the traditional or historical western theme, set anywhere west of the Mississippi River before the 20th century, ideally from 1850 to 1900." A spur is awarded for Best Historical Fiction, Best Juvenile Fiction and Best Short Fiction works.

‡WALLACE E. STEGNER FELLOWSHIP (III), Creative Writing Program, Stanford University, Stanford CA 94305. (415)497-2637. Contact: Kathy Ganas, program coordinator. Annually. 8 fellowships, unpublished or previously published fiction. Author must relocate to study at Stanford. Deadline: January 1. Entry fee $10. SASE for rules/entry forms.

***STORY TIME* SHORT-STORY CONTEST (I)**, Hutton Publications, Box 2377, Coeur d' Alene ID 83814. (208)667-7511. Contact: Linda Hutton, editor. Estab. 1982. Annual award. "To encourage short-story writers." Unpublished submissions. Award: $15 first prize; $10 second prize; $7.50 third prize. Entry deadline: March 1, June 1. Entry fee: $2. Looking for "tightly written plot and well-developed characters."

***SWALLOW'S TALE* SHORT FICTION CONTEST (II)**, Swallow's Tale Press/Magazine, Box 930040, Norcross GA 30093. (904)224-8859. Contact: Joe Taylor, editor. Annual award. "To publish a collection of short stories or novella and short stories of literary merit." The story entries may have been published in magazine form. Award: $500, 10 copies, discount on further copies, initial printing in hardcover and paper, national publicity. Deadline: December 20. Entry fee: $8.50. "All entrants receive a free copy of the winning book." Contest rules for SASE. Will accept novella length leader if mixed with short stories."

**‡TEXAS INSTITUTE OF LETTERS, SHORT STORY AWARD (III, IV)**, Library Associates of the William A. Blakley Library, University of Dallas, Box 8594, Waco TX 76717-8594. Contact: J.E. Weems, secretary-treasurer. Short stories, published within year. Requirements: for Texas authors (either born, now residing, or spent formative years in Texas), must supply info proving residency. Subject: Texas. Deadline: postmarked before January 15. SASE for rules and related material.

**‡TOWSON STATE UNIVERSITY PRIZE FOR LITERATURE (III)**, Towson State University Foundation, % Dean, College of Liberal Arts, Towson State University, Towson MD 21204. (301)321-2128. Contact: Annette Chappell, dean, college of Liberal Arts. Annually. Novels or short story collections, previously published. Requirements: not over 40, Maryland resident. Deadline: May 1. SASE for rules/entry forms.

**TRANSLATION CENTER AWARDS (II)**, The Translation Center, 307A Mathematics Bldg., Columbia University, New York NY 10027. Contact: Diane G. H. Cook, executive director. Annual awards. "For outstanding translation of a substantial part of a booklength *literary* work." Award: $1,000. Entry deadline: January 15. No entry fee. Write for application form.

**UNIVERSITY OF MISSOURI BREAKTHROUGH COMPETITION**, 200 Lewis Hall, Columbia MO 65211. Contact: Susan McGregor Denny, associate director. Biannual competition/ annual award. Entry fee is $10. Mss are read only in odd-numbered years. Award judged by professional writer or critic. Award: Publication in series. Looking for fiction, 96-124 pages. "In the past, most entries have been academics."

**JAMES F. VICTORIN MEMORIAL AWARD (IV)**, Dialogue Publications, Inc., 3100 Oak Park Ave., Berwyn IL 60402. (312)749-1908. Contact: Bonnie Miller, editor of fiction and poetry. Annual award. "To recognize the best short story published in *Dialogue* during the previous year." Previously published submissions in *Dialogue*. Award: $100. No entry fee. Publication of any story constitutes entry. ONLY BLIND OR VISUALLY HANDICAPPED ENTRANTS ARE ELIGIBLE.

**HAROLD D. VURSELL MEMORIAL AWARD (III)**, American Academy and Institute of Arts and Letters, 633 W. 155th St., New York NY 10032. (212)368-5900. Annual award. "To single out recent writing in book form that merits recognition for the quality of its prose style. It may be given for a work of fiction, biography, history, criticism, belles lettres, memoir, journal or a work of translation." Previously published submissions. Award: $5,000. Judged by 7-member jury composed of members of the Department of Literature of the American Academy and Institute of Arts and Letters. *No applications accepted.*

**EDWARD LEWIS WALLANT MEMORIAL BOOK AWARD (III)**, 3 Brighton Rd., West Hartford CT 06117. Sponsored by Dr. and Mrs. Irving Waltman in cooperation with the Hartford

Jewish Community Center. Contact: Mrs. Irving Waltman. Annual award. Memorial to Edward Lewis Wallant which offers incentive and encouragement to beginning writers. Published book the year before the award is conferred in the spring. Books may be submitted for consideration to Dr. Lothar Kahn, one of the permanent judges. Address: Central Conn. State University, New Britain CT 060500. Award: $250 plus award certificate. "Looking for creative work of fiction by an American which has significance for the American Jew. The novel (or collection of short stories) should preferably bear a kinship to the writing of Wallant. The award will seek out the writer who has not yet achieved literary prominence when published."

**WESTERN HERITAGE AWARDS (III)**, National Cowboy Hall of Fame, 1700 NE 63rd St., Oklahoma City OK 73111. (405)478-2250. Contact: W.H. Porter, public relations director. Annual award. "To honor outstanding quality in fiction, nonfiction, and art literature." Previously published submissions. Submissions are to be published during the previous calendar year. Award: The Wrangler, a replica of a C.M. Russell Bronze. Entry deadline: January 31. No entry fee. Entry forms or rules for SASE. Looking for "stories that best capture the spirit of the West."

**WESTERN STATES BOOK AWARDS**, Western States Arts Foundation, 207 Shelby St., Santa Fe NM 87501. (505)988-1166. Contact: Cheryl Alters, director. Estab. 1984. Biannual award. "Recognition for writers living in the West; encouragement of effective production and marketing of quality books published in the West; increase of sales and critical attention." Unpublished manuscripts submitted by publisher. Award: $2,500 for authors; $5,000 for publishers. Write for information on deadline. Contest rules for SASE.

**LAURA INGALLS WILDER AWARD (III)**, American Library Association/Association for Library Service to Children, 50 E. Huron St., Chicago IL 60611. Award offered every 3 years; next year 1986. "To honor a significant body of work for children for illustration, fiction or nonfiction." Award: Bronze Medal.

**LAURENCE L WINSHIP BOOK AWARD**, *The Boston Globe*, Boston MA 02107. (617)929-2649. Contact: Richard Collins, promotion director. Annual award. "To honor *The Globe*'s late editor who did much to encourage young talented New England authors." Previously published submissions from July 1 to July 1 each year. To be submitted by publishers. Award: $1,000. Deadline: June 30. Contest rules for SASE. Book must have some relation to New England—author, theme, plot or locale.

**WORD BEAT PRESS FICTION BOOK AWARD COMPETITION (I, II)**, Word Beat Press, Box 10509, Tallahassee FL 32302. Contact: Allen Woodman, editor. Estab. 1982. Annual award. "To publish quality collections of short stories or novellas. Stories previously published may be included, but credit must be given." Award: $100, 10 copies of publication, royalty contract, national publicity. All finalists, not just winner, will be considered for publication. Entry deadline: Postmarked by March 15. Entry fee: $5. Also include SASE and short bio. Looking for "40 to 90 typed, double-spaced manuscript pages of fiction. This can be any number of short stories or short-shorts. We will also consider novellas."

**‡WORDS AT WORK WRITING CONTEST**, Box 2547, Sedona AZ 86336. Contact: Linda Ann Stewart, secretary. Short stories (1,000 word limit) unpublished. Open to everyone. No age limits. Deadline: April 30, 1986. Winner announced June 15, 1986. Entry Fee $5. Prizes: $50 first place; $25-second; $15-third. SASE for rules.

**‡WORLD'S BEST SHORT STORY CONTEST**, English Department Writing Program, Florida State University, Tallahassee FL 32306. (904)644-4230. Contact: Jerome Stern, director. Annually. Short stories; unpublished, under 250 words. Open to all. Deadline: February 15. SASE for rules.

**WQ EDITORS' PRIZE (II, IV)**, *Cross-Canada Writers' Quarterly*, Box 277, Station F, Toronto, Ontario M4Y 2L7 Canada. Contact: Ted Plantos, editor. Annual award. "To encourage and publicize the best in new Canadian fiction writing." Unpublished submissions, under 3,000 words. Award: Over $1,500 in cash and book prizes, plus publication of the 1st and 2nd prize winner in *Cross-Canada Writers' Quarterly*. Entry deadline: June 30 each year. Details are announced in NOS. 1 & 2 of annual volume (winter and spring issues.) Entry fees are nominal. "Stories must demonstrate excellent handling of characterization, setting, plot and dialogue. Theme and approach must be fresh and original."

**WRITER'S DIGEST ANNUAL WRITING COMPETITION** (Short Story Division) (I, II), *Writer's Digest*, WD Writing Competition, 9933 Alliance Rd., Cincinnati OH 45242. (513)984-0717. Unpublished submissions. Entry deadline: Midnight May 31. All entries must be original, unpublished, and not previously submitted to a *Writer's Digest* contest. Short story: 2,000 words maximum, one entry only. No acknowledgment will be made of receipt of mss nor will mss be returned. Award: $1,000 grand prize, electronic typewriters, reference books, plaques, and certificates of recognition. Names of Grand Prize winner and top 100 winners are announced in the October issue of *Writer's Digest*. Send SASE to *WD* Writing Competition for rules or see January-May issues of *Writer's Digest*.

**THE WRITERS OF THE FUTURE CONTEST (I)**, L. Ron Hubbard, 2210 Wilshire Blvd., #343, Santa Monica CA 90403. (213)466-3310. Contact: Fred Harris. Estab. 1984. Quarterly. To honor original works of science fiction of short story or novellete form. Unpublished submissions. Award: 1st prize, $1,000; 2nd prize, $750; 3rd prize, $500. SASE for contest rules.

**YELLOW SILK MAGAZINE (II, IV)**, Annual Erotic Fiction Contest, Box 6374, Albany CA 94706. (415)841-6500. Contact: Lily Pond, editor. Estab. 1983. Annual award. "To encourage submission of more and better fiction." Unpublished submissions; no simultaneous submissions. Award: $200 plus publication. Editorial policy: "All persuasions; no brutality." Literary quality equally important as erotic content. Enclose SASE. Deadline October 23.

**YOUNG AMBASSADOR CONTEST (I, IV)**, *Young Ambassador* Magazine, Box 82808, Lincoln NE 68501. (402)474-4567. Contact: Nancy Bayne, managing editor. Annual contest. "To give teens (up to 19 years) an opportunity to use their talents and compete with their peers." Submissions must be original and previously unpublished. "Story must have spiritual emphasis. Up to 1,800 words." Award: "Payment for story comparable to our payment for regular freelance fiction." Two fiction categories: general fiction and Biblical fiction. Entry deadline: April 15. No entry fee. Entry forms or rules for SASE. Contest rules for 1986 in the October 1985 issue. "Only young people through age 19 are eligible."

**MORTON DAUWEN ZABEL AWARD (III)**, American Academy and Institute of Arts and Letters, 633 W. 155th St., New York NY 10032. (212)368-5900. Awarded annually, in rotation to a poet, writer of fiction, or critic. "To honor writers of progressive, original and experimental tendencies." Previously published submissions. No applications accepted. Award: $2,500.

---

66 *The ultimate prize in literature is unattainable. The curse for a writer is that the page can never be perfect. Despite revisions, a page is nearly always less than it can be. So a prize is always for incomplete work. A prize can never show what writers can really do, when they extend themselves and reach for the literary stratosphere.*
—*Geoff Hancock* 99

# Introducing: the literary agent

## by Michael Larsen

Writers, editors, and literary agents themselves conspire to perpetuate the greatest myth in publishing. It's hard to get an agent. Nonsense! It's easy to get an agent. What's hard is writing a salable book.

The moment you have a proposal or manuscript that's ready to sell, you will have no trouble finding an agent to sell it. In fact, finding an agent is getting easier all the time because agents are springing up around the country. *Literary Agents of North America: 1984-85 Marketplace* lists agents in 31 states and Canada. The challenge is to find a reputable, competent agent you will feel comfortable working with.

Here are four steps to finding an agent:

## Step 1: understand the business

If your book is strong enough, anybody can sell it because almost anybody will buy it. To become the best book it can be and earn you the most money, your book needs three ingredients: the best possible editor, the best possible publisher, and the best possible deal.

Editors have their own tastes, publishers their own character. They do certain kinds of books better than others. And while there may be more idealism in publishing than in any other business, editors and publishers vary in their ability and their sense of responsi-

---

*Michael Larsen worked for three major book publishers before establishing his San Francisco literary agency in 1972 with partner Elizabeth Pomada. In addition to teaching and speaking at writing seminars, the two agents work closely with beginning writers at workshops and conferences throughout the US. Larsen is the author of* California Publicity Outlets, Painted Ladies: San Francisco's Resplendent Victorians, *and most recently* How to Write a Book Proposal *and* Literary Agents: How to Get and Work With the Right One for You.

bility as much as agents and writers. There are editors who don't return phone calls, and publishers whose royalty statements can't be trusted or who don't do an effective job of publishing their books. Nor can a publisher's virtues be surmised from its size, its location, or its books.

Enter the agent.

## What an agent does

An agent is your mediator between you and the marketplace. Your agent reads your work and judges its salability. Your agent may be able to provide the editorial advice that can turn unsalable material into a winner. Your agent knows the editors and publishers to submit your project to, and, just as important, which to avoid. Your agent submits your manuscript as long as he or she feels that it is salable, until it is sold or until no potential publishers remain.

When your manuscript is sold, your agent negotiates the most favorable contract possible. The contract, which you must sign and approve, gives the agent the right to act on your behalf and receive income earned through the contract. Your agent deducts a commission and forwards the balance to you.

Your agent continues to serve as a liaison between you and your publisher on editorial, financial, production and promotional questions. Your agent is also your advocate in trying to resolve problems such as a late or rejected manuscript, your editor leaving, lack of promotion, or a faulty royalty statement.

Your agent may be able to get you writing assignments or come up with book ideas for you.

Whether or not you have a written agreement, your agent will normally expect to have the exclusive right to represent your work throughout the world in all forms and media. Before and often long after publication, your agent pursues subsidiary rights sales. For rights such as film or foreign rights, your agent may appoint co-agents. Large agencies have specialists in these areas.

By absorbing rejections and being a focal point for your business dealings, your agent frees you to write. Your agent can advise you on the direction of your career and, in what may be a desert of rejections, your agent can be an oasis of reassurance and encouragement.

## What an agent can't do

No agent can sell a book nobody will buy. Publishing is a subjective business and an agent's enthusiasm for a book, however genuine, may be misplaced. Timing is a fourth essential ingredient in a successful book, and if a manuscript reaches editors too soon or too late, it won't sell, regardless of how good it is. And unless it's a hot subject, publishers are increasingly reluctant to do "me-too" books that only duplicate what's already on the shelves.

Your agent may be your only agent, but you are not your agent's only client. Agents are continuously trying to divide their attention among all their clients while responding to an endless stream of letters, manuscripts and phone calls. You should communicate with your agent or expect contact only when it's necessary.

Your agent is not a publicist, a tax expert, a savings and loan, or a babysitter and shouldn't be expected to perform personal services for you. Enduring friendships do develop between writers and agents, however, and these relationships can blur the line of responsibility between duty and affection

# Why an agent can help you

As valuable sources of manuscripts, now and in the future, respected agents have more clout and credibility with editors than individual writers have.

Your subsidiary rights income will be greater if your agent, rather than your publisher, sells them. While your publisher will apply your subsidiary rights income against your advance, your agent will forward it to you as it's received.

Another essential asset for an agent is objectivity. It's been said that a lawyer who represents himself has a fool for a client. The same is true for a writer, which is why my partner and I both have agents for our books. When you write a book, you are too close to it to judge its quality or value, or to speak on its behalf with complete objectivity. Your agent can be objective.

The selling of your book deserves the same kind of professional care you lavish on your manuscript. And since publishing houses change hands and editors change jobs, your agent may be the only stable element in your career.

# Step 2: find the right agent

Literary agents are a remarkably diverse, independent, individualistic lot, partly because anybody can be a literary agent. All you need is a desk, office supplies, a telephone, and an address.

The small start-up costs, lack of licensing requirements (excepting some states which are now trying to establish licensing), and the glamorous aura of publishing attract aspiring agents. Consequently, agents vary in:

- their professional experience and knowledge of publishing and negotiating.
- how they like to receive queries
- how much of a manuscript they'll read
- how long they take to respond
- how involved they get in editing manuscripts
- how they approach publishers
- the publishers they deal with
- their commissions
- whether their agency agreement is oral or written
- and the amount of contact they like to have with their writers.

Literary agents also vary in their tastes and interests. Most can't afford to specialize and will consider any adult fiction and nonfiction books suitable for the general public. Some do consider your adult and children's books, scripts, poetry and short works.

# Reading fees

A new writer is particularly susceptible to being taken advantage of by a bad agent, a fate worse than having no agent at all. Some agents, for instance, make their living from reading and editing manuscripts rather than selling them.

There are, however, able, responsible agents who charge reading fees and may even edit your manuscript for a fee or larger commission. Agents, like editors, reject over 90% of what they see. New agents who haven't yet generated sufficient income from agenting may need a reading fee to compensate them for the time spent reading unsalable material. Some refund the fee if the book is accepted or when it is sold.

When Elizabeth and I started our agency, we wanted to see everything. After a year or so, we realized that we had read more than 150 complete manuscripts and found only two worth working with. To lessen the flow (and, we hoped naively, increase the quality) we decided to charge a nominal fee. Since Elizabeth was getting $25 to review books for the *San Francisco Chronicle*, we charged a $25 reading fee, refundable if we accepted the work. Alas, the gems—and refunded fees—were few and far between until finally we could no longer afford the time. We don't charge reading fees anymore, but we read only the first 50 pages and a synopsis of each completed manuscript—and the accept-ance-to-submission ratio is even slimmer than it was before.

If you're dead set against paying a reading fee, don't. Most agents don't charge one, but charging a fee doesn't automatically brand an agent an outcast.

## A living commission

Agenting originated in England about 100 years ago in response to the mistreatment of authors by publishers. An agent's commission was 10%.

Buffeted by rising costs, shrinking advances and royalties, lower bookstore sales, the proliferation of agents, and the greater difficulty of selling books to increasingly cau-tious publishers, independent agents (including this one) have recently begun to raise their commission to 15%. Agents are changing their commissions out of need, not greed, and are sometimes absorbing costs formerly charged to authors.

I believe that before the end of the decade, there will be few agents who are *not* charging 15%, at least for new writers.

You're looking for an agent you like and who can and wants to provide the represen-tation you need. If you find such a person, wouldn't it be a mistake to let 5% of your in-come get in the way of a satisfying relationship?

## When to look for an agent

The time to look for an agent is when you have a proposal or manuscript that is "100%," as well conceived and written as you can make it. Until you've written a novel, you can't prove that you can sustain plot and characterization for 200 pages, so a first novel should be finished.

Unless your short stories or articles consistently command four-figure sums, most agents will be unwilling to handle them because their commissions won't justify the time spent placing them. If an agent is representing you on a book, the agent may be willing to handle your less profitable work as a service.

## How to look for an agent

Here are five suggestions for finding an agent:

1. The publishing community. Ask writers you know or admire for recommenda-tions. Try writers groups, editors, writing teachers, booksellers, librarians, reviewers, and publishers' sales representatives.

2. SAR and ILAA. The Society of Author's Representatives and the Independent Literary Agents Association are the two groups of agents whose members are experi-enced and reputable. The SAR was founded in 1928 and comprises 55 of the larger and older agencies. Only New York agents may join. For a helpful brochure and membership list, send SASE to SAR, Box 650, Old Chelsea Station, New York City 10113.

Formed in the mid '70s, ILAA has fewer members generally from smaller, newer agencies (including mine) in and out of New York. Its list is available from IlAA, 55 5th Ave., 15th Floor, New York NY 10003.

3. *Literary Marketplace*, *Writer's Market*, *Fiction Writer's Market*, and *Literary*

*Agents of North America*. These annual compendiums, available in the library, have sections listing agents who have sold books; and *FWM* includes only those agents handling fiction. *LMP* provides only basic information.

For agents near you, try the Yellow Pages.

4. Book-related events. Writing classes, seminars, and conferences present opportunities to meet or learn about agents.

5. Books. Check the acknowledgment pages of your favorite books. Writers occasionally thank their agents in print.

## The Big Apple syndrome

Another myth about agenting that should be demolished is that an agent must be in New York. Agents don't sell books. Neither do writers. Books sell books. An editor reads a manuscript and decides if the book is worth publishing, and it makes no difference whether the manuscript arrives from across the street or across the country.

If editors like a book, they become the in-house agents for it. They share the manuscript with the key staff people to marshal support for the project. Then they usually have to justify buying it to other editors, company executives, and representatives from the sales, publicity and subsidiary rights departments at the next editorial board meeting.

Lunches help agents keep up to date on editors' needs and the latest gossip, and deals are certainly made over the Dover sole, but agents don't make their living over lunch; they make it by phone and by mail. During one of our periodic trips to New York, a paperback editor was wining and dining us at a chic midtown bistro. We were delighted when she informed us that she was ready to buy a historical romance series—and then speechless when she refused to negotiate the deal. She insisted that we wait until she returned to her office and then call her from a phone booth.

Because New York agents are closer to editors, they are more likely to hear an editor's latest ideas. So if getting assignments is important to you, you will be better off with a New York agent adept at ferreting them out.

But agents don't work for publishers; they work for writers. And when their publishers may be on a distant shore, many writers prefer an agent closer to home. Ability and compatibility count more than geography.

## Step 3: make the connection

Regardless of how they operate, all agents like to be queried properly, either by phone or, more commonly, by mail. Agents don't want to meet with writers until they have read something they want to handle.

If you're writing, follow the submission requirements stated by the individual agent. If submitting a query or proposal, keep it simple. Use one side of a page and include the idea for the book; its title, tone, style, structure; the number of pages and illustrations; the immediate and long-term markets for the book; what is ready for the agent to see; and the aspects of your personal, professional or literary background that will convince the agent to read your work.

Type the query immaculately and include your address, daytime phone number, and SASE.

Agents are used to multiple query letters, but if you plan to submit your work to more than one agent at a time, ask first. Most agents can't afford the luxury of reading what they may not be able to handle.

If an agent does request the full manuscript, find out how long the reading will take and call if you haven't heard by then. If you haven't heard in two months and are not satisfied with the reason why, ask for the manuscript back. Don't call just to see if the manuscript arrived or because you think nudging will help speed the process.

The more income agents make with their present roster of clients, the less eager they are to take on new writers and the harder it will be for you to break in. But I have never met an agent who wouldn't read a one-page query.

## Step 4: get together

If an agent likes your work and wants to represent you, what next?

Go see the agent if you can. Establishing a rapport in person is easier than over the phone. Visiting will also give you the chance to see the office and the books the agent has sold, and meet the staff.

The relationship between an agent and a writer is a working marriage with personal and professional aspects to it. There's no certainty the union will thrive until it does, but the chances for its success will be enhanced if, at the outset, you are familiar with your agent's ability, personality, and operating procedures. Know what the agent will do for you and what you need from an agent.

If there's a need to establish an agent's credentials, or if the information in a listing is scanty, these questions can help:

√How long have you been in business?
√How did you become an agent?
√Are you a member of SAR or ILAA?
√How many books have you sold?
√To what publishers?
√What kinds of books do you handle?
√Have you sold novels similar to mine? The same genre?
√How many editors do you deal with? How many publishers
√How large is your staff?
√How many clients do you represent?
√How do you handle film and foreign rights?
√What are your most successful books?

Taken together, the answers to these questions should convince you that you are talking to an experienced agent. The following questions will define your relationship with your agent.

√What is your commission?
√Do you have an agency agreement?
√What are the chances of selling my book? How long do you think it will take?
√How will you go about placing it?
√Does the book have subsidiary rights worth pursuing?
√When should I expect to hear from you?

On a personal level, your agent should have the same virtues that sustain any marriage: honesty, trust, consideration, patience, openness, courtesy, confidence, dependability, faith in you and your work, and passion and optimism tinged with fatalism. As in all things, you must trust your instincts. Everything your agent says and does on your behalf should make as much sense to you as it does to your agent. Always remember who works for whom. But at the same time, keep in mind that until the agent sells something for you, the agent is working for free, so it is not fair to abuse the agent's time.

Patience is an important virtue when dealing with an agent because selling your book may take years. It once took us four years to place a novel. So once your agent starts submitting your work, try to forget it exists. Write your next book.

If an editor rejects your manuscript it won't help your writing or your frame of mind to know. If the editor says something helpful (which happens rarely), your agent will tell you. If you feel compelled to see your rejection slips, just ask. Console yourself with the thought that good news travels fast.

Although in the past most agents did not put their agreements in writing, agency agreements are becoming the norm. An agreement solidifies the writer-agent relationship by clarifying what's expected of both parties.

Written or verbal, your understanding with your agent should cover:
- what the agent will handle
- who pays expenses
- how long the arrangement lasts
- commissions for book and subsidiary rights
- a method for ending the relationship
- the agent's rights after the agreement terminates.

If a problem arises and you both conscientiously but futilely try to solve it, you should have the right to fire your agent in a reasonable period of time.

## Go for the gold

Like publishers, agents should do a good job on the first book if they expect to handle the next one. Like publishers, agents start working with writers in the hope that they will forge permanent relationships that will grow more creative and profitable as the writers' careers develop. And like publishers, the hardest part of most agents' jobs is finding salable material.

There are more subjects to write about, more formats—hardcover, trade and mass-market paperbacks—for your books to be published in, more agents, more publishers (14,000 of them!), and more ways to make money from yur books than ever before.

If you are writing to meet the needs of the marketplace, this could be a golden age for you. A literary agent will make sure that you get your share of the gold.

---

❝ *I started writing stories because it's the best way to talk about religion. Jesus, Joseph, David . . . they were all storytellers. Stories appeal to the emotions and the whole personality, and not just the mind.*
—*Andrew M. Greeley* ❞

# Literary agents

In the listings of literary agents that follow, the information given pertains to fiction only, although the great majority of agents represented handle nonfiction writers also.

For years the standard agent's fee has been 10%. In the last few years, however, more and more agencies have raised their fees to 15% (occasionally there is a 12% fee) and for the first time we see an agent charging 25%. Such an increase is a reflection of the economic realities in keeping an agency going.

Although new talent is the lifeblood of the entire publishing industry, and even though a number of agencies represent beginning/published writers, most are interested in new novelists (seldom will an agent represent a writer of only short stories) *only* if they have publishing credits—that is, a substantial list of publications with magazines or a publisher. Therefore it is often more expeditious for a beginning writer to pursue a publisher or magazine directly without agent assistance—until he/she has more publishing experience.

Again this year we have listed those agents who *to our knowledge* do not charge a reading or prepublication fee of any kind. Some agents not listed here ask beginning, untested, unpublished writers to pay a reading fee, filing or processing fee, or manuscript fee—the terms vary. Our feeling is that an agent who is sincerely interested in developing or representing an author should be willing to read the queries and manuscripts that come in, and do the initial work necessary to find the special author he/she woul like to have as a client. We believe there should be no profit for agents from hopefuls who pay out sometimes considerable sums only to find that their manuscripts are rejected later for publication.

If in your correspondence with any of the agents listed you find that additional fees are required prior to an agent-client agreement or contract, please advise us and we will review the situation. We have not however, excluded those agencies requiring the writer to defray the costs of manuscript photocopying, postage or phone costs, and we have tried to apprise the reader of that information in the listing. We have also listed agencies that offer an *optional* service for a fee, e.g. manuscript criticism.

What literary agents are in total agreement on—and are adamant about—is the policy of return postage. Don't send checks or loose stamps, please, they say, and as Eleanor Merryman Roszel Rogers states, "Queries and unsolicited manuscripts should come with SASE; otherwise I shall not respond."

**CAROLE ABEL, LITERARY AGENT**, 160 W. 87th St., New York NY 10024. (212)724-1168. Contact: Carole Abel. Special interests: mainstream, women's, and thrillers/mystery. Send outline/proposal. Reviews fiction and nonfiction (50/50 fiction to nonfiction). Presently accepting new clients. Obtains clients via recommendation, some solicitation, conferences, some unsolicited mss and queries. New/unpublished writers: 25%. Agent's commission: 15%. Member of I.L-.A.A.

**DOMINICK ABEL LITERARY AGENCY, INC.**, 12C, 498 West End Ave., New York NY 10024. (212)877-0710. Adult fiction and nonfiction only. Query or send outline/proposal with SASE. (40-60% fiction to nonfiction). Occasionally accepts new clients, usually by referral. Agent's commission: 10%. Member of I.L.A.A.

**EDWARD J. ACTON, INC.**, 928 Broadway, New York NY 10100. (212)675-5400. Novels only. Special interest: mainstream. Send outline plus sample chapters. Also reviews nonfiction (50-50 fiction to nonfiction). Represents 100 writers. Obtains clients via recommendations of editors and present clients. Presently accepting new clients. New/beginning writers: 10%. Agent's commission: 15%. Members of I.L.A.A. Send all mss to Inge Hanson.

**MAXWELL ALEY ASSOCIATES**, 145 E. 35th St., New York NY 10016. (212)679-5377. Contact: Ruth Aley. Novels. Query with sample chapters with SASE. Also reviews nonfiction. Interested in quality fiction. Agent's commission: 15%. Member of I.L.A.A.

**JAMES ALLEN, LITERARY AGENT**, 538 E. Harford St., Milford PA 18337. (717)296-7266. Contact: James Allen. Novels only. Prefers "genre fiction more than mainstream, especially science fiction and fantasy, historical fiction, mysteries, and men's action/adventure." Query with letter and SASE, then send entire ms, "if I've expressed interest in seeing it." Also reviews nonfiction (80/20 fiction to nonfiction). Represents approximately 50 writers. Presently accepting new clients "on a *very* limited basis, preferably already-published authors." Obtains clients "by preference, through recommendation of someone whose opinion I respect; secondarily, by unsolicited queries." Agent's commission: 10% for domestic sales; 20% on dramatic-rights licenses; and 20% on foreign licenses through affiliates abroad.

**LINDA ALLEN, LITERARY AGENT**, 2881 Jackson St., San Francisco CA 94115. (415)921-6437. Contact: Linda Allen. Novels. Query. Also reviews nonfiction (50%/50% fiction to nonfiction). Represents 35-50 writers. Presently accepting new clients. Agent's commission: 12%.

**MARCIA AMSTERDAM AGENCY**, 41 W. 82nd St., New York NY 10024. (212)873-4945. Specializes in mainstream, women's, science fiction, children's, romance, mystery, young adult, occult, and adventure. Send outline plus first 3 chapters with SASE. Also considers nonfiction. Obtains clients via recommendations, conferences, queries. Presently accepting new clients. Interested in new/beginning novelists. Agent's commission: 10% domestic rights.

**THE ARTISTS AGENCY**, 10000 Santa Monica Blvd., Los Angeles CA 90067. (213)277-7779. Contact: Eric Rosenberg or Mickey Freiberg. Novels. Special interest: mainstream. Query. Also reviews nonfiction (50%/50% fiction to nonfiction). Represents 75 writers. Obtains new clients via recommendations, queries or unsolicited mss. New/unpublished writers: 10%. Agent's commission: 10%; 15% on beginning book writers.

**‡BARBARA BAUER LITERARY AGENCY**, 37 New Dorp Lane, Staten Island NY 10306. (718)356-3163. Contact: Barbara Bauer. Novels; novellas; short stories; short story collections. Special interest: "salable material." Send outline/proposal or outline plus sample chapters. Also reviews nonfiction. Presently accepting new clients. "We specialize in new and unpublished authors. We are authors' agents to the book publishing industry."

**BILL BERGER ASSOCIATES**, 444 E. 58th St., New York NY 10022. (212)486-9588. Fiction and nonfiction. Query; send outline/proposal or outline plus sample chapters with SASE. Agent's commission: 10%.

**THE BLAKE GROUP**, #105, 4300 N. Central Expressway, Dallas TX 75206. (214)828-2160. Contact: Lee B. Halff. Novels, novellas, short stories, and short story collections. Submit entire ms. Also reviews nonfiction. Accepts only top quality work. Agent's commission: 10% upon publication. "We charge for a comprehensive critique, or for editing; the latter only with a previous agreement with the author."

**HARRY BLOOM AGENCY**, #404, 1520 S. Beverly Glen Blvd., Los Angeles CA 90024. (213)556-3461. Contact: Patrice Dale. Novels. Special interests: mainstream, women's, romance, action, adventure and mystery. Send entire ms. Also reviews nonfiction (70%-30% fiction to nonfiction). Represents 15-20 writers. Obtains clients generally via recommendations and queries. Presently accepting new clients. New/unpublished writers: 25%. Agent's commission: 10%.

**‡REID BOATES LITERARY DEVELOPMENT**, 44 Mt. Ridge Dr., Wayne NJ 07470. (201)628-7523. Novels; novellas. Special interests: mainstream, popular adult, fiction and nonfiction. Agency represents 30 writers. Query. SASE. Generally obtains clients via personal recommendations. "Three quarters of my clients are new to books, although most have strong journalistic backgrounds." Agent's commission: 15%. "Fiction or nonfiction, the issue is clear writing; my taste runs to clear, clean prose that advances the storyline."

**GEORGES BORCHARDT INC.**, 136 E. 57th St., New York NY 10022. (212)753-5785. Novels. Special interest: literary fiction, nonfiction (3/1 nonfiction to fiction). Query, "but only if recommended by someone we know." Represents approximately 200 writers. Obtains clients via recommendations. Presently accepting new clients but very few. Interested in new/beginning novelists. New/beginning writers: 10%. Agent's commission: 10%. Member of S.A.R.

**BRANDT & BRANDT**, 1501 Broadway, New York NY 10036. (212)840-5760. Contact: Carl Brandt. "Send letter on background and what you are currently doing." Interested in new/beginning novelists. Agent's commission: 10%. Member of S.A.R.

**CURTIS BROWN ASSOCIATES LTD.**, Subsidiary of Curtis Brown, Ltd., New York, 10 Astor Place, New York NY 10003. (212)473-5400. No unsolicited material. Query. Presently accepting new clients. Interested in new/beginning novelists. Agent's commission: 10%. Member of S.A.R.

**NED BROWN INC.**, 407 N. Maple Dr., Beverly Hills CA 90210. East Coast: Lorna Brown, Vice-President, Ned Brown Inc., 185 Charter Oak Dr., New Canaan CT 06840. (203)966-2437. Full-length fiction and nonfiction. Send query with SASE. Presently accepting new clients "only if published commercially or recommended by another author or client." Agent's commission: 10%. Unpublished writers referred to Lorna Brown Literary Reading Service. (Editor's note: possible charge involved for beginners.)

**PEMA BROWNE LTD.**, 185 E. 85th St., New York NY 10028. (212)369-1925. Contact: Perry J. Browne. Fiction and nonfiction. Area of specialization: romance, mainstream, men's, women's, contemporary and historical romance, young adult, adventure, all paperback categories. Send query letter with synopsis and a couple of chapters with appropriate SASE. No checks for postage. Also reviews nonfiction (50/50 fiction to nonfiction). Represents approximately 20 writers. Obtains clients via editors and queries. Presently accepting new clients. Interested in new/beginning novelists. New/unpublished authors: 5%. Agent's commission: 15%. "Only wish to see queries as to manuscripts that have *not* been sent out to publishers or other agents!"

**FRANK BRUNOTTS**, 2744 San Carlos Dr., Walnut Creek CA 94598. (415)930-7980. Novels, novellas, short stories, and short story collections. Special interests: mainstream, literary fiction. Query or send entire ms. Also reviews nonfiction (50%/50% fiction to nonfiction). Represents about 10 writers. Obtains new clients via recommendations, solicitation, queries or unsolicited mss. Presently accepting new clients. New/unpublished writers: 90%. Agent's commission: 15%. Editorial services also offered for a fee.

**SHIRLEY BURKE AGENCY**, B-704, 370 E. 76th St., New York NY 10021. (212)861-2309. Contact: Shirley Burke. All types of novels. Specializes in romance, women's, mystery. Query; send outline/proposal with 2 chapters on request. Also nonfiction. Do not send mss. Interested mainly in writers who have been published previously. Represents about 25 writers. Obtains clients mainly via recommendation. Agent's commission: 15%.

**RUTH CANTOR**, Rm. 1005, 156 5th Ave., New York NY 10010. (212)243-3246. Novels. Special interests: mainstream, children's, women's, and science fiction mystery, suspense, *good* adventure stories; "not much true confession, cheap romances or potboilers." Query or send outline/proposal with SASE. Also reviews nonfiction (75%/25% fiction to nonfiction). Obtains new clients via recommendations or unsolicited mss. Presently accepting new clients. New/unpublished writers: varies. Agent's commission: 10%; 20% foreign sales.

**MARIA CARVAINIS AGENCY, INC.**, 235 West End Ave., New York NY 10023. (212)580-1559. Novels. Special interests: contemporary mainstream fiction, historicals, suspense, westerns, mysteries, nonfiction (popular science, business, etc.), and young adult novels. "I handle all kinds of fiction from serious to commercial." Query with SASE. No reply without SASE. No unsolicited mss will be considered or read. Also represents nonfiction (45% fiction to 40% nonfiction, 5% magazine fiction, "although this is always in flux.") "We also do film, TV and treatments, and we prefer you have previous credits in those areas." Selectively accepting new clients. Agent's commission: 15%. "I am a signatory to the Writers Guild of America, East Inc. and member-at-large of the Authors Guild Inc., the Author's League of America, Inc., and the Romance Writers of America."

**MARTHA CASSELMAN LITERARY AGENCY**, (formerly Martha Sternberg Literary Agency), 1263 12th Ave., San Francisco CA 94122. (415)665-3235. Contact: Martha Casselman. Adult fiction, nonfiction (30%/70% fiction to nonfiction). Query or, "if manuscript completed, synopsis, 50-60 pages, return envelope and postage. We will not review multiple submissions, either to other agents or publishers. Author must include an accounting of where book has previously been reviewed. No romances." Obtains new clients via recommendations and queries. Presently accepting new clients. New/unpublished writers: 40/60%. Agent's commission: 15%.

**‡SJ CLARK LITERARY AGENCY**, 756A San Jose Ave., San Francisco CA 94110. (415)285-7401. Contact: Sue Clark. Novels; short story collections. Special interests: mystery, mainstream, psychic, children's. Represents 8 writers. Query or send outline plus sample chapters. Also reviews nonfiction (75%-25% fiction to nonfiction). Obtains clients usually via word of mouth. Presently accepting new clients. New/unpublished writers: 90%. Agent's commission: 15%.

**HY COHEN LITERARY AGENCY**, 111 W. 57th St., New York NY 10019. (212)757-5237. Fiction and nonfiction. Specializes in "any and all" subjects. Send sample chapters with SASE ("if ms is to be returned"). Represents approximately 30 writers. Obtains writers via recommendation, conferences, unsolicited mss, and queries. New/unpublished writers: 95%. Agent's commission: 10%.

**RUTH COHEN, INC.**, Box 7626, Menlo Park CA 94025. (415)854-2054. Contact: Ruth Cohen. Special interests: juvenile and young adult fiction; adult fiction and nonfiction; genre fiction (mysteries, romances, westerns). "Have been especially successful with juvenile and young adult manuscripts and am always seeking professional and dedicated writers in these areas." Query or send outline plus sample chapters (opening 50 pages) and SASE. Represents 50 writers. Obtains new clients via query letters and client/editor recommendations. Presently accepting new clients. New/unpublished writers: 30%. Agent's commission: 10%. Member of I.L.A.A.

**JOYCE K. COLE LITERARY AGENCY**, Box 5139, Berkeley CA 94705. (415)548-9648. Contact: Joyce K. Cole. Novels, short story collections. Special interests: mainstream and literary; all genre fiction and young adult. Query or send outline plus sample chapters (up to 50 pages). Also reviews nonfiction (40%/60% fiction to nonfiction). Represents 50 writers. Obtains new clients via recommendations, conferences, and queries. Presently accepting new clients. New/unpublished writers: 30%. Agent's commission: 10%; 20% foreign sales.

**SHIRLEY COLLIER AGENCY**, 1127 Stradella Rd., Los Angeles CA 90077. (213)270-4500. Contact: Shirley Collier. Novels and biography. Prefers "good writing; no smut." Query first with SASE. Also reviews nonfiction (75%/25% fiction to nonfiction). Interested in new/beginning novelists when time permits. Writer must demonstrate a minimum number of sales to three top magazines. Agent's commission: 10%; foreign translations additional 10%.

**‡COLUMBIA LITERARY ASSOCS., INC.**, 7902 Nottingham Way, Ellicott City MD 21043. (301)465-1595. Contact: Linda Hayes. Novels. Special interest: mainstream and category, romance, popular historicals, family sagas, young-adult novels. Represents 30-40 writers. Query with synopsis plus first chapter and submission history (pubs/agents). SASE. Also reviews nonfiction (50%-50% fiction to nonfiction). Writer is billed for specific project expenses (shipping, long distance calls, photocopy). Obtains new clients via recommendations from others and queries. Presently accepting "a selected few" new clients. New/unpublished writers: ⅓. Agent's commission: 12-15%.

**‡DON CONGDON ASSOCIATES, INC.**, 177 E. 70th St., New York NY 10021. (212)570-9090. Contact: Michael Congdon. Novels; short stories; short story collections. Special interests: mainstream trade fiction; no juveniles, no romance. Represents 95 writers. Query. Also reviews nonfiction (40%-60% fiction to nonfiction). Obtains clients via recommendations from clients and editors. Presently accepting new clients "if previously published." New/unpublished writers 1%. Agent's commission: 10%. Member of S.A.R.

**MOLLY MALONE COOK LITERARY AGENCY, INC.**, Box 338, Provincetown MA 02657. (617)487-1931. Novels, short story collections. Query. "Queries and/or mss without return postage will not be acknowledged returned." Also reviews nonfiction (50/50 fiction to nonfiction).

**LIZ DARHANSOFF LITERARY AGENCY**, 1220 Park Ave., New York NY 10028. (212)534-2479. Novels only. Special interests: literary fiction. Query; send outline/proposal or outline plus sample chapters. Also reviews nonfiction. Represents 50 writers. Obtains clients via recommendations. Presently accepting new clients. New/beginning writers: 30%. Agent's commission: 10%. Member of I.L.A.A.

**JOAN DAVES**, 59 E. 54th St., New York NY 10022. (212)759-6250. Fiction and nonfiction. Query "with good information about the writer." Presently accepting new clients "but rarely." Interested in new/beginning novelists. Writer must demonstrate some prior credits or professional experience to be considered as client. Agent's commission: 10% domestic. Member of S.A.R.

**ANITA DIAMANT: THE WRITERS' WORKSHOP, INC.**, 310 Madison Ave., New York NY 10017. (212)687-1122. Novels and nonfiction (50/50). Specializes in anything of popular, general interest. Send query or outline/proposal with sample chapter with SASE. Represents approximately 100 writers. Currently accepting new clients. Obtains new clients mainly via recommendations. Agent's commission: 15% to $20,000; 10% thereafter. Member of S.A.R.

**CANDIDA DONADIO & ASSOCIATES, INC.**, 231 West 22nd St., New York NY 10011. "We do not read unsolicited mss; query first."

**JOSEPH ELDER AGENCY**, #6D, 150 W. 87th St., New York NY 10024. "Must query first, include SASE ('query' means query letter, not detailed outline, sample chapters)." Reviews book mss (75/25 fiction to nonfiction). Special interests: open. Represents 30 writers. Usually obtains clients via recommendations. Presently accepting new clients but very selectively. Writer need not demonstrate a number of sales "but it's very rare to take on a new client with no track record." Agent's commission: 10%. Member of I.L.A.A.

**JOHN FARQUHARSON LTD.**, Suite 1914, 250 W. 57th St., New York NY 10107. (212)245-1993. Attn: Jane Gelfman or Deborah Schneider. Novels. Special interests: mainstream, mysteries, literary novels; some romance and science fiction; no children's. Query by letter only with SASE. Also reviews nonfiction (50-50 fiction to nonfiction). Represents approximately 100-150 writers. Currently accepting only published authors, very few new clients. Obtains clients via recommendations, some queries. New/unpublished writers: 59%. Agent's commission: 10%. Member of S.A.R. and I.L.A.A.

**FLORENCE FEILER LITERARY AGENCY**, 1524 Sunset Plaza Dr., Los Angeles CA 90069. (213)652-6920, 659-0945. Novels. Special interests: most subjects. Query. Also reviews nonfiction (50-50 fiction to nonfiction). Represents approximately 50 writers. Obtains new clients via recommendations and "lectures given at various universities, colleges and writers' groups." Will handle only previously published authors. "I represent many published authors, fiction and nonfiction, film and television." Agent's commission: 10%.

**‡THE FILM/PUBLISHING GROUP AGENCY**, 11141 Wicks St., Sun Valley CA 91352. Contact: Vincent R. Ducette. Novels, biographies, autobiographies, manuscripts adaptable for books or films, plays; short story collections. Special interests: mainstream, children's, women's. Represents 15 writers. Query first. Also reviews nonfiction (85%-15% fiction to nonfiction). Obtains new clients via recommendations from others; solicitation; and queries. Presently accepting new clients. New/unpublished writers: 25%. Agent's commission: 10% domestic, 20% foreign. "Seeking new writers of present professional ability, high motivation and dedication as pro writers."

**THE FOLEY AGENCY**, 34 E. 38th St., New York NY 10016. (212)686-6930. Contact: Joan or Joe Foley. Novels. Query first with SASE. Also reviews nonfiction (30% fiction 70% nonfiction). Accepts very few new clients. Agent's commission: 10%.

**FRANKLIN/NATHAN AGENCY**, 386 Park Ave. S, New York NY 10016. (212)689-1842 or (212)685-0808. Contact: Ruth Nathan. Novels. Special interest: mainstream. Send outline/proposal. Represents approximately 20 writers. Obtains clients via recommendations and queries. Presently accepting new clients. Interested in new novelists. Agent's commission: 15%.

**JAY GARON-BROOKE ASSOCIATES, INC.**, 415 Central Park West, New York NY 10025. (212)866-3654. Contact: Jay Garon. "Mainstream, male action, adventure, frontier novels with authentic research, non-category horror novels, generational suspense sagas." Area of specialization: "whatever is selling at a given time; fiction and nonfiction." Query first; no phone calls. No magazine shorts or articles. Represents approximately 110 writers. Presently accepting new clients with credits via queries and recommendations only. New/unpublished writers: 10%. Agent's commission: 15% domestic; 30% foreign sales.

**‡MAX GARTENBERG, LITERARY AGENT**, 15 W. 44th St., New York NY 10036. (212)860-8451. Contact: Max Gartenberg. Novels. Special interests: mainstream, suspense and mystery novels. Represents 25 writers. Query. Also reviews nonfiction (50%-50% fiction to nonfiction). Obtains clients chiefly via queries and recommendations from others. Presently accepting new clients. "Approximately 20% of my sales each year are for new clients, who are rarely, however, unpublished writers." Agent's commission: 10%.

**GOODMAN ASSOCIATES**, 500 West End Ave., New York NY 10024. (212)873-4806. General adult fiction and nonfiction. Special interests: literary fiction, commercial contemporary novels, lead historicals, thrillers, mysteries. Limited interest in soft cover original genre books (romances, men's adventure, westerns, etc.). No science fiction, children's books, poetry, or short pieces. Written query; no unsolicited mss. Represents 50-60 writers. Accepting new clients on a very limited and selective basis. Agent's commission: 15% domestic; 20% foreign. Member of I.L.A.A.

**SANFORD J. GREENBURGER ASSOCIATES**, 55 5th Ave., New York NY 10003. (212)206-5600. Adult novels only (no short fiction, poetry). Send query letter and detailed description or approximately 50-page sample with synopsis of balance. Also reviews nonfiction (50/50 fiction to nonfiction). Presently accepting new clients. Interested in new/beginning novelists. Agent's commission: 15%. Member of I.L.A.A.

**REECE HALSEY AGENCY**, 8733 Sunset Blvd., Los Angeles CA. (213)OL2-2409. Query only with SASE. Also reviews nonfiction ("no set ratio"). Interested in new/beginning novelists but not presently accepting new clients. Agent's commission: 10%.

**JOHN HAWKINS & ASSOCIATES, INC.**, (formerly Paul R. Reynolds, Inc.), Suite 1600, 71 W. 23rd St., New York NY 10010. (212)807-7040. Novels, short stories and short story collections, periodicals, foreign rights, YA's and juvenile. Send cover letter, outline, samples. Also reviews nonfiction. Presently accepting new clients. Interested in new/beginning novelists. Agent's commission: 10%. Member of S.A.R.

**HEACOCK LITERARY AGENCY, INC.**, Suite 14, 1523 6th St., Santa Monica CA 90401. (213)451-8523 or 393-6227. Contact: James or Rosalie Heacock. Completed novels only by previously published authors. Query only if previously published. Must include SASE. Also reviews nonfiction (5/95% fiction to nonfiction). Represents 60-70 writers. Presently accepting new clients. Agent's commission: 15% of first $50,000 of earnings; thereafter 10%; 25% on foreign translations. Member of I.L.A.A. and Association of Talent Agents.

**HEINLE & HEINLE ENTERPRISES, INC.**, 29 Lexington Rd., Concord MA 01742. (617)369-4858. Contact: Beverly D. Heinle. Children's and young adult only. Prefers New England area writers. Query; then submit outline/proposal or outline plus sample chapters. Also reviews nonfiction (20%/80% fiction to nonfiction). Represents approximately 30 writers. Occasionally accepting new clients. Obtains clients via "word of mouth, listings." New/unpublished writers: 30%. Interested in previously published novelists. Agent's commission: 10%.

**‡HHM LITERARY AGENCY**, Box 1153, Rahway NJ 07065. (201)388-8167. Contact: Haes Hill Monroe. Novels. Special interests: mainstream, men's, women's, mystery. Represents 20 writers. Send query or outline plus sample chapters. Also reviews nonfiction (50%-50% fiction to nonfiction). Obtains new clients via recommendations from others; soliciation; via queries or unsolicited mss. Presently accepting new clients. "25% clients are unpublished." Agent's commission: 10% domestic, foreign 20%, dramatic 15%.

**FREDERICK HILL ASSOCIATES**, 2237 Union St., San Francisco CA 94123. (415)921-2910. Contact: Frederick Hill. Mainstream, fiction, young adult fiction and general nonfiction. No juveniles. Query. No unsolicited mss. Represents approximately 60 writers. Presently accepting new clients. Obtains clients mainly via recommendations, solicitations, and conferences. Agent's commission: 10%.

**HINTZ & FITZGERALD, INC. LITERARY AGENCY**, 207 E. Buffalo, Suite 211, Milwaukee WI 53202. (414)273-0300. Contact: Colleen Fitzgerald, Sandy Hintz. Novels. Special interests: mainstream, mysteries, thrillers and women's. Query or send outline/proposal. Also reviews nonfiction (75%/25% fiction to nonfiction). Represents 20 writers. Obtains new clients via recommendations from editors/authors; queries. Presently accepting new clients "but in small doses." New/unpublished writers: 10%. Agent's commission: 10%.

**‡THE INPRINT AGENCY**, 5495 Beltline Rd. #175, Dallas TX 75240. (214)661-1500. Contact: Henry Poirot, General Manager. Novels. Special interests: "all." Represents 12 writers. Query. Also reviews nonfiction (60%-40% fiction to nonfiction). "At the author's *request*, we provide editorial development." Obtains new clients via referrals. Presently accepting new clients. New/unpublished writers: 25%. Agent's commission: 15%, domestic and foreign. Member of I.L.A.A. "We are a new agency. We started in January, 1985."

**INTERNATIONAL CREATIVE MANAGEMENT**, 40 W. 57th St., New York NY 10019. (212)556-5600. Contact: Suzanne Gluck. Novels and novelettes. Query preferred; send outline plus sample chapters. Also reviews nonfiction. Presently accepting new clients. Interested in new/beginning novelists. Agent's commission: 10%; 15% British; 20% foreign. Unsolicited mss will not be accepted. Member of S.A.R.

**‡ASHER D. JASON ENTERPRISES, INC.**, 111 Barrow St., New York NY 10014. (212)929-2179. Contact: Asher Jason. Novels. Special interests: mainstream, women's, SF, romances, mystery, espionage. Represents 30 writers. Send outline plus 1 sample chapter. Also reviews nonfiction (25%-75% fiction to nonfiction). Obtains clients via referral, solicitation. Presently accepting new clients. New/unpublished writers: 25%. Agent's commission: 15%.

**JCA LITERARY AGENCY, INC.**, 242 W. 27th St., New York NY 10001. (212)807-0888. No short stories. Not presently accepting new clients. Photocopying charges only where applicable. Agent's commission: 10%. Member of S.A.R.

**JET LITERARY ASSOCIATES, INC.**, Suite 4A, 124 E. 84th St., New York NY 10028. (212)879-2578. Novels only. "Mainstream fiction and romances but author must have been published." Query with SASE. Also reviews nonfiction (50/50 fiction to nonfiction). Represents approximately 75 writers. Presently accepting new clients on a very selective basis. Obtains clients mainly via recommendations. New/unpublished writers: 10%. Agent's commission: 15%.

**‡KAMBRINA**, Box 16, Depoe Bay OR 97341. (503)764-3433. Contact: Kam Kavanaugh. Novels. Special interests: all adult fiction. Represents 37 writers. Query. Also reviews nonfiction (70-30% fiction to nonfiction). Obtains new clients via advertisement and referrals. Presently accepting new clients. New/unpublished writers: 80%. Agent's commission: 10%.

**VIRGINIA KIDD, LITERARY AGENT**, 538 E. Harford St., Milford PA 18337. (717)296-6205. Contact: Virginia Kidd. Novels, novellas, short stories, and short story collections. "I specialize in science fiction, but I do not limit myself to it." Query. Also reviews nonfiction (85%/15% fiction to nonfiction). Represents approximately 60 writers, 8 estates. "I receive queries all the time; I pass a very few on to the other four agents trained by me." Not presently accepting new clients. New/unpublished writers: "very few. Critieria are even more stringent within the last year. Our numbers are fewer, and everyone's list is full just now." Agent's commission: 10%.

**KIDDE, HOYT & PICARD**, 335 E. 51st St., New York NY 10022. (212)755-9461. Special interests: mainstream and literary fiction as well as romantic novels, some young adult. Query; send outline/proposal plus where published with what. Include postage for reply. Also represents published nonfiction authors (50 total). Interested in published authors only. Agent's commission: 10%.

**HARVEY KLINGER, INC.**, 301 W. 53rd St., New York NY 10019. (212)581-7068. Novels only. Query. Also reviews nonfiction (50-50 fiction and nonfiction). Presently accepting new clients. Interested in new/beginning novelists. Agent's commission: 15%.

**‡PAUL KOHNER, INC.**, 9169 Sunset Blvd., Los Angeles CA 90069. (213)550-1060. Contact: Gary Salt. Novels. Special interests: general fiction, likes true crime and mysteries; action *adventure*; no sci-fi, gothics or juveniles. Query. Also reviews nonfiction. Obtains clients via referrals. Presently accepting new clients. Agent's commission: 10%. "We mostly represent screen and TV writers. Some authors."

**‡BARBARA S. KOUTS, LITERARY AGENT**, 1465 3rd Ave., New York NY 10028. (212)628-0352. Contact: Barbara S. Kouts. Novels; novellas; short stories; short story collections. Special interests: literary, mainstream, women's, children's. Represents 50 writers. Query; send outline/proposal or outline plus 3 sample chapters. Also reviews nonfiction (50%-50% fiction to nonfiction). Obtains clients via recommendations from others, at conferences, by queries or unsolicited mss. Presently accepting new clients. New/unpublished writers: 90%. Agent's commission: 10%. Member I.L.A.A.

**‡LUCY KROLL AGENCY**, 390 West End Ave., New York NY 10024. (212)877-0556. Contact: Lucy Kroll, Kathe Telingator. Novels. Special interests: contemporary. Represents 25 writers (including playwrights and screenwriters). Query. Also reviews nonfiction (50%-50% fiction to nonfiction). Obtains new clients via recommendations from others; queries occasionally. "Not actively seeking new clients, but we take them on occasionally."

**BILL KRUGER LITERARY SERVICES**, Box 40887, St. Petersburg FL 33743. (813)381-5348. Contact: William F. Kruger. Novels, novelettes. Special interests: mainstream, science fiction, fantasy, adventure, intrigue, historical, young adult, and mystery. Query; submit outline plus 3 sample chapters. Also reviews nonfiction (3 to 1 fiction to nonfiction). Represents approximtely 25 writers. Obtains writers via recommendations, unsolicited mss, and queries. Presently accepting a few new clients. Interested in new/beginning novelists. New/unpublished writers: 50%. Agent's commission: 10% published writers, 15% nonpublished writers. "With non-published writers we request SASE until a sale is made; then it's on me."

**PETER LAMPACK AGENCY, INC.**, Suite 2015, 551 5th Ave., New York NY 10017. (212)687-9106. Novels, novelettes, motion pictures, television properties. Special interests: mainstream, women's, action/adventure, and literary fiction (but only if very accomplished). Written query only. Also reviews nonfiction (60/40 fiction to nonfiction). Represents approximately 75 writers. Presently accepting new clients. Interested in new/beginning novelists. New/beginning writers: 10%. Agent's commission: 15% US and Canada; 20% foreign rights.

**THE LANTZ OFFICE**, 888 7th Ave., New York NY 10106. (212)586-0200. Contact: Joy Harris. Special interest: mainstream. Also reviews nonfiction (50%/50% fiction to nonfiction). Represents 30 writers. Usually obtains new writers via recommendations and writer's conferences. Presently accepting new clients on limited basis. New/unpublished writers: 10%. Member of S.A.R.

**MICHAEL LARSEN/ELIZABETH POMADA LITERARY AGENTS**, 1029 Jones St., San Francisco CA 94109. Novels only. Query with SASE. "We don't really have special fiction interests. We read mainstream, women's contemporary fiction, romances, mysteries—anything we like. We do not handle children's or young adult books and do not adore westerns or science fiction." Also reviews nonfiction (E. Pomada does 90% fiction to 10% nonfiction; M. Larsen is just the reverse: 10% fiction to 90% nonfiction). Represents about 100 writers. "Clients come all ways—through recommendations from writers and editors, with queries, at conferences, and, most rarely, through our approaching them. New voices and new ideas are what we're looking for.

The quality of the writing, the freshness—and professionalism—count!" Presently accepting new clients. New/beginning writers: 50%. Agent's commission: 15%. Member of I.L.A.A.

**ELLEN LEVINE LITERARY AGENCY INC.**, Suite 1205, 432 Park Ave. S, New York NY 10016. (212)889-0620. Novels and nonfiction books. Query first; then outline (or sample chapters) if invited as a result of query. Approximately 50%-50% fiction/nonfiction. Presently accepting new clients if previously published. Agent's commission: 10%. Member of S.A.R and I.L.A.A.

**‡THE NORMA-LEWIS AGENCY**, 521 5th Ave., New York NY 10175. (212)751-4955. Contact: Norma Liebert. Novels; novellas. Special interest: children's books. Query. Also reviews nonfiction. Obtains clients via recommendations and queries. Presently accepting new clients. Agent's commission: 15%.

**‡PETER LIVINGSTON ASSOCIATES, INC.**, 947 Walnut St., Suite 800, Boulder CO 80302. (303)443-6877. Contact: Alice I. Price. Novels. Special interests: mainstream, thrillers, spy, adventure, mysteries. Represents about 100 writers active at any one time (fiction and nonfiction). Query or send brief outline plus 2 sample chapters. Also reviews nonfiction (30%-70% fiction to nonfiction). Obtains new clients mostly via recommendations from others, plus solicitation; at conferences; via queries or unsolicited mss. Presently accepting new clients. New/unpublished writers: 80%. Agent's commission: 15%. Member I.L.A.A. "We only handle full-length adult fiction with a potential for broad market appeal in hardcover edition through a major publisher."

**‡LONG ENTERPRISES**, Box 242108, Memphis TN 38124. Contact: Charles Long, Jr. Novels (primarily); short stories; short story collections. Special interests: horror/suspense (very interested), humor/satire, but not restricted. Represents 15 writers. Query first or send entire ms. Also reviews nonfiction (80%-20% fiction to nonfiction). Clients "now mostly people we know. Hope to get queries." Presently "in need of new clients!" New/unpublished writers: 90%. Agent's commission: 10%. "We accept photocopied manuscripts if readable, also computer disc containing manuscript if formatted for IBM PC, Zenith, IBM PC Jr., Sanyo 550, Apple II, Apple IIe, Radio Shack, Commodore 65, or Commodore 128."

**THE STERLING LORD AGENCY INC.**, 660 Madison Ave., New York NY 10021. (212)751-2533. Contact: Elizabeth Kaplan. Novels, nonfiction. Query first. Presently accepting new clients. Agent's commission: 10%. Member of S.A.R.

**BARBARA LOWENSTEIN ASSOCIATES**, Suite 714, 250 W. 57th St., New York NY 10107. (212)586-3825. Contact: Barbara Lowenstein or Eileen Fallon. Novels. Special interests: mainstream and romance. Query. Also reviews nonfiction. Presently accepting new clients. Agent's commission: 15%. Member of I.L.A.A.

**‡THE LUND AGENCY**, Suite 204, 6515 Sunset Blvd., Hollywood CA 90028. (213)466-8280. Contact: Cara Lund. Novels. Special interest: science fiction. Represents 20 writers. Send query/synopsis. Also reviews nonfiction (25%-75% fiction to nonfiction). Obtains new clients via recommendations from others and queries. Presently accepting new clients. New/unpublished writers: 20%. Agent's commission: 10-15%. "No unsolicited material will be read. Query letters only. SASE for answer. Short synopsis may be included."

**DONALD MacCAMPBELL INC.**, 12 E. 41st St., New York NY 10017. (212)683-5580. Novels only. Special interest: women's fiction. Query or send entire ms if encouraged on basis of query. Presently accepting no unpublished novelists. Agent's commission: 10% plus 5% on first sale.

**JANET WILKENS MANUS LITERARY AGENCY INC.**, Suite 906, 370 Lexington Ave., New York NY 10017. (212)685-9558. Novels, novellas, short stories, short story collections;

horror, mystery; hard and soft mainstream. Query; send outline/proposal or outline plus sample chapters. Also reviews nonfiction (50-50 fiction to nonfiction). Presently accepting new clients. Interested in new/beginning novelists. Agent's commission: 10% plus expenses. Member of I.L.A.A.

**ELAINE MARKSON LITERARY AGENCY**, 44 Greenwich Ave., New York NY 10011. (212)243-8480. Query letter first. *Do not* send unsolicited mss. "Authors should write to us (*don't call*) and we will respond." Also reviews nonfiction (about 50/50 fiction to nonfiction). Presently accepting new clients. ("Very rarely, but we do accept clients if we are very impressed with their potential.") Interested in new/beginning novelists. Agent's commission: 10%. Member of I.L.A.A.

**MARGARET McBRIDE LITERARY AGENCY**, Box 8730, La Jolla CA 92038. (619)459-0559. Contact: Winifred Golden, associate or Jane Duvall. Fiction and nonfiction for adult mainstream market. Prefers query letter. No unsolicited mss. Agent's commission: 15%. Member of I.L.A.A.

**RENATE B. McCARTER**, 823 Park Ave., New York NY 10021. Novels only. No science fiction. Query with SASE. No phone calls. Also reviews nonfiction (specializing in anthropology and archaeology). Interested in new novelists. Agent's commission: 10%.

**CLAUDIA MENZA LITERARY AGENCY**, 237 W. 11th St., New York NY 10014. (212)889-6850; (212) 741-3511. Contact: Claudia Menza. Novels and occasionally short story collections. "Fiction must set itself apart from the usual: prefer avant-garde, unique style with a good story. No children's or romance, nor strictly genre fiction." Query or send outline plus sample chapters. Also reviews quality nonfiction. Represents 25 writers. Presently accepting new clients. "Manuscripts must be accompanied by SASE or they cannot be returned." Agent's commission: 15%.

**HOWARD MORHAIM LITERARY AGENCY**, 501 5th Ave., New York NY 10017. (212)370-1585. Novels principally. Query. Also reviews nonfiction (70/30 fiction to nonfiction). Agent's commission: 10%. Member of I.L.A.A.

**WILLIAM MORRIS AGENCY, INC.**, 1350 Avenue of the Americas, New York NY 10019. (212)586-5100. Unsolicited authors send letter of inquiry with description of material and author's background. Reviews fiction and nonfiction. Very occasionally accepts new clients. Agent's commission: 10%. Member of S.A.R.

**HENRY MORRISON INC.**, Box 235, Bedford Hills NY 10507. (914)666-3500. Novels and screenplays only. Query only; no partials, no mss unless requested. Special interests: mainstream, some science fiction and mysteries. Also reviews nonfiction books. Represents 50 writers, mostly novelists. Accepting new clients only with recommendation and direct submission with queries. New/unpublished writers: 6%. Agent's commission: 15%.

**MORTON AGENCY INC.**, 1105 Glendon Ave., Los Angeles CA 90024. (213)824-4089. Novels, TV, and motion pictures. Special interest: mainstream. Query; send outline/proposal or outline plus sample chapters. Also reviews nonfiction (50-50 fiction to nonfiction). Represents 15-20 clients. Accepting new clients by recommendation only. New/unpublished writers: 15%. Agent's commission: 10%.

**MARVIN MOSS, INC.**, #601, 9200 Sunset Blvd., Los Angeles CA 90069. (213)274-8483. Novels. Mainstream, mystery, no children's books. Query. Also reviews nonfiction (50-50 fiction to nonfiction). Represents approximately 30 writers. Presently accepting new clients. Obtains clients mainly via recommendations. Agent's commission: 10%. "Will not accept any material without a release on our form. Interested in books that could be potential features or TV movies—but not ideas for TV series."

**MULTIMEDIA PRODUCT DEVELOPMENT, INC.**, Suite 724, 410 S. Michigan Ave., Chicago IL 60605. (312)922-3063. Contact: Jane Jordan Browne. Novels only. "Our focus is mainstream, but we also do genre books." Query with SASE. Also reviews nonfiction (65% nonfiction; 35% fiction). Represents approximately 75 writers. "Generally we obtain clients through the recommendation of other clients, and via conferences. However, we take on at least a few each year through unsolicited query letters." Presently accepting new clients. New/unpublished writers: approximately 10%. Agent's commission: 15%, 20% foreign rights. Member of I.L.A.A.

**JEAN V. NAGGAR LITERARY AGENCY**, 336 E. 73rd St., New York NY 10021. (212)794-1082. Novels and nonfiction. Special interests: mainstream fiction (literary and commercial), suspense, science fiction, women's, and mystery. Query with SASE. Represents 80 writers. Obtains clients via recommendations, solicited mss, queries, and writers' conferences. Presently accepting new clients only on a selective basis. Interested in some new/beginning novelists. Agent's commission: 15% domestic; 20% foreign authors. Member of I.L.A.A.

**CHARLES NEIGHBORS, INC.**, Suite 3607, 7600 Blanco Rd., San Antonio TX 78216. (512)342-5324. Novels only. Interested in "virtually everything except younger juvenile works (young adult OK—no picture books)." Send outline plus sample chapters, with SASE. Also reviews nonfiction (about 2 to 1 fiction to nonfiction). Represents about 50 writers. Obtains clients via recommendations from clients and editors: 65%; conferences: 25%; solicitation: 5%; queries: 3-5%. Presently accepting new clients. New/unpublished writers: 15%, "and I work very closely with them on rewriting and revising." Maintains New York branch office established in 1966 for frequent marketing trips. Texas office set up in 1982. Agent's commission: 15%.

**NEW WAVE, Author's Representative**, 2544 N. Monticello Ave., Chicago IL 60647. (312)342-3338. Contact: Gene Lovitz. Special interests: adult trade novels that deal with mainstream subjects; experimental (horror, mysteries, sex, gothic); and regency romances. Send queries with SASE. Also reviews nonfiction (50%/50% fiction to nonfiction). "No evaluation fee charges. We charge for editorial assistance *if the author so requests*." Represents over 300 writers including Joseph R. Rosenberger (*Death Merchant* series) and Paul H. Little (with 550 titles and 20 pseudonyms). Obtains new clients via referrals and directory listings mainly. Presently accepting new clients. New/unpublished writers: 75% (the idea of New Wave). Agent's commission: 10% domestic; 20% foreign. "We are now looking for 400-500 page historical romance novels with explicit sex, as well as non-hard-boiled mysteries *sans* super sex and violence that build on suspense instead of the seedy."

**THE BETSY NOLAN LITERARY AGENCY**, 215 Park Ave. S., New York NY 10003. (212)420-6000. Contact: Betsy Nolan; Michael Powers. Special interests: mainstream, humor, and women's ("but not romance"). Send outline/proposal. Also reviews nonfiction (25-75 fiction to nonfiction). Represents 30-40 writers. Presently accepting new clients. Obtains clients usually by word of mouth. New/beginning writers: 40%. Agent's commission: 15-25%.

**MARY NOVIK LITERARY AGENT**, 5519 Deerhorn Lane, North Vancouver, British Columbia V7R 4S8 Canada. Romance novels only. Area of specialization: contemporary category romance. No historical, mainstream or gothic novels. "Query letter with outline best. Include SASE, IRC." Presently accepting new clients. Agent's commission: 10% on North American sales, 20% on foreign. "Information about agency available if IRC or SASE sent (Canadian postage only or check to cover return postage)."

**HAROLD OBER ASSOCIATES, INCORPORATED**, 40 E. 49th St., New York NY 10017. (212)759-8600. Novels and general nonfiction. Reads all kinds, category and mainstream. Query first. About 75-25 fiction to nonfiction. Presently accepting new clients but very limited numbers. (Represents British agencies also.) Agent's commission: 10% US; 15% British; 20% other foreign. Member of S.A.R.

**FIFI OSCARD ASSOCIATES**, 19 W. 44th St., New York NY 10036. (212)764-1100. Contact: Ivy Fischer Stone. Novels and nonfiction. Presently accepting new clients. Query first. Writer must demonstrate a minimum number of sales for acceptance. Agent's commission: 15%. Member of S.A.R.

**JOHN K. PAYNE LITERARY AGENCY, INC.**, Room 1101, 175 5th Ave., New York NY 10010. (212)475-6447. Nonfiction and fiction. Query first. Agent's commission: 10%.

**RAY PEEKNER LITERARY AGENCY**, 3210 S. 7th St., Milwaukee WI 53215. Contact: Ray Puechner. Novels only. Special interests: mystery (private-eye), western (quality westerns), and young adult novels. Query. Also reviews nonfiction (80/20 fiction to nonfiction). Represents 50-60 writers. Not presently accepting new clients. Agent's commission: 10%.

**RODNEY PELTER, LITERARY AGENT**, 129 E. 61st St., New York NY 10021. (212)838-3432. Contact: Rodney Pelter. All fiction and nonfiction. Query with SASE, résumé and first 50 pages. Represents 15-25 writers. Obtains clients via recommendations, unsolicited mss, and queries. Presently accepting new clients. New/unpublished writers: "probably a majority." Agent's commission "varies, depending on size of the advance and is graduated downward in accordance with total earnings of each book."

**JOHN PICKERING ASSOCIATES**, 425 Riverside Dr., New York NY 10025. (212)662-0816. Contact: John Pickering, A. Elizabeth Davidson, or Charna Klau. Novels, novellas, and short story collections. Special interests: "experimental/innovative; women's and men's (urban/rural) interactions; mysteries and thrillers." Query. Also reviews nonfiction (50%/50% fiction to nonfiction). Represents 20 writers. Usually obtains clients via recommendations, "but I sometimes write to writers I admire, and am always glad for queries." Presently accepting new clients. New/unpublished writers: 20%. Agent's commission: 10%; standard split on foreign rights.

**FROMMER PRICE INC.**, 185 E. 85th St., New York NY 10028. (212)289-0589. Contact: Diana Price. Adult novels only. Area of specialization: mainstream/literary, women's fiction; no category. Query; send outline/proposal or outline plus sample chapters. Also reviews nonfiction (30/70 fiction to nonfiction). Represents 60 writers. Obtains clients generally via recommendations. Presently accepting new clients. New/unpublished writers: 5%. Agent's commission: 15%.

**THE AARON M. PRIEST LITERARY AGENCY INC.**, 565 5th Ave., New York NY 10017. (212)818-0344. Contact: Aaron Priest or Molly Friedrich. Fiction and nonfiction. Presently accepting new clients. Agent's commission: 10% (foreign mailing and copying charged to author). Send SASE with ms.

**‡HELEN REES LITERARY AGENCY**, 308 Commonwealth Ave., Boston MA 02116. (617)262-2401. Contact: Helen Rees. Novels. Special interests: mainstream, mysteries, literary. Agency represents 50 writers. Query. Also reviews nonfiction (15%-85% fiction to nonfiction). Obtains new clients via recommendations and solicitations. Presently accepting new clients. New/unpublished writers: 30%. Agent's commission: 15%. Member of I.L.A.A.

**RHODES LITERARY AGENCY, INC.**, 140 West End Ave., New York NY 10023. (212)580-1300. Contact: Joseph Rhodes. Novels. Query with SASE. Also reviews nonfiction (50%-50% fiction to nonfiction). Presently accepting new clients. Agent's commission: 10%. Member of I.L.A.A.

**THE ROBBINS OFFICE, INC.**, (formerly Robbins & Covey Association), 12th Floor, 2 Dag Hammarskjold Plaza, 866 2nd Ave., New York NY 10017. (212)223-0720. Novels and short story collections. Query first with SASE. "No unsolicited mss accepted. Only accepts material from previously published or referred writers." Also reviews nonfiction (1 to 3 fiction to nonfiction). Presently accepting new clients. Interested in new/beginning novelists. Agent's commission: 15%.

**MARIE RODELL-FRANCES COLLIN LITERARY AGENCY**, 110 W. 40th St., New York NY 10018. Area of specialization: general adult trade books. Query with SASE. 50-50 fiction to nonfiction. Agent's commission: 12%; 25% overseas. Member of S.A.R.

**ELEANOR MERRYMAN ROSZEL ROGERS**, 1487 Generals Highway, Crownsville MD 21032. (301)987-8166. Contact: E.M. Roszel. Special interests: mainstream, espionage, and children's; "no science fiction or Harlequin-types." Query first. Reviews fiction and nonfiction "about half and half." Represents 15-20 writers. Obtains clients via recommendations from publishers, other clients, and various reference books. Agent's commission: 10%. "Queries and unsolicited mss should come with SASE; otherwise I shall not respond."

**IRENE ROGERS LITERARY REPRESENTATION**, Suite 850, 9701 Wilshire Blvd., Beverly Hills CA 90212. (213)837-3511. Novels. Query or send outline/proposal. Also reviews nonfiction (50-50 fiction to nonfiction). Presently accepting new clients. "I accept only a few new clients each year, but am open to query." Interested in new/beginning novelists. Agent's commission: 10%.

**ROSENSTONE/WENDER**, 3 E. 48th St., New York NY 10017. (212)832-8330. Novels, novelettes, short stories, short story collections, plays and screenplays. Query. Does not accept unsolicited mss. Also reviews nonfiction (50/50 fiction to nonfiction). Presently accepting new clients. Agent's commission: 10%. Member of S.A.R.

**JANE ROTROSEN AGENCY**, 226 E. 32nd St., New York NY 10016. (212)889-7133. Agents: Jane Rotrosen Berkey; Donald Cleary; Andrea Cirillo; Margaret Ruley. Query with SASE. Fiction and nonfiction (60-40 fiction to nonfiction). Special interests: commercial fiction. Represents 130+ writers. "We are most interested in people who would like to make a career of writing. Many new clients are referred by authors already under representation." Presently accepting new clients. "We are certainly open to hearing from unpublished writers." Agent's commission: 15%. Member of I.L.A.A. Represented abroad and on the West Coast.

**RUSSELL & VOLKENING, INC.**, 50 W. 29th St., New York NY 10001. (212)684-6050. Novels, nonfiction and short stories. Send query letter with SASE. SASE for all mss also. Agent's commission: 10%. Member of S.A.R. Agents in all countries.

**GLORIA SAFIER, INC.**, 244 E. 53rd St., New York NY 10022. (212)838-4868. Contact: Teresa Cavanaugh. Novels. Query or send outline/proposal. Also reviews nonfiction (80%/20% fiction to nonfiction). Represents 30 writers. Usually obtains new clients via queries and recommendations. Presently accepting new clients. Agent's commission: 15%. Member of S.A.R.

**RAPHAEL SAGALYN, INC., LITERARY AGENCY**, 2813 Bellevue Terrace NW, Washington DC 20007. Member of I.L.A.A. "I am not accepting/encouraging unsolicited mss now."

**JOHN SCHAFFNER ASSOCIATES, INC.**, 114 E. 28th St., New York NY 10016. Query only. Presently accepting new clients. Agent's commission: 10%. Requires $5 for postage on return envelope. Member of S.A.R.

**HAROLD SCHMIDT LITERARY AGENCY**, 347 E. 53rd St., #LC, New York NY 10022. (212)752-7037. Contact: Harold Schmidt. Novels, novellas, short stories, and short story collections. "All polished, quality writing." Query with SASE. Also reviews nonfiction (60%/40% fiction to nonfiction). Represents 20 writers. Obtains new clients via recommendations from others and solicitations primarily. Interested in new/beginning clients. New/unpublished writers 25%. Agent's commission: 15% plus. "Once a client is accepted for representation, client is responsible for paying any necessary long distance calls, copying charges, messenger fees, etc. incurred by us in handling his/her work."

**ARTHUR P. SCHWARTZ**, 435 Riverside Dr., New York NY 10025. Novels only. Area of specialization: commercially-oriented fiction (i.e., frank, realistic sex and themes), adult-oriented romantic fiction, mainstream, family sagas, women's historical, contemporary romantic fiction, and science fiction. No "Harlequin" type books. Represents approximately 70 writers. Query. ("Do not register, certify or insure; retain original ms for your file. Enclose ms-size SASE.") Also reviews nonfiction (1-2 fiction to nonfiction). Presently accepting new clients. New/unpublished writers: ⅓ of total. Agent's commission: 12½%. Member of I.L.A.A.

**FRANCES SCHWARTZ LITERARY AGENCY**, Suite 413, 60 E. 42nd St., New York NY 10017. (212)661-2881. Fiction and nonfiction. Query by letter only with SASE. Presently accepting new clients.

**JAMES SELIGMANN AGENCY**, Suite 1101, 175 5th Ave., New York NY 10010. (212)477-5186. Novels and novelettes, mainstream; but absolutely no mysteries, science fiction, fantasy or suspense. Query; send outline/proposal or outline with sample chapters. Also reviews nonfiction (50-50 fiction to nonfiction). Represents approximately 50 writers. Accepting new clients via recommendations and queries. Agent's commission: 15%. Member of S.A.R.

**BOBBE SIEGEL, RIGHTS REPRESENTATIVE**, 41 W. 83rd St., New York NY 10024. (212)877-4985. Contact: Bobbe Siegel. Fiction and nonfiction. Special interests: mainstream, women's, science fiction, mystery, and literary. Query first. Also reviews nonfiction (65% fiction to 35% nonfiction). Represents about 60 writers. Obtains clients mainly via recommendations of authors and editors. Presently accepting new clients. New/unpublished writers: about 50%. Agent's commission: 15%. "We will suggest the names of very good editors who would be willing, for a fee, to either critique or work with an author on redoing a work."

**ROSALIE SIEGEL, INTERNATIONAL LITERARY AGENT, INC.**, 111 Murphy Dr., Pennington NJ 08534. (609)737-1007. Contact: Rosalie Siegel. Novels, novellas, short stories, short story collections. Special interests: mainstream, quality fiction, some young adult. Represents 35 writers. Query or send entire ms. Also reviews nonfiction (75%-25% fiction to nonfiction). "I am very selective about asking to see a manuscript; I read about 5 new manuscripts a week." Obtains clients via recommendations from other writers or editors. 50% new unpublished writers. Agent's commission: 10%. Member of I.L.A.A. "I run a one-woman agency, alone, with part-time secretarial help. Half my writers are European and therefore the American contingent is small. I'd like to have more American authors, but I've never found anything I really like from total strangers sending queries."

**‡EVELYN SINGER LITERARY AGENCY**, Box 594, White Plains NY 10602. Contact: Evelyn Singer. Novels. Special interests: good fiction/suspense, science fiction, contemporary romance/adult and young adult and children (no picture books). Represents over 75 writers. Query or send outline plus sample chapters. Also reviews nonfiction (25%-75% fiction to nonfiction). "We require SASE and/or stamped, self-addressed wrapper for ms. We do not return or answer unsolicited mail that has not enclosed SASE." Obtains clients via recommendations from editors and writers. Presently accepting new clients. New/unpublished writers: 20%. Agent's commission: 10%; 20% foreign and where co-agent is involved. "A professional-looking ms is helpful (typed, double-spaced)."

**ELYSE SOMMER, INC.**, Author's Representative, 962 Allen Lane, Box E, Woodmere LI NY 11598. (516)295-0046. Area of specialization: bestseller types: family sagas, some mysteries. No westerns, science fiction, futuristic books. Send outline plus 2 sample chapters with SASE. Entire manuscript should be available. "Send cover letter explaining status of ms—complete, partially finished, any previous marketing efforts." Also reviews nonfiction (1-4 fiction to nonfiction). Presently accepting new clients. Interested in new/beginning novelists and fiction only if "ms is unusual." Agent's commission: 10-15%. Member of I.L.A.A.

**PHILIP G. SPITZER LITERARY AGENCY**, 1465 3rd Ave., New York NY 10028. (212)628-0352. Novels. Query. Also reviews nonfiction (50-50 fiction to nonfiction). Seldom accepts new clients. Agent's commission: 10%. Member of S.A.R.

**CHARLES M. STERN ASSOCIATES**, Box 32742, San Antonio TX 78216. (512)349-6141. Novels, nonfiction and how-to. Special interests: mainstream, women's, romance, mystery and screenplays. Send query with SASE and/or send outline/proposal. Represents approximately 30+ writers. Obtains clients via recommendations and queries. Presently accepting new clients. Interested in new/unpublished novelists/writers. New/unpublished writers: 65%. Agent's commission: 15%. "Return postage must accompany every query or submission. Phone calls made to authors to discuss their work will be made collect."

**GLORIA STERN AGENCY**, 1230 Park Ave., New York NY 10028. (212)289-7698. Area of specialization: mainstream, women's, serious fiction suitable for original hardcover novel. Send short outline/proposal and writer's background and SASE for answer. Also reviews nonfiction (20-80% fiction to nonfiction). Represents 35 writers. Presently accepting few new clients (1/month). "Must have published articles or short stories and have some writing background. I am taking fewer first-fiction manuscripts." Obtains clients via recommendations and queries. Interested in new/beginning novelists. New/unpublished writers: 10%. Agent's commission: 10-15%. Member of I.L.A.A. Detailed critique for fee.

**LARRY STERNIG LITERARY AGENCY**, 742 Robertson St., Milwaukee WI 53213. Not presently accepting new clients.

**JO STEWART AGENCY**, 201 E. 66th St., New York NY 10021. (212)879-1301. Novels and nonfiction. Special interests: mainstream, women's, romance, and mystery/suspense. Presently accepting new clients. Obtains clients through other writers, editors and listings. Interested in new/beginning novelists. Agent's commission: 15%. Member of S.A.R.

**GUNTHER STUHLMANN AUTHOR'S REPRESENTATIVE**, Box 276, Becket MA 01223. Novels and nonfiction books (no unsolicited mss). Area of specialization: high quality; no SF/detective/adventure. Query with SASE. Presently accepting new clients but "very few, usually up-on recommendation." Interested in new/beginning novelists "if extremely talented." Agent's commission: 10% US and Canada; 15% Britain and Commonwealth; 20% elsewhere.

**‡THE LAURIE TAG AGENCY**, 1300 Seaport Lane, Alexandria VA 22314. (703)683-3736. Contact: Laurie Dustman Tag. Novels. Special interests: mainstream, women's, romance. Represents 25 writers. Sends outline plus 1 sample chapter. Also reviews nonfiction (30%-70% fiction to nonfiction). Obtains new clients via recommendations from current clients and editors. Presently accepting new clients. New/unpublished writers: 10%. Agent's commission: 10%.

**ROSLYN TARG LITERARY AGENCY, INC.**, 105 W. 13th St., New York NY 10011. (212)206-9390. Must send query letter with SASE. Presently accepting very few new clients. Considers both fiction and nonfiction. Agent's commission: 15% "on all new unpublished authors I take on." Member of S.A.R. and I.L.A.A.

**TEAL & WATT LITERARY AGENCY**, 2036 Vista Del Rosa, Fullerton CA 92631. (714)738-8333. Contact: Patricia Teal. Category novels only. Area of specialization: romance novels (sub-specialty). Send outline plus 3 sample chapters. Also reviews nonfiction (2-1 fiction to nonfiction). Presently accepting new clients. Agent's commission: 15%. SASE, a must!

**THOMPSON & CHRIS LITERARY AGENCY**, 3926 Sacramento St., San Francisco CA 94118. (415)386-2443. Contact: Teresa Chris. Novels. Special interests: mainstream and mystery. "A clear query with SASE first is appreciated," or send outline/proposal or outline plus sample chapters with SASE. Also reviews nonfiction (30%/70% fiction to nonfiction). Represents 45 writers. Obtains new clients via recommendations from clients and publishers. Presently accepting new clients. New/unpublished writers: 60%. Agent's commission: 15%; (foreign/film 15/20%).

**SUSAN URSTADT INC.,** 125 E. 84th St., New York NY 10028. (212)744-6605. Interested in quality fiction, both commercial and literary; also mysteries, young adult, and children's. No science fiction, romance or occult. Send query with outline/proposal; sample chapter and author bio. SASE. Also reviews nonfiction (25-75 fiction to nonfiction). Represents approximately 30 writers. Obtains clients generally via recommendations. Presently accepting new clients. Interested in new/beginning novelists "if very good." New/unpublished writers: 10-15%. Agent's commission: 10%. Member of I.L.A.A.

**VENICE LITERARY AGENCY,** 177 Golf Club Lane, Venice FL 33595. (813)493-2632. Contact: Jo Ann Moser. Novels, inspirational romances. "My field is in the Christian fiction romance line." Represents about 40 writers. Obtains clients usually via recommendations. Send entire ms with SASE. Presently accepting new clients. Interested in new/beginning novelists. New/unpublished writers: 25%. Agent's commission: 10%. "I like working with beginning writers; they are so eager to work and learn. I do not review any work that is offensive."

**AUSTIN WAHL AGENCY, INC.,** 342 Monadnock Bldg., 53 W. Jackson Blvd., Chicago IL 60604. (312)922-3331. Contact: Jason Liss. Motion picture properties and novels only. Send query with outline and first chapter. Specializes in contemporary novels, mysteries, romances, and westerns. Also handles nonfiction. No complete unsolicited mss. Represents 250 writers. Obtains clients usually via recommendations and queries, occasionally conferences. Author must have at least one recent book publication or film credit. Agent's commission: 10% motion pictures and 15% books.

**‡MARY JACK WALD ASSOCIATES, INC.,** Suite 325, 799 Broadway, New York NY 10003. (212)982-0072. Contact: Mary Jack Wald. Novels, short story collections. Special interests: mainstream and women's. Represents 40-50 writers including subsidiary rights. Send a query; then sample chapters. Also reviews nonfiction (50%-50% fiction to nonfiction). Obtains new clients via recommendations from others. Presently accepting new clients. The majority of clients are new/published writers. Agent's commission: 15%.

**JOHN A. WARE LITERARY AGENCY,** 392 Central Park West, New York NY 10025. (212)866-4733. Novels and short story collections. Special interests: mainstream, literary and mystery. Query letter first. Also reviews nonfiction (approximately 50-50 fiction to nonfiction). Represents 50 writers. Obtains new clients via recommendations from clients and editors, conferences, queries. Presently accepting new clients. New/unpublished writers: 50%. Agent's commission: 10%.

**CHERRY WEINER LITERARY AGENCY,** 28 Kipling Way, Manalapan NJ 07726. (201)446-2096. Partials and full-length mss marketed. Special interests: mainstream, women's, science fiction, romance, and mystery. Query only; no unsolicited manuscripts. Also does some nonfiction (85% fiction). Represents 50 writers. Obtains clients usually via recommendations. New/unpublished writers: 25%. Agent's commission: 15%.

**RHODA WEYR AGENCY,** 216 Vance St., Chapel Hill NC 27514. (919)942-0770. Novels. Query or send outline plus sample chapters. "The query letter should give any relevant information about the author and her/his work, publishing history, etc." Also represents nonfiction (about equal fiction to nonfiction). Presently accepting new clients. Interested in both fiction and nonfiction writers. Agent's commission: 10% for domestic; 20% foreign. Member of SAR and I.L.A.A. "Send letter/material, etc., with SASE—not checks and not just stamps!"

**‡RUTH WRESCHNER, AUTHORS' REPRESENTATIVE**, 10 W. 74th St., New York NY 10023. (212)877-2605. Contact: Ruth Wreschner. Novels; short story collections by well-known writers. Special interests: mainstream, both adult and young adult, women's, science fiction, historical fiction, thrillers, mysteries. Represents about 40 writers. Send query; outline/proposal; or outline plus sample chapters. Also reviews nonfiction. "I review both fiction and nonfiction but place far more nonfiction." Unpublished client pays photocopying expenses. Obtains clients mostly by recommendations; "sometimes I look for the right author for a saleable project, the latter, of course, for nonfiction." Presently accepting new clients. New unpublished writers about 80%. Agent's commission: 15%.

**WRITERS HOUSE, INC.**, 21 W. 26th St., New York NY 10010. Novels only. Area of specialization: contemporary, women's, thrillers, science fiction, fantasy, young adult, among others— "wonderful writing in all categories." Send outline plus 3 sample chapters and writing background. Also reviews nonfiction (75% fiction). Represents around 150 writers. Usually obtains clients via recommendations. Presently accepting a few new clients and also some juvenile illustrators. Interested in new novelists "who already have published short fiction or a novel or two." Member of I.L.A.A.

**WRITERS' PRODUCTIONS**, Box 5152, Westport CT 06881. (203)227-8199. Contact: David L. Meth. Book length fiction and nonfiction. Send outline plus sample chapters. Reviews "much more fiction." Presently accepting new clients. Interested in new/beginning novelists. Agent's commission: 15% domestic literary and dramatic sales—20% on foreign sales. "Send a sample of 25-50 pages only with SASE for return of ms. Clean, professional copies only. No phone calls, please. Literary quality fiction only. We have a special interest in work by Asian Americans; about Southeast Asia and the Far East. It should be insightful and sensitively written."

**‡MARY YOST ASSOCIATES**, 59 E. 54th St., New York NY 10022. (212)980-4988. Contact: Mary Yost. Novels. Special interests: mainstream, women's. Query or send outline plus 50 pages. Also reviews nonfiction (40%-60% fiction to nonfiction). Obtains new clients via recommendations from clients, editors, a few unsolicited mss. Presently accepting new clients. Agent's commission: 10%. Member of S.A.R.

**SUSAN ZECKENDORF ASSOC., INC.**, 171 W. 57th St., New York NY 10019. (212)245-2928. Contact: Susan Zeckendorf. Special interests: mainstream, women's, thrillers, mysteries, and literary fiction. Query; send outline/proposal or outline plus sample chapters. Reviews nonfiction (50% fiction). Represents 35 writers. Obtains clients via recommendations, solicitations, queries. Presently accepting new clients. New/unpublished writers: 50%. Agent's commission: 15%. Member of I.L.A.A.

**TOM ZELASKY LITERARY AGENCY**, 3138 Parkridge Crescent, Chamblee GA 30341. (404)458-0391. Novels, novelettes, short story collections. Special interests: romance, love and adventure stories, mainstream endeavors. Query or send outline/proposal with SASE. Also reviews nonfiction. Obtains clients mainly via queries, unsolicited mss, and listings. Presently accepting new clients. Interested in new/beginning novelists. New/unpublished writers: 75%. Agent's commission: 10-15%. "In some cases I provide criticism service concerning techniques used in writer's work. No fee is charged."

> " *The first page sells that book. The last page sells the next book.*
> —Mickey Spillane "

# Close-up

### David L. Meth
### Writers' Productions

In the past David Meth lived and worked in the Orient. While there he developed an interest in the people and culture, an interest that followed him back to the States and became an important part of his work.

Meth's work is a small literary agency, Writers' Productions, which he operates out of his home in Westport, Connecticut. The writers he represents are not trendy in their work. "I deal with a lot of material on the Orient, written by authors of Asian background." Meth also represents black writers. "I feel that these authors and this work are under represented."

Meth started Writers' Productions in 1981, picking up clients from press releases in various literary journals, word of mouth, and referrals from the New York based International Women's Writing Guild, which he still works with. "Like many agents, we came in the back door. I got started because of my interest in literature and writers." Meth, assisted only by his wife, handles 24 clients, mostly novelists—including Mary Monroe, JoAnne Brasil, and J. California Cooper. A small client list affords the opportunity for Meth to work on his writer/agent relationships. "I like the people to be my friends."

Meth works with his writers and their manuscripts on what he calls primary editing. If characters need filling out or a plot needs tightening, he works on such weaknesses with authors. This shaping and polishing takes place before a manuscript graces an editor's desk.

Writers' Productions doesn't charge reading fees. Meth feels agents should be in the business to sell books without charging fees. When a writer's manuscript is ready to sell, Meth queries the appropriate editor by phone, then by letter with the manuscript. New editor and publisher contacts are usually made through luncheons where Meth and editors explore the possibility of any common literary needs.

Meth advises new writers to work on their

manuscript "to the point where it's as perfect as it can be. Then, query agents." When writers query, they should include the first 25 or 30 pages of their manuscript, and a very brief cover letter. It is Meth's opinion that the most common problem with first novelists is their too often use of narrative to explain the story to the reader. "They don't let the characters reveal themselves through dialogue or plot."

Meth pitches manuscripts to commercial houses and independent presses which can offer advances to help his writers earn, or partially earn, a living and/or establish their reputation. Meth is working with JoAnne Brasil, who first published *Escape From Billy's Barbeque* with Alice Walker's Wild Trees Press, on her next novel. Also, St. Martin's Press will publish J. California Cooper's short story collection, *Homemade Love.*

One drawback in going to some publishers is having to overcome what Meth terms "commercial mentality." Editors might like the material he represents, but doubt its ability to sell. This brings up Meth's major concern: "The country is not being well represented in the publishing world, in terms of the diversity of its population." He says, "I would like to see editors and publishers start to look at America through different eyes, not just white Caucasian eyes."

*—Katherine Jobst*

# Category Index

The category index is a good starting point in your search for a market for your fiction.

Below you will find an alphabetized list of subjects containing the magazines, publishers and agents that buy or accept special categories of fiction. This year there are five sections represented individually—literary/little magazines, commercial periodicals, small press, commercial publishers and literary agents.

If you have a manuscript or an idea for a children's novel, for example, check the small press and commercial publishers (or agents) sections under Juvenile. After you have selected a possible publisher, look it up in the general index for the correct page number. Then find the listing and read it *carefully*.

The subject index is a very *general* guide to help save you time in your marketing process. Therefore we do not recommend that you use it exclusively. Many publications or presses, and particularly agents, are non-specific in their interests and prefer not to be listed—or limited—by categories; their specification may be *quality* fiction only, to include literary or mainstream work or all categories.

## Literary/Little Magazines

**Adventure** Allegheny Review; Amelia; Amherst Review; Artful Codger and Codgerette; Ball State Univ. Forum; Black Jack; Blueline; Breathless; Calli's Tales; Canadian Author & Bookman; Candle; Chunga Review; Cold-Drill; Cross Timbers Review; Cut Bank; Dan River; Door County Almanak; Earth's Daughters; Earthwise Quarterly; Event; Fag Rag; Fantasy Book; Fine Madness; Fighting Woman News; Footwork; Galactic Discourse; Green Feather; Hibiscus; Hob-Nob; Il Caffé; "In a Different Reality . . ."; Inky Trails Publication; Japanophile; Jeopardy; Journals of Regional Criticism; Joyful Noise; Little Balkans Review; Maat; Magical Blend; Menomonie Review; Merlyn's Pen; Muscadine; Negative Capability; New England Sampler; New Oregon Review; New Southern Literary Messenger; Nimrod; Passion For Industry; Permafrost; Potboiler; Prelude to Fantasy; Proof Rock; Pteranodon; The Pub; Pulpsmith; Queen's Quarterly; Rambunctious Review; Redneck Review of Literature; Reflect; RFD; River City Review; Roadwerk; Solome; Security Check; Sovereign Gold Literary; Space and Time; Orion; Street; Time to Pause; Uncle; Village Idiot; Villager; Vintage North West; Virginia Quarterly Review; Waves; Worlds of Wonder; Writer's Gazette; Writers West.

**Condensed Novel** Ball State Univ. Forum; Helicon Nine; Hob-Nob; Il Caffé; "In a Different Reality . . ."; Maat; Metamorfosis; Pinchpenny; The Pub; Security Check; Street; Vintage North West; Western Humanities Review; Wind Row.

**Confession** Allegheny Review; Amherst Review; Ball State Univ. Forum; Confrontation; Fag Rag; Handicap News; Il Caffé; Jeopardy; Mauscape; Passion For Industry; Processed World; Rambunctious Review; Spitball; Unspeakable Visions of the Individual; Village Idiot; Whiskey Island; Witt Review.

**Contemporary** Adrift; Agada; Ahnene Publications; Alaska Quarterly Review; Allegheny Review; Amelia; Amherst Review; Antaeus; Antietam Review; Antigonish Review; Antioch Review; Appalachee Quarterly; Arba Sicula; Arizona Quarterly; Artful Codger and Codgerette; Aura; Azorian Express; Backbone; Ball State Univ. Forum; B-City; Bellingham Review; Bellowing Ark; Beloit Fiction Journal; Black Jack; Black Scholar; Black Warrior Review; Bloomsbury Review; Blueline; Bogg; Bogus Review; Boston Review; Box 749; Breathless; Buff; California Quarterly; Callaloo; Calliope; Canadian Author & Bookman; Capilano Review; Central Park; Chariton Review; Chattahoochee Review; Chelsea; Chicago Review; Chiricu; Chunga Review; Cimarron Review; City Paper; Clifton; Clock Radio; Clockwatch Review; Cold-Drill; Colorado-North Review; Colorado Review; Confluent Education Journal; Confrontation; Corona; Cottonwood; Crab Creek Review; Cream City Review; Crescent Review; Critique; Crop Dust; Croton Review; Cut Bank; Dan River; Denver Quarterly; Descant; Descant [Canada]; Door County Almanak; Earth's Daughters; Earthwise Quarterly; Encounter; Epoch; Event; Exit; Farmer's Market; Fine Madness; FM Five; Florida Review; Fruition; Gamut; The Gamut; Gargoyle; Georgia Review; Grain; Green Feather; Greensboro Review; Handicap News; Hawaii Review; Helicon Nine; Hibiscus; Hill and Holler; Hob-Nob; Il Caffé; "In a Different Reality . . ."; Indiana Review; Inky Trails Publication; Inlet; Iowa Review; Jam To-Day; Jeopardy; Jewish Currents; Journal of Regional Criticism; Kalliope; Karamu; Kindred Spirit; Lake Street Review; Latin American Literary Review; Laurel Review; Limberlost Review; Little Balkans Review; Long Story; Loonfeather; Lost and Found Times; Maat; Maelstrom Review; Mati; Memphis State Review; Mendocino Review; Menomonie Review; Meridian; Midwest Arts & Literature; Milkweed Chronicle Journal; Minetta Review; Mississippi Review; Mississippi Valley Review; Missouri Review; Montana Review; Muscadine; Naked Man; Negative Capability; New America; New Laurel Review; New Oregon Review; New Orleans Review; New Southern Literary Messenger; NeWest Review; Nightsun; Nimrod; North American Mentor; North Country Anvil; North Dakota Quarterly; Northwest Review; NRG; Ohio Renaissance Review; Ohio Review; On the Edge; Oro Madre; Osiris, Overtone Series; Oyez Review; Painted Bridge Quarterly; Pale Fire Review; Parabola; Partisan Review; Passion For Industry; Permafrost; Piedmont Literary Review; Pig in a Pamphlet; Pikestaff Forum; Planet Detroit; Plaza; Portland Review; Potpourri Literary; Prairie Fire; Prairie Journal of Canadian Literature; Prelude to Fantasy; Primavera; Prism International; Processed World; Proofrock; Pteranodon; Ptolemy/Browns Mills Review; Puerto Del Sol; Quarterly West; Queen's Quarterly; Raddle Moon; Rag Mag; Rambunctious Review; Red Bass; Redneck Review of Literature; Reflect; River City Review; Salome; Samisdat; San Jose Studies; Sands; Security Check; Sewanee Review; Sez; Sing Heavenly Muse!; Skylark; Slipstream; Nebraska Review; Snapdragon; Sojourner; Sonoma Mandala; Soundings East; South Carolina Review; South Dakota Review; Southern Review; Southwest Review; Sou'wester; Spirit That Moves Us; Spitball; Star-Web Paper; Story Quarterly; Street; Strokes; Telescope; Texas Review; Time To Pause; Touchstone; Triquarterly; Uncle; Unicorn Quarterly; U.S. 1 Worksheets; Univ. of Portland Review; Univ. Of Windsor Review; Unmuzzled Ox; Unspeakable Visions of the Individual; Valley Grapevine; Village Idiot; Virginia Quarterly Review; Waves; Webster Review; West Branch; West Coast Review; Western Humanities Review; Westwind; Whiskey Island; James White Review; William and Mary Review; Wind Row; Witt Review; Working Classics; Writers' Forum; Writer's Gazette; Writers West; Xavier Review; X-It; Yale Review; Zone.

**Erotica** Adrift; Amelia; Bellingham Review; Bogg; Breathless; Central Park; Chattahoochee Review; Chiricu; Chunga Review; Clifton; Clock Radio; Cold-Drill; Comet Halley; Coydog Review; Crescent Review; Dan River; Day Tonight/Night Today; Earth's Daughters; Eidos; Erotic Fiction Quarterly; Fag Rag; Fat Tuesday; Fessender Review; Gay Chicago; Hysteria; Inkblot; Maat; Magic Changes; Manscape; New Oregon Review; New Southern Literary Review; Northern New England Review; On the Edge; Oro Madre; Overtone Series; Passion For Industry; Permafrost; Pig in a Pamphlet; Planet Detroit; Potboiler; Processed World; Proofrock; Ptolemy/ Browns Mills Review; Raddle Moon; Rambunctious Review; Red Bass; Samisdat; Sign of the Times; Slipstream; Sou'wester; Orion; Star-Web Paper; Unspeakable Visions of the Individual; Uroboros; Village Idiot; Whiskey Island; X-It; Yellow Silk.

**Ethnic** Adrift; Agada; Allegheny Review; Amelia; Amherst Review; Antietam Review; Arba Sicula; Aura; Azorian Express; Backbone; Ball State Univ. Forum; B-City; Bellingham Review; Bilingual Review; Black Jack; Black Scholar; Boston Review; Broomstick; Callaloo; Candle; Central Park; Chattahoochee Review; Chiricu; Chunga Review; Clifton; Cold-Drill; Colorado Review; Conditions; Confluent Educ. Journal; Coydog Review; Crescent Review; Cross Timbers Review; Cut Bank; Dan River; Day Tonight/Night Today; Earth's Daughters; Earthwise Quarterly; Epoch; Footwork; Gamut; Greenfield Review; Hawaii Review; Helicon Nine; Hill and Holler; Hysteria; Il Caffé; Inkblot; Jeopardy; Jewish Currents; Journal of Regional Criticism; Latin American Literary Review; Laurel Review; Little Balkans Review; Long Story; Maat; Malini; Manscape; Menomonie Review; Metamorfosis; Midland Review; Midstream; Midwest Arts & Literature; Minetta Review; Miorita; Muscadine; Musicworks; Negative Capability; New America; New People; New Southern Literary Review; NeWest Review; Nimrod; North Dakota Quarterly; Northern New England Review; Northward Journal; Notebook; Oro Madre; Overtone Series; Painted Bridge Quarterly; Pale Fire Review; Passion For Industry; Pennsylvania Review; Permafrost; Plaza; Processed World; Puerto Del Sol; RaJah; Rambunctious Review; Redneck Review of Literature; Reflect; Review, Latin American Literature and Art; River City Review; Roadwerk; San Jose Studies; Sez; Sing Heavenly Muse!; Skylark; Slipstream; Sojourner; Sonoma Mandala; South Carolina Review; South Dakota Review; Sou'wester; Spirit That Moves Us; Star-Web Paper; Street; Telescope; Valley Grapevine; Village Idiot; Virginia Quarterly Review; Waves; Western Humanities Review; Whiskey Island; Whispering Wind; Working Classics; Writers' Forum; Xavier Review; Yellow Silk; Zone.

**Experimental** Adrift; Agada; Ahnene Publications; Alaska Quarterly Review; Allegheny Review; Amelia; Amherst Review; Annex; Antietam Review; Antioch Review; Artful Dodge; Azorian Express; Backbone; Ball State Univ. Forum; B-City; Big Two-Hearted; Black Warrior Review; Bogg; Bogus Review; Boston Review; Bottomfish; Breathless; Buff; Cache Review; California Quarterly; Calliope; Capilano Review; Ceilidh; Central Park; Chattahoochee Review; Chicago Review; Chiricu; Chungar Review; Clock Radio; Clockwatch Review; Cold-Drill; Colorado Review; Comet Halley; Confluent Educ. Journal; Conjunctions; Corona; Coydog Review; Crescent Review; Cut Bank; Dan River; Day Tonight/Night Today; Dog River Review; Earth's Daughters; Expresso Tilt; Exquisite Corpse; Fat Tuesday; Fessender Review; Florida Review; Footwork; Fungi; Gamut; The Gamut; Gargoyle; Grain; Greensboro Review; Grue; Hawaii Review; Helicon Nine; Hysteria; Indiana Review; Inkblot; Iron Mountain; Jeopardy; Journal of Regional Criticism; Kairos; Kaleidoscope; Kindred Spirit; Labyris; Limberlost Review; Lionhead Publishing; Little Balkans Review; Lost and Found Times; Louisville Review; Maat; Madison Review; Menomonie Review; Meridian; Merlyn's Pen; Midland Review; Mid-American Review; Milkweed Chronicle Journal; Mind in Motion; Minetta Review; Mississippi Review; Mundus Artium; Musicworks; Naked Man; Nebo; Negative Capability; new renaissance; New Southern Literary Review; NeWest Review; Nexus; Nightsun; Nimrod; North Dakota Quarterly; Northern New England Review; Northwest Review; NRG; Ohio Review; Oikos; On the Edge; Oro Madre; Osiris; Overtone Series; Oyez Review; Painted Bridge Quarterly; Pale Fire Review; Pangloss Papers; Partisan Review; Passion For Industry; Pennsylvania Review; Permafrost; Pig in a Pamphlet; Planet Detroit; Plaza; Portland Review; Potboiler; Potpourri Literary; Prairie Fire; Prelude to Fantasy; Processed World; Proofrock; Ptolemy/Browns Mills Review; Puerto Del Sol; Quarry; Queen's Quarterly; Raddle Moon; Rag Mag; RaJah; Rambunctious Review; Red Bass; Redneck Review of Literature; Reflect; River City Review; Round Table; Sign of the Times; Skylark; Slipstream; Sojourner; Sonoma Mandala; South Dakota Review; Sou'wester; Spitball; Orion; Star-Web Paper; Street; Telescope; Timewarp; Touchstone; Uncle; Uroboros; Village Idiot; West Coast Review; Westwind; Whetstone; Whiskey Island; James White Review; White Walls; Wind Row; Wisconsin Academy Review; Wisconsin Review; Witt Review; Working Classics; Worlds of Wonder; Xavier Review; X-It; Yellow Silk; Zephyr; Zone.

**Fantasy** Agada; Ahnene Publications; Allegheny Review; Alpha Adventures SF&F; Amelia; Amherst Review; Argonaut; Aurora; Ball State Univ. Forum; B-City; Bellingham Review; Bifrost; Bogus Review; Both Sides Now; Box 749; Cache Review; Calli's Tales; Canadian Author &

Bookman; Candle; Chicago Review; Chiricu; Clifton; Cold-Drill; Confluent Educ. Journal; Corona; Crescent Review; Crosstown Rag; Cut Bank; Dan River; Dog River Review; Door County Almanak; Earth's Daughters; Earthwise Quarterly; Empire; Event; Exit; Expresso Tilt; Fag Rag; Fantasy & Terror; Fantasy Book; Fantasy Tales; Fighting Woman News; Fruition; Fungi; Galactic Discourse; Grue; Haunts; Helicon Nine; Hibiscus; Hob-Nob; Horizons SF; Hor-Tasy; Hysteria; In a Different Reality . . .; Inky Trails Publication; Inlet; Jeopardy; Journal of Regional Criticism; Kaleidoscope; Kalliope; Kindred Spirit; Little Balkans Review; Maat; Magic Changes; Magical Blend; Memphis State Review; Mendocino Review; Menomonie Review; Merlyn's Pen; Milkweed Chronicle Journal; Minas Tirith Evening-Star; Mississippi Review; Mundus Artium; Muscadine; Mythellany; Negative Capability; New England Sampler; New Laurel Review; New Oregon Review; NeWest Review; Nexus; North American Mentor; Northern New England Review; Ohio Renaissance Review; Oikos; On the Edge; Pale Fire Review; Pandora; Passion For Industry; Permafrost; Piedmont Literary Review; Pig in a Pamphlet; Portland Review; Potboiler; Prelude to Fantasy; Primavera; Processed World; Proofrock; Pteranodon; The Pub; Pulpsmith; Quarry; Queen's Quarterly; Raddle Moon; Rag Mag; RaJah; Rampant Guinea Pig; Reflect; River City Review; Salome; Sands; Security Check; SF International; Sing Heavenly Muse!; Skylark; Slipstream; Nebraska Review; Sojourner; Sonoma Mandala; Southern Humanities Review; Sou'wester; Space and Time; Orion; Star-Web Paper; Street; Threshold of Fantasy; Time to Pause; Timewarp; Uncle; Unicorn Quarterly; Village Idiot; Vintage Northwest; Waves; Weirdbook; Whiskey Island; Worlds of Wonder; Writer's Gazette; Writers West; Xavier Review; Yellow Silk; Zephyr.

**Feminist** Adrift; Alchemist; Allegheny Review; Amelia; Arizona Quarterly; Atlantis; Aura; Aurora; Backbone; Ball State Univ. Forum; B-City; Bellingham Review; Both Sides Now; Broomstick; Cache Review; Callaloo; Canadian Author & Bookman; Central Park; Chattahoochee Review; Chiricu; Clifton; Clock Radio; Cold-Drill; Communities: A Journal of Cooperation; Conditions; Confluent Education Journal; Confrontation; Corona; Coydog Review; Creative Woman; Crosstown Rag; Day Tonight/Night Today; Earth's Daughters; Event; Farmer's Market; Feminist Studies; Fighting Woman News; Fruition; Galactic Discourse; The Gamut; Gay Chicago; Heresies; Hurricane Alice; Hysteria; Jam To-Day; Jeopardy; Jewish Currents; Kairos; Kaleidoscope; Kalliope; Labyris; Little Balkans Review; Long Story; Maat; Mati; Mendocino Review; Menomonie Review; Merlyn's Pen; Midland Review; Moving Out; Negative Capability; New People; NeWest Review; Nexus; Nightsun; North Dakota Quarterly; Northern New England Review; Northwest Review; On the Edge; Overtone Series; Oyez Review; Painted Bridge Quarterly; Pale Fire Review; Passion For Industry; Pennsylvania Review; Permafrost; Plainswoman; Primavera; Processed World; RaJah; Red Bass; Room of One's Own; Salome; Samisdat; San Jose Studies; Sez; Sing Heavenly Muse!; Skylark; Slipstream; Sojourner; Sonama Mandala; Southern Humanities Review; Sou'wester; Spirit That Moves Us; Telewoman; Village Idiot; Virginia Quarterly Review; Working Classics; Yellow Silk; Zephyr; Zone.

**Gay** Adrift; Alchemist; Allegheny Review; Amelia; Amherst Review; Aurora; Backbone; B-City; Bellingham Review; Both Sides Now; Cache Review; Central Park; Chattahoochee Review; Chiricu; Clifton; Clock Radio; Cold-Drill; Confrontation; Corona; Coydog Review; Day Tonight/Night Today; Fag Rag; Feminist Studies; Fessender Review; Galactic Discourse; Gay Chicago; Hysteria; Little Balkans Review; Maat; Manscape; Mendocino Review; Menomonie Review; Merlyn's Pen; Midland Review; NeWest Review; Nexus; On the Edge; Overtone Series; Oyez Review; Painted Bridge Quarterly; Passion For Industry; Pennsylvania Review; Permafrost; Primavera; Processed World; Red Bass; RFD; Samisdat; San Jose Studies; Sez; Sign of the Times; Slipstream; Sonoma Mandala; Sou'wester; Spirit That Moves Us; Village Idiot; James White Review; Yellow Silk; Zone.

**Historical** Agada; Allegheny Review; Amelia; Amherst Review; Arba Sicula; Artful Codger and Codgerette; Atlantis; Backbone; Ball State Univ. Forum; B-City; Breathless; Cache Review; Callaloo; Calli's Tales; Candle; Central Park; Chattahoochee Review; Confluent Educ. Journal; Creative Years; Critique; Cross Timbers Review; Cut Bank; Dan River; Door County Almanak; Fag Rag; Fine Madness; Fruition; Handicap News; Helicon Nine; Japanophile; Jewish Currents; Journal of Regional Criticism; Joyful Noise; Little Balkans Review; Mendocino Review; Merlyn's Pen; Midland Review; Miorita; Mirage; Negative Capability; New England Sampler; New Oregon Review; New People; NeWest Review; North Country Anvil; North Dakota Quarterly; Northern New England Review; Notebook; Oro Madre; Overtone Series; Passion For Industry; Permafrost; Pilgrim Way; Portland Review; Processed World; Queen's Quarterly; RaJah; Rambunctious Review; Redneck Review of Literature; Reflect; Roadwerk; Skylark; Sovereign Gold Literary; Spitball; Street; Touchstone; Village Idiot; Villager; Vintage Northwest; Wisconsin Academy Review; Witt Review; Working Classics; Writers West; Xavier Review; Yesterday's Magazette; Zephyr; Zone.

**Horror** Ahnene; Allegheny Review; Alpha Adventures SF&F; Amherst Review; Argonaut; B-City; Bellingham Review; Cache Review; Canadian Author & Bookman; Cold-Drill; Dan River; Dark Visions; Eldritch Tales; Fantasy and Terror; Fantasy Book; Fantasy Macabre; Fantasy Tales; Footsteps; Fungi; The Gate; Grue; Haunts; Hawaii Review; Horizons SF; Horror Show; Hor-Tasy; Journal of Regional Criticism; Little Balkans Review; Living Color; Maat; Merlyn's Pen; Midland Review; New Oregon Review; Passion For Industry; Permafrost; Potboiler; The Pub; Pulpsmith; River City Review; Skylark; Space and Time; Orion; Street; Threshold of Fantasy; Timewarp; Uncle; Village Idiot; Waves; Weirdbook; Worlds of Wonder; Writer's Gazette.

**Humor/Satire** Agada; Ahnene; Allegheny Review; Alpha Adventures SF&F; Amelia; Amherst Review; Artful Codger and Codgerette; Aurora; Azorian Express; Backbone; Ball State Univ. Forum; B-City; Bellingham Review; Bifrost; Big Two-Hearted; Black Jack; Blueline Review; Bogg; Bogus Review; Boston Review; Both Sides Now; Box 749; Breathless; Broomstick; Cache Review; Callaloo; Canadian Author & Bookman; Candle; Chattahoochee Review; Chiricu; Chunga Review; Clifton; Clock Radio; Clockwatch Review; Cold-Drill; Confluent Educ. Journal; Confrontation; Corona; Coydog Review; Crab Creek Review; Creative Woman; Crescent Review; Cross Timbers Review; Crosstown Rag; Cut Bank; Dan River; Day Tonight/Night Today; DeKalb Literary Arts Journal; Dog River Review; Door County Almanak; Earth's Daughters; Earthwise Quarterly; Event; Express Tilt; Farmer's Market; Fat Tuesday; Fessender Review; Fine Madness; Florida Review; Freeway; Galactic Discourse; The Gamuet; Gargoyle; Goofus Office Gazette; Hawaii Review; Helicon Nine; Hibiscus; Hill and Holler; Hob-Nob; Holier Than Thou; Il Caffé; In a Different Reality . . .; Inky Trails Publication; Inlet; Japanophile; Jeopardy; Jewsih Currents; Journal of Polymorphous Perversity; Journal of Regional Criticism; Kaleidoscope; Kindred Spirit; Laurel Review; Little Balkans Review; Living Color; Lone Star; Maat; Mendocino Review; Menomonie Review; Meridian; Merlyn's Pen; Metamorfosis; Mind in Motion; Minetta Review; Mirage; Mississippi Review; Muscadine; Mythellany; Naked Man; New England Sampler; New Oregon Review; New People; new renaissance; New Southern Literary Review; NeWest Review; Nexus; Nit & Wit; North Country Anvil; North Dakota Quarterly; Northern New England Review; Notebook; Ohio Renaissance Review; Oikos; On the Edge; Oro Madre; Pale Fire Review; Pangloss Papers; Passion For Industry; Pegasus Review; Pennsylvania Review; Permafrost; Piedmont Literary Review; Pig in a Pamphlet; Pig Iron; Portland Review; Potboiler; Poultry; Prelude to Fantasy; Primavera; Processed World; Proofrock; Pteranodon; Ptolemy/Browns Mills Review; Pulpsmith; Queen's Quarterly; RaJah; Rambunctious Review; Red Bass; Redneck Review of Literature; Reflect; Right Here; River City Review; Roadwerk; Salome; Samisdat; San Jose Studies; Second Coming; Security Check; Signals; Sing Heavenly Muse!; Skylark; Slipstream; Nebraska Review; Sojourner; Sonoma Mandala; South Carolina Review; Southern Humanities Review; Space and Time; Spirit That Moves Us; Orion; Star-Web Paper; Story Quarterly; Sunrust; Threshold of Fantasy; Time to Pause; Touchstone; Uncle; Unicorn Quarterly; Uroboros; Village Idiot; Villager; Vintage Northwest; Virginia Quarterly Review; Wascana Review; Waves; Western Humanities Review; Whiskey Island; James White Review; William and Mary Review; Wisconsin Academy Review; Working Classics; Writer's Gazette; Writers West; X-It; Yellow Silk; Yesterday's Magazette; Zephyr.

**Juvenile** Black Scholar; Brillant Star/Child's Way; Busy Bees' News; Calli's Tales; Candle; Fruition; Inky Trails Publication; Mendocino Review; Muscadine; Mythellany; New People; Pilgrim Way; Right Here; Skylark; Sovereign Gold Literary; Stone Soup; Time to Pause.

**Lesbian** Adrift; Alchemist; Allegheny Review; Amelia; Amherst Review; Atlantis; Aurora; Backbone; Bellingham Review; Cache Review; Central Park; Chattahoochee Review; Chiricu; Clifton; Clock Radio; Cold-Drill; Common Lives/Lesbian Lives; Conditions; Confrontation; Corona; Coydog Review; Day Tonight/Night Today; Earth's Daughters; Feminist Studies; Galactic Discourse; Gay Chicago; Heresies; Hysteria; Kindred Spirit; Little Balkans Review; Maat; Mendocino Review; Menomonie Review; Merlyn's Pen; Midland Review; Moving Out; NeWest Review; Nexus; On the Edge; Overtone Series; Oyez Review; Painted Bridge Quarterly; Passion for Industry; Pennsylvania Review; Permafrost; Primavera; Processed World; Red Bass; Room of One's Own; Samisdat; San Jose Studies; Sez; Sign of the Times; Slipstream; Sojourner; Sonoma Mandala; Sou'wester; Spirit That Moves Us; Telewoman; Village Idiot; Working Classics; Yellow Silk; Zone.

**Mainstream** Ahnene; Allegheny Review; Amelia; Amherst Review; Ball State Univ. Forum; Bellowing Ark; Beloit Fiction Journal; Black Warrior Review; Bloomsbury Review; Boston Review; Cache Review; Chattahoochee Review; Chiricu; Chunga Review; City Paper; Clockwatch Review; Cold-Drill; Colorado Review; Coydog Review; Crescent Review; Dan River; Dog River Review; Expresso Tilt; Fine Madness; Florida Review; Gamut; The Gamut; Grain; Handicap News; Hibiscus; Il Caffé; In a Different Reality . . .; Indiana Review; Japanophile; Jeopardy; Journal of Regional Criticism; Little Balkans Review; Louisville Review; Maat; Menomonie Review; Meridian; Merlyn's Pen; Minetta Review; Naked Man; Nebo; New Oregon Review; NeWest Review; Nexus; Northern New England Review; On the Edge; Oro Madre; Overtone Series; Pale Fire Review; Potboiler; Prelude to Fantasy; Proofrock; Ptolemy/Browns Mills Review; Puerto Del Sol; Pulpsmith; Rag Mag; Rambunctious Review; Right Here; River City Review; Round Table; Sands; Skylark; Slipstream; Nebraska Review; Sonoma Mandala; Sou'wester; Spitball; Sunrust; Touchstone; Uncle; Village Idiot; Whetstone; Whiskey Island; Wind; Wisconsin Academy Review; Writer's Gazette; Writers West; X-It; Zephyr.

**Men's** Aura; Ball State Univ. Forum; Black Scholar; Canadian Author & Bookman; Chattahoochee Review; Cold-Drill; Dan River; Fag Rag; Maat; Menomonie Review; Minetta Review; Muscadine; New America; New Oregon Review; Northern New England Review; Parabola; Proofrock; Reflect; River City Review; San Jose Studies; Sez; Sign of the Times; Signals; Sonoma Mandala; Spirit That Moves Us; Uncle; Village Idiot; Virginia Quarterly Review; James White Review; Zone.

**Preschool/Picture Book** Brilliant Star/Child's Way; Calli's Tales; Corona; Inky Trails Publication; Magical Blend; Pilgrim Way; Sovereign Gold Literary; Time to Pause.

**Psychic/Supernatural/Occult** Agada; Alchemist; Allegheny Review; Alpha Adventures SF&F; Amherst Review; Aurora; Ball State Univ. Forum; Bellingham Review; Both Sides Now; Cache Review; Clifton; Confluent Educ. Journal; Corona; Crescent Review; Crosstown Rag; Dan River; Dog River Review; Earthwise Quarterly; Eldritch Tales; Fag Rag; Fantasy Book; Fantasy Tales; Fat Tuesday; Fessenden Review; Fungi; Galactic Discourse; The Gate; Grue; Haunts; Hob-Nob; Hysteria; In a Different Reality . . .; Inky Trails; Iron Mountain; Journal of Regional Criticism; Little Balkans Review; Maat; Magic Changes; Mendocino Review; Midland Review; Muscadine; Nebo; Negative Capability; New Mexico Humanities Review; New Oregon Review; New Southern Literary Review; Ohio Renaissance Review; On the Edge; Pale Fire Review; Passion for Industry; Permafrost; Piedmont Literary Review; Pilgrim Way; Portland Review; Prelude to Fantasy; Proofrock; The Pub; Reflect; Samisdat; Sands; Security Check; Skylark; Southern Humanities Review; Space and Time; Orion; Star-Web Paper; Street; Time to Pause; Timewarp; Uncle; Waves; Weirdbook; Whiskey Island; Worlds of Wonder; Writer's Gazette.

**Regional** Amelia; Amherst Review; Antietam Review; Arba Sicula; Arizona Quarterly; Artful Codger and Codgerette; Aura; Azorian Express; Backbone; Bellingham Review; Blueline Review; Boston Review; Cache Review; Callaloo; Candle; Caribbean Review; Chattahoochee Review; Chunga Review; Clifton; Clockwatch Review; Confluent Educ. Journal; Confrontation; Corona; Coydog Review; Crescent Review; Cross Timbers Review; Cross-Canada Writers' Quarterly; Dan River; Descant; Door County Almanak; Earthwise Quarterly; Event; Farmer's Market; Fruition; The Gamut; Greenfield Review; Hawaii Review; Hill and Holler; Hob-Nob; Hysteria; Jeopardy; Journal of Regional Criticism; Kalliope; Lake Street Review; Little Balkans Review; Loonfeather; Mendocino Review; Merlyn's Pen; Midland Review; Milkweed Chronicle Journal; Miorita; Mirage; Naked Man; Nebo; Negative Capability; New England Sampler; New Mexico Humanities Review; North Country Anvil; Northern New England Review; Notebook; Oikos; Oyez Review; Partisan Review; Pennsylvania Review; Piedmont Literary Review; Pilgrim Way; Plainswoman; Plaza; Prairie Journal of Canadian Literature; Processed World; Rag

Mag; Rambunctious Review; Redneck Review of Literature; River City Review; Samisdat; San Jose Studies; Sands; Sez; Skylark; Snapdragon; Snowy Egret; Sonoma Mandala; South Dakota Review; Southern Humanities Review; Sou'wester; Sunrust; Uncle; Waves; Westwind; Wisconsin Academy Review; Witt Review; Working Classics; Xavier Review.

**Religious/ Inspirational** Agada; Ahnene Publications; Ball State Univ. Forum; Both Sides Now; Creative Years; Critique; Handicap News; Hob-Nob; Inky Trails; Joyful Noise; Love Letters; Midstream; New England Sampler; North Portal; Pegasus Review; Pilgrim Way; Right Here; Sovereign Gold Literary; Studio Mystica; Time to Pause; Vintage Northwest; Writer's Gazette; Xavier Review; Yesterday's Magazette.

**Romance** Ahnene; Amherst Review; Arba Sicula; Aura; Ball State Univ. Forum; Cache Review; Canadian Author & Bookman; Corona; Crosstown Rag; Dan River; Earthwise Quarterly; Event; Gay Chicago; Handicap News; Hob-Nob; Il Caffé; In a Different Reality . . .; Inky Trails; Jeopardy; Journal of Regional Criticism; Mendocino Review; Merlyn's Pen; Negative Capability; Northern New England Review; Pilgrim Way; Proofrock; Pteranodon; Rambunctious Review; Salome; Security Check; Orion; Time to Pause; Village Idiot; Virgina Quarterly Review; Waves; Writer's Gazette.

**Science Fiction** Allegheny Review; Alpha Adventures SF&F; Amelia; Amherst Review; Argonaut; Artful Dodge; Atlantis; Aura; Aurora; Backbone; Ball State Univ. Forum; B-City; Bellingham Review; Bifrost; Bogg; Bogus Review; Cache Review; Callaloo; Canadian Author & Bookman; Candle; Ceilidh; Chicago Review; Chiricu; City Paper; Clifton; Cold-Drill; Comet Halley; Communities: A Journal of Cooperation; Confluent Educ. Journal; Confrontation; Cosmic Landscapes; Coydog Review; Crescent Review; Critique; Crosstown Rag; Dan River; Day Tonight/Night Today; Earthwise Quarterly; Empire; Event; Exit; Fantasy Book; Fighting Woman News; Galactic Discourse; Hibiscus; Hob-Nob; Holier Than Thou; Horizons SF; Hysteria; In a Different Reality . . .; Inlet; Jam To-Day; Jeopardy; Journal of Regional Criticism; Joyful Noise; Kaleidoscope; Kalliope; Kindred Spirit; Letters; Little Balkans Review; Maat; Magic Changes; Mati; Memphis State Review; Mendocino Review; Menomonie Review; Meridian; Merlyn's Pen; Midland Review; Mind in Motion; Muscadine; Mythellany; Nebo; Negative Capability; New Oregon Review; NeWest Review; Nexus; Nimrod; North American Mentor; Northern New England Review; Ohio Renaissance Review; Oikos; Pale Fire Review; Pandora; Passion In Industry; Permafrost; Piedmont Literary Review; Pig in a Pamphlet; Portland Review; Potboiler; Prelude to Fantasy; Primavera; Processed World; Pteranodon; Pulpsmith; Quarry; Queen's Quarterly; RaJah; Rampant Guinea Pig; Reflect; River City Review; Salome; Samisdat; Second Coming; Security Check; SF International; Skylark; Slipstream; Southern Humanities Review; Sovereign Gold Literary; Space and Time; Orion; Threshold of Fantasy; Timewarp; Uncle; Village Idiot; Whiskey Island; Wind Row; Wisconsin Academy Review; Worlds of Wonder; Writer's Gazette; Writers West; Yellow Silk; Zephyr; Zone.

**Senior Citizen/Retirement** Amelia; Arba Sicula; Artful Codger and Codgerette; Backbone; Broomstick; Cache Review; Candle; Confrontation; Corona; Creative Years; Dan River; Green's; Handicap News; Hob-Nob; Inky Trails; Jewish Currents; Joyful Noise; Mendocino Review; Moving Out; Negative Capability; Pilgrim Way; Reflect; Right Here; Senior Scribes; Sovereign Gold Literary; Time to Pause; Village Idiot; Vintage Northwest.

**Serialized/Excerpted Novel** Agada; Agni Review; Antaeus; Artful Dodge; Aurora; Ball State Univ. Forum; Bellingham Review; Bellowing Ark; Black Jack; Boston Review; Buff; Cache Review; Callaloo; Caribbean Review; Ceilidh; Central Park; Chiricu; Cold-Drill; Coydog Review; Day Tonight/Night Today; Fantasy Book; Farmer's Market; Fat Tuesday; Gamut; Gargoyle; Hob-Nob; Il Caffé; In a Different Reality . . .; Inkblot; Kaleidoscope; Kindred Spirit; Labyris; Memphis State Review; Mendocino Review; Montana Review; New Southern Literary Review; NeWest Review; Oikos; Overtone Series; Pale Fire Review; Passion For Industry; Pikestaff Forum; Planet Detroit; Prairie Journal of Canadian Literature; The Pub; Quarry; Red Bass; Roadwerk; Salome; Security Check; Skylark; South Dakota Review; Star-Web Paper; Story Quarterly; Street; Unspeakable Visions of the Individual; Virginia Quarterly Review; Webster Review; West Coast Review; Western Humanities Review; Westwind; Stephen Wright's Mystery Notebook; Writ; Xavier Review.

**Suspense/Mystery** Allegheny Review; Amelia; Amherst Review; Backbone; Ball State Univ. Forum; B-City; Bellingham Review; <u>Byline;</u> Cache Review; Candle; Cold-Drill; Crescent Review; Crosstown Rag; Dan River; Door County Almanak; Earthwise Quarterly; Exit; Galactic Discourse; Haunts; Hibiscus; Hob-Nob; In a Different Reality . . .; Inkblot; Inky Trails; Japanophile; Joyful Noise; Kaleidoscope; Letters; Little Balkans Review; Mendocino Review; Merlyn's Pen; <u>Minetta Review;</u> Muscadine; <u>Mystery Time;</u> Negative Capability; New England Sampler; New Oregon Review; Ohio Renaissance Review; Pale Fire Review; Passion For Industry; Potboiler; Prelude to Fantasy; Pteranodon; The Pub; Puerto Del Sol; Pulpsmith; Right Here; River City Review; Salome; Security Check; Sing Heavenly Muse!; Skylark; Spitball; Orion; Street; Time to Pause; Time Warp; Uncle; Village Idiot; Villager; Vintage Northwest; Waves; Whiskey Island; Wisconsin Academy Review; Stephen Wright's Mystery Notebook; Writer's Gazette; Writers West; Zephyr.

**Translations** Adrift; Agada; Agni Review; Alaska Quarterly Review; Amelia; Amherst Review; Annex; Antaeus; Antioch Review; Arba Sicula; Arizona Quarterly; Artful Dodge; Aurora; Backbone; Ball State Univ. Forum; Bellingham Review; Big Two-Hearted; Bogus Review; Boston Review; Box 749; Breathless; Cache Review; Callaloo; Caribbean Review; Ceilidh; Central Park; Chariton Review; Chelsea; Chiricu; Cold-Drill; Colorado Review; Columbia: A Mag. of Poetry & Prose; Comet Halley; Conditions; Confrontation Journal; Conjunctions; Crab Creek Review; Cut Bank; Denver Quarterly; Descant [Canada]; Dimension; Dog River Review; Earthwise Quarterly; Exit; Fighting Woman News; Florida Review; Footwork; Gamut; The Gamut; Gargoyle; Hawaii Review; Helicon Nine; Il Caffé; Inkblot; Jeopardy; Jewish Currents; Kairos; Little Balkans Review; Malini; Mati; Midland Review; Mid-American Review; Midwest Arts & Literature; Milkweed Chronicle Journal; Miorita; Mississippi Review; Montana Review; Mundus Artium; Negative Capability; New Laurel Review; New Orleans Review; new renaissance; Nexus; Nimrod; Northern New England Review; Northwest Review; On the Edge; Oro Madre; Overtone Series; Painted Bridge Quarterly; Parabola; Partisan Review; Passion For Industry; Pennsylvania Review; Permafrost; Portland Review; Prism International; Processed World; Proofrock; Ptolemy/Brown Mills Review; Puerto Del Sol; Quarry; Quarterly West; Raddle Moon; RaJah; Red Bass; Redneck Review of Literature; Roadwerk; Salome; Sands; Scandinavian Review; Snowy Egret; Sojourner; Sonoma Mandala; South Dakota Review; Sou'wester; Spirit That Moves Us; Star-Web Paper; Telescope; Touchstone; Translation; Triquarterly; Unmuzzled Ox; Village Idiot; Virginia Quarterly Review; Waves; Webster Review; West Branch; West Coast Review; Western Humanities Review; Westwind; Whiskey Island; James White Review; Wind Row; Witt Review; Writ; Xavier Review; Yale Literary; Yellow Silk; Zone.

**Western** Allegheny Review; Amelia; Amherst Review; Azorian Express; Ball State Univ. Forum; Black Jack; Canadian Author & Bookman; Cold-Drill; Crescent Review; Cross Timbers Review; Dan River; Earthwise Quarterly; Green Feather; Hibiscus; Inky Trails; Little Balkans Review; Merlyn's Pen; Mid-American Review; Mirage; Muscadine; Permafrost; Pteranodon; Pulpsmith; River City Review; Samisdat; Sing Heavenly Muse!; Skylark; Time to Pause; Uncle; Valley Grapevine; Village Idiot; Writer's Gazette; Writers West.

**Women's** Ahnene; Amelia; Aura; Aurora; Backbone; Ball State Univ. Forum; Black Scholar; Broomstick; Callaloo; Canadian Author & Bookman; Chattahoochee Review; Chiricu; Cold-Drill; Colorado Review; Conditions; Cottonwood; Coydog Review; Cut Bank; Day Tonight/Night Today; Earth's Daughters; Feminist Studies; Galactic Discourse; Gamut; Helicon Nine; Heresies; Iowa Woman; Jewish Currents; Kairos; Kalliope; Little Balkans Review; Maat; Menomonie Review; Minetta Review; Muscadine; Negative Capability; New America; New People; NeWest Review; Northern New England Review; On the Edge; Overtone Series; Pale Fire Review; Parabola; Pennsylvania Review; Portland Review; Proofrock; Queen's Quarterly; Red Bass; Reflect; Right Here; Room of One's Own; Salome; San Jose Studies; Sez; Sibyl-Child; Signals; Sonoma Mandala; Spirit That Moves Us; Star-Web Paper; Story Quarterly; Telewoman; Village Idiot; Vintage; Virginia Quarterly Review; Wisconsin Academy Review; Xavier Review; Zephyr; Zone.

**Young Adult/Teen** Orba Sicula; Black Scholar; Calli's Tales; Candle; Helicon Nine; Hob-Nob; Inky Trails; Little Balkans Review; Merlyn's Pen; Mythellany; New People; Portland Review; Purple Cow; Stone Soup; Time to Pause; Village Idiot.

**Canada** Ahnene; Alchemist; Antigonish Review; Atlantis; Canadian Author & Bookman; Canadian Fiction; Capilano Review; Cross-Canada Writers' Quarterly; C.S.P. World News; Dark Visions; Descant [Canada]; Event; Gamut; Grain; Green's Horizons SF; Hysteria; Musicworks; Northward Journal; Poor Man's Press; Potboiler; Prairie Fire; Prairie Journal of Canadian Literature; Prism International; Quarry; Queen's Quarterly; Raddle Moon; Room of One's Own; Rubicon; Timewarp; Univ. of Windsor Review; Wascana Review; Waves; West Coast Review; Whetstone; Writ; X-it.

# Commercial Periodicals

**Adventure** Alaska Outdoors; Alive!; Amazing Science Fiction; American Dane; American Newspaper Carrier; American Squaredance; Associate Reformed Presbyterian; Augusta Spectator; Banff Life; Bay & Delta Yachtsman; Bike Report; Boys' Life; Bread; Buffalo Spree; Cavalier; Chatelaine; Chesapeake Bay; Children's Digest; Christian Adventurer; Christian Life; Clubhouse; Cobblestone; Corvette Fever; Cosmopolitan; Crusader; Currents; Delta Scene; Dialogue; Discoveries; Easyriders; Espionage; Essence; Friend; Gent; Gospel Carrier; Hang Gliding; Hi-Call; High Adventure; Horse Illustrated; Indian Life; Jack and Jill; Leatherneck; Lighted Pathway; Magazine for Christian Youth; Messenger of the Sacred Heart; Motorcyclist; New Alaskan; New England Senior Citizen; New Methods; Night Cry; Nugget; On The Line; Penthouse; Playboy; Players; Pockets; Prime Times; Pro-Claimer; Ranger Rick's; Read; Road King; San Gabriel Valley; Saturday Evening Post; Stag; Student; Teenage; Torch Romances; Touch; Trailer Boats; Western People; Wisconsin Restaurateur; Working for Boys; Wyoming Rural Electric News; Young Ambassador; Young Judaean.

**Condensed Novel** Bakersfield Lifestyle; Bay & Delta Yachtsman; Campus Life; Friday of the Jewish Exponent; Inside Running; New Methods; Night Cry; Virtue.

**Confession** Crusader; Espionage; Essence; Friday of the Jewish Exponent; Secrets; Student.

**Contemporary** Associate Reformed Presbyterian; Atlantic Monthly; Augusta Spectator; Baltimore Jewish Times; Boys' Life; Buffalo Spree; Chatelaine; Christian Home; Cosmopolitan; Dialogue; Espionage; Esquire; Explorer; Family; Friday of the Jewish Exponent; Friend; Gambling Times; Gent; Good Housekeeping; Harper's Home Life; Indian Life; Inside; Insight; Junior Trails; Lighted Pathway; Living Message; Lutheran Journal; Mademoiselle; Magazine for Christian Youth; Mature Living; McCall's Moment; New Age Journal; New England Senior Citizen; New Methods; Night Cry; Northeast; Nugget; Omni; Other Side; Oui; Penthouse; Pioneer Woman; Playboy; Pockets; Prime Times; St. Anthony Messenger; St. Joseph's Messenger; San Gabriel Valley; Singlelife; Southern Exposure; Stag; Stories; Student; Teenage; Today's Christian Woman; Torch Romances; Trailer Boats; Virtue; Washington Post; Western People; Wisconsin Restaurateur; Woman's Day; Working Mother; YM.

**Erotica** Cavalier; First Hand; Fling; Gem; Genesis; Gent; Harvey for Loving People; New York Action, Philadelphia Action; Nugget; Penthouse; Pillow Talk; Players; Stag; Swank.

**Ethnic** Alive!; Aloha; American Dane; Americas; Ararat; Buffalo Spree; Christian Home; Clubhouse; Crusader; Espionage; First Hand; Festivals; Friday of the Jewish Exponent; Hadassah; Indian Life; Inside; Inside Kung Fu; Intimacy; Jewish Monthly; Jive; Magazine for Christian Youth; Moment; New England Senior Citizen; Other Side; Pockets; Prime Times; Reconstructionist; Southern Exposure; Stories; Student; Teenage; Teens Today; Touch; Wyoming Rural Electric News; Young Judaean.

**Experimental** Essence; Hang Gliding; Los Angeles Reader; New Methods; Other Side; Players; Rod Serling's the Twilight Zone; Southern Exposure; Teenage.

**Fantasy** Amazing Science Fiction; American Squaredance; Bay & Delta Yachtsman; Bike Report; Borderland; Campus Life; Chesapeake Bay; Corvette Fever; Dragon; Espionage; Essence; Fling; Genesis; Glad; Hang Gliding; Isaac Asimov's Science Fiction; Magazine for Christian Youth; Night Cry; Omni; Other Side; Oui; Playboy; Players; Pockets; Ranger Rick's; Read; Relix; Road King; Rod Serling's the Twilight Zone; Starwind; Trailer Boats; Woman's Day; Young Ambassador; Young Judaean.

**Feminist** Daughters of Sarah; Essence; Lighted Pathway; My Weekly; Other Side; Pioneer Woman; Playgirl; Southern Exposure; Wisconsin Restaurateur; Woman's Day.

**Gay** First Hand; Pillow Talk; Southern Exposure.

**Historical** American Dane; American Squaredance; Banff Life; Bay & Delta Yachtsman; Bike Report; Chesapeake Bay; Christian Adventurer; Clubhouse; Cobblestone; Currents; Daughters of Sarah; Delta Scene; Espionage; Explorer; Friday of the Jewish Exponent; Gospel Carrier; Hang Gliding; High Adventure; Indian Life; Inside Running; Jack and Jill; Jewish Monthly; Leatherneck; Lighted Pathway; Moment; New England Senior Citizen; New Methods; Players; Pockets; Pro-Claimer; Purpose; Southern Exposure; Stories; Washington Post; Wyoming Rural Electric News; Young Judaean.

**Horror** Borderland; Cavalier; Gent; Hang Gliding; Motorcyclist; Night Cry; Nugget; Omni; Penthouse; Playboy; Rod Serling's the Twilight Zone; Teenager.

**Humor/Satire** Alaska Outdoors; Alive!; Amazing Science Fiction; American Newspaper Carrier; American Squaredance; Augusta Spectator; Banff Life; Bay & Delta Yachtsman; Bike Report; Boys' Life; Buffalo Spree; Campus Life; Chatelaine; Chesapeake Bay; Corvette Fever; Delta Scene; Dialogue; Espionage; Essence; Friday of the Jewish Exponent; Friend; Gambling Times; Gem; Gent; Glad; Golf Journal; Hang Gliding; Harper's; Hi-Call; Home Life; Ideals; Inside; Inside Running; Jack and Jill; Jewish Monthly; Leatherneck; Lighted Pathway; Living Message; Magazine for Christian Youth; Mature Living; McCall's; Messenger of the Sacred Heart; Motorcyclist; My Weekly; New Alaskan; New England Senior Citizen; New York Action, Philadelphia Action; Nugget; Other Side; Oui; Playboy; Players; Prime Times; Ranger Rick's; Relix; Road King; St. Joseph's Messenger; San Gabriel Valley; Saturday Evening Post; Singlelife; Stag; Starwind; Stories; Student; Sunshine; 'Teen; Teenage; Teens Today; Tiger Beat; Trailer Boats; Virtue; Vista; Washington Post; Western People; Wisconsin Restaurateur; Woman's Day; Working for Boys; Wyoming Rural Electric News; Young Judaean.

**Juvenile** Action; American Dane; Associate Reformed Presbyterian; Boys' Life; Chickadee; Children's Playmate; Christian Home; Clubhouse; Cricket; Crusader; Discoveries; Friend; Highlights for Children; Horse Illustrated; Humpty Dumpty's; Ideals; Indian Life; Jack and Jill; Junior Trails; Lighted Pathway; Lollipops, Ladybugs and Lucky Stars; My Friend; Noah's Ark; Pockets; R-A-D-A-R; Ranger Rick's; Single Parent; Story Friends; Sunshine; Teens Today; Touch; Wisconsin Restaurateur; Woman's Day; Wonder Time; Working for Boys; Working Mother; Young Crusader; Young Judaean; YM.

**Lesbian** Harvey for Loving People; Oui; Pillow Talk; Southern Exposure.

**Mainstream** Espionage; Family; Magazine for Christian Youth; New England Senior Citizen; New Methods; Night Cry; Other Side; St. Joseph's Messenger; Teenage.

**Men's** Buffalo Spree; Cavalier; Dialogue; Easyriders; Fling; Gem; Genesis; Gent; Indian Life; Leatherneck; Lookout; Lutheran Journal; Mademoiselle; New York Action, Philadelphia Action; Night Cry; Nugget; Oui; Penthouse; Playboy; Purpose; Road King; Stag; Sunshine; Swank; Teenage; Wisconsin Restaurateur; Wyoming Rural Electric News.

**Preschool/Picture Book** Friend; Highlights for Children; Humpty Dumpty; Lollipops, Ladybugs and Lucky Stars; New Alaskan; Turtle.

**Psychic/Supernatural/Occult** Bay & Delta Yachtsman; Borderland; Currents; Dialogue; Espionage; Gent; Messenger of the Sacred Heart; Night Cry; Nugget; Penthouse; San Gabriel Valley; Rod Serling's the Twilight Zone; Teenage.

**Regional** Alaska Outdoors; Augusta Spectator; Banff Life; Bike Report; Chesapeake Bay; Cobblestone; Delta Scene; Georgia Journal; Gulfshore; Los Angeles Reader; Maine Life; New Alaskan; New Bedford; New Methods; Northeast; San Gabriel Valley; Washingtonian; Wisconsin Restaurateur; Wyoming Rural Electric News; Yankee; Young Ambassador.

**Religious/Inspirational** Alive! Alive Now!; American Newspaper Carrier; Associate Reformed Presbyterian; Bread; Christian Adventurer; Christian Home; Christian Life; Christian Living For Senior Highs; Church Musician; Clubhouse; Daughters of Sarah; Discoveries; Evangel; Explorer; Faith for the Family; Festivals; Friday of the Jewish Exponent; Friend; Glad; Good News; Gospel Carrier; Hi-Call; High Adventure; His; Home Life; Ideals; In Touch; Indian Life; Jewish Monthly; Junior Trails; Leatherneck; Lighted Pathway; Liguorian; Live; Living With Teenagers; Lookout; Lutheran Journal; Magazine for Christian Youth; Mature Living; Mature Years; Messenger of the Sacred Heart; Modern Liturgy; Moment; My Friend; Noah's Ark; North American Voice of Fatima; On The Line; Our Family; Pockets; Pro-Claimer; Purpose; Queen of All Hearts; R-A-D-A-R; St. Anthony Messenger; St. Joseph's Messenger; San Gabriel Valley; Saturday Evening Post; Seek; Shining Star; Southern Exposure; Story Friends; Straight; Student; Sunday Digest; Sunshine; Teens Today; Today's Christian Woman; Touch; Virtue; Woman's Day; Wonder Time; Working for Boys; Young Judaean.

**Romance** Affaire de Coeur; American Squaredance; Augusta Spectator; Bay & Delta Yachtsman; Chatelaine; Cosmopolitan; Delta Scene; Espionage; Explorer; Good Housekeeping; Hi-Call; Intimacy; Jive; Lutheran Journal; Magazine for Christian Youth; Messenger of the Sacred Heart; My Weekly; Playgirl; Prime Times; Publishers Syndication; St. Anthony Messenger; St. Joseph's Messenger; Saturday Evening Post; Secrets; Singlelife; 'Teen; Teenage; Teens Today; Tiger Beat; Torch Romances; Virtue; Woman's World; Wyoming Rural Electric News; Young Ambassador; YM.

**Science Fiction** Amazing Science Fiction; American Squaredance; Analog; Bakersfield Lifestyle; Bay & Delta Yachtsman; Boys' Life; Campus Life; Crusader; Currents; Dragon; Espionage; Explorer; Gent; Glad; Hang Gliding; Isaac Asimov's Science Fiction; Jack and Jill; Magazine for Christian Youth; Messenger of the Sacred Heart; Motorcyclist; New Methods; New York Action, Philadelphia Action; Night Cry; Nugget; Omni; Penthouse; Playboy; Players; Ranger Rick's; Read; Relix; Road King; Saturday Evening Post; Rod Serling's the Twilight Zone; Starwind; Trailer Boats; Wisconsin Restaurateur; Young Ambassador; Young Judaean.

**Senior Citizen/Retirement** Bakersfield Lifestyle; Bay & Delta Yachtsman; Bike Report; Liguorian; Lutheran Journal; Mature Living; Mature Years; My Weekly; New Alaskan; Our Family; St. Anthony Messenger; St. Joseph's Messenger; Sunshine; Working for Boys; Wyoming Rural Electric News.

**Serialized/Excerpted Novel** Amazing Science Fiction; Analog; Campus Life; Capper's Weekly; Essence; Family Circle; First Hand; Mademoiselle; Moment; My Weekly; Penthouse; Playgirl; Redbook; Virtue; Western People.

**Suspense Mystery** Alfred Hitchcock's Mystery Magazine; American Dane; American Newspaper Carrier; Associate Reformed Presbyterian; Augusta Spectator; Bakersfield Lifestyle; Bay & Delta Yachtsman; Bike Report; Boys' Life; Buffalo Spree; Chatelaine; Chesapeake Bay; Children's Digest; Christian Adventurer; Clubhouse; Cosmopolitan; Delta Scene; Dialogue; Discoveries; Ellery Queen's Mystery; Espionage; Gambling Times; Gent; Gospel Carrier; Hang Gliding; Hi-Call; High Adventure; Horse Illustrated; Jack and Jill; Messenger of the Sacred Heart; New Black Mask; New England Senior Citizen; Night Cry; Nugget; Other Side; Oui; Playboy; Pockets; Publishers Syndication International; Ranger Rick's; Read; Road King; 'Teen; Teenage; Torch Romances; Trailer Boats; Wisconsin Restaurateur; Woman's World; Young Judaean.

**Translations** Friday of the Jewish Exponent; Inside; Moment; Night Cry; Redbook; Young Judaean.

**Western** American Squaredance; Banff Life; Boys' Life; Clubhouse; Dialogue; Espionage; High Adventure; Horse Illustrated; Messenger of the Sacred Heart; New England Senior Citizen; New Methods; Penthouse; Playboy; Road King; San Gabriel Valley; Wisconsin Restaurateur; Wyoming Rural Electric News.

**Women's** Buffalo Spree; Christian Life; Cosmopolitian; Daughters of Sarah; Dialogue; Family Circle; Family; Good Housekeeping; Ideals; Indian Life; Lookout; Lutheran Journal; Lutheran Women; My Weekly; New York Action, Philadelphia Action; Night Cry; Pioneer Woman; Playgirl; Purpose; Sunshine; Teenage; Today's Christian Woman; Virtue; Wisconsin Restaurateur; Woman's Day; Working Mother; Wyoming Rural Electric News.

**Young Adult/Teen** Alive!; American Dane; American Newspaper Carrier; Associate Reformed Presbyterian; Boys' Life; Campus Life; Christian Adventurer; Christian Living For Senior Highs; Evangel; Gospel Carrier; Hi-Call; His; Home Life; Horse Illustrated; In Touch; Indian Life; Insight; Junior Trails; Lighted Pathway; Liguorian; Lookout; Los Angeles Reader; Lutheran Journal; Magazine for Christian Youth; Medical Detective; Noah's Ark; On The Line; Pro-Claimer; Read; Seventeen; Straight; 'Teen; Teenage; Teens Today; Tiger Beat; Wisconsin Restaurateur; Young Ambassador; YM.

**Canada** Banff Life; Borderland; Chatelaine; Chickadee; Indian Life; Living Message; Messenger of the Sacred Heart; Our Family; Western People.

# Small Press

**Adventure** Acheron; Aegina; Agapé; Ariadne; BookWrights; Book Publishers; Knights Press; Lace Publications; Lion; Longhorn; Mainespring; New Bedford; On the Move; Overlook; Quality; Ranger Associates; Second Chance; Somrie; Tres Amigos; Triple 'P'; Vimach Associates; John Westburg; Woodsong Graphics.

**Condensed Novel** Mosaic.

**Confession** Guernica; R&M Publishing.

**Contemporary** Acheron; Adler; Aegina; Agapé; Androgyne; Applezaba; Ariadne; Arsenal Pulp; BKMK; Bogus; Books for All Times; BookWrights; Book Publications; Broken Whisker; Brunswick; Carpenter; Chelsea Green; Commoner's Publishing Society; Coyote Love; Creative Concern; Cross-Cultural Communications; The Crossing; Curbstone; Dawnwood; Double M; Dragonsbreath; Fiction Collective; First East Coast Theatre; Fjord; Graphic Image; Griffon House; Guernica; Hermes House; Illuminations; Knights; Lace Publications; Lapis Educational; Little Balkans; Low-Tech; Maine Writers Workshop; Mainespring; Maize Press; Manic D Press; Morgan; New Bedford; New Rivers; New Seed; North Point; Ommations; Overlook; Owl Creek; Padre; Panjandrum; Paycock; Peachtree; Perivale; Pikestaff; Pineapple; Porcupine's Quill; Quality; Salt Lick; Sea Fog Press; Second Chance; Second Coming; Seven Buffaloes; Shameless Hussy; Somrie; Station Hill; Story; Studia Hispanica Editors; Sun & Moon; Teal; Tres Amigos; 22 Press; University of Illinois; Sherry Urie; John Westburg; Winglow; Woodsong Graphics; York; Zephyr.

**Erotica** Allegany Mountain; Creative Concern; Dragonsbreath; Guernica; Michael Kesend; Lace Publications; Maize Press; Peppermint Press; Perivale; Salt Lick; Somrie.

**Ethnic** Aegina; Akiba; Bilingual Review; Blind Beggar; Brunswick; Challenge; Commoner's Publishing Society; Council for Indian Education; Cross-Cultural Communications; Curbstone; Griffon House; Heritage; Hermes House; H.W.H. Creative Productions; Kar-Ben Copies; Kitchen Table; Knights; Lion; Little Balkans; Maize Press; Mina; New Seed; On The Move; Overlook; Pascal; Path; Perivale; R&M Publishing; Rossel; Salt Lick; Sea Fog Press; Seven Buffaloes; Shameless Hussy; Somrie; Story; Studia Hispanica Editors; Third World; Zephyr.

**Experimental** Acheron; Adler; Aegina; Allegany Mountain; Androgyne; Applezaba; Arsenal Pulp; BKMK; Blind Beggar; Bogus; BookWrights; Broken Whisker; Brunswick; Carpenter;

Commoner's Publishing Society; Coyote Love; Cross-Cultural Communications; Dimensionist; Dragonsbreath; Fiction Collective; First East Coast Theatre; Gay Sunshine; Illuminations; Lintel; Little Balkans; Low-Tech; Maize Press; Manic D Press; Mole; Morgan; New Rivers; North Point; Ommation; Overlook; Panjandrum; Path; Paycock; Perivale; Pikestaff; Pineapple; Proper Tales; Realities Library; Salt Lick; Second Chance; Shameless Hussy; The Smith; Somrie; Station Hill; Sun & Moon; Swank; Turnstone; 22 Press; Ultramarine; Unique Graphics; University of Illinois; Warlords and Wizards; John Westburg; Wingbow; Women's; York; Zephyr.

**Faction** Aegina; Applezaba; Erespin; Maine Writers Workshop; Mainespring; New Bedford; Quality; Somrie; Tres Amigos.

**Fantasy** Adler; Aegina; Andromeda; Ansuda; Applezaba; BookWrights; Brunswick; Carpenter; Commoner's Publishing Society; Curbstone; Dimensionist; Double M; Dragonsbreath; Erespin; H.W.H. Creative Productions; Knights; Lace Publications; Little Balkans; MTM; Overlook; Padre; Panjandrum; Parkhurst; Porcupine's Quill; Salt Lick; Shameless Hussy; Somrie; Space and Time; Steeldragon; Stillpoint; Tres Amigos; Triple 'P'; 22 Press; Ultramarine; Vimach Associates; Warlords and Wizards; John Westburg; George Whittell Memorial; W.W. Publications; Yith.

**Feminist** Aegina; Applezaba; Ariadne; Arsenal Pulp; Bookmakers; Brunswick; The Crossing; Curbstone; Double M; Firebrand; Frog in The Well; Gay Presses of New York; Guernica; Hermes House; Kitchen Table; Lapis Educational; Lintel; Metis; Mina; Naiad; New Seed; Ommation; Parkhurst; R&M Publishing; Salt Lick; Samisdat; Sea Fog Press; Shameless Hussy; Spinsters Ink; Triple 'P'; Wim; Wingbow; Zephyr.

**Gay** Aegina; Alyson; Applezaba; Arsenal Pulp; Banned Books; The Crossing; Curbstone; Gay Presses of New York; Gay Sunshine; Guernica; Knights; Lintel; Mina; Mogul; Motheroot; Salt Lick; Samisdat; Triple 'P'; Vimach Associates; Wim; Zephyr.

**Historical** Aegina; Agapé; Akiba; Ariadne; Bilingual Review; Binford & Mort; BKMK; BookWrights; Book Publishers; Brunswick; Challenge; Chelsea Green; Commoner's Publishing Society; Council for Indian Education; Curbstone; Double M; Erespin; Knights; Lace Publications; Library Research; Little Balkans; Longhorn; Maine Writers Workshop; Mainespring; Micah; Mosaic; New Rivers; New Seed; On The Move; Overlook; Path; Pineapple; Porcupine's Quill; Quality; Ranger Associates; Shameless Hussy; Somrie; Spiritual Fiction; Third World; Tres Amigos; University Editions; Sherry Urie; Vimach Associates; John Westburg; Woodsong Graphics; Zephyr.

**Horror** Aegina; Ansuda; Michael Kesend; Knights; Proper Tales; Salt Lick; Space and Time; Triple 'P'; Yith.

**Humor/Satire** Aegina; Allegany Mountain; Applezaba; Ariadne; Balance Beam; Bogus; BookWrights; Brunswick; Chelsea Green; Commoner's Publishing Society; Creative Concern; Creative With Words; Cross-Cultural Communications; Cube; Dragonsbreath; Erespin; Guernica; H.W.H. Creative Productions; Knights; Lace Publications; Little Balkans; Longhorn; Low-Tech; Mainespring; Mosaic; Overlook; Pacific Arts and Letters; Parkhurst; Paycock; Peppermint Press; Salt Lick; Second Coming; Shameless Hussy; Somrie; Tres Amigos; Vimach Associates; John Westburg; Woodsong Graphics; Zephyr.

**Juvenile** Acheron; Aegina; Agapé; Annick; Baker Street; Balance Beam; Binford & Mort; Blind Beggar; Brunswick; Carnival; Council for Indian Education; Creative Concern; Creative With Words; Cross-Cultural Communications; Dimensionist; Double M; Guernica; In Between; Kar-Ben Copies; Lollipop Power; Longhorn; Los Tres Osos; Maize Press; Mina; Mosaic; MTM; New Seed; Overlook; Pascal; Peppermint Press; Prairie; RDC Press; Rossel; Sea Fog Press; Shameless Hussy; Star Books; Stillpoint; Sunstone; Third World; Three Trees; Tree Frog; Unique Graphics; Vimach Associates; Warlords and Wizards; George Whittell Memorial; Woodsong Graphics.

**Lesbian** Alyson; Applezaba; Arsenal Pulp; Banned Books; The Crossing; Firebrand; Frog In The Well; Gay Presses of New York; Guernica; Kitchen Table; Lace Publications; Lintel; Metis; Mina; Mogul; Motheroot; Naiad; Salt Lick; Samisdat; Spinsters Ink; Triple 'P'; Vimach Associates; Wim; Women's; Zephyr.

**Mainstream** Adler; Aegina; Ansuda; Book Publishers; Brunswick; Commoner's Publishing Society; John Daniel; Michael Kesend; Little Balkans; Low-Tech; Morgan; Peachtree; Perivale; Second Chance; Sun & Moon; Tres Amigos; Ultramarine; University of Arkansas; Woodsong Graphics; Zephyr.

**Preschool/Picture Book** Andrew Mountain; Annick; Blind Beggar; Council for Indian Education; Creative Concern; Double M; In Between; Longhorn; Los Tres Osos; Peppermint Press; Third World; Women's.

**Psychic/Supernatural/Occult** Akiba; Ansuda; Brunswick; Dimensionist; Erespin; Guernica; Knights; Lapis Educational; Library Research; Lintel; Overlook; R&M Publishing; Salt Lick; Space and Time; Spiritual Fiction; Triple 'P'; Warlords and Wizards; Wingbow; Woodsong Graphics.

**Regional** Aegina; Binford & Mort; Brunswick; Chelsea Green; Commoner's Publishing Society; Council for Indian Education; Down East; First East Coast Theatre; Fjord; Frog in The Well; Kindred Joy; Lintel; Longhorn; Mosaic; New Seed; Padre; Peachtree; Peppermint Press; Perivale; Pineapple; Quintessence; St. Luke's; Samisdat; Somrie; Studia Hispanica Editors; Triple 'P'; University Editions; Sherry Urie; Wingbow; Zephyr.

**Religious/Inspirational** Aegina; Brunswick; Double M; Guernica; Illuminations; Kindred Joy; Lapis Educational; Micah; Millers River Publishing; Mosaic; R&M Publishing; Sea Fog Press; Spiritual Fiction; Star Books; Stillpoint; University of Arkansas; Sherry Urie.

**Romance** Aegina; Agapé; Book Publishers; Brunswick; Creative Concerns; Graphic Image; Guernica; H.W.H. Creative Productions; Knights; Lace Publications; Library Research; Mosaic; Triple 'P'; Woodsong Graphics.

**Science Fiction** Adler; Aegina; Andromeda; Balance Beam; Bogus; Brunswick; Carpenter; Commoner's Publishing Society; Dimensionist; Dragonsbreath; Erespin; H.W.H. Creative Productions; Knights; Lace Publications; Lion; Little Balkans; Maine Writers Workshop; Mainspring; Mina; MTM; Overlook; Padre; Panjandrum; Peppermint Press; Salt Lick; Second Coming Press; The Smith; Space and Time; Third World; Three Trees; Triple 'P'; 22 Press; Ultramarine; Unique Graphics; Warlords and Wizards; John Westburg; Woodsong Graphics; W.W. Publications; Zephyr.

**Short Story Collection** Adler; Aegina; Andromeda; Ansuda; Applezaba; Arsenal Pulp; Bilingual Review; Blind Beggar; Bogus; Books for All Times; Brunswick; Coyote Love; Creative With Words; Cube; John Daniel; Ecco; Exile; First East Coast Theatre; Frog in The Well; Graywolf; Hermes House; Intertext; Kitchen Table; Longhorn; Low-Tech; Micah; Morgan; North Point; Owl Creek; Padre; Path; Peachtree; Perivale; Proper Tales; Quality; RDC Press; Second Coming Press; Seven Buffaloes; Somrie; Still Point; Studia Hispanica Editors; Sun & Moon; Swamp; Third World; Triple 'P'; 22 Press; Ultramarine; Unique Graphics; University of Arkansas; Véhicule; Vimach Associates; Warlords and Wizards; George Whittell Memorial; Women's; Word Beat; Zephyr.

**Serialized/Excerpted Novel** Exile; Hermes House; Poet Galley; Word Beat;

**Suspense/Mystery** Acheron; Ansuda; Ariadne; Brunswick; Challenge; Creative Arts; Michael Kesend; Knights; Lace Publications; Library Research; Lion; MTM; New Bedford; Perseverance; Proper Tales; R&M Publishing; Second Chance Press; 22 Press; Sherry Urie; Vimach Associates; Woodsong Graphics.

**Translations** Adler; Aegina; Andromeda; Applezaba; Arsenal Pulp; Bilingual Review; BKMK; Blind Beggar; Bogus; Brunswick; Chelsea Green; Cross-Cultural Communications; Curbstone; Erespin; Fjord; Folder Editions; Gay Sunshine; Guernica; Hermes House; Lawrence Hill; H.W.H. Creative Productions; Intertext; Michael Kesend; Lace Publications; Manic D Press; Micah; New Rivers; North Point; On The Move; Overlook; Owl Creek; Panjandrum; Paycock; Perivale; Salt Lick; Sea Fog Press; Somrie; Station Hill; Studia Hispanica Editors; Sun & Moon; Swamp; Threshold; University Editions; University of Arkansas; Véhicule; York.

**War** Brunswick; Knights; Ranger Associates; Sea Fog Press; Vimach Associates; John Westburg.

**Western** Binford & Mort; Brunswick; Council for Indian Education; Erespin; Griffon House; Knights; Lace Publications; Little Balkans; Longhorn; Quality; Vimach Associates; John Westburg; Woodsong Graphics.

**Women's** Aegina; Agape; Ariadne; Arsenal Pulp; Blind Beggar; Book Publishers; Brunswick; The Crossing; Cube; Curbstone; Fjord; Frog in The Well; Guernica; Maize Press; Manic D Press; Metis; Motheroot; R&M Publishing; Salt Lick; Sea Fog Press; Shameless Hussy; The Smith; Spinsters Ink; Story; Sun & Moon; Sherry Urie; Véhicule; Wingbow; Women's; Woodsong Graphics; Zephyr.

**Young Adult/Teen** Acheron; Aegina; Akiba; Binford & Mort; Blind Beggar; Brunswick; Council for Indian Education; Creative Concern; Double M; Guernica; H.W.H. Creative Productions; Michael Kesend; Longhorn; Mainspring; Mosaic; MTM; New Seed; Peppermint Press; Perfection Form Company; Pineapple; Porcupine's Quill; Rossel; Sea Fog Press; Shameless Hussy; Sunstone; Third World; Three Trees; Tree Frog; Warlords and Wizards; George Whittell Memorial; Women's; Woodsong Graphics; W.W. Publications.

**Canada** Annick; Arsenal Pulp; Commoner's Publishing Society; Guernica; Peppermint Press; Porcupine's Quill; Prairie; Proper Tales; RDC Press; Three Trees; Tree Frog; Turnstone; Women's; York.

# Commercial Publishers

**Adventure** Avon; Bantam; Bethany House; Borealis; Broadman; Carroll & Graf; Crossway; Crown; Dahlstrom & Company; Dill; Dembner; Doubleday Canada; Fawcett; Bernard Geis; Holiday House; Holloway House; Holt, Rinehart & Winston; Houghton Mifflin; International University; Linden; McClelland and Stewart-Bantam Limited; McElderry/Atheneum; Marvel Comics; William Morrow; National Literary Guild; Naval Institute; New American Library; W.W. Norton; Pocket Books; Clarkson N. Potter; Random House; St. Martin's; Sharon; Simon & Pierre; SOS; Tor; TSR; University of Missouri; Vanguard; Vesta; Walker; Western; Word; Zebra.

**Confession** New American Library; W.W. Norton; St. Martin's.

**Contemporary** Alchemy; Apple; Bantam; Berkley; John F. Blair; Bookcraft; Borealis; Branden; Carroll & Graf; Crossway; Crown; Dahlstrom & Company; Dembner; Dorchester; Doubleday Canada; Douglas McIntyre; E.P. Dutton; Bernard Geis; David R. Godine; Harmony; Holiday House; Holloway House; Holt, Rinhart & Winston; Houghton Mifflin; International University; Alfred A. Knopf; Linden; Lodestar; McClelland and Stewart-Bantam Limited; McElderry/Atheneum; Mercury House; William Marrow; National Literary Guild; New American Library; W.W. Norton; Pelican; Philomel; Pocket Books; Poseidon; Clarkson N. Potter; Random House; Riverrun; St. Martin's; Sharon; Sierra Club; Simon & Pierre; Gibbs M. Smith; SOS; Stemmer House; Texas Monthly; Thorndike; University of Missouri; Vanguard; Vesta; Zebra.

**Erotica** Carroll & Graf; Greenleaf Classics; Holt, Rinehart & Winston; W.W. Norton; Pocket Books; St. Martin's.

**Ethnic** Bantam; John F. Blair; Branden; Dahlstrom & Company; Douglas McIntyre; David R. Godine; Holloway House; Holt, Rinehart & Winston; Pelican; Pocket Books; Stemmer House; Tex-

**as** Monthly; Three Continents; University of Missouri; Vesta; Winston-Derek.

**Experimental** George Braziller; Carroll & Graf; Columbia; Douglas & McIntyre; E.P. Dutton; McElderry/Atheneum; Mercury House; William Morrow; Mott Media; W.W. Norton; Riverrun; St. Martin's; Thorndike; Vesta.

**Faction** Doubleday Canada; Bernard Geis; Pocket Books; St. Martin's; Texas Monthly; Vesta.

**Fantasy** Avon; Baen; Bantam; Berkley; Berkley/Ace Science Fiction; Bluejay; Carroll & Graf; Daw; Delacorte Press for Young Readers; Holt, Rinehart & Winston; Houghton Mifflin; Linden; McElderry/Atheneum; Marvel Comics; Mott Media; National Literary Guild; W.W. Norton; St. Martin's; Sharon; Spectra; Tor; TSR; Vesta; Word.

**Feminist** Academy Chicago; Bantam; Bluejay; George Braziller; Douglas & McIntyre; Holt, Rinehart & Winston; Linden; William Morrow; Pocket Books; Press Gang; Quartet Books Ltd.; St. Martin's; University of Missouri; Vesta

**Gay** Bantam; Columbia; Douglas & McIntyre; Holt, Rinehart & Winston; William Morrow; National Literary Guild; New American Library; St. Martin's; Signet.

**Historical** Academy Chicago; Alchemy; Avon; Ballantine; Bantam; Bookcraft; Borealis; Broadman; Columbia; Crown; Dahlstrom & Company; Dembner; Denlinger's; Dorchester; Doubleday Canada; Douglas & McIntyre; Fawcett; David R. Godine; Harvest House; Holt, Rinehart & Winston; Houghton Mifflin; International University; Linden; McClelland and Stewart-Bantam; William Morrow; Mott Media; Naval Institute; New American Library; W.W. Norton; Pelican; Philomel; Pocket Books; Clarkson N. Potter; Presidio; Quartet Books Ltd.; Random House; St. Martin's; Simon & Pierre; SOS; Stemmer House; Texas Monthly; Vesta; Winston-Derek; Zebra.

**Horror** Bantam; Berkley; Crown; Dell; Dorchester; McClelland and Stewart-Bantam Limited; Marvel Comics; William Morrow; New American Library; W.W. Norton; Pocket Books; St. Martin's; Signet; Tor; TSR; Zebra.

**Humor/Satire** Alchemy; Bantam; Broadman; Crown; E.P. Dutton; David R. Godine; Holiday House; Holt, Rinehart & Winston; International University; Lodestar; Marvel Comics; William Morrow; Pelican; Pocket Books; Clarkson N. Potter; Prentice-Hall; Price/Stern/Sloan; Quartet Books Ltd.; St. Martin's; Sharon; Signet; Simon & Pierre; Texas Monthly; Thorndike; University of Missouri; Vanguard; Vesta; Western.

**Juvenile** Abingdon; Alchemy; Apple; Atlantic Monthly; Bethany House; Borealis; Bradbury; Branden; Broadman; Caedmon; Camelot; Carolrhoda; Childrens; Child's World; Clarion Books, Ticknor & Fields; Concordia; David C. Cook; Crossway; Crowell; Crown; Dahlstrom & Company; Delacorte Juvenile; Delacorte Press for Young Readers; Dell; Douglas & McIntyre; E.P. Dutton; Eakin; Farrar, Straus & Giroux; Gemstone; David R. Godine; Gospel Light; Green Tiger; Greenwillow; Grosset & Dunlap; Harcourt Brace Jovanovich; Harper & Row Junior Books; Herald; Holt, Rinehart & Winston; Ideals; Knopf Books for Young Readers; Little, Brown; Lodestar; McElderry/Atheneum; Macmillan; Marvel Comics; Mott Media; National Literary Guild; W.W. Norton; Oddo; Parker Brothers; Pelican; Philomel; Clarkson N. Potter; Prentice-Hall; Press Gang; Price/Stern/Sloan; Promise Romances; Random House; Scholastic; Scribner's, Books for Young Readers; Sharon; Simon & Pierre; Stemmer House; TSR; Vanguard; Vesta; Wanderer; Western; Albert Whitman; Winston-Derek; Yearling; Charlotte Zolotow.

**Lesbian** Bantam; Douglas & McIntyre; William Morrow; St. Martin's.

**Mainstream** Avon; Berkley; Carrol & Graf; Crown; Paul S. Ericksson; Bernard Geis; Holt, Rinehart & Winston; Houghton Mifflin; International University; Linden; McClelland and Stewart-Bantam Ltd.; Random House; SOS; Texas Monthly; Tor; Vesta.

**Men's** Avon; Fawcett.

**Preschool/Picture Book** Caedmon; Crowell; Farrar, Straus & Giroux; Greenwillow; Grosset & Dunlap; Harper & Row Junior Books; Houghton Mifflin; Knopf Books for Young Readers; Little, Brown; Oak Tree; Parker Brothers; Prentice-Hall; Random House; Sharon; Vesta; Western.

**Psychic/Supernatural/Occult** Avon; Bantam; Berkley; Bethany House; Dell; Dorchester; Fawcett; Bernard Geis; Holt, Rinehart & Winston; Houghton Mifflin; International University; Marvel Comics; New American Library; W.W. Norton; Pocket Books; St. Martin's; Signet; Vesta; Winston-Derek.

**Regional** Bethany House; John F. Blair; Columbia; Denlinger's; Miller; Stemmer House; Texas Monthly; Thorndike; Vesta; Winston-Derek.

**Religious/Inspirational** Abingdon; Accent; Augsburg; Ballantine/Epiphany; Bantam; Bethany House; Bookcraft; Branden; Bridge; Broadman; Concordia; David C. Cook; Crossway; Gospel Light; Harvest House; Herald; International University; Mott Media; National Literary Guild; Pelican; Promise Romances; Resource; Standard; Tyndale House; Vesta; Word; Zondervan.

**Romance** Accent; Avalon; Avon; Bantam; Berkley; Bookcraft; Branden; Crown; Dell; Dodd, Mead; Dorchester; Doubleday; Harlequin; Harvest House; Holloway House; Holt, Rinehart & Winston; Houghton Mifflin; International University; Loveswept; William Morrow; New American Library; W.W. Norton; Pocket Books; Second Chance at Love; Sharon; Signet; Silhouette; SOS; Sweet Dreams; Vesta; Walker; Word; Zebra; Zondervan.

**Science Fiction** Alchemy; Arbor House; Avon; Baen; Bantam; Berkley; Berkley/Ace Science Fiction; Bethany House; Bluejay; Crossway; Crown; Daw; Doubleday; Holiday House; Houghton Mifflin; International University; McElderry/ Atheneum; Marvel Comics; William Morrow; New American Library; Prentice-Hall; St. Martin's; Sharon; Spectra; Tor; TSR; Vesta.

**Short Story Collections** Branden; George Braziller; Crossway; Douglas & McIntyre; International University; Quartet Books Ltd.; Random House; Resource; Riverrun; Sharon; University of Georgia; Vesta.

**Suspense/Mystery** Academy Chicago; Avon; Bantam; Bethany House; Bluejay; Carroll & Graf; Dell; Dembner; Dodd, Mead; Dorchester; Doubleday; Doubleday Canada; E.P. Dutton; Fawcett; Bernard Geis; David R. Godine; Holt, Rinehart & Winston; Houghton Mifflin; International University; Alfred A. Knopf; Library of Crime Classics; Linden; Lodestar; McClelland and Stewart-Bantam Limited; McElderry/Atheneum; Marvel Comics; William Morrow; Mysterious Press; New American Library; W.W. Norton; Pocket Books; Prentice-Hall; Random House; St. Martin's; Sharon; Simon & Pierre; SOS; Texas Monthly; Tor; TSR; Vanguard; Vesta; Walker; Western; Word; Zebra.

**Translations** Academy Chicago; George Braziller; Columbia; Douglas & McIntyre; E.P. Dutton; Holt, Rinehart & Winston; International University; Mercury House; William Morrow; Quartet Books Ltd.; Riverrun; Simon & Pierre; Vesta.

**War** Avon; Bantam; Berkley; Carroll & Graf; Crown; Dell; Dorchester; E.P. Dutton; Holt, Rinehart & Winston; Houghton Mifflin; William Morrow; Naval Institute; New American Library; Pelican; Pocket Books; Presidio; St. Martin's; Stemmer House; University of Missouri; Vanguard; Vesta; Zebra.

**Western** Avalon; Avon; Ballantine; Bantam; Bookcraft; Holt, Rinehart & Winston; Marvel Comics; Miller; W.W. Norton; Pocket Books; Texas Monthly; Walker; Word.

**Women's** Avon; Ballantine; Bantam; Bookcraft; Broadman; Crown; Dorchester; Douglas & McIntyre; Fawcett; Harvest House; McClelland and Stewart-Bantam Ltd.; William Morrow; Mott Media; New American Library; Pocket Books; Clarkson N. Potter; Quartet Books Ltd.; Random House; St. Martin's; Sharon; Signet; Vesta; Word; Zondervan.

**Young Adult/Teen** Archway; Augsburg; Avon; Bantam; Bluejay; Borealis; Bradbury; Camelot; Carolrhoda; Clarion Books, Ticknor & Fields; Crossway; Crown; Dahlstrom & Company; Delacorte Press for Young Readers; Dell; Douglas & McIntyre; E.P. Dutton; Farrar Straus & Giroux; Flare; Gospel Light; Greenwillow; Harcourt Brace Jovanovich; Harper & Row Junior Books; Herald; Holt Rinehart & Winston; Knopf Books for Young Readers; McElderry/Atheneum; Macmillan; Marvel Comics; New American Library; W.W. Norton; Pelican; Philomel; Point Books; Press Gang; Scholastic; Scribner's; Scribner's, Books for Young Readers; Sharon; Signet; Silhouette; Simon & Pierre; Stemmer House; Sweet Dreams; Tor; TSR; Vanguard; Vesta; Albert Whitman; Winston-Derek; Yearling.

**Canada** Borealis; Doubleday Canada; Douglas & McIntyre; Harlequin, McClelland and Stewart-Bantam Ltd.; Macmillan of Canada; Press Gang; Simon & Pierre; Vesta.

# Agents

**Adventure** James Allen; Marcia Amsterdam; Harry Bloom; Pema Browne Ltd.; Ruth Cantor; Jay Garon-Brooke Assocs.; Paul Kohner; Bill Kruger; Peter Lampack; Peter Livingston Assocs.; Tom Zelasky.

**Contemporary** Pema Browne Ltd.; Maria Carvainis; Goodman Assocs.; Lucy Kroll; Michael Larsen/Elizabeth Pomada; Arthur P. Schwartz; Evelyn Singer; Austin Wahl; Writers House.

**Experimental** Claudia Menza; New Wave; John Pickering Assocs.

**Fantasy** James Allen; Bill Kruger; Writers House.

**Historical** James Allen; Maria Carvainis; Columbia Literary Assocs.; Goodman Assocs.; Bill Kruger; Ruth Wreschner.

**Horror** Long Enterprises; New Wave; The Betsy Nolan Literary Agency.

**Humor/Satire** Jay Garon-Brooke Assocs.; Long Enterprises; Janet Wilkens Manus.

**Juvenile** Marcia Amsterdam; Ruth Cantor; SJ Clark; Ruth Cohen; Joyce K. Cole; The Film/Publishing Group; Heinle & Heinle Enterprises; Barbara S. Kouts; Norma-Lewis.

**Mainstream** Carole Abel; Edward J. Acton; Marcia Amsterdam; The Artists Agency; Harry Bloom; Reid Boates; Pema Browne Ltd.; Frank Brunotts; Ruth Cantor; SJ Clark; Joyce K. Cole; Columbia Literary Assocs.; Don Congdon; John Farquharson Ltd.; The Film/Publishing Group; Franklin/Nathan; Jay Garon-Brooke Assocs.; Max Gartenberg; HHM Literary; Frederick Hill Assocs.; Hintz & Fitzgerald; Asher D. Jason Enterprises; Jet; Kidde, Hoyt & Picard; Barbara S. Kouts; Bill Kruger; Peter Lampack; The Lantz Office; Michael Larsen/Elizabeth Pomada; Peter Livingston Assocs; Barbara Lowenstein; Janet Wilkens Manus; Margaret McBride; Henry Morrison; Morton; Marvin Moss; Multimedia Product Development; Jean V. Naggar; New Wave; The Betsy Nolan Literary Agency; Frommer Price Inc.; Helen Rees; Eleanor Merryman Roszel Rogers; Arthur P. Schwartz; James Seligmann; Bobbe Siegel, Rights Representatives; Charles M. Stern Assocs.; Gloria Stern; Jo Stewart; The Laurie Tag Agency; Thompson & Chris; Mary Jack Wald; John A. Ware; Cherry Weiner; Ruth Wreschner; Mary Yost; Susan Zeckendorf Assoc.

**Men's** James Allen; Pema Browne Ltd.; Goodman Assocs.; HHM Literary; John Pickering Assocs.

**Juvenile** Eleanor Merryman Roszel Rogers; Susan Urstadt.

**Psychic/Supernatural/Occult** SJ Clark.

**Religious/Inspirational** Venice Literary.

**Romance** Marcia Amsterdam; Harry Bloom; Pema Browne Ltd.; Shirley Burke; Ruth Cohen; Columbia Literary Assocs.; John Farquharson Ltd.; Goodman Assocs.; Asher D. Jason Enterprises; Jet; Kidde, Hoyt & Picard; Michael Larsen/Elizabeth Pomada; Barbara Lowenstein; New Wave; Mary Novik; Arthur P. Schwartz; Evelyn Singer; Charles M. Stern Assocs.; Jo Stewart; The Laurie Tag Agency; Teal & Watt; Venice Literary; Austin Wahl; Cherry Weiner; Tom Zelasky.

**Science Fiction** James Allen; Marcia Amsterdam; Ruth Cantor; John Farquharson Ltd.; Asher D. Jason Enterprises; Virginia Kidd; Bill Kruger; The Lund Agency; Henry Morrison; Jean V. Naggar; Arthur P. Schwartz; Bobbe Siegel, Rights Representative; Evelyn Singer; Cherry Weiner; Ruth Wreschner; Writers House.

**Short Story Collections** Barbara Bauer; The Blake Group; Frank Brunotts; Don Congdon; Molly Malone Cook; The Film/Publishing Group; John Hawkins & Assocs.; HHM Literary; Barbara S. Kouts; Long Enterprises; Janet Wilkens Manus; Claudia Menza; John Pickering Assocs.; The Robbins Office; Rosenstone/Wender; Russell & Volkening, Inc.; Harold Schmidt; John A. Ware; Ruth Wreschner; Tom Zelasky.

**Suspense/Mystery** Carole Abel; James Allen; Marcia Amsterdam; Harry Bloom; Shirley Burke; Ruth Cantor; Maria Carvainis; SJ Clark; Ruth Cohen; John Farquharson Ltd.; Jay Garon-Brooke Assocs.; Max Gartenberg; Goodman Assocs.; HHM Literary; Hintz & Fitzgerald; Asher D. Jason Enterprises; Paul Kohner; Bill Kruger; Michael Larsen/Elizabeth Pomada; Peter Livingston Assocs.; Long Enterprises; Janet Wilkens Manus; Henry Morrison; Marvin Moss; Jean V. Nagger; New Wave; Ray Peekner; John Pickering Assocs.; Helen Rees; Eleanor Merryman Roszel Rogers; Bobbe Siegel, Rights Representative; Evelyn Singer; Charles M. Stern Assocs.; Jo Stewart; Thompson & Chris; Susan Urstadt; Austin Wahl; John A. Ware; Cherry Weiner; Ruth Wreschner; Writers House; Susan Zeckendorf Assocs.

**Western** Maria Carvainis; Ruth Cohen; Goodman Assocs.; Ray Peekner; Austin Wahl.

**Women's** Carole Abel; Marcia Amsterdam; Harry Bloom; Pema Browne Ltd.; Shirley Burke; Ruth Cantor; The Film/Publishing Group; HHM Literary; Hintz & Fitzgerald; Asher D. Jason Enterprises; Barbara S. Kouts; Peter Lampack; Michael Larsen/Elizabeth Pomada; Donald MacCampbell; Jean V. Naggar; The Betsy Nolan Literary Agency; John Pickering Assocs.; Frommer Price Inc.; Arthur P. Schwartz; Bobbe Siegel, Rights Representative; Charles M. Stern Assocs.; Gloria Stern; Jo Stewart; The Laurie Tag Agency; Mary Jack Wald; Cherry Weiner; Ruth Wreschner; Writers House; Mary Yost; Susan Zeckendorf Assocs.

**Young Adult/Teen** Marcia Amsterdam; Pema Browne Ltd.; Maria Carvainis; Ruth Cohen; Columbia Literary Assocs.; Heinle & Heinle Enterprises; Frederick Hill Assocs.; Kidde, Hoyt & Picard; Bill Kruger; Charles Neighbors; Ray Peekner; Evelyn Singer; Susan Urstadt; Ruth Wreschner; Writers House.

**Canada** Mary Novik.

# INDEX

## J

## K

## L

# M

# Q

# R

**X**

**Y**

**Z**

# Other Books of Interest

**Computer Books**
    **The Complete Guide to Writing Software User Manuals**, by Brad M. McGehee (paper) $14.95

**General Writing Books**
    **Beginning Writer's Answer Book**, edited by Polking and Bloss $14.95
    **Getting the Words Right: How to Revise, Edit and Rewrite**, by Theodore A. Rees Cheney $13.95
    **How to Write a Book Proposal**, by Michael Larsen $9.95
    **How to Write While You Sleep**, by Elizabeth Ross $12.95
    **Law & the Writer**, edited by Polking & Meranus (paper) $10.95
    **Knowing Where to Look: The Ultimate Guide to Research**, by Lois Horowitz $16.95
    **Pinckert's Practical Grammar**, by Robert C. Pinckert $12.95
    **Teach Yourself to Write**, by Evelyn Stenbock (paper) $9.95
    **The 29 Most Common Writing Mistakes & How to Avoid Them**, by Judy Delton $9.95
    **Writer's Block & How to Use It**, by Victoria Nelson $12.95
    **Writer's Encyclopedia**, edited by Kirk Polking $19.95
    **Writer's Guide to Research**, by Lois Horowitz $9.95
    **Writer's Market**, edited by Paula Deimling $19.95
    **Writer's Resource Guide**, edited by Bernadine Clark $16.95

**Magazine/News Writing**
    **Basic Magazine Writing**, by Barbara Kevles $15.95
    **Complete Guide to Writing Nonfiction**, by The American Society of Journalists & Authors $24.95
    **How to Write & Sell the 8 Easiest Article Types**, by Helene Schellenberg Barnhart $14.95
    **Writing Nonfiction that Sells**, by Samm Sinclair Baker $14.95

**Fiction Writing**
    **Creating Short Fiction**, by Damon Knight (paper) $8.95
    **Fiction Writer's Market**, edited by Jean Fredette $18.95
    **Handbook of Short Story Writing**, by Dickson and Smythe (paper) $7.95
    **How to Write & Sell Your First Novel**, by Oscar Collier with Frances Spatz Leighton $14.95
    **Storycrafting**, by Paul Darcy Boles $14.95
    **Writing Romance Fiction—For Love and Money**, by Helene Schellenberg Barnhart $14.95
    **Writing the Novel: From Plot to Print**, by Lawrence Block (paper) $8.95

**Special Interest Writing Books**
    **The Children's Picture Book: How to Write It, How to Sell It**, by Ellen E. M. Roberts $17.95
    **Complete Book of Scriptwriting**, by J. Michael Straczynski $14.95
    **The Craft of Comedy Writing**, by Sol Saks $14.95
    **How to Make Money Writing Fillers**, by Connie Emerson (paper) $8.95
    **How to Write a Play**, by Raymond Hull $13.95
    **How to Write the Story of Your Life**, by Frank P. Thomas $12.95
    **Mystery Writer's Handbook**, by The Mystery Writers of America (paper) $8.95
    **On Being a Poet**, by Judson Jerome $14.95
    **The Poet's Handbook**, by Judson Jerome (paper) $8.95
    **Poet's Market**, by Judson Jerome $16.95
    **Travel Writer's Handbook**, by Louise Zobel (paper) $9.95
    **TV Scriptwriter's Handbook**, by Alfred Brenner (paper) $9.95
    **Writing for Children & Teenagers**, by Lee Wyndham (paper) $9.95
    **Writing and Selling Science Fiction**, by Science Fiction Writers of America (paper) $7.95

**The Writing Business**
    **Complete Guide to Self-Publishing**, by Tom & Marilyn Ross $19.95
    **Complete Handbook for Freelance Writers**, by Kay Cassill $14.95
    **Editing for Print**, by Geoffrey Rogers $14.95
    **How to Get Your Book Published**, by Herbert W. Bell $15.95
    **How to Understand and Negotiate a Book Contract or Magazine Agreement**, by Richard Balkin $11.95
    **Literary Agents: How to Get & Work with the Right One for You**, by Michael Larsen $9.95

To order directly from the publisher, include $2.00 postage and handling for 1 book and 50¢ for each additional book. Allow 30 days for delivery.

**Writer's Digest Books, Dept. B, 9933 Alliance Rd., Cincinnati OH 45242**
Prices subject to change without notice.

# Writer's
## DIGEST
### THE WORLD'S LEADING MAGAZINE FOR WRITERS

How would you like to get:
- up-to-the-minute reports on new markets for your writings.
- professional advice from editors and writers about what to write and how to write it to maximize your opportunities for getting published.
- in-depth interviews with leading authors who reveal their secrets of success.
- expert opinion about writing and selling fiction, nonfiction, poetry and scripts.
- …all at a $7.00 discount?

(See other side for details.)

How You Can Break Into National Magazines